Sunset

COOKBOOK
classics

By the Editors of Sunset Books

Sunset Books • Menlo Park, California

Quick to prepare, yet elegant to serve, Fig-stuffed Turkey Roast (recipe on page 564) is seasoned with rosemary and mustard.

An Instant Kitchen Library!

Cookbook Classics is a compilation of eight of our most popular cookbooks over the past two decades. We hope you find both value and versatility in this collection. With a wide array of recipes to choose from, you're sure to discover menus for special occasions or practical dishes for weeknight meals.

In this one-stop cookbook you can choose from hundreds of delicious recipes, from taste-tempting appetizers to main entrées, vegetarian dishes, and elegant desserts. You'll also find numerous special features throughout the book. Some focus on creative menus and cooking tips, while others offer guidelines for healthy eating, or even advice on packing and sending cookies.

Most of the recipes in this volume are accompanied by a nutritional analysis prepared by Hill Nutrition Associates, Inc., of Florida. For those recipes with cooking times, keep in mind that the times are approximate and may vary depending on your expertise in the kitchen and the equipment you use.

SUNSET BOOKS
Vice President, General Manager: Richard A. Smeby
Vice President, Editorial Director: Bob Doyle
Production Director: Lory Day
Art Director: Vasken Guiragossian

STAFF FOR THIS BOOK
Research and Text
Sue Brownlee, Claire Coleman, Barbara E. Goldman, Karyn I. Lipman, Janeth Johnson Nix, Cynthia Scheer

Coordinating Editors
Kathryn Lescroart Detzer, Gregory J. Kaufman, Deborah Thomas Kramer, Linda J. Selden, Anne K. Turley

Contributing Editors
Ginger Smith Bate, Fran Feldman, Joan Griffiths, Rebecca LaBrum, Susan Warton

Design
Cynthia Bassett, Joe di Chiarro, Lea Damiano Phelps, Cynthia Hanson, Sandra Popovich, Susan Sempere

Illustrators
Sandra Bruce, Dick Cole, Susan Jaekel, Jacqueline Osborn, Kathy Parkinson, Liz Wheaton

Special Consultants
Kenneth N. Hall, Ph.D.
Extension Food Scientist and Professor of Nutritional Sciences
University of Connecticut
Patricia Kearney, R.D.
Stanford University Hospital

Production Coordinator
Patricia S. Williams

For additional copies of *Cookbook Classics* or any other Sunset book, call 1-800-526-511. Or see our web site at www.sunsetbooks.com

Cover: Angel Hair with Crab & Arugula (recipe on page 488). Cover design by Vasken Guiragossian. Photography by Noel Barnhurst. Food styling by George Dolese.

Contents

Sunset

Appetizers

By the Editors of
Sunset Books and
Sunset Magazine

Sunset Publishing Corporation ■ **Menlo Park, California**

CONTENTS

Cocktail Cream Puffs (recipe on page 75)

GREAT BEGINNINGS

Appetizers—creamy dips, chunky spreads, hot tidbits, and cold canapés —are delightful appetite enhancers. They can introduce a dinner, serve as between-meal snacks, or provide party sustenance all on their own.

Hors d'oeuvres should be enjoyed by both the guests and the cook. Literally "outside the main work," these additions to a basic menu don't have to overwhelm the cook with extra effort. Understanding what's involved can make even an all-appetizer event a breeze to prepare. The key to success is careful planning.

Variety. Plan to offer a varied assortment of appetizers that invites tasting a bit of everything. Your choices should include both hot and cold foods, keeping in mind, of course, your refrigerator, freezer, and oven space.

It's a good idea to contrast texture as well as temperature in your selections. Offer a balance between crunchy and smooth, delicate and dense. And mix appetizers that need to be passed with those that guests can serve themselves.

Plan on variety in flavors, too. Add spark with spices, but offer mild alternatives for the less adventuresome. Your company will also appreciate rich treats tempered by refreshingly light ones. And don't focus on a single taste; although everyone may enjoy basil, garlic, or lemon, use such flavorings as accents, rather than in every dish.

If you're planning a large appetizers-only party, serve at least one appetizer from each of the following categories: eggs and cheese; breads; meat and poultry; fish and shellfish; and vegetables and fruits. If you're choosing hors d'oeuvres to offer before dinner, try to complement the main course in taste, texture, and temperature.

Keep an eye on your selections so that colors harmonize with each other on your table. The fresh herbs, fruits, and vegetables you choose can brighten and tie together your presentation.

Quantity. For most cooks, the biggest problem is deciding how much food to prepare. Weather and time of day affect your guests' appetites: people tend to eat more in cold weather; appetites are also heartier in the early evening than in mid-afternoon. And be sure to keep in mind the rest of your menu. If you're planning a heavy dinner to follow, a few light appetizers (perhaps one passed, one serve-yourself) should suffice.

For an all-appetizer party, prepare at least two servings or pieces per person of each hors d'oeuvre you plan to pass; offer at least six different types of passed appetizers each

hour. Supplement them with food that guests can serve themselves, such as dips, spreads, and cheeses.

Time. You'll appreciate your event more—and so will your guests—if you're out of the kitchen and part of the party. Do your marketing well in advance and prepare as many dishes as possible ahead of time. Make sure you can easily handle those that require last-minute effort.

When you freeze, use specially designed freezer wraps and containers, and follow the storage guidelines in the recipe. Remember that recipes relying on potatoes, cooked noodles, rice, fried tortillas, and hard-cooked egg whites can change texture when frozen; emulsions, like mayonnaise and hollandaise, and foods in cream sauce are also not very successful freezer candidates.

Easy extras. Budgeting your time frees you for finishing touches. You'll be amazed at how effectively a few simple garnishes can dress up your dishes without taxing your patience or ability.

Cut carrots diagonally and fan them for a pretty floral effect. Run a fork down the sides of an unpeeled cucumber and then slice it crosswise for an attractive pattern. Thinly sliver both ends of green onion sections several times lengthwise and place in ice water until ready to use as flowers. Cut a lemon slice to the center and flip one end for a three-dimen-

sional presentation. Or try a star-topped mushroom: press the tip of a pointed knife five times around the center of each mushroom to form a star.

Beverages. Just as with food, your selection of beverages depends on the event, the weather, the time of day, and your taste. For a party lasting about two hours, figure about half a bottle of wine, 8 ounces of liquor, 1 quart of beer, or 16 ounces of mixed punch per person. Plan on about 32 servings from a gallon of nonalcoholic punch. Expect each guest to use two glasses and have plenty of ice: one 5-pound bag for every four guests.

Surprises. Impromptu gatherings and unexpected guests can challenge even the most organized host. Take some of the surprise out of spur-of-the-moment occasions by keeping some of the following on hand: assorted crackers, pocket bread, and tortillas; canned salmon, crab, anchovies, smoked oysters, and tuna; canned green chiles; Cheddar, jack, and cream cheese; sour cream, plain yogurt, and mayonnaise; soy sauce; liquid hot pepper seasoning; and cocktail-size paper napkins.

Enjoy! Careful planning allows you the luxury of relaxing and enjoying the event. Easy to prepare, not overly time-consuming, and always delicious, our recipes will put you in a party mood.

A WORD ABOUT OUR NUTRITIONAL DATA

For our recipes, we provide a nutritional analysis stating calorie count; grams of protein, carbohydrates, and total fat; and milligrams of cholesterol and sodium. Generally, the analysis applies to a single serving, based on the number of servings given for each recipe and the amount of each ingredient. If a range is given for the number of servings and/or the amount of an ingredient, the analysis is based on an average of the figures given.

The nutritional analysis does not include optional ingredients or those for which no specific amount is stated. If an ingredient is listed with a substitution, the information was calculated using the first choice.

For a celebration of many cuisines, dip Water-crisped Tortilla Chips (recipe on page 18) in Mexico's Chile con Queso (recipe on page 10); serve the flavors of Italy on breadsticks, bell peppers, or cucumber slices with Pesto Cheese Spread (recipe on page 22); and enjoy a taste of southern France with Baked Vegetables Provençal (recipe on page 30).

DIPS & SPREADS

Popular with guests as well as with the cook, dips and spreads offer the maximum in versatility and taste with the minimum of fuss. Most are easily prepared with just a few ingredients and can be made well ahead of time. And all look attractive at the party without requiring a lot of attention.

Choose from an assortment of hot and cold presentations—creamy dips, meaty pâtés, and zesty vegetable spreads. Whether you serve them with crunchy vegetables, crisp crackers, slices of crusty bread, or chunks of fresh fruit, they're sure to disappear in minutes.

GORGONZOLA PESTO

Preparation time: About 10 minutes

Assertive pesto becomes even bolder when teamed with Gorgonzola. Serve this zesty appetizer surrounded by radicchio leaves and zucchini spears.

 3 cups lightly packed fresh basil leaves
 ⅔ cup (about 6 oz.) lightly packed crumbled Gorgonzola cheese
 ¼ cup olive oil
 Salt and pepper

In a blender or food processor, whirl basil, cheese, and oil until puréed. Transfer to a small bowl. Season to taste with salt and pepper.

If made ahead, cover and refrigerate until next day. Serve at room temperature. Makes about ¾ cup.

Per tablespoon: 101 calories, 4 g protein, 3 g carbohydrates, 9 g total fat, 11 mg cholesterol, 199 mg sodium

Pictured on page 8

CHILE CON QUESO

Preparation time: About 20 minutes
Cooking time: About 10 minutes

Offer this melted cheese dip with tortilla chips or colorful red or green bell pepper strips.

 Water-crisped Tortilla Chips or Fried Tortilla Chips (recipes on page 16), optional
 2 tablespoons salad oil
 1 medium-size onion, finely chopped
 1 can (4 oz.) diced green chiles
 ⅓ cup heavy cream
 1 cup (4 oz.) shredded Longhorn Cheddar cheese
 Red or green bell peppers, stemmed, seeded, and cut into ½-inch-wide strips (optional)

Prepare Fried Tortilla Chips, if desired; set aside.

Heat oil in a 3- to 4-quart pan over medium heat. Add onion and cook, stirring, until soft (about 7 minutes). Add chiles and cream; cook, stirring, until hot. Reduce heat and add cheese, stirring until melted.

Pour into a chafing or fondue dish over a low flame or into a dish on an electric warming tray set on low. Offer with bell pepper strips and chips, if desired. Makes 2 cups.

Per tablespoon: 32 calories, 1 g protein, .5 g carbohydrates, 3 g total fat, 7 mg cholesterol, 45 mg sodium

RED PEPPER DIP

Preparation time: About 15 minutes
Cooking time: About 35 minutes

This colorful dip combines roasted red peppers, caramelized onions, and fresh thyme, showcasing them in a creamy ricotta and Parmesan cheese base. Good dippers include fresh vegetables, Cheese Wafers (recipe on page 44), and Polenta Triangles (recipe on page 46).

 3 tablespoons olive oil
 3 large onions, thinly sliced
 2 jars (7¼ oz. *each*) roasted red peppers
 2 teaspoons fresh thyme leaves or 1 teaspoon dry thyme leaves
 2 tablespoons tomato paste
 ½ cup *each* grated Parmesan cheese and ricotta cheese
 Thyme sprigs (optional)

Heat oil in a wide frying pan over medium heat. Add onions and cook, stirring occasionally, until golden and very soft (about 30 minutes).

Add red peppers, thyme leaves, and tomato paste; cook, stirring, for 5 more minutes. Let cool briefly.

In a blender or food processor, whirl red pepper mixture, Parmesan, and ricotta until puréed. Transfer to a bowl and garnish with thyme sprigs, if desired.

If made ahead, cover and refrigerate until next day. Serve cold or at room temperature. Makes about 4 cups.

Per tablespoon: 16 calories, .6 g protein, 1 g carbohydrates, 1 g total fat, 1 mg cholesterol, 20 mg sodium

HERBED CHEESE DIP

Preparation time: About 10 minutes
Chilling time: At least 2 hours

Three kinds of cheese enrich this sour cream–based dip. Make it up to five days before serving; offer with raw green beans or celery sticks.

 1 cup sour cream
 1 small package (3 oz.) cream cheese, at room temperature
 ¼ cup (about 2 oz.) crumbled unripened goat cheese, such as Bûcheron
 ¾ teaspoon dill weed
 ¼ teaspoon *each* dry sage, dry basil, and dry thyme leaves
 ¼ teaspoon freshly ground pepper
 1 clove garlic, minced or pressed
 ⅓ cup (3 oz.) crumbled blue-veined cheese

Beat sour cream, cream cheese, goat cheese, dill, sage, basil, thyme, pepper, and garlic until smooth and well blended. Stir in blue-veined cheese. Cover and refrigerate for at least 2 hours or up to 5 days. Makes about 1¾ cups.

Per tablespoon: 47 calories, 1 g protein, .7 g carbohydrates, 4 g total fat, 11 mg cholesterol, 68 mg sodium

CREAMY CRAB DIP

Preparation time: About 10 minutes

Spoon this luscious crabmeat dip into the centers of cold cooked artichokes for an impressive appetizer.

1 **large package (8 oz.) cream cheese, at room temperature**
2 **tablespoons** *each* **dry white wine and lemon juice**
1 **clove garlic, minced or pressed**
1 **teaspoon Dijon mustard**
½ **teaspoon Worcestershire**
¼ **cup thinly sliced green onions (including tops)**
½ **pound crabmeat**
 Salt and pepper

Beat cream cheese, wine, lemon juice, garlic, mustard, and Worcestershire until blended. Stir in onions and crab. Season to taste with salt and pepper. If made ahead, cover and refrigerate until next day. Makes about 2 cups.

Per tablespoon: 33 calories, 2 g protein, .3 g carbohydrates, 3 g total fat, 15 mg cholesterol, 47 mg sodium

SMOKED SALMON DIP

Preparation time: About 10 minutes

Accented with dill and onion, this creamy dip is an elegant starter. Endive spears are the perfect accompaniment for dipping.

1 **large package (8 oz.) cream cheese, at room temperature**
⅓ **cup (about 3 oz.) chopped smoked salmon or lox**
¼ **cup sour cream**
1 **tablespoon** *each* **lime juice and minced onion**
3 **tablespoons chopped fresh dill or 2 teaspoons dill weed**
 Dill sprigs (optional)
 Endive spears, washed and crisped (optional)

Beat cream cheese, salmon, sour cream, lime juice, and onion until well blended and fluffy. Mix in chopped dill. Transfer to a small bowl. If made ahead, cover and refrigerate for up to 3 days. Serve at room temperature.

If desired, garnish with dill sprigs and surround with endive. Makes about 1 cup.

Per tablespoon: 64 calories, 2 g protein, .7 g carbohydrates, 6 g total fat, 18 mg cholesterol, 86 mg sodium

CURRY-YOGURT DIP

Preparation time: About 10 minutes
Standing time: About 30 minutes

Tiny cooked shrimp are mixed with shredded zucchini in this light curry and yogurt combination. Make the dip just before serving and offer it with an assortment of raw vegetables.

1 **small zucchini (about 3 oz.), shredded**
 About 1 teaspoon salt
1 **cup plain yogurt**
½ **teaspoon curry powder**
¼ **cup thinly sliced green onions (including tops)**
½ **pound small cooked shrimp**
¼ **cup chopped cilantro (coriander)**
 Ground red pepper (cayenne)

Mix zucchini with 1 teaspoon of the salt. Let stand until zucchini is limp and liquid has drained from it (about 30 minutes). Rinse and drain, squeezing out as much water as possible.

Gently mix zucchini, yogurt, curry powder, onions, shrimp, and cilantro; season to taste with salt and pepper. Pour mixture into a bowl. Sprinkle with additional pepper, if desired. Makes 2⅓ cups.

Per tablespoon: 11 calories, 2 g protein, .5 g carbohydrates, .2 g total fat, 12 mg cholesterol, 33 mg sodium

DILL DIP

Preparation time: About 5 minutes
Chilling time: At least 4 hours

You can make this easy dill-accented dip with ingredients you have on hand. Cherry tomatoes, celery sticks, and cauliflowerets are the perfect partners.

⅔ **cup** *each* **mayonnaise and sour cream**
2 **tablespoons chopped parsley**
2½ **teaspoons** *each* **dill weed and finely chopped onion**

Mix mayonnaise and sour cream. Stir in parsley, dill, and onion until well blended. Cover and refrigerate for at least 4 hours or until next day. Makes about 1⅓ cups.

Per tablespoon: 67 calories, .3 g protein, .6 g carbohydrates, 7 g total fat, 7 mg cholesterol, 44 mg sodium

HORSERADISH DIP

Preparation time: About 5 minutes
Chilling time: At least 1 hour

This dip can do double duty at a barbecue. You can serve it with crisp, raw vegetables, such as jicama and cucumber, and offer it as a dipping sauce for grilled beef.

2 **cups plain yogurt**
¼ **cup minced green onions (including tops)**
½ **teaspoon** *each* **mustard seeds and cumin seeds**
1 **to 2 tablespoons prepared horseradish**

Stir together yogurt, onions, mustard seeds, cumin seeds, and horseradish. Cover and refrigerate for at least 1 hour or up to 3 days. Makes about 2½ cups.

Per tablespoon: 8 calories, .6 g protein, .9 g carbohydrates, .2 g total fat, .7 mg cholesterol, 9 mg sodium

MINT SAUCE

Pictured on page 64

Preparation time: About 15 minutes
Cooking time: About 30 seconds

Summertime parties call for a cool, refreshing dip like this one. Crisp, bright green pea pods complement the minty sour cream sauce in color, flavor, and texture.

- 1 **pound Chinese pea pods (snow or sugar peas), ends and strings removed (optional)**
- ¼ **cup *each* sour cream and mayonnaise**
- 2 **tablespoons coarsely chopped fresh mint leaves**

In a wide frying pan, cook peas, if used, in 2 inches boiling water just until bright green (about 30 seconds). Drain, immerse in ice water, and drain again. Set aside.

In a blender or food processor, whirl sour cream, mayonnaise, and mint until mint is finely chopped. Transfer to a small bowl and arrange on a platter with peas, if used. Makes about ½ cup.

Per tablespoon: 65 calories, .3 g protein, .5 g carbohydrates, 7 g total fat, 7 mg cholesterol, 43 mg sodium

SPRING ASPARAGUS DIP

Preparation time: About 10 minutes
Cooking time: About 2 minutes

Announce a special springtime event with this pale green vegetable dip. Accompany with red and yellow bell pepper strips for extra color and crunch.

- 1 **pound asparagus**
- 1 **green onion (including top), thinly sliced**
- 2 **tablespoons water**
- 1 **tablespoon salad oil**
- 1 **small package (3 oz.) cream cheese, at room temperature**
- ½ **cup sour cream**
- 1 **teaspoon lemon juice**
  Salt and pepper

Snap off and discard tough ends of asparagus; peel stalks, if desired. Cut asparagus into thin slices.

Combine asparagus, onion, water, and oil in a wide frying pan. Cover and cook over medium-high heat, stirring occasionally, until asparagus is tender crisp (about 2 minutes). Uncover and let cool briefly.

In a blender or food processor, whirl asparagus mixture, cream cheese, sour cream, and lemon juice until well blended. Season to taste with salt and pepper. Makes about 1½ cups.

Per tablespoon: 30 calories, .7 g protein, .7 g carbohydrates, 3 g total fat, 6 mg cholesterol, 13 mg sodium

SPINACH DIP

Preparation time: About 5 minutes
Chilling time: At least 2 hours

This simple dip can be put together in minutes and taken from the refrigerator when company comes. Serve with turnip slices, red bell pepper strips, and other raw vegetables.

- 1 **cup chopped cooked spinach or 1 package (10 oz.) frozen chopped spinach, thawed**
- ⅓ **cup coarsely chopped green onions (including tops)**
- ½ **cup lightly packed parsley sprigs**
- 1 **tablespoon lemon juice**
- 1 **cup sour cream**
- 1½ **teaspoons pepper**
- 2 **cloves garlic, minced or pressed**
  Salt

If using frozen spinach, drain well, squeezing out as much liquid as possible. Place spinach in a blender or

food processor with onions, parsley, lemon juice, sour cream, pepper, and garlic. Whirl until blended. Season to taste with salt. Cover and refrigerate for at least 2 hours or until next day. Makes 2 cups.

Per tablespoon: 18 calories, .4 g protein, .8 g carbohydrates, 2 g total fat, 3 mg cholesterol, 8 mg sodium

TARRAGON MAYONNAISE

Pictured on facing page

Preparation time: About 5 minutes

Fresh tarragon imparts a pungent flavor to this creamy herbed mayonnaise. You can make it up to two weeks before serving; offer it with crisp radishes and firm mushrooms.

- 1 **egg**
- 1 **tablespoon *each* Dijon mustard and tarragon vinegar**
- 2 **teaspoons lemon juice**
- 2 **tablespoons chopped fresh tarragon leaves or 1 teaspoon dry tarragon leaves**
- ¼ **teaspoon ground white pepper**
- ¾ **cup salad oil**
- ¼ **cup olive oil**
  Salt
  Tarragon sprigs (optional)

In a blender or food processor, whirl egg, mustard, vinegar, lemon juice, chopped tarragon, and pepper until well blended. Combine salad oil and olive oil. With motor running, add oil mixture, a few drops at a time at first, increasing to a slow, steady stream as mixture thickens. Season to taste with salt. If made ahead, cover and refrigerate for up to 2 weeks.

Transfer to a bowl. Garnish with tarragon sprigs, if desired. Makes about 1⅓ cups.

Per tablespoon: 96 calories, .3 g protein, .2 g carbohydrates, 11 g total fat, 10 mg cholesterol, 25 mg sodium

Autumn is the perfect time to offer herb-rich Tarragon Mayonnaise (recipe on facing page) and sweet-tart Apple Aïoli (recipe on page 14). Toast the harvest with Mulled Apple-Ginger Sparkler (recipe on page 91).

PIMENTO AÏOLI

Preparation time: About 5 minutes

Pimentos lend fiery orange color to this garlicky mayonnaise. Crisp, pale endive spears offer complementary taste, texture, and color.

- 1 jar (4 oz.) sliced pimentos, drained
- 1 large clove garlic
- ½ teaspoon dry mustard
- 2 teaspoons white wine vinegar
- 1 egg yolk
- ⅓ cup *each* olive and salad oil
  Salt

In a blender or food processor, whirl pimentos, garlic, mustard, vinegar, and egg yolk until blended. Combine olive oil and salad oil. With motor running, add oil mixture, a few drops at a time at first, increasing to a slow, steady stream as mixture thickens. Season to taste with salt. If made ahead, cover and refrigerate for up to 3 days. Makes about 1 cup.

Per tablespoon: 85 calories, .3 g protein, .5 g carbohydrates, 9 g total fat, 13 mg cholesterol, 2 mg sodium

Pictured on page 13
APPLE AÏOLI

Preparation time: About 5 minutes

Adding apple juice and lemon juice to aïoli gives the garlic dip a sweet-sour accent. Perfect for an autumn party, the dip is good with sliced pears and apples as well as with fresh vegetables.

- 3 tablespoons lemon juice
- 2 tablespoons thawed frozen apple juice concentrate
- 2 egg yolks
- 1 clove garlic, minced or pressed
  About ½ teaspoon ground cinnamon
- 1 cup salad oil

In a blender or food processor, whirl lemon juice, apple juice concentrate, egg yolks, garlic, and ½ teaspoon of the cinnamon until blended. With motor running, add oil, a few drops at a time at first, increasing to a slow, steady stream as mixture thickens.

Transfer to a bowl and sprinkle with additional cinnamon, if desired. Makes 1⅓ cups.

Per tablespoon: 101 calories, .3 g protein, .9 g carbohydrates, 11 g total fat, 20 mg cholesterol, 2 mg sodium

HOLLANDAISE

Preparation time: About 5 minutes
Cooking time: About 4 minutes

This quickly made hollandaise is delicious with crisp vegetables.

- 3 egg yolks, at room temperature
- 1½ tablespoons lemon juice
- ⅛ teaspoon ground red pepper (cayenne)
- 1 teaspoon Dijon mustard
- 1 cup (½ lb.) butter or margarine
  Salt

In a blender or food processor, whirl egg yolks, lemon juice, pepper, and mustard until blended; set aside. In a 1-quart pan, melt butter over medium heat until bubbling (do not let butter brown). With motor running, add butter to yolk mixture, a few drops at a time at first, increasing to a slow, steady stream as mixture thickens. Season to taste with salt. Makes about 1½ cups.

Per tablespoon: 76 calories, .4 g protein, .1 g carbohydrates, 8 g total fat, 47 mg cholesterol, 85 mg sodium

Hollandaise with Cucumber

Follow directions for **Hollandaise.** After seasoning, stir in 1 tablespoon *each* chopped **parsley** and **chives** and 1 small **cucumber,** peeled, seeded, and chopped. Makes about 2 cups.

Per tablespoon: 57 calories, .3 g protein, .2 g carbohydrates, 6 g total fat, 35 mg cholesterol, 64 mg sodium

TOASTED ALMOND MAYONNAISE

Preparation time: About 5 minutes
Cooking time: About 8 minutes

Take advantage of summer's bounty by offering baby vegetables, such as corn, carrots, and bok choy, with this rich mayonnaise. Toasted almonds add flavor to the egg yolk–based dip.

- Ground Toasted Almonds (recipe follows)
- 2 egg yolks
- 2 cloves garlic, minced or pressed
- 1½ tablespoons lemon juice
- ½ teaspoon sugar
- 1 to 4 tablespoons dry white wine
- 1 cup olive or salad oil
  Salt

Prepare Ground Toasted Almonds; set aside.

In a blender or food processor, whirl egg yolks, garlic, lemon juice, sugar, and 1 tablespoon of the wine until blended. With motor running, add oil, a few drops at a time at first, increasing to a slow, steady stream as mixture thickens. Stir in almonds. For a thinner consistency, add more wine. Season to taste with salt.

If made ahead, cover and refrigerate for up to 2 days. Makes 1½ cups.

Ground Toasted Almonds.
Spread ⅓ cup whole **unblanched almonds** in a 9- to 10-inch baking pan and bake in a 350° oven until golden under skin (about 8 minutes). Let cool. Whirl in a blender or food processor until finely ground.

Per tablespoon: 97 calories, .6 g protein, .6 g carbohydrates, 10 g total fat, 18 mg cholesterol, 1 mg sodium

BAGNA CAUDA

Preparation time: About 25 minutes
Cooking time: About 5 minutes

This northern Italian anchovy butter sauce (pronounced BAHN-yah COW-dah) contains more than a hint of garlic. Use it as a dip for fresh vegetables and crunchy bread.

- 1 cup (½ lb.) butter or margarine
- ½ cup olive oil
- 5 large cloves garlic, minced or pressed
- 2 tablespoons lemon juice
- 1½ teaspoons pepper
- 2 cans (2 oz. *each*) anchovy fillets

Heat butter, oil, garlic, lemon juice, and pepper in a 3- to 4-cup heatproof container over medium heat. Drain oil from anchovies into butter mixture; finely chop anchovies and stir into sauce.

Keep warm over a candle or alcohol flame, or reheat periodically; sauce may brown slightly, but do not let butter burn. Makes about 2 cups.

Per tablespoon: 94 calories, .9 g protein, .3 g carbohydrates, 10 g total fat, 17 mg cholesterol, 162 mg sodium

FISH ROE DIP

Preparation time: About 10 minutes
Chilling time: At least 2 hours

Red caviar is the key ingredient in this version of the Greek dip *taramasalata*. Crusty bread cubes and cucumber or zucchini slices are good scoopers.

- 4 sandwich-size slices white bread, crusts trimmed
- 1 small onion, grated
- 1 jar (4 oz.) red caviar, such as carp roe or red whitefish caviar, or 1 tube (about 3.3 oz.) red smoked carp roe paste
- ¼ cup lemon juice
- ½ cup *each* olive and salad oil

Soak bread in water to cover for 5 minutes; squeeze dry. In a blender or food processor, whirl bread, onion, caviar, and lemon juice until smooth. Combine olive oil and salad oil. With motor running, gradually add oil mixture, a few drops at a time at first, increasing to a slow, steady stream as mixture thickens. Cover and refrigerate for at least 2 hours or until next day. Makes 2 cups.

Per tablespoon: 77 calories, 1 g protein, 2 g carbohydrates, 7 g total fat, 21 mg cholesterol, 68 mg sodium

ASIAN EGGPLANT DIP

Preparation time: About 10 minutes
Cooking time: About 1 hour

Not for the timid, this eggplant purée is boldly seasoned with ginger, garlic, sesame oil, and chile. Serve on paper-thin crackers.

- 1 large eggplant (about 1½ lbs.), ends trimmed
- 2 cloves garlic
- 2 tablespoons soy sauce
- 2 tablespoons rice wine (mirin) or dry vermouth
- 1 tablespoon *each* minced fresh ginger, minced cilantro (coriander), and sesame oil
- ½ teaspoon crushed dried hot red chiles
  Salt

With a fork, pierce eggplant deeply in 10 to 12 places. Set in an 8- to 9-inch baking pan. Bake in a 350° oven until very soft when pressed (about 1 hour). Let cool. If desired, trim off and discard skin. Cut eggplant into large chunks.

Place eggplant, garlic, soy, wine, ginger, cilantro, oil, and chiles in a blender or food processor and whirl until fairly smooth; scrape container sides often. Season to taste with salt.

If made ahead, cover and refrigerate for up to 4 days. Serve at room temperature. Makes about 2 cups.

Per tablespoon: 13 calories, .3 g protein, 2 g carbohydrates, .4 g total fat, 0 mg cholesterol, 65 mg sodium

MOROCCAN EGGPLANT DIP

Preparation time: About 10 minutes
Cooking time: About 25 minutes
Chilling time: At least 2 hours

This versatile dip can be scooped on pumpernickel bread or served with fresh vegetables.

- 3 tablespoons olive oil
- 1 large eggplant (about 1½ lbs.), ends trimmed, diced
- 1 can (8 oz.) tomato sauce
- 2 cloves garlic, minced or pressed
- 1 large green bell pepper, stemmed, seeded, and chopped
- 1 tablespoon ground cumin
- ¼ teaspoon ground red pepper (cayenne)
- 2 teaspoons *each* sugar and salt
- ¼ cup red wine vinegar
- ¼ cup chopped cilantro (coriander)

Heat oil in a wide frying pan over medium heat. Add eggplant, tomato sauce, garlic, bell pepper, cumin, red pepper, sugar, salt, and vinegar. Cover and cook over medium heat for 20 minutes. Uncover, increase heat to high, and boil, stirring, until reduced to about 3 cups (about 5 more minutes). Let cool; then cover and refrigerate for at least 2 hours or until next day. Just before serving, stir in cilantro. Makes 3 cups.

Per tablespoon: 15 calories, .2 g protein, 2 g carbohydrates, .9 g total fat, 0 mg cholesterol, 121 mg sodium

Layer sour cream, green onions, bell peppers, and jack cheese over Guacamole (recipe on facing page) and easy-to-prepare Black Bean Dip (recipe on facing page); scoop up the Southwestern specialty with crisp jicama slices.

HUMMUS

Preparation time: About 5 minutes
Cooking time: About 3 minutes

This garlic-rich garbanzo dip can be made in minutes and is perfect at a barbecue. Offer Pita Crisps (recipe on page 18) with this Middle Eastern treat.

- ¼ **cup sesame seeds**
- 1 **can (15 oz.) garbanzo beans, drained (reserve liquid)**
- 4 **tablespoons olive oil**
- 3 **tablespoons lemon juice**
- 2 **cloves garlic**
  Salt and pepper

In a small frying pan, toast sesame seeds over medium heat, shaking pan often, until golden (about 3 minutes). Transfer seeds to a blender or food processor and add garbanzos, 2 tablespoons of the oil, lemon juice, garlic, and 6 tablespoons of the reserved garbanzo liquid. Whirl, adding more liquid if needed, until hummus is smooth but still thick enough to hold its shape. Season to taste with salt and pepper.

Transfer hummus to a shallow bowl. Drizzle with remaining 2 tablespoons oil. Makes 2 cups.

Per tablespoon: 38 calories, .9 g protein, 3 g carbohydrates, 2 g total fat, 0 mg cholesterol, 40 mg sodium

LAYERED KIDNEY BEAN DIP

Preparation time: About 15 minutes
Cooking time: About 4 minutes

You can build this multitiered dip quickly with marinated artichoke hearts and canned kidney beans. Let guests scoop up the dip with crisp celery sticks or Garlic Toast (recipe on page 18).

- 2 **teaspoons olive oil**
- 1 **clove garlic, minced or pressed**
- 2 **ounces prosciutto, chopped**
- 1 **tablespoon red wine vinegar**
- 1 **can (15½ oz.) kidney beans, drained (reserve liquid)**
- 1 **tablespoon minced fresh basil leaves**
- ⅛ **teaspoon pepper**
- 1 **jar (about 6 oz.) marinated artichoke hearts, drained and cut in half**
- 1 **cup (4 oz.) shredded provolone cheese**

Heat oil in a small frying pan over medium-high heat. Add garlic and prosciutto and cook, stirring, until prosciutto is crisp (about 4 minutes). Add vinegar and let cool.

In a large bowl, mash beans. Stir in ¼ cup of the reserved liquid from beans, prosciutto, basil, and pepper. Mound on a plate. Top with artichokes and sprinkle with cheese. Makes about 8 servings.

Per serving: 139 calories, 8 g protein, 11 g carbohydrates, 7 g total fat, 14 mg cholesterol, 567 mg sodium

Pictured on facing page
BLACK BEAN DIP

Preparation time: About 25 minutes
Cooking time: About 8 minutes

Serve this layered dip with jicama or tortilla chips (recipes on page 18).

- 1⅔ **cups Guacamole (recipe at right)**
- 6 **slices bacon, coarsely chopped**
- 1 **small onion, chopped**
- ½ **teaspoon chili powder**
- 1 **can (15 oz.) black beans, drained (reserve ⅓ cup of the liquid)**
- 1 **cup (4 oz.) shredded jack cheese**
- 1 *each* **small red and yellow bell peppers (or 2 of either), stemmed, seeded, and chopped**
- ¼ **cup thinly sliced green onions (including tops)**
  Jicama, peeled and cut into triangles (optional)
  Sour cream, cilantro (coriander) sprigs, and jalapeño chiles (optional)

Prepare Guacamole; set aside.

In an 8- to 10-inch frying pan, cook bacon, chopped onion, and chili powder over medium heat, stirring occasionally, until bacon is crisp (about 8 minutes). Drain and discard fat. Let cool.

In a large bowl, coarsely mash beans. Stir in reserved liquid and bacon mixture. Mound in center of a large plate; top with Guacamole. Sprinkle with cheese, bell peppers, and green onions. If desired, arrange jicama around edge and garnish dip with sour cream, cilantro, and chiles. Makes about 8 servings.

Per serving: 247 calories, 10 g protein, 18 g carbohydrates, 16 g total fat, 16 mg cholesterol, 534 mg sodium

Pictured on facing page
GUACAMOLE

Preparation time: About 10 minutes

Be sure to choose ripe, buttery avocados for this popular dip.

- 2 **large ripe avocados**
- 2 **to 3 tablespoons lemon or lime juice**
- 1 **clove garlic, minced or pressed**
- 1 **to 2 tablespoons chopped cilantro (coriander)**
- 2 **to 4 canned green chiles, seeded and chopped**
- 1 **medium-size tomato, peeled, seeded, and chopped**
  Minced jalapeño or serrano chiles (optional)
  Salt
  Cilantro (coriander) sprigs (optional)

Pit avocados and scoop out pulp; mash coarsely with a fork. Stir in lemon juice, garlic, chopped cilantro, green chiles, and tomato. Add jalapeño chiles to taste, if desired. Season to taste with salt.

Spoon into a bowl. Garnish with cilantro sprigs, if desired. Makes about 1⅔ cups.

Per tablespoon: 33 calories, .5 g protein, 2 g carbohydrates, 3 g total fat, 0 mg cholesterol, 52 mg sodium

Here's a simple way to add a special touch to a party with a minimum of fuss. Starting with purchased bread, corn tortillas, or even won ton skins, you can create savory toast rounds, crisp chips, or golden "crackers" to serve as holders for your favorite dips and spreads.

FRIED TORTILLA CHIPS

Preparation time: About 5 minutes
Cooking time: About 10 minutes

These all-purpose chips are the perfect scoop for Guacamole (recipe on page 17) or Salsa Fresca (recipe on facing page). For less fat, use our water-crisped variation.

> 12 **corn tortillas (6-in. diameter)**
> **Salad oil**
> **Salt**

Stack tortillas and cut into 6 wedges. In a deep 3- to 4-quart pan, heat about 1½ inches oil to 350°F on a deep-frying thermometer. Add tortillas, a batch at a time, and cook, turning occasionally, until crisp (about 30 seconds). Drain on paper towels. Season to taste with salt.

If made ahead, store in an airtight container for up to 2 days. Makes 6 dozen scoops.

Per scoop: 21 calories, .4 g protein, 2 g carbohydrates, 1 g total fat, 0 mg cholesterol, 9 mg sodium

Pictured on page 8
Water-crisped Tortilla Chips

Immerse 12 **corn tortillas** (6-in. diameter), one at a time, in water; drain briefly. Season to taste with **salt.** Stack and cut into 6 wedges. Arrange in a single layer on baking sheets. Bake in a 500° oven for 4 minutes. Turn and continue baking until crisp (about 1 more minute).

SIMPLE SCOOPS

If made ahead, store in an airtight container for up to 2 weeks. Makes 6 dozen scoops.

Per scoop: 11 calories, .4 g protein, 2 g carbohydrates, .2 g total fat, 0 mg cholesterol, 9 mg sodium

Pictured on page 21
GARLIC TOAST

Preparation time: About 5 minutes
Cooking time: About 3 minutes

Baguette slices brushed with garlic-flavored oil complement Prosciutto-topped Brie (recipe on page 20) and other spreads.

> 1 **clove garlic, minced or pressed**
> ¼ **cup olive oil**
> 2 **teaspoons finely chopped fresh oregano leaves or 1 teaspoon dry oregano leaves**
> 1 **small French baguette (8 oz.), sliced ¼ inch thick**

Mix garlic, oil, and oregano; set aside.

Place bread slices in a single layer on baking sheets. Broil about 4 inches below heat until golden (about 2 minutes). Remove from oven, turn, and brush tops with garlic mixture. Return to oven and continue broiling until lightly browned (about 1 more minute). Serve warm or at room temperature. Makes 2 dozen scoops.

Per scoop: 48 calories, .9 g protein, 5 g carbohydrates, 3 g total fat, .3 mg cholesterol, 55 mg sodium

PITA CRISPS

Preparation time: About 5 minutes
Cooking time: About 5 minutes

These crispy triangles are perfect with Hummus (recipe on page 17).

> 6 **pocket bread rounds (6-in. diameter)**
> 1 **clove garlic, minced or pressed**
> ¼ **cup olive oil**
> **Salt and pepper**

Split pocket breads to make 12 rounds. Combine garlic and oil and brush mixture over split sides. Season to taste with salt and pepper. Stack and cut into 6 to 8 wedges. Place in a single layer on baking sheets and bake in a 400° oven until crisp and golden (about 5 minutes). Makes 6 to 8 dozen scoops.

Per scoop: 18 calories, .4 g protein, 3 g carbohydrates, .7 g total fat, 0 mg cholesterol, 26 mg sodium

WON TON CRISPIES

Preparation time: About 5 minutes
Cooking time: About 10 minutes

Try this crisp cracker with Fresh Mushroom Pâté (recipe on page 30).

> 4 **tablespoons butter or margarine, melted**
> 20 **won ton skins**
> ½ **cup grated Parmesan cheese**

Brush 2 baking sheets with 1 tablespoon of the butter. Cut won ton skins in half; place about half the skins in a single layer on baking sheets. Brush with 1 more tablespoon butter; sprinkle with half the cheese. Bake in a 375° oven until golden (about 5 minutes). Repeat with remaining skins. Makes 40 scoops.

Per scoop: 25 calories, 1 g protein, 2 g carbohydrates, 2 g total fat, 4 mg cholesterol, 39 mg sodium

TROPICAL FRUIT SALSA

Preparation time: About 15 minutes

Fresh mango, pineapple, and honeydew are mixed into a colorful mélange enlivened with red pepper and cilantro. The dip can be stored for up to 2 days; it's delicious with barbecued chicken.

1 **firm-ripe mango, peeled and diced**
1 **cup *each* diced fresh pineapple and diced honeydew**
½ **cup diced red bell pepper**
⅓ **cup seasoned rice wine vinegar**
2 **tablespoons minced cilantro (coriander)**
½ **teaspoon crushed red pepper flakes**

Mix mango, pineapple, honeydew, bell pepper, vinegar, cilantro, and red pepper flakes. If made ahead, cover and refrigerate for up to 2 days. Makes 3½ cups.

Per tablespoon: 6 calories, 0 g protein, 2 g carbohydrates, 0 g total fat, 0 mg cholesterol, .7 mg sodium

TOMATILLO SALSA

Preparation time: About 20 minutes
Cooking time: About 15 minutes

Tomatillos combined with lime juice and chicken broth create a tangy alternative to traditional fresh salsa. Serve with thin slices of apple or jicama.

1¼ **pounds tomatillos, husks removed**
⅓ **cup chopped cilantro (coriander)**
1 **jalapeño or other small hot chile, stemmed**
¾ **cup regular-strength chicken broth**
⅓ **cup lime juice**
Salt

Rinse tomatillos. Arrange in a single layer on a baking sheet and bake in a 500° oven until slightly singed (about 15 minutes). Let cool.

In a blender or food processor, whirl tomatillos with cilantro and chile; stir in broth and lime juice. Season to taste with salt. If made ahead, cover and refrigerate for up to 2 days. Makes 3 cups.

Per tablespoon: 4 calories, .2 g protein, .6 g carbohydrates, .1 g total fat, 0 mg cholesterol, 16 mg sodium

SALSA FRESCA

Preparation time: About 10 minutes

It takes next to no time to make this classic Mexican condiment in the blender, but for a drier, chunkier texture, try making it by hand.

2 **cloves garlic**
½ **medium-size onion, quartered**
1 **or 2 jalapeño or other small hot chiles, stemmed and seeded**
¼ **cup lightly packed cilantro (coriander)**
1 **pound firm-ripe tomatoes, seeded**
2 **tablespoons salad oil**
Juice of 1 lime
Salt and pepper

To make in a blender or food processor: Whirl garlic, onion, chiles, cilantro, and tomatoes in a blender or food processor just until coarsely chopped. Add oil and lime juice; whirl until finely chopped. Season to taste with salt and pepper.

To make by hand: Using a sharp knife, mince garlic, onion, and chiles.

Finely chop cilantro and dice tomatoes. Combine in a nonmetallic bowl; add oil and lime juice. Season to taste with salt and pepper.

If made ahead, cover and refrigerate for up to 2 days. Makes 2 cups.

Per tablespoon: 11 calories, .1 g protein, .9 g carbohydrates, .9 g total fat, 0 mg cholesterol, 1 mg sodium

TOMATO RELISH

Preparation time: About 10 minutes
Cooking time: About 15 minutes

Blend tomatoes with fresh ginger, garlic, onion, and turmeric for an easy-to-prepare dip with an Asian accent. Serve with cucumber slices.

2 **to 4 small dried hot red chiles, stemmed and seeded**
2 **tablespoons water**
1 **large onion, quartered**
4 **cloves garlic**
2 **teaspoons chopped fresh ginger**
2 **tablespoons salad oil**
¼ **teaspoon turmeric**
1 **large can (28 oz.) tomatoes, drained**

In a blender or food processor, whirl chiles, water, onion, garlic, and ginger until puréed.

Heat oil in a wide frying pan over medium heat. Add onion mixture and turmeric and cook, stirring, until liquid has evaporated (about 5 minutes). Remove from heat.

Whirl tomatoes in blender until puréed. Add to onion mixture and cook, stirring occasionally, until reduced to about 2 cups (about 10 minutes). Serve at room temperature. Makes about 2 cups.

Per tablespoon: 15 calories, .3 g protein, 2 g carbohydrates, .9 g total fat, 0 mg cholesterol, 41 mg sodium

FETA CHEESE SPREAD

Preparation time: About 5 minutes

Nothing could be simpler, or tastier, than this three-ingredient cheese spread. Offer it with crusty Italian bread and prosciutto.

    8 ounces feta cheese, crumbled
    2 large packages (8 oz. *each*) cream
       cheese, at room temperature
    ½ cup whipping cream

Beat feta and cream cheese until blended. Stir in cream. If made ahead, cover and refrigerate for up to 5 days. Makes about 2½ cups.

Per tablespoon: 63 calories, 2 g protein, .6 g carbohydrates, 6 g total fat, 21 mg cholesterol, 98 mg sodium

MELTED BRIE IN CRUST

Preparation time: About 15 minutes
Cooking time: About 20 minutes

Bake Brie in a loaf of bread; then watch both the melted cheese and the container disappear.

    1 round or oval loaf French bread
       (about 1 lb.)
    ⅓ cup olive oil or melted butter
    2 cloves garlic, minced or pressed
    1 to 1½ pounds ripe Brie, Camem-
       bert, or St. André cheese, rind
       trimmed, if desired

Using a serrated knife and your fingers, remove center of bread in a single piece, leaving a shell about ½ inch thick on sides and bottom. Around rim of shell, make 1½-inch-deep cuts about 1½ inches apart. Cut bread pulled from loaf into 1½- by 2-inch chunks about ½ inch thick.

Mix oil and garlic. Brush inside of shell with about 3 tablespoons of the oil mixture; brush bread chunks with remaining mixture.

Cut cheese into chunks and place in bread shell. Place filled shell and bread chunks in a single layer on two 10- by 15-inch baking sheets. Bake in a 350° oven for 10 minutes. Remove bread chunks and let cool on a wire rack. Continue baking filled shell until cheese is melted (about 10 more minutes).

Place shell on a serving board; surround with toasted bread chunks. Makes about 1 dozen servings.

Per serving: 321 calories, 13 g protein, 21 g carbohydrates, 20 g total fat, 48 mg cholesterol, 517 mg sodium

MELTED BRIE WITH WINTER FRUITS

Preparation time: About 15 minutes
Soaking time: About 2 hours
Cooking time: About 25 minutes

A mixture of dried and fresh fruits soaked in wine is tucked into a round of Brie and then baked. Serve the elegant spread on toasted baguette slices.

    ¾ cup chopped pitted dates
    1 *each* small apple and small
       firm-ripe pear, peeled, cored,
       and diced
    ½ cup *each* currants and chopped
       pecans
    ⅓ cup rosé wine or apple juice
    1 whole firm-ripe Brie cheese
       (2 lbs.), chilled

Mix dates, apple, pear, currants, pecans, and wine. Set aside until fruit is softened (about 2 hours).

Cut cheese in half crosswise. Place a portion, cut side up, in a greased shallow baking dish just slightly larger than cheese. Spread with 2¼ cups of the fruit mixture. Cover with remaining cheese, cut side down. Spoon remaining fruit onto center of

cheese. (At this point, you may cover and refrigerate for up to 2 days.)

Bake, uncovered, in a 350° oven until cheese is melted at edges and warm in center (about 25 minutes). Makes about 16 servings.

Per serving: 256 calories, 12 g protein, 13 g carbohydrates, 18 g total fat, 57 mg cholesterol, 358 mg sodium

Pictured on facing page

PROSCIUTTO-TOPPED BRIE

Preparation time: About 10 minutes
Cooking time: About 12 minutes

There's a surprise hidden in this hot cheese spread: a layer of sun-dried tomatoes. Offer the baked Brie with celery sticks and garlicky French bread slices.

    1 whole firm-ripe Brie cheese
       (8 oz.), chilled
    3 tablespoons finely chopped
       dried tomatoes packed in oil,
       drained (reserve oil)
    1 ounce thinly sliced prosciutto,
       slivered

Cut cheese in half crosswise. Place a portion, cut side up, in a greased shallow baking dish just slightly larger than cheese. Spread with tomatoes. Cover with remaining cheese, cut side down. Mix prosciutto with 1 tablespoon of the reserved oil from tomatoes and mound over cheese. (At this point, you may cover and refrigerate until next day.)

Bake, uncovered, in a 350° oven until cheese is melted at edges and warm in center (about 12 minutes). Makes about 4 servings.

Per serving: 268 calories, 13 g protein, 2 g carbohydrates, 23 g total fat, 61 mg cholesterol, 742 mg sodium

Hot and cold cheese spreads are crowd pleasers.
Stuffed Camembert (recipe on page 22), filled with a
variety of cheeses and onions, and Prosciutto-topped
Brie (recipe on facing page), stuffed with dried tomatoes,
will disappear on crackers, celery, and Garlic Toast
(recipe on page 18).

LAZY LIPTAUER CHEESE

Preparation time: About 5 minutes

This version of the famous Austro-Hungarian cheese spread is made with a few shortcuts. The creamy blend is best served on dense-textured pumpernickel bread and topped with crisp dill pickle slices.

- 1 cup small curd cottage cheese
- 1 small package (3 oz.) cream cheese, at room temperature
- 2 teaspoons paprika
- 1 teaspoon *each* dry mustard and caraway seeds

Beat cottage cheese, cream cheese, paprika, mustard, and caraway seeds until smoothly blended. If made ahead, cover and refrigerate for up to 2 days. Makes about 1¼ cups.

Per tablespoon: 28 calories, 2 g protein, .6 g carbohydrates, 2 g total fat, 6 mg cholesterol, 59 mg sodium

WALNUT CHEESE SPREAD

Preparation time: About 10 minutes
Cooking time: About 8 minutes
Chilling time: At least 2 hours

Toasted walnuts add texture as well as flavor to this cream cheese and olive spread. You can make it up to 2 days in advance; serve with Pita Crisps (recipe on page 18).

- ½ cup chopped walnuts
- 10 pimento-stuffed green olives
- 1 large package (8 oz.) cream cheese, at room temperature
- 2 teaspoons liquid from olives
- 4 green onions (including tops), chopped

Spread walnuts in a shallow baking pan. Bake in a 350° oven until lightly browned (about 8 minutes). Let cool briefly.

Meanwhile, finely chop olives. Beat cream cheese with olive liquid until fluffy. Stir in nuts, olives, and onions. Cover and refrigerate for at least 2 hours or up to 2 days. Makes 1½ cups.

Per tablespoon: 52 calories, 1 g protein, .9 g carbohydrates, 5 g total fat, 10 mg cholesterol, 67 mg sodium

---

Pictured on page 8

PESTO CHEESE SPREAD

Preparation time: About 5 minutes
Cooking time: About 6 minutes

With purchased pesto sauce, you can whip up this tasty cheese spread in minutes. Serve with thick breadsticks and sliced vegetables.

- ⅓ cup pine nuts or slivered almonds
- 8 ounces ricotta cheese, at room temperature
- 8 ounces Neufchâtel cheese or mascarpone, at room temperature
- ⅓ cup pesto, purchased or homemade
  Salt
  Basil sprigs (optional)

Spread pine nuts in a shallow baking pan. Bake in a 350° oven until golden (about 6 minutes). Let cool briefly.

Meanwhile, beat ricotta, Neufchâtel, and pesto until well blended; season to taste with salt. Stir in half the nuts and mound in a bowl. If made ahead, cover and refrigerate until next day; store remaining nuts at room temperature.

Sprinkle with remaining pine nuts and garnish with basil, if desired. Serve at room temperature. Makes about 2 cups.

Per tablespoon: 45 calories, 2 g protein, 1 g carbohydrates, 4 g total fat, 8 mg cholesterol, 48 mg sodium

---

Pictured on page 21

STUFFED CAMEMBERT

Preparation time: About 15 minutes
Chilling time: At least 1 day

Camembert becomes the holder for a singular spread made with four different cheeses. Serve with a variety of your favorite crackers.

- 1 whole medium-ripe Camembert cheese (about 8 oz.), chilled
- 1 wedge (1¼ oz.) blue-veined cheese, crumbled, at room temperature
- 1 cup (4 oz.) shredded Cheddar cheese, at room temperature
- 1 small package (3 oz.) cream cheese, at room temperature
- 1 small clove garlic, minced or pressed
- 1 teaspoon *each* fresh basil and fresh oregano leaves or ½ teaspoon *each* dry basil and dry oregano leaves
- 1 tablespoon chopped parsley
- 2 tablespoons butter or margarine, at room temperature
- ¼ cup thinly sliced green onions (including tops)

With a sharp knife, cut around top of Camembert, about ¼ inch in from edge, cutting down about ½ inch into cheese. With a spoon, carefully scoop out cheese (including top rind), leaving a ¼-inch-thick shell. Wrap shell and refrigerate.

Place blue-veined cheese, Cheddar, cream cheese, and removed Camembert in a large bowl; then beat until smooth and creamy. Beat in garlic, basil, oregano, parsley, and butter; stir in onions. Mound cheese mixture in Camembert shell. Cover and refrigerate for at least a day or up to 4 days.

Serve at room temperature. Makes about 8 servings.

Per serving: 223 calories, 11 g protein, 1 g carbohydrates, 19 g total fat, 59 mg cholesterol, 468 mg sodium

CHÈVRE WITH MINT & CUMIN

Preparation time: About 5 minutes

Add a special touch to purchased cheese by drizzling it with extra-virgin olive oil. Serve with toasted baguette slices.

- 1 log- or cake-shaped unripened goat cheese (12 oz.), such as Bûcheron
- 3 tablespoons extra-virgin olive oil
- ½ teaspoon cumin seeds, crushed
- 2 tablespoons chopped fresh mint leaves
- ¼ teaspoon ground red pepper (cayenne) or to taste

Place cheese on a small plate. Drizzle with oil. Sprinkle with cumin, mint, and pepper. Makes about 6 servings.

Per serving: 267 calories, 11 g protein, 4 g carbohydrates, 23 g total fat, 52 mg cholesterol, 350 mg sodium

Pictured on page 53

PEPPERED CHÈVRE WITH PEARS

Preparation time: About 10 minutes

Roll fresh goat cheese in a savory blend of peppercorns, coriander, and lemon peel. Then spread the tangy coated log on pear slices.

- ½ teaspoon *each* black peppercorns, white peppercorns, and coriander seeds
- ½ teaspoon minced lemon peel (yellow part only)
- ½ teaspoon fresh lemon thyme leaves (optional)
- 1 log- or cake-shaped unripened goat cheese (4 oz.), such as Bûcheron
- 2 small firm-ripe Bartlett pears
  Lemon juice
  Lemon thyme sprigs (optional)
  Lemon wedges (optional)

In a spice grinder or blender, whirl black and white peppercorns, coriander, lemon peel, and, if desired, thyme leaves until seasonings form a coarse powder.

Transfer to wax paper. Roll cheese in mixture, pressing in seasonings on all sides. Core pears, cut each into 8 wedges, and sprinkle lightly with lemon juice.

Place cheese on a plate; garnish with thyme sprigs, if desired. Arrange pears and, if desired, lemon wedges beside cheese. Spread cheese on pear wedges. Makes 16 appetizers.

Per appetizer: 36 calories, 1 g protein, 3 g carbohydrates, 2 g total fat, 7 mg cholesterol, 44 mg sodium

NUT-STUDDED GARLIC-HERB CHEESE

Preparation time: About 10 minutes
Chilling time: At least 2 hours
Cooking time: About 8 minutes

You can make your own herb spread by adding savory and garlic to cream cheese. For extra appeal, shape the mixture into a ball and cover with almonds.

- 1 large package (8 oz.) cream cheese, at room temperature
- 3 tablespoons lemon juice
- 1 teaspoon dry winter or summer savory
- ¼ to ½ teaspoon freshly ground pepper
- 1 clove garlic, minced or pressed
- ½ cup slivered almonds

Beat cream cheese until smooth. Beat in lemon juice, savory, pepper, and garlic. Shape mixture into a ball, wrap in wax paper or plastic wrap, and refrigerate for at least 2 hours or up to 2 days.

Shortly before serving, spread almonds in a shallow pan. Bake in a 350° oven until golden (about 8 minutes); let cool. Stud top and sides of cheese with almonds. Serve at room temperature. Makes about 1¼ cups.

Per tablespoon: 60 calories, 2 g protein, 1 g carbohydrates, 6 g total fat, 12 mg cholesterol, 34 mg sodium

GORGONZOLA CHEESE TORTA

Preparation time: About 20 minutes
Chilling time: At least 1 hour

Butter-enriched cream cheese tempers the robust strength of Gorgonzola in this multitiered mold. Serve the simple spread with crisp crackers and sliced pears.

- 1 large package (8 oz.) cream cheese, at room temperature
- 1 cup (½ lb.) unsalted butter, at room temperature
- 12 ounces Gorgonzola or other blue-veined cheese, finely crumbled

Beat cream cheese and butter until very smoothly blended; set aside.

Cut two 18-inch squares of cheesecloth (or an 18-inch square of unbleached muslin); moisten with water, wring dry, and lay each out flat, one on top of the other. Use cloth to smoothly line a 4- to 5-cup straight-sided plain mold, such as a charlotte mold, loaf pan, or terrine; drape excess cloth over rim of mold.

Spread a third of the Gorgonzola in an even layer in mold. Top with a third of the cream cheese mixture, spreading evenly. Repeat layers, using all ingredients. Fold cloth over top and press down lightly to compact. Refrigerate for at least 1 hour or up to 5 days.

Grasp ends of cloth and lift torta from mold. Invert onto a plate and gently pull off cloth. Makes 16 servings.

Per serving: 226 calories, 6 g protein, .9 g carbohydrates, 23 g total fat, 63 mg cholesterol, 340 mg sodium

Easy on the host, Dried Tomato Torta (recipe on facing page) can be made well in advance of the party. Serve the creamy cheese spread on Pita Crisps (recipe on page 18) or crunchy baguette slices.

DRIED TOMATO TORTA

Pictured on facing page

Preparation time: About 20 minutes
Chilling time: About 20 minutes

Sun-dried tomatoes explain the bold color and unique flavor of this rich cheese spread. Serve on Garlic Toast (recipe on page 18) or toasted pita triangles and top with reserved tomato strips and basil leaves.

- 1 **large package (8 oz.) cream cheese, at room temperature**
- 1 **cup (½ lb.) unsalted butter, at room temperature**
- 1 **cup (about 4 oz.) freshly grated Parmesan cheese**
- ½ **cup dried tomatoes packed in oil, drained (reserve oil)**
  About 2 cups lightly packed basil leaves

Beat cream cheese, butter, and Parmesan cheese until very smoothly blended.

Cut 4 of the tomatoes into thin strips; set aside. In a blender or food processor, whirl remaining tomatoes, 2 tablespoons of the reserved oil from tomatoes, and about ½ cup of the cheese mixture until very smoothly puréed. Add purée mixture to cheese mixture and beat until blended. Cover and refrigerate until firm enough to shape (about 20 minutes).

Mound cheese on a platter. If made ahead, cover and refrigerate for up to 3 days.

Arrange basil and reserved tomato strips around torta. Makes 16 servings.

Per serving: 225 calories, 4 g protein, 3 g carbohydrates, 22 g total fat, 51 mg cholesterol, 320 mg sodium

BLACK CAVIAR PIE

Preparation time: About 25 minutes
Chilling time: At least 2 hours

A mustardy egg salad forms the crust of this creamy rich pie; black caviar tops the multilayered offering. Put thin slices of the pie on crackers or dark pumpernickel bread.

- 1 **jar (3 to 4 oz.) black lumpfish or whitefish caviar**
  Mustard Eggs (recipe follows)
- 1 **cup chopped green onions (including tops)**
- 1 **jar (2 oz.) sliced pimentos, drained**
- 1 **large package (8 oz.) cream cheese, at room temperature**
- ⅔ **cup sour cream**
  Dill sprigs
  Thin lemon slices

Empty caviar into a fine wire strainer and rinse with cold water; let drain. Cover and refrigerate. Meanwhile, prepare Mustard Eggs and spread in a 9-inch tart pan with a removable bottom. Sprinkle with onions and pimentos. Cover and refrigerate for 1 hour.

Mix cream cheese and sour cream until blended. Spoon about two-thirds of the mixture into pan. Using a pastry tube with a star tip, pipe remaining cream cheese mixture decoratively around edge. Cover and refrigerate for at least 1 hour or until next day.

Just before serving, remove sides of pan and spoon caviar into center of pie. Decorate with dill sprigs and lemon slices. Makes 16 servings.

Mustard Eggs. In a blender or food processor, whirl 6 **hard-cooked eggs;** ⅓ cup **butter** or margarine, at room temperature; 2 teaspoons *each* **Dijon mustard** and **white wine vinegar;** and 1 tablespoon chopped **fresh dill** or 1 teaspoon dill weed until smooth. Season to taste with **salt.**

Per serving: 151 calories, 5 g protein, 2 g carbohydrates, 14 g total fat, 146 mg cholesterol, 222 mg sodium

QUICK CHICKEN LIVER PÂTÉ

Preparation time: About 8 minutes
Cooking time: About 10 minutes
Chilling time: At least 3 hours

Present this smooth, thyme-accented spread in an attractive terrine or crock with thin slices of French bread alongside.

- 1 **cup (½ lb.) plus 2 teaspoons butter or margarine, at room temperature**
- 3 **green onions (including tops), thinly sliced**
- 1 **pound chicken livers**
- ½ **cup dry red wine**
- ¼ **teaspoon salt**
- ⅛ **teaspoon *each* dry thyme leaves and pepper**
- 2 **tablespoons chopped parsley**

In a wide frying pan, melt the 2 teaspoons butter over medium-high heat. Add onions and cook, stirring, until soft (about 3 minutes). Add chicken livers; cook, turning, until browned (about 3 more minutes). Stir in wine, salt, thyme, and pepper; reduce heat and simmer for 3 minutes. Stir in parsley.

Transfer mixture to a blender or food processor and whirl until smooth. Dice remaining 1 cup butter; with motor running, drop into blender, a few pieces at a time, and whirl until well combined. Cover and refrigerate for at least 3 hours or up to 4 days. Makes about 3 cups.

Per tablespoon: 48 calories, 2 g protein, .4 g carbohydrates, 4 g total fat, 52 mg cholesterol, 60 mg sodium

When the urge for a quick nibble strikes, you'll be glad to have these irresistible morsels on hand in the kitchen. All can be prepared in advance and stored from one day to two weeks before serving.

Whether you try seasoned nuts, candied popcorn, or crispy chips, you'll find these tempting edibles effortless to make. The hardest part is keeping enough of them around.

MAKE-AHEAD MUNCHIES

SWEET SPICED PISTACHIOS

Preparation time: About 5 minutes
Cooking time: About 10 minutes

Although delicious alone, pistachios become crisp sweets when glazed with melted sugar and spices.

- 1 **cup shelled salted pistachios**
- ¼ **cup sugar**
- ½ **teaspoon ground cinnamon**
- ½ **teaspoon ground mace or ground nutmeg**

In a wide frying pan, toast pistachios over medium heat, shaking pan often, until golden (about 5 minutes). Sprinkle with sugar, cinnamon, and mace. Cook, stirring, until sugar is melted and nuts are glossy (about 5 more minutes). Pour onto a sheet of foil and let cool. Break nuts apart. Store airtight for up to a week. Makes about 1½ cups.

Per ¼ cup: 156 calories, 4 g protein, 14 g carbohydrates, 10 g total fat, 0 mg cholesterol, 2 mg sodium

CANDIED WALNUTS

Preparation time: About 10 minutes
Cooking time: About 8 minutes

Sugar and soy sauce coat walnut halves with a dark, crunchy covering. You can make this Chinese treat in a wok or frying pan.

- 2 **cups (about 7 oz.) walnut halves**
- 1 **tablespoon soy sauce**
- ¼ **cup *each* granulated sugar and powdered sugar**
  Salad oil

SWEET & SPICY ALMOND BRITTLE

Preparation time: About 5 minutes
Cooking time: About 10 minutes

This sugar-glazed almond confection boasts a Southwestern accent: it's sparked with chili powder and ground red pepper.

- 1 **tablespoon chili powder**
- ½ **teaspoon *each* salt and ground red pepper (cayenne)**
- 3 **tablespoons salad oil**
- ½ **cup sugar**
- 2 **cups blanched almonds**

Combine chili powder, salt, and pepper. Set aside.

Heat oil in a wide frying pan over medium-high heat. Add sugar and cook, stirring, until sugar is melted and begins to turn golden (about 4 minutes). Add almonds and cook, stirring, until sugar is a rich caramel color (about 4 more minutes). Add chili powder mixture and cook, stirring, for 1 more minute; be careful not to scorch nuts.

Immediately pour almonds onto a large sheet of foil, spreading so nuts are in a single layer. Let harden. Break into small pieces. Store airtight for up to 2 weeks. Makes 4 cups.

Per ¼ cup: 155 calories, 4 g protein, 10 g carbohydrates, 12 g total fat, 0 mg cholesterol, 75 mg sodium

In a 3- to 4-quart pan, cook walnuts in 2 quarts boiling water for 3 minutes. Drain well. Return to pan and mix with soy. Then stir in granulated and powdered sugars.

In a wok or wide frying pan, heat about 1½ inches oil to 275°F on a deep-frying thermometer. Add nut mixture and cook, stirring often, until nuts are deep golden brown (about 5 minutes). Lift out with a slotted spoon and place on a chilled 10- by 15-inch baking pan. Using oiled chopsticks or forks, immediately separate nuts. Let cool. Blot off excess oil with paper towels. Break nuts apart, if necessary.

Immediately store airtight for up to a week. Makes 2 cups.

Per ¼ cup: 229 calories, 4 g protein, 15 g carbohydrates, 19 g total fat, 0 mg cholesterol, 131 mg sodium

SPICED PECANS

Preparation time: About 5 minutes
Cooking time: About 3 minutes

Pecans, a favorite in the South, benefit from spicy Southern seasonings. The result will be enjoyed anywhere.

- ½ **teaspoon *each* salt, paprika, and ground red pepper (cayenne)**
- 1 **teaspoon ground white pepper**
- 1 **tablespoon fresh or dry rosemary**
- 2 **tablespoons butter or margarine**
- 1 **tablespoon olive oil**
- 10 **ounces (about 2½ cups) pecan halves**
- 1 **tablespoon Worcestershire**
- ½ **teaspoon liquid hot pepper seasoning**

Combine salt, paprika, red pepper, white pepper, and rosemary. Set aside.

Heat butter and oil in a wide frying pan over medium-high heat. When butter is melted, add pecans and cook, stirring, until slightly darker in color (about 1 minute). Add Worcestershire, hot pepper seasoning, and salt mixture. Continue cooking, stirring, until pecans are well browned (about 1½ more minutes); be careful not to scorch nuts. Let cool. Store airtight for up to 2 days. Makes 2½ cups.

Per ¼ cup: 225 calories, 2 g protein, 6 g carbohydrates, 23 g total fat, 6 mg cholesterol, 156 mg sodium

CURRIED RAISINS, PEANUTS & BANANA CHIPS

Preparation time: About 5 minutes
Cooking time: About 2 minutes

This spicy dried fruit and nut combination blends curried raisins and banana chips with peanuts. Dust the lively party mix with nutmeg.

¼ **cup saiad oil**
1½ **teaspoons curry powder**
 1 **cup raisins**
 1 **cup** *each* **salted dry-roasted peanuts and dry banana chips**
    Ground nutmeg

Heat oil in a wide frying pan over medium-high heat. Add curry and cook, stirring, just until curry darkens slightly (about 30 seconds). Add raisins and cook, stirring, until puffed (about 1 more minute). Add peanuts and banana chips and cook, stirring, until coated. Pour onto paper towels. Blot gently with more paper towels and sprinkle with nutmeg. Store airtight until next day. Makes 3 cups.

Per ¼ cup: 174 calories, 4 g protein, 20 g carbohydrates, 11 g total fat, 0 mg cholesterol, 108 mg sodium

SWEET POTATO CHIPS

Preparation time: About 15 minutes
Cooking time: About 20 minutes

Here's a crunchy, distinctly sweeter alternative to regular potato chips. Be sure to cut the potatoes into uniform-size slices and cook in small batches.

 2 **large (about 2 lbs.** *total***) sweet potatoes or yams, peeled**
    Salad oil
    Salt

Rinse potatoes and pat dry. To cut slices about ¹⁄₁₆ inch thick, use a food slicer with an adjustable blade; push or hold potatoes crosswise to blade to cut rounds. For thicker, ⅛-inch slices, adjust blade on a manually operated slicer to this dimension or use slicing blade (about 3mm size) of a food processor and apply pressure lightly but evenly while cutting. Pat dry.

In a deep 3- to 4-quart pan, heat about 1½ inches oil to 300°F on a deep-frying thermometer. With a slotted spoon, lower potatoes, a spoonful at a time, into oil (do not crowd). Cook, turning about every 2 minutes, until chips are lightly browned (about 3 minutes for thin slices, longer for thicker ones). Lift out with a slotted spoon and drain on paper towels.

Season to taste with salt. Store airtight for up to 5 days. Makes about 3 quarts.

Per ¼ cup: 29 calories, .2 g protein, 3 g carbohydrates, 2 g total fat, 0 mg cholesterol, 2 mg sodium

BAKED CANDIED POPCORN

Preparation time: About 5 minutes
Cooking time: About 20 minutes

Peanuts lend added crunch to this favorite popcorn treat.

¼ **cup salad oil**
 1 **cup popcorn kernels**
1½ **cups salted or unsalted dry-roasted peanuts**
½ **cup (¼ lb.) butter or margarine**
½ **cup light or dark molasses**
½ **cup honey**

Heat oil in a 5- to 6-quart pan over medium-high heat. Add popcorn kernels, cover, and cook, shaking pan occasionally, until kernels have nearly stopped popping (about 6 minutes). Pour into a large bowl; discard any unpopped kernels. Stir in peanuts.

In same pan, melt butter over low heat. Add molasses and honey, increase heat to high, and cook, stirring, until bubbles begin to form (about 5 minutes); immediately pour over popped corn mixture, stirring to coat evenly.

Spread into two 10- by 15-inch baking pans. Bake in a 350° oven, stirring often, until coating is slightly darker (about 8 minutes, longer if margarine is used); switch pan positions halfway through cooking. Let cool. Store airtight for up to 3 days. Makes 6 quarts.

Per ¼ cup: 44 calories, .8 g protein, 5 g carbohydrates, 3 g total fat, 3 mg cholesterol, 30 mg sodium

CREAMY BRAUNSCHWEIGER APPETIZER

Preparation time: About 5 minutes
Chilling time: At least 4 hours

Spread this simplified pâté-like appetizer on pumpernickel or cocktail-size rye rounds.

½ **pound braunschweiger or other liver sausage, casing removed**
1 **cup sour cream**
1 **teaspoon Worcestershire**
6 **green onions (including tops), chopped**
  About ⅓ cup chopped parsley
3 **drops liquid hot pepper seasoning**
2 **to 3 tablespoons prepared horseradish**

Cut sausage into chunks. In a blender or food processor, whirl sausage, sour cream, Worcestershire, onions, ⅓ cup of the parsley, hot pepper seasoning, and horseradish until smooth and creamy. Transfer to a bowl. Cover and refrigerate for at least 4 hours or up to 2 days.

Garnish with additional parsley, if desired. Makes 2½ cups.

Per tablespoon: 34 calories, 1 g protein, .7 g carbohydrates, 3 g total fat, 11 mg cholesterol, 71 mg sodium

QUICK TUNA-ANCHOVY SPREAD

Preparation time: About 5 minutes
Marinating time: At least 20 minutes

By taking advantage of bottled dressing and other ingredients easily kept on hand, you can have this zesty spread ready to serve in less than half an hour.

1 **can (7 oz.) chunk-style tuna, drained**
1 **can (2 oz.) anchovy fillets, drained**
⅛ **teaspoon *each* dry mustard and dry oregano leaves**
  Dash of ground red pepper (cayenne)
1 **tablespoon pickle relish**
1 **teaspoon lemon juice**
¼ **cup bottled French dressing**
  Lemon slice (optional)
  Chopped parsley (optional)

Break tuna into bite-size pieces. Coarsely chop anchovies and add to tuna with mustard, oregano, pepper, pickle relish, lemon juice, and French dressing. Toss lightly. Transfer to a dish. Cover and refrigerate for at least 20 minutes or until next day.

Garnish with lemon and sprinkle with parsley, if desired. Makes about 2¼ cups.

Per tablespoon: 36 calories, 3 g protein, .8 g carbohydrates, 2 g total fat, 3 mg cholesterol, 161 mg sodium

POTTED SHRIMP WITH CHERVIL

Preparation time: About 25 minutes
Chilling time: At least 2 hours

A favorite for afternoon tea in England, this delicate shrimp butter is a perfect appetizer anytime. Try serving it with buttery crackers or toasted baguette slices.

¾ **pound small cooked shrimp**
½ **cup (¼ lb.) butter or margarine, at room temperature**
1½ **tablespoons lime or lemon juice**
¼ **teaspoon salt**
⅛ **teaspoon ground white pepper**
¼ **cup lightly packed fresh chervil**

In a blender or food processor, whirl shrimp, butter, lime juice, salt, and pepper until mixture is well combined. Add chervil and whirl until blended. Cover and refrigerate for at least 2 hours or until next day. Serve at room temperature. Makes about 2 cups.

Per tablespoon: 36 calories, 2 g protein, .1 g carbohydrates, 3 g total fat, 29 mg cholesterol, 70 mg sodium

DILLED SHRIMP MOUSSE

Preparation time: About 15 minutes
Cooking time: About 2 minutes
Chilling time: At least 4 hours

Use your favorite mold to showcase this creamy pink concoction. The dill-accented shrimp spread is delicious on thin slices of whole-grain bread.

¾ **cup tomato juice**
1 **envelope unflavored gelatin**
1 **cup sour cream**
¼ **teaspoon Worcestershire**
1 **tablespoon lemon juice**
1½ **teaspoons dill weed**
½ **pound small cooked shrimp**
16 **butter lettuce leaves, washed and crisped**
  Dill sprigs (optional)
1 **cinnamon stick (½ in. long), optional**

Pour tomato juice into a 1- to 1½-quart pan; sprinkle with gelatin and let stand for 5 minutes to soften. Place pan over low heat and cook, stirring, until gelatin is dissolved. Remove from heat and let cool.

In a bowl, beat gelatin mixture, sour cream, Worcestershire, lemon juice, and dill weed until well blended. Chop half the shrimp and add to sour cream mixture. Pour into a 2½- to 3-cup mold. Cover and refrigerate for at least 4 hours or until next day.

Unmold onto a plate. Arrange lettuce and remaining shrimp around mousse. Garnish with dill sprigs and cinnamon stick, if desired. Makes 2½ cups.

Per tablespoon: 66 calories, 5 g protein, 2 g carbohydrates, 4 g total fat, 45 mg cholesterol, 110 mg sodium

Holiday parties are easy to orchestrate when you offer a medley of simple-to-prepare spreads: Creamy Braunschweiger Appetizer (recipe on facing page), Dilled Shrimp Mousse (recipe on facing page), Sweet & Sour Onion Spread (recipe on page 31), and Quick Tuna-Anchovy Spread (recipe on facing page).

TURKEY RILLETTES

Preparation time: About 30 minutes
Cooking time: About 4 hours

The French make rillettes (pro-nounced ree-YET) with pork, duck, or goose and an abundance of fat. This leaner version is made with turkey thigh meat instead. Thick slices of French bread are the perfect ac-companiment.

- 3   to 3½ pounds turkey thighs
- ½   teaspoon *each* pepper and dry thyme leaves
- ¼   teaspoon *each* dry sage leaves and dry marjoram leaves
- 1   clove garlic, minced or pressed
- ¼   cup finely chopped shallots
- ⅔   cup dry white wine
- ¼   cup unsalted butter or marga-rine, at room temperature
      Salt

Place turkey in a 4- to 5-quart pan and add pepper, thyme, sage, marjo-ram, garlic, and shallots; pour in wine. Cover and bake in a 250° oven until meat falls apart when prodded with a fork (about 4 hours).

Drain and reserve juices, refriger-ate until cool, and then skim and dis-card fat. Meanwhile, discard skin and bones from turkey and shred meat; then chop.

Mix meat, juices, and butter until well blended. Season to taste with salt. Spoon mixture into a 5½- to 6½-cup terrine or crock.

If made ahead, cover and refriger-ate for up to 3 days. Serve at room temperature. Makes about 5½ cups.

Per tablespoon: 14 calories, 1 g protein, .1 g carbohydrates, .8 g total fat, 7 mg cholesterol, 6 mg sodium

---

Pictured on page 8
BAKED VEGETABLES PROVENÇAL

Preparation time: About 20 minutes
Cooking time: About 50 minutes

Eggplant, bell pepper, and onion are baked in olive oil and tossed with fresh tomatoes, parsley, and wine vinegar for a hearty vegetable mixture you can spread on Garlic Toast (recipe on page 18) or other toasted bread slices.

- 4   tablespoons olive oil
- 1   large eggplant (about 1½ lbs.), ends trimmed, cut in half lengthwise
- 1   large red bell pepper, cut in half, stemmed, and seeded
- 1   medium-size onion, cut in half
- 2   large pear-shaped tomatoes, coarsely chopped
- 2   tablespoons white wine vinegar
- ¼   cup chopped Italian parsley
      Salt and pepper
      Niçoise olives (optional)
      Italian parsley sprigs (optional)

Pour 2 tablespoons of the oil into a 10- by 15-inch baking pan. Lay egg-plant, bell pepper, and onion, cut sides down, in oil. Bake in a 350° oven until eggplant is very soft when pressed (about 50 minutes). Let cool briefly.

Trim off and discard skin from eggplant. Coarsely chop eggplant, bell pepper, and onion. Place in a strainer along with tomatoes; gently press out excess liquid. Transfer to a bowl. Stir in vinegar, chopped pars-ley, and remaining 2 tablespoons oil. Season to taste with salt and pepper.

If made ahead, cover and refriger-ate until next day. Serve at room tem-perature, stirring before serving.

Garnish with olives and parsley sprigs, if desired. Makes about 4 cups.

Per tablespoon: 11 calories, .1 g protein, .9 g carbohydrates, .8 g total fat, 0 mg cholesterol, .8 mg sodium

---

FRESH MUSHROOM PÂTÉ

Preparation time: About 15 minutes
Cooking time: About 15 minutes

This creamy spread works equally well on crackers, toast rounds, or crisp raw vegetables. Use fresh mushrooms: mild-flavored regular (button shaped), meaty shiitake, or a combination of both. Or experiment with another variety of your choice.

- ¼   cup butter or margarine
- ⅓   pound fresh mushrooms, such as regular, shiitake, or a com-bination, coarsely chopped
- ⅓   cup finely chopped onion
- 1   tablespoon dry sherry or regu-lar-strength chicken broth
- 1   small package (3 oz.) cream cheese, at room temperature
- ¼   cup minced parsley

In a wide frying pan, melt butter over medium heat. Add mushrooms and onion and cook, stirring often, until mushrooms are browned (about 15 minutes). Mix in sherry.

In a bowl, beat cream cheese and parsley until blended. Stir in mush-room mixture.

If made ahead, cover and refriger-ate for up to 3 days. Serve at room temperature. Makes 1 cup.

Per tablespoon: 49 calories, .7 g protein, 1 g carbohydrates, 5 g total fat, 14 mg cholesterol, 47 mg sodium

OLIVE PURÉE

Preparation time: About 5 minutes

With olives, anchovies, and capers in the cupboard, you can assemble this robust treat in minutes. Spread it on baguette slices and top with slivers of sun-dried tomatoes, if you like.

- 1 can (2¼ oz.) black ripe olives, drained
- ¼ cup drained capers
- 2 teaspoons Dijon mustard
- 5 drained canned anchovy fillets
- ¼ teaspoon *each* cracked bay leaves and dry thyme leaves
- 1 large clove garlic
- 1 tablespoon olive or salad oil

In a blender or food processor, whirl olives, capers, mustard, anchovies, bay, thyme, garlic, and oil until smoothly puréed. Serve at room temperature. Makes ½ cup.

Per tablespoon: 37 calories, .8 g protein, .6 g carbohydrates, 4 g total fat, 1 mg cholesterol, 299 mg sodium

SWEET & SOUR ONION SPREAD

Pictured on page 29

Preparation time: About 10 minutes
Cooking time: About 30 minutes

The slowly cooked sweet onions that go into this spread can be prepared a day in advance and then mixed with yogurt just before serving. Put out toasted pumpernickel bread for this lean, tangy-sweet appetizer.

- 2 tablespoons salad oil
- 3 large onions, thinly sliced
- 1 cup plain yogurt
- 1 tablespoon rice vinegar or cider vinegar
  Salt
  Coarsely ground pepper
  Cherry tomato halves (optional)
  Parsley sprigs (optional)

Heat oil in a wide frying pan over medium heat. Add onions and cook, stirring occasionally, until very soft (about 30 minutes). Let cool. (At this point, you may cover and refrigerate until next day; bring to room temperature before continuing.)

Mix onions, yogurt, and vinegar. Season to taste with salt. Spoon into a bowl and sprinkle with pepper. Garnish with tomato and parsley, if desired. Makes 2 cups.

Per tablespoon: 17 calories, .5 g protein, 2 g carbohydrates, 1 g total fat, .4 mg cholesterol, 5 mg sodium

ONION-CHEESE SPREAD

Preparation time: About 15 minutes
Cooking time: About 30 minutes

The sweet flavor of slowly cooked onions combines winningly with tangy goat cheese and prosciutto. Serve the warm spread on toasted cocktail-size rye bread.

- 2 tablespoons butter or margarine
- 3 large onions, thinly sliced
- 1 teaspoon fresh thyme leaves or ½ teaspoon dry thyme leaves
- 2 ounces thinly sliced prosciutto, slivered
- ¼ pound mild goat cheese, such as Montrachet or Bûcheron, crumbled

In a wide frying pan, melt butter over medium heat. Add onions and thyme and cook, stirring occasionally, until onions are very soft (about 30 minutes).

Add prosciutto and cheese and cook, stirring, until cheese is melted. Makes about 1 cup.

Per tablespoon: 55 calories, 2 g protein, 3 g carbohydrates, 4 g total fat, 12 mg cholesterol, 106 mg sodium

GINGER & MUSTARD SEED CHUTNEY

Preparation time: About 15 minutes
Cooking time: About 25 minutes

This bold tomato relish blends many seasonings into a sweet-sour, spicy balance. You can store the chutney in the refrigerator for up to three weeks. Spoon it over cream cheese and spread on crackers.

- 3 tablespoons salad oil
- 3 tablespoons mustard seeds
- 1 medium-size onion, finely chopped
- 1 cup *each* firmly packed brown sugar and red wine vinegar
- 3 medium-size tomatoes, cored, peeled, and chopped
- 2 tablespoons *each* minced fresh ginger and dark molasses
- 4 large cloves garlic, minced or pressed
- 1 stick cinnamon (2½ to 3 in. long)
- ½ teaspoon salt
- ¼ teaspoon whole cloves
- ¼ teaspoon ground red pepper (cayenne) or crushed dried hot red chiles
- ¼ cup finely chopped cilantro (coriander)

Heat oil in a 2- to 3-quart pan over medium-high heat. Add mustard seeds and cook, stirring often, until seeds begin to pop. Add onion and continue cooking, stirring, until soft (about 5 minutes).

Add sugar, vinegar, tomatoes, ginger, molasses, garlic, cinnamon, salt, cloves, and pepper. Boil gently, stirring occasionally, until mixture is reduced to 3 cups (about 10 minutes). Add cilantro and continue cooking, stirring occasionally, for 5 more minutes. Serve warm or at room temperature.

If made ahead, cool, cover, and refrigerate for up to 3 weeks. Makes about 3 cups.

Per tablespoon: 33 calories, .3 g protein, 6 g carbohydrates, 1 g total fat, 0 mg cholesterol, 26 mg sodium

Warm up your next party with our hot hors d'oeuvres.
Start with sausage- and spinach-stuffed Florentine
Mushrooms (recipe on page 67), Baked Shrimp with Garlic (recipe on page 63), and Summer Squash Squares
(recipe on page 34).

HOT MORSELS

Sweet or savory, the aroma of food cooking is an irresistible invitation to dine. Meat grilled to juicy perfection, stuffed vegetables hot from the steamer, and pastries browned in the oven greet guests warmly.

Happily for the cook, just because an appetizer is served hot (or allowed to cool just to room temperature) doesn't mean that it has to be fully prepared at the very last minute: meat can be marinated, vegetables filled, and dough formed all in advance. Still, it's the final introduction of heat that lends the welcome finishing touch.

SUPER NACHOS

Preparation time: About 30 minutes
Cooking time: About 30 minutes

This layered casserole of refried beans, meat, chiles, and cheese feeds a crowd. Tuck tortilla chips around the dish for an attractive presentation and easy eating.

½ pound *each* lean ground beef and chorizo sausage, casing removed; or 1 pound lean ground beef
1 large onion, chopped
  Salt
  Liquid hot pepper seasoning
1 or 2 cans (about 1 lb. *each*) refried beans
1 can (4 oz.) whole green chiles (for mildest flavor, remove seeds and pith), chopped
2 to 3 cups (8 to 12 oz.) shredded jack or mild Cheddar cheese
¾ cup prepared green or red taco sauce
  Fried Tortilla Chips (recipe on page 18) or packaged tortilla chips
  Garnishes (suggestions follow)

Crumble ground beef and sausage into a wide frying pan over medium heat. Add onion and cook, stirring, until meat is no longer pink (about 7 minutes). Discard fat; season to taste with salt and hot pepper seasoning.

Spread beans on a large heatproof platter. Top evenly with meat mixture. Sprinkle evenly with chiles and cheese, and drizzle with taco sauce. (At this point, you may cover and refrigerate until next day.)

Bake in a 400° oven until hot (about 20 minutes). Meanwhile, prepare Fried Tortilla Chips and garnishes of your choice.

Quickly garnish platter, mounding Guacamole and sour cream, if used, in center. Tuck chips around edges. If desired, keep hot on an electric warming tray. Makes about 1 dozen servings.

Garnishes. Prepare some or all of the following: About ¼ cup chopped **green onions** (including some tops), about 1 cup pitted **ripe olives, Guacamole** (recipe on page 17), about 1 cup **sour cream, cilantro** (coriander) or parsley **sprigs.**

Per serving: 366 calories, 18 g protein, 26 g carbohydrates, 20 g total fat, 43 mg cholesterol, 659 mg sodium

SCOTCH BAKED EGGS

Preparation time: About 15 minutes
Cooking time: About 30 minutes

Begin a Sunday brunch with this eye-catching sausage-and-egg combination. You can prepare the dish a day ahead and then bake it just before serving.

2½ pounds bulk pork sausage
8 hard-cooked eggs, chilled and shelled

Divide sausage into 8 equal portions. On wax paper, flatten each portion into a patty about ⅜ inch thick. With moistened hands, wrap an egg in each patty, smoothing surfaces until free of cracks. (At this point, you may cover and refrigerate until next day.)

Place sausage-wrapped eggs, slightly apart, in a shallow baking pan. Bake in upper third of a 450° oven until meat is no longer pink inside when cut (about 30 minutes). Drain briefly on paper towels. Cut in half crosswise. Makes 16 appetizers.

Per appetizer: 161 calories, 10 g protein, .6 g carbohydrates, 13 g total fat, 134 mg cholesterol, 467 mg sodium

Pictured on page 32
SUMMER SQUASH SQUARES

Preparation time: About 30 minutes
Cooking time: About 40 minutes
Cooling time: At least 15 minutes

Choose your favorite summer squash variety for this easy-to-prepare custardy dish.

¼ cup salad oil
1 small onion, finely chopped
1 clove garlic, minced or pressed
2½ cups shredded summer squash, such as crookneck, zucchini, or pattypan
6 eggs, lightly beaten
⅓ cup fine dry bread crumbs
½ teaspoon *each* salt, dry basil leaves, and dry oregano leaves
¼ teaspoon pepper
3 cups (12 oz.) shredded Cheddar cheese
½ cup grated Parmesan cheese
¼ cup sesame seeds
  Basil sprigs (optional)

Heat oil in a wide frying pan over medium-high heat. Add onion and cook, stirring, until soft (about 5 minutes). Add garlic and squash; cook, stirring, until squash is tender (about 3 more minutes). Set aside.

In a bowl, mix eggs, bread crumbs, salt, dry basil, oregano, pepper, and Cheddar; stir in squash mixture. Spread in a greased 9- by 13-inch baking dish. Sprinkle with Parmesan and sesame seeds. Bake in a 325° oven until set when touched in center (about 30 minutes). Let cool for at least 15 minutes.

Cut into 1-inch squares and arrange on a platter. Garnish with basil sprigs, if desired. Serve warm or at room temperature. Makes about 10 dozen appetizers.

Per appetizer: 24 calories, 1 g protein, .5 g carbohydrates, 2 g total fat, 14 mg cholesterol, 38 mg sodium

CHEESE-MUSHROOM FINGERS

◆

Preparation time: About 20 minutes
Cooking time: About 45 minutes
Cooling time: At least 15 minutes

Here's cheese custard for a crowd. Onion, bell pepper, and mushrooms bake along with jack and cottage cheese to a creamy consistency in these bite-size treats.

½ cup (¼ lb.) butter or margarine
1 pound mushrooms, sliced
1 large onion, chopped
2 cloves garlic, minced or pressed
1 large green bell pepper, seeded and chopped
10 eggs
2 cups small curd cottage cheese
4 cups (1 lb.) shredded jack cheese
½ cup all-purpose flour
1 teaspoon baking powder
¾ teaspoon *each* ground nutmeg, dry basil leaves, and salt

In a wide frying pan, melt butter over medium-high heat. Add mushrooms, onion, and garlic. Cook stirring, until onion is soft (about 7 minutes). Add bell pepper and cook, stirring, for 1 more minute; set aside.

In a large bowl, beat eggs, cottage cheese, jack, flour, baking powder, nutmeg, basil, and salt until blended; stir in mushroom mixture. Spread on a greased 10- by 15-inch rimmed baking sheet. Bake in a 350° oven until set when lightly touched in center (about 35 minutes). Let cool for at least 15 minutes.

Cut into ¾- by 2-inch fingers. Serve warm or at room temperature. Makes about 8 dozen appetizers.

Per appetizer: 43 calories, 3 g protein, 1 g carbohydrates, 3 g total fat, 29 mg cholesterol, 81 mg sodium

CRABBY JACK QUESADILLAS

◆

Preparation time: About 15 minutes
Cooking time: About 20 minutes

Flour tortillas with a crabmeat filling bake quickly into crisp quesadillas.

   Chile-Cilantro Sauce (recipe follows)
¼ pound crabmeat
2 cups (8 oz.) shredded jack cheese
1 cup thinly sliced green onions (including tops)
10 flour tortillas (7- to 8-in. diameter)

Prepare Chile-Cilantro Sauce; keep warm.

In a bowl, lightly mix crabmeat, cheese, and onions. Place 5 of the tortillas in a single layer on two 14- by 17-inch baking sheets. Evenly spread each with crab mixture to within ¾ inch of edges. Top with remaining tortillas.

Bake in a 450° oven until cheese is melted and tortillas are lightly browned (about 7 minutes). Cut each into 6 wedges.

Offer with sauce for dipping. Makes 2½ dozen appetizers.

Per appetizer: 71 calories, 4 g protein, 8 g carbohydrates, 2 g total fat, 10 mg cholesterol, 121 mg sodium

Chile-Cilantro Sauce. Place 4 medium-size fresh **Anaheim chiles** on a baking sheet. Broil 2 inches below heat, turning often, until browned and blistered (about 5 minutes); let cool. Pull off and discard skin, stems, and seeds. Chop coarsely.

In a blender or food processor, whirl chiles, ¼ cup **dry white wine**, 1 tablespoon **lemon juice**, and 1 medium-size **shallot**, chopped, until smooth. Pour into a 2- to 3-quart pan and boil over high heat, stirring, until reduced to ⅓ cup (about 5 minutes).

Return mixture to blender. Add 1 cup firmly packed **cilantro** (coriander) and whirl until smooth, scraping container sides often. With motor running, slowly add ¼ cup hot

melted **butter** or margarine, whirling until blended; scrape sides once or twice. Makes about 1 cup.

Per tablespoon: 29 calories, .2 g protein, .8 g carbohydrates, 3 g total fat, 8 mg cholesterol, 31 mg sodium

TOMATO-AVOCADO QUESADILLAS

◆

Preparation time: About 20 minutes
Cooking time: About 20 minutes

Tomatoes tame the heat of quesadillas filled with cheese, zucchini, chiles, and onion.

1⅔ cups Guacamole (recipe on page 17)
2 tablespoons salad oil
1 medium-size onion, finely chopped
2 teaspoons minced serrano or jalapeño chiles
1 cup finely chopped zucchini
8 whole wheat tortillas (9-in. diameter)
3 cups (12 oz.) shredded jack or mild Cheddar cheese
2 medium-size tomatoes, chopped

Prepare Guacamole; set aside.

Heat oil in a wide frying pan over medium heat. Add onion and chiles and cook, stirring, until onion is soft (about 7 minutes). Add zucchini and cook, stirring, until tender-crisp (about 4 more minutes).

Place 4 of the tortillas in a single layer on two 14- by 17-inch baking sheets. Evenly cover each with ¾ cup of the cheese and ¼ cup of the vegetable mixture. Top with remaining tortillas. Bake in a 450° oven until cheese is melted and tortillas are lightly browned (about 7 minutes). Cut each into 6 wedges. Top with tomatoes and Guacamole. Makes 2 dozen appetizers.

Per appetizer: 142 calories, 5 g protein, 11 g carbohydrates, 9 g total fat, 12 mg cholesterol, 205 mg sodium

APPETIZER MINI-QUICHES

Pictured on facing page

**Preparation time: About 1 hour
Cooking time: About 20 minutes**

Ham and chiles flavor the custard in these bite-size quiches.

**Flaky Pastry (recipe follows)
Ham & Green Chile Filling
(recipe follows)**
2 eggs
¾ cup sour cream

Prepare Flaky Pastry. On a floured board, roll dough ¹⁄₁₆ inch thick. Cut into 2-inch circles, rerolling scraps to make about 72 circles. Fit into bottoms and partway up sides of 1¾-inch muffin cups.

Prepare Ham & Green Chile Filling. Place a heaping teaspoon of the filling in each cup. Beat eggs lightly; beat in sour cream until smooth. Spoon about 1 teaspoon of the egg mixture into each cup.

Bake in a 375° oven until tops are lightly browned (about 20 minutes). Let cool for 5 minutes; then tip quiches out of pans. Serve warm or at room temperature.

If made ahead, let cool completely, wrap airtight, and refrigerate until next day; to reheat, spread quiches in a single layer in a shallow pan and place in a 350° oven until hot (about 10 minutes). Makes about 6 dozen appetizers.

Flaky Pastry. Mix 2 cups **all-purpose flour** and ½ teaspoon *each* **salt** and **chili powder**. Cut in ⅓ cup firm **butter** or margarine and ⅓ cup **solid vegetable shortening** until mixture resembles fine crumbs. Beat 1 **egg;** add enough cold **water** to make ¼ cup. Add to flour mixture, 1 tablespoon at a time, mixing until dough holds together. Shape into a ball.

Ham & Green Chile Filling. Mix ¾ cup finely diced cooked **ham** (about 3 oz.), 3 tablespoons chopped

canned **green chiles,** ¼ cup chopped **green onions** (including tops), and 1½ cups (6 oz.) shredded **jack cheese.**

Per appetizer: 48 calories, 2 g protein, 3 g carbohydrates, 3 g total fat, 15 mg cholesterol, 60 mg sodium

NIPPY CHEESE PUFFS

**Preparation time: About 15 minutes
Cooking time: About 35 minutes**

Here's a version of the classic French cheese puff, *gougère.*

1 cup water
½ cup (¼ lb.) butter or margarine
⅛ teaspoon ground nutmeg
1 cup all-purpose flour
4 eggs
1 cup (4 oz.) lightly packed finely shredded sharp Cheddar or Asiago cheese

In a 2- to 3-quart pan, stir water, butter, and nutmeg over medium-high heat until butter is melted. Add flour all at once, stirring until mixture leaves sides of pan and forms a ball (about 2 minutes). Remove from heat and transfer to a bowl; let cool briefly.

Add eggs, one at a time, beating well after each addition. Stir in ½ cup of the cheese. Drop by spoonfuls about 1½ inches in diameter onto greased baking sheets, spacing puffs about 2 inches apart. Sprinkle with remaining ½ cup cheese.

Bake in a 400° oven until golden brown (about 20 minutes). Turn off oven. Pierce each puff in several places. Return to oven until crisp (about 10 minutes). Makes about 3 dozen appetizers.

Per appetizer: 56 calories, 2 g protein, 3 g carbohydrates, 4 g total fat, 34 mg cholesterol, 53 mg sodium

ONION TARTS

**Preparation time: About 45 minutes
Cooking time: About 50 minutes**

Pimentos and ripe olives peek out from the latticework of these Spanish pies. Known as *tortas de cebollas,* they're an elegant addition to a tapas party.

⅓ cup olive or salad oil
3 large onions, thinly sliced
¼ teaspoon ground nutmeg
**½ teaspoon salt
Tart Shells (recipe follows)**
3 eggs, lightly beaten
¼ cup sliced ripe olives
2 to 3 tablespoons sliced pimentos

Heat oil in a wide frying pan over medium heat. Add onions, nutmeg, and salt; cook, stirring occasionally, until onions are very soft (about 30 minutes). Let cool. Meanwhile, prepare Tart Shells.

Combine onions and eggs; evenly pour mixture into shells. Trim dough about ½ inch above filling. On a floured board, roll out trimmings, cut into ¾-inch-wide strips, and weave over each tart to make a lattice topping. Fill spaces between lattices with olive and pimento slices. Bake in a 400° oven until pastry is golden (about 20 minutes); let cool briefly.

Cut each pie into 12 wedges. Makes 2 dozen appetizers.

Tart Shells. Mix 1⅔ cups **all-purpose flour** and ¼ teaspoon **salt.** Cut in ½ cup (¼ lb.) firm **butter** or margarine until mixture resembles fine crumbs. Stirring with a fork, gradually add 2 tablespoons **salad oil;** then add 2 to 4 tablespoons cold **water,** 1 tablespoon at a time, mixing until dough holds together. Shape into 2 equal-size balls. On a floured board, roll each ball into a 12-inch circle. Fit into two 8-inch pie pans.

Per appetizer: 121 calories, 2 g protein, 8 g carbohydrates, 9 g total fat, 37 mg cholesterol, 126 mg sodium

Guests will gobble up the golden goodies—Appetizer
Mini-Quiches (recipe on facing page)—in this basket.
They're perfect for a backyard barbecue or a more formal
dinner party.

Pictured on page 85
SMOKED SALMON & HERBED CHEESE TARTS

Preparation time: About 45 minutes
Chilling time: At least 30 minutes
Cooking time: About 12 minutes

Puff pastry forms the base for an easy-to-prepare filling of smoked salmon and herbed garlic cream cheese.

> 1 **sheet (half a 17¼-oz. package) frozen puff pastry, thawed**
> ⅓ **cup (about 3 oz.) shredded or finely chopped smoked salmon or lox**
> 4 **ounces cream cheese flavored with herbs and garlic, at room temperature**
> **Marjoram or parsley sprigs (optional)**

Unfold pastry sheet on a lightly floured board and roll into an 11-inch square. Cut into 2-inch circles, rerolling scraps to make about 36. Fit into bottoms and partway up sides of 1¾-inch muffin cups.

In a small bowl, mix salmon and cream cheese. Place a scant teaspoon of the mixture in each cup. Cover and refrigerate for at least 30 minutes or up to 2 hours.

Bake, uncovered, in a 450° oven until golden brown (about 12 minutes). Let cool for 5 minutes; then tip tarts out of pans.

Garnish each tart with marjoram, if desired. Makes about 3 dozen appetizers.

Per appetizer: 42 calories, 1 g protein, 3 g carbohydrates, 3 g total fat, 3 mg cholesterol, 66 mg sodium

SCALLOP TARTS

◆

Preparation time: About 20 minutes
Cooking time: About 25 minutes

Savory cheese pastry holds an elegant filling of sweet bay scallops.

> **Cheese Tart Shells (recipe follows)**
> ⅓ **cup *each* dry white wine and whipping cream**
> 2 **teaspoons lemon juice**
> 1 **teaspoon Dijon mustard**
> ¼ **teaspoon dry tarragon leaves**
> 1 **small shallot, finely chopped**
> ½ **pound bay scallops, rinsed and dried**
> 2 **tablespoons grated Parmesan cheese**

Prepare Cheese Tart Shells; set aside.

In a wide frying pan, bring wine, cream, lemon juice, mustard, tarragon, and shallot to a boil over medium-high heat. Add scallops and cook, stirring often, until opaque when cut (about 2 minutes). Remove from heat. Lift scallops from pan, drain, and spoon into tart shells.

Boil liquid in pan over high heat until reduced by about half (about 5 minutes). Spoon over scallops and sprinkle with cheese. Arrange tarts on a baking sheet. Bake in a 400° oven until hot (about 5 minutes). Makes 15 appetizers.

Cheese Tart Shells. Mix ¾ cup **all-purpose flour**, ⅓ cup finely shredded **Swiss cheese**, and 2 tablespoons **grated Parmesan cheese**. Cut in ¼ cup cold **butter** or margarine until mixture resembles coarse crumbs. Gradually add ½ teaspoon **Worcestershire** and 1½ to 3 tablespoons cold **water,** mixing until dough holds together. Shape into a ball.

Divide into 15 portions. Press each into a shallow 1½- to 2-inch tart pan. Pierce in several places with a fork and arrange on a baking sheet. Bake in a 400° oven until golden brown (about 12 minutes). Let cool; then carefully remove shells.

Per appetizer: 95 calories, 5 g protein, 6 g carbohydrates, 6 g total fat, 22 mg cholesterol, 101 mg sodium

Pictured on page 85
SHRIMP & FETA FILA TRIANGLES

◆

Preparation time: About 45 minutes
Cooking time: About 10 minutes

Delicate fila dough encases a creamy filling of feta cheese and tiny shrimp.

> **Shrimp & Feta Cheese Filling (recipe follows)**
> 6 **sheets fila pastry (about ¼ of a 1-lb. package), thawed if frozen**
> ½ **cup (¼ lb.) butter or margarine, melted**

Prepare Shrimp & Feta Cheese Filling; set aside.

Unroll pastry and lay flat; cut sheets in half crosswise. Brush a half-sheet with butter, keeping remaining fila covered with plastic wrap, and then cut half-sheet lengthwise into thirds. Place about 1½ teaspoons of the filling in an upper corner of each strip, fold corner down over filling, and then fold triangle over onto itself, continuing down length of strip.

Place triangles about 1½ inches apart on greased baking sheets, brush with butter, and cover with plastic wrap while shaping remaining triangles. (At this point, you may freeze until firm; then carefully stack in a rigid container, placing foil between layers, cover, and freeze for up to a month. Do not thaw before baking.)

Bake in a 375° oven until well browned and crisp (about 10 minutes; about 35 minutes if frozen). Serve hot or at room temperature. Makes 3 dozen appetizers.

Shrimp & Feta Cheese Filling. Mix 6 ounces **feta cheese,** crumbled; ½ pound **small cooked shrimp;** ⅛ teaspoon *each* **ground white pepper** and **dill weed;** and ¼ cup chopped **parsley.**

Per appetizer: 51 calories, 2 g protein, 2 g carbohydrates, 4 g total fat, 23 mg cholesterol, 106 mg sodium

COCKTAIL TURNOVERS

◆

**Preparation time: About 45 minutes,
plus at least 4 hours to chill pastry
Cooking time: About 25 minutes**

Offer a platter of these miniature,
meat-filled triangles for an inviting
and elegant light nibble with your
favorite beverage.

   **Cream Cheese Pastry (recipe
   follows)**
1 **small potato (about 5 oz.), finely
   chopped**
1 **small onion, finely chopped**
½ **pound lean ground beef**
1 **clove garlic, minced or pressed**
¼ **teaspoon *each* dry marjoram
   leaves and pepper**
½ **teaspoon dry oregano leaves**
1 **teaspoon salt**
1 **egg yolk beaten with 2
   tablespoons milk**

Prepare Cream Cheese Pastry.

   Mix potato, onion, beef, garlic,
marjoram, pepper, oregano, and salt;
set aside.

   On a floured board, roll pastry
into a rectangle ⅛ inch thick; cut into
2½-inch squares (you should have
about 48). Place 1 teaspoon of the
meat filling on each square. Fold
dough over to make a triangle, seal
edges with a fork, and brush with
egg mixture. Arrange on baking
sheets. Bake in a 350° oven until
golden brown (about 25 minutes).
Makes about 4 dozen appetizers.

Cream Cheese Pastry. Beat 1 large
package (8 oz.) **cream cheese** and 1
cup (½ lb.) **butter** or margarine, both
at room temperature, until smooth.
Beat in ½ teaspoon **salt.** Slowly mix
in 2 cups **all-purpose flour** to make a
stiff dough. Cover with plastic wrap
and refrigerate for at least 4 hours or
until next day.

*Per appetizer: 86 calories, 2 g protein,
5 g carbohydrates, 7 g total fat, 24 mg
cholesterol, 126 mg sodium*

EMPANADAS

◆

**Preparation time: About 30 minutes
Cooking time: About 45 minutes**

Bite-size turnovers are filled with a
sweet-tart meat and raisin mixture.

   **Cornmeal Pastry (recipe
   follows)**
1 **teaspoon butter or margarine**
½ **pound *each* ground beef and
   ground pork**
1 **large clove garlic, minced or
   pressed**
½ **cup *each* tomato purée and
   raisins**
¼ **cup dry sherry**
2 **teaspoons ground cinnamon**
½ **teaspoon ground cloves**
2 **tablespoons vinegar**
1 **tablespoon sugar**
¾ **cup slivered almonds**

Prepare Cornmeal Pastry. While pastry is chilling, melt butter in a wide
frying pan over medium heat.
Crumble meat into pan and cook,
stirring, until no longer pink (about 7
minutes). Drain off fat. Add garlic,
tomato purée, raisins, sherry, cinnamon, cloves, vinegar, and sugar.
Cook, stirring, until most of the liquid has evaporated (about 20 minutes). Stir in almonds; let cool.

   On a floured board, roll pastry ⅛
inch thick. Cut into 3-inch rounds.
Evenly spoon meat filling into each
circle. Moisten edges with water, fold
over, and seal with a fork. Arrange
on baking sheets. Bake in a 400° oven
until golden brown (about 15 minutes). Makes about 40 appetizers.

Cornmeal Pastry. Mix 2 cups **all-
purpose flour,** 1 cup **yellow cornmeal,** 1 tablespoon **baking powder,**
and ½ teaspoon **salt.** Cut in ¼ cup
cold **butter** or margarine until mixture resembles coarse meal. Beat 1
egg and ¾ cup **milk;** with a fork, stir
into flour mixture until dough holds
together. Gather dough into a ball
and knead lightly. Cover and refrigerate for 30 minutes.

*Per appetizer: 102 calories, 4 g protein,
11 g carbohydrates, 5 g total fat, 17 mg
cholesterol, 95 mg sodium*

HOT SPICED
APPLE CRÊPES

◆

**Preparation time: About 20 minutes
Cooking time: About 10 minutes**

Take advantage of purchased crêpes
to make this sweet autumn treat. Tart
apples laced with rum make a tempting filling.

1 **package (4 oz.) frozen prepared
   crêpes (6-in. diameter)**
1 **tablespoon butter or margarine
   About 2½ pounds tart apples,
   such as Granny Smith or Newtown Pippins, peeled, cored,
   and thinly sliced**
1 **tablespoon lemon juice**
1½ **teaspoons apple pie spice
   About ⅓ cup sugar**
2 **tablespoons rum or brandy
   (optional)**

Place crêpes in a baking pan. Cover
and bake in a 300° oven until crêpes
are warm and easy to separate (about
10 minutes).

   Meanwhile, melt butter in a wide
frying pan over medium heat. Add
apples, lemon juice, and apple pie
spice. Cook, turning occasionally, until apples are just tender when
pierced (about 4 minutes). Add sugar
to taste. Continue cooking, mixing
gently, until juices are syrupy (about
3 more minutes).

   Drizzle with rum, if desired, and
set aflame (not beneath an exhaust
fan or near flammable items), shaking pan gently until flames subside.
Continue cooking until most of the
liquid has evaporated.

   Evenly spoon filling onto a quarter of each crêpe; fold crêpes in half
and then in half again. Makes 10
appetizers.

*Per appetizer: 116 calories, 2 g protein,
25 g carbohydrates, 2 g total fat, 3 mg
cholesterol, 30 mg sodium*

Appetizer Pizza Squares (recipe on facing page) are a party success story. Simply cut the crisp crust topped with tomato sauce, cheese, artichokes, and salami into bite-size snacks.

APPETIZER PIZZA SQUARES

Pictured on facing page

**Preparation time: About 30 minutes
Cooking time: About 1 hour**

Refrigerated dough cuts down on preparation time for this artichoke-topped pizza, sure to be a party favorite.

Fresh Tomato Sauce (recipe follows)
1 **jar (6 oz.) marinated artichoke hearts**
2 **packages (10 oz. *each*) refrigerated pizza crust**
3 **cups (12 oz.) shredded whole-milk mozzarella cheese**
¼ **cup grated Parmesan cheese**
¼ **pound thinly sliced dry salami, cut into ½-inch-wide strips**

Prepare Fresh Tomato Sauce.

Meanwhile, drain artichokes, reserving marinade, and coarsely chop. Roll or pat crusts to fit into two 12-inch greased pizza pans (or one 17-inch pan). Brush dough with some of the reserved marinade. Spread with tomato sauce and sprinkle evenly with mozzarella and Parmesan. Evenly distribute artichokes and salami over top.

Bake on lowest rack of a 425° oven until crust is well browned (about 15 minutes for small pizzas, 25 minutes for large). Cut into about 2-inch pieces. Makes about 40 appetizers.

Fresh Tomato Sauce. Heat 2 tablespoons **olive oil** in a 2-quart pan over medium heat. Add 1 small **onion,** finely chopped, and cook, stirring often, until soft (about 7 minutes). Mix in 1 clove **garlic,** minced or pressed; 5 **pear-shaped tomatoes** (about ¾ lb. *total*), peeled and finely chopped; ¼ teaspoon *each* **salt** and **dry oregano leaves;** ½ teaspoon **dry basil leaves;** and ¼ cup **dry white wine.** Bring to a

boil; reduce heat, cover, and simmer for 20 minutes. Uncover and cook over medium-high heat, stirring often, until reduced to about 1 cup (about 15 more minutes).

Per appetizer: 86 calories, 4 g protein, 7 g carbohydrates, 4 g total fat, 9 mg cholesterol, 198 mg sodium

PESTO HOTS

**Preparation time: About 10 minutes
Cooking time: About 3 minutes**

This easy appetizer is ready to enjoy in minutes. Simply spread baguette slices with a basil-accented mayonnaise and brown under the broiler.

½ **cup *each* slivered fresh basil leaves and grated Parmesan cheese**
1 **small clove garlic, minced or pressed**
About 6 tablespoons mayonnaise
1 **small French baguette (8 oz.), sliced ¼ inch thick**

Stir together basil, Parmesan, garlic, and 6 tablespoons of the mayonnaise until well blended; add more mayonnaise, if necessary, to make a firm spreading consistency. Set aside.

Arrange bread slices in a single layer on a large baking sheet. Broil about 4 inches below heat until toasted on top (about 1 minute). Remove from broiler, turn, and spread untoasted sides with mayonnaise mixture, spreading to edges. Continue broiling until bubbling and lightly browned (about 2 more minutes). Makes 2 dozen appetizers.

Per appetizer: 59 calories, 2 g protein, 5 g carbohydrates, 3 g total fat, 4 mg cholesterol, 101 mg sodium

HERBED CHEESE CROUTONS

**Preparation time: About 20 minutes
Cooking time: About 12 minutes**

Watch these golden cheese cubes disappear as soon as you serve them hot from the oven. Try both versions for different flavor sensations.

About ⅓ of a 1-pound loaf unsliced day-old French bread
½ **to ¾ cup grated Parmesan or Romano cheese**
½ **cup (¼ lb.) butter or margarine, cut into pieces**
1 **clove garlic, minced or pressed**
¼ **teaspoon *each* dry thyme leaves, dry rosemary, summer savory, and paprika**

Slice bread about 1 inch thick; trim and discard crusts. Then cut into 1-inch cubes. Place cheese in a shallow bowl.

In an 8- to 10-inch frying pan, melt butter over low heat. Stir in garlic, thyme, rosemary, summer savory, and paprika; remove from heat. Dip bread cubes into butter mixture to coat on all sides; then roll in cheese.

Arrange in a single layer in a 10-by 15-inch baking pan. Bake in a 350° oven until crisp and golden brown (about 10 minutes). Makes about 2 dozen appetizers.

Per appetizer: 60 calories, 1 g protein, 3 g carbohydrates, 5 g total fat, 12 mg cholesterol, 112 mg sodium

Italian Herbed Cheese Croutons

Follow directions for **Herbed Cheese Croutons,** but omit rosemary, summer savory, and paprika. Instead, add ½ teaspoon **dry basil leaves** and ¼ teaspoon **dry oregano leaves.**

Per appetizer: 60 calories, 1 g protein, 3 g carbohydrates, 5 g total fat, 12 mg cholesterol, 112 mg sodium

A very versatile food, sandwiches can play many supporting roles—as hearty appetizers, between-meal snacks, or light meal starters. Different breads, fillings, serving temperatures, and styles make for an almost infinite variety of tastes.

Sandwiches can even announce the theme of a party, a special cuisine, or a certain mood. Whether you choose Olive Relish Poor Boy Sandwich Loaf for an on-the-go picnic, Spiedini alla Romana to begin an Italian feast, or Grilled Ham & Brie on Rye for easy snacking, our sandwiches are sure to please.

EGG & ONION TRIANGLES

Preparation time: About 10 minutes
Cooking time: About 3 minutes
Chilling time: At least 2 hours

Dense, dark pumpernickel is the perfect host for mustardy egg salad. Tart-sweet onions provide a flavorful finish.

        Pink Onions (recipe follows)
    4   hard-cooked eggs, finely chopped
    3   tablespoons sour cream
    2   teaspoons *each* Dijon mustard and mayonnaise
    1   teaspoon chopped fresh dill or ¼ teaspoon dill weed
        Salt and pepper
    4   slices thin, dense-textured pumpernickel bread
    2   green onions (including tops), thinly sliced

Prepare Pink Onions.

Mix eggs, sour cream, mustard, mayonnaise, and dill. Season to taste with salt and pepper. Evenly spread on bread slices. Cut each bread slice diagonally into quarters. Evenly mound Pink Onions over egg mix-

SATISFYING SANDWICHES

ture. Sprinkle with green onions. Makes 16 snack sandwiches.

Pink Onions. Thinly slice 1 small **red onion** (4 to 6 oz.). In a 1- to 1½-quart pan, bring 1½ cups **water** and 1 tablespoon **vinegar** to a boil over high heat. Add onion, pushing down to submerge. Return to a boil; then drain and place in a bowl. Stir in 2 teaspoons **salad oil,** 1 teaspoon **white wine vinegar,** and ¼ teaspoon *each* **dill seeds** and **mustard seeds.** Cover and refrigerate for at least 2 hours or until next day.

Per sandwich: 58 calories, 3 g protein, 5 g carbohydrates, 3 g total fat, 55 mg cholesterol, 85 mg sodium

RICE CAKES WITH RICOTTA-APRICOT PURÉE

Preparation time: About 15 minutes
Cooking time: About 1 minute (optional)

Rice cakes replace bread in these bite-size, ginger-spiced sandwiches. If desired, lightly broil them just before serving.

    1   cup dried apricots
    1   pound ricotta cheese
    4   teaspoons honey
    ½   teaspoon ground ginger
    36 miniature rice cakes (2-in. diameter)

Thinly sliver 6 of the apricots; reserve for garnish. Whirl remaining apricots in a food processor until minced. Add ricotta, honey, and ginger; whirl

until puréed. (Or mince apricots with a knife. Then beat with ricotta, honey, and ginger until blended.)

Evenly spread apricot mixture on rice cakes. Garnish with apricot slivers. Serve cold. Or, to serve warm, arrange in a single layer on a 12- by 15-inch baking sheet and broil about 4 inches below heat just until mixture begins to brown (about 1 minute). Makes 3 dozen snack sandwiches.

Per sandwich: 36 calories, 2 g protein, 5 g carbohydrates, .9 g total fat, 4 mg cholesterol, 18 mg sodium

GRILLED HAM & BRIE ON RYE

Preparation time: About 5 minutes
Cooking time: About 5 minutes

Rich-tasting Brie grilled with ham and slivered sweet onion lifts these ham and cheese sandwiches out of the ordinary.

    8   slices sourdough rye or regular rye bread
    8   thin slices Black Forest ham (7 oz. *total*)
    ½   pound firm-ripe Brie cheese, sliced
    ½   small red onion, thinly slivered

Make 4 sandwiches, using 2 slices of the bread, 2 slices of the ham, a quarter of the Brie, and a quarter of the onion for each.

Place a ridged grill pan, griddle, or wide frying pan over low heat until a drop of water dances on surface. Place sandwiches in pan. Cook, turning once, until browned on both sides (about 5 minutes). Cut each sandwich in half and serve hot. Makes 8 snack sandwiches.

Per sandwich: 201 calories, 14 g protein, 14 g carbohydrates, 10 g total fat, 43 mg cholesterol, 690 mg sodium

SPICED LENTILS IN POCKET BREADS

Preparation time: About 15 minutes
Cooking time: About 40 minutes

Pocket breads make handy holders for lentils mixed with chile, bay leaf, and cumin. Top with minty yogurt.

- 1 cup (7 oz.) lentils
- 1 quart water
- 1 bay leaf
- 1 small dried hot red chile
- 1 teaspoon cumin seeds
- ⅓ cup olive oil
- 3 tablespoons wine vinegar
- 1 clove garlic, minced or pressed
- ½ cup thinly sliced green onions (including tops)
- 1 cup chopped celery
-    Salt and pepper
-    Yogurt Sauce (recipe follows)
- 4 pocket bread rounds (6-in. diameter), cut in half

Sort lentils and discard any debris; rinse well and drain. Place in 3- to 4-quart pan with water, bay leaf, chile, and cumin seeds. Bring to a boil over high heat; reduce heat, cover, and simmer just until lentils are tender (about 40 minutes). Drain and let cool. Discard chile.

In a large bowl, mix oil, vinegar, and garlic; stir in lentils. (At this point, you may cover and refrigerate until next day.)

Just before serving, stir in onions and celery. Season to taste with salt and pepper.

Prepare Yogurt Sauce. Evenly spoon lentil mixture into each pocket bread half and offer with sauce. Makes 8 snack sandwiches.

Per sandwich: 257 calories, 10 g protein, 34 g carbohydrates, 9 g total fat, 0 mg cholesterol, 199 mg sodium

Yogurt Sauce. Mix 1 cup **plain yogurt,** 2 tablespoons chopped **fresh mint leaves,** and 2 tablespoons **golden raisins.** Makes 1¼ cups.

Per tablespoon: 10 calories, .6 g protein, 2 g carbohydrates, .2 g total fat, .7 mg cholesterol, 8 mg sodium

OLIVE RELISH POOR BOY SANDWICH LOAF

Preparation time: About 10 minutes

Fill a loaf of sourdough bread with salami, turkey, and Swiss cheese, and you have a hearty sandwich. Add two kinds of olives in a lemony vinaigrette, and you have a heroic one.

- ¼ cup olive oil
- 1½ tablespoons red wine vinegar
- 1 teaspoon grated lemon peel
- 1 clove garlic, minced or pressed
- ⅛ teaspoon coarsely ground pepper
- ½ cup *each* chopped ripe olives and pimento-stuffed green olives
- 1 long loaf sourdough French bread (1 lb.)
- 4 to 6 butter lettuce leaves, washed and crisped
- ¼ pound thinly sliced dry salami
- 6 ounces *each* thinly sliced cooked turkey breast and Swiss cheese
-    Red onion rings (optional)

Mix oil, vinegar, lemon peel, garlic, and pepper until well combined; stir in olives. Set aside.

Split bread in half lengthwise; pull out bread from top half, leaving about a ½-inch-thick shell (reserve crumbs for other uses).

Spread cut surfaces of both bread halves with olive mixture. Cover bottom half with lettuce leaves. Add salami, turkey, and cheese. Top with onion, if desired. Cover with top half of loaf.

Fasten sandwich at 2-inch intervals with wooden picks. Cut between picks. Makes 8 snack sandwiches.

Per sandwich: 382 calories, 20 g protein, 25 g carbohydrates, 22 g total fat, 47 mg cholesterol, 848 mg sodium

SPIEDINI ALLA ROMANA

Preparation time: About 15 minutes
Cooking time: About 20 minutes

Ham and cheese Italian style means prosciutto and mozzarella on Italian bread. Lightly battered and fried until golden, spiedini are served crisp and hot.

- 8 thin slices Italian or French bread, crusts trimmed
- 4 slices mozzarella cheese (about 2 oz. *total*)
- 8 thin slices prosciutto (about 3 oz. *total*)
- ¾ cup milk
- ⅓ cup all-purpose flour
- 2 eggs, lightly beaten
- ⅓ cup olive or salad oil

Make 4 sandwiches, using 2 slices of the bread, 1 slice of the cheese, and 2 slices of the prosciutto for each. Cut each into quarters and fasten with wooden picks. Place milk, flour, and eggs in separate shallow bowls.

Heat oil in an 8- to 10-inch frying pan over medium heat. Lightly dip each sandwich, coating all sides, in milk, then in flour, and finally in eggs. Cook sandwiches, a few at a time, turning once, until crusty and golden (about 5 minutes). Makes 16 snack sandwiches.

Per sandwich: 97 calories, 4 g protein, 5 g carbohydrates, 7 g total fat, 34 mg cholesterol, 168 mg sodium

CHEESE WAFERS

Preparation time: About 20 minutes
Cooking time: About 10 minutes

Sharp Cheddar cheese combines with dry mustard and ground red pepper to make a savory cracker.

- ⅔ **cup butter or margarine, at room temperature**
- ½ **cup shredded sharp Cheddar cheese**
- 1 **egg**
- ⅛ **teaspoon ground red pepper (cayenne)**
- ¼ **teaspoon dry mustard**
- ½ **teaspoon** *each* **salt and sugar**
- 1⅔ **cups all-purpose flour**

Beat butter and cheese. Add egg, pepper, mustard, salt, and sugar; beat until well blended. Gradually add flour, stirring until smooth. Shape dough into a ball.

Place dough, about half at a time, in a cooky press fitted with a sawtooth pattern and shape wafers, cutting at 1-inch intervals, on baking sheets. Bake in a 375° oven until golden (about 10 minutes). Serve warm or at room temperature. Makes about 4 dozen appetizers.

Per appetizer: 45 calories, .9 g protein, 3 g carbohydrates, 3 g total fat, 13 mg cholesterol, 58 mg sodium

Sesame Cheese Wafers

Follow directions for **Cheese Wafers,** but instead of cutting dough with a cooky press, divide dough in half and shape each portion into a smooth log about 1½ inches in diameter. For each portion, sprinkle 1½ tablespoons **sesame seeds** on wax paper. Roll log in seeds, pressing in lightly. Wrap in wax paper or plastic wrap and refrigerate for at least 2 hours or until next day.

Slice dough about ¼ inch thick and arrange rounds slightly apart on baking sheets. Bake as directed. Makes about 5 dozen appetizers.

Per appetizer: 39 calories, .8 g protein, 3 g carbohydrates, 3 g total fat, 10 mg cholesterol, 46 mg sodium

BABY DUTCH BABIES

Preparation time: About 15 minutes
Cooking time: About 15 minutes

Petite Dutch babies, a close relative of popovers, cradle a savory filling of cream cheese and chutney.

- 2 **tablespoons butter or margarine**
- 2 **eggs**
- ½ **cup** *each* **all-purpose flour and milk**
- 1 **small package (3 oz.) cream cheese**
- ¼ **cup chutney, chopped**

Divide butter evenly among twenty-four 1½-inch or twelve 2½-inch muffin cups. Place in a 425° oven until butter is melted (about 3 minutes).

Meanwhile, whirl eggs, flour, and milk in a food processor or blender until smooth. Cut cheese into cubes to equal number of muffin cups; set aside.

Evenly spoon batter into cups. Bake until bottoms are firm (2 minutes for small cups, 5 minutes for large cups). Remove from oven and quickly add 1 piece of the cheese and ½ teaspoon (for small cups) or 1 teaspoon (for large cups) of the chutney to each cup. Return to oven and continue baking until puffed (about 10 more minutes).

Let cool briefly; then remove from pans. Serve warm or at room temperature. Makes 2 dozen small or 1 dozen large appetizers.

Per appetizer (small): 46 calories, 1 g protein, 4 g carbohydrates, 3 g total fat, 25 mg cholesterol, 34 mg sodium

Pictured on facing page
CHEESE TWISTS

Preparation time: About 30 minutes
Cooking time: About 10 minutes

Light, flaky, and buttery—that's how to describe these cheese sticks, perfect openers for a sophisticated evening. Top the twists with sesame or poppy seeds.

- 1 **cup all-purpose flour**
- ½ **teaspoon** *each* **salt and ground ginger**
- ⅓ **cup butter or margarine**
- 1 **cup (4 oz.) shredded sharp Cheddar cheese**
- ½ **teaspoon Worcestershire**
- 2 **to 2½ tablespoons cold water**
- 1 **egg, beaten**
- 1 **tablespoon** *each* **sesame and poppy seeds**

Mix flour, salt, and ginger. Cut in butter until mixture resembles fine crumbs. Stir in cheese. Add Worcestershire to 1 tablespoon of the water and sprinkle over flour mixture. Mix lightly, adding remaining water as needed, until dough holds together. Shape into a flattened ball.

On a lightly floured board, roll dough into a 10-inch square. Brush with egg and cut in half. Sprinkle sesame seeds on 1 portion and poppy seeds on other portion. Then cut each portion into ½- by 5-inch strips. Holding each strip at ends, twist in opposite directions. Place about 1 inch apart on greased baking sheets.

Bake in a 400° oven until golden brown (about 10 minutes). Serve warm or at room temperature. Makes 40 appetizers.

Per appetizer: 41 calories, 1 g protein, 3 g carbohydrates, 3 g total fat, 12 mg cholesterol, 63 mg sodium

Let guests picnic on shallot- and sausage-accented Rice-stuffed Summer Squash (recipe on page 70), Spicy Chicken Wings (recipe on page 54) with blue cheese dip, and delicate Cheese Twists (recipe on facing page) topped with sesame and poppy seeds.

ZUCCHINI MADELEINES

Preparation time: About 30 minutes
Cooking time: About 25 minutes

This moist, cheese-laced variation on the French dessert cooky adds zucchini for texture and flavor. Serve right from the oven or at room temperature.

- 3 medium-size zucchini (about 1 lb. *total*), shredded
- 2 teaspoons salt
- 6 tablespoons olive oil
- 1 medium-size onion, chopped
- 1 cup all-purpose flour
- 1 tablespoon baking powder
- 5 eggs
- 2 tablespoons milk
- 1½ cups (about 6 oz.) freshly grated Parmesan cheese
- 1 clove garlic, minced or pressed
- 2 tablespoons chopped fresh basil leaves or 1 teaspoon dry basil leaves
- ¼ teaspoon pepper

Mix zucchini with salt. Let stand until zucchini is limp and liquid has drained from it (about 30 minutes). Rinse well and drain, squeezing out as much water as possible.

Meanwhile, heat 2 tablespoons of the oil in an 8- to 10-inch frying pan over medium-high heat. Add onion and cook, stirring, until soft (about 7 minutes); set aside.

In a large bowl, mix flour and baking powder. In another bowl, whisk eggs, milk, remaining 4 tablespoons oil, cheese, garlic, basil, and pepper until blended; add zucchini and onion and mix well. Stir into flour mixture just until evenly moistened.

Spoon batter into greased and floured madeleine pans (1½- or 2-tablespoon size) or tiny muffin pans (about 1½-in. diameter), filling to rims. Bake in a 400° oven until puffed and lightly browned (about 15 minutes for 1½-tablespoon size, 18 minutes for 2-tablespoon size, 20 minutes for small muffins). Let cool for 5 minutes; then invert pans to remove. Serve hot or at room temperature.

If made ahead, let cool completely, wrap airtight, and refrigerate until next day; freeze for longer storage. To reheat, lay madeleines (thawed, if frozen) in a single layer on baking sheets and place in a 350° oven until warm (about 5 minutes). Makes about 3 dozen appetizers.

Per appetizer: 65 calories, 3 g protein, 4 g carbohydrates, 4 g total fat, 33 mg cholesterol, 151 mg sodium

QUICK SALT STICKS

Preparation time: About 15 minutes
Cooking time: About 15 minutes

Take advantage of frozen puff pastry to make simple salt sticks, perfect for nibbling with dips and spreads. The sticks can be made ahead, chilled, and heated just before serving.

- 1 package (17¼ oz.) frozen puff pastry, thawed
- 1½ teaspoons caraway seeds
- 1 egg white, lightly beaten
- 1 teaspoon coarse (kosher-style) salt

Unfold pastry sheets and cut each into quarters; then cut each quarter into 2 triangles. Sprinkle evenly with caraway seeds.

Starting with longest side, roll each triangle into a stick. Place, center points down and several inches apart, on a 12- by 15-inch baking sheet. Brush lightly with egg white; sprinkle evenly with salt. Bake in a 400° oven until golden brown (about 15 minutes).

If made ahead, let cool on racks, wrap airtight, and refrigerate until next day. To reheat, lay on a baking sheet and place in a 400° oven until hot (about 5 minutes). Makes 16 appetizers.

Per appetizer: 132 calories, 2 g protein, 11 g carbohydrates, 9 g total fat, 0 mg cholesterol, 241 mg sodium

POLENTA TRIANGLES

Preparation time: About 10 minutes
Cooking time: About 18 minutes

Polenta, coarsely ground cornmeal traditionally used in Italian cooking, adds crunch to buttery flatbread triangles. Use freshly grated Parmesan cheese to give extra flavor to the cornbread, delicious alone or as a carrier for a dip or spread.

- ⅔ cup polenta or yellow cornmeal
- 1 cup all-purpose flour
- ½ cup (¼ lb.) butter or margarine
- ½ cup freshly grated Parmesan cheese
- 1 egg
- ¼ cup milk

In a food processor or bowl, combine polenta, flour, butter, and cheese. Whirl or rub with your fingers until mixture forms fine crumbs. Add egg and milk; whirl or stir just until moistened. Pat dough into a greased 9- by 13-inch pan.

Bake in a 400° oven until golden brown (about 18 minutes). Cut into about 2-inch squares; then cut each square diagonally in half. If made ahead, cool, cover, and let stand until next day. Makes 4 dozen appetizers.

Per appetizer: 40 calories, 1 g protein, 4 g carbohydrates, 2 g total fat, 10 mg cholesterol, 37 mg sodium

SLICED PEPPER STEAK IN MUSTARD SAUCE

Preparation time: About 5 minutes
Cooking time: About 10 minutes

Barbecue a thick sirloin steak en-crusted with peppercorns; then slice thinly, swirl in a mustardy butter sauce, and serve on sliced French bread.

- 2 teaspoons freeze-dried green peppercorns, coarsely crushed
- 1 pound top sirloin steak (about 1 in. thick), trimmed of fat
- 2 tablespoons butter or margarine
- 1 tablespoon Dijon mustard
- 1 tablespoon dry vermouth or dry white wine
- 1 small French baguette (8 oz.), sliced ½ inch thick

Sprinkle peppercorns over both sides of steak, pressing in lightly. Place steak on a lightly greased grill 4 to 6 inches above a solid bed of hot coals. (Or place steak on a rack in a broiler pan and broil about 3 inches below heat.) Cook, turning once, until done to your liking when cut (about 10 minutes for medium-rare).

Meanwhile, melt butter in a 3- to 4-cup pan on cooler part of grill (or over low heat); stir in mustard and vermouth.

Transfer steak to a rimmed platter; pour sauce over and around steak. Cut into thin, slanting slices, swirling pieces in sauce. Offer with bread slices. Makes 1 dozen appetizers.

Per appetizer: 123 calories, 9 g protein, 11 g carbohydrates, 5 g total fat, 26 mg cholesterol, 182 mg sodium

GINGERY MARINATED BEEF CUBES

Preparation time: About 5 minutes
Marinating time: At least 2 hours
Cooking time: About 7 minutes

Enjoy the gingery, peppery season-ings of this tender beef appetizer. Marinate the meat up to a day ahead; then quickly stir-fry the bite-size pieces.

- 1 tablespoon sesame seeds
- ¼ cup soy sauce
- 2 to 3 teaspoons minced fresh ginger
- 3 cloves garlic, minced or pressed
- 1 teaspoon *each* sugar and vinegar
- 2 green onions (including tops), thinly sliced
- ¼ to ½ teaspoon ground red pepper (cayenne)
  About 5 tablespoons salad oil
- 1½ pounds boneless beef sirloin, top round, or boneless chuck, cut into ¾-inch cubes

Toast sesame seeds in a small frying pan over medium heat, shaking pan frequently, until golden (about 3 minutes). In a bowl, mix sesame seeds, soy, ginger, garlic, sugar, vine-gar, onions, pepper, and 1 tablespoon of the oil. Add meat, stirring to coat. Cover and refrigerate for at least 2 hours or until next day.

Heat 2 more tablespoons of the oil in a wide frying pan over high heat. Add meat, half at a time, and cook, stirring, until done to your liking when cut (about 2 minutes for me-dium doneness). Repeat with remain-ing meat, adding remaining oil as needed.

Offer with wooden picks. Makes about 4 dozen appetizers.

Per appetizer: 59 calories, 3 g protein, .3 g carbohydrates, 5 g total fat, 10 mg cholesterol, 93 mg sodium

BARBECUED PRIME RIB BONES

Preparation time: About 5 minutes
Marinating time: About 2 hours
Cooking time: About 20 minutes

Meaty ribs flavored with a tangy mustard marinade make a hearty opener at an outdoor party.

> **About 6 pounds standing rib bones**
> **Mustard Marinade (recipe follows)**

Arrange meat in a large shallow bak-ing pan. Prepare Mustard Marinade and pour over ribs; turn to coat. Cover and let stand for about 2 hours.

Lift ribs from marinade, reserving marinade. Place on a lightly greased grill 4 to 6 inches above a solid bed of hot coals. (Or place ribs in a 10- by 15-inch baking pan and bake in a 425° oven.) Cook, turning frequently and brushing with marinade, until done to your liking when cut (about 20 minutes for medium-rare).

Cut between bones to separate ribs. Makes about 1 dozen appetizers.

Mustard Marinade. Combine ⅓ cup **Dijon mustard** and 2 table-spoons **red wine vinegar**. Beating constantly with a wire whisk, add ¼ cup **olive** or salad **oil**, a few drops at a time. Beat in 1 clove **garlic**, minced or pressed; ½ teaspoon *each* **dry thyme leaves** and **Worcestershire**; and ¼ teaspoon **pepper**.

Per appetizer: 322 calories, 15 g protein, 1 g carbohydrates, 28 g total fat, 60 mg cholesterol, 245 mg sodium

Begin a backyard barbecue with richly basted Down-home Baby Back Ribs (recipe on facing page), crispy coated Parmesan Zucchini Sticks (recipe on page 71), and tangy fresh Artichoke Hearts with Blue Cheese recipe on page 65).

BEEF CHIANG MAI

Preparation time: About 10 minutes
Cooking time: About 12 minutes

Cool, crisp lettuce leaves hold a warm, spicy beef mixture in this traditional dish from northern Thailand. Have your guests wrap their own meat bundles after topping them with sprigs of mint.

- ¼ cup short- or long-grain rice
- 1 pound lean ground beef
- 1 teaspoon *each* sugar and crushed red pepper
- ½ cup *each* thinly sliced green onions (including tops) and chopped fresh mint leaves
- 2 tablespoons chopped cilantro (coriander)
- ¼ cup lemon juice
- 1½ tablespoons soy sauce
  Small inner leaves from 2 large or 3 small heads butter lettuce, washed and crisped
  About 36 fresh mint sprigs

Place a wide frying pan or wok over medium heat. When pan is hot, add rice and cook, stirring, until golden (about 5 minutes). Remove from heat and transfer to a blender or food processor; whirl until finely ground. Set aside.

Return pan to heat. When wok is hot, crumble in beef and cook, stirring, until no longer pink (about 7 minutes). Stir in rice, sugar, pepper, onions, chopped mint, cilantro, lemon juice, and soy. Pour into a dish and surround with lettuce leaves and mint sprigs.

Spoon beef mixture onto lettuce leaves, top with a mint sprig, and roll up. Makes about 3 dozen appetizers.

Per appetizer: 124 calories, 7 g protein, 5 g carbohydrates, 8 g total fat, 28 mg cholesterol, 157 mg sodium

CRANBERRY COCKTAIL MEATBALLS

Preparation time: About 25 minutes
Cooking time: About 5 minutes

Just because these bite-size meatballs are served in cranberry sauce doesn't mean you have to save them for the holidays. Guests will enjoy their zesty flavor anytime, and you'll appreciate the ease of baking rather than sautéing them.

- 2 pounds lean ground beef
- 1 cup cornflake crumbs
- ⅓ cup finely chopped parsley
- 2 eggs, lightly beaten
- ¼ teaspoon pepper
- 1 clove garlic, minced or pressed
- ⅓ cup catsup
- 2 tablespoons *each* thinly sliced green onions (including tops) and soy sauce
- 1 can (1 lb.) whole berry cranberry sauce
- 1 bottle (12 oz.) tomato-based chili sauce
- 1 tablespoon *each* brown sugar and lemon juice

Thoroughly mix beef, cornflake crumbs, parsley, eggs, pepper, garlic, catsup, onions, and soy; shape into 1-inch balls (you should have about 75). Arrange, slightly apart, in shallow 10- by 15-inch baking pans. Bake in a 500° oven until lightly browned (about 5 minutes).

Meanwhile, in a 2- to 3-quart pan, cook cranberry sauce, chili sauce, sugar, and lemon juice over medium heat, stirring, until bubbling (about 3 minutes).

With a slotted spoon, transfer meatballs to a warm serving dish; pour sauce over meatballs. Offer with wooden picks. Makes about 75 appetizers.

Per appetizer: 48 calories, 3 g protein, 5 g carbohydrates, 2 g total fat, 13 mg cholesterol, 128 mg sodium

Pictured on facing page

DOWN-HOME BABY BACK RIBS

Preparation time: About 5 minutes
Cooking time: About 1 hour and 10 minutes

Pork spareribs are a perennial favorite, perfect for backyard barbecues with family and friends. A traditional molasses and catsup sauce accents the tender, juicy meat.

- 4 pounds pork spareribs (preferably baby back ribs)
- ½ cup water
- ¼ cup *each* catsup and light molasses
- 2 tablespoons soy sauce
- 2 cloves garlic, minced or pressed
- 1 teaspoon *each* dry mustard and ground ginger

Place ribs, overlapping slightly if necessary, in a 12- by 17-inch roasting pan; add water. Cover and bake in a 350° oven until tender when pierced (about 1 hour).

Shortly before ribs are done, combine catsup, molasses, soy, garlic, mustard, and ginger in a 1- to 1½-quart pan. Cook over medium heat, stirring, until hot; set aside.

Drain ribs, discarding liquid from baking pan. Brush all over with sauce. Place on a lightly greased grill 4 to 6 inches above a solid bed of medium coals. (Or place ribs on a rack in a broiler pan and broil about 4 inches below heat.) Cook, turning occasionally and brushing with remaining sauce, until well browned (about 10 minutes).

Cut between bones to separate. Makes about 1 dozen appetizers.

Per appetizer: 261 calories, 17 g protein, 6 g carbohydrates, 18 g total fat, 71 mg cholesterol, 287 mg sodium

Planning a party can be fun, especially when you choose a particular theme or celebrate a special occasion. When deciding on your appetizers, think about the taste, texture, temperature, and color of your choices, as well as the weather, time of day, and other food you'll be serving.

The menus we've created include spreads that showcase a particular ethnic cuisine, starters for an elegant dinner party, basic beginners for a lazy summer supper, and even hors d'oeuvres you can make with ingredients you have on hand when unexpected guests drop by.

To determine how many appetizers you'll need, follow the guidelines in "Great Beginnings" on pages 6–7.

APPETIZING MENUS

ELEGANT EVENING

Melted Brie with Winter Fruits, page 20

Turkey Rilletes, page 30

Zucchini Madeleines, page 46

Heavenly Mushrooms, page 66

Twice-baked Creamers, page 68

Tomato Tarts Niçoise, page 76

SPUR–OF–THE MOMENT PARTY

Hummus, page 15

Curried Raisins, Peanuts & Banana Chips, page 27

Quick Tuna-Anchovy Spread, page 28

Apricot & Almond-Butter Bites, page 83

Needles in a Haystack, page 83

Cherry Tomatoes with Smoked Oysters, page 86

Orange-Fennel Olives, page 94

ORIENTAL BANQUET

Asian Eggplant Dip, page 15

Gingery Marinated Beef Cubes, page 47

Chicken Yakitori, page 54

Phoenix-tail Shrimp, page 62

Marbled Tea Eggs, page 74

Thai Carrot Salad, page 92

Sesame Long Beans, page 92

SPRINGTIME CELEBRATION

Appetizer Mini-Quiches, page 36

Veal & Olive Terrine, page 78

Spinach-wrapped Chicken, page 79

Asparagus in Belgian Endive, page 89

Minted Peas & Almonds, page 94

Nut- & Cheese-filled Fruits, page 95

TAILGATE PICNIC

Apple Aïoli, page 14

Stuffed Camembert, page 22

Sweet Potato Chips, page 27

Creamy Braunschweiger Appetizer, page 28

Zucchini Frittata, page 75

Lean Terrine, page 81

Steeped Shrimp, page 87

Pickled Cucumbers, page 92

ITALIAN FEAST

Gorgonzola Pesto, page 10

Appetizer Pizza Squares, page 41

Baked Shrimp with Garlic, page 63

Florentine Mushrooms, page 67

Stuffed Pasta Shells Italiano, page 86

Meat-wrapped Fruits, page 95

EASY SUMMER SUPPER

Lazy Liptauer Cheese, page 22

Chili-baked Chicken Wings, page 79

Chilled Cucumber Cream Soup, page 83

Snap Pea Knots, page 94

Fruited Tabbouleh, page 94

Fresh Melon Pickles, page 95

MEXICAN BUFFET

Chile con Queso, page 10

Black Bean Dip, page 17

Salsa Fresca, page 19

Empanadas, page 39

Scallop Seviche, page 81

Jicama & Fresh Fruit Platter, page 95

SUNDAY BRUNCH

Tarragon Mayonnaise, page 12

Potted Shrimp with Chervil, page 28

Scotch Baked Eggs, page 34

Hot Spiced Apple Crêpes, page 39

Baby Dutch Babies, page 44

Turkey-Cheese Pinwheels, page 79

CHINESE PORK APPETIZERS

Preparation time: About 15 minutes
Marinating time: At least 1 hour
Cooking time: About 7 minutes

Cinnamon, cloves, and anise seeds in a soy-based sauce flavor lean boneless pork in this easy, Asian-inspired appetizer.

¼ **cup soy sauce**
2 **tablespoons salad oil**
2 **cloves garlic, minced or pressed**
1 **small dried hot red chile, crushed**
½ **teaspoon sugar**
¼ **teaspoon anise seeds**
⅛ **teaspoon *each* ground cinnamon and ground cloves**
2 **pounds lean boneless pork**

Mix soy, oil, garlic, chile, sugar, anise seeds, cinnamon, and cloves; set aside.

Cut pork into ¼- to ½-inch-thick strips about 1 inch wide (you should have about 48 strips). Add to soy mixture, stirring to coat. Cover and refrigerate for at least 1 hour or up to 2 hours, stirring several times.

Meanwhile, soak 24 bamboo skewers in hot water to cover for 30 minutes.

Thread 2 strips of meat onto each skewer. Place on a lightly greased grill 4 to 6 inches above a solid bed of medium coals. (Or place skewers on a rack in a broiler pan and broil about 4 inches below heat.) Cook, turning occasionally, until no longer pink in center when cut (about 7 minutes). Makes 2 dozen appetizers.

Per appetizer: 74 calories, 9 g protein, .3 g carbohydrates, 4 g total fat, 27 mg cholesterol, 150 mg sodium

Pictured on page 64

MEATBALLS WRAPPED IN BASIL LEAVES

Preparation time: About 35 minutes
Cooking time: About 10 minutes

Fresh basil and fennel seeds season grilled meatballs made from pork sausage. Wrap a whole basil leaf around each meatball for extra flavor and eye appeal.

For an alternative with less fat, try the variation using ground turkey.

1 **pound bulk pork sausage**
½ **cup minced fresh basil leaves**
1 **teaspoon crushed fennel seeds**
24 **large fresh basil leaves**

Soak 8 bamboo skewers in hot water to cover for 30 minutes.

Meanwhile, thoroughly mix sausage, minced basil, and fennel seeds. Shape into about 1-inch balls (you should have 24). Wrap a basil leaf around each meatball, lightly pressing it into meat so it sticks (leaf does not have to cover entire meatball). Thread 3 meatballs on each skewer.

Place on a greased grill 2 to 4 inches above a solid bed of hot coals. Cook, turning every 2 to 3 minutes, until no longer pink in center when cut (about 10 minutes). Makes 8 appetizers.

Per appetizer: 104 calories, 6 g protein, 1 g carbohydrates, 8 g total fat, 22 mg cholesterol, 349 mg sodium

Turkey Meatballs Wrapped in Basil Leaves

Follow directions for **Meatballs Wrapped in Basil Leaves,** but substitute 1 pound **ground turkey breast** for sausage. Do not grill; instead, place skewers on a rimmed baking sheet. Bake in a 450° oven, turning once, until meat is no longer pink in center when cut (about 8 minutes).

Per appetizer: 70 calories, 13 g protein, 1 g carbohydrates, 1 g total fat, 29 g mg cholesterol, 30 mg sodium

MEATBALLS & GINGER GLAZE

Preparation time: About 25 minutes
Cooking time: About 45 minutes

A sweet-sour sauce enlivened by a generous helping of fresh ginger coats meatballs made with ground pork, green onions, and crisp water chestnuts.

Ginger Glaze (recipe follows)
1 **can (about 8 oz.) water chestnuts, drained and finely chopped**
1 **cup chopped green onions (including tops)**
2 **pounds lean ground pork**
2 **tablespoons soy sauce**
2 **eggs, lightly beaten**
¾ **cup fine dry bread crumbs**
About 1 tablespoon salad oil

Prepare Ginger Glaze; set aside.

Thoroughly mix water chestnuts, onions, pork, soy, eggs, and bread crumbs. Shape into ¾-inch balls (you should have about 72).

Heat 1 tablespoon of the oil in a wide frying pan over medium heat. Add meatballs, about a third at a time, and cook, stirring, until well browned (about 10 minutes); add oil as needed. Remove meatballs and set aside. Clean pan.

Add glaze to pan, increase heat to high, and stir until glaze boils vigorously. Add meatballs, reduce heat, and simmer for 10 minutes. Offer with wooden picks. Makes about 6 dozen appetizers.

Ginger Glaze. Smoothly mix ½ cup **water** and ¼ cup **cornstarch.** Stir in 1 cup *each* **unsweetened pineapple juice** and **regular-strength beef broth,** ½ cup **cider vinegar,** ⅓ cup **sugar,** 1 tablespoon **soy sauce,** and 2 tablespoons minced **fresh ginger.**

Per appetizer: 42 calories, 3 g protein, 3 g carbohydrates, 2 g total fat, 15 mg cholesterol, 71 mg sodium

BARBECUED LAMB RIBS

Preparation time: About 10 minutes
Cooking time: About 25 minutes

Distinctive lamb spareribs grill to juicy tenderness cloaked in a tomato-based barbecue sauce. The ribs can also be broiled, if desired.

 1 tablespoon olive oil
 ½ cup finely chopped onion
 1 clove garlic, minced or pressed
 ¼ teaspoon *each* dry oregano leaves and ground cinnamon
 ⅛ teaspoon ground red pepper (cayenne)
 1½ teaspoons brown sugar
 1 tablespoon balsamic or cider vinegar
 ¼ cup catsup
 2 tablespoons dry red wine
 2 sections (2 to 2½ lbs. *total*) lamb spareribs, trimmed of fat

Heat oil in a 1- to 1½-quart pan over medium heat. Add onion and garlic and cook, stirring often, until soft (about 7 minutes). Add oregano, cinnamon, pepper, sugar, vinegar, catsup, and wine. Increase heat to high and boil, stirring, for 1 minute. Let cool briefly. (At this point, you may cool completely, cover, and refrigerate for up to 2 days.)

Brush ribs with sauce. Place on a lightly greased grill 4 to 6 inches above a solid bed of medium-hot coals. (Or place ribs on a rack in a broiler pan and broil about 3 inches below heat.) Cook, turning once and brushing with any remaining sauce, until browned (about 15 minutes for medium-rare).

Cut between bones to separate. Makes about 1½ dozen appetizers.

Per appetizer: 94 calories, 4 g protein, 2 g carbohydrates, 8 g total fat, 19 mg cholesterol, 49 mg sodium

---

Pictured on facing page

LAMB MEATBALLS WITH PINE NUTS

Preparation time: About 15 minutes
Cooking time: About 15 minutes

Meatballs made with ground lamb are covered with a sweet-sour sauce.

 1 egg, lightly beaten
 ½ teaspoon *each* salt and ground cinnamon
 1 clove garlic, minced or pressed
 2 tablespoons *each* fine dry bread crumbs and catsup
 1 tablespoon red wine vinegar
 ¼ cup pine nuts or slivered almonds
 1½ pounds lean ground lamb
 1 tablespoon olive oil
 1 small red onion, thinly slivered
 ½ cup Marsala or cream sherry
 2 teaspoons lemon juice
 Chopped parsley (optional)

Mix egg, salt, cinnamon, garlic, bread crumbs, catsup, and vinegar. Add nuts and lamb; mix lightly. Shape into 1-inch balls (you should have about 48). Arrange, slightly apart, in a baking pan. Bake in a 500° oven until well browned (about 10 minutes).

Meanwhile, heat oil in a wide frying pan over medium heat. Add onion and cook, stirring often, until soft (about 10 minutes). Remove pan from heat and set aside.

With a slotted spoon, transfer meatballs to a dish and keep warm. Discard fat from baking pan. Pour a little of the wine into pan, scraping browned bits free; add to onion mixture along with remaining wine and lemon juice. Boil over high heat, stirring, until reduced by about half. Pour over meatballs and sprinkle with parsley, if desired. Offer with wooden picks. Makes about 4 dozen appetizers.

Per appetizer: 42 calories, 3 g protein, .9 g carbohydrates, 3 g total fat, 15 mg cholesterol, 42 mg sodium

---

BLACKBERRY SHISH KEBABS

Preparation time: About 45 minutes
Marinating time: At least 4 hours
Cooking time: About 8 minutes

Blackberry syrup blends with soy sauce and fresh mint to create a complementary marinade for lamb. Grill the meat quickly—browned on the outside, but still pink in the center—for best flavor and texture.

 ½ cup blackberry syrup
 ¼ cup red wine vinegar
 2 tablespoons *each* soy sauce and chopped fresh mint leaves
 2 cloves garlic, minced or pressed
 ½ teaspoon pepper
 2 cans (about 8 oz. *each*) whole water chestnuts, drained
 1½ pounds lean boneless lamb (leg or shoulder), cut into 1-inch cubes

Mix syrup, vinegar, soy, mint, garlic, and pepper. Add water chestnuts and lamb, stirring to coat. Cover and refrigerate for at least 4 hours or until next day, stirring several times.

Soak 12 bamboo skewers in hot water to cover for 30 minutes. Lift meat and water chestnuts from marinade and thread alternately on skewers (to avoid splitting water chestnuts, rotate skewer as you pierce them).

Place on a lightly greased grill 4 to 6 inches above a solid bed of medium coals. (Or place skewers on a rack in a broiler pan and broil about 4 inches below heat.) Cook, turning occasionally, until meat is browned but still pink in center when cut (about 8 minutes). Makes 1 dozen appetizers.

Per appetizer: 137 calories, 13 g protein, 14 g carbohydrates, 3 g total fat, 38 mg cholesterol, 204 mg sodium

Welcome special company with cinnamon-accented
Lamb Meatballs with Pine Nuts (recipe on facing page),
savory Peppered Chèvre with Pears (recipe on page 23),
and pungent Garlic-buttered Mushrooms (recipe on
page 66).

SPICY CHICKEN WINGS

Pictured on page 45

Preparation time: About 15 minutes
Cooking time: About 45 minutes

Liquid hot pepper sauce and ground red pepper lend heat to these baked chicken wings. Serve with celery and sour cream–based blue cheese dip to help cool things off, if you wish.

- 4 **pounds chicken wings, cut apart at joints**
  Red Hot Sauce (recipe follows)
  Blue Cheese Dip (recipe follows), optional
- 2 **bunches celery (about 2 lbs. *total*), optional**

Discard wing tips or save for broth. Arrange chicken in 2 lightly greased 10- by 15-inch baking pans. Bake in a 400° oven until golden brown (about 30 minutes).

Meanwhile, prepare Red Hot Sauce. Remove pans from oven, drain off fat, and pour sauce over chicken, turning to coat well. Return pans to oven and continue baking, turning wings once or twice, until sauce is bubbling and edges of wings are crisp (about 15 more minutes).

Meanwhile, prepare Blue Cheese Dip and break celery stalks from head, if desired; remove leaves and set aside. Slice stalks lengthwise and place in a bowl.

Arrange chicken on a platter and garnish with reserved celery leaves, if used. Offer with celery stalks and cheese dip. Makes about 4 dozen appetizers.

Red Hot Sauce. Mix ½ cup *each* **vinegar** and **water,** ¼ cup **tomato paste,** 4 teaspoons **sugar,** 1 to 3 tablespoons (or to taste) **liquid hot pepper seasoning,** and 1 to 3 teaspoons (or to taste) **ground red pepper** (cayenne).

Per appetizer: 45 calories, 4 g protein, .8 g carbohydrates, 3 g total fat, 12 mg cholesterol, 39 mg sodium

Blue Cheese Dip. Coarsely mash ¼ pound **blue-veined cheese.** Stir in 1 cup **sour cream,** 1 teaspoon minced **garlic,** ½ teaspoon **dry mustard,** and ⅛ teaspoon **pepper.** If made ahead, cover and refrigerate for up to 3 days. Makes 1⅓ cups.

Per tablespoon: 43 calories, 2 g protein, .6 g carbohydrates, 4 g total fat, 9 mg cholesterol, 81 mg sodium

HOISIN CHICKEN WINGS

Preparation time: About 5 minutes
Marinating time: At least 1 hour
Cooking time: About 12 minutes

Take chicken drummettes, the meatiest portion of the wings, and marinate them in a bold blend of hoisin sauce, garlic, and sherry. Then quickly grill and watch them disappear.

- ⅓ **cup hoisin sauce**
- 2 **tablespoons dry sherry**
- 1 **tablespoon lemon juice**
- 1 **clove garlic, minced or pressed**
- 1½ **pounds chicken drummettes (meatiest part of wing)**

Mix hoisin, sherry, lemon juice, and garlic. Add chicken, turning to coat. Cover and refrigerate for at least 1 hour or until next day.

Lift chicken from marinade, reserving marinade. Place on a greased grill 4 to 6 inches above a solid bed of medium coals. Cook, turning occasionally and brushing with marinade, until meat near bone is no longer pink when cut (about 12 minutes). Makes about 1½ dozen appetizers.

Per appetizer: 45 calories, 5 g protein, .8 g carbohydrates, 2 g total fat, 20 mg cholesterol, 98 mg sodium

CHICKEN YAKITORI

Preparation time: About 30 minutes
Marinating time: About 15 minutes
Cooking time: About 12 minutes

A simple marinade of soy sauce and sherry flavors chicken thighs and livers. Thread the meat on separate skewers to take into account their different cooking times.

- ½ **cup soy sauce**
- ½ **cup cream sherry, sake, or mirin**
- 3 **tablespoons sugar**
- 6 **large chicken thighs, skinned and boned**
- ½ **pound chicken livers**
- 2 **bunches green onions (including tops), cut into 1½-inch lengths**

Soak 16 short bamboo skewers in hot water to cover for 30 minutes.

Meanwhile, in a 1- to 1½-quart pan, boil soy, sherry, and sugar over high heat; reduce heat, cover, and simmer for 3 minutes. Pour into a shallow baking pan and set aside.

Cut thighs into bite-size pieces. Cut each liver in half. Thread thigh meat and livers on separate skewers, including several onion pieces on each. Marinate in soy mixture, turning once or twice, for 15 minutes.

Lift skewers from marinade, reserving marinade. Place on a lightly greased grill 4 to 6 inches above a solid bed of low coals. Cook, turning occasionally and brushing with marinade, until livers are firm but still moist in center when cut (about 5 minutes) and thigh meat is no longer pink in center when cut (about 8 minutes). Makes 16 appetizers.

Per appetizer: 69 calories, 9 g protein, 3 g carbohydrates, 2 g total fat, 89 mg cholesterol, 297 mg sodium

CHICKEN SATAY

Preparation time: About 20 minutes
Marinating time: At least 1½ hours
Cooking time: About 14 minutes

Dip broiled chicken chunks in a spicy peanut sauce for a Southeast Asian treat.

- 1 **clove garlic, minced or pressed**
- 2 **tablespoons soy sauce**
- 1 **tablespoon salad oil**
- 1 **teaspoon** *each* **ground cumin and ground coriander**
- 2 **whole chicken breasts (about 2 lbs.** *total***), split, skinned, and boned**
  Basting Sauce (recipe follows)
  Peanut Sauce (recipe follows)

Mix garlic, soy, oil, cumin, and coriander. Cut chicken into ¾-inch chunks. Add to marinade, stirring to coat evenly. Cover and refrigerate for at least 1½ hours or up to 2 hours.

Meanwhile, prepare Basting Sauce and Peanut Sauce; set aside. Also, soak 16 bamboo skewers in hot water to cover for 30 minutes.

Thread 4 or 5 cubes of chicken on each skewer. Place on a rack in a broiler pan; brush with half the baste. Broil 4 to 6 inches below heat, turning once and brushing with remaining baste, until no longer pink in center when cut (about 10 minutes).

Offer with sauce for dipping. Makes about 16 appetizers.

Basting Sauce. Mix 3 tablespoons **lemon juice,** 2 tablespoons **soy sauce,** and ¼ teaspoon *each* **ground cumin** and **ground coriander.**

Per appetizer: 94 calories, 17 g protein, 1 g carbohydrates, 2 g total fat, 43 mg cholesterol, 435 mg sodium

Peanut Sauce. In a 1- to 1½-quart pan, boil 1 cup **water,** ⅔ cup **creamy** or crunchy **peanut butter,** and 2 cloves **garlic,** minced or pressed, over medium-high heat, stirring, until

thickened (about 4 minutes). Remove from heat and stir in 2 tablespoons firmly packed **brown sugar,** 1½ tablespoons **lemon juice,** 1 tablespoon **soy sauce,** and ¼ to ½ teaspoon **crushed red pepper.** Let cool to room temperature. Makes 1½ cups.

Per tablespoon: 57 calories, 3 g protein, 3 g carbohydrates, 4 g total fat, 0 mg cholesterol, 93 mg sodium

CHUTNEY CHICKEN ROLLS

Preparation time: About 15 minutes
Cooking time: About 15 minutes

Nestled in the center of tender chicken rolls is a tempting mixture of almonds and chutney.

- 2 **tablespoons light rum**
- 3 **tablespoons butter or margarine, melted**
  About ⅓ cup fine dry seasoned bread crumbs
- 3 **whole chicken breasts (about 3 lbs.** *total***), split, skinned, and boned**
- 6 **tablespoons Major Grey's chutney, chopped**
- 2 **tablespoons slivered almonds**

Combine rum and butter in a shallow dish. Pour crumbs onto wax paper.

Place each breast half between sheets of plastic wrap. Pound with a flat-surfaced mallet until ¼ inch thick. Lay skinned sides down. Place 1 tablespoon of the chutney and 1 teaspoon of the almonds in center of each. Roll up to enclose, fastening with wooden picks. Dip in rum mixture and coat with crumbs. Place in a baking pan and drizzle with any remaining rum mixture.

Bake in a 425° oven until no longer pink in center when cut (about 15 minutes). Cut rolls in half. Makes 1 dozen appetizers.

Per appetizer: 147 calories, 18 g protein, 8 g carbohydrates, 5 g total fat, 51 mg cholesterol, 182 mg sodium

CHILI CHICKEN CHUNKS

Preparation time: About 30 minutes
Cooking time: About 15 minutes

Chunks of chicken breast are fried in a crunchy cornmeal crust until golden, ready for dipping into Guacamole (recipe on page 15).

- 3 **whole chicken breasts (about 3 lbs.** *total***), split, skinned, and boned**
- ¾ **cup all-purpose flour**
- ¼ **cup yellow cornmeal**
- 2 **teaspoons chili powder**
- ½ **teaspoon** *each* **paprika and salt**
- ¼ **teaspoon** *each* **ground cumin and dry oregano leaves**
- ⅛ **teaspoon pepper**
- ¾ **cup beer**
  Salad oil

Cut chicken into 1- to 1½-inch chunks; set aside. In a bowl, mix flour, cornmeal, chili powder, paprika, salt, cumin, oregano, and pepper. Add beer and stir until smooth. Add chicken, stirring to coat evenly.

In a deep 3- to 4-quart pan, heat about 1½ inches oil to 350°F on a deep-frying thermometer. Lift chicken from batter, a piece at a time, and add to pan (do not crowd). Cook, stirring occasionally, until browned and no longer pink in center when cut (about 2 minutes). Drain on paper towels.

If made ahead, cool, cover, and refrigerate until next day; to reheat, lay chicken in a paper towel–lined pan and place in a 350° oven until hot (about 15 minutes).

Offer with wooden picks. Makes about 8 dozen appetizers.

Per appetizer: 22 calories, 2 g protein, 1 g carbohydrates, .9 g total fat, 5 mg cholesterol, 18 mg sodium

*Alternate chicken breasts with tropical fruits on bamboo
skewers and broil quickly for Curried Chicken & Fruit
Kebabs (recipe on facing page). You can use either papaya
or kumquats with chunks of banana and pineapple.*

CURRIED CHICKEN & FRUIT KEBABS

Pictured on facing page

Preparation time: About 25 minutes
Marinating time: At least 2 hours
Cooking time: About 12 minutes

Alternate tropical fruits with chunks of chicken breast on skewers. Your favorite oil and vinegar salad dressing enlivened by curry serves as a marinade.

  3   **whole chicken breasts (about 3 lbs. *total*), split, skinned, and boned**
  ¾   **cup bottled oil and vinegar salad dressing**
  2   **teaspoons curry powder**
  3   **medium-size green-tipped bananas**
  1   **medium-size papaya or 20 preserved kumquats, drained**
       About 2 cups fresh pineapple chunks
  ⅓   **cup honey**
       Lime wedges

Cut chicken into bite-size pieces (you should have at least 60). Mix salad dressing and curry powder; add chicken, stirring gently to coat. Cover and refrigerate for at least 2 hours or until next day.

Soak 20 bamboo skewers in hot water to cover for 30 minutes.

Shortly before cooking, peel bananas and cut into 1-inch slices; brush with marinade. Peel, halve, and seed papaya; cut into 1-inch cubes. Alternately thread chicken on skewers with 1 piece each pineapple, banana, and papaya. Stir honey into remaining marinade and brush over kebabs.

Broil 3 to 4 inches below heat, turning once and brushing with marinade, until chicken is no longer pink in center when cut (about 12 minutes). Offer with lime. Makes 20 appetizers.

Per appetizer: 138 calories, 11 g protein, 13 g carbohydrates, 5 g total fat, 26 mg cholesterol, 162 mg sodium

MUSSEL & CLAM APPETIZER

Preparation time: About 1 hour
Cooking time: About 30 minutes

A plate piled high with shelled mussels and clams invites guests to dig in! Red and green salsas top the shellfish served on toasted French bread.

  1   **cup Salsa Fresca (recipe on page 17)**
  1½   **cups Tomatillo Salsa (recipe on page 17)**
  3   **pounds mussels, scrubbed**
  1   **cup *each* dry white wine and water**
  2   **tablespoons lemon juice**
  1   **pound clams (suitable for steaming), scrubbed**
  3   **small French baguettes (8 oz. *each*), sliced ½ inch thick, lightly toasted**
       Lime wedges

Prepare Salsa Fresca and Tomatillo Salsa; set aside.

Discard any mussels that don't close when tapped. Pull beard (clump of fibers along side of shell) off each mussel with a quick tug.

In a 6- to 8-quart pan, simmer mussels, wine, water, and lemon juice, covered, over medium-high heat just until shells open (about 5 minutes). Lift out with a slotted spoon, discarding any mussels that don't open. Let cool. Meanwhile, add clams, about a third at a time, to pan, cover, and simmer just until open (about 8 minutes). Lift out with a slotted spoon, discarding any clams that don't open. Let cool.

Remove mussels and clams from shells and pile in a large plate. Spoon shellfish onto bread slices; top with salsas and a squeeze of lime. Makes about 3 dozen appetizers.

Per appetizer: 83 calories, 5 g protein, 12 g carbohydrates, 1 g total fat, 9 mg cholesterol, 161 mg sodium

GARLIC MUSSELS ON THE HALF SHELL

Preparation time: About 30 minutes
Cooking time: About 10 minutes

Steamed mussels on the half shell are easy and elegant hors d'oeuvres. Freshly grated Parmesan cheese and garlic top the succulent shellfish.

  1½   **pounds mussels, scrubbed**
  1   **cup dry white wine**
  ¼   **cup olive or salad oil**
  ⅓   **cup freshly grated Parmesan cheese**
  3   **large cloves garlic, minced or pressed**
  1   **tablespoon finely chopped parsley**

Discard any mussels that don't close when tapped. Pull beard (clump of fibers along side of shell) off each mussel with a quick tug.

In a 5- to 6-quart pan, simmer mussels and wine, covered, over medium-high heat just until shells open (about 5 minutes). Lift out with a slotted spoon, discarding any mussels that don't open.

When mussels are cool enough to handle, remove meat from shells, discarding half of each shell. Arrange remaining half shells in a single layer in a heatproof serving dish. Place a mussel in each shell. In a small bowl, stir together oil, 3 tablespoons of the cheese, and garlic; drizzle mixture over mussels.

Broil 4 inches below heat just until cheese begins to melt and mussels are hot (about 5 minutes). Sprinkle with parsley and remaining cheese. Offer with wooden picks. Makes about 3 dozen appetizers.

Per appetizer: 23 calories, 1 g protein, .4 g carbohydrates, 2 g total fat, 2 mg cholesterol, 33 mg sodium

Succulent seafood, hearty beef balls, creamy cheese dip, spicy potato rounds: this symphony of starters cooks in no time. Your microwave lets you orchestrate a variety of delicious overtures to a meal in just minutes.

SIZZLING CURRIED SHRIMP

Preparation time: About 15 minutes
Cooking time: 4½ to 6 minutes

Shrimp absorb the flavor of a piquant butter sauce while cooking to moist perfection in the microwave.

- ¼ cup butter or margarine
- 1 large clove garlic, minced or pressed
- 1½ teaspoons curry powder
- 1 teaspoon mustard seeds, slightly crushed
- ½ teaspoon crushed dried hot red chiles
  Chives (optional)
- 1 pound medium-size raw shrimp (about 36 per lb.), shelled and deveined
- 2 teaspoons lemon juice
- ¼ cup chopped cilantro (coriander) or sliced green onions (including tops)
  Salt

Place butter in a 9- to 10-inch microwave-safe baking dish. Microwave, uncovered, on **HIGH (100%)** for 1 to 1½ minutes or until melted.

Stir in garlic, curry powder, mustard seeds, and chiles. Microwave, uncovered, on **HIGH (100%)** for 30 more seconds.

Wrap and tie a chive around each shrimp, if desired. Add shrimp to dish and microwave, uncovered, on

MICROWAVE MEDLEY

HIGH (100%) for 3 to 4 minutes, stirring once or twice, or just until shrimp are bright pink. Stir in lemon juice and cilantro, and season to taste with salt. Offer with wooden picks. Makes about 3 dozen appetizers.

Per appetizer: 23 calories, 2 g protein, .2 g carbohydrates, 1 g total fat, 19 mg cholesterol, 28 mg sodium

ONIONS IN BASIL-PARMESAN BUTTER

Preparation time: About 10 minutes
Cooking time: 11 to 14 minutes

Tiny frozen onions cook quickly in the microwave. Toss them in basil-accented butter and serve them tucked into pocket bread wedges.

- 1 package (10 oz.) frozen small whole onions
- 2 tablespoons butter or margarine
- ¼ cup slivered fresh basil leaves or 1 tablespoon dry basil leaves
- ¼ cup grated Parmesan cheese
  Salt and pepper
- 5 or 6 pocket breads (6-in. diameter), cut into quarters

Place frozen onions in a shallow 9-inch microwave-safe dish. Dot with butter and sprinkle with basil. Microwave, uncovered, on **HIGH (100%)** for 8 to 10 minutes, stirring once or twice, or until onions are tender when pierced. Sprinkle with cheese and season to taste with salt and pepper.

If desired, microwave pocket bread quarters, 4 at a time, on **HIGH (100%)** for about 30 seconds or just until warm.

Spoon 2 or 3 onions and a little sauce into pocket bread wedges. Makes 20 to 24 appetizers.

Per appetizer: 62 calories, 2 g protein, 10 g carbohydrates, 1 g total fat, 4 mg cholesterol, 120 mg sodium

ZESTY BARBECUED MEATBALLS

Preparation time: About 15 minutes
Cooking time: 8 to 10 minutes

Choose your favorite barbecue sauce—from hickory-smoked to super-hot—for these meaty morsels, always popular party fare.

- 1 egg, lightly beaten
- 1 tablespoon Worcestershire
- ¼ cup *each* fine dry bread crumbs and thinly sliced green onions (including tops)
- 1 pound lean ground beef
- ½ cup prepared barbecue sauce

Mix egg, Worcestershire, bread crumbs, and onions. Add ground beef, mixing until well combined. Shape into 1-inch balls (you should have about 36). Arrange in a single layer in a microwave-safe 7- by 11-inch or 8-inch square dish.

Cover and microwave on **HIGH (100%)** for 5 minutes. Spoon off and discard drippings; rearrange meatballs, if necessary, so that uncooked ones are at outside of dish. Drizzle with barbecue sauce. Microwave, uncovered, on **HIGH (100%)** for 3 to 5 more minutes or until meatballs are no longer pink in center when cut. Stir gently to coat with sauce.

Offer with wooden picks. Makes about 3 dozen appetizers.

Per appetizer: 33 calories, 3 g protein, 1 g carbohydrates, 2 g total fat, 13 mg cholesterol, 45 mg sodium

HAM & PINEAPPLE PUPUS

Preparation time: About 15 minutes
Cooking time: 4½ to 6 minutes

Fresh pineapple takes these Hawaiian-inspired treats out of the ordinary. Substitute juicy pears for the pineapple for equally satisfying results.

¼ **pound thinly sliced baked ham**
   About 3 dozen 1-inch cubes fresh pineapple
¼ **cup catsup**
1 **teaspoon dry mustard**
2 **tablespoons soy sauce**
1 **tablespoon brown sugar**
1 **small clove garlic, minced or pressed**

Cut ham into 1-inch-wide strips. Wrap a strip around each pineapple cube, spearing with a wooden pick to secure.

In a small bowl, mix catsup, mustard, soy, sugar, and garlic. Drizzle a little of the sauce over each pupu, reserving remaining sauce.

Arrange pupus, about a dozen at a time, on a flat 9- to 10-inch microwave-safe plate. Microwave, uncovered, on **HIGH (100%)** for 1½ to 2 minutes, rotating plate a half-turn midway through cooking, or until ham is sizzling and pineapple is heated through.

Offer with remaining sauce for dipping. Makes about 3 dozen appetizers.

Per appetizer: 16 calories, .8 g protein, 2 g carbohydrates, .3 g total fat, 2 mg cholesterol, 124 mg sodium

Ham & Pear Pupus

Follow directions for **Ham & Pineapple Pupus,** but omit pineapple. Core 2 medium-size firm-ripe **pears** and cut each into 8 wedges; cut each wedge in half. Wrap a strip of ham around each half-wedge and continue as directed. Makes 32 appetizers.

Per appetizer: 17 calories, .9 g protein, 3 g carbohydrates, .4 g total fat, 2 mg cholesterol, 140 mg sodium

JALAPEÑO & BACON POTATOES

Preparation time: About 10 minutes
Cooking time: 13½ to 19 minutes

Melted jalapeño-flavored cheese and a sprinkling of bacon top tender potato rounds in this easily made hot hors d'oeuvre.

1 **pound small red thin-skinned potatoes (2-in. diameter), scrubbed**
4 **slices bacon**
1 **cup (4 oz.) lightly packed shredded jalapeño jack cheese**

Pierce each potato in several places with a fork. Arrange in a circle in a microwave oven. Microwave, uncovered, on **HIGH (100%)** for 6 to 8 minutes, rotating potatoes once, or until potatoes are tender when pierced. Let cool briefly.

Slice potatoes about ¼ inch thick. Arrange slices in a single layer on 2 flat 10-inch microwave-safe plates. Set aside.

Place bacon on several thicknesses of paper towels in a 7- by 11-inch microwave-safe baking dish or on a microwave-safe broiling rack; cover with a paper towel. Microwave on **HIGH (100%)** for 3½ to 6 minutes or until bacon is browned. Let cool briefly; then coarsely crush.

Place a rounded teaspoon of the cheese on each potato slice. Sprinkle with bacon. Microwave, uncovered, a plateful at a time, on **HIGH (100%)** for 2 to 2½ minutes or until cheese is melted and bubbling. Makes 3 to 3½ dozen appetizers.

Per appetizer: 24 calories, 1 g protein, 2 g carbohydrates, 1 g total fat, 4 mg cholesterol, 31 mg sodium

NEOCLASSIC CHEESE FONDUE

Preparation time: About 15 minutes
Cooking time: 5 to 10 minutes

Because it's made in the microwave, this version of Swiss fondue takes little time and attention.

1 **cup (4 oz.) *each* shredded aged Swiss (Emmenthaler) and Gruyère cheese**
2 **teaspoons cornstarch**
½ **teaspoon dry mustard**
¾ **cup dry white wine**
1 **tablespoon kirsch (optional)**
   Freshly grated nutmeg
   About 4 cups ½-inch cubes firm French bread

Lightly mix Swiss, Gruyère, cornstarch, and mustard; set aside.

Pour wine into a deep 1½- to 2-quart microwave-safe casserole. Microwave, uncovered, on **HIGH (100%)** for 2 to 5 minutes or just until wine begins to bubble. Remove from oven. Add cheese mixture, a handful at a time, stirring after each addition, until cheese is soft. Return to oven and microwave on **MEDIUM (50%)** for 3 to 5 minutes, stirring once or twice, or until fondue is thick and bubbly. Stir well. Blend in kirsch, if desired, and sprinkle with nutmeg.

Keep warm on an electric warming tray or over a candle warmer. Offer with bread cubes for dipping. Makes about 6 servings.

Per serving: 231 calories, 13 g protein, 16 g carbohydrates, 12 g total fat, 39 mg cholesterol, 269 mg sodium

SAUTÉED SQUID & SHIITAKE MUSHROOMS

Preparation time: About 20 minutes, plus 30 minutes to soak dried mushrooms
Cooking time: About 15 minutes

Quickly cook rings of squid and serve with shiitake mushrooms in a wine-enriched cream sauce on toast rounds. For an elegant presentation, garnish with raspberries, lemon peel, and mint.

1 **pound cleaned squid tubes (mantles)**
5 **large fresh or dried shiitake mushrooms (*each* 2- to 3-in. diameter)**
2 **tablespoons olive oil**
1 **cup *each* dry white wine and whipping cream**
3 **tablespoons raspberry vinegar or lemon juice**
½ **teaspoon freshly ground pepper**
  Salt
30 **slices cocktail rye bread, lightly toasted**
  Raspberries (optional)
  Long, thin shreds of lemon peel (optional)
  Mint sprigs (optional)

Cut squid tubes crosswise into ⅛- to ¼-inch-thick rings; set aside.

If using dried mushrooms, soak in warm water to cover until pliable (about 30 minutes); drain. Cut off and discard stems of fresh or dried mushrooms; slice caps thinly.

Heat oil in a wide frying pan over medium heat. Add mushrooms and cook, stirring, until soft (about 3 minutes). Lift out and set aside.

Add wine and cream to pan. Bring to a boil; reduce heat, add squid, and adjust heat so mixture barely simmers. Cook, stirring occasionally, until squid is tender (about 5 minutes). With a slotted spoon, lift out squid and add to mushrooms.

Increase heat to high and boil liquid in pan, stirring occasionally, until reduced to 1 cup (about 4 minutes). Return squid and mushrooms to pan; then remove from heat. Stir in vinegar and pepper; season to taste with salt.

Evenly spoon squid mixture onto toast slices. Garnish with raspberries, lemon peel, and mint, if desired. Makes 2½ dozen appetizers.

Per appetizer: 65 calories, 3 g protein, 5 g carbohydrates, 4 g total fat, 44 mg cholesterol, 49 mg sodium

HAWAII SCALLOP SKEWERS

Preparation time: About 25 minutes
Marinating time: At least 2 hours
Cooking time: About 8 minutes

Before you put on the steaks, quickly grill these colorful skewers of scallops, mushrooms, bacon, and bell peppers for a delicious meal opener. The soy marinade doubles as the basting sauce.

16 **scallops (1¼ to 1½ lbs. *total*)**
  Soy Marinade (recipe follows)
16 **medium-size to large mushrooms (about 1 lb. *total*)**
4 **slices bacon**
2 **small red bell peppers, seeded and cut into 1½-inch squares**

Rinse scallops and pat dry.

Prepare Soy Marinade and pour into a deep bowl; add scallops and mushrooms and turn to coat. Cover and refrigerate for at least 2 hours or up to 4 hours, turning several times. Meanwhile, soak 8 bamboo skewers in hot water to cover for 30 minutes.

In a wide frying pan, cook bacon over medium heat until partially cooked but still limp (about 3 minutes). Lift out and drain. Cut each slice into 4 pieces.

Lift scallops and mushrooms from marinade and drain briefly, reserving marinade. Thread scallops, mushrooms, bacon, and bell peppers alternately on skewers. Place on a well-greased grill 4 to 6 inches above a solid bed of hot coals. Cook, turning occasionally and brushing with marinade, until scallops are opaque inside when cut (about 5 minutes). Makes 8 appetizers.

Soy Marinade. Stir together ¼ cup **soy sauce**; 1 tablespoon *each* **lemon juice, dry sherry,** and **salad oil;** 2 cloves **garlic,** minced or pressed; and 1 teaspoon *each* **sugar** and minced **fresh ginger.**

Per appetizer: 117 calories, 16 g protein, 6 g carbohydrates, 3 g total fat, 29 mg cholesterol, 447 mg sodium

SHRIMP IN MINT LEAVES

Preparation time: About 35 minutes
Cooking time: About 4 minutes

Fresh mint leaves wrap and flavor shrimp coated with lemon and butter. Quickly barbecued, the succulent morsels are delicious hot off the grill.

24 **medium-size raw shrimp (about ⅔ lb. *total*), shelled and deveined**
3 **tablespoons lemon juice**
¼ **cup butter or margarine, melted**
24 **large fresh mint leaves**

Soak 12 bamboo skewers in hot water to cover for 30 minutes. Meanwhile, mix shrimp, lemon juice, and butter. Fold a mint leaf around each shrimp. Thread 2 shrimp closely together on each skewer. Brush with any remaining butter mixture.

Place shrimp on a greased grill 2 to 4 inches above a solid bed of hot coals. Cook, turning once, until shrimp are opaque when cut (about 4 minutes). Makes 1 dozen appetizers.

Per appetizer: 28 calories, 2 g protein, .2 g carbohydrates, 2 g total fat, 21 mg cholesterol, 35 mg sodium

Dress up your next dinner party with this elegant hors d'oeuvre, Sautéed Squid & Shiitake Mushrooms (recipe on facing page). The creamy canapé is served on rye rounds and garnished with fresh raspberries.

COCONUT SHRIMP

Preparation time: About 25 minutes
Marinating time: At least 30 minutes
Cooking time: About 10 minutes

Crisp shredded coconut coats butter-flied shrimp sizzled in hot oil. Look for coconut milk and panko (Japanese-style coarse bread crumbs) in Asian or other well-stocked supermarkets.

- 12 colossal-size shrimp (about 15 per lb.), shelled (leave tails on, if desired) and deveined
- 1   tablespoon dry sherry
- ⅛   teaspoon curry powder
- ¾   cup all-purpose flour
- 2   teaspoons cornstarch
- ½   teaspoon baking powder
- ½   cup canned or thawed frozen coconut milk; or ½ cup milk and ½ teaspoon coconut extract
- 2   to 3 tablespoons water
- 1½ cups sweetened shredded dry coconut
- ¾   cup panko or coarse fresh bread crumbs
     Salad oil
     Salt and pepper
     Mango chutney (optional)

Cut a slit almost completely through back of each shrimp. Mix sherry, curry powder, and shrimp. Cover and refrigerate for at least 30 minutes or until next day.

In a bowl, mix ½ cup of the flour, cornstarch, and baking powder. Stir in coconut milk and enough of the water to make a smooth, thin batter.

On wax paper, mix shredded coconut and panko. Put remaining ¼ cup flour on another piece of wax paper.

In a deep 3- to 4-quart pan, heat about 1½ inches oil to 350°F on a deep-frying thermometer. Laying shrimp flat, coat with flour, batter, and then panko mixture. Cook shrimp, 3 or 4 at a time, turning occasionally, until golden (about 1½ minutes). Skim oil often to remove browned bits. Drain on paper towels. Season to taste with salt and pepper.

Offer with chutney for dipping, if desired. Makes 1 dozen appetizers.

Per appetizer: 147 calories, 7 g protein, 13 g carbohydrates, 8 g total fat, 37 mg cholesterol, 93 mg sodium

PHOENIX-TAIL SHRIMP

Preparation time: About 30 minutes
Cooking time: About 25 minutes

Coated with a crunchy puff of batter, these deep-fried shrimp are ready for dipping in hot mustard or a sauce of your choice.

- 1   cup all-purpose flour
- 2½   teaspoons baking powder
- ¼   teaspoon salt
      Dash of ground white pepper
- 1   cup water
      Salad oil
- 1   pound medium-size raw shrimp (about 36 per lb.), shelled (leave tails on) and deveined
      Hot mustard (optional)

Combine flour, baking powder, salt, and pepper. Add water and stir until batter is smooth.

In a deep 3- to 4-quart pan, heat about 1½ inches oil to 350°F on a deep-frying thermometer. Holding shrimp by tail, dip into batter (do not dip tail) and cook, 3 or 4 at a time, turning occasionally, until golden (about 1¼ minutes). Drain on paper towels.

Offer with hot mustard for dipping, if desired. Makes about 3 dozen appetizers.

Per appetizer: 34 calories, 2 g protein, 3 g carbohydrates, 1 g total fat, 16 mg cholesterol, 60 mg sodium

CHEESE-FILLED SHRIMP

Preparation time: About 45 minutes
Cooking time: About 10 minutes

Plump shrimp are stuffed with cheese, wrapped with bacon, and deep-fried until golden for an impressive treat.

- 12 colossal-size raw shrimp (about 15 per lb.), shelled (leave tails on, if desired) and deveined
- 2   ounces jack cheese
- 6   slices bacon, cut in half cross-wise
     About ⅓ cup fine dry bread crumbs
     Salad oil
     Tomato-based cocktail sauce (optional)

Starting about ¼ inch from head end, cut along back of each shrimp to make a pocket about ¾ inch deep and 1½ inches long. In center of slit, make a ¼-inch cut through shrimp.

Cut cheese into twelve 1-inch triangles about ½ inch thick. Tuck a point of each cheese triangle into ¼-inch cut in each shrimp. Tightly wrap a half-slice of bacon around shrimp. Impale a slender wooden skewer through tail end of shrimp and then through bacon and cheese. (At this point, you may cover and refrigerate until next day.)

Place bread crumbs on wax paper. Coat shrimp with crumbs. In a deep 3- to 4-quart pan, heat about 1½ inches oil to 350°F on a deep-frying thermometer. Cook shrimp, 3 or 4 at a time, turning occasionally, until cheese begins to melt (about 1½ minutes). Drain on paper towels.

Offer with cocktail sauce for dipping, if desired. Makes 1 dozen appetizers.

Per appetizer: 93 calories, 7 g protein, 2 g carbohydrates, 6 g total fat, 44 mg cholesterol, 133 mg sodium

SHRIMP ON CABBAGE SQUARES

◆

Preparation time: About 40 minutes
Cooking time: About 8 minutes

Begin an Asian-inspired banquet with your own dim sum. Shrimp paste sparked with ginger and garlic steams on bite-size squares of napa cabbage.

   Fresh Shrimp Paste (recipe follows)
10   to 12 large napa cabbage leaves
48   julienne strips thinly sliced cooked ham (*each* about 1 in. long)
24   cilantro (coriander) leaves
     Soy sauce (optional)

Prepare Fresh Shrimp Paste; set aside.

   Cut off leafy portions of cabbage; cut stems into twenty-four 1½-inch squares. Reserve leaves and trimmings for other uses.

   In a wok or deep, wide pan, arrange cabbage squares on a rack over about 1 inch boiling water. Cover and steam over high heat just until cabbage is slightly wilted (about 2 minutes). Drain well.

   On each cabbage square, mound about 1½ teaspoons of the shrimp paste. Lightly press 2 ham strips and a cilantro leaf into shrimp paste. Place cabbage squares, slightly apart, on an 11- to 12-inch heatproof plate; cover with plastic wrap. (At this point, you may refrigerate for up to 8 hours.)

   Place plate on a rack over 1 inch boiling water in wok. Cover and steam over high heat just until shrimp paste feels firm when lightly pressed (about 6 minutes). Offer with soy for dipping, if desired. Makes 2 dozen appetizers.

Fresh Shrimp Paste. Shell and devein ½ pound medium-size **raw shrimp** (about 36 per lb.). In a food processor, combine shrimp; 2 **egg whites;** 1 tablespoon *each* **dry sherry** and minced **fresh ginger;** 1 clove **garlic,** minced or pressed; 2 teaspoons **cornstarch;** 1 teaspoon **sugar;** ½ teaspoon *each* **salt** and **sesame oil;** and ⅛ teaspoon **ground white pepper.** Whirl until mixture forms a smooth paste. (Or finely mince shrimp with a knife; then combine with remaining ingredients and beat until well blended and sticky.)

Per appetizer: 18 calories, 2 g protein, 1 g carbohydrates, .4 g total fat, 13 mg cholesterol, 90 mg sodium

BARBECUED SHRIMP

◆

Preparation time: About 15 minutes
Marinating time: At least 4 hours
Cooking time: About 4 minutes

Marinate shrimp in a sweet-sour sauce and then either grill or broil them for a speedy appetizer offering.

 1   can (8 oz.) tomato sauce
½   cup molasses
 1   teaspoon dry mustard
     Dash of liquid hot pepper seasoning
¼   cup salad oil
⅛   teaspoon dry thyme leaves
     Salt and pepper
 2   pounds medium-size raw shrimp (about 36 per lb.), shelled and deveined

Mix tomato sauce, molasses, mustard, hot pepper seasoning, oil, and thyme until well blended. Season to taste with salt and pepper. Add shrimp, turning to coat. Cover and refrigerate for at least 4 hours or until next day.

   Soak bamboo skewers in hot water to cover for 30 minutes. Lift out shrimp, reserving marinade, and thread on skewers. Place on a greased grill 6 inches above a solid bed of low-glowing coals. (Or place on a rimmed baking sheet and broil about 6 inches below heat.) Cook, brushing frequently with marinade and turning once, until shrimp are opaque when cut (about 4 minutes). Makes about 6 dozen appetizers.

Per appetizer: 24 calories, 2 g protein, 2 g carbohydrates, .9 g total fat, 16 mg cholesterol, 35 mg sodium

Pictured on page 32
BAKED SHRIMP WITH GARLIC

◆

Preparation time: About 15 minutes
Marinating time: At least 4 hours
Cooking time: About 10 minutes

With just five ingredients and some advance preparation, you can produce a delicious hot appetizer in minutes. Simply pop the marinated shrimp in the oven when your guests arrive.

½   cup olive oil
 1   clove garlic, minced or pressed
¼   teaspoon salt
 1   pound medium-size raw shrimp (about 36 per lb.), shelled and deveined
 1   tablespoon finely minced parsley
     Parsley sprigs (optional)

Mix oil, garlic, and salt. Add shrimp, turning to coat; sprinkle with minced parsley. Cover and refrigerate for at least 4 hours or until next day.

   Transfer to a 10- by 15-inch baking pan. Bake in a 375° oven until shrimp are opaque when cut (about 10 minutes). Arrange in a bowl. Garnish with parsley sprigs, if desired. Offer with wooden picks. Makes about 3 dozen appetizers.

Per appetizer: 37 calories, 2 g protein, .1 g carbohydrates, 3 g total fat, 16 mg cholesterol, 30 mg sodium

Your company will think you've fussed for hours, but
Mint Sauce (recipe on page 12) offered with pea pods,
Meatballs Wrapped in Basil Leaves (recipe on page 51),
and Eggplant & Goat Cheese Rolls (recipe on facing page)
are quick to prepare.

Pictured on facing page

EGGPLANT & GOAT CHEESE ROLLS

◆

Preparation time: About 15 minutes
Cooking time: About 13 minutes

Crisp watercress and tangy goat cheese are paired in an intriguing eggplant roll. Use Oriental eggplants, if you can find them; they're usually sweeter and have smaller seeds than the regular kind.

- 1   **pound Oriental eggplants (about 4 *total*) or regular eggplant, stems removed**
- 1½ **tablespoons olive oil**
- 3   **ounces soft goat cheese, such as Montrachet**
- 12 **to 16 watercress sprigs, washed and dried**

Cut eggplants lengthwise into ¼- to ⅓-inch-thick slices (if using regular variety, cut slices in half lengthwise). Brush both sides with oil and place in a single layer in large baking pans. Bake in a 450° oven for 8 minutes; turn and continue baking until very soft when pressed (about 5 more minutes). Remove from pans and let cool.

Place about ½ teaspoon of the cheese at an end of each eggplant slice; top with a sprig of watercress, letting leaves overhang edges. Roll up. Makes 12 to 16 appetizers.

Per appetizer: 43 calories, 1 g protein, 2 g carbohydrates, 3 g total fat, 6 mg cholesterol, 39 mg sodium

MEXICAN BARBECUED CORN

◆

Preparation time: About 5 minutes
Cooking time: About 8 minutes

Corn coblets are a wonderful introduction to a summer barbecue. Season the corn with chili and lime juice or with garlic, basil, and Parmesan.

- 2   **tablespoons salt**
- 1   **teaspoon *each* chili powder and ground cumin**
- 4   **medium-size ears corn, *each* cut into 3 chunks**
- ¼   **cup salad oil**
- 2   **limes, cut into wedges**

Mix salt, chili powder, and cumin; set aside.

Brush corn lightly with oil. Place on a lightly greased grill 4 to 6 inches above a solid bed of medium coals. Cook, turning occasionally, until kernels are lightly browned in several areas (about 8 minutes).

Offer with lime and salt mixture. Makes 1 dozen appetizers.

Per appetizer: 50 calories, 1 g protein, 7 g carbohydrates, 3 g total fat, 0 mg cholesterol, 1,105 mg sodium

Barbecued Corn with Basil Butter

Prepare and barbecue corn as directed for **Mexican Barbecued Corn,** but omit salt, chili powder, cumin, and limes.

Meanwhile, in a 1-quart pan, combine ½ cup (¼ lb.) **butter** or margarine; 1 clove **garlic,** minced or pressed; and 2 tablespoons chopped **fresh basil leaves** or 1 tablespoon dry basil leaves. Place on grill slightly away from coals and heat, stirring occasionally, until butter is melted. Place about ½ cup **grated Parmesan cheese** in a bowl.

Offer corn with butter mixture and cheese.

Per appetizer: 110 calories, 2 g protein, 6 g carbohydrates, 9 g total fat, 23 mg cholesterol, 145 mg sodium

Pictured on page 48

ARTICHOKE HEARTS WITH BLUE CHEESE

◆

Preparation time: About 30 minutes
Cooking time: About 20 minutes

Guests will enjoy these tiny artichoke halves topped with blue cheese.

- 2   **quarts water**
- 2   **tablespoons lemon juice or vinegar**
- 12 **small artichokes (*each* 2 in.-diameter) or 2 packages (10 oz. *each*) frozen artichoke hearts, thawed**
- ¼   **cup butter or margarine, at room temperature**
- 3   **ounces blue-veined cheese Lemon slices (optional)**

Combine water and lemon juice in a 5- to 6-quart pan. Remove and discard coarse outer leaves of fresh artichokes down to tender, pale yellow ones. Snip off thorny tips; trim stems to about ½ inch. (Or use 24 frozen artichoke halves.) As artichokes are trimmed, drop into water.

Bring water to a boil over high heat; reduce heat, cover, and simmer until artichoke bottoms are tender when pierced (about 10 minutes for either fresh or frozen artichokes). Drain; let cool. Cut whole artichokes in half lengthwise.

Arrange artichokes, cut sides up, in a baking pan. In a small bowl, mash butter and cheese until combined. Evenly spoon into artichokes. (At this point, you may cover and refrigerate until next day.)

Bake, uncovered, in a 350° oven just until cheese is melted (about 10 minutes). Garnish with lemon, if desired. Makes 2 dozen appetizers.

Per appetizer: 38 calories, 1 g protein, 2 g carbohydrates, 3 g total fat, 8 mg cholesterol, 80 mg sodium

Pictured on page 53
GARLIC-BUTTERED MUSHROOMS

Preparation time: About 15 minutes
Cooking time: About 5 minutes

Freshly grated Parmesan adds extra flavor to a shallot- and parsley-enriched garlic butter that fills grilled mushroom caps.

Serve with thin slices of French bread to soak up the buttery juices.

⅓ cup butter or margarine, at room temperature
1 small shallot, finely chopped
2 cloves garlic, minced or pressed
2 tablespoons *each* finely chopped parsley and freshly grated Parmesan cheese
⅛ teaspoon ground white pepper
12 large mushrooms (about 1½ lbs. *total*)
1 small French baguette (8 oz.), sliced ½ inch thick

Mix butter, shallot, garlic, parsley, cheese, and pepper until well blended.

Twist off mushroom stems; reserve for other uses. Evenly spoon butter mixture into mushroom caps.

In a barbecue with a lid, place mushrooms, butter sides up, on a lightly greased grill 4 to 6 inches above a solid bed of medium coals. Cover barbecue and open dampers. (Or place mushrooms on a rack in a broiler pan and broil about 6 inches below heat.) Cook until butter is melted and mushrooms begin to shrivel slightly (about 5 minutes). Offer with bread to absorb buttery juices. Makes 1 dozen appetizers.

Per appetizer: 119 calories, 3 g protein, 13 g carbohydrates, 6 g total fat, 15 mg cholesterol, 179 mg sodium

MISO GRILLED MUSHROOMS

Preparation time: About 15 minutes
Marinating time: At least 6 hours
Cooking time: About 5 minutes

Simply spear these hot mushrooms and dip them in a marinade made with sake, fresh ginger, and miso, a fermented soybean paste.

3 tablespoons miso
¼ cup sake or dry sherry
1 teaspoon grated fresh ginger
2 teaspoons honey
2 tablespoons lemon juice
2 tablespoons rice vinegar or distilled white vinegar
16 medium-size to large mushrooms (about 1 lb. *total*)
1 green onion (including top), thinly sliced

Mix miso, sake, ginger, honey, lemon juice, and vinegar until blended. Add mushrooms, stirring to coat. Cover and refrigerate for at least 6 hours or until next day.

Soak 8 bamboo skewers in hot water to cover for 30 minutes. Drain marinade into a small pan and set aside. Thread 2 mushrooms on each skewer and place on a lightly greased grill 4 to 6 inches above a solid bed of low-glowing coals. (Or place on a rack in a broiler pan and broil about 6 inches below heat.) Cook, brushing occasionally with marinade and turning once or twice, until browned (about 5 minutes).

Remove mushrooms from skewers. Heat remaining marinade, pour into a small bowl, and top with onion. Offer mushrooms with wooden picks. Makes 16 appetizers.

Per appetizer: 19 calories, 1 g protein, 4 g carbohydrates, .3 g total fat, 0 mg cholesterol, 119 mg sodium

HEAVENLY MUSHROOMS

Preparation time: About 20 minutes
Cooking time: About 15 minutes

A touch of black lumpfish caviar elevates these mushrooms out of the ordinary. Red onion and parsley add color to the dill-flavored cream cheese filling. Serve with your favorite Champagne or sparkling mineral water with a twist of lemon.

20 medium-size to large mushrooms (about 1¼ lbs. *total*)
¼ cup butter or margarine, melted
2 tablespoons black lumpfish caviar
1 large package (8 oz.) cream cheese, at room temperature
2 teaspoons fresh dill or 1 teaspoon dill weed
2 tablespoons minced red or white onion
⅓ cup minced parsley

Twist off mushroom stems; reserve for other uses. Pour butter into a 9-by 13-inch baking pan. Add mushrooms, turning to coat, and arrange in pan, cavity sides up.

Rinse caviar in a fine strainer under cold running water until water runs clear; let drain.

Beat cheese, dill, and onion until blended; stir in caviar. Evenly mound cheese mixture in mushroom caps. (At this point, you may cover and refrigerate until next day.)

Bake, uncovered, in a 350° oven until cheese mixture is lightly browned (about 15 minutes). Evenly sprinkle mushrooms with parsley. Makes 20 appetizers.

Per appetizer: 72 calories, 2 g protein, 2 g carbohydrates, 7 g total fat, 28 mg cholesterol, 83 mg sodium

FLORENTINE MUSHROOMS

Pictured on page 32

Preparation time: About 20 minutes
Cooking time: About 25 minutes

Mildly flavored Italian sausage mixed with spinach and two kinds of cheese—jack and ricotta—makes a hearty filling for mushroom caps.

 ¾ **pound mild Italian sausage, casing removed**
 1 **pound spinach, stems removed, washed and dried**
 1½ **tablespoons chopped fresh dill or 1 teaspoon dill weed**
 1½ **cups (6 oz.) shredded jack cheese**
 ½ **cup ricotta cheese**
 24 **medium-size to large mushrooms (about 1½ lbs. *total*)**
 ¼ **cup butter or margarine, melted Dill sprigs (optional)**

Crumble sausage into a wide frying pan over medium heat and cook, stirring occasionally, until no longer pink (about 7 minutes). With a slotted spoon, transfer to a bowl. Spoon off and discard all but 1 tablespoon of the drippings, reserving in pan.

Chop spinach leaves coarsely. Add to pan, cover, and cook until soft (about 1 minute). Drain well, pressing out moisture. Add to sausage; then lightly mix in chopped dill, jack, and ricotta.

Twist off mushroom stems; reserve for other uses. Pour butter into a 9- by 13-inch baking dish. Add mushrooms, turning to coat, and arrange in dish, cavity sides up. Evenly mound sausage mixture in caps. Bake in a 400° oven until hot (about 15 minutes).

Arrange on a platter. Garnish with dill sprigs, if desired. Makes 2 dozen appetizers.

Per appetizer: 98 calories, 5 g protein, 2 g carbohydrates, 8 g total fat, 21 mg cholesterol, 174 mg sodium

SHRIMP-STUFFED MUSHROOMS

Preparation time: About 10 minutes
Cooking time: About 20 minutes

Succulent mushroom caps hold a delicate shrimp filling accented with crunchy water chestnuts. You can steam this Asian-inspired appetizer in a wok or large frying pan.

 16 **medium-size to large mushrooms (about 1 lb. *total*)**
 ½ **teaspoon *each* salt and sugar**
 1 **tablespoon soy sauce**
 1 **cup regular-strength chicken broth
    Shrimp Filling (recipe follows)
    Parsley sprigs**
 1 **jar (2 oz.) sliced pimentos, drained (optional)**

Twist off mushroom stems; reserve for other uses. In a 1- to 1½-quart pan, bring mushroom caps, salt, sugar, soy, and broth to a boil over medium-high heat. Reduce heat and simmer for 10 minutes.

Meanwhile, prepare Shrimp Filling; set aside.

Remove mushrooms from broth; drain and let cool slightly. Evenly mound filling in mushroom caps. Arrange, cavity sides up, on 1 or 2 serving plates that will fit inside a wok or wide frying pan. (At this point, you may cover and refrigerate for up to 8 hours; bring to room temperature before steaming.)

Place plate on a rack in wok or pan over 1½ to 2 inches boiling water. Cover and steam until filling is cooked through (about 10 minutes). Garnish with parsley and, if desired, pimentos. Makes 16 appetizers.

Shrimp Filling. Beat 1 **egg white** until foamy. Blend 2 teaspoons *each* **dry sherry** and **cornstarch;** stir into egg white along with ½ teaspoon *each* **salt** and grated **fresh ginger.** Add ¼ cup finely chopped **water chestnuts**

and ½ pound **raw shrimp,** shelled, deveined, and finely chopped. Mix until blended.

Per appetizer: 27 calories, 3 g protein, 3 g carbohydrates, .4 g total fat, 18 mg cholesterol, 285 mg sodium

CRISP-FRIED ONIONS

Preparation time: About 20 minutes
Cooking time: About 25 minutes

These delicate, golden onion rings will disappear as soon as they're served, making everyone eager for more.

 2 **large onions (about 1 lb. *total*)**
 ½ **cup all-purpose flour
    Salad oil
    Salt**

Peel and thinly slice onions; separate into rings. Place flour in a bag, add onions, and shake to coat evenly.

In a deep 3- to 4-quart pan, heat about 1½ inches oil to 300°F on a deep-frying thermometer. Add onions, about a quarter at a time, and cook, stirring often, until golden (about 5 minutes). Oil temperature will drop at first and then rise as onions brown; regulate heat accordingly.

With a slotted spoon, lift out onions and drain on paper towels (discard any scorched bits).

If made ahead, let cool completely, package airtight, and refrigerate for up to 3 days; to reheat, spread in a single layer in a shallow pan and place in a 350° oven until hot (about 2 minutes).

Pile in a napkin-lined basket or on a plate; season to taste with salt. Makes about 8 servings.

Per serving: 93 calories, 1 g protein, 10 g carbohydrates, 5 g total fat, 0 mg cholesterol, 1 mg sodium

GLAZED ONIONS WITH CORN, PEPPERS & SHRIMP

◆

Preparation time: About 10 minutes
Cooking time: About 15 minutes

Balsamic vinegar provides a rich-tasting glaze for onions, corn, and roasted peppers. Top the vegetable mélange with tiny shrimp and green onions, and serve with baguette slices.

- 3 tablespoons olive oil
- 1 package (10 oz.) frozen tiny whole onions
- 1 cup whole-kernel corn, fresh or frozen
- 3 tablespoons balsamic or red wine vinegar
- 1 teaspoon sugar
- 1 jar (7 oz.) roasted peppers, drained and cut into ½-inch slivers
- ¼ pound small cooked shrimp
- ¼ cup chopped green onions (including some tops)
   Salt and pepper
- 1 small French baguette (8 oz.), sliced ¼ inch thick

Heat 1 tablespoon of the oil in an 8- to 10-inch frying pan over medium-high heat. Add whole onions and cook, stirring occasionally, until lightly browned (about 10 minutes). Reduce heat to medium; add corn, vinegar, and sugar. Cook, shaking pan often, until liquid has evaporated and onions are slightly browner (about 5 more minutes). Add roasted peppers and remaining 2 tablespoons oil, stirring until hot. Transfer to a bowl.

Scatter shrimp and green onions over vegetable mixture. Season to taste with salt and pepper. Offer with baguette slices. Makes about 2 dozen appetizers.

Per appetizer: 60 calories, 2 g protein, 8 g carbohydrates, 2 g total fat, 10 mg cholesterol, 70 mg sodium

---

Pictured on facing page

SALSA POTATO SKINS

◆

Preparation time: About 30 minutes
Cooking time: About 1¼ hours

These golden potato skins, coated with Cheddar and jack cheese, are almost a meal in themselves. Offer them with a green chile salsa for bite.

   Chile Salsa (recipe follows)
- 5 **large russet potatoes (about 3 lbs. *total*), scrubbed**
- ⅓ **cup butter or margarine, melted**
- ¾ **cup *each* shredded mild Cheddar and jack cheese**
   Cilantro (coriander) sprigs (optional)

Prepare Chile Salsa; set aside.

Pierce potatoes in several places with a fork. Bake in a 400° oven until soft when pressed (about 1 hour). Let potatoes stand until cool enough to handle. Cut each lengthwise into quarters. With a spoon, scoop out flesh, leaving a ⅛-inch-thick shell; reserve flesh for other uses.

Brush skins inside and out with butter. Place, skin sides down, in a single layer on a 12- by 15-inch baking sheet. Bake in a 500° oven until crisp (about 12 minutes). Remove from oven and evenly sprinkle with both Cheddar and jack.

Broil 4 inches below heat until cheese is melted (about 2 minutes). Arrange on a platter. Garnish with cilantro, if desired. Offer with salsa for dipping. Makes 20 appetizers.

Per appetizer: 115 calories, 3 g protein, 12 g carbohydrates, 6 g total fat, 16 mg cholesterol, 85 mg sodium

Chile Salsa. Stir together 1 can (8 oz.) **tomato sauce,** 1 can (4 oz.) diced **green chiles,** and ¼ cup chopped **green onions** (including tops). If made ahead, cover and refrigerate until next day. Makes 1½ cups.

Per tablespoon: 5 calories, .2 g protein, 1 g carbohydrates, 0 g total fat, 0 mg cholesterol, 103 mg sodium

---

TWICE-BAKED CREAMERS

◆

Preparation time: About 15 minutes
Cooking time: About 1 hour and 5 minutes

Potato purée seasoned with blue cheese and fresh chives fills small red potatoes, often called creamers, in this sophisticated version of twice-baked potatoes.

You can prepare this recipe up to 6 hours ahead of time. Serve the potatoes warm.

- 12 **small red thin-skinned potatoes (*each* 1- to 1½-in. diameter), scrubbed**
- 6 **ounces Gorgonzola cheese**
- 1 **tablespoon chopped chives or green onion (including top)**
- ¼ **teaspoon ground nutmeg**
   Salt and pepper

Pierce potatoes in several places with a fork and place in a 10- by 15-inch baking pan. Bake in a 350° oven until potatoes are soft when pressed (about 1 hour).

Let potatoes stand until cool enough to handle; then cut each potato in half and scoop out flesh, leaving a ¼-inch-thick shell all around. Place flesh in a bowl and add cheese, chives, and nutmeg. Mash until mixture is smooth.

Mound potato mixture in shells and place, filled sides up, in pan. (At this point, you may let stand for up to 2 hours at room temperature; or cover and refrigerate for up to 6 hours.)

Broil 4 to 6 inches below heat until centers are warm and tops are browned (about 4 minutes). Season to taste with salt and pepper. Makes 2 dozen appetizers.

Per appetizer: 44 calories, 2 g protein, 4 g carbohydrates, 2 g total fat, 5 mg cholesterol, 101 mg sodium

*Present Salsa Potato Skins (recipe on facing page)
temptingly hot from the broiler. The crisply baked skins
are sprinkled with shredded Cheddar and jack cheese,
and served with an easy-to-make salsa.*

CHEESE-STUFFED SQUASH BLOSSOMS

◆

Preparation time: About 30 minutes
Cooking time: About 15 minutes

Enjoy delicate squash blossoms with a zesty chile-cheese stuffing. Look for the blossoms during the summer in specialty produce stores or in Latin American or Mediterranean markets; use them within a day of purchase.

15 to 20 squash blossoms (*each about 3 in. long from base to tip*)
1 small package (3 oz.) cream cheese, at room temperature
1 tablespoon milk
⅓ cup grated Parmesan cheese
   Dash of ground black pepper
1½ tablespoons canned diced green chiles
   All-purpose flour
2 eggs
1 tablespoon water
   Salad oil

Rinse blossoms with cool water; shake off excess. Gently pat dry with paper towels. Trim off stems. Remove stamens, if necessary, to enlarge cavity before stuffing. Set aside.

Beat cream cheese, milk, Parmesan, pepper, and chiles until blended. Spoon about 1 teaspoon of the mixture into each blossom; twist tips to close. Roll in flour to coat lightly; set aside.

In a small bowl, beat eggs and water. Heat ¼ inch oil in a wide frying pan over medium-high heat. When oil is hot, use a fork to dip blossoms, one at a time, into egg mixture. Cook 2 or 3 at a time, turning occasionally, until golden (about 2 minutes). Drain on paper towels. Makes 15 to 20 appetizers.

Per appetizer: 49 calories, 2 g protein, 1 g carbohydrates, 4 g total fat, 30 mg cholesterol, 53 mg sodium

---

Pictured on page 45

RICE-STUFFED SUMMER SQUASH

◆

Preparation time: About 45 minutes
Cooking time: About 45 minutes

Scalloped summer squash make attractive holders for a rich filling of sausage, shallots, cheese, and rice.

24 small scalloped summer squash (2 lbs. *total*)
2 tablespoons olive oil
1 mild Italian sausage (about 3 oz.), casing removed
2 tablespoons finely chopped shallots
⅓ cup whipping cream
1 cup cooked rice
5 tablespoons grated Parmesan cheese

Cut about ½ inch from top of each squash; set tops aside. Carefully scoop out flesh, leaving a ¼-inch-thick shell. Finely chop flesh.

Heat oil in a wide frying pan over medium heat. Crumble sausage into pan, add shallots, and cook, stirring, until meat is no longer pink (about 7 minutes). Stir in chopped squash and cook, stirring, until hot (about 3 more minutes). Add cream, increase heat to high, and continue cooking, stirring often, until most of the liquid has evaporated (about 4 more minutes). Stir in rice. Remove from heat and stir in 3 tablespoons of the cheese.

Fill squash shells with meat mixture. Place, filled sides up, in a greased baking dish just large enough to hold them in a single layer. Sprinkle with remaining cheese. Replace squash tops at a slight angle. Cover dish with foil.

Bake in a 350° oven until squash are barely tender when pierced (about 30 minutes). Let cool briefly. Makes 2 dozen appetizers.

Per appetizer: 54 calories, 2 g protein, 4 g carbohydrates, 4 g total fat, 7 mg cholesterol, 47 mg sodium

---

PISTACHIO-TOPPED ZUCCHINI

◆

Preparation time: About 20 minutes
Cooking time: About 30 minutes

Crunchy pistachios combine with jack cheese, sautéed onions, and mustard seeds to create a tempting topping for sliced zucchini. Add whole pistachios for garnish.

2 medium-size zucchini (about 9 oz. *total*), ends trimmed
3 tablespoons olive oil
1 small onion, finely chopped
2 cloves garlic, minced or pressed
2 teaspoons mustard seeds
¾ cup shelled salted pistachios
1 egg
¾ cup shredded jack cheese

Cut each zucchini diagonally into 10 equal-size slices. Set aside.

Heat 1 tablespoon of the oil in a wide frying pan over medium-high heat. Add onion, garlic, and mustard seeds and cook, stirring often, until onion is lightly browned (about 5 minutes); let cool. Reserving 20 whole pistachios for garnish, chop remaining nuts and stir into onion mixture with egg and cheese.

Generously brush zucchini with remaining 2 tablespoons oil. Arrange, slightly apart, in a 10- by 15-inch baking pan. Bake in a 400° oven, turning after 5 minutes, until golden (about 10 minutes total). Remove from oven; reduce temperature to 325°.

Evenly spoon filling on zucchini. Top each with a whole pistachio. Bake until filling is light golden (about 15 more minutes). Makes 20 appetizers.

Per appetizer: 71 calories, 2 g protein, 2 g carbohydrates, 6 g total fat, 14 mg cholesterol, 64 mg sodium

PARMESAN ZUCCHINI STICKS

Pictured on page 48

Preparation time: About 35 minutes
Cooking time: About 25 minutes

Zucchini sticks are baked, rather than fried, to crisp perfection in a cheese-crumb crust seasoned with sage and rosemary.

- ⅔ cup grated Parmesan cheese
- ½ cup fine dry seasoned bread crumbs
- 1 teaspoon *each* ground sage and dry rosemary
- 2 eggs
- 5 medium-size zucchini (about 1½ lbs. *total*), ends trimmed
- 1 tablespoon olive or salad oil
  Salt
  Sage and rosemary sprigs (optional)

In a bowl, mix cheese, bread crumbs, ground sage, and dry rosemary; set aside. In another bowl, beat eggs until blended.

Cut each zucchini in half crosswise; then cut lengthwise into quarters. Add to eggs and mix gently. Lift out, one at a time, drain briefly, and roll in cheese mixture to coat evenly.

Lay sticks slightly apart in a greased 10- by 15-inch baking pan. Drizzle with oil. Bake in a 450° oven until coating is well browned and crusty (about 25 minutes). Season to taste with salt.

Arrange zucchini sticks in a serving dish and garnish with sage and rosemary sprigs, if desired. Makes 40 appetizers.

Per appetizer: 21 calories, 1 g protein, 2 g carbohydrates, 1 g total fat, 12 mg cholesterol, 68 mg sodium

CARAMELIZED GARLIC & CREAM CHEESE PRUNES

Preparation time: About 30 minutes
Cooking time: About 1¼ hours

Slow-roasting turns whole garlic heads into a surprisingly sweet seasoning that enhances the cream cheese filling for bacon-wrapped prunes.

   Caramelized Garlic Cloves (recipe follows)
- 30 pitted prunes (8 to 12 oz. *total*)
- ½ cup dry red wine
- 1 large package (8 oz.) cream cheese, at room temperature
- 15 slices bacon, cut in half

Prepare Caramelized Garlic Cloves.

In a 1- to 1½-quart pan, bring prunes and wine to a boil over medium heat. Reduce heat, cover, and simmer until prunes are plump (about 7 minutes). Drain; set aside.

Beat cream cheese and garlic cloves until smooth. Make a depression in center of each prune and fill each with about 1 teaspoon of the cheese mixture. Wrap a half-slice of bacon around each prune so ends are on bottom.

Set prunes, filled sides down, on a rack in a 10- by 15-inch broiler or baking pan. Broil about 4 inches below heat just until bacon begins to brown (about 3 minutes). Turn and continue broiling until bacon is crisp (about 3 more minutes). Let stand on rack in pan until cheese is slightly firm (about 2 minutes). Makes 2½ dozen appetizers.

Caramelized Garlic Cloves. Cut 2 large heads **garlic** (*each* about 2½ in. wide) in half crosswise about ⅓ of the way from root end. Pour 1 tablespoon **salad oil** into an 8- or 9-inch square baking pan. Place garlic, cut sides down, in pan. Bake in a 350° oven until center cloves are very soft when pressed and cut sides are browned (about 1 hour). Let cool.

Squeeze whole head to force out soft cloves (remove any bits of husk). If made ahead, cover and refrigerate for up to 3 days; freeze for longer storage. Makes about ¼ cup.

Per appetizer: 73 calories, 2 g protein, 7 g carbohydrates, 5 g total fat, 11 mg cholesterol, 74 mg sodium

BACON-WRAPPED DATES

Preparation time: About 10 minutes
Cooking time: About 10 minutes

How could something so simple be so delicious? Try this recipe and you'll see for yourself.

- 8 slices bacon, cut in half
- 16 pitted dates

Place bacon on a rimmed 10- by 15-inch baking sheet and broil about 6 inches below heat until partially cooked but still soft (about 2½ minutes). Let drain on paper towels. Discard excess fat from baking sheet.

Place a date at end of each bacon slice and roll up. Arrange, seam sides down, on baking sheet. Bake in a 400° oven until bacon is crisp and dates are hot (about 7 minutes). Makes 16 appetizers.

Per appetizer: 41 calories, 1 g protein, 6 g carbohydrates, 2 g total fat, 3 mg cholesterol, 51 mg sodium

Our selection of cold appetizers comes together for a festive atmosphere. Sample pistachio-topped Lean Terrrine (recipe on page 81); airy Savory Feta Cheesecake (recipe on page 75), and colorful Cherry Tomatoes with Smoked Oysters (recipe on page 86).

COLD BITES

Not everything that's delicious has to come hot from the oven. Many appetizers, such as glorious meat terrines, tempting marinated fish salads, and delectable vegetable combinations, actually taste best served either at room temperature or straight from the refrigerator.

Cold hors d'oeuvres have their advantages. Frequently, these selections don't require the host or hostess's attention at the last minute or during the party. They can be transported easily to locations far from the kitchen. Moreover, many cold choices wait patiently in the refrigerator for unexpected company or for between-meal snacks. And they're definitely a refreshing and welcome delight when the weather turns warm.

CREAMY DEVILED EGGS

◆

Preparation time: About 15 minutes
Chilling time: At least 1 hour

This basic deviled egg recipe mixes egg yolks with sour cream and mustard. The variations that follow offer some unusual twists on the familiar theme.

- 6 **hard-cooked eggs**, shelled and cut in half lengthwise
- 3 tablespoons **sour cream**
- ½ teaspoon **dry mustard**
  Dash of **ground red pepper (cayenne)** or **liquid hot pepper seasoning**
  Salt
  Parsley sprigs or slices of green or ripe **olives**

Remove yolks from eggs and mash with a fork. Stir in sour cream, mustard, and pepper until well blended. Season to taste with salt. Fill egg whites evenly with yolk mixture and garnish with parsley.

Arrange eggs in a single layer in a deep dish; cover and refrigerate for at least 1 hour or until next day. Makes 1 dozen appetizers.

Per appetizer: 45 calories, 3 g protein, .5 g carbohydrates, 3 g total fat, 108 mg cholesterol, 33 mg sodium

Anchovy Celery Eggs

Follow directions for **Creamy Deviled Eggs**, but omit mustard and salt. Add 1 teaspoon **anchovy paste** and 6 tablespoons finely chopped **celery** to yolk mixture.

Per appetizer: 47 calories, 3 g protein, .6 g carbohydrates, 3 g total fat, 108 mg cholesterol, 55 mg sodium

Dilled Eggs

Follow directions for **Creamy Deviled Eggs**, adding 2 tablespoons chopped **dill pickle** to yolk mixture.

Per appetizer: 45 calories, 3 g protein, .5 g carbohydrates, 3 g total fat, 108 mg cholesterol, 56 mg sodium

Caviar Eggs

Follow directions for **Creamy Deviled Eggs**, but omit mustard and garnish. Add 1 teaspoon **lemon juice** to yolk mixture. Garnish each egg half with ¼ teaspoon drained **red** or black **caviar**.

Per appetizer: 48 calories, 4 g protein, .5 g carbohydrates, 3 g total fat, 116 mg cholesterol, 53 mg sodium

Pictured on page 93

MARBLED TEA EGGS

◆

Preparation time: About 15 minutes
Cooking time: About 1 hour and 40 minutes
Chilling time: At least 8 hours

Here's a great way to begin an Asian-inspired feast. These eggs can be served quartered; or, to let guests admire their delicate marbling, you can leave them whole.

- 8 **eggs**
- 3 **black-tea bags** or 3 teaspoons **loose black tea**
- 2 tablespoons **soy sauce**
- 1 tablespoon **salt**
- 1 whole **star anise**; or 1 teaspoon **anise seeds** and 1 **cinnamon stick** (about 2 in. long)

Place eggs in a 5-quart pan and cover with cold water. Simmer over medium-high heat for 20 minutes. Drain; rinse eggs under cold running water until cool enough to handle. Gently crack shells with back of a spoon until there's a fine network of cracks, but do not remove shells.

Return eggs to pan. Add 4 cups water, tea, soy, salt, and star anise. Bring to a simmer over medium-high heat. Reduce heat and cook for 1 hour. Let cool; then refrigerate eggs in their cooking liquid for at least 8 hours or up to 2 days. Shell before serving. Makes 8 appetizers.

Per appetizer: 75 calories, 6 g protein, .7 g carbohydrates, 5 g total fat, 213 mg cholesterol, 243 mg sodium

PICKLED QUAIL EGGS & BABY BEETS

◆

Preparation time: About 15 minutes
Cooking time: About 7 minutes
Chilling time: At least 3 hours

Pickled eggs, a pub lunch staple, become appetizer fare when made with quail eggs. Remember to shake the eggs' container occasionally for consistent ruby-red color.

- **Hard-cooked Quail Eggs** (directions follow)
- 1 can (8¼ oz.) **pickled baby beets**
- 8 **black peppercorns**
- 2 tablespoons minced **red onion**
- 1 tablespoon chopped **fresh dill** or 1 teaspoon **dill weed**

Prepare Hard-cooked Quail Eggs.

Drain beet juice into a 1½- to 2-quart pan. Add peppercorns and bring to a boil over high heat. Meanwhile, place beets and eggs in a 4-cup jar. Let juice cool slightly. Then pour into jar, cover, and refrigerate for at least 3 hours or up to 2 days, shaking jar gently several times or inverting occasionally.

Drain off liquid and pour beets and eggs into a small bowl; sprinkle with onion and dill. Offer with wooden picks. Makes 10 to 12 appetizers.

Hard-cooked Quail Eggs. Place 10 to 12 **quail eggs** in a single layer in a 1- to 1½-quart pan. Cover with **water.** Bring to a boil over high heat; immediately reduce heat to hold water just below simmering and cook eggs for 5 minutes. Drain. Immerse eggs in cold water; then crack shells with back of a spoon and remove shells.

Per appetizer: 29 calories, 1 g protein, 4 g carbohydrates, 1 g total fat, 76 mg cholesterol, 56 mg sodium

SAVORY FETA CHEESECAKE

Pictured on page 72

Preparation time: About 20 minutes
Cooking time: About 45 minutes

No delicate dessert cake, this cheesecake boasts a distinctive feta cheese filling in a whole wheat pastry.

Whole Wheat Press-in Pastry
(recipe follows)
1 pound feta cheese
1 large package (8 oz.) cream
cheese, at room temperature
3 eggs
Whole Greek olives or thinly
sliced green onions (including
tops)
Oregano sprigs (optional)

Prepare Whole Wheat Press-in Pastry; set aside.

Cut feta and cream cheese into about 1-inch chunks. In a food processor or blender, whirl feta, cream cheese, and eggs until smooth. Pour into pastry. Bake in a 350° oven until center barely jiggles when gently shaken (about 20 minutes). Let cool to room temperature in pan on a wire rack. If made ahead, cover and refrigerate for up to 2 days; bring to room temperature before serving.

Remove pan sides. Garnish with olives and, if desired, oregano; cut into wedges. Makes 16 appetizers.

Whole Wheat Press-in Pastry.
Combine 1 cup **whole wheat flour** and 6 tablespoons firm **butter** or margarine, cut up. With your fingers, rub mixture together until butter lumps are no longer distinguishable. With a fork, stir in 1 **egg** and mix until dough forms a ball.

Press dough in a firm, even layer over bottom and about 1¾ inches up sides of a 9-inch round spring-form pan or cake pan with removable bottom. Bake in a 350° oven for about 20 minutes or until lightly browned. Use hot or cold.

Per appetizer: 206 calories, 8 g protein, 7 g carbohydrates, 17 g total fat, 106 mg cholesterol, 418 mg sodium

ZUCCHINI FRITTATA

Preparation time: About 20 minutes
Cooking time: About 1¼ hours
Chilling time: At least 2 hours

Flavored with fresh basil, parsley, sautéed onions, and Parmesan cheese, this baked zucchini omelet is chilled and served cold.

2 tablespoons olive oil
2 tablespoons butter or margarine
2 medium-size onions, finely
chopped
2 cloves garlic, minced or pressed
½ cup chopped parsley
8 medium-size zucchini (about 2¼
lbs. *total*), shredded
2 tablespoons chopped fresh basil
leaves or 1½ teaspoons dry
basil leaves
½ cup grated Parmesan cheese
Salt and pepper
16 eggs

Heat oil and butter in a wide frying pan over medium heat. Add onions, garlic, and parsley; cook, stirring often, until onions are soft (about 7 minutes). Add zucchini; cook, stirring, until liquid has evaporated (about 20 more minutes). Remove from heat and stir in basil and Parmesan; season to taste with salt and pepper.

In a large bowl, beat eggs until blended. Stir in zucchini mixture. Spread in a greased shallow 3-quart casserole. Bake in a 350° oven until firm in center when lightly touched (about 45 minutes). Let cool on a wire rack. Cover and refrigerate for at least 2 hours or until next day.

Cut into serving pieces. Makes 1 dozen appetizers.

Per appetizer: 170 calories, 11 g protein, 5 g carbohydrates, 12 g total fat, 291 mg cholesterol, 169 mg sodium

COCKTAIL CREAM PUFFS

Pictured on page 5

Preparation time: About 50 minutes
Cooking time: About 25 minutes
Chilling time: At least 2 hours

Tiny cream puffs elegantly cradle ginger-flavored chicken salad.

Gingered Chicken Salad
(recipe follows)
1 cup water
½ cup (¼ lb.) butter or margarine
1 cup all-purpose flour
4 eggs

Prepare Gingered Chicken Salad.

In a 2- to 3-quart pan, stir water and butter over medium-high heat until butter is melted. Add flour all at once, stirring until mixture leaves sides of pan and forms a ball (about 2 minutes). Remove from heat and transfer to a bowl; let cool briefly.

Add eggs, one at a time, beating well after each addition. Drop 1 tablespoon of the dough for each puff onto greased baking sheets, spacing puffs about 2 inches apart. Bake in a 400° oven until golden (about 20 minutes). Turn off oven. Pierce each puff in several places. Return to oven until crisp (about 10 minutes). Let cool on wire racks.

Split puffs horizontally. Evenly fill with chicken salad. Replace tops. If made ahead, cover and refrigerate for up to 2 hours. Makes about 3 dozen appetizers.

Gingered Chicken Salad. Mix ½ cup **mayonnaise**, ½ teaspoon **dry mustard,** and 1 teaspoon grated **fresh ginger** or ¼ teaspoon ground ginger. Stir in 2 cups chopped **cooked chicken,** ½ cup chopped and drained canned **water chestnuts,** and 2 **green onions** (including tops), thinly sliced. Cover and refrigerate for at least 2 hours or until next day.

Per appetizer: 82 calories, 3 g protein, 3 g carbohydrates, 6 g total fat, 39 mg cholesterol, 57 mg sodium

Pictured on facing page

TOMATO TARTS NIÇOISE

◆

Preparation time: About 55 minutes
Cooking time: About 50 minutes
Chilling time: At least 3 hours

Bring sunny Mediterranean flavors to your table with these savory tarts.

Cheese Pastry (recipe follows)
4 tablespoons olive oil
2 large onions, slivered
1 large can (28 oz.) tomatoes
½ teaspoon *each* sugar and dry rosemary
⅛ teaspoon *each* ground red pepper (cayenne) and black pepper
2 cloves garlic, minced or pressed
2 cans (2 oz. *each*) flat anchovy fillets
32 Niçoise or medium-size ripe olives
Rosemary sprigs (optional)

Prepare Cheese Pastry and divide into 8 equal portions; roll each out into a circle to fit 4-inch tart pans ¾ to 1 inch deep. Line pans with pastry, trimming edges even with top.

Heat 2 tablespoons of the oil in a wide frying pan over medium heat; add onions and cook, stirring occasionally, until golden and very soft (about 15 minutes). Evenly spoon onions into pastry-lined pans.

In pan, heat remaining 2 tablespoons oil slightly; add tomatoes (break up with a spoon) and their liquid, sugar, rosemary, red pepper, black pepper, and garlic. Cook over high heat, stirring occasionally, until mixture is reduced to about 2 cups (about 15 minutes). Evenly spoon into pastry. Arrange 2 anchovy fillets and 4 olives on each tart.

Bake in a 450° oven until well browned (about 20 minutes). Let stand for 10 minutes. Tip tarts out of pans and place on a rack to cool completely. Cover and refrigerate for at least 3 hours or until next day.

Arrange on a platter and garnish with rosemary sprigs, if desired. Makes 8 appetizers.

Cheese Pastry. Stir together 1½ cups **all-purpose flour**, ½ teaspoon **salt**, and ¼ cup **grated Parmesan cheese**. Cut in 4 tablespoons firm **butter** or margarine and 4 tablespoons **solid vegetable shortening** until mixture resembles coarse crumbs. With a fork, gradually stir in 2 to 3 tablespoons **cold water** until mixture holds together. Smooth into a flat ball.

Per appetizer: 351 calories, 8 g protein, 26 g carbohydrates, 24 g total fat, 30 mg cholesterol, 926 mg sodium

◆

CARPACCIO

◆

Preparation time: About 45 minutes
Freezing time: About 1½ hours

Carpaccio—thinly sliced raw beef—is wrapped around breadsticks.

1¼ pounds first-cut top round, trimmed of fat, if necessary
½ cup mayonnaise
⅓ cup Dijon mustard
1 teaspoon Worcestershire
2 teaspoons lime or lemon juice
Dash of ground red pepper (cayenne)
60 breadsticks
Lime or lemon wedges

Wrap meat and freeze just until firm (about 1½ hours). Meanwhile, mix mayonnaise, mustard, Worcestershire, lime juice, and pepper until smooth; cover and refrigerate.

Up to 2 hours before serving, use a food slicer to cut frozen beef across grain into paper-thin slices. (Or, using a very sharp knife, slice beef as thinly as possible; then place slices, a few at a time, between pieces of plastic wrap and pound with flat side of a mallet until paper thin.) As meat is prepared, arrange slices, separated by plastic wrap, in a large pan.

Cut each slice of beef in half lengthwise; wrap around a breadstick. Offer with sauce and lime. Makes about 5 dozen appetizers.

Per appetizer: 47 calories, 3 g protein, 4 g carbohydrates, 2 g total fat, 7 mg cholesterol, 91 mg sodium

Pictured on page 85

CHEDDAR CHEESE PUFFS

◆

Preparation time: About 1 hour
Cooking time: About 35 minutes

Smoked trout folded into horseradish-accented whipped cream creates the rich filling for delicate puffs.

1 cup water
½ cup (¼ lb.) butter or margarine
⅛ teaspoon ground nutmeg
1 cup all-purpose flour
4 eggs
½ cup lightly packed finely shredded sharp Cheddar cheese
Smoked Trout Mousse (recipe follows)

In a 2- to 3-quart pan, stir water, butter, and nutmeg over medium-high heat until butter is melted. Add flour all at once, stirring until mixture leaves sides of pan and forms a ball (about 2 minutes). Remove from heat and transfer to a bowl; let cool briefly.

Add eggs, one at a time, beating well after each addition. Stir in cheese. Drop by spoonfuls about 1½ inches in diameter onto greased baking sheets, spacing puffs about 2 inches apart. Bake in a 400° oven until golden (about 20 minutes). Turn off oven. Pierce each puff in several places. Return to oven until crisp (about 10 minutes). Let cool.

Meanwhile, prepare Smoked Trout Mousse. Split puffs horizontally. Evenly fill with mousse; then replace tops. If made ahead, cover and refrigerate for up to 2 hours. Makes about 3 dozen appetizers.

Smoked Trout Mousse. Beat 1 cup **whipping cream**, 1½ tablespoons **lemon juice**, and ⅛ teaspoon *each* **salt** and **ground white pepper** until stiff. Fold in 1 tablespoon **prepared horseradish** and ⅔ cup finely chopped boneless, skinless **smoked trout.**

Per appetizer: 73 calories, 2 g protein, 3 g carbohydrates, 6 g total fat, 42 mg cholesterol, 77 mg sodium

Summer calls for easy entertaining. Relax with refreshing Citrus Spritzer (recipe on page 90), chilled Tomato Tarts Niçoise (recipe on facing page), make-ahead Turkey-Cheese Pinwheels (recipe on page 79), and simple-to-prepare Snap Pea Knots (recipe on page 94).

FISHLESS SASHIMI

Preparation time: About 15 minutes
Marinating time: About 45 minutes

Lean beef tenderloin, flavored with a peppery oyster sauce marinade, replaces raw fish in this version of sashimi.

1 pound lean beef tenderloin, trimmed of fat
3 tablespoons *each* oyster sauce and lemon juice
¼ teaspoon *each* ground red pepper (cayenne) and finely chopped onion
  Chopped parsley

Cut beef into very thin slices; then cut slices into bite-size pieces. Place meat in a bowl and stir in oyster sauce, lemon juice, pepper, and onion. Cover and refrigerate until meat has lost all its bright red color (about 45 minutes).

Arrange meat pieces on a serving platter; sprinkle with parsley. Makes about 8 servings.

Per serving: 94 calories, 12 g protein, 2 g carbohydrates, 4 g total fat, 35 mg cholesterol, 300 mg sodium

PASTRAMI ROLL-UPS

Preparation time: About 10 minutes

This tasty appetizer is a snap to prepare. Simply roll thin slices of pastrami around horseradish-flavored cream cheese. You can substitute Lebanon bologna for the pastrami, if you like.

1 small package (3 oz.) cream cheese, at room temperature
¾ teaspoon prepared horseradish
¼ pound pastrami slices

Beat cream cheese and horseradish until smooth. Spread cheese mixture

evenly on pastrami slices; roll up jelly roll style. Cut into bite-size pieces. Makes about 16 appetizers.

Per appetizer: 26 calories, 2 g protein, .6 g carbohydrates, 2 g total fat, 9 mg cholesterol, 106 mg sodium

VEAL & OLIVE TERRINE

Preparation time: About 20 minutes
Cooking time: About 1½ hours
Chilling time: At least 8 hours

Slices of this delicate veal meatloaf display a layer of pimento-stuffed green olives. Plan to make this terrine ahead of time; the flavors need time to blend. Accompany with thin slices of French bread.

2 tablespoons butter or margarine
2 large onions, finely chopped
2 cloves garlic, minced or pressed
30 pimento-stuffed green olives
2 eggs
¼ cup fine dry bread crumbs
1 teaspoon dry basil leaves
½ teaspoon salt
⅛ teaspoon ground white pepper
¾ pound ground veal
½ pound ground pork
3 bay leaves

In a wide frying pan, melt butter over medium heat. Add onions and cook, stirring often, until soft (about 7 minutes). Stir in garlic; remove pan from heat and let cool briefly. Finely chop half the olives, reserving remaining olives whole.

In a large bowl, beat eggs. Mix in bread crumbs, basil, salt, and pepper. Add onion mixture, chopped olives, veal, and pork; mix until blended. Spread half the mixture in a deep, straight-sided 4½- to 5-cup terrine or baking pan. Arrange whole olives in 2 or 3 rows down length of pan. Spread remaining meat mixture over olives. Top with bay leaves.

Cover pan and place in a larger pan. Put in a 350° oven and pour scalding water into larger pan to a depth of at least 1 inch. Bake until

meat is firm when pressed and juices run clear when a knife is inserted in center (about 1 hour and 20 minutes). Let cool; then cover and refrigerate for at least 8 hours or up to 5 days.

Just before serving, remove and discard solid fat and bay leaves. Cut terrine into ¼-inch-thick slices and lift carefully from pan. Makes about 1 dozen appetizers.

Per appetizer: 136 calories, 11 g protein, 4 g carbohydrates, 8 g total fat, 78 mg cholesterol, 375 mg sodium

PROSCIUTTO & PEA BUNDLES

Preparation time: About 20 minutes
Cooking time: About 30 seconds

Quick cooking is the secret to these snap peas' crunch and color. Use flavored cream cheese for ease in preparing these attractive carrot-topped packages wrapped with prosciutto.

60 sugar snap peas, ends and strings removed
2 medium-size carrots, peeled
2 to 3 ounces thinly sliced prosciutto or cooked ham
1 package (4 oz.) onion-flavored spreadable cream cheese

In a wide frying pan, cook peas in 2 inches boiling water until bright green (about 30 seconds). Drain, immerse in ice water, and drain again. Set aside.

Cut carrots crosswise into thirds; cut each third into 10 matchstick-size pieces. Cut prosciutto into 60 strips.

Slice each pea along outside seam. Open slightly and push about ½ teaspoon of the cheese into each pea, smoothing cheese with back of a knife. Position a carrot stick on filling, hold in place, and wrap a prosciutto strip in a band around carrot and pea. Makes 5 dozen appetizers.

Per appetizer: 11 calories, .5 g protein, .8 g carbohydrates, .7 g total fat, 2 mg cholesterol, 36 mg sodium

SPINACH-WRAPPED CHICKEN

Preparation time: About 55 minutes
Cooking time: About 15 minutes
Chilling time: At least 1 hour

Wrap fresh spinach leaves around tender chunks of chicken and offer with mayonnaise accented with curry, chutney, and freshly grated orange peel.

2 whole chicken breasts (about 2 lbs. *total*)
1 can (14½ oz.) regular-strength chicken broth
¼ cup soy sauce
1 tablespoon Worcestershire
1 bunch spinach (about 1 lb.), stems removed, washed and dried
8 cups boiling water
Curry Mayonnaise (recipe follows)

In a 10-inch frying pan, combine chicken breasts, broth, soy, and Worcestershire. Bring to a boil over medium heat; reduce heat, cover, and simmer until meat in thickest part is no longer pink when cut (about 15 minutes).

Lift chicken from broth and let cool slightly. Remove and discard skin and bones; cut meat into 1-inch chunks.

Place spinach in a colander and pour boiling water over leaves; drain thoroughly. Let cool.

Place a chunk of chicken at stem end of a spinach leaf. Roll over once, fold leaf in on both sides, and continue rolling around chicken. Secure end of leaf with a wooden pick. Refrigerate for at least 1 hour or until next day.

Meanwhile, prepare Curry Mayonnaise. Offer with chicken for dipping. Makes about 4 dozen appetizers.

Per appetizer: 17 calories, 3 g protein, .3 g carbohydrates, .3 g total fat, 8 mg cholesterol, 39 mg sodium

Curry Mayonnaise. Mix ¼ cup *each* **mayonnaise** and **sour cream**, 2 teaspoons **curry powder**, 2 tablespoons chopped **Major Grey's chutney**, and 1 teaspoon **grated orange peel** until smoothly blended. Cover and refrigerate for at least 1 hour. Makes about ⅔ cup.

Per tablespoon: 62 calories, .3 g protein, 3 g carbohydrates, 6 g total fat, 6 mg cholesterol, 41 mg sodium

CHILI-BAKED CHICKEN WINGS

Preparation time: About 35 minutes
Cooking time: About 35 minutes
Chilling time: At least 4 hours

These mini-drumsticks—really the meaty joints of chicken wings—are covered with a crunchy, chili-spiked coating. Because they're served cold, they're perfect for an outdoor party.

2 tablespoons butter or margarine
1 tablespoon salad oil
¼ cup all-purpose flour
2 tablespoons yellow cornmeal
1½ teaspoons chili powder
½ teaspoon ground cumin
1¼ pounds (about 14) chicken drummettes (meatiest part of wing)

Combine butter and oil in a 10- by 15-inch baking pan. Set in a 400° oven to melt butter. Meanwhile, in a small bag, combine flour, cornmeal, chili powder, and cumin. Add chicken, about half at a time, to bag and shake to coat lightly with seasoned flour. Arrange in pan in a single layer, turning to coat with butter mixture.

Return pan to oven and bake until meat near bone is no longer pink when cut (about 30 minutes). Let cool; cover and refrigerate for at least 4 hours or until next day. Makes about 14 appetizers.

Per appetizer: 89 calories, 7 g protein, 3 g carbohydrates, 6 g total fat, 31 mg cholesterol, 46 mg sodium

Pictured on page 77
TURKEY-CHEESE PINWHEELS

Preparation time: About 20 minutes
Chilling time: At least 3 hours

Lean turkey breast slices swirl around vegetable-accented Neufchâtel cheese in this easy-to-make appetizer. You can make the flavorful pinwheels the day before you plan to serve them.

1 package (8 oz.) Neufchâtel cheese, at room temperature
1 tablespoon *each* chopped chives and prepared horseradish
2 tablespoons chopped Italian parsley
¼ teaspoon ground white pepper
1 medium-size carrot, finely shredded
2 tablespoons drained diced canned pimentos
Salt
1 package (8 oz.) sliced cooked turkey or ham
Italian parsley sprigs (optional)

Mix cheese, chives, horseradish, parsley, and pepper until smooth. Blend in carrot and pimentos. Season to taste with salt.

On each turkey slice, spread about 1 rounded tablespoon of the cheese mixture. Starting with a narrow end, roll each slice compactly to make a pinwheel. Place, seam sides down, in a single layer in a shallow pan. Cover and refrigerate for at least 3 hours or until next day.

Cut into 1-inch slices. Arrange on a platter and garnish with parsley sprigs, if desired. Makes about 3 dozen appetizers.

Per appetizer: 25 calories, 2 g protein, .5 g carbohydrates, 2 g total fat, 7 mg cholesterol, 75 mg sodium

A tangy lime-juice marinade "cooks" raw shellfish
for delicate Scallop Seviche (recipe on facing page).
Guests can spoon the salad into endive leaves and eat
out-of-hand.

LEAN TERRINE

Pictured on page 72

Preparation time: About 30 minutes
Cooking time: About 1¾ hours
Chilling time: At least 4 hours

Ground turkey and ham are combined with pistachios, onions, and fresh sage in this elegant but light version of meatloaf. Serve thin slices on crusty French bread.

- 2 tablespoons salad oil
- 2 large onions, finely chopped
- 3 cloves garlic, minced or pressed
- 2 tablespoons chopped fresh sage or 1 teaspoon dry sage leaves
- ¼ cup brandy
- 2 large eggs
- ½ cup soft bread crumbs
- ¼ teaspoon *each* ground nutmeg and ground white pepper
- ⅛ teaspoon ground allspice
- ½ cup *each* finely chopped cooked ham and salted pistachios
- 2 pounds ground turkey
  Sage sprigs (optional)

Heat oil in a wide frying pan over medium heat. Add onions and cook, stirring often, until soft (about 7 minutes). Stir in garlic and chopped sage. Remove pan from heat and add brandy; set aflame (not beneath an exhaust fan or near flammable items), shaking pan until flames die. Return to heat and stir until most of the liquid has evaporated; set aside.

In a large bowl, beat eggs. Mix in bread crumbs, nutmeg, pepper, allspice, ham, and pistachios (reserve some for garnish, if desired). Add onion mixture and turkey; mix until blended.

Spread in a 6- to 8-cup terrine or baking pan. Cover and place in a larger pan. Put in a 350° oven and pour scalding water into larger pan to a depth of at least 1 inch. Bake until meat is firm when pressed and juices run clear when a knife is inserted in center (about 1½ hours). Let cool; then cover and refrigerate for at least 4 hours or up to 2 days.

Garnish with sage sprigs and reserved nuts, if desired. Cut terrine into thin slices. Makes about 20 appetizers.

Per appetizer: 127 calories, 11 g protein, 3 g carbohydrates, 8 g total fat, 54 mg cholesterol, 109 mg sodium

CALICO FISH SALAD

Preparation time: About 20 minutes
Cooking time: About 10 minutes

Orange roughy is lightly tossed with mustard, tarragon, and a colorful array of vegetables.

- 1 pound orange roughy or sole fillets
- 3 tablespoons coarse-grained mustard
- ¼ cup celery leaves (optional)
- ⅔ cup *each* diced yellow bell pepper, tomato, and celery
- 2 tablespoons lemon juice
- 2 teaspoons minced fresh tarragon leaves or ½ teaspoon dry tarragon leaves
  Salt and pepper
- 16 inner romaine lettuce leaves, washed and crisped

Rinse fish and pat dry. Arrange in a single layer in an 8- to 9-inch square pan. Spread fillets with mustard and, if desired, top with celery leaves. Cover pan with foil.

Bake in a 400° oven just until fish looks just slightly translucent or wet inside when cut in thickest part (about 10 minutes). Let cool; discard celery leaves, if used. Add bell pepper, tomato, diced celery, lemon juice, and tarragon to fish, mixing gently with a fork and breaking fish into bite-size pieces. Season to taste with salt and pepper. If made ahead, cover and refrigerate until next day.

Place fish salad in a small bowl and surround with lettuce leaves for scooping. Makes 16 appetizers.

Per appetizer: 44 calories, 5 g protein, 1 g carbohydrates, 2 g total fat, 6 mg cholesterol, 52 mg sodium

SCALLOP SEVICHE

Pictured on facing page

Preparation time: About 25 minutes
Chilling time: At least 8 hours

To make seviche, raw fish—in this case, scallops—is marinated with lime juice until it looks and tastes as if poached. Present this refreshingly tangy fish salad with endive leaves for scooping.

- ½ pound sea or bay scallops
- ⅓ cup lime or lemon juice
- ¼ cup diced white onion
- 1 or 2 fresh jalapeño or serrano chiles, stemmed, seeded, and finely diced
- 2 tablespoons salad oil
- ½ teaspoon chopped fresh oregano leaves or ⅛ teaspoon dry oregano leaves
- ½ cup chopped yellow, green, or red bell pepper
- 2 teaspoons minced cilantro (coriander)
  Salt
  Oregano sprigs
  Lime halves or wedges
- 1 large head Belgian endive, separated into leaves, washed and crisped (optional)

Rinse scallops and pat dry. If using sea scallops, cut into ½-inch pieces.

In a large nonmetal bowl, stir together scallops, lime juice, onion, chiles, oil, and chopped oregano. Cover and refrigerate, stirring occasionally, for at least 8 hours or until next day.

Stir bell pepper and cilantro into scallop mixture; season to taste with salt. Pour into a serving bowl and garnish with oregano sprigs. Offer with lime halves and, if desired, endive leaves for scooping. Makes about 6 servings.

Per serving: 82 calories, 7 g protein, 3 g carbohydrates, 5 g total fat, 12 mg cholesterol, 64 mg sodium

Treats that can be prepared with a minimum of fuss and in little time are two times more pleasing. They get the cook out of the kitchen without a lot of effort and satisfy the hungry without a lot of waiting.

Whether after school, after work, before a party, or before a meal, these snacks can be made quickly.

RICE-CRUSTED MINI-PIZZAS

Preparation time: About 10 minutes
Cooking time: About 18 minutes

Crisp rice cakes take the place of traditional yeast dough for individual-size pizzas. Top each with red onion, salami, tomato, and three kinds of cheese to make a hearty snack that will please diners of all ages.

- 2 tablespoons olive oil
- 1 large red onion, thinly sliced
- 1 clove garlic, minced or pressed
- 1 teaspoon dry oregano leaves
- 12 rice cakes (3½-in. diameter)
- 1 package (3 oz.) sliced dry salami, cut into thin strips
- 2 medium-size tomatoes
- ½ cup grated Parmesan cheese
- 1 cup (4 oz.) *each* lightly packed shredded jack and provolone cheese

Heat oil in a wide frying pan over medium-high heat. Add onion and cook, stirring often, until soft and lightly browned (about 8 minutes). Stir in garlic and oregano; remove from heat.

Arrange rice cakes in a single layer on a 12- by 15-inch baking sheet. Top evenly with onion mixture and salami. Cut each tomato cross-

QUICK SNACKS

wise into 6 slices. Place a tomato slice on each pizza and sprinkle with Parmesan, jack, and provolone.

Bake pizzas in a 450° oven until cheese is melted (about 10 minutes). Makes 1 dozen snacks.

Per snack: 177 calories, 9 g protein, 11 g carbohydrates, 11 g total fat, 23 mg cholesterol, 339 mg sodium

PIZZA SNACKS MEXICANA

Preparation time: About 5 minutes
Cooking time: About 8 minutes

Made with tortillas, jack and Cheddar cheese, and green chiles, this snack is more like a Southwestern-style tostada than an Italian-style pizza.

- 3 large (10-in. diameter) flour tortillas
- 1½ cups *each* lightly packed shredded jack and Cheddar cheese
- 1 can (4 oz.) diced green chiles
  Prepared salsa

Place tortillas on 12- by 15-inch baking sheets. Sprinkle each with ½ cup of the jack and ½ cup of the Cheddar. Top evenly with chiles.

Bake tortillas, one at a time, in a 425° oven until crisp and golden brown (about 8 minutes). Cut each into 6 wedges and drizzle with salsa to taste. Makes about 1½ dozen snacks.

Per snack: 94 calories, 5 g protein, 5 g carbohydrates, 6 g total fat, 18 mg cholesterol, 183 mg sodium

MINTED YOGURT DIP

Preparation time: About 5 minutes

Fresh mint perks up a cumin-flavored yogurt dip. Serve it with red and yellow cherry tomatoes.

- 2 tablespoons lightly packed chopped fresh mint leaves or 1 tablespoon dry mint leaves
- ½ cup plain yogurt
- ¼ teaspoon ground cumin
- 24 cherry tomatoes

Mix mint, yogurt, and cumin until blended. If made ahead, cover and refrigerate until next day. Offer with cherry tomatoes for dipping. Makes 2 dozen snacks.

Per snack: 5 calories, .3 g protein, .8 g carbohydrates, .1 g total fat, .3 mg cholesterol, 4 mg sodium

TANGY EGG SALAD

Preparation time: About 5 minutes

When you substitute yogurt for mayonnaise in this egg salad, the results are light and refreshing.

- 4 hard-cooked eggs, shelled and chopped
- 3 tablespoons plain yogurt
- 1 tablespoon sweet pickle relish
- 2 teaspoons prepared mustard
  Salt and pepper
- 12 red leaf lettuce leaves, washed and crisped

Mix eggs, yogurt, relish, and mustard until blended. Season to taste with salt and pepper. Spoon into lettuce leaves. Makes 1 dozen snacks.

Per snack: 31 calories, 2 g protein, 1 g carbohydrates, 2 g total fat, 71 mg cholesterol, 44 mg sodium

CHILLED CUCUMBER CREAM SOUP

Preparation time: About 15 minutes

A blender or food processor makes this soup a snap to prepare. There's no cooking required, so the refreshingly cold result is perfect for a hot day. Serve it in mugs.

Make sure that the cucumbers, yogurt, and sour cream are well chilled before you begin.

- 3 **medium-size cucumbers (about 1½ lbs.** *total***), peeled and cut into cubes**
- 1 **clove garlic, cut in half**
- 3 **tablespoons** *each* **chopped parsley and chopped onion**
- 1 **cup regular-strength chicken broth**
- 3 **tablespoons white wine vinegar**
- 2 **cups plain yogurt**
- 1 **cup sour cream**
  Salt and pepper

In a blender or food processor, whirl cucumbers, garlic, parsley, onion, broth, and vinegar until well blended. Pour about half the mixture into a container; set aside.

Add 1 cup of the yogurt and ½ cup of the sour cream to cucumber mixture in blender; whirl until smooth. Transfer to a large bowl. Pour reserved cucumber mixture into blender container and add remaining 1 cup yogurt and ½ cup sour cream. Whirl until smooth.

Add to bowl and season to taste with salt and pepper. Makes about 8 servings (¾ cup each).

Per serving: 114 calories, 5 g protein, 8 g carbohydrates, 7 g total fat, 16 mg cholesterol, 183 mg sodium

APRICOT & ALMOND-BUTTER BITES

Preparation time: About 5 minutes

Almond butter, a sophisticated relative of peanut butter, is sandwiched between dried apricot halves in these deliciously simple snacks.

- 1 **package (6 oz.) dried apricots**
- ¼ **to ⅓ cup almond butter**

Set aside half the apricot halves. On cut side of each of the remaining apricot halves, evenly spread about ½ teaspoon of the almond butter. Top each with one of the remaining apricot halves, smooth side up. Makes about 2 dozen snacks.

Per snack: 36 calories, .7 g protein, 5 g carbohydrates, 2 g total fat, 0 mg cholesterol, 14 mg sodium

STRAWBERRY-BANANA SLURP

Preparation time: About 10 minutes

This fruit and yogurt smoothie is a refreshing way to grab a snack. Simply add a straw and drink up!

- 1 **cup plain yogurt**
- ½ **cup** *each* **orange juice and crushed ice**
- 2 **cups sliced, hulled strawberries**
- 1 **medium-size ripe banana, peeled and sliced**
- 2 **tablespoons sugar**

In a blender, whirl yogurt, orange juice, ice, strawberries, banana, and sugar until well blended. Makes 4 servings (about 1 cup each).

Per serving: 123 calories, 4 g protein, 26 g carbohydrates, 1 g total fat, 3 mg cholesterol, 41 mg sodium

NEEDLES IN A HAYSTACK

Preparation time: About 5 minutes

For a party treat or after-school nibble, simply pull string cheese into fine strips and mix them with crisp pretzel sticks.

- 1½ **ounces string cheese**
- 2 **ounces (about 1½ cups) pretzel sticks**

Pull cheese into fine strips 1/16 to 1/8 inch wide. Mix in a bowl with pretzels. Makes about 4 servings.

Per serving: 89 calories, 4 g protein, 13 g carbohydrates, 1 g total fat, 6 mg cholesterol, 313 mg sodium

HONEYED PEANUT BUTTER WRAP-UPS

Preparation time: About 5 minutes

This snack can bring out the child in almost anyone. It's the perfect pick-me-up for after school or after work.

- ¼ **cup creamy or crunchy peanut butter**
- 4 **lettuce leaves, washed and crisped**
- ¼ **cup raisins**
- 2 **tablespoons honey**

For each serving, spread 1 tablespoon of the peanut butter on a lettuce leaf. Sprinkle with 1 tablespoon of the raisins and top with ½ tablespoon of the honey. Wrap or roll lettuce leaf around filling. Makes 4 snacks.

Per snack: 156 calories, 5 g protein, 19 g carbohydrates, 8 g total fat, 0 mg cholesterol, 78 mg sodium

PICKLED HERRING

Preparation time: About 10 minutes
Marinating time: At least 1 day

Easy to prepare, this traditional Swedish dish must be made ahead. Serve it on slices of hearty dark bread with plenty of sour cream.

1½ cups or 2 jars (6 to 8 oz. *each*) marinated or wine-flavored herring fillet pieces
1 carrot, thinly sliced
1 small red onion, thinly sliced
1 teaspoon whole allspice, slightly crushed
⅓ cup distilled white vinegar
1 cup water
⅔ cup sugar
1 bay leaf

Drain liquid from herring. Alternate layers of herring, carrot, onion, and allspice in a deep 4-cup container until all are used. In a small bowl, stir together vinegar, water, and sugar; pour over herring. Tuck in bay leaf. Cover and refrigerate for at least a day or up to 4 days. Makes about 2½ dozen appetizers.

Per appetizer: 44 calories, 1 g protein, 6 g carbohydrates, 2 g total fat, 1 mg cholesterol, 83 mg sodium

CUCUMBER WITH GOLDEN CAVIAR

Preparation time: About 15 minutes

The holder is as elegant as the filling when you cut cucumbers into tulip-shaped cups to carry sour cream topped with golden caviar.

2 Japanese cucumbers or 1 long, slender English cucumber (about 1 lb. *total*)
¼ to ⅓ cup sour cream
¼ to ⅓ cup golden whitefish caviar or other caviar
Lime juice

Cut stem end of cucumber flat. Hold vertically; about 1½ inches up from flat end, insert a knife tip at a 45° angle and make 3 equally spaced cuts to center. Pull to release cup.

Trim pointed end flat and repeat cuts to make a total of 16 cups. (At this point, you may cover and refrigerate for up to 2 days.)

Spoon ½ to 1 teaspoon of the sour cream into each cucumber cup and top with ½ to 1 teaspoon of the caviar. Sprinkle with lime juice. Makes 16 appetizers.

Per appetizer: 24 calories, 1 g protein, 1 g carbohydrates, 2 g total fat, 29 mg cholesterol, 72 mg sodium

Pictured on facing page
SMOKED SALMON MAYONNAISE

Preparation time: About 15 minutes
Chilling time: At least 1 hour

Smoked salmon flavors fresh mayonnaise made in your blender or food processor. Spoon the elegant mixture on cucumber slices.

½ cup (about 4 oz.) chopped smoked salmon or lox
1 egg yolk
1½ tablespoons lemon juice
3 tablespoons salad oil
1 long, slender English cucumber (about 1 lb.), cut into ⅛-inch-thick slices
Finely chopped mild red onion

In a blender or food processor, whirl salmon, egg yolk, and lemon juice until puréed. With motor running, add oil in a thin, steady stream, mixing until smoothly blended. Cover and refrigerate for at least 1 hour or until next day.

Pipe or spoon about 1 teaspoon of the salmon mixture onto each cucumber slice. If made ahead, cover and refrigerate for up to 2 hours.

Arrange on a platter and sprinkle onion on top. Makes about 64 appetizers.

Per appetizer: 10 calories, .4 g protein, .2 g carbohydrates, .8 g total fat, 4 mg cholesterol, 14 mg sodium

CUCUMBER SALAD BOWLS

Preparation time: About 20 minutes

Simple and sophisticated accurately describes this appetizer. Smoked salmon, fresh dill, and sour cream are spooned into cucumber cups.

2 medium-size cucumbers (about 1 lb. *total*), cut into 1-inch-thick slices
¼ cup (about 2 oz.) chopped smoked salmon or lox
2 tablespoons sour cream
1 teaspoon prepared horseradish
1 tablespoon chopped fresh dill or ½ teaspoon dill weed
Dill sprigs (optional)

Using a melon baller, hollow out each cucumber slice, leaving an ¼-inch-thick bowl-shaped shell; reserve scooped-out portions. Drain shells upside down on paper towels.

Meanwhile, chop reserved cucumber; let stand in a colander for several minutes to drain well. In a small bowl, combine chopped cucumber, salmon, sour cream, horseradish, and chopped dill; mix lightly.

Mound salmon mixture into shells. Garnish with dill sprigs, if desired. If made ahead, cover and refrigerate for up to 30 minutes. Makes 10 to 12 appetizers.

Per appetizer: 17 calories, 1 g protein, 1 g carbohydrates, .8 g total fat, 2 mg cholesterol, 43 mg sodium

For a special occasion, serve Smoked Salmon Mayonnaise (recipe on facing page) on cucumber rounds. Offer with Cheddar Cheese Puffs (recipe on page 76), Shrimp & Feta Fila Triangles (recipe on page 38), and Smoked Salmon & Herbed Cheese Tarts (recipe on page 38).

STUFFED PASTA SHELLS ITALIANO

Preparation time: About 20 minutes
Cooking time: About 10 minutes

For a Mediterranean touch, add dried tomatoes and Italian parsley to tuna. Then fill oversize pasta shells with the sunny combination for an eat-with-your-fingers treat.

- 12 giant shell-shaped pasta (about 3 oz. *total*), *each* about 2½ inches long
- 2 tablespoons olive oil
- 1 can (6½ oz.) chunk light tuna, drained
- ¼ cup slivered dried tomatoes packed in oil, drained
- 1 tablespoon drained capers
- 1 hard-cooked egg, chopped
- 2 tablespoons mayonnaise
- 1 tablespoon sour cream
- 2 teaspoons Dijon mustard
- 2 tablespoons chopped Italian parsley
  Italian parsley sprigs

In a 5- to 6-quart pan, cook pasta in 3 quarts boiling water just until barely tender to bite (about 10 minutes); or cook according to package directions. Drain. Fill pan with about 2 quarts cold water. Add pasta and oil; when pasta is cool, drain well, shaking gently to remove water.

Combine tuna, dried tomatoes, capers, egg, mayonnaise, sour cream, mustard, and chopped parsley; mix until well blended. Spoon tuna mixture evenly into pasta shells. Arrange on a platter. If made ahead, cover and refrigerate until next day.

Garnish with parsley sprigs. Makes 1 dozen appetizers.

Per appetizer: 106 calories, 6 g protein, 6 g carbohydrates, 6 g total fat, 25 mg cholesterol, 219 mg sodium

---

Pictured on page 72

CHERRY TOMATOES WITH SMOKED OYSTERS

Preparation time: About 10 minutes

With a can of smoked oysters in the cupboard, you can easily make this quick treat. The unusual flavor combination is sure to bring raves from your guests.

- 2 baskets cherry tomatoes
- 1 can (3 oz.) tiny smoked oysters, drained
  Italian parsley sprigs (optional)
  Frisée (optional)

Remove stems from tomatoes. Slice each tomato vertically to within about ¼ inch of base; spread apart and slip in a smoked oyster and, if desired, parsley. Arrange on a platter and garnish with frisée, if desired. Makes about 40 appetizers.

Per appetizer: 4 calories, .3 g protein, .6 g carbohydrates, .1 g total fat, 2 mg cholesterol, 14 mg sodium

---

BELL PEPPER & OYSTER BOATS

Preparation time: About 20 minutes

Almost too pretty to eat: bright bell pepper strips cradle a creamy cheese blend topped with smoked oysters and fresh chives.

- 4 medium-size red bell peppers, stemmed and seeded
- 1 can (3¾ oz.) small smoked oysters, drained
- 2 small packages (3 oz. *each*) cream cheese, at room temperature
- 2 tablespoons lemon juice
- 1 teaspoon celery seeds
- 64 chive pieces (*each* 4 in. long)

Cut each bell pepper lengthwise into 8 equal strips. If necessary, cut larger oysters in half so you have 32 pieces.

Beat cream cheese, lemon juice, and celery seeds until smooth. Spread about 1 teaspoon of the mixture over end of each pepper strip. Top with 1 oyster piece and 2 chives. If made ahead, cover and refrigerate until next day. Makes 32 appetizers.

Per appetizer: 26 calories, .9 g protein, 1 g carbohydrates, 2 g total fat, 9 mg cholesterol, 38 mg sodium

---

CREAMY CRAB IN ENDIVE SPEARS

Preparation time: About 20 minutes

Fresh lime adds refreshing tang to a lightly blended combination of sour cream, cream cheese, and crabmeat.

- 1 small package (3 oz.) cream cheese, at room temperature
- 2 tablespoons sour cream
- 2 teaspoons lime or lemon juice
- ¼ teaspoon grated lime or lemon peel
- 2 tablespoons chopped chives
- ¼ pound crabmeat
  Salt and ground white pepper
  4 to 6 heads Belgian endive, separated into leaves, washed and crisped

Beat cream cheese, sour cream, and lime juice until fluffy. Mix in lime peel, chives, and crab; season to taste with salt and pepper.

Pipe or spoon a dollop of crab mixture into wide part of each endive leaf. Arrange on a platter in a starburst pattern, tips pointing outward. If made ahead, cover and refrigerate for up to 4 hours. Makes about 3½ dozen appetizers.

Per appetizer: 12 calories, .8 g protein, .3 g carbohydrates, .9 g total fat, 5 mg cholesterol, 14 mg sodium

CLAM-STUFFED SHELLS

Preparation time: About 20 minutes
Cooking time: About 10 minutes

A rich blend of horseradish, cream cheese, and clams is tucked into giant pasta shells for a convenient appetizer treat.

You can prepare the shells a day ahead.

- 32 **giant shell-shaped pasta (about 8 oz. *total*), *each* about 2½ inches long**
- 1 **tablespoon salad oil**
- 2 **large packages (8 oz. *each*) cream cheese, at room temperature**
- 3 **cloves garlic, minced or pressed**
- 2 **tablespoons prepared horseradish**
- ¼ **cup chopped parsley**
- 4 **cans (6½ oz. *each*) chopped clams, drained**
  Salt and coarsely ground pepper
  Parsley sprigs

In a 5- to 6-quart pan, cook pasta in 3 quarts boiling water just until barely tender to bite (about 10 minutes); or cook according to package directions. Drain. Fill pan with about 2 quarts cold water. Add pasta and oil; when pasta is cool, drain well, shaking gently to remove water.

Beat cheese, garlic, and horseradish until creamy. Stir in chopped parsley and clams. Season to taste with salt and pepper. Spoon clam mixture evenly into pasta shells. Arrange on a platter and sprinkle with more pepper. If made ahead, cover and refrigerate until next day.

Garnish with parsley sprigs. Makes 32 appetizers.

Per appetizer: 98 calories, 5 g protein, 7 g carbohydrates, 6 g total fat, 24 mg cholesterol, 57 mg sodium

STEEPED SHRIMP

Preparation time: About 45 minutes
Cooking time: About 3 minutes
Chilling time: At least 1 hour

Let guests enjoy succulent shrimp plain, seasoned in a highly spiced broth, or dipped in a flavored mayonnaise.

- ⅓ **cup vinegar**
- 1 **tablespoon *each* mustard seeds and cumin seeds**
- 2 **teaspoons black peppercorns**
- 8 **thin quarter-size slices fresh ginger**
- 10 **cilantro (coriander) sprigs (*each* about 4 in. long)**
- 10 **fresh mint sprigs (*each* about 4 in. long) or 2 tablespoons dry mint leaves**
- 2 **tablespoons olive oil**
- 2 **pounds medium-size raw shrimp (about 36 per lb.)**
  Mint-Ginger Vinegar (recipe follows)
  Seeded Mayonnaise (recipe follows)

In an 11- to 12-quart pan, combine 5 quarts water, vinegar, mustard seeds, cumin seeds, peppercorns, ginger, cilantro, mint, and oil. Cover and bring to a boil over high heat.

Add shrimp to pan. Cover and remove from heat. Let steep until shrimp are opaque when cut (about 2 minutes). Lift out shrimp and drain. Pour cooking liquid through a fine strainer; reserve seeds but discard liquid, ginger, mint sprigs, and cilantro. Let shrimp cool; then shell and devein. Cover and refrigerate for at least 1 hour or until next day.

Prepare Mint-Ginger Vinegar and Seeded Mayonnaise. Offer with shrimp for dipping. Makes about 6 dozen appetizers.

Per appetizer: 11 calories, 2 g protein, .1 g carbohydrates, .2 g total fat, 16 mg cholesterol, 15 mg sodium

Mint-Ginger Vinegar. Mix 1½ cups **rice** or cider **vinegar,** 3 tablespoons **sugar,** and 2 tablespoons minced **fresh ginger** until sugar is dissolved. Up to 2 hours before serving, add 2 tablespoons minced **cilantro** (coriander) and 2 tablespoons minced **fresh mint** or dry mint **leaves.** Makes about 2 cups.

Per tablespoon: 6 calories, 0 g protein, 2 g carbohydrates, 0 g total fat, 0 mg cholesterol, .1 mg sodium

Seeded Mayonnaise. Mix 2 cups **mayonnaise,** 3 tablespoons **lemon juice,** and reserved **seeds** from cooking liquid. Makes about 2 cups.

Per tablespoon: 101 calories, .3 g protein, .7 g carbohydrates, 11 g total fat, 8 mg cholesterol, 79 mg sodium

GINGERED SHRIMP & CUCUMBER

Preparation time: About 25 minutes
Marinating time: At least 1 hour

Tiny shrimp marinated in rice vinegar and topped with strips of tangy pickled red ginger perch atop cucumber slices in this light, nutritious offering.

- 2 **tablespoons rice vinegar**
- 1 **teaspoon sugar**
- 1 **tablespoon pickled ginger strips**
- ½ **pound tiny cooked shrimp**
- 1 **long, slender English cucumber (about 1 lb.), thinly sliced**

Stir together vinegar and sugar until sugar is dissolved. Mix in ginger and shrimp. Cover and refrigerate for at least 1 hour or up to 4 hours.

Arrange 1 or 2 shrimp and a bit of ginger atop each cucumber slice. Makes about 5 dozen appetizers.

Per appetizer: 5 calories, .8 g protein, .3 g carbohydrates, 0 g total fat, 7 mg cholesterol, 10 mg sodium

Present pretty pink packages wrapped with bright green chives; your guests will appreciate their edible gift, Shrimp with Tart Dipping Sauce (recipe on facing page).

Pictured on page 93
PARSLEY SHRIMP BALLS

Preparation time: About 35 minutes
Chilling time: About 2 hours

Tiny shrimp mixed with cheese and celery make attractive, bite-size appetizers that will please a crowd. Reserve some whole shrimp to use as decoration on top.

10 ounces small cooked shrimp or 2 cans (5 oz. *each*) shrimp
4 ounces Neufchâtel cheese, at room temperature
3 tablespoons finely chopped celery
1 clove garlic, minced or pressed
¼ teaspoon liquid hot pepper seasoning
1 teaspoon soy sauce
About ⅔ cup finely chopped parsley

Rinse and thoroughly drain shrimp; pat dry. Set aside 40 whole shrimp to use for garnish; coarsely chop remainder.

Beat cheese, celery, garlic, hot pepper seasoning, and soy until very smooth. Stir in chopped shrimp just until blended. Cover and refrigerate for about 1 hour or until easy to handle.

Sprinkle parsley on wax paper. For each appetizer, shape 1 teaspoon of the cheese mixture into a ball; then roll each ball in parsley until coated on all sides.

Spear reserved shrimp on wooden picks and stick a shrimp into each ball. Cover and refrigerate for at least 1 hour or until next day. Makes about 40 appetizers.

Per appetizer: 15 calories, 2 g protein, .2 g carbohydrates, .7 g total fat, 16 mg cholesterol, 37 mg sodium

Pictured on facing page
SHRIMP WITH TART DIPPING SAUCE

Preparation time: About 30 minutes
Cooking time: About 4 minutes

Plump pink shrimp neatly tied with bright green chives please the palate as well as the eye. Dip the shrimp in a tangy, shallot-flavored wine vinegar sauce.

Tart Dipping Sauce (recipe follows)
1 pound medium-size raw shrimp (about 36 per lb.), shelled and deveined
About 36 chives (*each* about 7 in. long)

Prepare Tart Dipping Sauce and set aside.

In a 6- to 8-quart pan, bring 4 cups water to boil over high heat. Add shrimp; reduce heat, cover, and simmer until shrimp are opaque when cut (about 3 minutes). Drain, immerse in cold water, and drain again. Set aside.

In a medium-size frying pan, cook chives in about 1 inch boiling water just until wilted (about 5 seconds); remove immediately with tongs. Tie a chive around center of each shrimp. If made ahead, cover and refrigerate for up to 4 hours.

Arrange shrimp in a dish. Offer with sauce for dipping. Makes about 3 dozen appetizers.

Per appetizer: 11 calories, 2 g protein, .1 g carbohydrates, .2 g total fat, 16 mg cholesterol, 15 mg sodium

Tart Dipping Sauce. Stir together ¼ cup *each* **dry white wine** and **white wine vinegar**, 1 tablespoon *each* minced **shallots** and **chives,** and ½ teaspoon **freshly ground pepper.** Makes about ½ cup.

Per tablespoon: 7 calories, 0 g protein, .5 g carbohydrates, 0 g total fat, 0 mg cholesterol, .5 mg sodium

ASPARAGUS IN BELGIAN ENDIVE

Preparation time: About 20 minutes
Cooking time: About 5 minutes

This elegant, appealing appetizer is easy to prepare. Make it to show off the early spring crop of asparagus while endive is still in season.

If endive isn't available, you can substitute small romaine lettuce leaves.

24 asparagus spears
24 large outer Belgian endive leaves (about 3 heads *total*) or small inner romaine leaves (about 2 heads *total*), washed and crisped
¼ cup olive or salad oil
2 tablespoons white wine vinegar
2 teaspoons Dijon mustard
Chopped parsley

Snap off and discard tough ends of asparagus. Peel stalks, if desired. Cut tips to same length as endive leaves; reserve remaining asparagus sections for other uses.

In a wide frying pan, bring 1 inch water to a boil over high heat. Add asparagus; reduce heat, cover, and simmer just until tender when pierced (about 5 minutes). Drain, immerse in ice water, and drain again. Place an asparagus spear in each endive leaf. (At this point, you may cover and refrigerate for up to 6 hours.)

Just before serving, whisk oil, vinegar, and mustard until blended. Pour into a small serving bowl and sprinkle with parsley. Offer with asparagus for dipping. Makes 2 dozen appetizers.

Per appetizer: 24 calories, .5 g protein, .7 g carbohydrates, 2 g total fat, 0 mg cholesterol, 13 mg sodium

Company's coming! You've planned every appetizer down to the last bite. here are party punches and sparkling spirits, warmed or chilled, to complement your choices. All will welcome guests to your party.

Consider your menu, the time of day, the weather, and, of course, the occasion when you choose your liquid refreshments. For help estimating how much to prepare, see "Great Beginnings" on pages 6–7.

Pictured on page 77

CITRUS SPRITZER

Preparation time: About 15 minutes

Full of spirit, this festive, nonalcoholic drink is a refreshing blend of citrus fruit and sparkling water.

- **4 to 5 large oranges**
- **2 to 3 large limes**
- **1 bottle (24 oz.) white grape juice About 3 cups sparkling mineral water**

With a vegetable peeler, cut 3 strips of peel (orange part only), each ½ inch by 3 inches, from 1 orange. Cut 2 strips of peel (green part only), each ½ inch by 3 inches, from 1 lime. Place peel in a pitcher and bruise with a wooden spoon.

Squeeze enough oranges to make 2 cups juice. From 1 lime, cut 5 thin center slices; cut in half and reserve. Squeeze enough of the remaining limes to make ¼ cup juice. Add orange juice, lime juice, and grape juice to pitcher and stir. (At this point, you may cover and refrigerate until next day.)

For each serving, fill glass with ice cubes, juice blend, and water, using about 2 parts juice to 1 part water. Garnish with a lime slice. Makes about 10 servings, ¾ cup each.

Per serving: 74 calories, .4 g protein, 18 g carbohydrates, .1 g total fat, 0 mg cholesterol, 7 mg sodium

PARTY BEVERAGES

◆

BANANA-CITRUS COOLER

Preparation time: About 5 minutes

This frothy, refreshing blend of tropical fruits takes no time to make. For a party with children, prepare it without the rum.

- **2 large ripe bananas, cut into chunks**
- **½ cup lime juice**
- **1 can (12 oz.) frozen pineapple-orange-banana juice concentrate**
- **1 bottle (1 pt. 12 oz.) chilled sparkling mineral water**
- **1¼ cups light rum (optional)**
- **1 lime, thinly sliced**

In a blender or food processor, smoothly purée bananas, lime juice, and concentrate. Pour into a 3-quart pitcher. Add water and, if desired, rum. Stir down foam. Pour into ice-filled glasses and garnish with lime slices. Makes about 12 servings, ¾ cup each.

Per serving: 84 calories, .3 g protein, 22 g carbohydrates, .1 g total fat, 0 mg cholesterol, 5 mg sodium

CRANBERRY-CITRUS COCKTAIL WITH RASPBERRY SWIZZLE

Preparation time: About 20 minutes
Freezing time: About 45 minutes
Cooking time: About 10 minutes

Raspberry swizzle sticks accent this warm, ruby-colored fruit punch, perfect for a holiday party.

- **1 package (12 oz.) frozen unsweetened raspberries, partially thawed**
- **1 bottle (64 oz.) cranberry juice cocktail**
- **1 *each* medium-size orange and lemon, thinly sliced**

Select 24 of the best-looking raspberries. Thread 3 berries on each of 8 thin wooden skewers. Lay skewers on a flat pan and freeze until berries are hard (about 45 minutes); for longer storage, cover and freeze for up to 5 days.

When remaining raspberries are thawed, press through a fine strainer into a 4- to 5-quart pan; discard seeds and pulp. To pan, add juice and orange and lemon slices. Stir over medium heat until steaming (about 10 minutes). Ladle into 8 tall heatproof glasses; add a skewer to each. Makes 8 servings, about 1 cup each.

Per serving: 178 calories, .8 g protein, 47 g carbohydrates, .8 g total fat, 0 mg cholesterol, 6 mg sodium

STRAWBERRY-GUAVA PUNCH WITH SORBET

Preparation time: About 20 minutes
Freezing time: About 1 hour

Fit for any festive occasion, this pink punch showcases strawberry sorbet and fresh strawberries. Offer spoons for the sorbet and fruit.

- **1 quart strawberries, rinsed and drained**
- **1 quart strawberry sorbet or sherbet**
- **1 can (6 oz.) frozen grapefruit juice concentrate**
- **2 bottles (1½ qts. *each*) guava fruit juice drink**
- **1 bottle (750 ml.) chilled sparkling wine or 1 bottle (1 pt. 12 oz.) chilled sparkling mineral water**

Place half the berries (use the prettiest ones, keeping hulls attached) on a flat pan without touching. Freeze until hard (about 1 hour); for longer storage, package airtight and freeze until next day. Put a 10- by 15-inch pan in freezer. When cold, scoop sorbet into 2-inch balls and place in pan. Freeze for 1 hour; for longer storage, cover airtight and freeze until next day.

Hull remaining berries. In a blender or food processor, smoothly purée berries and grapefruit concentrate. Pour into a 6- to 7-quart punch bowl. Add guava drink and wine; stir well. Add sorbet and frozen berries. Ladle into punch cups or wide-mouthed glasses. Makes about 24 servings, ¾ cup each.

Per serving: 145 calories, .5 g protein, 31 g carbohydrates, .2 g total fat, 0 mg cholesterol, 12 mg sodium

Pictured on page 13
MULLED APPLE-GINGER SPARKLER

Preparation time: About 5 minutes
Cooking time: About 35 minutes
Chilling time: At least 1 hour

Preserved ginger puts an extra punch in cinnamon-flavored apple juice. Just before serving, add sparkling wine or mineral water.

- 2 **cups apple juice**
- ½ **cup chopped preserved ginger in syrup (including syrup)**
- 8 **cinnamon sticks (*each* 2 to 3 in. long)**
- 2 **bottles (750 ml. *each*) chilled brut-style dry sparkling wine or 5 small bottles (10 oz. *each*) chilled sparkling mineral water**

In a 1- to 2-quart pan, boil apple juice, ginger, and cinnamon sticks over high heat, stirring occasionally, until reduced to 1 cup (about 30 minutes); watch closely to prevent scorching. Let cool; then cover and refrigerate for at least 1 hour or until next day. Pour into a small bowl and keep cold.

For each serving, spoon about 2 tablespoons of the apple-ginger syrup into a champagne flute or 6- to 8-ounce glass. Add a cinnamon stick and fill with wine. Makes about 8 servings, ¾ cup each.

Per serving: 161 calories, .3 g protein, 18 g carbohydrates, .1 g total fat, 0 mg cholesterol, 17 mg sodium

BUBBLING MARY

Preparation time: About 10 minutes

Not for the timid, this potent potion should be made with the driest sparkling wine available and fresh lime juice.

- 2 **cups cold tomato juice**
- 1 **teaspoon liquid hot pepper seasoning**
- 2 **tablespoons lime juice**
- 24 **pickled cocktail onions**
- 1 **medium-size lime, cut into 8 wedges**
- 1½ **bottles (750 ml. *each*) chilled brut-style dry sparkling wine or 4 small bottles (10 oz. *each*) chilled sparkling mineral water**

In a pitcher, mix tomato juice, hot pepper seasoning, and lime juice; keep cold. On each of 8 thin wooden skewers, thread 3 onions; place skewers in a tall glass. Put lime wedges in a dish.

For each serving, place an onion swizzle stick in a champagne flute or 8-ounce glass. Pour in ¼ cup of the juice mixture and fill with wine.

Squeeze and drop in a lime wedge and stir with a swizzle. Makes about 8 servings, ¾ cup each.

Per serving: 56 calories, .4 g protein, 3 g carbohydrates, 0 g total fat, 0 mg cholesterol, 152 mg sodium

HOT SPICED PUNCH

Preparation time: About 15 minutes
Chilling time: At least 12 hours
Cooking time: About 5 minutes

Special occasions—and cool nights—call for cups of warming liquid. This spicy drink can be made with grape or cranberry-apple juice.

- 8 **whole cardamom (optional)**
- ½ **teaspoon whole allspice**
- 3 **tablespoons chopped candied ginger**
- 4 **strips lemon peel (yellow part only), ½ inch by 3 inches**
- 1 **cinnamon stick (3 in. long)**
- 2 **bottles (25 oz. *each*) Gamay Beaujolais grape juice or 1 bottle (48 oz.) cranberry-apple juice cocktail**
- ⅓ **cup golden raisins**

Discard cardamom pods, if using. Place seeds in a stainless steel or glass bowl with allspice, ginger, and lemon peel. Slightly crush with a wooden spoon. Add cinnamon stick and juice. Cover and refrigerate for at least 12 hours or up to 2 days.

Pour juice through a strainer into a 2- to 3-quart pan; discard seasonings. Add raisins. Cover and place over medium heat just until hot (about 5 minutes). Serve warm. Makes about 12 servings, ½ cup each.

Per serving: 93 calories, .4 g protein, 23 g carbohydrates, .1 g total fat, 0 mg cholesterol, 6 mg sodium

THAI CARROT SALAD

Preparation time: About 25 minutes

Lettuce leaves hold mini-salads of finely shredded carrots, daikon, and radishes.

- 2 **cups lightly packed finely shredded carrots**
- 1 **cup lightly packed finely shredded daikon**
- ½ **cup lightly packed finely shredded red radishes**
- 2 **tablespoons fish sauce (*nuoc nam* or *nam pla*); or soy sauce to taste**
- 2 **tablespoons lime juice**
- ½ **teaspoon sesame oil**
- ¼ **teaspoon sugar**
  Lime slices
  About 16 small butter lettuce leaves (*each about 3 in. wide*), washed and crisped

Stir together carrots, daikon, radishes, fish sauce, lime juice, oil, and sugar. If made ahead, cover and refrigerate until next day.

Place vegetables in a small dish; garnish with lime slices. Place lettuce in a basket. Using a slotted spoon, scoop vegetables into lettuce leaves. Makes about 16 appetizers.

Per appetizer: 15 calories, .6 g protein, 2 g carbohydrates, .4 g total fat, 0 mg cholesterol, 7 mg sodium

PICKLED CUCUMBERS

Preparation time: About 10 minutes
Standing time: About 30 minutes
Chilling time: At least 30 minutes

These crunchy cucumbers should disappear in almost as little time as it takes to prepare them—and you can make them with ingredients readily at hand.

- 2 **large cucumbers (about ¾ lb. *each*), thinly sliced**
- 1 **teaspoon salt**
- ¼ **cup vinegar**
- 1 **teaspoon sugar**

In a large bowl, mix cucumbers and salt; let stand for about 30 minutes. Rinse well and drain. Return to bowl and stir in vinegar and sugar; cover and refrigerate for at least 30 minutes or until next day. Makes 8 servings.

Per serving: 13 calories, .4 g protein, 3 g carbohydrates, .1 g total fat, 0 mg cholesterol, 138 mg sodium

ONION KNOTS WITH PEANUT SAUCE

Preparation time: About 20 minutes
Cooking time: About 5 minutes

Tie blanched green onions into knots ready for dunking in a spicy sauce.

Peanut Sauce (recipe follows)
36 **green onions (including tops)**

Prepare Peanut Sauce; set aside.

Rinse onions and cut off roots. In a 5- to 6-quart pan, cook onions, a few at a time, in 3 quarts boiling water just until green ends are limp (about 20 seconds). Lift out, immerse in ice water, and drain.

Pull off and discard tough outside layers. Tie each onion in a knot so that white end protrudes about 1 inch; trim green end about 1 inch from knot. If made ahead, cover and refrigerate for up to 6 hours.

Offer with sauce for dipping. Makes 3 dozen appetizers.

Per appetizer: 4 calories, .3 g protein, .8 g carbohydrates, 0 g total fat, 0 mg cholesterol, .6 mg sodium

Peanut Sauce. Combine ¼ cup *each* **crunchy peanut butter** and **plum sauce** and 1 tablespoon *each* **lemon juice** and **soy sauce**. Season to taste

with **liquid hot pepper seasoning.** Makes about ½ cup.

Per tablespoon: 17 calories, .5 g protein, 2 g carbohydrates, .9 g total fat, 0 mg cholesterol, 38 mg sodium

SESAME LONG BEANS

Preparation time: About 30 minutes
Cooking time: About 13 minutes
Marinating time: At least 1 hour

The flavors of Asia—ginger, sesame oil, rice vinegar, and soy sauce—blend in a light marinade that perfectly suits Chinese long beans. Look for them in Asian markets or well-stocked supermarkets.

- 1 **tablespoon sesame seeds**
- ¾ **pound Chinese long beans, ends trimmed, cut into 6-inch lengths**
- 1 **teaspoon ground ginger**
- 1 **tablespoon sesame oil**
- 2 **tablespoons seasoned rice vinegar; or white wine vinegar mixed with 2 teaspoons sugar**
- 2 **tablespoons soy sauce**
- 3 **tablespoons sliced green onions (including tops)**

In a wide frying pan, toast sesame seeds over medium heat, shaking pan often, until golden (about 3 minutes). Remove from pan and let cool.

In pan, bring ¼ inch water to a boil over high heat. Add beans; reduce heat, cover, and simmer until tender when pierced (about 10 minutes). Drain, immerse immediately in ice water, and drain again.

In a bowl, stir together ginger, oil, vinegar, soy, and onions. Add beans, mixing to coat evenly. Cover and let stand for 1 hour, stirring several times. If made ahead, refrigerate until next day. Just before serving, drain beans. Makes about 40 appetizers.

Per appetizer: 10 calories, .3 g protein, 1 g carbohydrates, .5 g total fat, 0 mg cholesterol, 52 mg sodium

An Asian banquet begins with Marbled Tea Eggs (recipe on page 74), Thai Carrot Salad served in lettuce cups (recipe on facing page), Parsley Shrimp Balls (recipe on page 89), and Onion Knots with Peanut Sauce (recipe on facing page).

ORANGE-FENNEL OLIVES

Preparation time: About 10 minutes
Marinating time: 24 hours

Start with a jar of Greek-style olives and create something special: orange- and fennel-accented olives perfect with an apéritif.

- 1 jar (10 oz.) Greek-style olives packed in brine
- 1 teaspoon fennel seeds
- 6 strips orange peel (orange part only), *each* ½ inch by 2 inches
- 1 tablespoon sherry vinegar or red wine vinegar

Drain olives, reserving brine. Return half the olives to jar; add fennel seeds, orange peel, remaining olives, vinegar, and reserved brine. If liquid doesn't cover olives, add enough water to cover. Replace lid and let stand at room temperature for 24 hours, shaking occasionally. If made ahead, refrigerate for up to a month.

Drain olives, reserving orange peel, and place in a bowl with peel. Makes 8 servings.

Per serving: 121 calories, .8 g protein, 3 g carbohydrates, 13 g total fat, 0 mg cholesterol, 1,165 mg sodium

Pictured on page 77
SNAP PEA KNOTS

Preparation time: About 30 minutes
Cooking time: About 30 seconds

Quickly cooked snap peas retain their color and crunch. String cheese ties add a festive touch.

- ½ pound sugar snap peas
- 2 to 3 oz. string cheese

Snap off or trim ends of peas, pulling strings away from both sides. In a wide frying pan, cook peas in 1 inch boiling water until bright green (about 30 seconds). Drain, immerse in ice water, and drain again. (At this point, you may cover and refrigerate until next day.)

Separate cheese into strings slender enough to tie easily. Loosely tie a string of cheese around center of each pea. Makes about 4 dozen appetizers.

Per appetizer: 7 calories, .5 g protein, .7 g carbohydrates, .1 g total fat, .8 mg cholesterol, 11 mg sodium

MINTED PEAS & ALMONDS

Preparation time: About 15 minutes
Baking time: About 8 minutes

Guests can scoop this salad into lettuce leaves and enjoy the tasty mixture of peas, celery, and green onions in a minty yogurt dressing.

- 1 cup slivered almonds
- ⅓ cup mayonnaise
- ¼ cup plain yogurt or sour cream
- 1 teaspoon Dijon mustard
- 1 tablespoon chopped fresh mint leaves or 1 teaspoon dry mint leaves
- ¼ teaspoon salt
  Dash of ground red pepper (cayenne)
- 1 package (10 oz.) frozen tiny peas, thawed
- 2 stalks celery, finely chopped
- ¼ cup sliced green onions (including tops)
  About 24 butter lettuce leaves, washed and crisped

Spread almonds in a shallow pan. Bake in a 350° oven until golden (about 8 minutes). Set aside.

Stir together mayonnaise, yogurt, mustard, mint, salt, and pepper until blended. Add peas, celery, onions, and almonds; mix lightly. If made ahead, cover and refrigerate until next day.

Offer with lettuce leaves for scooping. Makes about 2 dozen appetizers.

Per appetizer: 66 calories, 2 g protein, 3 g carbohydrates, 5 g total fat, 2 mg cholesterol, 67 mg sodium

FRUITED TABBOULEH

Preparation time: About 1¼ hours
Cooking time: About 8 minutes
Chilling time: At least 1 hour

Dried apricots and dates give this crunchy cracked-wheat salad a whole new dimension. Wrap in a lettuce leaf for salad on-the-go.

- 1 cup *each* bulgur and cold water
- ¼ cup slivered almonds
- ⅓ cup *each* chopped pitted dates and slivered dried apricots
- ½ teaspoon ground cinnamon
- 2 tablespoons chopped fresh mint leaves or 1 tablespoon dry mint leaves
- 2 tablespoons salad oil
- 1 tablespoon *each* lemon juice and honey
  About 24 red leaf lettuce leaves, washed and crisped

Rinse bulgur several times. Combine with water and let stand for 1 hour. Drain any liquid that is not absorbed. Meanwhile, spread almonds in a shallow pan. Bake in a 350° oven until golden (about 8 minutes). Let cool.

Mix bulgur with almonds, dates, apricots, cinnamon, mint, and oil. Blend lemon juice and honey; stir into bulgur mixture. Cover and refrigerate for at least 1 hour or up to 3 days.

Offer with lettuce leaves for scooping. Makes about 2 dozen appetizers.

Per appetizer: 60 calories, 1 g protein, 10 g carbohydrates, 2 g total fat, 0 mg cholesterol, 2 mg sodium

FRESH MELON PICKLES

Preparation time: About 10 minutes
Chilling time: At least 2 hours

For a light fruit treat, pickle one of the many varieties of melon available during the summer months.

- ½ cup white wine vinegar
- 2 tablespoons sugar
- 1 teaspoon *each* minced fresh tarragon leaves, dill, and mint leaves, or ½ teaspoon *each* dry tarragon leaves, dill weed, and mint leaves
- 2 cups 1-inch melon cubes (casaba, Santa Claus, honeydew, Persian, or cantaloupe)

Mix vinegar, sugar, tarragon, dill, and mint until sugar is dissolved. Stir in melon cubes. Cover and refrigerate for at least 2 hours or until next day; stir occasionally. Makes 6 servings.

Per serving: 34 calories, .6 g protein, 8 g carbohydrates, .1 g total fat, 0 mg cholesterol, 7 mg sodium

PIctured on page 96

JICAMA & FRESH FRUIT PLATTER

Preparation time: About 30 minutes

For a piquant appetizer with a Southwestern accent, enjoy crunchy jicama and fresh fruit flavored with lime juice and chili powder.

- 1 medium-size jicama
  Fresh Fruit (suggestions follow)
- ⅔ cup lime juice
- 1 teaspoon salt
- 1 tablespoon chili powder

Peel jicama and rinse. Cut in half; then slice each half thinly. Prepare Fresh Fruit of your choice. Coat jicama and fruit well with lime juice; arrange separately on a platter. If made ahead, cover and refrigerate for up to 2 hours.

Combine salt and chili powder; sprinkle over jicama and fruit. Makes 10 servings.

Fresh Fruit. Choose from the following, using a total of 5 pounds: **Honeydew, cantaloupe,** and **watermelon** chunks or slices; sliced **papaya; mango** chunks; **orange** sections; sliced **kiwi fruit;** and sliced **green apple.**

Per serving: 130 calories, 2 g protein, 33 g carbohydrates, .7 g total fat, 0 mg cholesterol, 240 mg sodium

MEAT-WRAPPED FRUITS

Preparation time: About 30 minutes

Thinly sliced meats—domestic or imported—from an Italian delicatessen complement the flavor of fresh cantaloupe and pears.

- 1 medium-size cantaloupe
- ¼ pound thinly sliced prosciutto
- 2 pears, unpeeled
- ¼ cup lime or lemon juice
- ⅛ pound thinly sliced mild cooked coppa sausage
  Lime wedges (optional)

Cut cantaloupe in half lengthwise; discard seeds. Cut fruit from rind, discarding rind. Slice fruit into about 24 long, thin wedges. Cut prosciutto slices in half and wrap a half around each wedge. If made ahead, cover and refrigerate for up to 4 hours.

Cut pears in half lengthwise; discard seeds and cores. Cut into about 24 long, thin wedges; place in a bowl.

Pour lime juice over pears, turning to moisten. Cut coppa slices in half and wrap a half around each wedge. If made ahead, cover and refrigerate for up to 2 hours.

Offer with lime wedges to squeeze over cantaloupe, if desired. Makes about 4 dozen appetizers.

Per appetizer (cantaloupe): 16 calories, 1 g protein, 2 g carbohydrates, .5 g total fat, 3 mg cholesterol, 105 mg sodium

Per appetizer (pear): 19 calories, .6 g protein, 2 g carbohydrates, .9 g total fat, 2 mg cholesterol, 46 mg sodium

NUT- & CHEESE-FILLED FRUITS

Preparation time: About 15 minutes
Chilling time: At least 2 hours

You can change the flavor of this simple hors d'oeuvre by using kumquats or grapes instead of litchis and by substituting almonds or macadamias for the walnuts.

- 1 small package (3 oz.) cream cheese, at room temperature
- 1 tablespoon dry sherry
- 2 tablespoons chopped walnuts, almonds, or macadamias
- 1 can (1 lb. 4 oz.) litchi nuts, drained
  Parsley sprigs

Beat cream cheese and sherry until smooth. Stir in chopped nuts. Fill each litchi nut with about 1 teaspoon of the cheese mixture. Cover and refrigerate for at least 2 hours or until next day.

Garnish with parsley. Makes about 1½ dozen appetizers.

Per appetizer: 45 calories, .5 g protein, 6 g carbohydrates, 2 g total fat, 5 mg cholesterol, 25 mg sodium

Jicama & Fresh Fruit Platter (recipe on page 95) is a bountiful blend of colors and textures. Oranges, watermelon, honeydew, papaya, and jicama are cut into nibbling size, tossed with lime juice, and sprinkled with chili powder and salt for satisfying snacking.

Sunset

Home Canning

By the Editors of Sunset Books and Sunset Magazine

Sunset Publishing Corporation ● *Menlo Park, California*

98

Contents

Special Features

Basics of Canning

Easy techniques, equipment guide, safety tips

No matter where you live— in the city or country, in a high-rise apartment or a home surrounded by gardens—you can reap the rewards of canning. ● If you don't grow your own fruits and vegetables, just start with best-of-season produce purchased from a nearby supermarket, roadside stand, or farmers' market. If you do have a thriving garden, you'll experience the special satisfaction of putting up the crops you've carefully nurtured to ripe, wholesome goodness. You can choose your favorite varieties, too; perhaps you prefer a certain kind of tomato or peach that's not always available in local markets. What's more, canning home-grown fruits and vegetables is economical: if you have too much to eat fresh, preserve it to enjoy later. ● Whether you start with home-harvested or store-bought produce, canning is easy. Once you've gathered the equipment you need and mastered the basic techniques described in this chapter, you'll quickly convert that top-quality produce into a whole range of mouthwatering foods to savor at home or give as gifts: sparkling jams and jellies, meal-brightening chutneys, relishes, and sauces, and fruits and vegetables seasoned just right.

How Canning Preserves Food

There's no special magic to canning: you simply pack food into a jar fitted with a self-sealing lid, then heat the bottled food to a temperature high enough to destroy any microorganisms that could cause spoilage. Heat also causes gases in both food and jar to expand, driving out air. As the jar cools, a vacuum forms, pulling the lid down against the mouth to make a tight seal. Air and microorganisms cannot enter unless this seal is broken.

Two Kinds of Food, Two Canning Methods

For home canning purposes, all foods are considered either *acid* or *low-acid*. Acidity is stated in terms of a pH value: the lower the pH, the higher the acidity. Acid foods have a pH of 4.6 or lower, while a low-acid food's pH is above 4.6. Each type of food requires a different processing method.

Acid foods may be safely processed in a boiling water canner. Foods in this group include almost all fruits, tomatoes acidified with bottled lemon juice or citric acid, pickles, relishes, chutneys, jams, jellies, and preserves. (Figs are the exception among fruits: they're low-acid. But if acidified before canning, they too may be safely processed in a boiling water canner.)

Low-acid foods must be processed in a pressure canner. Foods classed as low-acid include meats, poultry, seafood, milk, and all vegetables except tomatoes.

Botulism & Other Dangers

You've undoubtedly heard of botulism, a deadly form of food poisoning resulting from a toxin produced by spores of the bacterium *Clostridium botulinum*. This organism has some peculiar characteristics. It thrives without air in sealed jars at temperatures between 40° and 120°F, cannot be destroyed in a reasonable amount of time in a boiling water canner at 212°F, and cannot always be detected when a jar is opened. It doesn't grow well in an acid environment, but flourishes when acidity is low. For this reason, low-acid foods must be processed in a pressure canner at 240°F to eliminate the risk of botulism. As a further safeguard, it's wise to boil all such foods for 10 minutes before serving (to destroy any toxin that may be present), even if the food doesn't look in the least suspicious. Add an additional minute of boiling time for each 1,000 feet of altitude, starting at 1,000 feet above sea level.

"Boil before eating" is also the rule for tomatoes and tomato-vegetable mixtures such as chili sauce; though these are usually acidified before processing, boiling assures you that they're absolutely safe.

Other types of food spoilage, usually resulting from a poor or broken jar seal, are more easily detected. If food smells bad, looks discolored, is slimy-textured or topped with cottony mold, or if you see an unsealed or bulging lid, rising bubbles, or cloudy liquid in the jar, discard the food without tasting it. When in doubt, throw it out!

To can food safely, you must always use the proper canning method and adhere exactly to the research-based processing times in this book. For more safety information, see "Guarding against Botulism" (page 121).

Equipment You'll Need

For successful canning, it's essential to use the right equipment. If you're a beginner, consider sharing equipment expenses with a friend. Then take turns canning or, better still, work together.

Boiling water canner. This type of canner is recommended for processing fruits, tomatoes acidified with bottled lemon juice or citric acid, pickles, relishes, chutneys, jams, jellies, and preserves. It has a metal basket or rack that holds jars off the bottom of the kettle, allowing heat to circulate properly. Your canner should be no more than 4 inches wider than the burner on which it is placed, and it must be flat-bottomed if the burner is electric.

If you don't want to invest in a boiling water canner, it's possible to improvise. Just use any covered kettle large enough to let you surround the jars with water and cover them by 1 to 2 inches, while still leaving 1 to 2 inches of air space between water and lid. A large stockpot with a cake rack set in the bottom works well.

Pressure canner. This is the *only* canner to use for safe canning of vegetables, meats, poultry, and seafood. A heavy kettle with a cover that locks down steam-tight, it's mounted with a safety valve, vent, and pressure indicator.

There are two types of pressure indicators: weighted gauge and dial gauge. A dial gauge has a needle that indicates pressure on a numbered face; it should be checked each year (most Cooperative Extension offices will do this for you) and replaced if it reads high or low by more than 1 pound. A weighted gauge automatically limits pressure by a control preset for 5, 10, or 15 pounds; it need not be checked.

Before using your pressure canner, insert a pipe cleaner or string through the vent to make sure that it's unobstructed. Then follow the manufacturer's directions for your canner, and the exact instructions in this book for the particular food you are canning.

For safe operation and results using our recommended processing times, you must use a pressure canner large enough to hold at least four 1-quart jars.

Canning jars. Made of tempered glass that withstands heat shock and rough treatment, canning jars are sold along with other canning supplies in supermarkets and hardware stores. Available in quart, pint, and half-pint sizes, they require a two-piece closure: a vacuum **lid** with a rubber sealant and a metal **ring band.**

Bands are reusable (unless they're bent or rusty), but lids are not; if reused, they'll often fail to seal properly. Unused lids more than 3 years old may also fail, so it's best to buy only a single year's supply at a time.

Old-fashioned canning jars with zinc caps or glass lids are not recommended for canning, nor are newer glass-domed jars with gaskets (it's difficult to determine if you have a seal). Metric jars aren't recommended either, since adequate safety testing has not yet been completed. Finally, avoid reusing jars which contained purchased foods such as mayonnaise and peanut butter. These jars have a greater tendency to break during the home-canning process than do canning jars, since they may have been weakened by metal spoons or knives used to remove their contents: even tiny scratches in the glass can cause cracking or breakage during processing.

Wide, heavy pans. For cooking jams, jellies, preserves, pickles, and tomato sauces, you'll need wide, heavy-bottomed pans in 6- to 8-quart and 8- to 10-quart sizes.

Jar funnel. This wide-mouth funnel makes jars easier to fill and keeps the sealing surfaces clean.

Jar lifter. Available where canning supplies are sold. Some types have heat-resistant handles to protect hands, as well as a soft plastic coating to keep jars from slipping.

Narrow nonmetallic spatula. Use to release trapped air bubbles in filled jars before sealing. A plastic knife also works well. Don't use a metal spatula or knife, which could scratch—and thus weaken—the jar.

Tongs. Use these to remove canning lids from hot water and place them on filled jars.

Measuring cups & spoons. Cup measures (both liquid and dry) and measuring spoons are necessary for accurate measuring.

Long-handled spoons & ladle. Wooden and metal spoons, a long-handled slotted spoon, and a ladle are required for preparing foods and filling jars.

Knives. Sharp paring and chopping knives are essential.

Vegetable brush & peeler. A stiff-bristled brush helps clean vegetables thoroughly; a good, sharp peeler is essential for removing peel from carrots, potatoes, and other vegetables.

Food mill. This sturdy sieve has a hand-turned paddle that crushes vegetables and fruits; the pulp is pressed through, while any seeds, skin, and fiber remain behind. A food mill is especially useful when you're canning tomatoes or preparing jams, jellies, or sauces from fruits with small seeds.

Jelly or candy thermometer. An invaluable aid in cooking jellies and jams to the correct temperature.

Jelly bag. Use a jelly bag to strain juice from softened pulp during jelly making. A cheesecloth-lined colander may also be used.

Colander. For draining fruits and vegetables after washing, then holding them until needed.

Kitchen scale. Essential for reliable canning when ingredients are given by weight. It's helpful to have a scale with a capacity up to 25 pounds.

Timer. A good kitchen timer ensures accurate processing times. Before using your timer, be sure to check it with a reliable timepiece.

Equipment for successful canning includes:
1) Boiling water canner
2) Weighted gauge pressure canner
3) Dial gauge pressure canner
4) Jelly bag 5) Colander 6) Food mill
7) Wide, heavy-bottomed 8-quart pan
8) Kitchen scale 9) Jar funnel 10) Pot holder
11) Long-handled spoons 12) Long-handled ladles
13) Measuring cups 14) Measuring spoons
15) Canning jars, lids, and ring bands
16) Vegetable brush 17) Vegetable peelers 18) Timer
19) Narrow nonmetallic spatula 20) Long-handled
wooden spoon 21) Candy thermometer
22) Tongs 23) Jar lifter 24) Knives

Packing It Right

You may fill jars by either the hot-pack or raw-pack (formerly called "cold-pack") method.

The hot-pack method is preferred for most foods, especially acid types that you'll process in a boiling water canner. When you use this method, you bring food to a boil, simmer it for a few minutes, then pack it loosely into hot jars along with any required hot liquid. Hot-packing shrinks food, removes air from its tissues, helps keep it from floating in jars, and lengthens its shelf life.

The raw-pack method calls for packing unheated prepared food tightly into hot jars, then covering it with hot liquid. Raw-packing is more likely to result in floating food than is hot-packing. In addition, air will be trapped in both the food and the jars, causing the food to discolor during storage more rapidly than hot-packed products do.

Though popular in the past, the old-fashioned *open-kettle method*—filling jars with hot food without further processing—is no longer recommended, since jars often fail to seal properly. Other unsafe canning methods include processing in conventional and microwave ovens and in dishwashers. Avoid steam canners as well; safe processing times for newer models have not been established.

Leaving Headspace

When you fill jars with food, it's important to leave *headspace*: empty space between the top of the food (or liquid) and the jar lid. Headspace is required both to allow food to expand as the jar is heated and to form a vacuum as the jar seals.

Each recipe in this book tells you how much headspace to leave. In general, allow ¼ inch for jams and jellies, ½ inch for fruits and tomatoes processed in a boiling water canner, and 1 to 1½ inches for low-acid foods processed in a pressure canner.

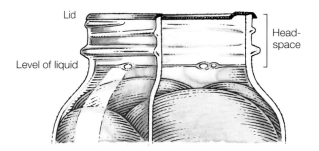

Testing the Seal

Once jars are processed, let them cool on a towel or rack for 12 to 24 hours. (Do not retighten ring bands after processing: seal failures may result.) After cooling, remove ring bands and check seals. You can do this in three ways (see illustrations on page 109).

■ Press the center of the lid. If it stays down when you release your finger, the seal is good; if it springs back, there's no seal.

■ Tap the lid with a spoon. A clear, high-pitched ringing sound indicates a good seal. If you hear a dull sound, either the lid is unsealed or you have a weak seal.

■ Raise the jar to eye level and look across the lid. If it curves down slightly in the center, it's sealed. If it's flat or bulging, it has failed to seal.

Reprocessing Unsealed Jars

If a jar has failed to seal, you have two choices. You can either refrigerate it and use the food within 2 or 3 days (*if* the food looks and smells right); or you can reprocess it within 24 hours. To reprocess, remove the lid and check the sealing surface for tiny nicks. If the jar isn't flawed, just add a new lid. If it is flawed, reheat the food, pack it in a prepared, hot new jar, and apply a new lid. Then reprocess, using the *same* processing time. Keep in mind that the food may turn out softer, with inferior color and flavor.

Storing Canned Food

Once you remove the ring bands and determine that the cooled jars have sealed, wash each jar and lid to remove any food residue; rinse and dry. Label and date the jars, then store them (with ring bands left off to prevent rusting) in a clean, cool, dark, dry place. Don't store canned foods in an uninsulated attic or a damp area; dampness can corrode metal lids, break seals, and allow contamination. And make sure your storage spot is cooler than 95°F, out of sunlight, and away from hot pipes, your range, and your furnace.

Though properly canned foods with intact jar seals may be stored indefinitely, use them within 1 year for optimal flavor, texture, and nutritional value.

High-altitude Canning

Processing times given in the charts and recipes in this book are for canning at sea level. If you live at an altitude above 1,000 feet, you must adjust processing times or canner pressure: at higher altitudes, atmospheric pressure is lower, and water boils at a lower temperature.

If you don't know your altitude, ask your local Cooperative Extension office or contact your local District Conservationist with the Soil Conservation Service. Then calculate proper canning times and pressures by consulting the following charts.

Processing Times for Boiling Water Canner at High Altitude

Altitude (feet)	Increase in time
0 – 1,000	No increase
1,001 – 3,000	Add 5 minutes
3,001 – 6,000	Add 10 minutes
6,001 – 8,000	Add 15 minutes
8,001 – 10,000	Add 20 minutes

Pressures for Dial & Weighted Gauge Canners at High Altitude

Altitude (feet)	Dial Gauge (PSI)	Weighted Gauge (PSI)*
0 – 1,000	11	10
1,001 – 2,000	11	15
2,001 – 4,000	12	15
4,001 – 6,000	13	15
6,001 – 8,000	14	15
8,001 – 10,000	15	15

Above 1,000 feet, operate weighted gauge canners at 15 pounds only. They cannot correct incrementally for higher altitudes.

Glossary

Acid foods. Foods with enough natural acid, or with enough additional acid such as vinegar or lemon juice, to result in a pH of 4.6 or lower. Fruits, acidified tomatoes, pickles, relishes, chutneys, jams, jellies, and preserves fall into this category. (Figs are an exception among fruits; they must be acidified before processing.)

Ascorbic acid. The chemical name for vitamin C. A commercially available form is often used in canning to keep peeled light-colored fruits and vegetables from browning. (Lemon juice is frequently used for the same purpose.)

Botulism. A deadly form of food poisoning, caused by a toxin produced by spores of the bacterium *Clostridium botulinum*. For more on botulism and how to prevent it, see page 121.

Citric acid. An acid derived from citrus fruits. It can be added to canned foods to increase acidity or to improve color and flavor.

Headspace. The unfilled space between the top of the food (or liquid) in a jar and the top of the jar.

Hot-pack method. A canning method that involves filling hot jars with hot precooked food before processing. It's the preferred method for processing foods in a boiling water canner.

Low-acid foods. Foods that contain little natural acid and have a pH above 4.6. This group includes meats, poultry, seafood, milk, vegetables, and some varieties of tomatoes. These foods must be processed in a pressure canner or acidified to a pH of 4.6 or lower before processing in a boiling water canner.

pH. A measure of acidity or alkalinity. Values range from 0 to 14; a pH of 7 is neutral. The lower the pH, the more acid the food.

Pickling. Adding enough vinegar or lemon juice to a low-acid food to bring its pH down to 4.6 or below. Properly pickled foods may be safely processed in a boiling water canner.

Raw-pack method. A canning method that involves filling hot jars with raw, unheated food prior to processing.

Venting (also called "exhausting"). Permitting excess air inside a pressure canner to escape before closing the vent or putting on the weighted gauge.

Home-canned fruits let you enjoy summer flavors all year long. Shown below right is a dish of Brandied Apricots (page 110) with Blackberry-Peach Topping (page 220) and sour cream. Jars on the tabletop include blackberries, pears, peaches, and more toppings; on the shelf are (left to right) Brandied Apricots, raspberries, pears, and Brandied Sweet Cherries (page 110).

Canning Fruits

Sweet summer flavors, homey sauces, brandied fruit

You can easily and confidently preserve fresh fruit in a boiling water canner. The hot-pack method (see "Packing It Right," page 104) is best for most fruits, though some cooks feel that raw-packing is preferable for small or soft types such as berries, cherries, apricots, and plums, since it minimizes crushing. ● Adding some sweetening helps fruit hold its shape and maintain its color and flavor; a very light syrup approximates the natural sugar content of many fruits. If you'd rather not use syrup, you may also can fruit in juice. Unsweetened apple, pineapple, and white grape juice are all good packing liquids, but the best choice is juice from the fruit being canned (to prepare juice, crush soft fruit, then heat and strain it). ● Packing fruit in water is another option, but water-packed fruits fall short on flavor, color, and texture. If you want to sweeten such fruits with an artificial sweetener, add it just before serving. ● No matter which pack you choose, start with fruit that's fully ripened, yet still firm. Examine it carefully to make sure it's free from bruises or soft spots, then rinse it well with cool water to remove any dirt or residues. ● To keep fruits such as pears, peaches, nectarines, and apples from turning brown when cut, treat them with an antidarkening agent (see "Protecting Fruit Colors," page 108).

1. Read the information about canning fruit on the preceding page. Check the fruit chart (pages 112 and 113) for instructions on the specific fruit you're canning. Prepare an antidarkening solution, if needed (see "Protecting Fruit Colors," below).

2. Get out boiling water canner, jars, new lids, ring bands, and other equipment you'll need (see pages 101 and 102). Jars must be free of nicks or cracks that might prevent sealing; ring bands must not be rusty, dented, or scratched. Be sure all equipment is clean and ready to use.

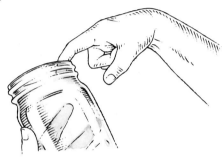

3. Wash jars; keep them hot in hot water to prevent breakage when filling with hot food. If jars will be processed for less than 10 minutes in the boiling water canner, you must sterilize them. To sterilize, cover with water and boil for 10 minutes; leave in hot water until filled.

Prepare lids according to manufacturer's directions; keep them hot in hot water. Check the manufacturer's advice concerning the ring bands you're using, then follow any preparation instructions printed on the box.

4. Place basket or rack in canner. Half-fill canner with hot water. Cover; bring water to a simmer. In a large teakettle or another pan, heat additional water to add later.

5. Prepare only enough fruit for one canner load at a time, following chart instructions. If necessary, treat fruit to prevent darkening (see below). Prepare syrup of your choice as directed on facing page; or heat fruit juice or water. Keep hot until ready to use.

6. Remove a jar from hot water. Stand it upright on a cloth towel.

To pack hot, bring syrup or other liquid to a boil. Add prepared fruit; cook briefly, or as directed. Pack hot fruit into prepared, hot jars (pack halves cavity side down, in overlapping layers); leave ½-inch headspace. Ladle or pour hot liquid over fruit, leaving directed headspace.

To pack raw, fill prepared, hot jars with raw fruit (pack halves cavity side down, in overlapping layers); leave ½-inch headspace. Cover with hot liquid, leaving ½-inch headspace, or as chart directs.

7. Gently run a narrow nonmetallic spatula between fruit and jar sides to release air bubbles; add more liquid, if necessary.

Protecting Fruit Colors

To keep apples, apricots, nectarines, peaches, and pears from darkening after cutting, drop the cut fruit into a commercial antidarkening mixture prepared according to the manufacturer's instructions; or use 1 teaspoon ascorbic acid (or enough crushed vitamin C tablets to equal 3,000 milligrams) to 1 gallon cold water.

8. Wipe jar rim and threads with a clean, damp cloth or paper towel to remove food particles that might prevent a seal. Lift a jar lid from hot water; place on jar, sealing side down. Firmly and evenly screw on ring band by hand; don't over-tighten. As each jar is filled, use jar lifter to place it on canner rack. Space jars so they don't touch each other or sides of canner. If needed, add more hot water to cover jars by at least 1 inch.

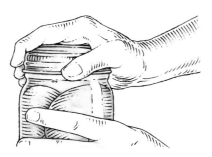

9. Cover canner; increase heat to high and bring water to a vigorous boil. Set timer for required processing time (see chart on pages 112 and 113); at altitudes above 1,000 feet, adjust times according to "Processing times for Boiling Water Canner at High Altitude" (page 105). Reduce heat to maintain a gentle boil throughout processing. Add more boiling water, if needed, to keep water level above jars.

10. When processing time is up, turn off heat. Immediately remove jars with jar lifter. Place jars at least 1 inch apart on a towel or rack, out of drafts. *Do not retighten bands.* Let cool for 12 to 24 hours.

11. When jars are cool, remove ring bands. (To loosen a band that sticks, cover it with a hot, damp cloth for 1 to 2 minutes.) Test seal as directed on page 104 and shown below. If a jar fails to seal, refrigerate it and use the food within 2 or 3 days—*if* it looks and smells right. Or reprocess as directed on page 104.

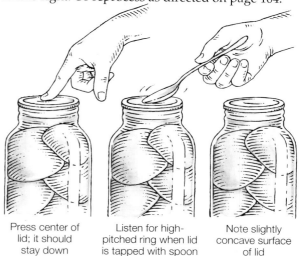

| Press center of lid; it should stay down | Listen for high-pitched ring when lid is tapped with spoon | Note slightly concave surface of lid |

12. Wash jars and lids to remove any food residue; rinse and dry. Label and date jars; store in a clean, cool, dark, dry place.

Syrups for Canning

Amounts make enough syrup to pack 8 or 9 pints or 4 quarts of fruit.

Type of Syrup	Water (Cups)	Sugar (Cups)
Very light	6½	¾
Light	5¾	1½
Medium	5¼	2¼
Heavy	5	3¼
Very heavy	4¼	4¼

To prepare syrup, combine sugar and water in a heavy-bottomed pan. Bring to a boil, stirring until sugar is dissolved; keep hot. You need ½ to ¾ cup syrup for each pint of fruit.

You may use a mild-flavored honey or light corn syrup in place of up to half the sugar, if you prefer. A higher proportion will mask the fruit flavor.

Many fruits, particularly sweeter varieties, are excellent when packed in lighter syrups. In general, use lighter syrups with sweeter fruits, heavier syrups with tarter fruits. Try a small amount of syrup first to see if you like it.

Home-style Applesauce

Pictured on facing page

Applesauce as *you* like it. Sweeten and spice it to taste, or leave it entirely plain. For a smoother sauce, whirl the cooked fruit in a food processor or blender before seasoning it and reheating to boiling. (For a new twist on this all-time favorite, don't pass up our winning pear and plum sauces.)

    9 pounds (about 27 medium-size) apples (such as
       Jonathan, McIntosh, Golden Delicious, or
       Gravenstein), peeled, cored, and sliced
 1½   cups water
    1 to 1½ cups sugar (optional)
    1 to 2 teaspoons ground cinnamon (optional)

Combine apples and water in a heavy-bottomed 8- to 10-quart pan. Bring to a boil over medium-high heat, stirring often. Reduce heat, cover, and simmer, stirring often, until apples are soft (about 30 minutes). Add sugar and cinnamon, if desired; bring to a boil. (Sauce will be slightly chunky; to remove larger lumps, whisk briefly with a wire whisk.)

Fill prepared, hot jars with hot sauce, leaving ½-inch headspace. Gently run a narrow nonmetallic spatula between sauce and jar sides to release air bubbles. Wipe rims and threads clean; top with hot lids, then firmly screw on bands. Process in boiling water canner for 15 minutes for pints, 20 minutes for quarts. Or omit processing and ladle sauce into freezer containers, leaving ½-inch headspace for pints, 1-inch headspace for quarts; apply lids. Let cool; freeze or refrigerate. Makes about 6 pints or 3 quarts.

Storage time. *Processed:* Up to 1 year. *Unprocessed:* Up to 1 week in refrigerator; up to 10 months in freezer.

Per ½ cup: 82 calories, 0 g protein, 21 g carbohydrates, 0 g total fat, 0 mg cholesterol, 0 mg sodium

Home-style Pear Sauce

Follow directions for **Home-style Applesauce,** but substitute 9 pounds **Bartlett pears** for apples, reduce water to 1 cup, and add 2 tablespoons **lemon juice.** After seasoning sauce, simmer, uncovered, until it thickens to the desired consistency. Makes about 4 pints or 2 quarts.

Per ½ cup: 139 calories, 1 g protein, 36 g carbohydrates, 1 g total fat, 0 mg cholesterol, 0 mg sodium

Home-style Plum Sauce

Follow directions for **Home-style Applesauce,** but substitute 9 pounds **plums** for apples. Rinse, pit, and slice; do not peel. Before seasoning sauce, whirl, a portion at a time, in a food processor or blender until smooth. Or put through a food mill or fine strainer. Makes about 6 pints or 3 quarts.

Per ½ cup: 88 calories, 1 g protein, 21 g carbohydrates, 1 g total fat, 0 mg cholesterol, 0 mg sodium

Brandied Apricots

Pictured on page 106

Fruits canned in brandy syrup have much the same heady flavor as those brandied in a stone crock. Serve the fruit plain or topped with vanilla yogurt, sour cream, or crème fraîche; or spoon it over ice cream or slices of pound cake.

    3 cups sugar
 2½   cups water
    6 pounds firm-ripe apricots
 1¼   to 1½ cups brandy

First, prepare syrup. Combine sugar and water in a heavy-bottomed 8- to 10-quart pan and bring to a boil over medium heat, stirring until sugar is dissolved. Keep hot.

Halve and pit apricots; treat to prevent darkening (see page 108). Drain apricots; add to hot syrup and bring to a boil. Pack (cavity side down, in overlapping layers) into prepared, hot pint jars.

Pour about ¼ cup hot syrup into each jar; then pour in 3 to 4 tablespoons brandy (the amount depends on your preference for a moderate or strong brandy flavor). Then fill jars with more hot syrup, leaving ½-inch headspace. Gently run a narrow nonmetallic spatula between fruit and jar sides to release air bubbles. Wipe rims and threads clean; top with hot lids, then firmly screw on bands. Process in boiling water canner for 20 minutes. Makes about 6 pints.

Storage time. Up to 1 year.

Per ½ cup: 177 calories, 1 g protein, 37 g carbohydrates, 0 g total fat, 0 mg cholesterol, 1 mg sodium

Brandied Sweet Cherries

Follow directions for **Brandied Apricots,** but substitute 6 pounds **dark sweet cherries** for apricots. Rinse, stem, and pit cherries. If desired, substitute **kirsch** for brandy. Process for 15 minutes. Makes about 6 pints.

Per ½ cup: 200 calories, 1 g protein, 42 g carbohydrates, 1 g total fat, 0 mg cholesterol, 0 mg sodium

Delicious fruit sauces add great flavor—and a pretty flourish—
to a variety of entrées. Here, pork tenderloin on a bed of noodles receives a
tangy assist from Home-style Plum Sauce. Home-style Applesauce (top left) is
another superb choice; or try making the same sauce with mellow pears.
All three sauce recipes are on the facing page.

111

Guide for Canning Fruits

You'll find recipes for syrups on page 109. Processing times are given for altitudes of 1,000 feet or below. Above 1,000 feet, you will need to increase times; see "Processing Times for Boiling Water Canner at High Altitude" (page 105). Before applying hot lids to filled jars, run a narrow nonmetallic spatula gently between fruit and jar sides to release trapped air bubbles.

Note: The suitable varieties noted for a number of fruits (apples, apricots, and peaches, for example) are meant only as general suggestions. The types listed are among the best choices for canning, but other kinds may also work well.

Fruit	Quantity to yield 1 pint	How to prepare	Processing time Pints	Quarts
Apples Golden Delicious, Granny Smith, Gravenstein, Jonathan, McIntosh, Newtown Pippin	1¼ to 1½ lbs.	Rinse, peel, and core; quarter or slice. Treat to prevent darkening (see page 12); drain. Prepare syrup or other packing liquid; add apples and boil gently for 5 minutes. Pack hot into prepared, hot jars; cover with hot liquid, leaving ½-inch headspace.	20 min.	20 min.
Apricots Castlebrite, Patterson, Royal-Blenheim, Tilton, Wenatchee	1 to 1¼ lbs.	You may leave apricots whole if tree-ripened (use varieties that hold their shape well); remove pits from apricots harvested before fully ripe. Rinse apricots; if desired, peel as directed for peaches. Halve or slice. Treat to prevent darkening (see page 12); drain. Prepare syrup or other packing liquid. *To pack hot*, bring apricots and syrup (or other liquid) to a boil. Pack hot into prepared, hot jars (place halves cavity side down, in overlapping layers). Cover with hot liquid, leaving ½-inch headspace. *To pack raw*, fill prepared, hot jars with apricots (place halves cavity side down, in overlapping layers). Cover with hot liquid, leaving ½-inch headspace.	20 min. / 25 min.	25 min. / 30 min.
Bananas		Canning not recommended.		
Berries (Except strawberries and cranberries, which are not recommended for canning)	¾ to 1½ lbs.	Rinse 1 to 2 quarts at a time. Drain, hull, and stem if necessary. For gooseberries, snip off tops and tails with scissors. Prepare syrup or other packing liquid and bring to a boil; pour ½ cup into each prepared, hot jar. *To pack hot* (for firm berries), heat berries in boiling water for 30 seconds; drain. Pack hot into jars. Cover with more hot liquid, leaving ½-inch headspace. *To pack raw*, fill jars with berries, shaking down gently while filling. Cover with more hot liquid, leaving ½-inch headspace.	15 min. / 15 min.	15 min. / 20 min.
Cherries, all varieties *Sweet:* Bing, Black Tartarian, Lambert, Rainier, Royal Ann *Sour:* Early Richmond, English Morello, Montmorency	1 to 1½ lbs.	Rinse and stem; pit, if desired. If pitted, treat sour cherries and light-colored varieties of sweet cherries to prevent darkening (see page 12); drain. If left unpitted, prick skins on opposite sides with a clean needle to prevent splitting. Prepare syrup or other packing liquid. *To pack hot*, bring cherries to a boil in syrup (or other liquid). Pack hot into prepared, hot jars. Cover with hot liquid, leaving ½-inch headspace. *To pack raw*, pour ½ cup hot syrup (or other liquid) into each prepared, hot jar. Fill jars with cherries, shaking down gently while filling. Cover with more hot liquid, leaving ½-inch headspace.	15 min. / 25 min.	20 min. / 25 min.
Figs Black Mission, Celeste, Kadota, Brown Turkey	¾ to 1½ lbs.	Avoid overripe figs. Rinse; do not peel or stem. Cover figs with water; bring to a boil and boil for 2 minutes. Drain. Prepare light syrup or other packing liquid. Add figs; boil gently for 5 minutes. **Add 2 tablespoons bottled lemon juice to each quart jar (1 tablespoon to each pint).** Pack hot figs into prepared, hot jars. Cover with hot liquid, leaving ½-inch headspace.	45 min.	50 min.
Grapefruit	2 lbs.	Use thoroughly ripe fruit. Cut off peel, including white membrane. Run a thin knife between pulp and skin of each segment; lift out whole segment. Remove any seeds. Prepare syrup or other packing liquid. Fill prepared, hot jars with fruit. Cover with hot liquid, leaving ½-inch headspace.	10 min.	10 min.

Fruit	Quantity to yield 1 pint	How to prepare	Processing time	
			Pints	Quarts
Grapes Any tight-skinned, slightly underripe seedless grapes, preferably harvested 2 weeks before reaching optimum eating quality	2 lbs.	Rinse and stem. Prepare light or medium syrup or other packing liquid. **To pack hot**, heat grapes in boiling water for 30 seconds; drain. Pack hot into prepared, hot jars. Cover with hot liquid, leaving 1-inch headspace.	10 min.	10 min.
		To pack raw, fill prepared, hot jars with grapes. Cover with hot liquid, leaving 1-inch headspace.	15 min.	20 min.
Lemons/Limes		Canning not recommended.		
Loquats	1½ to 2 lbs.	Rinse; remove stem and blossom ends. Halve and remove seeds. Prepare light syrup or other packing liquid; add loquats and boil gently for 3 to 5 minutes. Pack hot loquats into prepared, hot jars. Cover with hot liquid, leaving ½-inch headspace.	15 min.	20 min.
Melons		Freezing recommended (balls, cubes, or slices); see page 85.		
Nectarines Firebrite, Flavortop, Gold Mine, Panamint, Stanwick	1 to 1½ lbs.	Rinse; do not peel. Pit; halve or slice. Treat to prevent darkening (see page 12); drain. Prepare syrup or other packing liquid. **To pack hot**, bring fruit and syrup (or other liquid) to a boil. Pack hot into prepared, hot jars (pack halves cavity side down, in overlapping layers). Cover with hot liquid, leaving ½-inch headspace.	20 min.	25 min.
		To pack raw, fill prepared, hot jars with nectarines (pack halves cavity side down, in overlapping layers). Cover with hot liquid, leaving ½-inch headspace.	25 min.	30 min.
Oranges		Can as directed for grapefruit. Flavor is best when canned with equal parts grapefruit.		
Peaches Elberta, Halford, J.H. Hale, O'Henry, Redglobe, Redhaven, Rio Oso Gem	1 to 1½ lbs.	Rinse. To peel, dip firm-ripe peaches in boiling water for 1 to 1½ minutes to loosen skins. Dip in cold water; drain. Slip off skins. Pit, then halve or slice. Treat to prevent darkening (see page 108); drain. Prepare syrup or other packing liquid. **To pack hot,** follow hot-pack directions for nectarines. **To pack raw,** follow raw-pack directions for nectarines. (Note: Hot-packed peaches will generally be higher in quality than raw-packed fruit.)	20 min. 25 min.	25 min. 30 min.
Pears Bartlett	1 to 1½ lbs.	Rinse, peel, cut into halves or quarters, and remove cores. Treat to prevent darkening (see page 108); drain. Prepare syrup or other packing liquid; add pears and boil gently for 5 minutes. Pack hot into prepared, hot jars (pack halves cavity side down, in overlapping layers). Cover with hot liquid, leaving ½-inch headspace.	20 min.	25 min.
Pineapple	1 to 1½ lbs.	Rinse and peel; remove eyes and core. Slice or cube. Prepare syrup or other packing liquid; add pineapple and simmer for 10 minutes. Pack hot into prepared, hot jars. Cover with hot liquid, leaving ½-inch headspace.	15 min.	20 min.
Plums & fresh prunes Casselman, French Prune, Friar, Italian Prune, Laroda, Nubiana, Santa Rosa	1 to 1½ lbs.	Rinse and stem. Freestone varieties may be halved and pitted. If plums are left whole, prick skins on opposite sides with a clean needle to prevent splitting. Prepare syrup or other packing liquid. **To pack hot**, boil plums in syrup (or other liquid) for 2 minutes. Remove from heat, cover pan, and let stand for 20 to 30 minutes. Pack plums into prepared, hot jars (pack halves cavity side down, in overlapping layers). Cover with hot liquid, leaving ½-inch headspace.	20 min.	25 min.
		To pack raw, fill prepared, hot jars with plums, packing firmly (pack halves cavity side down, in overlapping layers). Cover with hot liquid, leaving ½-inch headspace.	20 min.	25 min.
Rhubarb	⅔ to 1 lb.	Rinse unpeeled stalks; cut into ½-inch lengths. Place in a large pan. Add ½ cup sugar for each 4 cups fruit; let stand for 3 to 4 hours. Heat gently just to a boil. Pack hot into prepared, hot jars; cover with hot cooking liquid, leaving ½-inch headspace.	15 min.	15 min.

Capture the robust flavor of red, ripe tomatoes by canning the fruit whole, halved, or crushed; or use your tasty crop as a base for zesty sauces. Surrounding a bowl of Meatless Pasta Sauce (page 120) are, from left, Barbecue Sauce (page 120), canned tomatoes (page 116), Salsa (page 118), and more Meatless Pasta Sauce.

Canning Tomatoes

Succulent tomatoes, spicy condiments, savory sauces

W hen the tomatoes in your garden ripen all at once, capture their sunny, full-bodied flavor with home canning. You can preserve the fruit whole or crushed, or use it in sauces, salsa, or spicy homemade catsup. ● Because some modern varieties are less acidic than older types, it's especially important to acidify tomatoes to minimize the risk of botulism. Just add bottled lemon juice or citric acid to each jar, in the amounts the recipe directs. Be aware that acidification is necessary even if you use a pressure canner (see basic tomato pack instructions, page 116), since the pressure canning times for tomatoes do not provide protection against botulism. ● When you prepare the recipes in this chapter, follow all instructions *explicitly*. If only pressure canning instructions are given, you *must* process in a pressure canner. Do not change processing times, preparation methods, or ingredient proportions. If you wish to add other ingredients or seasonings, wait until just before serving. And remember—for safety's sake, boil all home-canned tomatoes and tomato-vegetable mixtures for 10 minutes before eating; boil very thick mixtures for 15 to 20 minutes. Add an additional minute of boiling for every 1,000 feet of altitude, starting at 1,000 feet above sea level.

Step-by-Step Canning for Tomatoes

1. Choose firm-ripe tomatoes. Don't use overripe tomatoes with soft or wrinkled skins, tomatoes from dead or frost-killed vines, or those ripened in the house; these are all lower in acidity than firm, vine-ripened fruit, and thus carry a greater risk for botulism. (You may, however, safely can green tomatoes picked near maturity; follow the instructions for ripe tomatoes.)

2. Check recipe or pack instructions. If you will be using a boiling water canner, follow steps 2 through 4 on page 108. If you will be using a pressure canner, follow steps 2 and 3 on page 124.

3. Prepare just one canner load at a time. Rinse tomatoes gently but thoroughly; don't use detergent. Dip in boiling water until skins split (30 to 60 seconds), then dip in cold water. Slip off skins; cut out cores and any bruised or discolored areas. Prepare tomatoes and any other ingredients according to recipe or pack instructions.

4. Remove a jar from hot water; place upright on a cloth towel.

For tomatoes, add 2 tablespoons bottled lemon juice or ½ teaspoon citric acid to each quart jar (1 tablespoon juice or ¼ teaspoon citric acid to each pint jar). Add a little sugar to offset the tartness, if you like; you may also add salt. Fill jar according to pack instructions, leaving recommended headspace.

For tomato-vegetable mixtures, fill jar as recipe directs, leaving recommended headspace.

Gently run a narrow nonmetallic spatula between food and jar sides to release air bubbles; add more liquid, if necessary.

5. ***To process in a boiling water canner,*** follow steps 8 through 12 on page 109.

To process in a pressure canner, follow steps 7 through 13 on pages 124 and 125.

Basic Tomato Packs

Whether you can your tomatoes whole, halved, or crushed, you'll need an average of 3 pounds per quart. Rinse, peel, and core tomatoes, following the step-by-step instructions above; then proceed as directed below for the pack you're preparing. Note that it's necessary to adjust processing times or canner pressure at elevations higher than 1,000 feet; see page 105.

Crushed Tomatoes

Quarter tomatoes, then place a sixth of them in a large, heavy-bottomed non-aluminum pan. Heat quickly over high heat, crushing to release juice and stirring constantly to prevent scorching. Bring to a boil; gradually add remaining tomato quarters (do not crush). Boil gently, uncovered, for 5 minutes, stirring often.

Add 2 tablespoons bottled lemon juice or ½ teaspoon citric acid to *each* prepared, hot quart jar (1 tablespoon juice or ¼ teaspoon citric acid to *each* pint). *Don't* use fresh lemon juice; the acidity varies too much. If you wish to add salt, place 1 teaspoon in each quart jar, ½ teaspoon in each pint jar (or season to taste). Fill jars with hot tomatoes, leaving ½-inch headspace.

Process tomatoes in boiling water canner for 35 minutes for pints, 45 minutes for quarts. Or process in pressure canner for 15 minutes for pints and quarts (at 11 pounds pressure on dial gauge; 10 pounds for weighted gauge).

Whole or Halved Tomatoes

Leave tomatoes whole or cut into halves. Place in a large, heavy-bottomed non-aluminum pan and add enough water to cover. Bring to a boil; boil gently, uncovered, for 5 minutes.

Add 2 tablespoons bottled lemon juice or ½ teaspoon citric acid to *each* prepared, hot quart jar (1 tablespoon juice or ¼ teaspoon citric acid to *each* pint). *Don't* use fresh lemon juice; the acidity varies too much. If you wish to add salt, place 1 teaspoon in each quart jar, ½ teaspoon in each pint jar (or season to taste). Fill jars with hot tomatoes, leaving ½-inch headspace. Add hot cooking liquid, leaving ½-inch headspace.

Process tomatoes in boiling water canner for 40 minutes for pints, 45 minutes for quarts. Or process in pressure canner for 10 minutes for pints and quarts (at 11 pounds pressure on dial gauge; 10 pounds for weighted gauge).

Tomato Sauce

Use this tasty tomato sauce much as you would commercially canned sauce—in stews, soups, and casseroles, and as a base for pasta sauces.

- 10 pounds (about 20 large) firm-ripe tomatoes, peeled, cored, and quartered
- ¼ cup lightly packed chopped fresh basil
- 2 tablespoons chopped fresh oregano
- 5 cloves garlic, minced or pressed
- 2 to 4 tablespoons sugar
- 2 teaspoons salt (optional)
- ½ teaspoon freshly ground pepper
  About 3 tablespoons bottled lemon juice (1 tablespoon per pint jar)

In a heavy-bottomed 8- to 10-quart non-aluminum pan, combine tomatoes, basil, oregano, garlic, sugar, salt (if used), and pepper. Bring to a boil over high heat, stirring almost constantly; reduce heat and simmer, uncovered, stirring often, for 20 minutes. Put through a food mill or fine strainer, a portion at a time.

Return purée to pan and bring to a boil over high heat, stirring often. Then reduce heat and simmer, uncovered, stirring often, until sauce is thickened and reduced to about 6 cups (about 1½ hours); as sauce thickens, reduce heat and stir more often to prevent sticking.

Add 1 tablespoon bottled lemon juice to *each* prepared, hot pint jar. Fill jars with hot sauce, leaving ¼-inch headspace. Gently run a narrow nonmetallic spatula between sauce and jar sides to release air bubbles. Wipe rims and threads clean; top with hot lids, then firmly screw on bands. Process in boiling water canner for 35 minutes or in pressure canner for 15 minutes (at 11 pounds pressure on dial gauge; 10 pounds for weighted gauge). Or omit processing and ladle sauce into pint freezer containers, leaving ½-inch headspace; apply lids. Let cool; freeze or refrigerate. Makes about 3 pints.

Storage time. *Processed:* Up to 1 year. *Unprocessed:* Up to 1 week in refrigerator; up to 6 months in freezer.

Per tablespoon: 11 calories, 0 g protein, 2 g carbohydrates, 0 g total fat, 0 mg cholesterol, 4 mg sodium

---

Peeling Tomatoes

To peel tomatoes, dip them in boiling water until the skins split (30 to 60 seconds). Dip in cold water, then peel; the skins will slip off easily.

Mild Chili Sauce

Mild green chiles add a suggestion of heat to a sauce that's great over grilled hamburgers, barbecued chicken, and even scrambled eggs. If you'd prefer a little more heat, substitute jalapeño or serrano chiles for some of the Anaheim chiles.

- 7 pounds (about 14 large) firm-ripe tomatoes, peeled, cored, and quartered
- ¾ pound (about 4 large) fresh mild green chiles such as Anaheim, seeded (if desired) and chopped
- ½ pound onions, quartered
- 2 cloves garlic, halved
- 1½ cups sugar
- 3 cups cider vinegar (5% acidity)
- 1½ teaspoons *each* ground cinnamon and ground cloves
- 1 teaspoon ground ginger
  Salt and freshly ground pepper

In a large bowl, combine tomatoes, chiles, onions, and garlic. Purée vegetables in a blender or food processor, a portion at a time. Pour purée into a heavy-bottomed 8- to 10-quart non-aluminum pan and stir in sugar, vinegar, cinnamon, cloves, and ginger. Bring to a boil over high heat, stirring. Then reduce heat and simmer, uncovered, stirring occasionally, until sauce is thickened and reduced to 2 quarts (about 2 hours); as sauce thickens, reduce heat and stir more often to prevent sticking. Season to taste with salt and pepper.

Fill prepared, hot pint jars with hot sauce, leaving ¼-inch headspace. Gently run a narrow nonmetallic spatula between sauce and jar sides to release air bubbles. Wipe rims and threads clean; top with hot lids, then firmly screw on bands. Process in boiling water canner for 15 minutes. Or omit processing and ladle sauce into pint freezer containers, leaving ½-inch headspace; apply lids. Let cool; freeze or refrigerate. Makes about 4 pints.

Storage time. *Processed:* Up to 1 year. *Unprocessed:* Up to 3 weeks in refrigerator; up to 6 months in freezer.

Per tablespoon: 17 calories, 0 g protein, 4 g carbohydrates, 0 g total fat, 0 mg cholesterol, 2 mg sodium

Spicy Tomato Catsup

When you're overwhelmed with ripe tomatoes, try putting up a batch of homemade catsup. This version is seasoned with herbs, chiles, and sweet spices.

- 12 pounds (about 24 large) firm-ripe tomatoes, coarsely chopped
- 2 large onions, quartered
- 1 medium-size red bell pepper, seeded and cut into pieces
- 1 tablespoon *each* mustard seeds, whole black peppercorns, and dry basil
- 2 teaspoons whole allspice
- 2 small dried hot red chiles
- 1 large dry bay leaf
- 1 cinnamon stick (about 3 inches long)
- 1½ cups firmly packed brown sugar
- 1 tablespoon paprika
- 1 cup cider vinegar (5% acidity)
  Salt

In a large bowl, combine tomatoes, onions, and bell pepper. Smoothly purée vegetables in a blender or food processor, a portion at a time. Put through a food mill or fine strainer; you should have 6 quarts purée. Discard pulp left in food mill or strainer.

Pour purée into a heavy-bottomed 8- to 10-quart non-aluminum pan. Bring to a boil over medium-high heat; then boil gently, uncovered, stirring often, until reduced by about half (about 1 hour).

Tie mustard seeds, peppercorns, basil, allspice, chiles, bay leaf, and cinnamon stick in a washed square of cheesecloth. Add spice packet to purée. Add sugar and paprika; stir until well blended. Continue to boil gently over medium-high heat, uncovered, stirring occasionally, until catsup is very thick and reduced to 2 quarts (1½ to 2 hours); as catsup thickens, reduce heat and stir more often to prevent sticking. Stir in vinegar during last 10 to 15 minutes of cooking. Discard spice packet. Season to taste with salt.

Fill prepared, hot pint jars with hot catsup, leaving ¼-inch headspace. Gently run a narrow nonmetallic spatula between catsup and jar sides to release air bubbles. Wipe rims and threads clean; top with hot lids, then firmly screw on bands. Process in boiling water canner for 20 minutes. Or omit processing and ladle into pint freezer containers, leaving ½-inch headspace; apply lids. Let cool; freeze or refrigerate. Makes about 4 pints.

Storage time. *Processed:* Up to 1 year. *Unprocessed:* Up to 3 weeks in refrigerator; up to 6 months in freezer.

Per tablespoon: 20 calories, 0 g protein, 5 g carbohydrates, 0 g total fat, 0 mg cholesterol, 4 mg sodium

Salsa

Pictured on page 114 and on facing page

This red salsa is medium hot; if you prefer a tamer or more fiery sauce, you can adjust the proportions of mild and hot chiles (just be sure not to exceed 2 pounds of chiles *total*). Wear rubber gloves while handling chiles; or, if you work without gloves, wash your hands with soap and water before touching your face.

- 5 pounds (about 10 large) firm-ripe tomatoes, peeled, cored, and chopped
- 1 pound onions, chopped
- 1 pound (about 6 large) fresh mild green chiles such as Anaheim, seeded and chopped
- 1 pound (about 35) fresh green or red jalapeño chiles, seeded and chopped
- 1¼ cups cider vinegar (5% acidity)
- 2 teaspoons salt

In a heavy-bottomed 6- to 8-quart non-aluminum pan, combine tomatoes, onions, mild and jalapeño chiles, vinegar, and salt. Bring to a boil over high heat, stirring often; then reduce heat and simmer, uncovered, stirring occasionally, until thickened (about 15 minutes).

Fill prepared, hot pint jars with hot salsa, leaving ½-inch headspace. Gently run a narrow nonmetallic spatula between sauce and jar sides to release air bubbles. Wipe rims and threads clean; top with hot lids, then firmly screw on bands. Process in boiling water canner for 20 minutes. Or omit processing and ladle into pint freezer containers, leaving ½-inch headspace; apply lids. Let cool; freeze or refrigerate. Makes about 6 pints.

Storage time. *Processed:* Up to 1 year. *Unprocessed:* Up to 3 weeks in refrigerator; up to 6 months in freezer.

Per tablespoon: 5 calories, 0 g protein, 1 g carbohydrates, 0 g total fat, 0 mg cholesterol, 24 mg sodium

Take advantage of juicy summer tomatoes and mild and hot chiles to create your own signature salsa (facing page). Here, the lively sauce perks up a quesadilla stuffed with cheese, black beans, sliced green onion—and more salsa. By varying the chiles you use, you can make the sauce as tame or fiery as you like.

Meatless Pasta Sauce

Pictured on page 114

This robust sauce is wonderful as is, but if you like, you can stir in cooked ground meat just before serving. Do *not* increase the proportion of mushrooms, onion, or celery.

- 30 pounds (about ½ bushel) firm-ripe tomatoes, peeled, cored, and quartered
- 2 tablespoons olive oil
- 1 pound mushrooms, sliced
- 1 cup *each* chopped onion and chopped celery
- 6 cloves garlic, minced or pressed
- 2 tablespoons *each* dry basil, dry oregano, and parsley flakes
- ¼ cup firmly packed brown sugar
  Salt and freshly ground pepper

Place tomatoes in a heavy-bottomed 16-quart non-aluminum pan and bring to a boil over medium-high heat, stirring often. Then reduce heat and simmer, uncovered, for 20 minutes, stirring often. Put through a food mill or fine strainer; return to pan.

Heat oil in a wide frying pan over medium-high heat. Add mushrooms, onion, celery, and garlic; cook, stirring often, until onion is soft (about 10 minutes).

Add mushroom mixture, basil, oregano, parsley flakes, and sugar to tomato purée. Bring to a boil over medium-high heat. Then reduce heat and simmer, uncovered, stirring occasionally, until sauce is thickened and reduced by about half (about 6 hours); as sauce thickens, reduce heat and stir more often to prevent sticking. Season to taste with salt and pepper.

Fill prepared, hot jars with hot sauce, leaving 1-inch headspace. Gently run a narrow nonmetallic spatula between sauce and jar sides to release air bubbles. Wipe rims and threads clean; top with hot lids, then firmly screw on bands. Process in pressure canner for 20 minutes for pints, 25 minutes for quarts (at 11 pounds pressure on dial gauge; 10 pounds for weighted gauge). Or omit processing and ladle sauce into freezer containers, leaving ½-inch headspace for pints, 1-inch headspace for quarts; apply lids. Let cool; freeze or refrigerate. Makes about 10 pints or 5 quarts.

Storage time. *Processed:* Up to 1 year. *Unprocessed:* Up to 1 week in refrigerator; up to 6 months in freezer.

Per ½ cup: 83 calories, 3 g protein, 17 g carbohydrates, 2 g total fat, 0 mg cholesterol, 32 mg sodium

Barbecue Sauce

Pictured on page 114

Spicy-sweet barbecue sauce is great for slathering over grilled ribs, steak, or chicken.

- 12 pounds (about 24 large) firm-ripe tomatoes, peeled, cored, and quartered
- 2 cups chopped onions
- 2 cups chopped green bell peppers
- 1½ cups chopped celery
- 2 fresh hot red or green chiles (such as jalapeño or Fresno), seeded and minced
- 4 cloves garlic, minced or pressed
- 1½ cups firmly packed brown sugar
- 2½ cups cider vinegar (5% acidity)
- 1 tablespoon *each* dry mustard and paprika
- 1½ teaspoons ground red pepper (cayenne)
  About 1 teaspoon liquid hot pepper seasoning
  Salt

In a heavy-bottomed 8- to 10-quart non-aluminum pan, combine tomatoes, onions, bell peppers, celery, chiles, and garlic. Cook over medium-high heat, uncovered, stirring occasionally, until vegetables are soft (about 30 minutes). Put through a food mill or fine strainer, a portion at a time.

Return vegetable purée to pan and bring to a boil over medium-high heat; then boil gently, uncovered, stirring often, until reduced by about half (about 1 hour). Add sugar, vinegar, mustard, paprika, and red pepper. Continue to cook gently, uncovered, stirring often, until sauce is very thick and reduced to about 2½ quarts (about 1½ hours); as sauce thickens, reduce heat and stir more often to prevent sticking. Add hot pepper seasoning; season to taste with salt.

Fill prepared, hot pint jars with hot sauce, leaving ¼-inch headspace. Gently run a narrow nonmetallic spatula between sauce and jar sides to release air bubbles. Wipe rims and threads clean; top with hot lids, then firmly screw on bands. Process in boiling water canner for 20 minutes. Or omit processing and ladle into pint freezer containers, leaving ½-inch headspace; apply lids. Let cool; freeze or refrigerate. Makes about 5 pints.

Storage time. *Processed:* Up to 1 year. *Unprocessed:* Up to 3 weeks in refrigerator; up to 6 months in freezer.

Per tablespoon: 17 calories, 0 g protein, 4 g carbohydrates, 0 g total fat, 0 mg cholesterol, 5 mg sodium

Guarding against Botulism

Botulism is an especially dangerous form of food poisoning, caused by a toxin produced by spores of the bacterium *Clostridium botulinum.* Because these spores are extremely resistant to heat and favor a low-acid environment, they can thrive in improperly processed low-acid foods—often without producing discoloration or an "off" odor. Even a taste of food containing the botulinum toxin can prove fatal. Symptoms of botulism, usually appearing within 12 to 36 hours after contaminated food is consumed, include double vision, inability to swallow, and speech and respiratory difficulties. Medical treatment should be sought immediately; there are antitoxins.

How can you guard against botulism?

First, remember that for low-acid foods, safe processing means pressure canning: this is the only method to use for canning vegetables (see pages 126 through 129), meats, poultry, and seafood. Unlike processing in a boiling water canner, pressure canning at the correct time and pressure (temperature) destroys *C. botulinum* spores.

Second, keep in mind that though botulism rarely occurs in fruits or tomatoes, some tomato varieties have pH values in the low-acid range, slightly above 4.6 (as do figs). To can these foods safely in a boiling water canner, you must first acidify them with bottled lemon juice or citric acid. Likewise, be sure you follow recipes for pickles and relishes meticulously, always adding the proper amount of vinegar; if insufficiently acidified, these foods may not be safe to eat.

Third, always err on the side of caution. Do not even taste foods from jars that show signs of gas—a bulging lid, oozing from under the lid, or tiny upward-moving bubbles. Nor should you taste food that looks mushy or moldy, or gives off a disagreeable odor when the jar is opened.

Dispose of suspect food very carefully. If the jars are unopened (and no leakage has occurred), wrap them in a heavy garbage bag, then discard in the trash or bury in a landfill.

Unsealed, open, or leaking jars of low-acid foods or tomatoes must be detoxified before disposal. Carefully place both the jars and their lids in an 8-quart or larger pan; then wash your hands thoroughly. Slowly add enough water to the pan to cover the contents by 1 inch; avoid splashing as you pour. Cover the pan, bring the water to a boil, and boil for 30 minutes. Let the water and bottled food cool; then dispose of jars, lids, and food in the trash or bury them in the ground. Thoroughly scrub all equipment and counters. Wrap used sponges or dishcloths and discard them in the trash. Wash your hands thoroughly.

Fourth, as an additional safeguard, boil all home-canned low-acid foods, tomatoes, and tomato-vegetable mixtures (such as pasta sauce) for 10 minutes before eating; boil very thick mixtures for 15 to 20 minutes. Add an additional minute of boiling time for each 1,000 feet of altitude (starting at 1,000 feet above sea level).

And remember—

- Don't experiment or take shortcuts in home canning. Use only tested, approved methods.
- Use fresh, firm (not overripe), thoroughly washed vegetables. Can vegetables as soon as possible after you pick them.
- Use jars and lids made especially for home canning; discard cracked or nicked jars.
- Don't overpack foods. Putting too much food in a jar may result in underprocessing and spoilage.
- Never use lids a second time. Once the sealant on the lids has been through the processing stage, it may be ineffective for sealing again.
- Use only a pressure canner with an accurate gauge (have dial gauges tested annually). Process for the full required time at the correct pressure (temperature). Follow directions exactly, and make adjustments for high altitude (see "High-altitude Canning," page 105).
- Test each jar's seal before storing.
- Never use—or even taste—canned food that shows signs of spoilage.

Select fresh vegetables at peak quality, then can them to enjoy throughout the year.
The gleaming jars shown here contain (clockwise from right) sliced carrots,
roasted peppers (in a combination of red, yellow, and green), baby carrots, peas,
asparagus, beets, roasted red peppers, green beans, and whole-kernel corn.

Canning Vegetables

Garden-fresh, economical goodness

When your garden overflows with more produce than you and your family can eat fresh, put your canner to work and preserve that summertime bounty to enjoy later in the year. ● Fresh vegetables are easy to can—with nutritious, good-tasting results. But because these are low-acid foods, you do need to take special care: can all vegetables in a pressure canner under specific amounts of pressure, for specific times. *Never* can vegetables by the boiling water method; the processing temperature isn't high enough to kill botulism spores. ● Ready to begin? Start by choosing the best, freshest vegetables you can find. Rinse them well and scrub them with a vegetable brush. Then follow the instructions for the specific vegetable you're canning in our "Guide for Canning Vegetables," pages 126 through 129. You may season vegetables with salt, if you like, but it's not necessary for safety purposes. If you use a salt substitute, add it shortly before serving. ● And remember—for safety's sake, always boil home-canned vegetables for at least 10 minutes before eating; boil very thick mixtures for 15 to 20 minutes. Add an extra minute of boiling for each 1,000 feet of altitude, starting at 1,000 feet above sea level.

Step-by-Step Canning for Vegetables

1. Read the information about canning vegetables on the preceding page. Check the vegetable chart (see pages 126 through 129) for instructions on the specific vegetable you're canning.

2. Get out pressure canner, jars, *new* lids, ring bands, and other equipment you'll need (see pages 101 and 102). Jars must be free of nicks or cracks that might prevent sealing; ring bands must not be rusty, dented, or scratched. Be sure all equipment is clean and ready to use. Insert a pipe cleaner or string through your canner's vent to make sure that it's unobstructed.

3. Wash jars; keep hot in hot water to prevent breakage when filling with hot food. Prepare lids according to manufacturer's directions; keep hot in hot water. Check the manufacturer's advice concerning the ring bands you're using; then follow any preparation instructions printed on the box.

4. Prepare only enough vegetables for one canner load at a time, following chart instructions. If chart offers precooking as a choice (the hot-pack method), consider that precooking allows you to pack more food into jars and reduces the likelihood of floating food. If you run short of cooking liquid, you can use fresh boiling water to finish filling the jars. In general, you don't need to can vegetables with salt, but artichokes do require an acid-brine solution (see chart).

5. Pour 2 to 3 inches of hot water into pressure canner.

Remove a jar from hot water; stand it upright on a cloth towel. Fill with vegetables as instructed in chart, packing loosely enough for water to circulate between pieces without wasting space (a slotted spoon makes filling jars easier). Cover with hot cooking liquid, dividing it among jars (or cover with fresh boiling water); leave 1-inch headspace, or as chart directs.

6. Gently run a narrow nonmetallic spatula between vegetable and jar sides to release air bubbles; add more liquid, if necessary.

7. Wipe jar rim and threads with a clean, damp cloth or paper towel to remove food particles that might prevent a seal. Lift a jar lid from hot water; place on jar, sealing side down. Firmly and evenly screw on ring band by hand; don't overtighten. As each jar is filled, use jar lifter to place it on canner rack. Space jars so they don't touch each other or sides of canner.

8. Before processing, you must vent pressure canner to eliminate air inside. To do this, fasten canner lid securely, following manufacturer's instructions. Turn heat to high, leaving petcock open or weight off vent. Allow steam to escape steadily for 10 minutes. (If canner isn't vented in this way, trapped air could prevent the temperature from rising as high as necessary, resulting in underprocessing.)

After venting, close petcock or place weight over vent; bring canner to required pressure level. Start counting processing time. (For altitudes above 1,000 feet, see "Pressures for Dial & Weighted Gauge Canners at High Altitude," page 105.) Keep pressure steady for entire processing time by adjusting heat source. If pressure falls below required level, record the time it takes to return to the proper level; then add that many minutes to the total processing time.

9. When time is up, simply turn off heat if you are processing over a gas burner. If you are processing on an electric range, remove canner to an unheated range element—not to a cold surface. Canner will be heavy, but don't tilt it; toppled jars may not seal.

10. Let pressure fall to zero on its own. This will take 30 to 45 minutes. Cooling time is figured into safe processing times, so never try to speed the process by running the canner under cold water or opening the vent. When the dial gauge registers zero—or a gentle prodding of the weight produces no steam—slowly open petcock or remove weight. Open lid away from you to avoid steam burns. Remove jars with jar lifter.

11. Place jars at least 1 inch apart on a towel or rack out of drafts. *Do not retighten bands.* Let cool for 12 to 24 hours.

12. When jars are cool, remove ring bands (To loosen a band that sticks, cover it with a hot, damp cloth for 1 to 2 minutes.) Test seal as directed on page 104 and shown on page 109. If a jar fails to seal, refrigerate it and use the food within 2 or 3 days—*if* it looks and smells right. Or reprocess as directed on page 104.

13. Wash jars and lids to remove any food residue; rinse and dry. Label and date jars; store in a clean, cool, dark, dry place.

Guide for Canning Vegetables

Processing pressures for weighted and dial gauge canners are given for altitudes of 1,000 feet or below. If you live above 1,000 feet, you'll need to increase processing pressures; see "Pressures for Dial & Weighted Gauge Canners at High Altitude" (page 105).

You may add salt for flavor, if you like, but it's not necessary for safety. As a general rule, add ½ teaspoon per pint, 1 teaspoon per quart.

Before applying hot lids to the jars, don't forget to run a narrow nonmetallic spatula gently between the vegetable and the sides of the jar to release any trapped air bubbles.

Note: Not all vegetables are recommended for canning. Those not recommended include broccoli, Brussels sprouts, cabbage, cauliflower, cucumbers, eggplant, parsnips, rutabagas, and turnips.

Vegetables	Quantity to yield 1 quart	How to prepare	Processing time* Pints	Quarts
Small artichokes	35 to 40 (1¼-inch) or 20 to 30 (2-inch) trimmed whole small artichokes	Cut off thorny tops and stem ends. Remove coarse outer leaves, leaving only tender inner leaves. Precook for 5 minutes in boiling water to which you've added ¾ cup vinegar per gallon. Drain and discard cooking liquid. Fill prepared, hot jars with hot artichokes, leaving 1-inch headspace. Cover with boiling brine (¾ cup vinegar or lemon juice and 3 tablespoons salt per gallon water), leaving 1-inch headspace.	35 min.	40 min.
Asparagus	3 lbs.	Remove tough ends and scales. Rinse and drain. Cut stalks into lengths 1 inch shorter than jar; or cut stalks into 1- to 2-inch pieces. **To pack hot,** cover asparagus with boiling water. Bring to a boil; boil for 2 to 3 minutes. Loosely fill prepared, hot jars with hot asparagus. Cover with hot liquid, leaving 1-inch headspace; add salt, if desired. **To pack raw,** tightly fill prepared, hot jars with asparagus; don't crush pieces. Cover with boiling water, leaving 1-inch headspace; add salt, if desired.	30 min.	40 min.
Beans, fresh lima	4 lbs. (unshelled)	Shell and rinse beans. **To pack hot,** cover beans with boiling water; bring to a boil. Loosely fill prepared, hot jars with hot beans. Cover with hot liquid, leaving 1-inch headspace; add salt, if desired. **To pack raw,** loosely fill prepared, hot jars with beans; do not shake or press down. Cover with boiling water, leaving 1-inch headspace for pints. For quarts, leave 1½-inch headspace if beans are small, 1¼-inch headspace if they are large. Add salt, if desired.	40 min.	50 min.
Beans, snap Green, wax, Italian	2 lbs.	Rinse beans and trim ends; remove strings, if necessary. Leave whole, or cut into 1- to 1½-inch pieces. **To pack hot,** cover beans with boiling water. Bring to a boil; boil 5 minutes. Loosely fill prepared, hot jars with hot beans. Cover with hot liquid, leaving 1-inch headspace; add salt, if desired. **To pack raw,** tightly fill prepared, hot jars with beans. Cover with boiling water, leaving 1-inch headspace; add salt, if desired.	20 min.	25 min.
Beets	3 lbs.	To keep color from bleeding, leave root ends and 1 inch of tops on beets. Scrub well; don't peel. Cover with boiling water; boil until skins slip off easily (about 15 minutes). Dip in cold water. Remove skins; trim off stems and roots. Discard woody beets. Small beets (1 to 2 inches in diameter) may be left whole; cut medium-size or large beets into ½-inch cubes or ¼- to ½-inch-thick slices. Halve or quarter very large slices. Fill prepared, hot jars with beets. Cover with boiling water, leaving 1-inch headspace; add salt, if desired.	30 min.	35 min.

* 10 pounds pressure (weighted gauge canner)
11 pounds pressure (dial gauge canner)

*Canned roasted peppers add a bright, delicious finishing touch to a sandwich of
turkey, salami, and cheese on crusty bread. You'll find canning instructions for
both bell peppers and chiles on page 129.*

Vegetables	Quantity to yield 1 quart	How to prepare	Processing time* Pints	Quarts
Carrots	2½ lbs.	Rinse and peel. Leave baby carrots whole; slice or dice regular carrots. **To pack hot,** cover carrots with boiling water. Bring to a boil; boil gently for 5 minutes. Fill prepared, hot jars with hot carrots, leaving 1-inch headspace; add salt, if desired. **To pack raw,** tightly fill prepared, hot jars with carrots. Cover with boiling water, leaving 1-inch headspace; add salt, if desired.	25 min.	30 min.
Corn, cream style	Pints only; 2¼ lbs. (in husks) per pint	Discard husks and silk; rinse corn. Dip ears in boiling water for 4 minutes; then dip in cold water until cool enough to handle. With a sharp knife, cut corn from cob at about center of kernel. Then scrape cob, being careful not to scrape off any cob material. Add 2 cups boiling water to every 4 cups corn and scrapings. Bring to a boil. **Using pint jars only,** fill prepared, hot jars with hot corn mixture. Leave 1-inch headspace; add salt, if desired.	85 min.	
Corn, whole kernel	4½ lbs. (in husks)	Discard husks and silk; rinse corn. Dip ears in boiling water for 3 minutes; then dip in cold water until cool enough to handle. With a sharp knife, cut corn from cob at about three-fourths the depth of kernel. **Do not scrape cob.** **To pack hot,** add 1 cup of hot water to every 4 cups of kernels. Bring to a boil; boil gently for 5 minutes. Fill prepared, hot jars with hot corn and cooking liquid, leaving 1-inch headspace; add salt, if desired. **To pack raw,** loosely fill prepared, hot jars with raw kernels, leaving 1-inch headspace. Do not shake or press down. Cover with boiling water, leaving 1-inch headspace; add salt, if desired.	55 min.	85 min.
Greens (including spinach) Beet, collard, kale, mustard, spinach, turnip	4 lbs.	Rinse carefully, working with small amounts at a time. Drain; continue to rinse until water is clear and free of grit. Cut tough stems and midribs from leaves, then heat leaves in boiling water until wilted. Loosely fill prepared, hot jars with wilted leaves; cover with boiling water, leaving 1-inch headspace; add salt, if desired.	70 min.	90 min.
Mushrooms	Pints only; 2 lbs. per pint	Use small to medium-size commercial (button) mushrooms only. Trim off stems; cut out discolored parts. Soak in cold water for 10 minutes, then rinse. Leave small mushrooms whole; halve or quarter larger ones. Cover with water; bring to a boil and boil gently for 5 minutes. **Using pint jars only,** fill prepared, hot jars with hot mushrooms. Cover with fresh boiling water, leaving 1-inch headspace; add salt, if desired. For better color, add ⅛ teaspoon ascorbic acid or a 500-milligram tablet of vitamin C (crushed) to each jar.	45 min.	
Okra	1½ lbs.	Rinse tender young pods; trim ends. Leave whole or cut into 1-inch pieces. Cover okra with hot water and bring to a boil; boil gently for 2 minutes. Fill prepared, hot jars with hot okra. Cover with hot cooking liquid, leaving 1-inch headspace; add salt, if desired.	25 min.	40 min.
Peas, green	4½ lbs. (unshelled)	Shell and rinse tender young peas. **To pack hot,** cover peas with boiling water. Bring to a boil; boil for 2 minutes. Loosely fill prepared, hot jars with hot peas. Cover with hot liquid, leaving 1-inch headspace; add salt, if desired. **To pack raw,** loosely fill prepared, hot jars with raw peas. Do not shake or press down. Cover with boiling water, leaving 1-inch headspace; add salt, if desired.	40 min.	40 min.

* 10 pounds pressure (weighted gauge canner)
   11 pounds pressure (dial gauge canner)

Vegetables	Quantity to yield 1 quart	How to prepare	Processing time*	
			Pints	Quarts
Peppers, bell or chile	Pints only; 1 lb. per pint	Select your favorite green, red, or yellow peppers— either bell, mild or hot chile, or a mix. Choose firm peppers, never soft or bruised ones; rinse well. Leave small peppers whole; remove stems and seeds from large peppers. Cut 2 slits in each pepper. Place in a shallow pan and broil, turning as needed, until skins blister. To make peeling easier, cover tightly with foil or place in a plastic bag and close bag. Let stand for about 10 minutes, then peel. Quarter large peppers; flatten small whole peppers. **Using pint jars only,** add 1½ teaspoons bottled lemon juice to each prepared, hot jar. Fill jars loosely with peppers. Cover peppers with boiling water, leaving 1-inch headspace; add salt, if desired.	35 min.	
Potatoes, sweet	2½ lbs.	Choose small to medium-size potatoes. Rinse well; boil or steam until partially softened (15 to 20 minutes). Remove skins. Leave small potatoes whole; cut larger ones into pieces. **Do not mash or purée.** Fill prepared, hot jars with hot sweet potatoes; cover with boiling water or syrup of your choice (see "Syrups for Canning," page 109). Leave 1-inch headspace; add salt, if desired.	65 min.	90 min.
Potatoes, white	5 lbs.	Choose small to medium-size potatoes (1- to 2-inch diameter for canning whole).Rinse well. Peel; cut into ½-inch cubes, if desired. To prevent discoloration, place in an antidarkening solution (see page 108) as peeled or cut. Drain potatoes; cover with boiling water and bring to a boil. **For cubed potatoes,** boil for 2 minutes and drain; **for whole potatoes,** boil for 10 minutes and drain. Fill prepared, hot jars with hot potatoes. Cover with fresh boiling water, leaving 1-inch headspace; add salt, if desired.	35 min.	40 min.
Spinach *See* Greens (including spinach)				
Squash, summer Crookneck, zucchini, pattypan	1½ lbs.	Rinse squash and trim ends; do not peel. Cut into ½-inch-thick slices. Steam or boil for 2 to 3 minutes. Fill prepared, hot jars with hot squash. Cover with hot cooking liquid or fresh boiling water, leaving 1-inch headspace; add salt, if desired.	30 min.	40 min.
Squash, winter (including pumpkin) Banana, butternut, Hubbard, pumpkin	2¼ lbs.	Rinse squash and cut into halves or large pieces; scrape out all seeds and fibrous material. Peel. Cut into 1-inch-wide strips; then cut into 1-inch cubes. Cover with boiling water; bring to a boil and boil for 2 minutes. **Do not mash or purée.** Fill prepared, hot jars with hot squash cubes. Cover with hot liquid, leaving 1-inch headspace.	55 min.	90 min.

* 10 pounds pressure (weighted gauge canner)
11 pounds pressure (dial gauge canner)

The variety of preserves you can make is limited only by the size of your cupboard. Pictured here (clockwise from bottom right) are Raspberry-Plum Jam (page 137), Cranberry-Apple Jelly (page 153), Jalapeño Jelly (page 152), Apple Butter (page 139), Lime-Mint Jelly (page 152), and Citrus Marmalade (page 142).

Jams, Jellies & Preserves

Sparkling jams & jellies, fragrant butters, tangy marmalades

*I*t's one of life's simple pleasures: "putting up" preserves with distinctively fresh flavors you just can't get in store-bought products. Despite their different names, all fruit spreads—jams, jellies, marmalades, conserves, preserves, and butters—are pretty much alike. They're all just cooked fruit or juice, thickened to some degree and preserved with sugar. ● *Jellies* are clear, sparkling spreads made from strained fruit juice; they're tender, yet firm enough to hold their shape when turned out of the jar. *Marmalades* are soft jellies, generally containing suspended slivers of citrus peel or fruit. To make *jam*, you start with crushed or chopped fruit, then cook it until thick enough to spread, but not as stiff as jelly. *Preserves* are made with larger fruit pieces or small whole fruits, suspended in a clear, slightly jelled syrup. *Conserves* are much like jam, but they usually contain two or more fruits and often include raisins and nuts. *Butters* are simply fruit pulp and sugar, thickened to a good spreading consistency by long, slow cooking. ● The easy-to-make spreads on the following pages get their extra-special flavors from interesting fruit combinations—and from fresh, best-of-season produce you pick out yourself. Both sweet and savory, they'll shine on your table and delight the friends lucky enough to receive them as gifts.

Before You Begin

For success with jams, jellies, and preserves, start by reviewing the basic information below.

Ingredients & Techniques

Fruit. In general, use fresh, just-ripe fruit. If your recipe contains no added pectin, though, a fourth of the fruit should be slightly underripe; natural pectin content—and jelling ability—decrease as fruit ripens.

Pectin. Many recipes call for added pectin, in either liquid or dry form. *The two types require different procedures,* so always use the kind the recipe specifies. Buy fresh pectin yearly, since old pectin may result in poor jelling.

Sugar. Don't cut the sugar in recipes: you're likely to end up with syrup, not jam! If you'd like to make less-sweet preserves, try our reduced-sugar spreads (page 144) and dehydrated jams (page 204).

Recipe yields. Always prepare recipes just as they're written. *Don't* double recipes: larger volumes take longer to heat, and since heat destroys pectin, your jam may fail to jell.

Cooking times. Depending on your altitude, the cooking pan you use, and the humidity, your cooking times may differ from those in the recipe. For this reason, it's important to pay close attention to the doneness tests given in the instructions.

Sealing & processing. Paraffin is no longer recommended for sealing jars, since paraffin-sealed jam is more likely to spoil than processed jam. Always process preserves in a boiling water canner, *unless* you plan to freeze or refrigerate them. (For no-cook freezer jams, see "Quick-fix Jams," page 140.)

A Word about Proportions

Though all fruits except figs are considered acid foods (see page 101), the degree of acidity varies. Some kinds have enough acid and pectin to jell when cooked with sugar. Others are lower in pectin and acid; to make jams and jellies from these, you'll need to add pectin or an acid such as lemon juice (or both). In some recipes, fruits low in acid or pectin are combined with others that supply them in the right amounts. Follow directions exactly: for good flavor and consistency, you need the correct balance of fruit, sugar, acid, and pectin. Proper proportions are especially crucial when you're preparing jelly (see page 148).

Step-by-Step Canning for Jams

To can jams, preserves, conserves, butters, and marmalades, follow these steps.

1. Assemble and prepare equipment and sterilize jars, following steps 2 through 4 on page 108.

2. Rinse and sort fruit; do not use any that is overripe. Chop, slice, or crush fruit, or leave it whole, as the recipe directs. To crush berries, use a potato masher and crush just 1 to 2 cups at a time. To chop fruit with a food processor, use brief pulses, taking care not to purée fruit (purées may add too much liquid and fruit for a good jell).

3. In a large, heavy-bottomed pan, prepare jam according to recipe instructions, one batch at a time. *Do not double recipes;* it doesn't work. Bring fruit and any liquid to a boil over high heat, stirring frequently or constantly, as the recipe directs.

For jams (or other spreads) without added pectin, cook to the desired thickness, following recipe directions. Remember that jam will continue to thicken as it cools. (To find the jell point, see page 148.)

When added pectin is required, the type of pectin and the precise cooking time will be specified. Follow directions *exactly.* If the recipe tells you to bring a fruit mixture to a "full rolling boil," you're aiming for a hard boil that does not stop when the fruit is stirred.

When jam is done, remove it from the heat and skim off any foam. Remove a sterilized jar from the hot water. Place on a cloth towel. Ladle hot jam into hot, sterilized jar, leaving ¼-inch headspace.

4. Seal and process jars as directed in steps 8 through 12 on page 109, using the processing time specified in your recipe. At high altitudes, add an extra minute for each 1,000 feet above sea level.

5. If you choose not to process your jam, ladle it into clean freezer jars or freezer containers; rinse jars with hot water before filling them to prevent the hot jam from cracking the glass. Before refrigerating or freezing filled jars or containers, let them stand for 12 to 24 hours at room temperature; this gives the jam time to jell completely.

Classic Strawberry Jam

This old-fashioned strawberry jam is a breakfast-time classic. For a change, you might use half raspberries, half strawberries.

- 4 cups crushed strawberries (about 2 quarts whole berries)
- 4 cups sugar

Place crushed strawberries in a heavy-bottomed 8- to 10-quart pan. Stir in sugar until well blended. Bring to a boil over high heat, stirring constantly. Continue to boil, uncovered, stirring often, until mixture thickens and reaches the jell point (220°F)—10 to 15 minutes. As mixture thickens, reduce heat and stir more often to prevent sticking. Remove from heat and skim off any foam.

Ladle hot jam into hot, sterilized half-pint jars, leaving ¼-inch headspace. Wipe rims and threads clean; top with hot lids, then firmly screw on bands. Process in boiling water canner for 5 minutes. Or omit processing and ladle jam into freezer jars or freezer containers, leaving ½-inch headspace; apply lids. Let stand for 12 to 24 hours at room temperature; freeze or refrigerate. Makes about 4 half-pints.

Storage time. *Processed:* Up to 1 year. *Unprocessed:* Up to 1 month in refrigerator; up to 1 year in freezer.

Per tablespoon: 54 calories, 0 g protein, 14 g carbohydrates, 0 g total fat, 0 mg cholesterol, 0 mg sodium

Easy Strawberry Jam

Fresh-tasting and easy to prepare, this bright spread is bound to become a favorite.

- 4 cups crushed strawberries (about 2 quarts whole berries)
- 2 tablespoons lemon juice
- 1 box (1¾ or 2 oz.) dry pectin
- 6 cups sugar

In a heavy-bottomed 8- to 10-quart pan, mix strawberries, lemon juice, and pectin. Bring to a full rolling boil over high heat, stirring constantly. Quickly add sugar, still stirring. Return to a full rolling boil; then boil, stirring, for 1 minute. (If using a 2-oz. box of pectin, boil for 2 minutes.) Remove from heat and skim off any foam.

Ladle hot jam into hot, sterilized half-pint jars, leaving ¼-inch headspace. Wipe rims and threads clean; top with hot lids, then firmly screw on bands. Process in boiling water canner for 5 minutes. Or omit processing and ladle jam into freezer jars or freezer containers, leaving ½-inch headspace; apply lids. Let stand for 12 to 24 hours at room temperature; freeze or refrigerate. Makes about 6 half-pints.

Storage time. *Processed:* Up to 1 year. *Unprocessed:* Up to 1 month in refrigerator; up to 1 year in freezer.

Per tablespoon: 54 calories, 0 g protein, 14 g carbohydrates, 0 g total fat, 0 mg cholesterol, 0 mg sodium

Easy Strawberry-Peach Jam

Follow directions for **Easy Strawberry Jam,** but add ¼ cup **water** and substitute 2 cups peeled, pitted, crushed **peaches** (about 1½ lbs. peaches) for 2 cups of the strawberries. Makes about 6 half-pints.

Per tablespoon: 53 calories, 0 g protein, 14 g carbohydrates, 0 g total fat, 0 mg cholesterol, 0 mg sodium

Strawberry-Rhubarb Jam

Popular partners in pie fillings, sweet ripe strawberries and tart rhubarb are delicious together in jam.

- 1 pound rhubarb
- ¼ cup water
- About 4 cups strawberries
- 6 cups sugar
- 1 pouch (3 oz.) liquid pectin

Thinly slice unpeeled rhubarb stalks and place in a medium-size pan. Add water; bring to a boil over high heat. Reduce heat, cover, and simmer until rhubarb is limp (about 2 minutes), stirring once or twice. Drain rhubarb; then measure. Thoroughly crush strawberries; add enough crushed berries to rhubarb to make 3½ cups (pack fruit solidly into cup to measure). Turn fruit into a heavy-bottomed 8- to 10-quart pan. Stir in sugar until well blended.

Bring to a full rolling boil over high heat, stirring constantly; boil, stirring, for 1 minute. Remove from heat and stir in pectin all at once. Skim off any foam.

Ladle hot jam into hot, sterilized half-pint jars, leaving ¼-inch headspace. Wipe rims and threads clean; top with hot lids, then firmly screw on bands. Process in boiling water canner for 5 minutes. Or omit processing and ladle jam into freezer jars or freezer containers, leaving ½-inch headspace; apply lids. Let stand for 12 to 24 hours at room temperature; freeze or refrigerate. Makes about 8 half-pints.

Storage time. *Processed:* Up to 1 year. *Unprocessed:* Up to 1 month in refrigerator; up to 1 year in freezer.

Per tablespoon: 38 calories, 0 g protein, 10 g carbohydrates, 0 g total fat, 0 mg cholesterol, 0 mg sodium

Sweet Cherry Jam

Pictured on facing page

Here's a beautiful jam that's a superb choice for gift giving. A little kirsch adds complexity to the sweet cherry flavor.

- 4 cups pitted, finely chopped sweet cherries (about 3 lbs. cherries)
- ¼ cup *each* lemon juice and kirsch
- ½ teaspoon ground cinnamon
- 1 box (1¾ or 2 oz.) dry pectin
- 4½ cups sugar

In a heavy-bottomed 8- to 10-quart pan, mix cherries, lemon juice, kirsch, cinnamon, and pectin. Bring to a full rolling boil over high heat, stirring constantly. Quickly add sugar, still stirring. Return to a full rolling boil; then boil, stirring, for 2 minutes. (If using a 2-oz. box of pectin, boil for 4 minutes.) Remove from heat and skim off any foam.

Ladle hot jam into hot, sterilized half-pint jars, leaving ¼-inch headspace. Wipe rims and threads clean; top with hot lids, then firmly screw on bands. Process in boiling water canner for 5 minutes. Or omit processing and ladle jam into freezer jars or freezer containers, leaving ½-inch headspace; apply lids. Let stand for 12 to 24 hours at room temperature; freeze or refrigerate. Makes about 5 half-pints.

Storage time. *Processed:* Up to 1 year. *Unprocessed:* Up to 1 month in refrigerator; up to 1 year in freezer.

Per tablespoon: 59 calories, 0 g protein, 15 g carbohydrates, 0 g total fat, 0 mg cholesterol, 0 mg sodium

Peach-Orange Jam

Pictured on facing page

Aromatic ripe peaches combine with orange and lemon in a sprightly jam that's a perfect filling for jam tarts.

- 6 cups peeled, pitted, crushed peaches (about 4 lbs. peaches)
- ½ cup frozen orange juice concentrate, thawed
- ¼ cup lemon juice
- 5 cups sugar

In a heavy-bottomed 8- to 10-quart pan, mix peaches, orange juice concentrate, and lemon juice. Stir in sugar until well blended. Bring to a boil over high heat, stirring constantly. Continue to boil, uncovered, stirring often, until mixture thickens and reaches the jell point (220°F)—about 30 minutes. As mixture thickens, reduce heat and stir more often to prevent sticking. Remove from heat and skim off any foam.

Ladle hot jam into hot, sterilized half-pint jars, leaving ¼-inch headspace. Wipe rims and threads clean; top with hot lids, then firmly screw on bands. Process in boiling water canner for 5 minutes. Or omit processing and ladle jam into freezer jars or freezer containers, leaving ½-inch headspace; apply lids. Let stand for 12 to 24 hours at room temperature; freeze or refrigerate. Makes about 7 half-pints.

Storage time. *Processed:* Up to 1 year. *Unprocessed:* Up to 1 month in refrigerator; up to 1 year in freezer.

Per tablespoon: 42 calories, 0 g protein, 11 g carbohydrates, 0 g total fat, 0 mg cholesterol, 0 mg sodium

Easy Raspberry Jam

Pictured on facing page

It's hard to beat homemade raspberry jam—but our blackberry and boysenberry variations come close!

- 5 cups crushed raspberries (about 2 quarts whole berries)
- 1 tablespoon lemon juice
- 1 box (1¾ or 2 oz.) dry pectin
- 6½ cups sugar

In a heavy-bottomed 8- to 10-quart pan, mix raspberries, lemon juice, and pectin. (If you prefer seedless jam, heat the crushed berries until soft, then press them through a sieve or food mill before adding to pan with the lemon juice and pectin.) Bring mixture to a full rolling boil over high heat, stirring constantly. Quickly add sugar, still stirring. Return to a full rolling boil; then boil, stirring, for 1 minute. (If using a 2-oz. box of pectin, boil for 2 minutes.) Remove from heat and skim off any foam.

Ladle hot jam into hot, sterilized half-pint jars, leaving ¼-inch headspace. Wipe rims and threads clean; top with hot lids, then firmly screw on bands. Process in boiling water canner for 5 minutes. Or omit processing and ladle jam into freezer jars or freezer containers, leaving ½-inch headspace; apply lids. Let stand for 12 to 24 hours at room temperature; freeze or refrigerate. Makes about 7 half-pints.

Storage time. *Processed:* Up to 1 year. *Unprocessed:* Up to 1 month in refrigerator; up to 1 year in freezer.

Per tablespoon: 50 calories, 0 g protein, 13 g carbohydrates, 0 g total fat, 0 mg cholesterol, 0 mg sodium

Easy Blackberry or Boysenberry Jam

Follow directions for **Easy Raspberry Jam**, but substitute **blackberries** or boysenberries for raspberries. Makes about 7 half-pints.

Per tablespoon: 52 calories, 0 g protein, 13 g carbohydrates, 0 g total fat, 0 mg cholesterol, 0 mg sodium

Sparkling jam tarts are a lovely dessert—and they're easy to prepare, too. Start with dainty shells made from homemade or purchased pastry and baked in mini-muffin pans; then fill them with your favorite jams. We chose Sweet Cherry Jam, Peach-Orange Jam, and Easy Raspberry Jam (recipes on facing page).

Microwave Jams

Making jam in your microwave oven is quick and easy. You can even whip up a batch fresh in the morning to serve warm for breakfast. Just remember to store your jam in the refrigerator or freezer, since microwaving doesn't actually process jam the way a boiling water canner does.

To avoid boil-over, use an oversized container. We prefer a 2-quart glass measure; it's easy to remove from the oven, and the handle and spout simplify pouring the bubbly jam into jars. You can also use a 2½- to 3-quart ceramic or glass casserole, but this will get hot, so keep oven mitts handy.

Our basic recipe tells you how to make nine different fresh fruit jams. If you have an abundance of fruit, consider making several batches (don't multiply quantities; the recipe won't turn out properly). Or prepare measured amounts of fruit with sugar and flavorings, then freeze them. Later, thaw a portion and make fresh jam any time.

Because microwave ovens vary in power and wattage, your cooking times may differ somewhat from those given below.

Basic Microwave Jam

Fruit and flavorings (directions follow)

1½ cups sugar

Prepare fruit and flavorings; place in a 2-quart glass measure or 2½- to 3-quart casserole. Add sugar. Let stand until juices form (about 30 minutes).

Microwave, uncovered, on **HIGH (100%)** for 6 minutes or until mixture begins to boil. Stir well. Microwave on **HIGH (100%)** for 10 to 13 more minutes, stirring every 2 to 3 minutes. Spoon 1 tablespoon jam into a custard cup and refrigerate for 15 minutes; test consistency. For thicker jam, reheat jam to boiling, then microwave on **HIGH (100%)** for 2 more minutes; retest. Makes about 2 cups.

Storage time. Up to 1 month in refrigerator; up to 1 year in freezer.

Per tablespoon (approximate): 44 calories, 0 g protein, 11 g carbohydrates, 0 g total fat, 0 mg cholesterol, 0 mg sodium

Apricot. Rinse, pit, and chop about 1 pound **apricots** (you should have 2 cups). Add 2 tablespoons **lemon juice.**

Apricot-pineapple. Rinse, pit, and chop about ¾ pound **apricots** (you should have 1½ cups). Combine with ½ cup **crushed pineapple packed in its own juice** or ½ cup finely chopped fresh pineapple. Add 1 tablespoon **lemon juice.**

Berry. Rinse and crush 3½ cups **raspberries,** blackberries, boysenberries, or olallieberries; or use half raspberries and half of any of the blackberries. You should have 2 cups. Add 1 tablespoon **lemon juice.**

Blueberry. Rinse and slightly crush about 3 cups **blueberries** (you should have 2 cups). Add ¼ cup **lemon juice,** ½ teaspoon **grated lemon peel,** and ¼ teaspoon **ground cinnamon.**

Strawberry. Rinse and crush about 3½ cups hulled **strawberries** (you should have 2 cups). Add 1½ tablespoons **lemon juice.**

Cherry (sweet varieties). Rinse, pit, and quarter about 1 pound **cherries** (you should have 2 cups). Add ¼ cup **lemon juice** and ½ teaspoon each **grated lemon peel** and **ground cinnamon.**

Spiced fig-orange. Rinse 8 to 10 **figs;** clip off stems, then chop fruit (you should have 1½ cups). Combine with ½ cup peeled, seeded, chopped **orange.** Add 1½ teaspoons **grated orange peel,** 3 tablespoons **lemon juice,** and ¼ teaspoon *each* **ground cloves** and **ground cinnamon.**

Peach or nectarine. Rinse, peel, pit, and chop about 1⅓ pounds **peaches** or nectarines (you should have 2 cups). Add 1 tablespoon **lemon juice.** If desired, stir in 2 drops **almond extract** after cooking.

Peach-plum marmalade. Rinse, pit, and chop about ½ pound *each* **peaches** and **plums** (you should have 1½ cups *total*). Combine with ½ cup seeded, finely chopped unpeeled **orange.**

Raspberry-Plum Jam

Pictured on page 130

For pennywise raspberry jam, mix the berries—fresh or frozen—with more plentiful (and less expensive) plums. If you dice the plums with a food processor, be careful not to purée them.

- 2 **cups pitted, finely diced plums (about 1¼ lbs. plums)**
- 1½ **cups fresh raspberries; or 1½ cups unsweetened frozen raspberries, thawed**
- 5 **cups sugar**
- ¼ **cup lemon juice**
- 1 **pouch (3 oz.) liquid pectin**

In a heavy-bottomed 8- to 10-quart pan, mix plums and raspberries. Stir in sugar and lemon juice until well blended. Bring to a full rolling boil over high heat, stirring constantly. Stir in pectin all at once. Return to a full rolling boil; then boil, stirring, for 1 minute. Remove from heat and skim off any foam.

Ladle hot jam into hot, sterilized half-pint jars, leaving ¼-inch headspace. Wipe rims and threads clean; top with hot lids, then firmly screw on bands. Process in boiling water canner for 5 minutes. Or omit processing and ladle jam into freezer jars or freezer containers, leaving ½-inch headspace; apply lids. Let stand for 12 to 24 hours at room temperature; freeze or refrigerate. Makes about 6 half-pints.

Storage time. *Processed:* Up to 1 year. *Unprocessed:* Up to 1 month in refrigerator; up to 1 year in freezer.

Per tablespoon: 44 calories, 0 g protein, 11 g carbohydrates, 0 g total fat, 0 mg cholesterol, 0 mg sodium

Plum Jam

If you relish a touch of tart along with sweet, then use your favorite red- or purple-skinned plums to prepare this marvelous jam.

- 4 **cups pitted, finely diced plums (about 2½ lbs. plums)**
- 3½ **cups sugar**

Place plums in a heavy-bottomed 8- to 10-quart pan. Stir in sugar until well blended. Let stand for 1 hour, then bring to a boil over medium-high heat, stirring often. Continue to boil, uncovered, stirring often, until mixture thickens and reaches the jell point (220°F)—about 20 minutes. As mixture thickens, reduce heat and stir more often to prevent sticking. Remove from heat and skim off any foam.

Ladle hot jam into hot, sterilized half-pint jars, leaving ¼-inch headspace. Wipe rims and threads clean; top with hot lids, then firmly screw on bands. Process in boiling water canner for 5 minutes. Or omit processing and ladle jam into freezer jars or freezer containers, leaving ½-inch headspace; apply lids. Let stand for 12 to 24 hours at room temperature; freeze or refrigerate. Makes about 4 half-pints.

Storage time. *Processed:* Up to 1 year. *Unprocessed:* Up to 1 month in refrigerator; up to 1 year in freezer.

Per tablespoon: 51 calories, 0 g protein, 13 g carbohydrates, 0 g total fat, 0 mg cholesterol, 0 mg sodium

Cranberry-Orange Jam

Tangy, thick, orange-accented cranberry jam is just the thing to serve with your favorite roast poultry. For best flavor, store it for at least 1 week before using. (If you prefer a smooth and glistening jelly, pour the hot jam through a small sterilized metal strainer when you fill the jars.)

- 4 **cups (about 1 lb.) fresh or frozen cranberries**
- 3 **cups water**
- ¾ **cup orange juice**
- ¼ **cup lemon juice**
- 4 **cups sugar**
- 2 **pouches (3 oz. *each*) liquid pectin**

Place cranberries and water in a heavy-bottomed 8- to 10-quart pan. Bring to a boil over high heat; reduce heat and simmer, uncovered, until berries begin to pop (about 10 minutes). Drain well, reserving liquid. Place cranberries in a blender or food processor and whirl until smooth; add enough of the reserved liquid to berries to make 4 cups.

Return berry purée to pan. Stir in orange juice, lemon juice, and sugar until well blended. Bring to a full rolling boil over high heat, stirring constantly; then boil, stirring, for 1 minute. Remove from heat and stir in pectin all at once. Skim off any foam.

Ladle hot jam into hot, sterilized half-pint jars, leaving ¼-inch headspace. Wipe rims and threads clean; top with hot lids, then firmly screw on bands. Process in boiling water canner for 5 minutes. Or omit processing and ladle jam into freezer jars or freezer containers, leaving ½-inch headspace; apply lids. Let stand for 12 to 24 hours at room temperature; freeze or refrigerate. Makes about 6 half-pints.

Storage time. *Processed:* Up to 1 year. *Unprocessed:* Up to 1 month in refrigerator; up to 1 year in freezer.

Per tablespoon: 36 calories, 0 g protein, 9 g carbohydrates, 0 g total fat, 0 mg cholesterol, 0 mg sodium

Fresh bread spread with homemade preserves is an old-fashioned treat that will never go out of style. Our bread is topped with luscious, golden Papaya Butter; just as fragrant and delicious are Apple Butter (center) and Apricot Butter (right). All three recipes are on the facing page.

Apple Butter

Pictured on page 130 and facing page

Slow, even cooking is the secret of this aromatic butter's full flavor. If sweet Golden Delicious apples aren't available, you can use a tarter variety such as McIntosh, Jonathan, or Granny Smith, but you may want to add about ¼ cup more sugar.

- **4** **cups bottled unsweetened apple juice or apple cider**
- **4** **pounds (about 12 medium-size) Golden Delicious apples, peeled, cored, and sliced**
- **1½** **cups sugar**
- **2** **teaspoons ground cinnamon**

In a heavy-bottomed 8- to 10-quart pan, bring apple juice to a boil over high heat. Add apples; reduce heat to medium-low, cover, and simmer, stirring occasionally, until apples are soft enough to mash easily (about 30 minutes).

Stir in sugar and cinnamon until well blended. Cook, uncovered, mashing apples and stirring often, until mixture is thickened and reduced to 5 cups (about 1 hour); as mixture thickens, reduce heat and stir more often to prevent sticking.

Ladle hot apple butter into hot, sterilized half-pint jars, leaving ¼-inch headspace. Wipe rims and threads clean; top with hot lids, then firmly screw on bands. Process in boiling water canner for 5 minutes. Or omit processing and ladle into freezer jars or freezer containers, leaving ½-inch headspace; apply lids. Let stand for 12 to 24 hours at room temperature; freeze or refrigerate. Makes about 5 half-pints.

Storage time. *Processed:* Up to 1 year. *Unprocessed:* Up to 1 month in refrigerator; up to 1 year in freezer.

Per tablespoon: 32 calories, 0 g protein, 8 g carbohydrates, 0 g total fat, 0 mg cholesterol, 0 mg sodium

Apricot Butter

Pictured on facing page

Apples are doubtless the most popular choice for butters, but other fruits—apricots, in this case—are just as delicious.

- **3** **pounds apricots, pitted**
- **¼** **cup lemon juice**
- **3** **cups sugar**

Whirl apricots, a portion at a time, in a blender or food processor until smoothly puréed; you should have about 4 cups. Pour purée into a heavy-bottomed 8- to 10-quart pan. Stir in lemon juice and sugar until well blended. Bring mixture to a boil over high heat, stirring constantly. Continue to boil, uncovered, stirring often, until thickened (15 to 18 minutes); as mixture thickens, reduce heat and stir more often to prevent sticking.

Ladle hot apricot butter into hot, sterilized half-pint jars, leaving ¼-inch headspace. Wipe rims and threads clean; top with hot lids, then firmly screw on bands. Process in boiling water canner for 5 minutes. Or omit processing and ladle into freezer jars or freezer containers, leaving ½-inch headspace; apply lids. Let stand for 12 to 24 hours at room temperature; freeze or refrigerate. Makes about 5 half-pints.

Storage time. *Processed:* Up to 1 year. *Unprocessed:* Up to 1 month in refrigerator; up to 1 year in freezer.

Per tablespoon: 37 calories, 0 g protein, 9 g carbohydrates, 0 g total fat, 0 mg cholesterol, 0 mg sodium

Papaya Butter

Pictured on facing page

Capture the tropical essence of golden papayas with this soft-spreading preserve. A hint of lime heightens the exotic flavor.

- **3** **large ripe papayas (about 1¼ lbs. *each*)**
- **¼** **cup lime juice**
- **1** **teaspoon grated lime peel**
- **1½** **cups sugar**

Peel and halve papayas; scoop out seeds, then cut fruit into small chunks. Whirl papayas and lime juice, a portion at a time, in a blender or food processor until smoothly puréed. Pour purée into a heavy-bottomed 8- to 10-quart pan. Stir in lime peel and sugar until well blended. Bring to a boil over high heat; then reduce heat, partially cover pan, and simmer, stirring occasionally, for 15 minutes. Uncover pan and continue to simmer, stirring often, until mixture is thickened (about 15 more minutes); as mixture thickens, reduce heat and stir more often to prevent sticking.

Ladle hot papaya butter into hot, sterilized half-pint jars, leaving ¼-inch headspace. Wipe rims and threads clean; top with hot lids, then firmly screw on bands. Process in boiling water canner for 5 minutes. Or omit processing and ladle into freezer jars or freezer containers, leaving ½-inch headspace; apply lids. Let stand for 12 to 24 hours at room temperature; freeze or refrigerate. Makes about 4 half-pints.

Storage time. *Processed:* Up to 1 year. *Unprocessed:* Up to 1 month in refrigerator; up to 1 year in freezer.

Per tablespoon: 25 calories, 0 g protein, 6 g carbohydrates, 0 g total fat, 0 mg cholesterol, 1 mg sodium

Quick-fix Jams

*F*or year-round giving, few gifts are better than homemade jam. And with our no-fuss methods, you can easily make plenty. The short-cook technique uses dry pectin and a 2-minute cooking time; fresh-tasting freezer jam, made with liquid pectin, requires no cooking.

Whichever procedure you use, keep two rules in mind: *you can't double jam recipes, and you can't reduce the amount of sugar.* If you do, you may end up with fruit syrup instead of jam.

Short-cook Jam

Fruit of your choice (see chart)
Lemon juice (see chart)
1 **box (1¾ or 2 oz.) dry pectin**
Sugar (see chart)

To prepare jars and fruit, check yield for each fruit to determine how many canning jars you will need. Then follow steps 2 through 4 on page 108.

Rinse fruit; peel, seed, hull, or core as necessary. Cut into cubes. Mash fruit with a potato masher (or whirl briefly in a food processor, but do not purée).

In a heavy-bottomed 8- to 10-quart pan, mix fruit, lemon juice, and pectin. Bring to a full rolling boil over high heat, stirring constantly. Quickly add sugar, still stirring. Return to a full rolling boil; then boil, stirring, for exactly 2 minutes. Remove from heat and skim off any foam.

Ladle hot jam into hot, sterilized half-pint jars, leaving ¼-inch headspace. Wipe rims and threads

clean; top with hot lids, then firmly screw on bands. Process in boiling water canner for 5 minutes (see steps 8 through 12 on page 109). Or omit processing and ladle jam into freezer jars or freezer containers, leaving ½-inch headspace; apply lids. Let stand for 12 to 24 hours; then freeze or refrigerate.

Storage time. *Processed:* Up to 1 year. *Unprocessed:* Up to 1 month in refrigerator; up to 1 year in freezer.

Per tablespoon (approximate): 52 calories, 0 g protein, 14 g carbohydrates, 0 g total fat, 0 mg cholesterol, 1 mg sodium

No-cook Freezer Jam

Fruit of your choice (see chart)
Sugar (see chart)
1 **pouch (3 oz.) liquid pectin**
Lemon juice (see chart)

Rinse fruit; peel, seed, hull, or core as necessary. Cut fruit into cubes. Mash fruit with a potato masher (or whirl briefly in a food processor, but do not purée).

In a large bowl, thoroughly mix fruit and sugar; let stand for 10 minutes, stirring occasionally. Meanwhile, mix pectin and lemon juice; add to fruit mixture and stir (don't beat in air) for 3 minutes. Fill freezer jars or freezer containers with jam, leaving ½-inch headspace; apply lids. Let jam stand for 24 hours; then freeze or refrigerate.

Storage time. Up to 1 month in refrigerator; up to 1 year in freezer.

Per tablespoon (approximate): 42 calories, 0 g protein, 11 g carbohydrates, 0 g total fat, 0 mg cholesterol, 0 mg sodium

Short-cook Method (1¾- or 2-oz. box of pectin)					
FRUIT	AMT. OF FRUIT	MASHED FRUIT	LEMON JUICE	SUGAR	YIELD
Fig	3¼ lbs.	5 c. + ½ c. water	½ c.	7 c.	8½ c.
Mango	6 lbs.	4 c.	¼ c.	6 c.	6½ c.
Papaya	5 lbs.	4 c.	¼ c.	6 c.	6½ c.
Peach	3 lbs.	4 c.	¼ c.	6 c.	6¾ c.
Pear	3 lbs.	4 c.	¼ c.	5½ c.	6½ c.

No-cook Freezer Method (3-oz. pouch of pectin)					
FRUIT	AMT. OF FRUIT	MASHED FRUIT	LEMON JUICE	SUGAR	YIELD
Apricot	1 lb.	1½ c.	¼ c.	3 c.	4 c.
Berry	4 c.	2 c.	2 T.	4 c.	4¾ c.
Kiwi	1¼ lbs.	2¼ c.	¼ c.	4 c.	5 c.
Nectarine	1 lb.	1½ c.	¼ c.	3 c.	4 c.
Plum	1¼ lbs.	2¼ c.	2 T.	4 c.	5 c.

Caramel Spice Pear Butter

Caramelized sugar and a trio of sweet spices lend this fragrant pear butter its distinctive flavor. It's perfect for cool-weather breakfasts; try it on hot toast or English muffins.

7½	**pounds (about 15 large) firm-ripe Bartlett pears**
2	**cups water**
6	**cups sugar**
1½	**teaspoons ground cinnamon**
1	**teaspoon ground cloves**
½	**teaspoon ground ginger**
2	**tablespoons lemon juice**

Core pears, but do not peel them. Slice pears and place in a heavy-bottomed 8- to 10-quart pan. Add water; bring to a boil over medium-high heat. Then reduce heat to low, cover, and cook until pears are tender when pierced (about 30 minutes). Let cool slightly, then whirl in a food processor, a portion at a time, until finely chopped. Return to pan.

Place 1½ cups of the sugar in a wide frying pan. Cook over medium heat, stirring often, until sugar caramelizes to a medium-brown syrup. Immediately pour syrup into pan with chopped pears (syrup will sizzle and harden, but dissolve again as the mixture cooks). Stir in remaining 4½ cups sugar, cinnamon, cloves, and ginger until well blended.

Bring mixture to a boil over medium-high heat, stirring. Reduce heat and simmer, uncovered, stirring often, until thickened (about 45 minutes); as mixture thickens, reduce heat and stir more often to prevent sticking. Stir in lemon juice just before removing from heat.

Ladle hot pear butter into hot, sterilized half-pint jars, leaving ¼-inch headspace. Wipe rims and threads clean; top with hot lids, then firmly screw on bands. Process in boiling water canner for 5 minutes. Or omit processing and ladle into freezer jars or freezer containers, leaving ½-inch headspace; apply lids. Let stand for 12 to 24 hours at room temperature; freeze or refrigerate. Makes about 9 half-pints.

Storage time. *Processed:* Up to 1 year. *Unprocessed:* Up to 1 month in refrigerator; up to 1 year in freezer.

Per tablespoon: 45 calories, 0 g protein, 12 g carbohydrates, 0 g total fat, 0 mg cholesterol, 0 mg sodium

Spicy Tomato Marmalade

To those of us who think of tomato-based spreads as strictly savory condiments (catsup and chili sauce, for example), the idea of tomato jam is a bit peculiar. But when flavored with citrus and spices, tomatoes make a delicious marmalade.

8	**cups peeled, cored, coarsely chopped tomatoes (about 5 lbs. tomatoes)**
1	*each* **orange and lemon**
¼	**cup cider vinegar (5% acidity)**
1½	**teaspoons** *each* **ground cinnamon and ground allspice**
¾	**teaspoon ground cloves**
3	**cups sugar**

Place tomatoes in a heavy-bottomed 8- to 10-quart non-aluminum pan. Rinse orange and lemon; with a vegetable peeler, carefully remove thin outer peel. Cut peel into slivers and add to tomatoes. Holding fruit over a bowl to catch juice, cut off and discard remaining peel and white membrane from orange and lemon; coarsely chop fruit.

Add chopped orange and lemon (plus any juice) to tomatoes. Stir in vinegar, cinnamon, allspice, cloves, and sugar until well blended. Bring to a boil over high heat, stirring often. Then reduce heat and simmer, uncovered, stirring often, until thickened and reduced to about 4 cups (about 2 hours); as mixture thickens, reduce heat and stir more often to prevent sticking.

Ladle hot marmalade into hot, sterilized half-pint jars, leaving ¼-inch headspace. Wipe rims and threads clean; top with hot lids, then firmly screw on bands. Process in boiling water canner for 5 minutes. Or omit processing and ladle into freezer jars or freezer containers, leaving ½-inch headspace; apply lids. Let stand for 12 to 24 hours at room temperature; freeze or refrigerate. Makes about 4 half-pints.

Storage time. *Processed:* Up to 1 year. *Unprocessed:* Up to 1 month in refrigerator; up to 1 year in freezer.

Per tablespoon: 45 calories, 0 g protein, 11 g carbohydrates, 0 g total fat, 0 mg cholesterol, 3 mg sodium

Safe Seals

Unless you plan to refrigerate or freeze your jams, jellies, and preserves, always process them in canning jars with self-sealing lids and ring bands. Paraffin is no longer recommended for sealing, since air can enter beneath it and encourage molding. (Don't eat jams which have molded, even if only at the surface—the mold may not be as harmless as was once thought.)

Citus Marmalade

Pictured on page 130

Liven up breakfast breads with the fresh, sweet-tart flavor of this translucent golden spread.

  5 **medium-size oranges**
  2 **small lemons**
  3 **cups water**
  6 **cups sugar**
  ½ **cup lemon juice**

Rinse unpeeled oranges and lemons. Halve lengthwise; thinly slice crosswise, discarding seeds. Place slices in a heavy-bottomed 8- to 10-quart pan, add water, and press down fruit to make an even layer. Let stand for 8 to 24 hours at room temperature.

Bring fruit to a boil over high heat, stirring; reduce heat to low and cook, uncovered, stirring occasionally, for 40 minutes. Remove from heat; let stand for 4 hours. Stir in sugar; bring to a boil over high heat, stirring. Continue to boil, uncovered, stirring often, until mixture thickens and reaches the jell point (220°F)—about 20 minutes. As mixture thickens, reduce heat and stir more often to prevent sticking. Remove from heat and stir in lemon juice.

Ladle hot marmalade into hot, sterilized half-pint jars, leaving ¼-inch headspace. Wipe rims and threads clean; top with hot lids, then firmly screw on bands. Process in boiling water canner for 5 minutes. Or omit processing and ladle into freezer jars or freezer containers, leaving ½-inch headspace; apply lids. Let stand for 12 to 24 hours at room temperature; freeze or refrigerate. Makes about 7 half-pints.

Storage time. *Processed:* Up to 1 year. *Unprocessed:* Up to 1 month in refrigerator; up to 1 year in freezer.

Per tablespoon: 45 calories, 0 g protein, 12 g carbohydrates, 0 g total fat, 0 mg cholesterol, 1 mg sodium

Pineapple Marmalade

This exotic rendition of marmalade starts with fresh pineapple; minced ginger adds a zesty accent.

  1   **large orange**
  4½ **cups finely chopped fresh pineapple (chop with a knife, not a food processor)**
  2   **tablespoons minced fresh ginger**
  3   **cups sugar**

Rinse unpeeled orange; finely chop, discarding seeds. In a heavy-bottomed 6- to 8-quart pan, mix orange, pineapple, ginger, and sugar. Bring to a boil over high heat, stirring often; reduce heat to medium-low and cook, uncovered, stirring often,

until mixture thickens and reaches the jell point (220°F)—about 40 minutes. As mixture thickens, reduce heat and stir more often to prevent sticking.

Ladle hot marmalade into hot, sterilized half-pint jars, leaving ¼-inch headspace. Wipe rims and threads clean; top with hot lids, then firmly screw on bands. Process in boiling water canner for 5 minutes. Or omit processing and ladle into freezer jars or freezer containers, leaving ½-inch headspace; apply lids. Let stand for 12 to 24 hours at room temperature; freeze or refrigerate. Makes about 5 half-pints.

Storage time. *Processed:* Up to 1 year. *Unprocessed:* Up to 1 month in refrigerator; up to 1 year in freezer.

Per tablespoon: 37 calories, 0 g protein, 10 g carbohydrates, 0 g total fat, 0 mg cholesterol, 0 mg sodium

Lemon Marmalade

Pictured on facing page

Be careful to use *only* the thin, yellow outer layer of peel for this exquisite marmalade.

      About 12 large lemons
  ½ **cup water**
  5 **cups sugar**
  1 **pouch (3 oz.) liquid pectin**

Rinse unpeeled lemons. With a vegetable peeler, remove thin outer peel (colored part only); cut peel into slivers. Then squeeze juice from lemons. You should have 1¾ cups peel and 2 cups juice.

Place water, all the lemon peel, and ½ cup of the lemon juice in a heavy-bottomed 6- to 8-quart pan. Bring to a boil over high heat; then reduce heat, cover, and simmer, stirring occasionally, until peel is tender (about 25 minutes). Stir in sugar and remaining 1½ cups lemon juice. Bring to a full rolling boil over high heat, stirring. Remove from heat, cover, and let stand for 18 to 24 hours at room temperature.

Bring marmalade to a full rolling boil over high heat, stirring constantly. Quickly stir in pectin and return to a full rolling boil; boil, stirring, for 1 minute. Remove from heat and skim off any foam.

Ladle hot marmalade into hot, sterilized half-pint jars, leaving ¼-inch headspace. Wipe rims and threads clean; top with hot lids, then firmly screw on bands. Process in boiling water canner for 5 minutes. Or omit processing and ladle into freezer jars or freezer containers, leaving ½-inch headspace; apply lids. Let stand for 12 to 24 hours at room temperature; freeze or refrigerate. Makes about 5 half-pints.

Storage time. *Processed:* Up to 1 year. *Unprocessed:* Up to 1 month in refrigerator; up to 1 year in freezer.

Per tablespoon: 51 calories, 0 g protein, 13 g carbohydrates, 0 g total fat, 0 mg cholesterol, 0 mg sodium

Sweet-tart, shimmering, and translucent, Lemon Marmalade (facing page) is the perfect accompaniment for tea and crumpets. The marmalade is wonderful on English muffins, biscuits, scones, and toast, too.

143

Reduced-sugar Spreads

*A*lmost everyone enjoys sparkling, jewel-bright homemade jams and jellies. But if you're like many health-conscious cooks, you may be tempted to reduce the sugar in traditional spreads. Please don't! Cutting down on sugar (or using artificial sweetener) in regular recipes upsets the balance of fruit, pectin, acid, and sugar—and your jelly or jam may turn into syrup. It's better to use the modified pectins (labeled "light" or "less sugar") specially developed for making reduced-sugar jams and jellies. Preserves made with these pectins tend to taste less sweet than regular spreads and may have a firmer consistency.

Another good option is simply to follow tested recipes for low-sugar spreads, such as the two on this page. The first is an all-fruit treat that gets its sweetness from natural fructose; the refrigerator jelly calls for gelatin and artificial sweetener.

To develop your own all-fruit spreads, try boiling fruit pulp or finely chopped fruit (even unsweetened canned fruit) with frozen unsweetened juice concentrates (thawed). Long boiling makes these mixtures thicken to resemble jams, conserves, or fruit butters; if you like, add a little sugar or artificial sweetener. Just keep in mind that it may take you a while to come up with a combination you really like.

Because sugarless and reduced-sugar spreads don't have enough sugar to act as a preservative, you need to process them longer than regular jams and jellies—at least 15 minutes in a boiling water canner. Unprocessed spreads must be frozen; or you can store them in the refrigerator for up to 2 weeks.

Chunky Pear-Pineapple Spread

4 pounds pears, peeled, cored, and finely chopped
¼ cup lemon juice
1 large can (about 20 oz.) crushed pineapple packed in its own juice
1 can (12 oz.) frozen unsweetened apple juice concentrate, thawed

In a heavy-bottomed 8- to 10-quart pan, mix pears, lemon juice, undrained pineapple, and apple juice concentrate. Bring to a boil over medium-high heat, stirring constantly. Continue to boil gently, uncovered, stirring often, until spread is as thick as desired (about 45 minutes); as mixture thickens, reduce heat and stir more often to prevent sticking. If you prefer a smoother spread, whirl mixture, a portion at a time, in a blender or food processor; then return to pan and bring to a boil over medium-high heat, stirring constantly.

Ladle hot spread into prepared, hot half-pint jars, leaving ¼-inch headspace. Wipe rims and threads clean; top with hot lids, then firmly screw on bands. Process in boiling water canner for 15 minutes. Or omit processing and ladle into freezer jars or freezer containers, leaving ½-inch headspace; apply lids. Let the spread cool in jars at room temperature; freeze or refrigerate. Makes about 4 half-pints.

Storage time. *Processed:* Up to 1 year. *Unprocessed:* Up to 2 weeks in refrigerator; up to 1 year in freezer.

Per tablespoon: 32 calories, 0 g protein, 8 g carbohydrates, 0 g total fat, 0 mg cholesterol, 2 mg sodium

Refrigerator Grape Jelly

3 cups bottled unsweetened grape juice
2 tablespoons lemon juice
2 envelopes unflavored gelatin
1 tablespoon liquid artificial sweetener

In a heavy-bottomed 8- to 10-quart pan, mix grape juice, lemon juice, and gelatin. Bring to a full rolling boil over medium-high heat, stirring often; then boil, stirring, for 1 minute. Remove from heat; stir in artificial sweetener.

Ladle hot jelly into half-pint jars or refrigerator containers, leaving ¼-inch headspace; apply lids. Refrigerate. Do not freeze or process in a boiling water canner. Makes about 3 half-pints.

Storage time. Up to 2 weeks in refrigerator.

Per tablespoon: 11 calories, 0 g protein, 3 g carbohydrates, 0 g total fat, 0 mg cholesterol, 2 mg sodium

Peach-Pineapple-Orange Conserve

Reminiscent of marmalade, this piquant medley of golden fruits is great with baked ham or poultry. You can use either syrup- or juice-packed pineapple; the latter gives a less sweet preserve.

2 oranges
4 cups peeled, pitted, finely chopped peaches (about 3 lbs. peaches)
1 can (about 8 oz.) crushed pineapple
6 cups sugar

Rinse unpeeled oranges; then finely chop, discarding any seeds. Place oranges and peaches in a heavy-bottomed 8- to 10-quart pan. Stir in undrained pineapple and sugar until well blended. Bring to a boil over high heat, stirring. Reduce heat to medium-low and cook, uncovered, stirring often, until thickened (about 35 minutes); as mixture thickens, reduce heat and stir more often to prevent sticking.

Ladle hot conserve into hot, sterilized half-pint jars, leaving ¼-inch headspace. Wipe rims and threads clean; top with hot lids, then firmly screw on bands. Process in boiling water canner for 5 minutes. Or omit processing and ladle into freezer jars or freezer containers, leaving ½-inch headspace; apply lids. Let stand for 12 to 24 hours at room temperature; freeze or refrigerate. Makes about 10 half-pints.

Storage time. *Processed:* Up to 1 year. *Unprocessed:* Up to 1 month in refrigerator; up to 1 year in freezer.

Per tablespoon: 34 calories, 0 g protein, 9 g carbohydrates, 0 g total fat, 0 mg cholesterol, 0 mg sodium

Fresh Fig Conserve

The crunch of walnuts, the tang of orange peel, and the sweetness of figs make this richly colored conserve a deliciously memorable spread.

2½ pounds fresh figs
2½ cups sugar
⅓ cup lemon juice
1 tablespoon grated orange peel
¼ cup chopped walnuts

Clip off and discard fig stems; then chop figs and place in a heavy-bottomed 8- to 10-quart pan. Stir in sugar until well blended. Let stand for 1 hour.

Bring fig mixture to a boil over medium heat, stirring often. Then boil, uncovered, stirring often, until thickened (about 20 minutes); as mixture thickens, reduce heat and stir more often to prevent sticking. Stir in lemon juice, orange peel, and walnuts. Return mixture to a boil; then boil, stirring, for 3 minutes.

Ladle hot conserve into hot, sterilized half-pint jars, leaving ¼-inch headspace. Wipe rims and threads clean; top with hot lids, then firmly screw on bands. Process in boiling water canner for 5 minutes. Or omit processing and ladle into freezer jars or freezer containers, leaving ½-inch headspace; apply lids. Let stand for 12 to 24 hours at room temperature; freeze or refrigerate. Makes about 5 half-pints.

Storage time. *Processed:* Up to 1 year. *Unprocessed:* Up to 1 month in refrigerator; up to 1 year in freezer.

Per tablespoon: 37 calories, 0 g protein, 9 g carbohydrates, 0 g total fat, 0 mg cholesterol, 0 mg sodium

Rhubarb Conserve

This chunky conserve, dotted with raisins, dates, and nuts, is good in all ways: as a spread for toast, a relish with meats, or a topping for ice cream.

2½ pounds rhubarb
5½ cups sugar
2 oranges
1 lemon
1½ cups *each* raisins and snipped pitted dates
1 cup chopped walnuts

Dice unpeeled rhubarb stalks; you should have 4 cups. Place rhubarb in a heavy-bottomed 8- to 10-quart pan. Stir in sugar until well blended. Cover and let stand for 8 to 12 hours at room temperature.

Rinse and thinly slice unpeeled oranges and lemon; discard seeds, then cut slices into small pieces. Add orange and lemon pieces, raisins, and dates to rhubarb mixture. Bring to a boil over high heat, stirring. Then reduce heat and simmer, uncovered, stirring often, until thickened (35 to 40 minutes); as mixture thickens, reduce heat and stir more often to prevent sticking. About 5 minutes before removing from heat, stir in walnuts.

Ladle hot conserve into hot, sterilized half-pint jars, leaving ¼-inch headspace. Wipe rims and threads clean; top with hot lids, then firmly screw on bands. Process in boiling water canner for 5 minutes. Or omit processing and ladle into freezer jars or freezer containers, leaving ½-inch headspace; apply lids. Let stand for 12 to 24 hours at room temperature; freeze or refrigerate. Makes about 10 half-pints.

Storage time. *Processed:* Up to 1 year. *Unprocessed:* Up to 1 month in refrigerator; up to 1 year in freezer.

Per tablespoon: 42 calories, 0 g protein, 10 g carbohydrates, 0 g total fat, 0 mg cholesterol, 1 mg sodium

Who wouldn't appreciate a gift basket of home-canned savories? These tangy treats include Giardiniera (left; page 160), a beautiful mixed vegetable pickle, and Garlic Jelly (right; page 150), a savory accompaniment for cold meats. In the center of the basket is Apricot Chutney (page 167), a spicy partner for curries, meats, and cheese.

Apricot-Pear Conserve

The flavors of tangy dried apricots, lemon, and fresh pears blend harmoniously in this colorful conserve.

- 1 lemon
- 1 cup dried apricots, cut into thin slices
- 1 cup water
- 5 cups peeled, cored, chopped firm-ripe Anjou or Bosc pears (about 2½ lbs. pears)
- 4 cups sugar

Rinse unpeeled lemon and thinly slice; discard end pieces and any seeds. Place lemon slices in a small pan and stir in apricots and water. Bring mixture to a boil over high heat; reduce heat and simmer, uncovered, for 5 minutes. Remove mixture from heat and set aside.

Place pears in a heavy-bottomed 8- to 10-quart pan. Stir in sugar until well blended. Bring mixture to a boil over medium heat, stirring occasionally. Continue to boil gently, uncovered, stirring often, for 25 minutes; as mixture thickens, reduce heat and stir more often to prevent sticking. Stir in apricot mixture (including liquid); bring to a boil. Then boil, uncovered, stirring often, until reduced to about 5 cups (about 5 more minutes).

Ladle hot conserve into hot, sterilized half-pint jars, leaving ¼-inch headspace. Wipe rims and threads clean; top with hot lids, then firmly screw on bands. Process in boiling water canner for 5 minutes. Or omit processing and ladle into freezer jars or freezer containers, leaving ½-inch headspace; apply lids. Let stand for 12 to 24 hours at room temperature; freeze or refrigerate. Makes about 5 half-pints.

Storage time. *Processed:* Up to 1 year. *Unprocessed:* Up to 1 month in refrigerator; up to 1 year in freezer.

Per tablespoon: 50 calories, 0 g protein, 13 g carbohydrates, 0 g total fat, 0 mg cholesterol, 0 mg sodium

---

Using Commercial Fruits & Juices for Jams & Jellies

You can make excellent jams and jellies from purchased canned and frozen unsweetened fruits and juices. Commercial products may be low in pectin, though—so always add pectin as directed in the recipe (or, for juices, as instructed on page 148).

Quince & Orange Preserves

Bubbling down to glistening goodness, tart quinces are enhanced by orange quarters, cinnamon, and cloves.

- 8 small quinces (about 2 lbs. *total*)
  About 5½ cups water
- 3 cinnamon sticks (*each* about 2 inches long), broken in half
- 30 whole cloves
- 3 medium-size oranges
- 6 cups sugar
- 2 cups distilled white vinegar (5% acidity)

Peel and core quinces; place peels and cores in a 2-quart pan and add 4 cups of the water. Set aside. Pour about 1 inch of water (at least 1½ cups) into a heavy-bottomed 8- to 10-quart pan. Cut quinces into quarters; place in pan.

Bring contents of both the 2-quart pan and the 8- to 10-quart pan to a boil over high heat. Reduce heat, cover, and simmer until quince quarters are tender when pierced (about 30 minutes). Drain quince quarters. Strain cooking liquid from peels and cores; add 1½ cups strained liquid to quince quarters, then discard peels, cores, and remaining liquid.

Tie cinnamon sticks and cloves in a washed square of cheesecloth. Add to quinces. Rinse unpeeled oranges and thinly slice; discard any seeds, then quarter orange slices and add to quinces. Stir in sugar and vinegar until well blended. Bring mixture to a boil over medium heat. Then boil, uncovered, stirring often, until syrup is amber in color and slightly thickened (about 1 hour and 10 minutes); as syrup thickens, reduce heat and stir more often to prevent sticking. Syrup will continue to thicken as it cools. Remove spice packet.

Ladle hot preserves into hot, sterilized half-pint jars, leaving ¼-inch headspace. Wipe rims and threads clean; top with hot lids, then firmly screw on bands. Process in boiling water canner for 5 minutes. Or omit processing and ladle into freezer jars or freezer containers, leaving ½-inch headspace; apply lids. Let stand for 12 to 24 hours at room temperature; freeze or refrigerate. Makes about 8 half-pints.

Storage time. *Processed:* Up to 1 year. *Unprocessed:* Up to 1 month in refrigerator; up to 1 year in freezer.

Per tablespoon: 41 calories, 0 g protein, 11 g carbohydrates, 0 g total fat, 0 mg cholesterol, 0 mg sodium

How to Make Jelly

To make clear and sparkling jelly with a full, sweet flavor, you start by extracting juice from sound, ripe fruit, then strain it and boil it with sugar until it jells. For jellies with the right consistency—tender, yet firm enough to hold a jiggly shape—you'll need to use the right proportions of fruit, sugar, pectin, and acid. If the fruit you're using doesn't contain enough natural pectin and acid for jelly (see below), just add these ingredients to the juice as needed.

Pectin & Acid Contents of Fruits

Consult the lists below to check the pectin and acid content of the fruit you want to use.

Juice from these fruits usually contains enough pectin and acid for jelly: Tart apples, tart blackberries, crabapples, cranberries, red currants, gooseberries, lemons, limes, loganberries, most plums, quinces.

Juice from these fruits usually is low in acid or pectin: Sweet apples, sweet blackberries, sour and sweet cherries, elderberries, grapefruit, eastern Concord grapes, seedless grapes, loquats, oranges.

Juice from these fruits always needs added acid or pectin, or both: Apricots, blueberries, figs, western Concord grapes, guavas, nectarines, peaches, pears, pomegranates, prune plums, raspberries, strawberries.

Testing for Pectin

If the juice you're planning to use is too low in pectin, you'll wind up with runny jelly. To avoid this problem, test the juice—and make any necessary adjustments—before you start making your jelly.

To test the pectin content of fruit juice, combine 1 teaspoon of cooked fruit juice (see steps 2 through 4 on facing page) and 1 tablespoon of rubbing alcohol (70 percent alcohol) in a cup. Stir gently to make sure all the juice comes in contact with the alcohol. *Do not taste* this mixture—it's poisonous. Juices rich in pectin will form a solid, jellylike mass that can be picked up with a fork. Juices low in pectin will form only a few pieces of jellylike material. If more pectin is needed, you can either add commercial liquid pectin or mix the juice with another fruit juice that's higher in pectin. *Discard the alcohol test.*

If pectin is to be added, add 1 tablespoon liquid pectin to 1 cup juice. Test again for jelling. If more pectin is needed, add 1 more tablespoon; test again. Repeat until enough pectin has been added. Measure remaining juice; add pectin in the correct amount.

Testing for Acid

A tart juice is necessary for a good-tasting jelly. Compare the flavor of your cooked juice with that of a mixture of 1 teaspoon bottled lemon juice, 3 tablespoons water, and ½ teaspoon sugar. If your juice does not taste as tart as this lemon mixture, add 1 tablespoon lemon juice per cup of fruit juice.

Choosing Sweeteners

Besides contributing to the flavor of fruit spreads, sugar aids in jelling and acts as a preservative. Light corn syrup and mild-flavored honey may be used to replace part of the sugar in jams and jellies, but they tend to alter the texture and mask the fruit flavor; for best results, use tested recipes that specify honey or corn syrup. Likewise, use artificial sweeteners only when called for in a recipe.

Finding the Jell Point

If you're not using commercial pectin in your jelly, you need to test for doneness. There are three methods you can use. *The first two tests work for jam as well as for jelly; the third is for jelly only.*

Temperature test. The easiest way to tell whether your jelly has reached the jell point is to check its temperature with a jelly or candy thermometer: when it reaches 220°F (at sea level), it's ready. For each 1,000 feet of altitude above sea level, you'll need to subtract 2 degrees; at an elevation of 1,000 feet, for example, jelly is done at 218°F. The thermometer bulb must be completely covered with jelly, but it shouldn't touch the bottom of the pan. Read at eye level, and test your thermometer's accuracy in advance by placing it in boiling water.

Refrigerator test. Remove the pan from the heat; spoon about a tablespoon of boiling jelly onto a small chilled plate. Place in the refrigerator for 3 minutes, then push the jelly from the side; if it wrinkles and seems tender-firm, it's done.

Spoon or sheet test. Dip a cool metal spoon into the boiling fruit juice. Lift the spoon out of the steam and turn it so the juice runs off the side. When the juice begins to boil, it's light and syrupy; when it has almost reached the jell point, it becomes heavy and falls off the spoon two drops at a time. When the two drops form together and slide off the spoon in a sheet, the jelly is ready; remove it from the heat immediately. *This test does not work for jam.*

Remaking Runny Jelly

If your jelly ends up looking like syrup, you can try to remake it; work with just 4 cups at a time.

To remake with dry pectin. For each 4 cups of jelly, mix ¼ cup sugar, ½ cup water, 2 tablespoons bottled lemon juice, and 4 teaspoons dry pectin in a large, heavy-bottomed pan. Bring to a boil over high heat, stirring constantly; add jelly. Bring to a full rolling boil, stirring constantly; then boil, stirring, for 30 seconds. Remove from heat, skim off any foam, and ladle into hot, sterilized jars, leaving ¼-inch head-space. Process in boiling water canner for 5 minutes.

To remake with liquid pectin. For each 4 cups of jelly, mix ¾ cup sugar, 2 tablespoons bottled lemon juice, and 2 tablespoons liquid pectin in a bowl; set aside. In a large, heavy-bottomed pan, bring jelly just to a boil over high heat, stirring constantly. Remove from heat; quickly add pectin mixture. Bring to a full rolling boil over high heat, stirring constantly; then boil, stirring, for 1 minute. Remove from heat, skim off any foam, and ladle into hot, sterilized jars, leaving ¼-inch headspace. Process in boiling water canner for 5 minutes.

Step-by-Step Canning for Jelly

1. Assemble and prepare equipment and sterilize jars, following steps 2 through 4 on page 108.

2. Rinse fruit. Remove stems, hulls, blossom ends, and spoiled parts. Do not core or peel apples or other firm fruits; just cut them into small pieces. If fruit is soft, crush it to start the juice flowing.

3. To extract the juice, put crushed or cut-up fruit into a pan. For firm fruit such as apples, you'll need to add about 1 cup water for each pound of fruit; for semifirm fruit such as plums, add about ½ cup water per pound. Soft fruits usually don't need any additional water. Whatever the type of fruit, add only enough water to prevent scorching, since juice shouldn't be diluted any more than necessary.

4. Bring fruit to a boil over high heat; reduce heat to medium and cook, stirring to prevent scorching, until tender (5 to 10 minutes for grapes and berries, 20 to 25 minutes for apples and other firm fruits). Don't overboil; that reduces jelling strength.

Pour fruit mixture through four thicknesses of wet washed cheesecloth spread over a colander; or pour into a moistened jelly bag made of strong muslin. *Don't squeeze bag;* you'll get a cloudy jelly.

5. You can use one of two methods to make jelly.

The standard or long-cook method uses a little less sugar. Follow the directions on the facing page to test the cooked juice for its natural pectin and acid content; then supply more of either or both, as needed (see facing page).

Cook only 4 to 6 cups juice at a time, using a heavy-bottomed 8- to 10-quart pan. If you like, add ½ teaspoon margarine, butter, or salad oil to the juice to reduce foam (keep in mind that added fat may cause an "off" flavor to develop during long storage).

Bring the juice to a boil, then add the sugar and stir until dissolved. The amount of sugar you use depends upon the pectin and acid content of the juice.

In general, use ¾ to 1 cup sugar per cup of juice if the juice is naturally high in pectin; use ⅔ to ¾ cup sugar per cup of juice if the juice has only a moderate amount of natural pectin (see "Pectin & Acid Contents of Fruits," facing page).

Boil juice rapidly until the jell point is reached (see "Finding the Jell Point," facing page), then immediately remove the pan from the heat. Don't overcook; if you do, the jelly will lose flavor, color, and jelling ability.

The short-cook method, used in all our jelly recipes, depends on commercial pectin and requires a higher proportion of sugar. The boiling time, usually about 1 minute, cannot be varied from recipe or package directions. If the recipe tells you to bring the jelly mixture to a "full rolling boil," you want a hard boil that does not stop when the mixture is stirred. Follow recipe or package directions to cook your jelly, then remove the jelly from the heat at once.

6. Carefully skim off any foam from jelly. Remove a sterilized jar from the hot water. Stand it upright on a cloth towel. Ladle hot jelly into jar, leaving ¼-inch headspace.

7. Seal and process jars as directed in steps 8 through 12 on page 109, using the processing time specified in your recipe. At high altitudes, add an additional minute for each 1,000 feet above sea level.

8. If you choose not to process your jelly, ladle it into clean freezer jars or freezer containers; rinse jars with hot water before filling them to prevent the hot jelly from cracking the glass. Before storing filled jars or containers, let them stand for 12 to 24 hours at room temperature; this gives the jelly time to jell completely.

Ruby Wine Jelly

The wine lovers among your friends will enjoy this full-flavored jelly, superb with beef or lamb.

> 1¾ cups ruby port
> ¾ cup dry red wine, such as Cabernet Sauvignon
> 3 cups sugar
> 1 pouch (3 oz.) liquid pectin

In a heavy-bottomed 8- to 10-quart pan, mix port, dry red wine, and sugar. Stir over low heat until sugar is completely dissolved (about 5 minutes). Stir in pectin all at once; skim off any foam.

Ladle hot jelly into hot, sterilized half-pint jars, leaving ¼-inch headspace. Wipe rims and threads clean; top with hot lids, then firmly screw on bands. Process in boiling water canner for 5 minutes. Or omit processing and ladle jelly into freezer jars or freezer containers, leaving ½-inch headspace; apply lids. Let stand for 12 to 24 hours at room temperature; freeze or refrigerate. Makes about 5 half-pints.

Storage time. *Processed:* Up to 1 year. *Unprocessed:* Up to 1 month in refrigerator; up to 1 year in freezer.

Per tablespoon: 39 calories, 0 g protein, 8 g carbohydrates, 0 g total fat, 0 mg cholesterol, 1 mg sodium

Garlic or Shallot Jelly

Pictured on page 146

This bold-flavored jelly is a wonderful relish for meats; it's also good with cream cheese and crackers.

> ½ cup finely chopped garlic or shallots
> About 3 cups white wine vinegar (5% acidity)
> 1½ cups water
> 6 cups sugar
> 2 pouches (3 oz. *each*) liquid pectin

Combine garlic or shallots and 3 cups of the vinegar in a 2- to 2½-quart pan. Bring to a simmer over medium heat; simmer gently, uncovered, for 15 minutes. Remove from heat; pour into a glass jar. Cover and let stand for 24 to 36 hours at room temperature; then pour through a fine strainer into a bowl, pressing garlic or shallots with the back of a spoon to squeeze out as much liquid as possible. Discard residue. Measure liquid; if necessary, add vinegar to make 2 cups or boil liquid to reduce to 2 cups.

In a heavy-bottomed 8- to 10-quart pan, mix flavored vinegar, water, and sugar. Bring to a full rolling boil over medium-high heat, stirring. Stir in pectin all at once, return to a full rolling boil, and boil for 1 minute, stirring constantly. Remove from heat and skim off any foam.

Ladle hot jelly into hot, sterilized half-pint jars, leaving ¼-inch headspace. Wipe rims and threads clean; top with hot lids, then firmly screw on bands. Process in boiling water canner for 5 minutes. Or omit processing and ladle jelly into freezer jars or freezer containers, leaving ½-inch headspace; apply lids. Let stand for 12 to 24 hours at room temperature; freeze or refrigerate. Makes about 7 half-pints.

Storage time. *Processed:* Up to 1 year. *Unprocessed:* Up to 1 month in refrigerator; up to 1 year in freezer.

Per tablespoon: 43 calories, 0 g protein, 11 g carbohydrates, 0 g total fat, 0 mg cholesterol, 0 mg sodium

Apricot–Red Pepper Jelly

Pictured on facing page

You'll enjoy the combination of tangy-sweet dried apricots, red bell pepper, and feisty hot chiles in this jelly. It's fabulous with meat and poultry; or try it with cream cheese, as a spread for crackers.

> 1 package (about 6 oz.) dried apricots (about 1¼ cups), chopped
> ¾ cup chopped red bell pepper
> ¼ cup seeded, chopped fresh red Fresno chiles or red (or green) jalapeño chiles (4 to 6 medium-size chiles)
> 2½ cups cider vinegar (5% acidity)
> 1½ cups water
> 1 box (1¾ or 2 oz.) dry pectin
> 6 cups sugar

In a blender or food processor, whirl apricots, bell pepper, chiles, and 1¾ cups of the vinegar until fruit and vegetables are finely ground. Pour into a heavy-bottomed 8- to 10-quart pan. Rinse blender with the 1½ cups water and remaining ¾ cup vinegar; pour into pan. Stir in pectin; bring to a full rolling boil over high heat, stirring constantly. Quickly add sugar, still stirring. Return to a full rolling boil; then boil, stirring, for 1 minute. (If using a 2-oz. box of pectin, boil for 2 minutes.) Remove from heat and skim off any foam.

Ladle hot jelly into hot, sterilized half-pint jars, leaving ¼-inch headspace. Wipe rims and threads clean; top with hot lids, then firmly screw on bands. Process in boiling water canner for 5 minutes. Or omit processing and ladle jelly into freezer jars or freezer containers, leaving ½-inch headspace; apply lids. Let stand for 12 to 24 hours at room temperature; freeze or refrigerate. Makes about 6 half-pints.

Storage time. *Processed:* Up to 1 year. *Unprocessed:* Up to 1 month in refrigerator; up to 1 year in freezer.

Per tablespoon: 55 calories, 0 g protein, 14 g carbohydrates, 0 g total fat, 0 mg cholesterol, 0 mg sodium

Two savory pepper jellies add verve and flavor to a bountiful cold platter of sliced meats, goat cheese, vegetables, and lavosh (Armenian cracker bread). Apricot-Red Pepper Jelly (at left; recipe on facing page) and Jalapeño Jelly (page 152) are also good with cream cheese and crackers.

Jalapeño Jelly

Pictured on page 130 and page 151

Hot, spicy jalapeño jelly is a delightful Southwest-style condiment to serve with chicken, pork, or beef.

- ¼ **cup chopped green jalapeño chiles (4 to 6 medium-size chiles; remove half the seeds before chopping)**
- ¾ **cup chopped green bell pepper**
- 6 **cups sugar**
- 2½ **cups cider vinegar (5% acidity)**
- 2 **pouches (3 oz. *each*) liquid pectin**

In a blender or food processor, whirl chiles and bell pepper until finely ground. Place ground vegetables and any juice in a heavy-bottomed 8- to 10-quart pan. Stir in sugar and vinegar until well blended.

Bring to a full rolling boil over high heat, stirring constantly. Stir in pectin all at once. Return to a full rolling boil; then boil, stirring, for 1 minute. Remove from heat and skim off any foam.

Ladle hot jelly into hot, sterilized half-pint jars, leaving ¼-inch headspace. Wipe rims and threads clean; top with hot lids, then firmly screw on bands. Process in boiling water canner for 5 minutes. Or omit processing and ladle jelly into freezer jars or freezer containers, leaving ½-inch headspace; apply lids. Let stand for 12 to 24 hours at room temperature; freeze or refrigerate. Makes about 7 half-pints.

Storage time. *Processed:* Up to 1 year. *Unprocessed:* Up to 1 month in refrigerator; up to 1 year in freezer.

Per tablespoon: 42 calories, 0 g protein, 11 g carbohydrates, 0 g total fat, 0 mg cholesterol, 0 mg sodium

Lime-Mint Jelly

Pictured on page 130

Fresh lime juice and finely chopped mint combine in a jelly with an outstanding, delicately sweet flavor.

- 8 **to 10 limes**
- 4 **cups sugar**
- 1¾ **cups water**
- **Green food coloring (optional)**
- 1 **pouch (3 oz.) liquid pectin**
- 3 **tablespoons finely chopped fresh mint**

Rinse unpeeled limes. Grate thin outer peel (colored part only) from 5 limes; set aside. Squeeze enough limes (use remaining limes as needed) to make ¾ cup juice. Pour lime juice, sugar, and water into a heavy-bottomed 8- to 10-quart pan and stir until well blended. Bring to a boil over medium-high heat,

stirring occasionally. (At this point, stir in enough food coloring, if desired, to get the desired tint.)

Stir in pectin all at once. Add grated lime peel and mint. Bring to a full rolling boil; boil, stirring, for 1 minute. Remove from heat and skim off any foam.

Ladle hot jelly into hot, sterilized half-pint jars, leaving ¼-inch headspace. Wipe rims and threads clean; top with hot lids, then firmly screw on bands. Process in boiling water canner for 5 minutes. Or omit processing and ladle jelly into freezer jars or freezer containers, leaving ½-inch headspace; apply lids. Let stand for 12 to 24 hours at room temperature; then freeze or refrigerate. Makes about 5 half-pints.

Storage time. *Processed:* Up to 1 year. *Unprocessed:* Up to 1 month in refrigerator; up to 1 year in freezer.

Per tablespoon: 40 calories, 0 g protein, 10 g carbohydrates, 0 g total fat, 0 mg cholesterol, 0 mg sodium

Apple-Herb Jelly

Apple jelly with a whisper of herb flavor is a much-appreciated gift. To make plain apple jelly, don't boil the juice, add herbs, or strain the mixture; just begin by stirring in the lemon juice and sugar.

- 2 **cups bottled filtered unsweetened apple juice**
- ¼ **cup dry thyme, ⅓ cup dry basil, 2 tablespoons dry rosemary, or ¼ cup dry mint**
- 3 **tablespoons lemon juice**
- 3½ **cups sugar**
- 1 **pouch (3 oz.) liquid pectin**

In a heavy-bottomed 6- to 8-quart pan, bring apple juice to a boil. Remove from heat, stir in thyme, and cover. Let stand for 30 minutes (or 2 hours for basil; 15 minutes for rosemary; 10 minutes for mint).

Pour mixture through a jelly bag or a cheese-cloth-lined colander. Squeeze out and reserve all liquid; discard herbs. Rinse pan; return liquid to pan. Stir in lemon juice and sugar. Bring to a boil over high heat, stirring constantly. Pour in pectin all at once, bring to a full rolling boil, and boil, stirring, for 1 minute. Remove from heat and skim off any foam.

Ladle hot jelly into hot, sterilized half-pint jars, leaving ¼-inch headspace. Wipe rims and threads clean; top with hot lids, then firmly screw on bands. Process in boiling water canner for 5 minutes. Or omit processing and ladle jelly into freezer jars or freezer containers, leaving ½-inch headspace; apply lids. Let stand for 12 to 24 hours at room temperature; freeze or refrigerate. Makes about 4 half-pints.

Storage time. *Processed:* Up to 1 year. *Unprocessed:* Up to 1 month in refrigerator; up to 1 year in freezer.

Per tablespoon: 46 calories, 0 g protein, 12 g carbohydrates, 0 g total fat, 0 mg cholesterol, 1 mg sodium

Cranberry-Apple Jelly

Pictured on page 130

This shimmering, rosy jelly, subtly flavored with cranberry and apple juices, looks lovely on a holiday table.

- **2 cups bottled cranberry juice cocktail**
- **2 cups bottled unsweetened apple juice**
- **1 tablespoon lemon juice**
- **1 box (1¾ or 2 oz.) dry pectin**
- **4½ cups sugar**

In a heavy-bottomed 8- to 10-quart pan, mix cranberry juice cocktail, apple juice, lemon juice, and pectin. Bring to a full rolling boil over high heat, stirring constantly. Quickly add sugar, still stirring. Return to a full rolling boil; then boil, stirring, for 1 minute. (If using a 2-oz. box of pectin, boil for 2 minutes.) Remove from heat and skim off any foam.

Ladle hot jelly into hot, sterilized half-pint jars, leaving ¼-inch headspace. Wipe rims and threads clean; top with hot lids, then firmly screw on bands. Process in boiling water canner for 5 minutes. Or omit processing and ladle jelly into freezer jars or freezer containers, leaving ½-inch headspace; apply lids. Let stand for 12 to 24 hours at room temperature; freeze or refrigerate. Makes about 5 half-pints.

Storage time. *Processed:* Up to 1 year. *Unprocessed:* Up to 1 month in refrigerator; up to 1 year in freezer.

Per tablespoon: 52 calories, 0 g protein, 13 g carbohydrates, 0 g total fat, 0 mg cholesterol, 1 mg sodium

Quick Grape Jelly

Here's a bright grape jelly you can "put up" in a jiffy, at any time of year.

- **3 cups bottled unsweetened grape juice**
- **½ cup water**
- **1 tablespoon lemon juice**
- **1 package (1¾ or 2 oz.) dry pectin**
- **3½ cups sugar**

In a heavy-bottomed 8- to 10-quart pan, mix grape juice, water, lemon juice, and pectin. Bring to a full rolling boil over high heat, stirring constantly. Quickly add sugar, still stirring. Return to a full rolling boil; then boil, stirring, for 1 minute. (If using a 2-oz. box of pectin, boil for 2 minutes.) Remove from heat and skim off any foam.

Ladle hot jelly into hot, sterilized half-pint jars, leaving ¼-inch headspace. Wipe rims and threads clean; top with hot lids, then firmly screw on bands. Process in boiling water canner for 5 minutes. Or omit processing and ladle jelly into freezer jars or freezer containers, leaving ½-inch headspace; apply lids. Let stand for 12 to 24 hours at room temperature; then freeze or refrigerate. Makes about 4 half-pints.

Storage time. *Processed:* Up to 1 year. *Unprocessed:* Up to 1 month in refrigerator; up to 1 year in freezer.

Per tablespoon: 51 calories, 0 g protein, 13 g carbohydrates, 0 g total fat, 0 mg cholesterol, 1 mg sodium

Pomegranate Jelly

Pomegranate seeds provide the juice for this sweet-tart red jelly. Submerging the fruit in water makes it quite easy to separate seeds from peel and pulp, but it's still wise to allow extra time for preparation.

- **About 10 large pomegranates**
- **2 tablespoons lemon juice**
- **6 cups sugar**
- **1 pouch (3 oz.) liquid pectin**

Cut blossom end off each pomegranate and lightly score peel lengthwise, dividing fruit into quarters. Immerse fruit in a bowl of cool water; soak for 5 minutes. Holding fruit under water, break sections apart with your fingers and separate seeds from pulp; seeds will sink, and pulp and peel will float. Skim off pulp and peel; discard. Scoop up seeds, drain in a colander, and let dry on paper towels.

Whirl seeds, 1½ to 2 cups at a time, in a blender or food processor until liquefied. Set a colander in a bowl; line colander with moistened cheesecloth. Pour in purée and let juice drip through cloth. To speed the process, gather edges of cloth with rubber-gloved hands and twist *slowly* (juice tends to squirt) to extract liquid. You need 3½ cups juice *total*.

In a heavy-bottomed 8- to 10-quart pan, mix pomegranate juice, lemon juice, and sugar. Bring to a full rolling boil over medium-high heat, stirring constantly. Stir in pectin all at once. Return to a full rolling boil; then boil, stirring, for 1 minute. Remove from heat and skim off any foam.

Ladle hot jelly into hot, sterilized half-pint jars, leaving ¼-inch headspace. Wipe rims and threads clean; top with hot lids, then firmly screw on bands. Process in boiling water canner for 5 minutes. Or omit processing and ladle jelly into freezer jars or freezer containers, leaving ½-inch headspace; apply lids. Let stand for 12 to 24 hours at room temperature; freeze or refrigerate. Makes about 7 half-pints.

Storage time. *Processed:* Up to 1 year. *Unprocessed:* Up to 1 month in refrigerator; up to 1 year in freezer.

Per tablespoon: 53 calories, 0 g protein, 14 g carbohydrates, 0 g total fat, 0 mg cholesterol, 1 mg sodium

Brighten up your mealtimes with homemade pickles, relishes, and chutneys like these. The bottom shelf of the cupboard holds Quick Dill Pickles (page 157). On countertop are (clockwise from left) Sweet Pickle Sticks (page 160), Bread & Butter Pickles (page 157), Mango-Peach Chutney (page 166), Papaya-Plum Chutney (page 167), and Refrigerator Corn Relish (page 164).

154

Pickles, Relishes & Chutneys

Piquant pickles, tangy relishes, enticing chutneys

For streamlined pickle making, turn to these easy relishes, chutneys, and pickled vegetables. You'll find that your pickles taste best if left to stand for several weeks after processing—but if you want to sample the results of your efforts a bit sooner, try the quick refrigerator pickles on page 162. They're ready to eat within a day or two after you prepare them.● *Pickles* are most often made from cucumbers, but other vegetables and fruits are also delicious pickled. We've included a wide variety. ● *Relishes* are piquant blends of vegetables, fruits, spices, and vinegar. They're always welcome at casual meals—as embellishments for hot dogs, hamburgers, or grilled meats—and they're equally appropriate for more formal occasions. Cranberry-Pear Relish and Plum Relish, for example, are just right at your holiday table. ● *Chutneys*, made from fruit, vinegar, and spices, are a type of relish too; the flavor ranges from hot and spicy to mild and tangy. Chutneys are ideal accompaniments for Middle Eastern and Indian entrées, but you'll enjoy them with many other foods as well.

Pickling Fruits & Vegetables

Delicious pickles start with fresh produce. Choose the best fruits and vegetables you can find; then refrigerate them until you're ready to start pickling—preferably within 24 hours after you purchase (or pick) your produce.

Important Ingredients

Cucumbers should be firm, fresh, and unblemished. Use unwaxed young pickling cucumbers: they're smaller and spinier than ordinary garden cucumbers, and make crunchier pickles. Rinse any dirt from cucumbers, then pull off any blossoms that weren't removed by rinsing (the blossoms may contain an enzyme that causes pickles to soften).

Vinegar. To ensure safe pickles, the vinegar you use should always have an acidity of 5 percent; check the label. *Never* use homemade vinegars or those of unknown acidity. And don't boil vinegar solutions longer than necessary; if you do, their preserving properties, and thus the safety of your pickles, may be reduced. Cider and distilled white vinegars are both popular for pickling; cider vinegar is mellower in flavor but gives a darker product.

Water. Use soft water for pickling, since minerals in hard water adversely affect pickle quality. If your tap water isn't soft, buy bottled distilled water.

Salt. If possible, use canning or pickling salt; supermarkets carry canning salt seasonally, alongside the canning supplies. Table salt is an acceptable substitute, though it contains an anticaking additive (sodium silicoaluminate) that may make pickle brine slightly cloudy or leave a harmless precipitate. (Use only *noniodized* table salt, since the iodized type tends to darken pickles.) On the whole, though, most pickles made with table salt are indistinguishable from those put up with canning salt—and some canning salts also contain sodium silicoaluminate (check the label).

Salt is not necessary for the safety of the fresh-pack pickles in this chapter, and you'll even find several reduced-sodium recipes. Keep in mind, though, that cutting down on salt can affect texture and flavor slightly, with softer pickles the most frequent result. *Do not use salt substitutes in pickles.*

Sugar. Use granulated white sugar unless your recipe calls for another sweetener. Brown sugar tends to darken pickles.

Equipment You'll Need

Unless you intend to refrigerate and use your pickles within a short period of time, they must be processed in standard canning jars in a boiling water canner.

To prepare pickled products, use only stainless steel, unchipped enamel, or glass utensils. Copper may turn pickles an unappetizing off-green; iron turns them black. *Never* use galvanized containers; the interaction of acid or salt with zinc may cause the metal to dissolve partially, contaminating your pickles and rendering them inedible.

Step-by-Step Canning for Pickles

1. Read the preceding information on pickling. Check recipe instructions and gather the necessary ingredients. Assemble and prepare equipment and jars, following steps 2 through 4 on page 108.

2. Pickle vegetables and fruits as soon as possible after selecting them. Prepare just one canner load at a time; rinse produce well (don't use detergent). Follow recipe instructions carefully. *For safety's sake, do not alter the proportions of vinegar, vegetables and fruits, or water.*

3. In a large, heavy-bottomed stainless steel or unchipped enamel pan, bring the food to a boil and cook according to recipe instructions. Then remove a jar from the hot water. Stand it upright on a cloth towel; fill with hot food and liquid, leaving recommended headspace. *Avoid overpacking cucumbers and other vegetables;* you must leave space for the packing liquid, since it contains the acid that will make your pickles safe to eat. Gently run a narrow nonmetallic spatula between food and jar sides to release air bubbles; add more liquid, if necessary.

4. Seal and process jars as directed in steps 8 through 12 on page 109, processing jars for the time specified in your recipe. At high altitudes, add an additional minute for each 1,000 feet above sea level.

5. If you choose not to process condiments such as relishes and chutneys, you can ladle them into clean jars or refrigerator containers; rinse jars with hot water before filling them to prevent the hot food from cracking the glass. Before refrigerating filled jars or containers, let them cool completely.

Quick Dill Pickles

Pictured on page 154

Choose the freshest pickling cucumbers you can find: the fresher the cucumbers, the crisper the pickles. If you're watching the salt in your diet, you may want to try our reduced-sodium dills; the pickles may be somewhat softer, with a slightly different flavor.

    6 cups cider vinegar (5% acidity)
    6 cups soft tap water or bottled distilled water
    ½ cup canning salt or noniodized table salt
    ½ cup sugar
    9 small cloves garlic, peeled and halved
    6 fresh dill seed heads (*each* about 4 inches in diameter), separated into thirds (8 to 12 flowerets *each*)
    2 tablespoons mustard seeds
    6 pounds pickling cucumbers (*each* 3 to 4 inches long)

In a 5- to 6-quart stainless steel or unchipped enamel pan, combine vinegar, water, salt, and sugar; bring to a boil over medium-high heat.

Meanwhile, put 3 garlic-clove halves, 2 pieces of dill, and 1 teaspoon mustard seeds into each of 6 prepared, hot wide-mouth quart jars. Pack cucumbers firmly into hot jars, leaving ½-inch headspace. Top each jar with an additional piece of dill. Pour hot vinegar solution over cucumbers, leaving ½-inch headspace. Gently run a narrow nonmetallic spatula between cucumbers and jar sides to release air bubbles. Wipe rims and threads clean; top with hot lids, then firmly screw on bands. Process in boiling water canner for 15 minutes. Or omit processing; let stand for 12 to 24 hours at room temperature, then refrigerate. Makes 6 quarts.

Note: For firmer pickles, process pickles in boiling water canner for 30 minutes in water at 180° to 185°F (rather than in boiling water at 212°F). This process also prevents spoilage, but the water *must* remain within the specified temperature range for the entire 30 minutes. Use a candy or jelly thermometer to make sure the temperature is always at least 180°F; don't let it rise above 185°F, or your pickles may not have the desired firmness. (Do not use this method for other recipes in this book.)

Storage time. *Processed:* Up to 1 year. *Unprocessed:* Up to 1 month in refrigerator.

Per ¼ cup: 11 calories, 0 g protein, 3 g carbohydrates, 0 g total fat, 0 mg cholesterol, 550 mg sodium

Reduced-sodium Quick Dill Pickles

Follow directions for **Quick Dill Pickles**, but reduce salt to 2 tablespoons. Makes 6 quarts.

Per ¼ cup: 11 calories, 0 g protein, 3 g carbohydrates, 0 g total fat, 0 mg cholesterol, 138 mg sodium

Bread & Butter Pickles

Pictured on page 154

A forkful or two of this crisp, sweet-tart cucumber-onion mixture demonstrates why bread and butter pickles are so popular. Our version gets extra color and flavor from red bell pepper strips.

    4 pounds pickling cucumbers (*each* 4 to 6 inches long)
    1½ pounds onions, thinly sliced
    2 medium-size red bell peppers, seeded and cut into ¼-inch-wide strips
    ¼ cup canning salt or noniodized table salt
       Ice cubes or crushed ice
    3 cups cider vinegar (5% acidity)
    3 cups sugar
    2 tablespoons mustard seeds
    1½ teaspoons celery seeds
    1 teaspoon ground turmeric

Cut ends from cucumbers; then cut cucumbers into ¼-inch-thick slices. Place in a deep stainless steel, glass, or unchipped enamel bowl; mix in onions, bell peppers, and salt. Top with a 2- to 3-inch layer of ice cubes or crushed ice. Let stand for 3 hours, replenishing ice as needed.

In a heavy-bottomed 8- to 10-quart stainless steel or unchipped enamel pan, mix vinegar, sugar, mustard seeds, celery seeds, and turmeric. Bring to a boil over high heat. Drain and rinse vegetable mixture; add to hot vinegar solution and return to a boil. Pack hot into prepared, hot wide-mouth pint jars, leaving ½-inch headspace. Gently run a narrow nonmetallic spatula between pickles and jar sides to release air bubbles. Wipe rims and threads clean; top with hot lids, then firmly screw on bands. Process in boiling water canner for 10 minutes. Or omit processing; let stand for 12 to 24 hours at room temperature, then refrigerate. Makes about 7 pints.

Storage time. *Processed:* Up to 1 year. *Unprocessed:* Up to 1 month in refrigerator.

Per ¼ cup: 54 calories, 0 g protein, 14 g carbohydrates, 0 g total fat, 0 mg cholesterol, 472 mg sodium

Flavored Vinegars

Pictured on facing page

*I*t's easy to make your own flavored vinegars. Simply put fresh herbs and spices (or petals of edible flowers) in a decorative bottle or jar, then fill with wine vinegar and cork or cover tightly.

After the vinegar has mellowed in a cool, dark place for a time (usually about 3 weeks), it's ready to use or to give as a gift. Try it as a flavorful pick-me-up for salads, soups, or vegetables; or sprinkle it on cooked meat or seafood. Rose Petal Vinegar, infused with the fragrance of roses, is a lovely addition to fresh fruit salads.

Whether you keep the vinegar yourself or give it away, identify the flavor with a tag or label. Once opened, any of these vinegars should be stored in a cool, dark place and used within 4 months.

Herb Vinegar

2 to 4 rosemary sprigs (*each* about 5 inches long)
2 thyme sprigs (optional)
1 teaspoon whole black peppercorns
   White wine vinegar

Poke rosemary and, if desired, thyme sprigs into a 3½-cup bottle. Add peppercorns, then fill bottle with vinegar. Cork bottle and let stand in a cool, dark place for 3 weeks to develop flavor. Makes about 3½ cups.

Storage time. Up to 4 months.

Per tablespoon: 2 calories, 0 g protein, 1 g carbohydrates, 0 g total fat, 0 mg cholesterol, 0 mg sodium

Garlic–Green Onion Vinegar

Follow directions for **Herb Vinegar,** but substitute 4 cloves **garlic** (impale on a thin bamboo skewer, if desired) and 2 **green onions** (root ends and tops trimmed) for rosemary, thyme, and peppercorns. Makes about 3½ cups.

Per tablespoon: 3 calories, 0 g protein, 1 g carbohydrates, 0 g total fat, 0 mg cholesterol, 0 mg sodium

Basil-Oregano-Peppercorn Vinegar

Follow directions for **Herb Vinegar,** but substitute 2 **basil sprigs** and 4 **oregano sprigs** (*each* about 5 inches long) for rosemary and thyme. Substitute **red wine vinegar** for white wine vinegar, if desired. Makes about 3½ cups.

Per tablespoon: 2 calories, 0 g protein, 1 g carbohydrates, 0 g total fat, 0 mg cholesterol, 0 mg sodium

Spicy Chile Vinegar

Follow directions for **Herb Vinegar,** but substitute 4 **dry bay leaves,** 6 **small dried hot red chiles,** and 4 large cloves **garlic** (impale on a thin bamboo skewer, if desired) for rosemary, thyme, and peppercorns. Makes about 3½ cups.

Per tablespoon: 3 calories, 0 g protein, 1 g carbohydrates, 0 g total fat, 0 mg cholesterol, 0 mg sodium

Rose Petal Vinegar

2 cups lightly packed fresh rose petals, rinsed and drained (make sure the blossoms you use have never been sprayed with a pesticide)
3 cups white wine vinegar

Place rose petals in a wide-mouth quart jar with a tight-fitting lid. Add vinegar. Cover and let stand at room temperature until next day. Uncover and push petals down into vinegar; cover and let stand until petals are bleached and vinegar tastes of roses (about 3 more days). Strain, discarding petals; pour vinegar into a clean bottle. Cork bottle and store in a cool, dark place. Makes about 3 cups.

Storage time. Up to 4 months.

Per tablespoon: 2 calories, 0 g protein, 1 g carbohydrates, 0 g total fat, 0 mg cholesterol, 0 mg sodium

The gourmets on your gift list are sure to enjoy a bottle or two of flavored vinegar. Shown here are (left to right) Garlic-Green Onion Vinegar, Spicy Chile Vinegar, Rose Petal Vinegar, Herb Vinegar, and Basil-Oregano-Peppercorn Vinegar. The recipes are on the facing page.

Sweet Pickle Sticks

Pictured on page 154

Crisp, with a sweet-tart flavor, these pickle sticks perk up sandwich plates and give lunchboxes a lift.

- 4 **pounds pickling cucumbers** (*each* 3 to 4 inches long)
- 4 cups **cider vinegar (5% acidity)**
- 3 cups **sugar**
- 2 tablespoons **canning salt or noniodized table salt**
- 2 teaspoons **ground turmeric**
- 1 teaspoon **mustard seeds**

Cut ends from cucumbers; cut cucumbers lengthwise into quarters. Place cucumbers in a large stainless steel, glass, or unchipped enamel bowl; pour boiling water over them to cover. Let stand for 2 hours.

In a medium-size stainless steel or unchipped enamel pan, mix vinegar, sugar, salt, turmeric, and mustard seeds. Bring to a boil over high heat. Drain cucumber quarters and firmly pack them vertically into prepared, hot wide-mouth pint jars, leaving ½-inch headspace. Pour hot vinegar solution over cucumbers, leaving ½-inch headspace. Gently run a narrow nonmetallic spatula between cucumbers and jar sides to release air bubbles. Wipe rims and threads clean; top with hot lids, then firmly screw on bands. Process in boiling water canner for 10 minutes. Or omit processing; let stand for 12 to 24 hours at room temperature, then refrigerate. Makes about 5 pints.

Storage time. *Processed:* Up to 1 year. *Unprocessed:* Up to 1 month in refrigerator.

Per ¼ cup: 62 calories, 0 g protein, 17 g carbohydrates, 0 g total fat, 0 mg cholesterol, 330 mg sodium

Reduced-sodium Sweet Pickle Chips

Pictured on page 154

Whether or not you're cutting down on sodium, you'll enjoy these good-tasting pickles.

- 4 **pounds pickling cucumbers** (*each* 3 to 5 inches long)
- 4 cups **cider vinegar (5% acidity)**
- ½ cup **sugar**
- 1 tablespoon **canning salt or noniodized table salt**
- 1 tablespoon **mustard seeds**
  Canning Syrup (recipe follows)

Cut ends from cucumbers; then cut cucumbers into ¼-inch-thick slices. In a heavy-bottomed 8- to 10-quart stainless steel or unchipped enamel pan, mix vinegar, sugar, salt, and mustard seeds. Stir in cucumbers; cover and bring to a boil over medium-high heat. Reduce heat and simmer, covered, stirring occasionally, until cucumbers change from bright to dull green in color (about 5 minutes). Drain well.

While cucumbers are simmering, prepare Canning Syrup. When cucumbers are done, pack into prepared, hot wide-mouth pint jars, leaving ½-inch headspace. Pour hot syrup over cucumbers, leaving ½-inch headspace. Gently run a narrow nonmetallic spatula between cucumbers and jar sides to release air bubbles. Wipe rims and threads clean; top with hot lids, then firmly screw on bands. Process in boiling water canner for 10 minutes. Or omit processing; let stand for 12 to 24 hours at room temperature, then refrigerate. Makes about 5 pints.

Canning Syrup. In a medium-size pan, combine 3¼ cups **sugar**, 2 cups **cider vinegar (5% acidity)**, 1 tablespoon **whole allspice**, 2 teaspoons **celery seeds**, and 1 teaspoon **ground turmeric**. Bring to a boil over high heat.

Storage time. *Processed:* Up to 1 year. *Unprocessed:* Up to 1 month in refrigerator.

Per ¼ cup: 73 calories, 0 g protein, 19 g carbohydrates, 0 g total fat, 0 mg cholesterol, 23 mg sodium

Giardiniera

Pictured on pages 146 and 154

Great for the appetizer tray, these brightly colored mixed vegetable pickles are much like those you'll find in supermarkets and fancy food stores. If you enjoy spicy flavors, be sure to include the jalapeños (you can even use up to half a pound, if you like).

- 1 **pound baby carrots (or regular carrots)**
- 1 **pound celery**
- 1 **pound cauliflower flowerets**
- 1 **pound white boiling onions** (*each* ½ to 1 inch in diameter)
- 1 **pound** *each* **red and green bell peppers**
- ¼ **pound fresh jalapeño chiles (optional)**
- 6 **cloves garlic**
- 5 cups **distilled white vinegar (5% acidity)**
- 1½ cups **soft tap water or bottled distilled water**
- 1½ cups **sugar**
- ¼ cup **mustard seeds**
- 1 tablespoon **canning salt or noniodized table salt**

If using baby carrots, peel and cut in half lengthwise; then cut crosswise into 1½-inch-long pieces. If using regular carrots, peel and cut into 1½-inch-long julienne strips. Remove strings from celery; cut stalks in half lengthwise, then cut crosswise into 1½-inch-long pieces. Break cauliflower flowerets into 1½-inch pieces. Peel onions. Stem and seed bell peppers; then cut into ½- by 2-inch strips. If using chiles, leave whole; make 2 small slits in each one. Peel garlic and cut each clove in half.

In a heavy-bottomed 8- to 10-quart stainless steel or unchipped enamel pan, mix vinegar, water, sugar, mustard seeds, and salt. Bring to a boil, over high heat; then boil for 3 minutes. Add all vegetables except garlic. Bring to a boil (this will take about 10 minutes) stirring occasionally. Reduce heat to medium and cook, uncovered, pushing vegetables down into liquid occasionally, until vegetables are almost tender when pierced (about 10 minutes). Remove from heat.

Place 2 pieces of garlic in each prepared, hot wide-mouth pint jar. With a slotted spoon, remove vegetables from hot vinegar solution and distribute among jars, leaving ½-inch headspace. Pour remaining vinegar solution over vegetables in jars, leaving ½-inch headspace. Gently run a narrow nonmetallic spatula between vegetables and jar sides to release air bubbles. Wipe rims and threads clean; top with hot lids, then firmly screw on bands. Process in boiling water canner for 15 minutes. Or omit processing; let stand for 12 to 24 hours at room temperature, then refrigerate. Makes 6 pints.

Storage time. *Processed:* Up to 1 year. *Unprocessed:* Up to 1 month in refrigerator.

Per ¼ cup: 48 calories, 1 g protein, 11 g carbohydrates, 0 g total fat, 0 mg cholesterol, 152 mg sodium

Pickled Peppers

Pictured on page 154

Make your pickled peppers with sweet bells, hot or mild chiles, or some of each. Choose the color you like best, too: red, yellow, green, or a combination. If you use hot chiles, wear rubber gloves during preparation, since the oils can burn your skin.

- 6 **pounds bell peppers and/or fresh chiles**
- 4 **cups distilled white vinegar (5% acidity)**
- 4 **cups soft tap water or bottled distilled water**
- 1 **tablespoon canning salt or noniodized table salt**

Stem and seed bell peppers or large chiles; cut into 1-inch-wide strips. Leave smaller chiles whole; cut 2 small slits in each. In a heavy-bottomed 8- to 10-quart stainless steel or unchipped enamel pan, mix vinegar, water, and salt. Bring to a boil over high heat; add peppers, return to a boil, and remove from heat.

Pack hot peppers firmly into prepared, hot wide-mouth pint jars, leaving ½-inch headspace. Cover with hot vinegar solution, leaving ½-inch headspace. Gently run a narrow nonmetallic spatula between

peppers and jar sides to release air bubbles. Wipe rims and threads clean; top with hot lids, then firmly screw on bands. Process in boiling water canner for 10 minutes. Or omit processing; let stand for 12 to 24 hours at room temperature, then refrigerate. Makes about 7 pints.

Storage time. *Processed:* Up to 1 year. *Unprocessed:* Up to 1 month in refrigerator.

Per ¼ cup: 13 calories, 0 g protein, 3 g carbohydrates, 0 g total fat, 0 mg cholesterol, 119 mg sodium

Zucchini Pickles

What do you do with excess zucchini? There's zucchini bread, zucchini quiche, stuffed zucchini—and these easy pickles. They taste much like bread and butter pickles, and they're every bit as good with sandwiches, alongside salads, and as a snack.

- 5 **pounds medium-size zucchini, cut into ¼-inch-thick slices**
- 2 **pounds mild white onions, thinly sliced**
- ¼ **cup canning salt or noniodized table salt Ice water**
- 4 **cups cider vinegar (5% acidity)**
- 2 **cups sugar**
- 2 **tablespoons mustard seeds**
- 1 **tablespoon** *each* **celery seeds and ground turmeric**
- 2 **teaspoons ground ginger**
- 3 **cloves garlic, minced or pressed**

Place zucchini, onions, and salt in a large stainless steel, glass, or unchipped enamel bowl; cover with ice water and let stand for 1 to 2 hours. Drain, rinse well, and drain again.

In a heavy-bottomed 10- to 12-quart stainless steel or unchipped enamel pan, mix vinegar, sugar, mustard seeds, celery seeds, turmeric, ginger, and garlic. Bring to a boil over high heat, stirring to dissolve sugar; boil for 2 to 3 minutes. Stir in zucchini mixture, return to a boil, and boil for 2 more minutes.

Pack hot zucchini mixture into prepared, hot wide-mouth pint jars, leaving ½-inch headspace. Gently run a narrow nonmetallic spatula between pickles and jar sides to release air bubbles. Wipe rims and threads clean; top with hot lids, then firmly screw on bands. Process in boiling water canner for 10 minutes. Or omit processing; let stand for 12 to 24 hours at room temperature, then refrigerate. Makes about 8 pints.

Storage time. *Processed:* Up to 1 year. *Unprocessed:* Up to 1 month in refrigerator.

Per ¼ cup: 38 calories, 1 g protein, 9 g carbohydrates, 0 g total fat, 0 mg cholesterol, 414 mg sodium

No-fuss Pickling

When you're craving homemade pickles but don't have time for canning, try one of these recipes. The first is for freezer pickles; the other two can be quickly put together and stored in the refrigerator.

Sweet Freezer Chips

- 2½ pounds pickling or regular cucumbers
- 1 medium-size mild white onion, thinly sliced
- 2 tablespoons salt
- 8 cups ice cubes
- 4 cups sugar
- 2 cups cider vinegar (5% acidity)

Cut ends from cucumbers; then cut cucumbers into ⅛-inch-thick slices. Mix cucumbers, onion, and salt in a large bowl; cover mixture with ice cubes and refrigerate for 2 to 3 hours.

Drain off water and discard unmelted ice cubes; do not rinse vegetables. Pack cucumber and onion slices into 3 pint freezer jars or freezer containers, leaving ½-inch headspace.

In a 2-quart pan, mix sugar and vinegar; bring to a boil, stirring until sugar is dissolved. Pour just enough hot syrup over cucumbers to cover. Apply lids; let cool. To allow flavor to develop, freeze pickles for at least 1 week before serving. To thaw, let stand in refrigerator for at least 8 hours. Makes 3 pints.

Storage time: Up to 6 months in freezer.

Per ¼ cup: 138 calories, 0 g protein, 36 g carbohydrates, 0 g total fat, 0 mg cholesterol, 551 mg sodium

Pickled Maui Onions

- 2 medium-size Maui or other mild white onions
- 1½ cups water
- ¾ cup distilled white vinegar (5% acidity)
- ⅓ cup sugar
- 3 cloves garlic, pressed or minced
- 2 small dried hot red chiles
- 1 tablespoon salt

Cut onions into 1-inch chunks; separate chunks into layers. Place onions in a wide-mouth quart (or slightly larger) jar. In a 1- to 2-quart pan, mix water, vinegar, sugar, garlic, chiles, and salt; bring to a boil. Pour over onions; apply a leakproof lid to jar. Let onions cool. To allow flavor to develop, refrigerate onions for at least 3 days before serving, turning jar over occasionally. To serve, pour into a bowl; provide wooden picks for spearing onion pieces. Makes about 4 cups.

Storage time. Up to 1 month in refrigerator.

Per ¼ cup: 32 calories, 1 g protein, 8 g carbohydrates, 0 g total fat, 0 mg cholesterol, 415 mg sodium

Quick Refrigerator Cucumber Pickles

- 8 or 9 pickling cucumbers (*each* 3 to 4 inches long), 3 large regular cucumbers, or 2 long thin-skinned (English or Armenian) cucumbers
- 1 large red bell pepper, seeded and cut into ½-inch-wide strips
- 1 medium-size onion, thinly sliced
- 1 tablespoon salt
- 2 teaspoons dill seeds
- ¾ cup sugar
- ½ cup white wine vinegar (5% acidity)

Cut ends from cucumbers, then cut cucumbers into ¹⁄₁₆-inch-thick slices; you should have about 6 cups. In a large bowl, combine cucumbers, bell pepper, and onion. Sprinkle with salt and dill seeds; then stir well. Let stand for 1 to 2 hours, stirring occasionally.

In a small bowl, mix sugar and vinegar, stirring until sugar is dissolved; pour vinegar mixture over vegetables and mix gently. Ladle vegetable mixture into 4 pint canning jars; apply lids. To allow flavor to develop, refrigerate for at least 24 hours before serving. Makes 4 pints.

Storage time. Up to 3 weeks in refrigerator.

Per ¼ cup: 24 calories, 0 g protein, 6 g carbohydrates, 0 g total fat, 0 mg cholesterol, 207 mg sodium

Pickle-packed Beets

Delicious in salads or on their own as a side dish, these beet and onion pickles make a festive gift.

- 6 to 8 medium-size beets (about 2 lbs. *total*)
- 1 medium-size mild white onion, thinly sliced
- 1 cup distilled white vinegar (5% acidity)
- ⅔ cup sugar
- 1 clove garlic, minced or pressed (optional)

Scrub beets well, but do not peel; leave roots, 1 inch of stems, and skins intact to prevent "bleeding" during cooking. Place beets in a 5-quart pan; add water to cover. Bring to a boil over high heat; cover and boil until beets are tender throughout when pierced (20 to 45 minutes). Drain; let cool. Holding beets under running water, trim off roots and stems and slip off skins. Cut beets into ¼-inch-thick slices.

Firmly pack beet and onion slices in alternating layers into wide-mouth pint canning jars. In a small bowl, mix vinegar, sugar, and garlic (if used); stir until sugar is dissolved, then pour over beets and onion to fill jars. Cover jars tightly and shake well. To allow flavor to develop, refrigerate pickles for at least 1 day before serving. Makes about 2 pints.

Storage time. Up to 3 weeks in refrigerator.

Per ¼ cup: 54 calories, 1 g protein, 14 g carbohydrates, 0 g total fat, 0 mg cholesterol, 29 mg sodium

Spiced Apple Rings

A jar of sweet, spicy apple rings is a wonderful, inexpensive gift. You'll find that the cheery red color brightens up meals at any time of year.

- 6 cups sugar
- 1⅔ cups cider vinegar (5% acidity)
- 1 teaspoon red food coloring (optional)
- 4 cinnamon sticks (*each* about 3 inches long)
- 2 teaspoons whole cloves
- 4 pounds (about 12 medium-size) firm-ripe Golden Delicious apples, peeled and cored

In a heavy-bottomed 8- to 10-quart stainless steel or unchipped enamel pan, mix sugar, vinegar, food coloring (if used), cinnamon sticks, and cloves. Bring to a boil over medium-high heat; then reduce heat and simmer, uncovered, stirring often, for 10 minutes.

Cut apples crosswise into ⅓-inch-thick rings. Add to simmering syrup and cook, uncovered, turning occasionally, until apples are barely tender when pierced and are just turning translucent around edges (6 to 8 minutes).

With a fork, lift apples from syrup; evenly fill prepared, hot wide-mouth pint jars, leaving ½-inch headspace. Leaving spices in pan, ladle hot syrup into jars, leaving ½-inch headspace. Gently run a narrow nonmetallic spatula between apples and jar sides to release air bubbles. Wipe rims and threads clean; top with hot lids, then firmly screw on bands. Process in boiling water canner for 10 minutes. Or omit processing; let stand for 12 to 24 hours at room temperature, then refrigerate. Makes about 4 pints.

Storage time. *Processed:* Up to 1 year. *Unprocessed:* Up to 1 month in refrigerator.

Per ¼ cup: 175 calories, 0 g protein, 45 g carbohydrates, 0 g total fat, 0 mg cholesterol, 1 mg sodium

Spiced Pineapple Spears

If you're looking for new ways to enjoy fresh pineapple, try these unusual, spicy spears.

- 3 medium-size pineapples (3 to 3½ lbs. *each*)
- 1½ cups distilled white vinegar (5% acidity)
- 2 cups sugar
- 2 tablespoons whole cloves
- 1 tablespoon whole cardamom, lightly crushed
- 1 teaspoon whole allspice
- 3 cinnamon sticks (*each* about 3 inches long)
- 1 small dried hot red chile, seeded

Peel and core pineapples, reserving as much juice as possible. Cut pineapples into 3-inch-long, ½-inch-thick spears. Set aside. Measure reserved juice; add enough water to make 1½ cups liquid. Pour liquid into a heavy-bottomed 8- to 10-quart stainless steel or unchipped enamel pan; stir in vinegar, sugar, cloves, cardamom, allspice, cinnamon sticks, and chile. Bring to a boil over high heat; reduce heat, cover, and simmer for 15 minutes. Add half the pineapple spears; cover and simmer for 5 more minutes.

With a fork, lift spears from syrup and fill 2 prepared, hot wide-mouth pint jars, leaving ½-inch headspace. Leaving spices in pan, ladle hot syrup into jars, leaving ½-inch headspace. Gently run a narrow nonmetallic spatula between pineapple and jar sides to release air bubbles. Wipe rims and threads clean; top with hot lids, then firmly screw on bands.

Add remaining spears to syrup. Cover; simmer for 5 minutes. Fill 2 more jars as directed above.

Process in boiling water canner for 10 minutes. Or omit processing; let stand for 12 to 24 hours at room temperature, then refrigerate. Makes 4 pints.

Storage time. *Processed:* Up to 1 year. *Unprocessed:* Up to 1 month in refrigerator.

Per ¼ cup: 88 calories, 0 g protein, 23 g carbohydrates, 0 g total fat, 0 mg cholesterol, 2 mg sodium

Refrigerator Corn Relish

Pictured on page 154

A quick refrigerator version of an old-fashioned favorite, this colorful relish is a popular appetizer at picnics and barbecues—and a favorite accompaniment for frankfurters, hamburgers, and other meats.

- 1¼ cups distilled white vinegar (5% acidity)
- ¾ cup sugar
- 2½ teaspoons salt
- 1¼ teaspoons celery seeds
- ¾ teaspoon mustard seeds
- ½ teaspoon liquid hot pepper seasoning
- 8 cups fresh corn kernels (cut from about 10 large ears of corn)
- 1 *each* small green and red bell pepper, seeded and chopped
- 3 green onions, thinly sliced

In a heavy-bottomed 8- to 10-quart stainless steel or unchipped enamel pan, mix vinegar, sugar, salt, celery seeds, mustard seeds, hot pepper seasoning, and corn. Bring to a simmer over medium heat; simmer, uncovered, for 5 minutes. Remove from heat and let cool.

Stir bell peppers and onions into corn mixture. Pack into pint jars; cover tightly and refrigerate. Makes about 4 pints.

Storage time. Up to 1 month in refrigerator.

Per ¼ cup: 54 calories, 1 g protein, 13 g carbohydrates, 0 g total fat, 0 mg cholesterol, 180 mg sodium

Pickled Jicama

Enjoy crisp jicama in a piquant refrigerator pickle accented with cilantro, red pepper, dill, and mustard seeds.

- 2 pounds jicama, peeled and cut into 5-inch-long, ½-inch-thick sticks
- 4 teaspoons canning salt or noniodized table salt
- 1½ cups distilled white vinegar (5% acidity)
- ½ cup finely chopped onion
- ⅓ cup sugar
- 1 teaspoon *each* mustard seeds and dry dill weed
- ½ teaspoon crushed red pepper flakes
- 6 cilantro sprigs

Place jicama in a stainless steel, glass, or unchipped enamel bowl. Sprinkle with 1 tablespoon of the salt, then add enough water to cover. Stir until salt is dissolved, then let stand for 1 to 2 hours. Drain.

In a 2- to 3-quart stainless steel or unchipped enamel pan, mix vinegar, remaining 1 teaspoon salt, onion, and sugar. Bring to a boil over high heat; then boil for 1 minute.

Meanwhile, pack jicama sticks vertically into 2 hot wide-mouth pint jars. Place half *each* of the mustard seeds, dill weed, red pepper flakes, and cilantro in each jar. Pour hot vinegar solution into jars to cover jicama. Let cool, then cover jars tightly. To allow flavor to develop, refrigerate pickles for at least 1 day before serving. Makes 2 pints.

Storage time. Up to 1 month in refrigerator.

Per ¼ cup: 44 calories, 1 g protein, 10 g carbohydrates, 0 g total fat, 0 mg cholesterol, 554 mg sodium

Cranberry-Pear Relish

Add sparkle to your holidays with a zesty cranberry-pear relish that goes beautifully with turkey, baked ham, or roast pork (it's good in sandwiches, too). You'll want to make another batch as gifts for special friends.

- 3 pounds pears, peeled, cored, and cut into about 1-inch chunks
- 6 cups (about 1½ lbs.) fresh or frozen cranberries
- 2½ cups firmly packed brown sugar
- 1 cup orange juice
- ½ cup cider vinegar (5% acidity)
- 2 teaspoons minced fresh ginger

Coarsely chop pear chunks and cranberries by hand or in a food processor (do not purée). In a heavy-bottomed 8- to 10-quart pan, mix pears, cranberries, sugar, orange juice, vinegar, and ginger. Bring to a boil over medium-high heat, stirring constantly; then reduce heat and simmer, uncovered, stirring often to prevent sticking, until pears are tender to bite and relish is thickened (about 20 minutes).

Ladle hot relish into prepared, hot pint jars, leaving ½-inch headspace. Gently run a narrow nonmetallic spatula between relish and jar sides to release air bubbles. Wipe rims and threads clean; top with hot lids, then firmly screw on bands. Process in boiling water canner for 10 minutes. Or omit processing and ladle into jars or refrigerator containers, leaving ½-inch headspace; apply lids. Let cool, then refrigerate. Makes about 4 pints.

Storage time. *Processed:* Up to 1 year. *Unprocessed:* Up to 3 weeks in refrigerator.

Per ¼ cup: 101 calories, 0 g protein, 26 g carbohydrates, 0 g total fat, 0 mg cholesterol, 5 mg sodium

Plum Relish

Luscious flavor and attractive color make this sweet fruit relish a real standout. Serve it with baked ham, pork chops, grilled or roasted poultry, or curries.

- 2 **medium-size oranges**
- 5 **pounds plums, pitted and finely chopped**
- 3 **cups sugar**
- 1 **cup cider vinegar (5% acidity)**
- 1 **teaspoon ground cinnamon**

Rinse unpeeled oranges and grate off peel (colored part only); set peel aside. Holding fruit over a bowl to catch juice, cut off and discard remaining peel and all white membrane from oranges; coarsely chop fruit, discarding seeds.

In a heavy-bottomed 8- to 10-quart pan, mix grated orange peel, chopped oranges (plus any juice), plums, sugar, vinegar, and cinnamon. Bring to a boil over medium-high heat, stirring constantly; reduce heat and simmer, uncovered, stirring often to prevent sticking, until thickened (about 40 minutes).

Ladle hot relish into prepared, hot pint jars, leaving ½-inch headspace. Gently run a narrow nonmetallic spatula between relish and jar sides to release air bubbles. Wipe rims and threads clean; top with hot lids, then firmly screw on bands. Process in boiling water canner for 10 minutes. Or omit processing and ladle into jars or refrigerator containers, leaving ½-inch headspace; apply lids. Let cool, then refrigerate. Makes about 4 pints.

Storage time. *Processed:* Up to 1 year. *Unprocessed:* Up to 1 month in refrigerator.

Per ¼ cup: 116 calories, 1 g protein, 29 g carbohydrates, 0 g total fat, 0 mg cholesterol, 0 mg sodium

Red Pepper Relish

Pictured on page 154

This delicious blend of sweet red peppers and onions is a delightful gift—and a fantastic accompaniment to any grilled meat or poultry.

- 6 **pounds red bell peppers, seeded and cut into 1-inch squares**
- 3 **pounds onions, cut into 1-inch chunks**
- 4 **cups distilled white vinegar (5% acidity)**
- 3 **cups sugar**
- 2 **tablespoons canning salt or noniodized table salt**
- 1 **tablespoon mustard seeds**

Coarsely chop bell peppers and onions, a portion at a time, in a food processor; or put through a food chopper with a medium blade. Pour chopped vegetables into a heavy-bottomed 8- to 10-quart stainless steel or unchipped enamel pan. Mix in vinegar, sugar, salt, and mustard seeds. Bring to a boil over medium-high heat, stirring occasionally. Reduce heat to medium-low; boil gently, uncovered, stirring often to prevent sticking, until relish is thickened but still juicy (about 50 minutes).

Ladle hot relish into prepared, hot pint jars, leaving ½-inch headspace. Gently run a narrow nonmetallic spatula between relish and jar sides to release air bubbles. Wipe rims and threads clean; top with hot lids, then firmly screw on bands. Process in boiling water canner for 15 minutes. Or omit processing and ladle into jars or refrigerator containers, leaving ½-inch headspace; apply lids. Let cool, then refrigerate. Makes about 7 pints.

Storage time. *Processed:* Up to 1 year. *Unprocessed:* Up to 1 month in refrigerator.

Per ¼ cup: 63 calories, 1 g protein, 16 g carbohydrates, 0 g total fat, 0 mg cholesterol, 237 mg sodium

Papaya-Tomatillo Relish

Sweet papayas and tart tomatillos combine in this unique fruit relish. Try it hot or cold, with grilled lamb, pork chops, hamburgers, stews, or curries.

- 1 **tablespoon salad oil**
- ½ **small onion, thinly sliced**
- ¼ **teaspoon ground cinnamon**
- ⅛ **teaspoon ground red pepper (cayenne)**
- 1 **pound fresh tomatillos, husked, cored, and finely chopped**
- 1 **small ripe papaya (about ¾ lb.), peeled, seeded, and cut into ¼-inch chunks**
- ⅓ **cup cider vinegar (5% acidity)**
- ¼ **cup *each* firmly packed brown sugar and dried currants**

Heat oil in a wide frying pan over medium heat. Add onion, cinnamon, and red pepper; cook, stirring often, until onion is soft (about 7 minutes). Add tomatillos, papaya, vinegar, sugar, and currants. Bring to a boil over high heat; then boil, uncovered, stirring occasionally, until liquid has evaporated. Pack into hot half-pint jars or into a refrigerator container; cover tightly and refrigerate. Makes about 2 half-pints.

Storage time. Up to 3 weeks in refrigerator.

Per ¼ cup: 81 calories, 1 g protein, 16 g carbohydrates, 2 g total fat, 0 mg cholesterol, 3 mg sodium

Whole Cranberry–Orange Sauce

Traditional, tart, and luscious, this whole-berry cranberry sauce is accented with orange juice and sweetened with brown sugar.

- **4** cups (about 1 lb.) fresh or frozen cranberries
- **2** cups firmly packed brown sugar
- **3** tablespoons frozen orange juice concentrate, thawed
- **1¼** cups water

In a heavy-bottomed 6- to 8-quart pan, mix cranberries, sugar, orange juice concentrate, and water. Bring to a boil over high heat, stirring occasionally; then boil, uncovered, stirring occasionally, until almost all berries have split open (about 5 minutes).

Ladle hot sauce into prepared, hot half-pint or pint jars, leaving ½-inch headspace. Gently run a narrow nonmetallic spatula between sauce and jar sides to release air bubbles. Wipe rims and threads clean; top with hot lids, then firmly screw on bands. Process in boiling water canner for 10 minutes. Or omit processing and ladle into jars or refrigerator containers, leaving ½-inch headspace; apply lids. Let cool, then refrigerate. Makes about 4 half-pints or 2 pints.

Storage time. *Processed:* Up to 1 year. *Unprocessed:* Up to 3 weeks in refrigerator.

Per ¼ cup: 122 calories, 0 g protein, 31 g carbohydrates, 0 g total fat, 0 mg cholesterol, 9 mg sodium

Pear-Ginger Chutney

You'll enjoy this easy-to-make chutney with roast chicken or pork—and with curry, of course.

- **1** small lemon
- **1½** cups *each* sugar and cider vinegar (5% acidity)
- **½** cup *each* chopped onion and dried currants
- **1** clove garlic, minced or pressed
- **3** tablespoons minced fresh ginger
- **½** teaspoon ground allspice
- **5** pounds (about 10 large) firm-ripe Bartlett pears, peeled, cored, and cut into ¾-inch chunks

Rinse unpeeled lemon, then thinly slice; discard seeds. Place lemon slices in a heavy-bottomed 8- to 10-quart stainless steel or unchipped enamel pan and mix in sugar, vinegar, onion, currants, garlic, ginger, and allspice. Bring to a boil over medium-high heat, stirring occasionally. Reduce heat to medium-low and simmer, uncovered, stirring often, until a thin

syrup forms (about 15 minutes). Add pears; continue to cook, uncovered, stirring occasionally, until chutney is thickened (about 1¼ hours).

Ladle hot chutney into prepared, hot pint jars, leaving ½-inch headspace. Gently run a narrow nonmetallic spatula between chutney and jar sides to release air bubbles. Wipe rims and threads clean; top with hot lids, then firmly screw on bands. Process in boiling water canner for 15 minutes. Or omit processing and ladle into jars or refrigerator containers, leaving ½-inch headspace; apply lids. Let cool, then refrigerate. Makes about 3 pints.

Storage time. *Processed:* Up to 1 year. *Unprocessed:* Up to 3 weeks in refrigerator.

Per ¼ cup: 113 calories, 1 g protein, 30 g carbohydrates, 1 g total fat, 0 mg cholesterol, 1 mg sodium

Mango-Peach Chutney

Pictured on page 154

Mangoes make a delicious chutney. To reduce the cost, just extend the mangoes with fresh peaches in season.

- **1** lime
- **1½** cups *each* sugar and distilled white vinegar (5% acidity)
- **½** cup chopped onion
- **1** clove garlic, minced or pressed
- **1½** teaspoons ground cinnamon
- **1** teaspoon salt
- **½** teaspoon *each* ground cloves and allspice
- **⅛** to ¼ teaspoon ground red pepper (cayenne)
- **½** cup raisins
- **3** large ripe mangoes (about 2½ lbs. *total*)
- **2** pounds peaches

Rinse unpeeled lime, then thinly slice; discard seeds. Place lime slices in a heavy-bottomed 8- to 10-quart pan; mix in sugar, vinegar, onion, garlic, cinnamon, salt, cloves, allspice, red pepper, and raisins. Bring to a boil over high heat; then reduce heat to medium-low and simmer, uncovered, stirring occasionally to prevent sticking, until onion is limp and syrup is slightly thickened (about 15 minutes).

Meanwhile, peel mangoes; slice fruit off pits and cut into 1½-inch pieces (you should have about 3½ cups). Peel, pit, and slice peaches. Add mangoes and peaches to syrup and simmer, uncovered, stirring often to prevent sticking, until peaches are tender when pierced and chutney is thickened (about 30 minutes).

Ladle hot chutney into prepared, hot pint jars, leaving ½-inch headspace. Gently run a narrow nonmetallic spatula between chutney and jar sides to release air bubbles. Wipe rims and threads clean; top with hot lids, then firmly screw on bands. Process in boiling water canner for 15 minutes. Or omit processing and ladle into jars or refrigerator containers, leaving ½-inch headspace; apply lids. Let cool, then refrigerate. Makes about 3 pints.

Storage time. *Processed:* Up to 1 year. *Unprocessed:* Up to 3 weeks in refrigerator.

Per ¼ cup: 96 calories, 0 g protein, 25 g carbohydrates, 0 g total fat, 0 mg cholesterol, 93 mg sodium

Apricot Chutney

Pictured on page 146

This medium-hot chutney is superb with curries, lamb, and cheese. For a milder version, remove the seeds from the chiles before crushing them (or use fewer chiles than the recipe specifies).

    1 small lime
    1 cup *each* granulated sugar, firmly packed brown
       sugar, dried currants, and cider vinegar (5%
       acidity)
    1 tablespoon minced fresh ginger or ¾ teaspoon
       ground ginger
    1 teaspoon *each* dry mustard and ground allspice
    ¼ teaspoon salt
       Dash of ground cloves
    3 small dried hot red chiles, crushed
    ½ cup chopped onion
    1 small clove garlic, minced or pressed
    4 pounds apricots, pitted and quartered

Rinse unpeeled lime; then chop, discarding seeds. Place chopped lime in a heavy-bottomed 8- to 10-quart pan; mix in granulated sugar, brown sugar, currants, vinegar, ginger, mustard, allspice, salt, cloves, chiles, onion, and garlic. Bring to a boil over medium-high heat. Stir in apricots; return to a boil, stirring constantly. Reduce heat and simmer, uncovered, stirring often to prevent sticking, until slightly thickened (about 45 minutes).

   Ladle hot chutney into prepared, hot pint jars, leaving ½-inch headspace. Gently run a narrow nonmetallic spatula between chutney and jar sides to release air bubbles. Wipe rims and threads clean; top with hot lids, then firmly screw on bands. Process in boiling water canner for 15 minutes. Or omit processing and ladle into jars or refrigerator containers, leaving ½-inch headspace; apply lids. Let cool, then refrigerate. Makes about 4 pints.

Storage time. *Processed:* Up to 1 year. *Unprocessed:* Up to 1 month in refrigerator.

Per ¼ cup: 93 calories, 1 g protein, 23 g carbohydrates, 0 g total fat, 0 mg cholesterol, 3 mg sodium

Papaya-Plum Chutney

Pictured on page 154

Colorful papayas and red plums combine with raisins and sweet spices in an exotic-tasting chutney you'll enjoy all year round with curries, game, and poultry.

    1¼ cups cider vinegar (5% acidity)
    1¾ cups sugar
     ½ cup golden raisins
      2 cloves garlic, minced or pressed
      3 tablespoons chopped crystallized ginger
      1 cinnamon stick (about 3 inches long)
      1 teaspoon salt
     ⅛ to ¼ teaspoon ground red pepper (cayenne)
      2 medium-size ripe papayas (about 1 lb. *each*)
      2 pounds red plums

In a heavy-bottomed 8- to 10-quart pan, mix vinegar, sugar, raisins, garlic, ginger, cinnamon stick, salt, and red pepper. Bring to a boil over high heat, stirring often. Reduce heat to medium-low and simmer, uncovered, stirring occasionally to prevent sticking, until syrup is slightly thickened (about 15 minutes).

   Peel and halve papayas; scoop out seeds. Cut fruit into ½-inch chunks. Pit and quarter plums. Add papayas and plums to syrup and continue to simmer, uncovered, stirring occasionally, until papaya is tender when pierced and chutney is thickened (about 35 minutes). Discard cinnamon stick.

   Ladle hot chutney into prepared, hot pint jars, leaving ½-inch headspace. Gently run a narrow nonmetallic spatula between chutney and jar sides to release air bubbles. Wipe rims and threads clean; top with hot lids, then firmly screw on bands. Process in boiling water canner for 15 minutes. Or omit processing and ladle into jars or refrigerator containers, leaving ½-inch headspace; apply lids. Let cool, then refrigerate. Makes about 3 pints.

Storage time. *Processed:* Up to 1 year. *Unprocessed:* Up to 1 month in refrigerator.

Per ¼ cup: 104 calories, 1 g protein, 27 g carbohydrates, 0 g total fat, 0 mg cholesterol, 94 mg sodium

Questions & Answers

About canning...

Q. **Why do jars break during canning?**

A. Several explanations are possible. Jars with hairline cracks are likely to break during processing, as are commercial food jars (as opposed to those manufactured expressly for home canning). Breakage may also occur if hot food is placed in a cold jar, or when jars of unheated food are placed directly in boiling water in the canner.

Q. **What foods may be safely canned in a boiling water canner?**

A. All acid foods, such as fruits, acidified tomatoes, pickles, relishes, jams, and jellies.

Q. **What foods must always be canned in a pressure canner?**

A. All vegetables (except acidified tomatoes and pickled vegetables), meat, poultry, and seafood.

Q. **Is it normal for lids to make a popping sound after jars are removed from the canning kettle?**

A. Yes. The "pop" indicates that the sealing process is complete.

Q. **Is it all right to reuse canning lids?**

A. No. Because the sealing compound is damaged by the first use, lids may not seal again. Ring bands, however, may be used repeatedly if they're in good shape.

Q. **Can foods be processed in an oven or microwave oven?**

A. No. Jars may explode in conventional ovens; and in both conventional and microwave ovens, the bottled food may not heat evenly, possibly leading to spoilage.

Q. **Can food be reprocessed if the lid does not seal?**

A. Yes—as long as you reprocess within 24 hours. To reprocess, remove the lid and check the jar sealing surface for tiny nicks. If the jar is not flawed, just add a new lid; if it is flawed, reheat the food and pack it into a prepared, hot new jar, then apply a new lid. Reprocess, using the same processing time. (You may notice changes in the food's color and texture.)

Q. **What makes the undersides of metal canning lids turn dark?**

A. The natural acids and salts in some foods may corrode the metal, causing harmless brown or black deposits to form under the lid.

Q. **Is it all right to let jars cool in the boiling water canner in which they were processed?**

A. No. The food will keep right on cooking in the water—and will end up overcooked.

Q. **When foods are canned in half-pint jars, can processing time be reduced?**

A. No. You must process half-pints for the same amount of time as pints.

Q. **What causes sealed jars to come open during storage?**

A. Such failures may result from gas produced by microbes still alive in the food; in low-acid foods, it may indicate the growth of botulism bacteria. *Never eat food from such jars.*

About fruit...

Q. **Do fruits have to be canned in syrups made with white sugar?**

A. No. Fruit juice, water, or syrups made with honey may be used instead. Sugar improves flavor, stabilizes color, and helps fruit retain its shape. But fruit juice, particularly juice from the fruit being canned, is an excellent choice. (Commercial unsweetened juices are also good.) Honey often masks fruit flavor, so it's best not to substitute honey for more than half the sugar called for in a syrup. Water-packed fruit tends to be inferior in flavor, texture, and color.

Q. **When is ascorbic acid required during preparation for canning?**

A. When you're preparing any fruit that darkens when cut—apples, pears, peaches, and apricots, for example. Ascorbic acid (vitamin C), an antidarkening agent, retards the oxidation that browns these fruits.

Q. What causes fruits to float?

A. The syrup used may have been too heavy; or the fruit may have been overripe or packed too loosely into the jar. Hot-packed fruit is less likely to float.

Q. Why does fruit sometimes darken at the top of the jar?

A. Prepared cut fruit may have been exposed to the air too long, or it may not have been covered by liquid in the jar. This kind of darkening may also result if headspace is too great or if air bubbles are left in the jar.

About jams and jellies...

Q. Is it all right to double a favorite jam recipe?

A. No—you're inviting trouble. The larger quantity of fruit and juice requires too long a boiling period, destroying pectin and resulting in a product that will not jell.

Q. Should jelly be boiled slowly or rapidly?

A. Boil it rapidly. Slow boiling destroys the pectin in fruit juice.

Q. Why is my jelly too soft?

A. The mixture may have had too much juice, too much acid, or too little sugar; or it may have been heated too slowly for too long.

Q. Why is my jelly syrupy?

A. The mixture may have too little pectin or acid, or too much or too little sugar. Or you may have doubled the batch.

Q. Why is my jelly too stiff?

A. You may have used too much pectin or fruit that wasn't ripe enough; overcooking is another possible cause. Reduced-sugar jellies and jams made with modified ("light") pectins also tend to be stiff.

Q. Why is my jelly cloudy?

A. Jelly that stands too long before being poured into the jars may turn out cloudy. Cloudy jelly can also result if you didn't strain the juice well enough or if you squeezed the jelly bag; if you used underripe fruit; if

you cooked your jelly too long; or if you used a pectin containing an artificial sweetener.

About pickles...

Q. Why are my pickles hollow?

A. You may have used regular slicing cucumbers rather than pickling cucumbers; or the cucumbers may have been overmature or simply have had faulty growth. Or you may have waited too long between harvesting and pickling.

Q. What causes pickles to turn dark?

A. Minerals such as iron may have been present in the water or vinegar; or iron, zinc, copper, or brass utensils may have been used. Iodized table salt and ground spices will also cause darkening.

Q. Why did the garlic cloves in my pickles turn bluish green?

A. If metals such as iron, tin, or aluminum are present in your pans, water, or water pipes, they may react with pigments in the garlic to cause a color change. Some garlic has a naturally bluish tinge that becomes more evident after pickling. In any case, don't worry. Your pickles are safe to eat.

About vegetables...

Q. Are the vegetables safe to eat if the liquid in the jars has turned cloudy?

A. No. Spoilage may have occurred, and the food should not be eaten. See "Guarding against Botulism" (page 25) for information on how to dispose of spoiled food.

Q. Must I sterilize glass jars before canning vegetables and fruits?

A. No, not if you plan to process them in a pressure canner, or for 10 minutes or more in a boiling water canner. Just make sure they're clean—and to prevent breakage, rinse them with hot water before filling with hot food. But yes, you must sterilize jars by boiling them in water for 10 minutes if they will be processed for less than 10 minutes in a boiling water canner.

Q. Which vegetables should be packed loosely?

A. Corn, peas, and lima beans, all of which expand.

Freezing

Fresh-tasting foods for quick, convenient meals

*I*f you're like many busy cooks today, you've probably wondered how you'd ever manage without your freezer. ● Freezing is a great way to stock up on wholesome, delicious foods for your family. It lets you preserve fruit from your own trees, vegetables from your own garden, and made-from-scratch soups, sauces, main dishes, and desserts from your own kitchen. We offer a few recipes that freeze beautifully on pages 182 and 184, and you'll find many other superb choices—jams, preserves, chutneys, relishes, freezer pickles, and more—in earlier chapters. ● Of course, you'll want to keep some commercially frozen items on hand—but for most cooks, home-frozen foods have pride of place in the freezer. ● When you consider what to freeze, keep in mind what you like and how much food you really need. For help in choosing the best local fruit and vegetable varieties for freezing, consult your local Cooperative Extension office. ● Whatever you freeze, always start with top-quality foods and handle them under the most sanitary conditions. And to ensure that the quality stays high after thawing, use all frozen foods within the recommended storage time.

What Happens in Freezing?

When food is frozen quickly, its natural color and flavor are preserved. And as long as it's kept solidly frozen throughout the storage period, it won't spoil: bacteria, yeasts, and molds can't grow, and oxidation and enzyme activity slow down. Once food begins to thaw, however, enzyme action and growth of micro-organisms resume.

Freezing Basics

For successful home freezing, you'll need to follow a few simple rules.

Begin with quality. Freezing maintains quality, but can't improve it—so start with the best, freshest food you can find. Then prepare it under sanitary conditions and store it at 0°F or below.

Freeze it fast. During the freezing process, the water in food forms ice crystals that can puncture cell walls. If such puncturing occurs, the food's natural juices run out during thawing, resulting in a mushy texture. The faster food freezes, the smaller the ice crystals—and the better the texture upon thawing. To ensure quick freezing, turn the freezer to its coldest setting a day before freezing a significant amount of food; then place foods in a single layer in the coldest part of the freezer until frozen. To determine which shelves or positions are coldest, check the manufacturer's instructions. You'll usually use the nonremovable shelves in upright freezers; in chest freezers, a small compartment at one end is typically the coldest area. Once the foods are frozen solid, return the freezer setting to 0°F.

Changes in texture after thawing are most noticeable in fruits and vegetables with a high water content. Tomatoes, for example, always turn to mush if frozen raw, so it's best to cook them before freezing. If you're absolutely swamped with tomatoes, you can package and freeze some of them raw for cooking or seasoning, but you'll need to use them within 2 to 3 weeks; they deteriorate rapidly. To peel frozen tomatoes, hold them under cold water for a second or two; then slip off the skins.

Control enzyme activity. Though the freezing process naturally slows enzyme action, it doesn't work rapidly enough to preserve top quality. Thus, if vegetables and fruits are to maintain good flavor and color during storage, most of the enzymes they contain must be inactivated *before* freezing. In the case of vegetables, inactivation can be achieved by heat treatment (blanching). Blanching typically involves immersing the vegetable in boiling water for a short time, but you can also blanch vegetables in steam or in a microwave oven. To control enzyme activity in fruits, add an antioxidant (see "Protecting Fruit Colors," page 179) and sugar.

Prevent freezer burn. When frozen foods aren't packaged correctly, evaporation from the surface produces *freezer burn:* brownish or whitish areas that are dry, tough, and grainy. Foods damaged in this way are still safe to eat, but their texture is unappealing and they're less flavorful than properly stored foods. To prevent freezer burn, seal foods airtight in moisture- and vaporproof materials specifically designed for use in the freezer (see "Choosing the Right Packaging," page 172).

Avoid overload. Overloading your freezer slows down the freezing process, resulting in poor quality after thawing. Consult the manufacturer's guidelines for the maximum amount you can freeze at one time; typical freezers can handle no more than 2 pounds of food per cubic foot of space per 24 hours.

Avoid partial thawing and refreezing. Fluctuating temperatures cause the ice crystals in frozen foods to begin melting, then refreeze. With each such cycle, the crystals grow larger, damaging cell walls further and resulting in mushy thawed food. (Manual-defrost freezers maintain a more uniform temperature than frostless types do.)

About Your Freezer

A freezer is a long-term investment, so make your choice carefully. Consider the size of your family, how much (and what) you produce in your garden, and your available floor space.

Which Size to Buy?

Freezers come in many sizes, usually stated in cubic feet. Larger models are more energy efficient—*if* you use the space (obviously, you're wasting electricity if you're simply cooling empty shelves). You'll also save energy if you fill and empty your freezer several times a year; doing so just once annually raises your energy cost per package of food.

Which Type to Buy?

The three freezer types most commonly available are upright, chest, and freezer-refrigerator combinations. Units to be used for long-term storage must maintain a temperature of 0°F; some models (both newer and older types) do not, so check carefully with the salesperson before you buy.

Upright freezers are easy to load and unpack, and they take little floor space. However, a fair amount of cold air escapes each time you open the door.

Chest freezers are less expensive to buy and operate than are upright models, and they lose less cold air when opened. They do have drawbacks, though; they require more space than upright freezers, and they're difficult to load and unload unless equipped with lift-out or sliding baskets.

Freezer-refrigerator combinations, commonly found in most kitchens, vary in freezing reliability and efficiency. To maintain the ideal temperature of 0°F required for long-term food storage, the freezer component must be a true freezer, not merely a freezing compartment in the refrigerator.

Choosing the Right Packaging

The way a food is packaged directly affects its quality when thawed. The packaging you use should always be:

■ moisture- and vaporproof, odorless, and tasteless;

■ capable of protecting foods against absorption of "off" flavors and odors;

■ easy to seal;

■ easy to mark;

■ suitable in size;

■ in the case of wrappings, durable and pliable at low temperatures.

Two basic types of freezer packaging materials meet these criteria: first, rigid containers; and second, flexible bags and wraps.

Rigid plastic or glass containers are appropriate for freezing many foods, and most are reusable. In general, you need not leave headspace if you're filling the containers with dry foods or individually frozen pieces of food—but in all other cases, leave ½-inch headspace for pints, 1 inch for quarts. Always make sure the container lid fits tightly; if necessary, use freezer tape—designed to remain sticky at low temperatures—to reinforce the seal.

If you use plastic containers, you can usually transfer them directly from the freezer to a microwave oven to thaw the contents; just be sure to remove any tape from the container before microwaving.

Among glass containers, wide-mouth dual-purpose freezer/canning jars are the best choice. The sides are sloped, so the jar contents slide upward as they expand during freezing, and the wide openings make it easy to remove partially frozen food. Regular glass canning jars are another possibility, but don't use them for foods packed in water; water expands so much that it may crack or break the glass. Do not thaw foods stored in glass in a microwave oven, since microwaving can break jars.

Avoid freezing foods in cardboard cartons used for ice cream and milk. Unless you line them with a freezer bag or wrap, most of these aren't sufficiently moisture- and vaporproof for long-term storage.

Flexible freezer bags & wraps are good for packaging irregularly shaped foods.

Plastic freezer bags, designed especially for freezing, come in various sizes. *Never* use garbage or trash bags, since these contain chemicals not approved for use with foods. Once a bag has been filled, press out any air, beginning from the bottom of the bag and moving toward the top to prevent air from reentering. Then close the bags tightly, leaving ½-inch headspace. To make stacking easier, place the filled bags flat on the freezer shelves until they're solidly frozen; then stack.

Freezer wraps include plastic wrap, various types of coated or laminated freezer papers, and heavy-duty foil. If you use foil, keep in mind that it's relatively expensive, tears and punctures easily, and may pit if used with acid foods. Shape the wrap around the food to exclude as much air as possible; seal packages with freezer tape.

Thawing & Refreezing

Though some foods to be cooked can go straight from freezer to oven, most must be partially or completely thawed before use. When you thaw any food, leave it in its sealed package (unless otherwise instructed) to preserve nutrients and prevent darkening.

Thaw all poultry, meat, fish, and dairy products in the refrigerator; or thaw them in a microwave oven just prior to preparation. *Do not* defrost these foods at room temperature. Vegetables may be steamed or boiled still frozen; you may also thaw them in the refrigerator (but *not* at room temperature). Fruits are best thawed in the refrigerator, though you may thaw them at room temperature if they'll thaw in 2 hours or less. Baked goods such as bread and cookies may safely be thawed at room temperature.

Thaw only enough food for one meal, and once it's thawed, use it immediately. Don't hesitate to discard any food that smells or tastes odd: it could contain harmful microorganisms.

Food that has been partially thawed—whether intentionally or simply due to a freezer failure—may be refrozen as long as it still feels cold and contains ice crystals. Remember, though, that refrozen food will lose some quality and should be used as quickly as possible.

What about Power Failures?

If you have advance warning of a brownout or blackout, immediately turn your freezer to the coldest setting: the lower the temperature, the longer the food will stay frozen. A fully packed freezer will usually keep food frozen for 48 hours after a power failure, provided you avoid opening and closing the freezer door. Half-full freezers may not remain cold for over 24 hours.

Adding dry ice to your freezer helps food stay frozen longer. If added as soon as possible after the power goes off, a 50-pound quantity should keep the food temperature in a 20-cubic-foot freezer below freezing for 3 to 4 days in a full freezer, 2 to 3 days in a half-full (or emptier) one. Have the vendor prepare the ice for you in 2- to 3-inch pieces, and don't place these directly on packaged food. Instead, cover the food with heavy cardboard and arrange the ice on that. Don't touch dry ice with your bare hands; wear heavy gloves. Open the freezer door only to take food out or to add more dry ice. And to avoid any risk of carbon dioxide accumulation, make sure the room is well ventilated.

Tips for the Best Frozen Foods

As noted in "Freezing Basics" (page 171), it's crucial to start with fresh, top-quality products and to work under sanitary conditions. Also keep these hints in mind:

■ For each food, follow the relevant directions in the guides for freezing prepared foods, fruits, and vegetables. The instructions will tell you if the food should be packed dry or with added liquid; if it requires blanching or precooking; and if you need to add an antidarkening agent.

■ Pack foods tightly, leaving as little air in the package as possible. Leave the appropriate headspace, then seal securely; you may need to reinforce lids of rigid containers with freezer tape.

■ Label packages with the name of the product, the date, and the amount or number of servings.

■ Freeze packaged food immediately, placing food in single layers in the coldest part of your freezer (see "Freeze it fast," page 171). Leave a little space for air

circulation between and around packages. Once the packages are frozen, you can set them closer together or stack them.

■ Maintain a freezer temperature of 0°F or lower at all times. A freezer thermometer is invaluable in checking for the proper temperature.

■ Keep an inventory of the foods stored in your freezer; use them within the recommended storage period.

Foods That Don't Freeze Well

Certain foods do not freeze successfully and should not be stored in the freezer. Some of these are listed below.

FOOD	UNDESIRABLE CHARACTERISTICS WHEN THAWED
Cabbage, celery, cucumbers, radishes, salad greens	Waterlogged, limp, poor color and flavor
Cheese or crumb toppings for casseroles	Cheese turns tough, stringy; crumbs are soggy
Cream & custard fillings	Separated, lumpy, watery
Egg whites, cooked	Rubbery, tough
Fried foods	Less crisp or soggy
Gelatin	Tough; tends to weep
Icing containing egg whites	Tends to weep
Jam, jelly in sandwiches	Bread may be soaked
Mayonnaise, salad dressing	Separated
Meringue (in desserts)	Tough
Pasta, cooked	Rubbery, mushy, altered flavor
Potatoes, cooked	Waterlogged, soft, mealy
Rice, cooked	Mushy, altered flavor
Sauces made with milk	Separated or curdled
Sour cream, yogurt	Separated, watery

Guide for Freezing Prepared Foods

When you freeze foods such as soups, stews, or any other saucy or liquid mixture (creamed fish, for example), always leave headspace in the bag or container. In general, leave ½-inch headspace for pint containers, 1-inch headspace for quarts. If packing foods in plastic freezer bags, leave ½-inch headspace.

Dry foods and individually frozen food pieces do not require headspace.

When reheating foods in a microwave oven, *do not* heat them in freezer jars—the glass may break. You may, however, safely microwave foods frozen in most rigid plastic freezer containers.

Food	How to prepare & package	Freezer storage time at 0°F*	How to serve
Appetizers Cream puff shells; cheese rolls; cheese balls; open-faced sandwiches and canapés; dips, spreads, and fillings that contain cooked ham, seafood, cooked egg yolk mixtures, cheese, and avocado	Do not freeze appetizers that include mayonnaise, sour cream, yogurt, cooked egg whites, crisp vegetables, or tomatoes. Prepare other appetizers as usual, but do not combine cream puff shells or crisp toast bases with fillings before freezing. Freeze dips, spreads, and fillings in rigid freezer containers; freeze other appetizers in single layers on trays until solid, then tightly pack individually or in small quantities in moisture- and vaporproof plastic wrap, plastic freezer bags, heavy-duty foil, or shallow rigid freezer containers. Pack cream puff shells and crisp-base appetizers separately from other appetizers.	2 to 4 weeks	Thaw cream puff shells and crisp toast bases, still wrapped, for 2 to 3 hours at room temperature. You may need to recrisp them in the oven before serving. Thaw dips, spreads, and fillings in their containers in the refrigerator. Thaw appetizers containing meat, seafood, or vegetables, still wrapped, in the refrigerator. Unwrap other appetizers, arrange on serving trays, and thaw for about 1 hour at room temperature.
Biscuits	Prepare as usual and bake until light brown; let cool. Freeze unwrapped on trays until solid. Then pack in plastic freezer bags or heavy-duty foil, separating biscuits with wax paper or plastic wrap.	3 to 6 months	Thaw, still wrapped, for 30 to 45 minutes at room temperature. Or unwrap and heat in microwave oven, following manufacturer's instructions; or heat in foil wrapping in a 350° oven for 15 to 20 minutes.
Breads & rolls, yeast	Prepare and bake as usual; let cool. Pack in plastic freezer bags, moisture- and vaporproof plastic wrap, or heavy-duty foil.	3 months	Thaw, still wrapped, for about 1 hour at room temperature. Or unwrap and thaw in microwave oven, following manufacturer's instructions; or heat in foil wrapping in a 300° oven for about 20 minutes for bread, 5 to 10 minutes for rolls.
Breads, quick Coffeecake, gingerbread, nut and fruit breads	Prepare and bake as usual; let cool. Freeze unwrapped on a tray until solid; then pack in plastic freezer bags or heavy-duty foil.	3 to 4 months	Thaw, still wrapped, for about 1 hour at room temperature. Or unwrap and thaw in microwave oven, following manufacturer's instructions; or heat in foil wrapping in a 400° oven until heated through. (Slice nut and fruit breads while still partially frozen to prevent crumbling.)
Cakes & cupcakes Angel food, chiffon, and sponge cakes; shortening cakes (including chocolate, yellow, spice and pound)	Do not freeze cakes with cream or custard fillings, or with frostings containing egg white. Prepare as usual, but do not use synthetic vanilla; cut down on spices, especially cloves, in spice cakes. Bake as usual; remove from pans and let cool. Freeze unwrapped on a tray until solid. Then pack in moisture- and vaporproof plastic wrap or in plastic freezer bags. Store large whole cakes in a light box (if a tube pan has been used, fill hole in cake with crumpled plastic wrap). Store sliced cake with a double layer of plastic wrap between slices.	***Angel food, chiffon, and sponge cakes:*** 2 months ***Shortening cakes:*** 4 to 6 months	Unwrap. Thaw large cakes for 2 hours at room temperature, cupcakes for 30 to 45 minutes. To prevent beads of moisture from forming on frosted cakes, cover them with a large cake cover or pan that doesn't touch sides of cake.

* Food will be safe to eat after this time, but will lose quality

Food	How to prepare & package	Freezer storage time at 0°F*	How to serve
Casseroles, unbaked Fish, poultry, or meat with vegetables and/ or pasta	Prepare casserole mixture with less pepper, cloves, onion, and garlic than usual; flavors of these ingredients grow stronger during storage. Let cool. Spoon mixture into freezer-to-oven casserole dishes, leaving 1-inch headspace; seal lids with freezer tape. Or freeze in shallow foil containers until firm, then cover tightly with heavy-duty foil. Or freeze in foil-lined casserole dishes, then remove food from dish; wrap tightly in moisture- and vaporproof plastic wrap or heavy-duty foil or place in a plastic freezer bag.	2 to 4 weeks	*If stored in freezer-to-oven casserole dishes or shallow foil containers,* remove any tape from lids. Bake, still frozen, in a 400° oven for about 1¾ hours per quart. (Do not preheat oven.) Keep covered for first half of baking time, then uncover. *If not stored in ovenproof containers,* remove wrapping and slip frozen mixture into casserole dish in which it was originally frozen. Bake as directed above.
Cheesecake	Prepare and bake as usual. Freeze unwrapped on a tray until solid, then wrap in moisture- and vaporproof plastic wrap or in a large plastic freezer bag. Store in a light box or carton to prevent crushing.	2 to 4 months	Unwrap and thaw in refrigerator for 4 to 6 hours.
Cookies, baked or unbaked	**Baked cookies** Prepare and bake as usual; let cool. To prevent crushing, pack cookies in rigid freezer containers or in plastic freezer bags, with plastic wrap between layers and crumpled to fill spaces.	6 months	Thaw **crisp cookies,** still packaged, for 15 to 20 minutes at room temperature. (They will be less crisp than cookies baked from frozen dough.) Thaw **soft cookies** on a serving plate for about 15 minutes.
	Unbaked cookies (except meringue) **Refrigerator cookies.** Form dough into a roll. Slice, if desired. Wrap in moisture- and vaporproof plastic wrap or pack in plastic freezer bags.	3 to 6 months	Bake slices without thawing.
	Drop cookies. Drop onto a tray and freeze unwrapped until solid. Then pack in rigid freezer containers or plastic freezer bags, with plastic wrap between layers. Or simply pack bulk dough in rigid freezer containers or plastic freezer bags.	3 to 6 months	Bake formed cookies, still frozen, in a 400° oven. Thaw bulk dough, still packaged, at room temperature until soft enough to drop by teaspoonfuls onto a greased baking sheet.
Fish, flaked In cheese or tomato sauces	Prepare as usual, but keep fat to a minimum and slightly undercook any vegetables. Cool quickly by placing pan in ice water. Pack in rigid wide-mouth freezer containers, making sure that sauce covers fish.	2 to 4 months	Heat in microwave oven, following manufacturer's instructions. Or partially thaw in refrigerator; then remove from containers and heat over boiling water.
Fish, fried Pieces or sticks	Fry as usual, just until done. Let cool. Freeze unwrapped on trays until solid; then pack in plastic freezer bags or in moisture- and vaporproof plastic wrap.	1 to 2 months	Unwrap frozen pieces or sticks and place in a single layer in a well-greased baking pan. Bake, uncovered, in a 400° oven until fish is crisp and heated through (20 to 25 minutes; frozen fried fish may lose some crispness).
Fish cakes & balls, cooked	Let cool. Freeze unwrapped on a tray until solid. Then pack in rigid freezer containers, in moisture- and vaporproof plastic wrap, or in plastic freezer bags.	2 to 4 weeks	Unwrap and heat on a microwave-safe serving plate in microwave oven, following manufacturer's instructions.
Fish loaf, unbaked	Prepare as usual. Pack in loaf pan, but do not bake. Wrap in moisture- and vaporproof plastic wrap or place in a plastic freezer bag.	1 to 2 months	Thaw, still wrapped, for 1 to 2 hours in refrigerator. Unwrap and bake in a 450° oven for 15 minutes; reduce heat to 350° for remainder of baking time.

* Food will be safe to eat after this time, but will lose quality

Freezing   175

Food	How to prepare & package	Freezer storage time at 0°F*	How to serve
Frostings & fillings	Do not freeze fillings containing cream or eggs. Uncooked frostings based on powdered sugar freeze best. Cooked frostings may crack; those made with large amounts of granulated sugar may become grainy. Pack in rigid freezer containers.	1 to 2 months	Thaw in container in refrigerator.
Gravy	Because gravy tends to separate and curdle when thawed, it's best simply to freeze broth, then prepare gravy just before serving. If you do freeze gravy, add ¼ teaspoon unflavored gelatin to each quart of gravy to reduce curdling. Pour into rigid freezer containers.	2 to 3 months	Heat in microwave oven, following manufacturer's instructions. Or remove from containers and heat over boiling water, breaking up frozen blocks as gravy begins to thaw.
Meat & poultry, fried	Fry as usual, just until done. Let cool. Freeze unwrapped on trays until solid. Package pieces in plastic freezer bags or in moisture- and vaporproof plastic wrap.	1 to 3 months	Thaw, still wrapped, in refrigerator. Then unwrap, place in a shallow baking pan, and bake, uncovered, in a 350° oven until crisp and heated through (30 to 45 minutes; frozen fried meat and poultry may lose some crispness).
Meat & poultry, roasted	Roast as usual. Remove as much fat as possible. Turkey and other large birds should be cut off the bone to save space; smaller birds may be boned if you wish, but keep pieces large. Cured meats such as ham lose their color and become rancid more quickly than other meats. Sauce or broth helps keep meat from drying out and losing color. Pack **dry meat** (for short storage) in moisture- and vaporproof plastic wrap or heavy-duty foil. Pack **meat with sauce or broth** in rigid freezer containers, making sure that sauce or broth covers meat.	2 to 3 months	Thaw **dry meat,** still wrapped, in refrigerator. Or thaw or heat in microwave oven, following manufacturer's instructions. Or heat in foil wrapping in a 325° oven until heated through. Thaw **meat with sauce or broth** in refrigerator for 5 to 6 hours. Or heat in microwave oven, following manufacturer's instructions; or heat slowly on top of range or in oven until heated through.
Meat, fish, & poultry, creamed	Prepare as usual, using recipes fairly low in fat. Cool quickly by placing pan in ice water. Pack in rigid wide-mouth freezer containers.	2 to 3 months	Thaw in refrigerator. Then remove from containers and heat over boiling water or in microwave oven, following manufacturer's instructions.
Meat dishes, combination Stews; pasta sauce with meat, meatballs, or ravioli; meat with gravy	Prepare as usual, but keep fat to a minimum and omit potatoes; slightly undercook other vegetables. Cool combination dishes quickly by placing pan in ice water. Pack in freezer jars or in rigid freezer containers, making sure that sauce, broth, or gravy covers meat.	2 to 3 months	Partially thaw in refrigerator to prevent overcooking. Then remove from containers and heat over boiling water; or transfer to a baking dish and heat in a 400° oven until hot through. Or heat (if in rigid plastic containers) in microwave oven, following manufacturer's instructions.
Meat loaf	Prepare as usual. Bake or leave unbaked. Wrap in moisture- and vaporproof plastic wrap or place in a plastic freezer bag.	3 to 4 months	For **frozen unbaked loaf,** unwrap; if not frozen in pan, place in pan. Bake in a 350° oven for about 1½ hours. For **baked loaf:** to serve cold, thaw, still wrapped, in refrigerator. To reheat, unwrap frozen baked loaf, place in pan, and bake, uncovered, in a 350° oven for about 1 hour.
Muffins	Prepare and bake as usual; remove from pans and let cool. Freeze on trays until solid; then pack in plastic freezer bags or in heavy-duty foil.	3 to 4 months	Thaw, still wrapped, for about 1 hour at room temperature. Or unwrap and heat in microwave oven, following manufacturer's instructions; or heat in foil wrapping in a 300° oven for about 20 minutes.

* Food will be safe to eat after this time, but will lose quality

Food	How to prepare & package	Freezer storage time at 0°F*	How to serve
Pastry (Pie shells)	**Baked pastry** Prepare and bake as usual; let cool. Leave in pie pan; place in a plastic freezer bag or wrap in moisture- and vaporproof plastic wrap. Or freeze, unwrapped, on a tray until solid; remove from pan and freeze as above, storing in a light carton to prevent breakage.	2 to 3 months	Thaw, still wrapped, for 10 to 20 minutes at room temperature. Add filling.
	Unbaked pastry Prepare pastry or crumb crust as usual. Fit into pie pans. Prick pastry if you don't intend to bake it with a filling. Stack pans, separating them with double layers of plastic wrap. Cover top pie shell with an inverted paper plate for protection; tape edges to pan. Place stack in a large plastic freezer bag; or wrap in moisture- and vapor-proof plastic wrap. Or omit fitting into pans; instead, store rounds of pastry on lined cardboard, with a double layer of plastic wrap between each round and the next.	1½ to 2 months	Bake, still frozen, in a 475° oven until lightly browned. Or fill and bake as usual.
Pies	**Chiffon pie** Make with gelatin base. Freeze unwrapped on a tray until solid. Place in a plastic freezer bag or wrap in moisture- and vaporproof plastic wrap. Store in a light box or carton to prevent crushing.	2 to 4 weeks	Thaw, still wrapped, for 1 hour at room temperature.
	Fruit, mince, and nut pies, unbaked Do not freeze unbaked pecan pie. If desired, treat sliced light-colored fruits for pies with a commercial anti-darkening agent, following package directions. Prepare as usual, but add 1 extra tablespoon flour or tapioca or 1½ teaspoons cornstarch to very juicy fillings to prevent boil-over during baking. Do not cut slits in top crust. Freeze fruit pies in pans, using metal or other freezer-to-oven pie pans. Cover with an inverted paper plate for protection; tape edges to pan. Place in a plastic freezer bag; or wrap in moisture- and vaporproof plastic wrap.	2 to 4 months	Unwrap. Cut slits in top of frozen pie; cover edges with foil. Bake in a 450° oven for 15 minutes; reduce temperature to 375° and bake for 15 more minutes. Remove foil; bake until done (about 30 more minutes).
	Pumpkin pie, unbaked Prepare pie shell and filling as usual. Chill filling before adding it to unbaked pie shell. Package as for fruit pies.	1 month	Unwrap. Bake, still frozen, in a 400° oven for 10 minutes; then reduce oven temperature to 325° for remainder of baking time.
Pizza	Prepare as usual; do not bake. If topping is warm, let cool. Freeze unwrapped until solid. Pack in a plastic freezer bag or in moisture- and vaporproof plastic wrap.	1 month	Unwrap. Bake, still frozen, in a 450° oven for 10 to 20 minutes, depending on size.
Sandwiches	Use day-old bread; spread bread to edges with softened butter or margarine. Use cheese, meat, poultry, tuna, salmon, or peanut butter filling. Omit hard-cooked egg white, jellies, jams, mayonnaise, tomatoes, and crisp vegetables such as lettuce and celery. Wrap individually or in groups of the same type in moisture- and vapor-proof plastic wrap, then place in plastic freezer bags.	2 months	Thaw meat, poultry, or fish sand-wiches, still wrapped, for 1 to 2 hours in refrigerator. Thaw other sandwiches at room temperature. Frozen sandwiches in a lunchbox thaw in 3 to 4 hours and help keep other food cold.
Soups & purées	Omit potatoes. Use vegetables that freeze well, and undercook them slightly. (For cream soups, vegetables may be cooked and puréed.) Omit salt and thickening if soup is to be kept longer than 2 months. If possible, make a concentrate by using less liquid when cooking. Cool quickly by placing pan in ice water. Pour into rigid freezer containers. Or freeze in ice cube trays, then store cubes in plastic freezer bags.	1 to 3 months	Heat without thawing. Heat cream soups over boiling water; stir to keep smooth. If concentrated, add hot liquid. Add potatoes or other vegetables, if necessary. Heat vegetable purée over boiling water; then add milk or cream.
Waffles	Prepare as usual. Let cool. Wrap individually in moisture- and vaporproof plastic wrap; then pack in plastic freezer bags.	2 to 3 months	Unwrap; heat, still frozen, in a toaster or microwave oven, following manufacturer's instruc-tions. Or heat on a baking sheet in a 400° oven for 2 to 3 minutes.

* Food will be safe to eat after this time, but will lose quality

On a sweltering summer day, treat yourself to the cooling fruit flavors of raspberry, papaya, and pineapple ices. All three recipes are on page 182.

Freezing Fresh Fruits

Most fruits can be frozen; the chart on pages 180 and 181 lists the types that freeze best. Always select unblemished firm-ripe fruits, and remember to treat them with an antidarkening agent if needed. Work carefully but quickly, preparing just enough fruit to fill a few containers at a time.

Basic Fruit Packs

When you freeze fruit, you can pack it in syrup, with sugar, or with no sweetener at all. Syrup-packed fruits are usually best for uncooked desserts and sauces, while those frozen with sugar or packed entirely unsweetened are a better choice for cooking. Be aware that color, flavor, and texture change more rapidly when fruit is frozen unsweetened than when it's packed with sugar or syrup.

Packing fruit unsweetened. While many fruits are best frozen sweetened, others maintain high quality without sugar or syrup. Cranberries, raspberries, blueberries, and rhubarb are all good choices for freezing unsweetened. The technique is simple: just pack the fruit in rigid freezer containers, seal, and freeze. Or spread it on a tray, freeze uncovered until solid, and transfer to rigid containers or plastic freezer bags. This second method—freezing fruits or fruit pieces individually *before* packaging—makes it easy to remove just the amount you want at one time.

Unsweetened fruit can also be frozen in water or unsweetened fruit juice. The fruits usually aren't as plump as those frozen without liquid, and they'll take longer to thaw.

Packing fruit in pectin syrup. This lightly sweetened pack may help certain fruits—strawberries, cherries, and peaches, for example—retain better texture. To prepare the pectin syrup, combine one package (1¾ oz.) dry pectin with 1 cup water in a small pan. Bring to a boil; boil for 1 minute, stirring constantly. Add ½ cup sugar and stir until dissolved. Remove from heat, add enough cold water to make 2 cups liquid, and refrigerate. To use the syrup, pour it into a large bowl; add the fruit and stir until it's lightly coated with syrup, then pack.

Packing fruit in sugar. To freeze fruit in a *sugar pack* or *dry pack*—with sugar, but no liquid—spread it in a shallow pan and sprinkle with sugar (see chart, pages 180 and 181, for amounts). Gently mix until the fruit releases its juice and the sugar is dissolved.

Packing fruit in syrup. The syrups used to pack fruit for freezing can be made in different concentrations; to prepare them, simply mix the ingredients until well blended, then chill before using. (You may substitute honey for a fourth of the sugar.) When you pack the fruit, add enough cold syrup to cover it—usually ½ to ⅔ cup per pint.

Syrups for Freezing Fruits			
% Sugar	Water (in cups)	Sugar (in cups)	Yield (in cups)
20%	4	1	4¾
30%	4	1¾	5
40%	4	2¾	5⅓
50%	4	4	6

Protecting Fruit Colors

Some light-colored fruits have a tendency to darken after cutting. The chart on pages 180 and 181 specifies the treatment needed to preserve their color.

Ascorbic acid, sold in drugstores and health food stores, is one common antidarkening agent. Commercial antidarkening products containing ascorbic and/or citric acids (and often sugar) are also available; look for them in your supermarket. Lemon juice prevents darkening, too, but the quantity needed often makes the fruit too tart in flavor.

Antidarkening agents can be added to fruit in two ways. You can mix them into the packing syrup; or you can dissolve them in water, then sprinkle the solution over the fruit before packing. For syrup packs, you'll generally need ½ to ¾ teaspoon pure ascorbic acid per quart of 20 to 40 percent syrup. If you can't find pure ascorbic acid, you can substitute vitamin C tablets, keeping in mind that 1 teaspoon of ascorbic acid equals 3,000 milligrams of vitamin C. Crush the tablets thoroughly before using them.

Packaging & Headspace

Rigid plastic freezer containers and wide-mouth freezer/canning jars are good choices for any fruit pack. Freezer bags are also suitable for sugar-packed fruits and those packed unsweetened without liquid, but not convenient for fruits packed in syrup.

When packing unsweetened fruit frozen in individual pieces, you don't need to leave headspace. If you're using a sugar, juice, water, or syrup pack, leave ½-inch headspace for plastic freezer bags or pint containers, 1 inch for quarts. Do not freeze fruits with liquid in standard glass canning jars. Seal all containers tightly; label with the type of fruit and the date, then freeze. For easier stacking, freeze filled bags flat on freezer shelves until solid; then stack.

Guide for Freezing Fruits

The chart below indicates possible packs for a number of fruits. When packing, leave headspace as directed in "Packaging & Headspace" (page 179).

Unless otherwise noted, fruits of all kinds will keep for up to a year if solidly frozen.

Fruit & varieties	Quantity to yield 1 pint	How to prepare
Apples Golden Delicious, Granny Smith, Gravenstein, Jonathan, Newtown Pippin, Rome Beauty	1¼ to 1½ lbs.	For pies, use a sugar or dry pack. For uncooked desserts, use a syrup pack. For a firmer texture, steam sliced apples (1 lb. at a time) for 2 minutes. Cool in cold water; drain. Then pack in sugar or syrup. **To pack in sugar,** rinse, peel, core, and slice apples. As you work, coat them with a solution of ½ teaspoon ascorbic acid to 3 tablespoons cold water (about the amount you'll need per quart of fruit). Mix ½ cup sugar with each quart of fruit. Pack slices in plastic freezer bags or rigid freezer containers; press fruit down, leaving headspace. **To pack in syrup,** use a 20% to 40% syrup; add ½ teaspoon ascorbic acid per quart. Pour ½ cup cold syrup into each rigid pint freezer container. Rinse, peel, and core apples; slice directly into syrup. Press slices down; add syrup to cover, leaving headspace.
Apricots Royal-Blenheim, Tilton	1 to 1¼ lbs.	Rinse, halve, and pit. Dip fruit in boiling water for 30 seconds (this keeps skins from toughening). Cool in cold water; drain. Peel and slice, if desired. **To pack in syrup,** use a 20% to 40% syrup; add ¾ teaspoon ascorbic acid per quart. Pack apricots in rigid freezer containers; add cold syrup to cover, leaving headspace. **To pack in sugar,** dissolve ¼ teaspoon ascorbic acid in 3 tablespoons cold water. Mix this ascorbic acid solution and ½ cup sugar with each quart of fruit; stir until sugar is dissolved. Pack apricots and liquid in plastic freezer bags or rigid freezer containers; press down, leaving headspace.
Avocados Fuerte, Haas	4 medium-size	Pit, peel, and mash; as you mash, add 1 tablespoon lemon juice for every 2 avocados. Pack in plastic freezer bags or rigid freezer containers, leaving headspace. Store for up to 4 months.
Berries Raspberries, blackberries, boysenberries, loganberries, blueberries, huckleberries, elderberries; cranberries (unsweetened only)	¾ to 1½ lbs.	Rinse berries gently; drain. **To pack unsweetened,** spread berries on trays and freeze until solid, then transfer to plastic freezer bags or rigid freezer containers. **To pack in sugar,** use ¼ cup sugar per quart of raspberries; ½ cup sugar per quart of blueberries, elderberries, or huckleberries; and ¾ cup sugar per quart of blackberries, boysenberries, or loganberries. Mix gently until sugar is dissolved; fill plastic freezer bags or rigid freezer containers, leaving headspace. (To pack crushed berries, see "Fruit purées & sauces," below.) **To pack in syrup** (for berries to be served uncooked), place berries in rigid freezer containers and cover with cold 20% to 40% syrup, leaving headspace.
Cherries, sour Early Richmond, English Morello, Montmorency	1¼ to 1½ lbs.	Rinse, stem, and pit, working quickly to prevent color and flavor changes. **To pack in syrup,** use a 50% syrup; add ½ teaspoon ascorbic acid per quart. Pack cherries in rigid freezer containers; cover with cold syrup, leaving headspace. **To pack in sugar,** use ¾ cup sugar per quart of cherries; mix until sugar is dissolved. Pack in plastic freezer bags or rigid freezer containers, leaving headspace.
Cherries, sweet Bing, Black Tartarian, Lambert, Rainier, Royal Ann	1¼ to 1½ lbs.	Rinse, stem, and pit, working quickly to prevent color and flavor changes. **To pack in syrup,** use a 30% or 40% syrup; add ½ teaspoon ascorbic acid per quart. Pack cherries in rigid freezer containers; cover with cold syrup, leaving headspace. **To pack in sugar,** use ⅔ cup sugar per quart of cherries; mix until sugar is dissolved. Pack in plastic freezer bags or rigid freezer containers, leaving headspace. **To pack in pectin syrup,** cover fruit with cold pectin syrup (see page 179). Pack in rigid freezer containers, leaving headspace.
Figs Black Mission, Kadota	¾ to 1¼ lbs.	**To pack unsweetened,** rinse fully ripe fruit; remove stems. Pack in rigid freezer containers; cover with water (to which you have added ¾ teaspoon ascorbic acid per quart), leaving headspace. **To pack in syrup,** use a 20% to 40% syrup; add ¾ teaspoon ascorbic acid per quart. Pack figs in rigid freezer containers; cover with cold syrup, leaving headspace. Store unsweetened and syrup-packed figs for up to 6 months.
Fruit purées & sauces		Steam or simmer fruit until soft; then mash it, purée it in a blender, or press it through a strainer. Add sugar and/or lemon juice to taste. Heat mixture to 180°F; remove from heat and refrigerate until cold. Pack in rigid freezer containers, leaving headspace.

Fruit & varieties	Quantity to yield 1 pint	How to prepare
Grapefruit & oranges *Grapefruit:* Marsh *Oranges:* Any except navel	1½ to 2 lbs.	Rinse and peel, cutting deep enough to remove white membrane under rind. Holding fruit over a bowl to catch juice, cut between membranes to release segments. Remove and discard membranes and seeds from segments; reserve juice. *To pack in syrup,* use a 30% syrup made with reserved juice (and water, if needed). Pack in rigid freezer containers; cover with cold syrup, leaving headspace.
Mangoes Philippine, Hayden	2 or 3 medium-size	*To pack in syrup,* put ½ cup cold 20% or 30% syrup in each rigid pint freezer container. Rinse and peel mangoes; cut a slice off stem end. Then slice fruit (avoiding flesh near pit) directly into syrup. Press slices down; add more syrup to cover, leaving headspace. *To pack in sugar,* rinse and peel mangoes; cut a slice off stem end. Then slice fruit, avoiding flesh near pit. Place 5 to 6 cups mango slices in a shallow bowl; sprinkle with ½ cup sugar. Let stand for a few minutes, or until sugar is dissolved; mix gently. Pack in plastic freezer bags or rigid freezer containers, leaving headspace.
Melons Cantaloupe, casaba, Crenshaw, honeydew, Persian, watermelon	1 to 1¼ lbs.	Cut in half; cut off rind and scoop out seeds. *To pack in syrup,* use a 20% or 30% syrup, adding 1 teaspoon lemon juice per cup of syrup for flavor. Pour ½ cup cold syrup into each rigid pint freezer container. Cut melon into slices, cubes, or balls, dropping directly into syrup; add more syrup to cover, leaving headspace. Store for up to 6 months.
Oranges *See* Grapefruit & Oranges		
Peaches & nectarines *Peaches:* Elberta, J.H. Hale, O'Henry, Redglobe, Redhaven, Rio Oso Gem *Nectarines:* Flavortop, Gold Mine, Panamint, Stanwick	1 to 1½ lbs.	Do not peel nectarines. To peel peaches, dip in boiling water for 1 to 1½ minutes, then plunge into cold water; slip off skins. (For less "ragged" fruit, peel without boiling water dip.) *To pack in syrup,* use a 20% to 40% syrup; add ½ teaspoon ascorbic acid per quart of syrup. Pour ½ cup cold syrup into each rigid pint freezer container. Cut fruit into halves or slices directly into cold syrup; discard pits. Press fruit down; add more syrup to cover, leaving headspace. *To pack in sugar,* coat cut fruit with a solution of ¼ teaspoon ascorbic acid to 3 tablespoons cold water (about the amount you'll need per quart of fruit). Add ½ to ⅔ cup sugar to each quart of prepared fruit; stir gently until sugar is dissolved. Pack in plastic freezer bags or rigid freezer containers, leaving headspace. *To pack in pectin syrup or water,* cover cut fruit with cold pectin syrup (see page 179) or with cold water to which you've added 1 teaspoon ascorbic acid per quart. Leave headspace. Store water-packed peaches or nectarines for up to 6 months.
Pears		Not recommended for freezing.
Pineapple	1 to 1¼ lbs.	Peel; remove eyes and cores. Cut into wedges, cubes, sticks, or thin slices; or crush. *To pack unsweetened,* pack fruit tightly in rigid freezer containers (enough juice will squeeze out to fill spaces), leaving headspace. *To pack in syrup,* pack fruit in rigid freezer containers. Cover with cold 20% or 30% syrup, leaving headspace.
Plums & fresh prunes Casselman, El Dorado, French Prune, Italian Prune, Queen Ann, Satsuma	1 to 1½ lbs.	*To pack in syrup,* rinse and cut into halves or quarters; discard pits. Use a 20% to 40% syrup; add ½ teaspoon ascorbic acid per quart. Pack plums in rigid freezer containers and cover with cold syrup, leaving headspace. *To pack unsweetened,* leave whole. Rinse; dry well. Spread on a tray; freeze until solid. Pack in freezer bags or rigid freezer containers. Use cooked or in pies within 3 months.
Rhubarb	⅔ to 1 lb.	Rinse unpeeled rhubarb stalks and cut into pieces of the desired length. Immerse in boiling water; return to a boil and cook for 1 minute. Drain; cool quickly in ice water, then drain well. *To pack unsweetened,* pack tightly in rigid freezer containers, leaving headspace. Store for up to 6 months. *To pack in syrup,* pack rhubarb tightly in rigid freezer containers. Cover with cold 40% syrup, leaving headspace.
Strawberries Tioga, Tufts, Sequoia, Pajaro, Douglas, Aiko	¾ to 1½ lbs.	Rinse gently in cold water; drain and hull. *To pack in sugar,* leave berries whole (if small); or slice lengthwise. Add ⅔ cup sugar per quart of berries; mix gently until sugar is dissolved. Pack in freezer bags or rigid freezer containers, leaving headspace. (To pack crushed, see "Fruit purées & sauces," facing page.) *To pack in syrup,* pack whole berries in rigid freezer containers; cover with cold 30% or 40% syrup, leaving headspace. *To pack in pectin syrup or water,* cover fruit with cold pectin syrup (page 179) or with cold water to which you've added 1 teaspoon ascorbic acid per quart. Leave headspace.

Raspberry Ice

Pictured on page 178

You'll appreciate the fresh, sparkling flavor of this easy make-ahead dessert and its variations.

- **4 cups raspberries**
- **¾ cup sugar**
- **½ cup water**
- **1 tablespoon lemon juice**

In a food processor, purée berries. Press through a sieve; discard seeds. Return purée to food processor. Add sugar, water, and lemon juice; whirl to blend. Pour purée into divided ice cube trays, cover, and freeze until solid (at least 3 hours). Remove cubes from trays; use at once or transfer to plastic freezer bags and freeze for up to 3 weeks.

To prepare ice, whirl cubes, a portion at a time, in a food processor; use on-off pulses at first to break up cubes, then whirl continuously until mixture is smooth and slushy. (Or place all cubes in large bowl of an electric mixer; beat until smooth and slushy, increasing mixer speed from low to high as ice softens.) Spoon mixture into a 9-inch-square metal pan, cover airtight, and freeze until solid (at least 4 hours) or for up to 3 weeks.

To serve, let ice stand at room temperature until you can break it up with a spoon. Whirl in a food processor until smooth and free of ice crystals. Serve at once. Makes 6 servings (about 2¾ cups *total*).

Storage time. Up to 6 weeks in freezer (3 weeks as cubes, plus 3 weeks in pan after beating).

Per serving: 137 calories, 1 g protein, 24 g carbohydrates, 0 g total fat, 0 mg cholesterol, 0 mg sodium

Strawberry Ice

In a food processor, purée 4 cups hulled **strawberries**. Add ½ cup each **sugar** and **water** and 2 tablespoons **lemon juice**; whirl to blend. Freeze, beat, and serve as directed for **Raspberry Ice.** Makes 6 servings (about 3 cups *total*).

Per serving: 96 calories, 1 g protein, 24 g carbohydrates, 0 g total fat, 0 mg cholesterol, 2 mg sodium

Pineapple Ice

Peel and core 1 large **pineapple** (about 5 lbs.); cut into chunks. Purée fruit in a food processor, a portion at a time (you should have 4 cups). Add 1 cup **water**, 2 tablespoons **sugar**, and 2 tablespoons **lemon juice**; whirl to blend. Freeze, beat, and serve as directed for **Raspberry Ice.** Makes 10 servings (about 5 cups *total*).

Per serving: 41 calories, 0 g protein, 10 g carbohydrates, 0 g total fat, 0 mg cholesterol, 1 mg sodium

Papaya Ice

Peel, halve, and seed 1 large **papaya** (about 1¼ lbs.); cut into chunks. Purée in a food processor (you should have 1½ cups). Add 2 tablespoons **lime juice**, 3 tablespoons **sugar**, and ⅓ cup **water;** whirl to blend. Freeze, beat, and serve as directed for **Raspberry Ice.** Makes 3 servings (about 1⅔ cups *total*).

Per serving: 78 calories, 1 g protein, 20 g carbohydrates, 0 g total fat, 0 mg cholesterol, 4 mg sodium

Peach Pie Filling

Pictured on facing page

To vary this filling's flavor, omit the orange peel and orange juice; then increase the lemon juice in the filling to ¼ cup and add 1 teaspoon grated lemon peel.

- **2 quarts water**
- **¼ cup lemon juice**
- **6 pounds (about 18 medium-size) peaches**
- **2¼ cups sugar**
- **½ cup all-purpose flour**
- **1 teaspoon ground cinnamon**
- **¼ teaspoon ground nutmeg**
- **1 tablespoon grated orange peel**
- **¼ cup orange juice**

In a large bowl, mix water with 2 tablespoons of the lemon juice. Peel and pit peaches; slice directly into lemon water.

In a 6- to 8-quart pan, combine sugar, flour, cinnamon, nutmeg, orange peel, orange juice, and remaining 2 tablespoons lemon juice. Drain peaches; add to sugar mixture and stir gently. Let stand for 20 minutes. Then cook, uncovered, over medium heat, stirring often, until mixture begins to thicken (about 10 minutes). Let cool. Pack in rigid pint freezer containers or freezer jars, leaving ½-inch headspace; apply lids and freeze. Makes about 6 pints.

Storage time. Up to 6 months in freezer.

Per ½ cup (unbaked): 121 calories, 1 g protein, 31 g carbohydrates, 0 g total fat, 0 mg cholesterol, 1 mg sodium

Apple Pie Filling

Follow directions for **Peach Pie Filling,** but substitute 6 pounds **tart apples** (peeled, cored, and sliced) for peaches. Omit orange juice and peel, reduce sugar to 1¾ cups, reduce flour to ¼ cup, and increase cinnamon to 1½ teaspoons. Makes about 8 pints.

Per ½ cup (unbaked): 88 calories, 0 g protein, 23 g carbohydrates, 0 g total fat, 0 mg cholesterol, 1 mg sodium

With Peach Pie Filling (facing page) on hand in the freezer, it's easy to enjoy homemade peach pie all year long. Just thaw the filling in the refrigerator until it's spreadable, spoon it into a pastry shell, and bake.

Garden Marinara Sauce

Pictured on page 186

This made-from-scratch marinara sauce is great with pasta, but it also goes into two classic Italian appetizer relishes—Caponata and Peperonata (below).

¼ cup olive oil
3 large onions, coarsely chopped
3 or 4 cloves garlic, minced or pressed
6 pounds (15 to 18 medium-size) ripe tomatoes, peeled, cored, and chopped
1 cup lightly packed fresh basil leaves, chopped
½ to 1 tablespoon sugar
Salt and pepper

Heat oil in a wide frying pan over medium heat; add onions and garlic and cook, stirring often, until onions are soft (about 15 minutes). Add tomatoes and basil. Cook, uncovered, stirring occasionally, until sauce is reduced to 2 quarts (45 to 60 minutes); as sauce thickens, reduce heat and stir more often to prevent sticking. Add sugar; season to taste with salt and pepper.

Let sauce cool, then ladle into pint freezer jars or freezer containers, leaving ½-inch headspace; apply lids. Freeze or refrigerate. Makes about 4 pints.

Storage time. Up to 2 weeks in refrigerator; up to 6 months in freezer.

Per ½ cup: 80 calories, 2 g protein, 11 g carbohydrates, 4 g total fat, 0 mg cholesterol, 15 mg sodium

Caponata

Pictured on page 186

Peppers, olives, and creamy-textured eggplant combine with homemade marinara sauce in this Italian relish. Include it in an antipasto assortment; or serve it on its own, as a dip for pocket bread or butter lettuce leaves.

½ cup olive oil
1½ pounds eggplant (unpeeled), cut into ½-inch cubes
2 large red or green bell peppers, seeded and diced
1 large onion, chopped
1 clove garlic, minced or pressed
2½ cups Garden Marinara Sauce (this page)
1 cup sliced pimento-stuffed green olives or sliced ripe olives
Salt and pepper

Heat oil in a wide frying pan over medium heat. Add eggplant; cover and cook, stirring occasionally, until slightly softened (about 5 minutes). Uncover and cook, stirring often, until eggplant is browned (10 to 15 more minutes). Add bell peppers, onion, and garlic; cook, stirring, until onion is soft (about 10 minutes). Add Garden Marinara Sauce; cook, uncovered, until mixture is thick (about 10 more minutes). Stir in olives; season to taste with salt and pepper. Let caponata cool, then pack in pint freezer jars or freezer containers, leaving ½-inch headspace; apply lids. Freeze or refrigerate. Makes about 4 pints.

Storage time. Up to 2 weeks in refrigerator; up to 6 months in freezer.

Per ¼ cup: 57 calories, 1 g protein, 4 g carbohydrates, 5 g total fat, 0 mg cholesterol, 106 mg sodium

Peperonata

Pictured on page 186

This colorful blend of sweet red, green, and yellow peppers is a good meat relish and a tasty dip for crackers.

¼ cup olive oil
2 large onions, cut into 1-inch pieces, layers separated
2 cloves garlic, minced or pressed
About 10 medium-size bell peppers (use an assortment of red, yellow, and green peppers), seeded and thinly sliced (you should have 8 cups)
2½ cups Garden Marinara Sauce (this page)
Salt and pepper

Heat oil in a wide frying pan over medium heat. Add onions and cook, stirring, for 3 minutes. Add garlic, bell peppers, and Garden Marinara Sauce; cover and cook until peppers are tender when pierced (8 to 10 minutes). Season to taste with salt and pepper.

Let cool, then pack in pint freezer jars or freezer containers, leaving ½-inch headspace; apply lids. Freeze or refrigerate. Makes about 4 pints.

Storage time. Up to 2 weeks in refrigerator; up to 6 months in freezer.

Per ¼ cup: 38 calories, 1 g protein, 4 g carbohydrates, 2 g total fat, 0 mg cholesterol, 3 mg sodium

Freezing Vegetables

If you're a gardener with more fresh vegetables than you can use at home or give away, consider yourself lucky—those surplus peas, squash, and carrots can be frozen to enjoy later in the year.

For consistently excellent results, be careful to pick your vegetables at peak maturity and freeze them without delay. It's also important that your freezer maintain a temperature of 0°F or lower, without much fluctuation. The freezer compartments of many refrigerators do not meet this requirement, nor do some models of freezers, including both old and newer appliances.

About Blanching

Blanching—quick heating to inactivate enzymes and retard spoilage—helps preserve color, flavor, texture, and nutritive value. You'll need to blanch most vegetables before freezing them. The most common method involves a dip in boiling water, but you may also blanch in steam or in a microwave oven. Steam- and microwave-blanched vegetables often have a fresher flavor and retain more water-soluble vitamins than do those treated in boiling water, but water blanching is generally more effective in removing surface residues and microorganisms.

Regardless of the method you select, always adhere to the times recommended in the chart on pages 187 to 189. Blanching too briefly may allow continued enzyme activity, giving you a poor-quality product. Overblanching results in diminished nutritive value and loss of color and flavor.

To blanch vegetables in boiling water, you'll need an 8-quart or larger pan filled with about 1 gallon of rapidly boiling water (for greens, use 2 gallons of water). A blanching pot with a perforated basket and lid is ideal. Place about 1 pound of prepared raw vegetables at a time in a wire basket or metal colander (or in blanching pot basket); then immerse in the boiling water. Let the water return to a boil; then cover the pot and begin timing as directed in the chart on pages 187 to 189.

To blanch vegetables in steam, use a steam blanching pot or an 8-quart or larger pan with a tight-fitting lid and a wire or perforated basket that will hold food at least 3 inches off the pan bottom. Pour 2 inches of water into the pan, cover, and bring to a boil over high heat. Place 1 to 2 pounds of prepared raw vegetables in a single layer in the basket; cover.

When steam begins to flow from the pan, begin timing as directed in the chart on pages 187 to 189.

To blanch vegetables in a microwave oven, you'll need an oven at least 1 cubic foot in size. Use a 1-quart round microwave-safe glass casserole or other microwave-safe container of similar size. Add ¼ cup water and no more than 2 cups prepared raw vegetables (or no more than 4 cups leafy greens). Larger amounts of vegetables and water (or large vegetable pieces) increase blanching times. Cover the container with microwave-safe plastic wrap; don't use glass lids, since they, too, may increase blanching times unpredictably.

To determine the appropriate blanching time, you'll need to consider both the vegetable you're blanching and the characteristics of your microwave, since ovens differ in size, power levels, heating rates, and uniformity of heating. If you have a relatively new 650- to 700-watt, medium-size to large oven with a built-in microwave mixer or revolving turntable, use the times given for high-wattage ovens (see the chart on pages 187 to 189). Otherwise, use the times stated for low-wattage ovens. Always blanch on **HIGH (100%)** power.

To cool blanched vegetables, immediately plunge them into a large quantity of cold (60°F or lower) water; change the water frequently. Or place the vegetables in a colander under cold running water. As a rule of thumb, cool vegetables for about the same amount of time you blanched them. Drain vegetables thoroughly after cooling.

Packaging & Headspace

Loose vegetables are usually packed in plastic freezer bags, then often placed in cardboard freezer cartons to protect the bags and make stacking easier. Rigid freezer containers may also be used; they're especially convenient for purées.

Unless otherwise noted in the chart (pages 187 to 189), leave headspace in bags or containers. For plastic freezer bags, leave ½-inch headspace. After filling the bags, press out as much air as possible, beginning from the bottom of each bag and moving toward the top to prevent air from reentering. Seal the bags tightly.

If you're packing vegetables in plastic containers or freezer jars, leave ½-inch headspace for pints, 1 inch for quarts.

Label all containers with the type of vegetable and the date; then freeze at once.

The unbeatable flavors of sweet, red-ripe tomatoes and fresh basil guarantee that made-from-scratch Garden Marinara Sauce will win raves. Serve it over pasta—or use it in our Caponata or Peperonata. You'll find all three recipes on page 184.

Guide for Freezing Vegetables

For details on blanching methods and cooling techniques, see "About Blanching" (page 185). Consult "packaging & Headspace" (page 185) for instructions on how much headspace to leave.

Mushrooms and eggplant will keep well in the freezer for up to 3 months; all other vegetables keep for up to a year.

Vegetable	Quantity to yield 1 pint	How to prepare
Artichokes	20 to 25 (1- to 1¼-inch) trimmed whole small artichokes	Cut off thorny tops and stem ends. Remove coarse outer leaves, leaving only tender inner leaves. Rinse well. Blanch for 3 minutes in boiling lemon water (½ cup lemon juice per 2 quarts water). Cool; then drain and pack in plastic freezer bags or rigid freezer containers, leaving headspace.
Asparagus	1 to 1½ lbs.	Remove tough ends and scales; sort spears according to size. Rinse and drain. **For small spears,** blanch for 2 minutes in boiling water, 3 minutes in steam, 3 minutes in a high-wattage microwave oven, or 4 minutes in a low-wattage microwave oven. **For large spears,** blanch for 4 minutes in boiling water, 6 minutes in steam, 3 minutes in a high-wattage microwave oven, or 5 minutes in a low-wattage microwave oven. Cool; then drain and pack in plastic freezer bags or rigid freezer containers, leaving headspace.
Beans, fresh butter & lima	2 to 2½ lbs. (unshelled)	Shell and rinse beans; sort according to size. **For small beans,** blanch for 2 minutes in boiling water or for 3 minutes in steam. **For large beans,** blanch for 4 minutes in boiling water or for 6 minutes in steam. Cool; then drain and pack in plastic freezer bags or rigid freezer containers, leaving headspace.
Beans, snap Green, wax, Italian	⅔ to 1 lb.	Rinse beans and trim ends; remove strings, if necessary. Leave whole or cut into pieces of desired length. **For small beans (and thin cut pieces),** blanch for 2 minutes in boiling water, 3 minutes in steam, 3 minutes in a high-wattage microwave oven, or 4 minutes in a low-wattage microwave oven. **For large beans (and thick cut pieces),** blanch for 3 minutes in boiling water, 5 minutes in steam, 3 minutes in a high-wattage microwave oven, or 5 minutes in a low-wattage microwave oven. Cool; then drain and pack in plastic freezer bags or rigid freezer containers, leaving headspace.
Beets	1¼ to 1½ lbs.	To keep color from bleeding, leave root ends and 1 inch of tops on beets. Scrub well; don't peel. Cover with boiling water and boil gently until tender when pierced (20 to 45 minutes). Cool. Remove skins; trim off stems and roots. Leave small beets whole; slice or dice larger ones. Pack in plastic freezer bags or rigid freezer containers, leaving headspace.
Broccoli	1 lb.	Trim off outer leaves and tough stalk bases. Rinse broccoli. Trim flowerets from stalks; cut into pieces 1 to 2 inches in diameter. Cut tender stalks into ½-inch-thick pieces. Sort pieces according to size. If desired, soak for 30 minutes in salt water (¼ cup salt per gallon of cold water) to help remove insects; drain. **For small pieces,** blanch for 3 minutes in boiling water, 5 minutes in steam, 5 minutes in a high-wattage microwave oven, or 8 minutes in a low-wattage microwave oven. **For large pieces,** blanch for 4 minutes in boiling water, 6 minutes in steam, 5 minutes in a high-wattage microwave oven, or 8 minutes in a low-wattage microwave oven. Cool; drain and pack in plastic freezer bags or rigid freezer containers, leaving headspace.
Brussels sprouts	1 lb.	Trim off stalk bases and remove outer leaves. Rinse sprouts. Sort according to size. **For small sprouts,** blanch for 3 minutes in boiling water, 5 minutes in steam, 5 minutes in a high-wattage microwave oven, or 8 minutes in a low-wattage microwave oven. **For large sprouts,** blanch for 5 minutes in boiling water, 7 minutes in steam, 5 minutes in a high-wattage microwave oven, or 8 minutes in a low-wattage microwave oven. Cool; then drain and pack in plastic freezer bags or rigid freezer containers, leaving headspace.
Cabbage	1 to 1½ lbs.	Remove outer leaves. Rinse cabbage; cut into quarters or smaller wedges. **For quarters,** blanch for 4 minutes in boiling water or for 6 minutes in steam. **For smaller wedges,** blanch for 2 minutes in boiling water or for 3 minutes in steam. Cool; then drain and pack in plastic freezer bags or rigid freezer containers, leaving headspace.
Carrots	1¼ to 1½ lbs.	Rinse and peel. Leave small, tender carrots whole; cut others into ½-inch cubes or slices. **For diced or sliced carrots,** blanch for 2 minutes in boiling water, 3 minutes in steam, 5 minutes in a high-wattage microwave oven, or 7 minutes in a low-wattage microwave oven. **For whole carrots,** blanch for 5 minutes in boiling water, 8 minutes in steam, 5 minutes in a high-wattage microwave oven, or 7 minutes in a low-wattage oven. Cool; then drain and pack in plastic freezer bags or rigid freezer containers, leaving headspace.

Vegetable	Quantity to yield 1 pint	How to prepare
Cauliflower	1¼ lbs.	Break into 1- to 2-inch flowerets. Sort pieces according to size. If desired, soak for 30 minutes in salt water (¼ cup salt per gallon of cold water) to help remove insects; drain. **For small pieces,** blanch for 3 minutes in boiling water, 5 minutes in steam, 5 minutes in a high-wattage microwave oven, or 7 minutes in a low-wattage microwave oven. **For large pieces,** blanch for 5 minutes in boiling water, 7 minutes in steam, 5 minutes in a high-wattage microwave oven, or 7 minutes in a low-wattage microwave oven. Cool; then drain and pack in plastic freezer bags or rigid freezer containers, leaving headspace.
Corn	2 to 3 lbs. (in husks)	Discard husks and silk; rinse corn. **For whole-kernel corn,** blanch whole ears for 4 minutes in boiling water, 6 minutes in steam, 4 minutes in a high-wattage microwave oven, or 6 minutes in a low-wattage microwave oven. Drain; cool. Cut kernels from cobs with a sharp knife. Pack in plastic freezer bags, leaving headspace. **For cream-style corn,** blanch whole ears as for whole-kernel corn (above). Drain; cool. Cut kernels from cob with a sharp knife, then scrape remaining kernel tips and juice from cobs. Combine kernels, juice, and tips. Pack in plastic freezer bags, leaving headspace. **For corn on cob,** blanch **small ears** (less than 1¼-inch diameter) for 7 minutes in boiling water or for 10 minutes in steam. Blanch **medium-size ears** (1¼- to 1½-inch diameter) for 9 minutes in boiling water or for 13 minutes in steam. Blanch **large ears** (over 1½-inch diameter) for 11 minutes in boiling water or for 16 minutes in steam. Cool; then drain and pack in plastic freezer bags, leaving headspace.
Eggplant	1 to 1½ lbs.	Rinse, peel, and cut into ⅓-inch-thick slices. Blanch in boiling lemon water (½ cup lemon juice per gallon of water) for 4 minutes. Cool; then drain and pack in plastic freezer bags or rigid freezer containers, leaving headspace.
Ginger root	1 whole piece	Rinse and pat dry. No blanching required. Freeze whole in moisture- and vaporproof plastic wrap or in a small freezer bag. To use, grate or slice frozen root. Return unused portion to freezer.
Greens (including spinach) Beet, collard, kale, mustard, spinach, turnip	1 to 1½ lbs.	Rinse carefully, working with 2 to 3 pounds of greens at a time. Drain; continue to rinse until water is clear and free of grit. Cut tough stems from leaves; then tear or cut leaves into 2- to 4-inch pieces. Blanch for 2 minutes in boiling water, 3 minutes in steam, 4 minutes in a high-wattage microwave oven, or 6 minutes in a low-wattage microwave oven. Cool; then drain and pack in plastic freezer bags or rigid freezer containers, leaving headspace.
Mushrooms Commercial mushrooms only	1 to 1½ lbs.	Rinse well. Trim off stems and cut out discolored parts. Leave whole or slice. **For sliced mushrooms,** blanch for 3 minutes in boiling lemon water (½ cup lemon juice per gallon of water). **For whole mushrooms,** blanch for 6 minutes in boiling lemon water (½ cup lemon juice per gallon of water). Cool; then drain and pack in plastic freezer bags or rigid freezer containers, leaving headspace.
Okra	1 to 1½ lbs.	Rinse; trim ends, but don't open seed cells. Sort according to size. **For small pods,** blanch for 3 minutes in boiling water or for 5 minutes in steam. **For large pods,** blanch for 5 minutes in boiling water or for 8 minutes in steam. Cool; then drain and pack in plastic freezer bags or rigid freezer containers, leaving headspace.
Onions, yellow or white	1 lb.	Peel; remove outer layers until bulb is free of blemishes. Rinse. Chop; or leave small onions whole. No blanching required. Spread chopped or whole onions on trays and freeze for 4 to 6 hours. Pack in plastic freezer bags or rigid freezer containers. No headspace is needed.
Parsnips *See* Turnips, parsnips & rutabagas		
Peas, green or black-eyed	2 to 3 lbs. (unshelled)	Shell and rinse. Sort according to size. **For small peas,** blanch for 1½ minutes in boiling water, 3 minutes in steam, 4 minutes in a high-wattage microwave oven, or 6 minutes in a low-wattage microwave oven. **For large peas,** blanch for 2½ minutes in boiling water, 5 minutes in steam, 4 minutes in a high-wattage microwave oven, or 6 minutes in a low-wattage microwave oven. Cool; drain and pack in plastic freezer bags or rigid freezer containers, leaving headspace.
Peas, snow or sugar snap	⅔ to 1 lb.	Rinse. Remove ends and any strings from pods. Sort according to size. **For small pods,** blanch for 2 minutes in boiling water, 4 minutes in steam, 4 minutes in a high-wattage microwave oven, or 6 minutes in a low-wattage microwave oven. **For large pods,** blanch for 3 minutes in boiling water, 5 minutes in steam, 4 minutes in a high-wattage microwave oven, or 6 minutes in a low-wattage microwave oven. Cool; drain and pack in plastic freezer bags or rigid freezer containers, leaving headspace.

Vegetable	Quantity to yield 1 pint	How to prepare
Peppers, bell, all colors	1 to 2 lbs.	Rinse. Remove stems and seeds. Cut into rings or strips. Blanch for 2 minutes in boiling water or for 3 minutes in steam. Spread on trays and freeze until solid. Pack in plastic freezer bags or rigid freezer containers. No headspace is needed.
Peppers, hot chile	1 to 2 lbs.	Wear rubber gloves when preparing. Rinse and remove stems. No blanching required. Pack in plastic freezer bags or rigid freezer containers, leaving headspace.
Peppers, mild chile	1 to 2 lbs.	Wear rubber gloves when preparing. Rinse chiles; make two ¼-inch slits in each one. Place in a shallow pan and broil, turning as needed, until skins blister. To make peeling easier, cover tightly with foil or place in a plastic bag and close bag. Let stand for about 10 minutes, then peel. Discard stems and seeds. Flatten; or slice or dice. Spread on trays and freeze until solid. Pack in plastic freezer bags or rigid freezer containers. No headspace is needed.
Potatoes, sweet	1 to 1½ lbs.	Rinse well. No blanching required. Boil or steam until tender. Peel, halve, slice, or mash. Dip slices and halves in lemon water (½ cup lemon juice per quart of water); or add 1 tablespoon lemon juice to each pint of mashed sweet potatoes. Pack in rigid freezer containers, leaving headspace.
Potatoes, white French fries	1 to 2 lbs.	Cut peeled potatoes into ⅜-inch-thick strips. No blanching required. Soak for 1 minute in cold water. Drain, rinse, and pat dry with towels. Fry for about 5 minutes in hot oil (360°F) to cover. Drain on paper towels, let cool, and pack in plastic freezer bags, leaving headspace. To reheat, spread potatoes, still frozen, on baking sheets. Heat in a 475° oven for 5 to 6 minutes.
Rutabagas *See* Turnips, parsnips & rutabagas		
Spinach *See* Greens (including spinach)		
Squash, spaghetti	1 to 1½ lbs.	Rinse. No blanching required. Boil or bake until tender when pierced (about 45 minutes in boiling water, about 1 hour in a 350° oven). Let cool; then cut into halves, scoop out strands, and pack in rigid freezer containers, leaving headspace.
Squash, summer Crookneck, pattypan, zucchini	1 to 1¼ lbs.	Rinse squash and trim ends. Cut into ¼- to ½-inch-thick slices. Blanch for 3 minutes in boiling water or for 5 minutes in steam. Cool; then drain and pack in plastic freezer bags or rigid freezer containers, leaving headspace.
Squash, winter (including pumpkin) Banana, butternut, Hubbard, pumpkin	1 to 1½ lbs.	Rinse. Scrape out all seeds and fibrous material; cut into chunks or slices. No blanching required. Steam, boil, or bake until tender. Let cool; remove and discard skin. Purée flesh; pack in rigid freezer containers, leaving headspace.
Tomatoes		Rinse; dip for 30 to 60 seconds in boiling water. Cool and slip off skins. Quarter and simmer until tender (5 to 10 minutes). Press through a sieve, if desired. Let cool. Pack in rigid freezer containers, leaving headspace. Or freeze raw whole unpeeled tomatoes in rigid freezer containers for no longer than 2 to 3 weeks to use for cooking or seasoning. To peel, hold frozen tomatoes under cold water for a second or two; then slip off skins.
Turnips, parsnips & rutabagas	1¼ to 1½ lbs.	Rinse. Peel; cut into ½-inch pieces. Blanch for 3 minutes in boiling water, 5 minutes in steam, 4 minutes in a high-wattage microwave oven, or 6 minutes in a low-wattage microwave oven. Cool; then drain and pack in plastic freezer bags or rigid freezer containers, leaving headspace.
Vegetable mixes (for use in soups and stews)	1 to 1½ lbs.	Prepare each vegetable as specified above. Mix prepared vegetables and pack in plastic freezer bags or rigid freezer containers, leaving headspace.

Freezing Meat, Poultry & Seafood

What's for dinner? If you keep plenty of meat, poultry, and seafood in the freezer, you'll always have an answer to that question. The freezer can help with the food budget, too, when you take advantage of specials to stock up on favorite meats.

Buying Meat for Freezing

Select only fresh, high-quality meats. Remember that cured meats such as bologna and ham are best if used within a short period of time—1 to 3 months. Sliced bacon should be used within a month; if frozen longer, it tends to dry out and taste very salty after cooking.

How much to buy? The amount of meat you buy for freezing—not only the total poundage, but also the types of cuts and their size and weight—will depend on several factors. You'll need to consider your available freezer space, your family's needs, your budget, and the quantity your freezer can handle at one time (see the manufacturer's instructions). If you've purchased or plan to freeze a large amount of meat, it's best to have the market or a butcher cut, wrap, and freeze it. Slower home freezing can cause large ice crystals to form in the meat; these damage cell membranes, so that juices are lost during thawing.

Preparing Meat for the Freezer

Common notions notwithstanding, freezing neither tenderizes nor sterilizes meat. What it does do is reduce enzyme activity and stop the growth of bacteria and molds.

When you're cutting up meat to freeze yourself, make sure all utensils and cutting boards are spotlessly clean. Begin by chilling the meat; then cut it into pieces. To save freezer space, trim off excess fat before wrapping; remove bones from relatively bony pieces. Freeze meat in portions that suit your family's needs, remembering that smaller packages freeze and thaw more rapidly.

To package meat for freezing, use moisture- and vaporproof materials. Wrap all cuts closely, eliminating all air if possible; place a double thickness of freezer wrap or wax paper between chops, steaks, or ground meat patties so they won't stick together. Then pack the wrapped meat in plastic freezer bags or moisture- and vaporproof wrap. Be aware that packaged meat from the supermarket should be overwrapped at home before freezing, since typical see-through packaging is not moisture- and vapor-proof.

You can use two wrapping techniques: the drugstore wrap and the butcher wrap. Both are illustrated below.

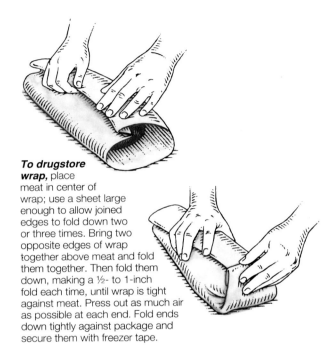

To drugstore wrap, place meat in center of wrap; use a sheet large enough to allow joined edges to fold down two or three times. Bring two opposite edges of wrap together above meat and fold them together. Then fold them down, making a ½- to 1-inch fold each time, until wrap is tight against meat. Press out as much air as possible at each end. Fold ends down tightly against package and secure them with freezer tape.

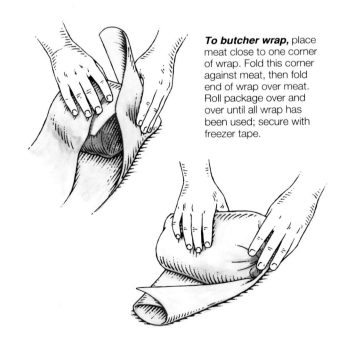

To butcher wrap, place meat close to one corner of wrap. Fold this corner against meat, then fold end of wrap over meat. Roll package over and over until all wrap has been used; secure with freezer tape.

For convenient storage and easier preparation at mealtime, cut large fish into steaks o
fillets and freeze in meal-size protions. Separate the pieces with a double thickness oʃ
freezer wrap or wax paper; then freeze in plastic freezer bags or wrap.
For more on preparing seafood for freezing, see page 192.

Label all packages with the cut of meat, the weight or number of servings, and the date. Then freeze at 0°F or below, making sure to leave space for air circulation between packages.

For recommended storage times at 0°F for different meats, check the chart below. Meat that has been partially thawed in the refrigerator can safely be refrozen, but you can expect some loss of quality.

Beef	
Ground & stew meat	3 to 4 months
Roasts & steaks	8 to 12 months

Lamb	
Ground & stew meat	3 to 4 months
Roasts & chops	6 to 9 months

Pork	
Ground sausage (patties or chunks) or link sausage	1 to 2 months
Roasts & chops	4 to 6 months
Pork & ham, smoked	1 to 3 months
Ham, fully cooked	1 to 2 months
Bacon, sliced	Up to 1 month

Preparing Poultry for the Freezer

Poultry can be frozen whole, halved, quartered, or in pieces. *Never* stuff whole poultry before freezing; the stuffing takes so long to cool during freezing—and to thaw and reheat during roasting—that spoilage and bacterial growth can occur.

Before freezing any poultry, rinse it well in cold water; pat dry with paper towels.

To freeze whole birds, start by freezing the giblets separately in a small plastic freezer bag or in moisture- and vaporproof plastic wrap; use them within 3 months, since they develop an "off" flavor if stored longer. (If you plan to use the poultry within 3 months, you can simply tuck the wrapped giblets into the body cavity; remember to remove them after thawing the bird.) Tie the drumsticks together at the tips; press the wings close to the body or tuck them behind the bird, akimbo-style. Then place each bird in a plastic freezer bag. To remove as much air as possible before sealing, submerge the bag in water up to the opening, then press it against the poultry.

Or simply press out as much air as you can with your hands.

You can also package each bird by placing it in the center of a sheet of moisture- and vaporproof wrap. Bring the long edges together over the bird and fold them down about 1 inch; continue to fold until the wrap is tight and flat over the bird. Force out air by pressing the wrap against the bird; then fold the corners of the wrap toward each other at each end of the bird, making a tight package. Secure with freezer tape.

To freeze poultry halves or quarters, separate the pieces with a double thickness of freezer wrap or wax paper, then place in plastic freezer bags. Or wrap and freeze pieces individually.

To freeze poultry pieces, separate the meaty pieces from the bony ones (bony parts can be used in soup). Spread the pieces in a single layer on a tray and freeze until solid, then place in plastic freezer bags. Or separate unfrozen pieces with a double layer of freezer wrap or wax paper, then pack the pieces close together in plastic freezer bags or moisture- and vaporproof plastic wrap. (The meat near the leg bones may darken, but its quality isn't affected.)

Store all poultry at 0°F for 6 to 12 months.

Preparing Seafood for the Freezer

To freeze fish and shellfish successfully, you must keep them cold after you purchase (or catch) them, then clean and freeze them as quickly as possible.

Freeze *small fish* whole, packaged in moisture- and vaporproof plastic wrap or plastic freezer bags. You may also pack them in rigid freezer containers, adding water to cover. Or place in plastic freezer bags in a large carton; fill the bags with water, leaving ¼-inch headspace, and seal.

Dress *medium-size fish* and package (individually or in meal-size quantities) in moisture- and vapor-proof plastic wrap or plastic freezer bags. Seal tightly, then place in a larger freezer bag.

You may cut *large fish* into steaks, fillets, or boned strips before freezing; package in meal-size quantities, separating pieces with double layers of freezer wrap or wax paper. Or store the fish whole, first glazing them for extra protection. To glaze, freeze the fish unwrapped, then dip it quickly in ice water to form a film of ice over the surface. Continue to dip until the ice glaze is ⅛ inch thick; if necessary, place the fish in the freezer between dippings to get a hard glaze. Package in a large plastic freezer bag and store in the coldest part of the freezer.

To prevent fatty fish such as tuna and salmon from darkening and turning rancid, dip the pieces in an ascorbic acid solution (2 tablespoons ascorbic acid to 1 quart water) for 20 seconds. Then package the fish in meal-size portions, separating pieces with double thicknesses of freezer wrap or wax paper; freeze quickly.

Shellfish is easy to freeze. For *shrimp,* remove heads, but do not shell; or remove entire shell, then devein. Freeze in a single layer on trays until solid, then package in plastic freezer bags.

Shuck or open *clams* and *oysters* and place in a colander to drain; reserve juices. Remove meat and rinse thoroughly and quickly in a solution of 1 tablespoon salt to 1 quart water; drain well. Pack meat in freezer jars or rigid freezer containers; barely cover with reserved juices (and more of the salt solution, if needed), leaving headspace. Freeze quickly. (Keep in mind that freezing changes the texture and flavor of oysters; they're best used in stews or casseroles.)

Prepare *crab* and *lobster* as soon as possible after purchase. Rinse the shellfish well and cook for 20 minutes; drain and let cool slightly, then pick meat from shells while still warm. Tightly pack meat in freezer jars or rigid freezer containers, removing as much air as possible. Leave headspace.

Scallops are usually purchased ready for freezing. Pack them in rigid freezer containers; barely cover with a solution of 1 tablespoon salt to 1 quart water, leaving headspace.

For recommended storage times at 0°F for various fish and shellfish, check the chart below.

Fish	
Fatty fish (tuna, salmon)	2 to 3 months
Lean fish (haddock, sole, trout)	6 to 8 months

Shellfish	
Crab & lobster, cooked	2 to 3 months
Oysters	4 to 6 months
Clams & scallops	4 to 6 months
Shrimp	6 to 8 months

Freezing Glossary

Antidarkening agent. Any antioxidant used to keep light-colored fruits (and some vegetables) from browning after cutting. Antidarkening agents commonly used on fruits to be frozen include ascorbic acid, citrus juice, and commercial products containing ascorbic and/or citric acids (and often sugar).

Blanching. The process of heating food quickly in boiling water or steam (or, in small amounts, in a microwave oven) to inactivate enzymes that can cause loss of color, flavor, and nutritive value. Most vegetables are blanched before freezing.

Dry pack. *See* Sugar pack.

Freezer burn. Damage caused by dehydration; often found in improperly packed frozen foods. Freezer-burned food is spotted with dry, grainy-textured, whitish or brownish areas.

Freezer wrap. Any moisture- and vaporproof wrap, including plastic wrap, coated or laminated paper, and heavy-duty foil.

Headspace. The unfilled space between the top of the food or liquid in a freezer container and the lid of the container.

Liquid pack. Fruit or vegetables packed for freezing in syrup or other liquid.

Moisture- and vaporproof packaging. Choices include both containers and wraps. You may use rigid plastic containers with tight-fitting lids; wide-mouth dual-purpose glass freezer/canning jars; plastic freezer bags with reclosable tops (or bags sealed with wire twist-ties or freezer tape); plastic wrap; coated or laminated paper; and heavy-duty foil.

Sugar pack. Fruit packed for freezing with sugar but without added liquid. Also called *dry pack.*

Syrup pack. Fruit packed for freezing with a syrup of sugar and water (or juice).

Freezing Fresh Herbs

Freezing is a good way to preserve tender herbs such as dill, chives, and tarragon. Simply rinse freshly picked herbs, carefully pat them dry, and freeze in small plastic freezer bags in amounts you'll use at one time. Because frozen herbs darken and become limp upon thawing, add them still frozen to the food you're seasoning.

Dried foods are marvelous to have on hand for snacking and for use in cooking. Shown on the tabletop are (clockwise from left) bell peppers (page 213), apples (page 208), plums (page 209), Dried Fruit Trail Mix (page 205), tomatoes (page 213), Barbecued Jerky (page 216), Teriyaki Turkey Jerky (page 217), peaches (page 209), mushrooms (page 213), apricots (page 208), and a plate holding Dried Fruits with Blue Cheese and High-energy Trail Logs (both on page 205). On the shelf above are fragrant dried herbs (see page 214).

Drying

Sweet dried fruits, colorful vegetables, hearty jerky

*T*hough recent years have seen a surge in the popularity of home drying, this method of food preservation is hardly new. Early American settlers made it through the winter on dried foods, as did the pioneers who traveled across the country to settle on the Western frontier. Sailors, too, relied on dried food supplies during long ocean voyages. ● Home-dried food is economical and easy to store. And with the advent of modern electric dehydrators, it's easy to prepare: you can dry food under sanitary conditions 24 hours a day, in any weather, with little watching or turning. Though dehydrators aren't inexpensive, in a few summers they often pay for themselves—with delicious dried fruits, fruit leathers, tomatoes, vegetables, and other foods for snacking and backpacking. ● Of course, if you live in a hot, dry climate, you may prefer to dry your food naturally out of doors. Many foods can also be dried successfully at very low temperatures in conventional or convection ovens. ● Home drying isn't as exact a science as canning or freezing; your results may vary depending on the weather, the type of pretreatment, and the particular drying method you choose. But with help from this book—and a little trial and error—you'll soon find the techniques that suit you best.

What Happens in Drying?

When you dry food, you remove moisture from it to inhibit the growth of microorganisms that might cause spoilage. Enzyme activity also slows, though it doesn't stop entirely. Keep in mind, however, that drying *doesn't* sterilize food: as soon as it has been rehydrated, microorganisms begin growing again.

Dried fruits retain only 15 to 20 percent of their original moisture, dried vegetables about 5 percent. As a natural consequence of this moisture loss, dried foods are much lighter in weight and take up far less space than do their fresh counterparts.

Drying Basics

To dry food, you need two things: increased temperature and dry, moving air.

The optimal drying temperatures given in this chapter are high enough to remove moisture from foods, yet not so high that the foods begin to cook. In general, vegetables are dried at 125° to 130°F, fruits at 135° to 140°F, and meats at 140° to 150°F. Be sure the temperature doesn't fall below the suggested level: if the air is overly cool, food dries too slowly and may spoil. Nor should you try to hurry things along by using higher temperatures, since foods (especially fruits) may "case harden"—cook and harden on the outside while remaining moist on the inside. Case-hardened food is low in quality and tends to turn moldy.

Dry, moving air first absorbs, then carries away the water released by drying food. The drier the air and the greater the airflow, the faster the food will dry. Calm, humid conditions, on the other hand, retard the drying process and increase the likelihood of spoilage.

Three Drying Methods

You can dry foods in the sun, in an electric dehydrator, or in a conventional or convection oven. Each method has its advantages and drawbacks; when you decide which technique to use, consider the amount of time and money you have to invest as well as the quantity of food you plan to dry. And remember: for successful results by any method, you'll need a combination of warm temperatures, low humidity, and good airflow.

Sun Drying

Sun drying is the earliest known form of food preservation, and most commercial dried fruits—apricots, prunes, raisins, and figs, for example—are still prepared in this age-old way. In fact, fruits are probably the best choice for drying outdoors, since they're high in sugar and acid (both natural preservatives) and thus less prone to spoilage. Vegetables, low in sugar and acid, are more likely to spoil; and meat's high protein content favors the growth of microorganisms unless heat and humidity can be strictly regulated. These foods are better dried inside, under the controlled conditions of a dehydrator or oven.

Where climate permits, sun drying is the least expensive of drying methods, and it lets you prepare large quantities at one time. It does require a fair amount of time and effort, though, and the food must be protected from insects and birds and covered at night. Sun drying is most feasible in regions where the humidity is low, air pollution is minimal, and the weather is sunny and hot (temperatures of 85°F or higher) for many days in a row.

To sun dry, use racks or screens safe for contact with food, such as those made from stainless steel or plastic with a nonstick coating. Do *not* use screening made of aluminum or copper; aluminum tends to corrode, discoloring the food, while copper increases oxidation of the food and destroys vitamin C. Also avoid galvanized metal screens coated with cadmium or zinc; these can leave harmful residues on food.

To ensure good air circulation, place your racks or screens on blocks, then cover them with a second screen or nylon netting as protection against birds and insects. (Don't let the top screen touch the food.)

For more detailed information on sun drying, contact your local Cooperative Extension office.

Drying in a Dehydrator

An electric dehydrator offers you the easiest, most reliable means of drying foods. A dehydrator is a box-shaped or cylindrical appliance that maintains a low, even temperature and circulates heated air (either horizontally or vertically, depending on the model) with a blower or fan. Most dehydrators are equipped with a thermostat and several trays. Some types are expandable, and those with many shelves allow you to dry more food at one time than an oven can handle.

Dehydrators generally yield excellent results, and they can be used all day long, in any weather, for any kind of food. They aren't cheap, though; prices range from $50 to $350, with $100 to $200 the average cost. But if you eat dried foods regularly and often take them along while backpacking and camping, you'll probably make up your investment in short order.

Sources for dehydrators include some hardware and department stores, mail-order and seed or garden supply catalogs, and natural food stores. You might also check the Yellow Pages of your telephone directory under "Dehydrating Equipment"; or call your Cooperative Extension office.

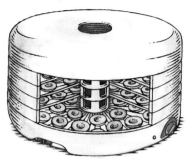

Electric dehydrators with vertical airflow (left) and horizontal airflow (below)

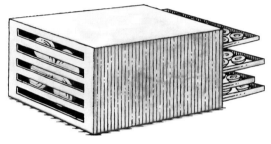

Dehydrator shopping tips. If you decide to buy a dehydrator, keep these questions in mind as you shop.

■ How well is the dehydrator constructed? Is the heating element enclosed for safety, and does it provide sufficient wattage for the entire drying area (about 70 watts per tray)? Are the walls insulated and easy to clean? Does the appliance have an enclosed thermostat? Is there a temperature control adjustable from 85° to 160°F? Is there a timer that can turn the dehydrator off to prevent scorching?

■ Does the fan or blower circulate heated air evenly over all of the food—and is it quiet? (Remember that you may be operating your dehydrator for long periods of time.)

■ Are the trays and inserts made of materials safe for contact with food, such as nylon, stainless steel, or plastic with a nonstick coating? Are there four to ten trays that can accommodate ample quantities of food? Are additional trays available? Can the trays be easily pulled forward or entirely removed? Are they easy to keep clean?

■ Is there a UL seal of approval? A 1-year warranty? Convenient service?

Oven Drying

If you can set your oven at a temperature between 120° and 150°F, you can use it for drying food. Unfortunately, many ovens have minimum settings of 200°F—too high for drying fruits and vegetables—but some modern conventional ovens may offer sufficiently low temperatures. Modern convection ovens can also be used for drying, and dehydrating accessories are often available for them; follow the manufacturer's advice. *The discussion below concerns conventional ovens only.*

Foods dry more rapidly in an oven than in the sun, but usually not as quickly as in a dehydrator, since most ovens lack a built-in fan to circulate air and carry away moisture. Oven drying also consumes more energy (and thus costs more) than dehydrator drying—and it can tie up your oven for hours at a time. Finally, oven-dried foods require a great deal of checking and tending as they dry.

Trays for oven drying should be 3 to 4 inches shorter than the oven from front to back, and narrow enough to clear the oven sides; you may use wire cooling racks placed on top of baking sheets or shallow baking pans. To permit proper air circulation, position the oven racks holding the trays 2 to 3 inches apart.

When you use a conventional oven for drying, you'll need to leave the door propped open by 2 to 6 inches; if you have an electric oven, make sure the upper (broiling) element is turned off. Because oven temperature varies when the door is open, place an oven thermometer next to the food; then adjust the oven temperature dial until the proper temperature is reached.

To improve air circulation, you can set a fan outside the oven door to one side, directing the airflow towards the oven opening. **Caution:** If you use a fan, be sure the oven and fan are attended throughout the drying period. If small children are present, don't use a fan at all; it can be dangerous.

One final note: *Never* oven-dry sulfured foods. Sulfur dioxide produces extremely irritating fumes and can also discolor the inside of your oven. You may, however, oven-dry foods dipped in a sodium bisulfite solution. (For more on sulfuring and sulfite dips, see pages 198 to 200.)

Equipment You'll Need

If you plan to use an electric dehydrator, you'll obviously need to start by buying that (see "Dehydrator shopping tips," at left). But almost all the other equipment you'll use is probably already in your kitchen: a scale for weighing ingredients, a colander for rinsing produce, a steamer (or a large pot and colander or wire basket) for blanching, a sharp knife or mandolin (or a food processor) for slicing, measuring cups and spoons, and a food processor or blender for puréeing fruit for leathers and dehydrated jams.

Packaging & Storing Dried Foods

Before packaging dried foods, make sure they're completely cool: warm food sweats, producing enough moisture for mold to grow. Dried fruits must be conditioned for 3 to 7 days before storage; see "Conditioning" (page 201).

Sun-dried foods in particular are susceptible to insect contamination, but dehydrators and oven-dried foods cooling indoors also attract flies and other pests. It's wise, therefore, to freeze all dried foods in plastic freezer bags for 48 hours to kill any insects or eggs that might be present. Once the food has been frozen, place it in clean, dry, insectproof containers, packing it as tightly as possible without crushing. Glass jars, metal cans or boxes, and rigid plastic containers with tight-fitting lids are all good choices—but don't place sulfured fruit in a metal can unless you've first enclosed it in a plastic bag (sulfur fumes react with metal and may cause the fruit to change color).

It's convenient to store dried foods in small heavy-duty plastic bags in amounts you'll use at one time. This kind of packaging is sensible from a freshness standpoint, too, since air and moisture enter each time you reopen packaged dried food, with a resulting decrease in quality. Just be sure to store bagged foods in one of the containers mentioned above (or in the refrigerator or freezer), since insects and rodents can penetrate plastic bags.

If stored in a cool, dry, dark area, dried foods will generally keep from 3 months to 1 year, depending on the particular food. Higher temperatures decrease maximum storage times; for example, most dried fruits store well for a year at 60°F, but only for 6 months at 80°F. Vegetables usually have about half this shelf life. Of course, refrigerated or frozen dried foods keep well longer.

Even foods that are very dry when stored can spoil if they reabsorb moisture, so check frequently to make sure your dried foods are still dry (glass jars make it easy to tell if there's moisture in the container). If the food looks at all moist, use it immediately; or redry and repackage it.

Drying Fresh Fruits

Naturally sweet and flavorful, nutritious dried fruits are delicious snacks and wonderful additions to cereals and baked goods. And when rehydrated, they're marvelous in sauces and toppings.

Preparing the Fruit

Assemble all the equipment you'll need for drying. Select fully ripe fruit in top condition, and prepare only as much as you can dry at one time. Just before processing, rinse the fruit well in cold water to remove dirt, insects, and insect eggs (you can't see the eggs, but if they're not washed away, they may hatch during storage).

As noted in our "Guide for Drying Fruits" (pages 208 and 209), most fruits dry more evenly and rapidly when sliced. When you cut them, keep in mind that lengthwise slicing yields fewer, larger pieces than crosswise slicing. If you like, you can dry peaches, shorten drying times, flatten the halves ("pop the backs") by pressing in the rounded side with your thumb to expose more surface. Dry the fruit skin side down, so juice will collect and dry in the cavity.

Some kinds of fruit can successfully be dried whole; be sure to pit them to hasten drying. Small whole fruits such as cherries, blueberries, cranberries, grapes, figs, and prune plums will dry faster if you first dip them in boiling water just long enough to crack ("check") the skins.

Many kinds, however, are best if pretreated to prevent *oxidation:* a chemical reaction that makes fruit darken when cut, diminishes flavor, and causes loss of vitamins A and C. A number of different pretreatments are described below; for advice on specific fruits, consult the chart on pages 208 and 209.

Pretreating Fruit

If you're drying fruit for long-term storage, you'll find that sulfuring it outdoors is the best way to preserve its color and flavor. Dipping fruit indoors in a sodium bisulfite solution is another excellent treatment. If you wish to avoid sulfur compounds, choose an alternative such as ascorbic acid, citric acid, or citrus juice; these often do a good job, though they're not as effective as sulfur.

Sulfuring. A very old and highly effective method, sulfuring preserves the fresh, natural appearance of

Scandinavian Dried Fruit Soup (page 206) offers a delicious blend on flavors. Start by simmering your favorite dried fruits with lemon slices, orange juice, and cinnamon; then add fresh pineapple chunks, honey, and a little rum. Serve the dessert hot or cold, topped with spoonfuls of vanilla yogurt and a sprinkling of cinnamon or nutmeg.

199

light-colored fruits, helps repel insects, inhibits mold growth, and speeds drying time. There are drawbacks, though. The process is time consuming and demands special care—and in addition, sulfured fruit may cause an allergic reaction in some asthmatics.

Fruit to be sulfured is usually placed on wooden trays in a "sulfur box"—often just a large cardboard box with two vents—set on concrete blocks over a shallow pit containing a pan of flowers of sulfur. (Also sold as "sublimed sulfur," flowers of sulfur are available in some pharmacies and in many garden supply stores.) The sulfur is burned briefly; then the box vents are closed and the fruit is exposed to the sulfur fumes for several hours. Finally, the sulfured fruit is dried outdoors in a dehydrator or in the sun. Because sulfur dioxide fumes are harmful when inhaled, sulfuring—as well as the drying of the treated fruit—must *always* be done outside, in an area with good air circulation. *Never* dry sulfured fruit indoors in an oven or dehydrator.

For detailed instructions on making a sulfur box and sulfuring fruit, contact your local Cooperative Extension office.

Sulfite dip. Sulfite dipping isn't as effective as sulfuring, but it's an excellent pretreatment nonetheless—and it can be done safely and easily indoors. Sulfite-dipped fruit can be dried indoors or out: in a dehydrator or an oven, or in the sun.

To prepare a sulfite dip, start by purchasing food-grade sodium bisulfite, sodium sulfite, or sodium metabisulfite from a wine-making supply store, pharmacy, or hobby shop. Dissolve ½ teaspoon sodium bisulfite, 1 teaspoon sodium sulfite, or 2 teaspoons sodium metabisulfite in a quart of cold water. (Sodium sulfite is half as strong as sodium bisulfite, sodium metabisulfite a fourth as strong.) Add the fruit to the solution; soak slices for up to 10 minutes, halves for up to 30 minutes. Then remove the fruit, rinse it lightly under cold running water, drain, and dry.

Ascorbic acid. Though less effective than sulfuring in preventing browning, pretreatment with ascorbic acid (vitamin C in powder form) yields nutritious, good-tasting fruit.

To prepare the dipping solution, dissolve 1 tablespoon pure crystalline ascorbic acid (sold in pharmacies and most health food stores) in a quart of cold water. Add the fruit and soak it for a few minutes; then drain well and dry. After using the solution two or three times, discard it and mix up a new batch.

Commercial antidarkening agents. Commercially marketed antidarkening agents are mixtures of ascorbic and/or citric acids (and often sugar) sold for use on fresh fruits to be canned or frozen. They're not as effective as ascorbic acid.

To prepare the dipping solution, dissolve 1½ tablespoons antidarkening agent in a quart of cold water. Add the fruit and soak it for a few minutes; then drain well and dry. After using the solution two or three times, discard it and mix up a new batch.

Citrus juices. Lemon and lime juices help prevent oxidation and preserve color, but they're only a sixth as effective as ascorbic acid.

To prepare the dipping solution, mix 1 cup lemon or lime juice with a quart of cold water. Soak the fruit for no more than 10 minutes; then drain well and dry. (You may use unsweetened pineapple juice in place of lemon or lime juice, but it doesn't enhance the fruit flavor as much as the other juices do.)

Citric acid. Citric acid is just an eighth as effective as ascorbic acid, and its tart taste may mask the fruit's flavor.

To prepare the dipping solution, dissolve 1 tablespoon citric acid in a quart of cold water. Add the fruit and soak it for a few minutes; then drain well and dry. After using the solution two or three times, discard it and mix up a fresh batch.

Honey-lemon dip. Honey is a natural preservative; lemon juice helps fruit keep its color. To prepare the dip, mix ½ cup honey with ½ cup water and the juice of one lemon. Heat slightly to dissolve the honey. Dip the fruit in the mixture, then drain well and dry.

Honey dip. Many store-bought dried fruits are honey dipped. To make the solution, dissolve 1 cup sugar in 3 cups hot water; let cool, then add 1 cup honey. Dip fruit in small batches; drain well and dry.

Blanching. Steam or water blanching slows oxidation and helps fruit retain its color—but it gives a less flavorful product than other methods, and the fruit has a slightly cooked taste and texture. For details on blanching techniques and times, contact your local Cooperative Extension office.

Drying the Fruit

Regardless of the drying method you use, it's important to arrange the fruit on trays or racks in a single layer, without letting the pieces touch or overlap.

To sun dry, start by reading "Sun Drying" (page 196). Arrange racks or screens in direct sun. Check the fruit frequently; move the racks when they become shaded. Unless you live where nights are relatively clear and evening temperatures remain within 20 degrees of midday highs, you'll need to take the drying racks to a porch or other sheltered place at night to keep the fruit from being dampened by dew. (Even if you can leave your racks out overnight, be sure to cover them loosely.)

After the fruit has dried for 2 or 3 days, place it in the shade for the remainder of the drying time; it will have a better flavor and color and retain more nutrients than it would if left in the sun throughout the drying process.

To dry fruit in a dehydrator, follow the manufacturer's instructions. In general, fruit should be dried at 135° to 140°F.

To dry fruit in a conventional oven, consult "Oven Drying" (page 197). Set the oven temperature at 140°F.

To dry fruit in a convection oven, follow the manufacturer's instructions.

Determining Dryness

The "Guide for Drying Fruits" (pages 208 and 209) gives specific dryness tests for a number of fruits. If you're preparing apricots, prunes, apples, or other types that you'll often eat without rehydrating, it's important not to dry them so long that they turn hard or brittle. To avoid overdrying, check the fruit frequently as it becomes drier: let a piece cool to room temperature, then cut it in half. Most types should remain pliable, but they shouldn't be sticky or show any visible pockets of moisture.

Conditioning

Dried fruit should always be "conditioned" to distribute any remaining moisture more evenly, reducing the possibility of mold.

To condition fruit, cool it to room temperature; then pack it loosely in plastic or glass containers with tight-fitting lids and let stand for 3 to 7 days. Over this period of time, the excess moisture in some pieces will be absorbed by drier fruit. Each day, shake the containers to separate the pieces, then check for condensation. If you see droplets or a mist of moisture on the container sides, the fruit should be redried.

After conditioning the fruit, package and store it as directed on page 198.

Using Dried Fruits

Dried fruits are superb "as is" for snacks, though you may wish to soften them slightly before eating. If the fruit is to be stewed or served as a sauce or topping, though, you'll need to reconstitute it in liquid (wait until it's as plump as you like before adding sugar, since sugar tends to hinder water absorption). And remember: the longer a fruit takes to dehydrate, the more time it will require to rehydrate.

To soften dried fruit for snacks. If the fruit is too firm for your taste, place it (in 1-cup quantities) in a plastic bag, sprinkle it with several drops of water, close the bag tightly, and refrigerate overnight.

To soften dried fruit for use in bread, cookie, and cake recipes. Steam for several minutes, then cut or slice as the recipe directs.

To rehydrate dried fruit. Spread the fruit in a shallow container and barely cover it with liquid, using about 1 cup liquid for each 2 cups fruit. The liquid you use may be water, fruit juice, fruit liqueur, wine, or brandy. Fruit usually rehydrates within a few hours; if more time is needed, cover the dish and refrigerate it to keep the fruit from fermenting. Add more liquid if necessary—but for best flavor and texture, keep the liquid you add to a minimum.

To cook rehydrated fruit in liquid. If you want to cook fruit after it has been rehydrated, simmer it, covered, in any remaining soaking liquid (the liquid contains vitamins and other nutrients from the fruit). If necessary, add a small amount of water or juice to keep the fruit from scorching. Sugar should be added only when the fruit is nearly done.

To cook dried fruit in liquid. Un-rehydrated dried fruit can be cooked on the rangetop, in an electric slow cooker, or in a microwave oven. The amount of liquid you'll need depends on how you plan to use the fruit. If you'll be serving it in a compote or topping, use about 1 cup liquid to 1 cup fruit; if it's going into a pie, cobbler, dough, or batter, start with $2/3$ to $3/4$ cup liquid per cup of fruit, then add more liquid as needed to achieve the desired consistency.

To cook dried fruit on the range, bring the liquid to a boil and add the fruit; then reduce heat, cover, and simmer until fruit is tender (usually 10 to 15 minutes).

To cook dried fruit in a slow cooker or microwave oven, follow the manufacturer's instructions.

It's easy to make sweet leathers from puréed fresh fruits—especially if you have a dehydrator. Shown here are strawberry, raspberry, peach, apricot, plum, and pear-pecan fruit rolls, all prepared according to the recipe on the facing page.

202

Fresh Fruit Leather

Pictured on facing page

Sweet fruit leathers are especially easy to dry in a dehydrator, but sun drying also works well—as long as the temperature is 85°F or higher and the relative humidity 60 percent or lower. Our recipe makes 10-inch squares of leather; if you'd like to make larger pieces or prepare several leathers at a time, just increase the amount of purée proportionately.

Fruit Purée (choices and directions follow)
Finely chopped nuts or shredded coconut (optional)

Prepare drying surface for dehydrator or sun drying.

Dehydrator drying. If your dehydrator has special trays for leather, prepare them according to the manufacturer's instructions. Or cover each drying tray with a sheet of plastic wrap, extending it over tray edges; secure with tape. Preheat dehydrator.

Sun drying. Start early in the day. Cover rimmed 10- by 15-inch baking pans or other shallow pans with plastic wrap (one continuous sheet per pan), extending it over tray edges; secure wrap to underside of pans with tape. Set pans in full sun, on a level surface such as a table.

Once drying surface has been prepared, prepare purée (or purées) of your choice. To make each leather, pour 1 cup purée onto prepared surface and spread to about 10 inches square. (You may need to double the amount of purée for some dehydrator trays intended especially for leathers.) Layer of purée should be about ⅜ inch thick; make it slightly thicker around edges to ensure that leather dries evenly, without brittle edges. If desired, lightly sprinkle purée with nuts or coconut.

Dry purée until leathery, pliable, and no longer tacky to touch; it should peel off drying surface with no sticky spots. Dehydrator-dried purées are usually ready in 5 to 10 hours; sun-dried purées take 1 to 2 days. To keep purées clean during sun drying, suspend cheesecloth over them, supporting it with 2-by-4s on each side. If purées aren't dry by day's end, bring them indoors; return to sun the next day.

While leather is still warm, roll it up jelly roll style in plastic wrap, enclosing the wrap. Or cut it into snack-size strips and wrap each piece in plastic wrap; store pieces flat or roll up. Store in an airtight container; for longer storage, place in plastic freezer bags or rigid freezer containers and refrigerate or freeze.

Makes 1 (10-inch-square) leather (2 servings) from each cup of purée.

Fruit Purée. It's not necessary to peel most fruits, but peeled fruits make smoother leather. Rinse all fruit well; pat dry (drain berries on paper towels). To purée, whirl fruit (plus lemon juice, spices, and/or sweetener) in a blender until very smooth, scraping down sides of container as needed.

Because the drying process concentrates natural sugars, many fruits don't need sweetening. If you do use a sweetener, sugar is fine—as long as you plan to freeze your leathers or eat them within a few weeks. But if you intend to store them at room temperature (or in the refrigerator) for over a week or two, sweeten them with honey or corn syrup, since sugar-sweetened leather may become grainy.

Each fruit choice below yields 1 cup purée.

Apple. In a 1½- to 2-quart pan, combine 2½ cups cored, sliced **apples** with ⅓ cup **apple juice** or water. Bring to a boil; reduce heat, cover, and simmer until apples are soft when mashed (about 10 minutes). Let cool slightly. Purée with 1 tablespoon **lemon juice**, about 2 tablespoons **honey**, light corn syrup, or sugar, and ¼ teaspoon **ground cinnamon** (optional); add a few tablespoons **apple juice**, if needed, to give purée the consistency of cake batter.

Apricot. Purée 1½ cups halved, pitted **apricots** with 1 tablespoon **lemon juice** and about 3 tablespoons **honey**, light corn syrup, or sugar.

Cherry. Pit about 1½ cups **sweet cherries**. Purée with 1 tablespoon **lemon juice**.

Peach or nectarine. Purée 2 cups sliced **peaches** or nectarines with 1 tablespoon **lemon juice** and about 2 tablespoons **honey**, light corn syrup, or sugar.

Pear. Juicy Bartletts are best. Purée 2 cups cored, sliced **pears** with 1 tablespoon **lemon juice**.

Plum. Purée 1½ cups sliced **plums** with 1 tablespoon **lemon juice** and about 2 tablespoons **honey**, light corn syrup, or sugar.

Raspberry or blackberry (blackberries include boysenberries, olallieberries, and loganberries). Purée about 2 cups **berries** with 1 tablespoon **lemon juice** and about ¼ cup **honey**, light corn syrup, or sugar. Press through a fine strainer; discard seeds.

Strawberry. Hull 1¼ to 1½ cups **strawberries** and purée with 1 tablespoon **lemon juice** and about 2 tablespoons **honey**, light corn syrup, or sugar.

Storage time. Up to 2 months at room temperature; up to 6 months in refrigerator; up to 1 year in freezer.

Per serving (approximate): 134 calories, 1 g protein, 35 g carbohydrates, 1 g total fat, 0 mg cholesterol, 3 mg sodium

Naturally Sweet No-cook Jams

Naturally sweet dehydrated jams are easy to make. Just purée your choice of fruit, then let it dry in a dehydrator or an oven—or in the sun, provided the temperature is 85°F or higher and the relative humidity 60 percent or lower. As moisture evaporates from the purée, it thickens to a jamlike consistency. The process usually takes 2 to 4 hours in a dehydrator or oven; sun drying requires a day or two.

Dehydrated Jam

Fruit Purée (choices and directions follow)
Sugar, honey, and/or lemon juice (optional)

Following the directions below, prepare a drying tray or container for dehydrator, oven, or sun drying. Then prepare purée and proceed as directed for each method. Once an hour, carefully scrape jam from edges of tray or pan with a rubber spatula and stir well; then spread evenly again. Let dry until jam is almost as thick as you prefer; it will thicken further as it cools. Spoon jam into a container and stir in a little more sugar, honey, and/or lemon juice, if desired. Cover; freeze or refrigerate.

Dehydrator drying. If your dehydrator has a door and removable drying trays, place a pie pan or other shallow baking pan on tray. Or make a container to fit the dimensions of your dehydrator tray, using a double thickness of heavy-duty foil; pinch foil container together at corners to secure. Spray pan or foil container with vegetable oil cooking spray before adding purée.

If your dehydrator has drying trays that stack over a heat source on the bottom and includes a special tray for fruit leathers and sauces, prepare tray according to manufacturer's instructions.

Pour purée onto tray and spread to a thickness of ⅜ inch. Use temperature recommended for drying fruit in your dehydrator (usually 135° to 140°F).

Oven drying. Lay a continuous sheet of parchment paper in a shallow baking pan (about 10 by 15 inches); paper should extend beyond pan edge.

Pour purée into pan and spread to a thickness of ⅜ inch. Heat oven to 120° to 130°F; place pan in oven. Prop oven door open several inches to allow moisture to escape; check oven temperature periodically with an oven thermometer.

Sun drying. Use a glass, metal, or plastic pan (about 9 by 13 inches). Pour purée into pan and spread evenly. Cover pan with plastic wrap, leaving about 1 inch along one long side uncovered. Place pan in full sun, on a level surface such as a table. If purée isn't sufficiently thickened by day's end, cover and refrigerate it overnight; return to sun the next day.

Purées dried by any method make about 1 cup apricot, berry, peach, or plum jam, ½ cup melon jam.

Fruit Purée. For best flavor, start with fully ripe, top-quality fruit. Rinse all fruit well; pat dry (drain berries on paper towels). To purée, whirl fruit (plus any lemon juice, sugar, or honey) in a blender until smooth, scraping down sides of container as needed. Each fruit choice below yields 2 cups purée.

Apricot. Purée 3 cups halved, pitted **apricots** with 1 tablespoon **lemon juice** and 2 to 4 tablespoons **sugar** or honey.

Melon. Cut peeled, seeded **cantaloupe,** Persian, or honeydew melon into chunks; purée enough melon to make 2 cups. Blend in 2 tablespoons **lemon juice** and 1 to 2 tablespoons **sugar** or honey.

Peach or nectarine. Purée 4 cups sliced peeled **peaches** or unpeeled nectarines with 1 tablespoon **lemon juice** and 2 to 4 tablespoons **sugar** or honey.

Plum. Purée 3 cups sliced **plums** or prune plums with 2 to 4 tablespoons **sugar** or honey. Pour purée into a 2-quart pan. Bring to a simmer, stirring occasionally; cover and simmer for 2 minutes. Let cool slightly.

Raspberry or blackberry (blackberries include boysenberries, olallieberries, and loganberries). Purée 4 cups **berries;** press through a fine strainer and discard seeds. Blend in 1 tablespoon **lemon juice** and 4 to 6 tablespoons **sugar.**

Strawberry. Hull 3 cups **strawberries** and purée with 1 tablespoon **lemon juice** and 2 to 4 tablespoons **sugar.**

Storage time. Up to 1 week in refrigerator; up to 6 months in freezer.

Per tablespoon (approximate): 27 calories, 0 g protein, 6 g carbohydrates, 0 g total fat, 0 mg cholesterol, 1 mg sodium

Dried Fruit Trail Mix

Pictured on page 194

A handful of this fruity mix is great on the trail or any time you want a treat. You can substitute other favorite fruits, either home-dried or purchased at a supermarket or health food store, for the selections below. Try dried cherries or cranberries in place of raisins or use mango slices instead of papaya.

- 1 cup *each* dried papaya slices and banana chips
- 1 cup unsweetened shredded coconut
- ½ cup *each* dark and golden raisins
- ⅔ cup chopped pitted dates
- ½ cup chopped dried apricots

Cut papaya slices into bite-size pieces; break banana chips into bite-size pieces. Place in a large bowl and add coconut, raisins, dates, and apricots. Toss gently until well blended. Package in airtight containers; or place in serving-size plastic bags, then in an airtight container. Makes about 5 cups.

Storage time. Up to 2 weeks at room temperature; up to 4 months in refrigerator; up to 1 year in freezer.

Per ½ cup: 207 calories, 2 g protein, 44 g carbohydrates, 5 g total fat, 0 mg cholesterol, 7 mg sodium

High-energy Trail Logs

Pictured on page 194

Backpackers will applaud these hearty little nuggets of energy. They're great as at-home snacks, too; stored airtight, they'll keep in the refrigerator for several weeks.

- 1¼ cups walnut pieces
- ¼ cup dry-roasted cashews
- 6 dried black figs
- ½ cup pitted dates
- ½ cup golden or dark raisins
- ¼ cup dried apples
- ½ teaspoon lemon juice
- 1 tablespoon dark or light rum
- 2 tablespoons powdered sugar or about ½ cup sweetened flaked coconut

Using a food processor or a food chopper fitted with a fine blade, grind walnuts, cashews, figs, dates, raisins, and apples. Turn into a bowl and mix thoroughly. Blend in lemon juice and rum.

To shape logs, scoop out mixture in 1-tablespoon portions; roll each portion into a ¾- by 2-inch log. Roll logs in sugar or coconut, arrange in a single layer, and let stand, uncovered, for 1 to 2 days to dry. Then cover airtight and refrigerate. To carry on the trail, wrap logs individually in foil or plastic wrap. Makes about 2½ dozen logs.

Storage time. Up to 3 weeks in refrigerator.

Per log: 68 calories, 1 g protein, 9 g carbohydrates, 4 g total fat, 0 mg cholesterol, 2 mg sodium

Dried Fruits with Blue Cheese

Pictured on page 194

The simplest of appetizers, these fruit treats are a great contribution to a buffet table or a nice beginning for a casual get-together. Top each piece with a cashew, walnut, or pecan; or sprinkle with minced fresh mint.

- 32 dry-roasted cashews, walnut halves, or pecan halves; or about 3 tablespoons minced fresh mint
- 5 ounces blue-veined cheese such as cambozola or Gorgonzola
- 1 small package (about 3 oz.) cream cheese, at room temperature
- ½ teaspoon ground white or black pepper
- 32 pieces dried fruit (use apricot, peach, or pear halves, whole pitted prunes, or some of each fruit)

Toast nuts in a small frying pan over medium heat until golden brown (about 4 minutes), stirring occasionally. Pour out of pan and let cool.

In a small bowl, beat together blue cheese, cream cheese, and pepper (or whirl in a food processor). Spread cheese mixture evenly over fruit pieces. (At this point, you may cover and refrigerate until next day.)

To complete appetizers, press a nut into cheese on each piece of fruit or sprinkle cheese with mint. Arrange fruit, cheese side up, on a platter. If made ahead, cover and refrigerate. Makes 32 appetizers.

Storage time. Up to 1 day in refrigerator before topping with nuts; up to 4 hours in refrigerator after topping.

Per appetizer: 39 calories, 1 g protein, 3 g carbohydrates, 3 g total fat, 6 mg cholesterol, 70 mg sodium

Scandinavian Dried Fruit Soup

Pictured on page 199

Dried fruits and chunks of fresh pineapple combine with orange juice in this refreshing Scandinavian-style dessert.

- 2½ cups mixed dried fruit, such as apples, apricots, peaches, and prunes, cut into bite-size pieces
- ½ cup raisins or dried cherries
- ½ lemon, thinly sliced and seeded
- 1 cinnamon stick (about 3 inches long)
- 3½ cups water
- 2 cups orange juice
- 1½ cups fresh pineapple chunks; or 1½ cups pineapple chunks packed in their own juice, drained
- ⅔ to ¾ cup honey
- ⅛ teaspoon salt (optional)
- ⅓ cup rum or brandy
- 1 tablespoon cornstarch blended with 2 tablespoons cold water
  Vanilla yogurt or sour cream

In a 3-quart pan, combine dried fruit, raisins, lemon slices, cinnamon stick, water, and orange juice; bring to a boil over high heat. Reduce heat to medium-low, cover, and simmer for 10 to 15 minutes. Then remove from heat and stir in pineapple, honey, salt (if desired), and rum. Let stand for 10 minutes to blend flavors and let fruit soften.

Return pan to heat; then blend cornstarch mixture into soup. Cook over medium-low heat, stirring, until liquid is bubbly, clear, and thickened. Remove cinnamon stick and lemon slices. Serve soup hot; or cover and refrigerate to serve cold. Top with spoonfuls of yogurt. Makes 10 servings.

Storage time. Up to 2 days in refrigerator.

Per serving: 247 calories, 2 g protein, 61 g carbohydrates, 0 g total fat, 0 mg cholesterol, 9 mg sodium

Chopping Dried Fruit

To chop dried fruit more easily, occasionally dip your scissors or knife in hot water or coat the blades lightly with salad oil. Freeze dried fruit before chopping it in a food processor or blender.

Fettuccine with Dried Tomatoes & Mushrooms

Pictured on facing page

Intensely flavored dried tomatoes and mushrooms lend zest to this colorful pasta dish. You can use any kind of dried mushrooms; we suggest button or shiitake.

- 1 ounce (about 2 cups lightly packed) dried sliced mushrooms, such as button or shiitake
- 2 ounces (about 1½ cups) dried sliced beefsteak-type tomatoes; or 2 ounces (about 1½ cups) dried pear-shaped (Roma-type) tomatoes, coarsely chopped
- 1 *each* medium-size zucchini and crookneck squash
- 8 ounces dry fettuccine
- 2 tablespoons olive oil
- 2 cloves garlic, minced
- ¼ cup dry white wine
- 1 tablespoon chopped fresh basil or 1 teaspoon dry basil
- 1 tablespoon chopped fresh tarragon or ½ teaspoon dry tarragon
- ¼ teaspoon *each* crushed red pepper flakes and salt
- ½ cup grated Parmesan cheese

Place mushrooms in a medium-size bowl; place tomatoes in another medium-size bowl. Add cold water to cover each vegetable; let stand until vegetables are soft (about 1 hour). Drain off any liquid; set vegetables aside. Cut zucchini and crookneck squash into ¼-inch-thick slices; then cut each slice into thirds. Set aside.

In a 6- to 8-quart pan, cook fettuccine according to package directions just until tender to bite. Meanwhile, heat oil in a wide frying pan over high heat; add mushrooms, zucchini, crookneck squash, and garlic. Cook, stirring, until zucchini is tender-crisp to bite (2 to 3 minutes). Mix wine, basil, tarragon, red pepper flakes, and salt; pour over vegetables and toss to heat through.

Drain pasta; return to cooking pan. Add vegetable mixture and tomatoes and toss to mix. Transfer to a large platter; sprinkle with cheese. Makes 6 servings.

Storage time. Best when served immediately, but you may cover and refrigerate for up to 1 day, then reheat (add cheese just before serving).

Per serving: 262 calories, 10 g protein, 36 g carbohydrates, 8 g total fat, 41 mg cholesterol, 233 mg sodium

*Dried tomato slices and shiitake mushrooms bring vibrant and earthy flavors to
a combination of tender pasta strands, fresh summer squash, and herbs. For a satisfying
lunch or supper, you might serve Fettuccine with Dried Tomatoes & Mushrooms (facing page)
with a crisp salad, warm bread, and dry white wine.*

Guide for Drying Fruits

For details on sulfuring and other preteatments, see "Pretreating Fruit" (page 198). When treating fruits with sulfite or other dip, don't soak them for more than a few minutes; oversoaking causes a decrease in nutritional value. If you're drying fruit halves, keep in mind that they'll take longer to dry than slices do.

Fruit & best types for drying	How to prepare	Treatment before drying	Test for dryness*
Apples Firm varieties such as Granny Smith, Gravenstein, Jonathan, Newtown Pippin, Rome Beauty	Rinse, peel, cut off both ends, core, and cut into ¼- to ⅜-inch-thick slices.	Dip in sulfite solution, ascorbic acid solution, or citrus juice dip. Or sulfur fruit, using 2 teaspoons sulfur per pound of cut fruit.	Soft, leathery, pliable
Apricots Royal-Blenheim, Tilton	Rinse, halve, and pit. If drying fruit as halves, press halves to flatten. Otherwise, cut halves into ¼-inch-thick slices.	Dip in sulfite solution, ascorbic acid solution, or citrus juice dip. Or sulfur fruit, using 1 teaspoon sulfur per pound of cut fruit.	Pliable, with no areas of moisture
Bananas	Choose fruit that's solid yellow or slightly speckled with brown. Peel; cut into ¼- to ⅜-inch-thick slices.	Treatment optional; may dip in honey-lemon or honey dip.	Pliable to crisp
Berries	Blackberries, boysenberries, huckleberries, and raspberries are not recommended for drying; they're too full of seeds and take too long to dry. They do, however, make good fruit leathers; see page 203.		
Blueberries	Choose large, firm, fully ripe berries with deep blue color. Rinse and remove stems.	Dip in boiling water until skins crack. Dip briefly in ice water; drain on paper towels.	Leathery and pliable
Cherries, all varieties *Sweet:* Bing, Lambert, Royal Ann *Sour:* Early Richmond, Montmorency	Rinse and remove stems. Pit fruit and leave whole; or halve and pit.	Treatment optional; may dip in boiling water until skins crack.	Leathery and pliable, with no areas of moisture
Citrus peel Peels of grapefruit, kumquat, lemon, lime, orange, tangerine	Peel from thick-skinned navel oranges is better than that from thin-skinned Valencias. If fruit is marked "color added," do not dry its peel. Rinse well to remove surface residues. Pare off colored part of peel only, avoiding bitter white pith beneath.	No treatment necessary.	Crisp
Coconut	Choose fresh coconut, heavy for its size. Pierce eyes and pour out milk; crack nut with a hammer. Remove meat; discard outer skin. Grate or slice thinly.	No treatment necessary.	Crisp
Cranberries	Rinse.	Treatment optional; may dip in boiling water until skins crack.	Shriveled, with no areas of moisture
Figs Black Mission, Kadota, Calimyrna	Use tree-ripened figs; when fully ripe and ready for drying, they fall to the ground. Rinse; halve or leave whole.	Treatment optional; may dip in boiling water until skins crack.	Leathery outside, but still pliable. Slightly sticky inside, but not wet

* Cool a piece before testing

Fruit & best types for drying	How to prepare	Treatment before drying	Test for dryness*
Grapes (for raisins) Green or red seedless varieties	Rinse and remove stems; leave whole or halve.	Treatment optional; may dip in boiling water until skins crack.	Leathery, with wrinkled, raisinlike texture; no areas of moisture
Melons, all varieties	Avoid overripe fruit. If using watermelon, cut lengthwise into quarters. Cut quarters into ¼- to ⅜-inch-thick slices; then cut slices into 2-inch pieces as you remove rind and seeds. If using other melons, halve, seed, and peel; cut into ¼-inch-thick slices, then into 2-inch pieces.	No treatment necessary.	Soft and pliable, with no areas of moisture (very sweet melons will be slightly sticky)
Nectarines Flamekist, Flavortop, Red Diamond	Rinse; no need to peel. Halve and pit. If drying fruit as halves, press halves to flatten. Otherwise, cut halves into ⅜-inch-thick slices.	Dip in sulfite solution, ascorbic acid solution, or citrus juice dip. Or sulfur fruit, using 2 teaspoons sulfur per pound of cut fruit.	Soft and pliable, with no areas of moisture
Peaches Elberta, Flavorcrest, O'Henry, Redtop	Rinse and peel; halve and pit. If drying fruit as halves, press halves to flatten. Otherwise, cut halves into ⅜-inch-thick slices.	Dip in sulfite solution, ascorbic acid solution, or citrus juice dip. Or sulfur fruit, using 2 teaspoons sulfur per pound of cut fruit.	Soft and pliable, with no areas of moisture
Pears Bartlett	Rinse, peel if desired, halve, and core. If drying fruit as halves, press halves to flatten. Otherwise, cut halves into ¼-inch-thick slices.	Dip in sulfite solution, ascorbic acid solution, or citrus juice dip. Or sulfur fruit, using 2½ teaspoons sulfur per pound of cut fruit.	Soft and pliable, with no areas of moisture
Pineapple	Use only fully ripe fruit. Rinse; peel, then cut out eyes and core. Cut crosswise into ½-inch-thick rings.	No treatment necessary.	Leathery but not sticky
Plums, most varieties	Rinse. Do not peel; do not dry fruit whole. Halve and pit. If drying fruit as halves, press halves to flatten. Otherwise, cut halves into ¼- to ⅜-inch-thick slices.	No treatment necessary.	Leathery and pliable, with no areas of moisture
Prune plums (for prunes) French, Italian	Rinse. Do not peel. Halve and pit; press halves to flatten. Prunes may also be dried whole, but will take 4 times as long as halved fruit. If you are sun-drying whole fruit, pit it; then dip it in boiling water until skins crack.	No treatment necessary.	Leathery and pliable, with no areas of moisture
Strawberries	Choose red, fully ripe berries. Rinse gently and hull. Cut into ½-inch-thick slices.	No treatment necessary.	Leathery and pliable, with no areas of moisture

* Cool a piece before testing

Drying Vegetables

Vegetables are easily dried at home in a dehydrator. Oven drying is acceptable, too, though it's more complicated and time consuming than dehydrator drying. Sun drying is best avoided—because vegetables are low in sugar and acid, they tend to spoil under uncontrolled outdoor conditions.

Preparing the Vegetables

If possible, get vegetables ready for drying immediately after harvesting, preparing only as much as you can dry at one time. Rinse vegetables thoroughly in cold water, but don't soak them—that depletes minerals and vitamins. Peel vegetables, then cut out any woody, fibrous, decayed, or bruised areas. Cut or slice each type of vegetable as directed in the chart on pages 212 and 213, keeping pieces uniform in size so they'll dry at the same rate.

About Blanching

Many vegetables must be blanched before drying. *Blanching*—quick heating to inactivate enzymes—prevents deterioration during drying and storage; it also sets color and shortens drying and rehydrating time by relaxing cell walls, allowing moisture to escape and re-enter more rapidly.

To blanch vegetables, you may dip them in boiling water or steam them briefly. Steam-blanched vegetables retain more nutrients than do those treated in boiling water, but water blanching is faster and generally more effective in removing surface residues and microorganisms.

To blanch vegetables in boiling water, you'll need an 8-quart or larger pan filled with about 1 gallon of rapidly boiling water (for leafy greens, use 2 gallons of water). A blanching pot with a perforated basket and lid is ideal. Place about 1 pound of prepared raw vegetables at a time in a wire basket or metal colander (or in blanching pot basket); then immerse in the boiling water. Let the water return to a boil; then cover the pan and begin timing as directed in the chart on pages 212 and 213.

To blanch vegetables in steam, use a steam blanching pot or an 8-quart or larger pan with a tight-fitting lid and a wire or perforated basket that will hold food at least 3 inches off the pan bottom. Pour 2 inches of water into the pan, cover, and bring to a boil over high heat. Place 1 to 2 pounds of prepared raw vegetables in a single layer in the basket; cover. When steam begins to escape from pan, begin timing as directed in the chart on pages 212 and 213.

To cool blanched vegetables, lift them from the pan and immediately plunge into a large quantity of cold (60°F or lower) water. Cool them just long enough to stop the cooking action; *do not* cool to room temperature (the heat remaining in the vegetables allows them to start drying faster). If you plan to dry the vegetables in a dehydrator, pour them directly onto a dehydrator tray held over a sink; wipe any excess water from the tray underside. If you're oven-drying the vegetables, pour them onto paper towels to drain, then quickly transfer to trays or baking pans.

Drying the Vegetables

Whatever drying method you use, it's important to arrange the vegetables on trays in a single layer, without letting the pieces touch or overlap. Don't dry strong-flavored vegetables such as garlic, onions, and chiles with milder kinds; you'll end up with onion-flavored celery, garlicky green beans, and so on. Also avoid drying onions or garlic in the house, since the odor will permeate upholstery, draperies, and clothing. Instead, place the dehydrator on a covered porch or patio or in a garage.

To dry vegetables in a dehydrator, follow the manufacturer's instructions; a temperature of 125° to 130°F is recommended for most vegetables. Drying time will vary from about 4 to 14 hours.

To dry vegetables in a conventional oven, consult "Oven Drying" (page 197). Preheat oven to 120° to 140°F (temperatures above 140°F will reduce tenderness and cause loss of nutrients).

To dry vegetables in a convection oven, follow the manufacturer's instructions.

Determining Dryness

As the vegetables become drier, check them often to avoid scorching. When ready to store, most types are crisp and brittle; check the chart (pages 212 and 213).

Packaging & Storage

Store your dried vegetables as directed in "Packaging & Storing Dried Foods" on page 198. At cool room temperature, they'll keep well for about 6 months.

Chips, Flakes & Powders

When chopped or ground into flakes or powder, dried vegetables make flavorful bases for soups and sauces—and super seasonings for salads, cooked vegetables, and other foods. You can enjoy dried vegetable slices whole, too, as crisp and nutritious snacks.

Vegetable Chips

Wholesome and low in calories, vegetable chips are a tasty alternative to commercial deep-fried potato and corn chips. To prepare them, slice vegetables thinly before drying, using a food processor, mandolin, or sharp knife. Then serve them as is or with a favorite dip.

Beets, carrots, summer squash, tomatoes, and zucchini all make great chips. Zucchini and other squash chips are especially flavorful if dipped in barbecue sauce or sprinkled with seasoned salt before drying. Or try sprinkling ¼-inch-thick firm-ripe tomato slices with a little salt and, if you like, a bit of dry basil before drying.

Vegetable Flakes

Crushed or chopped into flakes, dried vegetables make excellent soup bases and seasonings. To prepare the flakes, use a blender, rolling pin, or wooden mallet. The vegetables must be really crisp before chopping, and the chopping equipment (particularly if you're using a blender) must be very dry. Because flaked vegetables have a shorter shelf life and lose nutritional value more rapidly than do sliced or whole dried vegetables, prepare them in small amounts—only as much as you'll use within a month. Then store them in small airtight containers such as empty spice bottles or baby food jars.

To use your vegetable flakes, try these ideas:

- Sprinkle the flakes over green salads to add color and crunch. Tomato and carrot flakes are especially good served this way.
- Create your own soup and dip mixes by combining a variety of vegetable flakes.

Vegetable Powders

Vegetable powders are finer than flakes. To prepare them, simply grind dried vegetables in a blender, food processor, or food mill until powdery; make sure the vegetables are crisp and the grinding equipment very dry. Store as for vegetable flakes (at left).

To use vegetable powders, try these ideas:

- Use homemade onion and garlic powders in place of commercial products.
- Make seasoned salts by mixing herb and vegetable powders with table salt. Equal parts of celery powder and salt make celery salt; one part garlic powder to four parts salt gives you garlic salt.
- Use vegetable powders to flavor sauces and cream soups. For each cup of soup or sauce, mix about 1 tablespoon vegetable powder and ¼ cup boiling water; let stand for about 15 minutes, then add to soup or sauce.
- Use tomato powder to make tomato sauce and paste. (Tomato powder is very concentrated: just 1 tablespoon is equivalent to about 1 medium-size fresh tomato.) To make tomato paste, mix 1¼ cups water and 1 cup tomato powder in a blender; whirl until smooth. For tomato sauce, use 1¾ cups water to 1 cup tomato powder.
- Make your own single-serving instant soups: mix about 1 tablespoon of your favorite vegetable powder with 4 teaspoons instant nonfat dry milk. Stir in 1 cup boiling water, then season to taste with salt, pepper, and herbs. You can prepare the soup in a large mug or small bowl; or, for more flavor, mix it in a small pan and simmer for a few minutes before serving.
- Keep vegetable broth mix on hand to use as a seasoning and for quick, nourishing snacks. Just powder any combination of vegetables, such as carrots, celery, green beans, peas, peppers, spinach, tomatoes, mushrooms, onion, garlic, and/or parsley; include favorite dry herbs, too. To make each cup of broth, combine about 1 tablespoon vegetable powder with 1 cup of boiling water.

Guide for Drying Vegetables

For details on blanching methods, see "About Blanching" (page 210).

To rehydrate dried vegetables, soak them in cold water, vegetable juice, or broth; most will rehydrate within an hour or two. If they need over 2 hours (or if you plan to soak them overnight), refrigerate them.

To speed up rehydration, you can soak the vegetables in boiling water. Or omit soaking and add the vegetables directly to stews and soups (they'll be a bit less tender than if they'd been soaked).

Vegetable	Best for drying	How to prepare	Test for dryness*
Artichokes	Tender hearts only	Rinse hearts and cut into ⅛-inch-wide strips. To blanch, heat in boiling solution of 3 cups water and ¼ cup lemon juice for 6 to 8 minutes.	Brittle
Asparagus	Tender tips, slender green stalks	Rinse stalks well; break off tough ends and halve large tips. Cut stalks into 1-inch pieces. Blanch for 3½ to 4½ minutes in boiling water, for 4 to 5 minutes in steam.	Leathery to brittle
Beans, snap	Tender varieties with crisp, thick walls and small seeds	Rinse. Cut off ends; then cut beans diagonally into short pieces. Blanch for 2 minutes in boiling water, for 2 to 2½ minutes in steam. (You may freeze beans for 30 to 40 minutes after blanching for better texture.)	Very dry, brittle
Beets	Small, tender beets	To keep color from bleeding, leave root ends and 1 inch of tops on beets. Scrub well; don't peel. Cover with boiling water and boil gently until tender when pierced (25 to 35 minutes). Cool. Remove skins; trim off stems and roots. Cut beets into ⅛-inch-thick strips. No further blanching required.	Tough, leathery
Broccoli	Young, fresh stalks	Trim off outer leaves and tough stalk bases. Rinse broccoli. Quarter stalks lengthwise. If desired, soak for 30 minutes in salt water (¼ cup salt per gallon of water) to help remove insects; drain. Blanch for 2 minutes in boiling water, for 3 to 3½ minutes in steam.	Brittle
Cabbage		Remove outer leaves. Rinse cabbage; then quarter and core. Cut into ⅛-inch-wide strips. Blanch until wilted: 1½ to 2 minutes in boiling water, 2½ to 3 minutes in steam.	Tough to brittle
Carrots	Crisp, tender carrots only	Rinse and peel. Cut into ⅛-inch-thick slices or strips. Blanch for 3½ minutes in boiling water, for 3 to 3½ minutes in steam.	Tough, leathery
Cauliflower		Rinse and break into small flowerets. If desired, soak for 30 minutes in salt water (¼ cup salt per gallon of water) to help remove insects; drain. Blanch for 3 to 4 minutes in boiling water, for 4 to 5 minutes in steam.	Tough to brittle
Celery	Crisp, tender stalks relatively free from strings	Rinse and slice. Blanch for 2 minutes in boiling water or steam.	Brittle
Corn	Young, tender ears in milk stage	Discard husks and silk; rinse corn. Blanch until milk does not exude when kernels are cut: 4 to 5 minutes in boiling water, 5 to 6 minutes in steam. Cut kernels from cob after blanching.	Dry, brittle
Eggplant *See* Squash, summer (& eggplant)			
Garlic		Peel and finely chop garlic cloves. No blanching required. Odor is pungent; dry outdoors in protected area in dehydrator.	Brittle
Greens (including spinach)	Young, tender leaves of chard, kale, spinach, and turnip	Rinse carefully. Drain; continue to rinse until water is clear and free of grit. Cut tough stems from leaves. Blanch for 1½ minutes in boiling water, for 2 to 2½ minutes in steam.	Brittle

* Cool a piece before testing

Vegetable	Best for drying	How to prepare	Test for dryness*
Horseradish		Rinse; remove all small rootlets and stubs. Peel or scrape roots. Grate. No blanching required.	Very dry and powdery
Mushrooms	*Commercial mushrooms only. Do not dry mushrooms gathered in the wild, which may be poisonous*	Use young, medium-size mushrooms with small closed caps. Rinse well, but quickly. Trim off tough stems. Cut tender stems into short sections. Do not peel small mushrooms or "buttons"; you may peel and slice large mushrooms. Blanch for 3 minutes in boiling water, for 3 to 4 minutes in steam.	Very dry and leathery
Okra		Rinse; trim ends. Cut pods crosswise into ⅛- to ¼-inch-thick slices. No blanching required.	Tough to brittle
Onions	Onions with strong aroma and flavor	Rinse and peel onions; cut into ⅛- to ¼-inch-thick slices. No blanching required. Odor is pungent; dry outdoors in protected area in dehydrator.	Brittle
Parsley		Rinse well. Separate clusters. Discard long or tough stems. No blanching required.	Brittle, flaky
Peas, green	Young, tender peas of a sweet variety (mature peas become tough and mealy)	Shell. Blanch for 2 minutes in boiling water, for 3 minutes in steam.	Crisp, wrinkled
Peppers, bell or chile		If preparing chiles, wear rubber gloves. Rinse. Remove stems and seeds. Cut bell peppers into ½-inch squares or ⅛-inch-wide strips. No blanching required. 　　Cut chiles into ½-inch squares; or dry whole outside if you live in a hot, sunny, dry climate. No blanching required. Do not dry hot chiles with other vegetables in a dehydrator.	Brittle
Potatoes, white		Rinse well; peel. Cut into ¼-inch-thick julienne strips or ⅛-inch-thick slices. Blanch for 5 to 6 minutes in boiling water, for 6 to 8 minutes in steam.	Brittle
Spinach *See* Greens (including spinach)			
Squash, summer (& eggplant)	Crookneck, zucchini, pattypan; eggplant	Rinse squash or eggplant and trim ends. Cut into ¼-inch-thick slices. Blanch for 1½ minutes in boiling water, for 2½ to 3 minutes in steam.	Brittle
Squash, winter (including pumpkin)	Banana, Hubbard, pumpkin	*For banana squash,* rinse and peel; cut into ¼-inch-thick strips. Blanch for 2 minutes in boiling water, for 3 minutes in steam. *For Hubbard squash and pumpkin,* cut into pieces. Scrape out all seeds and fibrous material. Cut into 1-inch-wide strips; peel strips and cut crosswise into ⅛-inch-thick slices. To blanch, steam until tender when pierced.	Tough to brittle
Tomatoes	Firm-ripe tomatoes with good color, no green spots	*For beefsteak-type tomatoes,* rinse and core. If desired, peel: dip in boiling water until skins crack (30 to 60 seconds), then dip in cold water and slip off skins. Cut crosswise into ¼-inch-thick slices; using a salt shaker, sprinkle with a tiny amount of salt to set color. No blanching required. *For small pear-shaped (Roma-type) tomatoes,* rinse and peel (see above). Halve; or, for large tomatoes, quarter or cut into ¼-inch-thick slices. Using a salt shaker, sprinkle with a tiny amount of salt to set color. No blanching required. Dry all tomatoes in a dehydrator for best results.	Slightly leathery

* Cool a piece before testing

Drying Fresh Herbs

*I*f your garden has provided you with more herbs than you can use fresh, you may want to dry some for later use. The process is simple: you just expose leaves or seeds to warm, dry air until their moisture is gone. We give instructions for drying herbs in open air or in a microwave or convection oven; don't try to use a conventional oven, since you're almost certain to end up with scorched herbs.

In most cases, you should harvest herbs for drying when the flowers first open.

Bunch drying is an easy way to dry long-stemmed herbs such as marjoram, sage, savory, mint, parsley, basil, and rosemary. Cut long stalks and rinse them in cool water; discard any dead or yellowed leaves. Then tie small bunches of herbs together by the stem ends. To keep dust from collecting on the leaves, place each bunch inside a paper bag before hanging; gather the top of the bag and tie the herb stems so the leaves hang freely inside the bag. For ventilation, cut out the bottom of the bag or punch air holes in the sides. Then hang the herbs—leafy ends down—in a warm, dry place (either inside or outdoors) not exposed to direct sunlight.

An even temperature in the range of 70° to 90°F is best for drying. Be sure there's good air circulation around the drying herbs—don't hang them against a wall. If you dry herbs outside, bring them in at night so the dew won't dampen them.

After a week or two, the herbs should be crackling dry. Carefully remove the leaves without breaking them; they retain flavor longer if left whole until ready to use. Store airtight.

Tray drying works well for seeds and large-leafed herbs; it's also the best choice for types with short stems that are difficult to tie together for hanging. Dry the herbs on shallow-rimmed trays covered with cheesecloth; or arrange them on wire racks set atop trays.

Rinse the herbs in cool water; shake off excess moisture.

To dry leaves, either remove them from their stems or leave them attached. Spread only one layer of leaves (loose or still on stems) on each tray: if you attempt to dry too much at once, air won't reach all the herbs evenly and they'll take longer to dry. Put the trays in a warm, dry, well-ventilated place not exposed to direct sunlight.

Every few days, stir or turn the leaves gently to assure even, thorough drying. Depending on the temperature and humidity, it should take the herbs a week or so to dry completely; if you're drying them outside, bring them in at night so the dew won't dampen them. When the leaves are crisp and thoroughly dry, take them off the trays and store airtight.

To dry seeds, spread them on trays in a thin layer and dry as for leaves. Once they're dry, carefully rub the seed capsules through your hands, gently blowing away chaff. Store airtight.

Microwave ovens let you dry herbs quickly. Rinse herbs in cool water; shake off excess moisture (if you put wet herbs in a microwave, they'll cook, not dry). Put no more than 4 or 5 herb branches in the oven, arranging them between 2 paper towels. Microwave on **HIGH (100%)** for 2 to 3 minutes; remove herbs from oven. If they're not brittle and dry, microwave on **HIGH (100%)** for 30 more seconds. Place herbs on a rack and let cool; then store airtight.

Convection ovens can also be used for drying herbs, though there is some flavor loss at higher temperatures. Use the lowest oven setting possible and leave the oven door ajar by about ½ inch. Rinse herbs in cool water; shake off excess moisture. Then prepare as for tray drying. Herbs usually dry in 1 to 3 hours; start checking after the first 45 minutes. To test for doneness, rub a few leaves to see if they crumble readily. Store airtight.

How to Make Jerky

Like other dried foods, meat jerky—tough, leathery strips of dried meat—was a staple for pioneers and "mountain men" in times past. Today, beef jerky is still a favorite among backpackers, skiers, and campers—and a popular snack for armchair sports fans, too. Modern jerky is prepared in an electric dehydrator or oven; sun drying, the technique favored in pioneer days, presents too great a risk of spoilage or contamination.

Though most of the following recipes call for beef, we also offer instructions for making turkey-breast jerky. Compared to jerky made with trimmed beef flank steak, it has less fat. It also has a more brittle texture, since poultry is fairly fibrous.

If you like, you can prepare beef jerky with game instead—but if you do, freeze the meat before drying for at least 30 days at 0°F as a precaution against disease.

The leaner the meat you use for jerky, the better: a lower fat content means a longer shelf life. As a first step for any jerky, trim and discard all visible fat and connective tissue from the meat; partially freeze it (to make slicing easier), then cut it into thin (⅛- to ¼-inch-thick) strips about 1 inch wide. Cut with the grain if you like a chewy jerky, across the grain if you prefer a more tender, brittle product.

Properly dried beef or game jerky should crack, but not break, when bent; turkey jerky, however, will crack and break.

Once the jerky has been dried, let it cool; then pack it in a rigid freezer container or plastic freezer bag and freeze for 72 hours at 0°F. Then store it in an airtight, insectproof container for up to 3 weeks in a cool, dark, dry place. Or, to maintain flavor and prolong shelf life, refrigerate or freeze.

Basic Jerky

You can use this recipe for lean cuts of beef such as flank steak, round steak, or brisket; it's good with venison, too.

- 1½ **pounds lean boneless meat (see recipe introduction, above), trimmed of all fat and connective tissue**
- ¼ **cup soy sauce**
- 1 **tablespoon Worcestershire**
- ½ **teaspoon onion powder**
- ¼ **teaspoon *each* pepper, garlic powder, and liquid smoke**
  Vegetable oil cooking spray

Freeze meat until firm but not hard; then cut into ⅛- to ¼-inch-thick slices.

In a medium-size glass, stoneware, plastic, or stainless steel bowl, combine soy sauce, Worcestershire, onion powder, pepper, garlic powder, and liquid smoke. Stir to dissolve seasonings. Add meat and mix until all surfaces are thoroughly coated. Cover tightly and refrigerate for at least 6 hours or until next day, stirring occasionally; recover tightly after stirring.

Drying the jerky. Depending upon the drying method you're using, evenly coat dehydrator racks or metal racks with cooking spray; if oven drying, place racks over rimmed baking pans.

Lift meat from bowl, shaking off any excess liquid. Arrange meat strips close together, but not overlapping, on racks.

Dehydrator drying. Arrange trays according to manufacturer's directions and dry at 140°F until a piece of jerky cracks, but does not break, when bent (8 to 10 hours; let jerky cool for 5 minutes before testing).

Oven drying. Set oven at 140° to 200°F (the lower, the better—the lowest your oven allows). Place racks at least 4 inches away from (above or below) heat source. Prop oven door open by about 2 inches. Dry until a piece of jerky cracks, but does not break, when bent (4 to 7 hours; let jerky cool for 5 minutes before testing).

Pat off any beads of oil from jerky. Let jerky cool completely on racks; remove from racks, place in a rigid freezer container, and freeze for 72 hours. Then store in airtight, insectproof containers in a cool, dry place; or freeze or refrigerate. Makes about ¾ pound.

Storage time. Up to 3 weeks at room temperature; up to 4 months in refrigerator; up to 8 months in freezer.

Per ounce: 94 calories, 12 g protein, 1 g carbohydrates, 4 g total fat, 28 mg cholesterol, 398 mg sodium

Barbecued Jerky

Pictured on page 194

If you love barbecue, you'll appreciate this jerky. It's great for taking along on a backpacking or camping trip; you'll also enjoy it for at-home snacking.

- 1½ **pounds flank or lean top round steak, trimmed of all fat and connective tissue**
- ½ **cup catsup**
- ⅓ **cup red wine vinegar**
- ¼ **cup firmly packed brown sugar**
- 1½ **teaspoons** *each* **dry mustard and onion powder**
- 1 **teaspoon salt**
- ½ **teaspoon garlic powder**
- ¼ **teaspoon ground red pepper (cayenne)**
  Vegetable oil cooking spray

Freeze meat until firm but not hard; then cut into ⅛- to ¼-inch-thick slices.

In a medium-size glass, stoneware, plastic, or stainless steel bowl, combine catsup, vinegar, sugar, mustard, onion powder, salt, garlic powder, and red pepper. Stir to dissolve seasonings. Add meat and mix until all surfaces are thoroughly coated. Cover tightly and refrigerate for at least 6 hours or until next day, stirring occasionally; recover tightly after stirring. Then proceed as directed in "Drying the jerky" for Basic Jerky (page 215). Makes about ¾ pound.

Storage time. Up to 3 weeks at room temperature; up to 4 months in refrigerator; up to 8 months in freezer.

Per ounce: 119 calories, 12 g protein, 8 g carbohydrates, 4 g total fat, 28 mg cholesterol, 345 mg sodium

Texas-style Jerky

Cayenne, black pepper, and chili powder give this jerky its slightly hot flavor.

- 1 **pound lean top round steak, trimmed of all fat and connective tissue**
- 1 **tablespoon salt**
- 1 **teaspoon** *each* **black pepper, chili powder, garlic powder, and onion powder**
- ¼ **teaspoon** *each* **ground red pepper (cayenne) and liquid smoke**
- ½ **cup water**
  Vegetable oil cooking spray

Freeze meat until firm but not hard; then cut into ⅛- to ¼-inch-thick slices.

In a medium-size glass, stoneware, plastic, or stainless steel bowl, combine salt, black pepper, chili powder, garlic powder, onion powder, red pepper, liquid smoke, and water. Stir to dissolve seasonings. Add meat and mix until all surfaces are thoroughly coated. Cover tightly and refrigerate for at least 6 hours or until next day, stirring occasionally; recover tightly after stirring. Then proceed as directed in "Drying the jerky" for Basic Jerky (page 215). Makes about ½ pound.

Storage time. Up to 3 weeks at room temperature; up to 4 months in refrigerator; up to 8 months in freezer.

Per ounce: 78 calories, 13 g protein, 1 g carbohydrates, 2 g total fat, 32 mg cholesterol, 857 mg sodium

Paniolo Beef Jerky

In Hawaii, a cowboy is called a *paniolo*—hence this jerky's name. Ginger and lime bring a taste of the islands to the marinade; crushed red pepper adds a little heat.

- 1½ **pounds flank steak, trimmed of all fat and connective tissue**
- ¼ **cup lime juice**
- 2 **tablespoons** *each* **reduced-sodium soy sauce and Worcestershire**
- 1 **tablespoon grated fresh ginger**
- 1 **teaspoon crushed red pepper flakes**
- ¼ **teaspoon coarsely ground black pepper**
- ⅛ **teaspoon liquid smoke**
  Vegetable oil cooking spray

Freeze meat until firm but not hard; then cut into ⅛- to ¼-inch-thick slices.

In a medium-size glass, stoneware, plastic, or stainless steel bowl, combine lime juice, soy sauce, Worcestershire, ginger, red pepper flakes, black pepper, and liquid smoke. Stir to dissolve seasonings. Add meat and mix until all surfaces are thoroughly coated. Cover tightly and refrigerate for at least 6 hours or until next day, stirring occasionally; recover tightly after stirring. Then proceed as directed in "Drying the jerky" for Basic Jerky (page 215). Makes about ¾ pound.

Storage time. Up to 3 weeks at room temperature; up to 4 months in refrigerator; up to 8 months in freezer.

Per ounce: 95 calories, 12 g protein, 1 g carbohydrates, 4 g total fat, 28 mg cholesterol, 170 mg sodium

Teriyaki Turkey Jerky

Pictured on page 194

For a modern twist on a very old tradition, try jerky made from lowfat turkey.

- **1 pound boned, skinned turkey breast or turkey tenderloins, trimmed of all fat and connective tissue**
- **¼ teaspoon *each* onion powder and garlic powder**
- **½ cup water**
- **¼ cup reduced-sodium soy sauce**
- **2 teaspoons Worcestershire**
- **2 tablespoons firmly packed brown sugar**
- **1 teaspoon pepper**
- **½ teaspoon liquid smoke**
- **Vegetable oil cooking spray**

Freeze turkey until firm but not hard; then cut into ⅛- to ¼-inch-thick slices.

In a medium-size glass, stoneware, plastic, or stainless steel bowl, combine onion powder, garlic powder, water, soy sauce, Worcestershire, sugar, pepper, and liquid smoke. Stir to dissolve seasonings. Add turkey and mix until all surfaces are thoroughly coated. Cover tightly and refrigerate for at least 6 hours or until next day, stirring occasionally; recover tightly after stirring.

Drying the jerky. Depending on the drying method you're using, evenly coat dehydrator racks or metal racks with cooking spray; if oven drying, place racks over rimmed baking pans.

Lift turkey from bowl, shaking off any excess liquid. Arrange strips close together, but not overlapping, on racks.

Dehydrator drying. Arrange trays according to manufacturer's directions and dry at 140°F until a piece of jerky cracks and breaks when bent (4½ to 6 hours; let jerky cool for 5 minutes before testing).

Oven drying. Set oven at 140° to 200°F (the lower, the better—the lowest your oven allows). Place racks at least 4 inches away from (above or below) heat source. Prop oven door open by about 2 inches. Dry until a piece of jerky cracks and breaks when bent (4 to 6 hours; let jerky cool for 5 minutes before testing).

Pat off any beads of oil from jerky. Let jerky cool completely on racks; remove from racks, place in a rigid freezer container, and freeze for 72 hours. Then store in airtight, insectproof containers in a cool, dry place; or freeze or refrigerate. Makes about ½ pound.

Storage time. Up to 3 weeks at room temperature; up to 4 months in refrigerator; up to 8 months in freezer.

Per ounce: 85 calories, 15 g protein, 5 g carbohydrates, 0 g total fat, 35 mg cholesterol, 557 mg sodium

Drying Glossary

Antidarkening agent. Any antioxidant used to keep light-colored fruits from browning after cutting. Antidarkening agents commonly used on fruits to be dried include sulfur, sulfite dips, ascorbic acid, citric acid, commercial formulas containing ascorbic and/or citric acids (and often sugar), and citrus juice.

Blanching. The process of heating food quickly in boiling water or steam to inactivate enzymes that can cause loss of color, flavor, and nutritive value. Most vegetables are blanched before drying.

Case harden (usually used to describe fruit). To form a hard shell on the outside, trapping moisture inside and resulting in deterioration. Case hardening often results from drying fruit at too high a temperature.

Dehydrating (drying). Removing moisture from food by exposing it to warm temperatures and moving air. The term is often used to refer to the process of drying foods in an electric dehydrator.

Dehydrator. An electric appliance, usually relatively small, used for drying foods at home. It maintains a low, even temperature and circulates heated air with a blower or fan.

Oven drying. Drying foods in a conventional or convection oven set at a low temperature.

Oxidation. A chemical reaction to oxygen that makes fresh produce darken when cut, diminishes flavor, and causes loss of vitamins A and C.

Sulfiting. Pretreating fruit by soaking cut pieces in a solution of water and sodium bisulfite, sodium sulfite, or sodium metabisulfite.

Sulfuring. Pretreating fruit by exposing cut pieces to the fumes of burning sulfur.

Sun drying. Drying foods (primarily fruits) by exposing them, usually in cut pieces, to the sun.

Syrups, Toppings & Cordials

Refreshing syrups, unique toppings, dried fruit cordials

*H*ome-canned fruits and jewel-bright jams let you enjoy summertime flavors all year long. But there are other ways to capture the essence of summer, too—with mellow cordials, luscious toppings, and brilliant-hued Italian fruit syrups. ● The syrups make refreshing drinks when mixed with sparkling water or wine; or you can freeze them to make sorbetlike *granitas*. ● To make our fabulous toppings, use your boiling water canner. You'll find that the fruity sauces, some lightly spiked with liqueur, are wonderful with ice cream, sorbet, waffles, and pancakes. And don't pass up our rich Caramel Pecan Topping—it's great to have on hand in the refrigerator, ready to use in tempting sundaes or to spoon over French toast. ● If you have dried fruit in your cupboard, try mixing it with a little wine, brandy, and sugar; let the mixture mellow for a few weeks, then sip the liqueur and enjoy the spirited fruit on ice cream or cake.

Italian Fruit Syrups

The summery sweetness of ripe berries, plums, or citrus fruits comes through with flair in these enticing syrups. Mix a few spoonfuls with sparkling water or white wine for a refreshing drink, or freeze a half-and-half blend of water and syrup to make sorbetlike *granita*.

Because the syrups are fermented, their flavors are especially intense. The yeast-fruit mixture, which bubbles and froths for several days, looks dull at first; but when you cook it before bottling, it brightens and takes on a jewel-like clarity.

2 pounds ripe strawberries, raspberries, blueberries, peaches, or plums; or 2 cups orange, lemon, or lime juice

2 packages active dry yeast

1 teaspoon sugar (if using lemon or lime juice)
Sugar, water, and lemon juice (amounts for each fruit or juice choice follow)

Choose fruit or juice from the list above. Hull strawberries; pit (do not peel) and slice peaches or plums. Whirl fruit in a food processor or blender until puréed. Press raspberry purée through a fine strainer to remove seeds. Measure purée; the amount you need for each fruit is listed at right.

Pour purée or juice into a 3-quart or larger glass, ceramic, or stainless steel bowl. Sprinkle with yeast; if using lemon or lime juice, add 1 teaspoon sugar. Stir to moisten yeast. Cover bowl with a dishtowel or paper towel and set aside at room temperature to ferment, stirring occasionally. Mixture will bubble and rise in bowl; when bubbles no longer appear when mixture is stirred, fermentation is complete. The process takes about 2 days for juices, 3 to 4 days for purées.

Line a colander with 3 or 4 thicknesses of moistened cheesecloth, making sure squares of cloth are large enough to hang over sides of colander. Set colander over a 6- to 8-quart stainless steel or unchipped enamel pan. Pour purée or juice through cheesecloth; bring together corners of cloths and twist to extract juice. (You may have to scrape purée from cloth in order to force out as much juice as possible.) Discard pulp and any seeds; remove colander from pan.

To pan, add sugar, water, and lemon juice as specified for each fruit purée or juice. Bring to a boil over high heat; boil, uncovered, until reduced to amount specified for each fruit or juice (15 to 20 minutes).

Let syrup cool completely, then pour into a 1- to 2-quart glass container. Cover tightly and refrigerate for up to 6 months. A harmless sediment may form at bottom of container; to keep syrup clear, do not shake container. Makes 3½ to 7 cups, depending on fruit or juice used.

Fruit Purée or Juice. Check the listings below to see how much purée you need for each fruit and to find out how much sugar, water, and lemon juice each choice requires.

Strawberry. You should have 2½ to 2¾ cups purée. Use 6 cups **sugar**, 4 cups **water**, and 1½ cups **lemon juice**; boil down to 7 cups.

Blueberry, plum, or peach. You should have about 2 cups purée. Use 4½ cups **sugar**, 3 cups **water**, and 1 cup plus 2 tablespoons **lemon juice**; boil down to 5¼ cups.

Orange, lemon, or lime juice (2 cups). Use 4½ cups **sugar** and 3 cups **water**. *For orange juice only,* also add 1 cup plus 2 tablespoons **lemon juice**. Boil down to 5¼ cups.

Raspberry. You should have 1½ cups strained purée. Use 3 cups **sugar**, 2 cups **water**, and ¾ cup **lemon juice**. Boil down to 3½ cups.

Storage time. Up to 6 months in refrigerator.

Per tablespoon (approximate): 46 calories, 0 g protein, 12 g carbohydrates, 0 g total fat, 0 mg cholesterol, 1 mg sodium

Water Cooler

Partially fill an 8- to 10-ounce glass with **ice**. Fill glass with **sparkling or plain water** and ¼ cup (or to taste) **Italian Fruit Syrup**. Makes 1 serving.

Per serving: 184 calories, 1 g protein, 47 g carbohydrates, 0 g total fat, 0 mg cholesterol, 4 mg sodium

Italian Wine Cooler

Add 2 tablespoons (or to taste) **Italian Fruit Syrup** to ½ to ⅔ cup chilled **dry white wine**. Makes 1 serving.

Per serving: 182 calories, 0 g protein, 25 g carbohydrates, 0 g total fat, 0 mg cholesterol, 9 mg sodium

Granita

Combine equal parts **water** and **Italian Fruit Syrup**. Freeze until almost hard. With an electric mixer or a food processor, beat to a coarse slush; serve as a dessert or between courses.

Per ½ cup: 184 calories, 0 g protein, 47 g carbohydrates, 0 g total fat, 0 mg cholesterol, 4 mg sodium

Garden Lemon Syrup

This sweet, lemony syrup is delicious on pancakes, waffles, or ice cream; you can also stir it into chilled sparkling water for a refreshing beverage.

    2 cups lemon juice
    3 cups sugar

In a heavy-bottomed 6- to 8-quart pan, combine lemon juice and sugar. Bring to a boil over medium heat, stirring until sugar is dissolved. Then reduce heat and simmer, uncovered, for 6 minutes, stirring often. Remove from heat and let cool. Pour into freezer jars or freezer containers, leaving ½-inch headspace; apply lids. Freeze or refrigerate. Makes about 3 half-pints.

Storage time. Up to 1 month in refrigerator; up to 6 months in freezer.

Per tablespoon: 50 calories, 0 g protein, 13 g carbohydrates, 0 g total fat, 0 mg cholesterol, 2 mg sodium

Blackberry-Peach Topping

Pictured on page 106

Fresh blackberries and peaches combine in this luscious, homey topping. If you like, you can also use unsweetened frozen fruit; let it stand just until thawed before adding it to the sugar mixture.

    3 cups sugar
    ½ cup water
    2 tablespoons lemon juice
    ¼ teaspoon ground cinnamon
    4 cups crushed blackberries (about 2 quarts whole berries)
    4 cups peeled, pitted, crushed peaches (about 2¾ lbs. peaches)

In a heavy-bottomed 8- to 10-quart pan, mix sugar, water, lemon juice, and cinnamon. Bring to a boil over medium heat, stirring constantly (about 8 minutes). Add blackberries and peaches; increase heat to medium-high and return to a boil, stirring constantly (about 12 minutes). Then boil, uncovered, for 5 more minutes, stirring constantly. Mixture should be slightly thinner than the consistency you prefer at room temperature.

Ladle hot topping into prepared, hot jars, leaving ½-inch headspace. Gently run a narrow nonmetallic spatula between topping and jar sides to release air bubbles. Wipe rims and threads clean; top with hot lids, then firmly screw on bands. Process in boiling water canner for 10 minutes. Or omit processing and

ladle into freezer jars or freezer containers, leaving ½-inch headspace; apply lids. Let cool; freeze or refrigerate. Makes about 10 half-pints or 5 pints.

Storage time: *Processed:* Up to 1 year. *Unprocessed:* Up to 1 week in refrigerator; up to 10 months in freezer.

Per ¼ cup: 84 calories, 0 g protein, 22 g carbohydrates, 0 g total fat, 0 mg cholesterol, 0 mg sodium

Raspberry-Peach Topping

Follow directions for **Blackberry-Peach Topping,** but substitute 4 cups crushed **raspberries** (about 2 quarts whole berries) for blackberries. Makes about 10 half-pints or 5 pints.

Per ¼ cup: 81 calories, 1 g protein, 21 g carbohydrates, 0 g total fat, 0 mg cholesterol, 0 mg sodium

Plum-Marnier Topping

This delectable fresh plum sauce, flavored with a hint of orange liqueur, makes a superb topping for ice cream, sorbet, or fresh fruit.

    8 cups pitted, chopped unpeeled plums
      (about 5 lbs. plums)
    3 cups sugar
    ½ cup water
    1 tablespoon grated orange peel
    ¼ cup orange-flavored liqueur

In a heavy-bottomed 8- to 10-quart pan, mix plums, sugar, water, and orange peel. Bring to a boil over medium heat, stirring constantly; boil, uncovered, for 5 minutes. Transfer mixture to a blender or food processor, a portion at a time; whirl until smooth. Return to pan and bring to a boil over medium-high heat, stirring often. Continue to boil until thickened (5 to 10 more minutes). Add liqueur and boil, stirring often, for 3 more minutes.

Ladle hot topping into prepared, hot jars, leaving ½-inch headspace. Gently run a narrow nonmetallic spatula between topping and jar sides to release air bubbles. Wipe rims and threads clean; top with hot lids, then firmly screw on bands. Process in boiling water canner for 10 minutes. Or omit processing and ladle into freezer jars or freezer containers, leaving ½-inch headspace; apply lids. Let cool; freeze or refrigerate. Makes about 6 half-pints or 3 pints.

Storage time. *Processed:* Up to 1 year. *Unprocessed:* Up to 1 week in refrigerator; up to 10 months in freezer.

Per ¼ cup: 135 calories, 0 g protein, 33 g carbohydrates, 0 g total fat, 0 mg cholesterol, 0 mg sodium

Easy Cherry-Amaretto Topping

Lots of plump sweet cherries go into a topping that's a snap to make at any time of year. You don't even need to thaw the cherries before you begin.

- **4 pounds frozen pitted dark sweet cherries**
- **3 cups sugar**
- **1 tablespoon lemon juice**
- **¼ cup amaretto liqueur**

In a heavy-bottomed 8- to 10-quart pan, mix cherries, sugar, and lemon juice. Cook over low heat, stirring occasionally, until cherries thaw (10 to 15 minutes). Then bring to a boil over high heat, stirring occasionally (about 15 minutes). Reduce heat to medium-high and continue to cook until syrup is slightly thickened and mixture has the consistency of a thick sauce (about 35 minutes). Add liqueur and cook, stirring often, for 3 more minutes.

Ladle hot topping into prepared, hot jars, leaving ½-inch headspace. Gently run a narrow nonmetallic spatula between topping and jar sides to release air bubbles. Wipe rims and threads clean; top with hot lids, then firmly screw on bands. Process in boiling water canner for 10 minutes. Or omit processing and ladle into freezer jars or freezer containers, leaving ½-inch headspace; apply lids. Let cool; freeze or refrigerate. Makes about 6 half-pints or 3 pints.

Storage time. *Processed:* Up to 1 year. *Unprocessed:* Up to 1 week in refrigerator; up to 10 months in freezer.

Per ¼ cup: 154 calories, 1 g protein, 38 g carbohydrates, 1 g total fat, 0 mg cholesterol, 0 mg sodium

Caramel Pecan Topping

Ideal for spooning over ice cream, this topping is just as good with waffles, pancakes, and French toast. If you like, you can add a little light or dark rum before stirring in the nuts.

- **3 cups firmly packed brown sugar**
- **1½ cups light corn syrup**
- **1 cup water**
- **¼ cup light or dark rum (optional)**
- **2½ cups coarsely chopped toasted pecans**

In a heavy-bottomed 6- to 8-quart pan, mix sugar, corn syrup, and water. Bring to a boil over medium heat, stirring constantly; reduce heat to medium-low and simmer for 5 minutes. Add rum, if desired, stirring well; then stir in pecans.

Ladle hot topping into prepared, hot jars, leaving ½-inch headspace. Gently run a narrow nonmetallic spatula between topping and jar sides to release air bubbles. Wipe rims and threads clean; top with hot lids, then firmly screw on bands. Process in boiling water canner for 10 minutes. Or omit processing and ladle into hot jars; apply lids. Let cool; then refrigerate. Makes about 6 half-pints or 3 pints.

Storage time. *Processed:* Up to 1 year. *Unprocessed:* Up to 1 month in refrigerator.

Per ¼ cup: 237 calories, 1 g protein, 43 g carbohydrates, 8 g total fat, 0 mg cholesterol, 38 mg sodium

Dried Fruit Cordials

Dried apricots, peaches, pears, or prunes soaked in a mixture of sweetened white wine and brandy make fruity cordials that mellow with age. Because the fruit softens any harshness, you can use inexpensive wine and brandy. Sip the liqueur; serve the soaked fruit over ice cream or pound cake.

- **1 pound dried apricots, prunes (with pits), pears, or peaches**
- **1 bottle (750 ml.) or 3⅓ cups dry white wine**
- **1 cup brandy**
- **2 cups sugar**

Place fruit in a 2-quart glass, ceramic, or stainless steel container. Stir in wine, brandy, and sugar until well blended. Cover tightly. Let stand for at least 1 week at room temperature to allow flavors to develop; stir occasionally during the first few days to dissolve sugar.

After 1 week, apricots, prunes, and pears should be soft; peaches should still be slightly firm. After 3 to 4 weeks, the cordial's fruit flavor will reach maximum intensity. After about 6 weeks, fruit should be removed if it has become too soft. (If you'd like to give a cordial as a gift, transfer it to 1 or 2 decanters or other attractive glass containers.) Makes about 6 cups fruit-cordial mixture.

Storage time. Up to 6 weeks at room temperature for fruit-cordial mixture; indefinitely for cordial alone.

Per ½ cup fruit-cordial mixture: 312 calories, 1 g protein, 57 g carbohydrates, 0 g total fat, 0 mg cholesterol, 7 mg sodium

Sunset
Vegetarian Cooking

By the Editors of
Sunset Books
and
Sunset Magazine

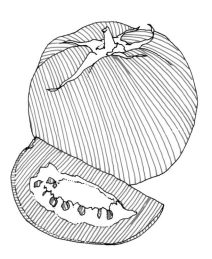

Sunset Publishing Corp. • Menlo Park, California

Contents

Going Vegetarian

We've heard many reasons for going vegetarian. Some people are just looking for a change of pace from meat and potatoes. Some want to save money. Some want the health advantages of a low-cholesterol, high-fiber diet. Others have religious or philosophical reasons for not eating meat. And there are also those who want to do something about the global food problem.

But whether you want to save money, save your heart, save animals, or save the world from food shortage, you'll need good recipes that sustain your interest in going vegetarian.

And good recipes are the heart of this vegetarian cook book.

We've selected contrasting tastes, colors, and textures and created recipes and menus for dishes that appeal to both eye and appetite. You'll find recipes drawn from the world's great cuisines: Italian pasta dishes, Indian curry dishes, French egg and cheese dishes, and Oriental and Middle Eastern vegetable entrées that will be revelations to your taste buds.

We issue our recipes as irresistible invitations to those who rarely have a meatless meal, as well to those who already know that vegetarian fare is neither fad food nor bland and boring. There are recipes for strict vegetarians who eat neither eggs nor dairy products, and recipes for the ovo-lacto vegetarians, who include eggs and dairy products in their diets.

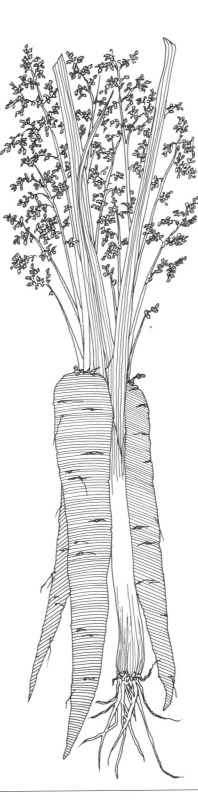

We think the greatest number of our readers are those who consider themselves part-time vegetarians. Part-time vegetarians enjoy a wide variety of foods and are usually on the lookout for meatless recipes that are exciting and thoroughly satisfying. They don't calculate every amino acid molecule. They shop in ordinary grocery stores and devote ordinary amounts of time to meal preparation; but they aim for extraordinary results with a minimum of fuss.

Indeed, extraordinary results with minimum fuss has been the controlling idea throughout this cook book. Ease of preparation and availability of ingredients were main concerns as we selected recipes. You'll see many recipes in each chapter that fall into the "quick and easy" category. Most ingredients can be purchased at your supermarket. Wheat berries (whole grains of wheat) and soybeans are about the only exceptions. Of course, you may prefer shopping for staples in a health food store, and buying stone-ground flours and cold-pressed oils; the choice is always yours.

Looking ahead

A glance through the chapters in this book should convince even the most skeptical carnivore that vegetarian cooking means far more than bowls of gruel with alfalfa sprouts sprinkled on top.

Starting with salads and appetizers, you'll find unusual side-dish salads and magnificent whole-meal salads.

For a balanced meal, you might want to try the Perfect Protein Salad (page 236) or the Bulgur Supper Salad (page 240). They're both good examples of combining necessary nutrients with a minimum of fuss to present fresh, attractive meals.

In the soup chapter, you'll find a full range of recipes—from family fare like hearty Garden Fresh Minestrone (page 253), to soups guaranteed to impress your guests, such as Cheddar Sherry Soup (page 248), or Almond Soup Gratinée (page 245).

Moving to cheese and egg dishes, you'll discover a stunning collection of omelets, soufflés, and quiches, plus such extraordinary creations as Zesty Tomato Fondue (page 265), Fila Cheese Squares (page 263), and Meringue-topped Vegetable Custard (page 263).

The chapter called "Greens, Grains & Other Good Entrées" takes us to the center of vegetarian cooking—recipes built on the nutritional staples of grains, legumes, and green and yellow vegetables. It also takes us on a discovery trip around the world, with ports of call in Greece, Italy, the Middle East, Japan, and Mexico. And if you've never attempted Indian cooking, here's your opportunity. For incentive, check the photograph on page 283 to see how spectacularly colorful an Indian vegetarian meal can be.

Stir-frying and steaming, two excellent methods for cooking all kinds of vegetables, are featured in the vegetable side-dish chapter. Besides instructions in these basic techniques, we've included a collection of combination vegetable dishes, such as Cauliflower with Broccoli Sauce (page 290) and Curried Carrots with Fruit (page 290).

(Continued on page 228)

 ## Just a Few Questions, Please...

Won't I get tired of eating nothing but vegetables?
Of course. Anyone would grow tired of eating just spinach and broccoli, but vegetarian cooking includes much more than vegetables. Vegetarian menus include plentiful amounts of legumes and grains, in addition to green and yellow vegetables, and fruit. Many vegetarians also eat eggs and dairy products.

What do you mean by "legumes and grains"?
Legumes are dried beans and peas, including split peas, lentils, soybeans, and a wide variety of red, white, and black beans. Grains are the seeds of cereal plants—wheat, corn, oats, rice, millet, barley, rye. (No, you don't eat them whole, though whole wheat grains, called wheat berries, are delicious.) Most whole grains are milled and made into a variety of different foods—bread, pasta, crêpes, and tortillas, to name a few. Eaten together, legumes and grains are the main source of protein for vegetarians who don't eat eggs and dairy products.

Won't I get fat by eating all those carbohydrates?
Carbohydrates, by themselves, probably won't cause you to gain weight. Eating more calories than you burn is what really pushes up the pounds. Naturally, if you eat too much of a good thing—even whole grain bread—you'll get fat. But before you cut out nutrient-rich whole grains, cut down on excess sugar and fat to lower the number of calories you consume.

Don't I need meat for protein?
No. By weight, soybeans and cheese are better sources of protein than meat and fish. In terms of protein quality, eggs and milk rank above meat. By combining grains and legumes, you can create a protein of higher quality than meat or fish.

Is it true that a meatless diet is good for my health?
That depends. If your doctor has told you to cut down on cholesterol and saturated fats, one way to do it is to cut back on meat; cholesterol appears only in animal products, not in plants. Eggs and whole milk products are also high in cholesterol, so cut back on them, too.

Should I go "cold turkey" on cold turkey, roast beef, and my favorite meats and fish?
We recommend a gradual approach to going vegetarian. For instance, you might want to cut back just on the quantity of meat you serve per meal, or serve meatless meals one, two, or three days a week.

In the beginning, most people who go vegetarian rely on quiches, omelets, cheese pizzas, and the more familiar bean dishes. Gradually, though, they try more adventuresome entrées and international vegetarian dishes.

What makes a meal memorable? Good friends and good conversation, artful presentation of even the simplest dish, and exciting contrasts of texture, taste, and color.

You're on your own for the friends and conversation, but on these two pages we have lots of suggestions for the food. You'll find an international selection of menus, from Mexico to the Orient, plus appealing nonethnic menus. Most are for vegetarians who eat eggs and dairy products. Strict vegetarians will be interested in the Oriental Dinner and the Three-course Vegan Special.

Brunch with Ease

The luscious casserole here can be composed in a jiffy or made ahead, and the bread and dessert are definitely make-ahead items. So on the day you serve this brunch, the only dish you'll have to prepare is Tomatoes Provençal. The ricotta dessert is a do-it-yourself affair that your guests will especially enjoy.

Creamy Spinach-Artichoke Casserole (page 281)
Pebble-top Oatmeal Bread (page 293)
Tomatoes Provençal (page 290)
Brandied Ricotta with Fruit (page 311)

Quiche-Plus for Lunch or Supper

All the "plus" items on this menu are make-ahead dishes. The salad and dessert need to be made ahead—the salad has to marinate and the dessert must be chilled for at least 2 hours. The soup and bread can be made a day in advance, if you like; we suggest treating them as a first course. You might bring the Wheat Berry Batter Bread to the table on a small bread board and slice it there—a nourishing beginning for a cool-weather meal. Then serve the salad alongside the golden wedges of quiche.

Double Mushroom Soup (page 247)
Wheat Berry Batter Bread (page 293)
Golden Cauliflower Quiche (page 261)
Tarragon Vegetable Salad (page 237)
Lemon Yogurt Sponge Torte (page 310)

Lunch or Supper for Summer's End

Family-pleasing menus are always welcome. This one is perfect for late summer or early fall. It contrasts the wonderful seasonal flavors of fresh corn, pears, grapes, and peaches.

Tomato Corn Chowder (page 249)
Casserole Cheese Bread (page 297)
Pear & Grape Slaw (page 237)
Honey Peach Cobbler (page 311)

Dinner from the Middle East

The seasonings are mild but intriguing in this composition of dishes. You can start off with the soup and bread or with the stuffed chard and carrots, whichever you prefer. A simple green salad is optional.

Lemony Lentil Soup (page 250)
Butter-topped Whole Wheat Bread (page 293)
Stuffed Chard or Grape Leaves (page 279)
Steamed Carrots and Crookneck Squash with Savory Cheese Sauce (page 289)
Tossed Green Salad
Yogurt Cheesecake with Dates (page 309)

Winter Picnic

Here's hearty food to warm you during a cold day's outing. You can pack the kettle of hot chili beans in an insulated chest or wrap newspapers and a blanket around it to keep it warm. The hot chocolate can be carried in a thermos, and the tortillas can be wrapped in foil and heated over a grill or camp stove. If the day is too gloomy, you can always heat everything at home and picnic in front of the fireplace.

Layered Chili (page 269)
Whole Wheat Tortillas (page 301)
Hot Chocolate
Juicy Apples
Chewy Bran Bars (page 314)

Three-course Vegan Special

A "vegan" is a strict vegetarian who avoids not only meat, but eggs and dairy products as well. We've designed this menu especially for vegans; though the recipe for soybean soup calls for a little milk, vegetable stock can be used just as well. The soup makes a protein-packed first course, followed by a three-part main course.

Soybean Soup, Bistro-style (page 250)
Cracked Wheat Pilaf
Curried Carrots with Fruit (page 290)
Steamed Broccoli or Green Beans (page 289)
Honey Crunch Baked Apples (page 311) or Orange Slices with Shredded Coconut

Company Dinner

You'll have to invest some culinary effort in this menu, but the results are impressive. Here's a short cut you can take with the cannelloni: fry the eggplant slices a day ahead, then cover and refrigerate them until you're ready to fill and bake them. You may want to omit the egg garnish from the salad, since it's quite substantial without the egg. Or if red bell peppers are out of season, you can substitute a mixed green salad for the colorful first course.

Roasted Pepper & Tomato Salad (page 234)
Bread Sticks
Eggplant Cannelloni (page 274)
Rice or Risotto
Steamed Italian Green Beans or Swiss Chard (page 289)
Marzipan Torte (page 309)

Italian Dinner

This family dinner can be served in three or four courses, depending on when you serve the salad. Some people prefer salad before or after the lasagne dish; others like it alongside the hearty entrée.

For a more elaborate meal, you can make the first-course caponata part of a large antipasto platter composed of cheeses, bread sticks, fresh and pickled vegetables, olives, and whatever else Italian strikes your fancy.

Caponata (page 233)
Lasagne Swirls (page 273) or Vegetable Lasagne (page 273)
Simple Green Salad
Garlic Bread
Sherried Cream with Fruit (page 312)

Mexican Dinner

A good warm-weather menu, this mildly spiced Mexican dinner starts and ends with cooling dishes—a gazpacho for starters and a refreshing fruit with sherbet for dessert. You can buy refried beans, or make your own "refritos" by mashing cooked pinto beans and cooking them with salad oil, butter, or margarine. You can fry your own strips of tortillas, too, or buy tortilla chips.

Make-ahead Gazpacho (page 255)
Chiles Rellenos Casserole (page 271)
Refried Beans
Fried Tortilla Chips (page 252)
Lettuce, Onion & Orange Salad
Cantaloupe Melba (page 313)

Oriental Dinner

This menu allows you to prepare the piquant soybeans and the rice ahead of time. Have the asparagus washed and cut before you serve the soup. When everyone's through with the soup, you stir-fry the asparagus (it takes only a couple of minutes), then serve the soybeans, rice, and asparagus together.

Strict vegetarians may want to substitute a fruit dessert for the Sesame Poundcake, which contains eggs.

Hot & Sour Soup (page 249)
Sweet & Sour Soybeans (page 271)
Brown Rice
Stir-fried Asparagus or Broccoli (page 288)
Sesame Poundcake (page 308)

The breads chapter will make you hungry for a freshly baked slice of Maple-Molasses Bread (page 296) or a herculean sandwich built on your own Honey-Wheat Buns (page 295). Besides quick breads and yeast breads—all chock-full of wholesome whole grains—there are four special pages full of breakfast ideas. Included are recipes for waffles, pancakes, and quick breakfast beverages, plus some revolutionary breakfast ideas, such as Apricot-Almond Sandwiches (page 303) and Peanut Honey Crisps (page 302).

Ready for dessert? A dish of Honey Peach Cobbler (page 311) served hot with vanilla ice cream, perhaps? Or maybe we could tempt you with Ricotta Cheesecake (page 309), a super-rich Marzipan Torte (page 309), or a cooling scoop of Fresh Berry Ice (page 312) and a sliver of Sesame Poundcake (page 308).

Vegetarian cooking bland and boring? We rest our case.

Special features

Every recipe in this cookbook has a special feature—namely, a list of the grams of protein, grams of carbohydrate, milligrams of cholesterol, and number of calories per serving. We offer the information as a resource for those on various diets, or for those simply interested in the approximate nutritional breakdown of recipes.

The numbers were computed with data based on the United States Department of Agriculture's Handbook No. 456. Where a choice of ingredients is given—for instance, most recipes call for butter *or* margarine—the calculations were based on the first item. Of course, if you use margarine instead of butter, the amount of cholesterol per serving will be lower than the amount listed.

Other special features are scattered throughout the book. You'll find out how to make cheese and yogurt (pages 266 and 267), and how to cope with meat eaters in your family (page 287). For menu suggestions, turn to pages 226 and 227).

Nutrition—knowing what counts

Ours is an age fascinated by analysis and calculation. Even in the kitchen, people are counting like crazy: counting calories, counting cholesterol, counting carbohydrate. And vegetarians—whether full-time or part-time—have to count protein amino acids, right?

Well, not really. Vegetarian cooking doesn't require burdensome homework or recondite information. After all, people have been eating meatless meals for centuries. It's not a strange, exotic way of cooking, nor is it a gimmick diet.

Most vegetarians we know take a moderate approach to counting nutrients. Many of them do little or no nutritional calculation. When we asked vegetarians if they calculate protein intake, a typical response was, "We started out tallying protein grams, but relaxed once we caught on to the idea of protein complementing and realized how easy it was. In a very short time, it just came naturally."

Every vegetarian we've talked and cooked with heartily agrees that all the nutritional calculating in the world won't add up to a hill of soybeans if you and your family don't like what you're cooking. "It's good for you; it's got 10 grams of protein" is no argument if, as the kids say, it tastes yucky. That's why this book features good-tasting, good-looking recipes rather than large doses of nutritional information.

Your grandmother was right

The old-fashioned nutritional advice your grandmother gave still holds: namely, eat a varied, balanced diet. That's the key to menu planning and good general nutrition whether you eat meat or not. In our society, if you eat a variety of foods in a balanced diet, it's extremely unlikely that you're eating too little protein, or too little of almost any nutrient.

A balanced, varied diet of vegetarian foods includes grains (breads, cereals, pasta), legumes (dried beans, peas), vegetables (especially the dark green leafy ones), fruits, dairy products, and eggs.

Each of these food families contributes to a balance of important nutrients: protein, carbohydrate, fats, vitamins, and minerals. Strict vegetarians shun not only meat but also dairy products and eggs. They eat leafy green vegetables for calcium and combine grains, legumes, and vegetables for protein; and many take vitamin supplements for "insurance."

Here's a brief review of important nutrients and nutritional considerations in vegetarian cooking.

Carbohydrate. Carbohydrate is one of the two main sources of energy for physical activity (the other is fat). If we don't eat enough carbohydrate, our versatile body machinery draws eventually on its protein, possibly taking it away from tissue-building and other vital tasks. Grains, legumes, vegetables, and fruits provide carbohydrate in the form of starches and sugars.

"Won't all those caloric starches and sugars make me fat?" That's the most common question asked about the plentiful carbohydrates in a vegetarian diet. The simple answer is no. Consuming more calories than you use makes you fat. Of itself, neither carbohydrate nor any other class of nutrients will add pounds to most people.

If calories are a concern, the best approach is to make every calorie count nutritionally. When you're planning menus, choose sources of carbohydrate that are high in nutrients. This means limiting sweets, sweeteners, and alcohol—they have little to offer other than calories. Instead, concentrate on fruits, vegetables, and other foods that are packed with vitamins and minerals. In a vegetarian diet, beans and grains are important sources of protein as well as carbohydrates.

Beans, rice, breads, pasta, and potatoes aren't by themselves terribly caloric. But beans baked with salt pork and brown sugar, rice dripping with butter, bread slathered with jam, pasta loaded with butter and cheese, and potatoes weighed down with sour cream—there are your excess calories.

Fats. Fats are fattening, aren't they? Indeed, they can be. Fats have more calories per ounce than any other kind of food, but you'd be in trouble if you tried to eliminate them entirely: the fat-soluble vitamins—A, D, K, and E—could not perform their roles, and you'd lack an essential nutrient called linoleic acid.

Fats from animal sources tend to be solid and saturated. Cholesterol, a fatlike substance, is found only in animal fats and animal tissue. If you're turning to meatless menus to cut down on saturated fat and cholesterol, you'll also want to cut down on butter, cheese, whole milk, and eggs (one of the highest sources of cholesterol).

Fats from plant sources tend to be liquid and polyunsaturated. The richest sources of linoleic acid are plant-source fats, especially safflower oil, corn oil, cottonseed oil, and soy oil. When recipes in this book call for "salad oil," you can take your choice.

Vitamins & minerals. Because vitamin B-12 and riboflavin can be in short supply in a strict (no eggs, no dairy products) vegetarian diet, vitamin supplements are recommended. Vegetarians who eat dairy products and eggs usually can satisfy their B-12 and riboflavin needs with a couple of glasses of milk a day, or with milk and an egg or ½ cup of cottage cheese a day.

For excellent sources of vitamins, plus calcium and iron, check the chart on this page. The foods

Nutrition-packed Foods

Vitamins & Minerals	Main Sources
A	carrots, butternut squash, Hubbard squash, sweet potato, cantaloupe, dark leafy greens, papaya, broccoli, red bell pepper, apricots
D	fortified milk, egg yolk (also sunlight)
E	unsaturated oils (especially walnut, sunflower, and safflower), almonds, filberts, walnuts, wheat germ, beet greens, spinach, sweet potato
C	papaya, broccoli, red and green bell pepper, Brussels sprouts, kale, citrus juice, cantaloupe, strawberries, oranges, cauliflower
Thiamin (B-1)	brewer's yeast, whole wheat flour, pinto beans, green peas, wheat germ, soybeans, wheat berries, barley, navy beans, spinach
Riboflavin (B-2)	cottage cheese, milk, yogurt, collards, broccoli, mushrooms, Camembert cheese, okra, butternut squash, asparagus
Niacin	tofu, soybeans, cottage cheese, bulgur wheat, collards, navy beans, fresh and dried peas, pinto beans, kidney beans, lentils
B-6	soybeans, kale, spinach, bananas, buckwheat flour, lentils, garbanzos, pinto beans, black-eyed peas, avocado
Folacin	spinach, brewer's yeast, soybeans, garbanzos, kidney beans, limas, oranges, rye flour, sweet potato, whole wheat flour
B-12	cottage cheese, milk, egg, cheese (such as Edam, Camembert, blue, Cheddar, mozzarella), yogurt
Calcium	dairy products, collards, bok choy, kale, mustard greens, broccoli, okra, tofu, soybeans, corn tortillas
Iron	prune juice, black beans, garbanzos, pinto beans, navy beans, limas, soybeans, lentils, spinach, dried peas

listed as the "main sources" aren't the only sources, but they're the foods most worth considering when you're planning meals for maximum nutrition.

Protein. From the tips of your toenails to the hair on your head, you're protein. Protein means "holding first place" and it is, literally, what holds you together. It's an essential part of your muscles, skin, connective tissue, enzymes, hormones—not to mention hair and nails. The protein you eat keeps all your complex systems in good repair, and it's crucial for children's growth.

The U.S. Recommended Daily Allowance for protein is 46 grams for adult women and 54 grams for men. (Just for comparison, a cup of creamed cottage cheese has 18.6 grams protein; one large egg has 6.5 grams; and 1 cup cooked soybeans has 20 grams.)

Protein from an animal source, especially milk and eggs, contains essential amino acids (those our bodies can't produce themselves) in the proportions our bodies need. That's why animal-source proteins are called complete proteins.

Protein from plant sources, though, with one major exception, has an incomplete amount of one or more essential amino acids. The

exception is soybeans, which provide virtually complete protein). The amino acid present in a limited amount is called the *limiting amino acid* because it limits the usability of the whole protein. For example, if one essential amino acid is 75 percent complete, only 75 percent of the protein can be utilized.

By combining a food that's low in one or two amino acids with a food that's complete in those amino acids, you'll create a high-quality protein combination comparable to animal-source protein. This is called *protein complementing.* Any animal-source protein will complete an incomplete plant protein. Or you can combine two plant-source proteins.

Combining plant sources to make a high-quality, complete protein is part of the kitchen wisdom of most traditional cultures—tortillas and beans, rice and beans, lentil soup and wheat bread, tofu and rice. Even the American kitchen, in its short history, has produced some classic variations on the theme of complementary proteins: macaroni and cheese, a peanut butter sandwich with a glass of milk; beans with cornbread.

Mixing & matching protein

The chart on this page combines the traditional knowledge of food families with the modern contribution of amino acid analysis. By combining foods from different columns, you'll be able to create varieties of high-quality protein.

The chart lists sources of protein according to their limiting amino acids. The first column includes foods that have virtually no limiting

amino acid: dairy products, eggs, and soybeans. They can be used as high-quality protein sources by themselves or as a boost to any food in any of the other columns.

The other columns each contain foods low in a certain essential amino acid. To make a complete protein, you combine a food from one of these columns with a different food from one of the others.

You'll notice that families of plant foods tend to be low in the same amino acids. Looking down the columns, you see the two main plant families for protein: grains and legumes. The strengths of grains make up for the weaknesses of legumes, and vice versa. To take you a long way toward meeting your daily protein needs, combine a grain food from the second column with a legume from the third or fourth column.

The vegetables, nuts, and seeds also contribute protein to your diet, though their contribution is less than that from grains and legumes.

Mix & Match for Complete Protein

Combine Different Foods From Any Two Columns

No Limiting Amino Acid	Low in Lycine	Low in Sulfur-carrying Amino Acids	Low in Tryptophan

Dairy products
  Cheese (except cream cheese)
  Cottage cheese
  Milk, all types, including powdered
  Yogurt
Eggs
  Whole, and egg whites
Legumes
  Soybeans
  Soybean curd (tofu)
  Soy milk
Grains
  Wheat germ
Nuts
  Walnuts, black
	Legumes
	  Peanuts
	Grains
	  Barley
	  Buckwheat
	  Bulgur wheat
	  Cornmeal
	  Millet
	  Oats
	  Rice
	  Rye
	  Wheat
	Nuts & Seeds
	  Almonds
	  Brazil nuts
	  *Cashews
	  Coconut
	  Filberts
	  Pecans
	  Pumpkin seeds
	  Sunflower seeds
	  Walnuts, English
	Vegetables
	  Asparagus
	  Beet greens
	  Corn
	  Kale
	  Mushrooms
	  *Potato
	  Sweet potato
	  Yams
		Legumes
		  Beans, dried (black, pinto, red, white)
		  Black-eyed peas, dried
		  Garbanzos
		  Lentils
		  Limas
		  Mung beans
		  *Peanuts
		Nuts
		  Filberts
		Vegetables
		  Asparagus
		  Beans, green
		  Beet greens
		  Broccoli
		  Brussels sprouts
		  Mushrooms
		  Parsley
		  Peas, green
		  Potatoes
		  Soybeans
		  Swiss chard
			Legumes
			  *Beans, dried (black, pinto, red, white)
			  Garbanzos
			  Limas
			  Mung beans
			  *Peanuts
			Grains
			  Cornmeal
			Nuts
			  Almonds
			  Brazil nuts
			  *Walnuts, English
			Vegetables
			  Corn
			  Beet greens
			  Mushrooms
			  Peas, green
			  *Swiss chard

*Indicates foods containing more than 90 percent of ideal amount.

What's missing? There are so many beautiful good foods to serve vegetarian-style, it's easy to forget about meat.

Salads & Appetizers

Delicate, ruffled lettuce leaves, bold-colored beets and carrots, glorious red peppers, creamy-white mushrooms, fruits of all varieties—there's really nothing in a farmers' market of produce that can't go into a salad or appetizer.

In the face of such a wealth of possibilities, our selection of recipes for this chapter was particularly difficult. We narrowed our testing to foods with a certain spunky character that we felt would go well with other vegetarian fare.

When you start improvising on your own—and many of the best salads and appetizers are improvised from fresh ingredients you just happen to have on hand—you'll want to follow the same guidelines we use in testing. First of all, use the freshest possible ingredients. Then, think in terms of contrasts and select a variety of shapes, colors, tastes, and textures. Finally, present your salads and appetizers in the most beautiful and appealing way possible.

The first four recipes in this chapter are appetizers. You'll find an elegant Mushroom Almond Pâté (page 233), a lively Italian eggplant Caponata (page 233), a three-layered Vegetable Terrine (page 233), and Hummus (page 234).

After the appetizer recipes comes a banquet of side-dish and whole-meal salads. Some use spring and summertime ingredients, others include winter vegetables, still others are made of produce that's available all year.

For a simple supper, you might want to tease the palate with Mushroom, Blue Cheese & Walnut Salad (page 234) before serving a plain omelet. Or maybe you'll choose to do all the work a day ahead and prepare a magnificent platter of cooked marinated vegetables, called Vegetables à la Grecque (page 236). You can follow the vegetables with delicious Baked Brie (page 265).

In contrast to our side-dish salads that provide mainly vitamins, minerals, and fiber, our whole-meal salads generally live up to their name and provide a balanced whole meal to serve with bread or rolls.

But what about serving just a plain tossed green salad? Fine! More power to the greens! Freshness is the key in all salads and is especially appreciated when just one or two types of lettuce or other greens are used. In general, the more delicate the ingredients, the more delicate the dressing should be. At the end of the chapter, you'll find two dressings for mixed greens, and a low-calorie dressing that's delightful on fresh fruit.

Mushroom Almond Pâté

For occasions that call for an elegant appetizer, try this well-seasoned pâté. Serve it from a crock with crackers for an hors d'oeuvre. As a first course, it can be sliced and presented on plates along with crusty bread and tiny sweet gherkins, if you wish.

- 1 cup slivered almonds
- ¼ cup butter or margarine
- 1 small onion, chopped
- 1 clove garlic, minced or pressed
- ¾ pound mushrooms, sliced
- ¾ teaspoon salt
- ½ teaspoon thyme leaves
- ⅛ teaspoon white pepper
- 2 tablespoons salad oil

Spread almonds in a shallow pan and toast in a 350° oven for about 8 minutes or until lightly browned.

Melt butter in a wide frying pan over medium-high heat. Add onion, garlic, mushrooms, salt, thyme, and pepper. Cook, stirring occasionally, until onion is soft and most of pan juices have evaporated.

In a food processor or blender, whirl almonds to form a paste. With motor running, add oil and whirl until creamy. Add mushroom mixture and whirl until pâté is smooth. Makes eight ¼-cup servings.

Per serving: 4 grams protein, 6 grams carbohydrate, 35 milligrams cholesterol, 234 calories.

Vegetable Terrine

Here's a superb appetizer—exclusively yours from Ma Maison, a Los Angeles restaurant so celebrated it has an unlisted phone number. You make a combination of carrots and mushrooms for the bottom and top layers, and use a spinach mixture for the center layer. Eggs and Swiss cheese bind the colorful vegetables and make it easy to slice.

- 8 tablespoons (¼ lb.) butter
- 8 medium-size (2 lbs.) carrots, cut in ½-inch slices
- ½ pound mushrooms, sliced
- 1 package (10 oz.) frozen chopped spinach, thawed
- 5 eggs
- 1 cup (4 oz.) shredded Swiss cheese
- 1 teaspoon salt
- ½ teaspoon pepper
- ⅛ teaspoon ground nutmeg

Melt 4 tablespoons of the butter in a wide frying pan over medium-high heat. Add carrots and cook, stirring, for 2 minutes. Reduce heat to low; cover and simmer carrots until tender (about 15 minutes). Coarsely chop carrots and set aside in a large mixing bowl.

In the same pan, cook mushrooms in 2 more tablespoons of the butter until mushrooms are limp and all liquid has evaporated. Coarsely chop mushrooms and add to carrots. Let cool.

Squeeze as much liquid as possible from spinach. In same pan, cook spinach in the remaining 2 tablespoons butter for 2 minutes. Let cool.

In a bowl, beat together 4 of the eggs. Add cheese, salt, pepper, and nutmeg; mix well. Stir into cooled carrot-mushroom mixture. Beat remaining egg lightly, then combine with spinach. Fold lengthwise into thirds a 15-inch length of foil. Line bottom and both ends of a 9 by 5-inch loaf pan with foil. Generously butter foil and pan sides. Spread half the carrot mixture in pan. Cover with spinach mixture. Spread remaining carrot mixture over top.

Cover pan tightly with foil and set in a larger pan containing at least 1 inch of scalding water. Bake in a 400° oven until a knife inserted in center comes out clean (about 1 hour and 15 minutes). Remove from oven and let stand for 10 minutes. Run a knife around sides of pan. Invert onto a serving platter and carefully lift off foil. Cut in slices and serve warm or at room temperature. Makes 8 servings.

Per serving: 11 grams protein, 14 grams carbohydrate, 207 milligrams cholesterol, 269 calories.

Caponata

Enjoy an Italian-style first course—spoon this piquant eggplant mixture onto crisp lettuce and pass around crusty bread. Caponata would also be good as part of an antipasto selection.

- 2 cups diced celery
- ½ cup olive oil
- 1 medium-size unpeeled eggplant, cut in ¾-inch cubes
- 1 large onion, chopped
- ⅓ cup wine vinegar
- 1 teaspoon sugar
- 2 large tomatoes, peeled and diced
- 1 cup water
- 1 tablespoon capers
- ¼ cup sliced pimento-stuffed olives
- 1 can (about 2¼ oz.) sliced ripe olives, drained
- 2 tablespoons minced parsley
  Salt (optional)

In a wide frying pan over medium heat, cook celery in oil, stirring occasionally, until soft. Remove with a slotted spoon and set aside.

Add eggplant to pan and cook, stirring, until it is lightly browned and tender enough to mash easily. Add onion and continue cooking until onion is soft. Remove eggplant and onion with a slotted spoon and add to celery.

Add to pan the vinegar, sugar, tomatoes, and water; cook, stir-

...Caponata (cont'd.)

ring occasionally, for 5 minutes.

Return vegetables to pan. Stir in capers, olives, and parsley. Reduce heat and simmer, uncovered, until most of liquid evaporates (about 20 minutes). Add salt to taste, if desired. Cool, cover, and chill until next day or for as long as 1 week. Bring to room temperature before serving. Makes 8 servings.

Per serving: 2 grams protein, 8 grams carbohydrate, no cholesterol, 166 calories.

Hummus

(Pictured on page 278)

For a classic presentation of this Middle Eastern dish, spread hummus on a rimmed plate. Make a design with a spatula, then drizzle olive oil over it. Or simply garnish hummus with parsley. Pocket bread makes a fine accompaniment.

1 can (15 oz.) garbanzos
¼ cup tahine (sesame paste), or ¼ cup toasted sesame seeds and 2 tablespoons olive oil
3 tablespoons lemon juice
1 large clove garlic, cut in thirds
¼ teaspoon ground cumin
Salt and pepper
Optional garnishes: Olive oil or chopped parsley

Drain garbanzos, reserving liquid. Put garbanzos into a blender or food processor. Add tahine (or toasted sesame seeds and olive oil), lemon juice, garlic, cumin, and ¼ cup of the garbanzo liquid. Whirl, adding more garbanzo liquid if needed, until mixture is smooth and the consistency of heavy batter. Season to taste with salt and pepper. Garnish as suggested above. Makes 12 servings, 2 tablespoons per serving.

Per serving: 4 grams protein, 11 grams carbohydrate, no cholesterol, 97 calories.

Mushroom, Blue Cheese & Walnut Salad

Marinated fresh mushrooms, zesty blue cheese, and crunchy walnuts make a lively first-course salad. For a meal that is well balanced, both nutritionally and esthetically, follow the salad with a simple omelet.

¼ cup olive oil or salad oil
2 teaspoons dry basil leaves
½ teaspoon salt
⅛ teaspoon *each* pepper and paprika
2 teaspoons Dijon mustard
5 teaspoons white wine vinegar
½ pound mushrooms, sliced
2 green onions (including tops), thinly sliced
⅔ cup broken walnut pieces
4 ounces blue-veined cheese, coarsely crumbled
4 cups bite-size pieces of romaine or butter lettuce leaves
About 10 cherry tomatoes, whole or halved

In a salad bowl, combine oil, basil, salt, pepper, paprika, mustard, and vinegar. Beat with a fork until blended. Mix in mushrooms and green onions; let stand at room temperature to marinate for at least 30 minutes.

Add walnut pieces, blue cheese, lettuce, and cherry tomatoes and toss lightly. Makes 4 servings.

Per serving: 12 grams protein, 12 grams carbohydrate, 25 milligrams cholesterol, 407 calories.

Roasted Pepper & Tomato Salad

(Pictured on facing page)

Late summer is the time to enjoy this Mediterranean-inspired roasted pepper salad. If you've

never tried a roasted pepper, you're likely to be pleasantly intrigued by its nutty, mellow flavor and tender-crisp texture.

This salad is an excellent appetizer, but it also makes a marvelous full meal accompanied by a cheese board, iced tea or wine, and crusty bread.

6 large red or green bell peppers or a combination of both
5 large tomatoes (about 2½ lbs.)
20 pitted ripe olives
¼ cup olive oil
½ teaspoon salt
¼ teaspoon pepper
1 teaspoon ground cumin
4 cloves garlic, minced or pressed
1 tablespoon chopped parsley
Lettuce leaves
6 hard-cooked eggs

Set whole peppers in a shallow pan and place in broiler so that peppers are about 1 inch from heat source. Broil, turning frequently with tongs, until peppers are well blistered and charred on all sides. Then place in a paper bag, close bag tightly, and let peppers sweat for 15 to 20 minutes to loosen skins. Cool and strip off skins. Cut peppers in half and remove and discard stems and seeds. Cut peppers into strips roughly ½ by 1 inch and place in a bowl.

Peel tomatoes and cut in half; remove and discard seeds. Cut into bite-size pieces and add to peppers along with olives.

In another bowl, combine oil, salt, pepper, cumin, garlic, and parsley; stir well to blend. Stir into

(Continued on page 236)

Red peppers are hot, right? Not when they're mellow red bell peppers roasted to bring out their nutlike flavor. Enjoy them in Roasted Pepper & Tomato Salad (recipe on this page), accompanied by assorted cheeses and French bread.

. . . Roasted Pepper & Tomato Salad (cont'd.)

pepper mixture; taste and add more salt and pepper, if desired.

Cover salad and let stand at room temperature for about 4 hours, or refrigerate for as long as two days (but bring to room temperature before serving).

To serve, line individual plates with lettuce leaves and mound pepper mixture onto lettuce. Garnish each salad with eggs, cut in halves or quarters. Makes 6 servings.

Per serving: 10 grams protein, 13 grams carbohydrate, 352 milligrams cholesterol, 245 calories.

Perfect Protein Salad

Here's a beautifully composed salad. It's brimming with delightful textures, colors, and tastes — and it's packed with protein. You can serve it as a main course or side dish.

  2 large heads butter lettuce
10 medium-size mushrooms
  1 medium-size carrot, sliced
  ½ cup Spanish-style peanuts
  3 tablespoons chopped parsley
  2 tablespoons *each* wheat germ, sunflower seeds, and unsweetened granola-type cereal
  ½ cup *each* bean sprouts and shredded jack cheese
  ¾ cup plain yogurt
  3 tablespoons salad oil
  1½ tablespoons lemon juice
    Salt and pepper
  1 small avocado
  2 hard-cooked eggs, quartered

Line a large serving bowl with outer leaves of lettuce. Tear inner leaves into bite-size pieces. Place in bowl and mix with mushrooms, carrot, and peanuts. Sprinkle in parsley, wheat germ, sunflower seeds, cereal, sprouts, and cheese.

In a small bowl, blend yogurt, oil, and lemon juice. Pour dressing over salad; toss gently. Season to taste with salt and pepper. Peel, pit, and slice avocado. Garnish salad with eggs and avocado slices. Makes 6 servings.

Per serving: 12 grams protein, 14 grams carbohydrate, 54 milligrams cholesterol, 315 calories.

Vegetables à la Grecque

The French style of simmering a variety of vegetables in the Greek manner (with herbs, lemon juice, and oil) and marinating them in this same sauce, concentrated, results in a superbly seasoned salad.

The basic recipe suits a wide range of vegetables, and though it takes more time to cook a variety, rather than a single vegetable, that's part of the fun. Cook vegetables that appeal to you, then arrange them handsomely on a platter.

  3½ cups water
  6 tablespoons lemon juice
  ¾ cup dry white wine
  ½ cup olive oil
  1½ teaspoons salt
  2 bay leaves
  2 cloves garlic, cut in thirds
  1 shallot or 1 large green onion, chopped
  6 whole black peppers
  1 teaspoon *each* dry tarragon and thyme leaves
    Vegetables (directions follow)
  2 tablespoons chopped parsley

In a large Dutch oven or other wide pan, place water, lemon juice, wine, oil, salt, and bay leaves. In a tea ball or cheesecloth bag, enclose garlic, shallot, peppers, tarragon, and thyme; add to pan. Bring to a boil, then lower heat; cover and simmer for 10 minutes.

Add vegetables and cook according to directions that follow. With a slotted spoon, remove vegetables as they are cooked and place in a shallow pan. When all vegetables are cooked, remove tea ball or cheesecloth bag from pan and discard herbs. Increase heat to medium and cook broth until reduced to one cup; cool slightly, then spoon sauce over vegetables.

Cover and refrigerate for at least 4 hours or as long as 3 days. To serve, lift vegetables from sauce, arrange on a platter, and garnish with parsley. Makes 8 servings.

Per serving (including all vegetables listed below): 4 grams protein, 17 grams carbohydrate, no cholesterol, 211 calories.

Summer squash. Remove ends from 2 small crookneck squash and slice squash in half lengthwise. Remove ends from 3 small zucchini and slice in half lengthwise; cut each half again lengthwise. Add to broth, cover, and simmer until crisp-tender (about 5 minutes).

Carrots. Peel 3 carrots and slice on the diagonal about ½-inch thick. Add to broth; cover and simmer until crisp-tender (about 7 minutes).

Leeks. Cut 3 leeks in half lengthwise, then cut into 4-inch lengths; discard coarse leaves. Wash thoroughly to remove sand. Add to broth; cover and simmer until tender (about 7 minutes).

Eggplant. Cut 1 small (¾ lb.) unpeeled eggplant in half lengthwise, then slice into 1-inch-thick strips. Add to broth; cover and simmer until tender (about 7 minutes).

Mushrooms. Remove ends from ½ pound small mushrooms; wash mushrooms. Add to broth; cover and simmer until barely tender (about 3 minutes).

Bell pepper (red or green).   Seed and cut 3 peppers into 1-inch-wide strips. Add to broth; cover and simmer until barely tender (about 5 minutes).

Onions.   Trim and peel 8 small boiling onions. Add to broth; cover and simmer until tender (7 to 9 minutes).

Celery hearts.   Remove ends from 3 celery hearts and cut off tops to make 4-inch-long pieces; cut each piece in half lengthwise. Add to broth; cover and simmer until tender (about 15 minutes).

Tarragon Vegetable Salad

Take a hint from French cooks and marinate cooked vegetables for a delicious salad. Because the frozen peas and carrots are only thawed, not cooked, they taste and look extraordinarily fresh in this recipe.

½ cup olive oil or salad oil

3 tablespoons white wine vinegar

1 tablespoon chopped parsley

1 teaspoon *each* salt and tarragon leaves

2 teaspoons Dijon mustard

½ teaspoon pepper

1 shallot, finely chopped (or ¼ cup chopped green onion)

1 pound small thin-skinned potatoes

1 pound green beans, cut in 1-inch lengths

1 pound turnips, peeled and cut in ½-inch squares

2 packages (10 oz. *each*) frozen mixed carrots and peas, thawed

Lettuce leaves

About 8 cherry tomatoes

Stir together oil, vinegar, parsley, salt, tarragon, mustard, pepper, and shallot; set aside.

Place potatoes in 1 inch boiling water; cover and cook just until tender when pierced (about 20

minutes); drain. When cool enough to handle, peel and cut into ¼-inch-thick slices.

Meanwhile, steam green beans over boiling water for about 7 minutes or until crisp-tender. Rinse with cold water and drain well. Steam turnips over boiling water for about 8 minutes or until tender when pierced. Rinse with cold water and drain well.

In a large bowl, combine potatoes, beans, turnips, and thawed carrots and peas. Pour dressing over all and stir gently. Cover and chill for at least 8 hours or until next day; stir occasionally.

About 1 hour before serving, line a shallow serving dish with lettuce leaves and halve the cherry tomatoes. Mound salad in center of lettuce and garnish with tomato halves. Let stand at room temperature until serving time. Makes 8 servings.

Per serving: 5 grams protein, 25 grams carbohydrate, no cholesterol, 237 calories.

Turkish Eggplant Salad

You bake an eggplant until it collapses, then mix the pulp with green pepper and yogurt for a calorie-lean salad. You might feature it as a first course, garnished with tomato, onion rings, and romaine spears.

1 large (about 1½ lbs.) eggplant

1 tablespoon *each* olive oil and lemon juice

1 clove garlic, minced or pressed

1 medium-size green pepper, seeded and finely chopped

1 cup plain yogurt

Salt and pepper

Romaine lettuce leaves

3 tomatoes

1 small red onion

2 tablespoons chopped parsley

With a fork, pierce skin of eggplant. Place eggplant in a rimmed pan. Bake in a 400° oven for 1 hour or until very soft. Cool. Split in half and scoop out pulp into a bowl. Mash pulp with a fork. Mix in oil, lemon juice, garlic, green pepper, yogurt, and salt and pepper to taste. Cover and chill for 2 hours.

To serve, arrange romaine leaves on individual salad plates. Mound eggplant in center of each. Cut tomatoes in wedges. Thinly slice onion and separate into rings. Surround salad with tomato wedges and top with onion rings and parsley. Makes 6 servings.

Per serving: 4 grams protein, 13 grams carbohydrate, 3 milligrams cholesterol, 87 calories.

Pear & Grape Slaw

Orange-flavored yogurt enfolds this luscious mixture of grapes, pears, cabbage, celery, and green onions.

4 cups finely shredded cabbage

2 green onions (including tops), thinly sliced

1 stalk celery, thinly sliced

2 cups seedless grapes

¼ cup slivered almonds

1 carton (8 oz.) orange-flavored yogurt

3 firm ripe Bartlett pears

Salt and pepper

2 tablespoons finely chopped crystallized ginger

(Continued on page 239)

...Pear & Grape Slaw (cont'd.)

In a serving bowl, combine cabbage, green onion, celery, and grapes; cover and chill to crisp.

Spread almonds in a shallow pan and toast in a 350° oven for about 8 minutes or until lightly browned.

Just before serving, place yogurt in a bowl. Halve, core, and thinly slice pears into yogurt; stir lightly, making sure each slice is coated to keep pears from darkening. Mix pears and yogurt into the salad and season to taste with salt and pepper. Sprinkle toasted nuts and ginger over top. Makes 8 servings.

Per serving: 3 grams protein, 28 grams carbohydrate, 1 milligram cholesterol, 139 calories.

Salad-in-a-Boat

(Pictured on facing page)

A creamy, crunchy mixture of vegetables and eggs sails forth in a puffy pastry boat—an ingenious way to launch a main-dish salad. You can bake the cheese-flavored pastry boat a day ahead. You can even fill the boat several hours before serving, since the layer of spinach keeps the salad mixture from soaking into the crust.

⅔ cup water
5 tablespoons butter or margarine
¼ teaspoon salt
⅔ cup all-purpose flour
3 eggs
¾ cup (3 oz.) shredded Swiss cheese
1½ cups small spinach leaves
Egg-Vegetable Salad (recipe follows)
8 cherry tomatoes

Summertime fare with a flair—that's Salad-in-a-Boat (recipe above). It's an attractive, easy-to-make entrée, shown here with Sesame Pound Cake (recipe on page 308) and a cooling blend of equal parts mint tea and orange juice.

In a 2-quart pan, bring water, butter, and salt to a boil. When butter melts, remove pan from heat and add flour all at once. Beat until well blended.

Return pan to medium heat and stir rapidly for 1 minute or until a ball forms in middle of pan and a film forms on bottom of pan. Remove pan from heat and beat in eggs, one at a time, until mixture is smooth and glossy. Add cheese and beat until well mixed. Spoon into a greased 9-inch round pan with removable bottom or spring-release sides. Spread evenly over bottom and up sides of pan.

Bake crust in a 400° oven for 40 minutes or until puffed and brown; turn off oven. With a wooden pick, prick crust in 10 to 12 places; leave in closed oven for about 10 minutes to dry. Remove pan from oven and cool completely. Remove crust from pan.

Prepare egg-vegetable salad. Line bottom and sides of boat with spinach leaves. Cut each tomato in half. Pile egg salad over spinach and garnish with cherry tomatoes. Cut boat in thick wedges. Makes 6 servings.

Per serving (including salad): 18 grams protein, 19 grams carbohydrate, 436 milligrams cholesterol, 483 calories.

Egg-Vegetable Salad. In a bowl, stir together ½ cup **mayonnaise,** 1 teaspoon **Dijon mustard,** and ¼ teaspoon ground **cumin.** Stir in 1 cup thinly sliced raw **cauliflower,** ¼ pound raw **mushrooms** (thinly sliced), 1 cup frozen **peas** (thawed), 1 cup thinly sliced **celery,** and 2 **green onions** and tops (thinly sliced). Coarsely chop 6 **hard-cooked eggs;** gently fold into vegetable mixture.

Zucchini Fiesta Salad

Introduce your favorite Mexican entrée with this spring-fresh salad.

Bright green zucchini and pretty yellow crookneck squash mix with distinctive Mexican ingredients—cumin, green chilies, and avocado—for a fiesta of flavors.

½ pound *each* small zucchini and crookneck squash, cut crosswise in ¼-inch-thick slices
2 tablespoons lemon juice
¼ cup salad oil
½ teaspoon salt
Dash *each* of pepper and ground cumin
1 green onion (including top), thinly sliced
⅓ cup diced green chilies
⅓ cup pimento-stuffed olives, cut in half crosswise
1 small package (3 oz.) cream cheese, cut in ¾-inch cubes
1 small avocado
Lettuce leaves
Fresh coriander (cilantro) sprigs

Steam zucchini and crookneck squash over boiling water until crisp-tender (about 3 minutes). Plunge into ice water to cool; drain well.

In a large bowl, combine lemon juice, oil, salt, pepper, and cumin. Add drained squash and stir lightly; chill for 30 minutes. Add onion, chilies, olives, and cheese. Peel and pit avocado; cut into small cubes. Add to salad and mix lightly.

To serve, arrange lettuce leaves on 4 salad plates. Mound equal portions of salad on each plate. Garnish each salad with a sprig of coriander. Makes 4 servings.

Per serving: 5 grams protein, 10 grams carbohydrate, 24 milligrams cholesterol, 335 calories.

Vegetable-Herb Salad

For a show-off salad that can steal the scene at a party or on a buffet, assemble this salad in a glass serving bowl so each colorful layer can be seen. You can serve it after an hour's chilling or make it a day ahead—it won't wilt.

4 cups shredded iceberg lettuce

⅔ cup chopped parsley

1 green or red bell pepper, seeded and coarsely chopped

2 cups coarsely chopped cauliflower or broccoli

3 stalks celery, thinly sliced

2 *each* large carrots and zucchini, shredded

1 package (10 oz.) frozen peas, thawed

1 cup *each* mayonnaise and plain yogurt

2 tablespoons Dijon mustard

1 teaspoon *each* dry rosemary, dry basil, and oregano leaves

2 teaspoons garlic salt

½ teaspoon pepper

2½ cups (10 oz.) shredded Cheddar cheese

2 green onions (including tops), thinly sliced

⅓ cup sunflower seeds

In a shallow 4-quart serving dish, place lettuce in an even layer. Distribute parsley, green pepper, cauliflower, celery, carrots, zucchini, and peas in even layers over lettuce. Mix mayonnaise, yogurt, mustard, rosemary, basil, oregano, garlic salt, and pepper. Spread evenly over top. Sprinkle cheese and onions over dressing, then sprinkle sunflower seeds over all. Cover and chill up to 24 hours. Makes 12 servings.

Per serving: 10 grams protein, 9 grams carbohydrate, 38 milligrams cholesterol, 288 calories.

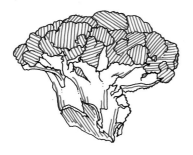

Zucchini & Apple Salad

Fruit and vegetables make a crisp combination that's perfect as a side dish with blintzes, kugel, or any noodle-and-cheese dish. Prepare the salad ahead of time so the flavors have a chance to blend.

⅓ cup salad oil

1 tablespoon lemon juice

2 tablespoons white wine vinegar

1 teaspoon *each* sugar and dry basil

About ¾ teaspoon salt

¼ teaspoon pepper

3 medium-size red or golden Delicious apples

½ medium-size red onion, thinly sliced lengthwise

1 green pepper, seeded and cut into matchstick pieces

1 pound zucchini, thinly sliced

In a large salad bowl, combine oil, lemon juice, vinegar, sugar, basil, salt, and pepper. Core and dice unpeeled apples and add to dressing; coat apples well with dressing. Add onion, green pepper, and zucchini. Stir lightly. Cover and chill.

Just before serving, mix salad again until well combined. Taste and add more salt if needed. Makes 8 servings.

Per serving: 1 gram protein, 10 grams carbohydrate, no cholesterol, 122 calories.

Tabbuli

It's worth growing a pot of mint just to make this classic fresh-tasting Middle Eastern salad. Traditionally, the bulgur is just soaked in water, but we like to cook it lightly to intensify the wheaty flavor. Be careful not to overcook it, though—the bulgur should still have crunch.

Spinach and Feta Quiche (page 261) would go well with tabbuli, as would Feta Cheese Squares (page 263) or Stuffed Grape Leaves (page 279).

1 cup bulgur wheat

1 cup water

⅓ cup olive oil or salad oil

¼ cup lemon juice

1 teaspoon *each* salt and ground allspice

1 cup chopped green onions (including tops)

¼ cup chopped fresh mint leaves

1 cup chopped parsley

½ cup cooked garbanzo beans

2 tomatoes, finely diced

1 head romaine lettuce, washed and chilled

Bring bulgur and water to a boil in a covered pan. Immediately reduce heat and simmer covered, for 5 minutes or until liquid is absorbed; bulgur should still be crunchy. Turn bulgur into a bowl and mix in oil, lemon juice, salt, and allspice. Cool.

Add onions, mint, parsley, garbanzos, and tomatoes. Mix together lightly. Cover and chill for 1 hour or until next day.

To serve, line a platter with large outer romaine leaves; pile tabbuli in center. Arrange inner romaine leaves on a separate serving plate. To eat tabbuli, take inner leaf of romaine and use it to scoop up each bite. Makes 6 servings.

Per serving: 11 grams protein, 50 grams carbohydrate, no cholesterol, 363 calories.

Bulgur Supper Salad

The toasty whole-grain flavor of bulgur—quick-cooking cracked wheat—goes well with all kinds of vegetables. Here it's tossed with a spicy mustard dressing and mixed with artichoke hearts, carrots, celery, green pepper, and onions for a splendid whole-meal salad.

2 cups water
¾ teaspoon salt
1 vegetable-flavored bouillon cube
1 cup bulgur wheat
Mustard Dressing (recipe follows)
1 jar (6 oz.) marinated artichoke hearts
1 large carrot, shredded
2 stalks celery, thinly sliced
1 green pepper, seeded and diced
2 green onions (including tops), thinly sliced
½ cup chopped parsley
About 8 lettuce leaves
3 hard-cooked eggs, quartered
2 medium-size tomatoes, cut in wedges
4 ounces sharp Cheddar or Swiss cheese, cut into julienne strips
About ¼ cup pitted ripe olives

In a 3-quart pan, bring water, salt, and vegetable bouillon cube to boiling. Stir in bulgur. Reduce heat; cover and simmer for 15 minutes.

Meanwhile prepare Mustard Dressing. Drain marinade from artichokes into dressing, mixing it well. Dice artichokes and set aside.

Turn hot cooked bulgur into a bowl, add dressing, and stir gently. Let stand until cool. Stir in artichokes, carrot, celery, green pepper, onions, and parsley. Cover and refrigerate for 2 hours or until next day.

Arrange lettuce on a serving platter or individual plates. Mound salad on lettuce; surround with eggs and tomatoes. Sprinkle cheese over top and garnish with olives. Makes 8 servings.

Per serving (including dressing): 10 grams protein, 26 grams carbohydrate, 108 milligrams cholesterol, 682 calories.

Mustard Dressing. In a bowl, combine 4 tablespoons *each* **salad oil** and **lemon juice**, 1 teaspoon *each* dry **basil** and **oregano** leaves, ½ teaspoon **pepper**, 1 clove **garlic** (minced or pressed), and 1 tablespoon **Dijon mustard.**

Russian Potato Salad

Potato salad is pale, soft, and bland, right? Wrong. Not when it's Russian! Then it's colorful, crisp, and tangy because it's full of apples, carrots, pickled beets, red onion, green pepper—and, of course, potatoes.

1 pound thin-skinned potatoes
Caper Dressing (recipe follows)
2 medium-size apples, unpeeled
3 medium size carrots, thinly sliced
1 small red onion, chopped
1 medium-size green pepper, seeded and cut into strips
1 can (1 lb.) pickled beets, drained and diced

Place potatoes in 1-inch boiling water; cover and cook just until tender when pierced (20 to 25 minutes).

Meanwhile, prepare dressing in a large bowl. Drain potatoes, cool, peel, and dice directly into dressing. Also dice apples into dressing (to prevent browning). Add carrots, onion, green pepper, and beets. Stir lightly. Cover and refrigerate for 6 hours or until next day. Makes 10 servings.

Per serving (including dressing): 2 grams protein, 18 grams carbohydrate, no cholesterol, 173 calories.

Caper Dressing. Stir together 3 tablespoons *each* **white wine vinegar** and **capers**, ½ cup **salad oil**, 2 teaspoons **sugar**, 1 teaspoon *each* **dry mustard** and **salt**, ½ teaspoon **dill weed**, and ¼ teaspoon *each* **pepper** and **paprika.**

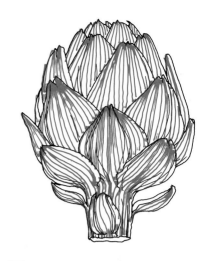

Quick Artichoke Pasta Salad

(Pictured on page 243)

The liquid from marinated artichoke hearts turns into a zingy dressing for this marvelously simple macaroni salad. It's delicious served with a frittata or Vegetarian Joe (page 264), or with a minestrone soup.

4 ounces (about 1 cup) salad macaroni or other medium-size pasta
1 jar (6 oz.) marinated artichoke hearts
¼ pound mushrooms, quartered
1 cup cherry tomatoes, halved
1 cup medium-size pitted ripe olives
1 tablespoon chopped parsley
½ teaspoon dry basil leaves
Salt and pepper

Cook macaroni according to package directions; drain well, rinse with cold water, and drain again. Turn into a large bowl.

Add artichokes and their liquid, mushrooms, cherry tomatoes, olives, parsley, and basil; toss gently. Cover and refrigerate for at least 4 hours or until next day. Before serving, season with salt and pepper to taste. Makes 6 servings.

Per serving: 5 grams protein, 21 grams carbohydrate, no cholesterol, 123 calories.

Chili-spiced Bean Salad

This spicy variation on the three-bean salad theme includes corn and green chilies. You can pour the chili-seasoned dressing over the salad and chill it overnight, if you like.

> **Chili Dressing (recipe follows)**
> 1 can (1 lb. *each*) red kidney beans, pinto beans, and garbanzos
> 1 can (1 lb.) whole kernel corn
> 1 large stalk celery, thinly sliced
> 5 green onions (including tops), thinly sliced
> ¼ cup chopped parsley
> 1 can (4 oz.) diced green chilies
> Lettuce leaves

Prepare dressing and reserve.

Drain kidney beans, pinto beans, and garbanzos into a colander, rinse with cold water, drain, and turn into a salad bowl. Drain corn; add to beans along with celery, green onions, parsley, and chilies. Pour over dressing and mix lightly. Cover and refrigerate for 4 hours or until next day. Stir lightly before serving. Garnish with lettuce leaves. Makes 8 servings.

Per serving (including dressing): 13 grams protein, 44 grams carbohydrate, no cholesterol, 354 calories.

Chili Dressing. In a bowl, combine ¾ cup **salad oil**, ¼ cup **wine vinegar**, 1 clove **garlic** (minced or pressed), 1 teaspoon *each* **salt**, **chili powder**, and **oregano** leaves, ¼ teaspoon ground **cumin**, and a dash of **pepper**. Stir to blend well.

Lemon-Yogurt Dressing

Here's a low-calorie boiled dressing that's delightful on fruit salads.

Display a variety of fruit — melon crescents, pineapple spears, orange slices, pear quarters, grapes — in rows on a serving platter and offer the dressing in a separate bowl.

> ½ cup sugar
> 1 tablespoon cornstarch
> ¼ teaspoon salt
> ⅔ cup water
> 1 teaspoon grated lemon peel
> ⅓ cup lemon juice
> 2 eggs
> 1 cup plain yogurt

In a pan, blend sugar, cornstarch, and salt. Stir in water, lemon peel, and lemon juice. Cook, stirring, over medium heat until mixture boils and thickens.

In a small bowl, lightly beat eggs. Stir some of the hot sauce into eggs, then stir all into mixture in pan; heat, stirring, for 1 minute. Remove from heat and cool for 10 minutes, stirring occasionally. Cover and refrigerate for as long as 5 days. Just before serving, fold in yogurt. Makes about 2 cups

Per tablespoon: .6 grams protein, 4 grams carbohydrate, 16 milligrams cholesterol, 22 calories.

Lemon-Thyme Dressing

You use lemon juice instead of vinegar to mingle with thyme and lots of minced parsley in this refreshing dressing. It's perfect on salad greens.

> ½ cup salad oil
> 1½ teaspoons grated lemon peel
> ¼ cup lemon juice
> 1 small clove garlic, minced or pressed
> 1¼ teaspoons sugar
> ¾ teaspoon thyme leaves
> ½ teaspoon salt
> ⅛ teaspoon pepper
> ⅓ cup chopped parsley

In a container, combine oil, lemon peel, lemon juice, garlic, sugar, thyme, salt, and pepper; blend well. Just before serving, stir in parsley. Cover and refrigerate for as long as 1 week. Makes about 1 cup.

Per tablespoon: .07 grams protein, .8 grams carbohydrate, no cholesterol, 63 calories.

Toasted Sesame Seed Dressing

This nutlike dressing is good on any simple mixed green salad. For fewer calories, use sour half-and-half in place of sour cream.

> 2 tablespoons sesame seeds
> ¼ cup olive oil or salad oil
> 1 tablespoon *each* lemon juice and honey
> 1 teaspoon curry powder
> 1 cup sour cream or sour half-and-half
> Salt and pepper

Spread sesame seeds in a frying pan and cook over medium heat, shaking pan occasionally, until seeds turn golden and begin to pop (2 to 3 minutes); let cool.

In a container, stir together oil, lemon juice, honey, toasted sesame seeds, curry, sour cream, and salt and pepper to taste. Cover and refrigerate for at least 1 hour or as long as 5 days. Makes about 1½ cups.

Per tablespoon (made with sour cream): .4 grams protein, .5 grams carbohydrate, 4 milligrams cholesterol, 44 calories.

Artichoke marinade acts like the genie in the jar for Quick Artichoke Pasta Salad (recipe on page 241), granting your wish for a well-seasoned instant salad dressing. It's delicious served with wedges of Zucchini Frittata (recipe on page 257).

Soups for Starters or Full Meals

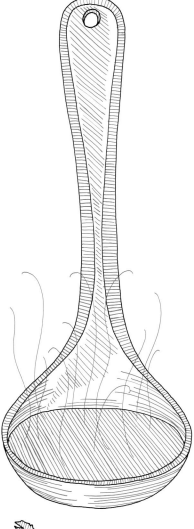

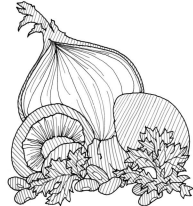

Discovering—or rediscovering—homemade soup is one of the delights of vegetarian cooking. That's why we've included a chapter devoted to soups of all kinds: meal-in-a-bowl soups, soups high in protein, soups packed with vegetables, soups that are creamy or spicy or chilled. This chapter is, in short, a veritable celebration of soups.

Of course, serving soup isn't obligatory, but we find that a meatless menu naturally places more emphasis on breads, salads, and soups.

Selecting a soup to go with two or three other vegetarian dishes is just a matter of exercising your good food sense. Nutrition, flavor, texture, and your own preferences are the most important considerations. For instance, it makes good sense to serve a tomato-based chunky vegetable soup with a smooth egg and cheese dish, rather than with a tomato-based chunky vegetable dish. This vegetable soup provides vitamins and minerals as well as some protein; the cheese and egg dish contains a large amount of complete protein.

If you do want to serve two vegetable dishes and avoid cheese and eggs, see to it that one dish contains legumes and the other a grain to make a complete protein. You might purée the soup to provide a contrasting texture, and sprinkle sunflower seeds or nuts on top. Of course, you wouldn't season everything with the same herbs or to the same degree. Remember, the same esthetic principles apply for meals as for any sensuous event; sameness is monotonous; contrast is exciting. As for nutrition, the breakdown (per serving) of protein, carbohydrate, cholesterol, and calories at the end of each recipe provides some guidelines for menu planning.

Some soups are substantial enough to be the entrée, with only a light salad and perhaps some bread to round out the meal. And if you serve soup as a solo dish for supper, you serve up a bit of word history—at root, soup and supper are the same.

One of our favorite solo soups, the colorful Aztec Soup (page 252), starts with a simple base of corn and squash. Each guest then adds to his or her bowl from an assortment of condiments—fried tortilla strips, pine nuts, grated cheese, pumpkin seeds, diced avocado.

Of course, any main-dish soup can be served in small portions as part of an ensemble of vegetarian foods. The converse doesn't always work as well, though. Some soups, such as Potato Yogurt Soup (page 248), wouldn't be filling enough for a whole meal. Others, such as Chilled Cucumber Soup (page 255), would be too rich to serve in large portions.

Vegetarian Soup Stocks

Most of the soup recipes in this chapter call for a vegetable stock. The quickest way to prepare the amount of stock you'll need is to buy instant vegetable stock base in cubes or granules (labeled as vegetable-flavored instant bouillon or vegetarian-style instant bouillon).

For each cup of vegetable stock specified in our recipes, dissolve 1 teaspoon vegetable-flavored granules or 1 cube vegetable stock base in 1 cup boiling water.

If you have a little more time, you might want to try the recipe for Quick Vegetable Stock that follows. And, if you're inclined to be super-thrifty, you can save vegetable peelings and make a grand soup stock following the suggestions for Save-It-Up Vegetable Stock.

Quick Vegetable Stock. Made from fresh vegetables, this stock takes much less cooking time than meat stock. Here's the traditional French way to prepare a flavorful all-vegetable stock. Scrub and coarsely chop 3 large **carrots,** 1 large **turnip,** and 2 stalks **celery.** Peel and chop 2 large **onions.** Melt 2 tablespoons **butter** in an 8-quart pan over medium-high heat. Add chopped vegetables and cook, stirring occasionally, until vegetables turn golden (about 15 minutes).

Add 3 quarts **water,** 2 teaspoons **salt,** 6 large sprigs **parsley,** ½ **bay leaf,** and 1 teaspoon **thyme leaves.** Cover and bring to a boil. Reduce heat and simmer for 1½ hours. Strain and discard vegetables. Makes 2½ quarts stock.

You can adjust the seasoning to suit your taste by adding 2 cloves peeled garlic, several peppercorns, or your favorite herbs. You can freeze extra stock for future soups.

Save-It-Up Vegetable Stock. This too is a thrifty, delicious base for soups. You make it by cooking the parings and trimmings saved from vegetables served during the week. You can also save up the cooking water from boiled or steamed vegetables—it's full of vitamins and minerals.

Save cooking and soaking water in a covered container in the refrigerator or freezer. Save parings and trimmings in a large plastic bag in the refrigerator.

Since most soup recipes in this chapter are best with a mildly flavored stock, you'll probably want to avoid using trimmings from pungent vegetables, such as cabbage and broccoli. Here are a few save-up suggestions: tips of green beans; ends of zucchini, crookneck squash, mushrooms, carrots, and asparagus stalks; potato peels, parsley stems, tomato trimmings, pea pods, wilted celery stalks, green onion tops, green pepper stems and seeds, wilted or outer leaves of lettuce, and spinach and chard stems.

When you have a quart or more of parings and trimmings, coarsely chop them, then place in a large pan and cover with cold water (or cover with the cooking water you've saved). The more chopped vegetable bits and pieces you use in proportion to the water, the stronger the stock. Salt lightly to bring out the flavor, then bring to a boil. Reduce heat; cover and simmer for 30 minutes.

If you want, you can add herbs to the stock—half a bay leaf, a pinch of thyme, a sprig of parsley. For a double-strength vegetable broth, you can use the save-it-up vegetable stock in place of water when you make the quick vegetable stock.

Almond Soup Gratinée

A large bowl of almond soup bubbling under a golden crust of cheese makes a heart-warming meal on a wintry day. You can prepare the broth ahead of time, but once you combine it with the eggs, you should complete the final steps.

Then you might serve it with a platter of Greek-style marinated vegetables (page 236) or a crisp green salad and a light red wine.

> **About 1 tablespoon butter or margarine**
> **4 slices French bread, cut ¾ inch thick**
> **1 cup blanched slivered almonds**
> **2 large cloves garlic, minced or pressed**
> **6 cups vegetable stock (recipe at left)**
> **Salt and pepper**
> **2 eggs**
> **1 cup (4 oz.) shredded Swiss or Gruyère cheese**
> **Paprika**

Butter both sides of bread and place in a single layer on a baking sheet. Bake in a 350° oven for 10 minutes or until bread is lightly browned; turn and lightly brown the other side.

Meanwhile, reserving 1 tablespoon of the almonds, spread remaining almonds in a shallow pan and toast in a 350° oven for about 8 minutes or until lightly browned. Let cool until crisp, then whirl with garlic in a blender or food processor until nuts are very finely chopped.

Place nuts in a 3-quart pan; add stock. Bring to a boil, then cover and simmer for 15 minutes. Add salt and pepper to taste. Beat eggs lightly. Remove soup from heat and, stirring constantly, stir eggs into soup.

Ladle hot soup into 4 individual ovenproof soup bowls (2 to 2½-cup size). Set a piece of toasted French bread on top of soup in each bowl and sprinkle equally with shredded cheese, the reserved almonds, and paprika.

Place bowls in a 425° oven for 10 minutes; then broil about 4 inches from heat until cheese and almonds brown. Makes 4 servings.

Per serving: 29 grams protein, 27 grams carbohydrate, 212 milligrams cholesterol, 488 calories.

Finnish Summer Soup

(Pictured on facing page)

Summer's most tender offerings—petite new peas, baby carrots, tiny onions, new potatoes—bob in a light cream soup. For a luncheon, you could serve moderate-size portions of this delightful soup with an array of decorated open-faced sandwiches. For supper you could serve larger portions accompanied by a bread-and-cheese platter.

- 2 cups water
- 4 to 6 small thin-skinned potatoes, peeled and halved
- 1 teaspoon salt
- ⅛ teaspoon white pepper
- 2 tablespoons butter or margarine
- 6 small boiling onions, or 6 green onions (including tops), cut into 3-inch lengths
- 12 very young fresh baby carrots (½ pound) or 1 package (8 oz.) frozen whole baby carrots
- ½ pound fresh young green beans, cut into 1-inch lengths, or 1 package (9 oz.) frozen cut green beans
- 2 cups fresh, shelled, tiny peas or 1 package (10 oz.) frozen tiny green peas
- 2 cups half-and-half (light cream)
- 3 tablespoons all-purpose flour

Heat water to boiling in a wide 5-quart pan; add potatoes. Reduce heat; cover and simmer for 5 minutes. Add salt, pepper, butter, onions, carrots, and green beans; simmer for 8 more minutes. Add peas and cook for another 2 minutes or until vegetables are crisp-tender.

Finnish Summer Soup (recipe above) features tender-crisp baby vegetables in light cream. Perfect post-sauna soup partners are open-faced sandwiches of cream cheese on rye, decorated with sliced vegetables.

In a small bowl, stir together half-and-half and flour until smooth; stir into simmering vegetables. Cook, stirring, until soup is slightly thickened (about 5 minutes). Makes five 1⅔-cup servings.

Per serving: 9 grams protein, 34 grams carbohydrate, 49 milligrams cholesterol, 292 calories.

Double Mushroom Soup

"It's like sipping the essence of mushrooms!" That's our favorite reaction to this fragrant soup. You make it with both dried and fresh mushrooms and just a touch of garlic, paprika, and thyme. Your guests will enjoy sipping this soup while waiting for a soufflé to finish cooking.

- ½ cup dried mushrooms
- 1 cup warm water
  About 3 cups vegetable stock (page 245)
- 2 tablespoons butter or margarine
- 1 small onion, coarsely chopped
- 1 clove garlic, minced or pressed
- ½ pound fresh mushrooms, sliced
- 3 tablespoons all-purpose flour
- ½ teaspoon paprika
- ¼ teaspoon thyme leaves
  Salt
  About ⅓ cup plain yogurt or sour cream

Cover dried mushrooms with water and let stand for 30 minutes. Remove mushrooms; cut off and discard stems. Thinly slice mushrooms and set aside. Measure soaking water (discarding any sandy portion at the bottom) and add enough stock to make a total of 4 cups liquid; reserve.

In a 3-quart pan over medium-high heat, melt butter. Add onion, garlic, and fresh mushrooms; cook,

stirring occasionally, until vegetables are golden and pan juices have evaporated. Stir in flour, paprika, and thyme. Add reserved stock mixture and dried mushrooms. Cook, stirring, until soup thickens slightly. Reduce heat; cover and simmer for 30 minutes.

In a blender or food processor, purée soup, a portion at a time, until smooth. Add salt to taste. Garnish each serving with a spoonful of yogurt or sour cream. Makes four 1-cup servings.

Per serving: 3 grams protein, 12 grams carbohydrate, 26 milligrams cholesterol, 146 calories.

Creamy Herbed Walnut Soup

An exquisite walnut flavor tinged with thyme and basil makes this soup a sophisticated first course, to be followed, perhaps, by a butter-lettuce salad and your favorite quiche.

- 1½ cups coarsely chopped walnuts
  Water
- 2 cups milk
- ½ bay leaf
- ¼ teaspoon *each* thyme leaves and dry basil
- 2 tablespoons chopped parsley
- 2 tablespoons butter or margarine
- 1 medium-size onion, sliced
- 1 large stalk celery, thinly sliced
- 2 tablespoons whole wheat flour
- 3 cups vegetable stock (page 245)
- 2 tablespoons dry sherry
  Salt and pepper
  Finely chopped chives or green onion

In a pan over medium heat, cover walnuts with water and bring to a boil; boil for 3 minutes. Drain,

... *Creamy Herbed Walnut Soup (cont'd.)*

rinse with cold water, and drain again. Pour milk over drained nuts and add bay, thyme, basil, and parsley; heat to scalding. Cover and set aside for 20 minutes.

Meanwhile, in a 3-quart pan over medium heat, melt butter. Add onion and celery and cook, stirring occasionally, for 5 minutes. Stir in flour and cook for 1 more minute. Gradually stir in stock; cook, stirring, until soup boils. Reduce heat; simmer for 10 minutes.

Remove bay leaf from milk-nut mixture; add mixture to soup. In a blender or food processor, purée soup, a portion at a time, until smooth. Return soup to pan and stir in sherry. Add salt and pepper to taste. Reheat without boiling.

Sprinkle each serving with chives. Makes seven 1-cup servings.

Per serving: 7 grams protein, 10 grams carbohydrate, 20 milligrams cholesterol, 255 calories.

Curried Peanut Soup

Since this soup contains an unusual combination of flavors, we expected a mixed reaction from our taste-testers. But they were enthusiastic: "It's wonderful! The crunchy peanuts on top and the mild curry flavor are marvelous."

It's an easy soup to make, especially if you have a cup of cooked brown rice left from another meal.

3 tablespoons butter or margarine
1 small onion, finely chopped
1 medium-size carrot, finely chopped
1 large stalk celery, finely chopped
1 teaspoon curry powder
2 tablespoons whole wheat flour
4 cups vegetable stock (page 245)
½ cup peanut butter
2 tablespoons catsup
2 teaspoons Worcestershire
1 cup cooked brown rice
About ½ cup *each* sour cream and chopped peanuts

In a 3-quart pan over medium heat, melt butter. Add onion, carrot, and celery and cook, stirring occasionally, until vegetables are soft (about 10 minutes). Stir in curry powder and cook for 1 minute. Stir in flour and cook for 1 more minute. Gradually stir in stock. Reduce heat; cover and simmer for 15 minutes.

Stir in peanut butter, catsup, and Worcestershire until smooth. Add rice and simmer, uncovered, for 5 minutes. Garnish each serving with a spoonful of sour cream and peanuts. Makes four 1⅓-cup servings.

Per serving: 12 grams protein, 20 grams carbohydrate, 35 milligrams cholesterol, 414 calories.

Cheddar Sherry Soup

Here you are in an intimate country inn...mellow candlelight, a table to one side of a glowing hearth. For openers, the innkeeper suggests a bowl of Cheddar Sherry Soup—perfect. Can you have the recipe?

The innkeeper is only too happy to share the recipe (below). Don't forget the port and walnuts for dessert.

4 tablespoons butter or margarine
1 large stalk celery, finely chopped
1 large carrot, finely chopped
3 green onions (including tops), thinly sliced
3 tablespoons all-purpose flour
3 cups vegetable stock (page 245)
1 cup milk
2 cups (8 oz.) shredded sharp Cheddar cheese
¼ cup dry or cream sherry
White pepper
Ground nutmeg
Chopped parsley

In a 3-quart pan over medium heat, melt butter. Add celery and carrot and cook, stirring occasionally, for 5 minutes. Add onions and cook for 3 minutes. Stir in flour and cook for 1 more minute. Gradually stir in stock and cook, stirring, until soup thickens slightly. Reduce heat; cover and simmer for 10 minutes.

Add milk and cheese to soup and cook, stirring, until cheese is melted. Add sherry, then stir in pepper and nutmeg to taste. Garnish with chopped parsley. Makes four 1¼-cup servings.

Per serving: 17 grams protein, 12 grams carbohydrate, 100 milligrams cholesterol, 403 calories.

Potato Yogurt Soup

One of the light classics in our soup repertoire, Potato Yogurt Soup is a sprightly prelude to either an egg-and-cheese entrée or a vegetable-and-grain main course. Cucumber and lettuce are the surprise ingredients that add a touch of spring to this puréed soup.

3 tablespoons butter or margarine
1 cucumber, peeled, seeded, and cut into thick slices
3 medium-size thin-skinned potatoes, peeled and cut into 1-inch chunks
2 cups coarsely sliced lettuce
4 green onions (including tops), thinly sliced
3 cups vegetable stock (page 245)
1 teaspoon dill weed
1½ cups milk
2 tablespoons cornstarch
1 cup plain yogurt
Salt and white pepper
Fresh dill sprigs or chopped parsley

In a 3-quart pan over medium heat, melt butter. Add cucumber and potatoes and cook, stirring, for 4 minutes. Add lettuce, onions, stock, and the 1 teaspoon dill. Simmer, covered, until potatoes are tender (about 25 minutes).

In a blender or food processor, purée soup, a portion at a time, until smooth. Return to pan and stir in milk.

In a small bowl, combine cornstarch and yogurt; stir into soup. Cook, stirring, over medium heat, until hot and thickened. Season to taste with salt and pepper.

Garnish each serving with a sprig of fresh dill or a sprinkling of chopped parsley. Makes six 1⅓-cup servings.

Per serving: 5 grams protein, 20 grams carbohydrate, 26 milligrams cholesterol, 175 calories.

Hot & Sour Soup

White pepper makes it hot; vinegar makes it sour. This piquant hot-sour combination is a gift to the world's treasury of great soups from the Szechwan region of China. You can use the soup as a warmup for an Oriental feast, or serve it as the main event.

½ cup dried mushrooms
1 cup warm water
About 3 cups vegetable stock (page 245)
1 tablespoon dry sherry
½ cup sliced bamboo shoots, cut in matchstick pieces, or ½ cup sliced water chestnuts
4 ounces tofu, diced
½ cup frozen peas, thawed
2 tablespoons white wine vinegar
1 tablespoon soy sauce
2 tablespoons cornstarch
¼ cup water
½ to ¾ teaspoon white pepper
1 teaspoon sesame oil
1 egg, lightly beaten
2 green onions (including tops), cut into 1-inch diagonal slices
Salt

Cover mushrooms with water and let stand for 30 minutes. Remove mushrooms; cut off and discard stems. Thinly slice mushrooms and set aside. Measure soaking water (discard any sandy portion at the bottom) and add enough stock to make a total of 4 cups liquid. Place in a 2-quart pan and add sherry, bamboo shoots, and sliced mushrooms. Bring to a boil, then reduce heat; cover and simmer for 15 minutes. Add tofu, peas, wine vinegar, and soy; heat for 3 minutes.

In a small bowl, stir together cornstarch and the ¼ cup water. Add to soup and cook, stirring, until slightly thickened. Turn off heat. Add pepper and sesame oil. Stirring continuously, slowly pour egg into soup. Sprinkle with onion; add salt to taste. Makes four 1½-cup servings.

Per serving: 6 grams protein, 10 grams carbohydrate, 63 milligrams cholesterol, 95 calories.

Tomato Corn Chowder

Here's a marvelous summertime chowder, mellow and sweet from the freshest corn you can find. Removing the corn kernels is messy, but not difficult. You can serve this pretty and filling soup with thick slices of whole wheat bread and a fruit salad with cottage cheese.

4 large ears corn on the cob
3 tablespoons butter or margarine
1 medium-size onion, chopped
1 clove garlic, minced or pressed
1 stalk celery, thinly sliced
1 large carrot, thinly sliced
2 small potatoes, peeled and diced
3 medium-size tomatoes, seeded and coarsely chopped
1 teaspoon salt
¼ teaspoon white pepper
½ teaspoon dry basil
3 cups vegetable stock (page 245)
1 cup half-and-half (light cream)
About ½ cup alfalfa sprouts or chopped parsley

With a sharp knife, cut corn off cob, leaving kernel bases attached. With back of knife, scrape cob to extract the creamy pulp. Reserve.

In a 5-quart pan over medium heat, melt butter. Add onion, garlic, celery, and carrot; cook, stirring occasionally, until vegetables are soft (about 10 minutes). Add potatoes, tomatoes, salt, pepper, basil, stock, and reserved corn to pan. Reduce heat; cover and simmer until potatoes are fork-tender (about 30 minutes). Add half-and-half and heat through without boiling. Garnish each serving with sprouts or parsley. Makes six 1⅔-cup servings.

Per serving: 5 grams protein, 24 grams carbohydrate, 35 milligrams cholesterol, 204 calories.

Soybean Soup, Bistro-style

With protein-packed, cooked soybeans from your freezer, you can make a quick meal that needs only the accompaniment of green salad and whole wheat bread.

> **6 medium-size leeks, or 2 medium-size onions, chopped**
> **3 tablespoons butter or margarine**
> **1 small onion, chopped**
> **1 large stalk celery, sliced**
> **1 medium-size carrot, thinly sliced**
> **1 medium-size turnip, peeled and diced**
> **2½ cups cooked soybeans, (page 269)**
> **4 cups vegetable stock (page 245)**
> **¼ teaspoon thyme leaves**
> **Salt and white pepper**
> **1 cup milk or half-and-half (light cream)**
> **¼ cup chopped watercress or parsley**
> **Lemon slices**

Trim root ends and tough outer leaves from leeks. Slit each leek lengthwise, rinse between layers, then thinly slice.

In a 5-quart pan over medium heat, melt butter. Add leeks and onion (or use all onion), celery, and carrot. Cook, stirring, until onion is soft (about 10 minutes). Add turnip, soybeans, stock, and thyme. Reduce heat; cover and simmer until vegetables are tender (about 40 minutes).

In a blender or food processor, purée soup, a portion at a time, until smooth. Return soup to pan. Add salt and pepper to taste. Stir in milk and reheat without boiling. Garnish with watercress and lemon slices. Makes six 1⅓-cup servings.

Per serving: 11 grams protein, 19 grams carbohydrate, 23 milligrams cholesterol, 212 calories.

Cuban Black Bean Soup

For a light meal, accompany this soup with cheese-topped corn tortillas. For a larger feast, offer portions of the soup as a first course to be followed by enchiladas or chiles rellenos.

> **Marinated Rice (directions follow)**
> **4 tablespoons olive oil or salad oil**
> **2 medium-size onions, finely chopped**
> **2 medium-size green peppers, seeded and finely chopped**
> **5 large cloves garlic, minced or pressed**
> **About 3 cups vegetable stock (page 245)**
> **1½ teaspoons *each* ground cumin and oregano leaves**
> **2 tablespoons vinegar**
> **About 6 cups cooked black or red beans (page 269)**
> **Salt**

Prepare marinated rice. Set aside for 1 hour or until next day; bring to room temperature before serving.

Heat oil in a 5-quart pan over medium heat. Add onions, green peppers, and garlic; cook, stirring, until limp. Add stock, cumin, oregano, vinegar, and beans. Cover and simmer for 30 minutes, adding more stock if desired for thinner consistency. Add salt to taste.

Serve in bowls, adding a generous spoonful of the cool rice to each bowl of hot soup. Makes six 1⅔-cup servings.

Per serving: 17 grams protein, 60 grams carbohydrate, no cholesterol, 467 calories.

Marinated Rice. Thinly slice 3 **green onions** (including tops). Combine with 2 cups cooked **white rice**, 1 **tomato** (finely chopped), and 3 tablespoons *each* **olive oil** and **white wine vinegar**. Cover and chill.

Lemony Lentil Soup

Lemon is the perfect accent for lentils and Swiss chard — the main ingredients in this meal-in-a bowl soup from Lebanon. Enjoy it as an entrée accompanied by black bread and cucumbers with yogurt.

> **1½ cups lentils**
> **8 cups vegetable stock (page 245)**
> **1 large potato**
> **2 bunches (about 1½ pounds) Swiss chard**
> **1 medium-size onion, finely chopped**
> **4 tablespoons olive oil or salad oil**
> **½ cup coarsely chopped fresh coriander (cilantro), or ½ cup chopped parsley plus ¾ teaspoon ground coriander**
> **3 cloves garlic, minced or pressed**
> **Salt**
> **¼ teaspoon pepper**
> **½ teaspoon ground cumin**
> **3 tablespoons lemon juice**
> **Lemon slices**

Rinse lentils; sort through and discard any foreign material. Drain well. Combine lentils and stock in an 8-quart pan; cover and bring to simmering.

Peel potato and cut into ½-inch cubes; add to lentils. Cover and simmer for 20 minutes. Slice chard leaves and stems crosswise in ½-inch wide strips. Add to soup, cover, and continue simmering until lentils are tender (about 20 more minutes).

(Continued on page 252)

Razzle-dazzle your taste buds with Sweet & Sour Borscht (recipe on page 253). Then follow the ruby-red soup with plump Potato-Onion Blintzes (recipe on page 276) topped with sour cream, green onion slices, and poppy seeds.

In a small frying pan over medium heat, cook onion in oil, stirring occasionally, until onion is soft and golden (about 10 minutes). Add to onion ⅓ cup of the fresh coriander (or ⅓ cup of the parsley-coriander mixture) along with garlic and cook for 1 to 2 minutes.

Add onion mixture to soup during the last 5 minutes of cooking. Stir in salt to taste, pepper, cumin, and lemon juice. Garnish soup with lemon slices and remaining chopped coriander or parsley-coriander mixture. Makes six 1⅔-cup servings.

Per serving: 16 grams protein, 43 grams carbohydrate, no cholesterol, 310 calories.

Broccoli Barley Soup

Thick enough to be called a porridge, but full of the fresh taste of broccoli and rosemary, this is a good soup to serve on a brisk day. You could present it with an egg dish for a substantial dinner, or serve it with bread and cheese for a lighter supper.

    3 tablespoons butter or
      margarine
    2 medium-size onions,
      chopped
    2 cloves garlic, minced or
      pressed
    ¼ pound mushrooms, sliced
    ½ teaspoon dry rosemary
    6 cups vegetable stock
      (page 245)
    ¾ cup pearl barley
    1 pound broccoli
    2 tablespoons cornstarch
    ¼ cup water
    2 cups milk
      Salt and pepper
      About ⅓ cup grated
      Parmesan cheese

In a 5-quart pan over medium-high heat, melt butter. Add onions, gar-

lic, and mushrooms. Cook, stirring frequently, until onion is soft (about 5 minutes). Add rosemary, stock, and barley and bring to a boil. Reduce heat; cover and simmer until barley is tender (about 45 minutes).

Meanwhile, remove broccoli flowerets and cut into bite-size pieces. Peel stems and thinly slice. When barley is tender, increase heat and add broccoli stems and pieces. Cook, covered, until broccoli is just tender and still bright green (about 10 minutes).

In a small bowl, stir together cornstarch and water. Add to soup along with milk and cook, stirring, until soup boils and thickens. Add salt and pepper to taste. Sprinkle each serving lightly with Parmesan cheese. Makes six 1⅔-cup servings.

Per serving: 10 grams protein, 36 grams carbohydrate, 33 milligrams cholesterol, 265 calories.

Aztec Soup

By far the most unusual soup in this chapter, Aztec Soup glows with the golden-orange colors of squash and corn. And that's just the basic soup—the background, as it were. At the table you pass bowls of condiments (pine nuts, walnuts, fried tortilla pieces, grated cheese, pumpkin seeds, diced avocado) and let family or guests compose their own soup to suit their individual tastes.

To complete the meal, you might want to include a bowl of refried beans; fresh fruit would be excellent for dessert.

    Fried Tortilla Pieces
    (directions follow)
    3 tablespoons butter or
      margarine
    ⅔ cup (about 3 oz.) pine nuts
    ¾ cup walnut halves
    1 large onion, coarsely
      chopped
    2 cloves garlic, minced or
      pressed
   12 cups vegetable stock
      (page 245)
    4 cups diced, peeled butternut,
      acorn, or hubbard squash
    2 packages (10 oz. *each*) frozen
      corn
    ¾ cup toasted shelled pumpkin
      seeds
    1 large avocado
    3 cups (12 oz.) shredded jack
      cheese

Fry tortilla pieces.

In an 8-quart pan over medium heat, melt 1 tablespoon of the butter. Add pine nuts and walnuts and cook, stirring, until golden (about 2 minutes). Remove nuts; reserve.

Melt the remaining 2 tablespoons butter in pan and cook onion and garlic until onion is golden. Add stock and squash and bring to boiling. Reduce heat; cover and simmer until squash is tender (10 to 15 minutes). Add corn and cook for 5 more minutes. Sprinkle with pumpkin seeds just before serving. Peel and dice avocado.

Arrange avocado, reserved nuts, cheese, and tortilla pieces in bowls. Pass condiments at the table to add to the soup. Makes ten 2-cup servings.

Per serving (including tortillas): 20 grams protein, 38 grams carbohydrate, 44 milligrams cholesterol, 543 calories.

Fried Tortilla Pieces. Arrange 8 **corn tortillas** in a stack and cut into 6 equal wedges. Pour about ½ inch **salad oil** in a deep 2 or 3-quart pan and set on medium-high to high heat. When oil is hot enough to make a piece of tortilla sizzle, add tortilla pieces, a handful at a time, and stir to separate. Cook until crisp (1 to 1½ minutes); lift from oil with slotted spoon and drain on paper towels.

Garden Fresh Minestrone

Minestrone means "big soup," and that's exactly what this recipe makes—a generous quantity of main-dish soup. While minestrone is a traditional dish, there is no definitive way to prepare it. The best minestrone is the one filled with your family's favorite seasonal vegetables.

3 medium-size leeks, or 1 medium-size onion, chopped

2 cloves garlic, minced or pressed

3 tablespoons olive oil or salad oil

8 cups vegetable stock (page 245)

1 can (1 pound) kidney beans

6 cups prepared fresh vegetables (such as diced turnips and potatoes; sliced carrots, celery, zucchini, and crookneck squash; green beans cut in 1-inch lengths; and shelled peas)

½ teaspoon *each* dry basil, oregano leaves, and dry rosemary

¼ cup tomato paste

½ cup elbow macaroni

2 cups shredded cabbage, spinach, or chard

Salt and pepper

About ½ cup grated Parmesan cheese

Trim root ends and tough outer leaves from leeks; slit each leek lengthwise, rinse between layers, then thinly slice.

In a 6-quart kettle over medium heat, cook leeks and garlic in oil, stirring occasionally, for 5 minutes. Add stock, beans and their liquid, vegetables, basil, oregano, and rosemary; bring to simmering.

Reduce heat; cover and cook for 30 minutes.

Stir in tomato paste and macaroni and continue simmering for 15 minutes or until macaroni is tender. Add cabbage and cook, covered, just until it wilts (about 5 more minutes). Season to taste with salt and pepper. Pass Parmesan at the table. Makes eight 2-cup servings.

Per serving: 11 grams protein, 36 grams carbohydrate, 5 milligrams cholesterol, 243 calories.

Sweet & Sour Borscht

(Pictured on page 251)

This jewel of a soup shimmers with the ruby-red of beets and the bright vermilion of carrots. You can serve it with cheese and black bread for lunch or a light supper; or serve it before a main course like blintzes.

3 medium-size beets with leafy tops

2 tablespoons salad oil

1 small onion, chopped

2 large carrots, diced

2 cups coarsely shredded red or green cabbage

¼ cup lemon juice

2½ tablespoons sugar

½ teaspoon dill weed

6 cups vegetable stock (page 245)

Salt and pepper

About ½ cup plain yogurt or sour cream

Cut off beet tops. Cut off and discard stems and any wilted leaves. Coarsely chop remaining leaves. Peel beets and shred coarsely; set aside.

Heat oil in a 5-quart pan over medium heat. Add onion and carrots and cook, stirring occasionally, until vegetables are soft (about 10 minutes). Add beets and tops, cabbage, lemon juice, sugar, dill, and

stock; bring to simmering. Reduce heat to low; cover and simmer until beets and cabbage are tender (about 45 minutes). Season with salt and pepper to taste.

Garnish each serving with yogurt. Makes six 1⅔-cup servings.

Per serving: 2 grams protein, 14 grams carbohydrate, 9 milligrams cholesterol, 137 calories.

Fresh Vegetable Basil Soup

(Pictured on page 254)

Chock-full of good crunchy vegetables, this soup speaks with an Italian accent. You might follow it with other Italian favorites, like an antipasto platter and a frittata.

3 tablespoons butter or margarine

1 medium-size onion, chopped

1 large stalk celery, sliced

1 large carrot, sliced ⅛-inch thick

1 large thin-skinned potato

2 large tomatoes

4 cups vegetable stock (page 245)

3 tablespoons coarsely chopped fresh basil or 1 teaspoon dry basil

½ small head cauliflower, broken into flowerets

2 small zucchini, sliced ¼ inch thick

½ pound fresh green peas, shelled

Salt and pepper

About ½ cup grated Parmesan cheese

In a 5-quart pan over medium heat, melt butter. Add onion, celery, and carrot; cook, stirring occasionally, until vegetables are soft but not brown (about 10 minutes).

Meanwhile, peel potato and cut into ½-inch cubes. Peel and dice tomatoes; you should have 2 cups. Add potato, tomatoes, stock, and

(Continued on page 255)

...Fresh Vegetable Basil Soup (cont'd.)

basil to pan. Bring to a boil, then cover and simmer for 15 minutes.

Add cauliflower and zucchini and simmer for 10 more minutes. Add peas and simmer for another 5 minutes or until all vegetables are tender. Season to taste with salt and pepper. Pass Parmesan cheese at the table to sprinkle onto soup. Makes six 1⅔-cup servings.

Per serving: 9 grams protein, 21 grams carbohydrate, 24 milligrams cholesterol, 178 calories.

Make-ahead Gazpacho

It's a sip of cool pleasure on a sun-dappled day. It's a taste-tempting way to start a party. It's gazpacho, the easiest make-ahead soup a cook can concoct to begin a meal.

> 2 cups *each* vegetable stock (page 245) and tomato juice
> 2 tablespoons *each* lemon juice and green taco sauce
> 1 teaspoon sugar
> ½ teaspoon garlic salt
> ⅛ teaspoon pepper
> 1 cucumber, peeled, seeded, and coarsely chopped
> 1 green pepper, seeded and diced
> 4 large tomatoes, peeled and coarsely chopped
> 3 green onions (including tops), thinly sliced

In a 3-quart pan over medium heat, combine stock, tomato juice, lemon juice, taco sauce, sugar, garlic salt, and pepper. Leave uncovered and bring to a boil. Stir in cucumber, green pepper, tomatoes, and onion; bring mixture, uncovered, to a boil again. Remove from heat and cool. Cover

Abbondanza! That means abundance in Italian, and that's the word for Fresh Vegetable Basil Soup (recipe on page 253). It's made with an abundance of fresh vegetables and a rich seasoning of basil.

and refrigerate until well chilled. Makes six 1-cup servings.

Per serving: 3 grams protein, 14 grams carbohydrate, no cholesterol, 64 calories.

Almond Buttermilk Soup

If you were dining in Denmark, you might be served this lightly sweetened, chilled buttermilk soup topped with clouds of fluffy meringue and colorful berries.

> 2 cups berries (strawberries, raspberries, or blackberries)
> Honey or sugar
> 2 eggs
> ¼ cup sugar
> ⅛ teaspoon almond extract
> 2½ cups buttermilk
> ¼ cup sliced almonds

Rinse berries, drain, and, if using strawberries, slice; set aside ½ cup to use as garnish. Put remaining berries in a serving bowl and drizzle with honey or sprinkle with sugar (about 1 tablespoon); set aside.

Separate eggs; put whites into a small bowl, yolks into a large bowl. Beat egg whites until fluffy. Gradually add 2 tablespoons of the sugar and continue to beat until the mixture holds stiff peaks; reserve.

Beat egg yolks until lemon colored; gradually add the remaining 2 tablespoons sugar along with almond extract. Beat until thick and smooth. Stir in buttermilk.

Pour buttermilk mixture over berries in serving bowl. Top with reserved egg whites and berries; garnish with almonds. Serve at once, or cover and chill up to 2 hours.

To serve, ladle soup and a portion of meringue and berries into each bowl. Makes four 1-cup servings.

Per serving: 11 grams protein, 28 grams carbohydrate, 129 milligrams cholesterol, 220 calories.

Chilled Cucumber Soup

You start this soup by making an unsweetened custard. Then whisk in sour cream and add finely chopped cucumber. As an opener for a warm-weather dinner, offer small glass bowls of this soup. Or serve it for lunch accompanied by toasted rye bread that's topped with sautéed mushrooms, covered with Swiss cheese, and broiled.

> 3 eggs
> 2 cups milk
> 1 cup sour cream
> 2 medium-size cucumbers
> 1 cup vegetable stock (page 245)
> ½ cup dry white wine
> 1 green onion (including top), finely chopped
> 1 tablespoon chopped pimento
> ½ teaspoon dill weed
> Salt
> About 2 tablespoons grated Parmesan cheese

In a small bowl, beat eggs lightly. In top of a double boiler over direct heat, heat milk to scalding. With a fork, gradually blend milk into eggs. Return mixture to top of double boiler, place over simmering water, and cook, stirring constantly, until custard coats a metal spoon in a velvety smooth layer. Remove from heat and cool. Stir sour cream into cooled custard.

Cut a dozen thin slices of unpeeled cucumber for garnish; reserve. Peel, seed, and finely chop remaining cucumber. Stir into custard mixture along with stock, wine, onion, pimento, and dill. Add salt to taste. Chill thoroughly.

Serve cold in small bowls. Garnish each serving with cucumber slices and a sprinkling of Parmesan cheese. Makes five 1-cup servings.

Per serving: 10 grams protein, 11 grams carbohydrate, 188 milligrams cholesterol, 238 calories.

Main Dishes with Eggs & Cheese

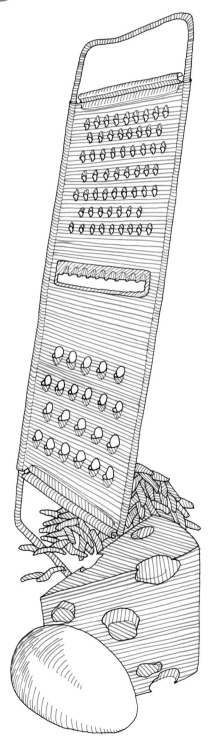

For the part-time vegetarian and anyone just looking for a change of pace from meat entrées, cheese and egg dishes are a natural choice. They're instantly appealing to the whole family—even confirmed meat eaters—and many of them are spectacular enough for party fare.

While there's nothing out of the ordinary about serving a plain omelet, soufflé, or quiche, you'll find this chapter's collection of recipes extraordinary. There's an open-faced Country Omelet (page 257) that's topped with a luscious mixture of diced potatoes, onions, Swiss cheese, and parsley, plus a scoop of sour cream and a crunchy garnish of walnut halves. Definitely out of the ordinary! But it's easy to make—you don't even have to fold the omelet; just cut it in wedges and serve it from the pan.

In the soufflé category, you'll find a Camembert Soufflé (page 260) that has the traditional high-rising shape, and a Broccoli Soufflé Roll (page 260) that's not only unusually delicious, but unusually shaped—it looks like a jelly roll.

The versatile quiche has four representatives in this chapter. Our Spinach & Feta Quiche (page 261) is a good choice to serve cold with a classic Greek salad. The Russian Quiche (page 262), chock-full of onions and mushrooms spiked with a touch of horseradish, would be delicious paired with the Sweet & Sour Borscht (page 253). Or you might like to whip up the Golden Cauliflower Quiche baked in an oatmeal pastry shell (page 261), or go for a quiche with no pastry shell at all—the Mushroom Crust Quiche (page 262).

As a special feature, there's a section on homemade cheese and yogurt. We find making yogurt a great moneysaver, and the cheese made from yogurt is a revelation in tangy freshness. This feature also includes two recipes for raita (page 267)—a refreshing mixture of yogurt, chopped vegetables, and spices, that goes especially well with Indian curries.

Eggs contain an amazing amount of cholesterol—252 milligrams per large egg. If you should be limiting your intake of cholesterol, you'll want to limit the number of egg dishes you eat.

Many kinds of cheese, too, have substantial amounts of cholesterol (28 milligrams in 1 ounce of Swiss cheese) and a lot of calories (105 calories in 1 ounce of Swiss cheese). But with cheeses like Swiss, Cheddar, and jack, or hard cheese like Parmesan, a little can go a long way to add protein to your menu—not to mention calcium, an essential nutrient found in abundance in cheese.

Cheese & Basil Omelet

Basil is a wonderful herb to combine with eggs and cheese. In this recipe, you cook the egg mixture in butter and garlic, then sprinkle with basil and—surprise—blue cheese. For a quick family supper, you can serve this omelet with sliced tomatoes and Whole Wheat Crescent Rolls (page 293). For a heartier meal, you might start off with a bowl of Potato Yogurt Soup (page 248).

> 8 eggs
> 3 tablespoons water
> ½ teaspoon salt
> ¼ teaspoon pepper
> 2 tablespoons butter or margarine
> 1 large clove garlic, minced or pressed
> 3 ounces blue-veined cheese, coarsely crumbled
> 3 tablespoons chopped fresh basil leaves or 1 tablespoon dry basil

Beat eggs lightly with water, salt, and pepper.

Heat a 10-inch omelet pan or frying pan with sloping sides over medium-high heat. Add butter and garlic and stir until butter melts; tilt pan so butter coats bottom and sides. Pour in egg mixture and cook, gently lifting cooked portion to allow uncooked egg to flow underneath. Gently shake pan to keep omelet free.

When top of omelet is almost set but still moist, sprinkle with cheese and basil. Continue to shake pan and lift omelet edges until there is no more liquid, but top still looks moist and creamy.

Tilting pan over a serving plate, shake pan to slide half the omelet onto plate; with a flick of the wrist, fold over remaining omelet. Makes 4 servings.

Per serving: 18 grams protein, 2 grams carbohydrate, 542 milligrams cholesterol, 295 calories.

Country Omelet

This omelet is served from the frying pan and cut into wedges like a pie. The topping is scrumptious— a mixture of lightly browned diced potato, onions, Swiss cheese, and parsley, with a scoop of sour cream in the center. Don't forget our favorite part—a garnish of walnuts.

> 3 tablespoons butter or margarine
> ¼ cup walnut halves
> 1 small thin-skinned potato, diced
> ¼ cup chopped onion
> 4 eggs
> ¼ cup diced Swiss cheese
> 2 tablespoons shredded Swiss cheese
> 1 tablespoon chopped parsley
> Salt
> About ¼ cup sour cream

Melt 1½ tablespoons of the butter in a wide frying pan over medium heat. Add walnuts and cook until lightly browned (about 1 or 2 minutes). Remove nuts with a slotted spoon and set aside. Reduce heat to medium-low. Add potato and onion and cook, stirring, until potato is soft but only lightly browned (about 10 minutes). Remove from pan and set aside; keep warm.

Remove any particles from pan, then melt remaining 1½ tablespoons butter over medium-low heat. Beat eggs lightly; add to pan and cook, gently lifting cooked portion to allow uncooked egg to flow underneath. When top of omelet is almost set but still moist, sprinkle evenly with potato-onion mixture, diced cheese, shredded cheese, parsley, and salt to taste. Mound sour cream in center of omelet. Garnish with toasted walnuts.

Cut in wedges and serve from pan. Makes 4 servings.

Per serving: 16 grams protein, 10 grams carbohydrate, 307 milligrams cholesterol, 375 calories.

Zucchini Frittata

(Pictured on page 243)

A frittata is a flat omelet with a medley of vegetables and herbs mixed into it. This recipe calls for zucchini and chard, but you can substitute any summer squash for the zucchini, and spinach for the chard.

> 2 tablespoons salad oil
> 1 small onion, finely chopped
> 1 clove garlic, minced or pressed
> 2 large Swiss chard leaves (including stems), coarsely chopped
> 1 medium-size zucchini, coarsely chopped
> 6 eggs
> ⅛ teaspoon pepper
> ¼ teaspoon *each* dry basil and oregano leaves
> 1 cup (3 oz.) grated Parmesan cheese

Heat oil in a wide frying pan over medium-high heat. Add onion, garlic, chard, and zucchini; cook, stirring occasionally, until vegetables are soft (about 5 minutes). Remove from heat and let cool slightly.

Beat eggs lightly with pepper, basil, and oregano. Stir in cheese and vegetables. Pour into a greased 9-inch pie pan. Bake in a 350° oven for 25 to 30 minutes or until puffed and browned. Serve hot or at room temperature. Makes 6 servings.

Per serving: 14 grams protein, 4 grams carbohydrate, 269 milligrams cholesterol, 204 calories.

Mayan Egg Tortillas

Toasted pumpkin seeds and chilies flavor the sauce for this delicious dish. You can prepare the sauce ahead of time and refrigerate it until time to spoon it over the lightly scrambled eggs wrapped in whole wheat tortillas. You may want to seve these tortillas with a platter of fresh fruit garnished with lime wedges, and mugs of hot cinnamon-spiced chocolate.

8 ounces (about 1½ cups) toasted shelled pumpkin seeds

½ cup vegetable stock (page 245)

3 tablespoons lemon juice

1 clove garlic, cut into thirds

3 tablespoons diced canned green chilies

½ teaspoon *each* salt and pepper

½ pint (1 cup) whipping cream

8 large whole wheat tortillas (page 301)

8 eggs

2 tablespoons milk

2 tablespoons butter or margarine

2 green onions (including tops), chopped

In a blender or food processor, whirl pumpkin seeds until coarsely chopped; turn out half the chopped seeds and set them aside. Add stock, lemon juice, garlic, chilies, salt, and pepper to remaining seeds and whirl until well mixed. Add cream and whirl briefly to blend. Stir in remaining seeds. If made ahead, cover sauce and refrigerate.

Stack tortillas, wrap in foil, and place in a 325° oven for 6 to 8 minutes or until heated through and softened. If tortillas are very fresh, do not heat them; just bring to room temperature.

Beat eggs lightly with milk. Melt butter in a wide frying pan over medium-low heat. Pour in egg mixture and cook, gently lifting cooked portion to allow uncooked egg to flow underneath, until eggs are barely set and top is still moist.

Spoon ⅛ of the scrambled eggs down center of each tortilla; top each with about 2 tablespoons of the sauce. Roll to enclose filling; arrange, seam side down, in a shal-low baking dish. Spoon remaining sauce over top.

Broil 4 to 6 inches from heat until sauce is heated through and tortillas are flecked with brown. Sprinkle with green onions before serving. Makes 8 servings.

Per serving: 18 grams protein, 25 grams carbohydrate, 319 milligrams cholesterol, 500 calories.

Crunchy Egg Patties

Tofu goes international in this recipe. It combines with Italian and Chinese vegetables and turns up in small patties or frittatas. You can't taste the tofu, but it makes the egg mixture creamy and soft, and boosts the protein content.

About 8 ounces tofu

1 teaspoon *each* dry sherry and soy sauce

1 small stalk celery, chopped

1 green onion (including top), finely chopped

½ cup shredded zucchini

4 small mushrooms, thinly sliced

¼ pound bean sprouts

¾ teaspoon salt

Dash of pepper

2 tablespoons grated Parmesan cheese

6 eggs

Drain tofu and pat dry with paper towels. Crumble into a large bowl; stir in sherry and soy and let stand for 5 minutes. Add celery, onion, zucchini, mushrooms, bean sprouts, salt, pepper, and cheese; mix lightly. Lightly beat eggs, then stir into vegetable mixture.

Heat a griddle or large frying pan over medium-high heat; grease well. Spoon mixture, about ¼ cup for each patty, onto griddle. From the bowl, spoon about 2 more tablespoons of only the liquid egg over each patty and distribute evenly over vegetables. Cook until egg is set and bottoms of patties are golden brown. Turn with a spatula and cook other sides until browned. Keep warm in a 200° oven until all patties are cooked. Makes 5 servings, 2 patties each.

Per serving: 13 grams protein, 3 grams carbohydrate, 305 milligrams cholesterol, 147 calories.

Puffy Herb Omelet

Beating egg whites and yolks separately makes a light, puffy omelet. After the herb-filled creation finishes cooking, you fold it in half and tuck in fresh sprouts—either alfalfa sprouts or blanched bean sprouts.

Cheddar Cheese Sauce (recipe follows)

5 eggs, separated

¼ cup milk

½ teaspoon salt

2 tablespoons chopped parsley

1 tablespoon chopped fresh or freeze-dried chives

1 teaspoon dill weed

¼ teaspoon *each* dry mustard, pepper, and garlic salt

1½ tablespoons butter or margarine

1 cup alfalfa sprouts

Prepare Cheddar Cheese Sauce.

Beat egg whites until stiff, moist peaks form. In a separate bowl,

(Continued on page 260)

For luscious simplicity, just top a round of brie with butter and sliced almonds, heat it until the cheese is hot and fluid, and serve it as an entrée. Your guests will relish their role—scooping up the melted cheese with French bread. Offer fruit, too—such as grapes, pears, and apples. The recipe for Baked Brie is on page 265.

beat egg yolks until very thick; stir in milk, salt, parsley, chives, dill weed, mustard, pepper, and garlic salt. Gently fold egg yolk mixture into whites until blended.

In a 10-inch omelet pan or frying pan with sloping sides and heat-resistant handle, melt butter over medium heat; tilt pan to coat bottom and sides. Pour egg mixture into pan and smooth surface gently. Reduce heat to low and cook until lightly browned on bottom (5 to 7 minutes); lift edge of omelet with a spatula to test.

Place pan in a 325° oven for 10 to 12 minutes or until a knife inserted in the center comes out clean.

Run a spatula around edge of omelet. Tip pan and slide spatula under omelet to loosen; fold omelet in half and slip onto a heated plate.

With a spatula, lift top edge gently and quickly tuck sprouts into fold. To serve, cut into wide slices; pass hot Cheddar Cheese Sauce at the table. Makes 4 servings.

Per serving (including cheese sauce): 11 grams protein, 5 grams carbohydrate, 334 milligrams cholesterol, 186 calories.

Cheddar Cheese Sauce. In a pan, combine 1 can (10¾ oz.) condensed **Cheddar cheese soup,** ¼ cup **milk** or dry white wine, and several dashes of **Worcestershire sauce.** Stir over medium heat until smooth and bubbly.

Camembert Soufflé

A bottle of champagne waiting on ice, soft music, a bouquet of sweetheart roses on the table... For that kind of mood, whether it be a late evening supper or a Sunday brunch, you need a special dish like Camembert Soufflé. Its extra rich taste and creamy texture come from just a small wedge of Camembert cheese.

Butter or margarine
Grated Parmesan cheese
4 **tablespoons butter or margarine**
¼ **teaspoon ground nutmeg**
⅛ **teaspoon ground red pepper (cayenne)**
3 **tablespoons all-purpose flour**
1⅓ **cups milk**
2 **teaspoons Dijon mustard**
2 **tablespoons dry sherry**
4 **ounces ripe Camembert cheese, rind removed**
1¼ **cups (5 oz.) shredded Gruyère, Samsoe, or Swiss cheese**
5 **eggs, separated**
¼ **teaspoon *each* cream of tartar and salt**

Preheat oven to 375°. Generously butter a 2-quart soufflé dish or casserole. Sprinkle with Parmesan cheese, turning dish to coat bottom and sides; set aside.

Melt the 4 tablespoons butter in a 3-quart pan over medium heat. Add nutmeg and red pepper. Blend in flour and cook, stirring, until bubbly. Gradually pour in milk and continue cooking and stirring until sauce boils and thickens. Add mustard, sherry, Camembert cheese, and Gruyère cheese; stir just until cheeses are melted. Set aside.

In a small bowl, beat egg yolks. Gradually stir ¼ cup of the cheese sauce into egg yolks, then stir mixture back into cheese sauce. Return to heat and cook, stirring, for 1 minute.

In a large bowl, combine egg whites, cream of tartar, and salt. Beat until short, moist peaks form. Fold ¼ cup of the beaten whites into cheese sauce. Slowly fold sauce into remaining whites. Pour into prepared soufflé dish.

Bake in the preheated 375° oven for 35 to 40 minutes or until top is browned and center feels firm when lightly touched. Serve immediately. Makes 6 servings.

Per serving: 17 grams protein, 4 grams carbohydrate, 286 milligrams cholesterol, 324 calories.

Broccoli Soufflé Roll

First you bake the egg mixture in a jelly roll pan until the egg is light and puffy. Then you spread it with a cheese-broccoli filling, roll it up, and—voilà!—an impressive entrée ready to be sliced. And this is one soufflé that won't let you down. You can leave it in a warm oven for up to half an hour before serving.

1 **pound broccoli**
6 **tablespoons butter or margarine**
¾ **cup all-purpose flour**
About 1 teaspoon dry mustard
About ½ teaspoon salt
3 **cups milk**
4 **eggs**
½ **cup milk**
1 **cup (4 oz.) shredded Cheddar or Longhorn cheese**

Cut broccoli into small flowerets and thinly slice stems. Steam over boiling water just until crisp-tender (4 to 6 minutes). Chop broccoli and set aside.

Preheat oven to 325°. Line the bottom of a greased jelly roll pan with foil; grease and lightly flour foil and set pan aside.

Melt butter in a 3-quart pan over medium heat. Stir in the ¾ cup flour, 1 teaspoon of the mustard, and ½ teaspoon of the salt. Cook, stirring, until flour is bubbly. Gradually pour in the 3 cups milk and continue cooking and stirring until sauce is smooth and thickened (8 to 10 minutes). Measure out 1 cup of this sauce and set aside.

Separate eggs. Beat yolks lightly and gradually beat in all but the 1 cup reserved sauce. Beat egg whites until short, stiff, moist peaks form; fold into egg yolk mixture. Pour into prepared pan. Bake in the preheated 325° oven for 35 to 40 minutes or until soufflé is golden brown and center springs back when lightly touched.

Meanwhile, in a pan over medium heat, combine the 1 cup reserved sauce and the ½ cup milk. Stir in cheese and cook, stirring, until cheese is melted. Sprinkle with more mustard and salt, if desired. Measure out 1 cup of the cheese sauce and combine with chopped broccoli.

When soufflé is done, immediately invert onto a clean towel. Starting at one narrow end, spread broccoli mixture over three-fourths of the soufflé. Using towel for support, roll up soufflé to enclose filling; place, seam side down, on a serving platter. (If not served at once, place in a 200° oven for as long as 30 minutes.) Reheat remaining cheese sauce over low heat, then pour over roll or serve individual slices and pour sauce over each. Makes 8 servings.

Per serving: 17 grams protein, 23 grams carbohydrate, 195 milligrams cholesterol, 368 calories.

Golden Cauliflower Quiche

Tender-crisp cauliflower, lots of Longhorn cheese, toasted almonds, and a creamy custard add up to a quiche with some delicious differences. Though you can use any pastry recipe for the 9-inch pie shell, we especially enjoy Oatmeal Pastry with this filling.

Oatmeal Pastry for a 9-inch deep-dish pie shell (page 307)

- 1 small head (about 1 lb.) cauliflower
- ½ cup slivered almonds
- 2 eggs
- ½ cup *each* milk and mayonnaise
- 2 cups (8 oz.) shredded Longhorn cheese
- ⅛ teaspoon *each* pepper and ground nutmeg

On a lightly floured board, roll out pastry about ⅛ inch thick. Fit into a deep 9-inch pie pan; crimp edge. Bake in a preheated 400° oven for 10 minutes. Let cool.

Meanwhile, break cauliflower into flowerets and cut into ½-inch-thick pieces. (You should have 4 cups.) Steam over boiling water until just crisp-tender (about 4 minutes). Drain, plunge into cold water to cool, then drain again.

Spread almonds in a shallow pan and toast in a 350° oven for about 8 minutes or until lightly browned. Place cauliflower in bottom of pastry shell and sprinkle with toasted almonds.

In a blender or food processor, whirl eggs, milk, and mayonnaise until smooth. Add 1¼ cups of the cheese, along with pepper and nutmeg, and whirl briefly to mix. Pour over cauliflower and nuts in pastry shell. Sprinkle with remaining ¾ cup cheese.

Bake on bottom rack of a 350° oven for 30 to 35 minutes or until a knife inserted in center comes out clean. Let stand on a wire rack for 10 minutes before serving. Makes 6 servings.

Per serving: 19 grams protein, 29 grams carbohydrate, 179 milligrams cholesterol, 586 calories.

Spinach & Feta Quiche

Spinach and feta cheese are often paired in Greek cooking and wrapped in flaky fila dough. Here they're cooked instead in a buttery whole wheat pastry shell. On a warm day, you may want to start your meal with chilled Make-ahead Gazpacho (page 255) and serve the quiche cooled, accompanied by a classic Greek salad or fresh fruit. For cooler weather, you can serve the quiche hot, with a cup of Potato Yogurt Soup (page 248).

Whole Wheat Pastry for a single crust 9-inch pie (page 307)

- 1 package (10 oz.) frozen chopped spinach
- 6 ounces feta cheese, crumbled
- ½ cup cottage cheese
- 6 green onions (including tops), sliced
- 1 tablespoon olive oil
- 1 teaspoon dry basil
- ½ teaspoon pepper
- ¼ teaspoon garlic salt
- 4 eggs
- ½ cup milk

Roll out pastry about ⅛ inch thick on a lightly floured board. Fit into a 9-inch pie pan; crimp edge. Bake in a preheated 400° oven for 10 minutes. Let cool.

Squeeze out as much liquid as possible from spinach; set aside. In a blender or food processor, whirl feta cheese, cottage cheese, onions, oil, basil, pepper, and garlic salt until smooth. Add eggs and milk and blend well. Add spinach and whirl briefly to mix. Pour into pastry shell.

Bake in a 400° oven for 20 minutes; reduce temperature to 350° and bake for 15 to 20 more minutes or until a knife inserted in center comes out clean. Let stand on a wire rack for 10 minutes or bring to room temperature before cutting into wedges to serve. Makes 6 servings.

Per serving: 18 grams protein, 31 grams carbohydrate, 245 milligrams cholesterol, 423 calories.

Mushroom-crust Quiche

Looking for a change-of-pace quiche? Try a change of crust. In this egg and cheese pie, mushrooms mixed with wheat germ and whole wheat bread crumbs take the place of the usual pastry crust. A simple butter lettuce salad makes a good accompaniment for a light supper.

> 5 tablespoons butter or margarine
> ½ pound mushrooms, coarsely chopped
> ⅓ cup fine dry whole wheat bread crumbs
> 2 tablespoons wheat germ
> ¾ cup (7 or 8) chopped green onions (including tops)
> 2 cups (8 oz.) shredded Swiss or jack cheese
> 1 cup cottage cheese
> 3 eggs
> ¼ teaspoon *each* thyme and marjoram leaves
> Paprika

In a wide frying pan over medium heat, melt 3 tablespoons of the butter. Add mushrooms and cook until limp. Remove pan from heat and stir in bread crumbs and wheat germ. Turn into a well-greased 9-inch pie pan and press evenly onto bottom and sides.

In the same pan, melt the remaining 2 tablespoons butter. Add

onions and cook until soft. Spread onions over crust and sprinkle evenly with shredded cheese. In a blender or food processor, whirl cottage cheese, eggs, thyme, and marjoram until smooth. Pour into crust and sprinkle with paprika.

Bake in a 350° oven for 25 to 30 minutes or until a knife inserted in center comes out clean. Let stand on a wire rack for 10 minutes before serving. Makes 6 servings.

Per serving: 21 grams protein, 9 grams carbohydrate, 201 milligrams cholesterol, 345 calories.

Russian Quiche

Onion, mushrooms, Swiss cheese, yogurt, and touch of horseradish make a tangy filling for this quiche. Sweet & Sour Borscht (page 253) would provide a tantalizing counterpoint of flavors. Or you can serve this substantial but not overly rich quiche with a beet or cucumber salad in dill-seasoned dressing.

> 9-inch unbaked pastry shell, 1½ inches deep
> 1 tablespoon butter or margarine
> 1 small onion, chopped
> ¼ pound mushrooms, sliced
> ½ teaspoon thyme leaves
> 1 cup (4 oz.) shredded Swiss cheese
> 3 eggs
> 1 cup plain yogurt
> 2 tablespoons all-purpose flour
> ½ teaspoon prepared horseradish
> ¼ teaspoon *each* salt and dry mustard
> Paprika

Bake pastry shell in a preheated 450° oven for 7 to 10 minutes or until lightly browned. Let cool.

Meanwhile, melt butter in a wide frying pan over medium heat. Add onion and mushrooms and cook until onion is soft. Stir in thyme and let cool.

Sprinkle cheese evenly into pastry shell. Spoon onion mixture into shell. Beat eggs slightly, then stir in yogurt, flour, horseradish, salt, and mustard until well blended. Pour over mushroom layer. Sprinkle with paprika.

Bake in a 375° oven for 40 to 45 minutes or until filling is puffed and browned and a knife inserted in center comes out clean. Let stand on a wire rack for 10 minutes before serving. Makes 6 servings.

Per serving: 12 grams protein, 34 grams carbohydrate, 159 milligrams cholesterol, 320 calories.

Creamy Eggs & Sweet Onions

Slowly sautéed in butter, the onion slices in this creamy egg dish take on a golden hue and mellow sweetness. For a simple meal—similar to those enjoyed in French country homes—serve the eggs with crusty bread and fried potatoes, followed by a crisp green salad and fruit.

> 1¼ pounds small boiling onions
> 2 tablespoons butter or margarine
> 6 hard-cooked eggs
> ¼ cup all-purpose flour
> 2 cups milk
> Salt and pepper

Cut onions in half through stem, then thinly slice. Melt butter in a heavy 3-quart pan over medium heat. Add onions and cook, stirring frequently, until soft but not browned (about 25 minutes).

Meanwhile, cut eggs into ½-inch-thick slices; set aside.

When onions are soft, gradually sprinkle in flour, stirring to mix well. Slowly pour in milk and cook, stirring, until sauce boils and thickens. Add salt and pepper to taste. Gently stir in all but 4 or 5 egg slices and cook until heated through. Garnish with reserved egg slices before serving. Makes 4 servings.

Per serving: 17 grams protein, 26 grams carbohydrate, 414 milligrams cholesterol, 338 calories.

Meringue-topped Vegetable Custard

Surprise! Lemon pie doesn't have a monopoly on meringue. For this savory vegetable custard dish, you make a meringue topping with grated Cheddar cheese folded into beaten egg whites. The topping, sprinkled lightly with sesame seeds, bakes to an appealing golden hue and forms an airy "crust" over the mixed vegetables beneath.

    2 tablespoons butter or
      margarine
    6 medium-size (2 lbs. total)
      zucchini, shredded
    1 large green pepper, seeded
      and chopped
    1 large onion, chopped
    1 teaspoon *each* salt and dry
      basil
    ¼ teaspoon *each* ground
      nutmeg and pepper
    2 tablespoons all-purpose flour
    ½ pint (1 cup) sour cream
    6 eggs, separated
    4 cups (1 lb.) shredded
      Cheddar cheese
    2 tablespoons sesame seeds

Melt butter in a wide frying pan over medium-high heat. Add zucchini, green pepper, onion, salt, basil, nutmeg, and pepper. Cook, stirring often, until liquid evaporates (about 12 minutes). Add flour and cook for 1 minute. Let cool.

Beat together sour cream and egg yolks. Stir in vegetable mixture and 2 cups of the cheese. Spread in a well-buttered shallow 2-quart casserole. Beat egg whites until stiff, moist peaks form. Fold in remaining 2 cups cheese and spread over vegetable-custard mixture. Sprinkle with sesame seeds.

Bake in a 350° oven for about 55 minutes or until a knife inserted in center comes out clean. Let stand for 10 minutes before serving. Makes 8 servings.

Per serving: 23 grams protein, 12 grams carbohydrate, 243 milligrams cholesterol, 428 calories.

Fila Cheese Squares

Food for Greek gods! You make this version of Greek pie—called *borek*—by spreading layers of fila dough with a seasoned mixture of feta and ricotta cheeses. You bake it to a buttery gold color, let it cool slightly, then cut it into squares. It makes a marvelous meal accompanied by a platter of Vegetables à la Grecque (page 236). For an Olympian feast, include Stuffed Grape Leaves (page 279) too.

    1 cup ricotta cheese
    8 ounces feta cheese, crumbled
    1 small package (3 oz.) cream
      cheese, softened
    2 tablespoons all-purpose flour
    2 eggs
    ½ teaspoon ground nutmeg
    ¼ teaspoon white pepper
    ½ cup chopped parsley
    9 to 12 sheets (about ½ lb.) fila
      dough, each about 16 by 24
      inches
    ½ cup butter, melted

With an electric mixer, beat ricotta, feta, and cream cheese with flour, eggs, nutmeg, and pepper until well blended. Stir in parsley.

Cut fila in half crosswise, then cover loosely to keep from drying out. With a pastry brush, coat bottom of a 9 by 13-inch baking pan with butter. Line pan with a sheet of fila. Brush fila lightly in a few places with melted butter. Cover with another sheet of fila and brush lightly with butter. Repeat until you have used half the fila.

Spread cheese mixture evenly over fila. Cover with another sheet of fila and brush lightly with butter; repeat with remaining fila. Brush top with remaining butter. (At this point, you may cover and refrigerate until next day.)

Just before baking, score top layer of fila with a sharp knife, marking off serving-size pieces: 2½ by 3-inch rectangles for entrée servings, or smaller pieces for appetizers.

Bake, uncovered, in a 375° oven for 35 minutes or until top of pastry is golden and crisp. Makes 15 entrée servings.

Per entrée serving: 6 grams protein, 10 grams carbohydrate, 60 milligrams cholesterol, 140 calories.

Fettuccine with Four Cheeses

Fontina, Bel Paese, and Gorgonzola blend to make a divine cheese sauce for this classic Italian dish. Parmesan, the fourth cheese, is tossed with the noodles and also passed around the table. All you need to complete a light meal is a crisp salad or vegetable vinaigrette. For dessert, serve a piquant Italian ice or fresh fruit.

    3 tablespoons butter or
      margarine
 1½ tablespoons all-purpose flour
    ⅛ teaspoon ground nutmeg
      Dash of white pepper
    1 cup half-and-half (light
      cream)
    ½ cup vegetable stock
      (page 245)
    ⅓ cup *each* shredded fontina
      and Bel Paese cheeses
    ⅓ cup crumbled Gorgonzola
      cheese
    8 ounces medium-wide noodles
    ¾ cup grated Parmesan cheese

(Continued on next page)

...Fettuccine with Four Cheeses (cont'd.)

In a 2-quart pan over medium heat, melt 1½ tablespoons of the butter. Mix in flour, nutmeg, and pepper; cook, stirring, until bubbly. Slowly stir in half-and-half and stock; cook, stirring constantly, until sauce boils and thickens. Mix in fontina and Bel Paese cheeses; cook, stirring, until cheeses are melted and sauce is smooth. Stir in Gorgonzola cheese until blended; place pan over simmering water to keep sauce warm.

Cook noodles according to package directions. Drain well. Toss noodles lightly with remaining 1½ tablespoons butter and ½ cup of the Parmesan cheese. Spoon noodles onto serving plates. Top each serving with an equal amount of hot cheese sauce and the remaining ¼ cup Parmesan cheese. Makes 4 servings.

Per serving: 24 grams protein, 48 grams carbohydrate, 152 milligrams cholesterol, 584 calories.

Vegetarian Joe

A garden of vegetables goes into this variation of Joe's Special. Eggs and tofu provide the protein. It's delicious served with whole wheat toast or muffins.

½ **pound Italian green beans *or* 1 package (9 oz.) frozen Italian green beans, thawed**

1 **cup sliced cauliflower**

1 **package (10 oz.) frozen chopped spinach, thawed**

About 8 ounces tofu

1 **tablespoon *each* olive oil and butter**

1 **medium-size onion, chopped**

2 **cloves garlic, minced or pressed**

¼ **pound mushrooms, sliced**

½ **teaspoon *each* dry basil and oregano leaves**

½ **teaspoon *each* salt and vegetable-flavored granules**

6 **eggs**

½ **cup grated Parmesan cheese**

Remove ends and strings from beans; cut into 1½-inch lengths. Steam fresh beans and cauliflower over boiling water until crisp-tender (4 to 5 minutes). If using frozen beans, just drain well; do not cook. Squeeze spinach to remove excess moisture. Drain tofu, pat dry with paper towels, and cut into ¾-inch cubes.

Heat oil and butter in a wide frying pan over medium-high heat. Add onion, garlic, and mushrooms; cook, stirring occasionally, until onion is soft. Add beans, cauliflower, spinach, basil, oregano, salt, and granules. Reduce heat to medium-low and cook until heated through.

Beat eggs until blended; pour over vegetable mixture. Add tofu. Cook, gently lifting cooked portion to allow uncooked egg to flow underneath; cook until eggs are softly set. Sprinkle Parmesan cheese over individual servings. Makes 6 servings.

Per serving: 16 grams protein, 11 grams carbohydrate, 268 milligrams cholesterol, 228 calories.

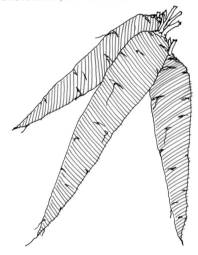

Filled Oven Pancake

Oven pancakes—often called Dutch Babies—are usually baked until puffy around the edges. Then they're filled. In this version, though, you first cook the mushroom-and-onion filling in an ovenproof frying pan, then pour the pancake batter over the filling. The result is a generous puffy entrée that you can serve hot, right from the oven, for brunch or dinner. A chewy whole wheat bread and fruit salad would make perfect accompaniments.

About 5 tablespoons butter or margarine

½ **pound mushrooms, sliced**

1 **small onion, chopped**

1 **teaspoon dry basil**

¾ **teaspoon salt**

¼ **teaspoon *each* pepper and ground nutmeg**

4 **eggs**

1 **cup *each* milk and all-purpose flour**

⅓ **cup grated Parmesan cheese**

About ½ cup sour cream

¼ **cup thinly sliced green onions (including tops)**

In a 10 or 11-inch frying pan with an ovenproof handle, melt 3 tablespoons of the butter. Add mushrooms and onion and cook, stirring, until mushrooms are lightly browned. Stir in basil, salt, pepper, and nutmeg. Tip pan to estimate drippings, then add enough butter to make about 5 tablespoons fat.

In a blender or food processor, whirl eggs for 1 minute. With motor running, gradually pour in milk, then slowly add flour; whirl for 30 seconds. (Or, with a rotary beater, beat eggs until light; gradually beat in milk, then flour.)

Place pan with mushroom mixture in a 425° oven until pan is hot and butter is melted and bubbly. Remove pan from oven. Quickly pour in batter, sprinkle with cheese, and return to oven. Bake for 20 to 25 minutes or until puffy and browned. Top with sour cream and sprinkle with green onions. Serve immediately. Makes 4 servings.

Per serving: 23 grams protein, 37 grams carbohydrate, 340 milligrams cholesterol, 545 calories.

Corn Chili Strata

You build up a strata in layers: in this case, a layer of whole wheat bread, a layer of corn, a layer of zucchini, and a layer of chilies and jack cheese. Then you pour a custard mixture over the top and refrigerate the strata until the next day, if you like. The result is a custardy vegetable casserole sure to become a family favorite. It's also an excellent dish to serve buffet style or take to a potluck.

6 slices whole wheat bread

1 to 1½ tablespoons butter or margarine, softened

1 can (1 lb.) whole kernel corn, drained

2 cups thinly sliced zucchini or crookneck squash

1 can (4 oz.) diced green chili peppers

2 cups (8 oz.) shredded jack, Longhorn, or mild Cheddar cheese

4 eggs

2 cups milk

½ teaspoon salt

⅛ teaspoon pepper

Trim crusts from bread. Lightly spread slices with butter and fit into a lightly buttered 7 by 11-inch baking dish. Distribute corn in an even layer over bread, then arrange zucchini evenly over corn. Sprinkle chilies and cheese evenly over zucchini.

Beat eggs lightly, then beat in milk, salt, and pepper. Pour egg mixture over cheese. Cover and refrigerate for at least 4 hours or overnight.

Bake, uncovered, in a 375° oven for 30 to 40 minutes or until lightly browned and puffed; a knife inserted in center should come out clean. Let stand for 10 minutes before cutting into squares to serve. Makes 6 servings.

Per serving: 21 grams protein, 26 grams carbohydrate, 244 milligrams cholesterol, 372 calories.

Zesty Tomato Fondue

"Dive in!" That's the way to introduce this Italian-style fondue to your family and friends. It's a dish that's fun to serve any time, even at a small dinner party or out camping.

For diving in, we suggest dunking cubes of crusty French or sourdough bread, and dipping cooked artichoke leaves, lightly steamed whole baby carrots, green beans, broccoli, and cauliflower. For meat-eaters, you can offer oven-browned meatballs or pieces of cooked Italian sausages.

2 tablespoons butter or margarine

1 medium-size onion, finely chopped

1 clove garlic, minced or pressed

1 small can (about 8 oz.) stewed tomatoes

½ teaspoon dry basil

¼ teaspoon oregano leaves

⅛ teaspoon pepper

2 cups (8 oz.) shredded Longhorn cheese

¼ cup grated Parmesan cheese

1 tablespoon cornstarch

Melt butter in a 2-quart pan over medium heat. Cook onion and garlic, stirring occasionally, until

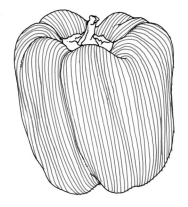

golden. Add tomatoes (break up with a spoon), basil, oregano, and pepper. Heat to simmering. Meanwhile, combine Longhorn and Parmesan cheeses with cornstarch.

Reduce heat to low and add cheese mixture, a handful at a time, stirring until cheeses are melted and blended. Transfer to fondue pot or chafing dish and keep warm over heat source. Serve with bread and vegetables for dipping. Makes 4 servings.

Per serving: 18 grams protein, 10 grams carbohydrate, 80 milligrams cholesterol, 337 calories.

Baked Brie

(Pictured on page 259)

Baked Brie is similar to *beignet au fromage* (deep-fried cheese), only simpler to prepare. You can use these same directions for a larger Brie to serve more people. Precede this elegant entrée with Tarragon Vegetable Salad (page 237) or Vegetables à la Grecque (page 236). Spread the hot Brie on slices of French bread, accompanied by grapes and sliced pears or apples. Then, with white wine, toast *bon appetit* to your friends.

2 tablespoons butter, softened

About 7 ounces whole ripe Brie or Camembert cheese with rind

2 tablespoons sliced almonds

Preheat oven to 350°.

Spread butter over top and sides of cheese. Place cheese on an ovenproof rimmed serving plate. Sprinkle almonds over top.

Bake in the preheated 350° oven for 12 to 15 minutes or until cheese just begins to melt. Makes 3 servings.

Per serving: 11 grams protein, 1 gram carbohydrate, 67 milligrams cholesterol, 240 calories.

Tangy, fresh flavor is the special bonus of making your own cheese and yogurt. Homemade cheese is marvelously light, delicate, and creamy. Homemade yogurt is thick, tangy, and velvety, far surpassing anything you've ever tasted from a carton. And besides tasting heavenly, both these foods are strong sources of protein.

Making cheese and yogurt is really quite simple. The only special equipment you'll need is a thermometer that will measure 170° to 175°F for cheese and 100° to 120°F for yogurt; a variety of such thermometers are available in cookware departments.

Making & Serving Cream Cheese

Kept refrigerated, this homemade cheese stays fresh for about a week. If you make more than you can use in that time, you can freeze the remainder. When you're ready to use it, let it thaw completely, then beat with an electric mixer.

Serve the cheese with fruit, or spread it on warm English muffins, toasted bagels, or sliced nut bread. Season it with herbs for an appetizer dip, or make it into one of the two desserts that follow the basic recipe.

Fresh Cream Cheese.   In a heavy 6 to 8-quart kettle, combine 4 quarts **whole milk** and 1 quart **cultured buttermilk.** Attach a thermometer inside the kettle and place kettle over medium to medium-high heat; stir occasionally to prevent scorching. Too-frequent stirring breaks up the curds almost as fast as they form; you should stir gently, only every 5 to 10 minutes.

When the temperature reaches 170°, reduce heat to low and keep temperature between 170° and 175°.

Meanwhile, line a colander with 3 or 4 thicknesses of cheesecloth wrung out in cold water. Set colander inside a bowl beside the kettle of milk. When thick white curds separate from the watery whey, use a slotted spoon to scoop the curds into the colander.

When most of the curds have been removed, pour remaining curds and whey into colander. (Reserve whey—which contains some vitamins and protein—for making bread or soup, if you wish.) Allow curds to drain for 2 to 3 hours. Scrape them into a bowl and mix in **salt** to taste. For a supersmooth texture, whirl in a blender or food processor. Makes 4 cups or 2 pounds cheese.

Per ounce (2 tablespoons): 4 grams protein, 1 gram carbohydrate, 18 milligrams cholesterol, 57 calories.

Fresh Cheese Cheesecake.   In a blender or food processor, place 2 **eggs,** 1 pound (2 cups) **fresh cream cheese,** 1 cup **sugar,** 1 teaspoon grated **lemon peel,** 3 tablespoons **lemon juice,** and ½ teaspoon *each* **vanilla** and **salt.** Whirl until very smooth.

Pour into a well-buttered 8-inch layer cake pan (one with a solid bottom) and set inside a baking pan. Pour ½ inch boiling water into baking pan. Bake in 325° oven until a knife inserted in center comes out clean (45 to 55 minutes).

Remove from water, cool slightly, then turn onto a serving plate. Serve at room temperature or chilled. If desired, garnish with fruit. Makes 8 servings.

Per serving: 12 grams protein, 40 grams carbohydrate, 99 milligrams cholesterol, 298 calories.

Mascarpone.   In a bowl, beat until smooth: ½ pound (1 cup) **fresh cream cheese,** ¼ cup **powdered sugar,** 2 tablespoons **half-and-half** (light cream), and 2 tablespoons **orange-flavored liqueur** (or 1 tablespoon frozen orange juice concentrate, undiluted). Mound on a serving plate. Serve with fresh **apricot halves.** Makes 4 servings.

Per serving: 11 grams protein, 24 grams carbohydrate, 35 milligrams cholesterol, 233 calories.

Making & Serving Yogurt

Given a little patience and the right temperature, yogurt almost makes itself. Then, if you like, you can take the delicious, creamy result and move along to further adventures. You can drain it to make cheese, or you can blend it with flavorings to make an Indian *raita* to cool the palate alongside a curry or any other hot and spicy dish.

The important factor in making successful yogurt is keeping the milk culture at a fairly constant temperature (about 115°) until it thickens. Yogurt bacteria are killed by higher temperatures; below 90° they become inactive.

Today many commercial yogurt makers are available that provide the right amount of heat. Also a variety of home methods will keep the milk warm. Here are two reliable methods.

Electric frying pan method.   Use a bowl or several canning jars for the yogurt containers. Set containers inside a deep kettle, then set the kettle inside an electric frying pan or on an electric griddle.

To preheat this system, fill yogurt containers with warm water (about 115°), then set containers inside the kettle, and fill the kettle with 115° water. Place a thermometer in the water surrounding the yogurt containers and turn the appliance setting to warm (or whatever setting will keep the water at 115°).

Cover the kettle with a lid or, if the containers are large, with a tent of foil. You can also set a folded bath towel on top of the foil to help hold in heat. Let stand while you heat milk and add starter (directions follow).

When mixture is ready, remove yogurt containers, pour out their water, and replace with milk mixture; return containers to the kettle. The yogurt will develop the most even consistency if the surrounding water is the same level as the yogurt inside the containers.

Leave containers undisturbed until yogurt has set (3½ to 5 hours). If water temperature should go as high as 120°, ladle out some of the water from the kettle, replace with cold water, and lower heat setting as needed. Refrigerate yogurt until cold and firm.

Vacuum bottle method.   Preheat a 1 or 2-quart wide-mouth vacuum bottle by filling it with warm water (about 115°). Cap the bottle and let stand while you heat milk and add starter (directions follow). When mixture is ready, pour water out of container and immediately replace it with milk mixture. Replace cap tightly and leave undisturbed for about 4 hours. Check, and if yogurt has not set, recap and test again every ½ hour. When set, remove lid, loosely cover, and refrigerate.

Thick Homemade Yogurt.   Pour 2 cups low-fat milk into a pan and place over medium heat. Heat to scalding (185°). Remove from heat and cool; discard skin. Meanwhile combine 1¼ cups **water** and 1⅓ cups **instant nonfat dry milk** powder and stir until smooth. Add this to the cooling milk, then check its temperature.

As soon as the mixture cools to 115°, stir in ¼ cup **plain commercial yogurt** until smooth. Transfer mixture to preheated yogurt container. Keep warm as directed for the method you are using. When set, usually in 3½ to 5 hours, remove from heat and refrigerate, covered, until cold. After the first batch, you can use your own yogurt for a starter as long as it is fresh—not more than a week old. Makes 1 quart.

Per ½-cup serving: 7 grams protein, 10 grams carbohydrate, 8 milligrams cholesterol, 81 calories.

Yogurt Cheese.   Wring out a clean dishcloth or 3 or 4 thicknesses of cheesecloth (cut 20 inches square) in cold water. Line a colander with the cloth. Spoon in 1 quart **thick homemade yogurt.** Twist ends of cloth together to close. Place colander in your sink (or set in a larger bowl) and let drain at room temperature for 24 hours or until yogurt is consistency of cream cheese. Cover and refrigerate. Makes 1½ cups.

Per tablespoon: 1.3 grams protein, 2 grams carbohydrate, 3 milligrams cholesterol, 19 calories.

Mint & Coriander Raita (*pictured on page 283*).   In a bowl, combine 2 cups **plain yogurt,** ¼ cup chopped fresh **mint leaves,** ¼ cup chopped **red onion,** 2 tablespoons chopped fresh **corainder** (cilantro), 1 tablespoon minced canned **green chili pepper,** and **salt** to taste. makes 8 servings.

Cucumber & Tomato Raita (*pictured on page 283*).   In a bowl, combine 2 cups **plain yogurt;** 1 medium-size **cucumber,** peeled, seeded, and chopped; 1 large **tomato,** peeled and chopped; 1 teaspoon ground **cumin;** ½ teaspoon **paprika;** and **salt** to taste. Makes 8 servings.

Per serving: 2 grams protein, 4 grams carbohydrate, 4 milligrams cholesterol, 34 calories.

Greens, Grains & Other Good Entrées

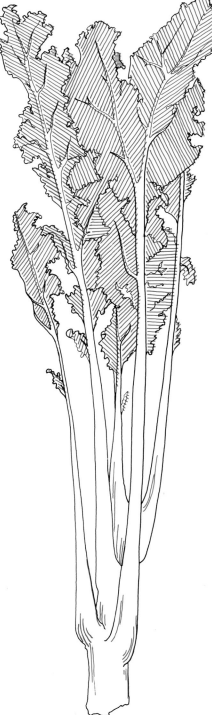

"What goes in that empty space on my plate where the meat used to be?"

A delicious entrée from this chapter, that's what! The question "Where's the meat?" won't even arise when you're serving such dishes as Eggplant Cannelloni (page 274) that uses slices of eggplant to enclose a savory cheese and mushroom filling. And you certainly won't hear it when you offer a meal-in-itself slice of Whole Wheat Zucchini Pizza (page 274), or a delicious Vegetable Kebab (page 277).

In fact, Vegetable Kebabs elicited this inquiry from one of our taste-test panelists: "What kind of meat is on the kebabs?" There wasn't any meat, of course. The well-seasoned, marinated chunks of grilled mushrooms and eggplant were simply satisfying replacements for meat.

Speaking of meat replacements, we haven't included any recipes for meat substitutes, sometimes called meat analogues — "burgers" made of processed soy, "meat loaves" made of nuts and beans. Our feeling is that if you're going vegetarian, you might as well enjoy the many virtues of grains, beans, and vegetables for themselves, rather than attempt to cook dishes that supposedly resemble meat in taste and texture.

That's why this chapter is a veritable kitchens-of-the-world tour. From Mexico's kitchen come the Green Enchiladas (page 271) and Chiles Rellenos Casserole (page 271), and you'll also recognize a south-of-the-border accent in Bulgur Mexicana (page 272) and Sonora Pizza (page 272). From Italy's kitchen comes inspiration for Lasagne Swirls (page 273) and Ricotta Gnocchi (page 273).

From India, we're pleased to include India-spiced Eggplant (page 282), Savory Fried Rice (page 284), and Vegetable Curry (page 282) — a royal feast, indeed. Traveling yet farther East, we bring back Sweet & Sour Soybeans (page 271), Savory Vegetables & Tofu (page 281), and Sesame Tofu Sticks (page 279).

Many of the dishes in this section need merely the addition of a simple green salad or perhaps a little soup and bread, with fruit for dessert, to make a complete meal. The Bulgur Mexicana and Eggplant Cannelloni, as well as Layered Chili (page 269), are in that category.

You'll find other entrées that need to share the spotlight. Sesame Tofu Sticks, for example, are excellent with steamed or stir-fried vegetables (pages 288 and 289); and the Armenian Vegetable Casserole (page 280), a Middle-eastern version of ratatouille, is best served over a pilaf of bulgur wheat or mixed grains. Another example is the Vegetable Kebabs, so delicious served with the exotic combination of dried apricots, dates, and rice known as Fruited Rice Pilaf (page 287).

Cooking Beans

Beans are about the best nutrition bargain going. Low in cost, they provide thiamin, riboflavin, niacin, iron, and calcium. When complemented by grains or dairy products, they're a main source of high-quality protein for vegetarians.

The simplest cooking directions are to sort through the beans and discard any bad ones, then rinse well, drain, and gently boil, uncovered, in three times their volume of water until tender.

For some beans, cooking "until tender" can take a considerable length of time. If you prefer, you can shorten their cooking time by soaking them according to one of the following methods.

Quick soaking. In a kettle, combine 6 to 8 cups **hot water** with 1 pound **dry beans.** Bring to a boil over high heat and continue to boil for 2 minutes. Remove from heat and let soak, covered, for 1 hour before draining.

Long soaking. In a kettle, combine 6 to 7 cups **cold water** with 1 pound **dry beans.** Add 2 teaspoons **salt,** (it helps beans absorb water evenly). Let soak for at least 3 to 4 hours or until next day. Drain before cooking.

To cook soaked beans. In a kettle, bring 6 to 7 cups water to a boil. Add drained, soaked beans. Boil gently, partially covered, until tender. (See list of legumes at right for cooking times.) Add water if needed to keep beans covered. Add salt to taste (up to 2 teaspoons) when beans are tender. Drain excess water when done; reserve for soups or stews, if desired.

Beans double in size; 1 pound dry beans yields about 4 cups cooked beans. We prefer to cook a large quantity of beans and freeze whatever we don't plan to use right away.

The following list of legumes (mostly beans) contains a brief description as well as recommended cooking time *after soaking* for each item. Note that lentils and split peas do not need soaking.

Black beans. Robust flavor; popular in South American cooking. 1 to 1½ hours.

Black-eyed peas. Smooth texture, pealike flavor; good mixed with other vegetables. 1 to 1½ hours.

Garbanzos (chick peas, ceci). Firm texture, nutlike flavor; naturals for minestrone, salads. 2 to 2½ hours.

Great Northern beans. Mild flavor; good in soups, and combined with other vegetables. 1 to 1½ hours.

Kidney beans. Firm texture, meaty flavor; hold shape well in chili dishes and other casseroles. 1½ to 2 hours.

Lentils. No soaking needed. Mild flavor blends well with many different foods, spices. 40 to 45 minutes.

Limas, baby. Versatile; use like other white beans in soups, casseroles. 1 to 1½ hours.

Pink, pinto, and red beans. Hearty flavor; great for barbecue-style beans, Mexican cooking, soups, casseroles. 1½ to 2 hours.

Soybeans. Strong-flavored, near-perfect protein source. Refrigerate while soaking. 3 to 3½ hours.

Split peas, green and yellow. No soaking; good for soups, side dishes. 40 to 45 minutes.

White beans (navy), small. Hold their shape when cooked; classic for baked beans. 1 to 1½ hours.

Layered Chili

(Pictured on page 270)

This is no timid chili. It's liberally spiced without being too hot. To serve, you pass special pink onions, cheese, and a variety of toppings to layer on each steaming bowl. As a shortcut, you can use canned kidney beans.

4 large onions, chopped
1 large green pepper, seeded and chopped
3 tablespoons salad oil
1 tablespoon *each* mustard seeds and chili powder
1 teaspoon *each* cumin seeds and unsweetened cocoa
¼ teaspoon ground cinnamon
1 can (about 1 lb.) tomatoes
5 cups cooked kidney beans plus 1½ cups cooking liquid or water, or 3 cans (about 1 lb. size) kidney beans, undrained, and 1 cup water
1 can (6 oz.) tomato paste
Salt
Pink Onions (recipe follows)
Relish toppings (suggestions follow)
2 limes or lemons, cut in wedges

In a 5 or 6-quart kettle, cook onions and green pepper in oil over medium-high heat, stirring occasionally, until onions are golden and pepper is soft. Add mustard seeds and cook, stirring, for 1 minute. Add chili powder, cumin seeds, cocoa, cinnamon, tomatoes (break up with a spoon) and their liquid, beans and their liquid, and tomato paste. Reduce heat and simmer rapidly, uncovered, for about 40 minutes or until most of the liquid has cooked away and chili is thickened; stir frequently to prevent scorching.

Season with salt to taste (not necessary if using canned beans). Pass pink onions, relish toppings, and lime wedges to layer on top of chili. Makes 6 servings.

Per serving (including pink onions and relishes): 28 grams protein, 69 grams carbohydrate, 37 milligrams cholesterol, 563 calories.

Pink Onions. In a 1-quart pan over high heat, bring 2 cups **water** and 1½ tablespoons **vinegar** to a boil. Add 1 large **red onion** (thinly sliced) and push down into liquid. (Use white onion if red is not available, but it won't turn pink.) Return to a boil and cook, uncovered, over

(Continued on page 271)

...Layered Chili (cont'd.)
medium heat for 2 to 3 minutes. Drain onion and let cool. In a bowl, stir together onion, 1½ teaspoons **vinegar**, 1 tablespoon **salad oil**, ½ teaspoon **mustard seeds**, ¼ teaspoon **cumin seeds**, and **salt** to taste. Serve at room temperature, or cover and chill until ready to serve.

Relish toppings. Arrange in containers 3 medium-size **tomatoes** (chopped), 1 can (7 oz.) diced **green chilies**, 1 medium-size **cucumber** (peeled and chopped), 1 cup sliced **green onions** (including tops), and 2 cups (8 oz.) shredded **Cheddar cheese.**

Sweet & Sour Soybeans

Pineapple chunks and a bevy of fresh vegetables combine with soybeans in a pert sweet-sour sauce. It's delicious over rice.

> **Sweet-Sour Sauce (recipe follows)**
> 2 tablespoons salad oil
> 1 large onion, cut in 1-inch squares
> 2 large carrots, cut in ¼-inch slices
> 1 clove garlic, minced or pressed
> 1 green pepper, seeded and cut into 1-inch squares
> ¾ cup fresh pineapple chunks, or canned pineapple chunks, drained
> 2 tomatoes, cut in wedges

2½ cups cooked soybeans (page 269)

Prepare sweet-sour sauce and reserve.

Ladle up a steaming bowl of Layered Chili (recipe on page 269). Then make it live up to its name—pile on layers of cheese and other condiments. A wedge of Quick Corn Bread (recipe on page 298) complements the chili and completes the protein.

Heat oil in a wide frying pan over high heat; add onion, carrots, and garlic and cook, stirring, for about 3 minutes or until vegetables are crisp-tender. Add green pepper and cook for 1 minute. Add pineapple, tomatoes, and soybeans and cook for 2 minutes or until hot. Stir sweet-sour sauce, pour into pan, and continue to cook, stirring, until sauce bubbles and thickens. Makes 6 servings.

Per serving: 10 grams protein, 72 grams carbohydrate, no cholesterol, 391 calories.

Sweet-Sour Sauce. In a bowl, combine 1½ tablespoons *each* **cornstarch, soy sauce,** and **dry sherry;** ½ cup *each* **brown sugar** and **wine vinegar;** and ⅓ cup **vegetable stock** (page 245).

Green Enchiladas

Spinach and green chilies in a creamy sauce account for the "green" in this recipe. The enchiladas themselves are corn tortillas wrapped around a mild cheese and onion filling.

> 1 tablespoon salad oil
> 2 large onions, chopped
> ¼ teaspoon salt
> Salad oil
> 12 corn tortillas
> 3 cups (12 oz.) shredded jack cheese
> 1 package (10 oz.) frozen chopped spinach, thawed
> 2 green onions (including tops), sliced
> 1 can (4 oz.) diced green chili peppers
> 1 can (10½ oz.) condensed cream of mushroom soup
> ½ pint (1 cup) sour cream

Heat the 1 tablespoon oil in a wide frying pan over medium heat. Add onions and cook until soft (about 5 minutes). Stir in salt; set pan aside.

In a small frying pan, heat a little oil over medium heat. One at a time, dip tortillas in oil for a few seconds on each side or just until soft; drain briefly. Across the middle of each tortilla, sprinkle 2 tablespoons *each* cooked onion and shredded cheese. Roll to enclose. Place tortillas, seam side down, in a greased shallow 9 by 13-inch baking pan.

Squeeze spinach to remove excess moisture. In a blender or food processor, purée spinach, green onions, chili peppers, soup, and sour cream until smooth. Pour sauce over tortillas. Sprinkle remaining cheese over all.

Bake, uncovered, in a 350° oven for 30 minutes or until hot and bubbly. Makes 12 enchiladas.

Per enchilada: 11 grams protein, 22 grams carbohydrate, 39 milligrams cholesterol, 273 calories.

Chiles Rellenos Casserole

Instead of stuffing and frying the chili peppers in true chiles rellenos fashion, you cover them with two kinds of cheese and bake them in a puffy batter. For a south-of-the-border dinner, serve the casserole with refried beans, warm tortillas, and a salad of greens, oranges, and red onions.

> 2 cans (7 oz. *each*) whole green chili peppers
> 3 cups (12 oz.) shredded sharp Cheddar cheese
> 4 green onions (including tops), thinly sliced
> 3 cups (12 oz.) shredded mozzarella cheese
> 6 eggs
> 3 cups milk
> ¾ cup all-purpose flour
> ¼ teaspoon salt
> 2 cans (7 oz. *each*) green chili salsa

(Continued on next page)

...*Chiles Rellenos Casserole (cont'd.)*

Split chili peppers lengthwise and remove seeds and pith. Spread chilies in a single layer in a greased 9 by 13-inch baking dish. Sprinkle Cheddar cheese, green onions, and 1½ cups of the mozzarella cheese over chilies.

In a bowl, beat eggs, milk, flour, and salt together until smooth. Pour over chilies and cheese. Bake in a 325° oven for 50 minutes or until a knife inserted in custard comes out clean.

Meanwhile, mix salsa with the remaining 1½ cups mozzarella cheese. Sprinkle over casserole and return to oven for 10 minutes or until cheese melts. Let stand for 5 minutes before serving. Makes 10 servings.

Per serving: 32 grams protein, 21 grams carbohydrate, 268 milligrams cholesterol, 474 calories.

Sonora Pizza

This Mexican-flavored pizza has enough elements to make a great entrée: crisp-fried whole wheat tortillas, refried beans, cheese, chilies, crunchy vegetables, and a crown of sour cream. You assemble the base before you heat it in the oven. Then, if you wish, you can set out the condiments and let everyone be creative.

Salad oil

8 large whole wheat tortillas (page 301)
Spicy Tomato Sauce (recipe follows)

1 can (1 lb.) refried beans

1 can (4 oz.) *each* diced green chili peppers and chopped ripe olives

1 large onion, chopped

3 cups (12 oz.) shredded jack cheese or Cheddar cheese

About 3 cups shredded lettuce

About 1 cup thinly sliced radishes

About ½ cup sour cream

1 cup alfalfa sprouts

Place a 10-inch frying pan over medium heat. Pour oil into pan to a depth of ½ inch and heat to 375° on a deep-frying thermometer. Fry one tortilla at a time, turning quickly several times with 2 wide spatulas, until bubbly and just golden (about 30 seconds total). Lift tortilla and let excess oil drain back into pan; drain on paper towels. If fried ahead, cool, package airtight in plastic bags, and store up to 2 days at room temperature.

Prepare spicy tomato sauce.

To assemble pizza, gently spread unheated beans in an even layer over each tortilla. Top each with about 2 tablespoons of the tomato sauce. Sprinkle chili peppers, olives, and onion over tortillas, then top with shredded cheese. Arrange on baking sheets.

Bake tortillas in a 350° oven until beans are hot and cheese is bubbly (7 to 10 minutes). Pass individual bowls of lettuce, radishes, sour cream, and alfalfa sprouts to be spooned over individual servings. Makes 8 servings.

Per serving: 20 grams protein, 41 grams carbohydrate, 69 milligrams cholesterol, 499 calories.

Spicy Tomato Sauce. In a pan over low heat, combine 1 can (15 oz.) **tomato sauce,** 2 cloves **garlic** (minced or pressed), 1½ teaspoons **chili powder,** and ½ teaspoon *each* **salt, oregano** leaves, and ground **cumin.** Simmer, uncovered, for 10 minutes.

Bulgur Mexicana

Here's a main-dish pilaf that's fast to prepare and fun to eat. The flavors will remind you of Spanish rice, and the dish is served like a tostada with a selection of condiments on top. Make-ahead Gazpacho (page 255) would be the perfect first course for this entrée.

2 tablespoons butter or margarine

1 medium-size onion, chopped

1 cup bulgur wheat

1 large stalk celery, thinly sliced

½ green or red bell pepper, seeded and diced

1 teaspoon chili powder

¾ teaspoon ground cumin

2¼ cups vegetable stock (page 245)
Salt and pepper
Condiments (suggestions follow)

Melt butter in a wide frying pan over medium heat. Add onion and bulgur and cook, stirring occasionally, until onion is soft and bulgur is golden (7 to 8 minutes). Stir in celery, bell pepper, chili powder, and cumin and cook for 2 minutes. Pour in stock and bring to a boil. Reduce heat to low; cover and simmer until all liquid is absorbed (about 20 minutes). Season to taste with salt and pepper.

To serve, mound bulgur mixture on a platter or individual plates. At the table, offer condiments, each in a separate bowl. Makes 4 servings.

Per serving (including condiments): 17 grams protein, 48 grams carbohydrate, 54 milligrams cholesterol, 469 calories.

Condiments. Prepare 1 cup *each* shredded **Cheddar cheese** and **alfalfa sprouts;** ⅓ cup *each* sliced **green onions** (including tops), **sunflower seeds,** and **sour cream;** 2 **tomatoes** (diced); and **bottled taco sauce.**

Lasagne Swirls

Here's meatless magic with pasta. Instead of layering wide lasagna noodles in a baking dish, you wrap them around a low fat, high protein ricotta cheese filling. The result is a platter of pinwheels that are as pretty as they are delicious.

16 packaged lasagne noodles
   Boiling salted water
 2 packages (10 oz. *each*) frozen chopped spinach, thawed
 2 cups (6 oz.) grated Parmesan cheese
2⅔ cups ricotta cheese
 1 teaspoon *each* salt and pepper
 ½ teaspoon ground nutmeg
 2 cloves garlic, minced or pressed
 1 large onion, chopped
 3 tablespoons olive oil or salad oil
 2 large cans (15 oz. *each*) tomato sauce
 ¼ cup dry red wine
 ½ teaspoon *each* dry basil and oregano leaves

Cook noodles in a large kettle of boiling salted water according to package directions. Drain, rinse with cold water, and drain again.

Squeeze spinach to remove excess moisture. In a bowl, mix spinach with 1½ cups of the Parmesan cheese. Add ricotta, salt, ½ teaspoon of the pepper, and nutmeg; mix together. Spread about ¼ cup of this cheese mixture along entire length of each noodle; roll noodles up. Butter two 9 by 13-inch baking dishes. In each dish stand rolled noodles on end so they do not touch.

In a wide frying pan over medium heat, cook garlic and onion in olive oil until onion is soft. Add tomato sauce, wine, basil, oregano, and the remaining ½ teaspoon pepper. Simmer, uncovered, for 10 minutes. Pour sauce around noodles. If made ahead, cover and refrigerate.

Bake, covered, in a 350° oven for about 30 minutes (40 minutes, if refrigerated) or until heated through. Remove from oven and sprinkle lasagne evenly with remaining ½ cup Parmesan cheese. Makes 16 swirls.

Per swirl: 16 grams protein, 25 grams carbohydrate, 58 milligrams cholesterol, 281 calories.

Vegetable Lasagne

Your guests may never guess that this vegetable-laden lasagne is meatless. Cheese supplies a good deal of the protein, and you can add more by using whole wheat noodles.

 ⅓ cup olive oil or salad oil
 1 large onion, chopped
 2 cloves garlic, minced or pressed
 1 medium-size unpeeled eggplant (about 1 lb.), diced
 ¼ pound mushrooms, sliced
 1 can (about 1 lb.) Italian-style tomatoes
 1 can (8 oz.) tomato sauce
 ½ cup dry red wine
 1 medium-size carrot, shredded
 ¼ cup chopped parsley
 2 teaspoons oregano leaves
 1 teaspoon *each* dry basil and salt
 ¼ teaspoon pepper
16 packaged whole wheat or regular lasagne noodles
   Boiling salted water
 2 cups (1 lb.) ricotta cheese
 2 cups (8 oz.) shredded mozzarella cheese
1½ cups (4½ oz.) grated Parmesan cheese

Heat oil in a wide frying pan over medium heat. Add onion, garlic, eggplant, and mushrooms and cook, stirring frequently, for 15 minutes. Add tomatoes and their liquid (break up tomatoes with a spoon), tomato sauce, wine, carrot, parsley, oregano, basil, salt, and pepper. Bring to a boil, then reduce heat and simmer, covered, for 30 minutes. Uncover and continue cooking until sauce is thick. You should have 5 cups sauce; set aside.

Cook noodles in a large kettle of boiling salted water according to package directions. Drain, rinse with cold water, and drain again.

Butter a 9 by 13-inch baking dish. Spread about ¼ of the sauce in dish. Arrange ⅓ of the noodles in an even layer over sauce. Dot noodles with ⅓ of the ricotta. Sprinkle with ⅓ of the mozzarella, then with ¼ of the Parmesan cheese. Repeat this layering two more times. Spread remaining sauce evenly over top and sprinkle with remaining Parmesan cheese. If made ahead, cover and refrigerate.

Bake, uncovered, in a 350° oven until hot and bubbly (40 to 50 minutes). Cut in squares to serve. Makes 10 servings

Per serving (made with whole wheat noodles): 26 grams protein, 44 grams carbohydrate, 20 milligrams cholesterol, 504 calories.

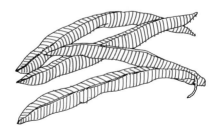

Ricotta Gnocchi

Think of these ricotta dumplings as vegetarian meatballs. They're firm, but tender and delicious. Serve them with tomato sauce on spaghetti, rice, or polenta (cooked cornmeal). If you prepare them ahead, or have any left over, reheat by steaming over boiling water for 5 minutes or by browning in butter.

(Continued on next page)

...Ricotta Gnocchi (cont'd.)

Fresh Tomato Sauce (recipe follows)
1 egg
1 cup (8 oz.) ricotta cheese
½ cup fine dry bread crumbs
¾ cup grated Parmesan cheese
¼ teaspoon garlic salt
Dash of pepper
⅛ teaspoon ground nutmeg
½ teaspoon dry basil
1 package (10 oz.) frozen chopped spinach, thawed
All-purpose flour
Boiling salted water

Prepare fresh tomato sauce.

In a large bowl, beat egg. Add ricotta and mix well. Stir in bread crumbs, ½ cup of the Parmesan, garlic salt, pepper, nutmeg, and basil. Squeeze spinach to remove excess moisture. Stir spinach into ricotta mixture. Shape mixture into 1½-inch balls. Roll in flour to coat lightly.

Drop balls gently into a large kettle of boiling salted water. When water returns to a boil, adjust heat so water boils *very* gently. Cook for 10 minutes. Meanwhile, reheat fresh tomato sauce. Remove balls with a slotted spoon, drain well, and place in a serving dish. Pour tomato sauce over gnocchi; sprinkle with the remaining ¼ cup Parmesan. Makes 4 servings.

Per serving (including fresh tomato sauce): 20 grams protein, 22 grams carbohydrate, 113 milligrams cholesterol, 322 calories.

Fresh Tomato Sauce. In a 2-quart pan over medium heat, melt 1½ tablespoons **butter** or margarine. Add 1 medium-size **onion** (chopped) and cook until soft. Add 2 large **tomatoes** (peeled and finely chopped), 1 cup **vegetable stock** (page 245), ½ teaspoon dry basil, ¼ teaspoon **salt** and a dash of **pepper**. Bring to a boil over high heat and cook for 10 minutes, stirring frequently; then reduce heat to medium and continue to cook, stirring occasionally, until sauce has thickened.

Whole Wheat Zucchini Pizza

(Pictured on facing page)

First you prepare a chewy whole wheat crust topped with an amply spiced tomato sauce. Then you pile up the goodies—artichoke hearts, cheese, zucchini, olives, and on and on.

1 package active dry yeast
1½ cups warm water (about 110°)
2 tablespoons salad oil
1 teaspoon *each* salt, sugar, dry basil, and oregano leaves
¼ cup wheat germ
1½ cups *each* all-purpose flour and whole wheat flour
All-purpose flour for kneading
Tomato Sauce (recipe follows)
2 medium-size zucchini, thinly sliced
½ green or red bell pepper, seeded and thinly sliced
4 green onions (including tops), thinly sliced
1 can (2¼ oz.) sliced ripe olives
1 can (14 oz.) artichoke hearts, drained and quartered
3 cups (12 oz.) shredded jack cheese
¼ cup grated Parmesan cheese

In a large bowl, dissolve yeast in water. Add oil, salt, sugar, basil, oregano, wheat germ, and all-purpose flour. Beat until smooth (about 3 minutes, if using electric mixer). Using a heavy-duty mixer or wooden spoon, beat in whole wheat flour until dough holds together.

Turn out onto a lightly floured board and knead until dough is smooth and elastic (about 5 minutes). Turn over in a greased bowl, cover, and let rise in a warm place until dough has doubled in size (about 45 minutes). Meanwhile, prepare tomato sauce.

Punch dough down and divide in half. Roll out each half to form a 14-inch circle, then transfer each

circle onto a greased 14-inch pizza pan. One at a time, bake on next-to-bottom rack of a 450° oven for about 7 minutes or just until bottom of crust starts to brown. During baking, watch carefully and prick any bubbles that form. Remove from oven and set aside.

To assemble pizza, spread tomato sauce over crust. Arrange zucchini, bell pepper, green onions, olives, and artichoke quarters over sauce. Sprinkle jack cheese and Parmesan over all.

Bake in a 450° oven for 12 to 15 minutes or until cheese melts. Cut hot pizzas in wedges to serve. Makes 2 pizzas; each serves 6.

Per serving: 22 grams protein, 50 grams carbohydrate, 44 milligrams cholesterol, 464 calories.

Tomato Sauce. In a wide frying pan over medium heat, cook 1 large **onion** (chopped) in 2 tablespoons **olive oil** or salad oil until soft. Stir in 1 can (15 oz.) **tomato sauce**, 1 can (6 oz.) **tomato paste**, ½ cup **red wine**, 1 teaspoon *each* **oregano** leaves and dry **basil**, and ½ teaspoon **salt**. Simmer, uncovered, for 10 minutes.

Eggplant Cannelloni

Thin, browned slices of eggplant replace the usual pasta or crêpe wrapping in this light but luscious dish. To complete the meal, serve a whole-grain pilaf and a green salad.

(Continued on page 276)

Supper in a single slice— *Whole Wheat Zucchini Pizza (recipe on this page) has it all—a chewy crust, rich tomato sauce with a double order of cheeses, then vegetables galore.*

1 large (about 1½ lbs.) eggplant
1 egg
⅔ cup milk
3 tablespoons salad oil
¼ cup whole wheat flour
1¼ cups (5 oz.) shredded jack cheese
½ cup ricotta cheese
¾ cup grated Parmesan cheese
⅔ cup coarsely chopped fresh mushrooms
2 eggs, lightly beaten
2 tablespoons chopped parsley
⅛ teaspoon *each* salt and pepper
   Fresh Tomato Sauce (page 274)

Remove stem from eggplant. Cut unpeeled eggplant lengthwise in slices ¼ inch thick. You should have 12 large slices; save small pieces for another use.

In a pie pan, beat until smooth the 1 egg, milk, 1 tablespoon of the oil, and flour. Place a wide frying pan on medium heat and add 1 tablespoon of the oil. Or set an electric griddle at 350° and add oil as needed. One at a time, dip eggplant slices in batter and drain briefly. Place slices in a single layer in pan and cook for about 10 minutes on each side or until lightly browned and very soft when pressed. Adding more oil as needed, repeat until all eggplant is cooked.

In a bowl, combine jack and ricotta cheeses, ½ cup of the Parmesan, mushrooms, the 2 eggs, parsley, salt, and pepper. Divide mixture into 12 equal portions. Spoon 1 portion across center of each eggplant slice; fold narrow end of slice over filling and roll to enclose. Arrange eggplant cannelloni, seam side down, in a single layer in a shallow 3-quart casserole. If made ahead, cover and refrigerate until next day.

Prepare fresh tomato sauce. Just before baking, spoon sauce over eggplant. Bake, uncovered, in a 375° oven for 15 to 20 minutes (25 minutes, if refrigerated) or until hot throughout.

To serve, sprinkle with the remaining ¼ cup Parmesan cheese. Makes 6 servings.

Per serving (including sauce): 19 grams protein, 16 grams carbohydrate, 181 milligrams cholesterol, 372 calories.

Whole Wheat Crêpes

Tender crêpes with their rich, whole wheat flavor make fine wrappers for sweet or savory fillings. Be sure you let the batter sit for at least an hour before cooking the crêpes so the bran in the whole wheat flour has a chance to soften.

With a batch of these made ahead and stored in the freezer, you have the handy starting point for a variety of entrées.

3 eggs
1 cup milk
⅔ cup whole wheat flour
   About 4 teaspoons butter or margarine

In a blender or food processor (or with a wire whip or electric mixer), blend eggs and milk; add flour and blend until smooth. Let stand at room temperature for 1 hour.

Place a 6 or 7-inch crêpe pan or other flat-bottomed frying pan over medium heat. When hot, add ¼ teaspoon of the butter and swirl to coat surface. Stir batter and pour about 2 tablespoons (all at once) into hot pan; immediately lift and tilt pan so batter covers entire bottom of pan. (Don't worry if there are a few little holes.) Return to heat and cook until surface appears dry and edge is lightly browned. With a spatula, turn and brown other side. Turn out onto a plate, stacking crêpes as made. If made ahead, cool, then place wax paper between each crêpe; package airtight (in quantities you expect to use) and refrigerate for as long as 3 days or freeze for longer storage. Allow crêpes to

come to room temperature before separating; they tear if cold. Fill crêpes as desired and roll or fold to enclose. Makes about 16 crêpes.

Per crêpe: 2 grams protein, 4 grams carbohydrate, 58 milligrams cholesterol, 67 calories.

Potato-Onion Blintzes

(Pictured on page 251)

For these savory blintzes, you enclose mashed potatoes and onions in whole wheat crêpes. The little packets, browned in butter, can be topped with sour cream or yogurt and your choice of poppy, sesame, sunflower, or pumpkin seeds. Potato-Onion Blintzes are the natural companions of Sweet & Sour Borscht (page 253).

About 16 whole wheat crêpes (recipe at left)
2 tablespoons butter or margarine
1 large onion, finely chopped
2 cups mashed, unseasoned potatoes (3 medium-size potatoes)
1 egg
½ teaspoon salt
   White pepper
   About 4 tablespoons butter or margarine
   About 1 cup sour cream or plain yogurt
   Finely chopped chives or green onion
   Poppy seeds, sesame seeds, sunflower seeds, or pumpkin seeds

Prepare crêpes.

In a small frying pan over medium heat, melt butter. Add onion and cook, stirring occasionally, until golden brown (about 15 minutes). Stir into mashed potatoes. Beat egg and stir into potatoes along with salt and a dash of pepper.

For each blintz, place a crêpe,

browned side up, on a flat surface. Spoon about 2 tablespoons of the potato mixture onto center of crêpe. Fold opposite sides over center so they overlap slightly, then fold bottom up over sides and roll over top to enclose. Place, folded side down, on a pan or tray. Repeat until all crêpes are filled. If made ahead, cover and refrigerate until next day.

Before serving, melt 2 table-spoons of the butter in a wide fry-ing pan over medium heat. Place blintzes, folded sides down, in pan. Cook, turning carefully, until both sides are browned. Add more but-ter, about 1 tablespoon at a time, as needed, and brown remaining blintzes. Keep warm in a low oven until all are cooked. Serve hot with sour cream, chives, and your choice of seeds. Makes 16 blintzes.

Per blintz: 4 grams protein, 5 grams carbohydrate, 26 milligrams cholesterol, 111 calories.

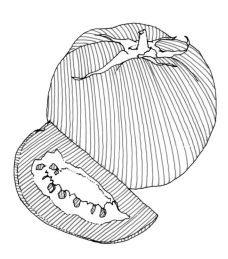

Mushroom-Broccoli Stroganoff

Spinach noodles and fresh vege-tables team up for a family-pleasing casserole. Sour cream and two kinds of cheese give this entrée its tangy richness.

2 tablespoons butter or margarine
1 large onion, chopped
½ pound mushrooms, sliced
2 tablespoons lemon juice
½ teaspoon *each* salt and dry basil
½ pint (1 cup) sour cream
1 cup (4 oz.) *each* shredded jack cheese and Cheddar cheese
About 1½ pounds broccoli
1 package (12 oz.) spinach noodles
Boiling salted water
⅓ cup chopped walnuts or sunflower seeds

Melt butter in a wide frying pan over medium heat. Add onion and mushrooms and cook, stirring oc-casionally, until soft (about 8 min-utes). Remove from heat and stir in lemon juice, salt, basil, sour cream, and ½ cup *each* of the jack cheese and Cheddar cheese. Mix until blended, then set aside.

Cut broccoli into small flowerets and thinly slice stems. Steam broc-coli just until crisp-tender (about 5 minutes). Cook noodles in a large kettle of boiling salted water ac-cording to package directions; drain.

In a large bowl, combine sour cream mixture, noodles, and broc-coli. Turn into a shallow 3-quart baking dish.

Bake casserole, covered, in a 350° oven for 30 minutes (40 min-utes, if refrigerated). Remove from oven, sprinkle remaining cheese and walnuts over top, and continue baking, uncovered, for about 5 minutes or until cheese melts. Makes 8 servings.

Per serving: 20 grams protein, 46 grams carbohydrate, 64 milligrams cholesterol, 461 calories.

Savory Kugel

This baked noodle dish originated with a Russian-Jewish version of unsweetened noodle pudding.

Spinach noodles give it color and there's a touch of seasoning to spark the flavor.

8 ounces packaged spinach noodles
Boiling salted water
1½ cups large curd cottage cheese
1 cup (½ pint) sour cream
1 clove garlic, minced or pressed
3 green onions (including tops), thinly sliced
1 teaspoon Worcestershire
¼ teaspoon liquid hot pepper seasoning
2 tablespoons butter or margarine, melted
½ cup grated Parmesan cheese

Cook noodles in a large kettle of boiling salted water according to package directions. Drain, rinse with cold water, and drain again.

In a bowl, combine cottage cheese, sour cream, garlic, green onions, Worcestershire, hot pepper seasoning, and melted butter. Gently stir in noodles. Turn mixture into a greased 1½-quart casserole. Sprinkle Parmesan cheese over top. Bake, covered, in a 350° oven for about 30 minutes or until heated through. Makes 6 servings.

Per serving: 17 grams protein, 33 grams carbohydrate, 69 milligrams cholesterol, 334 calories.

Vegetable Kebabs

(Pictured on page 278)

If you are serving meat eaters as well as vegetarians at your next barbecue, plan on Vegetable Kebabs for everyone. It's hard for even a meat-and-potato buff to re-sist them. To accompany these skewers of herb-marinated vege-tables, you might serve a Greek-style salad of crisp greens, to-matoes, olives, and feta cheese, along with pilaf and garlic bread.

(Continued on page 279)

Vegetable Kebabs (cont'd.)

1 **small unpeeled eggplant (about ¾ lb.), cut into 2-inch cubes**

2 **large carrots, cut into ½-inch slices**

About 1 dozen small thin-skinned potatoes (2 inches in diameter)

3 **medium-size zucchini, cut crosswise into 1-inch slices**

2 **small red or green bell peppers, seeded and cut into 1-inch squares**

1 **large onion, cut in wedges and layers separated**

About 16 whole large mushrooms

Herb Marinade (recipe follows)

Salt

Cook eggplant in 1 inch boiling water for 3 minutes; drain. Cook carrots in 1 inch boiling water until crisp-tender (about 6 minutes); drain. Cook unpeeled potatoes in 1 inch boiling water just until tender (about 20 minutes); drain and cut in half.

Place eggplant, carrots, potatoes, zucchini, bell peppers, onion, and mushrooms in a plastic bag. Prepare herb marinade; pour over vegetables. Seal bag and refrigerate for 2 hours or until next day.

Drain and reserve marinade from vegetables. Onto 8 sturdy metal skewers, alternately thread vegetables. Place on a lightly greased grill 4 to 6 inches above a solid bed of low-glowing coals. Cook, turning often and basting with reserved marinade, for 10 to 15 minutes or until vegetables are tender. Sprinkle lightly with salt before serving. (Remaining marinade

Everything tastes better when it's grilled outdoors—including herb-marinated vegetable Kebabs (recipe on page 277 and above). Add Fruited Rice Pilaf (recipe on page 287), and Hummus (recipe on page 234) to scoop up with whole wheat pocket bread, and you have a perfect Middle Eastern vegetarian barbecue.

can be refrigerated up to 2 weeks and used again.) Makes 4 servings of 2 skewers each.

Per serving: 12 grams protein, 71 grams carbohydrate, no cholesterol, 385 calories.

Herb Marinade. In a bowl, combine ¾ cup **salad oil;** ¼ cup **white wine vinegar;** 2 cloves **garlic** (minced or pressed); 1 teaspoon *each* **Dijon mustard, dry basil,** and **oregano** leaves; ½ teaspoon *each* **marjoram** leaves and **dry rosemary;** and ¼ teaspoon **pepper.**

Stuffed Chard or Grape Leaves

These toothsome little rolls take on a different character depending on their wrapper. Chard wrappers have a pleasant bitter flavor that contrasts with the filling of fruit, nuts, and rice. Grape leaves lend a more pickled, winy flavor.

¼ **cup olive oil or salad oil**

¼ **cup pine nuts or slivered almonds**

2 **large onions, chopped**

½ **cup chopped parsley**

2 **cups cooked brown rice**

½ **cup raisins**

4 **teaspoons dill weed**

½ **teaspoon *each* salt and ground cinnamon**

¾ **teaspoon ground allspice**

⅛ **teaspoon ground red pepper (cayenne)**

1 **tablespoon lemon juice**

40 **small or 20 large Swiss chard leaves, or 1 jar (8 oz.) grape leaves**

2 **tablespoons water**

Heat oil in a wide frying pan over medium heat; add nuts and cook, stirring, until golden. Remove nuts with a slotted spoon and set aside. Add onions to pan and cook, stirring frequently, until golden brown (15 to 20 minutes). Add parsley and cook for 2 minutes. Remove

pan from heat and stir in rice, raisins, dill, salt, cinnamon, allspice, red pepper, and lemon juice. Stir gently to blend.

If using chard, wash leaves, cut off stems, and save for another use. Cut large leaves in half lengthwise; leave small leaves whole. Drop leaves into a large kettle of boiling water and blanch for 1 minute; drain. Plunge leaves into a bowl of cold water to cool, then drain again. Spread leaves, veined side down, on a flat surface. Place 1 scant tablespoon filling near stem end, fold in leaf's sides, and roll up.

If using grape leaves, drain, rinse with cold water, and drain again. Spread leaves, veined side up, on a flat surface; cut off stems. Place 1 scant tablespoon filling near stem end, fold sides in, then roll up.

Arrange filled leaves, seam side down, in a single layer in a greased baking pan. Sprinkle with the water. If made ahead, cover and refrigerate. Bake, covered, in a 350° oven for about 25 minutes (35 minutes, if refrigerated) or until hot. Makes 8 servings.

Per serving: 5 grams protein, 29 grams carbohydrate, no cholesterol, 206 calories.

Sesame Tofu Sticks

Marinated in teriyaki sauce and coated in a sesame seed mixture, these tofu sticks come out crusty on the outside but remain creamy on the inside. Steamed or stir-fried vegetables and rice or pilaf would go well with this dish.

About 1 pound medium-firm tofu

Teriyaki Sauce (recipe follows)

½ **cup whole wheat flour**

¼ **cup sesame seeds**

2 **tablespoons salad oil**

3 **green onions (including tops), thinly sliced**

(Continued on next page)

...Sesame Tofu Sticks (cont'd.)

Place tofu in a colander and let drain for 10 minutes. Meanwhile, prepare teriyaki sauce. Cut tofu in domino-shaped pieces and marinate in teriyaki sauce for 15 minutes, turning to coat well. Meanwhile, combine flour and sesame seeds. Lift tofu from marinade, drain briefly, then dip in flour mixture to coat all sides.

Heat 1 tablespoon of the oil in a wide frying pan over medium heat; add half the tofu and cook until lightly browned (about 4 minutes on each side). Remove from pan and keep warm. Add the remaining 1 tablespoon oil to cook the remaining tofu. Serve warm, sprinkled with green onion, and pass remaining teriyaki sauce for dipping. Makes 4 servings.

Per serving: 14 grams protein, 12 grams carbohydrate, no cholesterol, 293 calories.

Teriyaki Sauce. Combine ⅓ cup **soy sauce,** 2 tablespoons *each* **sugar** and **dry sherry,** ¾ teaspoon grated **fresh ginger** or ¼ teaspoon ground ginger, and 2 cloves **garlic** (minced or pressed).

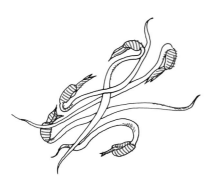

Mushroom Cabbage Rolls

We found the long, broad leaves of Chinese cabbage easier to roll than regular cabbage. If you can't buy Chinese cabbage, core a whole head of regular cabbage and steam it for 5 minutes. When it's cool, carefully peel off the large outer leaves to use in this recipe.

1 large head (about 3 lbs.) Chinese cabbage (napa cabbage)
1 tablespoon *each* salad oil and butter or margarine
1 pound mushrooms, sliced
1 large onion, chopped
1 clove garlic, minced or pressed
1½ cups cooked wheat berries (page 293) or cooked brown rice
½ teaspoon salt
   Dash of pepper
1 cup (4 oz.) shredded jack cheese
⅓ cup grated Parmesan cheese
   Fresh Tomato Sauce (page 274) or 1 jar (about 15 oz.) meatless marinara sauce

Cut off core end of cabbage and remove torn outer leaves. Separate remaining leaves and select 12 large ones (save inside leaves for another use). In a large kettle of boiling salted water, cook 3 or 4 of these large leaves at a time just until limp (about 2 minutes). Lift from water and let drain and cool.

Heat salad oil and butter in a wide frying pan over medium-high heat. Add mushrooms, onion, and garlic; cook, stirring occasionally, until vegetables are soft and pan juices have evaporated. Stir in wheat berries, salt, and pepper; cook for 1 minute. Remove pan from heat and stir in jack cheese and Parmesan.

Spoon an equal amount of filling onto base of each leaf, and roll halfway to enclose. Fold sides in, then continue rolling up. Place rolls, seam side down, in a shallow 2-quart baking dish. If made ahead, cover and refrigerate.

Bake, covered, in a 350° oven for 30 minutes (40 minutes, if refrigerated) or until hot throughout. Heat tomato sauce or marinara sauce to spoon over each serving. Makes six servings of 2 rolls each.

Per serving (including fresh tomato sauce): 15 grams protein, 27 grams carbohydrate, 30 milligrams cholesterol, 259 calories.

Armenian Vegetable Casserole

French cooks have their ratatouille; Armenian cooks have this hearty vegetable dish, called *tourlu.* You can serve it in wide soup bowls with a mound of yogurt on top to melt down into the marvelous juices.

½ pound green beans
1 medium-size (about 1 lb.) eggplant, unpeeled, and cut into 1-inch cubes
2 large onions, cut into 1-inch cubes
3 medium-size carrots, cut into ¾-inch-thick slanting slices
2 large stalks celery, cut into ½-inch thick slices
1 large red or green bell pepper, seeded, cut into 1-inch squares
2 large thin-skinned potatoes, peeled and cut into 1½-inch cubes
1 can (about 1 lb.) pear-shaped tomatoes
¼ cup olive oil or salad oil
½ cup catsup
   About 2 teaspoons salt
1½ teaspoons *each* sugar and dry basil
¼ teaspoon pepper
3 small zucchini
1 cup plain yogurt

Snap off ends of beans and cut into 2-inch lengths. Combine in a 5-quart or larger casserole with eggplant, onions, carrots, celery, bell pepper, and potatoes.

Drain juice from tomatoes into casserole. Chop tomatoes and add to casserole, along with olive oil, catsup, salt, sugar, basil, and pepper; stir gently. Cover casserole and bake in a 350° oven for 1½ hours or until vegetables are almost tender, removing lid and basting vegetables with juices about *every* 30 minutes.

Meanwhile, remove ends of zucchini; cut zucchini into ½-inch slices. Remove casserole from oven and gently mix in zucchini. Return to oven and bake, uncovered, for 20 to 30 minutes or until vegetables are tender. Serve hot or at room temperature with a generous spoonful of yogurt on each serving. Makes 8 servings.

Per serving: 6 grams protein, 29 grams carbohydrate, 2 milligrams cholesterol, 198 calories.

Savory Vegetables & Tofu

(Pictured on page 294)

Try cooking your vegetables the Chinese way—in seasoned liquid. It lets vegetables keep their color while they absorb flavor from the liquid. To serve, arrange the vegetables in a ring and place a tofu-mushroom mélange in the center.

About 1 pound medium-firm tofu

Cooking Sauce (recipe follows)

½ **teaspoon salt**

1 **pound broccoli, green beans, or carrots**

4 **cups water**

1 **teaspoon** *each* **salt and sugar**

2 **quarter-size slices fresh ginger, crushed**

1 **tablespoon** *each* **salad oil and dry sherry**

4 **tablespoons salad oil**

¼ **pound mushrooms, quartered**

1 **tablespoon dry sherry**

½ **teaspoon sugar**

Place tofu in a colander and let drain for 15 minutes. Meanwhile, prepare cooking sauce and set aside. Cut tofu in domino-shaped pieces, and place between paper towels; gently press out excess water. Sprinkle with the ½ teaspoon salt and set aside.

If you use broccoli, cut off flowerets (if large, cut in half) and slash stems. Peel thick stalks and thinly slice. If you use green beans,

remove ends and strings; cut in 2-inch-long slanting slices. If you use carrots, cut in ¼-inch-thick slanting slices.

In a 3-quart pan over medium heat, place water, the 1 teaspoon *each* salt and sugar, ginger, and the 1 tablespoon *each* oil and sherry. Bring to a simmer.

Heat 2 tablespoons of the salad oil in a wide frying pan over high heat. Add mushrooms and cook, stirring, until golden. Add sherry and the ½ teaspoon sugar and cook until liquid evaporates; remove mushrooms and set aside. Reduce heat to medium and add the remaining 2 tablespoons oil. Add tofu and cook until flecked with brown (about 3 minutes on each side). Return mushrooms to pan. Stir cooking sauce, pour into pan, and cook, stirring gently, until sauce bubbles and thickens. Keep hot.

Bring seasoned water to a boil. Drop in vegetables. Cook until crisp-tender (about 4 minutes); drain, then discard ginger. To serve, arrange vegetables around edges of a serving platter. Pour tofu mixture into center. Makes 4 servings.

Per serving: 14 grams protein, 15 grams carbohydrate, .4 milligrams cholesterol, 299 calories.

Cooking Sauce. In a bowl, blend ½ cup **vegetable stock** (page 245), 2 tablespoons **soy sauce,** 1 tablespoon **dry sherry,** 1 teaspoon **sugar,** 2 teaspoons **cornstarch,** and ¼ teaspoon **sesame oil.**

Creamy Spinach-Artichoke Casserole

Just to prove once again that vegetarian cooking doesn't have to be time-consuming, here's a quick but elegant casserole that can be assembled ahead and baked when your guests arrive.

1 **jar (6½ oz.) marinated artichoke hearts**

¼ **pound mushrooms, thinly sliced**

1 **small onion, chopped**

1 **clove garlic, minced or pressed**

2 **packages (10 oz.** *each***) frozen chopped spinach, thawed**

1 **can (10½ oz.) condensed cream of mushroom soup**

½ **cup sour cream**

2 **eggs, beaten**

¼ **teaspoon** *each* **oregano leaves, ground nutmeg, and white pepper**

½ **teaspoon lemon juice**

1 **cup crushed seasoned croutons**

Drain artichoke hearts, reserving marinade; set artichokes aside. Place marinade in a wide frying pan and add mushrooms, onion, and garlic. Cook over medium-high heat, stirring occasionally, until onion is limp. Remove pan from heat.

Squeeze spinach to remove moisture. Add spinach to mushroom mixture along with soup, sour cream, eggs, oregano, nutmeg, pepper, and lemon juice. Stir until well blended.

Spoon half the spinach mixture into a greased 1½-quart shallow casserole. Arrange artichokes on top and spoon remaining spinach mixture over them. Sprinkle crushed croutons over the top. Bake, uncovered, in a 325° oven for 35 to 40 minutes or until custard is set. Let stand for 5 minutes before serving. Makes 6 servings.

Per serving: 7 grams protein, 17 grams carbohydrate, 96 milligrams cholesterol, 171 calories.

Almond-Rice Stuffed Peppers

Brown rice or wheat berries give the stuffing for these peppers a satisfying chewiness. You might

...Almond-Rice Stuffed Peppers (cont'd.)

serve them with steamed broccoli and Quick Corn Bread (page 298). Double Mushroom Soup (page 247) would be a good first course.

3 large red or green bell peppers
Boiling water
2 cups cooked brown rice or wheat berries (page 293)
¾ cup chopped almonds
2 green onions (including tops) thinly sliced
1 large tomato, peeled, seeded, and chopped
¼ cup chopped parsley
1½ cups (6 oz.) shredded Cheddar cheese
2 eggs, lightly beaten
½ teaspoon each Worcestershire and dry basil
Garlic salt
Pepper

Cut peppers lengthwise through stems; remove stems and seeds. Drop pepper halves into boiling water; boil, uncovered, for 2 minutes, then plunge into cold water and drain well.

Stir together rice, almonds, green onions, tomato, parsley, 1 cup of the cheese, eggs, Worcestershire, basil, and garlic salt and pepper to taste. Mound mixture into pepper shells. Place peppers in a shallow baking pan; sprinkle tops equally with remaining ½ cup cheese. If made ahead, cover and refrigerate.

Bake, uncovered, in a 375° oven for about 35 minutes (45 minutes, if refrigerated) or until filling is piping hot. Makes 6 servings.

Per serving: 15 grams protein, 22 grams carbohydrate, 112 milligrams cholesterol, 320 calories.

India-spiced Eggplant
(Pictured on facing page)

In India, most curried foods are seasoned with individual spices rather than curry powder, and this eggplant dish is no exception. The various spices meld into a flavor that's distinctive, delicious, and not overly hot. This is especially good topped with raita—a yogurt-based salad (page 267).

1 large eggplant or 2 small ones (2 pounds *total*)
2 tablespoons salad oil
½ teaspoon cumin seeds
1 tablespoon minced fresh ginger
1 medium-size red onion, coarsely sliced
1 teaspoon turmeric
½ green pepper, seeded and coarsely chopped
2 teaspoons ground coriander
1 teaspoon *each* ground cumin, paprika, and salt
¼ teaspoon black pepper
1 large tomato, peeled and chopped
¼ cup water
¼ cup coarsely chopped fresh coriander (cilantro)

Place whole eggplant in a shallow pan and bake in a 400° oven until very soft (about 50 minutes). Cool slightly. Cut a slit in eggplant and scoop out pulp; discard large seed pockets, skin, and stem. Coarsely chop pulp; place in a colander to drain.

Heat oil in a wide frying pan over medium heat. Add cumin seeds, ginger, and onion and cook, stirring occasionally, until onion is soft. Stir in turmeric, green pepper, coriander, ground cumin, paprika, salt, pepper, and tomato. Cook, stirring occasionally, until tomato releases its juices (about 5 minutes). Add water and bring to a simmer. Reduce heat to low and simmer, uncovered, for 10 minutes. Stir in chopped eggplant and cook for 5 minutes to heat through and blend flavors. Just before serving, stir in coriander. Makes 6 servings.

Per serving: 2 grams protein, 11 grams carbohydrate, no cholesterol, 80 calories.

Vegetable Curry
(Pictured on facing page)

This Indian curry takes easily to improvisation. You start with a basic method of cooking and combination of spices, then add vegetables that appeal to you. If you cook vegetables other than those suggested here, and the textures vary, add the firmest vegetables to the pan first. Then, toward the end of the cooking time, add the more tender vegetables.

2 tablespoons salad oil
1 large onion, coarsely chopped
1 teaspoon *each* salt and curry powder
½ teaspoon pepper
¼ teaspoon *each* ground ginger and cumin
⅛ teaspoon ground red pepper (cayenne)
2 bay leaves
2 medium-size carrots, cut into ¼-inch slices
½ pound green beans, cut into 2-inch lengths
1 red or green bell pepper, seeded and cut into 1-inch pieces
½ small cauliflower, separated into flowerets
½ pound broccoli, separated into flowerets, stems peeled and sliced
½ pound butternut or banana squash, peeled and cut into 1-inch pieces
¾ cup water

Pour oil into a 5-quart pan and place over medium heat. Add

(Continued on page 284)

Feast from India features, clockwise from top left, deep-fried bread called Puris (page 301), Vegetable Curry (above), India-spiced Eggplant (at left) encircled by fried mint leaves, and Savory Fried Rice (page 284). Small bowls contain Raita— Mint & Coriander, and Cucumber & Tomato; recipes are on page 267.

...Vegetable Curry (cont'd.)

onion and cook, stirring occasionally, until soft. Stir in salt, curry powder, pepper, ginger, cumin, and red pepper; cook for 1 minute. Add bay leaves, carrots, beans, bell pepper, cauliflower, broccoli, squash, and water. Cover and bring to a boil; reduce heat and simmer until vegetables are just tender (about 20 minutes). Remove cover, increase heat, and cook for a few minutes to reduce pan juices by one-half. Remove bay leaves before serving. Makes 6 servings.

Per serving: 5 grams protein, 33 grams carbohydrate, no cholesterol, 127 calories.

Savory Fried Rice

(Pictured on page 283)

This spicy rice and vegetable dish from India is a dazzling yellow, thanks to turmeric. Savory Fried Rice can be an entrée on its own, or it can share the honors with steamed vegetables or a curried dish.

1½ cups long-grain rice
  6 whole cloves
  3 whole black peppers
  ¼ teaspoon turmeric
  ½ teaspoon salt
2½ cups water
  6 whole cardamom seeds
  2 small leeks
  2 tablespoons butter or
      margarine
  1 medium-size carrot,
      shredded
  1 cup frozen peas, thawed
  ¼ cup *each* cashews and raisins
  3 hard-cooked eggs, cut in
      wedges (optional)

Place rice, cloves, black peppers, turmeric, salt, and water in a 2-quart pan. Crush cardamom seeds slightly with your fingers and add both husks and seeds to rice.

Cover pan and bring to a boil over high heat. Reduce heat to low and simmer, covered, until rice is tender and liquid is absorbed (about 20 minutes).

Meanwhile, wash and trim leeks. Cut crosswise in ½-inch-thick slices; use the tender part of the green tops as well as the white. Separate the white part into rings. Melt butter in a wide frying pan over medium heat. Add leeks and carrot and cook, stirring occasionally, for 5 minutes. Add peas, cashews, and raisins and cook for 3 minutes.

When rice is cooked, stir in leek mixture. Turn onto a serving platter and garnish with egg wedges if desired. Makes 6 servings.

Per serving (including eggs): 9 grams protein, 49 grams carbohydrate, 138 milligrams cholesterol, 321 calories.

Baked Lentils with Cheese

Lentils and vegetables bake together in this well-seasoned casserole. During the last few minutes, you stir in cheese to complement the taste—and the protein.

  1 package (12 oz.) lentils,
      rinsed
  2 cups water
  1 bay leaf
  2 teaspoons salt
  ¼ teaspoon *each* pepper, and
      marjoram, sage, and thyme
      leaves
  2 large onions, chopped
  2 cloves garlic, minced or
      pressed
  1 can (about 1 lb.) tomatoes
  2 large carrots, cut in
      ⅛-inch-thick slices
  1 stalk celery, thinly sliced
  1 green pepper, seeded and
      chopped
  2 tablespoons chopped parsley
1½ cups (6 oz.) shredded sharp
      Cheddar cheese

Place lentils in a shallow 3-quart casserole or 9 by 13-inch baking dish along with water, bay leaf, salt, pepper, marjoram, sage, thyme, onions, garlic, and tomatoes (break up with a spoon) and their liquid.

Bake, covered, in a 375° oven for 30 minutes. Remove from oven and stir in carrots and celery. Cover and bake for about 40 more minutes or until vegetables are tender. Remove from oven and stir in green pepper and parsley; sprinkle cheese on top. Return to oven and bake, uncovered, for 5 more minutes or until cheese is melted. Makes 6 servings.

Per serving: 26 grams protein, 55 grams carbohydrate, 28 milligrams cholesterol, 402 calories.

Ricotta-stuffed Squash

(Pictured on page 286)

The favorite flavors of Italian cooking season this ricotta-spinach filling for zucchini, crookneck, or pattypan squash. A whole-grain pilaf or buttered pasta sprinkled with Parmesan cheese would be excellent with this dish.

  8 crookneck or zucchini
      squash (*each* about 6 inches
      long), or 8 large pattypan
      squash
  2 tablespoons butter or
      margarine
  1 small onion, finely chopped
  1 clove garlic, minced or
      pressed
  1 package (10 oz.) frozen
      chopped spinach, thawed
  2 eggs
  2 cups (1 lb.) ricotta cheese
  ¼ cup grated Parmesan cheese
  1 tablespoon chopped parsley
  ½ teaspoon *each* salt, dry basil,
      and oregano leaves
      Dash of pepper
      Tomato Sauce (recipe
      follows)

Trim ends off squash; cut squash in half lengthwise. With a teaspoon scoop out seeds and part of pulp (save pulp for soup stock), leaving shells ½ inch thick. Steam squash shells over boiling water until crisp-tender (about 5 minutes). Plunge in cold water, drain well, and set aside.

In a small frying pan over medium heat, melt 1 tablespoon of the butter. Add onion and garlic and cook, stirring occasionally, until onion is limp. Squeeze spinach to remove excess moisture. Add spinach to onion mixture and cook for 1 minute; let cool.

In a bowl, combine eggs with ricotta, stirring until well blended. Stir in Parmesan, parsley, salt, basil, oregano, pepper, and spinach mixture. Allowing about 3 tablespoons filling per squash, mound filling inside squash shells. Arrange filled shells in shallow baking pans. Melt the remaining 1 tablespoon butter; brush over cut surfaces of squash. If made ahead, cover and refrigerate.

Bake, uncovered, in a 350° oven for about 20 minutes (30 minutes, if refrigerated) or until filling is piping hot. While squash is baking, prepare tomato sauce to spoon over squash before serving. Makes 8 servings.

Per serving (including tomato sauce): 13 grams protein, 10 grams carbohydrate, 95 milligrams cholesterol, 184 calories.

Tomato Sauce. In a 1-quart pan, simmer together for 5 minutes 1 can (15 oz.) **tomato sauce,** 2 tablespoons chopped **parsley,** 1 clove **garlic** (minced), 1 teaspoon **dry basil,** ½ teaspoon **oregano leaves,** and **salt** and **pepper** to taste.

 # Recipe Adaptations for Meat Eaters

Many of the recipes in this book can be adapted for meat eaters. We point this out because many people looking into vegetarian cooking for health or budget reasons want to reduce the amount of meat in their diets, but don't want to eliminate it completely. Some continue to eat small quantities of all types of meat; others confine themselves to chicken and fish.

Sometimes only one or two members of a household want to eat meatless meals. Teenagers interested in vegetarian diets are often confronted with the practical objection that it's too much trouble to cook two separate kinds of food. This leaves them to fend for themselves or glower through family meals and make disparaging remarks about carnivores.

Here are some suggestions for adapting the recipes in this book to satisfy families with a member who eats to the beat of a different drum. The adaptations will also please those cutting back, but not eliminating meat from their diet. An added bonus is that most of the adaptations are budget stretchers making good use of leftover meat. Remember that the addition of meat will invalidate the nutritional data which follows each recipe, increasing protein, cholesterol, and calories.

Soups. For the vegetarian in the family, reserve a portion of soup before adding meat. We suggest adding 1 cup shredded cooked pork to Hot & Sour Soup (page 249); 1 can (8 oz.) minced clams, drained, to Tomato Corn Chowder (page 249); 1 cup diced cooked ham to Lemony Lentil Soup (page 250); sliced and browned Italian sausage to Fresh Vegetable Basil Soup (page 253)

Salads. Add 1 cup diced cooked chicken to all or part of Zucchini Fiesta Salad (page 239). Fill half the Salad-in-a-Boat (page 239) with your favorite chicken or ham salad, half with egg salad. Serve the Bulgur Supper Salad (page 240) surrounded by pieces of roast chicken or slices of roast beef or lamb. Add 1 cup small cooked shrimp to Quick Artichoke Pasta Salad (page 241). Garnish half of Perfect Protein Salad (page 236) with slivers of roast beef.

Entrées. Most vegetarian entrées can be served in smaller portions of accompany roast beef, chicken, lamb, or fish. You can add diced cooked chicken or beef to Almond-Rice Stuffed Peppers (page 281). Add cooked ground beef to Bulgar Mexicana (page 272), Mushroom Cabbage Rolls (page 280), or Cracked Wheat Vegetable Pilaf (page 287). Green Enchiladas (page 271) can be filled with cooked chicken or ground beef; Sonora Pizza (page 272) can have a layer of cooked ground beef added to the toppings.

Stir-fry strips of beef to accompany Savory Vegetables & Tofu (page 281), or marinate chicken wings in the same teriyaki sauce you use for Sesame Tofu Sticks (page 279), then bake.

Cooked ground lamb can be rolled up in some of the Stuffed Chard or Grape Leaves (page 279). You can make Whole Wheat Zucchini Pizza (page 274) as a combination order; half vegetarian, half pepperoni or sausage. Layered Chili (page 269) can be made *con carne* with ground beef.

Cracked Wheat Vegetable Pilaf

Soaking instead of cooking is a traditional Middle Eastern way to prepare bulgur—that way the grains stay separate and slightly chewy, even when baked in this colorful pilaf.

- 1 cup bulgur wheat
- 1 cup boiling vegetable stock (page 245)
- 2 tablespoons chopped parsley
- ¼ cup diced green or red bell pepper or carrot
- 3 green onions (including tops), thinly sliced
- 2 cups (8 oz.) shredded Cheddar or jack cheese
- 1 cup whole kernel corn, cut off cob, or frozen and thawed
- 1 egg, lightly beaten
- 1 can (8 oz.) tomato sauce
- 1 teasoon dry basil
- ½ teaspoon *each* oregano leaves and garlic salt
- ¼ teaspoon pepper

In a large bowl, combine bulgur and stock. Stirring occasionally, let stand for about 1 hour or until liquid is absorbed. Stir in parsley, bell pepper, onions, cheese, corn, and egg. Add tomato sauce, basil, oregano, garlic salt, and pepper and stir gently. Spoon into a shallow greased 1½-quart casserole. Cover and bake in a 350° oven until heated through (25 to 30 minutes). Makes 6 servings.

Per serving: 15 grams protein, 14 grams carbohydrate, 80 milligrams cholesterol, 312 calories.

Like a sunburst of flavor, arrangement of Ricotta-stuffed Squash (recipe on page 284) around Brown Rice & Carrot Pilaf (recipe on this page) radiates the warmth of good cooking. Pass tomato sauce to spoon over the squash.

Stuffed Zucchini

Stuff extra large zucchini with Cracked Wheat Vegetable Pilaf for an impressive main dish.

Cracked Wheat Vegetable Pilaf (preceding recipe)
3 large zucchini, *each* about 10 inches long and 2 inches wide

Prepare pilaf to the point of baking.

Trim ends of zucchini; cut each zucchini in half lengthwise. Using a spoon, scoop out seeds. Mound pilaf into zucchini halves; place in two 9 by 13-inch pans. Pour about ¼ inch water into each pan.

Bake zucchini, uncovered, in a 375° oven for 35 to 40 minutes or until tender and pilaf is hot. Makes 6 servings.

Per serving: 17 grams protein, 22 grams carbohydrate, 80 milligrams cholesterol, 351 calories.

Fruited Rice Pilaf

(Pictured on page 278)

Brown rice, raisins, dried apricots, dates, and cashews—what a wonderful mixture. You can serve it with Vegetable Kebabs or simply surround it with golden chunks of steamed butternut squash. A yogurt side dish of raita (page 267) would be perfect.

- 1 cup long-grain brown rice
- ½ teaspoon salt
- 2 cups vegetable stock (page 245)
- 2 tablespoons butter or margarine
- ¼ cup cashews
- ¼ cup *each* raisins and coarsely chopped dried apricots and pitted dates

In a 2-quart pan, combine rice, salt, and vegetable stock. Cover and bring to a boil over high heat. Reduce heat to low; and simmer until rice is tender and liquid is absorbed (about 45 minutes).

Meanwhile, in a small frying pan over medium-low heat, melt butter. Add nuts and cook until golden. Remove from pan with a slotted spoon and set aside. Add raisins, apricots, and dates to pan and cook, stirring, for 2 minutes.

When rice is cooked, stir in dried fruits; cover and let stand for 5 minutes. Stir in nuts just before serving. Makes 6 servings.

Per serving: 4 grams protein, 39 grams carbohydrate, 12 milligrams cholesterol, 230 calories.

Brown Rice & Carrot Pilaf

(Pictured on facing page)

Onion and carrot give a pleasant sweetness to this easy pilaf. If you wish to add a crunchy texture, stir in sprouts just before serving.

- 3 tablespoons butter or margarine
- 1 large onion, finely chopped
- 1 cup coarsely shredded carrots
- 1 cup long-grain brown rice
- 2½ cups vegetable stock (page 245)
- ½ teaspoon salt
- ½ cup chopped parsley
- 2 cups bean sprouts (optional)

Melt butter in a 2-quart pan over medium-high heat. Add onion and carrots and cook until onion is soft (about 5 minutes). Stir in rice; continue to cook, stirring, until rice begins to brown slightly. Add stock and salt; cover and simmer until rice is tender and liquid is absorbed (about 45 minutes). Stir in parsley and sprouts, if used, just before serving. Makes 6 servings.

Per serving (including sprouts): 4 grams protein, 32 grams carbohydrates, 31 milligrams cholesterol, 198 calories.

Vegetable Side Dishes

Because ideas for preparing and serving vegetables are always welcome, we've gathered in this section some recipes for quick sauces to dress plain vegetables, and for vegetable combination dishes to give variety to your menus. First, though, we explain in detail two important cooking methods—stir-frying and steaming—that can be adapted to almost any fresh vegetable.

How to Stir-fry

As a technique for cooking vegetables, stir-frying is one of the best. A wok is the traditional piece of equipment to use, but a wide frying pan works, too. You begin by cutting your vegetables into uniform shapes—usually thin slices or pieces that will cook in a few minutes.

To stir-fry, place a wok or wide frying pan over high heat. When the pan is hot, add 1 to 2 tablespoons salad oil for each 1 pound of cut vegetables, and swirl the oil around the pan. When the oil is hot, you can add seasonings, if you wish—such as 1 clove minced garlic and ½ teaspoon minced fresh ginger—and cook just until fragrant. Then add the cut vegetables

and stir-fry for 1 minute to coat them with oil. If you don't wish to add seasonings, add the vegetables to the pan as soon as the oil is hot.

What you do next depends on the vegetable. With a few, such as bean sprouts or tomato or onion wedges, you continue cooking for about another minute. Most vegetables, though, need a little liquid to become tender. Pour in 1 to 3 tablespoons water; then cover and continue cooking until vegetables are crisp-tender. Plan on 2 to 3 minutes for asparagus, bok choy, green peppers, snow peas, and zucchini. More dense vegetables, such as broccoli, carrots, cauliflower, and green beans, should be cooked for 3 to 5 minutes.

If the pan appears dry, add a few more drops water; cover and continue cooking until crisp-tender. You want the vegetables to steam lightly, not to simmer in liquid. The cooking times and amounts of water should be used as flexible guidelines, because the way you cut a vegetable and the intensity of the heat you use both affect the cooking time.

If you wish to cook several vegetables and the textures are different, add firmer vegetables to the pan first and partially cook; then add the more tender vegetables near the end of the cooking time. Better yet, you can cook each vegetable separately and combine them for reheating and blending of flavors.

When the vegetable is cooked, season to taste with salt, pepper, and your favorite herbs; then serve piping hot. Or if you like to serve vegetables in the Chinese manner with a light sauce, combine ½ cup vegetable stock (page 245), 1 tablespoon cornstarch, and 2 teaspoons soy sauce. Add this to the pan of hot cooked vegetables and cook, stirring, until the sauce bubbles and thickens (about 30 seconds).

Cooking with Steam

While stir-frying is very active cooking, the opposite is true of steaming. You simply place vegetables *over* boiling water, then cover and let them steam for about the same length of time you would cook vegetables *in* the boiling water. Because swirling vapors, rather than water, tenderize the vegetables, there's little loss of vitamins and minerals.

Many types of steaming equipment are available, from compartmentalized steamers that let you steam several vegetables at a time, to bamboo steaming baskets that you set in a wok. One of the least expensive steamers is a collapsible metal steaming basket that you place inside another cooking pot.

Steamed vegetables have a light flavor. They need little seasoning to emphasize their freshness. If you wish, you can sprinkle them with salt, pepper, and herbs before cooking, or season them after cooking; finally, top them with butter or dress them with a flavorful sauce.

If you plan to serve steamed vegetables in a cold salad, or if you intend to marinate them for a first course, cool them quickly in cold water after cooking, then drain and refrigerate them.

Vegetable Sauces

To give a finished look and extra flavor to hot steamed vegetables, dress them with one of the following hot or cold sauces. For scale watchers, we've included some low-calorie variations of traditional sauces, too.

Herbed Tofu Sauce. Drain ½ carton (1-lb. 6-oz. size) **medium-firm tofu.** Pat tofu dry, place in a blender or food processor, and purée until completely smooth (about 5 minutes). Stir in 1¼ teaspoons **celery salt,** 1 tablespoon chopped **parsley,** ½ cup sliced **green onions,** 2 teaspoons **Dijon mustard,** 1 teaspoon prepared **horseradish,** ½ teaspoon **dill weed,** ¼ teaspoon **onion powder,** and 2 cloves **garlic,** pressed. Cover and refrigerate for at least 1 day to blend flavors. Serve cold. Makes 1¼ cups sauce.

Per tablespoon: 3 grams protein, 1 gram carbohydrate, no cholesterol, 28 calories.

Savory Cheese Sauce. In a blender or food processor, place 1 cup **cottage cheese,** ½ cup **plain yogurt,** 1 tablespoon **lemon juice,** 1 teaspoon **sugar,** ¼ teaspoon *each* **salt** and **dill weed,** a dash of **pepper,** and 2 tablespoons *each* chopped **onion** and chopped **parsley.** Purée until mixture is smooth. Serve cold. Makes 1½ cups.

Per tablespoon: 1.5 grams protein, 1 gram carbohydrate, 2 milligrams cholesterol, 13 calories.

Green Herb Sauce (*pictured on page 291*). In a blender, place ½ cup packed **watercress** leaves and small stems (or spinach leaves), ½ cup packed **parsley** sprigs, 1 large **shallot** or 1 large green onion and top (sliced), ½ teaspoon *each* **tarragon** and **thyme** leaves, ½ teaspoon **salt,** ¾ teaspoon **dry mustard,** 2 tablespoons **white wine vinegar,** and 1 **egg;** whirl until liquefied. With motor running,

begin pouring 1 cup **salad oil** into blender in a small stream; add oil very slowly at first, then a little faster as sauce begins to thicken. Serve cold. Makes 1⅔ cups.

Per tablespoon: .5 grams protein, .5 grams carbohydrate, 9 milligrams cholesterol, 82 calories.

Parmesan Sour Cottage Sauce (*pictured on page 291*). Place 1 pint (2 cups) **cottage cheese** in a fine wire strainer. Hold under cold running water and stir gently until water runs clear; let drain for about 20 minutes. Place cheese in a blender or food processor and add ¼ cup **skim milk** and 2 tablespoons **lemon juice.** Purée until completely smooth (about 5 minutes). Stir in ¼ cup grated **Parmesan** cheese and 2 tablespoons minced **green onion.** Serve cold. Makes 1½ cups.

Per tablespoon: 3 grams protein, 1 gram carbohydrate, 5 milligrams cholesterol, 25 calories.

Broiled Cheese Topping. In a bowl, combine ½ cup **mayonnaise,** ¼ cup grated **Parmesan cheese,** 2 tablespoons chopped **parsley,** and 2 teaspoons **lemon juice.** Beat 2 **egg whites** just until stiff, moist peaks form; fold into mayonnaise mixture. Spread topping evenly over 2 pounds hot steamed **vegetables,** such as green beans, broccoli, or asparagus. Broil, 6 to 8 inches from heat, until topping is golden brown. Serve hot. Makes 6 servings.

Per serving (including topping and vegetable): 5 grams protein, 9 grams carbohydrate, 16 milligrams cholesterol, 188 calories.

Yogurt Hollaindaise (*pictured on page 291*). In the top of a double boiler, stir together 1 cup plain **yogurt** and 2 **whole eggs.** Add ¾ teaspoon **salt,** 1 teaspoon **sugar,** and ¼ teaspoon **liquid hot pepper seasoning.** Place over barely simmering water and cook, stirring constantly, until thickened (8 to 10 minutes). Serve hot.

(Continued on next page)

If made ahead, reheat, stirring, in top of double boiler over hot (not boiling) water. Makes 1⅓ cups.

Per tablespoon: 1 gram protein, 1 gram carbohydrate, 25 milligrams cholesterol, 14 calories.

Vegetable Combinations

The following recipes combine two vegetables or a vegetable with fruit, and they're especially delicious with grain entrées.

Curried Carrots with Fruit. Cut 4 **carrots** in ¼-inch-thick slanting slices; you should have 3 cups carrots. Drain 1 can (11 oz.) **mandarin oranges,** reserving 3 tablespoons of the liquid.

In a wide frying pan over medium-high heat, melt 2 tablespoons **butter** or margarine. Add carrots and reserved orange liquid. Cook, covered, until carrots are tender and most of liquid has evaporated (about 6 minutes).

In a cup, stir together 1 teaspoon **curry powder,** ½ teaspoon **salt,** and 1 teaspoon **lemon juice** until blended. Stir into carrots along with 1 cup whole seedless **grapes.** Cover and cook just until heated through. Stir in orange segments and 1 **green onion** (thinly sliced). Makes 6 servings.

Per serving: 1 gram protein, 17 grams carbohydrate, 12 milligrams cholesterol, 105 calories.

Stewed Tomatoes with Cheese. Drain a large (28-oz.) can **tomatoes** into a 2-quart pan. Coarsely chop tomatoes and add to pan. Cook, uncovered, over medium-high heat until a third of the liquid has evaporated. Season to taste with **salt** and **pepper.** Have ready ½ cup *each* diced **jack cheese** and **whole wheat croutons** and 2 tablespoons diced **green pepper.**

Just before serving, reheat tomatoes, add cheese, croutons, and green pepper, and stir just until cheese begins to melt. Makes 4 servings.

Per serving: 6 grams protein, 11 grams carbohydrate, 14 milligrams cholesterol, 106 calories.

Tomatoes Provençal. In a bowl, combine 1 tablespoon *each* finely chopped **garlic** (about 3 large cloves), chopped **parsley,** and fine dry **whole wheat bread crumbs,** ⅛ teaspoon **salt,** and a dash of **pepper.**

Core and halve 4 medium-size **tomatoes.** Squeeze gently to remove seeds and juice. Place tomatoes, cut side up, in a small baking dish. Drizzle with 1 tablespoon **olive oil** or salad oil. Bake, uncovered, in a 400° oven for 10 minutes. Sprinkle crumb mixture over tomatoes and continue baking for 15 minutes longer or until tomatoes are soft throughout. Makes 4 servings.

Per serving: 1.5 grams protein, 6 grams carbohydrate, .5 milligrams cholesterol, 57 calories.

Sun-gold Sprouts & Onions. Peel ½ pound small **white boiling onions;** score root end of each onion with a small cross. Wash and trim ½ pound **Brussels sprouts;** score stem end of each sprout with a small cross. Cut 1 small **carrot** crosswise into thin slices.

In a 3-quart pan over medium heat, bring 3 cups **water,** ½ teaspoon **salt,** and 1 teaspoon **sugar** to a boil. Add onions, reduce heat, and simmer, uncovered, for 15 minutes. Add sprouts and carrot and continue cooking, uncovered, for 8 minutes or until sprouts are crisp-tender. Drain. Add 1 tablespoon **butter** or margarine and a **dash** of pepper. Makes 4 servings.

Per serving: 3.5 grams protein, 11 grams carbohydrate, 9 milligrams cholesterol, 77 calories.

Winter Squash with Apples. Seed, peel, and cut 1 pound **winter squash** (acorn, butternut, banana, or Hubbard) into ½-inch cubes. You should have 4 cups. Peel and core 1 **apple** and cut into ½-inch cubes. Melt 3 tablespoons **butter** or margarine in a wide frying pan over medium-high heat. Add squash, apple, ¼ cup **water,** and 2 teaspoons **lemon juice.** Cover and cook, stirring occasionally, just until tender and liquid is absorbed (4 to 5 minutes). Stir in ¼ cup firmly packed **brown sugar,** ¼ teaspoon *each* **salt** and **ground cinnamon,** and ⅛ teaspoon **ground nutmeg.** Garnish with ¼ cup toasted sliced **almonds** just before serving. Makes 6 servings.

Per serving: 2 grams protein, 21 grams carbohydrate, 18 milligrams cholesterol, 154 calories.

Cauliflower with Broccoli Sauce. Remove flowerets from 1 pound **broccoli;** peel stems and slice. Steam stems and flowerets over boiling water until tender (10 to 12 minute). Place broccoli in a blender and add ¼ cup **vegetable stock** (page 245), ½ cup **sour cream,** 1 tablespoon **lemon juice,** and ⅓ cup grated **Parmesan cheese.** Whirl until smooth. Season to taste with **salt** and **white pepper.**

Separate 1 medium-size head **cauliflower** into flowerets. Steam over boiling water until crisp-tender (10 to 12 minutes). Reheat broccoli sauce over low heat, then spoon sauce over cauliflower. Sprinkle ¼ cup **sunflower seeds** over the top. Makes 6 servings.

Per serving: 9 grams protein, 13 grams carbohydrate, 13 milligrams cholesterol, 122 calories.

A simple hot steamed vegetable— the freshest the season has to offer— goes to dinner in style with a special sauce. Clockwise from top right, you see Parmesan Sour Cottage Sauce, Yogurt Hollandaise, and Green Herb Sauce. The recipes are on page 289.

Breads & Breakfast

Moments to cherish: Buttering a still-warm slice of Wheat Berry Batter Bread (page 293) that's been filling your kitchen with an enticing aroma as it bakes. Passing around a platter of high-rising Cheddar Cheese Popovers (page 300). Tucking into a stack of Oatmeal Pancakes topped with Blueberry Sauce (page 304). Watching butter and syrup melt into the little indented squares on golden, light-textured Orange Yogurt Waffles (page 305).

This chapter is devoted to proving that it's pure pleasure to eat the nourishing-good whole grains so important in a vegetarian diet. The first section features breads, rolls, and muffins that can be part of almost any meal. Then the chapter focuses on breakfast foods, including granola-type cereals and some blender-quick breakfast beverages, as well as pancakes and waffles.

The collection of breads includes recipes for novices, plus recipes for more experienced bakers. Both beginners and old hands at bread baking will find the Whole Wheat Single-rising Dough (page 293) so versatile it might become their standard recipe for a variety of breads and rolls.

For sandwiches, you'll want to sample the attractive Pebble-top Oatmeal Bread (page 293), and the lightly sweetened Maple-Molasses Bread (page 296).

If you want a bread with fruit in it, bake Anadama Bread (page 297), flavored with dates and banana; or try Apple Brown Bread (page 298), a quick bread that's delicious with cream cheese.

For breads with extra protein from cheese, there's a no-knead Casserole Cheese Bread (page 297) that bakes in individual loaves, and Honey-Wheat Buns (page 295) made with cottage cheese and bulgur wheat.

One of our special favorites is Chinese Steamed Buns (page 296). They're made with whole wheat flour and filled with a savory mixture of mushrooms and cashews. The buns are perfect with stir-fried vegetables.

Most of the recipes in this chapter call for whole wheat flour. You can use either the stone ground type (found in health food stores) or the standard whole wheat flour usually found in supermarkets. We find that stone ground whole wheat flour makes a denser loaf that takes a little longer to rise than the standard whole wheat flour. Freshness of the flour is also an important factor in successful bread baking: the fresher the flour—whether stone ground or standard—the better your final baked product will be.

Wheat Berry Batter Bread

If you're new to bread making and need the encouragement of fast results, this is the loaf for you. There's no kneading, and the golden-crusted result is a fine-textured bread studded with whole wheat kernels, called wheat berries.

Because wheat berries take time to precook, and can be used in so many ways, it makes sense to pre-cook at least a cupful at a time. This will produce far more wheat berries than you'll need for one recipe, but you can use the extra cooked berries in pilaf or soup, or freeze them in small quantities for future loaves.

1½ cups all-purpose flour
1 tablespoon sugar
½ teaspoon salt
1 package active dry yeast
1 cup warm water (about 110°)
½ cup cooked, drained, wheat berries (directions follow)
¾ cup whole wheat flour
Cornmeal
1 tablespoon melted butter or margarine

In a bowl, combine all-purpose flour, sugar, salt, and yeast. Gradually beat in the warm water, then beat until dough is very elastic (about 3 minutes at medium speed if using electric mixer). Add wheat berries. Gradually beat in whole wheat flour (at low speed with electric mixer); dough should be very soft and elastic. Cover and let rise in a warm place until doubled (about 45 minutes).

Stir dough down with a wooden spoon. Grease a 4 by 8-inch loaf pan and coat with cornmeal; invert pan and shake out excess. Spoon dough into pan and spread in an even layer. Bake in a 375° oven for about 1 hour or until a skewer inserted in center of loaf comes out clean and crust is golden brown. Brush top with melted butter. Makes 1 loaf; cut into 16 slices.

Per slice: 2 grams protein, 15 grams carbohydrate, 2 milligrams cholesterol, 75 calories.

To precook wheat berries. In a large pan, combine 1 cup **wheat berries** and 5 cups **water.** Cover and let stand for at least 8 hours or until next day. (Or cover pan and bring to a boil over highest heat; boil for 2 minutes, then remove from heat and let stand, still covered, for 1 hour.)

Without draining wheat, bring to a boil over high heat. Reduce heat and simmer until tender (about 1½ hours). Drain well (save liquid for soup stock) and cool. Cover and store in refrigerator or freezer (thaw before using). Makes about 3 cups.

Pebble-top Oatmeal Bread

You can shape this even-textured bread into loaves or rolls to be crowned with an attractive pebble topping of rolled oats.

1 package active dry yeast
¼ cup warm water (about 110°)
¼ cup molasses
4 tablespoons butter or margarine
2 teaspoons salt
¼ cup firmly packed brown sugar
2½ cups regular or quick-cooking rolled oats
1 cup *each* boiling water and cold water
4½ to 5 cups all-purpose flour
3 tablespoons milk

In a small bowl, combine yeast, the warm water, and 1 tablespoon of the molasses; let stand until bubbly (about 15 minutes). In a large bowl, combine butter, remaining molasses, salt, brown sugar, 2 cups of the oats, and boiling water; stir until butter melts. Add cold water

and yeast mixture. Beat in 4 cups of the flour, 1 cup at a time.

Turn dough out onto a floured board; knead until smooth and elastic (10 to 20 minutes), adding flour as needed to prevent sticking. Turn dough over in a greased bowl; cover and let rise in a warm place until doubled (about 1 hour). Punch dough down; knead briefly on a floured board to release air.

To make loaves, divide dough in half and shape each half into a loaf; place in greased 9 by 5-inch loaf pans.

To make rolls, divide dough into 20 equal pieces. Shape each piece into a smooth ball. Place balls about 2 inches apart on greased baking sheets and flatten slightly.

Soften remaining ½ cup rolled oats in milk; dot over tops of loaves or buns. Cover and let rise in a warm place until doubled (about 45 minutes).

Bake loaves in a 350° oven for about 1 hour or until bread sounds hollow when tapped. Turn out on a rack to cool. Bake buns in a 350° oven until lightly browned (15 to 18 minutes). Makes 2 loaves (cut 18 slices per loaf) or 20 buns.

Per slice: 3 grams protein, 19 grams carbohydrate, 8 milligrams cholesterol, 102 calories.

Per bun: 5 grams protein, 34 grams carbohydrate, 13 milligrams cholesterol, 183 calories.

Whole Wheat Single-rising Dough

Even a dedicated bread baker appreciates a yeast dough as speedy as this one—it rises only once.

Its versatility is also a boon. You can bake all of the dough at once or refrigerate it for later baking. You can make the herb and cheese variation that follows the basic recipe. And you can make either dough into loaves or crescent rolls.

(Continued on page 295)

3 cups *each* all-purpose flour and whole wheat flour

½ cup wheat germ

2 packages active dry yeast

1 cup warm water (about 110°)

3 tablespoons sugar

3 teaspoons salt

1 cup warm milk (about 110°)

⅓ cup melted butter or margarine

2 eggs, lightly beaten

In a bowl, mix together all-purpose flour, whole wheat flour, and wheat germ. In a large bowl, dissolve yeast in the warm water. Add sugar, salt, milk, butter, and eggs. Beat in 3 cups of the flour mixture, 1 cup at a time, then beat until dough is elastic (about 5 minutes at medium speed if using electric mixer).

With a heavy-duty mixer or wooden spoon, gradually beat in remaining flour mixture. Dough should be soft, but not too sticky to knead; add additional all-purpose flour if necessary to prevent sticking. Turn dough out onto a floured board and knead just until smooth. Divide in half.

Shape, let rise, and bake dough as suggested below; or turn dough over in a well-greased bowl, cover, and refrigerate for as long as 24 hours. Makes 2 butter-topped loaves (cut 18 slices per loaf) or 48 crescent rolls.

Per slice: 4 grams protein, 17 grams carbohydrate, 21 milligrams cholesterol, 104 calories.

Per crescent roll: 3 grams protein, 14 grams carbohydrate, 19 milligrams cholesterol, 94 calories.

Herb Cheese Dough. Prepare dough as directed above, but when you add eggs, also add 1 teaspoon *each* **oregano** and **basil leaves**; ½ teaspoon *each* **savory leaves, thyme leaves,** and **garlic powder**; ¼ teaspoon **pepper**; and ¼ cup *each* **instant toasted onion** and grated **Parmesan cheese.**

Butter-topped Loaves. Divide dough (wheat or herb) in half and shape each half into a smooth loaf. Place in 2 greased 5 by 9-inch loaf pans. Cover and let rise in a warm place until dough has risen 1 inch above pan rims (about 1½ hours).

Butter a razor blade or sharp knife and make a ¼-inch-deep slash lengthwise down tops of loaves. Drizzle each slash with 1 tablespoon melted **butter** or margarine. Bake in a 375° oven for 45 minutes or until browned. Turn out onto a rack.

Crescent Rolls. Divide dough (wheat or herb) into 4 equal portions; shape each into a smooth ball. On a floured board, roll out each ball into a 12-inch circle, brush with 1 tablespoon melted **butter** or margarine, and cut into 12 equal wedges. Starting from the wide end, roll up each wedge toward the point. Place rolls, points down, 2 inches apart on well-greased baking sheets. Curve each roll slightly and brush lightly with 1 **egg white** beaten with 1 tablespoon **water.** Sprinkle lightly with **sesame seeds,** if desired. Cover and let rise in a warm place until very puffy (about 45 minutes).

Bake in a 400° oven for about 15 minutes or until golden. Cool on wire racks.

Honey-Wheat Buns

Caution! Sandwich construction site ahead. You can build a sandwich really worth munching if you have these buns and your favorite sandwich fixings. The buns are made with cottage cheese, so they have an extra boost of protein. For an unusual sandwich filling, try chopped, cooked artichoke hearts, tomato slices, and sprouts.

1 cup *each* bulgur wheat and boiling water

2 packages active dry yeast

½ cup warm water (about 110°)

⅓ cup honey

2 tablespoons salad oil

1 tablespoon salt

1½ cups small curd cottage cheese

3 eggs

About 6½ cups whole wheat flour

In a large bowl, stir together bulgur and boiling water; let cool to lukewarm. Meanwhile, dissolve yeast in the warm water and stir into bulgur. Add honey, oil, salt, cottage cheese, and eggs; mix well. Gradually add 3 cups of the flour, beating well after each addition.

With a heavy-duty mixer or wooden spoon, beat in enough of the remaining flour (about 3 cups) to form a stiff dough. Turn dough out onto a floured board and knead briefly as you shape dough into a smooth ball; dough will be a little sticky. Turn dough over in a greased bowl, cover, and let rise in a warm place until doubled (about 1½ hours).

Punch down dough, turn out onto a floured board, and divide into 20 equal pieces. Shape each piece into a smooth ball by kneading briefly on floured board; dough will still be a little sticky.

Place balls about 2 inches apart on greased baking sheets and flatten slightly. Cover lightly and let stand in a warm place until puffy and almost doubled (about 45 minutes).

Bake buns in a 375° oven until lightly browned (about 12 to 15 minutes). Let cool on wire racks, then package airtight or freeze to store. Makes 20 buns.

Per bun: 10 grams protein, 40 grams carbohydrate, 51 milligrams cholesterol, 230 calories.

Mushrooms and cashews inside, flavorful whole wheat on the outside —they're Chinese Steamed Buns (recipe on page 296), an excellent choice to serve with Savory Vegetables & Tofu (recipe on page 281) or any stir-fried dish.

Maple-Molasses Bread

A slice of this round loaf when it's fresh from the oven is pure bliss; toasted, it's even better.

- 2 tablespoons sugar
- 1½ cups warm water (about 110°)
- 1 package active dry yeast
- ⅓ cup maple or maple-flavored syrup
- ⅓ cup *each* molasses (dark or light) and salad oil
- 1 teaspoon salt
- 3½ cups all-purpose flour
  - About 4 cups whole wheat flour
- 1 cup raisins
  - Salad oil
- 1 egg white beaten with 1 teaspoon water

In a large bowl, dissolve sugar in the warm water. Stir in yeast and let stand for 5 minutes. Blend in maple syrup, molasses, oil, and salt. Beat in all-purpose flour, 1 cup at a time, then beat until dough pulls away from bowl in stretchy strands (about 10 to 15 minutes at medium speed if using electric mixer). With a heavy-duty mixer or wooden spoon, gradually beat in 3 cups of the whole wheat flour.

Turn dough out on a floured board and knead until smooth and elastic (10 to 15 minutes), adding more whole wheat flour as needed to prevent sticking. Gradually knead in raisins during the last 5 minutes of kneading time. Turn dough over in a greased bowl; cover and let rise in a warm place until doubled (about 2 hours).

Punch dough down and turn onto a lightly floured board. Divide dough in half; shape each half into a smooth ball and place in a greased 8-inch pie pan. Lightly brush tops with salad oil; cover and let rise in a warm place until doubled (45 minutes to 1 hour).

Brush egg white mixture over loaves. Bake in a 375° oven for 30 minutes or until loaves are dark golden and sound hollow when tapped. Cool in pan for 10 minutes, then turn out onto racks to cool completely. Makes 2 loaves; cut 18 slices per loaf.

Per slice: 3 grams protein, 26 grams carbohydrate, no cholesterol, 136 calories.

Chinese Steamed Buns

(Pictured on page 294)

The buns are flavorful whole wheat. The filling is a marvelous mixture of mushrooms, cashews, and other goodies prepared with fresh ginger, a little garlic, and soy sauce. You can steam them or bake them; either way, they're superb.

- 1 package active dry yeast
- 1 cup warm water (about 110°)
- 1 tablespoon sugar
- 2 tablespoons salad oil
- 1 teaspoon salt
  - About 2¾ cups whole wheat flour
  - Mushroom-Cashew Filling (recipe follows)
- 1 tablespoon butter or margarine (for baked buns)

In a large bowl, dissolve yeast in the warm water; blend in sugar, oil, and salt. Let stand until bubbly (about 15 minutes). Add flour and mix until dough holds together. Place dough on a lightly floured board and knead until smooth and elastic (about 8 to 10 minutes). Turn dough over in a greased bowl; cover and let rise in a warm place until doubled (about 1 hour).

Meanwhile prepare mushroom-cashew filling; let cool and set aside.

Turn dough out onto a lightly floured board and knead for 1 minute. Cut dough into 12 equal pieces.

Roll each piece into a round about 4½ inches in diameter. Press outside edge of round to make it slightly thinner than the rest of the dough. Place about 2 tablespoons filling in center of each round. Pull edges of dough up around filling and twist to seal.

For steamed buns, place each bun, twisted side down, on a 2-inch square of foil and place on a cooky sheet. Cover and let rise in a warm place until puffy and light (about 30 minutes). Set with foil, in a single layer in a steamer over boiling water. Cover and steam for 15 minutes. Serve warm; or let cool, then wrap and refrigerate or freeze. To reheat, steam buns until hot (about 5 to 10 minutes).

For baked buns, place buns about 2 inches apart on a greased cooky sheet. Cover and let rise in a warm place until puffy and light (about 30 minutes). Melt butter; brush over tops. Bake in a 350° oven until bottoms of buns turn golden brown (about 15 minutes). Makes 12 buns.

Per steamed bun: 6 grams protein, 26 grams carbohydrate, no cholesterol, 195 calories.

Per baked bun: 6 grams protein, 26 grams carbohydrate, 3 milligrams cholesterol, 200 calories.

Mushroom-Cashew Filling. Prepare the following: ¼ pound **mushrooms,** chopped; 1 small **onion,** chopped; 1 clove **garlic,** minced or pressed; 1 teaspoon minced **fresh ginger;** ½ cup coarsely chopped **bamboo shoots;** ¾ cup coarsely chopped **cashews;** and 2 **green onions,** including tops, thinly sliced. In a bowl, combine 3 tablespoons **soy sauce,** 1 tablespoon **dry sherry,** 1 teaspoon **sugar,** ¼ cup **water,** and 1 tablespoon **cornstarch.**

Heat 1 tablespoon **salad oil** in a wide frying pan over high heat. Add mushrooms, onion, garlic, and ginger and stir-fry for 3 minutes. Add bamboo shoots, cashews, and green onions and cook for 2 minutes. Pour in soy mixture and cook, stirring, until sauce bubbles and thickens. Stir in 1 teaspoon **sesame oil.** Remove pan from heat; cool.

Anadama Bread

Legend has it that Anna's disgruntled New England husband muttered "Anna, damn her" as he recombined the unimaginative ingredients of Anna's dinner—cornmeal and molasses—to make this bread. We say, "Anna, bless her," and add bananas and dates to make a bread that's just perfect when you spread it with cream cheese.

1½ cups whole wheat flour
¾ cup cornmeal
¾ teaspoon salt
½ teaspoon baking soda
1 package active dry yeast
2½ tablespoons salad oil
⅓ cup light molasses
1 cup plus 2 tablespoons very warm water (120° to 130°)
   About 3 cups all-purpose flour
½ cup mashed ripe banana
1 cup diced pitted dates
   About 1 teaspoon cornmeal

In a large bowl, mix together whole wheat flour, the ¾ cup cornmeal, salt, baking soda, and yeast. Stir in oil, molasses, and the warm water; beat (at medium speed for 2 minutes if using electric mixer). Add ¼ cup of the all-purpose flour and beat (at high speed for 2 minutes with electric mixer). With a heavy duty mixer or wooden spoon, stir in the banana and about 2½ cups of the all-purpose flour—enough to make a stiff dough.

Turn dough out onto a floured board and knead until smooth, adding all-purpose flour as necessary to prevent sticking. Knead dates into dough, a portion at a time. Turn dough over in a greased bowl. Cover and let rise in a warm place until doubled (about 1½ hours).

Grease a 9-inch pie pan and sprinkle with the 1 teaspoon cornmeal. Punch down dough, knead a few times, then shape into a smooth ball. Place in pie pan; cover and let rise in a warm place until almost doubled (about 45 minutes).

Bake in a 375° oven until browned (35 to 40 minutes). Turn out onto a rack to cool. Makes 1 large loaf; cut in 20 slices.

Per slice: 4 grams protein, 35 grams carbohydrate, no cholesterol, 173 calories.

Casserole Cheese Bread

Baked in one-cup custard or soufflé dishes, this recipe turns out six miniature loaves. Both Cheddar and Parmesan cheeses go into the dough, then more Cheddar is sprinkled on top to give each loaf a golden crown.

1 package active dry yeast
¼ cup warm water (about 110°)
¾ cup milk
1 tablespoon butter or margarine
1 tablespoon instant minced onion
2 tablespoons sugar
1 teaspoon salt
1 egg
   About 1¼ cups all-purpose flour
   About 1⅛ cups whole wheat flour
1½ cups (6 oz.) shredded Cheddar cheese
⅓ cup grated Parmesan cheese

In a bowl, sprinkle yeast over the warm water. In a pan over medium heat, combine milk, butter, onion, and sugar. Heat to 110°. Blend into yeast mixture. Add salt and egg and mix well. Gradually beat in 1⅛ cups of the all-purpose flour and all of the whole wheat flour, adding a little more all-purpose flour if necessary to make a stiff, sticky dough. Stir in 1 cup of the Cheddar cheese and all the Parmesan cheese. Cover and let rise in a warm place until almost doubled (about 1 hour).

Stir dough down and divide equally among 6 greased 1-cup baking dishes (such as custard or soufflé dishes). Cover and let rise in a warm place until almost doubled (20 to 30 minutes). Sprinkle tops with the remaining ½ cup Cheddar cheese. Bake in a 350° oven until richly browned (about 30 minutes). Remove bread from dishes and cool. Makes 6 servings.

Per serving: 17 grams protein, 42 grams carbohydrate, 85 milligrams cholesterol, 369 calories.

Golden Swiss Cheese Loaves

There's so much cheese in this bread that a slice of it, toasted, tastes like a grilled cheese sandwich. It's a natural partner for soups and salads and makes a wonderful sandwich with avocado, sprouts, and tomato.

2 packages active dry yeast
1½ cups warm water (about 110°)
2 tablespoons sugar
4 tablespoons butter or margarine, melted and cooled
1 teaspoon liquid hot pepper seasoning
¼ cup wheat germ
   About 4½ to 5 cups all-purpose flour
¾ cup shredded Swiss cheese
⅓ cup grated Parmesan cheese
   Melted butter or margarine

(Continued on next page)

...Golden Swiss Cheese Loaves (cont'd.)
In a large bowl, dissolve yeast in the warm water. Stir in sugar, the 4 tablespoons melted butter, hot pepper seasoning, wheat germ, and 2 cups of the flour. Beat, scraping bowl often for 4 minutes (at medium speed if using electric mixer). Add 1 more cup of the flour and beat (for 4 more minutes at high speed with electric mixer).

With a heavy-duty mixer or wooden spoon, beat in enough of the remaining flour (about 1½ cups) to form a soft dough that is not too sticky to knead. Turn out onto a floured board and knead until smooth, adding remaining flour as needed to prevent sticking. Turn dough over in a greased bowl; cover and let rise in a warm place until doubled (about 1½ hours).

Punch down dough and gradually knead in Swiss cheese and all but about 2 tablespoons of the Parmesan cheese. Divide dough in half; shape each half into a smooth loaf and place in a greased 4 by 8-inch loaf pan. Cover and let rise in a warm place until loaves have risen slightly above pan rims (about 2 hours).

Brush lightly with melted butter and sprinkle with remaining Parmesan cheese. Bake in a 350° oven until loaves are browned and sound hollow when tapped (30 to 35 minutes). Turn out onto racks to cool completely. Makes 2 loaves; cut 16 slices per loaf.

Per slice: 3 grams protein, 15 grams carbohydrate, 8 milligrams cholesterol, 97 calories.

Graham Yogurt Bread

Here is a nutritious, even-textured bread that bakes in three 1-pound vegetable or fruit cans (*not* coffee cans). Tightly wrapped and stored in the refrigerator, these loaves stay fresh for about 5 days. This bread is especially good lightly toasted.

- 2 cups graham flour or whole wheat flour
- ½ cup all-purpose flour
- 2 teaspoons baking soda
- 1 teaspoon salt
- 2 cups plain yogurt
- ½ cup molasses (dark or light)
- 1 cup raisins
- ½ cup chopped walnuts

Remove one end from each of three 1-pound cans (see introduction above); rinse, dry, and grease cans well. In a large bowl, stir together graham flour, all-purpose flour, baking soda, and salt until thoroughly blended. Stir in yogurt, molasses, raisins, and walnuts; mix well. Distribute batter evenly among cans.

Bake in a 350° oven for about 1 hour or until a wooden skewer inserted in center of loaves comes out clean. Cool in cans for about 10 minutes; then turn out and stand loaves upright on a rack to cool completely. Makes 3 small loaves; cut 6 slices per loaf.

Per slice: 4 grams protein, 26 grams carbohydrate, 2 milligrams cholesterol, 137 calories.

Quick Corn Bread

(Pictured on page 270)

High and light, moist and tender, with a hint of sweetness...this corn bread can be stirred together in minutes when you want a hot bread to serve with dinner.

- 1 cup *each* baking mix (biscuit mix) and yellow cornmeal
- 3 teaspoons baking powder
- 2 eggs
- 1 cup milk
- ⅓ cup honey
- 4 tablespoons butter or margarine, melted and cooled

In a large bowl, stir together baking mix, cornmeal, and baking pow-

der. In a small bowl, beat eggs lightly; stir in milk, honey, and butter. Pour egg mixture into dry ingredients and mix just until moistened.

Turn batter into a well-greased 8-inch square or round baking pan. Bake in a 400° oven for 25 to 30 minutes or until a wood skewer inserted in center comes out clean. Cut into squares or wedges and serve warm. Makes 9 servings.

Per serving: 5 grams protein, 31 grams carbohydrate, 76 milligrams cholesterol, 224 calories.

Apple Brown Bread

Bits of fresh apple dot this wholesome molasses-flavored brown bread. A moist loaf, it slices more easily the day after it's baked.

- ½ cup (¼ lb.) butter or margarine
- ½ cup firmly packed brown sugar
- 1 egg
- ½ cup dark molasses
- 2 cups all-purpose flour
- 1½ cups graham flour or whole wheat flour
- ½ cup wheat germ
- 2 teaspoons baking soda
- 1 teaspoon *each* baking powder and salt
- 2 cups buttermilk
- 2 cups finely chopped, unpeeled, tart apples
- 1 cup chopped walnuts

In a large bowl, beat together butter and brown sugar until light and

Daisy-bright start in the morning ... light-textured Oatmeal Pancakes with Blueberry Sauce (recipe on page 304) contain rolled oats and wheat germ; Orange Froth (recipe on page 303) combines milk, eggs, and orange juice for high nutrition.

creamy. Beat in egg; then stir in molasses until blended. In another bowl, stir together all-purpose flour, graham flour, wheat germ, baking soda, baking powder, and salt until thoroughly blended.

Add dry ingredients alternately with buttermilk to creamed mixture; after each addition mix just until blended. Stir in apples and nuts. Spoon batter into 2 greased and flour-dusted 4 by 8-inch loaf pans.

Bake in a 350° oven for about 1½ hours or until bread begins to pull away from sides of pans and a wooden skewer inserted in center comes out clean. Let cool in pans for 10 minutes; then turn out onto a rack to cool completely. Makes 2 loaves; cut 16 slices per loaf.

Per slice: 3 grams protein, 20 grams carbohydrate, 17 milligrams cholesterol, 141 calories.

Cottage Cheese Muffins

Cottage cheese adds moistness to these whole grain muffins; cornmeal gives them an intriguingly crunchy texture.

1½ cups all-purpose flour
½ cup buckwheat or whole wheat flour
1 cup yellow cornmeal
4½ teaspoons baking powder
¼ teaspoon salt
3 tablespoons sugar
2 eggs
1 cup *each* small curd cottage cheese and buttermilk
⅓ cup salad oil

In a large bowl, combine all-purpose flour, buckwheat flour, cornmeal, baking powder, salt, and sugar; mix well. In a small bowl, beat eggs lightly; mix in cottage cheese, buttermilk, and oil. Make a well in center of flour mixture and add liquid ingredients all at once.

Stir with a fork just enough to blend ingredients.

Spoon into well-greased 2 to 3-inch muffin cups, filling them about two-thirds full. Bake in a 400° oven until golden brown (about 20 minutes). Turn out of pans onto a rack. Makes 2 dozen muffins.

Per muffin: 4 grams protein, 14 grams carbohydrate, 23 milligrams cholesterol, 107 calories.

Cheddar Cheese Popovers

A big crisp popover, hot from the oven, makes the perfect partner to a bowl of soup or a main-dish salad for lunch or supper.

1 cup all-purpose flour
½ teaspoon Mexican seasoning (or ¼ teaspoon chili powder and a dash *each* ground cumin, garlic powder, and oregano leaves)
¼ teaspoon garlic salt
1 tablespoon melted butter or margarine
1 cup milk
3 eggs
1 cup (4 oz.) shredded sharp Cheddar cheese
¼ cup finely chopped ripe olives

Preheat oven to 375°.

In a bowl, combine flour, Mexican seasoning, and garlic salt. Add butter, milk, and eggs and beat,

scraping bowl frequently, until very smooth (about 2½ minutes at medium-high speed if using electric mixer). Beat in cheese and olives.

Evenly distribute batter in 12 well-greased ½-cup-size containers (muffin tins or ovenproof glass custard cups). Bake on center rack in the preheated 375° oven for 45 to 50 minutes or until well browned and firm to touch. Remove from containers and serve hot.

If you like popovers to be especially dry, loosen from pan but leave sitting at an angle in cups; prick popovers' sides with a skewer and let stand in the turned-off oven with door slightly ajar for 8 to 10 minutes. Makes 12 popovers.

Per popover: 6 grams protein, 9 grams carbohydrate, 78 milligrams cholesterol, 122 calories.

Sesame Swirls

If your family favors biscuits, you might want to serve these easy-to-make dinner rolls filled with toasted sesame seeds.

2 tablespoons butter or margarine
½ cup sesame seeds
2½ cups all-purpose flour
2½ teaspoons baking powder
1 teaspoon salt
½ cup butter or margarine
1 cup sour cream
½ cup milk
1 egg, lightly beaten

Melt the 2 tablespoons butter in a small frying pan over medium heat. Add sesame seeds and cook, stirring, until toasted; set aside to cool.

In a bowl, stir together flour, baking powder, and salt until well blended. With a pastry blender or 2 knives, cut the ½ cup butter into flour mixture until it resembles coarse crumbs. In a separate bowl, stir together sour cream and milk. Add to flour mixture, blending gently. Turn out on a lightly floured board and knead gently about 5 times.

Roll out dough to a rectangle about 15 inches long, 12 inches wide, and ¼ inch thick. Brush with half the beaten egg, then spread with toasted sesame seeds. Starting with long side, roll up jelly-roll fashion; pinch edge to seal. Cut roll with a floured knife into 1-inch slices and place slices, cut side up, on a lightly greased baking sheet. Brush slices with remaining egg.

Bake in a 425° oven for about 15 minutes or until lightly browned. Makes 16 biscuits.

Per biscuit: 4 grams protein, 17 grams carbohydrate, 46 milligrams cholesterol, 199 calories.

Whole Wheat Tortillas

These versatile flat breads can be served hot and soft from the griddle, deep-fried until crisp, or used in Mexican cookery.

2 cups whole wheat flour
½ teaspoon salt
4 tablespoons butter or margarine
½ cup lukewarm water
All-purpose flour

Combine whole wheat flour and salt in a mixing bowl. With a pastry blender or 2 knives, cut butter into flour mixture until it resembles fine crumbs. Add water gradually, tossing with a fork to mix. Turn out onto a board and knead for a minute or two until well mixed. Shape into a ball; cover and let rest for 15 minutes.

Divide and shape dough into 8 balls for 9-inch tortillas, 12 balls for 6-inch tortillas. Keep balls covered to prevent them from drying out. On a board lightly dusted with all-purpose flour, roll out one ball at

a time as thin as possible. As each tortilla is shaped, place in a pre-heated ungreased heavy frying pan or on a griddle over medium-high heat. Almost immediately, blisters should appear. Use a wide spatula to press gently but firmly all over the top. Blisters will form over most of surface as you press. Turn and cook to brown the other side.

Stack cooked tortillas in a tightly covered dish or wrap tightly in foil to keep them soft. Serve while still warm; or cool tortillas, wrap airtight, and refrigerate.

To reheat tortillas, wrap with foil, and heat in a 350° oven for 15 minutes. Makes 8 large tortillas or 12 small tortillas.

Per large tortilla: 4 grams protein, 21 grams carbohydrate, 18 milligrams cholesterol, 150 calories.

Chapaties

Four minutes is all it takes to cook this simple wheat-flavored bread that accompanies almost every meal in India. Mild in flavor and slightly chewy, chapaties are a delicious balance to hot spicy foods, hearty soups, and crisp salads.

2 cups whole wheat flour
1 teaspoon salt
About ⅔ cup warm water

In a bowl, stir together flour and salt. With a fork, gradually stir in water until a crumbly dough forms. With your hands, work dough until it holds together. Add a few more drops water, if needed. On a floured board, knead dough until it is smooth but still sticky (about 3 minutes). Wrap airtight in plastic wrap and let rest for 30 minutes.

Divide and shape dough into 16 smooth balls and flatten each ball with your hand. On a floured board, roll each flattened ball into a circle about 5 inches in diameter. Stack circles, separated by sheets of wax paper. If made ahead, seal

in a plastic bag, and refrigerate until next day.

Preheat an ungreased heavy frying pan or griddle over medium-low heat. Place rounds of dough in pan. After about 1 minute, top surface of dough will darken slightly. Use a wide spatula to press directly on top of dough; blisters will gradually appear on top. When bottom browns lightly (about 2 minutes), turn bread over and bake until lightly browned on other side (about 2 minutes more). Serve hot. Makes 16 chapaties.

Per chapatie: 2 grams protein, 11 grams carbohydrate, no cholesterol, 50 calories.

Puris

(Pictured on page 283)

These little Indian breads start out like chapaties, but instead of baking them on a griddle, you deep-fry them in hot oil. Each round puffs up like a balloon and becomes crisp.

Chapatie dough (preceding recipe)
Salad oil

Prepare chapatie dough. Roll out pieces of dough on board lightly rubbed with salad oil rather than flour.

In a deep pan at least 6 inches in diameter, pour salad oil to a depth of 1½ inches and heat to 350° on a deep-frying thermometer. Place one puri at a time in the hot oil. In a few seconds it will bubble up to the surface and start to inflate unevenly like a balloon. With a slotted spoon, very gently press puri against side or bottom of pan so it will inflate completely. Turn over and continue cooking until golden brown (about 1 minute). Remove and drain on paper towels. Serve warm. Makes 16 puris.

Per puri: 2 grams protein, 11 grams carbohydrate, no cholesterol, 98 calories.

Up at 5 a.m. Deep knee bends while feeding cat. Milk goat. Grind wheat. Make four-course breakfast.

What? That's not your morning routine? Yours is a quick cup of coffee and a dash for the door? Well, we're not going to mention the early bird, worms, being healthy, wealthy, and wise, or any other of those adages guaranteed to make those who resent mornings even more resentful. We're just going to offer some recipes and breakfast ideas for food so tempting, you'll want to get up in the morning to try them.

On the next four pages you'll find innovative breakfast suggestions, as well as traditional breakfast foods. Most vegetarians are very nutrition conscious and want every calorie to count. They prefer whole grains in their breads, cereals, and pancakes instead of refined flour; and that's what you'll find in our recipes.

Cereal Suggestions

Granola-type cereals give you grains, dried fruit, and nuts in crunchy combination. The next two recipes, sweetened with honey and baked at low temperatures, are delicious with milk, or eaten dry as a snack or portable breakfast. Then we offer a recipe for hot cereal that combines the nutrients of grains, milk, eggs, and fruit in one bowl.

Spiced Fruit Granola. In a large bowl, combine 3½ cups regular or quick-cooking **rolled oats;** 1 cup *each* chopped **walnuts,** shredded **coconut,** and slivered **almonds;** ½ cup *each* **wheat germ** and **sesame seeds;** 1 teaspoon **ground cinnamon;** and ½ teaspoon **ground cloves.** In a small bowl, stir together ¼ cup *each* **salad oil** and **honey,** and 2 tablespoons grated **orange peel.** Pour over oat mixture and stir to coat evenly.

Spread mixture in two large baking pans. Bake, uncovered, in a 200° oven, stirring occasionally, for about 55 minutes or until lightly toasted. Cool completely, then stir in ½ cup *each* **raisins** and chopped **dried apricots.** Cover and store at room temperature. Makes 8 cups.

Per ⅓ cup serving: 5 grams protein, 19 grams carbohydrate, no cholesterol, 204 calories.

Puffed Cereal Granola. In a large bowl, combine 6 ounces (about 13 cups) unsweetened **puffed cereal** (corn, rice, wheat, or millet), 1 cup **sunflower seeds,** and 1 cup *each* coarsely chopped **peanuts** and **cashews.** In a small bowl, stir together 2 tablespoons **vanilla** and ½ cup *each* **honey, water,** and **salad oil.** Pour over cereal mixture and stir to coat evenly.

Spread mixture in two large baking pans. Bake, uncovered, in a 275° oven, stirring occasionally, for about 45 minutes or until golden. Cool completely, then stir in 2 cups chopped **dried apples** and ½ cup chopped **dates,** figs, or pitted prunes. Cover and store at room temperature. Makes 10 cups.

Per ⅓ cup serving: 3 grams protein, 19 grams carbohydrate, no cholesterol, 154 calories.

Hot Cereal with Fruit. In a pan, bring to a boil 1½ cups **water;** 1 cup **rye flakes,** wheat flakes, or rice flakes; and ½ teaspoon **salt.** Cover, reduce heat, and simmer until liquid is absorbed.

Meanwhile, lightly beat 2 **eggs** with ½ cup **milk** and 1 cup **applesauce.** Stir some hot cereal into egg mixture, then return all to pan. Also stir in ½ cup chopped pitted **dates** or dried apricots and ¼ cup toasted **coconut** or sliced almonds. Heat, stirring, until hot. Serve with milk or light cream. Makes 4 servings.

Per serving: 8 grams protein, 41 grams carbohydrate, 131 milligrams cholesterol, 255 calories.

Breakfast Sandwiches

Sandwiches are a slightly unorthodox but delicious substitute for the usual morning fare. Here are several ideas for wake-up sandwiches.

Peanut Honey Crisps. In a bowl, blend 3 tablespoons *each* **peanut butter,** softened **butter** or margarine, and **honey.** Spread evenly on 8 slices toasted **whole wheat bread.** Place side by side on a baking sheet; sprinkle evenly with 2 tablespoons **sesame seeds.** Bake in a 325° oven for 10 minutes; then broil 4 inches from heat until lightly toasted (about 45 seconds). Cut each slice in half. Makes 8 servings.

Per serving: 5 grams protein, 20 grams carbohydrate, 15 milligrams cholesterol, 170 calories.

Grilled Fruit & Cheese Sandwich. For each sandwich, use 2 slices **whole wheat bread** or oatmeal bread, 2 or 3 slices peeled **apple** or pear (cut ¼ inch thick), 2 slices (½ oz. *each*) **Cheddar** or jack cheese, and 1 teaspoon softened **butter** or margarine. Butter one side of each slice of bread. To assemble each sandwich, lay 1 bread slice, buttered side down, on a flat surface and top bread with a slice of cheese; place fruit slices over cheese, cover with another slice of cheese, then top with bread (buttered side up). Bake in heated grill until bread is toasted and cheese is melted. Or cook in a wide frying pan over medium heat, turning as needed, until browned on each side.

Per sandwich: 12 grams protein, 26 grams carbohydrate, 42 milligrams cholesterol, 276 calories.

Apricot-Almond Sandwiches. In a pan, combine 1½ cups **dried apricots** and 1 cup **water.** Cover and simmer for 25 to 30 minutes. If there is still water in pan, uncover and continue cooking until apricots are very soft and most of the water has evaporated. Remove from heat, mash, and stir in ½ to ¼ cup firmly packed **brown sugar.** Then stir in ½ cup chopped **almonds.** Spread 8 slices of **whole wheat bread** or toast with **cream cheese.** Spread apricot-almond filling on top. Makes 8 servings.

Per serving: 6 grams protein, 34 grams carbohydrate, 7 milligrams cholesterol, 209 calories.

Totally Wild Breakfasts

If it's breakfast foods you dislike in the morning, fix what you do like to eat. Where is it written that you can't have a bean burrito for breakfast, or a bowl of hot soup instead of cereal, or even finish up last night's supper?

Or how about breakfast cookies? Half-cup Cookies (page 314) and Chewy Bran Bars (page 314) can be nutrition-packed take-along breakfast treats. The only catch to breakfast cookies is that you have to make them ahead of time. Also, you have to have the willpower not to eat them all at once.

Breakfast Beverages

You can select from a variety of ingredients — milk, yogurt, honey, fruit, juice, eggs — to make nutritious breakfast beverages. So bring out your blender and try one of these quick concoctions.

Strawberry Banana Smoothie. In a blender, whirl until smooth: 1 cup *each* cracked **ice** and **plain yogurt;** 2 cups sliced **strawberries;** 1 **banana,** peeled and sliced; and 2 tablespoons **honey.** Makes 4 servings.

Per serving: 3 grams protein, 25 grams carbohydrate, 6 milligrams cholesterol, 170 calories.

Tropical Smoothie. In a blender, whirl until smooth: 1 cup *each* cracked **ice** and **plain yogurt;** 1 can (8 oz.) **unsweetened crushed pineapple,** drained; 1 **banana,** peeled and sliced; and 1 tablespoon **honey.** Makes 3 servings.

Per serving: 3 grams protein, 27 grams carbohydrate, 6 milligrams cholesterol, 125 calories.

Orange Froth (*pictured on page 299*). In a blender, whirl until smooth: 1 cup *each* **milk** and **water,** ¼ cup **sugar,** 1 teaspoon **vanilla,** 1 can (6 oz.) **frozen orange juice concentrate** (undiluted), 2 **eggs,** and 10 **ice cubes** (crushed). Makes 4 servings.

Per serving: 7 grams protein, 37 grams carbohydrate, 135 milligrams cholesterol, 219 calories.

Strawberry Nog. In a blender, whirl until smooth: 2½ cups sliced **strawberries,** 1 can (6 oz.) **frozen orange juice concentrate** (undiluted), 1½ cups **milk,** ¼ cup **sugar,** 1 teaspoon **vanilla,** 2 **eggs,** and 10 **ice cubes** (crushed). Makes 6 servings.

Per serving: 6 grams protein, 31 grams carbohydrate, 93 milligrams cholesterol, 182 calories.

Cool Apple Nog. In a blender, whirl until smooth: 1 can (12 oz.) **frozen apple juice concentrate** (undiluted), 2 **eggs,** ¼ teaspoon grated **lemon peel,** 1 tablespoon **lemon juice,** ⅛ teaspoon **ground cinnamon,** dash of **ground nutmeg,** ½ cup **milk,** and 10 **ice cubes**

(Continued on next page)

(crushed). Garnish each serving with fresh **mint sprigs.** Makes 4 servings.

Per serving: 5 grams protein, 32 grams carbohydrate, 131 milligrams cholesterol, 179 calories.

Pancakes, Waffles, French Toast & Quick Breads

Airy-light, but packed with nutrition, the following pancakes, waffles, French toast, and quick breads are deliciously persuasive arguments for morning meals.

Oatmeal Pancakes *(pictured on page 299).* In a bowl, combine 1 cup regular or quick-cooking rolled oats, 1 cup **whole wheat flour,** ¼ cup *each* **wheat germ** and **nonfat dry milk powder,** 1 teaspoon **baking soda,** ¼ teaspoon **salt,** and 1 tablespoon brown sugar. In another bowl, combine 2 **eggs** (lightly beaten), 2 cups **buttermilk,** and 4 tablespoons **butter** or margarine (melted and cooled). Add all at once to dry ingredients and stir until well blended.

Preheat a griddle or large frying pan over medium heat; grease lightly. Spoon batter, about ¼ cup for each cake, onto griddle; spread batter to make 5-inch circles. Cook until tops are bubbly and appear dry; turn and cook other sides until lightly browned. Makes 16 pancakes.

Per pancake: 3 grams protein, 12 grams carbohydrate, 42 milligrams cholesterol, 185 calories.

Blueberry Sauce *(pictured on page 299).* In a pan, combine ⅓ cup **sugar** and 1 tablespoon **cornstarch;** add 2 cups fresh or frozen and thawed **blueberries,** 2 tablespoons **lemon juice,** and ⅓ cup **water.** Cook over medium heat, stirring, until mixture is thickened. Serve warm or cold over pancakes, waffles, or French toast. Makes 2 cups sauce.

Per 2 tablespoons: .14 grams protein, 7 grams carbohydrate, no cholesterol, 29 calories.

Cottage Cheese Pancakes with Applesauce. Break 3 **eggs** into a blender or food processor. Add 1 cup **small curd cottage cheese** and whirl until blended. Add 2 tablespoons **salad oil,** ¼ cup **whole wheat flour,** and ¼ teaspoon **salt;** whirl until smooth.

Preheat a griddle or large frying pan over medium heat; grease lightly. Pour batter, about ¼ cup for each cake, onto griddle. Cook until tops are bubbly and appear dry; turn and cook other sides until lightly browned.

While pancakes are cooking, heat 1 cup **applesauce** over medium heat. Spoon 2 tablespoons warm sauce over each pancake and sprinkle lightly with **cinnamon.** Makes 8 pancakes.

Per pancake (including applesauce): 6 grams protein, 4 grams carbohydrate, 83 milligrams cholesterol, 71 calories.

Walnut Wheat Griddle Cakes. In a bowl, stir together 1 cup **whole wheat flour,** ⅓ cup **soy flour,** ¾ teaspoon **salt,** and 3 teaspoons **baking powder.** In another bowl, combine 2 **eggs** (lightly beaten), 1¼ cups **milk,** 2 tablespoons **honey,** and ⅓ cup **salad oil.** Pour all at once into flour mixture and stir until smooth. Stir in ½ cup chopped **walnuts.**

Preheat a griddle or large frying pan over medium heat; grease lightly. Pour batter, about ¼ cup for each cake, onto griddle to make 4-inch circles; space them well apart (they spread). Cook until tops are bubbly and appear dry; turn and cook other sides until lightly browned. Makes 1 dozen pancakes.

Per pancake: 5 grams protein, 13 grams carbohydrate, 46 milligrams cholesterol, 153 calories.

Cornmeal Waffles. Separate 2 **eggs.** Place yolks in a large bowl; place whites in a small bowl and reserve. Beat yolks together with 2 cups **buttermilk.** In another bowl, combine 1 cup **whole wheat flour,** ¾ cup **cornmeal,** 2 teaspoons **baking powder,** 1 teaspoon **baking soda,** ½ teaspoon **salt,** 2 tablespoons **sugar,** and ¼ cup **wheat germ.** Gradually add flour mixture to yolk mixture, blending until smooth. Stir in 6 tablespoons **butter** or margarine (melted and cooled).

Beat the reserved egg whites just until stiff, moist peaks form; fold into batter just until blended. Bake waffles in a preheated waffle iron according to manufacturer's directions. Makes 1 dozen 4-inch square waffles.

Per waffle: 5 grams protein, 18 grams carbohydrate, 61 milligrams cholesterol, 155 calories.

Orange Yogurt Waffles. Separate 4 **eggs.** Place yolks in a large bowl; place whites in a small bowl and reserve. Beat yolks together with 2 cups **plain yogurt,** 1 tablespoon grated **orange peel,** ¼ cup **orange juice,** 2 tablespoons **sugar,** ¼ teaspoon **ground nutmeg,** and 6 tablespoons **butter** or margarine (melted and cooled); beat until blended.

In another bowl, combine 1 cup **all-purpose flour,** ¾ cup **whole wheat flour,** ¼ cup **wheat germ,** 1 teaspoon *each* **baking powder** and **salt,** and 2 teaspoons **baking soda.** Gradually stir flour mixture into yolk mixture just until moistened; do not beat.

Beat the reserved egg whites just until stiff, moist peaks form; fold into batter. Bake waffles in a preheated waffle iron according to manufacturer's directions. Makes 1 dozen 4-inch square waffles.

Per waffle: 6 grams protein, 20 grams carbohydrate, 105 milligrams cholesterol, 182 calories.

Bran Wheat Waffles. Separate 2 **eggs.** Place yolks in a large bowl; place whites in a small bowl and reserve. Beat yolks together with 1½ cups **milk,** ¼ cup firmly packed **brown sugar,** and ⅓ cup **butter** or margarine (melted and cooled).

In another bowl, combine ⅔ cup *each* **all-purpose flour** and **whole wheat flour,** ¾ cup **unprocessed bran,** 1 tablespoon **baking powder,** and ½ teaspoon **salt.** Gradually add flour mixture to yolk mixture, blending until smooth.

Beat the reserved egg whites just until stiff, moist peaks form; fold into batter just until blended. Bake waffles in a preheated waffle iron according to manufacturer's directions. Makes eight 4-inch waffles.

Per waffle: 6 grams protein, 25 grams carbohydrate, 85 milligrams cholesterol, 195 calories.

Cashew French Toast. In a blender, place ¾ cup **milk,** ½ cup **cashews,** 3 tablespoons chopped pitted **dates** or moist-pack dried apricots, and a dash of **salt.** Whirl until smooth. Pour into a pie pan.

Dip 3 slices whole wheat or oatmeal **bread,** one at a time, in milk-nut mixture to coat each side. Melt 1 tablespoon **butter** or margarine in a wide frying pan over medium heat. Place dipped bread in pan and cook until browned on bottoms. Turn and brown other sides. Repeat, with 3 more slices bread and remaining milk-nut mixture, adding more butter to pan as needed. Sprinkle with **powdered sugar** before serving. Makes 6 slices.

Per slice: 6 grams protein, 23 grams carbohydrate, 17 milligrams cholesterol, 203 calories.

Apricot Bran Scones. In a bowl, stir together 1 cup *each* **all-purpose** and **whole wheat flour,** ¼ cup **sugar,** 4 teaspoons **baking powder,** and 2 cups **bran flake cereal.** With a pastry blender or two knives, cut in 4 tablespoons **butter** or margarine until mixture resembles coarse crumbs. Stir in 2 **eggs** (lightly beaten), ⅓ cup **milk,** and ½ cup chopped moist-pack **dried apricots** or pitted prunes. Turn out onto a floured board and knead about 6 times; divide dough into thirds.

On a greased baking sheet, pat each third into a 5-inch circle about ½ inch thick. With a floured knife, cut each round into 6 wedges (leave wedges in place). Bake in the middle of a 400° oven for 15 to 20 minutes or until lightly browned. Separate wedges before serving. Makes 18 scones.

Per scone: 3 grams protein, 19 grams carbohydrate, 36 milligrams cholesterol, 116 calories.

Gold Surprise Muffins. In a large bowl, beat together ¼ cup **butter** or margarine and ¼ cup firmly packed **brown sugar** until creamy. Add 2 **eggs** and beat until light and fluffy. Add 1 tablespoon *each* **lemon juice** and **water** and 1 cup lightly packed, finely shredded **carrots.** Stir until well blended.

In another bowl, combine 1 cup all-purpose **flour,** 2 teaspoons **baking powder,** ½ teaspoon **salt,** ¼ teaspoon **ground ginger,** and 2 tablespoons **wheat germ.** Add to carrot mixture. Stir just enough to moisten all the dry ingredients. Spoon batter into greased 2½-inch muffin cups, filling each about ⅔ full.

Bake in a 400° oven for about 18 minutes or until tops spring back when lightly touched. Makes 10 muffins.

Per muffin: 3 grams protein, 17 grams carbohydrate, 65 milligrams cholesterol, 133 calories.

Sweet Endings

As you can see by the big ice cream cone in the middle of this page, sweets and desserts are just as much fun for vegetarians as anyone else. In fact, desserts often play an important nutritional role in vegetarian menus.

We've included a range of desserts in this chapter, from fairly calorie-conscious goodies, such as Ricotta Cheesecake (page 309), to flagrantly rich sweets, such as Marzipan Torte (page 309). You'll find desserts that appeal to the child in you—for instance, Frozen Fruit Yogurts (page 312) and Half-cup Cookies (page 314). And there are desserts that appeal to the sophisticated gourmand side of you—Figs Romanoff (page 311) and Glazed Peach Crêpes (page 310), to name a couple.

Besides old-time favorites like Honey Peach Cobbler (page 311) and Honey Crunch Baked Apples (page 311), we've come up with some new twists on old themes—for instance, cool refreshing Cantaloupe Melba (page 313) and Strawberry Sundae (page 313) made with strawberries in several forms: puréed, sliced, and whole.

Overall, you'll notice that refined sugar makes a limited appearance in these recipes. Fruit and honey are frequently used as sweeteners. Wherever possible, whole wheat flour is used in cookies, cakes, and pies. Fresh fruit is used in abundance for lighter desserts.

We're especially fond of Brandied Ricotta with Fruit (page 311). It's a model of simplicity and superior nutrition. You simply beat ricotta cheese with flavorings and a little sugar, mound it on a platter, and chill. Serving it is the fun part. You surround the ricotta mixture with sliced fresh fruit and simple butter cookies and let your guests make their own fruit-cheese-and-cooky open-faced sandwiches.

If you prefer the even simpler classic finale of cheese and fresh fruit, here are some combinations to consider: pears with Gorgonzola; aged Parmesan with dried figs; pineapple with Monterey jack; peaches with ricotta and a dusting of freshly grated nutmeg; Port du Salut and melon; strawberries with Neufchâtel; grapes with Brie or Camembert; apples with Bel Paese; plums with Cheddar.

For a special fruit and cheese treat, try making your own fresh cheese (directions on page 266) to serve with fresh raspberries, strawberries, blackberries, nectarines, or peaches. Homemade yogurt (page 266) with fruit is another light ending that provides nutritional bonuses and satisfies your sweet tooth as well.

Apple Custard Pie

A pie that's both apple and custard? That's the best of both worlds. The oatmeal crust is also excellent for quiches and fruit pies. For a crunchier filling, you can shred the apples without peeling them.

**Oatmeal Pastry
(recipe follows)**
4 **eggs**
¾ cup **sugar**
4 **tablespoons butter or margarine, melted and cooled**
1 **teaspoon vanilla**
½ **teaspoon grated lemon peel**
¼ teaspoon *each* **ground cinnamon and nutmeg**
About 3 large Golden Delicious apples

Roll out pastry dough and fit into a 9-inch pie pan; flute edge, then set aside.

Lightly beat eggs; add sugar and beat until well blended. Stir in butter, vanilla, lemon peel, cinnamon, and nutmeg.

Peel apples, if *desired;* coarsely shred apples. You should have about 3 cups lightly packed apples. Stir apples into egg mixture; turn filling into unbaked pastry shell.

Bake pie on the lowest rack of a 425° oven for 10 minutes. Reduce temperature to 350° and bake for 35 to 40 minutes or until a knife inserted in center comes out clean. Cool on a rack for 10 minutes. Serve warm or chilled. Makes 6 servings.

Per serving (including pastry): 8 grams protein, 54 grams carbohydrate, 234 milligrams cholesterol, 471 calories.

Oatmeal Pastry. In a bowl, mix together 1 cup **all-purpose flour** and ⅓ cup regular or quick-cooking **oats.** With a pastry blender or 2 knives, cut 7 tablespoons cold **butter** or margarine into flour mixture until it resembles coarse crumbs.

With a fork, gradually blend in 2 to 3 tablespoons **cold water.** Press pastry into a ball with your hands. On a floured board, roll out dough ⅛ inch thick. Fit pastry into a 9-inch pie pan (at least 1¼ inches deep).

Pear Crumble Pie

This recipe could be the source of the expression "easy as pie." All you have to do is slice pears and toss them with a little sugar and lemon juice, put them in a pie shell, and add an easy spiced topping.

**Whole Wheat Pastry
(recipe follows)**
**Spiced Topping
(recipe follows)**
5 **medium-size pears**
½ cup **sugar**
1 **teaspoon grated lemon peel**
3 **tablespoons lemon juice**

Roll out pastry dough and fit into a 9-inch pie pan; flute edge, then set aside. Prepare topping and set aside.

Peel, halve, core, and slice pears. Lightly toss pear slices with the sugar, lemon peel, and lemon juice. Arrange in unbaked pastry shell. Sprinkle topping over pears.

Bake pie in a 400° oven for 45 minutes or until pears are tender. Serve warm or chilled. Makes 6 servings.

Per serving (including pastry): 6 grams protein, 77 grams carbohydrate, 73 milligrams cholesterol, 552 calories.

Whole Wheat Pastry. In a bowl, mix together 1 cup **whole wheat flour** and ¼ teaspoon **salt.** With a pastry blender or 2 knives, cut 6 tablespoons **butter** into flour mixture until it resembles coarse crumbs.

With a fork, gradually blend in

just enough **whipping cream** (about 2 tablespoons) to moisten dough. Press pastry into a ball with your hands. On a board floured with **all-purpose flour,** roll out dough ⅛ inch thick. Fit pastry into a 9-inch pie pan (at least 1¼ inches deep).

Spiced Topping. In a bowl, combine ½ cup *each* **whole wheat flour** and **sugar,** ½ teaspoon *each* **ground ginger** and **ground cinnamon,** ¼ teaspoon **ground mace,** and ¼ cup finely chopped **walnuts.** With a pastry blender or 2 knives, cut ⅓ cup **butter** or margarine into flour mixture until it resembles coarse crumbs.

Carrot Cake

Carrot cake is a "can't miss" dessert, and this chewy, tortelike version is just delicious; yet it's not nearly as rich as traditional carrot cakes.

2 **cups lightly packed, shredded raw carrots**
1 **cup raisins**
1½ **cups** *each* **sugar and water**
⅓ **cup butter or margarine**
1 **cup all-purpose flour**
1½ **teaspoons baking soda**
½ **teaspoon** *each* **salt, ground cloves, and ground allspice**
1 **teaspoon** *each* **ground nutmeg and ground cinnamon**
1 **cup whole wheat flour**
1 **teaspoon vanilla**
1 **cup chopped walnuts**

Place carrots, raisins, sugar, water, and butter in a 3-quart pan and bring to a simmer over medium heat; continue to simmer, uncovered, for 5 minutes. Remove from heat and let cool.

In a bowl, sift together all-purpose flour, baking soda, salt, cloves, allspice, nutmeg, and cinnamon; stir in whole wheat flour.

(Continued on next page)

Stir dry ingredients into cooled carrot mixture until flour is moist. Stir in vanilla and walnuts. Spoon into a greased 9-inch square baking pan.

Bake in a 350° oven for 35 minutes or until a wooden pick inserted in center comes out clean. Cool on a rack for 10 minutes. Serve warm or at room temperature. Makes 12 servings.

Per serving: 5 grams protein, 53 grams carbohydrate, 16 milligrams cholesterol, 318 calories.

Sesame Poundcake

(Pictured on page 238)

Sesame seeds and sesame oil richly flavor this moist poundcake. For best flavor, make it a day ahead and refrigerate; but serve at room temperature.

⅓ **cup sesame seeds**

¾ **cup (1½ sticks) butter or margarine, softened**

1 **cup sugar**

4 **eggs**

2 **cups all-purpose flour**

½ **teaspoon salt**

1 **teaspoon baking powder**

½ **cup milk**

1 **teaspoon *each* vanilla, sesame oil, and grated lemon peel**

In a wide frying pan over medium heat, toast sesame seeds, shaking pan frequently, until seeds are golden (about 2 minutes); set aside.

With an electric mixer, beat together butter and sugar until creamy. Add eggs, one at a time, beating well after each addition.

In another bowl, sift together flour, salt, and baking powder; stir in all but 1 tablespoon of the sesame seeds. In a large measuring cup, combine milk, vanilla, sesame

oil, and lemon peel. To the butter mixture, add flour mixture alternately with milk mixture, stirring well after each addition; *do not beat or overstir.*

Pour batter into a well-greased and flour-dusted 9-inch tube pan with a removable bottom or a 5 by 9-inch loaf pan. Sprinkle top with the remaining 1 tablespoon seeds.

Bake in a 325° oven for 1 hour or until a wooden pick inserted in center comes out clean. Cool on wire rack. Makes 16 slices.

Per slice: 3 grams protein, 19 grams carbohydrate, 91 milligrams cholesterol, 199 calories.

Carob-Orange Cake

Frankly, we don't think carob tastes like chocolate—it's delicious in its own right, especially when paired with orange flavoring. Here, carob chips go into the batter as well as on top of this moist, single-layer cake.

½ **cup (¼ lb.) butter or margarine, softened**

1 **cup firmly packed brown sugar**

2 **eggs**

1 **teaspoon vanilla**

1 **tablespoon grated orange peel**

1 **cup *each* whole wheat flour and all-purpose flour**

1½ **teaspoons baking powder**

1 **teaspoon baking soda**

½ **teaspoon salt**

1 **cup buttermilk**

1½ **cups (8 oz.) carob baking chips, coarsely chopped**

¼ **cup chopped walnuts**

With an electric mixer, beat together butter and brown sugar until creamy. Add eggs, vanilla, and orange peel; beat until fluffy.

In a separate bowl, mix together

whole wheat flour, all-purpose flour, baking powder, baking soda, and salt. Add to butter mixture alternately with the buttermilk, mixing well after each addition. Stir in 1 cup of the chopped carob chips. Mix thoroughly.

Pour batter into a greased 9-inch square baking pan. Combine remaining ½ cup chopped carob chips with nuts and scatter evenly over batter.

Bake in a 350° oven for about 45 minutes or until a wooden pick inserted in center comes out clean. Cool on a rack for 10 minutes. Serve warm or at room temperature. Makes 9 servings.

Per serving: 7 grams protein, 50 grams carbohydrate, 89 milligrams cholesterol, 424 calories.

Whole Wheat Yogurt Poundcake

Just a thin slice of this orange-flavored poundcake will satisfy your sweet tooth. Offer it plain or with frozen yogurt or chilled fruit spooned over each serving.

1 **cup (½ lb.) butter or margarine, softened**

2 **cups firmly packed brown sugar**

1 **teaspoon *each* grated orange peel and vanilla**

3 **eggs**

2 **cups whole wheat flour**

¼ **cup wheat germ**

¼ **teaspoon baking soda**

½ **teaspoon salt**

1 **cup orange-flavored or plain yogurt**

½ **cup granola-type cereal**

With an electric mixer, beat together butter and sugar until creamy. Beat in orange peel and vanilla. Add eggs, one at a time, beating well after each addition.

In another bowl, stir together whole wheat flour, wheat germ, baking soda, and salt. Add to butter mixture alternately with yogurt, mixing well after each addition.

Pour batter into a greased and flour-dusted 10-inch tube pan with removable bottom. Sprinkle granola over top.

Bake in a 325° oven until a wooden pick inserted in center comes out clean (about 1 hour). Cool in pan on rack. Makes 12 servings.

Per serving: 6 grams protein, 53 grams carbohydrate, 113 milligrams cholesterol, 383 calories.

Yogurt Cheesecake with Dates

This delicious cheesecake is made without the usual eggs or gelatin. You simply combine cream cheese, honey, and yogurt, then chill the mixture in a sesame crumb crust overnight so it will be firm enough to slice.

Sesame Crumb Crust (recipe follows)

1 large package (8 oz.) cream cheese, softened

3 tablespoons honey

1 cup plain yogurt

1 teaspoon *each* vanilla and grated orange peel

½ cup *each* chopped pitted dates and sliced almonds

Prepare and bake crust; let cool.

In a bowl, beat cream cheese with honey until fluffy. Gradually mix in yogurt until smooth. Stir in vanilla and orange peel. Turn into prepared crust and spread evenly. Sprinkle dates and almonds evenly over filling. Cover and refrigerate until next day, or freeze.

Serve well chilled. If frozen, thaw for about 20 minutes to serve partially frozen, or allow to thaw completely in refrigerator. Makes 8 servings.

Per serving: 7 grams protein, 30 grams carbohydrate, 57 milligrams cholesterol, 345 calories.

Sesame Crumb Crust. In a bowl, mix together ¾ cup **dry whole wheat bread crumbs,** ¼ cup **wheat germ,** 2 tablespoons *each* **sugar** and **sesame seeds,** and 5 tablespoons melted **butter** or margarine. Press mixture firmly into bottom and sides of a 9-inch pie pan. Bake in a 375° oven for 8 minutes.

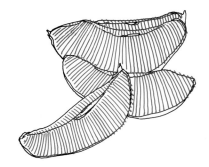

Marzipan Torte

Marzipan is a time-honored confection of ground almonds, sugar, and egg whites. You usually see it around holiday time made into tiny fruits and animals, but here marzipan flavors the filling of a rich torte. Look for cans or tubes of almond paste in supermarkets or gourmet specialty shops.

Marzipan Filling (recipe follows)

1⅓ cups all-purpose flour

1 teaspoon baking powder

½ cup (¼ lb.) butter or margarine, softened

⅓ cup sugar

1 egg

½ cup raspberry jam

Prepare filling and set aside.

In a bowl, stir together flour and baking powder. In a large mixing bowl, beat together butter and sugar until creamy. Add egg and beat until light and fluffy. Stir in flour mixture and mix well.

Firmly press dough in an even layer in a 9-inch spring-form pan. Spread ¼ cup of the jam over the dough. Spread filling in an even layer over the jam.

Bake in a 350° oven for 50 minutes or until a knife inserted in center comes out clean. Spread remaining ¼ cup jam over the top. Serve chilled. Makes 16 servings.

Per serving: 5 grams protein, 30 grams carbohydrate, 83 milligrams cholesterol, 315 calories.

Marzipan Filling. In a mixing bowl, beat together ½ cup (¼ lb.) softened **butter** or margarine and ⅔ cup **sugar** until creamy. Add 1 can (8 oz.) **almond paste** and ½ teaspoon **almond extract** and beat until smooth. Beat in 2 **eggs,** one at a time, until well blended.

Ricotta Cheesecake

Here's a splendid cheesecake that doesn't have too many calories. For a simpler version with even fewer calories, eliminate the crust —just coat the buttered pan with wheat germ.

Nutty Crumb Crust (recipe follows), or 2 teaspoons butter or margarine and ¼ cup toasted wheat germ

3 eggs

3 cups (1½ pounds) ricotta cheese

⅔ cup sugar

⅓ cup *each* sour cream and cornstarch

1 teaspoon *each* baking powder and vanilla

3 tablespoons butter or margarine, melted and cooled

2 teaspoons grated lemon peel

2 cups whole strawberries

(Continued on next page)

Prepare and bake crust. Or spread the 2 teaspoons butter over bottom and sides of a 9-inch cake pan with removable bottom, then sprinkle with wheat germ.

In a blender or food processer, whirl eggs, cheese, sugar, and sour cream until smooth. Blend cornstarch and baking powder; add to cheese mixture with vanilla, butter, and lemon peel. Whirl mixture until well blended. (Or use an electric mixer to prepare filling.) Turn filling into prepared pan.

Bake in a 325° oven for 55 to 60 minutes or until a knife inserted in center comes out clean. Cool on a rack; cover and refrigerate. Garnish each slice with a few strawberries. Makes 12 servings.

Per serving (with Nutty Crumb Crust): 10 grams protein, 29 grams carbohydrate, 105 milligrams cholesterol, 297 calories.

Per serving (with Wheat Germ Crust): 9 grams protein, 21 grams carbohydrate, 95 milligrams cholesterol, 216 calories.

Nutty Crumb Crust. Blend together 1¼ cups finely crushed **graham cracker crumbs,** ¼ cup *each* finely minced **almonds** and melted **butter** or margarine, and 2 tablespoons **sugar.** Press evenly into bottom and sides of a 9-inch cake pan with removable bottom. Bake in a 325° oven for 8 minutes; cool.

Glazed Peach Crêpes

Sliced peaches accented with lemon, nutmeg, and brandy are cooked until tender, then used as a filling and topping for tender whole wheat crêpes. If you use frozen peaches, look for bags of slices that are unsweetened and individually frozen.

As a variation, you could use sliced apples, nectarines, apricots, or pears in place of the peaches.

8 **Whole Wheat Crêpes (page 276)**
2 **tablespoons butter or margarine**
6 **medium-size peaches, peeled and cut in ½-inch-thick slices, or 6 cups unsweetened frozen peach slices, partially defrosted**
1 **teaspoon grated lemon peel**
1 **tablespoon lemon juice**
⅛ **teaspoon ground nutmeg**
½ **cup sugar**
2 **tablespoons brandy**
½ **cup sour cream**

Prepare crêpes and set aside.

Melt butter in a wide frying pan over medium heat. Add peaches, lemon peel, lemon juice, and nutmeg. Cook, gently turning occasionally with a wide spatula, until peaches begin to soften (about 7 minutes). Sprinkle in sugar and cook, stirring gently, for 2 minutes longer. Warm brandy in a small pan, ignite (*not* beneath an exhaust fan or flammable items), then spoon flaming liquid over peaches. Continue cooking until liquid is thickened. Remove from heat and cool slightly.

To assemble, spoon 3 tablespoons filling across lower third of each crêpe and roll to enclose. Place filled crêpes, seam side down, in a lightly buttered baking dish. Spoon remaining filling over top.

Cover and bake in a 325° oven for 25 minutes or until crêpes are heated through. Top each crêpe with a spoonful of sour cream before serving. Makes 8 crêpes.

Per crêpe: 4 grams protein, 29 grams carbohydrate, 65 milligrams cholesterol, 204 calories.

Lemon Yogurt Sponge Torte

Your guests will know they're special when you serve this tangy light torte. It has a layer of delicate cake, a filling of lemon yogurt, another layer of cake, then a topping of whipped cream and coconut.

1 **cup shredded coconut**
4 **eggs, separated**
¾ **cup sugar**
1½ **tablespoons lemon juice**
1 **teaspoon baking powder**
½ **teaspoon grated lemon peel**
½ **cup all-purpose flour**
2 **cups lemon-flavored yogurt**
¾ **cup whipping cream**
1 **tablespoon sugar**
Lemon slices for garnish

Spread coconut on a large baking sheet and bake in a 350° oven for 4 minutes or until golden. Lightly grease a 10 by 15-inch jelly roll pan. Line pan with wax paper; grease the paper.

In a small bowl, beat together egg yolks, ½ cup of the sugar, lemon juice, and baking powder until thick and lemon-colored. Stir in lemon peel and ½ cup of the coconut.

In a large bowl, beat egg whites until soft peaks form. Gradually beat in the remaining ¼ cup sugar until stiff peaks form. Gently fold egg yolk mixture and flour into beaten whites until blended. Pour into prepared pan, spreading evenly. Bake in a 375° oven for 10 to 12 minutes or until top springs back when lightly touched.

Place a piece of wax paper on a large rack (or two smaller racks). Invert cake on rack and peel off paper used in baking; cool.

Cut cake into two layers. Place one layer on a serving platter and spread with yogurt. Set remaining cake layer on yogurt. Whip cream just until stiff; flavor with the 1 tablespoon sugar. Spread whipped cream over top of cake and sprinkle with the remaining ½ cup coconut. Garnish with lemon slices. Chill for at least 2 hours or overnight. Makes 9 servings.

Per serving: 7 grams protein, 37 grams carbohydrate, 136 milligrams cholesterol, 304 calories.

Figs Romanoff

Fresh figs folded into a mixture of ice cream and whipped cream, then garnished with grated chocolate is a sophisticated sweet concoction.

2 pounds fresh figs
2 tablespoons curaçao or orange juice
1 pint vanilla ice cream
½ pint (1 cup) whipping cream
1 tablespoon sugar
¼ cup grated sweet chocolate

Peel figs, if desired, and cut in halves; arrange in a shallow bowl and sprinkle with curaçao. Cover and chill.

About 10 minutes before serving, remove ice cream from freezer to soften. Whip cream until thick and sweeten with sugar. Fold ice cream into whipped cream. Fold in figs. Spoon into small dessert bowls or goblets. Sprinkle chocolate over each serving. Makes 8 servings.

Per serving: 4 grams protein, 37 grams carbohydrate, 46 milligrams cholesterol, 312 calories.

Honey Peach Cobbler

Here's a homey dessert of peaches baked with a topping of whole wheat and honey. We think it's best served warm with vanilla ice cream.

6 medium-size peaches, peeled, and cut in ½-inch-thick slices, or 6 cups unsweetened frozen peach slices, partially defrosted
2 tablespoons *each* cornstarch and water
3 tablespoons lemon juice
½ cup honey
Whole Wheat & Honey Topping (recipe follows)
1 pint vanilla ice cream

Place peaches in a shallow 3-quart baking dish. In a bowl, mix cornstarch and water. Add lemon juice and honey; stir until blended, then stir into peaches.

Prepare topping as directed and drop by spoonfuls onto fruit mixture. Bake in a 400° oven for 30 to 35 minutes or until well browned. Serve warm or cool, and accompany with ice cream. Makes 8 servings.

Per serving (including ice cream): 6 grams protein, 64 grams carbohydrate, 33 milligrams cholesterol, 348 calories.

Whole Wheat & Honey Topping. In a bowl, stir together 1¼ cups **whole wheat flour,** 2 teaspoons **baking powder,** ½ teaspoon *each* **salt** and **ground cinnamon,** and ¼ teaspoon **ground nutmeg.** With a pastry blender or 2 knives, cut 4 tablespoons cold **butter** or margarine into flour mixture until it resembles coarse crumbs. Combine ½ cup **milk** and ¼ cup **honey;** stir into flour mixture just until blended.

Honey Crunch Baked Apples

Warm or cool, these granola-filled baked apples are delicious topped with cream. Choose a good baking apple such as Rome Beauty, Pippin, or Golden Delicious.

6 large baking apples
⅓ cup *each* granola-type cereal (page 302 or purchased) and chopped dates
¼ cup chopped walnuts or almonds
½ teaspoon ground cinnamon
¼ teaspoon ground nutmeg
2 teaspoons lemon juice
⅓ cup honey
3 tablespoons butter or margarine, melted
¾ cup apple juice or water
1 cup half-and-half (light cream)

Peel apples, if desired, and core; stand upright in a 9-inch square baking pan. To make filling, combine granola, dates, walnuts, cinnamon, nutmeg, lemon juice, and 3 tablespoons of the honey. Spoon equal amounts of filling into center of each apple (pack filling in lightly). Combine the remaining honey with butter and apple juice; pour over apples.

Cover and bake in a 350° oven for 30 minutes. Remove cover and bake, basting with pan juices several times, until apples are tender when pierced (about 35 minutes longer). Serve warm or cooled. At the table, pass a pitcher of cream to pour over each apple. Makes 6 servings.

Per serving (including cream): 3 grams protein, 49 grams carbohydrate, 35 milligrams cholesterol, 316 calories.

Brandied Ricotta with Fruit

For elegance with ease, this dessert reigns supreme. You just beat ricotta cheese with flavorings and sugar, chill, then surround with cookies and fruit slices. Your guests spread the cheese mixture on their choice of fruit and cookies, or make their own open-faced cooky sandwiches.

1 pint (2 cups) ricotta cheese
¼ cup powdered sugar
2 tablespoons brandy
¼ teaspoon ground cinnamon
8 plums or small peaches or 2 dozen unhulled whole large strawberries
2 dozen mildly sweet cookies, such as petit beurre

(Continued on next page)

With an electric mixer, beat together ricotta, powdered sugar, brandy, and cinnamon until smooth. Mound cheese mixture on a serving plate and swirl in a cone shape; cover lightly and chill for several hours.

To serve, surround with halved plums, small peach halves, or strawberries and accompany with cookies. To eat, spread on fruit and cookies. Makes 8 servings.

Per serving (including fruit and cookies): 8 grams protein, 26 grams carbohydrate, 31 milligrams cholesterol, 215 calories.

Sherried Cream with Fruit

This no-fuss dessert is elegant enough to serve your best company. You make a creamy pudding flavored with sherry, then layer it with fresh fruit in stemmed glasses.

⅓ **cup sugar**

2 **tablespoons cornstarch**

⅛ **teaspoon salt**

2 **cups milk**

¼ **cup cream sherry or apple juice**

2 **egg yolks, lightly beaten**

2 **tablespoons butter or margarine**

1 **teaspoon vanilla**

About 1½ cups seedless red or green grapes, diced fresh pineapple, or sliced nectarines

In a 2-quart pan, stir together sugar, cornstarch, and salt. Gradually add milk and sherry until well blended. Set mixture over medium heat and cook, stirring constantly, until it boils; boil for 1 minute. Remove from heat.

Stir part of the hot sauce into beaten yolks, then return all to pan and cook for 30 seconds. Remove from heat and stir in butter and vanilla until butter is melted.

Layer spoonfuls of pudding and fruit in 4 stemmed glasses. If you use nectarines, be sure you end top layer with pudding so fruit will not darken. Chill until ready to serve. Makes 4 servings.

Per serving: 6 grams protein, 38 grams carbohydrate, 161 milligrams cholesterol, 285 calories.

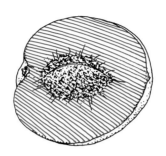

Fresh Berry Ice

This refreshing fruit ice is lighter than ice cream, cooler than sherbet, and packed with fresh fruit flavor. Best of all, with a tray of frozen fruit purée cubes ready in the freezer, you can whip up this low calorie dessert in minutes to serve one person or four.

It is best to make the ice into slush with a food processor. We give directions for using an electric mixer too, though the end result may be coarser and softer, and you may need to freeze the slush until it firms up.

3 **cups boysenberries, blackberries or olallieberries**

¾ **cup *each* water and sugar**

3 **tablespoons lemon juice**

In a blender or food processor, whirl berries until puréed. Pour through a sieve to remove seeds. Combine purée with water, sugar, and lemon juice. Mix well so sugar is dissolved. Freeze purée in divided ice cube trays. When purée is frozen, transfer cubes to plastic bags if you wish; return to freezer.

To serve, remove desired number of frozen purée cubes from

freezer and let stand for about 5 minutes at room temperature. With a food processor, whirl about 4 to 6 cubes at a time, using on-off bursts to break up the ice. Then process continuously until velvety. Spoon into serving containers and serve at once.

If you don't have a food processor, place ice cubes in a mixing bowl and smash them into small pieces with a wooden spoon. Then beat with an electric mixer until smooth—slowly at first, then gradually increasing to higher speeds. Beat purée into slush. Serve immediately. If texture is too soft, spoon into serving containers, then store in freezer until slush attains desired firmness. Makes 4 servings.

Per serving: 1.4 grams protein, 50 grams carbohydrate, no cholesterol, 203 calories.

Frozen Fruit Yogurts

Here's great party fun! Bring out the ice cream freezer and let everyone take a turn cranking out fruit-flavored frozen yogurt.

Sweetened fruit mixture (suggestions follow)

3 **eggs, separated**

¼ **teaspoon *each* salt and cream of tartar**

¼ **cup sugar**

2 **quarts plain yogurt**

From the suggestions below, select the sweetened fruit mixture of your choice. Combine the suggested amounts of fruit, sugar, and honey (if used) in a 3-quart pan and bring to a boil, stirring, over high heat. Reduce heat to medium and cook, stirring constantly, until fruit softens and partially disintegrates (1 to 4 minutes). Remove from heat; stir in fruit juices, spices, and flavorings.

In a small bowl, lightly beat egg

yolks; stir in about ½ cup of the hot fruit mixture. Then stir yolk mixture into fruit mixture; cool to room temperature.

In a large mixing bowl, beat egg whites until frothy; add salt and cream of tartar and beat until soft peaks form. Gradually add the ¼ cup sugar and continue beating until stiff peaks form.

Turn yogurt into a 5-quart or larger bowl; fold fruit mixture into yogurt until well blended. Then gently fold yogurt-fruit mixture into egg whites. At this point, you can cover and refrigerate for several hours. When ready to process, transfer to a gallon-size or larger, hand-crank or electric ice cream freezer.

Assemble freezer according to manufacturer's directions, using about 4 parts ice to 1 part rock salt. When hand-cranking becomes difficult or electric motor stalls, remove the dasher. Once the yogurt has been turned and frozen, you can store the metal container in the freezer compartment of your refrigerator until serving time. Makes 1 gallon.

Apricot-orange. Use 4 cups thinly sliced unpeeled ripe **apricots,** 2 cups **sugar,** 2 tablespoons **lemon juice,** ½ cup **orange juice,** 1 teaspoon grated **orange peel,** and 4 teaspoons **vanilla.**

Per cup frozen apricot-orange yogurt: 5.5 grams protein, 40 grams carbohydrate, 56 milligrams cholesterol, 203 calories.

Banana-honey. Measure 4 cups thinly sliced ripe **bananas,** then coarsely mash them. Also use 1¼ cups **sugar,** ¾ cup **honey,** 3 tablespoons **lemon juice,** and 2 tablespoons **vanilla.**

Per cup frozen banana-honey yogurt: 5.5 grams protein, 46 grams carbohydrate, 56 milligrams cholesterol, 224 calories.

Peach. Use 4 cups sliced peeled **peaches,** 2 cups firmly packed **brown sugar,** 3 tablespoons **vanilla,** and ¾ teaspoon *each* **ground nutmeg** and **cinnamon.**

Per cup frozen peach yogurt: 5 grams protein, 40 grams carbohydrate, 56 milligrams cholesterol, 202 calories.

Raspberry. Use 4 cups lightly packed fresh (or unsweetened frozen and thawed) **raspberries,** 2 cups **sugar,** and 4 teaspoons *each* **lemon juice** and **vanilla.**

Per cup frozen raspberry yogurt: 5.5 grams protein, 38 grams carbohydrate, 56 milligrams cholesterol, 198 calories.

Broiled Pineapple & Bananas

Served hot with sour cream, this dish of glazed bananas is a delicious winter dessert to serve when other fresh fruit is scarce.

- 3 **ripe bananas**
- 6 **slices fresh or canned pineapple**
- ⅓ **cup firmly packed brown sugar**
- 2 **tablespoons butter or margarine**
- 1 **tablespoon lemon juice**
- ½ **cup sour cream**

Peel each banana and cut in half lengthwise, then crosswise, to make 4 pieces. You will have 12 pieces in all, 2 for each serving.

Arrange banana and pineapple in a single layer in a baking dish. Sprinkle brown sugar over the top, dot with butter, and sprinkle with lemon juice. Broil about 8 inches from heat, basting several times, until fruit is glazed (5 to 7 minutes). While still hot, arrange 2 pieces of banana and 1 piece of pineapple in each of 6 dessert dishes. Top each with a dollop of sour cream and spoon some of the hot butter sauce over the sour cream. Makes 6 servings.

Per serving: 1.5 grams protein, 37 grams carbohydrate, 20 milligrams cholesterol, 214 calories.

Strawberry Sundae

Fresh strawberries take three different shapes in this dessert— puréed for sauce, sliced to top the ice cream, and whole for garnish.

- 6 **cups whole strawberries**
- **About ½ cup sugar**
- 2 **tablespoons orange-flavored liqueur (optional)**
- ½ **cup whipping cream**
- 1 **tablespoon sugar**
- 3 **cups strawberry ice cream**

In a blender or food processor, whirl about 1½ cups of the strawberries until puréed; you should have 1 cup purée. Pour through a sieve to remove seeds. Stir ¼ cup of the sugar, along with liqueur (if used) into purée and mix well; cover and chill.

Set aside 8 whole berries for garnish. Slice remaining berries and sweeten with remaining ¼ cup sugar; cover and chill.

Just before serving, whip cream until thick. Sweeten with the 1 tablespoon sugar.

For each serving, place a scoop of ice cream in a small dessert bowl or goblet. Spoon about ½ cup sliced strawberries over ice cream and drizzle with about 2 tablespoons chilled strawberry sauce. Top with a dollop of whipped cream and a whole strawberry. Makes 8 servings.

Per serving (including liqueur): 3 grams protein, 33 grams carbohydrate, 36 milligrams cholesterol, 231 calories.

Cantaloupe Melba

Raspberry sherbet in goblets lined with sliced cantaloupe and topped with Melba sauce would make a memorable finale for a menu featuring an egg and cheese dish.

(Continued on next page)

2 cups fresh raspberries or
   unsweetened frozen
   raspberries, defrosted
⅓ cup sugar
2 tablespoons orange-flavored
   liqueur or raspberry-flavored
   brandy (optional)
2 small cantaloupes
3 cups raspberry sherbet

In a blender or food processor, whirl raspberries until puréed. Pour through a sieve to remove seeds. Stir sugar and liqueur (if used) into purée and mix well; cover and chill.

Halve cantaloupes and remove seeds; peel and cut into thin slices. Line each of 8 small dessert bowls or goblets with 3 or 4 melon slices. Top melon with a scoop of sherbet and pour 2 tablespoons chilled raspberry sauce over sherbet. Makes 8 servings.

Per serving (including liqueur): 2 grams protein, 45 grams carbohydrate, no cholesterol, 186 calories.

Half-cup Cookies

These crunchy drop cookies are nutritious enough for an on-the-go breakfast when coupled with a glass of milk.

2 cups whole wheat flour
1 teaspoon baking powder
¾ teaspoon salt
1 teaspoon ground cinnamon
2 eggs
¼ cup milk
½ teaspoon vanilla
½ cup *each* peanut butter,
   honey, and lightly packed
   brown sugar
½ cup (¼ lb.) butter or
   margarine, softened
½ cup semisweet chocolate or
   carob baking chips
½ cup chopped cashews,
   toasted almonds, or walnuts
½ cup *each* flaked coconut,
   raisins, and granola-type
   cereal

Combine whole wheat flour, baking powder, salt, and cinnamon; set aside.

In a large bowl, place eggs, milk, and vanilla; beat with an electric mixer. Beat in peanut butter, honey, brown sugar, and butter until creamy.

Stir in flour mixture until blended, then stir in chocolate chips, nuts, coconut, raisins, and granola until blended.

Drop batter, 1 heaping teaspoon at a time, about 1 inch apart on lightly greased baking sheets. Bake in a 375° oven for about 10 minutes or until cookies are golden on the bottom. Cool on rack. Makes 5 dozen cookies.

Per cooky: 2 grams protein, 10 grams carbohydrate, 13 milligrams cholesterol, 87 calories.

Freezer Date Cookies

There's no sugar added—dates and coconut give these cookies natural sweetness, and walnuts add crunch.

½ cup (¼ lb.) butter or
   margarine, softened
1 egg
2 teaspoons vanilla
1 cup all-purpose flour
1 teaspoon baking powder
¼ teaspoon salt
1 cup *each* chopped pitted
   dates, shredded coconut, and
   chopped walnuts

With an electric mixer, beat butter with egg and vanilla until smooth. In a separate bowl, combine flour, baking powder, and salt. Gradually add flour mixture to creamed mixture; beat until blended. Stir in dates, coconut, and walnuts.

Form dough into two 1½-inch rolls and wrap in wax paper or foil; chill in freezer until firm enough to slice easily (about 2 hours) or for as long as 1 month.

With a sharp knife, cut rolls into ⅜-inch-thick slices. Place slices on a lightly greased cooky sheet and bake in a 350° oven for about 12 minutes or until golden. Cool on rack. Makes 5 dozen cookies.

Per cooky: 1 gram protein, 5 grams carbohydrate, 9 milligrams cholesterol, 53 calories.

Chewy Bran Bars

These are no-bake cookies made with peanut butter, raisins, and whole bran cereal. They're perfect after-school treats or breakfast take-alongs for hurried mornings.

2 tablespoons butter or
   margarine
¼ cup *each* peanut butter and
   firmly packed brown sugar
½ cup honey
1½ cups chopped walnuts
2 teaspoons ground cinnamon
1 teaspoon vanilla
⅛ teaspoon salt
½ cup raisins or chopped pitted
   prunes or dates
2 cups whole bran cereal

In a heavy 3-quart pan, combine butter, peanut butter, brown sugar, and honey. Cook over low heat, stirring constantly, just until mixture begins to boil. Remove from heat. Add walnuts, cinnamon, vanilla, and salt; stir until blended. Stir in raisins and bran cereal and mix until well coated.

Turn mixture into a well buttered 8 or 9-inch square pan.

With a buttered spatula, firmly press mixture into an even layer. Let cool until mixture begins to firm up (about 5 minutes). Cut into bars and let cool thoroughly. Store airtight at room temperature. Makes 16 bars.

Per bar: 4 grams protein, 24 grams carbohydrate, 4 milligrams cholesterol, 185 calories.

Sunset

Poultry
COOK BOOK

By the Editors of
Sunset Books and Sunset Magazine

Sunset Publishing Corporation ■ Menlo Park, California

Contents

SPECIAL FEATURES

Serving Up Poultry

WHOLE & HALVES & QUARTERS &

BREASTS & LEGS & THIGHS & WINGS &

DRUMMETTES & GROUND &

Chicken and turkey were once reserved for Sunday suppers and holiday feasts. Today, though, both birds come to the table any day of the week, any time of year—and not just as whole poultry. The chicken and turkey pieces so widely available in modern markets have made poultry a favorite for everyday meals.

APPEALING ASSETS

Why are poultry parts so popular among today's busy cooks? First of all, chicken and turkey pieces allow quick and easy preparation; boned, skinned pieces and ground poultry in particular get meals off to a fast start.

Convenience isn't the only asset poultry offers—it's an economical choice, as well. Of course, price varies with the pieces you choose: cost per pound is less for whole birds, higher for boneless, skinless breast meat. The best buy for you depends in part on your dining habits. If you prefer light meat, you'll cut down on waste, and thus ultimately spend less, by purchasing only breasts. Likewise, keep in mind the yield per pound for various parts. According to USDA figures, a whole chicken is 53% edible meat; breasts are 63% edible, thighs 60%, drumsticks 53%, wings 30%, and back and neck 27%.

Poultry's popularity can also be traced to the health benefits it offers. It's a good source of protein and is generally lower in calories than most red meats, particularly if you opt for skinless white meat. Skinned chicken and turkey breast also contain less saturated fat than most red meats, a strong selling point for diners watching their cholesterol. The nutritional values of several poultry types are summarized in the chart below.

NUTRITIONAL VALUES OF POULTRY

Portion: 3 ounces cooked	Calories	Protein (g)	Total fat (g)	Saturated fat (g)	Cholesterol (mg)
CHICKEN					
Breast, meat and skin, roasted	168	25	7	2	71
Breast, meat only, roasted	140	26	3	1	72
Thigh, meat and skin, roasted	210	21	13	4	79
Thigh, meat only, roasted	178	22	9	3	81
Drumstick, meat and skin, roasted	184	23	9	3	77
Drumstick, meat only, roasted	146	24	5	1	79
Liver, simmered	134	21	5	2	537
TURKEY					
Breast, meat and skin, roasted	161	24	6	2	63
Breast, meat only, roasted	131	25	2	1	59
Leg, meat and skin, roasted	177	24	8	3	72
Leg, meat only, roasted	157	24	6	2	75
Giblets (gizzard, heart, liver), simmered	142	23	4	1	356
Ground, regular, cooked	195	21	12	3	59
GOOSE					
Meat and skin, roasted	259	21	19	6	77
Meat only, roasted	202	25	11	4	82
DUCK					
Meat and skin, roasted	287	16	24	8	71
Meat only, roasted	171	20	10	4	76

Finally, poultry is wonderfully versatile. Serve it as an appetizer, in a salad, soup, or sandwich, as a main course or a snack, hot or cold. Choose it for your fanciest party or homiest supper; present it simply or with an elaborate sauce. Cook it any way you like: baked, braised, broiled, barbecued, sautéed, steeped, steamed, smoked, stir-fried. Season it with hot chiles or sweet spices, with citrus juices, wine, soy sauce, or mustard. For any cook, poultry offers almost limitless possibilities.

■ POULTRY TYPES

Almost all markets offer both fresh chicken and turkey; some stores also feature a selection of other poultry, such as game hens and quail.

BROILERS. Also called frying chickens and broiler-fryers, broilers account for about 90% of all the chicken marketed in the United States. And for good reason, too—they're the perfect all-purpose birds, suitable for roasting, simmering, and grilling as well as for broiling and frying. Broilers are usually about 7 weeks old and typically weigh 3 to 3½ pounds, although weights may range from 2½ to 5 pounds. You can purchase these chickens whole, cut up, and as individual parts.

ROASTERS. In general, all chickens weighing 5 pounds or more are classed as roasters. The average roaster weight is 5 to 6 pounds, though some birds may be as heavy as 8 pounds. Usually about 2½ months old, these chickens provide more servings than broilers do; they're a good choice if you're planning a roast chicken dinner for a big party.

CAPONS. A capon is a surgically desexed male chicken. Meaty and tender, capons are excellent for roasting. They're usually about 4 months old and weigh about 9½ pounds.

HEAVY HENS. Weighing in at 4½ to 6 pounds, these chickens aren't much heavier than broilers or roasters; they are, however, a good deal older (about 15 months), less tender, and less available in markets. Heavy hens are also called stewing hens—and as that name implies, they're best in slowly simmered dishes such as stews and soups.

TURKEYS. Whole turkeys range in weight from 8 to 36 pounds. Generally, birds under 16 pounds are hens, while those over 16 pounds are toms. Hens and toms don't differ in flavor or texture, but heavier birds typically do have a higher proportion of meat to bone. Almost all commercially sold turkeys are labeled "young" turkeys; they're usually 4 to 6 months old.

Birds under 4 months old are sold as fryer-roaster turkeys. Age does affect quality: the younger the turkey, the milder and more tender the meat.

OTHER BIRDS. Cornish game hens, ducks, geese, pheasants, quail, and squab are discussed in special features throughout this book.

■ POULTRY PIECES

Both chicken and turkey are sold as individual parts and as ground meat.

BREASTS. You'll find *chicken breast halves* sold in several ways: boneless and skinless (about 4 oz. per breast half); skinned, but with the bone in (6 to 6½ oz. per breast half, yielding 4 oz. meat); and complete with bones and skin (about 8 oz. per breast half, yielding 4 oz. meat). Many of the recipes in this book use skinless, boneless breast halves, also called fillets and typically sold four to a package.

Boned turkey breast half (or roast) is sold with or without the skin. *Bone-in turkey breast* is also available, usually with the skin on; it yields about a pound of meat for every 1¼ to 1⅓ pounds weight (with skin).

Turkey breast slices (or cutlets) are thin (⅛- to ⅜-inch) crosswise slices cut from boned, skinned breast.

Turkey tenderloin (or fillet) is a boneless whole muscle from the inside center of a breast half. Large tenderloins, weighing about 8 ounces, are usually sold two to a package; smaller ones come three or four to a package. When split lengthwise, tenderloins may be labeled "tenderloin steaks."

Chicken or turkey breast strips (sometimes called stir-fry strips, tenders, or chicken tenderloins) are boneless pieces ready to use for stir-frying.

THIGHS & LEGS. *Chicken thighs* are available boned and skinned, usually in 1-pound packages; they're also sold with bones and skin. To get a pound of meat, you'll need to buy 1¾ to 2 pounds bone-in, skin-on thighs.

Turkey thigh is sold boned (usually two thighs to a package) and bone-in. One medium-size bone-in thigh (about 1½ lbs.) yields 1 pound meat.

Whole chicken legs (thighs with drumsticks attached) are usually sold two to a package; they weigh about 8 ounces each.

Chicken drumsticks typically come six to a package; each piece weighs about 4 ounces. *Turkey drumsticks* weigh 1 to 1¼ pounds each and are generally sold three to a package.

WINGS. You'll usually find *chicken wings* 10 to 12 to a 2-pound package; *drummettes*, the meatiest part of the

For a festive autumn supper, offer Grilled Quail with Pasta (recipe on page 418). The juicy butterflied birds, hot from the grill, are served atop wide pasta ribbons tossed with fresh Roma tomatoes, mushrooms, and smoky pancetta.

wing, come about 15 to a 1¼-pound package. *Turkey wings* generally weigh about 12 ounces each and are sold two to a package.

GROUND POULTRY. Both *ground chicken* and *ground turkey* consist primarily of dark meat. Ground turkey resembles ground beef in flavor and texture, while ground chicken has a milder flavor and a pastier, moister texture. For ground poultry that's lower in fat and calories, buy ground skinned breast meat (you may need to have your meat market grind it for you).

■ PURCHASING POULTRY

Make sure any fresh poultry you buy has been kept refrigerated. When purchasing prepackaged poultry, select trays with little or no liquid in the bottom. If the packaged poultry you choose is frozen, avoid torn packages and those containing frozen liquid; both these conditions may be signs of moisture loss or of partial thawing and refreezing, leading to a decrease in the quality of the meat.

When buying whole chicken and turkey, look for plump birds with smooth, tight skin. Turkeys should have cream-colored skin; a chicken's skin color may range from nearly white to deep yellow, depending on the bird's diet, its age, and the methods used in processing.

In general, buy about 1 pound of whole chicken per serving; allow 1 pound of whole turkey per serving (2 pounds if you want ample leftovers).

■ STORING POULTRY

Fresh poultry should be cooked within 2 days of purchase; if you can't use it within that time, freeze it (see the chart below for storage times).

To refrigerate poultry, leave it in the market's wrap to avoid introducing bacteria by repeated handling. (If the wrapping is torn, though, do replace it with wax paper, plastic wrap, or foil.) Place the poultry in the coldest part of the refrigerator. If you plan to stuff a whole bird, keep poultry and stuffing *separate* for refrigeration.

To freeze poultry, enclose it in heavy freezer paper, plastic wrap, or foil; to prevent freezer burn, be sure the wrap is airtight. Label and date all packages, and use older items first. Don't stuff whole birds before freezing them.

■ THAWING POULTRY

The safest way to thaw all poultry is simply to let it stand, well wrapped, in the refrigerator. Allow 12 to 16 hours for a whole chicken and 4 to 9 hours for chicken parts, depending on the size and number in package. For whole turkey, allow 1 to 2 days if the bird weighs 8 to 12 pounds; allow 2 to 3 days for a 12- to 16-pound bird, 3 to 4 days for a 16- to 20-pounder, and 4 to 5 days for a 20- to 24-pounder. Turkey parts take 1 to 2 days.

If you must thaw poultry quickly, enclose it in a watertight plastic bag, then place in cold water;

■ COLD STORAGE OF POULTRY

Product	Refrigerator (Days at 40°F)	Freezer (Months at 0°F)
FRESH POULTRY		
Chicken and turkey (whole)	1 to 2	12
Chicken and turkey pieces	1 to 2	9
Duck and goose (whole)	1 to 2	6
Giblets	1 to 2	3 to 4
COOKED POULTRY		
Covered with broth or gravy	1 to 2	6
Pieces not in broth or gravy	3 to 4	4
Cooked poultry dishes	3 to 4	4 to 6
Fried chicken	3 to 4	4

Source: A Quick Consumer Guide to Safe Food Handling, United States Department of Agriculture Food Safety and Inspection Service, September 1990

change the water frequently. You can also thaw poultry in your microwave oven according to the manufacturer's instructions. *Do not thaw poultry in warm water or at room temperature:* bacteria can develop rapidly under these conditions.

◼ TESTING FOR DONENESS

The type of bird, the cut, and the cooking method will all influence the test you use to determine doneness. For chicken and turkey, one technique that works well in almost all cases is to cut the meat in the thickest part (or to the bone); it should no longer be pink in the center (or near the bone). *Note:* Birds such as goose and pheasant may require special tests; refer to our features for help.

For a whole chicken or turkey, a meat thermometer offers the most accurate doneness test. You can either insert a regular thermometer before roasting or check the temperature occasionally with an instant-read thermometer. Consult your thermometer well before the suggested total cooking time is up: because the rate of cooking varies with a bird's shape, even birds of identical weight may be done at different times. Check birds weighing less than 12 pounds at least 30 minutes before they should be done, larger birds at least 1 hour ahead. Then read the thermometer again about every 15 minutes until the desired temperature is reached.

To check breast temperature, insert the thermometer straight down through the thickest part of the breast until it touches the bone; or insert it horizontally, about halfway between the wing joint and the tip of the breastbone. A 160°F reading means the breast is done (the concurrent temperature in the center of the thickest part of the breast, *not* touching the bone, will be 170°F).

To check thigh meat, insert the thermometer into the thigh between body and leg, almost to the thigh joint; it should read 180° to 185°F. Usually, but not always, the breast is done before the thigh (the drumstick will be done in either case). In this instance, remove the bird from the oven when the breast is done; carve the breast, then continue to cook the thighs, skin side down, in a shallow pan in a 450° oven until the meat near the bone is no longer pink (about 10 more minutes).

◼ SAFETY GUIDELINES

All poultry is a potential host for the organisms that cause spoilage and food poisoning. To avoid problems, be sure you follow proper storage, cooking, and handling procedures. Remember that the bacteria, yeasts, and molds that cause food to spoil grow more rapidly at higher temperatures; for this reason, it's wise—especially if the weather is hot—to make poultry the last item on your shopping list, and then get it home and into the refrigerator quickly. If your trip home is a long one, consider taking along a cooler with frozen ice packs to hold your purchases. Be aware that spoilage organisms continue to grow even in food refrigerated at 40°F or lower; luckily, though, most such "bugs" make themselves known. If poultry has an off odor or looks bad, throw it out.

Unfortunately, the bacteria that cause food poisoning don't announce their presence so clearly: most of them can't be seen, smelled, or tasted. The best way to protect yourself against these organisms is to keep cold foods cold and hot foods hot. At low refrigerator temperatures (40°F or lower), most food poisoning bacteria don't grow; at the high temperatures (160° to 212°F) reached in roasting, baking, boiling, and frying, they're killed. Typical holding temperatures for cooked food (at least 140°F) keep bacteria from growing, but don't kill them; and when cooked food is left to stand, the possibility for bacterial growth rises rapidly as the food drops to room temperature. Be sure you keep poultry cold until cooking. Refrigerate leftovers as quickly as possible, always storing stuffing separately; and in any case, never let cooked food stand at room temperature for more than 2 hours.

Finally, take steps to prevent the spread of bacteria. After working with raw poultry, thoroughly wash your hands, tools, and work surfaces with hot, soapy water. To sanitize work surfaces and tools, treat them with diluted chlorine bleach (2 to 3 teaspoons of bleach per quart of water) and rinse well.

ABOUT OUR NUTRITIONAL DATA

For our recipes, we provide a nutritional analysis stating calorie count; grams of protein, carbohydrates, total fat, and saturated fat; and milligrams of cholesterol and sodium. Generally, the analysis applies to a single serving, based on the number of servings given for each recipe and the amount of each ingredient. If a range is given for the number of servings and/or the amount of an ingredient, the analysis is based on an average of the figures given.

The nutritional analysis does not include optional ingredients or those for which no specific amount is stated. If an ingredient is listed with a substitution, the information was calculated using the first choice.

*A golden, creamy purée of carrot, onion, and pan juices makes a simple
sauce for rosemary-fragrant Roast Chicken & Potatoes (recipe on page 326).
Fresh Brussels sprouts are a bright and tasty accompaniment for the
crisp-crusted potatoes, sweet garlic cloves, and tender meat.*

Plump Birds & Cut-up Pieces

ROASTED & BRAISED & BARBECUED &

STUFFED & HERBED & SAUCED & GLAZED &

DRESSED & BASTED & NOODLED & CASSEROLED &

■ *Pictured on page 324*

ROAST CHICKEN & POTATOES

Preparation time: About 15 minutes

Roasting time: 1 to 1¼ hours

No matter how crisp and delicious the bird, a bowl of lumpy gravy can put a damper on a roast chicken dinner. But no need to worry here: just cook carrots and onions with the chicken, then blend the vegetables and pan juices to make a foolproof, flavorful sauce.

- 1¼ **pounds small thin-skinned potatoes (*each* 1½ to 2 inches in diameter), scrubbed and cut in half**
- 1 **small onion, cut in half**
- 1 **small carrot, quartered**
- ½ **cup garlic cloves, peeled**
- 1 **teaspoon minced fresh rosemary or ½ teaspoon dry rosemary**
- ¼ **cup butter or margarine, cut into small chunks**
- 1 **chicken (4 to 4½ lbs.)**
- ¾ **to 1 cup regular-strength chicken broth**
  Salt and pepper

Place potatoes (cut side down), onion, carrot, and garlic cloves in a 9- by 13-inch baking pan. Sprinkle with rosemary and dot with butter.

Reserve chicken neck and giblets for other uses; pull off and discard lumps of fat from chicken. Rinse chicken inside and out, pat dry, and place, breast up, atop vegetables. Roast, uncovered, in a 400° oven for 30 minutes; brush chicken with pan juices. Return to oven. Continue to roast, basting often, until meat near thighbone is no longer pink; cut to test (30 to 45 more minutes).

Tilt chicken to drain juices from cavity into pan. Transfer chicken, potatoes, and half the garlic to a platter; keep warm.

Scrape onion, carrot, remaining garlic, and pan juices into a food processor or blender; whirl until smoothly puréed, adding enough broth to make a pourable sauce. Pour sauce into a small serving bowl. Serve chicken and vegetables with sauce; add salt and pepper to taste. Makes 4 servings.

Per serving: 967 calories, 66 g protein, 34 g carbohydrates, 62 g fat, 21 g saturated fat, 277 mg cholesterol, 583 mg sodium

ROAST CHICKEN WITH BEETS, SQUASH & ONIONS

Preparation time: About 15 minutes

Roasting time: 1 to 1¼ hours

Small whole onions plus a pair of unexpected vegetables—beets and banana squash—roast alongside an herb-seasoned whole chicken in this one-pan supper.

- 4 **small beets (*each* about 1½ inches in diameter), tops removed, scrubbed (leave root ends intact)**
- 8 **small onions (*each* about 1 inch in diameter), unpeeled**
- ¼ **cup olive oil**
- 2 **teaspoons *each* fresh thyme and rosemary leaves (or 1 teaspoon *each* dry leaves)**
- 1 **chicken (3½ to 4 lbs.)**
- 12 **ounces banana or Hubbard squash, peeled and cut into 2-inch chunks**
  Thyme or rosemary sprigs

Place beets and onions in opposite corners of a shallow 12- by 15-inch roasting pan. In a bowl, mix oil, thyme leaves, and rosemary leaves; brush some of the mixture over vegetables. Bake in a 375° oven for 10 minutes.

Increase oven temperature to 400°. Reserve chicken neck and giblets for other uses; pull off and discard lumps of fat from chicken. Rinse chicken inside and out, pat dry, and place, breast up, in center of pan. Place squash in an empty corner of pan. Brush chicken and vegetables with remaining oil mixture. Roast, uncovered, basting often with pan juices, until beets are tender when pierced and until meat near chicken thighbone is no longer pink; cut to test (45 minutes to 1 hour). Lift vegetables from pan with a slotted spoon; set aside. Tilt chicken to drain juices from cavity into pan; discard juices.

To serve, trim root ends from beets. Transfer chicken and vegetables to a platter and garnish with thyme sprigs. Makes 4 servings.

Per serving: 734 calories, 56 g protein, 17 g carbohydrates, 49 g fat, 12 g saturated fat, 192 mg cholesterol, 228 mg sodium

COUSCOUS WITH ROAST CHICKEN & VEGETABLES

Preparation time: About 20 minutes

Roasting time: 1 to 1¼ hours

When you roast a chicken, you get both a crisp golden bird and a bonus of savory pan juices. Here, we combine the juices with broth, couscous, and a variety of vegetables to create an appetizing, colorful supper.

- 1 **chicken (3½ to 4 lbs.)**
  Pepper
- 1 **small head fennel (about 1 lb.), base trimmed and coarse stalks cut off (reserve green leaves)**
- 2 **tablespoons olive oil**
- 1 **small head garlic**
- 4 **medium-size zucchini (about 1½ lbs. *total*), cut into 1-inch-thick slices**
- 2 **large carrots (about 12 oz. *total*), cut into 1-inch-thick slices**
- 1 **large red bell pepper (about 6 oz.), seeded and cut into chunks**
- 1 **large red onion, cut into eighths**
- 3 **cups regular-strength chicken broth**
- 2 **cups couscous**
  Salt

Reserve chicken neck and giblets for other uses; pull off and discard lumps of fat from chicken. Rinse chicken inside and out, pat dry, and place, breast up, on a rack in a 9- by 13-inch baking pan. Sprinkle liberally with pepper.

Rinse fennel and cut into 1-inch chunks.

Pour oil into a 10- by 15-inch baking pan. Place fennel, whole garlic, zucchini, carrots, bell pepper, and onion in pan; turn to coat with oil.

Roast chicken and vegetables, uncovered, in a 400° oven for 1 to 1¼ hours, switching pan positions halfway through roasting. Vegetables should be soft and beginning to blacken at edges; meat near thighbone should no longer be pink (cut to test).

Separate garlic into cloves; set aside. Coarsely chop vegetables; set aside. Tilt chicken to drain juices from cavity into pan. Transfer chicken to a platter; keep warm.

Skim and discard fat from pan juices. Add broth to pan and bring to a boil over high heat. Squeeze garlic cloves from skins into pan. Stir in couscous and vegetables. Cover, remove from heat, and let stand until liquid is absorbed (about 5 minutes). Spoon couscous around chicken; garnish with reserved fennel leaves and season to taste with salt. Makes 4 servings.

Per serving: 994 calories, 71 g protein, 98 g carbohydrates, 35 g fat, 8 g saturated fat, 165 mg cholesterol, 1,033 mg sodium

FIVE-SPICE ROAST CHICKEN

Preparation time: About 10 minutes

Roasting time: 1¼ to 1½ hours

Chinese spices quickly cooked together with soy and sherry season this flavorful roast chicken and the sauce that goes with it. Steamed broccoli and brown rice are good accompaniments for the meal.

- 1 **teaspoon salad oil**
- 1½ **teaspoons Chinese five-spice; or ½ teaspoon *each* anise seeds and ground ginger and ¼ teaspoon *each* ground cinnamon and ground cloves**
- 3 **tablespoons soy sauce**
- 1 **tablespoon *each* sugar and dry sherry**
- 1 **clove garlic, minced**
- 1 **large chicken (4½ to 5 lbs.)**
- 3 **tablespoons minced green onions (including tops)**

In a small pan, stir oil with five-spice over medium heat until hot. Add soy, sugar, sherry, and garlic.

Reserve chicken neck and giblets for other uses; pull off and discard lumps of fat from chicken. Rinse chicken inside and out, pat dry, and place, breast up, on a rack in a 9- by 13-inch baking pan. Rub generously with five-spice mixture. Pour remaining mixture into chicken cavity.

Roast, uncovered, in a 400° oven until meat near thighbone is no longer pink; cut to test (1¼ to 1½ hours). Tilt chicken to drain juices from cavity into pan, then transfer bird to a platter. Stir pan juices to scrape up browned bits. Pour juices into a small pitcher, skim off fat, and add onions. Offer sauce with chicken. Makes 4 servings.

Per serving: 603 calories, 66 g protein, 6 g carbohydrates, 34 g fat, 9 g saturated fat, 209 mg cholesterol, 967 mg sodium

CHICKEN & NOODLES WITH PIMENTOS

Preparation time: About 20 minutes

Cooking time: About 1¼ hours

Bite-size pieces of roast chicken are tossed with pasta and slivered fresh pimentos in a piquant, orange-scented cream sauce. Garnish the dish with fresh cilantro leaves and crumbled crisp chicken skin (you can omit the skin, if you like).

1 **chicken (3½ to 4 lbs.)**
1 **large orange (about 8 oz.)**
2 **large fresh pimentos or red bell peppers (about 12 oz. *total*), seeded and cut into thin strips**
2 **cups whipping cream**
1 **teaspoon crushed dried hot red chiles**
   Salt and pepper
1 **package (9 or 10 oz.) fresh fettuccine or tagliarini**
½ **cup fresh cilantro (coriander) leaves**

Reserve chicken neck and giblets for other uses; pull off and discard lumps of fat from chicken. Rinse chicken inside and out, pat dry, and place, breast up, in a 9- by 13-inch baking pan. Roast, uncovered, in a 400° oven until meat near thighbone is no longer pink; cut to test (about 1 hour). Tilt chicken to drain juices from cavity into pan. Set chicken

aside. Scrape juices, including browned bits, into a 10- to 12-inch frying pan; set aside.

When chicken is cool enough to handle, pull off skin in large pieces; place, fat side down, on a rack in baking pan. Return to 400° oven and roast, uncovered, until very crisp (about 15 minutes).

Meanwhile, remove and discard chicken bones; tear meat into bite-size pieces and set aside. With a zester, remove peel (colored part only) from orange. (Or use a vegetable peeler, then cut peel into fine strands with a knife.) Reserve orange for other uses.

Add pimentos to pan juices in frying pan; cook over medium-high heat, stirring often, until pimentos are slightly softened (about 3 minutes). Add cream, chiles, and half the orange peel. Increase heat to high and boil until reduced by half (about 5 minutes). Add chicken meat and cook just until hot; season to taste with salt and pepper.

Meanwhile, cook fettuccine according to package directions just until tender to bite. Drain well. Add pasta to chicken mixture; remove from heat and mix lightly, using 2 forks. Transfer to a deep platter. Crumble chicken skin over pasta; garnish with cilantro and remaining orange peel. Makes 6 servings.

Per serving: 570 calories, 37 g protein, 30 g carbohydrates, 33 g fat, 18 g saturated fat, 232 mg cholesterol, 129 mg sodium

■ *Pictured on facing page*

HOT & SWEET CHICKEN

Preparation time: About 10 minutes

Cooking time: About 55 minutes

A tangy, citrus-based sauce does double duty in this dish. You use part of it to coat a cut-up chicken during baking, then mix the rest with the pan juices to spoon over the cooked meat and hot, fluffy rice.

1 **tablespoon grated orange peel**
1 **cup orange juice**
3 **tablespoons lemon juice**
2 **tablespoons Worcestershire**
1 **tablespoon Dijon mustard**
½ **teaspoon liquid hot pepper seasoning**
½ **cup red currant jelly**
1 **chicken (3 to 3½ lbs.), cut up**
3 **cups hot cooked rice**
1 **tablespoon cornstarch mixed with 2 tablespoons water**

In a 1- to 1½-quart pan, combine orange peel, orange juice, lemon juice, Worcestershire, mustard, hot pepper seasoning, and jelly. Stir over medium heat until jelly is melted.

Rinse chicken and pat dry. Then arrange chicken, except breast pieces, skin side up in a shallow 12- by 15-inch roasting pan; brush with some of the orange sauce. Bake, uncovered, in a 400° oven for 20 minutes, basting with sauce after 10 minutes. Add breast pieces. Continue to bake, basting often, until meat near thighbone is no longer pink; cut to test (about 25 more minutes).

Arrange chicken and rice on a platter; keep warm. Skim and discard fat from pan juices; then add remaining orange sauce to pan. Add cornstarch mixture and bring to a boil over high heat, stirring. Serve sauce with chicken and rice. Makes 4 servings.

Per serving: 741 calories, 49 g protein, 81 g carbohydrates, 23 g fat, 6 g saturated fat, 143 mg cholesterol, 358 mg sodium

Clusters of sautéed chanterelles and fans of snow peas frame a
platter of Hot & Sweet Chicken (recipe on facing page). The baked chicken
pieces are basted and sauced with a tart, tempting blend of citrus
juices, hot pepper, and currant jelly.

OVEN-BARBECUED CHICKEN

Preparation time: About 10 minutes

Cooking time: About 50 minutes

There's no need to light the grill to make this super-saucy chicken—you cook it right in your oven. Chili-sparked pineapple juice glazes and flavors the pieces as they bake.

    3 tablespoons firmly packed brown sugar
    1 tablespoon cornstarch
    ¾ cup pineapple juice
    3 tablespoons catsup
    ¼ cup cider vinegar
    1 tablespoon chili powder
    1 teaspoon ground ginger
    ⅛ teaspoon ground allspice
    1 tablespoon soy sauce
    2 cloves garlic, minced or pressed
    1 chicken (about 3½ lbs.), cut up

In a 1- to 1½-quart pan, mix sugar and cornstarch. Stir in pineapple juice, catsup, vinegar, chili powder, ginger, allspice, soy, and garlic. Bring to a boil over high heat, stirring. Remove from heat.

Rinse chicken and pat dry. Then arrange chicken, except breast pieces, skin side down in a foil-lined shallow 10- by 15-inch baking pan. Brush some of the sauce over chicken.

Bake, uncovered, in a 400° oven for 20 minutes. Turn chicken pieces over. Add breast pieces, skin side up, to pan; brush all chicken with remaining sauce. Continue to bake until skin is well browned and meat near thighbone is no longer pink; cut to test (about 25 more minutes). Makes 4 servings.

Per serving: 516 calories, 49 g protein, 24 g carbohydrates, 24 g fat, 7 g saturated fat, 154 mg cholesterol, 557 mg sodium

ROAST CHICKEN & FIGS

Preparation time: About 10 minutes

Cooking time: About 55 minutes

Sweet fresh figs complement roasted chicken quarters flavored with a simple orange juice and honey baste. You can use either black or green figs; both kinds are available in June and again from August until early September.

    1 chicken (3 to 3½ lbs.), quartered
    1 teaspoon grated orange peel
    ½ cup *each* orange juice and regular-strength chicken broth
    1 tablespoon honey
   12 large or 24 small ripe figs, stems trimmed

Rinse chicken, pat dry, and place, skin side up, in a shallow 12- by 15-inch roasting pan. Roast, uncovered, in a 375° oven for 40 minutes. Skim and discard fat from pan.

In a bowl, mix orange peel, orange juice, broth, and honey. Add figs; mix gently to coat.

With a slotted spoon, lift figs from bowl and spoon into pan alongside chicken. Then spoon juice mixture over chicken. Continue to roast until figs are hot and chicken meat near thighbone is no longer pink; cut to test (about 10 more minutes).

Spoon sauce from roasting pan into a 1- to 2-quart pan. Turn off oven; return roasting pan with chicken and figs to oven to keep warm. Boil sauce over high heat until reduced to ½ cup (about 3 minutes).

Divide chicken and figs equally among 4 dinner plates; top with sauce. Makes 4 servings.

Per serving: 564 calories, 46 g protein, 45 g carbohydrates, 23 g fat, 6 g saturated fat, 143 mg cholesterol, 259 mg sodium

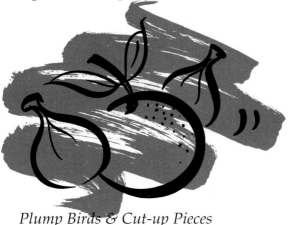

CHICKEN-RICE-TOMATILLO BAKE

Preparation time: About 10 minutes

Cooking time: About 1 hour and 5 minutes

Chicken pieces bake on a rice pilaf with a difference: it's treated to tangy tomatillos, ground cumin, and cilantro. To accompany the dish, offer fresh corn on the cob coated with melted butter and sprinkled with cracked black pepper.

- 1 chicken (about 3½ lbs.), cut up
- 2 tablespoons salad oil
- 1 medium-size onion, chopped
- 1 clove garlic, minced or pressed
- 1 cup long-grain white rice
- 1 can (18 oz.) tomatillos
  About 1 cup regular-strength chicken broth
- 1 can (4 oz.) whole green chiles, thinly sliced crosswise
- 1 teaspoon ground cumin
- 2 tablespoons minced fresh cilantro (coriander)
  Cilantro (coriander) sprigs

Rinse chicken and pat dry. Heat oil in a 12- to 14-inch frying pan over medium-high heat. Add chicken pieces, a portion at a time; cook, turning as needed, until browned on all sides (about 6 minutes). Remove chicken from pan; set aside. Pour off and discard all but 2 tablespoons of the drippings.

Add onion, garlic, and rice to reserved drippings in pan; cook, stirring often, until rice is golden (about 5 minutes). Set aside.

Drain liquid from tomatillos and add enough of the broth to make 2 cups. Cut each tomatillo in half. In a 9- by 13-inch baking dish, mix broth mixture, tomatillos, chiles, cumin, minced cilantro, and rice mixture.

Arrange chicken, except breast pieces, skin side up atop rice. Bake, uncovered, in a 350° oven for 15 minutes. Add breast pieces and any accumulated juices. Continue to bake, uncovered, until meat near thighbone is no longer pink; cut to test (about 30 more minutes). Garnish with cilantro sprigs. Makes 4 servings.

Per serving: 717 calories, 53 g protein, 45 g carbohydrates, 35 g fat, 9 g saturated fat, 159 mg cholesterol, 717 mg sodium

CHICKEN SANTA FE

Preparation time: About 10 minutes

Cooking time: About 1¼ hours

Spicy yet not too hot, this dinner should please anyone with a taste for Southwest cooking. It features plenty of green chiles and just a touch of hot taco sauce; you can add more sauce to taste.

- 1 large can (7 oz.) whole green chiles
- 1 chicken (about 3½ lbs.), cut up
- 2 slices bacon
- 1 large onion, cut into eighths
- 2 cloves garlic, minced or pressed
- ½ cup *each* dry white wine and regular-strength chicken broth
- 1 tablespoon prepared hot taco sauce
- ¼ teaspoon ground cumin
  Salt and pepper

Dice half the chiles; cut remaining chiles lengthwise into thin strips. Set aside in separate piles. Rinse chicken, pat dry, and set aside.

Cook bacon in a 12- to 14-inch frying pan or 5- to 6-quart pan over medium heat until crisp. Lift out; drain on paper towels. Increase heat under pan to medium-high. Add chicken pieces, a portion at a time, to bacon drippings; cook, turning as needed, until browned on all sides (about 6 minutes). Remove from pan and set aside. Pour off and discard all but 2 tablespoons of the drippings.

Add onion and garlic to reserved drippings in pan; cook, stirring often, until onion is soft and layers are separated. Crumble bacon; add to onion along with diced chiles, wine, broth, taco sauce, and cumin. Mix well. Add chicken and any accumulated juices to sauce, arranging chicken pieces skin side up. Spoon some of sauce up over chicken, then arrange chile strips over chicken.

Reduce heat, cover, and simmer until meat near thighbone is no longer pink; cut to test (about 30 minutes). With a slotted spoon, lift chicken from pan and place on a platter; keep warm. Boil sauce over high heat until reduced by about half. Spoon sauce around chicken. Season to taste with salt and pepper. Makes 4 servings.

Per serving: 679 calories, 53 g protein, 7 g carbohydrates, 48 g fat, 14 g saturated fat, 210 mg cholesterol, 799 mg sodium

The garnish tells the story: this dish is spicy! Browned chicken simmers
with tomatoes, carrots, sweet currants, and fresh chiles to make a sensational
stew. Serve Chicken with Currants & Jalapeños (recipe on facing page) with
colorful accompaniments: corn with onion and red pepper, and a cool salad
of apples, jicama, and pomegranate seeds in lime juice.

■ *Pictured on facing page*

CHICKEN WITH CURRANTS & JALAPEÑOS

Preparation time: About 10 minutes

Cooking time: About 1 hour and 5 minutes

Turn chicken stew from standard to sassy with the heated addition of fresh jalapeños. Dried currants add a sweet accent and soak up some of the spicy sauce.

1	**chicken (about 4 lbs.), cut up**
¾	**teaspoon paprika**
2	**tablespoons olive oil or salad oil**
5	**cloves garlic, minced or pressed**
2	**fresh jalapeño chiles, seeded and minced**
1	**large onion, chopped**
2	**medium-size carrots, sliced**
4	**ounces mushrooms, sliced**
1	**can (14½ oz.) stewed tomatoes**
½	**teaspoon ground cumin**
½	**teaspoon fines herbes or dry thyme leaves**
¾	**cup dry white wine or regular-strength chicken broth**
½	**cup dried currants**

Rinse chicken, pat dry, and sprinkle all over with paprika. Heat oil in a 4- to 5-quart pan over medium-high heat. Add chicken pieces, a portion at a time; cook, turning as needed, until browned on all sides (about 6 minutes). Remove from pan and set aside.

Add garlic, chiles, onion, and carrots to pan. Cook, stirring often, until vegetables begin to brown lightly (about 12 minutes). Add mushrooms, tomatoes, cumin, fines herbes, wine, and currants; then add chicken and any accumulated juices. Bring to a boil. Then reduce heat and simmer, uncovered, until meat near thighbone is no longer pink; cut to test (about 40 minutes). Makes 4 servings.

Per serving: 853 calories, 61 g protein, 31 g carbohydrates, 54 g fat, 14 g saturated fat, 232 mg cholesterol, 524 mg sodium

BRAISED CHICKEN WITH GARLIC, TOMATOES & POTATOES

Preparation time: About 15 minutes

Cooking time: About 55 minutes

Two *dozen* garlic cloves? That alarming number may be enough to make you flinch and promptly turn the page. But give this meal a try—you'll be surprised by its deliciously mellow flavor. The secret lies in cooking the cloves without cutting them.

1	**chicken (about 3½ lbs.), cut up**
2	**tablespoons salad oil**
24	**large cloves garlic, peeled**
4	**large firm-ripe pear-shaped tomatoes (about 12 oz. *total*), cut in half lengthwise**
1	**cup *each* dry white wine and regular-strength chicken broth**
4	**small thin-skinned potatoes (*each* 1½ to 2 inches in diameter), scrubbed and cut in half**
	Salt and pepper

Rinse chicken and pat dry. Heat oil in a 12- to 14-inch frying pan or 5- to 6-quart pan over medium-high heat. Add chicken pieces, a portion at a time; cook, turning as needed, until browned on all sides (about 6 minutes). Remove from pan and set aside.

Reduce heat to medium; add garlic and tomato halves, cut side down, to pan. Cook until tomatoes are lightly browned (about 2 minutes). Lift out tomatoes; set aside.

Add chicken and any accumulated juices to pan, then add wine, broth, and potatoes. Bring to a boil; then reduce heat, cover, and simmer until potatoes are tender when pierced (about 25 minutes). Set tomatoes on top of chicken. Continue to simmer, covered, until meat near thighbone is no longer pink; cut to test (about 5 more minutes). With a slotted spoon, lift out chicken, garlic, potatoes, and tomatoes; place on a platter and keep warm.

Boil pan juices over high heat until reduced to about 1 cup (about 5 minutes). Pour over chicken. Season to taste with salt and pepper. Makes 4 servings.

Per serving: 742 calories, 54 g protein, 21 g carbohydrates, 48 g fat, 13 g saturated fat, 203 mg cholesterol, 453 mg sodium

Feature

COOK'S CHOICE—CHICKEN OR TURKEY

Today's markets offer a wide selection of skinless, boneless cuts of chicken and turkey—and that presents plenty of options for creative cooks. You'll be able to devise all sorts of appetizing recipes, many of them low in fat and quick to cook. With appropriate attention to preparation, it's even possible to interchange chicken and turkey in some dishes. Such a substitution is easiest for ground meat (see pages 405 to 423), but on these two pages, we offer suggestions for roasting, steeping, barbecuing, and stir-frying chicken or turkey breasts, thighs, or tenderloins.

Note: We used chicken breast to calculate our preparation times, cooking times, and nutritional data.

ROASTED THAI NUGGETS

Preparation time: About 15 minutes

Roasting time: About 12 minutes

> Thai Sauce (page 419)
> 1 **pound skinless, boneless chicken or turkey**
> 3 **tablespoons minced fresh cilantro (coriander)**
> 2 **teaspoons coarsely ground pepper**
> 6 **cloves garlic, minced**

Prepare Thai Sauce and refrigerate.

Rinse poultry and pat dry. *If using chicken breast halves,* cut each diagonally across the grain into 2 equal pieces; tuck thin ends under. *If using chicken thighs,* roll each into a compact shape. *If using turkey breast or thigh,* cut into 8 equal-size pieces no thicker than 1½ inches. *If using turkey tenderloins,* split lengthwise, cutting away tendon in center; divide into 8 equal-size pieces.

Mix cilantro, pepper, and garlic. Rub mixture over poultry, then place pieces well apart in an ungreased shallow 10- by 15-inch baking pan.

Roast, uncovered, in a 500° oven until meat is lightly browned and no longer pink in center; cut to test. Allow about 12 minutes for chicken breast, 18 minutes for chicken thigh, 10 minutes for turkey breast or ten-

derloin, and 15 minutes for turkey thigh. Serve with Thai Sauce. Makes 4 servings.

Per serving without sauce: 134 calories, 27 g protein, 2 g carbohydrates, 1 g fat, 0 g saturated fat, 66 mg cholesterol, 75 mg sodium

STEEPED POULTRY IN ROLLS

Preparation time: About 15 minutes

Cooking time: About 25 minutes

> 1 **pound skinless, boneless chicken or turkey**
> 4 **cups water**
> 2 **cups regular-strength chicken broth**
> ¼ **cup chili powder**
> ¼ **cup firmly packed brown sugar**
> 2 **teaspoons dry oregano leaves**
> 1 **star anise or 1 teaspoon anise seeds**
> 3 **tablespoons *each* olive oil and red wine vinegar**
> 2 **tablespoons *each* chopped fresh cilantro (coriander) and minced green onion (including top)**
> 4 **French rolls (*each* 6 inches long), split**
> **Butter lettuce leaves, washed and crisped**

Rinse poultry and pat dry. Place all pieces to be pounded between 2 sheets of plastic wrap. *If using chicken breast halves or thighs,* cook as is. *If using a 1-pound turkey breast piece,* cut across the grain into 1-inch-thick slices. *If using turkey tenderloins or turkey thigh,* pound with a flat-surfaced mallet until ½ to ¾ inch thick.

In a 4- to 5-quart pan with a tight-fitting lid, combine water, broth, chili powder, sugar, oregano, and anise; bring to a boil. Remove from heat and immediately add poultry pieces, opened out as flat as possible. Cover pan and let stand until meat is no longer pink in center; lift from water and cut to test (do not lift cover until ready to test). Allow about 20 minutes for all poultry cuts; if meat is not done, return to water, cover, and let steep for about 2 more minutes.

Drain meat, reserving 2 cups of the steeping liquid. Boil reserved 2 cups liquid over high heat until reduced to ⅓ cup; as liquid becomes concentrated, watch carefully to prevent scorching. Serve meat warm; or, to serve cold, cover meat and liquid separately and refrigerate for up to 2 days.

To serve, prepare a dressing by mixing reduced liquid with oil, vinegar, cilantro, and onion. Cut poultry pieces across the grain into thin, slanting slices. Moisten cut surfaces of rolls with dressing; fill rolls with meat and lettuce. Makes 4 servings.

Per serving: 414 calories, 32 g protein, 39 g carbohydrates, 14 g fat, 2 g saturated fat, 68 mg cholesterol, 596 mg sodium

GRILLED ROMAINE WRAPS

Preparation time: About 15 minutes

Grilling time: About 20 minutes

    Green Dressing (recipe follows)
1 pound skinless, boneless chicken or turkey
2 large, 4 medium-size, or 8 small romaine lettuce leaves (size depends on poultry used; see instructions below)
4 thin slices prosciutto (about 2½ oz. *total*)
    Salt and pepper

Prepare Green Dressing and set aside. Rinse poultry and pat dry; set aside.

In a 10- to 12-inch frying pan, bring 1 inch water to a boil. Plunge lettuce into water for 1 minute. Lift out; immerse in cold water until cool. Drain and pat dry.

If using chicken breast halves, wrap each piece in 1 slice prosciutto and 1 medium-size lettuce leaf. *If using chicken thighs,* roll each into a compact shape and wrap in a half-slice of prosciutto and 1 small lettuce leaf. *If using a 1-pound turkey breast piece or thigh,* cut into 4 equal-size logs (each 1 to 1½ inches thick); wrap each in 1 slice prosciutto and 1 medium-size lettuce leaf. *If using large turkey tenderloins,* wrap each in 2 slices prosciutto and 1 large lettuce leaf.

Place wrapped poultry on a grill 4 to 6 inches above a solid bed of medium coals. Cook, turning occasionally, until meat in thickest part is no longer pink; cut to test. Allow about 20 minutes for chicken or turkey breast, about 25 minutes for turkey tenderloin, chicken thigh, or turkey thigh.

To serve, cut meat across the grain into 1-inch-thick slices; arrange on 4 dinner plates. Add Green Dressing, salt, and pepper to taste. Makes 4 servings.

Per serving without dressing: 160 calories, 31 g protein, 0 g carbohydrates, 3 g fat, 1 g saturated fat, 76 mg cholesterol, 342 mg sodium

GREEN DRESSING. In a blender or food processor, combine ⅓ cup **olive oil** or salad oil, ¼ cup **white wine vinegar,** 2 tablespoons minced **onion,** 1 tablespoon minced **parsley,** and 2 teaspoons *each* minced **fresh sage and thyme leaves** (or ¾ teaspoon *each* dry leaves). Whirl until puréed. Makes ½ cup.

Per tablespoon: 81 calories, 0 g protein, 1 g carbohydrates, 9 g fat, 1 g saturated fat, 0 mg cholesterol, 0 mg sodium

STIR-FRIED POULTRY

Preparation time: About 15 minutes

Cooking time: About 6 minutes

1 pound skinless, boneless chicken or turkey
¾ cup regular-strength chicken broth
1 tablespoon lemon juice
2 tablespoons drained capers
2 to 3 tablespoons olive oil or salad oil
1 small onion, cut into 1-inch squares
    About 4 cups washed, crisped arugula, watercress, or Belgian endive

Rinse poultry and pat dry. Place all pieces to be pounded between 2 sheets of plastic wrap. *If using chicken or turkey stir-fry strips or chicken tenderloins,* cook as is. *If using chicken breast halves, chicken thighs, or turkey breast slices,* pound with a flat-surfaced mallet until about ¼ inch thick. *If using turkey tenderloins,* split lengthwise, cutting away tendon in center; then cut across the grain into ¼-inch-thick slices. *If using turkey thigh,* cut across the grain into ¼-inch-thick slices. Cut all larger poultry pieces into 1-inch squares.

To prepare sauce, mix broth, lemon juice, and capers in a small bowl. Set aside.

Heat 1 tablespoon of the oil in a 12- to 14-inch frying pan or wok over high heat. Add onion; cook, stirring, until browned at edges (about 2 minutes). Pour onion into a bowl. Add 1 more tablespoon oil to pan; then add half the poultry in a single layer. Cook until meat begins to brown (about 1 minute). Then turn pieces over and continue to cook until no longer pink in center; cut to test (about 30 more seconds). Add to onion in bowl. Repeat to cook remaining poultry, adding more oil if needed to prevent sticking.

Pour sauce into pan, stir to scrape up browned bits, and boil until reduced to ¼ cup. Remove pan from heat and stir in poultry mixture. Distribute greens equally on 4 dinner plates; spoon poultry mixture over greens. Makes 4 servings.

Per serving: 212 calories, 28 g protein, 2 g carbohydrates, 10 g fat, 2 g saturated fat, 66 mg cholesterol, 384 mg sodium

CHILI-GLAZED CHICKEN WITH PEAS

Preparation time: About 5 minutes

Grilling time: About 40 minutes

Try serving iced tea and margaritas with this lime- and chili-charged chicken. A buttery baste helps keep the pieces moist—and makes them especially flavorful, too.

    1 chicken (3 to 3½ lbs.), cut up
    ⅓ cup butter or margarine, melted
    2 cloves garlic, minced or pressed
    1 teaspoon chili powder
    ¼ teaspoon *each* ground cumin and grated
       lime peel
    2 tablespoons lime juice
    2 pounds peas in the pod
    2 tablespoons water

Rinse chicken and pat dry. In a small pan, stir together butter, garlic, chili powder, cumin, lime peel, and lime juice. Brush generously over chicken.

Arrange chicken, except breast pieces, skin side up on a lightly greased grill 4 to 6 inches above a solid bed of medium coals. Cook for 15 minutes, turning and basting frequently with butter mixture. Place breast pieces on grill. Continue to cook, turning and basting often, until meat near thighbone is no longer pink; cut to test (about 25 more minutes).

Meanwhile, rinse peas; then place in a cast-iron frying pan or Dutch oven and add water. Cover with lid or foil; place on grill next to chicken during last 15 minutes of cooking, stirring peas every 5 minutes. Let guests shell their own peas to eat alongside chicken. Makes 4 servings.

Per serving: 599 calories, 49 g protein, 14 g carbohydrates, 38 g fat, 16 g saturated fat, 184 mg cholesterol, 299 mg sodium

BARBECUED TURKEY

Preparation time: 15 minutes, plus 30 minutes to heat coals

Grilling time: 4 to 4½ hours

It's easy to roast a big turkey out on the patio if you grill it by indirect heat in a covered barbecue. Fresh rosemary sprigs on the hot coals add an appealing aroma to the barbecued bird.

    1 turkey (20 to 22 lbs.)
    2 teaspoons poultry seasoning
    ¼ teaspoon pepper
    1 cup port
    1 large onion, quartered
    2 large carrots (about 12 oz. *total*), cut into
       chunks
    2 stalks celery, cut into chunks
    1 clove garlic, quartered
    3 or 4 rosemary sprigs (*each* 3 to 4 inches
       long)

Open or remove lid from a covered barbecue; open bottom dampers. Pile about 50 long-burning briquets on fire grate and ignite them. Let briquets burn until hot (about 30 minutes). Using long-handled tongs, bank about half the briquets on each side of fire grate; then place a metal drip pan in center. Set cooking grill in place 4 to 6 inches above pan; lightly grease grill.

Reserve turkey neck and giblets for other uses; pull off and discard lumps of fat from turkey. Rinse turkey inside and out; pat dry. Combine poultry seasoning and pepper. Sprinkle some of mixture into neck and body cavities; rub remaining mixture over skin. Place turkey on its breast and spoon 1 to 2 tablespoons of the port into neck cavity; bring skin over opening and skewer cavity shut. Turn turkey on its back and place onion, carrots, celery, and garlic in body cavity.

Place turkey, breast up, on grill directly above drip pan. Pour about ⅓ cup of the remaining port into body cavity; cover barbecue and adjust dampers as necessary to maintain an even heat. Cook until a meat thermometer, inserted straight down through thickest part of breast until it touches the bone, registers 160°F; or cook until meat near thighbone is no longer pink (cut to test). Total time will be 4 to 4½ hours.

Several times during cooking, place a rosemary sprig on the coals to add fragrance as it smolders. During last hour, brush turkey with port several times, using all remaining port. When turkey is done, discard stuffing. Makes 16 to 18 servings.

Per serving: 448 calories, 77 g protein, 1 g carbohydrates, 12 g fat, 4 g saturated fat, 202 mg cholesterol, 197 mg sodium

*Keep company busy at your next barbecue with our Chili-glazed
Chicken with Peas (recipe on facing page). Between bites of spicy butter-basted
chicken, guests shell and enjoy fresh peas steamed in a kettle on the grill.*

337

Preparation time: About 1½ hours

Cooking time: 3¼ to 3¾ hours

When it comes to roast turkey, doubling the pleasure means doubling the opportunity to eat stuffing! This plump bird is sure to please; it's filled with a richly seasoned wild rice stuffing, while a lighter brown rice dressing bakes alongside.

> **Wild & Tame Rice Stuffings (recipe follows)**
> **Brown Turkey Gravy (recipe on facing page)**
> 1 **turkey (12 to 14 lbs.)**
> **About 3 tablespoons olive oil**
> **Parsley, rosemary, or thyme sprigs**

Prepare Wild & Tame Rice Stuffings; set aside.

Reserve turkey neck for other uses. Rinse turkey giblets; begin preparing Brown Turkey Gravy.

Pull off and discard lumps of fat from turkey. Rinse turkey inside and out, pat dry, and fill breast and body cavities with wild rice–chard stuffing. Skewer cavities shut. Rub bird all over with oil; then place, breast down, on a V-shaped rack set in a 12- by 15-inch roasting pan.

Roast, uncovered, in a 350° oven for 1 hour; remove from oven. Tilt bird to drain juices into pan; then turn breast up. Continue to roast until a meat thermometer, inserted straight down through thickest part of breast until it touches the bone, registers 160°F; or roast until meat near thighbone is no longer pink (cut to test). Additional time will be 2 to 2½ hours.

About 1 hour before turkey is done, place brown rice–spinach stuffing in a greased shallow 2- to 2½-quart baking dish. Cover tightly and bake until very hot in center (about 1 hour).

Remove skewers from turkey; spoon stuffing into a wide, shallow serving bowl, mounding it on one side.

Mound brown rice–spinach stuffing in bowl on other side. Place turkey on a platter. Keep turkey and stuffing warm while you finish gravy. Garnish turkey and stuffing with herbs; offer gravy to spoon over meat and stuffing. Makes 8 to 12 servings.

Per serving turkey without dressing or gravy: 488 calories, 85 g protein, 0 g carbohydrates, 14 g fat, 4 g saturated fat, 224 mg cholesterol, 215 mg sodium

WILD & TAME RICE STUFFINGS. In a 1- to 2-quart pan, bring 1½ cups **water** to a boil over high heat. Add ½ cup **wild rice,** rinsed and drained. Also, in a 3- to 4-quart pan, bring 3 cups **water** to a boil over high heat; add 1¾ cups **long-grain brown rice.** Reduce heat under both pans, cover, and simmer until rices are tender to bite (about 45 minutes). Drain.

While rices are cooking, place 1½ ounces **dried porcini mushrooms** (cèpes) in a bowl and add 1⅓ cups **hot water.** Let stand until mushrooms are limp (about 20 minutes), then gently squeeze mushrooms in the water to help release any grit. Lift out mushrooms, chop, and set aside. Pour soaking liquid into another container, taking care not to disturb residue in bottom of bowl. Save liquid for gravy; discard residue.

Place two 10- to 12-inch frying pans over medium-high heat. Into one pan, crumble ⅓ pound **hot Italian sausage** (casings removed); into other pan, crumble ⅓ pound **mild Italian sausage** (casings removed). Cook, stirring often to break sausage into small bits, until lightly browned (about 5 minutes). With a slotted spoon, transfer to paper towels to drain; then place each kind of sausage in a separate large bowl.

To each frying pan, add 2 tablespoons **olive oil** or salad oil and 1 medium-size **onion,** chopped.

To pan in which hot sausage was cooked, also add porcini mushrooms; 4 ounces **button mushrooms,** sliced; 3 cloves **garlic,** minced or pressed; and 1½ to 2 tablespoons *each* minced **fresh marjoram leaves** and minced **fresh sage** (or about 2 teaspoons *each* dry leaves). To other frying pan, add 1½ tablespoons *each* minced **fresh marjoram leaves** and minced **fresh sage** (or about 2 teaspoons *each* dry leaves) and 1¼ cups sliced **celery.** Cook, stirring often, until vegetables in both pans are very soft (about 10 minutes).

Meanwhile, rinse 8 ounces **Swiss chard;** drain and chop. Also remove stems and any wilted leaves from 12 ounces **spinach;** rinse remaining leaves, drain, and chop.

Add chard to pan with mushrooms, spinach to pan with celery. Cook, stirring often, until greens are wilted and liquid has evaporated (4 to 6 minutes).

To bowl with hot sausage, add chard mixture, wild rice, 2 cups of the brown rice, ½ cup grated **Parmesan cheese,** and ½ cup **dry white wine.** To bowl with mild sausage, add spinach mixture, remaining brown rice, ½ cup grated **Parmesan cheese,** ¼ cup **dry white wine,** and ½ cup **regular-strength chicken broth.** Mix contents of both bowls well; season to taste with **salt** and **pepper.** If made ahead, cover and refrigerate for up to 1 day. Makes 12 cups.

Per ½ cup of wild rice–chard stuffing: 153 calories, 6 g protein, 16 g carbohydrates, 8 g fat, 3 g saturated fat, 12 mg cholesterol, 196 mg sodium

Per ½ cup of brown rice–spinach stuffing: 154 calories, 6 g protein, 16 g carbohydrates, 8 g fat, 3 g saturated fat, 12 mg cholesterol, 218 mg sodium

BROWN TURKEY GRAVY. Wrap and refrigerate **turkey liver;** place remaining **turkey giblets** in a 3- to 4-quart pan. Add 1 medium-size **onion,** quartered; 1 large stalk **celery,** chopped; 2 **dry bay leaves;** ½ teaspoon **dry thyme leaves;** 5 cups **water;** and **soaking liquid from porcini mushrooms** (reserved from stuffing).

Bring to a boil over high heat; then reduce heat, cover, and simmer until gizzard is very tender when pierced (about 2¼ hours). Add liver to pan; simmer for 15 more minutes.

Pour broth through a fine strainer; discard vegetables and giblets. Measure broth; you should have 5 cups. If necessary, boil broth over high heat to reduce; or add **regular-strength chicken broth** to increase amount. Return strained broth to cooking pan.

After turkey is done, pour fat and drippings from roasting pan into a glass measuring cup. Let stand until fat rises to surface, then ladle out and discard all but ¼ cup of the fat. Add this reserved fat and drippings to roasting pan; stir or whisk over medium-high heat, scraping up browned bits. Then scrape mixture into pan of broth.

In a small bowl, stir together ½ cup **cornstarch** and 1 cup **dry white wine** or regular-strength chicken broth until smooth. Add to broth in pan. Bring to a boil over high heat, whisking or stirring constantly. Pour into a bowl or gravy boat. Makes 6 cups.

Per tablespoon: 11 calories, 0 g protein, 1 g carbohydrates, 1 g fat, 0 g saturated fat, 2 mg cholesterol, 1 mg sodium

BLACK BEAN TURKEY CASSOULET

Preparation time: About 25 minutes

Cooking time: About 3¼ hours

Cassoulet is traditionally prepared with goose or duck and white beans, but our version—made with black beans and turkey pieces—is every bit as satisfying and hearty. It's the perfect meal for winter parties; just add a tossed salad and dark beer.

      3   **large onions**
      4   **ounces sliced bacon, chopped**
      2   **parsley sprigs**
      2   **dry bay leaves**
      2   **teaspoons dry thyme leaves**
      4   **cloves garlic, minced or pressed**
  1½   **pounds dried black beans**
      2   **pounds boneless pork shoulder or butt (trimmed of excess fat), cut into 1-inch chunks**
      6   **cups regular-strength chicken broth**
      1   **small turkey (about 8 lbs.), cut up**
      1   **pound garlic sausages**
   ½   **cup (¼ lb.) butter or margarine**
      2   **cups coarse soft bread crumbs**

Coarsely chop one of the onions; place in a 7- to 8-quart pan and add bacon. Cook over medium-high heat, stirring often, until onion is soft (about 7 minutes). Add parsley, bay leaves, thyme, and half the garlic; cook, stirring often, until garlic is soft (about 2 minutes). Remove from heat.

Sort beans and discard any debris. Rinse beans well, drain, and add to onion mixture along with pork; then stir in broth. Bring to a boil; reduce heat, cover, and simmer, stirring occasionally, until beans mash easily (about 2½ hours).

Meanwhile, place remaining 2 onions (unpeeled) in a shallow baking pan. Bake, uncovered, in a 350° oven until soft when pressed (about 1½ hours). Let cool; peel and cut lengthwise into quarters.

Also rinse turkey and pat dry. Then arrange turkey (skin side up) and sausages in a single layer in a shallow 10- by 15-inch baking pan. Bake, uncovered, in a 350° oven until meat near turkey thighbone is no longer pink; cut to test (about 50 minutes; turn meats after 30 minutes). Remove meats from pan with a slotted spoon; cut sausages into ¼-inch-thick diagonal slices.

Melt butter in a 10- to 12-inch frying pan over medium-high heat. Add crumbs and remaining garlic; stir until crumbs are light brown (about 3 minutes).

Divide bean mixture between two 4-quart casseroles; mix half each of the onions, turkey pieces, and sausages into each. Sprinkle evenly with crumbs. Bake, uncovered, in a 350° oven until hot and golden brown on top (about 30 minutes). Makes 16 servings.

Per serving: 762 calories, 64 g protein, 33 g carbohydrates, 41 g fat, 15 g saturated fat, 210 mg cholesterol, 865 mg sodium

For a meal that's simple to prepare and simply delicious,
serve steamed baby bok choy and red potatoes alongside Baked
Chicken Breasts with Pears (recipe on page 342). You poach the fruit in
pear brandy while the soy-coated chicken breasts bake.

Tender Breast Meat

BUNDLED & BREADED & FRUITED & CHEESED &

SAUTÉED & CHUTNEYED & STEAMED & SMOKED &

CREAMED & ROLLED & GINGERED & BROILED &

STEWED & SCENTED & KEBABED & SLICED &

HERB-BAKED CHICKEN BREASTS

Preparation time: About 10 minutes

Marinating time: At least 1 hour or up to 1 day

Cooking time: About 1 hour and 10 minutes

A simple marinade accented with thyme and rosemary dresses up chicken breasts for Sunday supper. Onions and bright bell peppers bake alongside the chicken; you might round out the meal with a bowl of fluffy mashed potatoes.

- 6 skinless, boneless chicken breast halves (about 1½ lbs. *total*)

  Herb Marinade (recipe follows)
- 2 large onions, sliced crosswise
- 2 *each* large red and yellow bell peppers (1½ to 2 lbs. *total*), seeded and slivered
- 3 tablespoons olive oil
- ½ cup *each* regular-strength chicken broth and dry red wine

Rinse chicken, pat dry, and place, skinned side up, in a shallow 10- by 15-inch baking pan. Prepare Herb Marinade; brush over chicken. Cover and refrigerate for at least 1 hour or up to 1 day.

Place onions and bell peppers in a 12- by 17-inch baking pan; drizzle evenly with oil. Bake, uncovered, on lower rack of a 450° oven for 45 minutes, stirring occasionally. Place pan of chicken on upper rack of oven. Continue to bake, stirring vegetables occasionally, for about 20 more minutes. Vegetables should be soft when pierced and browned at edges; chicken meat in thickest part should no longer be pink (cut to test). With a slotted spoon, transfer onions, peppers, and chicken to a platter; cover and keep warm.

Skim any fat from chicken pan juices; add broth and wine. Boil over high heat, stirring to scrape up browned bits, until reduced to ½ cup (about 5 minutes). Spoon sauce over chicken. Makes 6 servings.

HERB MARINADE. In a small bowl, stir together 3 tablespoons **olive oil**, 1 tablespoon **balsamic vinegar** or red wine vinegar, 1½ teaspoons *each* **dry rosemary** and **dry thyme leaves,** and ¼ teaspoon coarsely ground **pepper.**

Per serving: 296 calories, 28 g protein, 11 g carbohydrates, 16 g fat, 2 g saturated fat, 66 mg cholesterol, 162 mg sodium

■ *Pictured on page 340*

BAKED CHICKEN BREASTS WITH PEARS

Preparation time: About 5 minutes

Cooking time: About 20 minutes

Chicken breasts, a little soy sauce, some sliced pears—the dish may sound too plain, but wait until you taste it! These aren't just any pears; they're first poached in fragrant brandy, then tossed with the meat and pan juices to make a memorable meal.

- 6 skinless, boneless chicken breast halves (about 1½ lbs. *total*)
- 3 tablespoons soy sauce
- 4 teaspoons cornstarch
- 1 cup pear-flavored brandy or apple juice
- 2 medium-size firm-ripe pears

  Parsley sprigs

  Salt and pepper

  Lime wedges

Rinse chicken and pat dry; then arrange, skinned side up, in a 9- by 13-inch baking pan. Drizzle evenly with soy. Bake, uncovered, in a 450° oven, basting occasionally, until meat in thickest part is no longer pink; cut to test (about 20 minutes).

Meanwhile, place cornstarch in a 1½- to 2-quart pan; smoothly stir in brandy. Peel and core pears, then cut lengthwise into ½-inch-thick slices. Add pears to pan and bring to a boil over medium-high heat, mixing gently. Then reduce heat, cover, and simmer until pears are tender when pierced (about 5 minutes).

When chicken is done, add pear mixture to baking pan; gently shake pan to mix pears and chicken. Transfer chicken, pears, and sauce to a platter and garnish with parsley. Season to taste with salt and pepper; offer lime wedges to squeeze over individual servings. Makes 6 servings.

Per serving: 248 calories, 27 g protein, 23 g carbohydrates, 2 g fat, 0 g saturated fat, 66 mg cholesterol, 588 mg sodium

PLUM CHICKEN

Preparation time: About 10 minutes

Baking time: About 25 minutes

"Spicy" and "succulent" are the words that describe this quick-to-cook entrée. Bottled plum sauce sparked with ginger and anise glazes the juicy chicken. Serve with brown rice and a green vegetable—perhaps snap beans, snow peas, or broccoli.

- 4 skinless, boneless chicken breast halves (about 1 lb. *total*)
- 1 cup Oriental plum sauce
- ¼ cup minced onion
- 2 tablespoons lemon juice
- 1 tablespoon reduced-sodium soy sauce
- 1 teaspoon grated lemon peel
- ½ teaspoon *each* dry mustard and ground ginger
- ¼ teaspoon *each* pepper and liquid hot pepper seasoning
- ¼ teaspoon anise seeds, crushed

Rinse chicken, pat dry, and place, skinned side up, in a 9- by 13-inch or other shallow 3-quart baking dish. In a small bowl, stir together plum sauce, onion, lemon juice, soy, lemon peel, mustard, ginger, pepper, hot pepper seasoning, and anise seeds. Pour over chicken.

Bake chicken, uncovered, in a 400° oven until meat in thickest part is no longer pink; cut to test (about 25 minutes). Baste chicken halfway through baking. To serve, transfer chicken to a platter; spoon sauce on top. Makes 4 servings.

Per serving: 353 calories, 27 g protein, 58 g carbohydrates, 2 g fat, 0 g saturated fat, 66 mg cholesterol, 243 mg sodium

DIJON BAKED CHICKEN

Preparation time: About 20 minutes

Baking time: About 25 minutes

When only the best will do, choose this recipe. Boneless breast halves are coated with white wine and Dijon mustard, rolled in fresh bread crumbs seasoned with parsley and Parmesan, and baked until golden. Serve hot; or chill, then serve cold for an elegant picnic entrée.

- 2 cups soft bread crumbs
- ½ cup grated Parmesan cheese
- ¼ cup chopped parsley
- ½ cup (¼ lb.) butter or margarine, melted
- ⅛ teaspoon ground red pepper (cayenne)
- ½ cup Dijon mustard
- ¼ cup dry white wine
- 2 tablespoons minced shallots
- 1 teaspoon dry thyme leaves
- 8 skinless, boneless chicken breast halves (about 2 lbs. *total*)

In a shallow pan or wide, shallow rimmed plate, combine crumbs, cheese, parsley, butter, and red pepper. In another shallow pan, mix mustard, wine, shallots, and thyme.

Rinse chicken and pat dry; coat with mustard mixture, then dip in crumb mixture. Arrange chicken pieces slightly apart in a greased shallow baking pan. Bake, uncovered, in a 400° oven until chicken is golden brown on outside and meat in thickest part is no longer pink; cut to test (about 25 minutes). Makes 8 servings.

Per serving: 302 calories, 30 g protein, 9 g carbohydrates, 16 g fat, 9 g saturated fat, 101 mg cholesterol, 791 mg sodium

EASY OVEN-FRIED CHICKEN

Preparation time: About 10 minutes

Marinating time: About 20 minutes

Baking time: About 20 minutes

Looking for an alternative to fried chicken? Baking is easier on the cook and more healthful for the diner. A little cornmeal adds an appealing crunch to the well-seasoned coating for these tender chicken breasts.

- 4 **skinless, boneless chicken breast halves (about 1 lb. *total*)**
- 2 **tablespoons dry sherry**
- 2 **cloves garlic, minced or pressed**
- ½ **cup soft whole wheat bread crumbs**
- 2 **tablespoons cornmeal**
- ½ **teaspoon salt**
- 1 **teaspoon paprika**
- ½ **teaspoon *each* pepper, dry sage leaves, dry thyme leaves, and dry basil leaves**
- 1 **teaspoon salad oil**

Rinse chicken and pat dry. In a shallow bowl, combine sherry and garlic. Add chicken, turn to coat, and let stand for about 20 minutes.

In a wide, shallow rimmed plate, combine crumbs, cornmeal, salt, paprika, pepper, sage, thyme, and basil. Dip each chicken piece in crumb mixture to coat.

Brush a shallow 10- by 15-inch baking pan with oil. Arrange chicken in pan. Bake, uncovered, in a 450° oven until meat in thickest part is no longer pink; cut to test (about 20 minutes). Serve hot or cold. Makes 4 servings.

Per serving: 175 calories, 27 g protein, 8 g carbohydrates, 3 g fat, 1 g saturated fat, 66 mg cholesterol, 382 mg sodium

■ *Pictured on facing page*

CHICKEN BREASTS WITH CHEESE & CHILES

Preparation time: About 10 minutes

Baking and broiling time: About 32 minutes

Piled high with creamy avocado, crisp bacon, and melted jack cheese, these chicken breasts offer a sensational medley of tastes and textures.

- 4 **skinless, boneless chicken breast halves (about 1 lb. *total*)**
- 1 **cup (4 oz.) shredded jack cheese**
- 1 **can (4 oz.) diced green chiles**
- ½ **cup chopped green onions (including tops)**
- 4 **slices bacon, crisply cooked, drained, and crumbled**
- 1 **medium-size firm-ripe avocado**
- 1 **cup sour cream (optional)**

Rinse chicken, pat dry, and place, skinned side up, in an 8- by 12-inch baking pan. Cover tightly with foil and bake in a 350° oven for 15 minutes. Meanwhile, mix cheese and chiles.

After chicken has baked for 15 minutes, remove foil. Top each piece equally with cheese mixture, patting to hold in place. Sprinkle evenly with onions and bacon.

Return to oven and continue to bake, uncovered, until cheese is melted and meat in thickest part is no longer pink; cut to test (about 15 more minutes). Then broil about 4 inches below heat until lightly browned (about 2 minutes).

Pit avocado, then peel and slice. To serve, arrange avocado over chicken; serve with sour cream, if desired. Makes 4 servings.

Per serving: 358 calories, 37 g protein, 6 g carbohydrates, 21 g fat, 3 g saturated fat, 96 mg cholesterol, 505 mg sodium

Here's a way to have supper in the Southwest without even leaving home. Corn sticks, black bean salad, baked papaya with lime juice, and icy sangrita are just the right partners for avocado-topped Chicken Breasts with Cheese & Chiles (recipe on facing page).

345

MACADAMIA CHICKEN

Preparation time: About 10 minutes

Cooking time: About 20 minutes

For a hint of Hawaii, serve up honey-sweetened chicken and fresh pineapple with a macadamia nut topping. Cooked spinach makes a colorful bed for the meat and fruit.

- 4 skinless, boneless chicken breast halves (about 1 lb. *total*)
- 1 piece pineapple (about 2 lbs.), peeled, cored, and cut crosswise into 4 equal slices (weight of peeled pineapple will be about 1 lb.)
- ¼ cup Dijon mustard
- 3 tablespoons honey
- 1 tablespoon *each* salad oil and lime juice
- 2 packages (10 oz. *each*) frozen chopped spinach
- 2 tablespoons chopped salted macadamia nuts

  Salt and pepper

Rinse chicken and pat dry. Place chicken (skinned side up) and pineapple side by side on rack of a 12- by 14-inch broiling pan. In a bowl, mix mustard, honey, oil, and lime juice; spoon half the mixture evenly over chicken and pineapple. Bake, uncovered, in a 450° oven until meat in thickest part is no longer pink; cut to test (about 20 minutes).

Meanwhile, cook spinach according to package directions; keep warm. Also warm remaining mustard mixture in a small pan over high heat.

To serve, place spinach on a platter, top with chicken and pineapple, and drizzle with mustard mixture. Sprinkle with macadamias and season to taste with salt and pepper. Makes 4 servings.

Per serving: 341 calories, 31 g protein, 36 g carbohydrates, 10 g fat, 1 g saturated fat, 66 mg cholesterol, 649 mg sodium

MELTDOWN CHICKEN BUNDLES

Preparation time: About 35 minutes

Baking time: About 20 minutes

Tucked inside rolled chicken breasts is an appetizing surprise: jalapeños and jack cheese. Fine bread crumbs blended with Parmesan cheese and chili powder make a crisp, golden coating for the baked bundles.

- 8 skinless, boneless chicken breast halves (about 2 lbs. *total*)
- 4 pickled jalapeño chiles
- 4 ounces jack cheese
- ¼ cup fine dry bread crumbs
- 2 tablespoons grated Parmesan cheese
- 1 teaspoon chili powder
- ¼ teaspoon *each* ground cumin and pepper
- 6 tablespoons butter or margarine, melted

Rinse chicken and pat dry. Place each breast half between 2 sheets of wax paper; pound with a flat-surfaced mallet to a thickness of about ¼ inch. Set chicken aside.

Stem and seed jalapeños, then cut each jalapeño lengthwise into ¼-inch-wide strips. Cut jack cheese into 8 equal strips.

In a wide, shallow rimmed plate, combine crumbs, Parmesan cheese, chili powder, cumin, and pepper.

To assemble each chicken bundle, place a strip of cheese and an eighth of the jalapeños on a pounded chicken breast half. Roll chicken around filling to enclose; coat roll with butter, then with crumb mixture.

Arrange rolls, seam side down, in a shallow 10- by 15-inch baking pan. Drizzle evenly with any remaining butter. Bake, uncovered, in a 425° oven until meat is no longer pink and filling is hot in center; cut to test (about 20 minutes). Makes 8 servings.

Per serving: 275 calories, 31 g protein, 3 g carbohydrates, 15 g fat, 6 g saturated fat, 103 mg cholesterol, 397 mg sodium

BROCCOLI-STUFFED CHICKEN BREASTS

Preparation time: About 45 minutes

Baking and broiling time: About 17 minutes

Top these chicken rolls with Swiss cheese and slip them under the broiler just until lightly browned; then let guests cut the golden bundles open to reveal the bright green broccoli-mushroom stuffing inside.

- 1 tablespoon salad oil
- ½ cup minced shallots
- 1 pound mushrooms, minced
- 2 cups broccoli flowerets
- 2 tablespoons Madeira
- 2 tablespoons grated Parmesan cheese
- ½ cup shredded Swiss cheese
- 6 skinless, boneless chicken breast halves (about 1½ lbs. *total*)

Heat oil in a 10- to 12-inch frying pan over medium heat. Add shallots and mushrooms; cook, stirring occasionally, until shallots are soft (about 5 minutes). Add broccoli and Madeira; cover and cook, stirring occasionally, until broccoli is tender-crisp to bite (about 5 minutes). Remove from heat and stir in Parmesan cheese and ¼ cup of the Swiss cheese. Let cool.

Rinse chicken and pat dry. Place each breast half between 2 sheets of plastic wrap; pound with a flat-surfaced mallet to a thickness of about ¼ inch.

In center of each breast half, mound a sixth of the broccoli mixture. Roll chicken around filling to enclose. Set rolls, seam side down, in a greased 9- by 13-inch baking pan. Sprinkle with remaining ¼ cup Swiss cheese.

Bake, uncovered, in a 450° oven until meat is no longer pink and filling is hot in center; cut to test (about 15 minutes). Then broil chicken 4 to 6 inches below heat until cheese is golden brown (about 2 minutes). Makes 6 servings.

Per serving: 232 calories, 33 g protein, 9 g carbohydrates, 7 g fat, 3 g saturated fat, 76 mg cholesterol, 145 mg sodium

CHICKEN BREASTS WITH FETA CHEESE

Preparation time: About 15 minutes

Cooking time: About 10 minutes

Fresh lemon juice and salty feta cheese give sautéed chicken a distinctive tang. Add a simple rice pilaf and steamed tiny artichokes for a satisfying Mediterranean meal.

- 8 ounces feta cheese, crumbled
- ¼ cup chopped fresh oregano leaves
- 6 skinless, boneless chicken breast halves (about 1½ lbs. *total*)
- 1 tablespoon butter or margarine
- 1 tablespoon salad oil
  Juice of 1 lemon

In a small bowl, combine cheese and oregano; set aside.

Rinse chicken and pat dry. Place each breast half between 2 sheets of plastic wrap; pound with a flat-surfaced mallet to a thickness of about ¼ inch. In center of each breast half, mound a sixth of the cheese mixture. Fold chicken over filling to enclose.

Melt butter in oil in a 12- to 14-inch frying pan over medium-high heat. Add chicken and lemon juice. Cook, turning as needed, until meat is golden brown on both sides and no longer pink in center, and cheese filling is hot; cut to test (about 10 minutes). Makes 6 servings.

Per serving: 265 calories, 32 g protein, 2 g carbohydrates, 14 g fat, 8 g saturated fat, 105 mg cholesterol, 515 mg sodium

Flavorful Chicken in Port Cream with Fettuccine (recipe on facing page) deserves to be shown off at your next party—perhaps with a side dish of steamed asparagus. Chopped dried tomatoes and a cup of wine give the sauce its rich, rosy color.

CHICKEN BREASTS WITH PARMESAN PESTO

Preparation time: About 20 minutes

Cooking time: About 10 minutes

Pesto is usually tossed with pasta, but that doesn't mean you can't use it in other ways too. Here, we enclose the basil-rich sauce in pounded chicken breasts. Garnish the dish with blooming basil sprigs from your garden or a produce market.

- 6 skinless, boneless chicken breast halves (about 1½ lbs. *total*)
- 1 cup lightly packed fresh basil leaves
- ¾ cup grated Parmesan cheese
- ¼ cup olive oil
- 1 small clove garlic
- 1½ tablespoons butter or margarine
- 1½ tablespoons olive oil
  About ⅓ cup all-purpose flour
  Basil sprigs

Rinse chicken and pat dry. Place each breast half between 2 sheets of plastic wrap; pound with a flat-surfaced mallet to a thickness of about ¼ inch. Set aside.

In a blender or food processor, combine basil leaves, cheese, the ¼ cup oil, and garlic; whirl to form a thick paste. Then mound a sixth of the pesto in center of each pounded chicken breast half; roll chicken around pesto to enclose.

Melt butter in the 1½ tablespoons oil in a 12- to 14-inch frying pan over medium-high heat. Dip each chicken roll in flour and shake off excess; add chicken to pan. Cook, turning as needed, until meat is golden brown on all sides and no longer pink in center, and filling is hot; cut to test (about 10 minutes). Transfer to a serving dish and garnish with basil sprigs. Makes 6 servings.

Per serving: 338 calories, 32 g protein, 8 g carbohydrates, 20 g fat, 6 g saturated fat, 81 mg cholesterol, 290 mg sodium

■ *Pictured on facing page*

CHICKEN IN PORT CREAM WITH FETTUCCINE

Preparation time: About 5 minutes, plus about 1 hour to soak tomatoes

Cooking time: About 20 minutes

Pasta couldn't be better served than by sautéed chicken in a port-infused cream sauce flecked with chunks of dried tomatoes. Offer plenty of crisp-crusted bread to soak up the extra sauce.

- ¾ cup dried tomatoes
- 6 skinless, boneless chicken breast halves (about 1½ lbs. *total*)
- 3 tablespoons butter or margarine
- 1 cup port
- 1½ cups whipping cream
- 1 package (9 oz.) fresh fettuccine or 8 ounces dry fettuccine
  Salt and pepper
  Tarragon sprigs

In a small bowl, soak tomatoes in warm water to cover until soft (about 1 hour). Drain well, chop coarsely, and set aside.

Rinse chicken and pat dry. Melt butter in a 12- to 14-inch frying pan over medium-high heat. Add chicken and cook, turning as needed, until well browned on both sides and no longer pink in center; cut to test (about 10 minutes). Remove from pan and keep warm.

To pan drippings, add port and cream. Increase heat to high and bring mixture to a boil; boil, stirring occasionally, until large, shiny bubbles form (about 10 minutes). Meanwhile, cook fettuccine according to package directions just until tender to bite. Drain well; transfer to a deep platter and keep warm.

Add tomatoes to cream mixture; then add chicken and any accumulated juices. Season to taste with salt and pepper. Spoon chicken and sauce over fettuccine; garnish with tarragon sprigs. Makes 6 servings.

Per serving: 519 calories, 34 g protein, 36 g carbohydrates, 27 g fat, 16 g saturated fat, 198 mg cholesterol, 179 mg sodium

MINI-HEN MEALS

Cornish game hens can truly be called mini-chickens. Developed from the Cornish breed of chicken, these little birds weigh in at just 1¼ to 1½ pounds—the perfect size for one or two servings. And because their meat is so mild in flavor, game hens are compatible with all sorts of seasonings, sauces, and marinades.

For an elegant evening, try butterflied hens brushed with a mustard coating and roasted with rosemary; if you're planning a romantic dinner for two, simmer a single bird in red wine sauce with carrots, onions, and spinach. Family and guests alike will enjoy roasted birds with an unusual vegetable "hash" featuring yams and jicama. Grilled hens with a flavorful balsamic marinade are another sure success.

■ *Pictured on page 439*

GAME HENS WITH MUSTARD CRUST

Preparation time: About 15 minutes

Roasting time: About 25 minutes

- ¼ cup butter or margarine, melted
- ¼ cup Dijon mustard
- 1 tablespoon minced fresh rosemary; or 1 tablespoon dry rosemary, crumbled
- 2 cloves garlic, minced or pressed
- 4 Cornish game hens (1¼ to 1½ lbs. *each*), thawed if frozen
  Rosemary sprigs (optional)
  Salt and pepper

In a small bowl, stir together butter, mustard, minced rosemary, and garlic. Set aside.

Reserve game hen necks and giblets for other uses. With poultry shears or a knife, split hens lengthwise along one side of backbone. Pull hens open; place, skin side up, on a flat surface and press firmly, cracking bones slightly, until hens lie reasonably flat. Rinse hens and pat dry. Coat both sides of each hen with mustard mixture; then set hens, skin side up, slightly apart in 2 shallow 10- by 15-inch baking pans.

Roast, uncovered, in a 350° oven, switching positions of pans halfway through baking, until meat near thighbone is no longer pink; cut to test (about 25 minutes). Transfer hens to a platter or dinner plates. Garnish with rosemary sprigs, if desired; season to taste with salt and pepper. Makes 4 servings.

Per serving: 783 calories, 75 g protein, 3 g carbohydrates, 50 g fat, 18 g saturated fat, 274 mg cholesterol, 794 mg sodium

GAME HEN DINNER FOR TWO

Preparation time: About 15 minutes

Cooking time: About 35 minutes

- 1 Cornish game hen (about 1½ lbs.), thawed if frozen
- 2 tablespoons butter or margarine
- 6 small onions (*each* about 1 inch in diameter), peeled
- 1 cup regular-strength beef broth
- ½ cup dry red wine
- 1 tablespoon Dijon mustard
- ½ teaspoon dry basil leaves
- 3 slender carrots, cut in half crosswise
- 8 ounces spinach

Reserve game hen neck and giblets for other uses. With poultry shears or a knife, split hen in half, cutting lengthwise through breastbone and along one side of backbone. Rinse hen and pat dry.

Melt butter in a 12- to 14-inch frying pan over medium heat. Add game hen halves and onions; cook, turning as needed, until well browned on all sides (about 15 minutes). Remove hen halves and onions from pan; set aside.

Add broth to pan and boil over high heat, stirring to scrape up browned bits, until reduced to ⅓ cup. Blend in wine, mustard, and basil.

Return hen halves and onions to pan; add carrots. Reduce heat, cover, and simmer until meat near thighbone is no longer pink; cut to test (about 15 minutes). Meanwhile, discard stems and any wilted leaves from spinach; wash and drain remaining leaves.

Mound hen halves, onions, and carrots to one side of pan. Push spinach into broth and stir until wilted. Serve hen halves and vegetables with broth. Makes 2 servings.

Per serving: 700 calories, 48 g protein, 19 g carbohydrates, 48 g fat, 17 g saturated fat, 205 mg cholesterol, 1,023 mg sodium

ROAST GAME HENS WITH VEGETABLE HASH

Preparation time: About 20 minutes

Roasting time: About 1 hour

2 **Cornish game hens (1¼ to 1½ lbs. *each*), thawed if frozen**

3 **tablespoons lemon juice**

3 **tablespoons olive oil or salad oil**

2 **teaspoons minced fresh rosemary; or 2 teaspoons dry rosemary, crumbled**

1 **clove garlic, minced or pressed**

1 **small jicama (about 1 lb.), peeled and cut into ½-inch cubes**

2 **large yams or sweet potatoes (about 1 lb. *total*), scrubbed and cut into ½-inch cubes**

1 **large red or yellow bell pepper (about 6 oz.), seeded and diced**

1 **large onion, coarsely chopped**

1 **package (10 oz.) frozen baby lima beans, thawed**

Salt and pepper

Rosemary sprigs

Reserve game hen necks and giblets for other uses. With poultry shears or a knife, split hens lengthwise through breastbone and along one side of backbone. Rinse hens and pat dry.

In an 12- by 17-inch roasting pan, mix lemon juice, oil, minced rosemary, and garlic. Turn hen halves in oil mixture to coat; lift out and set aside. Add jicama, yams, bell pepper, and onion to pan; stir to coat.

Roast vegetables, uncovered, in a 425° oven for 30 minutes. Stir in beans. Lay hen halves, skin side up, on vegetables and continue to roast, uncovered, until meat near thighbone is no longer pink; cut to test (about 30 more minutes).

Transfer hen halves to a large platter; spoon vegetables alongside. Season to taste with salt and pepper. Garnish with rosemary sprigs. Makes 4 servings.

Per serving: 664 calories, 35 g protein, 60 g carbohydrates, 32 g fat, 7 g saturated fat, 103 mg cholesterol, 153 mg sodium

GRILLED GAME HENS

Preparation time: About 20 minutes

Marinating time: At least 1 hour or up to 1 day

Grilling time: About 30 minutes

Balsamic Marinade (recipe follows)

4 **Cornish game hens (about 1¼ lbs. *each*), thawed if frozen**

2 **medium-size zucchini (about 12 oz. *total*), cut diagonally into ½-inch-thick slices**

2 **medium-size crookneck squash (about 8 oz. *total*), cut diagonally into ½-inch-thick slices**

1 **large red bell pepper (about 6 oz.), seeded and cut into 1½-inch squares**

8 **large mushrooms, stems trimmed**

8 **large shallots (about 8 oz. *total*), peeled
Salt**

Prepare Balsamic Marinade; set aside.

Reserve game hen necks and giblets for other uses. With poultry shears or a knife, split hens lengthwise through breastbone. Pull hens open; place, skin side up, on a flat surface and press firmly, cracking bones slightly, until hens lie reasonably flat.

Place hens in a large heavy-duty plastic bag. Place zucchini, crookneck squash, bell pepper, mushrooms, and shallots in a second heavy-duty plastic bag. Pour half the marinade into each bag; seal bags and turn over several times to coat hens and vegetables with marinade. Set bags in a large, shallow baking pan or dish. Refrigerate for at least 1 hour or up to 1 day, turning bags over occasionally.

Drain hens and vegetables; reserve marinade. Using a pair of parallel metal skewers (at least 12 to 15 inches long), thread 2 hens from wing to wing and from thigh to thigh to hold them flat. Repeat to skewer remaining 2 hens, using another pair of skewers. Then thread each kind of vegetable separately on 5 additional 12- to 15-inch metal skewers.

Place birds (skin side up) and vegetables on a lightly greased grill 4 to 6 inches above a solid bed of medium coals. Cook, turning often and basting with marinade, until meat near thighbone is no longer pink; cut to test (about 30 minutes).

To serve, push foods off skewers. Season to taste with salt. Makes 4 servings.

BALSAMIC MARINADE. In a bowl, stir together ⅔ cup **balsamic vinegar** or red wine vinegar, 4 teaspoons **Dijon mustard**, 2 teaspoons minced **parsley**, 2 teaspoons minced **fresh thyme leaves** or about ¾ teaspoon dry thyme leaves, and ⅛ teaspoon **pepper**.

Per serving: 685 calories, 73 g protein, 19 g carbohydrates, 35 g fat, 10 g saturated fat, 220 mg cholesterol, 292 mg sodium

CALIFORNIA CHICKEN SEAFOOD

Preparation time: About 15 minutes

Cooking time: About 30 minutes

Does the chicken complement the seafood—or are the scallops and shrimp added to enhance the chicken? One thing's for sure: the cognac-laced cream sauce tastes wonderful with everything.

8	ounces medium-size raw shrimp (about 48 per lb.)
	Shrimp Stock (recipe follows)
2	tablespoons butter or margarine
1	tablespoon salad oil
6	skinless, boneless chicken breast halves (about 1½ lbs. *total*)
4	ounces scallops, rinsed well and drained
¾	cup whipping cream
¼	cup cognac or brandy
	Whole chives
	Salt and pepper

Shell and devein shrimp, reserving shells for Shrimp Stock. Cover and refrigerate shrimp; prepare Shrimp Stock.

Melt butter in oil in a 12- to 14-inch frying pan over medium-high heat. Add chicken and cook, turning as needed, until well browned on both sides and no longer pink in center; cut to test (about 10 minutes). Remove chicken from pan and keep warm.

If using sea scallops, cut them into ½-inch chunks. Add scallops and shrimp to pan. Cook, stirring often, until shrimp are opaque throughout; cut to test (about 3 minutes). Remove from pan; set aside. Add Shrimp Stock, cream, and cognac to pan and boil over high heat, stirring frequently, until sauce is reduced to about ¾ cup and large, shiny bubbles form (about 5 minutes).

Reduce heat to medium. Return chicken and any accumulated juices, shrimp, and scallops to pan. Turn to coat with sauce. Arrange in a serving dish and garnish with chives; season to taste with salt and pepper. Makes 6 servings.

SHRIMP STOCK. In a 2- to 3-quart pan, combine **reserved shrimp shells** and 1 cup *each* **dry white wine** and **regular-strength chicken broth.** Bring to a boil over high heat; boil, uncovered, until liquid is reduced by half. Pour through a fine strainer; discard shells. Return stock to pan and boil until reduced to about ½ cup.

Per serving: 321 calories, 37 g protein, 2 g carbohydrates, 18 g fat, 9 g saturated fat, 162 mg cholesterol, 365 mg sodium

DOUBLE CHEESE CHICKEN BREASTS

Preparation time: About 15 minutes

Cooking time: About 4 minutes

Chicken is treated to cheese times two—first coated with a Parmesan crust, then covered with melted mozzarella. Choose colorful accompaniments for this quick-to-cook dish; sliced tomatoes and steamed zucchini are good selections.

4	skinless, boneless chicken breast halves (about 1 lb. *total*)
4	slices white bread, torn into pieces
¼	cup *each* chopped parsley and grated Parmesan cheese
	About ¼ teaspoon *each* salt and pepper
1	large egg, lightly beaten
	About 2 tablespoons salad oil
½	cup shredded mozzarella cheese

Rinse chicken and pat dry. Place each breast half between 2 sheets of plastic wrap; pound with a flat-surfaced mallet to a thickness of about ¼ inch. Set aside.

Place bread in a blender or food processor and whirl to form coarse crumbs. In a wide, shallow rimmed plate, combine crumbs, parsley, Parmesan cheese, salt, and pepper. Dip each pounded chicken breast half in egg; then press into crumb mixture to coat well.

Heat 2 tablespoons of the oil in a 12- to 14-inch frying pan over medium-high heat. Add chicken and cook, turning as needed, until golden on both sides (about 3 minutes); add a little more oil, if necessary. Sprinkle each piece with 2 tablespoons of the mozzarella cheese; cover pan and continue to cook just until cheese is melted. Makes 4 servings.

Per serving: 333 calories, 35 g protein, 13 g carbohydrates, 15 g fat, 5 g saturated fat, 135 mg cholesterol, 494 mg sodium

When scallops and shrimp combine with chicken, the result is a
culinary success story: California Chicken Seafood (recipe on facing page).
Credit a creamy-rich, cognac-infused sauce for this meal's winning flavor.
Accompany with warm sourdough bread and steamed green beans
topped with toasted almonds.

353

PASTA & CHICKEN IN SWEET-SOUR TOMATO SAUCE

Preparation time: About 10 minutes

Cooking time: About 25 minutes

Sautéed chicken strips surround a bed of linguine for this elegant, easy main dish. Family and friends may not be able to guess what goes into the rich tomato sauce, but they're sure to enjoy the contrasting flavors.

- 3 tablespoons olive oil
- 1 medium-size onion, thinly sliced
- 2 tablespoons pine nuts or slivered blanched almonds
- 2 cloves garlic, minced or pressed
- 6 medium-size pear-shaped tomatoes (about 12 oz. *total*), chopped
- 1 tablespoon *each* firmly packed brown sugar and dried currants
- 2 tablespoons cider vinegar
- ½ teaspoon ground allspice
- ¾ cup dry red wine
- 4 skinless, boneless chicken breast halves (about 1 lb. *total*)
- 8 ounces dry linguine or 1 package (9 oz.) fresh linguine
  Salt and pepper
  Chopped parsley

Heat 2 tablespoons of the oil in a 10- to 12-inch frying pan over medium heat. Add onion and pine nuts and cook, stirring, until onion is soft (about 10 minutes). Stir in garlic, tomatoes, sugar, currants, vinegar, allspice, and wine. Adjust heat so mixture boils gently. Continue to cook, uncovered, stirring occasionally, until sauce is slightly thickened (about 15 minutes).

Meanwhile, rinse chicken and pat dry. Brush on all sides with remaining 1 tablespoon oil. Place a ridged cooktop grill pan over medium heat; heat until a drop of water dances on the surface. Place chicken on hot pan and cook, turning as needed, until well browned on both sides and no longer pink in center; cut to test (about 10 minutes).

While chicken is cooking, cook linguine according to package directions just until tender to bite. Drain well.

Season tomato sauce to taste with salt and pepper. Add linguine and mix lightly, using 2 forks. Transfer to a deep platter. Cut chicken across the grain into ½-inch-wide strips; arrange around edge of linguine. Sprinkle with parsley. Makes 4 servings.

Per serving: 497 calories, 36 g protein, 55 g carbohydrates, 15 g fat, 2 g saturated fat, 66 mg cholesterol, 89 mg sodium

CHICKEN BREASTS WITH BLUEBERRIES

Preparation time: About 5 minutes

Cooking time: About 21 minutes

Just half a cup of blueberries makes a definite contribution to the taste—and the color—of this dish. The sauce features apricot jam to enhance the berries' sweetness; mustard and wine vinegar add tang.

- 4 skinless, boneless chicken breast halves (about 1 lb. *total*)
- 1 tablespoon salad oil
- ½ cup apricot jam
- 3 tablespoons Dijon mustard
- ½ cup frozen unsweetened blueberries
- ⅓ cup white wine vinegar
  Watercress sprigs

Rinse chicken and pat dry. Heat oil in a 10- to 12-inch frying pan over medium-high heat. Add

chicken; cook, turning as needed, until lightly browned on both sides (about 6 minutes).

Meanwhile, in a small bowl, stir together jam and mustard. Spread jam mixture over browned chicken; sprinkle with blueberries. Reduce heat to low, cover, and cook until meat in thickest part is no longer pink; cut to test (about 10 minutes; turn chicken over after 5 minutes). With a slotted spoon, lift chicken and blueberries to a platter; keep warm.

Add vinegar to pan, increase heat to high, and bring to a boil. Boil, stirring occasionally, until sauce is thickened (about 5 minutes). Pour sauce over chicken; garnish with watercress. Makes 4 servings.

Per serving: 290 calories, 27 g protein, 33 g carbohydrates, 6 g fat, 1 g saturated fat, 66 mg cholesterol, 416 mg sodium

SPICED CHICKEN WITH CAPERS

Preparation time: About 10 minutes

Cooking time: About 22 minutes

The old adage "opposites attract" may not always hold true—but the contrasting flavors of this dish will certainly bring your guests back for more. The sweetness of cinnamon, cloves, and raisins beautifully complements the tartness of capers and orange juice. Serve over rice, if you like.

- 4 skinless, boneless chicken breast halves (about 1 lb. *total*)
- 2 tablespoons salad oil
- 1 large onion, thinly sliced
- 2 cloves garlic, minced or pressed
- ¼ teaspoon *each* ground cinnamon and ground cloves
- ½ cup orange juice
- 2 tablespoons raisins
- 1 tablespoon drained capers
- Parsley sprigs (optional)
- Salt and pepper

Rinse chicken and pat dry. Heat oil in a 10- to 12-inch frying pan over medium-high heat. Add chicken and cook, turning as needed, until lightly browned on both sides (about 6 minutes). Remove from pan and set aside.

Add onion and garlic to pan; cook, stirring often, until onion is lightly browned (about 6 minutes). Stir in cinnamon, cloves, orange juice, raisins, and capers. Return chicken and any accumulated juices to pan. Reduce heat to low, cover, and simmer until meat in thickest part is no longer pink; cut to test (about 10 minutes; turn chicken over after 5 minutes).

Transfer chicken and sauce to a serving dish and garnish with parsley, if desired. Season to taste with salt and pepper. Makes 4 servings.

Per serving: 229 calories, 27 g protein, 11 g carbohydrates, 8 g fat, 1 g saturated fat, 66 mg cholesterol, 131 mg sodium

CREAMY CHICKEN ROULADES

Preparation time: About 20 minutes

Cooking time: About 15 minutes

Looking for "company's coming" chicken? These cheese-filled rolls in sour cream–white wine sauce will be welcomed by the most discriminating diner.

- 4 skinless, boneless chicken breast halves (about 1 lb. *total*)
- ½ cup shredded mozzarella cheese
- 3 tablespoons butter or margarine
- 1 clove garlic, minced or pressed
- 2 teaspoons chopped parsley
- 3 tablespoons dry white wine
- ¼ cup all-purpose flour
- ¼ teaspoon *each* paprika and pepper
- ½ cup regular-strength chicken broth
- ½ cup sour cream
- Salt

Rinse chicken and pat dry. Place each breast half between 2 sheets of plastic wrap; pound with a flat-surfaced mallet to a thickness of about ¼ inch. Top each piece of chicken with 2 tablespoons of the cheese, 1 teaspoon of the butter, a fourth of the garlic, ½ teaspoon of the parsley, and 1 teaspoon of the wine. Roll chicken around filling to enclose, securing rolls with wooden picks.

In a paper or plastic bag, combine flour, paprika, and pepper. Shake chicken pieces in bag to coat evenly with flour mixture; shake off excess. Reserve remaining flour mixture.

Melt remaining butter in a 10- to 12-inch frying pan over medium heat. Add chicken and cook, turning as needed, until lightly browned on all sides (about 6 minutes). Add broth. Reduce heat, cover, and simmer until meat is no longer pink and filling is hot; cut to test (about 6 minutes). With a slotted spoon, transfer chicken to a platter; remove wooden picks.

Blend remaining wine with 1 teaspoon of the reserved flour mixture; stir wine mixture into sour cream, then whisk mixture into pan juices. Cook over high heat, stirring, until sauce just comes to a boil. Pour sauce over chicken. Season to taste with salt. Makes 4 servings.

Per serving: 337 calories, 31 g protein, 8 g carbohydrates, 19 g fat, 11 g saturated fat, 113 mg cholesterol, 354 mg sodium

Guests will never guess this entrée is a diet-conscious diner's delight—but saucy Apricot–Dijon Mustard Chicken (recipe on facing page) served over the "super grain" quinoa is both low in fat and high in protein. Complete the menu with dinner rolls and a salad of butter lettuce, mandarin oranges, red onions, walnuts, and watercress in vinaigrette.

STUFFED CHICKEN BREASTS WITH CHUTNEY

Preparation time: About 35 minutes

Cooking time: About 15 minutes

Here's a low-fat meal elegant enough for a party. Tender chicken is wrapped around a stuffing of fresh spinach, sautéed garlic, and onions, then simmered in a tangy chutney sauce.

  1 **tablespoon olive oil**
  2 **cloves garlic, minced or pressed**
  1 **large onion, chopped**
2¼ **cups chopped spinach leaves**
  8 **skinless, boneless chicken breast halves (about 2 lbs.** *total***)**
  1 **tablespoon balsamic vinegar**
  ½ **cup low-sodium chicken broth**
  ¼ **cup chopped chutney**

Heat oil in a 12- to 14-inch frying pan over medium-high heat. Add garlic and onion and cook, stirring occasionally, until onion is soft (about 7 minutes).

Add 2 cups of the spinach; remove from heat and let cool.

Rinse chicken and pat dry. Place each breast half between 2 sheets of plastic wrap; pound with a flat-surfaced mallet to a thickness of about ¼ inch. In center of each breast half, mound an eighth of the spinach mixture; roll chicken around filling to enclose. Place chicken rolls in pan used for spinach mixture.

In a small bowl, mix vinegar, broth, and chutney. Pour over chicken. Bring to a simmer over medium heat. Cover and simmer until meat is no longer pink and filling is hot; cut to test (about 8 minutes). With a slotted spoon, lift chicken from pan and place on a platter; keep warm.

Boil pan juices over high heat, stirring occasionally, until reduced to ½ cup (about 5 minutes); then pour over chicken. Garnish with remaining ¼ cup spinach. Makes 8 servings.

Per serving: 174 calories, 27 g protein, 8 g carbohydrates, 3 g fat, 1g saturated fat, 66 mg cholesterol, 107 mg sodium

■ *Pictured on facing page*

APRICOT–DIJON MUSTARD CHICKEN

Preparation time: About 5 minutes

Cooking time: About 25 minutes

Creating a meal that's wholesome *and* irresistibly appetizing can be a challenge. This flavorful dish fills the bill: boneless chicken breasts are simmered in apricot nectar and Dijon mustard, then served on seasoned quinoa. (You'll find this high-protein grain in health food stores and well-stocked supermarkets.)

  6 **skinless, boneless chicken breast halves (about 1½ lbs.** *total***)**
  1 **can (12 oz.) apricot nectar**
  3 **tablespoons Dijon mustard**
  3 **cups regular-strength chicken broth**
1½ **cups quinoa**
  2 **tablespoons minced fresh basil leaves**
     Basil sprigs
     Lime halves and wedges

Rinse chicken and pat dry; set aside.

In a 12- to 14-inch frying pan, combine apricot nectar and mustard; bring to a boil over high heat. Then place chicken breasts, skinned side down, in pan. Reduce heat to medium-low, cover, and simmer until meat in thickest part is no longer pink; cut to test (about 15 minutes; turn chicken pieces over after 10 minutes).

Meanwhile, in a 2- to 3-quart pan, bring broth to a boil over high heat. Stir in quinoa; reduce heat, cover, and simmer until grain is tender and liquid is absorbed (about 15 minutes).

Fluff quinoa with a fork; pour onto a platter. With a slotted spoon, lift chicken from pan and place atop quinoa; cover and keep warm. Boil pan juices over high heat, partially covered, until reduced to 1 cup (about 5 minutes); then pour over chicken. Sprinkle with minced basil; garnish with basil sprigs and lime halves. Accompany with lime wedges to squeeze over meat. Makes 6 servings.

Per serving: 344 calories, 34 g protein, 40 g carbohydrates, 5 g fat, 1 g saturated fat, 66 mg cholesterol, 820 mg sodium

CHICKEN ON COOL GREENS

Preparation time: About 15 minutes

Marinating time: At least 30 minutes or up to 1 day

Cooking time: About 15 minutes

A generous helping of minced shallots goes into a mustardy vinaigrette that doubles as a marinade for chicken and a dressing for your choice of greens. Just broil the marinated boneless breasts, cut them into strips, and serve warm over a crisp salad.

4 **boneless chicken breast halves (about 1¼ lbs. *total*)**

⅓ **cup salad oil or olive oil**

3 **tablespoons white wine vinegar**

1 **tablespoon Dijon mustard**

1 **clove garlic, minced or pressed**

¼ **cup minced shallots**

8 **to 10 cups bite-size pieces washed, crisped mixed salad greens, such as chicory, leaf lettuce, arugula, butter lettuce, and escarole**

Salt and pepper

Rinse chicken and pat dry. Set aside.

In a small bowl, prepare dressing by mixing oil, vinegar, mustard, garlic, and shallots. Place chicken in a large bowl and pour ¼ cup of the dressing over it; turn chicken to coat. Cover and refrigerate for at least 30 minutes or up to 1 day. Also cover and refrigerate remaining dressing.

Drain chicken; discard marinade. Place chicken, skin side up, on rack of a 10- by 15-inch broiling pan. Broil about 4 inches below heat, turning as needed to brown evenly, until meat in thickest part is no longer pink; cut to test (about 15 minutes).

Shortly before chicken is done, mix greens with remaining dressing. Divide salad equally among 4 dinner plates. Cut each chicken breast half across the grain into ½-inch-wide strips; arrange one sliced half atop each serving of salad. Season to taste with salt and pepper. Makes 4 servings.

Per serving: 338 calories, 30 g protein, 4 g carbohydrates, 22 g fat, 4 g saturated fat, 81 mg cholesterol, 171 mg sodium

CHINESE NOODLE SALAD WITH FIVE-SPICE CHICKEN

Preparation time: About 15 minutes

Grilling time: About 15 minutes

Warm barbecued chicken breasts and cool pasta rest side by side on a bed of crisp spinach leaves. The Asian-accented dressing features rice vinegar, sesame oil, and fragrant five-spice.

Five-spice Dressing (recipe follows)

10 **ounces (3 cups; part of a 14-oz. package) fresh Chinese-style noodles**

½ **cup chopped fresh cilantro (coriander)**

1 **tablespoon grated fresh ginger**

½ **teaspoon grated lemon peel**

4 **skinless, boneless chicken breast halves (about 1 lb. *total*)**

4 **to 6 cups spinach leaves, washed and crisped**

¼ **cup thinly sliced green onions (including tops)**

Prepare Five-spice Dressing; set aside.

In a 5- to 6-quart pan, cook noodles in 3 quarts boiling water just until tender to bite (about 2 minutes). Drain, immerse in cold water until cool, drain again, and place in a large bowl. Add ⅓ cup of the dressing; then gently mix in cilantro, ginger, and lemon peel. Set aside.

Rinse chicken and pat dry. Place on a lightly greased grill 4 to 6 inches above a solid bed of medium-hot coals. Cook, turning once and basting several times with the remaining dressing, until meat in thickest part is no longer pink; cut to test (about 15 minutes). Remove chicken to a board and cut across the grain into ½-inch-wide strips.

Line 4 dinner plates with spinach. Top equally with warm chicken and noodles, arranging separately. Sprinkle with onions. Makes 4 servings.

FIVE-SPICE DRESSING. In a small bowl, combine 2 tablespoons **seasoned rice vinegar** (or 2 tablespoons rice vinegar and 1 teaspoon sugar); 1 tablespoon *each* **soy sauce, Oriental sesame oil,** and **lemon juice;** 1 clove **garlic,** minced or pressed; ½ teaspoon **Chinese five-spice** (or ¼ teaspoon *each* anise seeds and ground ginger and ⅛ teaspoon *each* ground cinnamon and ground cloves); and ¼ cup **salad oil.**

Per serving: 510 calories, 33 g protein, 44 g carbohydrates, 20 g fat, 3g saturated fat, 149 mg cholesterol, 409 mg sodium

SMOKED CHICKEN SALAD WITH MANGO DRESSING

Preparation time: About 15 minutes, plus 30 minutes to heat coals and 20 minutes to soak wood chips

Marinating time: At least 4 hours or up to 1 day

Grilling time: About 20 minutes

Greet guests with fruity flavor and fragrance when you prepare this very special salad.

  1 tablespoon *each* chopped fresh ginger and grated orange peel
  ⅓ cup *each* soy sauce, orange juice, and oyster sauce
  8 skinless, boneless chicken breast halves (about 2 lbs. *total*)
     Mango Dressing (recipe follows)
     About 1 cup fruit wood chips, such as cherry or apple, soaked in water for 20 minutes and drained
  4 quarts bite-size pieces washed, crisped mixed salad greens, such as watercress, leaf lettuce, and butter lettuce
  1 *each* medium-size red and yellow bell pepper, seeded and thinly sliced

In a large bowl, combine ginger, orange peel, soy, orange juice, and oyster sauce. Rinse chicken and pat dry; add to marinade and turn to coat. Cover and refrigerate for at least 4 hours or up to 1 day, turning several times.

Prepare Mango Dressing and set aside.

Prepare a covered barbecue for grilling by indirect heat as directed for Barbecued Turkey on page 336. After banking coals, sprinkle each pile of coals with half the wet wood chips. Set cooking grill in place 4 to 6 inches above drip pan; lightly grease grill.

Drain chicken; place on grill directly above drip pan. Cover barbecue; adjust dampers as necessary to maintain an even heat. Cook chicken until meat in thickest part is no longer pink; cut to test (about 20 minutes). Cut across the grain into ½-inch-wide strips.

To serve, divide greens among 8 dinner plates. Arrange chicken and bell peppers over greens. Offer Mango Dressing to add to taste. Makes 8 servings.

Per serving without dressing: 150 calories, 28 g protein, 4 g carbohydrates, 2 g fat, 0 g saturated fat, 66 mg cholesterol, 378 mg sodium

MANGO DRESSING. Peel 2 ripe **mangoes** (about 1½ lbs. *total*). Slice fruit from pits; discard pits. Place fruit in a blender or food processor; add ⅓ cup **orange juice** and 2 tablespoons *each* **Oriental sesame oil** and **balsamic vinegar.** Whirl until smooth. Makes 2 cups.

Per tablespoon: 18 calories, 0 g protein, 3 g carbohydrates, 1 g fat, 0 g saturated fat, 0 mg cholesterol, 0 mg sodium

CHICKEN PICADILLO

Preparation time: About 45 minutes

Baking time: About 1½ hours

Hearty, piquant, colorful, and low in fat, this stew would be hard to improve!

  1 tablespoon olive oil
  1½ pounds skinless, boneless chicken breasts, cut into 1½-inch chunks
  1 large onion, chopped
  2 cloves garlic, minced or pressed
  1 medium-size green bell pepper, seeded and chopped
  1 large can (15 oz.) no-salt-added tomato sauce
  1 cup dry white wine
  1 fresh jalapeño chile, thinly sliced, seeded
  1½ teaspoons dry oregano leaves
  1 teaspoon dry thyme leaves
  1½ pounds small red thin-skinned potatoes (*each* 1½ to 2 inches in diameter)
  ½ cup pimento-stuffed olives, thinly sliced
  ½ cup raisins
  1 cup frozen peas, thawed
  ¼ cup slivered blanched almonds

Heat oil in a 12- to 14-inch frying pan over medium heat. Add chicken and cook, stirring often, until browned on all sides (about 6 minutes). Transfer chicken to a 4- to 5-quart casserole.

Add onion, garlic, and bell pepper to pan; cook, stirring occasionally, until onion is soft (about 10 minutes). Add tomato sauce, wine, chile, oregano, and thyme; cook, stirring occasionally, until sauce comes to a boil. Boil gently, uncovered, for 5 minutes. Scrub and quarter unpeeled potatoes.

Pour sauce over chicken; add potatoes, olives, and raisins. Cover and bake in a 375° oven until potatoes are tender when pierced (about 1½ hours). Stir in peas and almonds. Makes 6 servings.

Per serving: 380 calories, 33 g protein, 44 g carbohydrates, 9 g fat, 1 g saturated fat, 66 mg cholesterol, 402 mg sodium

SAKE-STEAMED CHICKEN BREASTS WITH RICE

Preparation time: About 10 minutes

Marinating time: At least 30 minutes or up to 2 hours

Cooking time: About 12 minutes

You can use a fork, chopsticks, or just your fingers for this light meal. Dip each bite of meat in horseradish-spiked soy sauce before eating.

 6 **skinless, boneless chicken breast halves (about 1½ lbs. *total*)**

 ½ **cup sake or rice vinegar**

 ½ **teaspoon salt**

 1 **small head iceberg lettuce (about 1¼ lbs.), separated into leaves, washed, and crisped**

 About ¼ cup soy sauce

 About 1 tablespoon prepared horseradish

 Hot cooked rice

 Slivered green onions (including tops) or black sesame seeds

 Lemon wedges

Rinse chicken and pat dry. In a bowl, stir together sake and salt until salt is dissolved. Add chicken; turn to coat, then cover and refrigerate for at least 30 minutes or up to 2 hours. Drain chicken; discard marinade. Arrange chicken in a single layer in a 10- or 11-inch glass pie dish or rimmed plate. Cover dish with wax paper or foil; set dish on a rack in a large pan above 1 to 2 inches of boiling water. Cover and steam until meat in thickest part is no longer pink; cut to test (about 12 minutes).

While chicken is cooking, place 1 or 2 large lettuce leaves on each of 6 dinner plates. Finely cut remaining lettuce into long, thin shreds; pile equally onto whole leaves. Also, for each plate, pour about 2 teaspoons of the soy into a tiny bowl and add about ½ teaspoon of the horseradish; set bowl on plate.

Cut chicken across the grain into ½-inch-wide strips. Spoon rice alongside lettuce and divide chicken among plates; sprinkle with onions or sesame seeds and garnish with lemon wedges.

To eat, squeeze lemon into soy-horseradish sauce; dip chicken into sauce and eat with rice and shredded lettuce. Or tear lettuce leaves into large portions and wrap up bits of sauce-dipped chicken, rice, and shredded lettuce to eat out of hand. Makes 6 servings.

Per serving: 152 calories, 28 g protein, 5 g carbohydrates, 2 g fat, 0 g saturated fat, 66 mg cholesterol, 861 mg sodium

■ *Pictured on facing page*

CHICKEN JAMBALAYA

Preparation time: About 45 minutes

Baking time: About 45 minutes

When the weather calls for a "tummy warmer," try this Cajun-inspired casserole, heated up with a full tablespoon of pepper.

 1 **tablespoon salad oil**

 8 **ounces Canadian bacon, diced**

 1½ **pounds skinless, boneless chicken breasts, cut into bite-size chunks**

 1 **large onion, chopped**

 3 **cloves garlic, minced or pressed**

 2 **large green bell peppers (about 12 oz. *total*), seeded and chopped**

 1 **cup chopped celery**

 6 **large tomatoes (about 2 lbs. *total*), chopped**

 1 **large can (15 oz.) no-salt-added tomato sauce**

 2 **dry bay leaves, crumbled**

 1 **teaspoon dry thyme leaves**

 2 **teaspoons white pepper**

 1 **teaspoon ground red pepper (cayenne)**

 ½ **cup chopped parsley**

 1½ **cups long-grain white rice**

 3 **cups low-sodium chicken broth**

Heat oil in a 12- to 14-inch frying pan over medium heat. Add Canadian bacon and chicken; cook, stirring often, until browned on all sides (about 6 minutes). Transfer to a 4- to 5-quart casserole.

Add onion, garlic, bell peppers, and celery to pan. Cook, stirring occasionally, until onion is soft (about 10 minutes). Add tomatoes, tomato sauce, bay leaves, thyme, white and red pepper, and parsley; bring to a boil, stirring. Boil gently, uncovered, for 5 minutes.

Pour sauce over chicken; stir in rice and broth. Cover and bake in a 375° oven until rice is tender to bite (about 45 minutes). Makes 6 servings.

Per serving: 472 calories, 42 g protein, 57 g carbohydrates, 8 g fat, 2 g saturated fat, 85 mg cholesterol, 684 mg sodium

Heat up your next party with Chicken Jambalaya (recipe on facing page). Our version of the Cajun classic boasts chunks of chicken breast, bell pepper, tomato, onion, and a tongue-tingling touch of cayenne.

CHICKEN STROGANOFF

Preparation time: About 15 minutes, plus about 1 hour to soak tomatoes

Cooking time: About 25 minutes

Here's an unusual version of a classic company dish. Chicken stands in for beef, rice replaces the traditional noodles, and the sour cream sauce is accented with grated fresh ginger and chopped dried tomatoes. To coat the chicken quickly and easily, shake it together with the flour mixture in a paper or plastic bag.

- ½ cup dried tomatoes
- ¼ cup all-purpose flour
- ¼ teaspoon pepper
- 1 pound skinless, boneless chicken breasts, cut into ½-inch cubes
- 3 tablespoons butter or margarine
- 3 tablespoons salad oil
- 1 medium-size onion, chopped
- 8 ounces mushrooms, sliced
- 2 cloves garlic, minced or pressed
- 1 teaspoon cornstarch mixed with 2 teaspoons water
- 1 cup sour cream
- ½ cup regular-strength chicken broth
- 1 cup dry white wine
- ½ teaspoon *each* grated fresh ginger and dry thyme leaves

- 2 tablespoons dry sherry
  Hot cooked rice
  Chopped parsley

In a small bowl, soak tomatoes in warm water to cover until soft (about 1 hour). Drain well, chop coarsely, and set aside.

In a paper or plastic bag, combine flour and pepper. Shake chicken in bag to coat evenly with flour mixture; shake off excess.

Melt 1½ tablespoons of the butter in 1½ tablespoons of the oil in a 10- to 12-inch frying pan over medium-high heat. Add chicken and cook, stirring often, until no longer pink in center; cut to test (about 5 minutes). Remove from pan with a slotted spoon and set aside.

In pan, melt remaining 1½ tablespoons butter in remaining 1½ tablespoons oil. Add onion, mushrooms, and garlic; cook, stirring often, until mushrooms are lightly browned (about 15 minutes). Meanwhile, stir cornstarch mixture into sour cream.

Stir broth, wine, ginger, thyme, and sherry into pan. Bring to a boil, stirring; then add tomatoes, chicken, and sour cream mixture. Bring to a boil, stirring. Serve over rice and sprinkle with parsley. Makes 4 servings.

Per serving: 512 calories, 32 g protein, 21 g carbohydrates, 33 g fat, 15 g saturated fat, 114 mg cholesterol, 333 mg sodium

STIR-FRIED CHICKEN WITH SORREL

Preparation time: About 20 minutes

Cooking time: About 10 minutes

Fresh sorrel contributes a lemony tartness to this chile-heated stir-fry. Just as appealing as the flavor is the eye-catching medley of colors: white chicken strips, bright greens, and shiny black olives.

- 5 cups lightly packed sorrel leaves, washed, stems removed
- 3 tablespoons salad oil
- 1 pound skinless, boneless chicken breasts, cut across the grain into ½-inch-wide strips
- 3 cloves garlic, minced or pressed
- 1 small onion, chopped
- ½ teaspoon crushed dried hot red chiles
- 1 can (3½ oz.) pitted ripe olives, drained
- ¼ cup grated Parmesan cheese

Cut sorrel leaves crosswise into 1-inch strips; set aside.

Heat 2 tablespoons of the oil in a wok or 12- to 14-inch frying pan over high heat. Add chicken. Cook, stirring often, until no longer pink in center; cut to test (about 4 minutes). Remove chicken from pan with a slotted spoon and set aside.

Heat remaining 1 tablespoon oil in pan. Add garlic and onion; cook, stirring, until onion is lightly browned (about 4 minutes). Add chiles, olives, and sorrel; cook just until sorrel is wilted. Stir in chicken and 2 tablespoons of the cheese; sprinkle with remaining 2 tablespoons cheese. Makes 4 servings.

Per serving: 283 calories, 29 g protein, 5 g carbohydrates, 16 g fat, 3 g saturated fat, 70 mg cholesterol, 385 mg sodium

CHICKEN BURROS

Preparation time: About 15 minutes

Cooking time: About 25 minutes

Cut into these hot tortilla-wrapped packages and discover a super-satisfying blend of chicken, celery, and mushrooms in a spicy-sweet tomato sauce. Try tossing black beans and bell pepper strips in a simple vinaigrette to serve alongside.

Burro Sauce (recipe follows)
About ½ cup salad oil
1 clove garlic, minced or pressed
1 small dried hot red chile
8 ounces skinless, boneless chicken breast, cut into ½-inch cubes
1 tablespoon dry sherry
½ cup finely chopped celery
2 green onions (including tops), thinly sliced
4 medium-size mushrooms, sliced
4 large flour tortillas (*each* about 10 inches in diameter)
4 ounces Cheddar cheese, cut into thin strips

Prepare Burro Sauce and set aside.

Heat 2 tablespoons of the oil in a 10- to 12-inch frying pan over medium-high heat; add garlic and chile.

Cook, stirring, until chile turns almost black. Discard chile. Add chicken and sherry. Cook, stirring often, until meat is no longer pink in center; cut to test (about 4 minutes). Remove from pan with a slotted spoon and set aside.

Add 1 tablespoon more oil to pan; then add celery and cook, stirring, for 2 minutes. Add onions and mushrooms and cook, stirring, for 2 more minutes. Return chicken to pan, add Burro Sauce, and stir over low heat until hot. Remove from heat.

To shape each burro, lay a tortilla flat. Spoon a fourth of the filling near one edge and top with a fourth of the cheese strips. Fold tortilla edge up over filling, then fold in sides and roll to enclose filling.

Rinse pan and wipe dry. Heat 2 tablespoons more oil in pan over medium-high heat; then add one burro and cook until browned on all sides (about 3 minutes). Remove from pan. Repeat to cook remaining burros, adding remaining oil to pan as needed. Makes 4 servings.

BURRO SAUCE. In a small bowl, stir together ¼ cup **catsup**, 1½ teaspoons **honey**, 1 teaspoon **Worcestershire**, 1 clove **garlic**, minced or pressed, and 2 or 3 drops **liquid hot pepper seasoning.**

Per serving: 573 calories, 25 g protein, 34 g carbohydrates, 38 g fat, 10 g saturated fat, 63 mg cholesterol, 629 mg sodium

GINGER CHICKEN & YAMS

Preparation time: About 30 minutes

Cooking time: About 10 minutes

Candied yams in a stir-fry? That's just about what you get when matchstick strips of yams are cooked with chicken in a gingery brown sugar–sherry sauce. Green and red onions make the dish even more colorful.

Cooking Sauce (recipe follows)
2 tablespoons olive oil or salad oil
1 pound yams, peeled and cut into matchstick-size strips
1 small red onion, cut into eighths, layers separated
1 pound skinless, boneless chicken breasts, cut into ½-inch cubes
2 tablespoons minced fresh ginger
⅓ cup minced green onions (including tops)

Prepare Cooking Sauce and set aside.

Heat 1 tablespoon of the oil in a wok or 12- to 14-inch frying pan over medium heat. Add yams and red onion; cook, stirring often, until vegetables are just tender to bite (about 5 minutes). Spoon onto a platter, cover loosely, and keep warm.

Increase heat to high and heat remaining 1 tablespoon oil in pan. Add chicken and ginger. Cook, stirring often, until meat is no longer pink in center; cut to test (about 4 minutes). Return yams and red onion to pan, add Cooking Sauce, and bring to a boil, stirring. Then stir in green onions and serve. Makes 4 servings.

COOKING SAUCE. In a small bowl, stir together 3 tablespoons *each* **soy sauce, dry sherry,** and **water;** 1 tablespoon firmly packed **brown sugar;** and 1½ teaspoons **cornstarch.**

Per serving: 336 calories, 29 g protein, 36 g carbohydrates, 8 g fat, 1 g saturated fat, 66 mg cholesterol, 857 mg sodium

Chicken in a Squash Shell (recipe on facing page) shows off stir-fried chicken and vegetables in nutty-sweet acorn squash "bowls." For a refreshing accent, top each serving with tart yogurt and a sprinkling of green onions.

CHICKEN IN A SQUASH SHELL

Preparation time: About 25 minutes

Cooking time: About 40 minutes

A sophisticated version of chicken in a basket, this meal is served in acorn squash halves.

    2 **small acorn squash (about 1 lb.** *each)*
       Soy-Ginger Sauce (recipe follows)
    1 **tablespoon salad oil**
    1 **pound skinless, boneless chicken breasts, cut into ½-inch cubes**
    1 **small onion, finely chopped**
    ½ **cup** *each* **finely diced jicama and red bell pepper**
    2 **small firm-ripe tomatoes, peeled and finely diced**
    1 **teaspoon Sichuan peppercorns, toasted (see below) and coarsely ground; or ½ teaspoon black pepper**
    ¼ **cup chopped green onions (including tops)**
       Plain low-fat yogurt (optional)

Cut each squash in half lengthwise and scoop out seeds. Place halves, cut side down, in an oiled 9- by 13-inch baking pan. Bake, uncovered, in a 400° oven until tender when pierced (about 40 minutes).

About 20 minutes before squash is done, prepare Soy-Ginger Sauce and set aside. Then heat oil in a wok or 12- to 14-inch frying pan over medium-high heat; add chicken. Cook, stirring often, until meat is no longer pink in center; cut to test (about 5 minutes). Remove from pan with a slotted spoon. Add finely chopped onion, jicama, bell pepper, tomatoes, and peppercorns to pan; cook, stirring often, for 5 minutes. Add sauce and bring to a boil, stirring. Stir in chicken.

Place each squash half in an individual bowl; fill with chicken mixture. Offer green onions and, if desired, yogurt to add to taste. Makes 4 servings.

SOY-GINGER SAUCE. Mix 2 tablespoons *each* **soy sauce** and **dry sherry;** ¾ cup **regular-strength chicken broth;** 1 tablespoon *each* **cornstarch** and firmly packed **brown sugar;** and 1 teaspoon finely minced **fresh ginger.**

Per serving: 283 calories, 30 g protein, 30 g carbohydrates, 5 g fat, 1 g saturated fat, 66 mg cholesterol, 786 mg sodium

CHICKEN WITH CHILI PASTE

Preparation time: About 20 minutes

Cooking time: About 8 minutes

Fragrant ground peppercorns and a paste of crushed chiles provide the heat you expect from a Sichuan stir-fry. Offer rice alongside to temper the fiery flavor.

       Cooking Sauce (recipe follows)
    ½ **teaspoon ground toasted Sichuan peppercorns (directions follow)**
   12 **ounces skinless, boneless chicken breast, cut into 3-inch-long slivers**
    1 **tablespoon cornstarch**
    2 **tablespoons rice wine or dry sherry**
    2 **tablespoons salad oil**
    2 **tablespoons slivered fresh ginger**
    1 **tablespoon minced garlic**
   1½ **to 2 teaspoons chili paste**
    ½ **cup bamboo shoots, cut into slivers**
    2 **stalks celery, cut into 2-inch-long slivers**

Prepare Cooking Sauce and ground toasted peppercorns; set aside. In a large bowl, mix chicken, cornstarch, and wine. Set aside.

Heat 1 tablespoon of the oil in a wok or 12- to 14-inch frying pan over high heat. Add ginger and garlic; cook, stirring, until garlic is golden. Add chili paste, bamboo shoots, and celery; cook, stirring, for 1 minute. Remove from pan with a slotted spoon.

Heat remaining 1 tablespoon oil in pan; add chicken mixture and cook, stirring often, until chicken is no longer pink (about 2 minutes). Return vegetables to pan, add Cooking Sauce, and stir until sauce boils. Sprinkle with peppercorns. Makes 3 servings.

COOKING SAUCE. Mix 2 tablespoons **rice wine** or dry sherry, 1 tablespoon **soy sauce,** 1 tablespoon **rice vinegar** or white wine vinegar, and 1 teaspoon *each* **sugar, Oriental sesame oil,** and **cornstarch.**

GROUND TOASTED SICHUAN PEPPERCORNS. Place 1 tablespoon **Sichuan peppercorns** in a 6- to 8-inch frying pan. Pick out and discard any debris. Cook over medium heat until peppercorns are fragrant and lightly toasted (about 3 minutes), shaking pan often. Finely crush with a mortar and pestle (or whirl in a blender). Makes 2 teaspoons.

Per serving: 282 calories, 28 g protein, 15 g carbohydrates, 12 g fat, 2 g saturated fat, 66 mg cholesterol, 521 mg sodium

MICROWAVE MATCHUPS

If you have a microwave oven, you have just the help you need to put dinner on the table extra-fast. Cooking takes mere minutes; cleanup is usually quicker, too. Microwaved meals also offer health benefits: nutrients are retained well, and you can often use less fat than you would for conventional cooking.

As the recipes on these pages prove, poultry takes especially well to microwaving. Try chicken breasts topped with capers and anchovies, or enjoy mustard-sauced dark meat over hot vermicelli. When the occasion calls for something fancy, serve tender turkey steaks wrapped around a creamy spinach filling. Or choose turkey tenderloins masked in a rich-tasting raspberry glaze made without a bit of oil or butter.

CHICKEN BREASTS WITH ANCHOVIES & RED PEPPERS

Preparation time: About 5 minutes

Marinating time: At least 30 minutes or up to 4 hours

Microwaving time: About 10 minutes

Standing time: 2 minutes

> 6 **skinless, boneless chicken breast halves (about 1½ lbs. *total*)**
> ¼ **cup dry vermouth**
> 2 **tablespoons olive oil**
> 1 **tablespoon lemon juice**
> ½ **teaspoon grated lemon peel**
> 1 **clove garlic, minced or pressed**
> 1 **small red bell pepper, seeded and cut into thin strips**
> 6 **canned flat anchovy fillets, drained and coarsely chopped**
> 1 **teaspoon drained capers**
> 1 **tablespoon chopped parsley**

Rinse chicken and pat dry. In a wide, shallow bowl, stir together vermouth, oil, lemon juice, lemon peel, and garlic. Add chicken and turn to coat; then cover

and refrigerate for at least 30 minutes or up to 4 hours. Drain chicken; reserve marinade.

In a 10- to 11-inch microwave-safe baking dish, arrange chicken in a single layer, positioning thickest parts of breasts toward outside of dish. Cover and microwave on **HIGH (100%)** for about 6 minutes, giving dish a quarter-turn every 1½ minutes. Let stand, covered, for 2 minutes. Meat in thickest part should no longer be pink; cut to test. Remove chicken from dish and set aside.

Add marinade and bell pepper to dish. Microwave, uncovered, on **HIGH (100%)** for 3 minutes or until pepper is tender-crisp to bite, stirring every minute. Return chicken to dish, arranging it in a single layer; spoon sauce and peppers up over chicken. Sprinkle with anchovies and capers. Microwave, uncovered, on **HIGH (100%)** for 1 minute or until heated through. Sprinkle with parsley. Makes 6 servings.

Per serving: 182 calories, 27 g protein, 2 g carbohydrates, 6 g fat, 1 g saturated fat, 68 mg cholesterol, 235 mg sodium

MUSTARD CHICKEN CHUNKS WITH VERMICELLI

Preparation time: About 5 minutes

Microwaving time: About 17 minutes

> 1½ **pounds boneless chicken thighs, skinned**
> 1½ **tablespoons butter or margarine**
> 1 **small clove garlic, minced or pressed**
> 1 **teaspoon mustard seeds, coarsely crushed**
> ¼ **teaspoon dry tarragon leaves**
> ⅓ **cup dry white wine**
> 2 **teaspoons Dijon mustard**
> ¼ **cup sliced green onions (including tops)**
> ½ **cup sour cream**
> 8 **to 10 ounces dry vermicelli, cooked according to package directions and drained (keep hot)**

Rinse chicken and pat dry. Preheat a 2- to 2½-quart or 10-inch-square microwave browning dish on **HIGH (100%)** for 4½ minutes. Using oven mitts, carefully remove dish to a heatproof surface. Add butter; swirl dish to coat bottom with butter. Immediately add chicken thighs in a single layer. Wait until sizzling stops; then turn chicken over and sprinkle evenly with garlic, mustard seeds, and tarragon. Cover and microwave on **HIGH (100%)** for 5 minutes, giving dish a half-turn after 2½ minutes. Meat in thickest part should no longer be pink; cut to test. Remove chicken from dish and set aside.

Stir wine and mustard into liquid in dish. Microwave, uncovered, on **HIGH (100%)** for 5 minutes or until mixture comes to a boil and browns slightly at edges.

Return chicken to dish; stir in onions and sour cream. Microwave, uncovered, on **HIGH (100%)** for 2 minutes or until sauce is heated through, stirring after 1 minute. Serve over hot cooked vermicelli. Makes 4 servings.

Per serving: 493 calories, 34 g protein, 50 g carbohydrates, 17 g fat, 8 g saturated fat, 126 mg cholesterol, 246 mg sodium

Rinse turkey and pat dry. Place each steak between 2 sheets of plastic wrap; pound with a flat-surfaced mallet to a thickness of about ¼ inch.

In a bowl, mix spinach, 1 cup of the cheese, and 3 tablespoons of the mushroom sauce. Place a fourth of the filling at one end of each pounded turkey steak; roll to enclose. Place rolls, seam side down, in remaining sauce in baking dish; spoon some of the sauce up over rolls.

Cover and microwave on **HIGH (100%)** for 5 minutes. Rearrange rolls, bringing those in center to ends of dish; cover and microwave on **HIGH (100%)** for 5 minutes. Sprinkle remaining ½ cup cheese over rolls. Microwave, uncovered, on **HIGH (100%)** for 2 minutes or until cheese is melted and turkey is no longer pink; cut to test.

To serve, place one roll on each of 4 dinner plates. Cut each roll diagonally into ½-inch-thick slices; then arrange slices on plates so stuffing shows. Spoon a fourth of the sauce over and around each serving. Makes 4 servings.

Per serving: 438 calories, 50 g protein, 10 g carbohydrates, 22 g fat, 13 g saturated fat, 150 mg cholesterol, 440 mg sodium

FLORENTINE TURKEY ROLLS

Preparation time: About 15 minutes

Microwaving time: About 22 minutes

- 1½ tablespoons butter or margarine
- 4 ounces mushrooms, thinly sliced
- 1½ tablespoons all-purpose flour
- ⅛ teaspoon *each* ground nutmeg and white pepper
- ½ cup *each* regular-strength chicken broth, dry white wine, and half-and-half
- 4 turkey breast steaks (about 5 oz. *each*), cut ½ inch thick
- 1 package (10 oz.) frozen chopped spinach, thawed and squeezed dry
- 1½ cups (6 oz.) shredded Swiss cheese

Place butter in a shallow 2- to 2½-quart microwave-safe baking dish. Microwave, uncovered, on **HIGH (100%)** for 30 to 35 seconds or until butter is melted. Add mushrooms and stir to coat with butter. Microwave, uncovered, on **HIGH (100%)** for 3 minutes, stirring once. Blend flour, nutmeg, and pepper into mushroom mixture. Gradually stir in broth, wine, and half-and-half to make a smooth sauce. Microwave, uncovered, on **HIGH (100%)** for 6 minutes or until sauce boils and thickens, stirring every 2 minutes.

RASPBERRY-GLAZED TURKEY TENDERLOINS

Preparation time: About 5 minutes

Microwaving time: 6 to 7 minutes

- 2 turkey breast tenderloins (about 6 oz. *each*)
- ¼ cup seedless red raspberry jam
- 3 tablespoons raspberry vinegar
- 2 tablespoons Dijon mustard
- 1 teaspoon grated orange peel
- ¼ teaspoon dry thyme leaves
  Salt

Rinse turkey and pat dry. In a shallow 2- to 2½-quart microwave-safe baking dish, stir together jam, vinegar, mustard, orange peel, and thyme until well blended. Add turkey; turn to coat well with sauce.

Cover and microwave on **HIGH (100%)** for 3 minutes. Brush turkey with sauce; then arrange with uncooked portions toward outside of dish. Microwave, uncovered, on **HIGH (100%)** for 3 to 4 minutes or until meat in thickest part is no longer pink; cut to test. Season to taste with salt. Makes 2 servings.

Per serving: 325 calories, 40 g protein, 32 g carbohydrates, 4 g fat, 1 g saturated fat, 105 mg cholesterol, 569 mg sodium

CHICKEN ON A STICK WITH COUSCOUS

Preparation time: About 30 minutes

Marinating time: At least 30 minutes or up to 4 hours

Grilling time: About 10 minutes

Cut the heat of a summer afternoon with this quick-cooking barbecue. You can thread the chicken on metal or bamboo skewers; if you choose bamboo skewers, soak them in hot water for 30 minutes before grilling.

Cumin-Garlic-Yogurt Sauce (recipe follows)
⅓ cup lemon juice
⅓ cup olive oil or salad oil
¼ cup dry white wine
6 cloves garlic, minced or pressed
2 dry bay leaves, crumbled
1¼ pounds skinless, boneless chicken breasts, cut into ¾-inch cubes
2½ cups low-sodium chicken broth
1¾ cups couscous
½ cup sliced green onions (including tops)
Salt and pepper

Prepare Cumin-Garlic-Yogurt Sauce; refrigerate. In a bowl, combine lemon juice, oil, wine, garlic, and bay leaves. Add chicken, stir to coat, cover, and refrigerate for at least 30 minutes or up to 4 hours.

Lift chicken from marinade and drain briefly; reserve marinade. Thread chicken equally on 8 metal skewers. Place chicken on a lightly greased grill 4 to 6 inches above a solid bed of medium-hot coals. Cook, basting with marinade and turning as needed, until meat is lightly browned on outside and no longer pink in center; cut to test (about 10 minutes).

Meanwhile, in a 2- to 3-quart pan, bring broth to a boil over medium-high heat; stir in couscous. Cover, remove from heat, and let stand until liquid is absorbed (about 5 minutes). Stir in onions; season to taste with salt and pepper.

To serve, fluff couscous with a fork; then spoon couscous onto a platter and top with chicken skewers. Serve with sauce to add to taste. Makes 4 servings.

Per serving without sauce: 553 calories, 44 g protein, 63 g carbohydrates, 12 g fat, 2 g saturated fat, 82 mg cholesterol, 137 mg sodium

CUMIN-GARLIC-YOGURT SAUCE. In a bowl, stir together 1½ cups **plain low-fat yogurt;** 2 tablespoons minced **fresh cilantro** (coriander); 1 clove **garlic,** minced or pressed; and 1 teaspoon **cumin seeds.** Cover and refrigerate for at least 15 minutes or until next day. Makes about 1½ cups.

Per tablespoon: 9 calories, 1 g protein, 1 g carbohydrates, 0 g fat, 0 g saturated fat, 1 mg cholesterol, 10 mg sodium

CHILI CHICKEN CHUNKS

Preparation time: About 20 minutes

Cooking time: About 15 minutes

Chips are the usual dippers for guacamole, but chicken chunks do just as well. Coat the meat in a spicy, cornmeal-crunchy beer batter before frying.

¾ cup all-purpose flour
¼ cup yellow cornmeal
2 teaspoons chili powder
½ teaspoon *each* paprika and salt
¼ teaspoon *each* ground cumin and dry oregano leaves
⅛ teaspoon pepper
¾ cup beer
1½ pounds skinless, boneless chicken breasts, cut into 1½-inch chunks
Salad oil
Homemade or purchased guacamole

In a bowl, mix flour, cornmeal, chili powder, paprika, salt, cumin, oregano, and pepper. Add beer and stir until smooth. Add chicken pieces to batter and stir to coat evenly.

In a deep 3- to 4-quart pan, heat 1 to 1½ inches of oil to 350°F on a deep-frying thermometer. Lift chicken from batter, a piece at a time, and add to oil. Fill pan with a single layer of chicken; do not crowd pan. Cook, stirring occasionally, until chicken is richly browned on outside and no longer pink in center; cut to test (about 2 minutes). As chicken is cooked, lift it from pan with a slotted spoon; drain on paper towels.

To serve, mound chicken in a napkin-lined basket; offer guacamole alongside. Makes 8 to 10 servings.

Per serving: 194 calories, 19 g protein, 12 g carbohydrates, 7 g fat, 1 g saturated fat, 44 mg cholesterol, 178 mg sodium

Dinner will be off the grill and on the table in no time when
you prepare Chicken on a Stick with Couscous (recipe on facing
page). The garlicky barbecued chicken chunks are served with a
cool, cilantro-seasoned yogurt sauce.

FAJITA CHICKEN SKEWERS

Preparation time: About 15 minutes

Marinating time: At least 1 hour or up to 8 hours

Grilling time: About 10 minutes

Fajitas come off the grill faster if you start with marinated chicken chunks. Don't let the amount of spices scare you; the seasonings flavor the meat perfectly.

- ½ cup *each* lime juice and salad oil
- ¼ cup *each* beer and firmly packed brown sugar
- 1 large onion, thinly sliced
- 1 clove garlic, minced or pressed
- 2 fresh jalapeño chiles, seeded and minced
- 2 tablespoons *each* ground cumin and paprika
- 1 tablespoon Worcestershire
- 1 teaspoon pepper
- 1 pound skinless, boneless chicken breasts, cut into ¾-inch cubes
- 8 flour tortillas (*each* about 8 inches in diameter)

Shredded Cheddar cheese, homemade or purchased guacamole, and sour cream (optional)

In a large bowl, combine lime juice, oil, beer, sugar, onion, garlic, chiles, cumin, paprika, Worcestershire, and pepper. Add chicken and stir to coat; cover and refrigerate for at least 1 hour or up to 8 hours.

Drain chicken; discard marinade. Thread chicken equally on 4 metal skewers. Sprinkle each tortilla with a few drops of water; then stack tortillas and wrap in heavy-duty foil.

Place chicken on a lightly greased grill 4 to 6 inches above a solid bed of hot coals. Place tortillas at edge of grill (not above coals). Cook, turning chicken and tortillas occasionally, until tortillas are warm and chicken is lightly browned on outside and no longer pink in center; cut to test (about 10 minutes).

To eat, place chicken on a tortilla; top with cheese, guacamole, and sour cream, if desired. Roll to enclose, then eat out of hand. Makes 4 servings.

Per serving: 440 calories, 33 g protein, 54 g carbohydrates, 9 g fat, 1 g saturated fat, 66 mg cholesterol, 507 mg sodium

CHICKEN & WATERMELON WITH HERBS

Preparation time: About 25 minutes

Marinating time: 1 to 2 hours

Grilling time: About 12 minutes

Grilled chicken shares the spotlight—as well as a minty orange sauce—with skewers of crisp, juicy melon. Cook and company alike will appreciate the small, almost seedless, red- or yellow-fleshed watermelons now available in many markets.

- **Orange-Herb Sauce (recipe follows)**
- ⅓ cup orange juice
- 1 teaspoon ground coriander
- 2 pounds skinless, boneless chicken breasts, cut into 1½-inch cubes
- 1 piece seedless or seed-in watermelon (about 2 lbs.), rind removed
- **Salt and pepper**

Prepare Orange-Herb Sauce and refrigerate.

In a bowl, mix orange juice and coriander. Add chicken, stir to coat, cover, and refrigerate for 1 to 2 hours. Drain chicken, discarding marinade; thread chicken equally on 8 metal skewers. Cut watermelon into 1-inch cubes; thread equally on 8 skewers.

Place chicken on a lightly greased grill 4 to 6 inches above a solid bed of hot coals. Cook, turning as needed, until lightly browned on outside and no longer pink in center; cut to test (about 12 minutes).

Arrange chicken and watermelon on individual plates; offer Orange-Herb Sauce to pour over meat and fruit. Makes 8 servings.

Per serving without sauce: 146 calories, 27 g protein, 5 g carbohydrates, 2 g fat, 0 g saturated fat, 66 mg cholesterol, 75 mg sodium

ORANGE-HERB SAUCE. In a small bowl, stir together 1 cup **orange juice**; ½ teaspoon grated **orange peel**; 1 clove **garlic**, minced or pressed; 1 tablespoon finely chopped **fresh mint** or dry mint leaves; 1 tablespoon finely chopped **fresh dill** or 1 teaspoon dry dill weed; 1 tablespoon finely chopped **fresh cilantro** (coriander); and 1 tablespoon **balsamic vinegar** or red wine vinegar. Makes about 1¼ cups.

Per tablespoon: 6 calories, 0 g protein, 1 g carbohydrates, 0 g fat, 0 g saturated fat, 0 mg cholesterol, 0 mg sodium

YAKITORI CHICKEN & VEGETABLES

Preparation time: About 20 minutes

Marinating time: At least 1 hour or up to 8 hours

Grilling time: About 30 minutes

A simple soy marinade, nippy with fresh ginger, seasons every part of this meal—skewered chicken chunks, fresh shiitake mushrooms, and slender Oriental eggplants. Slash the eggplants before grilling so the flavors can really sink in.

- 2 tablespoons sesame seeds
- 1 pound skinless, boneless chicken breasts, cut into ¾-inch cubes
  Sherry-Soy Marinade (recipe follows)
- 6 medium-size Oriental eggplants
- 18 large fresh shiitake mushrooms or button mushrooms

Toast sesame seeds in a small frying pan over medium heat until golden (about 3 minutes), shaking pan often. Set aside.

Place chicken in a bowl. Prepare Sherry-Soy Marinade; pour ¼ cup of the marinade over chicken and mix gently to coat (reserve remaining marinade). Cover and refrigerate for at least 1 hour or up to 8 hours.

Drain chicken; discard any marinade left in bowl. Thread chicken equally on 6 metal skewers. Set aside.

Slash each eggplant lengthwise or crosswise in 4 or 5 places, making cuts ⅓ inch deep and spacing them evenly. Cut mushroom stems flush with caps.

Place eggplants on a lightly greased grill 4 to 6 inches above a solid bed of hot coals. Cook, turning often, until eggplants are slightly charred and very soft when pressed (about 30 minutes).

After eggplants have cooked for 20 minutes, start cooking mushrooms and chicken. Dip mushrooms in reserved marinade, drain briefly, and set on grill. Cook for 5 minutes; turn over and continue to cook until softened and lightly browned (about 5 more minutes). At the same time you place mushrooms on grill, place chicken on grill and cook, turning as needed, until meat is lightly browned on outside and no longer pink in center; cut to test (about 10 minutes).

Arrange chicken, mushrooms, and eggplants on a shallow platter. Pull each eggplant apart at a slash to expose flesh. Moisten chicken and vegetables with marinade and sprinkle with sesame seeds. Pass any remaining marinade at the table. Makes 6 servings.

SHERRY-SOY MARINADE. In a small bowl, stir together ⅓ cup **dry sherry**, 3 tablespoons *each* **soy sauce** and **Oriental sesame oil**, and 1½ teaspoons finely minced **fresh ginger.**

Per serving: 252 calories, 23 g protein, 21 g carbohydrates, 10 g fat, 1 g saturated fat, 44 mg cholesterol, 578 mg sodium

BARBECUED CHICKEN & POTATO KEBABS

Preparation time: About 45 minutes

Grilling time: About 12 minutes

Here's a hearty and unusual version of chicken on a stick. Cubed chicken, precooked small potatoes, and mushrooms are threaded on skewers and basted with homemade barbecue sauce as they grill.

- 1 tablespoon salad oil
- 1 medium-size onion, chopped
- 1 clove garlic, minced or pressed
- 1 can (8 oz.) tomato sauce
- ½ cup red wine vinegar
- ¼ cup firmly packed brown sugar
- 1 tablespoon Worcestershire
- 8 small red thin-skinned potatoes (*each 1½ to 2 inches in diameter*), scrubbed
- 24 mushrooms (about 1 lb. *total*)
- 1 pound skinless, boneless chicken breasts, cut into 1½-inch cubes

Heat oil in a 3-quart pan over medium heat. Add onion and garlic; cook, stirring often, until onion is soft (about 10 minutes). Add tomato sauce, vinegar, sugar, and Worcestershire. Bring to a boil; then reduce heat and simmer, uncovered, until thickened (about 20 minutes), stirring occasionally to prevent sauce from sticking.

Meanwhile, cook potatoes in boiling water to cover until barely tender when pierced (about 10 minutes); drain.

Thread potatoes, mushrooms, and chicken equally on 4 sturdy metal skewers. Place skewers on a lightly greased grill 4 to 6 inches above a solid bed of hot coals. Cook, turning as needed and basting several times with sauce, until meat is longer pink in center; cut to test (about 12 minutes). Makes 4 servings.

Per serving: 347 calories, 32 g protein, 44 g carbohydrates, 6 g fat, 1 g saturated fat, 66 mg cholesterol, 475 mg sodium

Roast Turkey Breast with Dried Fruit & Cranberries (recipe on facing page) is a perfect meal for a brisk fall day. Choose your favorite dried fruit for the sauce; we opted for apricot halves. Braised leeks and puréed winter squash complete the feast.

ROAST TURKEY BREAST WITH DRIED FRUIT & CRANBERRIES

Preparation time: About 10 minutes

Roasting time: About 1 hour

A turkey breast half is just the right size to feed a hungry group of six. To complement the meat, choose dried apricots, peaches, prunes, or figs; or use some of each kind.

- 1 **turkey breast half (about 3 lbs.)**
- 1 **pound (about 2 cups) dried apricots, peaches, pitted prunes, or figs; or use a combination**
- 1 **cup apple juice**
- 1 **cup low-sodium chicken broth**
- 1 **cup fresh or frozen cranberries**
- 2 **tablespoons firmly packed brown sugar**

Rinse turkey and pat dry. Place, skin side up, in a 9-by 13-inch baking pan. Surround with dried fruit; pour apple juice over fruit. Tightly cover pan with foil. Roast in a 400° oven for 40 minutes. Uncover; add broth and cranberries to pan, then sprinkle in 1 tablespoon of the sugar. Continue to roast, uncovered, basting turkey with pan juices 2 or 3 times, until meat in thickest part is no longer pink; cut to test (about 20 more minutes).

Transfer turkey to a platter; with a slotted spoon, arrange fruit around meat. Add remaining 1 tablespoon sugar to pan juices; boil over medium-high heat until sauce is thickened (about 5 minutes). Spoon sauce over turkey and fruit. Makes 6 servings.

Per serving: 550 calories, 48 g protein, 58 g carbohydrates, 15 g fat, 4 g saturated fat, 133 mg cholesterol, 249 mg sodium

TURKEY ROAST WITH HERB HEART

Preparation time: About 20 minutes

Roasting time: About 2 hours

Looking for an elegant entrée that doesn't require hours of effort? Layer fresh parsley, thyme, fontina cheese, and prosciutto over a boned turkey breast; then fold the meat around the filling, tie it to secure, and slip it into the oven. The result is a richly flavored roast with an aromatic "heart" of green herbs.

- 1 **boned turkey breast (about 4 lbs.)**
- ¼ **cup chopped parsley**
- 2 **tablespoons minced fresh thyme leaves or 2 teaspoons dry thyme leaves**
- **Salt and pepper**
- 2 **ounces *each* thinly sliced fontina cheese and thinly sliced prosciutto**
- 3 **or 4 thyme or parsley sprigs (*each* 3 to 4 inches long)**
- 1⅓ **cups regular-strength chicken broth**
- ½ **cup dry white wine**
- 1½ **tablespoons cornstarch mixed with 3 tablespoons water**

On a board, lay three 18-inch-long pieces of cotton string parallel to each other and about 2 inches apart. Rinse turkey and pat dry; then place turkey atop strings, setting it skin side down and perpendicular to strings.

Sprinkle turkey evenly with parsley, minced thyme, salt, and pepper. Lay cheese and prosciutto over surface, overlapping slices. Fold over one side of breast; then turn whole breast over, so top side faces up. Tuck any excess skin underneath.

Arrange thyme sprigs on top of turkey. Bring ends of strings over turkey and tie to secure. Then cut a few more strings and tie turkey roast lengthwise a few times to make neat and compact.

Place roast, skin side up, on a rack in a 12- by 15-inch roasting pan. Roast, uncovered, in a 325° oven until meat in thickest part is no longer pink; cut to test (about 2 hours). Transfer turkey to a platter and remove strings. Let rest for about 15 minutes (keep warm).

Add broth and wine to drippings in roasting pan. Set over high heat and stir to scrape up browned bits; add cornstarch mixture and bring to a boil, stirring. Offer sauce to spoon over sliced meat. Makes 8 to 10 servings.

Per serving without sauce: 300 calories, 43 g protein, 1 g carbohydrates, 13 g fat, 4 g saturated fat, 113 mg cholesterol, 276 mg sodium

Per tablespoon sauce: 3 calories, 0 g protein, 0 g carbohydrates, 0 g fat, 0 g saturated fat, 0 mg cholesterol, 41 mg sodium

TURKEY TONNATO

Preparation time: About 15 minutes

Roasting time: About 2 hours

Chilling time: At least 4 hours or up to 2 days

Terrific when the temperature soars, this version of an Italian classic features cold turkey with a rich, creamy tuna-caper sauce. It's the perfect make-ahead meal; you can prepare both meat and sauce early in the morning or even a few days in advance.

- 1 **boned, rolled, and tied turkey breast (about 4 lbs.)**
- 1 **small onion, finely chopped**
- ½ **cup dry white wine**
- 2 **tablespoons butter or margarine, melted**
  Tonnato Sauce (recipe follows)
- 4 **hard-cooked eggs, halved**
- 4 **medium-size tomatoes, cut into wedges**
  Watercress sprigs

Rinse turkey and pat dry; place, skin side up, in a shallow roasting pan. In a small bowl, mix onion, wine, and butter; pour over turkey. Roast turkey, uncovered, in a 325° oven until meat in thickest part is no longer pink; cut to test (about 2 hours).

Transfer turkey from pan to a plate; reserve pan drippings. Let turkey cool; then cover and refrigerate for at least 4 hours or up to 2 days.

Meanwhile, skim and discard fat from pan drippings. Stir to scrape up browned bits, then pour drippings into a measuring cup. Add water, if needed, to make ½ cup. Use drippings to prepare Tonnato Sauce.

To serve, remove strings and skin from turkey. Thinly slice meat and arrange on a platter; garnish with eggs, tomatoes, and watercress. Offer Tonnato Sauce to add to taste. Makes 8 to 10 servings.

Per serving without sauce: 251 calories, 46 g protein, 3 g carbohydrates, 5 g fat, 2 g saturated fat, 217 mg cholesterol, 120 mg sodium

TONNATO SAUCE. In a blender or food processor, combine the ½ cup **drippings;** 1 can (about 7 oz.) **oil-packed tuna,** drained; 2 tablespoons *each* drained **capers** and **lemon juice;** and 1 clove **garlic,** halved. Whirl until puréed. Pour sauce into a bowl, cover, and refrigerate for at least 4 hours or up to 2 days. Makes about 1½ cups.

Per tablespoon: 21 calories, 2 g protein, 0 g carbohydrates, 1 g fat, 0 g saturated fat, 3 mg cholesterol, 51 mg sodium

STEAMED TURKEY BREAST WITH HERB MAYONNAISE

Preparation time: About 15 minutes

Cooking time: About 1½ hours

Chilling time: At least 4 hours or up to 2 days

Moist, tender turkey—the product of careful steaming—makes a simple supper or super sandwiches. Serve the juicy meat with our Green Herb Mayonnaise, easily made by blending purchased mayonnaise with watercress, parsley, and green onions.

- 1 **turkey breast half (about 3 lbs.)**
- 6 **parsley sprigs**
- 1 **small onion, thinly sliced**
  Green Herb Mayonnaise (recipe follows)

Tear or cut a sheet of heavy-duty foil large enough to enclose turkey. Rinse turkey, pat dry, and place, skin side up, on foil. Top turkey with parsley and onion; wrap in foil. Place on a rack in a large pan above 1 to 2 inches of boiling water. Cover and steam (adding water, if necessary) until meat near bone is no longer pink; cut to test (about 1½ hours).

Meanwhile, prepare Green Herb Mayonnaise.

Remove turkey from pan; unwrap completely. Discard parsley and onion. When turkey is cool enough to handle, remove skin and bones. Cover turkey and refrigerate for at least 4 hours or up to 2 days.

To serve, thinly slice turkey and arrange on a platter. Offer Green Herb Mayonnaise to add to taste. Makes 6 servings.

Per serving without mayonnaise: 290 calories, 56 g protein, 0 g carbohydrates, 6 g fat, 2 g saturated fat, 130 mg cholesterol, 128 mg sodium

GREEN HERB MAYONNAISE. In a food processor, combine 1 cup *each* lightly packed **watercress sprigs** and **parsley sprigs;** ⅓ cup sliced **green onions** (including tops); 1 clove **garlic;** and ¼ teaspoon **dry rosemary.** Whirl until minced. (Or mince watercress, parsley, onions, and garlic; add rosemary.) Blend in ½ cup **mayonnaise.** Cover and refrigerate for at least 30 minutes or up to 2 days. Makes about 1¼ cups.

Per tablespoon: 42 calories, 0 g protein, 1 g carbohydrates, 4 g fat, 1 g saturated fat, 3 mg cholesterol, 34 mg sodium

BARBECUED TURKEY BREAST WITH PEACHES & CHUTNEY

Preparation time: 15 minutes, plus 30 minutes to heat coals

Grilling time: About 1¼ hours

Forget the expected at your next barbecue. Instead of the usual hamburgers, hot dogs, and steaks, offer up a succulent boneless turkey breast glazed with puréed chutney. The green onions and fresh peaches that grill alongside the turkey are another delightful surprise.

- ⅔ cup Major Grey's chutney
- 1 teaspoon minced fresh ginger
- 1 turkey breast half (about 3 lbs.), skinned and boned
- 3 firm-ripe fresh peaches; or 6 canned peach halves, drained
- 2 tablespoons lemon juice (if using fresh peaches)
- 6 to 8 green onions
  Salt

Prepare a covered barbecue for grilling by indirect heat as directed for Barbecued Turkey on page 336.

In a blender, whirl ⅓ cup of the chutney with ginger until smoothly puréed. Coarsely chop remaining ⅓ cup chutney and set aside. Rinse turkey, pat dry, and brush all over with some of the puréed chutney.

Place turkey on lightly greased grill directly above drip pan. Cover barbecue and adjust dampers as necessary to maintain an even heat. Cook, brushing occasionally with puréed chutney, until meat in thickest part is no longer pink; cut to test (about 1¼ hours).

Meanwhile, immerse fresh peaches in boiling water for about 30 seconds; lift from water and let cool for 1 minute. Peel, halve, and pit; then coat with lemon juice to prevent darkening. Cut root ends from onions, peel off outer layer, and trim tops, leaving about 4 inches of green leaves.

About 10 minutes before turkey is done, lay peach halves (cut side down) and onions on grill over coals. Cook, turning once and brushing several times with puréed chutney, until peaches are hot and onion tops are wilted (about 10 minutes).

Arrange turkey on a platter; surround with peaches and onions. Slice meat and serve with chopped chutney; season to taste with salt. Makes 6 servings.

Per serving: 282 calories, 35 g protein, 27 g carbohydrates, 3 g fat, 1 g saturated fat, 78 mg cholesterol, 140 mg sodium

BARBECUED TURKEY SALTIMBOCCA

Preparation time: About 15 minutes

Grilling time: About 6 minutes

The aroma of fresh sage can attract a crowd in record time. Fortunately, these ham- and cheese-topped turkey slices can be grilled in mere minutes, allowing the cook to pacify any hungry hordes quickly.

- 1 turkey breast half (about 3 lbs.), skinned and boned
- 1 large clove garlic, cut in half
- 2 teaspoons olive oil
- 20 large fresh sage leaves
- 4 ounces thinly sliced prosciutto
- 4 ounces thinly sliced Swiss cheese

Rinse turkey, pat dry, and cut across the grain into 10 slices, each about ½ inch thick. Rub each slice all over with cut garlic, then rub with oil. Press one sage leaf onto one side of each turkey slice. Cut prosciutto and cheese into equal-size pieces; you need one prosciutto slice and one cheese slice for each turkey slice. Set aside.

Place turkey, sage side up, on a lightly greased grill 4 to 6 inches above a solid bed of hot coals. Cook for 3 minutes, then turn slices over. Quickly top each piece with a slice of prosciutto, a slice of cheese, and another sage leaf. Cover barbecue and adjust dampers (or cover with a tent of heavy-duty foil). Continue to cook until meat is no longer pink in center; cut to test (about 3 more minutes). Using a wide metal spatula, transfer turkey to individual plates. Makes 5 servings.

Per serving: 355 calories, 52 g protein, 2 g carbohydrates, 14 g fat, 6 g saturated fat, 128 mg cholesterol, 648 mg sodium

Tender Breast Meat   375

CREAMY PESTO TURKEY

Preparation time: About 20 minutes

Cooking time: About 20 minutes

When you deserve a treat, there's no better reward than this rich combination of pasta, turkey, and pine nuts in a creamy basil-scented sauce.

- 3 tablespoons pine nuts
  Pesto Sauce (recipe follows)
- 8 ounces dry shell-shaped pasta
- 1 tablespoon olive oil
- 1 pound skinless, boneless turkey breast, cut into ¼- by 2-inch strips
- ¼ cup dry white wine
- 1 cup whipping cream
- ¼ teaspoon ground nutmeg

Toast pine nuts in a small frying pan over medium-low heat until lightly browned (about 3 minutes), shaking pan often. Prepare Pesto Sauce, using 2 tablespoons of the pine nuts; set Pesto Sauce and remaining 1 tablespoon pine nuts aside.

Cook pasta according to package directions just until tender to bite. Drain well and set aside.

Heat oil in a 12- to 14-inch frying pan over medium-high heat. Add turkey and cook, stirring often, until no longer pink in center; cut to test (about 3 minutes). Remove turkey from pan and set aside. Add Pesto Sauce and wine to pan; cook over medium heat, stirring occasionally, until bubbly (about 2 minutes). Stir in cream and bring to a full rolling boil, stirring often. Add nutmeg, pasta, and turkey; mix lightly and sprinkle with remaining 1 tablespoon pine nuts. Makes 4 servings.

PESTO SAUCE. In a blender or food processor, combine 2 tablespoons **toasted pine nuts;** 1 clove **garlic,** coarsely chopped; 1 cup lightly packed **fresh basil leaves;** ¼ cup grated **Parmesan cheese;** 2 tablespoons **olive oil;** and ¼ cup **butter.** Whirl until well combined, scraping sides of container several times.

Per serving: 800 calories, 41 g protein, 49 g carbohydrates, 50 g fat, 23 g saturated fat, 172 mg cholesterol, 313 mg sodium

WESTERN TURKEY CASSEROLE

Preparation time: About 15 minutes

Baking time: About 40 minutes

Here's a savory Southwestern-style meal that's sure to warm up a chilly evening. Layers of green chiles, spicy sautéed turkey, and cheese custard add up to a hearty one-dish dinner.

- 2 tablespoons salad oil
- 1 pound skinless, boneless turkey breast, cut into ¼- by 2-inch strips
- 1 small onion, chopped
- 1 cup prepared taco sauce
- 2 cups (8 oz.) shredded jack cheese
- ¼ cup all-purpose flour
- 4 large eggs
- ¾ cup milk
- 2 large cans (7 oz. *each*) whole green chiles

Heat oil in a 10- to 12-inch frying pan over medium heat; add turkey and onion. Cook, stirring often, until turkey is white on outside but still pink in center; cut to test (about 5 minutes). Stir in taco sauce, remove from heat, and set aside.

In a bowl, mix cheese and flour; then beat in eggs and milk. Slice chiles open and remove any seeds.

Cover bottom of a greased shallow 9-inch-square baking dish with half the chiles. Top with half the turkey mixture, then half the cheese mixture. Repeat layers, using remaining ingredients.

Bake, uncovered, in a 350° oven until golden brown on top (about 40 minutes). Let stand for about 5 minutes before serving. Makes 6 servings.

Per serving: 389 calories, 33 g protein, 15 g carbohydrates, 22 g fat, 3 g saturated fat, 226 mg cholesterol, 1,008 mg sodium

Classic pesto sauce, turkey breast, pasta seashells, pine nuts, and
cream add up to a deliciously memorable treat. Serve Creamy Pesto Turkey
(recipe on facing page) with ripe cherry tomatoes—first heated in olive oil with
tender sautéed garlic cloves, then sprinkled with Italian parsley.

TURKEY CURRY

Preparation time: About 20 minutes

Cooking time: About 15 minutes

Create your own curry powder with a fragrant blend of seasonings, including ginger, chiles, coriander, cumin, and fennel—then use it to season tender turkey breast strips. Add cream and broth, serve over rice, and top with crunchy cashews for a flavorful treat.

- 2 tablespoons salad oil
- ¼ cup minced shallots
- 1 clove garlic, minced or pressed
- 1 tablespoon grated fresh ginger
- 1 teaspoon *each* crushed dried hot red chiles, ground coriander, ground cumin, and ground turmeric
- ½ teaspoon fennel seeds
- 1 pound skinless, boneless turkey breast, cut into ¼- by 2-inch strips
- 1 cup *each* regular-strength chicken broth and whipping cream
- 2 cups hot cooked rice
- ½ cup unsalted roasted cashews

Heat oil in a 12- to 14-inch frying pan over medium-high heat. Add shallots and garlic and cook, stirring occasionally, until shallots are soft (about 6 minutes). Add ginger, chiles, coriander, cumin, turmeric, and fennel seeds. Cook, stirring, for 1 minute.

Add turkey. Cook, stirring often, until meat is no longer pink in center; cut to test (about 3 minutes). Remove turkey from pan and set aside.

Add broth and cream to pan; cook, stirring occasionally, until slightly thickened (about 5 minutes). Stir in turkey. Serve over rice; garnish with cashews. Makes 4 servings.

Per serving: 617 calories, 35 g protein, 39 g carbohydrates, 36 g fat, 15 g saturated fat, 137 mg cholesterol, 351 mg sodium

TURKEY SUMMER SQUASH STIR-FRY

Preparation time: About 15 minutes

Cooking time: About 8 minutes

To the cook, "stir-fry" is a synonym for "quick meal"—and this ginger-sparked dish is no exception. Succulent chunks of turkey are tossed together with tender-crisp squash strips in a tempting beer sauce.

- Cooking Sauce (recipe follows)
- 1 tablespoon *each* cornstarch and rice wine
- 1 pound skinless, boneless turkey breast, cut into ¾-inch cubes
- 2 tablespoons salad oil
- 1 clove garlic, minced or pressed
- 1 teaspoon grated fresh ginger
- 4 medium-size crookneck squash (about 1 lb. *total*), cut into short, thin strips

Prepare Cooking Sauce; set aside. In a bowl, stir together cornstarch and wine; add turkey and stir to coat. Set aside.

Heat oil in a 12- to 14-inch frying pan over medium-high heat; add garlic and ginger and stir once. Add turkey and cook, stirring often, until no longer pink in center; cut to test (about 5 minutes). Remove turkey and set aside. Add squash and cook, stirring often, until tender-crisp to bite (about 2 minutes). Return turkey to pan, then stir in Cooking Sauce and cook, stirring, until sauce boils and thickens. Makes 4 servings.

COOKING SAUCE. In a small bowl, stir together 1½ tablespoons **cornstarch,** 1 teaspoon **sugar,** ½ cup **regular-strength chicken broth,** ¼ cup **beer,** and 1 tablespoon **rice wine.**

Per serving: 250 calories, 28 g protein, 12 g carbohydrates, 9 g fat, 1 g saturated fat, 70 mg cholesterol, 203 mg sodium

TURKEY CHILI

Preparation time: About 15 minutes

Cooking time: About 50 minutes

Chili fanatics may not even deign to call this "chili": after all, it contains beans and soy sauce, and there's not a scrap of beef to be found. Nonetheless, even the purists will probably be back for seconds! Serve with your favorite toppings.

- 2 tablespoons salad oil
- 1 medium-size onion, chopped
- 1 small green bell pepper, seeded and chopped
- 1 clove garlic, minced or pressed
- 1½ pounds skinless, boneless turkey breast, cut into bite-size chunks
- 1 small can (about 8 oz.) tomatoes, drained and chopped
- 2 cans (about 15 oz. *each*) kidney beans, drained
- 1 large can (15 oz.) tomato sauce
- 2 tablespoons soy sauce
- 1½ tablespoons chili powder
- ½ teaspoon *each* ground cumin, dry sage leaves, and dry thyme leaves

  Toppings (suggestions follow)

Heat oil in a 4- to 5-quart pan over medium-high heat; add onion, bell pepper, and garlic. Cook, stirring often, until onion is soft (about 7 minutes). Remove from pan and set aside.

Increase heat to high. Add half the turkey and cook, stirring often, until no longer pink in center; cut to test (about 5 minutes). Remove from pan; set aside. Repeat to cook remaining turkey.

Return onion mixture and all turkey to pan. Then add tomatoes, beans, tomato sauce, soy, chili powder, cumin, sage, and thyme. Bring to a boil; reduce heat, cover, and simmer until chili is thick and flavors are well blended (about 30 minutes; uncover for last 5 minutes).

Ladle hot chili into bowls; offer toppings to embellish individual servings. Makes 6 servings.

TOPPINGS. Offer **lime wedges,** sliced **green onions** (including tops), shredded **jack or Cheddar cheese,** and chopped **tomatoes.**

Per serving: 310 calories, 32 g protein, 29 g carbohydrates, 8 g fat, 1 g saturated fat, 70 mg cholesterol, 1,247 mg sodium

GRILLED TURKEY CHUNKS PICCATA

Preparation time: About 15 minutes

Marinating time: At least 30 minutes or up to 2 hours

Grilling time: About 15 minutes

Searching for simple summer fare? Try tender, caper-topped turkey chunks freshened with a lemon-pepper marinade. Grill zucchini halves alongside the skewered meat.

- 3 tablespoons capers with liquid
- ½ cup lemon juice
- 2 tablespoons olive oil
- ¼ teaspoon pepper
- 2 pounds skinless, boneless turkey breast, cut into 1-inch cubes
- 4 medium-size zucchini (about 1½ lbs. total)

  Lemon wedges

Drain caper liquid into a shallow dish; cover drained capers and refrigerate. Stir lemon juice, oil, and pepper into caper liquid. Add turkey and stir to coat. Cover and refrigerate for at least 30 minutes or up to 2 hours.

Drain turkey; reserve marinade. Thread turkey equally on 6 metal skewers. Cut each zucchini in half lengthwise; coat zucchini with marinade.

Place turkey and zucchini on a lightly greased grill 4 to 6 inches above a solid bed of medium coals. Cook, turning as needed and basting several times with marinade, until turkey is no longer pink in center; cut to test (about 15 minutes). Sprinkle with drained capers; offer lemon wedges to squeeze over meat. Makes 6 servings.

Per serving: 233 calories, 37 g protein, 5 g carbohydrates, 7 g fat, 1 g saturated fat, 94 mg cholesterol, 219 mg sodium

Hungry guests will greet dinner with glee when they see this hearty dish!
A savory tomato sauce, thick with big chunks of turkey, crowns squares of
cheese-topped polenta. Accompany our Broiled Turkey with Baked Polenta
(recipe on page 394) with an oregano-seasoned summer squash sauté.

Succulent Legs & Thighs

SKEWERED & STUFFED & WINED & MINTED &

STIR-FRIED & CRUMBED & CURRIED & GRILLED &

TOMATOED & MUSHROOMED & OVEN-FRIED &

OVEN-FRIED BUTTERMILK CHICKEN LEGS

Preparation time: About 10 minutes

Baking time: About 45 minutes

Shake a leg—or rather legs—and get this main course in the oven in minutes: simply toss chicken in a bag with a buttermilk-tangy crumb coating. Bake acorn squash and small russet potatoes alongside for an almost effortless dinner.

- ½ **cup fine dry bread crumbs**
- ¼ **cup dry buttermilk**
- ½ **teaspoon *each* dry thyme leaves and dry oregano leaves**
- 6 **whole chicken legs (about 3 lbs. *total*)**
- 3 **tablespoons butter or margarine, melted**
  Salt and pepper

In a paper or plastic bag, combine crumbs, dry buttermilk, thyme, and oregano. Rinse chicken and shake off most of the moisture; then shake chicken in bag to coat evenly with crumb mixture.

Arrange chicken legs slightly apart in a greased shallow 10- by 15-inch baking pan. Drizzle with butter. Bake, uncovered, in a 400° oven until coating is brown and crisp and meat near thighbone is no longer pink; cut to test (about 45 minutes). Season to taste with salt and pepper. Makes 6 servings.

Per serving: 398 calories, 32 g protein, 7 g carbohydrates, 26 g fat, 9 g saturated fat, 154 mg cholesterol, 262 mg sodium

CRANBERRY CHICKEN

Preparation time: About 10 minutes

Baking time: About 1 hour

A sweet-tart cranberry glaze elevates easy baked chicken from ordinary to extra-special. And because the recipe works well with both fresh and frozen berries, you can enjoy it all year long. You might round out the meal with French fries and a tossed salad.

- 1 **tablespoon butter or margarine**
- 1 **small onion, chopped**
- 6 **whole chicken legs (about 3 lbs. *total*), skinned if desired**
- ⅔ **cup catsup**
- ⅓ **cup firmly packed brown sugar**
- 1 **tablespoon cider vinegar**
- 1 **teaspoon dry mustard**
- 1½ **cups fresh or frozen cranberries**

Place butter in a shallow 10- by 15-inch baking pan; set pan in a 400° oven until butter is melted. Stir in onion. Bake, uncovered, until onion is pale gold (about 15 minutes), stirring occasionally. Meanwhile, rinse chicken and pat dry.

Push onion to one side of pan; arrange chicken in a single layer in pan (not on top of onion). Continue to bake, uncovered, for 25 more minutes; stir onion occasionally.

In a bowl, stir together catsup, sugar, vinegar, mustard, and cranberries. Spoon browned onions out of pan and stir them into cranberry mixture; space chicken evenly in pan, then top evenly with cranberry mixture. Continue to bake until cranberry mixture is slightly caramelized and chicken meat near thighbone is no longer pink; cut to test (about 20 more minutes). Makes 6 servings.

Per serving: 422 calories, 31 g protein, 24 g carbohydrates, 22 g fat, 7 g saturated fat, 143 mg cholesterol, 472 mg sodium

BAKED CHICKEN WITH TOMATO-CHEESE PASTA

Preparation time: About 10 minutes

Cooking time: About 45 minutes

Company casserole or family feast? This meal fits either role. Top small pasta seashells with diced tomatoes and a luscious, creamy-rich blend of Neufchâtel cheese, butter, and Parmesan; offer basil-sprinkled baked chicken on top or alongside.

- 4 to 6 whole chicken legs (2 to 3 lbs. *total*)
- 8 ounces dry small shell-shaped or round pasta
- 1 tablespoon olive oil
- 1 large package (8 oz.) Neufchâtel or cream cheese, at room temperature
- ½ cup (¼ lb.) unsalted butter or margarine, at room temperature
- ⅓ cup grated Parmesan cheese
- 3 medium-size pear-shaped tomatoes (about 6 oz. *total*), chopped
- 1 tablespoon chopped fresh basil leaves or 1 teaspoon dry basil leaves
  Basil sprigs

Rinse chicken, pat dry, and arrange in a single layer in a shallow baking pan. Bake, uncovered, in a 400° oven for 35 minutes.

Meanwhile, cook pasta according to package directions just until tender to bite. Drain; place in a shallow 2- to 3-quart baking dish, lightly mix in oil, and set aside.

In a medium-size bowl, combine Neufchâtel cheese, butter, and ¼ cup of the Parmesan cheese; beat with an electric mixer until well blended. Mound cheese mixture in center of pasta; sprinkle tomatoes over cheese mixture.

When chicken has baked for 35 minutes, place cheese-topped pasta in oven. Bake, uncovered, until pasta is hot in center and meat near chicken thighbone is no longer pink; cut to test (about 10 minutes). Arrange chicken over pasta around edge of baking dish. Sprinkle with chopped basil and remaining Parmesan cheese; garnish with basil sprigs. Makes 4 to 6 servings.

Per serving: 763 calories, 42 g protein, 37 g carbohydrates, 49 g fat, 24 g saturated fat, 191 mg cholesterol, 385 mg sodium

SAUTÉED CHICKEN WITH CORINTH GRAPES

Preparation time: About 5 minutes

Cooking time: About 37 minutes

Black Corinth grapes, frequently marketed as "champagne grapes," add an elegant touch to this dinner-for-two version of classic chicken Véronique. You simmer whole chicken legs in a sweet white wine–cream sauce, then add clusters of grapes to the cooking pan.

You'll find Black Corinth grapes in markets and produce shops from mid-July to mid-October.

- 2 whole chicken legs (about 1 lb. *total*)
- 1 tablespoon butter or margarine
- 1 tablespoon olive oil
- ½ cup late-harvest sweet white wine, such as Johannisberg Riesling
- ½ cup whipping cream
- 2 clusters Black Corinth grapes (*each* about 1½ inches wide and 4 inches long)
  Salt and pepper

Rinse chicken and pat dry. Melt butter in oil in a 10- to 12-inch frying pan over medium-high heat. Add chicken and cook, turning as needed, until

browned on both sides (about 6 minutes). Reduce heat to medium-low, cover, and continue to cook until meat near thighbone is no longer pink; cut to test (about 25 more minutes). Transfer chicken to dinner plates; keep warm.

Pour off and discard fat from pan, then pour in wine and boil over high heat until reduced to 2 tablespoons (about 3 minutes). Stir in cream. Place grapes in pan and reduce heat to medium; cook, turning clusters several times, until grapes are slightly softened and sauce is slightly thicker (about 3 minutes).

Place grapes alongside chicken, then pour sauce over both. Season to taste with salt and pepper. Makes 2 servings.

Per serving: 601 calories, 31 g protein, 17 g carbohydrates, 46 g fat, 20 g saturated fat, 185 mg cholesterol, 181 mg sodium

CHICKEN WITH OLIVES & PINE NUTS

Preparation time: About 10 minutes

Cooking time: About 45 minutes

Fit for a festival! The sunny Mediterranean flavor of chicken simmered with fresh sage and salty green olives should cheer up any crowd. Toasted pine nuts accent the dish.

⅔ **cup pine nuts**

8 *each* **chicken drumsticks and thighs (about 4 lbs.** *total***), skinned**

1 **tablespoon butter or margarine**

1 **tablespoon olive oil**

2 **cups drained unpitted Spanish-style olives**

5 **fresh sage leaves or 1 teaspoon dry sage leaves**

¼ **cup water**
Fresh sage leaves (optional)

Toast pine nuts in a 12- to 14-inch frying pan over medium-low heat until golden brown (about 7 minutes), shaking pan often. Remove nuts from pan and set aside.

Rinse chicken and pat dry. Melt butter in oil in pan over medium-high heat. Add chicken, a portion at a time; cook, turning as needed, until browned on all sides (about 6 minutes).

Pour off and discard fat from pan, then return pine nuts and all chicken (and any accumulated juices) to pan. Add olives, the 5 sage leaves (or all the dry sage), and water. Bring to a simmer. Then reduce heat to medium-low, cover, and simmer until meat near thighbone is no longer pink; cut to test (about 25 minutes).

Transfer chicken mixture to a platter; garnish with sage leaves, if desired. Makes 8 servings.

Per serving: 271 calories, 29 g protein, 2 g carbohydrates, 17 g fat, 3 g saturated fat, 105 mg cholesterol, 935 mg sodium

---

■ *Pictured on facing page*

MUSTARD CHICKEN & PASTA

Preparation time: About 10 minutes

Cooking time: About 1 hour

The Dijon mustard sauce alone is enough to make this meal a hit. Half-and-half and a rich-tasting broth from simmered chicken contribute to the wonderful flavor. You can serve the chicken and sauce over any pasta shapes; try tricolor *radiatore* for an unusual touch.

6 **whole chicken legs (about 3 lbs.** *total***)**

2 **cups regular-strength chicken broth**

¼ **cup butter or margarine**

¼ **cup all-purpose flour**

1 **cup half-and-half or milk**

2 **tablespoons Dijon mustard**

½ **teaspoon dry thyme leaves**
Salt and pepper

12 **ounces dry pasta shapes, such as radiatore**

¼ **cup finely chopped parsley**
Parsley sprigs

Rinse chicken and pat dry; then place in a wide, heavy 4- to 5-quart pan. Add broth and bring to a boil over medium-high heat. Reduce heat, cover,

and simmer for 30 minutes. Lift out chicken and set aside. Skim and discard fat from broth, then measure out 1¾ cups broth. Reserve remaining broth for other uses.

In pan used to cook chicken, melt butter over medium heat. Blend in flour and cook, stirring, until bubbly. Remove from heat; gradually stir in the 1¾ cups broth, then half-and-half, until blended. Return to heat and continue to cook, stirring, until mixture boils and thickens. Blend in mustard and thyme; season to taste with salt and pepper.

Remove and discard skin from chicken. Place chicken in sauce and simmer, uncovered, until meat near thighbone is no longer pink; cut to test (about 15 minutes).

Meanwhile, cook pasta according to package directions just until tender to bite. Drain well and mound in center of a serving dish or deep platter.

Lift chicken from sauce and arrange around edge of platter. Stir chopped parsley into sauce; pour sauce over pasta and chicken. Garnish with parsley sprigs. Makes 6 servings.

Per serving: 517 calories, 36 g protein, 49 g carbohydrates, 19 g fat, 9 g saturated fat, 139 mg cholesterol, 669 mg sodium

Spoil your family with a special meal: Mustard Chicken & Pasta
(recipe on facing page). Succulent chicken legs and tricolor pasta shapes are
cloaked in a rich, parsley-flecked mustard cream sauce. Alongside, serve
baby carrots tossed with butter and fresh thyme.

TANDOORI BARBECUED CHICKEN

Preparation time: About 15 minutes, plus 30 minutes to heat coals

Marinating time: At least 1 hour or up to 1 day

Grilling time: About 40 minutes

Tandoori chicken translates beautifully to your backyard barbecue. Marinate whole legs in a tart blend of yogurt, lime, and spices, then grill them slowly over indirect heat. Serve with rice pilaf and sliced tomatoes.

- 2 tablespoons white wine vinegar
- ¼ cup lime juice
- ½ teaspoon *each* crushed dried hot red chiles and cumin seeds
- 1 teaspoon ground turmeric
- 1½ teaspoons paprika
- ¼ cup chopped fresh cilantro (coriander)
- 3 cloves garlic
- 1 tablespoon minced fresh ginger
- ¼ cup chopped parsley
- 1 cup plain low-fat yogurt
- 6 to 8 whole chicken legs (3 to 4 lbs. *total*)

In a blender or food processor, combine vinegar, lime juice, chiles, cumin seeds, turmeric, paprika, cilantro, garlic, ginger, and parsley. Whirl until smoothly puréed. Turn mixture into a large bowl, add yogurt, and mix well.

Rinse chicken and pat dry. Make a cut through to thigh and drumstick bones along entire length of each leg. Add chicken to yogurt mixture; turn to coat well. Cover and refrigerate for at least 1 hour or up to 1 day.

Prepare a covered barbecue for grilling by indirect heat as directed for Barbecued Turkey on page 22.

Drain chicken; reserve yogurt marinade. Then arrange chicken on lightly greased grill directly above drip pan. Cover barbecue and adjust dampers as necessary to maintain an even heat. Cook chicken, basting often with marinade, until meat near thighbone is no longer pink; cut to test (about 40 minutes). Makes 6 to 8 servings.

Per serving: 275 calories, 30 g protein, 2 g carbohydrates, 15 g fat, 4 g saturated fat, 104 mg cholesterol, 110 mg sodium

CURRY CHICKEN WITH CURRANTS

Preparation time: About 10 minutes

Cooking time: About 40 minutes

This uncomplicated curry offers proof positive that a minimum of ingredients can yield maximum flavor. Chicken thighs, chopped onion and bell pepper, and currants simmer together in a tomato-based sauce; salted almonds add a crunchy accent.

- 3 pounds chicken thighs
  About ¾ cup all-purpose flour
- 2 tablespoons salad oil
- 1 large onion, chopped
- 1 large green bell pepper (about 6 oz.), seeded and chopped
- 2 cloves garlic, minced or pressed
- 1 tablespoon curry powder
- 1 can (14½ oz.) tomatoes
- 1 teaspoon liquid hot pepper seasoning
- ½ cup dried currants
  Salt
- ½ cup chopped salted roasted almonds

Rinse chicken and pat dry. Roll in flour to coat; shake off excess.

Heat oil in a 12- to 14-inch frying pan over medium-high heat. Add chicken, a portion at a time; cook, turning as needed, until browned on all sides (about 6 minutes). Remove from pan and set aside. Add onion, bell pepper, garlic, and curry powder; reduce heat to low and cook, stirrring, until vegetables are limp (about 7 minutes).

Add tomatoes (break up with a spoon) and their liquid, hot pepper seasoning, and currants; then add chicken and any accumulated juices. Bring to a boil. Reduce heat, cover, and simmer until meat near bone is no longer pink; cut to test (about 20 minutes). Skim and discard fat from sauce; season to taste with salt. Spoon chicken and sauce into a serving dish and garnish with almonds. Makes 6 servings.

Per serving: 624 calories, 37 g protein, 30 g carbohydrates, 40 g fat, 9 mg saturated fat, 151 mg cholesterol, 375 mg sodium

BRAISED TERIYAKI CHICKEN

Preparation time: About 10 minutes

Cooking time: About 45 minutes

This version of teriyaki chicken is simmered, not grilled, so the meat is extra-juicy. The sauce features the familiar soy and garlic—but you'll also taste onion, red bell pepper, white wine (not the usual sherry), and even sweet raisins.

8 **chicken thighs (about 2 lbs.** *total***), skinned**

1 **tablespoon butter or margarine**

1 **tablespoon olive oil or salad oil**

1 **medium-size onion, chopped**

1 **medium-size red bell pepper, seeded and chopped**

2 **cloves garlic, minced or pressed**

2 **small dried hot red chiles**

¾ **cup dry white wine**

¼ **cup soy sauce**

½ **cup raisins**

Cilantro (coriander) sprigs

Rinse chicken and pat dry. Melt butter in oil in a 10- to 12-inch frying pan over medium-high heat. Add chicken, a portion at a time; cook, turning as needed, until browned on all sides (about 6 minutes). Remove from pan and set aside.

Add onion, bell pepper, and garlic to pan; cook, stirring often, until onion is soft (about 7 minutes). Add chiles, wine, and soy; stir to blend. Push vegetables to sides of pan. Arrange chicken in center of pan; add any accumulated juices.

Bring to a boil over high heat. Then reduce heat, cover, and simmer until meat near bone is no longer pink; cut to test (about 20 minutes).

With a slotted spoon, transfer chicken and vegetables to a platter and keep warm. Skim and discard fat from sauce; stir in raisins, then boil sauce over high heat until reduced to about ½ cup (about 5 minutes). Remove and discard chiles, if desired. Pour sauce over chicken and garnish with cilantro. Makes 4 servings.

Per serving: 291 calories, 28 g protein, 20 g carbohydrates, 12 g fat, 4 g saturated fat, 115 mg cholesterol, 1,175 mg sodium

ESCABÈCHE OF CHICKEN

Preparation time: About 10 minutes

Cooking time: About 45 minutes

Serve up a taste of Spain with this entrée! Small whole onions and succulent chicken thighs simmer in a spicy red wine sauce made piquant with a splash of sherry vinegar.

8 **chicken thighs (about 2 lbs.** *total***), skinned**

2 **tablespoons olive oil**

Escabèche Sauce with Onions (recipe follows)

Salt

Rinse chicken and pat dry. Heat oil in a 10- to 12-inch frying pan over medium-high heat. Add chicken, a portion at a time; cook, turning as needed, until browned on all sides (about 6 minutes). Remove from pan and set aside.

Use pan (with any remaining oil and chicken drippings in it) to prepare Escabèche Sauce with Onions. Add chicken and any accumulated juices to sauce; bring to a boil over high heat. Then reduce heat, cover,

and simmer until meat near bone is no longer pink; cut to test (about 20 minutes).

With a slotted spoon, transfer chicken and whole onions to a platter; keep warm. Skim and discard fat from sauce; then boil sauce over high heat until reduced to 1 cup (about 3 minutes). If desired, remove and discard bay leaf, chiles, and cinnamon stick. Pour sauce over chicken. Season to taste with salt. Makes 4 servings.

ESCABÈCHE SAUCE WITH ONIONS. To pan used to brown chicken, add 2 or 3 cloves **garlic,** minced; 1 small **onion,** chopped; 1 **dry bay leaf;** 3 **small dried hot red chiles;** 6 **dry juniper berries;** 1 **cinnamon stick** (about 3 inches long); and ½ teaspoon *each* **ground coriander** and **dry thyme leaves.** Cook over medium heat, stirring often, until onion is soft (about 7 minutes). Then stir in 1 tablespoon **tomato paste,** ⅔ cup **dry red wine,** ⅓ cup **regular-strength chicken broth,** ¼ cup **sherry vinegar** or red wine vinegar, and 1 package (10 oz.) **frozen small whole onions.** Stir to mix well.

Per serving: 287 calories, 27 g protein, 11 g carbohydrates, 12 g fat, 2 g saturated fat, 107 mg cholesterol, 235 mg sodium

There's something for everyone in our Brown Rice Paella (recipe
on facing page). Chicken thighs, chorizo, pork, shrimp, and even oysters
mingle in this hearty company entrée. Offer lots of crunchy-crusted
bread to soak up the saffron-flavored broth.

BROWN RICE PAELLA

Preparation time: About 15 minutes

Cooking time: About 2 hours

Thinking of a special dinner? Think paella: Saffron-scented rice studded with chicken, sausage, and shellfish. Our version calls for brown rice, adds pork shoulder, and omits the usual mussels or clams, but your tastebuds won't object to the twist on tradition.

    2   to 3 tablespoons olive oil
    8   small onions (*each* about 1 inch in
        diameter), quartered
    1   pound boneless pork shoulder or butt
        (trimmed of excess fat), cut into ½-inch
        cubes
    8   chicken thighs (about 2 lbs. *total*),
        skinned
   12   ounces chorizo sausages, casings removed
    2   cups long-grain brown rice
  ¹⁄₁₆ teaspoon powdered saffron
    4   cups regular-strength chicken broth,
        heated
    1   can (14½ oz.) stewed tomatoes
    1   jar (4 oz.) sliced pimentos, drained
    ½   cup chopped parsley
    1   pound tiny cooked and shelled shrimp
    1   jar (10 oz.) small Pacific oysters (optional)

Heat 2 tablespoons of the oil in a 6- to 8-quart pan over medium heat. Add onions; cook, stirring often, until lightly browned (about 5 minutes). Remove from pan and set aside. Add pork to pan; cook, stirring often, until browned (about 20 minutes). Remove from pan and set aside.

Rinse chicken; pat dry. Add to pan, a portion at a time; cook, turning as needed, until browned on all sides (about 8 minutes), adding more oil if needed to prevent sticking. Remove from pan; set aside. Add chorizo to pan and crumble with a spoon; cook, stirring often, until browned (about 15 minutes). Spoon off and discard all but 3 tablespoons of the drippings. Add rice to pan; stir until opaque (about 8 minutes).

Moisten saffron with 2 tablespoons of the hot broth. Add saffron mixture to pan along with remaining broth, onions, and pork; stir well. Bring to a boil over high heat; reduce heat, cover, and simmer for 20 minutes. Stir in tomatoes, then add chicken and any accumulated juices. Cover and continue to simmer until rice is tender to bite and chicken meat near bone is no longer pink; cut to test (about 20 more minutes).

Add pimentos, parsley, shrimp, and (if desired) oysters and their liquid. Stir gently to mix; cover. Cook over lowest heat for 5 minutes. Makes 8 servings.

Per serving: 588 calories, 47 g protein, 43 g carbohydrates, 24 g fat, 7 g saturated fat, 230 mg cholesterol, 1,026 mg sodium

CHICKEN WITH BARLEY & PECANS

Preparation time: About 10 minutes

Cooking time: About 1 hour and 20 minutes

This one-dish dinner qualifies as true comfort food—with a touch of style. Toasted pecans top a soothing blend of barley, chicken, and mushrooms in broth.

    8   chicken thighs (about 2 lbs. *total*),
        skinned
    3   tablespoons olive oil or salad oil
    ½   cup pecan halves
    1   large onion, chopped
    1   pound mushrooms, thinly sliced
    1   cup pearl barley
    2   cloves garlic, minced or pressed
    3   cups regular-strength chicken broth
    2   tablespoons minced parsley

Rinse chicken, pat dry, and set aside. Heat 1 tablespoon of the oil in a 10- to 12-inch frying pan over medium-low heat. Add pecans and cook, stirring, until nuts have a toasted flavor and are golden inside; break a nut to test (about 7 minutes). Remove from pan with a slotted spoon and set aside.

Increase heat to medium-high; heat 1 tablespoon more oil in pan. Add chicken, a portion at a time; cook, turning as needed, until browned on all sides (about 6 minutes). Remove from pan and set aside.

Heat remaining 1 tablespoon oil in pan. Add onion and mushrooms; cook, stirring often, until onion is soft (about 7 minutes). Add barley and garlic; cook, stirring, until barley starts to turn golden (about 2 minutes). Add broth; bring to a boil. Reduce heat, cover, and simmer for 20 minutes. Add chicken and any accumulated juices; cover. Continue to simmer until barley is tender to bite and chicken meat near bone is no longer pink; cut to test (about 30 more minutes). Top with pecans and parsley. Makes 4 servings.

Per serving: 575 calories, 37 g protein, 51 g carbohydrates, 26 g fat, 4 g saturated fat, 107 mg cholesterol, 862 mg sodium

OVEN-SMOKED POULTRY

When you crave succulent hickory-scented chicken but don't feel like firing up the barbecue, use the oven instead. "Oven-smoking" simply takes advantage of liquid smoke, a pale chestnut-colored liquid sold in supermarkets alongside Worcestershire and other seasoning sauces. Though it doesn't preserve food as true smoking does, liquid smoke imparts the same savory flavor.

Liquid smoke really is made from smoke. The smoke from burning wood is caught in tubes, where it cools and condenses; the resulting liquid is then filtered and bottled. Hickory wood is the most common source of liquid smoke, but you may find other "flavors"—mesquite, for example—in specialty markets.

Oven-smoking is a simple process. Choose a tight-lidded pan and a rack that will fit inside it; pour a few tablespoons of liquid smoke into the pan, place the poultry of your choice on the rack, and cook. The food essentially steams as it bakes, absorbing flavor as the liquid smoke evaporates. To adjust the "smokiness" of your poultry, vary the amount of liquid smoke used, keeping in mind that the flavor grows stronger as the food cools. Because liquid smoke's aroma can fill your kitchen, you may prefer to do your oven-smoking the day before serving—you want your family and guests to be enticed by the fragrance, not knocked out cold. Oven-smoked poultry keeps in the refrigerator for 2 days; be sure to wrap it securely, so it won't flavor the foods stored around it.

The following instructions and chart present the basics of oven-smoking. We also suggest a tempting use for smoked chicken breasts: a luncheon salad of chicken, toasted pecans, and crisp greens with a sweet-tangy orange vinaigrette.

Basic directions for oven-smoking: Pour 3 tablespoons **liquid smoke** into a 5- to 6-quart pan. Set a perforated or wire rack in pan. Arrange **poultry** of your choice (see chart at left below) in a single layer on rack; tightly cover pan. Bake in a 350° oven until poultry tests done (see chart for times and tests). If made ahead, let cool; then cover and refrigerate for up to 2 days.

SMOKED CHICKEN SALAD

Preparation time: About 40 minutes, plus 2 hours to chill chicken

Cooking time: About 7 minutes

> Orange Vinaigrette (recipe follows)
> 1 tablespoon butter or margarine
> ¾ cup pecan halves
> 6 cups bite-size pieces washed, crisped mixed salad greens, such as butter lettuce, romaine lettuce, and watercress
> 4 smoked chicken breast halves (see chart at left below), chilled

Prepare Orange Vinaigrette; set aside. Melt butter in a 10- to 12-inch frying pan over medium-low heat. Add pecans and cook, stirring occasionally, until nuts have a toasted flavor and are golden inside; break a nut to test (about 7 minutes). Drain on paper towels. Arrange salad greens equally on 4 dinner plates; sprinkle evenly with pecans.

Cut each breast half into ¼-inch-thick slanting slices. On each plate, arrange one sliced breast half alongside greens, fanning out slices. Spoon Orange Vinaigrette over greens and chicken. Makes 4 servings.

ORANGE VINAIGRETTE. In a bowl, mix ¼ cup **orange juice**, 2 tablespoons *each* **white wine vinegar** and **salad oil**, 1 tablespoon thinly slivered or shredded **orange peel**, 2 teaspoons *each* **honey** and **Dijon mustard**, and ½ teaspoon coarsely ground **pepper**.

Per serving: 372 calories, 36 g protein, 10 g carbohydrates, 21 g fat, 4 g saturated fat, 93 mg cholesterol, 211 mg sodium

Poultry	Maximum amount or size	Cooking time
Skinless, boneless chicken breast halves	4 breast halves (about 4 oz. each)	About 20 minutes*
Whole chicken legs	4 legs (about 2 lbs. total)	About 40 minutes**
Whole chicken	3 to 3½ pounds	About 1¼ hours**
Cornish game hens	2 (2½ lbs. total)	About 1 hour**

*Done when meat in thickest part is no longer pink; cut to test.
**Done when meat near thighbone is no longer pink; cut to test.

GRILLED ASIAN CHICKEN

Preparation time: About 15 minutes

Marinating time: At least 4 hours or up to 1 day

Grilling time: About 30 minutes

A paste of garlic, cilantro, and black peppercorns packs a powerful punch. Slipped beneath the skin of chicken thighs before grilling, it flavors the meat more thoroughly than any baste could.

- 8 **chicken thighs (about 2 lbs.** *total***)**
- 6 **cloves garlic**
- ½ **cup fresh cilantro (coriander) leaves**
- 2 **teaspoons whole black peppercorns**
- 2 **teaspoons soy sauce**
- 1 **teaspoon sugar**
- 5 **tablespoons salad oil**
- 1 **tablespoon wine vinegar**

Rinse chicken, pat dry, and set aside.

In a blender or food processor, whirl garlic, cilantro, and peppercorns until finely chopped. Add soy, sugar, and ¼ cup of the oil; whirl to form a paste. Measure out 1½ tablespoons of the paste; cover and refrigerate. Rub remaining paste evenly all over chicken, slipping some under skin. Cover and refrigerate for at least 4 hours or up to 1 day.

Place chicken, skin side up, on a lightly greased grill 4 to 6 inches above a solid bed of medium coals. Cook, turning often, until meat near bone is no longer pink; cut to test (about 30 minutes). Mix reserved paste, vinegar, and remaining 1 tablespoon oil; spoon over chicken. Makes 4 servings.

Per serving: 401 calories, 30 g protein, 2 g carbohydrates, 30 g fat, 7 g saturated fat, 109 mg cholesterol, 214 mg sodium

APPLE COUNTRY CHICKEN

Preparation time: About 10 minutes

Cooking time: About 40 minutes

Curried chicken goes country when Golden Delicious apples and cider are added to the cooking pan. This dish can be ready to serve in under an hour; top it with spoonfuls of tart yogurt, if you like.

- 3 **pounds chicken thighs, skinned**
- 1½ **teaspoons curry powder**
- 2 **large Golden Delicious apples, cored and chopped**
- 1 **large onion, chopped**
- 1 **cup cider or apple juice**
- 1 **cup regular-strength chicken broth**
- 1 **tablespoon lemon juice**
- 4 **ounces mushrooms, sliced**
- 1 **tablespoon all-purpose flour**
- 2 **tablespoons sliced green onion (including top)**
- 1 **cup plain yogurt (optional)**

Rinse chicken, pat dry, and set aside.

Place curry powder in a 12- to 14-inch frying pan or 5- to 6-quart pan; stir over medium heat until slightly darker in color (about 4 minutes). Add apples, chopped onion, cider, ½ cup of the broth, lemon juice, and mushrooms; bring to a boil over high heat. Add

chicken, reduce heat, cover, and simmer until meat near bone is no longer pink; cut to test (about 30 minutes). With a slotted spoon, transfer chicken to a platter. Keep warm.

Skim and discard fat from chicken cooking liquid. Blend flour and remaining ½ cup broth; add to pan. Boil over high heat, stirring often, until reduced to 3 cups. Pour sauce over chicken. Garnish with green onion; add yogurt to taste, if desired. Makes 6 servings.

Per serving: 233 calories, 27 g protein, 18 g carbohydrates, 6 g fat, 1 g saturated fat, 107 mg cholesterol, 279 mg sodium

CURRIED TURKEY DRUMSTICKS

Preparation time: About 15 minutes

Grilling time: About 55 minutes

No arguments over who gets the drumsticks this time — there's one for every member of the family. Flavor the turkey with a ginger-sparked curry butter before grilling; offer crunchy peanut sauce at the table.

- ¼ **cup butter or margarine, at room temperature**
- 4 **teaspoons curry powder**
- ¼ **teaspoon** *each* **ground ginger and ground cloves**
   Dash of pepper
- 4 **turkey drumsticks (about 1¼ lbs.** *each***)**
- ¼ **cup butter or margarine, melted**
   Peanut-Chile Sauce (recipe follows)

In a small bowl, blend room-temperature butter, curry powder, ginger, cloves, and pepper. Set aside.

Rinse turkey and pat dry. Carefully peel back skin on each drumstick and spread butter mixture evenly over meat. Pull skin back into place and secure with small metal skewers.

Place drumsticks on a lightly greased grill 4 to 6 inches above a solid bed of medium coals. Cover barbecue and adjust dampers (or cover with a tent of heavy-duty foil). Cook, turning as needed to cook evenly and basting often with melted butter, until meat near bone is no longer pink; cut to test (about 55 minutes).

Meanwhile, prepare Peanut-Chile Sauce. Pass sauce at the table to spoon over individual servings. Makes 4 servings.

Per serving without sauce: 794 calories, 79 g protein, 1 g carbohydrates, 51 g fat, 23 g saturated fat, 300 mg cholesterol, 451 mg sodium

PEANUT-CHILE SAUCE. In a small bowl, stir together ½ cup *each* **apple juice** and **crunchy peanut butter;** then stir in 1 teaspoon **crushed dried hot red chiles.** Makes about 1 cup.

Per tablespoon: 51 calories, 2 g protein, 3 g carbohydrates, 4 g fat, 1 g saturated fat, 0 mg cholesterol, 39 mg sodium

STUFFED TURKEY THIGHS

Preparation time: About 15 minutes

Baking time: About 1 hour

For holiday flavor without the fuss, bake boned turkey thighs stuffed with a savory celery and onion dressing. The casually festive entrée takes only about an hour to cook.

- 2 **turkey thighs (about 2 lbs.** *each***), boned**
- 2 **cups coarsely crushed packaged stuffing mix**
- ½ **cup finely chopped celery**
- 3 **tablespoons** *each* **chopped parsley and thinly sliced green onions (including tops)**
- ¼ **cup butter or margarine, melted**
- ½ **teaspoon poultry seasoning**
- ½ **cup regular-strength chicken broth**

Rinse turkey and pat dry; set aside.

In a large bowl, combine stuffing mix, celery, parsley, onions, butter, poultry seasoning, and broth.

To stuff turkey thighs, place them, skin side down, on a flat surface. Spoon about ¼ cup of the stuffing in center of each thigh where bone was removed. Bring meat up over stuffing and secure skin with metal skewers along 2 sides. Tuck more stuffing into open end; then secure skin across it with another skewer, completely enclosing meat and stuffing in a neat bundle. Wrap any remaining stuffing in foil.

Place turkey and foil-wrapped stuffing on a baking sheet. Bake, uncovered, in a 350° oven until meat in thickest part is no longer pink; cut to test (about 1 hour). To serve, remove skewers from turkey and cut each thigh crosswise into thick slices. Transfer extra stuffing from foil to a small bowl and serve alongside turkey. Makes 6 servings.

Per serving: 332 calories, 27 g protein, 18 g carbohydrates, 17 g fat, 7 g saturated fat, 107 mg cholesterol, 569 mg sodium

Serve a spicy, easy-to-make peanut sauce over Curried Turkey
Drumsticks (recipe on facing page) at your next patio party. Cool tabbouli
and grilled pineapple slices and red bell pepper halves complete a
casual, colorful menu.

■ *Pictured on page 380*

BROILED TURKEY WITH BAKED POLENTA

Preparation time: About 15 minutes

Broiling time: About 25 minutes

Baking time: About 50 minutes

A cool autumn day calls for a warm, colorful supper. Try bite-size pieces of broiled turkey thigh in a bright tomato and bell pepper sauce, served over crunchy, cheese-topped polenta.

- 2 pounds turkey thighs
- 1 onion, finely chopped
- 1 green bell pepper, seeded and chopped
- 1 can (14½ oz.) stewed tomatoes
- 1 can (8 oz.) tomato sauce
- ½ cup dry white wine
- 1 teaspoon *each* dry oregano leaves and dry basil leaves
- 5 cups regular-strength chicken broth
- 1½ cups polenta or yellow cornmeal
- ¼ cup butter or margarine, diced
- ½ cup grated Parmesan cheese

Rinse turkey and pat dry. Then arrange, skin side down, in a 9- by 13-inch baking pan. Broil about 4 inches below heat, turning once, until meat near bone is no longer pink; cut to test (about 25 minutes). Remove turkey from pan and set aside. To pan, add onion, bell pepper, tomatoes, tomato sauce, wine, oregano, and basil; mix well.

In a greased 9-inch-square baking pan, stir together broth, polenta, and butter.

Bake vegetable mixture and polenta, uncovered, in a 350° oven, stirring vegetables occasionally, until vegetables are very soft and have formed a thick sauce, and almost all polenta liquid has been absorbed (about 45 minutes).

Remove and discard skin and bones from turkey; cut meat into bite-size pieces. Stir meat into vegetable sauce; sprinkle cheese over polenta. Continue to bake, uncovered, until all polenta liquid has been absorbed (about 5 more minutes). Serve turkey and sauce over portions of polenta. Makes 6 servings.

Per serving: 446 calories, 29 g protein, 37 g carbohydrates, 20 g fat, 9 g saturated fat, 88 mg cholesterol, 1,484 mg sodium

SICHUAN TURKEY THIGH SCALOPPINE

Preparation time: About 15 minutes

Cooking time: About 15 minutes

If you think scaloppine always means veal and Italian flavors, you'll find this recipe unusual all the way around. The meat is pounded turkey thigh; the seasonings of garlic, fresh ginger, and Sichuan chili are Asian. You might serve the spicy sautéed slices with steamed rice and bok choy.

- 2½ pounds turkey thighs
- 3 tablespoons soy sauce
- 2 tablespoons Sichuan chili sauce or Chinese hot bean paste (or use pepper to taste)
  - About 3 tablespoons olive oil or salad oil
- 2 tablespoons minced shallots
- 1 tablespoon *each* minced garlic and minced fresh ginger
- ⅓ cup water

Pull off and discard turkey skin. Rinse turkey and pat dry; then place, skin side down, on a flat surface and find the thick bone with your fingers. Run a sharp knife along bone to cut meat free in a large, neat piece; lift bone with your other hand as you

cut. Discard bone. Cut meat into 6 equal-size pieces; lay any small scraps of meat in center of big pieces.

Place each turkey piece between 2 sheets of plastic wrap; pound with a flat-surfaced mallet to a thickness of about ¼ inch.

Mix soy and chili sauce; rub on both sides of turkey pieces (keep small scraps of meat in place on larger pieces). Set aside.

Heat 1 tablespoon of the oil in a 10- to 12-inch frying pan over medium-high heat. Add shallots, garlic, and ginger; cook, stirring, just until shallots are golden (about 3 minutes). Remove from pan with a slotted spoon and set aside. Heat 1 tablespoon more oil in pan; add turkey in a single layer (do not crowd pan). Cook until edges of turkey pieces turn white (about 2 minutes). Then turn and cook until meat is no longer pink in center; cut to test (about 2 minutes). Transfer cooked turkey to a platter and keep warm. Repeat to cook remaining turkey, adding more oil as necessary to prevent sticking.

Add water and shallot mixture to pan; stir to scrape up browned bits. Heat through, then pour over turkey. Makes 4 to 6 servings.

Per serving: 251 calories, 27 g protein, 4 g carbohydrates, 13 g fat, 3 g saturated fat, 97 mg cholesterol, 813 mg sodium

STIR-FRIED TURKEY SALAD

Preparation time: About 25 minutes

Cooking time: About 7 minutes

Stir-fried bacon slivers and turkey strips warm up this main-course salad. Pour the meat over tomato, avocado, and crisp butter lettuce, then toss with an assertive mustard dressing. Hot, crusty bread completes a hearty meal-in-minutes.

  2 **pounds turkey thighs**

12 **cups bite-size pieces washed, crisped butter lettuce**

  1 **large tomato, cut into wedges**

  1 **large avocado, pitted, peeled, and sliced**

¼ **cup thinly sliced green onions (including tops)**

    Mustard Dressing (recipe follows)

  4 **slices bacon, cut into thin slivers**

¼ **cup grated Parmesan cheese**

Skin and bone turkey as directed for Sichuan Turkey Thigh Scaloppine (page 394). Cut meat into ¼- by 2-inch julienne strips and set aside.

Arrange lettuce, tomato, avocado, and onions in a large salad bowl. Set aside. Prepare Mustard Dressing; set aside.

Cook bacon in a wok or 12- to 14-inch frying pan over medium-high heat until crisp (about 4 minutes). With a slotted spoon, remove bacon from pan and set aside. Pour off and discard all but 1 tablespoon of the drippings.

Increase heat to high. Add turkey to drippings in pan and cook, stirring often, until lightly browned on outside and no longer pink in center; cut to test (about 3 minutes). Pour turkey and pan juices over salad; then pour dressing over salad. Add cheese and bacon; toss to mix. Makes 4 to 6 servings.

MUSTARD DRESSING. In a small bowl, stir together ¼ cup **salad oil,** 3 tablespoons *each* **mayonnaise** and **red wine vinegar,** 1 tablespoon **Dijon mustard,** and 1 teaspoon **dry thyme leaves.**

Per serving: 449 calories, 26 g protein, 8 g carbohydrates, 35 g fat, 7 g saturated fat, 92 mg cholesterol, 398 mg sodium

SKEWERED TURKEY

Preparation time: About 15 minutes

Marinating time: At least 1 hour or up to 1 day

Grilling time: About 15 minutes

Guests will think they're dining on lamb when you serve turkey flavored by a mint jelly marinade. The meat needs to soak for at least an hour, but if you like, you can marinate it up to a full day before grilling. Serve the sizzling-hot skewers with fluffy rice.

  2 **pounds turkey thighs**

¼ **cup** *each* **salad oil and dry white wine**

¼ **cup mint jelly, melted**

¼ **teaspoon grated lime peel**

  1 **tablespoon lime juice**

⅛ **teaspoon pepper**

    Hot cooked rice

Skin and bone turkey as directed for Sichuan Turkey Thigh Scaloppine (page 80); cut meat into 1-inch chunks.

In a bowl, stir together oil, wine, jelly, lime peel, lime juice, and pepper. Then add turkey and stir to coat. Cover and refrigerate for at least 1 hour or up to 1 day, stirring several times.

Drain turkey; reserve marinade. Thread meat equally on 4 metal skewers. Place skewers on a lightly greased grill 4 to 6 inches above a solid bed of medium coals. Cook, turning as needed and basting several times with marinade, until turkey is well browned on outside and no longer pink in center; cut to test (about 15 minutes).

To serve, mound rice on a platter; top with skewered turkey. Makes 4 servings.

Per serving: 249 calories, 26 g protein, 7 g carbohydrates, 12 g fat, 3 g saturated fat, 97 mg cholesterol, 106 mg sodium

Big appetites call for plates piled high with mashed potatoes, cole slaw, and Oven-fried Turkey Wings (recipe on page 403). A crisp cornmeal crust seasoned with marjoram and paprika makes this meaty, down-home main course extra satisfying.

Saucy Wings & Drummettes

CRUSTED & SPICED & CHILIED & GLAZED &

MARINATED & DIPPED & BREADED & SIMMERED &

CHILI-BAKED CHICKEN WINGS

Preparation time: About 10 minutes

Baking time: About 30 minutes

A golden, crunchy coating with just the right amount of chili seasoning makes these baked drummettes (the meatiest part of the wing) perfect party fare. Serve them hot or cold.

- **2 tablespoons butter or margarine**
- **1 tablespoon salad oil**
- **1¼ pounds chicken drummettes (about 15 drummettes)**
- **¼ cup all-purpose flour**
- **2 tablespoons yellow cornmeal**
- **1½ teaspoons chili powder**
- **½ teaspoon ground cumin**

Place butter and oil in a shallow 10- by 15-inch baking pan. Set pan in a 400° oven until butter is melted.

Meanwhile, rinse drummettes and pat dry; set aside. In a paper or plastic bag, combine flour, cornmeal, chili powder, and cumin. Shake drummettes in bag to coat lightly with flour mixture; arrange in a single layer in pan, turning to coat with butter mixture.

Bake, uncovered, until meat near bone is no longer pink; cut to test (about 30 minutes). Serve hot. Or, to serve wings cold, let cool; then cover and refrigerate for at least 4 hours or until next day. Makes about 15 appetizers.

Per appetizer: 83 calories, 6 g protein, 3 g carbohydrates, 5 g fat, 2 g saturated fat, 29 mg cholesterol, 43 mg sodium

GLAZED CHICKEN WINGS ORIENTAL

Preparation time: About 25 minutes

Baking time: About 45 minutes

Two-step baking turns out chicken wings that are crisp and saucy at the same time. Serve them as an appetizer; or, for a full meal, allow three or four wings per person and offer hot rice and Chinese pea pods alongside.

- **2 teaspoons water**
- **½ cup cornstarch**
- **2 pounds chicken wings**
- **1 large egg**
- **1 tablespoon salad oil**
- **½ cup *each* sugar and regular-strength chicken broth**
- **½ cup rice vinegar or white wine vinegar**
- **¼ cup catsup**
- **1 teaspoon soy sauce**
- **2 cloves garlic, minced or pressed**

In a small dish, stir together water and 2 teaspoons of the cornstarch. Set aside.

Cut off and discard chicken wingtips; then rinse chicken and pat dry. In a shallow pan, beat egg until blended. Dip wings in egg to coat, then dip in remaining cornstarch to coat lightly. Pour oil into a shallow 10- by 15-inch baking pan; set pan in a 450° oven until oil is hot. Then arrange wings in a single layer in pan. Bake, uncovered, until lightly browned on bottom (about 20 minutes). Turn wings over; continue to bake,

uncovered, until lightly browned on other side (about 20 more minutes). Remove baking pan from oven; drain off fat.

When wings are nearly done, prepare sauce. In a 1½- to 2-quart pan, mix sugar, broth, vinegar, catsup, soy, and garlic. Bring to a boil over high heat; boil, stirring, until reduced to ¾ cup. Stir cornstarch mixture and add to broth mixture; bring to a rolling boil, stirring constantly.

Brush all the sauce over wings. Continue to bake, uncovered, until sauce is bubbly (about 5 more minutes). Makes about 1 dozen appetizers.

Per appetizer: 151 calories, 8 g protein, 13 g carbohydrates, 7 g fat, 2 g saturated fat, 42 mg cholesterol, 158 mg sodium

Feature

CHICKEN LIVER CREATIONS

If you like the hearty, robust flavor of chicken livers, you'll want to add these two recipes to your files. Both dishes showcase livers at their best: cooked just until browned outside, but still pink inside.

COUNTRY CHICKEN LIVERS

Preparation time: About 15 minutes

Cooking time: About 40 minutes

> About 1 pound mustard greens
> 8 slices thick-cut bacon, cut into halves
> 1 pound chicken livers, drained, cut into halves
> 1 large onion, sliced
> 8 ounces mushrooms, sliced
> 1 tablespoon *each* dry white wine and Worcestershire

Wash and drain mustard greens. Discard tough stems; cut leaves into wide strips and set aside.

Cook bacon in a 10- to 12-inch frying pan over medium heat until crisp (about 10 minutes); lift out and drain. Pour off and discard all but 3 tablespoons of the drippings, then pour 1 tablespoon of the reserved drippings into a 5- to 6-quart pan and set aside.

Add chicken livers to remaining 2 tablespoons drippings in frying pan. Cook over medium-high heat, turning as needed, until browned on outside but still pink in center; cut to test (about 5 minutes). Remove livers from pan and set aside.

Add onion and mushrooms to frying pan; pour in wine and Worcestershire. Cover and cook for 15 minutes, then uncover and continue to cook until almost all liquid has evaporated (about 10 more minutes). Meanwhile, place the 5- to 6-quart pan over medium-high heat; add mustard greens and stir until wilted. Mound greens in center of a platter and keep warm.

Return livers to frying pan with onion and mushrooms; cook, stirring, just until heated through. Spoon liver mixture around greens; garnish with bacon. Makes 4 servings.

Per serving: 393 calories, 32 g protein, 15 g carbohydrates, 23 g fat, 8 g saturated fat, 523 mg cholesterol, 548 mg sodium

LIVERS WITH PEA PODS

Preparation time: About 10 minutes, plus 15 minutes to stand

Cooking time: About 5 minutes

> 1 pound chicken livers, drained, quartered
> 1 tablespoon *each* soy sauce and dry sherry
> 1 tablespoon minced fresh ginger
> Cooking Sauce (recipe follows)
> 2 tablespoons salad oil
> 8 ounces Chinese pea pods (also called snow peas), ends and strings removed
> 6 green onions (including tops), cut into 2-inch lengths
> Hot cooked rice

In a bowl, combine chicken livers, soy, sherry, and 2 teaspoons of the ginger. Stir gently to mix; then let stand for 15 minutes. Meanwhile, prepare Cooking Sauce and set aside.

Heat oil in a wok or 12- to 14-inch frying pan over high heat. Add pea pods, remaining 1 teaspoon ginger, and onions; cook, stirring, until pea pods turn bright green and are tender to bite (about 1 minute). Remove from pan with a slotted spoon and set aside.

Add livers and their marinade to pan. Cook, stirring, until livers are browned on outside but still pink in center; cut to test (about 3 minutes). Return pea pod mixture to pan; then add Cooking Sauce. Cook, stirring, just until ingredients are well blended and sauce is thickened. Serve over rice. Makes 4 servings.

COOKING SAUCE. In a small bowl, stir together 2 tablespoons *each* **soy sauce** and **dry sherry** and 1 teaspoon *each* **sugar** and **cornstarch.**

Per serving: 252 calories, 23 g protein, 14 g carbohydrates, 11 g fat, 2 g saturated fat, 498 mg cholesterol, 866 mg sodium

SPICY CHICKEN WINGS

Preparation time: About 15 minutes

Baking time: About 45 minutes

Our version of this popular appetizer makes enough to let a crowd keep coming back for more. True fire-eaters will enjoy the super-hot nibbles served plain—but most diners will appreciate the chance to soothe their tastebuds with side-snacks of celery sticks and cool, creamy blue cheese dip.

    4 **pounds chicken wings, cut apart at joints**
       Red Hot Sauce (recipe follows)
       Blue Cheese Dip (optional; recipe follows)
    2 **bunches celery (about 2 lbs. *total*), optional**

Discard chicken wingtips. Rinse remaining wing pieces and pat dry, then arrange in a single layer in 2 lightly greased shallow 10- by 15-inch baking pans. Bake, uncovered, in a 400° oven until golden brown (about 30 minutes).

Meanwhile, prepare Red Hot Sauce. Remove pans from oven, drain off fat, and pour sauce over chicken; turn chicken to coat well. Then continue to bake, uncovered, turning wings once or twice, until sauce is bubbly and edges of wings are crisp (about 15 more minutes).

Meanwhile, if desired, prepare Blue Cheese Dip and break celery stalks from bunches; remove leaves and set aside. Slice stalks lengthwise and place in a bowl.

Arrange chicken on a platter. If using celery and Blue Cheese Dip, garnish chicken with reserved celery leaves; offer with celery stalks and dip. Makes about 4 dozen appetizers.

RED HOT SAUCE. In a small bowl, stir together ½ cup *each* **distilled white vinegar** and **water,** ¼ cup **tomato paste,** 4 teaspoons **sugar,** 1 to 3 tablespoons (or to taste) **liquid hot pepper seasoning,** and 1 to 3 teaspoons (or to taste) **ground red pepper** (cayenne).

Per appetizer without dip: 45 calories, 4 g protein, 1 g carbohydrates, 3 g fat, 1 g saturated fat, 12 mg cholesterol, 39 mg sodium

BLUE CHEESE DIP. In a bowl, coarsely mash 4 ounces **blue-veined cheese.** Stir in 1 cup **sour cream,** 1 teaspoon minced **garlic,** ½ teaspoon **dry mustard,** and ⅛ teaspoon **pepper.** If made ahead, cover and refrigerate for up to 3 days. Makes 1⅓ cups.

Per tablespoon: 43 calories, 2 g protein, 1 g carbohydrates, 4 g fat, 2 g saturated fat, 9 mg cholesterol, 81 mg sodium

BASIL PARMESAN CHICKEN WINGS

Preparation time: About 20 minutes

Baking time: About 30 minutes

Here's a great way to start an Italian feast. Coat chicken drummettes with garlic butter, then roll in cheese- and basil-seasoned crumbs and bake until crisp.

    ¼ **cup butter or margarine**
    2 **tablespoons salad oil**
    1 **clove garlic, minced or pressed**
    1 **cup soft bread crumbs**
    2 **tablespoons finely chopped parsley**
    ½ **cup grated Parmesan cheese**
    ¼ **cup grated Romano cheese**
    1 **teaspoon dry basil leaves**
  1½ **pounds chicken drummettes (about 18 drummettes)**

In a frying pan or other shallow pan, combine butter, oil, and garlic. Stir over low heat until butter is melted. In another shallow pan or wide, shallow rimmed plate, combine crumbs, parsley, Parmesan cheese, Romano cheese, and basil.

Rinse drummettes and pat dry. Dip each drummette in butter mixture to coat; then roll in crumb mixture to coat.

Arrange chicken in a single layer in a lightly greased shallow 10- by 15-inch baking pan. Bake, uncovered, in a 400° oven until meat near bone is no longer pink; cut to test (about 30 minutes). Makes about 1½ dozen appetizers.

Per appetizer: 99 calories, 6 g protein, 1 g carbohydrates, 7 g fat, 3 g saturated fat, 31 mg cholesterol, 114 mg sodium

*Serve Spicy Chicken Wings (recipe on facing page) at
your next appetizer party—and start the evening off with a bang!
A tomato-based hot sauce, fiery with cayenne and liquid hot pepper
seasoning, coats the wings as they bake.*

HOT CHILI CHICKEN WINGS

Preparation time: About 10 minutes

Cooking time: About 45 minutes

Combine soy sauce with chili oil, add garlic and fresh ginger, and simmer drummettes in the mixture until it's reduced to a thick (and incendiary!) glaze. Serve hot, or refrigerate and serve cold the next day.

2 **pounds chicken drummettes (about 24 drummettes)**

2 **tablespoons salad oil**

¼ **cup soy sauce**

2 **tablespoons rice wine or dry sherry**

2 **tablespoons sugar**

1 **teaspoon chili oil or 2 small dried hot red chiles**

4 **quarter-size slices fresh ginger**

2 **cloves garlic**

2 **green onions, roots and tops trimmed**

1 **cup water**

Rinse drummettes and pat dry. Heat salad oil in a 10- to 12-inch frying pan over medium-high heat. Add drummettes, a portion at a time; cook, turning as needed, until browned on all sides (about 6 minutes).

Return all chicken to pan; add soy, wine, sugar, chili oil, ginger, garlic, onions, and water. Bring to a boil. Then reduce heat, cover, and simmer until meat near bone is no longer pink; cut to test (about 20 minutes). Uncover and bring to a boil; boil, turning chicken often, until sauce is reduced and thick enough to coat chicken (about 10 minutes). If made ahead, let cool; then cover and refrigerate until next day. Serve hot or cold. Makes about 2 dozen appetizers.

Per appetizer: 60 calories, 5 g protein, 2 g carbohydrates, 4 g fat, 1 g saturated fat, 21 mg cholesterol, 193 mg sodium

GRILLED MUSTARD WINGS & RIBS

Preparation time: About 10 minutes

Marinating time: At least 4 hours or up to 1 day

Grilling time: About 20 minutes

Forget the utensils at your next patio party: these are strictly finger foods. Chicken wings and meaty beef ribs, bathed in a mustardy marinade, cook together on the grill.

Mustard Marinade (recipe follows)

3 **pounds chicken wings**

3 **pounds beef ribs, cut into separate ribs**

Prepare Mustard Marinade; set aside. Cut off and discard chicken wingtips; then rinse chicken and pat dry.

Place chicken and ribs in separate large heavy-duty plastic bags. Pour half the marinade into each bag. Seal bags and turn over several times to coat meat with marinade; then set bags in a large, shallow baking pan or dish. Refrigerate for at least 4 hours or up to 1 day, turning bags over several times.

Drain chicken and ribs; reserve marinade. Place meats on a lightly greased grill 4 to 6 inches above a solid bed of medium-hot coals. Cook chicken, turning occasionally and basting with marinade, until browned on outside and no longer pink near bone; cut to test (about 20 minutes). Cook ribs, turning and basting, until browned on outside but still slightly pink near bone; cut to test (about 15 minutes). Makes 6 servings.

MUSTARD MARINADE. In a bowl, stir together 1 cup **Dijon mustard,** 1 cup **dry white wine** or regular-strength chicken broth, 2 tablespoons *each* **salad oil** and **honey,** 2 teaspoons **dry tarragon leaves,** and 2 cloves **garlic,** minced or pressed.

Per serving: 608 calories, 43 g protein, 6 g carbohydrates, 45 g fat, 15 g saturated fat, 145 mg cholesterol, 727 mg sodium

■ *Pictured on page 396*

OVEN-FRIED TURKEY WINGS

Preparation time: About 15 minutes

Baking time: About 40 minutes

Cornmeal-crunchy turkey wings are fun to pick up and eat with your fingers—and they're easy to "fry" in the oven.

     6 **turkey wings (about 5 lbs. *total*)**
 1¼ **cups yellow cornmeal**
     2 **tablespoons paprika**
     1 **tablespoon dry marjoram leaves**
     1 **teaspoon pepper**
     1 **large egg**
     2 **tablespoons water**
        About 5 tablespoons butter or margarine, melted
        Salt

With your hands, force joints of each turkey wing open until they snap; then cut wings apart at joints.

Discard wingtips. Rinse remaining wing pieces and pat dry.

In a wide, shallow rimmed plate, mix cornmeal, paprika, marjoram, and pepper. In a shallow pan, beat egg and water to blend.

Dip wing pieces in egg mixture to coat; then dip in cornmeal mixture to coat well (pat coating on lightly for an extra-thick crust). Arrange pieces, slightly apart, in a single layer in an oiled shallow 10- by 15-inch baking pan.

Bake, uncovered, in a 400° oven for 15 minutes; drizzle evenly with butter. Continue to bake, uncovered, until meat near bone in thickest part of wing is no longer pink; cut to test (about 25 more minutes). Season to taste with salt. Makes 6 servings.

Per serving: 688 calories, 68 g protein, 24 g carbohydrates, 34 g fat, 13 g saturated fat, 327 mg cholesterol, 279 mg sodium

HOISIN TURKEY WINGS

Preparation time: About 10 minutes

Marinating time: At least 1 hour or up to 1 day

Grilling time: About 45 minutes

A few simple ingredients and half a dozen turkey wings add up to an easy entrée that leaves you with plenty of time to relax. Accompany the barbecued turkey with grilled green onions and fresh fruit salad.

     1 **cup hoisin sauce**
 ⅓ **cup dry sherry**
 ¼ **cup lemon juice**
     3 **cloves garlic, minced or pressed**
     6 **turkey wings (about 5 lbs. *total*)**

In a shallow pan or dish, combine hoisin, sherry, lemon juice, and garlic. Cut off and discard turkey wingtips; then rinse turkey, pat dry, and add to marinade. Turn to coat. Cover and refrigerate for at least 1 hour or up to 1 day.

Drain turkey; reserve marinade. Place turkey on a lightly greased grill 4 to 6 inches above a solid bed of medium-hot coals. Cook, turning occasionally and

basting with marinade, until meat near bone in thickest part of wing is no longer pink; cut to test (about 45 minutes). Makes 6 servings.

Per serving: 513 calories, 65 g protein, 8 g carbohydrates, 23 g fat, 6 g saturated fat, 265 mg cholesterol, 850 mg sodium

When our Sour Cream Meatballs (recipe on page 406) are on the menu, expect guests to linger over lunch. Serve the delicate meatballs over your favorite pasta shapes; we chose bowties. Spinach-stuffed tomatoes make a colorful side dish.

Versatile Ground Meat

CRUMBLED & SEASONED & PEPPERED & BAKED &

NUTTED & POCKETED & PATTIED & LAYERED &

LOAFED & SCENTED & SANDWICHED & STACKED &

405

■ Pictured on page 404

SOUR CREAM MEATBALLS

Preparation time: About 15 minutes

Cooking time: About 40 minutes

Novices and accomplished cooks alike will present this dish with pride. Delicate ground chicken meatballs flavored with rye bread crumbs and a hint of mustard are first browned, then simmered in a rich tomato–sour cream sauce.

- 1½ **pounds ground chicken**
- 1 **cup rye bread crumbs**
- 1 **small onion, finely chopped**
- ⅓ **cup finely chopped parsley**
- 1 **large egg**
- 1 **teaspoon dry mustard**
- ¼ **teaspoon pepper**
- 2 **tablespoons salad oil**
- 1½ **cups regular-strength chicken broth**
- 1 **can (6 oz.) tomato paste**
- 2 **cups sour cream**
-     **Hot cooked pasta**

In a large bowl, combine chicken, crumbs, onion, ¼ cup of the parsley, egg, mustard, and pepper. Mix thoroughly; then shape into 1-inch balls.

Heat oil in a 12- to 14-inch frying pan over medium-high heat. Add meatballs, a portion at a time; do not crowd pan. Cook, turning often, until no longer pink in center; cut to test (about 10 minutes).

In a 4-quart pan, blend broth and tomato paste; bring to a boil over medium-high heat. Gradually stir in sour cream. Reduce heat to medium-low, add meatballs, and simmer, uncovered, stirring occasionally, for 15 minutes. Serve over pasta and sprinkle with remaining parsley. Makes 6 servings.

Per serving: 447 calories, 26 g protein, 14 g carbohydrates, 32 g fat, 13 g saturated fat, 163 mg cholesterol, 662 mg sodium

SUNSHINE STUFFED PEPPERS

Preparation time: About 55 minutes

Baking time: About 30 minutes

Quick cure for rainy day blues: Sunny bell peppers stuffed with tomatoes, chicken, and provolone cheese. The bright red "surprise packages," their filling seasoned with garlic, oregano, fennel seeds, and chiles, will wake up your palate and lift your spirits.

- 8 **medium-size red bell peppers**
- 2 **tablespoons salad oil**
- 2 **large onions, sliced**
- 3 **cloves garlic, minced or pressed**
- 1½ **pounds ground chicken**
- ¾ **cup chopped Italian parsley**
- 1 **teaspoon *each* dry oregano leaves and fennel seeds**
- ¼ **teaspoon crushed dried hot red chiles**
- 2 **small tomatoes, peeled and chopped**
- 8 **ounces provolone cheese, cut into ½-inch cubes**
- 1 **cup cooked brown rice**

Cut off and discard stem ends of bell peppers, then remove seeds. If necessary, trim bases of peppers so they will stand upright. In a 6- to 8-quart pan, bring 3 to 4 quarts water to a boil over high heat. Add peppers and cook for 2 minutes, then lift out and plunge into cold water to cool. Drain and set aside.

Heat oil in a 12- to 14-inch frying pan over medium heat. Add onions and garlic and cook, stirring occasionally, until onions are soft (about 10 minutes). Add chicken and cook, stirring often, until no longer pink (about 10 minutes). Remove from heat and let cool; then mix in parsley, oregano, fennel seeds, chiles, tomatoes, cheese, and rice.

Fill peppers equally with chicken mixture and arrange upright in a shallow 1½-quart baking dish. Bake, uncovered, in a 350° oven until cheese is melted and stuffing is lightly browned on top (about 30 minutes). Makes 8 servings.

Per serving: 324 calories, 24 g protein, 14 g carbohydrates, 19 g fat, 7 g saturated fat, 90 mg cholesterol, 325 mg sodium

TARRAGON CHICKEN TURNOVERS

Preparation time: About 1 hour

Baking time: About 15 minutes

Give your family or friends some extra attention of the edible kind—put together an individual main-dish pie for each person. Brush your favorite pastry with tarragon mustard; then fill with ham, cheese, chicken, and mushrooms, and bake.

- 2 **tablespoons butter or margarine**
- 2 **tablespoons** *each* **minced onion and minced shallots**
- 8 **ounces mushrooms, chopped**
- 1 **pound ground chicken**
- 2 **ounces cooked ham, finely chopped**
- 2 **tablespoons finely chopped parsley**
- ¼ **teaspoon pepper**
- ¼ **cup whipping cream**
- 1 **cup (4 oz.) shredded Swiss cheese**
  Pastry for 2 double-crust 9-inch pies
- ¼ **cup tarragon mustard**
- 1 **large egg yolk beaten with 2 tablespoons milk**

Melt butter in a 12- to 14-inch frying pan over medium-high heat. Add onion, shallots, and mushrooms; cook, stirring often, until onion and shallots are golden brown (about 15 minutes). Add chicken and ham; cook, stirring often, until chicken is no longer pink (about 5 minutes). Add parsley, pepper, and cream; continue to cook until mixture is thickened (about 5 minutes). Remove from heat, let cool, and stir in cheese.

On a lightly floured board, roll out pastry to a thickness of ⅛ inch. Cut out eight 6-inch circles. Brush each circle evenly with 1½ teaspoons of the mustard, then mound an eighth of the chicken mixture in center of each circle. Fold pastry over filling, press edges to seal, and brush with egg yolk mixture. Place turnovers, slightly apart, on a baking sheet. Bake, uncovered, in a 425° oven until lightly browned (about 15 minutes). Makes 8 servings.

Per serving: 494 calories, 21 g protein, 27 g carbohydrates, 33 g fat, 12 g saturated fat, 107 mg cholesterol, 438 mg sodium

CHICKEN EGGPLANT PARMESAN

Preparation time: About 45 minutes

Baking time: About 25 minutes

It's time to add another version of hearty, ever-popular eggplant *parmigiana* to your recipe files. The meaty to-mato sauce is made with ground chicken; the egg-plant slices are oven-browned, not fried, letting you use a minimum of oil.

- **Oven-browned Eggplant (recipe follows)**
- 1 **tablespoon olive oil**
- 1½ **pounds ground chicken**
- 2 **cloves garlic, minced or pressed**
- 1 **large can (15 oz.) tomato sauce**
- 2 **teaspoons dry oregano leaves**
- 1 **teaspoon dry thyme leaves**
- ½ **teaspoon dry marjoram leaves**
- 1 **cup (about 5 oz.) grated Parmesan cheese**
- ¼ **cup chopped Italian parsley**

Prepare Oven-browned Eggplant; set aside.

While eggplant is baking, heat oil in a 12- to 14-inch frying pan over medium-high heat. Add chicken and garlic; cook, stirring often, until chicken is no longer pink (about 5 minutes). Stir in tomato sauce, oregano, thyme, and marjoram; reduce heat to medi-um-low and simmer for about 5 minutes. Remove from heat.

Arrange half the Oven-browned Eggplant in a shallow 2- to 2½-quart baking dish. Cover with half the chicken-tomato sauce; sprinkle with ½ cup of the cheese. Repeat layers, using remaining eggplant, sauce, and cheese. Sprinkle with parsley. Cover and bake in a 375° oven for 20 minutes; then uncover and continue to bake until lightly browned (about 5 more minutes). Makes 6 servings.

OVEN-BROWNED EGGPLANT. Cut 1 large **egg-plant** (about 1¾ lbs.) into ¼-inch-thick slices. Brush slices with **olive oil** (you'll need about ⅓ cup). Ar-range slices in a single layer in 2 shallow baking pans. Bake, uncovered, in a 425° oven until browned (about 25 minutes), turning slices over halfway through bak-ing to brown evenly. Season to taste with **salt** and **pepper.**

Per serving: 467 calories, 32 g protein, 15 g carbohydrates, 31 g fat, 9 g saturated fat, 113 mg cholesterol, 966 mg sodium

SWEET SPICE CHICKEN & ORZO

Preparation time: About 10 minutes

Cooking time: About 1¾ hours

Not your typical tomato sauce, this chunky, slow-simmered blend of bacon, onions, celery, and chicken is richly seasoned with herbs and sweet spices. Serve it with tiny rice-shaped pasta.

- 4 **ounces sliced bacon, chopped**
- 1 **pound ground chicken**
- 4 **medium-size onions, chopped**
- 2 **cloves garlic, minced or pressed**
- 1 **cup finely chopped celery**
  Spice Blend (recipe follows)
- 2 **tablespoons finely chopped parsley**
- 3 **large cans (15 oz. *each*) tomato sauce**
- 1 **can (6 oz.) tomato paste**
- 2 **tablespoons red wine vinegar**
- 1 **pound dry orzo or other tiny pasta shapes**

Cook bacon in a 5- to 6-quart pan over medium-high heat until lightly browned (about 10 minutes), stirring occasionally. Spoon off and discard all but 2 tablespoons of the drippings. Then add chicken and cook, stirring often, until no longer pink (about 5 minutes). Add onions, garlic, and celery; cook, stirring often, until onions are very soft (about 20 minutes). Meanwhile, prepare Spice Blend.

To chicken mixture, add Spice Blend, parsley, tomato sauce, tomato paste, and vinegar. Bring to a boil; then reduce heat to medium-low and simmer, uncovered, until sauce is thickened and flavors are blended (about 1 hour).

Cook orzo according to package directions just until tender to bite. Drain well; place in a large, shallow serving bowl and top with chicken-tomato sauce. Mix lightly. Makes 8 to 10 servings.

SPICE BLEND. In a small bowl, mix 1 tablespoon firmly packed **brown sugar;** ½ teaspoon *each* **ground cinnamon, dry oregano leaves, pepper, dry sage leaves,** and **dry thyme leaves;** and ¼ teaspoon *each* **ground cloves** and **ground nutmeg.**

Per serving: 387 calories, 20 g protein, 57 g carbohydrates, 10 g fat, 3 g saturated fat, 47 mg cholesterol, 1,136 mg sodium

CHICKEN IN CREAMY PEANUT SAUCE

Preparation time: About 10 minutes

Cooking time: About 15 minutes

It may be ready in minutes, but it's not missing a thing! This stir-fry has it all—fantastic flavor, and speed and ease of preparation. The spicy peanut sauce, packed with meat and vegetables, is served with soba noodles (or use whole wheat spaghetti, if you like).

Creamy Peanut Sauce (recipe follows)
- 1 **tablespoon salad oil**
- 1 **large onion, sliced**
- 1 **clove garlic, minced or pressed**
- 1½ **pounds ground chicken**
- 12 **ounces dry soba noodles**
- 2 **cups shredded napa cabbage**
- ¼ **cup chopped green onions (including tops)**

Prepare Creamy Peanut Sauce and set aside.

Heat oil in a 12- to 14-inch frying pan over medium-high heat. Add sliced onion and garlic; cook, stirring often, until onion is soft (about 7 minutes). Add chicken and cook, stirring often, until no longer pink (about 5 minutes).

Meanwhile, cook soba according to package directions just until barely tender to bite. Drain well, place in a large, shallow serving bowl, and keep warm.

Add Creamy Peanut Sauce and cabbage to chicken mixture; bring to a boil, stirring. Stir chicken mixture into drained soba; sprinkle with green onions. Makes 6 servings.

CREAMY PEANUT SAUCE. In a bowl, stir together ½ cup *each* **low-sodium chicken broth** and **reduced-sodium soy sauce;** ¼ cup *each* **creamy peanut butter** and **hoisin sauce;** 1 tablespoon **sugar;** and ½ teaspoon **crushed dried hot red chiles.**

Per serving: 500 calories, 33 g protein, 54 g carbohydrates, 18 g fat, 4 g saturated fat, 94 mg cholesterol, 1,734 mg sodium

A cluster of your favorite fresh herbs garnishes Sweet Spice
Chicken & Orzo (recipe on facing page). Served over rice-shaped pasta,
the tempting tomato sauce is thick with chicken, celery, onion, and bacon.
A mixed green salad with cucumber slices and tangy feta cheese offers
a refreshing contrast to the richly flavored main course.

EXTRAORDINARY DUCK ENTRÉES

Duck demands attention and praise at your dinner table. Rich-tasting Peking or Long Island duck, the most popular and widely available variety, is often sold both fresh and frozen in supermarkets. Wild or farm-raised mallard duck is leaner and stronger in flavor than the Peking type; you can order it from specialty markets or—in season—request it from a hunter friend.

When preparing Peking duck for roasting, prick the skin all over with a fork to let the fat drain out; then prick again every 15 minutes throughout the cooking time to allow continued release of fat. For extra-crisp skin, separate the skin from the breast meat by sliding a spoon between the two before roasting.

The recipes we offer here cover several cooking styles and presentations. Our golden roast Duck in Fruit Sauce, basted with honey butter and served with mixed dried fruit and sweet-sour red cabbage, is a beautiful entrée that's sure to take the chill off winter weather. In spring or summer, you may want to try our salad of shredded duck and mixed greens in a tarragon mustard vinaigrette; it can be made with home-cooked or purchased Chinese barbecued duck. To usher in autumn, serve wild duck—first marinated in chile-accented soy sauce, then quickly grilled.

DUCK IN FRUIT SAUCE

Preparation time: About 15 minutes

Cooking time: About 2¾ hours

1	duck (4½ to 5 lbs.), thawed if frozen
¼	cup butter or margarine
½	cup honey
¼	cup firmly packed brown sugar
1	package (8 oz.) mixed dried fruit
1⅓	cups water
	Sweet-Sour Red Cabbage (recipe follows)

Reserve duck neck and giblets for other uses. Pull off and discard lumps of fat from duck; then rinse duck inside and out and pat dry. Secure neck skin to back with a small metal skewer; bend wings akimbo.

With a fork, prick duck skin all over. Then place duck, breast down, on a rack in a 12- by 15-inch roasting pan. Roast, uncovered, in a 350° oven for 1 hour. Turn duck breast up and continue to roast, uncovered, for 45 more minutes.

Meanwhile, melt butter in a 1- to 1½-quart pan over medium heat. Stir in honey and sugar; cook, stirring, until sugar is dissolved. Remove from heat and set aside.

Place dried fruit in another 1- to 1½-quart pan, add water, and bring to a boil. Cover, remove from heat, and let stand until duck is ready. Also prepare Sweet-Sour Red Cabbage and set aside.

After duck has roasted for 1¾ hours, siphon off and discard all fat from roasting pan. Reduce oven temperature to 300°. Continue to roast duck until meat near thighbone is no longer pink; cut to test (about 45 more minutes). During first 20 minutes, baste duck 3 or 4 times with butter-honey mixture.

Transfer duck to a platter; discard fat in roasting pan. Pour remaining butter-honey mixture into pan; bring to a boil over medium-high heat, stirring to scrape up browned bits. Reduce heat to low. Drain fruit and turn gently in roasting pan to warm and mix with sauce. Also reheat Sweet-Sour Red Cabbage.

Spoon fruit sauce around duck on platter; serve duck and fruit with cabbage. Makes 4 servings.

Per serving without cabbage: 1,110 calories, 41 g protein, 84 g carbohydrates, 70 g fat, 27 g saturated fat, 203 mg cholesterol, 254 mg sodium

SWEET-SOUR RED CABBAGE. Core and finely shred 1 medium-size head **red cabbage** (about 2 lbs.). Place cabbage in a 5- to 6-quart pan and add ½ cup **water**, ⅓ cup **cider vinegar**, 1 tablespoon *each* **granulated sugar** and firmly packed **brown sugar,** and ¼ teaspoon **pepper.** Bring to a boil over high heat; then reduce heat, cover, and simmer, stirring occasionally, until cabbage is very tender to bite (about 40 minutes). Uncover and boil rapidly, stirring, until any liquid has evaporated. Makes 4 cups.

Per cup: 77 calories, 3 g protein, 19 g carbohydrates, 0 g fat, 0 g saturated fat, 0 mg cholesterol, 21 mg sodium

DUCK & GREENS IN VINAIGRETTE

Preparation time: About 35 minutes

Baking time: About 2½ hours

Cooked Duck (recipe follows); or 1 Chinese barbecued duck (2 to 2½ lbs.)

House Dressing (recipe follows)

8 to 12 ounces green or red leaf lettuce, separated into leaves, washed, and crisped

About 8 ounces *each* escarole and chicory (or 1 pound escarole or chicory), separated into leaves, washed, and crisped

About 8 ounces radicchio, separated into leaves, washed, and crisped

Salt and pepper

Prepare Cooked Duck. Pull meat from duck; discard skin and bones. Tear meat into thin shreds.

Prepare House Dressing and set aside.

Line a salad bowl with large lettuce leaves. Tear remaining lettuce into bite-size pieces; coarsely chop escarole and chicory. Add torn lettuce, escarole, chicory, and radicchio to bowl. Top greens with duck, add House Dressing, and mix well. Season to taste with salt and pepper. Makes 6 to 8 servings.

COOKED DUCK. Use 1 **duck** (4½ to 5 lbs.), thawed if frozen. Reserve duck neck and giblets for other uses; pull off and discard lumps of fat from duck. Rinse duck inside and out; pat dry.

Wrap duck in foil and place in a 9- by 13-inch baking pan. Bake in a 350° oven until meat is tender enough to pull easily from bones (about 2½ hours). Unwrap and let cool.

HOUSE DRESSING. In a small bowl, stir together 1 teaspoon **dry tarragon leaves,** 1 tablespoon **mustard**

seeds, ¼ cup **Dijon mustard,** ½ cup **balsamic vinegar** or red wine vinegar, ½ cup **olive oil** or salad oil, and 1 small **red onion,** thinly slivered.

Per serving: 580 calories, 25 g protein, 8 g carbohydrates, 50 g fat, 13 g saturated fat, 98 mg cholesterol, 355 mg sodium

GRILLED MALLARD DUCKS WITH SOY

Preparation time: About 45 minutes

Marinating time: At least 30 minutes or up to 2 hours

Grilling time: About 10 minutes

4 wild or farm-raised mallard ducks (1½ to 2 lbs. *each*)

3 cloves garlic, minced or pressed

¾ cup light soy sauce

¼ teaspoon crushed dried hot red chiles

2 lemons, cut into wedges

½ cup canned lingonberries, drained

About 2 cups watercress sprigs, washed and crisped

With poultry shears or a heavy knife, cut ducks in half lengthwise. Remove backbones. Cut off wings.

On each duck half, start at edge of breast and slide a small, sharp knife parallel to bone, cutting meat free from bones of breast and back. Then cut thigh from body, so you end up with boned body meat with a leg attached. Trim off any loose skin flaps. If breast fillets fall free, reserve them.

Reserve wings and bones for stock, if desired. Rinse duck halves and pat dry. Press breast fillets back in place, if necessary.

Place duck halves in a large heavy-duty plastic bag. Add garlic, soy, and chiles. Seal bag and turn over several times to coat duck halves with marinade. Place bag in a large, shallow baking pan or dish; refrigerate for at least 30 minutes or up to 2 hours, turning bag over several times.

Drain duck; discard marinade. Then lay duck halves out flat, skin side down, on a lightly greased grill 4 to 6 inches above a solid bed of hot coals. Cook, turning as needed to brown evenly, until breast meat in thickest part is pinkish-red but no longer wet-looking; cut to test (about 10 minutes). Place duck on a platter.

To serve, garnish duck with lemon wedges, lingonberries, and watercress. Makes 4 servings.

Per serving: 1,099 calories, 60 g protein, 22 g carbohydrates, 86 g fat, 29 g saturated fat, 254 mg cholesterol*

*Sodium data not available.

Easy to prepare and simple to serve, Layered Turkey Enchiladas (recipe on facing page) are good for you, too! To assemble the tempting tower, just stack corn tortillas with a blend of ground turkey, chiles, cheese, tomatoes, and salsa. Serve with simmered pinto beans and more salsa, if you like.

SUMMER CHICKEN STIR-FRY

Preparation time: About 10 minutes, plus 1 hour to soak bulgur

Cooking time: About 12 minutes

Summer meals can present a dilemma. When the weather's sultry, you don't want to spend much time in the kitchen—but you still may be in the mood for a hot dinner. Solve the problem with this simple combination of ground chicken, zucchini, and carrots, easily stir-fried in under 15 minutes. There's no need to steam rice to go alongside; you serve the dish over bulgur that's soaked, not cooked, to tenderness.

  1 **cup bulgur (cracked wheat)**
  2 **cups boiling water**
    Cooking Sauce (recipe follows)
  2 **tablespoons olive oil or salad oil**
  3 **cloves garlic, minced or pressed**
  1 **pound ground chicken**
  2 **cups thinly sliced carrots**
  2 **small zucchini, thinly sliced**
  1 **tablespoon minced fresh ginger**
  ⅓ **cup water**
  ½ **cup thinly sliced green onions (including tops)**

In a bowl, stir together bulgur and the 2 cups boiling water; set aside until almost all liquid has been absorbed (about 1 hour). Drain.

Prepare Cooking Sauce and set aside.

Heat oil in a wok or 12- to 14-inch frying pan over high heat. Add garlic and chicken; cook, stirring often, until chicken is lightly browned (about 5 minutes). Remove chicken mixture from pan and set aside.

To pan, add carrots, zucchini, ginger, and the ⅓ cup water; stir to scrape up browned bits. Cover; cook until vegetables are tender to bite (about 5 minutes), stirring often. Then uncover and boil until almost all liquid has evaporated. Add chicken mixture and Cooking Sauce; bring to a boil, stirring.

Spoon bulgur onto plates; top with chicken mixture and sprinkle with onions. Makes 4 servings.

COOKING SAUCE. In a small bowl, stir together ½ cup **regular-strength chicken broth,** 2 tablespoons **soy sauce,** and 1 tablespoon **cornstarch.**

Per serving: 409 calories, 27 g protein, 38 g carbohydrates, 18 g fat, 4 g saturated fat, 94 mg cholesterol, 758 mg sodium

■ *Pictured on facing page*

LAYERED TURKEY ENCHILADAS

Preparation time: About 15 minutes

Baking time: About 1 hour and 20 minutes

These quick, low-fat enchiladas are something like a savory layer cake: you stack up corn tortillas and an appetizing filling of ground turkey breast, green chiles, Cheddar cheese, and mild salsa. To serve the "cake," simply cut it into wedges.

  1 **pound ground skinned turkey breast**
  1 **large can (7 oz.) diced green chiles**
  1 **medium-size onion, chopped**
  1 **cup (4 oz.) shredded extra-sharp Cheddar cheese**
  1 **cup prepared mild green chile salsa**
  1½ **cups chopped pear-shaped tomatoes**
  8 **corn tortillas (***each* 6 to 7 inches in diameter**)**

In a bowl, mix turkey, chiles, onion, ¾ cup of the cheese, ½ cup of the salsa, and 1 cup of the tomatoes. Divide into 7 equal portions.

Place a tortilla in a shallow 9- to 10-inch-diameter baking pan; cover evenly with one portion of the turkey mixture. Repeat layers to use remaining tortillas and turkey mixture, finishing with a tortilla. Then cover with remaining ¼ cup cheese, ½ cup salsa, and ½ cup tomatoes.

Cover with foil and bake in a 400° oven for 40 minutes. Uncover and continue to bake until turkey is no longer pink; cut to center of stack to test (about 40 more minutes). Let stand for 5 minutes, then cut into wedges. Makes 4 to 6 servings.

Per serving: 341 calories, 31 g protein, 30 g carbohydrates, 11 g fat, 5 g saturated fat, 80 mg cholesterol, 821 mg sodium

TURKEY-PISTACHIO APPETIZER CUPS

Preparation time: About 1 hour

Baking time: About 12 minutes

Looking for an appetizer with a difference? Fresh mint makes a fragrant and flavorful impact on mushrooms stuffed with ground turkey. These tasty mouthfuls are just right for parties, since you can get them all ready to bake a full day in advance.

40 **mushrooms (about 2 lbs. *total*), *each* 1½ to 2 inches in diameter**

3 **tablespoons soy sauce**

1 **tablespoon olive oil or salad oil**

1 **small onion, finely chopped**

½ **cup finely chopped salted roasted pistachio nuts**

8 **ounces ground turkey**

1 **tablespoon cornstarch**

1 **large egg white**

3 **tablespoons fine dry bread crumbs**

¼ **cup chopped fresh mint**

Carefully break off mushroom stems; mince stems and set aside.

Arrange a third of the mushrooms, stemmed side up, in a 10- to 12-inch frying pan. Sprinkle with 1 ta-

blespoon of the soy. Cook over medium heat until mushroom cups contain liquid (about 3 minutes), then turn mushrooms over and continue to cook until pan is almost dry (about 3 more minutes). Transfer cooked mushrooms, stemmed side up, to an oiled 9- by 13-inch baking dish. Repeat to cook remaining mushrooms in 2 batches, using remaining 2 tablespoons soy.

To frying pan, add oil, onion, and minced mushroom stems. Cook over medium-high heat, stirring often, until onion is soft and all liquid has evaporated (about 7 minutes). Add pistachios and cook, stirring, until mixture is lightly browned; then remove from heat and let cool.

To onion mixture, add turkey, cornstarch, egg white, crumbs, and mint; mix well. Divide mixture into 40 equal portions and shape each into a ball. Set a ball in each mushroom cap and press down to settle firmly in place. (At this point, you may cover and refrigerate for up to 1 day.)

Bake mushrooms, uncovered, in a 500° oven until turkey-pistachio stuffing is no longer pink in center; cut to test (about 12 minutes; about 17 minutes if refrigerated). Serve hot. Makes 40 appetizers.

Per appetizer: 31 calories, 2 g protein, 2 g carbohydrates, 2 g fat, 0 g saturated fat, 4 mg cholesterol, 101 mg sodium

APPLE TURKEY LOAF

Preparation time: About 25 minutes

Baking time: About 1 hour

This moist, apple-filled meat loaf tastes marvelous between thick slices of crunchy-crusted bread. For an especially lean loaf, we've used ground skinned turkey breast in place of regular ground turkey.

1 **tablespoon butter or margarine**

2 **tart green-skinned apples, such as Granny Smith, peeled, cored, and chopped**

1 **medium-size onion, chopped**

1½ **pounds ground skinned turkey breast**

1½ **teaspoons dry marjoram leaves**

1 **teaspoon *each* dry thyme leaves, dry sage leaves, and pepper**

½ **cup chopped parsley**

2 **large egg whites**

½ **cup *each* fine dry bread crumbs and nonfat milk**

Melt butter in a 10- to 12-inch frying pan over medium heat. Add apples and onion; cook, stirring occasionally, until onion is soft (about 10 minutes). Remove from heat and let cool; then scrape into a large bowl and mix in turkey, marjoram, thyme, sage, pepper, parsley, egg whites, crumbs, and milk. Pat mixture evenly into a 5- by 9-inch loaf pan.

Bake loaf, uncovered, in a 350° oven until browned on top and no longer pink in center; cut to test (about 1 hour). Drain fat from loaf pan, then invert pan and turn loaf out onto a platter. Serve hot. Or, to serve cold, let cool; then cover and refrigerate for up to 1 day. Makes 6 servings.

Per serving: 224 calories, 30 g protein, 15 g carbohydrates, 4 g fat, 2 g saturated fat, 76 mg cholesterol, 188 mg sodium

SHEPHERD'S PIE

Preparation time: About 45 minutes

Baking time: About 20 minutes

Beneath its creamy mashed potato topping, this one-dish dinner holds a surprise: a filling made with ground turkey, not the traditional minced lamb.

- 2 pounds russet potatoes, scrubbed
- 2 tablespoons salad oil
- 1 large onion, chopped
- 2 cloves garlic, minced or pressed
- ½ cup finely chopped celery
- 8 ounces mushrooms, sliced
- 1½ pounds ground turkey
- 2 teaspoons dry sage leaves
- 1 teaspoon dry thyme leaves
- ½ teaspoon *each* dry marjoram leaves and dry mustard
- 8 ounces carrots, shredded
- ½ cup chopped parsley
- 1 cup regular-strength chicken broth
- ¼ cup milk
- ½ cup (¼ lb.) butter or margarine, at room temperature
- ¼ teaspoon white pepper
- 1 teaspoon salt

Place whole unpeeled potatoes in a 3-quart pan and add enough water to cover. Bring to a boil over high heat; then reduce heat, cover, and boil gently until potatoes are tender throughout when pierced (about 30 minutes).

Meanwhile, heat oil in a 12- to 14-inch frying pan over medium-high heat. Add onion, garlic, celery, and mushrooms; cook, stirring often, until onion is soft (about 7 minutes). Add turkey and cook, stirring often, until no longer pink (about 5 minutes). Add sage, thyme, marjoram, and mustard; cook for 1 minute. Add carrots, parsley, and broth. Bring to a boil over high heat, then boil until liquid has evaporated (about 10 minutes). Transfer to a 3-quart casserole.

Drain potatoes; peel and mash with milk, butter, pepper, and salt. Spread over turkey mixture. Bake, uncovered, in a 375° oven until lightly browned (about 20 minutes). Makes 6 servings.

Per serving: 512 calories, 25 g protein, 37 g carbohydrates, 30 g fat, 13 g saturated fat, 126 mg cholesterol, 837 mg sodium

TURKEY LASAGNE

Preparation time: About 1 hour

Baking time: About 25 minutes

Ground turkey in the herbed tomato sauce makes for a lasagne that's a bit leaner than the usual dish.

- 1 package (8 oz.) dry lasagne noodles
- 12 ounces carrots, cut into ¼-inch-thick slices
- 1 pound zucchini, cut into ¼-inch-thick slices
- 2 tablespoons olive oil or salad oil
- 1 medium-size onion, chopped
- 1 teaspoon *each* dry basil leaves, dry thyme leaves, and dry oregano leaves
- 8 ounces ground turkey
- 1 jar (32 oz.) marinara sauce
- 2 packages (10 oz. *each*) frozen chopped spinach, thawed and squeezed dry
- 1 cup (8 oz.) ricotta cheese
- 3 cups (12 oz.) shredded mozzarella cheese
- ¼ cup grated Parmesan cheese

In a 5- to 6-quart pan, bring 3 quarts water to a boil over high heat. Add noodles and carrots; cook for 6 minutes. Add zucchini; continue to cook until noodles are just tender to bite (about 4 more minutes). Drain well; set vegetables and noodles aside separately.

Heat oil in same pan over medium-high heat. Add onion, basil, thyme, and oregano. Cook, stirring often, until onion is soft (about 7 minutes). Add turkey and cook, stirring occasionally, until no longer pink (about 5 minutes). Stir in marinara sauce; remove from heat.

Mix spinach and ricotta cheese; set aside.

Spread a third of the sauce in a shallow 2½- to 3-quart baking dish. Arrange half the noodles over sauce. Top noodles evenly with half *each* of the carrots, zucchini, spinach mixture, and mozzarella cheese. Repeat layers; then spread with remaining sauce. Sprinkle with Parmesan cheese.

Set baking dish in a shallow 10- by 15-inch baking pan to catch any drips. Bake lasagne, uncovered, in a 400° oven until hot in center (about 25 minutes). Let stand for 5 minutes before serving. Makes 6 servings.

Per serving: 627 calories, 35 g protein, 60 g carbohydrates, 30 g fat, 12 g saturated fat, 86 mg cholesterol, 1,403 mg sodium

SPEEDY CHILI WITH CORNMEAL DUMPLINGS

Preparation time: About 10 minutes

Cooking time: About 50 minutes

Cumin-seasoned cornmeal dumplings flecked with shredded cheese steam atop the chili they complement. For a change of pace, substitute red kidney beans or black beans for the cannellini.

2 tablespoons salad oil
1 large onion, chopped
1 clove garlic, minced or pressed
1 pound ground turkey
3 tablespoons chili powder
1 large can (28 oz.) tomatoes
2 cans (about 15 oz. *each*) cannellini (white kidney beans), drained
1 can (4 oz.) diced green chiles
Dumpling Dough (recipe follows)

Heat oil in a 4- to 5-quart pan over medium-high heat. Add onion and garlic and cook, stirring often, until onion is soft (about 7 minutes). Add turkey and cook, stirring often, until no longer pink (about 5 minutes). Add chili powder, tomatoes (break up with a spoon) and their liquid, cannellini, and chiles. Bring to a boil; reduce heat to medium-low and simmer, uncovered, for 15 minutes.

Meanwhile, prepare Dumpling Dough.

After chili has simmered for 15 minutes, drop dough onto chili in about 2-tablespoon portions. Cover and simmer until dumplings are dry in center; cut to test (about 20 minutes). Makes 4 to 6 servings.

DUMPLING DOUGH. In a bowl, combine 1 cup **all-purpose flour**, ¼ cup **yellow cornmeal**, 1½ teaspoons **baking powder**, and ½ teaspoon *each* **ground cumin, dry sage leaves**, and **dry thyme leaves**. In another bowl, beat together 1 large **egg**, ½ cup **milk**, 1 tablespoon **salad oil**, and ½ cup shredded **Cheddar cheese**. Add egg mixture to flour mixture; stir just until moistened.

Per serving: 593 calories, 36 g protein, 62 g carbohydrates, 23 g fat, 6 g saturated fat, 124 mg cholesterol, 1,290 mg sodium

■ *Pictured on facing page*

TURKEY BURGERS WITH TOMATO SALAD

Preparation time: About 15 minutes

Cooking time: About 15 minutes

Enjoy this warm-weather meal for two outdoors on the patio. The dill-seasoned yogurt sauce is doubly refreshing—use half of it to dress the cucumber-tomato salad, the rest to top the moist burgers.

Yogurt Sauce (recipe follows)
1 medium-size red onion
1 teaspoon salad oil
8 ounces ground turkey
½ teaspoon ground cumin
Freshly ground pepper
¼ cup water
2 tablespoons white wine vinegar or sherry vinegar
2 whole wheat pocket breads (*each* about 6 inches in diameter)
1 small cucumber (about 6 oz.), peeled and thinly sliced
2 small tomatoes, sliced

Prepare Yogurt Sauce and refrigerate. Cut onion in half horizontally. Chop one half; thinly slice remaining half, separate into rings, and set aside.

In a 12- to 14-inch nonstick frying pan, combine chopped onion and oil. Cook over medium-high heat, stirring often, until onion is soft (about 7 minutes). Transfer to a bowl. Let cool slightly, mix with turkey and cumin, and season to taste with pepper. Shape mixture into 2 patties.

Place patties in pan and cook over medium-high heat, turning once, until browned on both sides (about 8 minutes). Pour off fat. Add water and vinegar. Reduce heat, cover, and simmer until almost all liquid has evaporated and patties are no longer pink in center; cut to test (about 7 more minutes).

Meanwhile, wrap pocket breads in foil and place in a 250° oven until hot (about 15 minutes). Also mix cucumber, onion rings, tomatoes, and half the Yogurt Sauce in a salad bowl.

Offer turkey patties with pocket breads, tomato salad, and remaining Yogurt Sauce. Makes 2 servings.

YOGURT SAUCE. In a small bowl, stir together 1 cup **plain nonfat yogurt**, ¼ cup **white wine vinegar** or sherry vinegar, and 2 tablespoons **dry dill weed**.

Per serving: 498 calories, 35 g protein, 57 g carbohydrates, 15 g fat, 4 g saturated fat, 59 mg cholesterol, 539 mg sodium

Ready for a different take on the familiar meat on a bun? Try Turkey Burgers with Tomato Salad (recipe on facing page). Heated pocket breads hold seasoned meat patties and a simple combination of cucumber, red onion, and tomatoes in a dill-seasoned yogurt sauce. Corn on the cob, fresh fruit, and lemonade complete a casual supper for two.

Feature

QUAIL & SQUAB SAMPLER

Pamper your dinner guests with some individual attention: serve them rich-tasting, all-dark-meat quail or squab. Just one squab is enough for a serving, but you'll usually want to allow two quail per person.

Sautéed quail in a buttery-smooth balsamic vinegar sauce make an impressive main course for your next small gathering. Grilled quail are just right for a patio party; try them with *pappardelle* (wide fettuccine) in fresh tomato-mushroom sauce.

Squab is especially tempting when soaked in a spicy marinade before roasting, then topped with tart lemon sauce. Or serve the birds skewered and grilled, acccompanied with a garlicky sweet-hot sauce.

QUAIL WITH ROSEMARY & BALSAMIC VINEGAR SAUCE

Preparation time: About 5 minutes

Cooking time: About 50 minutes

- 8 quail (about 4 oz. *each*), thawed if frozen
- ¼ cup butter or margarine
- ¾ cup regular-strength beef broth
- ½ cup balsamic vinegar
- 1 tablespoon chopped fresh rosemary leaves or 1 teaspoon dry rosemary

Reserve quail necks and giblets for other uses. Rinse quail inside and out; pat dry.

Melt 2 tablespoons of the butter in a 10- to 12-inch frying pan over medium-high heat. Add quail, about 4 at a time; do not crowd pan. Cook, turning as needed, until deep golden brown on all sides (about 20 minutes). Breast meat should be cooked through but still pink near bone; cut parallel to wing joint to test. Transfer quail to a serving dish and keep warm.

To pan, add broth, vinegar, and rosemary. Boil over high heat until reduced to ½ cup (about 5 minutes). Add remaining 2 tablespoons butter; reduce heat to medium and stir until butter is smoothly blended into sauce. Pour sauce over quail. Makes 4 servings.

*Per serving: 499 calories, 40 g protein, 1 g carbohydrates, 36 g fat, 14 g saturated fat, 380 mg sodium**

■ *Pictured on page 321*

GRILLED QUAIL WITH PASTA

Preparation time: About 20 minutes

Cooking time: About 35 minutes

- 2 ounces sliced pancetta or bacon, diced
- 6 tablespoons olive oil
- 1 medium-size onion, thinly sliced
- 8 ounces mushrooms, quartered
- 2 cloves garlic, minced or pressed
- 6 medium-size pear-shaped tomatoes (about 12 oz. *total*), chopped
- ¼ cup slivered fresh sage leaves or 2 teaspoons dry sage leaves
- 1 cup dry white wine
- 8 quail (about 4 oz. *each*), thawed if frozen
  Coarsely ground pepper
- 1 package (8½ oz.) dry pappardelle, 10 to 12 ounces fresh pappardelle, or 8 ounces dry extra-wide egg noodles
  Salt
  Sage sprigs and lemon wedges

Cook pancetta in a wide frying pan over medium heat until crisp. Remove from pan with a slotted spoon; drain and set aside. To pan drippings, add ¼ cup of the oil, then onion and mushrooms. Increase heat to medium-high and cook, stirring often, until mushrooms are lightly browned (about 5 minutes). Stir in garlic, tomatoes, slivered sage, and wine. Boil gently, uncovered, stirring occasionally, until sauce is slightly thickened (about 10 minutes).

Reserve quail necks and giblets for other uses. Then, with poultry shears or a knife, split quail lengthwise along one side of backbone. Pull quail open; place, skin side up, on a flat surface and press firmly, cracking bones slightly, until birds lie reasonably flat. Rinse quail and pat dry. Brush well with remaining 2 tablespoons oil; sprinkle with pepper.

Place quail, skin side down, on a lightly greased grill 4 to 6 inches above a solid bed of hot coals. Cook, turning as needed, until breast meat is cooked through but still pink near bone; cut parallel to wing joint to test (about 8 minutes). Lift from grill; keep warm.

Cook pasta according to package directions just until barely tender to bite. Drain well. Add pancetta to tomato sauce; season to taste with salt. Add pasta and mix lightly, using 2 spoons. Transfer to a large platter. Surround pasta with quail. Garnish with sage sprigs and lemon wedges. Makes 4 servings.

Per serving: 918 calories, 52 g protein, 52 g carbohydrates, 56 g fat, 13 g saturated fat, 230 mg sodium*

SQUAB WITH LEMON SAUCE

Preparation time: 15 minutes, plus 1 hour to marinate

Roasting time: About 20 minutes

    4 squab (12 to 16 oz. *each*), thawed if frozen
    ¼ cup *each* soy sauce and dry sherry
    2 tablespoons Oriental sesame oil
    2 teaspoons honey
    1 teaspoon Chinese five-spice; or ¼ tea-
       spoon *each* crushed anise seeds and
       ground cinnamon, cloves, and ginger
       Lemon Sauce (recipe follows)

Reserve squab necks and giblets for other uses. With poultry shears or a knife, split squab lengthwise along one side of backbone. Pull squab open; place, skin side up, on a flat surface and press firmly, cracking bones slightly, until birds lie reasonably flat. Rinse squab, pat dry, and place in a large heavy-duty plastic bag.

In a bowl, mix soy, sherry, oil, honey, and five-spice; pour over squab. Seal bag; turn over several times to coat birds with marinade. Place bag in a large, shallow baking pan or dish; refrigerate for at least 1 hour or up to 1 day, turning bag over occasionally.

Drain squab; reserve marinade. Place squab, skin side up, on a rack in a 12- by 15-inch roasting pan. Roast, uncovered, in a 500° oven, brushing several times with marinade, until breast meat is cooked through but still pink near bone; cut parallel to wing joint to test (about 20 minutes). Meanwhile, prepare Lemon Sauce. Top squab with Lemon Sauce. Makes 4 servings.

Per serving without sauce: 968 calories, 58 g protein, 3 g carbohydrates, 78 g fat, 27 g saturated fat, 515 mg sodium*

LEMON SAUCE. Cut 2 large thin-skinned **lemons** into halves. Thinly slice one half; discard end pieces and any seeds. Set slices aside. Squeeze juice from remaining 3 lemon halves; you will need ¼ cup.

Heat 1 teaspoon **salad oil** in an 8- to 10-inch frying pan over high heat. Add 4 quarter-size slices **fresh ginger;** stir for 30 seconds. Add lemon slices, 1 cup **regular-strength chicken broth,** 3 tablespoons **sugar,** and the ¼ cup **lemon juice.** Bring to a boil; then reduce heat and simmer, uncovered, for 2 minutes.

Mix 1 tablespoon **cornstarch** with 2 tablespoons **water.** Pour into sauce and cook, stirring, until sauce boils and thickens. Add ½ to 1 teaspoon **soy sauce.** Discard ginger slices. Use sauce hot. Makes 1¼ cups.

Per tablespoon: 14 calories, 0 g protein, 3 g carbohydrates, 0 g fat, 0 g saturated fat, 0 mg cholesterol, 62 mg sodium

SQUAB, THAI STYLE

Preparation time: About 1 hour

Grilling time: About 20 minutes

       Thai Sauce (recipe follows)
    8 squab (12 to 16 oz. *each*), thawed if frozen
    ½ cup minced fresh cilantro (coriander)
    ⅓ cup coarsely ground pepper
   24 cloves garlic, minced or pressed

Prepare Thai Sauce and refrigerate. Reserve squab necks and giblets for other uses. With poultry shears or a knife, split squab lengthwise through breastbone. Pull squab open; place, skin side up, on a flat surface and press firmly, cracking bones slightly, until birds lie reasonably flat. Rinse; pat dry.

Thread squab on sturdy 18-inch metal skewers as follows. Force one skewer into drumstick and through thigh, then under backbone, through other thigh, and out other drumstick. Run a second skewer parallel to the first, forcing it through one side of breast and middle section of one wing, then over backbone, through middle section of other wing, and out other side of breast. Each pair of 18-inch skewers holds 2 or 3 squab.

Mash together cilantro, pepper, and garlic; rub evenly over squab. Place squab on a lightly greased grill 4 to 6 inches above a solid bed of medium coals. Cook, turning as needed, until breast meat is cooked through but still pink near bone; cut parallel to wing joint to test (about 20 minutes). Serve with Thai Sauce. Makes 8 servings.

Per serving without sauce: 948 calories, 59 g protein, 6 g carbohydrates, 75 g fat, 27 g saturated fat, 4 mg sodium*

THAI SAUCE. In a blender or food processor, combine 1 can (8 oz.) **tomato sauce,** 3 tablespoons firmly packed **brown sugar,** 6 cloves **garlic,** ⅛ to ½ teaspoon **ground red pepper** (cayenne), and ¼ cup **cider vinegar.** Whirl until blended. Add 1¼ cups **golden raisins** and ⅓ cup **water;** whirl to chop raisins coarsely. Pour sauce into a 2- to 3-quart pan; boil over high heat, stirring, until reduced to 1½ cups. Let cool, then cover and refrigerate until cold. Makes about 1½ cups.

Per tablespoon: 34 calories, 0 g protein, 9 g carbohydrates, 0 g fat, 0 g saturated fat, 0 mg cholesterol, 59 mg sodium

*Cholesterol data not available.

Serve Turkey Parmesan with Spaghetti (recipe on facing page)
once, and you're bound to get requests for an encore! Cheese-topped
ground turkey patties, a simple tomato sauce, and pasta add up
to a guaranteed family favorite.

SPICY SAUSAGE

Preparation time: About 10 minutes

Cooking time: About 5 minutes

Some people think that breakfast just isn't breakfast without a few sizzling sausage patties. Unfortunately, the usual pork sausage doesn't fit the low-fat diets many of us are trying to establish. You can still start the day with the flavors you like, though: just make your own fragrant sausage from turkey breast, pepper, and fresh sage and rosemary.

1 **pound ground skinned turkey breast**
1 **teaspoon chopped fresh rosemary**
2 **teaspoons chopped fresh sage**
½ **teaspoon freshly ground pepper**

In a large bowl, combine turkey, rosemary, sage, and pepper. Form mixture into 8 patties, each 3 inches in diameter and about ¼ inch thick. Place patties in a 12- to 14-inch frying pan (preferably nonstick) and cook over high heat for 1 minute; then turn patties over and continue to cook for 1 more minute. Reduce heat. Continue to cook, turning occasionally, until patties are golden brown on outside and no longer pink in center; cut to test (about 3 more minutes). Makes 4 servings.

Per serving: 130 calories, 27 g protein, 0 g carbohydrates, 2 g fat, 1 g saturated fat, 70 mg cholesterol, 76 mg sodium

■ *Pictured on facing page*

TURKEY PARMESAN WITH SPAGHETTI

Preparation time: About 15 minutes

Cooking time: About 50 minutes

Spaghetti and meatballs? Veal Parmesan? This family favorite has elements of both. Herb-rich turkey patties boasting a double cheese coating of mozzarella and Parmesan are served on a bed of spaghetti with a tempting tomato-onion sauce.

Tomato-Onion Sauce (recipe follows)
1 **large egg**
½ **cup soft bread crumbs**
1⅓ **cups (about 7 oz.) grated Parmesan cheese**
½ **teaspoon poultry seasoning**
1 **pound ground turkey**
1 **tablespoon butter or margarine**
1 **tablespoon olive oil**
4 **slices mozzarella cheese (3 oz. *total*)**
8 **ounces dry spaghetti**
Italian parsley sprigs (optional)

Prepare Tomato-Onion Sauce; keep warm over lowest heat.

In a medium-size bowl, beat egg until blended. Add crumbs, ⅓ cup of the Parmesan cheese, and poultry seasoning; stir until blended. Add turkey; mix lightly until well combined. Shape turkey mixture into 4 patties, each about 4 inches in diameter.

Melt butter in oil in a 12- to 14-inch frying pan over medium-high heat. Add turkey patties and cook, turning once, until browned on both sides (about 8 minutes). Transfer patties to a shallow baking or broiling pan. Spread each patty with 2 tablespoons of the Tomato-Onion Sauce; then top each with 1 slice of the mozzarella cheese and 1 tablespoon of the remaining Parmesan cheese.

Just before broiling patties, cook spaghetti according to package directions just until tender to bite. Drain well, transfer to a deep platter, and keep warm.

Broil turkey patties about 4 inches below heat until cheeses are melted and lightly browned (about 3 minutes).

To serve, spoon remaining Tomato-Onion Sauce over spaghetti, then top with turkey patties. Garnish with parsley, if desired. Offer remaining ¾ cup Parmesan cheese to add to taste. Makes 4 servings.

TOMATO-ONION SAUCE. Heat 2 tablespoons **olive oil** or salad oil in a 2-quart pan over medium heat. Add 1 medium-size **onion,** finely chopped; 2 teaspoons **dry oregano leaves;** 1 **dry bay leaf;** and 1 large clove **garlic,** minced or pressed. Cook, stirring often, until onion is soft but not browned (about 10 minutes). Stir in 1 large can (15 oz.) **tomato sauce.** Bring to a boil; then reduce heat, cover, and simmer for 20 minutes, stirring occasionally.

Per serving: 764 calories, 46 g protein, 57 g carbohydrates, 39 g fat, 14 g saturated fat, 154 mg cholesterol, 1,323 mg sodium

CHUNKY TURKEY SAUCE WITH PENNE

Preparation time: About 15 minutes

Cooking time: About 1¾ hours

When the weather is cold and you'd rather cozy up to a fire than venture outdoors, try this hearty pasta meal. Once you've started the sauce, you can settle down with a favorite book and keep an eye on the simmering pot. (Don't skimp on the cooking time; the flavor improves as the sauce boils down.)

      2 tablespoons olive oil
      1 large onion, finely chopped
      1 clove garlic, minced or pressed
      1 medium-size green bell pepper, seeded and finely chopped
      2 medium-size carrots, finely shredded
      8 ounces mushrooms, thinly sliced
      2 tablespoons chopped parsley
      2 teaspoons dry basil leaves
      1 teaspoon dry rosemary
      1 pound ground turkey
      2 large cans (28 oz. *each*) pear-shaped tomatoes
      1 large can (12 oz.) tomato paste
      ½ cup dry red wine
      1 dry bay leaf
      1 pound dry penne

Heat oil in a 4- to 5-quart pan over medium-high heat. Add onion, garlic, bell pepper, carrots, mushrooms, parsley, basil, and rosemary. Cook, stirring often, until vegetables are soft (about 15 minutes). Remove vegetables from pan, transfer to a bowl, and set aside.

Add turkey to pan; cook over medium-high heat, stirring often, until no longer pink (about 5 minutes). Return vegetables to pan; add tomatoes (break up with a spoon) and their liquid, tomato paste, wine, and bay leaf. Increase heat to high and bring mixture to a boil; then reduce heat to medium-low, cover, and boil gently, stirring often, for 30 minutes. Uncover and continue to cook, stirring occasionally, until sauce is reduced to 8 cups (about 45 more minutes). Remove and discard bay leaf.

Cook penne according to package directions just until tender to bite. Drain well. Place in a large, shallow serving bowl, top with sauce, and mix lightly. Makes 8 servings.

Per serving: 424 calories, 22 g protein, 65 g carbohydrates, 10 g fat, 2 g saturated fat, 41 mg cholesterol, 726 mg sodium

SPAGHETTI SQUASH WITH CREAMY TURKEY

Preparation time: About 10 minutes

Cooking time: About 1¼ hours

If your dinner guests haven't encountered spaghetti squash before, they'll marvel at the magical way it separates into long, pastalike strands. The mild vegetable "spaghetti" is the perfect partner for a delicate, nutmeg-scented meat sauce.

      1 spaghetti squash (2 to 3 lbs.)
      2 tablespoons olive oil
      ¼ cup finely chopped shallots
      1 pound ground turkey
      ¼ cup butter or margarine
      1 cup whipping cream
      ½ cup dry white wine
      1 cup (about 5 oz.) grated Parmesan cheese
      ½ teaspoon ground nutmeg

Pierce spaghetti squash in several places with a fork; then place in a shallow baking pan. Bake, uncovered, in a 350° oven until shell gives when pressed (about 1¼ hours; turn squash over after 45 minutes). Keep warm until ready to serve.

About 20 minutes before squash is done, heat oil in a 10- to 12-inch frying pan over medium-high heat. Add shallots and cook, stirring often, for 1 minute. Add turkey and cook, stirring often, until no longer pink (about 5 minutes). Add butter, cream, and wine; stir to melt butter. Reduce heat to medium-low and simmer, uncovered, stirring occasionally, until thickened (about 10 minutes). Stir in cheese and nutmeg.

Cut baked squash in half; scrape out and discard seeds. Loosen squash strands with a fork, then scoop strands out onto a rimmed platter. Spoon sauce over squash. Makes 6 servings.

Per serving: 503 calories, 25 g protein, 13 g carbohydrates, 38 g fat, 19 g saturated fat, 139 mg cholesterol, 627 mg sodium

MINCED TURKEY IN LETTUCE

Preparation time: About 15 minutes, plus 30 minutes to soak mushrooms

Cooking time: About 8 minutes

Nestled in crisp lettuce cups, this speedy stir-fry of turkey and vegetables is bursting with flavor. The meal is just as good with ground chicken or with thin strips of turkey or chicken breast.

   Cooking Sauce (recipe follows)
3   **medium-size dried shiitake mushrooms** (*each* about 2 inches in diameter)
1   **tablespoon salad oil**
2   **cloves garlic, minced or pressed**
1½ **teaspoons grated fresh ginger**
½   **teaspoon crushed dried hot red chiles**
1   **pound ground skinned turkey breast**
1   **can (about 8 oz.) sliced bamboo shoots, drained and minced**
1   **can (about 8 oz.) water chestnuts, drained and minced**
6   **green onions (including tops), minced**
½   **cup frozen peas, thawed**
12 **large lettuce leaves**
   Hoisin sauce (optional)

Prepare Cooking Sauce and set aside. Soak mushrooms in warm water to cover for 30 minutes, then drain. Cut off and discard stems; squeeze caps dry, thinly slice, and set aside.

   Heat oil in a 10- to 12-inch frying pan over medium-high heat. Add garlic, ginger, and chiles; stir once. Then add turkey and cook, stirring often, until no longer pink (about 5 minutes). Remove turkey mixture from pan and set aside.

   Add bamboo shoots, water chestnuts, onions, and mushrooms to pan; cook, stirring, for 2 minutes. Return turkey mixture to pan along with peas. Then stir in Cooking Sauce and cook, stirring, until sauce is thickened.

   To serve, coat center of a lettuce leaf with hoisin, if desired. Spoon some of the turkey mixture on top, then roll up and eat out of hand. Makes 6 servings.

COOKING SAUCE. In a small bowl, stir together 2 teaspoons **cornstarch**, 1 tablespoon **dry sherry**, 2 tablespoons *each* **reduced-sodium soy sauce** and **water,** and ½ teaspoon **sugar.**

Per serving: 163 calories, 20 g protein, 12 g carbohydrates, 4 g fat, 1 g saturated fat, 47 mg cholesterol, 272 mg sodium

SORREL-SCENTED BROTH WITH TURKEY

Preparation time: About 25 minutes

Cooking time: About 10 minutes

Hot broth and the lemony accent of sorrel seem perfectly suited to crisp autumn days. Celebrate the season with this soup—there's sorrel in both the simple broth and the tender meatballs.

¾   **cup lightly packed sorrel leaves, washed, stems removed**
2   **or 3 slices white bread, crusts removed**
1   **pound ground turkey**
1   **large egg**
8   **cups regular-strength chicken broth**
⅛   **teaspoon white pepper**
   About ½ teaspoon salt (or to taste)
4   **strips lemon peel (colored part only),** *each* ½ **by 4 inches**
2   **medium-size carrots, cut into julienne strips**
2   **to 3 tablespoons lemon juice**

Finely chop half the sorrel leaves. Cut remaining leaves into thin shreds. Set sorrel aside.

   Tear bread into small pieces and whirl in a blender or food processor to make ¾ cup fine crumbs. In a large bowl, mix crumbs, chopped sorrel, turkey, egg, ¼ cup of the broth, pepper, and salt.

   In a 5- to 6-quart pan, combine lemon peel and remaining 7¾ cups broth. Bring to a boil over high heat. Drop turkey mixture into boiling broth in tablespoon-size portions, then add carrots. Reduce heat, cover, and simmer until turkey meatballs are no longer pink in center; cut to test (about 5 minutes). Skim and discard fat from broth; remove and discard lemon peel, if desired. Add lemon juice.

   Ladle meatballs and soup into 6 wide soup bowls; sprinkle sorrel shreds over each serving. Makes 6 servings.

Per serving: 215 calories, 20 g protein, 10 g carbohydrates, 11 g fat, 2 g saturated fat, 74 mg cholesterol, 1,615 mg sodium

Convenient Cooked Poultry

DICED & CHUNKED & CHILLED & TOSSED &

DRESSED & SOUPED & SHREDDED & MINCED &

WRAPPED & SLAWED & SANDWICHED & STACKED &

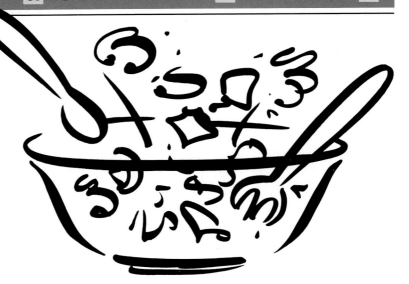

The family will urge you to roast a turkey just so they can enjoy
the leftovers in Turkey Pot Pie (recipe on page 438). Peppery cream cheese
pastry covers a savory blend of cooked poultry, yams, kale, and leeks.
You won't need elaborate accompaniments—try a green salad or perhaps
a dish of sweet peas tossed with enoki mushrooms.

CHICKEN & LEMON GRASS SOUP

Preparation time: About 15 minutes

Cooking time: About 35 minutes

Lemon grass adds its citrusy flavor and fragrance to many Thai and Vietnamese dishes. The bulbous-based stalks, quite similar in appearance to green onions, are sold in most Asian grocery stores and in many larger supermarkets. Here, lemon grass combines with some distinctly non-Asian ingredients—among them jalapeños and avocado—in an appetizing first-course soup.

> 1 stalk fresh lemon grass
> 1 large can (49½ oz.) regular-strength chicken broth
> ⅛ teaspoon freshly ground pepper
> 1 fresh jalapeño chile, seeded and minced
> 1 clove garlic, minced or pressed
> ½ cup thinly sliced green onions (including tops)
> ½ cup chopped fresh cilantro (coriander)
> 1 medium-size firm-ripe tomato, seeded and coarsely chopped
> 2 cups bite-size pieces cooked chicken or turkey
> 1 medium-size firm-ripe avocado

Trim and discard root end and leaves from lemon grass; peel off and discard coarse outer layers of stalk. In a 4- to 5-quart pan, combine lemon grass, broth, pepper, chile, and garlic. Bring to a boil over high heat; then reduce heat, cover, and simmer for 30 minutes. Discard lemon grass. Stir in onions, cilantro, tomato, and chicken; heat through.

Pit, peel, and chop avocado. Evenly divide avocado among 6 soup bowls; then ladle soup over avocado. Makes 6 servings.

Per serving: 179 calories, 18 g protein, 5 g carbohydrates, 10 g fat, 2 g saturated fat, 42 mg cholesterol, 1,063 mg sodium

HOT CHICKEN & SAVOY SALAD

Preparation time: About 25 minutes

Frilly ornamental kale, also known as salad savoy, adds color to this main-course salad. The sweet leaves hold their texture and tint when heated briefly; tossed with shredded chicken and sliced oranges, they make the perfect meal for a dark, chilly day.

> 12 ounces salad savoy
> 2 large oranges (about 1 lb. *total*)
> 2 tablespoons white wine vinegar
> 1 teaspoon minced fresh rosemary; or 1 teaspoon dry rosemary, crumbled
> 1 clove garlic, minced or pressed
> ¼ to ½ teaspoon crushed dried hot red chiles
> ⅓ cup salad oil
> ¼ cup thinly sliced green onions (including tops)
> 1½ cups shredded cooked chicken
> Salt and pepper

Remove and discard tough stems from salad savoy; wash and drain leaves, then tear into bite-size pieces (you should have about 8 cups). Set aside.

Grate enough peel from one orange to make 1 teaspoon. In a small dish, mix grated orange peel, vinegar, rosemary, garlic, and chiles; set aside. Then, using a sharp knife, cut peel and all white membrane from both oranges. Thinly slice oranges crosswise; cut each slice in half.

Heat oil in a 12- to 14-inch frying pan or 5- to 6-quart pan over medium-high heat. Add onions and cook, stirring, until limp (about 2 minutes). Add vinegar mixture and salad savoy; cook, stirring, just until leaves begin to wilt slightly (about 1 minute).

Remove savoy mixture from heat; turn into a large bowl, arrange oranges and chicken on top, and toss to mix. Season to taste with salt and pepper. Makes 4 servings.

Per serving: 341 calories, 19 g protein, 19 g carbohydrates, 22 g fat, 3 g saturated fat, 47 mg cholesterol, 85 mg sodium

CHICKEN-GRAPEFRUIT SALAD ON AVOCADOS

Preparation time: About 15 minutes

Presented on buttery avocado halves and topped with juicy pink grapefruit, this refreshing salad will keep the cook out of the kitchen and the company at the table. Fresh tarragon and a pinch of cayenne pepper enliven the creamy dressing that coats celery, green onions, and chunks of chicken.

Tarragon-Pepper Dressing (recipe follows)
2 cups bite-size pieces cooked chicken breast
½ cup thinly sliced celery
¼ cup thinly sliced green onions (including tops)
3 large firm-ripe avocados
1 tablespoon lemon juice
2 large pink grapefruits
6 medium-size red leaf lettuce leaves, washed and crisped

Prepare Tarragon-Pepper Dressing; add chicken, celery, and onions and mix to coat with dressing. Set aside.

Halve, pit, and peel avocados; coat with lemon juice. Using a sharp knife, cut peel and all white membrane from grapefruits; then cut segments free and set them aside.

Place a lettuce leaf on each of 6 salad plates; set an avocado half, pitted side up, on lettuce on each plate. Spoon a sixth of the chicken salad over each avocado half, then top salads equally with grapefruit segments. Makes 6 servings.

TARRAGON-PEPPER DRESSING. In a large bowl, mix ⅓ cup *each* **mayonnaise** and **sour cream**, 2 teaspoons **white wine vinegar**, 1 tablespoon chopped **fresh tarragon leaves** or 1 teaspoon dry tarragon leaves, 1 teaspoon minced **parsley**, ⅛ teaspoon **ground red pepper** (cayenne), and ¼ teaspoon **black pepper.**

Per serving: 430 calories, 19 g protein, 19 g carbohydrates, 33 g fat, 7 g saturated fat, 53 mg cholesterol, 133 mg sodium

CHERIMOYA CHICKEN SALAD

Preparation time: About 10 minutes

Don't let its reptilian appearance scare you away! Beneath the cherimoya's leathery, almost scaly-looking skin is fragrant flesh with a custardy texture and a pineapple-banana flavor. Cut into wedges, the sweet fruit complements chicken chunks and thin cucumber slices in a tart lemon dressing.

¼ cup olive oil or salad oil
¼ cup lemon juice
1½ teaspoons *each* grated lemon peel and sugar
½ teaspoon pepper
1½ cups bite-size pieces cooked chicken breast
1 piece (about 7 inches long) European-style cucumber (about 8 oz.), quartered lengthwise, then thinly sliced
3 green onions (including tops), thinly sliced
8 medium-size butter lettuce leaves, washed and crisped
1 ripe cherimoya (about 12 oz.), quartered lengthwise
Lemon wedges
Salt

In a large bowl, stir together oil, lemon juice, lemon peel, sugar, and pepper; spoon out 2 tablespoons of this dressing and reserve. Add chicken to remaining dressing in bowl, then stir in cucumber and onions.

Arrange 2 lettuce leaves on each of 4 dinner plates; top leaves with equal amounts of salad. Set a cherimoya wedge on each plate; drizzle fruit evenly with the reserved 2 tablespoons dressing, then garnish with lemon wedges. Season to taste with salt. Makes 4 servings.

Per serving: 282 calories, 18 g protein, 19 g carbohydrates, 16 g fat, 2 g saturated fat, 45 mg cholesterol, 45 mg sodium

This is definitely not the same old salad! Creative but surprisingly simple, Lemon Chicken Salad in Radicchio (recipe on facing page) combines pine nuts, fresh lemon wedges, chicken, and radicchio with a touch of oil. Serve with iced tea, warm herb bread, and your favorite marinated beans.

LEMON CHICKEN SALAD IN RADICCHIO

Preparation time: About 20 minutes, plus at least 1 hour to crisp radicchio

Brighten up the buffet with a colorful chicken salad served in purple-red radicchio leaves. Because the salad is so simple, it's important to use a flavorful, good-quality olive oil, such as a fruity extra-virgin variety.

> 2 **heads radicchio (about 1 lb.** *total*), *each* **3 to 4 inches in diameter**
> ¼ **cup pine nuts**
> 1 **large lemon, thinly sliced**
> 2 **cups minced cooked chicken breast**
> 2 **tablespoons extra-virgin olive oil**
>   **Salt and pepper**

Remove 8 large radicchio leaves; rinse leaves and radicchio heads. Wrap in paper towels, enclose in a plastic bag, and refrigerate until crisp (at least 1 hour) or for up to 2 days.

Spread pine nuts in an 8- or 9-inch-diameter baking pan. Toast, uncovered, in a 350° oven until lightly browned (about 8 minutes), shaking pan occasionally. Set aside.

Discard seeds from lemon slices. Cut 2 slices into quarters and set aside. Cut each remaining slice into 10 wedges. In a large bowl, mix small lemon wedges with pine nuts, chicken, and oil. (At this point, you may cover and refrigerate until next day.)

Finely shred radicchio heads; discard cores. Mix shredded radicchio with chicken mixture, then season to taste with salt and pepper.

Set reserved radicchio leaves on a large platter; mound chicken salad equally in leaves. Garnish with reserved lemon quarter-slices. Makes 6 to 8 servings.

Per serving: 143 calories, 15 g protein, 5 g carbohydrates, 8 g fat, 1 g saturated fat, 34 mg cholesterol, 37 mg sodium

OLIVE-PECAN CHICKEN SLAW

Preparation time: About 15 minutes

Cole slaw? How ordinary! Well, not always. This main-dish slaw does feature the requisite shredded cabbage and slightly sweetened dressing, but it also holds apple chunks, ripe olives, chicken, and crisp butter-toasted pecans. Line the salad bowl with whole cabbage leaves for an attractive presentation.

> 2 **teaspoons butter or margarine**
> ½ **cup pecan halves**
>   **Lemon-Mustard Dressing (recipe follows)**
> 2 **cups shredded green cabbage**
> 1½ **cups bite-size pieces cooked chicken breast**
> 1 **medium-size Red Delicious apple, cored and diced**
> 1 **jar (2 oz.) diced pimentos, drained**
> 1 **can (2¼ oz.) sliced ripe olives, drained**
> ¼ **cup thinly sliced celery**
>   **Salt**

Melt butter in a 8- to 10-inch frying pan over medium-low heat. Add pecans and cook, stirring occasionally, until nuts smell toasted and look golden inside; break a nut to test (about 7 minutes). Set aside on paper towels to drain.

Prepare Lemon-Mustard Dressing. Then add cabbage, chicken, apple, pimentos, olives, and celery to dressing; stir to blend. Sprinkle pecans over salad; season to taste with salt. Makes 4 servings.

LEMON-MUSTARD DRESSING. In a salad bowl, stir together ½ cup **mayonnaise,** 2 tablespoons **lemon juice,** 1 teaspoon **Dijon mustard** or regular prepared mustard, ½ teaspoon **sugar,** and ¼ teaspoon **pepper.**

Per serving: 455 calories, 19 g protein, 15 g carbohydrates, 37 g fat, 6 g saturated fat, 67 mg cholesterol, 410 mg sodium

GLORIOUS GOOSE & PHEASANT

Dinner is always a celebration if you serve goose or pheasant: when these birds come to the table, it's a safe bet that the cook has put some careful planning—and often a lot of time—into the meal. Happily, our recipes reward both cooks and diners for that extra effort.

If you're after a truly magnificent feast, offer a rich roast goose, stuffed with herbed cabbage. Roast pheasant is impressive, too; try it with a creamy white wine and chanterelle sauce. For a special meal for two, offer sautéed pheasant breasts with lime-pistachio butter and cranberry sauce.

Both goose and pheasant are usually sold frozen, but you can buy them fresh in some supermarkets during the holiday season or order them almost all year round from specialty meat markets or game farms.

GOLDEN GOOSE WITH CABBAGE-APPLE STUFFING

Preparation time: About 1 hour

Roasting time: 2 to 3 hours

- 1 **goose (8 to 12 lbs.), thawed if frozen**
- 2 **medium-size lemons**
- 1 **tablespoon olive oil or salad oil**
- 1½ **pounds green cabbage, cored and finely shredded**
- 4 **cups coarsely chopped peeled Golden Delicious apples**
- 1 **cup golden raisins**
- ¾ **cup chopped parsley**
- ½ **teaspoon *each* dry marjoram leaves, dry thyme leaves, dry chervil leaves, dry sage leaves, and ground allspice**
- ½ **cup unsweetened white grape juice or apple juice**
  Pepper
  Parsley sprigs and lemon wedges

Reserve goose neck and giblets for other uses. Pull off and discard lumps of fat from goose. Rinse goose inside and out; pat dry. With a fork, prick skin all over goose at about 1½-inch intervals. Cut one of the lemons in half. Rub and gently squeeze one half all over inside of goose; set remaining lemon half and whole lemon aside.

Heat oil in a 5- to 6-quart pan over medium-high heat. Add cabbage and apples; cover and cook, stirring occasionally, until cabbage is wilted (about 8 minutes). Remove from heat and stir in raisins, chopped parsley, marjoram, thyme, chervil, sage, and allspice. Grate peel from remaining whole lemon and stir into cabbage mixture. Then squeeze juice from this lemon and stir into grape juice; set aside.

Stuff body and neck cavities of goose with cabbage mixture; skewer cavities closed. Rub outside of goose with remaining lemon half; sprinkle goose all over with pepper. Place goose, breast down, on a V-shaped rack in a 12- by 17-inch roasting pan. Cover goose with a tent of foil, sealing foil to pan edges.

Roast goose in a 350° oven for 1 hour. Uncover; siphon off and discard fat from pan. Turn goose breast up and insert a meat thermometer in thickest part of a drumstick (not touching bone). Continue to roast, uncovered, siphoning off fat and basting bird with grape juice mixture every 30 minutes, until thermometer registers 175°F (1 to 2 more hours).

Transfer goose to a large platter. Remove skewers, then spoon stuffing out onto platter next to bird. Garnish with parsley sprigs and lemon wedges. Makes 6 to 8 servings.

Per serving: 1,101 calories, 80 g protein, 34 g carbohydrates, 71 g fat, 22 g saturated fat, 283 mg cholesterol, 239 mg sodium

PHEASANTS & CHANTERELLES

Preparation time: About 20 minutes

Cooking time: About 1 hour

- 2 **pheasants (about 2½ lbs.** *each)***, thawed if frozen**
- 2 **tablespoons salad oil**
- 1 **cup** *each* **coarsely chopped onion, carrots, and celery**
- 10 **dry juniper berries**
- 6 **whole cloves**
- 1 **clove garlic, minced or pressed**
- 1 **teaspoon minced fresh sage leaves or ¼ teaspoon dry sage leaves**
   About 3 cups water
- 4 **slices bacon**
   Mushroom Sauce (recipe follows)
   Salt and white pepper

Remove and rinse pheasant necks; reserve giblets for other uses. Rinse birds inside and out; pat dry.

Heat oil in a 12- to 14-inch frying pan over medium-high heat. Add whole birds and necks; cook, turning as needed, until browned on all sides (about 10 minutes). Place birds, breast up, on a rack in a 12-by 15-inch roasting pan; set aside.

Leave necks in frying pan; then add onion, carrots, celery, juniper berries, cloves, garlic, and sage to pan. Cook over medium heat, stirring often, until onion is soft. Add 3 cups of the water. Bring to a boil over high heat; then boil until liquid is reduced by half (about 10 minutes). Pour mixture through a fine strainer; discard vegetables and necks. Measure strained stock; you need 1 cup. If necessary, boil to reduce to 1 cup or add water to increase amount. Skim and discard fat from stock; set stock aside for Mushroom Sauce.

Drape pheasants with bacon. Roast, uncovered, in a 400° oven, basting often with pan juices, until breast meat is white with a touch of pink near bone (about 30 minutes). To test, cut to breastbone parallel to wing joint; meat should look moist, not soft and wet.

While pheasants are roasting, prepare Mushroom Sauce. When pheasants are done, pour any pan juices into Mushroom Sauce; heat sauce through and season to taste with salt and pepper. Remove bacon from pheasants. With poultry shears or a heavy knife, cut each pheasant in half lengthwise along backbone and through breastbone. Place pheasant halves on a platter; top with Mushroom Sauce. Makes 4 servings.

MUSHROOM SAUCE. In frying pan used to brown pheasants, melt 2 tablespoons **butter** or margarine over medium-high heat. Add ¾ teaspoon minced **garlic,** 1 tablespoon minced **shallot,** and 3 cups (9 oz.) **chanterelles** or thinly sliced button mushrooms.

Cook, stirring often, until mushrooms are lightly browned and all liquid has evaporated (about 5 minutes). Stir 2 tablespoons **all-purpose flour** into mushroom mixture; smoothly stir in **reserved vegetable-pheasant stock** and 1 cup **dry white wine.** Boil, uncovered, stirring often, until reduced by a third (about 5 minutes). Add ½ cup **whipping cream** and bring to a boil. Remove from heat.

Per serving: 1,259 calories, 116 g protein, 12 g carbohydrates, 81 g fat, 28 g saturated fat, 444 mg sodium*

PHEASANT BREASTS WITH PISTACHIO BUTTER

Preparation time: About 20 minutes

Cooking time: About 6 minutes

   Pistachio Butter (recipe follows)
- 2 **pheasant breast halves (about 6 oz.** *each)***, breastbone removed (may have wing joint attached)**
- ½ **teaspoon coarsely ground pepper**
- 2 **tablespoons butter or margarine**
- ¾ **cup fresh or frozen cranberries**
- 1 **tablespoon sugar**
   Parsley sprigs (optional)

Prepare Pistachio Butter; set aside.

Rinse pheasant and pat dry. If wing joints are attached, cut them off and set aside. Pull off and discard all skin and fat from breast halves. Place each breast half between 2 sheets of plastic wrap; pound with a flat-surfaced mallet to a thickness of ⅛ to ¼ inch. Sprinkle meat with pepper.

Melt butter in a 10- to 12-inch frying pan over medium-high heat. When butter sizzles, add pounded breast halves and wing sections. Cook, turning as needed, until breasts are lightly browned on both sides but still slightly pink in center; cut to test (about 4 minutes). Place a breast half on each dinner plate. Top each serving with Pistachio Butter; keep warm.

To pan with wing sections, add cranberries and sugar. Reduce heat to low and cook, stirring often, until berries just begin to pop (about 1 minute). Spoon cranberries equally onto breast pieces beside Pistachio Butter. Add a wing section to each plate; garnish with parsley, if desired. Makes 2 servings.

PISTACHIO BUTTER. Mince ¼ cup **salted roasted pistachio nuts.** Place in a small bowl and add 2 tablespoons **butter** or margarine (at room temperature), 1 tablespoon minced **parsley,** ¼ teaspoon grated **lime peel,** and 1 teaspoon **lime juice.** Mix well.

Per serving: 585 calories, 48 g protein, 16 g carbohydrates, 37 g fat, 17 g saturated fat, 297 mg sodium*

*Cholesterol data not available.

CHINESE HOT & SOUR CHICKEN NOODLE SALAD

Preparation time: About 10 minutes

Cooking time: About 15 minutes

Here's a tempting cold pasta salad that fits right into a healthful diet. Chile-flavored oil mixed with soy and a generous splash of mellow rice vinegar dresses linguine, cool cucumber slices, and shredded chicken breast.

> 8 **ounces dry linguine**
>
> 3 **tablespoons salad oil**
>
> ¾ **teaspoon crushed dried hot red chiles**
>
> 1 **tablespoon Sichuan peppercorns, toasted and ground (see page 365); or 1 tablespoon whole black peppercorns, ground**
>
> ⅓ **cup rice vinegar or cider vinegar**
>
> 2 **tablespoons reduced-sodium soy sauce**
>
> ¼ **cup chopped fresh cilantro (coriander)**
>
> 1 **small cucumber, thinly sliced**
>
> 1½ **cups shredded cooked chicken breast**

Cook linguine according to package directions just until tender to bite. Drain; immerse in cold water until cool, then drain well again. Set aside.

Heat oil in a 6- to 8-inch frying pan over low heat. Add chiles; cook just until chiles begin to brown (about 3 minutes). Let cool, then add ground peppercorns, vinegar, soy, and cilantro.

In a shallow dish, arrange a bed of linguine; cover with cucumber and chicken. Pour dressing evenly over salad and mix to blend. Makes 4 servings.

Per serving: 407 calories, 25 g protein, 47 g carbohydrates, 13 g fat, 2 g saturated fat, 45 mg cholesterol, 345 mg sodium

■ *Pictured on facing page*

BARBECUE CHICKEN PIZZA PIE

Preparation time: About 50 minutes

Baking time: About 25 minutes

Are you ready for pizza pie, Southern style? Skip the traditional tomato sauce and mozzarella cheese; instead, top the crust with homemade barbecue sauce, chicken, jack cheese, and bell pepper. Serve with a simple salad for down-home satisfaction.

> **Barbecue Sauce (recipe follows)**
>
> 1 **package (10 oz.) refrigerated pizza dough; or 1 package (1 lb.) frozen white bread dough, thawed**
>
> 2 **cups diced or shredded cooked chicken**
>
> 1 **large red bell pepper, seeded and thinly sliced**
>
> 2 **cups (8 oz.) shredded plain or chile-seasoned jack cheese**
>
> **Cilantro (coriander) sprigs**

Prepare Barbecue Sauce; set aside.

Press dough over bottom and up sides of a lightly greased 14-inch-diameter pizza pan or shallow 10- by 15-inch baking pan. Pierce dough with a fork at 2-inch intervals. Bake on bottom rack of a 400° oven until light golden (about 10 minutes).

In a bowl, mix chicken and Barbecue Sauce. Spread mixture evenly over baked crust. Arrange bell pepper over chicken mixture, then sprinkle evenly with cheese. Return to oven and bake on bottom rack until cheese is bubbly (about 15 minutes). Garnish with cilantro. Cut into wedges or rectangles to serve. Makes 6 servings.

BARBECUE SAUCE. Melt 2 tablespoons **butter** or margarine in a 10- to 12-inch frying pan over medium heat. Add 1 large **onion,** thinly sliced; cook, stirring occasionally, until onion is golden brown (about 25 minutes). Add ½ cup *each* **catsup** and **tomato-based chili sauce,** ¼ cup **cider vinegar,** and 1 tablespoon *each* **molasses** and **Worcestershire.** Bring to a boil over high heat; then reduce heat and simmer, uncovered, for 10 minutes. If made ahead, let cool; then cover and refrigerate for up to 2 days.

Per serving: 457 calories, 28 g protein, 39 g carbohydrates, 20 g fat, 3 g saturated fat, 85 mg cholesterol, 1,079 mg sodium

If you like barbecued chicken and pizza, why not enjoy both in one dish?
Barbecue Chicken Pizza Pie (recipe on facing page) may not be traditional, but
that doesn't lessen its appeal. Sweetened with molasses and spiced with chiles,
the pie is complemented by chunky potato salad and dill-seasoned okra.

433

CHICKEN-BROCCOLI QUICHE WITH ALMONDS

Preparation time: About 30 minutes

Baking time: About 45 minutes

Take advantage of the chicken you saved from yesterday's dinner to create a new meal tonight. An easy pat-in pastry crust holds a rich, nutmeg-scented custard filled with chicken, broccoli, and Gruyère—so good that no one will even think "leftovers"!

> Pat-in Crust (recipe follows)
> 8 ounces broccoli
> 3 large eggs
> 1 cup half-and-half or milk
> ¼ teaspoon *each* ground nutmeg and pepper
> 1 cup finely chopped cooked chicken
> 1 cup (4 oz.) shredded Gruyère or Swiss cheese
> 2 tablespoons sliced almonds

Prepare Pat-in Crust; set aside. Reduce oven temperature to 350°.

Trim and discard tough ends of broccoli stalks; then peel and thinly slice remainder of stalks. Cut flowerets into about ¾-inch pieces. Then arrange all broccoli on a rack in a 2- to 3-quart pan above 1 inch of boiling water. Cover and steam until broccoli is tender when pierced (about 5 minutes). Let cool.

In a bowl, beat eggs, half-and-half, nutmeg, and pepper until blended. In another bowl, mix broccoli, chicken, and cheese; spread evenly in crust. Pour egg mixture over chicken mixture; sprinkle with almonds. Bake in a 350° oven until center appears set when pan is gently shaken (about 45 minutes). Let stand for at least 15 minutes before cutting into wedges. Makes 6 servings.

PAT-IN CRUST. In a 9-inch pie pan, combine 1½ cups **all-purpose flour** and ½ cup (¼ lb.) **butter** or margarine, cut into chunks. Rub together with your fingers until mixture resembles fine crumbs. Add 1 large **egg;** stir until dough clings together. Then press dough evenly over bottom, sides, and rim of pie pan. Bake on bottom rack of a 375° oven until pale golden (about 10 minutes).

Per serving: 496 calories, 23 g protein, 29 g carbohydrates, 33 g fat, 18 g saturated fat, 239 mg cholesterol, 309 mg sodium

CHICKEN ENCHILADA BAKE

Preparation time: About 20 minutes

Baking time: About 30 minutes

How can such a hearty and richly flavored casserole be perfect fare for the diet-conscious diner? Simple— the tortillas are baked (not fried), the meat is skinless chicken breast, and the sauce is made with low-sodium broth and low-fat yogurt. Top with Cheddar cheese for an extra taste treat.

> 12 corn tortillas (*each* 6 to 7 inches in diameter)
> 5 medium-size tomatoes, peeled and thinly sliced
> 2 cups shredded cooked chicken breast
> 1 cup thinly sliced green onions (including tops)
> 1 tablespoon butter or margarine
> 2 tablespoons all-purpose flour
> 2 cups low-sodium chicken broth
> 1 cup plain low-fat yogurt
> 1 can (4 oz.) diced green chiles
> ½ cup finely shredded Cheddar cheese

Dip tortillas, one at a time, in water; let drain briefly. Stack tortillas; cut stack into 8 wedges. Then spread a third of the tortilla wedges in a 9- by 13-inch baking pan. Top with half the tomatoes; cover with half *each* of the chicken and onions. Repeat layers, ending with tortillas. Set aside.

Melt butter in a 2- to 3-quart pan over medium heat. Add flour and cook, stirring, until bubbly. Whisk in broth and bring to a boil. Remove from heat, add yogurt and chiles, and whisk until smooth. Pour over tortillas in baking pan.

Cover and bake in a 375° oven for 20 minutes. Uncover, sprinkle with cheese, and continue to bake, uncovered, until cheese is melted (about 10 more minutes). Makes 8 servings.

Per serving: 254 calories, 19 g protein, 28 g carbohydrates, 8 g fat, 3 g saturated fat, 43 mg cholesterol, 291 mg sodium

CHICKEN CARBONARA

Preparation time: About 10 minutes

Cooking time: About 20 minutes

Adding pine nuts and diced chicken to classic pasta *carbonara* creates a delightful new tradition. Serve with lightly dressed salad greens and crisp whole wheat bread sticks.

- ½ **cup pine nuts**
- 4 **slices bacon, chopped**
- 8 **ounces dry linguine or 1 package (9 oz.) fresh linguine**
- 4 **eggs (room temperature)**
- ½ **cup grated Parmesan cheese**
- ⅓ **cup whipping cream**
- ¼ **cup chopped parsley**
- ¼ **cup chopped fresh basil leaves or 2 tablespoons dry basil leaves**
- 3 **cloves garlic, minced or pressed**
- 1½ **cups diced cooked chicken**
- 1 **to 2 tablespoons butter or margarine**

Toast pine nuts in a 10- to 12-inch frying pan over medium-low heat until lightly browned (about 3 minutes), shaking pan often. Remove from pan and set aside in a large bowl. Increase heat to medium; add bacon to pan and cook, stirring often, until browned (about 7 minutes). Lift out bacon with a slotted spoon; place in bowl with nuts. Reserve drippings in pan.

Cook linguine according to package directions just until tender to bite. Drain well.

While pasta is cooking, add eggs, cheese, cream, parsley, basil, garlic, and chicken to bacon and pine nuts. Beat until well mixed.

To reserved bacon drippings in frying pan, add enough butter to make ¼ cup; melt butter in drippings over medium heat. Add linguine, then egg mixture. Mix lightly, using 2 forks, just until linguine is well coated and heated through. Makes 4 servings.

Per serving: 755 calories, 40 g protein, 49 g carbohydrates, 46 g fat, 17 g saturated fat, 316 mg cholesterol, 508 mg sodium

MINI TURKEY TAMALES

Preparation time: About 1¼ hours

Cooking time: About 45 minutes

Substituting squares of foil for the standard corn husk wrappers cuts down on the time it takes to prepare tamales. Filled with a robust mixture of salsa, olives, and turkey, these savory little bundles can be served as a main course or an appetizer.

- 2 **cups dehydrated masa flour (corn tortilla flour)**
- 1¼ **cups regular-strength chicken broth**
  Salt
- ½ **cup salad oil**
- 2 **cups finely diced cooked turkey or chicken**
- ½ **cup pitted ripe olives, coarsely chopped**
- 1 **medium-size onion, finely chopped**
- ½ **cup prepared green chile salsa**

Cut thirty 6-inch-square pieces of foil. In a large bowl, combine masa flour, broth, ½ teaspoon salt, and oil; stir together to make a thick paste. Spread about 1½ tablespoons of the paste in a 3-inch square in center of each piece of foil.

In a bowl, mix turkey, olives, onion, and salsa; season to taste with salt. Spoon about 1½ tablespoons of the filling down center of each masa-dough square. Fold foil edges together so masa edges meet; then seal all sides.

Stack wrapped tamales, arranging loosely so steam can circulate, in a large pan on a rack above at least 1 inch of boiling water. Cover; adjust heat to keep water at a steady boil. Cook, adding boiling water as needed to maintain water level, until masa dough is firm to touch; unwrap a tamale to test (about 45 minutes). Makes 30 small tamales, 6 main dish servings.

Per serving: 406 calories, 18 g protein, 32 g carbohydrates, 23 g fat, 3 g saturated fat, 36 mg cholesterol, 643 mg sodium

Yesterday's turkey gets dressed up for today's dinner with the help of juicy orange slices and an easy sour cream sauce. Served over fresh cheese- or meat-filled spinach pasta, Turkey with Tortellini & Oranges (recipe on facing page) is worthy of your most important company.

■ *Pictured on facing page*

TURKEY WITH TORTELLINI & ORANGES

Preparation time: About 25 minutes

Cooking time: About 20 minutes

Pick out a pretty serving platter—this main dish really deserves to be shown off! Orange slices surround fresh tortellini and turkey chunks topped with a chive-sprinkled sour cream sauce.

- 3 **large oranges (about 1½ lbs. *total*)**
- 7 **cups regular-strength chicken broth**
- 1½ **pounds fresh cheese- or meat-filled plain or spinach tortellini**
- 3 **cups diced or shredded cooked turkey**
- 2 **teaspoons celery seeds**
- 2 **cups sour cream**
- ¼ **cup snipped chives**

Using a vegetable peeler, cut a 6-inch-long, 1-inch-wide strip of peel (colored part only) from one of the oranges. Cut strip into long, thin shreds and set aside. Then, using a sharp knife, cut peel and all white membrane from all 3 oranges. Cut each orange crosswise into 6 slices; set slices aside.

In a 5- to 6-quart pan, bring broth to a boil over high heat. Add tortellini and cook just until tender to bite (about 4 minutes; or time according to package directions). With a slotted spoon, lift out tortellini and transfer to a platter; keep warm.

To broth in pan, add turkey, celery seeds, and shredded orange peel; cook just until turkey is heated through. Lift out turkey with a slotted spoon and arrange atop tortellini. Place sour cream in a small pan, then stir in 3 tablespoons of the chives and ½ cup of the hot broth (reserve remaining broth for other uses). Stir broth–sour cream mixture over low heat just until hot, then spoon over turkey. Sprinkle with remaining 1 tablespoon chives; arrange orange slices around turkey and pasta. Makes 6 servings.

Per serving: 694 calories, 46 g protein, 68 g carbohydrates, 27 g fat, 11 g saturated fat, 150 mg cholesterol, 1,752 mg sodium

TURKEY QUICHE

Preparation time: About 35 minutes

Baking time: About 30 minutes

Leftovers are cause for culinary celebration when you transform yesterday's roast turkey and stuffing into filling and crust for today's quiche. Layered with cheese, onions, and mushrooms, this creamy, custardy pie is a satisfying and thrifty supper.

- 5 **large eggs**
- 2½ **to 3 cups leftover bread stuffing; or half of a 6-ounce package bread stuffing mix, prepared according to package directions**
- 1 **cup (4 oz.) shredded Gruyère or Swiss cheese**
- 1 **cup diced cooked turkey or chicken**
- ¼ **cup thinly sliced green onions (including tops)**
- ½ **cup sliced mushrooms**
- 1 **cup half-and-half**
  Salt and pepper

In a bowl, beat one egg until blended; then add stuffing and mix well. Press stuffing mixture over bottom and up sides of a greased 10-inch pie pan or deep quiche pan or dish. Bake, uncovered, on lowest rack of a 425° oven until stuffing is crisp and dry to the touch (about 15 minutes). Remove from oven; reduce oven temperature to 350°.

Sprinkle cheese over bottom and sides of stuffing crust, then top crust evenly with turkey, onions, and mushrooms.

In bowl used to prepare stuffing crust, beat remaining 4 eggs to blend; then stir in half-and-half and season to taste with salt and pepper. Pour over turkey and vegetables. Bake on lowest rack of oven until filling appears set when pan is gently shaken (about 30 minutes). Let stand for at least 10 minutes before cutting into wedges. Makes 6 servings.

Per serving: 464 calories, 23 g protein, 26 g carbohydrates, 30 g fat, 15 g saturated fat, 272 mg cholesterol, 725 mg sodium

■ *Pictured on page 425*

TURKEY POT PIE

Preparation time: About 30 minutes

Cooking time: About 30 minutes

The rich cream cheese pastry crust for this pie bakes separately while the turkey-vegetable filling cooks on your stove.

>   Parmesan-Pepper Pastry (recipe follows)
>   1   tablespoon butter or margarine
>   ½   cup thinly sliced leeks (white part only)
>   2½ cups regular-strength chicken broth
>   ½   cup Madeira or regular-strength chicken broth
>   1   pound yams or sweet potatoes, peeled and cut into ½-inch cubes
>   ½   teaspoon *each* dry sage leaves and dry thyme leaves
>   3   tablespoons cornstarch mixed with 3 tablespoons water
>   8   ounces kale, washed, stems removed, and leaves chopped
>   3   cups bite-size pieces cooked turkey

Prepare Parmesan-Pepper Pastry.

While pastry is baking, melt butter in a 5- to 6-quart pan over medium heat. Add leeks; cook, stirring, until soft (about 3 minutes). Add broth, Madeira, yams, sage, and thyme. Bring to a boil; reduce heat, cover, and simmer until yams are tender when pierced (about 20 minutes). Stir cornstarch mixture into broth. Add kale and turkey; bring to a boil, stirring.

Pour turkey mixture into casserole used to shape pie crust. Loosen hot pastry from foil on baking sheet; then slide it onto turkey mixture. To serve, break through pastry with a spoon, dipping out filling with pastry. Makes 6 servings.

PARMESAN-PEPPER PASTRY. In a food processor, combine 1 cup **all-purpose flour,** ½ cup grated **Parmesan cheese,** ½ teaspoon **pepper,** and 1 large package (8 oz.) **cream cheese,** cut into large chunks. Whirl until dough forms a ball.

On a 12- by 15-inch sheet of foil, invert a shallow 2- to 2½-quart casserole. With tip of a knife, lightly trace around edge of casserole. Set casserole aside.

In center of outline, pat pastry out ½ inch thick; lightly dust with **all-purpose flour.** Roll pastry out until it extends ¼ inch beyond outline. Fold edge of pastry under ¼ inch; crimp edge. With a sharp knife or cookie cutter, make one or more cutouts through pastry; take care not to tear foil. With a fork, pierce pastry at ½-inch intervals just inside edge (to keep pastry from puffing excessively as it bakes).

Slide pastry on foil onto a 12- by 15-inch baking sheet. Bake, uncovered, in a 350° oven until golden (about 30 minutes). Use hot.

Per serving: 502 calories, 31 g protein, 45 g carbohydrates, 21 g fat, 12 g saturated fat, 106 mg cholesterol, 697 mg sodium

CHINESE STIR-FRIED TURKEY

Preparation time: About 20 minutes

Marinating time: At least 30 minutes or up to 1 day

Cooking time: About 7 minutes

At the end of a tiring day, this zippy stir-fry wakes up the tastebuds without wearing out the cook.

>   Spiced Marinade (recipe follows)
>   3   cups shredded cooked turkey or chicken
>   2   tablespoons salad oil
>   1½ tablespoons minced fresh ginger
>   2   cloves garlic, thinly sliced
>   3   small dried hot red chiles
>   2   cups shredded napa cabbage
>   3   stalks celery, sliced diagonally
>   1   cup 1-inch pieces green onions (including tops)
>   1½ cups julienne strips jicama

Prepare Spiced Marinade. Stir in turkey, cover, and refrigerate for at least 30 minutes or up to 1 day.

Heat oil in a wok or 12- to 14-inch frying pan over medium-high heat. Add ginger, garlic, and chiles; stir until garlic is golden (about 1½ minutes). Add cabbage, celery, onions, and jicama; cook, stirring, until celery is barely tender-crisp to bite (about 3 minutes). Add turkey mixture; stir until sauce comes to a full boil. Discard chiles, if desired. Makes 4 servings.

SPICED MARINADE. In a large bowl, stir together 1 cup **regular-strength chicken broth;** 2 tablespoons **cornstarch;** 2 tablespoons *each* **soy sauce** and **oyster sauce;** 2 tablespoons **dry sherry** or regular-strength chicken broth; 1 tablespoon **Oriental sesame oil;** and ½ teaspoon *each* **anise seeds** and **ground cinnamon.**

Per serving: 354 calories, 35 g protein, 17 g carbohydrates, 16 g fat, 3g saturated fat, 82 mg cholesterol, 1,232 mg sodium

*Good looks aren't everything, but they certainly make Game Hens
with Mustard Crust (recipe on page 350) even more appealing. A mustard
coating enriched with garlic and rosemary gives the butterflied birds a
flavor every bit as wonderful as their tempting appearance.*

Sunset

Fresh Ways with
Pasta

By the Editors of
Sunset Books
and
Sunset Magazine

 Sunset Publishing Corporation ▪ Menlo Park, California

Contents

Special Features

Introduction

The very first Italian word you ever learned may well have been "spaghetti," or perhaps "macaroni." These two favorites, along with the multitude of additional varieties you've probably encountered over the years, are collectively known as "pasta."

Though there's no doubt that Italian cooks made pasta famous, it plays a part in other national cuisines as well. In the pages that follow, you'll find not only numerous Italian specialties, but also tantalizing variations inspired by the cooking of other European cultures, Asia, and Latin America.

Pasta's popularity is easy to understand. It's fun to choose from the scores of forms, creative to dream up combinations of pasta with all sorts of sauces and dressings. And the final result is invariably wonderful to eat. Many pasta entrées can be cooked in mere minutes—and what's more, the price is usually right.

Pasta Variety

Many a good cook makes tender egg pasta at home, either by hand or with the aid of a food processor and pasta machine. If you'd like to turn out your own fresh pasta, try the Egg Pasta on page 446—and don't forget the colorful variations on page 444. You can cut any of these pastas into noodles of any width, including lasagne strips and cannelloni squares.

What if you don't have the time or desire for pasta making? Drop into a pasta shop—you'll find freshly made noodles as well as filled pastas such as ravioli and tortellini, all sold in bulk. Many supermarkets also offer a tempting variety of refrigerated packaged fresh pasta, both plain and fancy; in the freezer case, you'll come upon ravioli and their cousins—plump tortellini, lunette, anolini, and pansotti. (Look for plain, unsauced ravioli, then add your family's favorite embellishments.)

However enticing, fresh noodles and filled shapes are by no means the entire pasta picture. Dry pasta, available in myriad forms, underlies some of the most delectable dishes of all. Each kind has its special attractions — smooth cream sauces cling to curves, zesty seasonings fill hollows, rich broths invite tiny pasta bits. The selection is especially abundant in an Italian delicatessen, but any supermarket offers plenty of good options for the dry pastas specified in our recipes.

For those truly interested in exploring the vast pasta world, gourmet shops and mail-order sources offer premium-priced dry pasta in numerous shapes and a wide range of exotic flavors, from artichoke to wild mushroom.

Cooking Pasta Perfectly

By now, we've all heard that the ideal state for cooked pasta is summed up in the succinct Italian phrase *al dente*—"to the tooth," or tender but still firm. To achieve such perfectly cooked pasta, start by using plenty of water: pasta in an abundance of rapidly boiling water is unlikely to stick to itself or to the pan. Be sure to choose a cooking pan that can comfortably hold the amount of boiling water you will need.

For each 8 ounces dry pasta, bring 3 quarts water to a rapid boil. Add 1 tablespoon salt, if desired (for more pasta, increase the amount of water only). Then add the pasta to the boiling water. When you cook spaghetti or other pasta that's longer than the pan is deep, hold the bunch of pasta by one end, then gently push the other end into the boiling water until the strands soften enough to submerge. Stir only if the pasta needs to be separated. Keep the water boiling continuously and cook the pasta, uncovered, according to the cooking time specified in the recipe.

Cooking time varies with the pasta's size and shape—the thinner and moister the pasta, the shorter the cooking time. Our recipes specify the time it took our testers. But because one manufacturer's spaghetti may cook faster than another's, it's always wise to check the cooking time specified on the package. And of course, you'll want to use your own judgment. A quick, reliable test for doneness is simply to lift a piece or strand from the pan and quickly bite into it; if it's al dente, it's done. Pasta that breaks easily against the side of the pan when prodded with a spoon has probably been cooked too long.

If the pasta is destined for a baked casserole, shorten the cooking time by a few minutes to allow for additional cooking in the oven.

As soon as the pasta is al dente, drain it quickly and continue according to the recipe. Rinse cooked pasta only if you're going to use it in a salad or need to cool lasagne noodles in order to handle them. Pasta that will be served at once should not be rinsed; to keep it as hot as possible, have a warm platter or plates—and your family or guests—ready and waiting. (Don't worry about excess water clinging to the drained pasta, it will blend in with the sauce.)

How Much to Cook?

As a general rule, 2 ounces dry pasta make about 1 cup cooked pasta or 1 serving. Spaghetti and macaroni products approximately double in volume upon cooking, but packaged egg noodles don't expand quite that much. Fresh pasta is much moister than the dry product, so you'll need a greater weight for each serving—3 to 3½ ounces to make 1 cup (about 1 serving).

A kitchen scale allows you to weigh out pasta most accurately, but if you don't have one, you can measure by eye—just estimate the proportion of a package needed.

Pasta Nutrition

Pasta is low in fat and sodium; it's a good source of complex carbohydrates, and enriched pastas provide B-vitamins and iron. The durum wheat from which most pasta is made is high in protein. Finally, pasta's calorie content is lower than you may have assumed—2 ounces of uncooked spaghetti or macaroni provide less than 210 calories.

A Word about Our Nutritional Data

For our recipes, we provide a nutritional analysis stating calorie count; grams of protein, carbohydrates, and total fat; and milligrams of cholesterol and sodium. Generally, the analysis applies to a single serving, based on the number of servings given for each recipe and the amount of each ingredient. If a range is given for the number of servings and/or the amount of an ingredient, the analysis is based on an average of the figures given.

The nutritional analysis does not include optional ingredients or those for which no specific amount is stated. If an ingredient is listed with a substitution, the information was calculated using the first choice.

Colorful Flavored Pastas

Added to fresh pasta dough, puréed vegetables or herbs give homemade fettuccine, tagliarini, or even lasagne eye-catching color and extra flavor. You'll find that herbs such as basil and chives contribute an especially sprightly taste.

After making any of these colorful doughs, follow the directions on page 447 for rolling and cutting by hand or using a roller-type pasta machine (the dough may be too stiff to feed through an extrusion-type machine).

All these fresh pastas cook quickly. Allow just 1 to 3 minutes—depending on the thinness of the pasta—in a generous quantity of boiling water.

Fresh Herb Pasta

Pictured on facing page

1 cup firmly packed fresh basil leaves, oregano or marjoram sprigs (woody stems removed), or coarsely chopped chives or garlic chives
1 large egg
1 tablespoon water
About 2 cups all-purpose flour

In a food processor, whirl herb of your choice with egg and water until puréed. Add 1 cup of the flour to herb purée in food processor. Whirl until dough forms a smooth, elastic ball (2 to 3 minutes). If dough feels sticky, add about 1 tablespoon more flour and whirl until blended. Wrap dough in plastic wrap and let rest for about 30 minutes. Roll and cut as directed on page 447, using additional flour as needed. Makes 8 to 10 ounces uncooked pasta (about 4 servings).

Per serving: 286 calories, 10 g protein, 56 g carbohydrates, 2 g total fat, 53 mg cholesterol, 19 mg sodium

Red Bell Pepper Pasta

Pictured on facing page

4 large red bell peppers (about 2 lbs. *total*)
About 2½ cups all-purpose flour
1 large egg

Arrange peppers in a single layer in a 9- or 10-inch square baking pan. Bake, uncovered, in a 500° oven, turning occasionally, until skins are blackened on all sides (40 to 50 minutes). Then cover peppers with foil and let stand until cool (about 30 minutes).

Remove and discard pepper skins, stems, and seeds. Whirl peppers in a blender or food processor until puréed; pour purée into a 1- to 2-quart pan. Cook over medium heat, stirring often, until reduced to ½ cup (about 10 minutes). Let cool.

In a food processor, combine pepper purée, 2 cups of the flour, and egg. Whirl until dough forms a ball (at least 30 seconds). If dough feels sticky, add 2 tablespoons more flour; process until dough forms a ball again (at least 30 more seconds). Divide dough into 6 equal parts; wrap each in plastic wrap and let rest for at least 10 minutes.

Roll and cut as directed on page 447, using additional flour as needed. Makes about 1 pound uncooked pasta (4 to 6 servings).

Per serving: 234 calories, 8 g protein, 46 g carbohydrates, 2 g total fat, 43 mg cholesterol, 18 mg sodium

Spinach Pasta

½ of a 10-ounce package frozen chopped spinach, thawed; or about ½ cup cooked fresh spinach
2 large eggs
1½ to 2 cups all-purpose flour

Squeeze spinach dry and measure it; you need ¼ cup. In a food processor, combine spinach, eggs, and 1½ cups of the flour. Whirl until dough forms a smooth, elastic ball (1 to 2 minutes); if dough feels sticky, add more flour, 1 tablespoon at a time, and whirl until blended. Wrap dough in plastic wrap and let rest for 10 minutes.

Roll and cut as directed on page 447, using additional flour as needed. Makes about 12 to 14 ounces uncooked pasta (about 4 servings).

Per serving: 273 calories, 11 g protein, 49 g carbohydrates, 3 g total fat, 106 mg cholesterol, 59 mg sodium

Pine Nut–Butter Sauce

Pictured on facing page

½ cup (¼ lb.) butter or margarine
1 medium-size red bell pepper (about 5 oz.), seeded and thinly slivered
¼ cup pine nuts

Melt butter in a medium-size frying pan over medium heat. Add bell pepper and cook, stirring often, until limp but not brown (4 to 6 minutes). Stir in pine nuts and cook until lightly toasted (2 to 3 minutes). Makes enough sauce for about 1 pound uncooked fresh pasta (4 to 6 servings).

Per serving: 206 calories, 2 g protein, 2 g carbohydrates, 22 g total fat, 50 mg cholesterol, 188 mg sodium

*Three colors of homemade fettuccine mingle in
this bright first course. Combine equal quantities of
Fresh Herb Pasta, Red Bell Pepper Pasta, and Egg Pasta,
then drizzle with hot Pine Nut-Butter Sauce. The
recipes are on the facing page and page 446.*

Tender, springy fresh pasta dough is perfect for noodles of all sizes. To alter the flavor and texture, you can use whole wheat or semolina flour for up to half of the all-purpose flour.

Remember that the amount of liquid any flour can absorb will vary with the flour's natural moisture content and with the air temperature and humidity. In fact, you really won't know just how much water you need until you start working with the dough—so add water gradually, always paying close attention to the dough's texture.

Following we present two recipes for making egg pasta. In the first, the dough is mixed and kneaded by hand. The second recipe utilizes the food processor, which reduces mixing time to seconds and kneading time from 10 minutes to two or three. With either recipe, the dough can be rolled and cut by hand or with a pasta machine.

It's best to cook homemade pasta right away, but if you make more than you need, let it stand until dry but still pliable (30 minutes to 1 hour). Then enclose in a plastic bag; refrigerate for up to 2 days or freeze for up to 2 months. Do not thaw pasta before cooking.

The pasta-making techniques described here are also appropriate for the colorful flavored pasta doughs on page 444.

Egg Pasta

Pictured on page 445

About 2 cups all-purpose flour
2 large eggs
3 to 6 tablespoons water

Mound 2 cups of the flour on a work surface or in a large bowl and make a deep well in the center. Break eggs into well. With a fork, beat eggs lightly; then stir in 2 tablespoons of the water. Using a circular motion, begin to draw in flour from sides of well. Add 1 more tablespoon water and continue to mix until all flour is evenly moistened. If necessary, add more water, 1 tablespoon at a time. When dough becomes too stiff to stir easily, use your hands to finish mixing. Pat dough into a ball and knead a few times to help flour absorb liquid. Clean and lightly flour work surface.

If you plan to use a rolling pin, knead dough by hand: flatten dough ball slightly, then fold farthest edge toward you. With your fingertips or the heel of your hand, press and push dough away from you, sealing the fold. Rotate dough a quarter turn and continue folding-pushing motion, making a turn each time. Knead with a gentle, rhythmic motion until dough is smooth and elastic (about 10 minutes). Cover dough and let it rest for 20 minutes.

If you plan to use a pasta machine (manual or electric), first knead dough by hand, sprinkling with flour if needed, until no longer sticky (3 to 4 minutes).

With rolling pin or pasta machine, roll and cut dough by hand or by machine, as directed on facing page.

Machine-rolled dough makes about 32 pieces lasagne or about 4 cups cooked medium-wide (machine-cut) noodles (14 to 16 oz. uncooked). Yield of hand-rolled noodles may vary.

Per cup cooked pasta: 279 calories, 10 g protein, 51 g carbohydrates, 3 g total fat, 106 mg cholesterol, 33 mg sodium

Homemade Egg Pasta

Food Processor Pasta

About 2 cups all-purpose flour
2 large eggs
About ¼ cup water

Combine 2 cups of the flour and eggs in a food processor; whirl until mixture looks like cornmeal (about 5 seconds). With motor running, pour ¼ cup of the water through feed tube and whirl until dough forms a ball. Dough should be well blended but not sticky. If dough feels sticky, add a little flour and whirl to blend; if it looks crumbly, add another teaspoon or two of water. If processor begins to slow down or stop—a good indication that dough is properly mixed—turn off motor and proceed to next step.

Turn out dough onto a floured work surface and knead a few times, just until smooth.

If you plan to use a rolling pin, cover dough and let it rest for 20 minutes.

If you plan to use a pasta machine (manual or electric), you can roll dough out immediately.

With rolling pin or pasta machine, roll and cut dough as directed on facing page.

Machine-rolled dough makes about 32 pieces lasagne or about 4 cups cooked medium-wide (machine-cut) noodles (14 to 16 oz. uncooked). Yield of hand-rolled noodles may vary.

Per cup cooked pasta: 279 calories, 10 g protein, 51 g carbohydrates, 3 g total fat, 106 mg cholesterol, 33 mg sodium

Pasta by Hand

Once you've kneaded the dough and let it rest, you're ready to roll it out.

Rolling. Keeping unrolled portions of dough covered, roll out a fourth of the dough into a rectangle about 1/16 inch thick with a rolling pin. If dough is sticky, turn and flour both sides as you roll. Transfer rolled strip to a lightly floured surface or cloth and let stand, uncovered, while you roll remaining portions. Let each strip dry until it feels leathery but still pliable (5 to 10 minutes).

Cutting. Place a strip of rolled pasta dough on a lightly floured board and sprinkle with flour. Starting at narrow end, roll up jelly roll fashion and cut crosswise into slices as wide as you want the pasta. Fettuccine is about 1/4 inch wide, tagliarini about 1/8 inch wide; lasagne is about 2 inches wide.

Pasta by Machine

The following general directions apply to both manual and electric pasta machines. (Because pasta machines differ slightly in size and function depending upon the brand,

always consult the manufacturer's directions as well.)

Kneading and rolling. Keeping the unrolled portions covered, flatten a fourth of the dough slightly; flour it, then feed it through widest roller setting. Fold dough into thirds and feed it through rollers again. Repeat folding and rolling process 8 to 10 times or until dough is elastic. If dough feels at all damp or sticky, flour both sides each time it's rolled.

When dough is smooth and pliable, set rollers one notch closer together and feed dough through. Flour dough if it is damp or sticky. Repeat rolling, setting rollers closer each time, until dough is a long strip of the desired thinness. Cut strip in half crosswise for easy handling; place pieces on a lightly floured surface or cloth and let stand, uncovered, while you roll remaining portions. Let each strip dry until it feels leathery but still pliable (5 to 10 minutes).

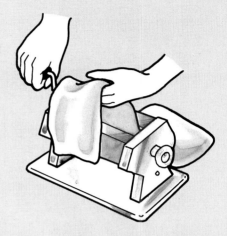

Cutting. Feed each strip through the medium-wide blades for fettuccine or through the narrow blades for thin noodles or tagliarini. Some machines have attachments for wide and narrow lasagne, but lasagne can also be cut easily by hand.

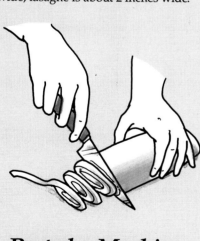

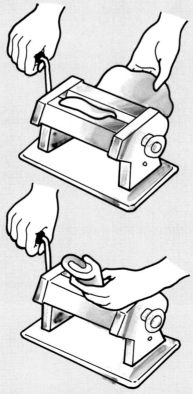

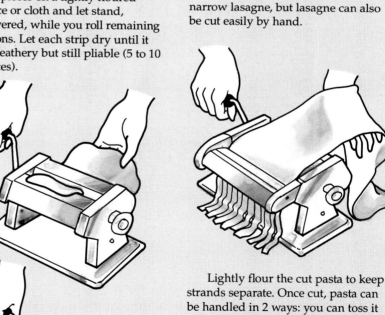

Lightly flour the cut pasta to keep strands separate. Once cut, pasta can be handled in 2 ways: you can toss it in a loose pile, or you can carefully gather the strands as they emerge from the machine (or have someone else gather them) and lay them in neat rows.

For a cozy supper or weekend lunch, enjoy steaming
bowls of bacon-flecked Ravioli & Cabbage Soup (recipe
on facing page) and crusty bread at the fireside or
around the TV.

Soups

Pasta in some form is a familiar addition to a bowl of steaming soup—golden egg noodles swirled through rich chicken broth, or an edible alphabet in disarray among the peas and carrots in a thick beef stock. Today, pasta in all shapes and sizes plays a prominent role in soups as satisfying as they are distinctive. Plump ravioli and tortellini mingle with a profusion of colorful vegetables; noodles and thin spaghetti strands lend welcome substance to light yogurt-enriched or clear broth. Tiny rice-shaped orzo, big seashells, or ruffly bow ties join hearty beans to supply cold-weather comfort.

Pictured on facing page
Ravioli & Cabbage Soup

Preparation time: About 20 minutes

Cooking time: 20 to 35 minutes

Fresh, frozen, or dry ravioli cook to plumpness in a simple bacon-seasoned broth for a nourishing lunch or supper soup.

- 4 ounces sliced bacon (about 5 slices), cut into ½-inch pieces
- 1 small onion, finely chopped
- 2 cloves garlic, minced or pressed
- 1 tablespoon chopped parsley
- 2 quarts regular-strength beef broth
- 2 cups water
- 1 large carrot (about 3 oz.), thinly sliced
- 1 pound (about 24) fresh or frozen ravioli; or 1 package (7 oz.) dry raviolini
- 2 cups shredded cabbage
  Grated Parmesan cheese

In a 5- to 6-quart pan, cook bacon over medium heat until translucent and limp. Add onion; continue to cook, stirring, until onion and bacon are lightly browned (about 5 more minutes). Discard all but 1 tablespoon of the bacon drippings; then stir garlic and parsley into bacon-onion mixture. Add broth, water, and carrot. Increase heat to high and bring to a boil. Separate any ravioli that are stuck together, then add ravioli to boiling broth. Reduce heat to medium and boil gently, uncovered, stirring occasionally, until ravioli are just tender to bite (about 10 minutes for fresh, 12 minutes for frozen, or 25 minutes for dry; or time according to package directions). Stir in cabbage during last 5 minutes of cooking. Serve with cheese to add to taste. Makes 4 to 6 servings.

Per serving: 473 calories, 20 g protein, 33 g carbohydrates, 28 g total fat, 90 mg cholesterol, 1,945 mg sodium

Tortellini Soup

Preparation time: About 25 minutes

Cooking time: About 15 minutes

Tortellini in brodo, the familiar Italian first-course soup, is transformed into a sturdy main dish when you add chicken, fresh spinach, red bell pepper, mushrooms, and rice.

    About 12 ounces spinach, rinsed well
3 **large cans (49½ oz. each) regular-strength chicken broth**
1 **package (9 oz.) fresh cheese-filled spinach tortellini**
1 **whole chicken breast (about 1 lb.), skinned, boned, and cut into ½-inch pieces**
8 **ounces mushrooms, sliced**
1 **medium-size red bell pepper (about 5 oz.), seeded and finely chopped**
1 **cup cooked rice**
2 **teaspoons dry tarragon**
    Salt and freshly ground pepper
    Grated Parmesan cheese

Pat spinach dry. Remove and discard stems; chop leaves coarsely and set aside.

In an 8- to 10-quart pan, bring broth to a boil over high heat. Add tortellini, return to a gentle boil, and cook, uncovered, just until tender to bite (4 to 6 minutes; or time according to package directions). Add spinach, chicken, mushrooms, bell pepper, rice, and tarragon. Return to a boil, then reduce heat so soup simmers. Cover and simmer until chicken is no longer pink in center; cut to test (about 2 minutes). Season to taste with salt and pepper. Serve with cheese to add to taste. Makes 10 to 12 servings.

Per serving: 180 calories, 15 g protein, 20 g carbohydrates, 5 g total fat, 27 mg cholesterol, 1,826 mg sodium

Chicken-Noodle Yogurt Soup

Preparation time: About 15 minutes

Cooking time: 30 to 35 minutes

A great warm-up on chilly days, this sprightly soup gets its pleasantly tart flavor from lowfat yogurt. Before stirring the yogurt into the soup, blend it with a little cornstarch to keep it from separating.

1 **tablespoon salad oil**
1 **large onion, finely chopped**
1 **teaspoon dry thyme leaves**
¼ **teaspoon each pepper and dry dill weed**
3 **cloves garlic, minced or pressed**
4 **or 5 parsley sprigs**
3 **small carrots (about 5 oz. total), thinly sliced**
2 **quarts regular-strength chicken broth**
4 **ounces dry medium-wide egg noodles**
2 **cups cubed cooked chicken or turkey**
1 **cup plain lowfat yogurt**
1 **tablespoon cornstarch**
6 **green onions (including tops), thinly sliced**

Heat oil in a 5- to 6-quart pan over medium heat; add chopped onion, thyme, pepper, and dill weed. Cook, stirring often, until onion is soft (6 to 8 minutes). Stir in garlic; then add parsley, carrots, and broth and bring to a boil. Reduce heat, cover, and boil gently until carrots are tender to bite (12 to 15 minutes).

Remove and discard parsley; increase heat to high and add noodles. Cook, uncovered, until noodles are just tender to bite (8 to 10 minutes; or time according to package directions). Add chicken.

In a medium-size bowl, smoothly blend yogurt and cornstarch. Gradually blend in about 1 cup of the hot broth mixture; then stir broth-yogurt mixture back into soup and bring to a boil, stirring. Garnish with green onions. Makes 6 servings.

Per serving: 282 calories, 22 g protein, 26 g carbohydrates, 10 g total fat, 62 mg cholesterol, 1,417 mg sodium

■ *To Microwave:* In a 4- to 5-quart microwave-safe casserole or tureen, mix oil, chopped onion, thyme, pepper, dill weed, and garlic. Microwave, covered, on **HIGH (100%)** for 6 to 8 minutes or until onion is soft, stirring twice. Stir in parsley, carrots, and ½ cup of the broth. Microwave, covered, on **HIGH (100%)** for 4 to 5 minutes or until carrots are almost tender when pierced. Remove and discard parsley; add remaining 7½ cups broth and noodles. Microwave, covered, on **HIGH (100%)** for 20 to 25 minutes or until noodles are almost tender to bite, stirring twice.

In a medium-size bowl, smoothly blend yogurt and cornstarch. Blend in 1 cup of the hot broth; stir broth-yogurt mixture and chicken into soup. Microwave, covered, on **HIGH (100%)** for 3 minutes. Let stand, covered, for 2 minutes. Stir well before serving; garnish with green onions.

Fresh Pea & Pasta Broth

Preparation time: About 10 minutes

Cooking time: About 10 minutes

Crunchy emerald sugar snap peas share the spotlight with slender strands of capellini in this light soup. Star anise and ginger flavor the broth.

  4 ounces sugar snap peas or Chinese pea pods (also called snow or sugar peas), ends and strings removed
  1 large can (49½ oz.) regular-strength chicken broth
  2 whole star anise; or ¼ teaspoon crushed anise seeds and 2 cinnamon sticks (*each 2 inches long*)
  ¾ teaspoon grated fresh ginger
  1 ounce dry thin pasta, such as capellini or coil vermicelli

Cut peas diagonally into ¼- to ½-inch-wide slices. Set aside.

In a 4- to 5-quart pan, combine broth, star anise, and ginger. Bring to a boil over high heat. Add pasta; return to a boil and cook, uncovered, just until pasta is tender to bite (about 3 minutes; or time according to package directions). Add peas; return to a boil. Remove whole spices, then serve soup immediately. Makes 6 servings.

Per serving: 61 calories, 3 g protein, 8 g carbohydrates, 2 g total fat, 0 mg cholesterol, 1,036 mg sodium

■ ***To Microwave:*** Cut peas as directed. In a 4-quart microwave-safe casserole or tureen, combine broth, star anise, and ginger. Microwave, covered, on **HIGH (100%)** for 12 to 15 minutes or until mixture comes to a boil. Add pasta; microwave, covered, on **HIGH (100%)** for 4 to 6 minutes or until pasta is almost tender to bite, stirring once. Add peas; microwave, covered, on **HIGH (100%)** for 2 minutes. Let stand, covered, for 2 minutes.

Winter Green Minestrone

Preparation time: About 30 minutes

Cooking time: About 2½ hours

Mustard greens and kale or cabbage add freshness to a classic supper. To preserve the greens' bright color and brisk flavor, stir the sliced leaves into the pot just minutes before serving.

  3 quarts water
  3 pounds smoked ham hocks or shanks
  1 pound thin-skinned potatoes
     Chicken bouillon cubes (optional)
  ½ cup dry elbow macaroni or anelli
  4 to 5 ounces mustard greens, rinsed well and drained
  5 to 6 ounces green or red kale or green, Savoy, or napa cabbage, rinsed well and drained
  1 package (10 oz.) or 2 cups frozen tiny peas
     Salt and pepper
     Grated Parmesan cheese

In an 8- to 10-quart pan, combine water and ham hocks. Bring to a boil over high heat. Reduce heat, cover, and simmer until meat is tender when pierced (about 2 hours). Then lift out ham hocks and let stand until cool enough to handle. Pull meat from bones in bite-size shreds; discard skin, fat, and bones. Return meat to broth. (At this point, you may let cool, then cover and refrigerate for up to 2 days.)

Skim and discard fat from broth, then return broth to a boil over high heat. Meanwhile, scrub potatoes well; cut into ½-inch cubes. Taste broth; if desired, add bouillon cubes to enrich flavor. Add potatoes and macaroni to broth. Reduce heat, cover, and boil gently until potatoes are tender when pierced (10 to 15 minutes).

Meanwhile, cut mustard greens crosswise into ½-inch strips to make about 3 cups. Cut off and discard coarse stems from kale; cut leaves into shreds to make 1 quart. Add greens and peas to soup; then increase heat to medium-high and boil, uncovered, just until greens are wilted (2 to 3 minutes). Season to taste with salt and pepper. Serve with cheese to add to taste. Makes 6 to 8 servings.

Per serving: 208 calories, 13 g protein, 26 g carbohydrates, 6 g total fat, 28 mg cholesterol, 708 mg sodium

Pictured on facing page

White Bean, Pasta & Sausage Soup

Preparation time: 10 to 15 minutes

Cooking time: 2 ¼ to 2 ¾ hours

Thick with beans and shell-shaped pasta, this hearty soup makes a comforting supper dish. Serve with warm, crusty bread and a dessert of cheese and fresh fruit.

   1½   **cups (about 8 oz.) dried Great Northern or small white beans**
     8   **ounces spicy Italian sausages**
     1   **large onion, chopped**
     3   **cloves garlic, minced or pressed**
     1   **large carrot (about 3 oz.), finely chopped**
     2   **tablespoons dried currants**
     1   **teaspoon dry basil**
   1½   **quarts regular-strength chicken broth**
     3   **cups water**
     1   **can (14½ oz.) pear-shaped tomatoes**
     1   **cup (about 3 oz.) dry large shell-shaped pasta**
         Grated Parmesan cheese

Sort beans and discard any debris; rinse well and drain. Set beans aside.

Remove and discard casings from sausages, then crumble meat in large chunks into a 5- to 6-quart pan. Cook over high heat, stirring occasionally, until lightly browned (3 to 5 minutes). Discard all but 2 tablespoons of the fat. Add onion, garlic, and carrot; cook, stirring often, until onion begins to soften (2 to 3 minutes). Stir in beans, currants, basil, broth, and water. Bring to a boil; reduce heat, cover, and boil gently until beans are tender to bite (2 to 2½ hours).

Add tomatoes (break up with a spoon) and their liquid, then stir in pasta. Return to a boil; cover and boil gently until pasta is just tender to bite (about 12 minutes; or time according to package directions). Skim off and discard fat from soup. Serve soup with cheese to add to taste. Makes 4 to 6 servings.

Per serving: 448 calories, 23 g protein, 55 g carbohydrates, 16 g total fat, 30 mg cholesterol, 1,684 mg sodium

Pistou Soup with Sausage

Preparation time: About 35 minutes

Cooking time: About 1 hour and 20 minutes

This substantial whole-meal soup takes its name from *pistou*, a colorful Niçoise variation on pesto. You blend garlic, tomato paste, cheese, parsley, basil, and olive oil, then stir the pungent mixture into the soup as seasoning.

     1   **pound leeks**
     8   **ounces linguisa sausages, cut into ½-inch-thick slices**
     1   **cup chopped carrots**
     ½   **cup dried split peas**
   1½   **cups diced thin-skinned potatoes**
   1½   **quarts** *each* **regular-strength chicken broth and water**
         Pistou (recipe follows)
     8   **ounces green beans, cut into 1-inch lengths**
     3   **ounces dry spaghetti, broken into 2-inch pieces**

Cut off and discard all but 3 inches of green tops from leeks. Split leeks lengthwise and rinse well, then thinly slice crosswise. Set aside.

In a 6- to 8-quart pan, brown sausages over medium-high heat, stirring often. Discard all but 1 tablespoon of the fat. Add leeks and carrots; cook, stirring occasionally, until leeks are soft (about 8 minutes). Meanwhile, sort peas and discard any debris; rinse well and drain. To sausage-vegetable mixture, add peas, potatoes, broth, and water. Bring to a boil; reduce heat, cover, and boil gently until peas are soft to bite (about 1 hour). Meanwhile, prepare Pistou and set aside.

Add Pistou, beans, and spaghetti to soup. Increase heat to medium-high, bring to a boil, and boil until spaghetti is just tender to bite (6 to 8 minutes; or time according to package directions). Makes 8 servings.

Pistou. Combine 4 cloves **garlic** (minced or pressed), 1 can (6 oz.) **tomato paste,** ¾ cup grated **Parmesan cheese,** ¼ cup minced **parsley,** 1½ tablespoons **dry basil,** and ⅓ cup **olive oil.** Mix until well blended.

Per serving: 393 calories, 16 g protein, 35 g carbohydrates, 22 g total fat, 27 mg cholesterol, 1,285 mg sodium

Plump pasta shells (conchiglie) mingle with vegetables and spicy sausage in hearty White Bean, Pasta & Sausage Soup (recipe on facing page). Balance the soup's richness with a dessert of seasonal fresh fruit.

Pinto Bean
& Pasta Soup

Preparation time: About 15 minutes

Cooking time: About 2½ hours

One of the most traditional of Italian soups is *pasta e fagioli*—pasta and beans cooked together in a thick, hearty broth. Smoky with bits of bacon, this version uses dried pinto beans or fresh red-and-white speckled cranberry beans.

8 ounces (about 1¼ cups) dried pinto beans; or 2½ cups fresh-shelled cranberry beans (2½ lbs. unshelled)
1 pound sliced bacon, cut into 1-inch pieces
1 large onion, coarsely chopped
3 stalks celery, cut into ½-inch-thick slices
6 cloves garlic, minced or pressed
2 teaspoons dry oregano leaves
2 quarts water
1 can (14½ oz. to 1 lb.) tomatoes
2 ounces dry fettuccine, broken into 2-inch pieces
Salt and pepper
Freshly grated Parmesan cheese

If using dried beans, sort beans and discard any debris; rinse well and drain. Set beans aside.

In a 5- to 6-quart pan, cook bacon over medium-low heat until crisp, stirring often. Lift out, drain, crumble, and set aside. Discard all but ¼ cup of the drippings.

To reserved drippings, add onion, celery, garlic, and oregano. Cook, stirring, for 5 minutes. Add dried or fresh-shelled beans and water. Increase heat to high and bring to a boil; reduce heat, cover, and boil gently until beans are tender to bite (about 2 hours for dried beans, 45 minutes to 1 hour for fresh-shelled beans).

Add tomatoes (break up with a spoon) and their liquid. Stir in fettuccine, cover, and boil gently, stirring occasionally, just until tender to bite (8 to 10 minutes; or time according to package directions). Season to taste with salt and pepper. Serve with bacon and cheese to add to taste. Makes 6 to 8 servings.

Per serving: 328 calories, 14 g protein, 33 g carbohydrates, 16 g total fat, 28 mg cholesterol, 452 mg sodium

Red Bean
& Lamb Soup

Preparation time: About 20 minutes

Cooking time: About 3½ hours

Rice-shaped pasta or *orzo* (similar shapes are called *riso* and *seme di melone*) lends substance to this full-meal soup. You'll detect Greek influences in the flavors of mint, rosemary, cinnamon, and lemon—and in the garnish of crumbled feta cheese.

8 ounces (about 1¼ cups) dried red kidney beans, pinto beans, or pink beans
¼ cup salad oil
4 lamb shanks (about 4 lbs. *total*), cracked
2 medium-size onions, chopped
½ cup finely chopped fresh mint or 2 tablespoons dry mint
½ teaspoon *each* dry rosemary and ground cinnamon
2 quarts water
⅓ cup (about 2 oz.) dry rice-shaped pasta
2 tablespoons tomato paste
4 cloves garlic, minced or pressed
3 tablespoons lemon juice
Salt and pepper
4 ounces feta cheese, crumbled into ½-inch pieces
Lemon wedges

Sort beans and discard any debris; rinse well and drain. Set beans aside.

Heat 2 tablespoons of the oil in a 6- to 8-quart pan over medium heat. Add lamb shanks and brown evenly on all sides (about 20 minutes). Lift lamb from pan; add remaining 2 tablespoons oil, onions, mint, rosemary, and cinnamon. Cook for 5 minutes, stirring often.

Return lamb to pan; add beans and water. Bring to a boil. Reduce heat, cover, and boil gently until meat is very tender and pulls easily from bones (about 3 hours).

Skim and discard fat from soup, then stir in pasta, tomato paste, garlic, and lemon juice. Cover and continue to cook until pasta is tender to bite (about 10 minutes; or time according to package directions). Season to taste with salt and pepper. Serve with cheese and lemon wedges to season soup to taste. Makes 6 to 8 servings.

Per serving: 490 calories, 48 g protein, 30 g carbohydrates, 19 g total fat, 129 mg cholesterol, 337 mg sodium

Mediterranean Pasta Soup

Preparation time: About 20 minutes

Cooking time: About 2½ hours

It all adds up to mealtime satisfaction in wintery weather: *tripolini* (tiny ruffled bow ties) combined with small white beans, vegetables, and just enough crumbled Italian sausage to lend a mildly spicy flavor. Sprinkle chopped tomato and shredded Swiss cheese atop each serving to taste.

- ½ cup (about 3½ oz.) dried small white beans
- 4 ounces mild Italian sausages
- 1 small onion, finely chopped
- 2 cloves garlic, minced or pressed
- 1½ teaspoons dry thyme leaves
- ¼ teaspoon pepper
- 3 quarts regular-strength chicken broth
- 1 teaspoon grated lemon peel
- 2 small carrots (about 3 oz. *total*), cut lengthwise into quarters, then thinly sliced crosswise
- 2 stalks celery, finely chopped
- 1 cup (about 4½ oz.) dry tripolini or small shell-shaped pasta
- 1 small tomato (about 4 oz.), cut into ½-inch cubes (optional)
- 1 cup (4 oz.) shredded Swiss cheese (optional)

Sort beans and discard any debris; rinse well and drain. Set beans aside.

Remove and discard casings from sausages, then crumble meat into a 4- to 5-quart pan. Cook over medium heat, stirring often, until lightly browned (about 4 minutes). Add onion, garlic, thyme, and pepper; cook, stirring occasionally, until onion begins to brown (about 5 minutes). Add beans, broth, and lemon peel. Increase heat to high and bring to a boil. Reduce heat, cover, and boil gently until beans are tender to bite (about 2 hours).

Add carrots, celery, and pasta. Increase heat to high and bring to a boil. Cover, reduce heat, and boil gently until carrots and pasta are just tender to bite (8 to 10 minutes; or time according to package directions).

Ladle soup into bowls. Offer tomato and cheese, if desired, to sprinkle over soup to taste. Makes 6 to 8 servings.

Per serving: 243 calories, 12 g protein, 30 g carbohydrates, 9 g total fat, 12 mg cholesterol, 1,859 mg sodium

Hoppin' John Soup

Preparation time: About 30 minutes

Cooking time: About 3 hours and 20 minutes

Named for a traditional Southern dish, this soup features black-eyed peas and greens along with tiny soup pasta such as stars (*stelline* or *stellette*) or circles (*occhi di pernice*—"partridge eyes").

- 8 ounces (about 1¼ cups) dried black-eyed peas or baby lima beans
- 3 tablespoons salad oil
- 1 pound *each* turnips and carrots, diced
- 1 medium-size red bell pepper (about 5 oz.), seeded and chopped
- ½ to 1 teaspoon crushed dried hot red chiles
  About 2 pounds smoked ham hocks or shanks
- 2 quarts water
- ⅓ cup (about 2 oz.) dry tiny star- or circle-shaped pasta
- 8 ounces mustard greens, rinsed well and drained

Sort peas and discard any debris; rinse well and drain. Set peas aside.

Heat oil in a 6- to 8-quart pan over medium heat. Add turnips, carrots, bell pepper, and chiles; cook for 5 minutes, stirring often. Add ham hocks, peas, and water. Increase heat to high and bring to a boil. Reduce heat, cover, and boil gently until meat is very tender and pulls easily from bones (about 3 hours).

Skim and discard fat from soup, then stir in pasta. Cover and cook until pasta is tender to bite (about 10 minutes; or time according to package directions). Meanwhile, chop greens; stir into soup just before serving. Makes 6 to 8 servings.

Per serving: 307 calories, 17 g protein, 39 g carbohydrates, 10 g total fat, 18 mg cholesterol, 507 mg sodium

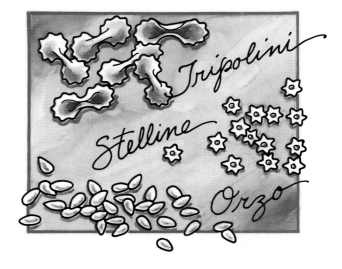

Sizzling and smoky from the barbecue, hot chicken is a delicious foil for cool vegetables and gemelli (pasta twists). Serve Grilled Chicken & Pasta Primavera (recipe on facing page) on a spring evening, accompanied with warm corn sticks and iced tea.

Salads

*V*ersatile and adaptable, salads based on pasta range from elegant first courses such as Stir-fried Asparagus & Scallops on Cool Pasta to casual potluck contributions like Antipasto Pasta Salad. You can serve them at room temperature or cold, and some—Hot Pasta & Tuna Salad, for example—are even brought forth steaming hot.

Virtually any size or shape of pasta can slip temptingly into a salad; choices in this chapter include plump tortellini, svelte vermicelli, and engaging little corkscrews. We've even concocted a memorable salad with won ton wrappers—they're cut into strips, baked until crisp, and topped with fresh spinach and chicken in a sesame dressing.

Pictured on facing page

Grilled Chicken & Pasta Primavera Salad

Preparation time: About 25 minutes

Cooking time: About 30 minutes

You'll enjoy the tantalizing hot and cold contrasts of this colorful salad, a good choice for a warm-weather main dish.

Balsamic Dressing (page 458)

8 ounces dry gemelli or other bite-size pasta twists or spirals

½ cup frozen peas, thawed

¼ cup thinly sliced green onions (including tops)

2 whole chicken breasts (about 1 lb. *each*), skinned, boned, and split

2 medium-size carrots (about 4 oz. *total*), thinly sliced

12 ounces asparagus, tough ends snapped off, spears cut into ½-inch-long pieces (keep stems and tips separate)

4 ounces mushrooms, thinly sliced

Red oak leaf lettuce leaves or small inner red leaf lettuce leaves, washed and crisped

Slivered green onions (including tops)

Prepare Balsamic Dressing and set aside.

In a 5- to 6-quart pan, cook pasta in 3 quarts boiling water just until tender to bite (8 to 10 minutes); or cook according to package directions. Drain, rinse with cold water, and drain well again. Place pasta in a large bowl and lightly mix in peas, sliced onions, and ½ cup of the dressing. Set aside.

Rinse chicken and pat dry, then brush on all sides with some of the remaining dressing. Place on

457

a greased grill 4 to 6 inches above a solid bed of medium-hot coals. Cook, brushing with remaining dressing and turning once, until meat in thickest part is no longer pink; cut to test (18 to 20 minutes *total*).

Meanwhile, in a medium-size pan, bring 2 cups of water to a boil over high heat. Add carrots. Return water to a boil, then add asparagus stems; return to a boil again and add asparagus tips. Return water to a boil a third time and boil vegetables for 1 minute; then drain, rinse with cold water, and drain well again. Lightly mix blanched vegetables and mushrooms into pasta mixture.

Line 4 dinner plates with lettuce. Divide pasta mixture among plates; garnish with slivered onions. Slice each chicken breast half crosswise into ½-inch-wide strips, cutting on a slight diagonal. Arrange hot chicken attractively to one side of pasta salad on each plate; serve at once. Makes 4 servings.

Balsamic Dressing. Combine 3 tablespoons **balsamic vinegar,** 1 large clove **garlic** (minced or pressed), ½ teaspoon **crushed dried hot red chiles,** 2 tablespoons grated **Parmesan cheese,** and ½ cup **olive oil.** Mix until well blended; season to taste with **salt,** if desired, and freshly ground **pepper.**

Per serving: 670 calories, 46 g protein, 52 g carbohydrates, 31 g total fat, 88 mg cholesterol, 176 mg sodium

Crisp Won Ton Salad

Preparation time: About 35 minutes

Baking time: About 6 minutes

Cooking time: About 20 minutes

Ready-made won ton wrappers—sliced, buttered, and baked—make a crisp bed for this hot main-dish salad of stir-fried vegetables and chicken with fresh spinach.

Gemelli

Crisp Won Ton Strips (recipe follows)
Sesame-Lemon Dressing (recipe on facing page)

- 12 ounces spinach, rinsed well
- 5 teaspoons salad oil
- 1 small onion, thinly sliced
- ½ cup thinly sliced celery
- 1 large carrot (about 3 oz.), cut into 1-inch-long matchstick pieces
- 1 tablespoon finely chopped fresh ginger
- 2 tablespoons water
- 1 whole chicken breast (about 1 lb.), skinned, boned, and cut into ¼-inch-thick bite-size strips
- 1 can (about 5 oz.) sliced water chestnuts, drained
- ½ cup salted roasted peanuts
- ½ cup thinly sliced green onions (including tops)

Prepare Crisp Won Ton Strips and Sesame-Lemon Dressing; set aside. Pat spinach dry. Remove and discard stems; cover and refrigerate leaves while preparing salad.

Place a wide frying pan or wok over medium heat. When pan is hot, add 2 teaspoons of the oil, then the sliced small onion; cook, stirring occasionally, until onion is pale golden (2 to 3 minutes). Add celery, carrot, ginger, and water; cover and cook, stirring occasionally, until carrot is tender-crisp to bite (3 to 4 minutes). Transfer the vegetable mixture to a bowl and set aside.

Add 2 teaspoons more oil to pan and increase heat to high. Add half the chicken strips. Cook until browned on bottom, then stir-fry until meat is opaque throughout; cut to test (about 3 minutes). Add chicken to vegetables. Heat remaining 1 teaspoon oil in pan; add remaining chicken and cook as just directed. Then pour chicken-vegetable mixture from bowl back into pan; add water chestnuts, peanuts, and 3 tablespoons of the dressing. Stir-fry until hot (about 3 minutes).

Divide spinach among 4 or 5 dinner plates; top with Crisp Won Ton Strips. Spoon hot chicken mixture over won tons; sprinkle with green onions. Offer remaining dressing to add to salad to taste. Makes 5 servings.

Crisp Won Ton Strips. Cut 1 package (7 oz.; or use half of a 14-oz. package) **won ton wrappers** into ½-inch-wide strips. Melt about 1 tablespoon **butter** or margarine. Brush a baking sheet lightly with some of the melted butter; arrange won ton strips close together in a single layer on baking sheet, then brush lightly with a little more butter.

Bake, uncovered, in a 375° oven until light golden (about 6 minutes). Pour onto a rack to cool. Repeat to bake remaining strips. If made ahead, package cooled strips airtight and store at room temperature for up to 2 days.

Per serving of salad (without dressing): 373 calories, 24 g protein, 38 g carbohydrates, 15 g total fat, 40 mg cholesterol, 263 mg sodium

Sesame-Lemon Dressing. Combine ½ cup **seasoned rice vinegar** (or ½ cup rice vinegar or white wine vinegar mixed with 1½ teaspoons sugar); 2 tablespoons *each* **soy sauce** and **Oriental sesame oil;** 1 tablespoon **lemon juice;** and ⅛ teaspoon **chili oil** or ground red pepper (cayenne). Mix until well blended. Makes about ¾ cup.

Per tablespoon of dressing: 25 calories, 0.2 g protein, 1 g carbohydrates, 2 g total fat, 0 mg cholesterol, 172 mg sodium

Hot Pasta & Tuna Salad

Preparation time: About 15 minutes

Cooking time: About 15 minutes

Ripe olives, roasted peppers, and a chile-caper dressing brighten this hot main-dish salad. Use oil- or water-packed tuna, as you prefer.

    Chile Dressing (recipe follows)
 12 ounces dry large shell-shaped pasta
  1 tablespoon olive oil
  1 jar (7 oz.) roasted red peppers, drained and cut into thin strips
 ⅓ cup finely chopped parsley
  1 can (3½ oz.) pitted ripe olives, drained
  1 large can (12½ oz.) chunk-style tuna, drained
    Salt and freshly ground pepper

Prepare Chile Dressing and set aside.

In a 5- to 6-quart pan, cook pasta in 3 quarts boiling water just until tender to bite (about 12 minutes); or cook according to package directions. Drain well and set aside.

While pasta is cooking, heat oil in a wide frying pan over medium-high heat. Add roasted peppers, parsley, olives, and tuna. Stir gently until hot (about 2 minutes). Mix in half the dressing.

In a large bowl, lightly mix pasta and remaining dressing. Add tuna mixture; lift with 2 spoons to mix gently. Season to taste with salt and pepper. Makes 6 servings.

Chile Dressing. Combine ⅓ cup **olive oil,** 3 tablespoons **wine vinegar,** 2 tablespoons drained **capers,** ½ teaspoon **crushed dried hot red chiles,** and 2 cloves **garlic** (minced or pressed). Mix well.

Per serving: 446 calories, 23 g protein, 46 g carbohydrates, 19 g total fat, 22 mg cholesterol, 397 mg sodium

Stir-fried Asparagus & Scallops on Cool Pasta

Preparation time: 10 minutes

Cooking time: 10 to 15 minutes

For an elegant first course, top thin pasta strands with a refreshing combination of scallops and sliced asparagus in a light rice vinegar dressing.

  8 ounces dry capellini or coil vermicelli
  8 ounces bay scallops or sea scallops, rinsed and drained
  3 tablespoons salad oil
  1 pound asparagus, tough ends snapped off, spears cut diagonally into ¼-inch-thick, 1½- to 2-inch-long slices
  3 tablespoons water
  1 clove garlic, minced or pressed
  1 tablespoon minced fresh ginger
 ½ cup rice vinegar; or ½ cup white wine vinegar mixed with 1 teaspoon sugar
  2 tablespoons sugar
  1 teaspoon *each* soy sauce and Oriental sesame oil

In a 5- to 6-quart pan, cook capellini in 3 quarts boiling water just until barely tender to bite (about 3 minutes); or cook according to package directions. Drain, rinse with cold water, and drain well again. Place in a shallow dish. If using sea scallops, cut scallops into ½-inch pieces. Set aside.

Place a wok or wide frying pan over high heat. Add 1 tablespoon of the salad oil, then asparagus; stir to coat with oil. Add 3 tablespoons water; cover and cook just until asparagus is tender-crisp to bite (2 to 3 minutes). Lift out asparagus and spoon over pasta.

Add remaining 2 tablespoons salad oil, garlic, ginger, and scallops to pan. Cook, stirring, until scallops are opaque throughout; cut to test (2 to 3 minutes). Add vinegar, sugar, soy, and sesame oil; cook, stirring, just until sugar is dissolved. Pour over pasta mixture. If made ahead, cover and refrigerate for up to 4 hours. Makes 4 to 6 servings.

Per serving: 326 calories, 15 g protein, 44 g carbohydrates, 10 g total fat, 15 mg cholesterol, 144 mg sodium

Pictured on facing page

Tortellini, Shrimp & Pesto Salad

Preparation time: About 15 minutes

Cooking time: 5 to 20 minutes

Chilling time: At least 1 hour

Here's a salad that's perfect for picnics and potlucks. You can make it the night before, then refrigerate it to let the flavors blend. Both fresh and dry tortellini work well in this recipe.

Pesto Dressing (recipe follows)
1 package (9 oz.) fresh tortellini or 1 package (7 or 8 oz.) dry tortellini
1 medium-size red bell pepper (about 5 oz.), seeded and cut into thin bite-size strips
6 ounces tiny cooked and shelled shrimp

Prepare Pesto Dressing and set aside.

In a 4- to 5-quart pan, cook tortellini in 3 quarts boiling water just until tender to bite (4 to 6 minutes for fresh tortellini, 15 to 20 minutes for dry); or cook according to package directions. Drain, rinse with cold water, and drain well again.

In a large bowl, lightly mix the tortellini, Pesto Dressing, bell pepper strips, and shrimp. Cover mixture and refrigerate for at least 1 hour or up to 8 hours. Makes 4 servings.

Pesto Dressing. In a blender or food processor, combine 1 cup lightly packed **fresh basil leaves** (or ¾ cup fresh parsley leaves and 2 tablespoons dry basil); 1 large clove **garlic,** coarsely chopped; ½ cup grated **Parmesan cheese;** 2½ tablespoons **red wine vinegar;** and ½ cup **olive oil.** Whirl until puréed.

Per serving: 538 calories, 24 g protein, 35 g carbohydrates, 34 g total fat, 126 mg cholesterol, 569 mg sodium

Antipasto Pasta Salad

Preparation time: About 30 minutes

Cooking time: About 40 minutes

The brightly colored ingredients of an Italian appetizer—fresh vegetables, shiny black olives, prosciutto, and Parmesan cheese—join pasta spirals in a raspberry vinaigrette.

Cooked Artichoke Hearts (recipe follows) or 1 can (8½ oz.) artichoke hearts packed in water, drained
10 ounces dry bite-size pasta twists or spirals such as rotelle or fusilli
Raspberry Vinaigrette (recipe follows)
3 cups broccoli flowerets
1 cup pitted ripe olives
4 ounces mushrooms, thinly sliced
1 cup quartered cherry tomatoes
2 ounces prosciutto or cooked ham, cut into thin bite-size strips
1 cup (about 5 oz.) finely shredded Asiago or Parmesan cheese

If using fresh artichokes, prepare Cooked Artichoke Hearts and set aside.

In a 5- to 6-quart pan, cook pasta in 3 quarts boiling water just until tender to bite (12 to 15 minutes); or cook according to package directions. Drain, rinse with cold water, and drain well again. While pasta is cooking, prepare Raspberry Vinaigrette and set aside.

Steam broccoli, covered, on a rack over 1 inch of boiling water until barely tender when pierced (about 5 minutes). Rinse with cold water and drain well.

In a large bowl, combine pasta, broccoli, artichokes, olives, mushrooms, tomatoes, prosciutto, cheese, and Raspberry Vinaigrette; mix lightly. If made ahead, cover and refrigerate for up to 8 hours. Makes 8 to 10 servings.

Cooked Artichoke Hearts. Break tough outer leaves from 10 small **artichokes** (*each* about 2 inches in diameter), leaving only the pale, edible inner leaves. Trim and discard thorny tips of leaves; peel bases of artichokes. In a large pan, cook artichokes, uncovered, in 2 quarts **boiling water** until tender when pierced (about 20 minutes). Drain well; when cool enough to handle, cut into quarters.

Raspberry Vinaigrette. Combine ½ cup **raspberry vinegar,** ⅔ cup **olive oil,** 1½ teaspoons **dry basil,** and ¼ teaspoon **pepper.** Mix until well blended.

Per serving: 391 calories, 14 g protein, 31 g carbohydrates, 24 g total fat, 14 mg cholesterol, 484 mg sodium

*Make the most of summer's abundance of fragrant fresh
basil—whirl it into an aromatic dressing for easy
Tortellini, Shrimp & Pesto Salad (recipe on facing page).
Tote the salad along to your next picnic; it's great for
dining al fresco.*

461

Penne with Tomato & Basil Mignonette

Preparation time: About 10 minutes

Cooking time: 15 to 20 minutes

Standing time: About 15 minutes

The sweet summer flavor of vine-ripened tomatoes permeates *al dente* pasta in this lean and refreshing red, white, and green salad.

- 2 **tablespoons pine nuts**
  Basil Mignonette Dressing (recipe follows)
- 8 **ounces dry penne or other small tube-shaped pasta, such as pennette or mostaccioli**
- 2 **large tomatoes (about 12 oz. *total*), seeded and chopped**
  Salt (optional)
  Fresh basil sprigs

Stir pine nuts in a small frying pan over medium-low heat until lightly browned (about 3 minutes). Set nuts aside. Prepare Basil Mignonette Dressing and set aside.

In a 5- to 6-quart pan, cook pasta in 3 quarts boiling water just until tender to bite (10 to 12 minutes); or cook according to package directions. Drain, rinse with cold water, and drain well again.

In a large bowl, lightly mix pasta, dressing, and tomatoes; season to taste with salt, if desired. Let stand at room temperature for about 15 minutes. Mix lightly; sprinkle with pine nuts and garnish with basil sprigs, then serve. Makes 4 to 6 servings.

Basil Mignonette Dressing. Combine ¼ cup **dry white wine;** 2 tablespoons *each* **lemon juice,** finely chopped **shallot,** and slivered **fresh basil leaves;** and ¼ teaspoon freshly ground **pepper.** Mix until well blended.

Per serving: 211 calories, 7 g protein, 39 g carbohydrates, 3 g total fat, 0 mg cholesterol, 9 mg sodium

Sesame Noodle Salad

Preparation time: About 30 minutes

Cooking time: About 15 minutes

Chilling time: At least 2 hours

Thin noodles flecked with sesame seeds and stir-fried vegetables make a good picnic accompaniment to cold roast chicken.

- **Sesame Seed Dressing (recipe on facing page)**
- 8 **medium-size fresh or dried shiitake mushrooms or large fresh regular mushrooms**
- 8 **ounces dry vermicelli (not coil vermicelli)**
- 3 **tablespoons salad oil**
- 2 **teaspoons minced fresh ginger**
- 4 **ounces green beans, cut diagonally into ¼-inch-thick slices**
- 2 **medium-size carrots (about 4 oz. *total*), cut into 1-inch-long matchstick pieces**
- 2 **medium-size crookneck squash (about 8 oz. *total*), cut into 1-inch-long matchstick pieces**
- 1 **tablespoon *each* soy sauce and dry sherry**
  Salt
- 2 **or 3 green onions, ends trimmed**

Prepare Sesame Seed Dressing and set aside.

If using dried mushrooms, soak in warm water to cover until soft and pliable (20 to 30 minutes). Cut off and discard stems; set caps aside. If using fresh mushrooms, set caps aside and cut stems into thin strips.

Meanwhile, in a 5- to 6-quart pan, cook vermicelli in 3 quarts boiling water just until tender to bite (8 to 10 minutes); or cook according to package directions. Drain, rinse with cold water, and drain well again. Transfer to a large bowl and set aside.

Heat 2 tablespoons of the oil in a wide frying pan over high heat. Add ginger, beans, carrots, squash, and slivered fresh mushroom stems. Stir-fry just until vegetables are barely tender-crisp to bite (1 to 1½ minutes). Lift vegetables from pan and add to vermicelli.

Reduce heat to medium. Add remaining 1 tablespoon oil, soy, sherry, and mushroom caps to pan. Cover pan if using dried mushrooms; leave uncovered if using fresh mushrooms. Cook, turning occasionally, until mushrooms have absorbed all liquid (about 2 minutes). Set aside.

Add Sesame Seed Dressing to vermicelli mixture, then mix lightly. Season to taste with salt. Cover and refrigerate, stirring occasionally, for at least 2 hours or until next day. Garnish with mushroom caps and whole green onions. Makes 4 to 6 servings.

Sesame Seed Dressing. Heat ¼ cup **salad oil** in a wide frying pan over medium-low heat. Add 3 tablespoons **sesame seeds** and cook, uncovered, until golden (about 2 minutes). Remove from heat and let cool slightly.

Combine ⅓ cup **sugar**, ½ cup **distilled white vinegar**, and 2 tablespoons **dry sherry**; stir until sugar is dissolved. Blend sesame-oil mixture into sugar mixture.

Per serving: 288 calories, 8 g protein, 45 g carbohydrates, 9 g total fat, 0 mg cholesterol, 218 mg sodium

Broccoli, Pasta & Bean Salad

Preparation time: About 10 minutes

Cooking time: About 15 minutes

A mustard-seasoned olive oil and red wine vinegar dressing brings together the flavors of pasta and vegetables in this simple salad.

- 1 **pound broccoli**
- 2 **cups (about 6 oz.) dry large shell-shaped pasta**
- ½ **cup olive oil**
- ¼ **cup red wine vinegar**
- 1 **tablespoon Dijon mustard**
- ½ **teaspoon dry basil**
- 1 **can (about 15 oz.) red kidney beans, drained and rinsed**
  Salt and pepper

Trim and discard tough ends from broccoli stalks. Thinly slice tender portion of stalks crosswise; cut tops into bite-size flowerets. Set all broccoli aside.

In a 5- to 6-quart pan, cook pasta in 3 quarts boiling water just until barely tender to bite (10 to 12 minutes); or cook according to package directions. Drop broccoli into boiling water and cook just until it turns bright green (1 to 2 minutes). Drain pasta and broccoli, rinse with cold water, and drain well again.

While pasta and broccoli are cooking, combine oil, vinegar, mustard, and basil in a large bowl. Mix until well blended, then add drained pasta, broccoli, and beans; mix gently. Season to taste with salt and pepper. If made ahead, cover and refrigerate for up to 2 hours. Makes 6 to 8 servings.

Per serving: 279 calories, 7 g protein, 28 g carbohydrates, 16 g total fat, 0 mg cholesterol, 300 mg sodium

Summertime Pasta Salad

Preparation time: About 25 minutes

Chilling time: At least 2 hours

Cooking time: 12 to 15 minutes

This salad is so flavorful you won't notice that it's made without oil. Pasta twists and an abundance of summer vegetables are accented with savory herbs and grated Parmesan cheese.

- 3 **small tomatoes (about 12 oz. *total*), peeled and chopped**
- 1 **cup *each* thinly sliced green onions (including tops), finely chopped celery, finely chopped green bell pepper, and diced zucchini**
- 2 **cloves garlic, minced or pressed**
- 3 **tablespoons white wine vinegar**
- 1 **tablespoon sugar**
- ⅓ **cup chopped fresh basil**
- 1 **teaspoon chopped fresh rosemary**
- ½ **to 1 teaspoon chopped fresh oregano**
  Salt and coarsely ground pepper
- 8 **ounces dry bite-size pasta twists or spirals such as rotelle or fusilli**
- ⅓ **to ⅔ cup grated Parmesan cheese**

In a large bowl, combine tomatoes, onions, celery, bell pepper, zucchini, garlic, vinegar, sugar, basil, and rosemary. Mix lightly, then season to taste with oregano, salt, and pepper; mix well. Cover and refrigerate for at least 2 hours or for up to 8 hours.

Shortly before serving, in a 5- to 6-quart pan, cook pasta in 3 quarts boiling water just until tender to bite (12 to 15 minutes); or cook according to package directions. Drain, rinse with cold water, and drain well again. Pour into a serving bowl or rimmed platter.

To serve, spoon tomato mixture over pasta; mix lightly with 2 forks, then sprinkle with 2 tablespoons of the cheese. Serve with remaining cheese to add to taste. Makes 8 servings.

Per serving: 161 calories, 7 g protein, 28 g carbohydrates, 2 g total fat, 5 mg cholesterol, 132 mg sodium

A quartet of flavorful vegetables tops fresh green pasta in
Parsley Pesto Grilled Vegetables & Spinach Fettuccine
(recipe on facing page). The pungent pesto doubles as a
baste for the vegetables and a sauce for the noodles.

Vegetables & Cheese

*L*iberal quantities of bright vegetables and sharp or mellow cheeses are favorite additions to pasta of all sorts, in dishes that can enliven your menus throughout the year. Fascinating first courses, substantial main dishes, winning side dishes—you'll find them all among the appealing choices in this chapter. Pasta and vegetable lovers will applaud our updated lasagne (it's meatless), plump tortellini in a creamy sauce thick with mushrooms, and a fresh new version of popular pasta primavera.

For some novel ways with pesto, see page 471; we show you how to make the famous sauce with a variety of herbs and greens. And for a taste of trompe l'oeil, have a look at the ingenious ways vegetables can masquerade as pasta (page 482).

Pictured on facing page

Parsley Pesto Grilled Vegetables & Spinach Fettuccine

Preparation time: About 10 minutes

Cooking time: About 15 minutes

For a colorful vegetarian meal from the barbecue, arrange savory grilled vegetables over a mound of tender green fettuccine. If you'd like to add meat, serve juicy Italian sausages as an accompaniment; put them on the grill before you add the first vegetables.

Parsley Pesto (page 466)
4 small zucchini (10 to 12 oz. *total*)
2 small Japanese eggplants (about 8 oz. *total*), halved lengthwise
4 small pear-shaped (Roma-type) tomatoes (about 6 oz. *total*), halved lengthwise
1 medium-size red onion, unpeeled, quartered
1 package (9 oz.) fresh green fettuccine
½ cup whipping cream
⅓ to ½ cup grated Parmesan cheese

Prepare Parsley Pesto; set aside.

Cutting toward stem end, slice each zucchini lengthwise into thin strips, leaving strips attached at stem so they can be fanned out. Brush cut surfaces of zucchini, eggplants, tomatoes, and onion with some of the pesto.

Place vegetables, cut sides down, on a greased grill 4 to 6 inches above a bed of medium-hot coals. Cook until vegetables are just tender when pierced (about 3 minutes for tomatoes, 4 to 5 minutes for zucchini, and 8 to 10 minutes for eggplant and onion). As each vegetable is cooked, remove it from grill and keep warm.

In a 5- to 6-quart pan, cook fettuccine in 3 quarts boiling water just until tender to bite (3 to 4 minutes); or cook according to package directions. Drain well.

In a wide frying pan, combine cream and remaining Parsley Pesto; bring to a boil over high heat. Remove from heat; quickly add pasta and mix lightly, using 2 spoons. Divide among 4 dinner plates. Arrange vegetables over pasta, spreading zucchini into fans. Serve with cheese to add to taste. Makes 4 servings.

Parsley Pesto. In a food processor or blender, combine 1½ cups lightly packed **Italian (flat-leaf) parsley**, ¾ cup grated **Parmesan cheese,** ⅔ cup **olive oil,** and 3 cloves **garlic,** coarsely chopped; whirl until smoothly puréed. Season to taste with **salt** and freshly ground **pepper.**

Per serving: 756 calories, 22 g protein, 47 g carbohydrates, 55 g total fat, 124 mg cholesterol, 517 mg sodium

Vermicelli with Vegetable Sauce

Preparation time: 15 to 20 minutes

Cooking time: About 50 minutes

This slowly simmered, vegetable-rich red sauce is so filled with savory flavor that you'll never even miss the meat.

- 2 tablespoons olive oil or salad oil
- 1 medium-size onion, finely chopped
- 1 teaspoon *each* dry basil, dry tarragon, fennel seeds, and dry oregano leaves
- 1 clove garlic, minced or pressed
- 1 small zucchini (about 3 oz.), thinly sliced
- 4 ounces mushrooms, thinly sliced
- 1 small green bell pepper (about 4 oz.), seeded and finely chopped
- ½ cup dry red wine
- 1 pound (about 3 medium-size) tomatoes, peeled, seeded, and chopped
- 1 can (6 oz.) tomato paste
- 1 teaspoon sugar
  Salt and pepper
- 10 to 12 ounces dry vermicelli (not coil vermicelli) or spaghettini
- ½ to ¾ cup grated Parmesan cheese

Heat oil in a 3- to 3½-quart pan over medium heat. Add onion, basil, tarragon, fennel seeds, and oregano; cook, stirring often, until onion begins to soften (about 5 minutes). Stir in garlic, zucchini, mushrooms, and bell pepper. Cook, stirring often, until mushrooms begin to brown (8 to 10 minutes).

Add wine, tomatoes, tomato paste, and sugar. Increase heat to high and bring mixture to a boil; reduce heat, cover, and simmer until sauce is thick (about 35 minutes), stirring occasionally. Season to taste with salt and pepper.

When sauce is almost done, in a 5- to 6-quart pan, cook vermicelli in 3 quarts boiling water just until tender to bite (8 to 10 minutes); or cook according to package directions. Drain pasta well, then divide among 6 dinner plates and top with sauce. Serve with cheese to add to taste. Makes 6 servings.

Per serving: 330 calories, 13 g protein, 53 g carbohydrates, 8 g total fat, 7 mg cholesterol, 390 mg sodium

Seashells with Cauliflower Sauce

Preparation time: About 12 minutes

Cooking time: About 25 minutes

For a hearty winter main dish, stir cauliflower and little pasta seashells into a bright tomato-wine sauce; pass Parmesan cheese to sprinkle on top.

- ¼ cup olive oil
- ½ teaspoon dry thyme leaves
- 1 medium-size onion, thinly sliced
- 1 medium-size carrot (about 2 oz.), coarsely shredded
- 2 cloves garlic, minced or pressed
- 1 large can (28 oz.) pear-shaped tomatoes
- ½ cup dry white wine
- 8 ounces dry small shell-shaped pasta
- 2 cups coarsely chopped cauliflower
  Salt and freshly ground pepper
  Chopped parsley
- ⅓ to ½ cup grated Parmesan cheese

Heat oil in a wide frying pan over medium heat. Add thyme, onion, and carrot; cook, uncovered, stirring often, until onion is soft but not brown (about 5 minutes). Stir in garlic, tomatoes (break up with a spoon) and their liquid, and wine. Bring to a boil; reduce heat, cover, and boil gently for 10 minutes. Then uncover, increase heat to medium-high, and cook, stirring occasionally, until sauce is thick (about 10 minutes).

Meanwhile, in a 5- to 6-quart pan, cook pasta in 3 quarts boiling water just until tender to bite (10 to 12 minutes); or cook according to package directions. Drain well. While pasta is cooking, steam cauliflower, covered, on a rack over 1 inch of boiling water until barely tender when pierced (about 5 minutes); remove from heat and set aside.

Season sauce to taste with salt and pepper. Add pasta and cauliflower to sauce; mix lightly. Sprinkle with parsley. Serve with cheese to add to taste. Makes 4 servings.

Per serving: 440 calories, 14 g protein, 59 g carbohydrates, 17 g total fat, 7 mg cholesterol, 496 mg sodium

Straw & Hay in Tomato Cream

Preparation time: About 15 minutes

Cooking time: About 20 minutes

Known as *paglia e fieno* in Italian, this colorful dish combines thinly cut yellow and green pasta. Look for the pasta in your supermarket, in either the dry pasta section or the refrigerator case.

 1 tablespoon olive oil
 5 medium-size pear-shaped (Roma-type) tomatoes (10 to 12 oz. *total*), seeded and chopped
 1 clove garlic, minced or pressed
 2 tablespoons chopped fresh basil or 1 teaspoon dry basil
 ¼ teaspoon salt
 ⅛ teaspoon ground white pepper
 ½ cup dry white wine
 8 ounces dry yellow and green tagliarini or 4½ ounces (half of a 9-oz. package) *each* fresh yellow and green linguine
 1 cup whipping cream
 1 tablespoon lemon juice
   Fresh basil sprigs
 ⅓ to ½ cup grated Parmesan cheese

Heat oil in a wide frying pan over medium heat; add tomatoes, garlic, chopped basil, salt, white pepper, and wine. Bring to a boil over medium-high heat. Cook, uncovered, stirring often, until tomatoes are soft and almost all liquid has evaporated (8 to 10 minutes). Transfer mixture to a food processor or blender and whirl until puréed; return to pan.

In a 5- to 6-quart pan, cook pasta in 3 quarts boiling water just until tender to bite (6 to 7 minutes for dry pasta, 1 to 2 minutes for fresh); or cook according to package directions. Drain well.

While pasta is cooking, stir cream and lemon juice into tomato purée. Bring to a boil over high heat, stirring often; cook until sauce boils and thickens slightly (about 3 minutes).

Divide pasta among shallow bowls or rimmed plates; spoon sauce over each serving. Garnish with basil sprigs. Serve with cheese to add to taste. Makes 2 main-dish or 4 first-course servings.

Per main-dish serving: 942 calories, 25 g protein, 98 g carbohydrates, 50 g total fat, 146 mg cholesterol, 643 mg sodium

Bucatini, Amatrice Style

Preparation time: About 10 minutes

Cooking time: 20 to 25 minutes

Cooked in the manner favored in a small town north of Rome, the pasta in this classic dish is a thin, hollow tube in the shape of a drinking straw. You may find it labeled *bucatini, perciatelli,* or (in a thinner version) *perciatellini*.

 4 ounces sliced pancetta or bacon, cut into ½- by 1-inch strips
   Olive oil or salad oil (if needed)
 1 large onion, finely chopped
 ½ teaspoon crushed dried hot red chiles
 1 clove garlic, minced or pressed
 1 can (14½ oz.) pear-shaped tomatoes
 ⅓ cup dry white wine
 2 tablespoons chopped parsley
 8 ounces dry bucatini or other thin pasta tubes
   Salt
 ⅓ to ½ cup grated Parmesan cheese

In a wide frying pan, cook pancetta over medium heat until it is crisp and lightly browned, stirring often. Lift out, drain, and set aside. Measure the drippings; add oil, if needed, to make ¼ cup.

To drippings, add onion and chiles. Stir until onion is soft but not brown (6 to 8 minutes). Add garlic, tomatoes (break up with a spoon) and their liquid, wine, and parsley. Boil gently until slightly thickened (10 to 15 minutes); stir occasionally.

Meanwhile, in a 5- to 6-quart pan, cook bucatini in 3 quarts boiling water just until tender to bite (about 10 minutes); or cook according to package directions. Drain well and place on a deep platter.

Mix pancetta into sauce; season to taste with salt. Spoon sauce over pasta; mix lightly, using 2 forks. Serve with cheese to add to taste. Makes 2 main-dish or 4 first-course servings.

Per main-dish serving: 861 calories, 29 g protein, 102 g carbohydrates, 37 g total fat, 41 mg cholesterol, 1,006 mg sodium

Pictured on facing page

Baked Tomato Spaghetti

Preparation time: About 20 minutes

Baking time: 55 to 70 minutes

Cooking time: 10 to 12 minutes

Baked Roma-type tomatoes and fresh basil make a savory sauce for spaghetti in this Florentine first course. Long cooking partially dries the tomatoes, intensifying their sweetness.

- 12 medium-size firm-ripe pear-shaped (Roma-type) tomatoes (about 1¾ lbs. *total*)
  Salt and pepper
- 3 to 6 cloves garlic, minced
- ½ cup chopped parsley
- ½ cup olive oil
- 1 pound dry spaghetti
- 2 tablespoons butter or margarine, at room temperature
- ½ cup whole fresh basil leaves or 2 tablespoons dry basil
  Grated Parmesan cheese (optional)

Cut tomatoes in half lengthwise; set, cut sides up, in a shallow 9- by 13-inch baking pan or dish. Sprinkle lightly with salt and pepper. Mix garlic, ⅓ cup of the parsley, and 2 tablespoons of the oil; pat mixture over cut sides of tomatoes. Drizzle with 2 tablespoons more oil. Bake, uncovered, in a 425° oven until browned on top (55 to 70 minutes; pan juices may become very dark).

When tomatoes are almost done, in a 6- to 8-quart pan, cook spaghetti in 4 quarts boiling water just until tender to bite (10 to 12 minutes); or cook according to package directions.

Meanwhile, in a warm large serving bowl, place butter, remaining parsley, remaining ¼ cup oil, basil, and 4 of the baked tomato halves. Remove and discard most of the skin from the 4 halves; coarsely mash halves.

Drain spaghetti well; add to tomato mixture and mix lightly, using 2 forks. Add remaining baked tomato halves and pan juices. Mix gently; season to taste with salt and pepper. Serve with cheese, if desired. Makes 6 to 8 first-course servings.

Per serving: 434 calories, 10 g protein, 55 g carbohydrates, 20 g total fat, 9 mg cholesterol, 46 mg sodium

Wide Noodles in Tomato-Cheese Sauce

Preparation time: About 15 minutes

Cooking time: About 15 minutes

The broad egg noodles featured in this distinctive dish are called *pappardelle* in Italy; you may be able to find them in stores featuring imported foods. (If you make your own fresh pasta, just cut it half the width of lasagne.) Here, the noodles are served in a creamy tomato sauce with mozzarella—a combination the Italians call *pappardelle al telefono*, describing the way the cheese stretches out like a telephone cord when you lift the pasta.

- 2 tablespoons butter or margarine
- ⅓ cup finely chopped onion
- 2 tablespoons chopped fresh basil or 1 teaspoon dry basil
- 4 medium-size pear-shaped (Roma-type) tomatoes (about 8 oz. *total*), peeled, seeded, and chopped
- 1 clove garlic, minced or pressed
- ½ cup whipping cream
- 1 package (8½ oz.) dry pappardelle (wide fettuccine), 10 to 12 ounces fresh pappardelle, or 8 ounces dry extra-wide egg noodles
  Salt and ground white pepper
- 1 cup (4 oz.) shredded whole-milk mozzarella cheese
- ⅓ to ½ cup grated Parmesan cheese

Melt butter in a wide frying pan over medium heat. Add onion and cook, stirring occasionally, until soft but not brown (about 3 minutes). Stir in basil, tomatoes, garlic, and cream. Cook, uncovered, stirring often, until tomatoes are soft (6 to 8 minutes). Transfer to a food processor or blender; whirl until smooth. Return sauce to pan; set aside.

In a 5- to 6-quart pan, cook pasta in 3 quarts boiling water just until barely tender to bite (3 to 4 minutes for dry pappardelle, about 2 minutes for fresh pappardelle, 4 to 6 minutes for noodles); or cook according to package directions. Drain well.

Meanwhile, reheat sauce over low heat. Season to taste with salt and white pepper. Sprinkle with mozzarella cheese. Heat without stirring just until cheese is melted (about 3 minutes). Add pasta; mix lightly, using 2 spoons. Serve with Parmesan cheese to add to taste. Makes 4 first-course servings.

Per serving: 505 calories, 18 g protein, 49 g carbohydrates, 27 g total fat, 134 mg cholesterol, 338 mg sodium

Baked fresh Roma tomatoes replace the traditional slow-cooked sauce in this light, lively Baked Tomato Spaghetti (recipe on facing page). Spicy fresh basil balances the sweetness of the tomatoes.

Linguine with Zucchini

Preparation time: 12 to 15 minutes

Cooking time: 6 to 10 minutes

When time is short, try this quick entrée—*al dente* linguine topped with shredded zucchini in a two-cheese sauce.

- 3 tablespoons salad oil
- 6 medium-size zucchini (about 1½ lbs. total), coarsely shredded (5 to 6 cups)
- 3 large cloves garlic, minced or pressed
- 10 to 12 ounces fresh linguine or 8 ounces dry linguine
- ¼ cup chopped parsley
- ¼ cup butter or margarine
- ½ cup half-and-half
- ½ cup grated Parmesan cheese
- 1½ cups (6 oz.) shredded jack cheese
  Salt and freshly ground pepper

Heat oil in a wide frying pan over high heat. Add zucchini and garlic; cook, stirring, just until zucchini is tender-crisp to bite (3 to 4 minutes). Reduce heat to low.

While zucchini is cooking, in a 5- to 6-quart pan, cook linguine in 3 quarts boiling water just until tender to bite (1 to 2 minutes for fresh pasta, 8 to 10 minutes for dry); or cook according to package directions. Drain well and set aside.

To zucchini mixture, add parsley, butter, and half-and-half; stir lightly until butter is melted. Add pasta, Parmesan cheese, and jack cheese. Mix lightly, using 2 forks. Season to taste with salt and pepper. Makes 4 servings.

Per serving: 691 calories, 28 g protein, 51 g carbohydrates, 43 g total fat, 179 mg cholesterol, 572 mg sodium

■ *To Microwave:* Decrease oil to 1 tablespoon. In a 3- to 3½-quart microwave-safe casserole, mix oil, zucchini, and garlic. Microwave, covered, on **HIGH (100%)** for 5 to 6 minutes or until tender-crisp to bite, stirring 2 or 3 times. Stir in parsley, butter, and half-and-half. Microwave, covered, on **HIGH (100%)** for 2½ to 3 minutes or until butter is melted, stirring once. Meanwhile, cook and drain linguine as directed in recipe. Mix pasta and cheeses lightly into zucchini mixture; microwave, covered, on **HIGH (100%)** for 2 minutes. Let stand, covered, for 1 minute, then season to taste with salt and pepper.

Angel Hair Primavera

Preparation time: About 20 minutes

Cooking time: About 15 minutes

Green and golden spring vegetables in profusion make this delicate dish a seasonal treat.

- 8 ounces asparagus, tough ends snapped off, spears cut into bite-size pieces
- 1 medium-size or large yellow pattypan squash (4 to 6 oz.), cut into thin bite-size pieces
- 1 cup small broccoli flowerets
- 4 ounces Chinese pea pods (also called snow or sugar peas), ends and strings removed
- 2 tablespoons pine nuts
- 3 tablespoons butter or margarine
- 4 ounces mushrooms, thinly sliced
- 2 ounces thinly sliced prosciutto, cut into strips (optional)
- ¼ cup thinly sliced green onions (including tops)
- 1 clove garlic, minced or pressed
- 1 cup whipping cream
- ⅓ cup dry white wine
- ⅛ teaspoon *each* ground nutmeg and ground white pepper
- 6 ounces dry capellini or 1 package (9 oz.) fresh angel hair pasta
- ½ to ¾ cup grated Parmesan cheese

In a 3- to 4-quart pan, cook asparagus, squash, and broccoli in about 1 quart boiling water, uncovered, for 2 minutes. Add pea pods; cook just until water returns to a boil. Drain vegetables and set aside.

Stir pine nuts in a wide frying pan over medium-low heat until nuts are lightly browned (about 3 minutes), then remove from pan and set aside.

Increase heat to medium. Melt butter in pan; add mushrooms and cook, stirring, until they begin to brown (3 to 5 minutes). Add prosciutto (if used), onions, and garlic; continue to cook, stirring often, until onions are soft and bright green (1 to 2 minutes). Add cream, wine, nutmeg, and white pepper. Increase heat to high and bring to a boil; boil, stirring occasionally, for 2 minutes.

Meanwhile, in a 5- to 6-quart pan, cook pasta in 3 quarts boiling water just until tender to bite (about 3 minutes for dry pasta, 1 to 2 minutes for fresh); or cook according to package directions. Drain well.

To cream mixture, add vegetables, pine nuts, and ⅓ cup of the cheese, then stir gently just until heated through. Remove from heat. Using 2 forks, stir in pasta until lightly coated with sauce. Serve with additional cheese to add to taste. Makes about 3 main-dish or 5 first-course servings.

Per main-dish serving: 702 calories, 22 g protein, 58 g carbohydrates, 45 g total fat, 131 mg cholesterol, 431 mg sodium

The enticing aroma alone is enough to explain the magic of pesto. Fabled as the synthesis of the sunny flavors and fragrances of Liguria (the hilly coastal region near Genoa), it's actually a simple, quick-to-make paste of fresh basil, Parmesan cheese, and olive oil. In its classic version, the mixture is pulverized with a mortar and pestle—hence the name *pesto*, which means "pounded" in Italian. But a food processor or blender gets the ingredients together far more quickly and uniformly.

Taking liberties with the traditional preparation technique is just one of the ways you can vary this pungent green sauce. Many cooks wouldn't consider making pesto without garlic; others routinely add pine nuts or walnuts, toasted or plain. (To toast nuts for any of the following recipes, stir pine nuts or coarsely chopped walnuts in a frying pan over medium-low heat until lightly browned, about 3 minutes.) Another way to vary pesto is to use other fresh herbs or greens in place of or in addition to basil. To prepare the herbs or greens, rinse them well, then drain and pat dry.

To serve any of these pesto sauces with pasta, add 6 to 8 tablespoons of the pesto and ¼ cup butter or margarine (at room temperature) to 4 cups hot cooked fettuccine, spaghetti, linguine, or similar pasta. Mix lightly; serve with grated Parmesan cheese and additional pesto to add to taste.

To store pesto, refrigerate or freeze it. It will darken slightly as it stands; covering the top with a thin layer of oil will help preserve the color.

Pasta with Pesto

Classic Pesto

2 cups lightly packed fresh basil leaves
1 cup (about 5 oz.) grated Parmesan cheese
½ to ⅔ cup olive oil
1 or 2 cloves garlic (optional)

In a blender or food processor, whirl basil, cheese, ½ cup of the oil, and garlic (if used) until smoothly puréed; add more oil, if needed. If made ahead, cover and refrigerate for up to 5 days; or freeze in small portions. Makes about 1½ cups.

Per tablespoon: 79 calories, 3 g protein, 1 g carbohydrates, 7 g total fat, 5 mg cholesterol, 111 mg sodium

Basil-Cilantro Pesto

Follow directions for **Classic Pesto,** but decrease basil to 1½ cups and add ½ cup firmly packed **fresh cilantro (coriander) leaves.** Decrease cheese to ¾ cup. Increase garlic to 3 cloves. Add 2 tablespoons *each* **pine nuts** and coarsely chopped **walnuts** (toasted, if desired). Makes about 1¼ cups.

Per tablespoon: 84 calories, 2 g protein, 1 g carbohydrates, 8 g total fat, 2 mg cholesterol, 57 mg sodium

Cilantro Pesto

Follow directions for **Classic Pesto,** but omit basil; instead, use 2 cups firmly packed **fresh cilantro (coriander) leaves.** Decrease cheese to ½ cup, decrease oil to ¼ cup, and use only 1 clove garlic. Add ¼ cup **pine nuts** (toasted, if desired) and 1 teaspoon grated **lime peel;** season to taste with **salt.** Makes about ¾ cup.

Per tablespoon: 71 calories, 2 g protein, 0.6 g carbohydrates, 7 g total fat, 3 mg cholesterol, 63 mg sodium

Spinach-Herb Pesto

Follow directions for **Classic Pesto,** but omit basil; instead, use 1½ cups lightly packed **spinach leaves** and ¼ cup lightly packed **fresh tarragon, thyme, marjoram, or oregano leaves** (tough stems discarded). Decrease cheese to ½ cup. Makes about 1 cup.

Per tablespoon: 84 calories, 1 g protein, 0.4 g carbohydrates, 9 g total fat, 2 mg cholesterol, 52 mg sodium

Dried Tomato Pesto

Follow directions for **Classic Pesto,** but add ¼ cup chopped drained **dried tomatoes packed in oil.** Decrease cheese to ½ cup. Use 2 cloves garlic. Makes about 1¼ cups.

Per tablespoon: 81 calories, 1 g protein, 2 g carbohydrates, 8 g total fat, 2 mg cholesterol, 103 mg sodium

Linguine with Morels & Asparagus

Preparation time: About 10 minutes

Soaking time: About 45 minutes

Cooking time: 12 to 15 minutes

In a spectacular gathering of gastronomic treasures, spring asparagus and flavorful morels lend elegance to golden, creamy pasta.

- ½ to 1 cup (½ to 1 oz.) dried morel mushrooms
- 12 ounces asparagus, tough ends snapped off, spears cut into 1-inch-long pieces
- 2 tablespoons pine nuts
- 3 tablespoons butter or margarine
- 2 tablespoons finely chopped shallot
- 1 cup whipping cream
- 6 ounces dry linguine or 1 package (9 oz.) fresh linguine
- 2 tablespoons 1-inch-long chive strips
- 1 teaspoon chopped fresh thyme or ¼ teaspoon dry thyme leaves
  Salt
  Chive blossoms or other small edible flower petals (optional)
- ⅓ to ½ cup grated Parmesan cheese

Place mushrooms in a medium-size bowl; cover with hot water. Let stand until soft (about 45 minutes). Drain, reserving ½ cup of the soaking liquid. Cut mushrooms lengthwise into halves or quarters; pat dry and set aside.

Steam asparagus, covered, on a rack over 1 inch of boiling water until barely tender when pierced (3 to 4 minutes). Remove asparagus from pan and set aside.

Stir pine nuts in a wide frying pan over medium-low heat until lightly browned (about 3 minutes); remove from pan and set aside. Increase heat to medium. Melt butter in pan, then add mushrooms and shallot. Cook, stirring often, until mushrooms are lightly browned (4 to 5 minutes). Add reserved ½ cup mushroom soaking liquid and cream. Increase heat to high, bring mixture to a boil, and boil, stirring often, until liquid is reduced by about a third.

Meanwhile, in a 5- to 6-quart pan, cook linguine in 3 quarts boiling water just until tender to bite (8 to 10 minutes for dry pasta, 1 to 2 minutes for fresh); or cook according to package directions. Drain well and divide among wide, shallow bowls.

To sauce, add chive strips, thyme, and asparagus; stir just until heated through. Season to taste with salt. Spoon over linguine; sprinkle with pine nuts and chive blossoms (if used). Serve with cheese to add to taste. Makes 4 first-course servings.

Per serving: 499 calories, 13 g protein, 41 g carbohydrates, 33 g total fat, 96 mg cholesterol, 270 mg sodium

Pasta with Swiss Chard

Preparation time: About 15 minutes

Cooking time: About 35 minutes

Toasted pecans, crisp bacon, and ribbons of Swiss chard dress up short tube-shaped pasta such as *penne, mostaccioli,* or *ziti* in this savory main course.

- 1 pound Swiss chard or kale, rinsed well
- 1 cup pecan halves
- ¾ cup (6 oz.) firmly packed chopped bacon
- 3 cloves garlic, minced or pressed
- ¼ to ½ teaspoon crushed dried hot red chiles
- 8 to 10 ounces dry small tube-shaped pasta such as penne, mostaccioli, or ziti
- 2 teaspoons Dijon mustard
- 2 tablespoons white wine vinegar
- 1½ cups (about 7½ oz.) freshly grated Parmesan or Romano cheese

Trim and discard ends of chard stems; then cut off remainder of stems at base of each leaf. Thinly slice stems and leaves, keeping them separate. (If using kale, cut off and discard coarse stems; slice leaves thinly.) Set chard or kale aside.

Stir pecans in a wide frying pan over medium heat until lightly browned (8 to 10 minutes); remove from pan and set aside. Add bacon to pan; cook, stirring often, until crisp and brown (about 10 minutes). Lift out, drain, and set aside. Discard all but 3 tablespoons of the drippings. Add chard stems, garlic, and chiles to drippings; cook, stirring often, until stems are limp (about 10 minutes). Add chard leaves (or all the kale) and stir until tender to bite (about 5 minutes).

Meanwhile, in a 5- to 6-quart pan, cook pasta in 3 quarts boiling water just until tender to bite (10 to 12 minutes); or cook according to package directions. Drain well.

In a warm large serving bowl, combine pasta, mustard, and vinegar. Using 2 spoons, lightly mix in cheese, then greens and bacon. Sprinkle with pecans. Makes 4 to 6 servings.

Per serving: 767 calories, 31 g protein, 57 g carbohydrates, 47 g total fat, 54 mg cholesterol, 1,212 mg sodium

Among the most aromatic and full-flavored of wild mushrooms, crinkly morels perfume creamy Linguine with Morels & Asparagus (recipe on facing page). You'll find the morels in specialty food markets.

Linguine with Double Mushroom Sauce

Preparation time: About 10 minutes

Cooking time: About 20 minutes

To make this stylish first course, combine familiar brown or white button mushrooms with one or more unusual, subtly flavored varieties, such as shiitake or oyster mushrooms or angel trumpets.

> 8 ounces mushrooms (choose 2 or 3 different kinds; see suggestions in recipe introduction above)
>
> ⅓ cup olive oil
>
> 1 clove garlic, minced or pressed
>
> ½ cup dry white wine
>
> 1 package (9 oz.) fresh linguine or 6 ounces dry linguine
>
> 1 small pear-shaped (Roma-type) tomato (about 1½ oz.), seeded and finely chopped
>
> ¼ cup chopped Italian (flat-leaf) parsley
> Salt and freshly ground pepper

Cut any large mushrooms into quarters or halves. Heat oil in a wide frying pan over medium heat. Add mushrooms and cook, stirring often, until they begin to brown (about 10 minutes). Stir in garlic. Add wine, bring to a boil, and boil gently until liquid is reduced by about half (3 to 5 minutes).

Meanwhile, in a 5- to 6-quart pan, cook linguine in 3 quarts boiling water just until tender to bite (1 to 2 minutes for fresh pasta, 8 to 10 minutes for dry); or cook according to package directions. Drain pasta well.

Stir tomato and parsley into mushroom mixture just until heated through (about 1 minute). Season to taste with salt and pepper. Remove from heat and add pasta. Mix lightly, using 2 spoons. Makes 4 first-course servings.

Per serving: 362 calories, 9 g protein, 39 g carbohydrates, 20 g total fat, 75 mg cholesterol, 24 mg sodium

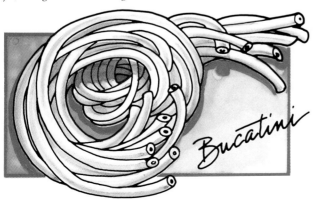

Bucatini

Tortellini with Mushroom-Cheese Sauce

Preparation time: About 15 minutes

Cooking time: 15 to 20 minutes

Start with ready-made tortellini, fresh, frozen, or dried—then add a garlic-and basil-accented mushroom sauce, mellowed with cream cheese.

> 1 package (12 oz.) frozen tortellini, 12 ounces fresh tortellini, or 1 package (7 or 8 oz.) dry tortellini
>
> 1 tablespoon butter or margarine
>
> 1 pound mushrooms, finely chopped
>
> 3 cloves garlic, minced or pressed
>
> 1 tablespoon minced fresh basil leaves or ½ teaspoon dry basil
>
> 2 small packages (3 oz. *each*) cream cheese
>
> ¾ cup milk
> Parsley sprigs

In a 5- to 6-quart pan, cook tortellini in 3 quarts boiling water just until tender to bite (15 to 20 minutes for frozen tortellini, 4 to 6 minutes for fresh, 15 to 20 minutes for dry); or cook according to package directions. Drain well.

While tortellini are cooking, melt butter in a wide frying pan over medium-high heat. Add mushrooms, garlic, and basil; cook, stirring often, until all liquid has evaporated and mushrooms are beginning to brown (10 to 12 minutes). Add cream cheese and milk; stir until cheese is melted and sauce comes to a gentle boil.

Remove sauce from heat, add tortellini, and mix lightly, using 2 spoons. Garnish with parsley. Makes 4 main-dish or 6 first-course servings.

Per main-dish serving: 486 calories, 21 g protein, 43 g carbohydrates, 26 g total fat, 61 mg cholesterol, 479 mg sodium

Fettuccine Emmenthaler

Preparation time: About 5 minutes

Cooking time: 3 to 4 minutes

This refined version of pasta and cheese makes a satisfying main dish; serve it with your favorite green vegetable.

10 ounces fresh thin fettuccine or 8 ounces dry thin fettuccine

½ cup (¼ lb.) butter or margarine, melted

2 cups (8 oz.) shredded Emmenthaler or Swiss cheese

Freshly ground pepper

Chopped parsley

In a 5- to 6-quart pan, cook fettuccine in 3 quarts boiling water just until tender to bite (3 to 4 minutes for fresh pasta, 7 to 8 minutes for dry); or cook according to package directions. Drain well; transfer to a wide bowl or deep platter.

Immediately add butter and 1 cup of the cheese to hot pasta; rapidly lift pasta with 2 forks to blend in melting cheese. Sprinkle on remaining 1 cup cheese a little at a time, lifting pasta to mix in well. Sprinkle with pepper and parsley. Makes 4 servings.

Per serving: 622 calories, 25 g protein, 41 g carbohydrates, 40 g total fat, 198 mg cholesterol, 401 mg sodium

Capellini with Broccoli Cream Sauce

Preparation time: 10 to 15 minutes

Cooking time: About 10 minutes

Serve this simple but luxurious pasta dish with crisp bread sticks and an Italian white wine, such as pinot grigio or soave.

1½ pounds broccoli

1 package (10 oz.) dry capellini or coil vermicelli

6 tablespoons butter or margarine

⅓ cup water

2 cups whipping cream

¼ teaspoon ground nutmeg

2 cups (about 10 oz.) freshly grated Parmesan cheese

Trim and discard tough ends from broccoli stalks. Peel stems; finely chop broccoli, reserving a few whole flowerets for garnish. Set aside.

In a 5- to 6-quart pan, cook capellini in 3 quarts boiling water just until tender to bite (about 3 minutes); or cook according to package directions. Drain, rinse with cold water, and drain well again.

Melt butter in a wide frying pan over medium-high heat; add all broccoli and ⅓ cup water. Cover and cook until broccoli is tender when pierced (about 5 minutes); remove flowerets from pan and set aside.

Add cream and nutmeg to remaining broccoli in pan; bring to a boil, then add pasta. Cook, mixing lightly with 2 spoons, just until mixture is hot and cream clings to pasta. Remove from heat, sprinkle with 1¼ cups of the cheese, and mix lightly again.

Transfer pasta to a warm deep platter. Sprinkle with 3 to 4 tablespoons more cheese and garnish with broccoli flowerets. Serve with remaining cheese to add to taste. Makes 6 servings.

Per serving: 714 calories, 27 g protein, 43 g carbohydrates, 49 g total fat, 152 mg cholesterol, 921 mg sodium

Lasagne Packets

Preparation time: About 10 minutes

Baking time: 10 to 15 minutes

Instant lasagne, a dry pasta product that needs only brief moistening to be ready to use, speeds up the preparation of this hearty baked entrée.

4 to 6 sheets (*each* about 7 inches square) instant lasagne noodles

1 package (10 oz.) frozen chopped spinach, thawed

2 cloves garlic, minced or pressed

1 teaspoon Italian herb seasoning or ¼ teaspoon *each* dry basil and dry oregano, thyme, and marjoram leaves

1½ cups prepared (refrigerated or bottled) pasta sauce, such as marinara, Bolognese, roasted red pepper, or shrimp sauce

1 pound ricotta or small-curd cottage cheese

½ cup grated Parmesan, Romano, or Asiago cheese

Pour 2 quarts hottest tap water into a 5- to 6-quart pan. Add lasagne and let stand until pliable (about 5 minutes).

Meanwhile, squeeze as much liquid as possible from spinach. In a bowl, mix spinach, garlic, herb seasoning, ½ cup of the pasta sauce, ricotta cheese, and ¼ cup of the Parmesan cheese.

Drain lasagne sheets well, then place on a flat surface. Scoop an equal amount of spinach mixture onto center of each. Fold all 4 corners of each sheet to center over filling, pulling corners together to make snug packets. Set packets, folded sides down, in a greased 9- by 13-inch baking dish. Moisten tops of packets evenly with remaining 1 cup sauce; sprinkle with remaining ¼ cup Parmesan cheese.

Bake, uncovered, in a 400° oven until packets are heated through; cut to test (10 to 15 minutes). Makes 4 to 6 servings.

Per serving: 305 calories, 20 g protein, 31 g carbohydrates, 11 g total fat, 34 mg cholesterol, 533 mg sodium

A favorite pasta from Italy's Adriatic coast, cup-shaped
orecchiette are perfectly designed to hold sauces and
seasonings. In Orecchiette with Spinach & Garlic (recipe
on facing page), they gain emphatic flavor from olive oil
that's scented with garlic and piqued with hot chiles.

Vegetable Lasagne

Preparation time: About 25 minutes

Cooking time: About 20 minutes

Baking time: About 25 minutes; 50 minutes if refrigerated

All the hearty flavor of a classic lasagne, but none of the meat! This bright, fresh version features a variety of vegetables and a trio of cheeses.

- 8 ounces dry lasagne
- 4 large carrots (about 12 oz. *total*), cut into ¼-inch-thick slices
- 3 large zucchini (about 1 lb. *total*), cut into ¼-inch-thick slices
- 2 tablespoons olive oil or salad oil
- 1 medium-size onion, finely chopped
- 8 ounces mushrooms, thinly sliced
- 1 teaspoon *each* dry basil, thyme leaves, and oregano leaves
- 1 jar (32 oz.) marinara sauce
- 2 packages (10 oz. *each*) frozen chopped spinach, thawed
- 8 ounces ricotta cheese
- 3 cups (12 oz.) shredded mozzarella cheese
- ¼ cup grated Parmesan cheese

In a 5- to 6-quart pan, cook lasagne and carrots in 3 quarts boiling water for 6 minutes. Add zucchini; continue to cook just until lasagne is tender to bite (4 to 5 more minutes). Drain well; set lasagne and vegetables aside separately.

In same pan, heat oil over high heat; add onion, mushrooms, basil, thyme, and oregano. Cook, stirring often, until onion is soft and all liquid has evaporated (5 to 8 minutes). Remove from heat, stir in marinara sauce, and set aside.

Squeeze as much liquid as possible from spinach. Mix spinach and ricotta cheese; set aside.

Spread a third of the sauce in a shallow 2½- to 3-quart baking dish. Arrange half the lasagne over sauce. Add half each of the blanched carrots and zucchini, spinach mixture, and mozzarella cheese. Repeat layers, using half the remaining sauce and all the remaining lasagne, carrots, zucchini, spinach mixture, and mozzarella. Spread remaining sauce on top, then sprinkle with Parmesan cheese. (At this point, you may cover baking dish and refrigerate for up to a day.)

Set baking dish in a shallow rimmed baking pan to catch any drips. Bake, uncovered, until hot in center. Bake freshly made lasagne in a 400° oven for about 25 minutes; bake refrigerated lasagne in a 350° oven for about 50 minutes. Let stand for about 5 minutes before serving. To serve, cut into squares. Makes 6 servings.

Per serving: 586 calories, 29 g protein, 63 g carbohydrates, 27 g total fat, 59 mg cholesterol, 1,367 mg sodium

Pictured on facing page

Orecchiette with Spinach & Garlic

Preparation time: 15 to 20 minutes

Cooking time: About 15 minutes

Some people see fanciful shapes in clouds, but Italians find them in pasta. You might take round, shallow *orecchiette* for diminutive berets, but their Italian name indicates that they're meant to be seen as little ears.

- 2 bunches (about 12 oz. *each*) spinach, rinsed well and drained
- 12 ounces dry orecchiette or ruote (wheel-shaped pasta)
- ⅓ cup olive oil
- 6 cloves garlic, minced or pressed
- ½ teaspoon crushed dried hot red chiles
  Salt
- ⅓ to ½ cup grated Parmesan cheese

Remove and discard spinach stems; chop leaves coarsely and set aside.

In a 6- to 8-quart pan, cook orecchiette in 4 quarts boiling water just until tender to bite (12 to 15 minutes); or cook according to package directions. Just before pasta is done, stir in spinach. Cook, uncovered, stirring to distribute spinach, just until water returns to a full boil. Drain pasta and spinach.

While pasta is cooking, heat oil in a wide frying pan over medium heat. Stir in garlic and chiles. Cook, uncovered, until garlic turns opaque (about 2 minutes). Add pasta and spinach to pan; mix lightly, using 2 spoons. Season to taste with salt. Serve with cheese to add to taste. Makes 6 first-course servings.

Per serving: 363 calories, 12 g protein, 47 g carbohydrates, 15 g total fat, 4 mg cholesterol, 170 mg sodium

Pasta with Peppers & Onions

Preparation time: About 20 minutes

Cooking time: About 30 minutes

Your choice of red, yellow, or orange bell peppers enlivens a creamy, walnut-sprinkled sauce for fettuccine. (For an especially eye-catching entrée, you might combine all three colors of peppers.)

  ¼ **cup butter or margarine**
  ⅓ **cup coarsely chopped walnuts**
  2 **large onions, thinly sliced**
  3 **medium-size red, yellow, or orange bell peppers (about 1 lb. *total*), seeded and cut into ¼-inch-wide strips**
  8 **ounces dry fettuccine or 10 to 12 ounces fresh fettuccine**
  ½ **cup *each* regular-strength chicken broth and whipping cream**
  ⅛ **teaspoon ground nutmeg**
  ½ **cup grated Parmesan cheese**
      Salt and pepper

Melt 1 tablespoon of the butter in a wide frying pan over medium-low heat. Add walnuts and cook, stirring often, until lightly toasted (about 2 minutes). Lift out and set aside. Add remaining 3 tablespoons butter, onions, and bell peppers to pan; cook, stirring often, until onions are very soft and light golden (20 to 25 minutes).

Meanwhile, in a 5- to 6-quart pan, cook fettuccine in 3 quarts boiling water just until tender to bite (8 to 10 minutes for dry pasta, 3 to 4 minutes for fresh); drain well.

To bell pepper mixture, add broth, cream, and nutmeg. Increase heat to high and bring to a full boil. Reduce heat to low; add fettuccine and cheese. Mix lightly, using 2 forks. Season to taste with salt and pepper, then sprinkle with walnuts. Makes 4 servings.

Per serving: 570 calories, 15 g protein, 54 g carbohydrates, 33 g total fat, 125 mg cholesterol, 447 mg sodium

Orecchiette

Garbanzo Pasta

Preparation time: 10 to 15 minutes

Cooking time: 10 to 12 minutes

You can put this spirited main dish together in a hurry, using ingredients you probably already have on hand in the pantry and refrigerator.

  8 **ounces dry spaghetti**
  4 **ounces sliced bacon (about 5 slices), cut into ½-inch pieces**
  3 **tablespoons olive oil or salad oil**
  1 **medium-size onion, finely chopped**
  3 **cloves garlic, minced or pressed**
  1 **can (15 oz.) garbanzo beans, drained**
  ¾ **cup regular-strength beef broth**
  ¼ **teaspoon crushed dried hot red chiles**
  ½ **cup finely chopped parsley**
  ½ **cup grated Parmesan cheese**

In a 5- to 6-quart pan, cook spaghetti in 3 quarts boiling water just until tender to bite (10 to 12 minutes); or cook according to package directions. Drain well.

While spaghetti is cooking, in a wide frying pan, cook bacon over medium heat until crisp. Lift out, drain, and set aside. Discard all but 2 tablespoons of the drippings. Add oil, onion, and garlic to drippings. Cook, stirring often, until onion is soft but not brown (about 5 minutes). Add garbanzos, broth, chiles, and parsley. With a spoon, mash garbanzos slightly. Bring to a boil, then add pasta. Mix lightly, using 2 spoons, until pasta is hot.

Transfer pasta mixture to a serving dish. Sprinkle with cheese and mix lightly. Sprinkle with bacon. Makes 4 servings.

Per serving: 583 calories, 20 g protein, 71 g carbohydrates, 24 g total fat, 19 mg cholesterol, 823 mg sodium

■ ***To Microwave:*** Cook pasta as directed in recipe. Place bacon pieces in a single layer on several layers of paper towels; cover with another paper towel. Microwave on **HIGH (100%)** for 4 to 5 minutes or until bacon is brown; set aside. In a 3- to 3½-quart microwave-safe casserole, combine oil, onion, and garlic. Microwave, covered, on **HIGH (100%)** for 4 to 5 minutes or until onion is soft, stirring once or twice. Add garbanzos, broth, chiles, and parsley; mash garbanzos slightly with a spoon. Microwave, covered, on **HIGH (100%)** for 3½ to 5 minutes or until mixture is hot and bubbling, stirring once. Mix in pasta, cover, and let stand for 1 minute. Sprinkle with Parmesan cheese and mix lightly; then sprinkle with bacon.

Tagliarini with Chèvre & Olives

Preparation time: About 15 minutes

Cooking time: 12 to 15 minutes

Cream, chicken broth, and distinctively flavored goat cheese mingle in a rich sauce for tagliarini. Crisp pine nuts and tangy olives accent the dish.

¼ **cup pine nuts**

2 **cups** *each* **whipping cream and regular-strength chicken broth**

8 **to 12 ounces soft, unripened chèvre (trimmed of coating, if necessary)**

½ **cup Spanish-style or Niçoise olives, pitted and chopped**

8 **ounces dry tagliarini or 10 to 12 ounces fresh tagliarini**

¼ **cup butter or margarine, melted**

1 **tablespoon grated orange peel**

3 **tablespoons chopped chives**
Whole chives

Stir pine nuts in a medium-size frying pan over medium-low heat until lightly browned (about 3 minutes); set aside.

In a 4- to 5-quart pan, combine cream and broth. Bring to a boil over high heat; boil, uncovered, stirring occasionally, until reduced to 1½ cups. Reduce heat to low and whisk in about half of the cheese, adding enough to develop a rich cheese flavor; stir in olives and keep warm.

Meanwhile, in a 5- to 6-quart pan, cook tagliarini in 3 quarts boiling water just until tender to bite (6 to 7 minutes for dry pasta, 2 to 3 minutes for fresh); or cook according to package directions. Drain well, then return to pan over low heat. Add pine nuts, butter, and 2 teaspoons of the orange peel. Mix lightly, using 2 forks.

Pour sauce into a warm serving bowl; mound pasta in center. Crumble remaining cheese and sprinkle over pasta with chopped chives and remaining 1 teaspoon orange peel. Garnish with whole chives. Makes 6 first-course servings.

Per serving: 668 calories, 18 g protein, 36 g carbohydrates, 52 g total fat, 153 mg cholesterol, 1,004 mg sodium

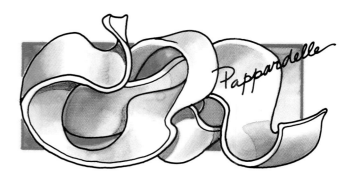

Red, White & Green Pasta

Preparation time: About 10 minutes

Cooking time: 30 to 35 minutes

Display the three colors of the Italian flag in this mellow dish. Sautéed white onions and red bell peppers are moistened with broth and lemon juice, then served over green fettuccine.

1 **tablespoon butter or margarine**

1 **tablespoon salad oil**

2 **large onions, thinly sliced**

1 **clove garlic, minced or pressed**

2 **large red bell peppers (about 1 lb.** *total***), seeded and cut into thin strips**

8 **ounces dry green fettuccine or 10 to 12 ounces fresh green fettuccine**

⅓ **cup regular-strength chicken or beef broth**

1 **tablespoon lemon juice**
Salt and freshly ground pepper

¼ **cup chopped fresh basil**

½ **to ¾ cup grated Parmesan cheese**

Melt butter in oil in a wide frying pan over medium-low heat. Stir in onions and garlic; cook, stirring often, until onions are very soft and light golden (20 to 25 minutes). Increase heat to medium, add bell peppers, and cook, stirring often, until peppers are just limp (8 to 10 minutes).

Meanwhile, in a 5- to 6-quart pan, cook fettuccine in 3 quarts boiling water just until tender to bite (8 to 10 minutes for dry pasta, 3 to 4 minutes for fresh); or cook according to package directions. Drain well, transfer to a warm bowl or deep platter, and keep warm.

Add broth and lemon juice to onion mixture; increase heat to high and bring to a boil. Season to taste with salt and pepper. Stir in basil. Spoon sauce in a broad stripe down center of pasta; using 2 forks, mix lightly at the table. Serve with cheese to add to taste. Makes 4 to 6 first-course servings.

Per serving: 270 calories, 12 g protein, 33 g carbohydrates, 10 g total fat, 66 mg cholesterol, 319 mg sodium

Pictured on facing page

Pasta Pilaf

Preparation time: About 10 minutes

Cooking time: About 20 minutes

For a side dish that's delicious with grilled fish or roast chicken, dress tiny rice-shaped pasta with a creamy tomato sauce. You'll find the pasta labeled *orzo, riso,* or *seme di melone.*

- 2 tablespoons butter or margarine
- 1 large onion, finely chopped
- 1 large clove garlic, minced or pressed
- 2 medium-size tomatoes (about 10 oz. *total*), peeled, seeded, and chopped
- 1 teaspoon dry basil
- ¼ cup water
- 1 cup (about 8 oz.) dry rice-shaped pasta
- ¾ cup frozen peas
- ½ cup whipping cream
- ½ to ⅔ cup grated Parmesan cheese
   Salt and pepper

Melt butter in a wide frying pan over medium heat. Add onion and garlic; cook, stirring occasionally, until onion is soft but not brown (5 to 7 minutes). Add tomatoes, basil, and ¼ cup water; reduce heat, cover, and simmer for 10 minutes.

Meanwhile, in a 5- to 6-quart pan, cook pasta in 3 quarts boiling water just until tender to bite (about 10 minutes); or cook according to package directions. Drain well.

Add peas and cream to tomato mixture. Increase heat to high and bring to a boil; mix in pasta. Remove from heat and stir in ¼ cup of the cheese. Season to taste with salt and pepper. Serve with remaining cheese to add to taste. Makes 4 to 6 side-dish servings.

Per serving: 361 calories, 12 g protein, 43 g carbohydrates, 16 g total fat, 46 mg cholesterol, 261 mg sodium

■ *To Microwave:* In a 3-quart microwave-safe casserole, combine butter, onion, and garlic. Microwave, covered, on **HIGH (100%)** for 4 to 5 minutes or until onion is soft, stirring 2 or 3 times. Stir in tomatoes, basil, and 2 tablespoons water. Microwave, covered, on **HIGH (100%)** for 8 to 10 minutes or until tomatoes are very soft, stirring twice. Meanwhile, cook pasta as directed in recipe. Add peas and cream to tomato mixture. Microwave, uncov-

ered, on **HIGH (100%)** for 3 to 4 minutes or until mixture comes to a boil. Stir in pasta, cover, and let stand for 2 minutes. Stir in ¼ cup of the cheese; season to taste with salt and pepper. Serve with remaining cheese to add to taste.

Toasted Cabbage with Noodles

Preparation time: About 15 minutes

Cooking time: 35 to 40 minutes

Wide egg noodles mingle with buttery cabbage and onions in this homey, old-fashioned side dish. It's a good accompaniment for a juicy pork roast.

- 1 small head green cabbage (about 1½ lbs.)
- ½ cup (¼ lb.) butter or margarine
- 1 large onion, finely chopped
- 1 clove garlic, minced or pressed
- 2 tablespoons sugar
- 8 ounces dry wide egg noodles
   Salt and pepper

Cut cabbage into fine shreds, discarding core; you should have about 2 quarts. Set aside.

Melt butter in a wide frying pan over medium heat. Add onion and garlic and cook, stirring occasionally, until onion is soft but not brown (5 to 7 minutes). Add cabbage; continue to cook, stirring often, until cabbage is softened and turns a brighter green (about 5 minutes). Sprinkle with sugar; continue to cook, stirring often, until cabbage takes on an amber color and begins to brown lightly (about 25 more minutes).

Shortly before cabbage is done, in a 5- to 6-quart pan, cook noodles in 3 quarts boiling water just until tender to bite (7 to 9 minutes); or cook according to package directions. Drain well.

In a wide, shallow serving bowl or deep platter, combine noodles and cabbage mixture; mix lightly, using 2 forks. Season to taste with salt and pepper. Makes 4 to 6 side-dish servings.

Per serving: 397 calories, 8 g protein, 46 g carbohydrates, 21 g total fat, 92 mg cholesterol, 210 mg sodium

Enfolded in a creamy fresh tomato sauce and mixed
with bright green peas, rice-shaped orzo is transformed
into a Pasta Pilaf (recipe on facing page)—an ideal
accent for an unadorned main dish such as roast
chicken or broiled fish steaks.

Pasta of a different persuasion, spaghetti squash (with pulp that naturally separates into slender strands) and zucchini (cut into long, slim ribbons) can be fanciful stand-ins for vermicelli or linguine. Top them with sauces and butters designed to complement their mild flavor and tender-crisp texture.

To bake a 2- to 3-pound spaghetti squash, pierce it in several places with a fork, then place it in a rimmed baking pan. Bake, uncovered, in a 350° oven until shell gives when pressed (1¼ to 1½ hours; turn squash after 45 minutes). Keep warm until ready to serve.

To microwave a 2- to 3-pound spaghetti squash, cut it in half length-wise; scrape out and discard seeds. Place squash halves, cut sides up, in a 9- by 13-inch microwave-safe baking dish. Cover with plastic wrap. Microwave on **HIGH (100%)** for 15 to 20 minutes or until squash is tender when pierced, rotating each piece a half-turn after 5 minutes. Let stand, covered, for 5 minutes.

Spaghetti Squash with Turkey Sauce

- 1 spaghetti squash (2 to 3 lbs.)
- 1 pound ground turkey
- 1 medium-size red or green bell pepper (about 5 oz.), seeded and diced
- 4 ounces mushrooms, thinly sliced
- 1 can (4 oz.) diced green chiles
- 1 jar (about 15 oz.) spaghetti sauce
- ½ teaspoon Italian herb seasoning or ⅛ teaspoon *each* dry basil and dry oregano, thyme, and marjoram leaves
  Salt and ground red pepper (cayenne)
  About ¾ cup grated Parmesan cheese

Great Pretenders:
Vegetables as Pasta

Bake or microwave squash as directed at left. Meanwhile, crumble turkey into a wide frying pan; cook over medium-high heat, stirring, until pink color is almost gone. Add bell pepper and mushrooms; cook, stirring often, until mushrooms are lightly browned (about 10 minutes). Stir in chiles, spaghetti sauce, and herb seasoning. Season to taste with salt and red pepper. Reduce heat and boil gently, uncovered, for 8 to 10 minutes.

Cut baked squash in half; scrape out and discard seeds.

Loosen squash strands with a fork and scoop out onto a warm rimmed platter. Spoon sauce over squash. Serve with cheese to add to taste. Makes 6 servings.

Per serving: 305 calories, 21 g protein, 24 g carbohydrates, 15 g total fat, 59 mg cholesterol, 749 mg sodium

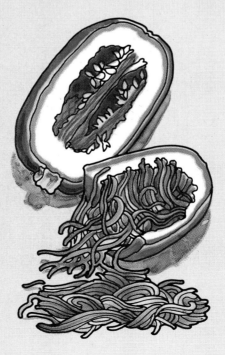

Spaghetti Squash Lasagne

- 2 spaghetti squash (about 2 lbs. *each*)
- 1 pound lean ground beef
- 1 clove garlic, minced or pressed
- 4 ounces mushrooms, sliced
- 1½ teaspoons dry basil
- 1½ teaspoons Italian herb seasoning or ½ teaspoon *each* dry basil, dry oregano leaves, and dry thyme or marjoram leaves
- ½ teaspoon salt
- 1 can (15 oz.) tomato purée
- ½ cup dry red wine or water
- 3 medium-size zucchini (about 12 oz. *total*), shredded
- 4 cups (1 lb.) shredded Cheddar cheese
- ½ to ¾ cup grated Parmesan cheese

Bake or microwave squash as directed at left. Meanwhile, crumble beef into a wide frying pan; cook over medium heat, stirring, until browned. Spoon off and discard fat. Add garlic and mushrooms; cook, stirring, until mushrooms are soft. Stir in basil, herb seasoning, salt, tomato purée, and wine. Reduce heat and boil gently, uncovered, for 10 to 15 minutes.

Cut baked squash in half; scrape out and discard seeds.

Loosen squash strands with a fork. Place strands from one whole squash in a greased shallow 3-quart baking dish. Lightly mix zucchini and Cheddar cheese; spoon half the mixture over squash. Cover with half the meat sauce. Repeat layers, using remaining spaghetti squash, zucchini mixture, and meat sauce.

Bake, covered, in a 350° oven until hot and bubbly (about 30 minutes). Serve with Parmesan cheese to add to taste. Makes 6 servings.

Per serving: 579 calories, 39 g protein, 19 g carbohydrates, 39 g total fat, 130 mg cholesterol, 1,163 mg sodium

Spaghetti Squash with Lime-Basil Sauce

1 spaghetti squash (2 to 3 lbs.)
1 quart lightly packed fresh basil leaves
½ cup olive oil or salad oil
2 cups (about 10 oz.) grated Parmesan cheese
2 tablespoons sugar
3 cloves garlic, quartered
¼ cup lime juice

Bake or microwave squash as directed on facing page. Meanwhile, in a blender or food processor, combine basil, oil, 1 cup of the cheese, sugar, garlic, and lime juice. Whirl until smoothly puréed. Set mixture aside.

Cut baked squash in half; scrape out and discard seeds.

Loosen squash strands with a fork and scoop out into a warm serving bowl. Add basil sauce and mix lightly, using 2 forks. Serve with remaining cheese to add to taste. Makes about 6 side-dish servings.

Per serving: 473 calories, 23 g protein, 25 g carbohydrates, 33 g total fat, 37 mg cholesterol, 909 mg sodium

Onion-Dill Spaghetti Squash

1 spaghetti squash (2 to 3 lbs.)
¼ cup butter or margarine
2 medium-size onions, coarsely chopped
1 teaspoon dill seeds
2 tablespoons vinegar
1 cup sour cream
2 small zucchini (about 6 oz. total), coarsely shredded

Bake or microwave squash as directed on facing page. Meanwhile, melt butter in a wide frying pan over medium heat. Add onions and dill seeds; cook, stirring often, until onions are very soft and light golden (about 20 minutes). Stir in vinegar and sour cream. Remove from heat and keep warm.

Cut baked squash in half; scrape out and discard seeds.

Loosen squash strands with a fork and scoop out into frying pan with onion mixture; add zucchini. Place over medium heat and mix lightly, using 2 spoons, just until heated through. Makes 4 to 6 side-dish servings.

Per serving: 255 calories, 4 g protein, 18 g carbohydrates, 20 g total fat, 45 mg cholesterol, 148 mg sodium

Zucchini Spaghetti with Veal Sauce

Savory Veal Sauce (recipe follows)
8 large zucchini (about 3 lbs. *total*)
¼ cup salad oil
3 large cloves garlic, minced or pressed
1 to 2 tablespoons butter or margarine, at room temperature
Pepper
½ to ¾ cup grated Parmesan cheese

Prepare Savory Veal Sauce. Meanwhile, using a knife or Oriental shredder, cut zucchini into long, very thin slivers (if using shredder, draw zucchini full length across coarse shredding blade).

Heat 2 tablespoons of the oil in a wide frying pan over medium-high heat. Add half each of the zucchini and garlic. Cook, lifting and gently stirring with 1 or 2 wide spatulas, just until tender-crisp to bite (3 to 4 minutes). Mound zucchini in the center of a deep platter; keep warm.

Heat remaining 2 tablespoons oil in pan; cook remaining zucchini and garlic and add to zucchini mixture on platter. Top with butter; season to taste with pepper.

Spoon sauce around but not over zucchini. Serve with cheese to add to taste. Makes 4 servings.

Savory Veal Sauce. In a wide frying pan, combine 1 tablespoon **olive oil**; 1 small **onion,** finely chopped; ½ cup finely chopped **green bell pepper;** 1 medium-size **carrot** (about 2 oz.), finely shredded; 3 **mushrooms,** thinly sliced; 1 tablespoon chopped **parsley;** 1 clove **garlic** (minced or pressed); 1 teaspoon **dry basil;** and ½ teaspoon *each* **dry rosemary** and **dry oregano leaves.** Cook over medium-high heat, stirring often, until onion is soft (about 5 minutes).

Crumble 1 pound **ground veal** or lean ground beef into pan and cook, stirring often, until lightly browned. Add 1 large can (28 oz.) **pear-shaped tomatoes** (break up with a spoon) and their liquid, 1 can (6 oz.) **tomato paste,** ⅓ cup **dry red wine,** and 1 **dry bay leaf;** bring to a boil. Adjust heat so mixture boils gently; cook, stirring occasionally, until sauce is thickened (about 20 minutes).

Season sauce to taste with **salt** and **pepper.** Discard bay leaf.

Per serving: 572 calories, 36 g protein, 34 g carbohydrates, 35 g total fat, 116 mg cholesterol, 1,072 mg sodium

*Fresh dill punctuates the vodka-enhanced
sauce that swathes Penne with Smoked Salmon
(recipe on facing page). To serve this distinctive pasta
dish as an entrée, add a salad of mixed greens
and a whole-grain bread.*

Seafood

As accomplices in delicious dining, pasta and seafood are perfect partners. The muted flavor of pasta balances and enhances—but never overpowers—the delicacy of fish and shellfish. For examples of this subtle sophistication, sample such combinations as *Penne with Smoked Salmon, Fettuccine with Calamari,* and *Angel Hair with Shrimp & Mint Butter Sauce.*

Another acknowledged advantage of the pasta-seafood alliance is the thriftiness pasta brings to the match. Hearty, satisfying dishes like *Grilled Swordfish with Stir-fried Noodles* and *Barbecued Crab with Spaghetti* vividly demonstrate pasta's renowned ability to stretch far costlier ingredients.

Pictured on facing page

Penne with Smoked Salmon

Preparation time: About 10 minutes

Cooking time: 10 to 12 minutes

Vodka emphasizes the flavor of a creamy, tomato-dotted sauce for silken smoked salmon and pasta tubes. Serve the dish as a first course, or present it as the entrée with tender-crisp green beans and a simple salad.

> 12 ounces dry small tube-shaped pasta such as penne, mostaccioli, or ziti
>
> 2 tablespoons olive oil
>
> 1 small shallot, thinly sliced
>
> 4 small pear-shaped (Roma-type) tomatoes (about 6 oz. *total*), peeled, seeded, and chopped
>
> ⅔ cup whipping cream
>   Pinch of ground nutmeg
>
> 2 tablespoons chopped fresh dill or ½ teaspoon dry dill weed
>
> ⅓ cup vodka
>
> 4 to 6 ounces sliced smoked salmon or lox, cut into bite-size strips
>   Ground white pepper
>   Fresh dill sprigs

In a 6- to 8-quart pan, cook pasta in 4 quarts boiling water just until tender to bite (10 to 12 minutes); or cook according to package directions. Drain well.

While pasta is cooking, heat oil in a wide frying pan over medium-low heat. Add shallot and cook, stirring often, until soft but not brown (about 3 minutes). Stir in chopped tomatoes, cover, and simmer for 5 minutes. Add cream, nutmeg, chopped dill, and vodka. Increase heat to high and bring to a full boil; boil for 1 minute.

Add pasta to sauce and mix lightly, using 2 spoons, until pasta is well coated. Remove from heat, add salmon, and mix lightly. Season to taste with white pepper and garnish with dill sprigs. Makes 4 servings.

Per serving: 541 calories, 18 g protein, 67 g carbohydrates, 22 g total fat, 53 mg cholesterol, 297 mg sodium

Tuna Carbonara

Preparation time: About 15 minutes

Cooking time: 10 to 12 minutes

This colorful dish is a good choice for a spur-of-the-moment supper. The cooked vermicelli is coated with beaten egg, helping the cheese, bell pepper strips, and tuna to cling to it.

- 8 ounces dry vermicelli (not coil vermicelli)
- 2 tablespoons olive oil
- 2 tablespoons butter or margarine
- 1 large red bell pepper (about 8 oz.), seeded and cut into thin bite-size strips
- 3 cloves garlic, minced or pressed
- 1 can (9¼ oz.) chunk-style tuna, drained
- 4 eggs, beaten until blended
- 1 cup (about 5 oz.) grated Parmesan cheese
- ¼ cup chopped parsley
  Salt and pepper

In a 5- to 6-quart pan, cook vermicelli in 3 quarts boiling water just until tender to bite (8 to 10 minutes); or cook according to package directions. Drain well.

While pasta is cooking, heat oil and butter in a wide frying pan over medium-high heat. Add bell pepper and garlic; cook, stirring often, until pepper is soft (6 to 8 minutes).

Add vermicelli and tuna to frying pan; mix lightly, using 2 forks, just until mixture is heated through. Remove from heat; then add eggs, cheese, and parsley. Mix lightly, lifting with 2 forks, until pasta is well coated with sauce. Season to taste with salt and pepper. Makes 4 servings.

Per serving: 653 calories, 45 g protein, 48 g carbohydrates, 30 g total fat, 282 mg cholesterol, 1,024 mg sodium

Fresh Tuna Puttanesca

Preparation time: About 15 minutes

Cooking time: About 20 minutes

Grilled tuna stars in a savory dish that's just right for a summer evening. In Italian cooking, *gnocchi*—the pasta specified—are usually little dumplings made from semolina or mashed potatoes. This entrée, though, uses dry gnocchi—fluted shapes rather like large shells, with ridges and hollows that are perfect for holding the fresh tomato sauce.

- 5 tablespoons olive oil
- 1 medium-size onion, thinly sliced
- 1 teaspoon crushed dried hot red chiles
- 2 cloves garlic, minced or pressed
- 6 medium-size pear-shaped (Roma-type) tomatoes (about 12 oz. *total*), chopped
- ¾ cup dry white wine
- ¼ cup sliced pitted ripe olives
- 1 tablespoon drained capers
- 1½ teaspoons minced fresh oregano leaves or ½ teaspoon dry oregano leaves
- 8 ounces dry gnocchi-shaped pasta
- 1 pound tuna fillets or steaks, about ½ inch thick
  Salt and freshly ground pepper
- ¼ cup chopped Italian (flat-leaf) or curly-leaf parsley

Heat ¼ cup of the oil in a wide frying pan over medium heat. Add onion and chiles; cook, stirring often, until onion is soft (about 5 minutes). Stir in garlic, tomatoes, wine, olives, capers, and oregano. Adjust heat so mixture boils gently. Continue to cook, uncovered, stirring occasionally, until sauce is slightly thickened (10 to 15 minutes).

Meanwhile, in a 5- to 6-quart pan, cook pasta in 3 quarts boiling water just until tender to bite (10 to 12 minutes); or cook according to package directions. Drain well.

While pasta is cooking, rinse tuna, pat dry, and cut into serving-size pieces. Brush on all sides with remaining 1 tablespoon oil. Place a ridged cooktop grill pan over medium-high heat; heat until a drop of water dances on the surface. Place fish on hot pan and cook, turning once, until fish is just slightly translucent or wet inside; cut in thickest part to test (about 4 minutes *total*).

Season tomato sauce to taste with salt and pepper; stir in parsley. Slice tuna across the grain into bite-size strips. Place pasta in a warm serving bowl; top with sauce. Arrange tuna around edge. Makes 4 servings.

Per serving: 567 calories, 35 g protein, 50 g carbohydrates, 25 g total fat, 43 mg cholesterol, 175 mg sodium

Grilled Swordfish with Stir-fried Noodles

Preparation time: About 25 minutes

Marinating time: At least 30 minutes

Cooking time: About 20 minutes

Tender swordfish steaks are soaked in a flavorful soy marinade, then grilled and served on a bed of colorful, chile-seasoned Chinese noodles.

- ¼ **cup soy sauce**
- 2 **tablespoons seasoned rice vinegar (or 2 tablespoons rice or white wine vinegar mixed with ⅜ teaspoon sugar)**
- 1 **tablespoon Oriental sesame oil**
- 1 **to 1½ pounds swordfish steaks, ¾ to 1 inch thick**
- ¼ **cup salad oil**
- 2 **medium-size onions, thinly sliced**
- 3 **medium-size carrots (7 to 8 oz. *total*), coarsely shredded**
- 1 **medium-size red bell pepper (about 5 oz.), seeded and cut into thin bite-size strips**
- 1 **or 2 *each* small fresh hot red and green chiles, seeded and finely chopped**
- 3 **cloves garlic, minced or pressed**
- 1 **tablespoon grated fresh ginger**
- 1 **cup lightly packed fresh cilantro (coriander) leaves**
- 1 **package (14 oz.) fresh Chinese-style noodles**
- ½ **cup unsalted dry-roasted peanuts**

In a shallow baking dish, mix soy, vinegar, and sesame oil. Rinse swordfish, pat dry, and cut into serving-size pieces. Place fish in soy mixture and turn to coat well. Cover and refrigerate for at least 30 minutes or up to 1 hour.

Heat 2 tablespoons of the salad oil in a wide frying pan over medium heat. Add onions, carrots, bell pepper, and chiles. Cook, stirring often, until vegetables are tender-crisp to bite (about 5 minutes). Stir in garlic and ginger; cook for 30 more seconds. Add cilantro; cook and stir for a few seconds, just until cilantro turns bright green. Lift vegetable mixture from pan and set aside. Reserve pan.

In a 6- to 8-quart pan, cook noodles in 4 quarts boiling water just until barely tender to bite (2 to 3 minutes); or cook according to package directions. Drain well, rinse with hot water, and drain again.

Lift swordfish from baking dish, reserving marinade. Place an oiled ridged cooktop grill pan over medium heat; heat until a drop of water dances on the surface. Then place fish on hot pan and cook, turning once, until fish is just slightly translucent or

wet inside; cut in thickest part to test (7 to 10 minutes *total*).

Heat remaining 2 tablespoons salad oil in reserved frying pan over medium-high heat. Add noodles and peanuts. Cook, turning gently with 2 spoons, just until noodles are hot (1 to 2 minutes). Add stir-fried vegetables and reserved marinade. Cook, stirring gently, until heated through. Arrange noodle-vegetable mixture on a platter; arrange fish on top. Makes 4 to 6 servings.

Per serving: 628 calories, 38 g protein, 59 g carbohydrates, 28 g total fat, 138 mg cholesterol, 966 mg sodium

Fettuccine with Calamari

Preparation time: About 10 minutes

Cooking time: About 15 minutes

Cook the squid for this garlic-accented pasta main dish very briefly—just until the meat is opaque white. Overcooking can make the delicate shellfish unpleasantly tough.

- 1 **pound cleaned squid tubes (mantles) and tentacles**
- ⅓ **cup olive oil**
- 1 **large red onion, thinly sliced and separated into rings**
- 1 **package (9 oz.) fresh fettuccine or 8 ounces dry fettuccine**
- 3 **large cloves garlic, minced or pressed**
- 1 **tablespoon lemon juice**
- ¼ **cup finely chopped parsley**
  Salt and freshly ground pepper
  Lemon wedges

Cut squid tubes crosswise into ½-inch-wide strips; set squid strips and tentacles aside.

Heat oil in a wide frying pan over medium heat. Add onion and cook, stirring often, until very soft but not brown (8 to 10 minutes).

Meanwhile, in a 5- to 6-quart pan, cook fettuccine in 3 quarts boiling water until tender to bite (3 to 4 minutes for fresh pasta, 8 to 10 minutes for dry); or cook according to package directions. Drain well.

To onion, add garlic and squid strips and tentacles; cook, stirring constantly, just until squid is opaque (2 to 3 minutes). Mix in lemon juice. Add fettuccine and half the parsley; mix gently, using 2 spoons, until heated through. Season to taste with salt and pepper. Sprinkle with remaining parsley and garnish with lemon wedges. Makes 4 servings.

Per serving: 473 calories, 27 g protein, 44 g carbohydrates, 21 g total fat, 339 mg cholesterol, 71 mg sodium

Angel Hair with Crab & Arugula

Preparation time: About 5 minutes

Cooking time: About 15 minutes

Crab lovers will adore this light, simple showcase for their favorite shellfish. Delicate angel hair pasta is topped with a combination of green onions, tiny cherry tomatoes, wilted arugula, and sweet crabmeat, all flavored with a touch of lemon peel and a splash of dry vermouth.

- 6 ounces dried angel hair pasta (capellini)
- 2 tablespoons butter or margarine
- 1 clove garlic, minced or pressed
- ½ cup thinly sliced green onions
- 1½ teaspoons finely shredded lemon peel
- 1 cup whole tiny cherry tomatoes; or 1 cup halved regular-size cherry tomatoes

- ⅓ cup dry vermouth
- 8 ounces cooked crabmeat
- 1 tablespoon lemon juice
- 2½ cups lightly packed arugula sprigs, cut into 2-inch-wide strips
  Salt and freshly ground pepper
  Lemon wedges

In a covered 3- to 4-quart pan, bring about 2 quarts water to a boil over high heat. Add pasta and cook, uncovered, until just tender to bite (about 5 minutes); or cook according to package directions.

Meanwhile, melt 1 tablespoon of the butter in a wide frying pan over medium-high heat. Add garlic, onions, lemon peel, tomatoes, and vermouth. Bring to a boil, stirring often; then reduce heat and simmer, uncovered, until tomatoes are slightly softened (about 5 minutes).

To pan, add crab, lemon juice, arugula, and remaining 1 tablespoon butter. Stir gently just until crab is heated through and arugula is barely wilted (about 2 more minutes). Season to taste with salt and pepper.

Drain pasta well and return to cooking pan. Top with crab sauce and toss gently with 2 forks until lightly mixed. Divide between 2 warm dinner plates. Offer lemon wedges to squeeze over pasta to taste.

Per serving: 606 calories, 15 g total fat, 8 g saturated fat, 144 mg cholesterol, 461 mg sodium, 71 g carbohydrates, 4 g fiber, 36 g protein, 226 mg calcium, 5 mg iron

Seafood in Parchment

Preparation time: About 25 minutes

Cooking & baking time: About 30 minutes

Effortlessly elegant, this parchment-wrapped main dish showcases succulent shellfish in tomato sauce.

- 6 tablespoons olive oil
- 1 clove garlic, minced or pressed
- 1 can (15 oz.) tomato purée
- ½ cup dry white wine
- 2 tablespoons drained capers
- ½ cup finely chopped parsley
  Salt and pepper
- 8 ounces sea scallops, rinsed, drained, and cut crosswise into ½-inch-thick slices
- 12 medium-large raw shrimp (31 to 35 per lb.), shelled and deveined
- 12 small hard-shell clams in shells, suitable for steaming, scrubbed
- 12 mussels in shells, scrubbed, beards pulled off
- 6 ounces dry linguine

Heat 2 tablespoons of the oil in a 2- to 3-quart pan over medium-high heat. Add garlic and stir until soft (about 1 minute). Add tomato purée, wine, capers, and ¼ cup of the chopped parsley. Bring to a boil; then reduce heat and boil gently, uncovered, until sauce is slightly thickened (about 10 minutes). Season to taste with salt and pepper; set aside.

Cut 4 rectangles of cooking parchment, each 15 by 24 inches. Place scallops and shrimp in centers of rectangles; place clams and mussels alongside. Pour tomato sauce over scallops and shrimp.

To seal each packet, bring together short ends of parchment and fold over by 1 inch; then fold over by 1 inch a second time. Fold the open ends under 2 or 3 times; tuck under packet. Place packets in a single layer in a large, shallow rimmed baking pan.

Bake in a 425° oven until clams and mussels pop open (about 15 minutes). To check, open one end of one packet; if necessary, reseal and continue baking.

Meanwhile, in a 5- to 6-quart pan, cook linguine in 3 quarts boiling water just until tender to bite (8 to 10 minutes); or cook according to package directions. Drain well and place in a warm serving bowl. Mix in remaining ¼ cup oil and remaining ¼ cup chopped parsley; keep warm.

Transfer packets, seam sides up, to 4 dinner plates. At the table, open packets; fold back parchment and tuck under. Add linguine to each packet alongside seafood. Makes 4 servings.

Per serving: 518 calories, 32 g protein, 46 g carbohydrates, 24 g total fat, 152 mg cholesterol, 779 mg sodium

Freshly cooked linguine completes each serving of Seafood in Parchment (recipe on facing page). Each fragrant little package holds oven-steamed scallops, shrimp, clams, and mussels in a tomato-wine sauce.

Capellini

Angel Hair with Shrimp & Mint Butter Sauce

Preparation time: About 30 minutes

Cooking time: 12 to 15 minutes

Refreshingly minty, this combination of shrimp and very thin pasta is a fine dish for an elegant warm-weather dinner.

- 6 tablespoons butter or margarine
- ½ teaspoon grated lemon peel
- ½ cup lightly packed fresh mint leaves
- 1 pound medium-size raw shrimp (35 to 45 per lb.), shelled and deveined
- 8 ounces dry capellini or 1 package (9 oz.) fresh angel hair pasta
- 1 cup dry white wine
  Thin lemon wedges
  Fresh mint sprigs

In a food processor or blender, whirl ¼ cup of the butter, lemon peel, and the ½ cup mint leaves until well blended; set aside. If made ahead, cover and refrigerate for up to 1 day.

In a wide frying pan, melt remaining 2 tablespoons butter over medium heat. Add shrimp and cook, stirring, until opaque throughout; cut to test (3 to 4 minutes). Lift out shrimp and keep warm. Reserve drippings in pan.

In a 5- to 6-quart pan, cook capellini in 3 quarts boiling water just until tender to bite (about 3 minutes for dry pasta, 1 to 2 minutes for fresh); or cook according to package directions. Drain well.

While pasta is cooking, add wine to drippings in frying pan; bring to a boil over high heat. Boil, stirring, until reduced to ⅓ cup (about 5 minutes). Add mint butter (all in one chunk) and stir quickly until butter is completely blended into sauce. Stir in shrimp and remove from heat.

Divide pasta among 4 wide, shallow bowls. Spoon shrimp mixture over pasta. Garnish with lemon wedges and mint sprigs. Makes 4 servings.

Per serving: 463 calories, 26 g protein, 44 g carbohydrates, 20 g total fat, 186 mg cholesterol, 316 mg sodium

Tricolor Pasta with Brandied Shrimp

Preparation time: About 30 minutes

Cooking time: About 10 minutes

Thin strands of golden, spinach-green, and rosy tomato-flavored linguine mingle vividly with juicy shrimp flamed in a buttery sauce with sliced fresh mushrooms.

- 6 tablespoons butter or margarine
- 2 tablespoons lemon juice
- 1 pound medium-size raw shrimp (35 to 45 per lb.), shelled, deveined, and butterflied
- ¼ cup brandy
- ½ teaspoon *each* dry tarragon and Worcestershire
- ¼ teaspoon ground ginger
- 1 teaspoon Dijon mustard
- 6 ounces mushrooms, thinly sliced
  Salt
- 1 package (9 oz.) fresh tricolor linguine
  Chopped parsley

Melt 3 tablespoons of the butter in a wide frying pan over medium heat. Stir in lemon juice; cook, stirring, until bubbly. Add shrimp and cook, stirring often, until opaque throughout; cut to test (3 to 4 minutes). Meanwhile, heat brandy in a small pan over low heat until barely warm to the touch. Carefully pour brandy over shrimp; ignite at once. Stir gently until flames are gone. Lift out shrimp and set aside.

To drippings in pan, add remaining 3 tablespoons butter, tarragon, Worcestershire, ginger, and mustard. Stir until well combined. Increase heat to medium-high. Add mushrooms and cook, stirring often, until lightly browned (about 3 minutes). Return shrimp to pan and stir lightly just until heated through (about 1 minute). Season to taste with salt.

Meanwhile, in a 5- to 6-quart pan, cook linguine in 3 quarts boiling water just until tender to bite (about 4 minutes); or cook according to package directions. Drain well.

Divide pasta among 4 heated dinner plates, then spoon shrimp sauce over pasta. Garnish with parsley. Makes 4 servings.

Per serving: 450 calories, 28 g protein, 39 g carbohydrates, 21 g total fat, 261 mg cholesterol, 377 mg sodium

Scallops & Green Noodles

Preparation time: About 25 minutes

Cooking time: 12 to 15 minutes

Barely cooked slivers of carrot, bell pepper, and green onion add color and crisp texture to this creamy blend of spinach noodles and scallops.

- 2 **large carrots (6 to 8 oz. *total*)**
- 1 **large red bell pepper (about 8 oz.), quartered and seeded**
- 8 **green onions (including tops)**
- 1 **pound sea scallops, rinsed and drained**
- ½ **cup (¼ lb.) butter or margarine**
- ⅔ **cup dry white wine**
- 1½ **cups whipping cream**
- 1 **package (9 oz.) fresh green fettuccine or 8 ounces dry green fettuccine**
- **Salt and pepper**
- **Freshly grated nutmeg**

Cut carrots, bell pepper, and onions into slivers ⅛ inch thick and 2 to 3 inches long. Set aside in separate piles. Cut scallops into ¼-inch-thick slices; set aside.

Melt 2 tablespoons of the butter in a wide frying pan over high heat. Add carrots and cook, stirring, until slightly limp (about 1 minute); lift out and set aside. Add 1 tablespoon more butter and bell pepper; cook, stirring, until slightly limp (about 1 minute). Lift out and add to carrots. Add onions and 1 tablespoon more butter; stir just until hot (30 to 45 seconds). Add to carrots and pepper; set aside.

Add wine to pan and bring to a boil. Add scallops, reduce heat, cover, and simmer until scallops are opaque throughout; cut to test (2 to 3 minutes). Lift scallops from pan with a slotted spoon and add to vegetables; keep warm.

Add cream to liquid in pan, increase heat to high, and bring to a full boil. Boil, uncovered, until reduced to 1¾ cups. Reduce heat to low, then add remaining ¼ cup butter and stir until smoothly blended into sauce.

While you are finishing sauce, in a 5- to 6-quart pan, cook fettuccine in 3 quarts boiling water just until tender to bite (3 to 4 minutes for fresh pasta, 5 to 7 minutes for dry); or cook according to package directions. Drain well. Add pasta to hot cream sauce; mix lightly, using 2 forks. Add scallops and vegetables and mix gently. Season to taste with salt, pepper, and nutmeg. Makes 4 to 6 servings.

Per serving: 642 calories, 26 g protein, 39 g carbohydrates, 44 g total fat, 220 mg cholesterol, 421 mg sodium

Ginger Linguine with Smoked Scallops

Preparation time: About 5 minutes

Smoking time: 12 to 15 minutes

Cooking time: 10 to 12 minutes

The woodsy flavor of oven-smoked scallops blends hauntingly with fresh ginger and cream in this rich sauce for linguine.

- 1 **pound scallops, rinsed and patted dry**
- 3 **tablespoons liquid smoke**
- 8 **ounces dry linguine or 1 package (9 oz.) fresh linguine**
- 1½ **tablespoons *each* tarragon wine vinegar and grated fresh ginger**
- ¼ **cup thinly sliced shallots**
- 1 **cup whipping cream**
- ½ **cup dry white wine**
- 1 **teaspoon Dijon mustard**
- **Chopped parsley**

If scallops are large, cut them into bite-size pieces. Pour liquid smoke into a 5- to 6-quart pan with ovenproof handles. Set a perforated or wire rack in pan. Arrange scallops in a single layer on rack and cover tightly. Bake in a 350° oven until scallops are opaque throughout; cut to test (12 to 15 minutes). If made ahead, let scallops cool; then cover and refrigerate for up to 1 day.

While scallops are smoking, in another 5- to 6-quart pan, cook linguine in 3 quarts boiling water just until tender to bite (8 to 10 minutes for dry pasta, 1 to 2 minutes for fresh); or cook according to package directions. Drain well.

While pasta is cooking, combine vinegar, ginger, and shallots in a wide frying pan over high heat; cook until vinegar has evaporated (about 1 minute). Add cream, wine, and mustard. Bring to a full boil; then boil, uncovered, stirring often, until sauce is reduced to 1¼ cups. Reduce heat to medium; add scallops and mix lightly until heated through (1 to 2 minutes). Add linguine; mix lightly, using 2 spoons. Sprinkle with parsley. Makes 4 servings.

Per serving: 496 calories, 28 g protein, 50 g carbohydrates, 20 g total fat, 104 mg cholesterol, 245 mg sodium

Bake pasta corkscrews beneath a fluffy
blanket of cream cheese and butter, then top them with
golden chicken legs to make this family-style feast:
Tomato-Cheese Pasta with Baked Chicken
(recipe on facing page).

Poultry

C hicken and noodles—to single out one well-known combination—illustrate the enduring popularity of pasta and poultry. Whether you choose familiar fettuccine or fanciful cockscombs, whether the meat is chicken, turkey, or something a bit more exotic, the finished dish is bound to be a hit.

And though the typical recipe calls for pasta as a foundation and poultry as the crowning touch, it's perfectly possible to vary the scheme. In Orzo-stuffed Roast Chicken & Vegetables, for example, tiny rice-shaped pasta is hidden within the cavity of a roast chicken. In Mexican Chicken Lasagne, the poultry is layered between the pasta ribbons; and in Won Ton Ravioli, ground chicken fills plump little pasta pillows.

Pictured on facing page

Tomato-Cheese Pasta with Baked Chicken

Preparation time: About 10 minutes

Cooking time: 8 to 10 minutes

Baking time: About 45 minutes

Bake chicken legs until they're almost done, then open the oven and slip in the pasta—a casserole of spiral-shaped *cavatappi* blanketed with snowy whipped cheese and dotted with diced tomatoes.

- 4 to 6 whole chicken legs, thighs attached (2 to 3 lbs. *total*)
- 8 ounces dry corkscrew-shaped pasta (cavatappi)
- 1 tablespoon olive oil
- 1 large package (8 oz.) Neufchâtel or cream cheese, at room temperature
- ½ cup (¼ lb.) unsalted butter or margarine, at room temperature
- ⅓ cup grated Parmesan cheese
- 3 medium-size pear-shaped (Roma-type) tomatoes (about 6 oz. *total*), chopped
- 1 tablespoon chopped fresh basil or 1 teaspoon dry basil
  Fresh basil sprigs

Rinse chicken legs, pat dry, and place, skin sides up, in a single layer in a shallow rimmed baking pan. Bake, uncovered, in a 400° oven for 35 minutes.

Meanwhile, in a 5- to 6-quart pan, cook pasta in 3 quarts boiling water just until tender to bite (8 to 10 minutes); or cook according to package direc-

493

tions. Drain; place in a shallow 2- to 3-quart baking dish, lightly mix in oil, and set aside.

In a medium-size bowl, combine Neufchâtel cheese, butter, and ¼ cup of the Parmesan cheese; beat with an electric mixer until well blended. Mound cheese mixture over center of pasta; sprinkle tomatoes over cheese mixture.

When chicken has baked for 35 minutes, place cheese-topped pasta in oven. Bake, uncovered, until pasta is hot in center and meat near chicken thigh-bone is no longer pink; cut to test (about 10 minutes). If desired, arrange chicken over pasta around edge of baking dish. Sprinkle with chopped basil and remaining Parmesan cheese; garnish with basil sprigs. Makes 4 to 6 servings.

Per serving: 763 calories, 42 g protein, 37 g carbohydrates, 49 g total fat, 191 mg cholesterol, 383 mg sodium

Orzo-stuffed Roast Chicken & Vegetables

Preparation time: About 45 minutes

Cooking time: About 15 minutes

Roasting time: 1 to 1¼ hours

Tiny rice-shaped pasta cooked in chicken broth with fresh chard and flavorful dried mushrooms makes a tempting dressing for a plump whole chicken. You'll find the pasta sold under several names, among them *orzo* and *riso*.

Creste di galli

Orzo & Chard Stuffing (recipe follows)
1 large frying chicken (3½ to 4 lbs.)
2 medium-size onions, unpeeled, cut lengthwise into quarters
4 large carrots (about 1 lb. *total*), cut lengthwise into quarters
¼ cup olive oil
1 tablespoon lemon juice
2 cloves garlic, minced or pressed
1 teaspoon dry rosemary, crumbled
 Lemon wedges

Prepare Orzo & Chard Stuffing; set aside to cool slightly.

Remove chicken neck and giblets; reserve for other uses, if desired. Remove and discard lumps of fat from chicken cavity. Rinse chicken inside and out; pat dry. Fill cavity with stuffing; close cavity with skewers. Spoon remaining stuffing into a greased 2- to 3-cup casserole, cover, and set aside.

Place chicken, breast up, in a shallow roasting pan. Surround with onions and carrots. Mix oil, lemon juice, garlic, and rosemary; brush some of the mixture generously over chicken, then drizzle remainder over vegetables. Roast, uncovered, in a 375° oven until a meat thermometer inserted in thickest part of chicken thigh (not touching bone) registers 185°F or until meat near thighbone is no longer pink; cut to test (1 to 1¼ hours). Vegetables should be tender when pierced. Bake stuffing in casserole for last 10 to 15 minutes.

Transfer chicken and vegetables to a serving platter. Garnish with lemon wedges. To serve, spoon out stuffing and carve chicken. Serve chicken and stuffing with vegetables. Makes 4 to 6 servings.

Orzo & Chard Stuffing. In a medium-size bowl, soak ½ cup (about ½ oz.) **dried mushrooms** in **hot water** to cover until soft (20 to 30 minutes). Drain well; cut off and discard any hard stems. Set mushrooms aside. Coarsely chop 4 **Swiss chard leaves** (about 3 oz. *total*) to make about 2 cups, lightly packed; set aside.

Heat 2 tablespoons **olive oil** in a 2-quart pan over medium heat. Add 1 small **onion,** finely chopped; cook, stirring often, until soft but not brown (about 5 minutes). Stir in mushrooms and 1 cup (about 8 oz.) **dry rice-shaped pasta.** Add 1 can (14½ oz.) **regular-strength chicken broth.** Bring to a boil; reduce heat and boil gently, uncovered, stirring occasionally, until broth is absorbed but pasta is still slightly chewy (8 to 10 minutes). Stir in chard. Season to taste with **salt** and **pepper.** Cover and let stand until slightly cooled (about 15 minutes).

Per serving: 744 calories, 49 g protein, 49 g carbohydrates, 38 g total fat, 132 mg cholesterol, 555 mg sodium

Rooster Crests with Mustard Chicken

Preparation time: 5 minutes

Cooking time: About 55 minutes

This isn't exactly a traditional American dish, but you'll still be reminded of your grandmother's Sunday stewed chicken and noodles! Whole chicken legs are simmered in a creamy sauce enlivened with a sophisticated mustard, then served atop whimsically shaped pasta cockscombs (*creste di galli*). Serve with Sunday-dinner favorites—fresh peas and hot, buttery biscuits with honey.

- 6 **whole chicken legs, thighs attached (2½ to 3 lbs.** *total***)**
- 2 **cups water**
- 2 **chicken bouillon cubes**
- ¼ **cup butter or margarine**
- ¼ **cup all-purpose flour**
- 1 **cup milk or half-and-half**
- 2 **tablespoons Dijon mustard**
- ½ **teaspoon dry thyme leaves**
   Salt and pepper
- 1 **package (12 oz.) dry rooster-crest pasta**
- ¼ **cup finely chopped parsley**

Rinse chicken and pat dry; then place in a wide, heavy 4- to 5-quart pan with water and bouillon cubes. Bring to a boil over medium-high heat, stirring as needed to dissolve bouillon cubes. Reduce heat, cover, and simmer for 30 minutes. Lift out chicken and set aside. Skim and discard fat from broth, then measure out 1¾ cups broth. Reserve remaining broth for other uses.

In pan used to cook chicken, melt butter over medium heat. Blend in flour and cook, stirring constantly, until bubbly. Remove from heat; gradually stir in the 1¾ cups broth, then milk, until blended. Return to heat and continue to cook, stirring, until mixture boils and thickens. Blend in mustard and thyme; season to taste with salt and pepper.

Remove and discard skin from chicken. Place chicken in sauce and simmer, uncovered, until chicken is tender and meat near thighbone is no longer pink; cut to test (about 15 minutes).

Meanwhile, in a 6- to 8-quart pan, cook pasta in 4 quarts boiling water just until tender to bite (8 to 10 minutes); or cook according to package directions. Drain well and mound in center of a warm deep platter.

Lift chicken from sauce and arrange around edge of platter. Stir parsley into sauce; pour sauce over pasta and chicken. Makes 6 servings.

Per serving: 472 calories, 33 g protein, 50 g carbohydrates, 15 g total fat, 121 mg cholesterol, 672 mg sodium

Spaghetti with Chicken Chili Sauce

Preparation time: About 30 minutes

Cooking time: About 1 hour

The distinctive aroma is reminiscent of *chili con carne*—but here, traditional chili seasonings go into a pungent sauce for spaghetti and gently poached, shredded chicken.

- 1 **frying chicken (3 to 3½ lbs.), quartered**
- 2 **tablespoons butter or margarine**
- 1 **large onion, finely chopped**
- 2 **cloves garlic, minced or pressed**
- 2½ **teaspoons chili powder**
- 2 **teaspoons ground cumin**
- 3 **cans (15 oz.** *each***) tomato purée**
- 1 **pound dry spaghetti**
- 2 **cups (8 oz.) shredded jack cheese**

Rinse chicken and pat dry. Place in a deep 5- to 6-quart pan and add enough water to barely cover. Bring to a boil over medium-high heat. Reduce heat, cover, and simmer until meat near thighbone is no longer pink; cut to test (about 30 minutes). Lift out chicken and let cool slightly; reserve broth for other uses. Remove and discard chicken skin and bones; tear meat into bite-size pieces and set aside.

Melt butter in a wide frying pan over medium heat. Add onion and cook, stirring often, until soft but not brown (about 5 minutes). Mix in garlic, chili powder, cumin, and tomato purée. Reduce heat and simmer, uncovered, for 15 minutes.

Meanwhile, in a 6- to 8-quart pan, cook spaghetti in 4 quarts boiling water just until tender to bite (10 to 12 minutes); or cook according to package directions. Drain well and place in a warm large serving bowl.

About 5 minutes before spaghetti is done, add chicken to sauce and simmer just until hot. Spoon sauce over spaghetti; serve with cheese to add to taste. Makes 6 servings.

Per serving: 719 calories, 48 g protein, 80 g carbohydrates, 23 g total fat, 122 mg cholesterol, 1,113 mg sodium

Chicken & Noodles with Pimentos

Preparation time: About 25 minutes

Roasting time: About 1¼ hours

Cooking time: About 10 minutes

The familiar combination of chicken and noodles sheds its homey, everyday image here! Fettuccine and roast chicken mingle with cream and colorful fresh pimento, orange zest, and cilantro.

1 large frying chicken (3½ to 4 lbs.)
1 large orange (about 8 oz.)
2 large fresh pimentos or red bell peppers (about 12 oz. *total*), seeded and cut into thin strips
2 cups whipping cream
1 teaspoon crushed dried hot red chiles
  Salt and pepper
1 package (9 or 10 oz.) fresh fettuccine or tagliarini
½ cup fresh cilantro (coriander) leaves

Remove chicken neck and giblets; reserve for other uses, if desired. Remove and discard lumps of fat from chicken cavity. Rinse chicken inside and out; pat dry. Place chicken, breast up, in a shallow roasting pan. Roast, uncovered, in a 400° oven until a meat thermometer inserted in thickest part of thigh (not touching bone) registers 185°F or until meat near thighbone is no longer pink; cut to test (about 1 hour). Drain juices from chicken into roasting pan; set chicken aside. Scrape drippings, including browned bits, from pan and reserve.

When chicken is cool enough to handle, pull off skin in large pieces; place, fat side down, on a rack in roasting pan. Return to 400° oven and bake, uncovered, until very crisp (15 to 20 minutes).

Meanwhile, remove and discard chicken bones; tear meat into bite-size pieces and set aside. With a zester, remove peel (colored part only) from orange. (Or use a vegetable peeler, then cut peel into fine strands with a knife.) Reserve orange for other uses.

Combine pan drippings and pimentos in a wide frying pan; cook over medium-high heat, stirring often, until pimentos are slightly softened (3 to 5 minutes). Add cream, chiles, and half the orange peel. Increase heat to high and boil until reduced by half (about 5 minutes). Add chicken meat and cook just until hot; season to taste with salt and pepper.

Meanwhile, in a 5- to 6-quart pan, cook fettuccine in 3 quarts boiling water just until tender to bite (3 to 4 minutes); or cook according to package directions. Drain well. Add pasta to chicken mixture, remove from heat, and mix lightly, using 2

forks. Transfer to a warm deep platter. Crumble chicken skin over pasta; garnish with cilantro and remaining orange peel. Makes about 6 servings.

Per serving: 731 calories, 38 g protein, 30 g carbohydrates, 51 g total fat, 265 mg cholesterol, 157 mg sodium

Pictured on facing page

Oven Chicken & Linguine

Preparation time: About 10 minutes

Baking time: About 45 minutes

Cooking time: About 10 minutes

For this one-dish meal, bake chicken thighs until golden, then toss linguine and spinach with the pan drippings.

½ cup (¼ lb.) butter or margarine
1 medium-size onion, thinly sliced
2 cloves garlic, minced or pressed
1 tablespoon dry basil
½ teaspoon crushed dried hot red chiles
8 chicken thighs (about 2½ lbs. *total*)
2 packages (10 oz. *each*) frozen chopped spinach, thawed
8 ounces dry linguine
1 cup (about 5 oz.) grated Parmesan cheese
  Salt
1 small orange (about 6 oz.), cut into wedges
  Fresh basil sprigs

Melt butter in a 10- by 15-inch shallow rimmed baking pan in a 400° oven. Remove pan from oven; stir onion, garlic, dry basil, and chiles into butter. Rinse chicken and pat dry; then place, skin side down, in butter mixture and turn to coat. Bake, uncovered, until meat near bone is no longer pink; cut to test (about 45 minutes). Meanwhile, squeeze as much liquid as possible from spinach.

Ten minutes before chicken is done, in a 5- to 6-quart pan, cook linguine in 3 quarts boiling water just until tender to bite (8 to 10 minutes); or cook according to package directions. Drain well.

Lift chicken from baking pan and keep warm. Add spinach to pan and stir over medium heat to scrape up browned bits. Remove from heat. Add linguine and cheese; mix lightly, using 2 forks. Season to taste with salt.

Mound linguine mixture on dinner plates; arrange chicken alongside. Garnish with orange wedges and basil sprigs. Makes 4 to 6 servings.

Per serving: 866 calories, 51 g protein, 40 g carbohydrates, 56 g total fat, 263 mg cholesterol, 865 mg sodium

For an appealing one-dish meal, try these tender
chicken thighs accompanied by chile-dotted pasta with
spinach and cheese. A squeeze of orange adds the
finishing touch to Oven Chicken & Linguine
(recipe on facing page).

Purchased won ton, egg roll (spring roll), and pot sticker (*gyoza*) wrappers can help you turn out Italian ravioli, cannelloni, and tortellini at record speed. You omit the time-consuming step of making, rolling, and cutting fresh pasta dough, yet the results are still impressive and delicious. In fact, you might even prefer ready-made to homemade wrappers, since some purchased varieties are thinner than homemade pasta. The thinness also makes them fragile, though—so handle them gently when cooking and saucing.

Because these Asian wrappers are generous in size, they hold more filling than their classic counterparts, making rather large versions of each pasta specialty.

Won ton and other wrappers are sold in the produce section of most supermarkets; you'll also find them in Asian markets.

Shiitake & Cheese Cannelloni

2 ounces (2½ to 3 cups) dried shiitake mushrooms
1½ pounds button mushrooms, thinly sliced
7 tablespoons butter or margarine
1 clove garlic, minced or pressed
3 tablespoons white wine vinegar
1½ tablespoons soy sauce
⅔ cup dry sherry
1½ tablespoons minced fresh ginger
1¼ teaspoons dry mustard
1¾ teaspoons ground coriander
¼ cup all-purpose flour
1½ cups regular-strength chicken broth
¾ cup milk
3 cups (12 oz.) shredded Münster cheese
8 egg roll wrappers, *each* about 6 inches square

Won Ton Ravioli & More

In a medium-size bowl, soak shiitake mushrooms in warm water to cover until soft and pliable (20 to 30 minutes). Drain and rinse well. Cut off and discard stems; set aside 8 small caps for garnish. Thinly slice remaining caps and add to sliced button mushrooms.

Melt ¼ cup of the butter in a 5- to 6-quart pan over medium-high heat. Add sliced mushrooms and garlic; cook, stirring often, until liquid has evaporated and mushrooms are browned (about 25 minutes). Add vinegar, soy, ⅓ cup of the sherry, 1 tablespoon of the ginger, ¾ teaspoon of the mustard, and 1 teaspoon of the coriander. Cook, stirring, until liquid has evaporated (about 5 minutes); set aside.

Melt remaining 3 tablespoons butter in a 3- to 4-quart pan over medium-high heat. Blend in flour, remaining 1½ teaspoons ginger, remaining ½ teaspoon mustard, and remaining ¾ teaspoon coriander. Cook, stirring constantly, until bubbly. Remove from heat and gradually stir in broth and milk. Return to heat and continue to cook, stirring, until sauce comes to a rapid boil (about 3 minutes). Remove from heat and add 2 cups of the cheese and remaining ⅓ cup sherry; stir until cheese is melted. Mix 1 cup of the sauce into mushrooms.

Place egg roll wrappers on a flat surface. Spoon an eighth of the mushroom mixture along one end of each, then roll up wrapper from that end to enclose filling.

Spread ½ cup of the sauce in a 9-by 13-inch baking dish; place cannelloni in sauce, side by side and seam side down. Spoon remaining sauce evenly over cannelloni to cover;

sprinkle with remaining 1 cup cheese. Garnish with reserved shiitake caps. (At this point, you may cover and refrigerate for up to 1 day.)

Bake, uncovered, in a 425° oven until cannelloni are hot in center and sauce is bubbly (10 to 20 minutes). Makes 4 servings.

Per serving: 790 calories, 34 g protein, 57 g carbohydrates, 50 g total fat, 189 mg cholesterol, 1,548 mg sodium

Won Ton Ravioli

Chicken & Prosciutto Filling (facing page)
About 6 dozen won ton wrappers (about 1 lb. *total*)
1 egg white, beaten just to blend Mushroom-Tomato Sauce (facing page)
¾ to 1 cup grated Parmesan cheese

Prepare Chicken & Prosciutto Filling. Place a won ton wrapper on a flat surface (cover remaining wrappers with plastic wrap to prevent drying). Place 1 rounded tablespoon filling on wrapper; spread evenly to within about ⅜ inch of edges. Brush edges with egg white. Cover with another wrapper and press edges well to seal. If desired, use a pastry wheel to trim edges decoratively; discard trimmings.

Repeat to make more ravioli, using remaining filling; as ravioli are completed, place in a single layer in flour-dusted shallow baking pans and cover with plastic wrap. (At this point, you may cover and refrigerate for up to 4 hours. Or freeze ravioli in baking pans until firm, then transfer to containers and store in freezer for up to 1 month.)

Prepare Mushroom-Tomato Sauce. When sauce is almost done, in a 6- to 8-quart pan, cook ravioli, about half at a time, in 4 quarts gently boiling water just until they are tender to bite (about 5 minutes if fresh, 6 minutes if frozen). Lift ravioli from water with a slotted spoon and place on warm plates or a deep platter; spoon Mushroom-Tomato Sauce over each layer of ravioli. Serve with cheese to add to taste. Makes 6 servings (about 3 dozen ravioli).

Chicken & Prosciutto Filling.
Coarsely chop 6 ounces thinly sliced **prosciutto** or ham. Remove and discard bones and skin from 1 pound **chicken breasts;** cut meat into ½-inch pieces. Melt 2 tablespoons **butter** or margarine in a wide frying pan over medium heat. Add 1 large **onion,** chopped; cook, stirring often, until onion is soft (6 to 8 minutes). Add chicken and cook, stirring, until it loses its pink color (about 3 minutes). Mix in prosciutto, then whirl the mixture in a food processor until coarsely ground (or chop finely with a knife). Mix in 2 **egg yolks,** ⅔ cup grated **Parmesan cheese,** 8 ounces **ricotta cheese,** and ⅛ to ¼ teaspoon **ground nutmeg;** season to taste with **salt** and **ground white pepper.** If made ahead, cover and refrigerate for up to 8 hours.

Mushroom-Tomato Sauce.
Melt 3 tablespoons **butter** or margarine in a wide frying pan over medium heat. Stir in ½ cup chopped **shallots** or onion and 1 pound **mushrooms,** thinly sliced. Cook, stirring often, until mushrooms are lightly browned. Stir in 2 tablespoons **tomato paste,** 1 teaspoon **dry basil,** and 2 cups *each* **dry vermouth** and **regular-strength chicken broth.** Increase heat to high and bring to a boil. Cook, stirring often, until reduced to 3 cups. Reduce heat to low. (At this point, you may let cool, then cover and refrigerate for up to 1 day. Reheat before continuing.)

Add 1 cup (½ lb.) **butter** or margarine to sauce; stir constantly until

butter is smoothly blended into sauce (butter thickens sauce). Serve at once.

Per serving: 903 calories, 48 g protein, 63 g carbohydrates, 52 g total fat, 333 mg cholesterol, 1,670 mg sodium

Pot Sticker Tortellini

Sausage-Spinach Filling (recipe follows)
6 **to 7 dozen thin pot sticker (***gyoza***) or won ton wrappers (about 1 lb.** *total***)**
1 **egg white, beaten just to blend Cream Sauce (recipe follows)**
2 **tablespoons butter or margarine**
1¾ **to 2 cups (9 to 10 oz.) grated Parmesan cheese**
Freshly grated nutmeg

Prepare Sausage-Spinach Filling.

Fill wrappers a few at a time. (If using won ton wrappers, use a 3- to 3¼-inch round cookie cutter to cut several wrappers at a time; discard trimmings.) Cover remaining wrappers with plastic wrap to prevent drying.

To shape tortellini, place about 1 teaspoon of the filling in center of a wrapper; moisten edge of wrapper with egg white, fold wrapper in half, and press edges together to seal. Bring ends together to overlap; moisten with egg white and press to seal. Repeat to make more tortellini, using remaining filling; as tortellini are

completed, place in a single layer in flour-dusted shallow baking pans and cover with plastic wrap. (At this point, you may cover and refrigerate for up to 4 hours. Or freeze tortellini in baking pans until firm, then transfer to containers and store in freezer for up to 1 month.)

Prepare Cream Sauce.

In a 6- to 8-quart pan, cook tortellini, half at a time, in 4 quarts gently boiling water just until tender to bite (about 4 minutes if fresh, 6 minutes if frozen). Lift tortellini from water with a slotted spoon and add to Cream Sauce along with butter and 1 cup of the cheese. Turn tortellini gently in sauce until coated. Sprinkle with nutmeg; serve with remaining ¾ to 1 cup cheese to add to taste. Makes 6 servings.

Sausage-Spinach Filling.
Remove and discard casings from 6 ounces **mild Italian sausages.** Crumble meat into a wide frying pan over medium-low heat. Cook, stirring often, until lightly browned. Remove from heat; spoon off and discard drippings. Squeeze as much liquid as possible from 1 package (10 oz.) thawed **frozen chopped spinach.** Combine sausage, spinach, 8 ounces **ricotta cheese,** 1 **egg yolk,** ½ cup grated **Parmesan cheese,** ⅛ teaspoon **pepper,** and ¾ teaspoon *each* crushed **fennel seeds** and **dry oregano leaves.** If made ahead, cover and refrigerate for up to 8 hours.

Cream Sauce.
In a wide frying pan, combine 3 cups **whipping cream** and ⅛ teaspoon **ground nutmeg.** Bring to a boil over high heat, then boil until large shiny bubbles form all over and sauce is reduced by about a third. Keep warm over lowest heat, stirring occasionally.

Per serving: 891 calories, 36 g protein, 51 g carbohydrates, 61 g total fat, 320 mg cholesterol, 973 mg sodium

Dried tomatoes add a toasty-sweet accent to
Chicken in Port Cream with Fettuccine (recipe on facing
page). Steamed fresh asparagus is a good accompaniment
for this elegant entrée.

Pasta & Chicken with Sweet-Sour Tomato Sauce

Preparation time: About 15 minutes

Cooking & grilling time: About 20 minutes

Distinctively seasoned with allspice, currants, and pine nuts, this fresh tomato sauce is delightful with tender linguine and strips of grilled chicken.

- 5 tablespoons olive oil
- 1 medium-size onion, thinly sliced
- 2 tablespoons pine nuts or slivered almonds
- 2 cloves garlic, minced or pressed
- 6 medium-size pear-shaped (Roma-type) tomatoes (about 12 oz. *total*), chopped
- 1 tablespoon *each* firmly packed brown sugar and dried currants
- 2 tablespoons cider vinegar
- ½ teaspoon ground allspice
- ¾ cup dry red wine
- 2 whole chicken breasts (about 1 lb. *each*), skinned, boned, and split
- 8 ounces dry linguine or 1 package (9 oz.) fresh linguine
  Salt and pepper
  Chopped parsley

Heat ¼ cup of the oil in a wide frying pan over medium heat. Add onion and pine nuts and cook, stirring, until onion is soft (about 5 minutes). Stir in garlic, tomatoes, sugar, currants, vinegar, allspice, and wine. Adjust heat so mixture boils gently. Continue to cook, uncovered, stirring occasionally, until sauce is slightly thickened (12 to 15 minutes).

Meanwhile, rinse chicken and pat dry. Brush on all sides with remaining 1 tablespoon oil. Place a ridged cooktop grill pan over medium heat; heat until a drop of water dances on the surface. Place chicken on hot pan and cook, turning once, until well browned on outside and no longer pink in center; cut chicken in thickest part to test (about 10 minutes *total*).

While chicken is cooking, in a 5- to 6-quart pan, cook linguine in 3 quarts boiling water just until tender to bite (8 to 10 minutes for dry pasta, 1 to 2 minutes for fresh); or cook according to package directions. Drain well.

Season tomato sauce to taste with salt and pepper. Add linguine and mix lightly, using 2 forks. Transfer to a warm deep platter. Cut chicken into ½-inch-wide strips; arrange around edge of linguine. Sprinkle with parsley. Makes 4 servings.

Per serving: 592 calories, 43 g protein, 55 g carbohydrates, 22 g total fat, 86 mg cholesterol, 108 mg sodium

---

Pictured on facing page

Chicken in Port Cream with Fettuccine

Soaking time: About 1 hour

Preparation time: 3 to 5 minutes

Cooking time: About 30 minutes

An unusual combination of ingredients produces decidedly elegant results in this simple-to-make dish. Be sure to use *dry* dried tomatoes, not the kind packed in olive oil.

- ¾ cup dried tomatoes
- 3 whole chicken breasts (about 1 lb. *each*), skinned, boned, and split
- 3 tablespoons butter or margarine
- 1 cup port
- 1½ cups whipping cream
- 1 package (9 oz.) fresh fettuccine or 8 ounces dry fettuccine
  Salt and pepper
  Fresh tarragon sprigs

In a small bowl, soak tomatoes in warm water to cover until soft (about 1 hour). Drain well, chop coarsely, and set aside.

Rinse chicken; pat dry. Melt butter in a wide frying pan over medium-high heat. Add chicken and cook, turning once, until well browned on outside and no longer pink in center; cut in thickest part to test (about 10 minutes *total*). Lift out chicken and keep warm.

To pan drippings, add port and cream. Increase heat to high and bring to a boil; boil, uncovered, stirring occasionally, until large, shiny bubbles form (10 to 15 minutes). Meanwhile, in a 5- to 6-quart pan, cook fettuccine in 3 quarts boiling water just until tender to bite (3 to 4 minutes for fresh pasta, 8 to 10 minutes for dry); or cook according to package directions.

While pasta is cooking, mix tomatoes, chicken, and any chicken juices into cream mixture; season to taste with salt and pepper.

Drain fettuccine well; transfer to a warm deep platter. Top with chicken mixture, then garnish with tarragon sprigs. Makes 6 servings.

Per serving: 541 calories, 41 g protein, 32 g carbohydrates, 27 g total fat, 217 mg cholesterol, 195 mg sodium

Pictured on front cover

Farfalle with Grilled Chicken & Pesto Cream

Preparation time: About 15 minutes

Cooking time: 15 to 20 minutes

How would you describe the shape of the pasta in this creamy green combination? The Italians see these little noodles as butterflies or *farfalle*; to others, they may look more like bow ties.

- 2 **tablespoons pine nuts**
  Minted Pesto Butter (recipe follows)
- 2 **whole chicken breasts (about 1 lb. *each*), skinned, boned, and split**
- 1 **tablespoon olive oil**
- 10 **ounces dry bow-shaped pasta**
- ¼ **cup dry white wine**
- 1 **cup whipping cream**
  Salt
- 2 **tablespoons chopped roasted red pepper**
  Fresh basil sprigs
- ⅓ **to ½ cup grated Parmesan cheese**

Stir pine nuts in a small frying pan over medium-low heat until lightly browned (about 3 minutes). Prepare Minted Pesto Butter, using 1 tablespoon of the pine nuts; set Minted Pesto Butter and remaining 1 tablespoon pine nuts aside.

Rinse chicken and pat dry. Brush on all sides with oil. Place a ridged cooktop grill pan over medium heat; heat until a drop of water dances on the surface. Place chicken on hot pan and cook, turning once, until well browned on outside and no longer pink in center; cut in thickest part to test (about 10 minutes *total*). Cut chicken into ½-inch-wide bite-size strips.

While chicken is cooking, in a 5- to 6-quart pan, cook pasta in 3 quarts boiling water just until tender to bite (about 10 minutes); or cook according to package directions. Drain well and set aside.

In a wide frying pan, combine Minted Pesto Butter and wine. Cook over medium heat, stirring occasionally, until bubbly (about 2 minutes). Stir in cream and bring to a full rolling boil, stirring often. Season sauce to taste with salt, then add roasted pepper, pasta, and chicken; mix lightly, using 2 spoons. Sprinkle mixture with remaining 1 tablespoon toasted pine nuts and garnish with basil sprigs. Serve with Parmesan cheese to add to taste. Makes 4 to 6 servings.

Minted Pesto Butter. In a blender or food processor, combine 1 tablespoon of the **toasted pine nuts;**

1 clove **garlic,** coarsely chopped; ½ cup *each* lightly packed **parsley sprigs** and **fresh basil leaves;** 2 tablespoons coarsely chopped **fresh mint leaves;** 1 **green onion** (including top), sliced; ⅛ teaspoon **pepper;** a pinch of **ground nutmeg;** 2 tablespoons **olive oil;** and ¼ cup **butter** or margarine, melted. Whirl until well combined, scraping sides of container several times.

Per serving: 711 calories, 40 g protein, 45 g carbohydrates, 41 g total fat, 205 mg cholesterol, 319 mg sodium

Fettuccine Verde with Chicken

Preparation time: About 25 minutes

Cooking time: About 20 minutes

Give leftover chicken a delicious encore with this colorful pasta dish. It's good with warm garlic bread and a ruffly green salad in a tart vinaigrette.

- 3 **tablespoons olive oil**
- 1 **large onion, thinly sliced**
- 8 **ounces mushrooms, thinly sliced**
- 2 **cloves garlic, minced or pressed**
- ¼ **cup butter or margarine**
- 1 **package (3 oz.) thinly sliced ham, cut into julienne strips**
- 1 **medium-size tomato (about 5 oz.), chopped**
- 1 **teaspoon dry basil**
- 1 **package (9 oz.) fresh green fettuccine or 8 ounces dry green fettuccine**
- 2 **cups shredded cooked chicken**
- ½ **cup *each* whipping cream and chopped parsley**
- ½ **cup dry white wine or dry sherry**
- ⅛ **teaspoon ground nutmeg**
  Salt and pepper
  About ½ cup grated Parmesan cheese

Heat oil in a wide frying pan over medium-high heat. Add onion and cook, stirring often, until lightly browned (6 to 8 minutes). Add mushrooms and continue to cook, stirring, until lightly browned. Add garlic, butter, ham, tomato, and basil; bring to a gentle boil, then reduce heat and boil gently, uncovered, for 5 minutes.

In a 5- to 6-quart pan, cook fettuccine in 3 quarts boiling water just until tender to bite (3 to 4 minutes for fresh pasta, 8 to 10 minutes for dry); or cook according to package directions. Drain well.

While fettuccine is cooking, add chicken, cream, parsley, wine, and nutmeg to mushroom-ham mixture. Mix gently until hot, then add fettuccine and mix lightly, using 2 forks. Season to taste with salt

and pepper. Serve with cheese to add to taste.
Makes 4 servings.

Per serving: 721 calories, 41 g protein, 42 g carbohydrates, 44 g total fat, 219 mg cholesterol, 755 mg sodium

Mexican Chicken Lasagne

Preparation time: About 30 minutes

Cooking time: About 20 minutes

Baking time: 45 to 50 minutes; 55 minutes if refrigerated

This dish certainly *looks* Italian—but when you cut into its bubbling depths, the spicy aroma lets everyone know that the flavor is Mexican.

Chile-Cheese Filling (recipe follows)
2 tablespoons salad oil
1 medium-size onion, chopped
2 cloves garlic, minced or pressed
1 medium-size red bell pepper (about 5 oz.), seeded and chopped
2 jars (1 lb. *each*) mild chile salsa
½ teaspoon pepper
2 tablespoons chili powder
1 teaspoon ground cumin
10 ounces dry lasagne
4 cups bite-size pieces cooked chicken
1 cup (4 oz.) shredded sharp Cheddar cheese
1 cup (4 oz.) shredded jack cheese

Prepare Chile-Cheese Filling and set aside.

Heat oil in a 4- to 5-quart pan over medium heat; add onion, garlic, and bell pepper. Cook, stirring often, until onion is soft but not brown (8 to 10 minutes). Add salsa, pepper, chili powder, and cumin; bring to a boil. Reduce heat and boil gently, uncovered, stirring often, until mixture is reduced to 1 quart (about 10 minutes).

Meanwhile, in a 5- to 6-quart pan, cook lasagne in 3 quarts boiling water just until tender to bite (about 10 minutes); or cook according to package directions. Drain, rinse with cold water, and drain well again.

Arrange half the lasagne over bottom of a 9- by 13-inch baking dish; spread with half the Chile-Cheese Filling, then cover with half the chicken. Spoon half the sauce over chicken; sprinkle with ½ cup each of the Cheddar and jack cheeses. Repeat layers, using remaining lasagne, filling, chicken, sauce, and shredded cheeses. (At this point, you may cover and refrigerate for up to 1 day.)

Bake, covered, in a 375° oven until lasagne is bubbly and hot in center (45 to 50 minutes; 55 minutes if refrigerated). Uncover and let stand for 5 minutes; cut into squares to serve. Makes 9 servings.

Chile-Cheese Filling. Combine 2 cups **small-curd cottage cheese, 2 eggs,** ⅓ cup chopped **parsley,** and 1 can (4 oz.) **diced green chiles.** Mix well.

Per serving: 469 calories, 36 g protein, 36 g carbohydrates, 20 g total fat, 134 mg cholesterol, 1,138 mg sodium

Chicken Carbonara

Preparation time: About 15 minutes

Cooking time: About 20 minutes

Beaten eggs, cream, and Parmesan cheese make the golden sauce that brings this creamy pasta and chicken dish together.

½ cup pine nuts
4 slices bacon (about 3 oz. *total*), chopped
8 ounces dry linguine or 1 package (9 oz.) fresh linguine
4 eggs (room temperature)
½ cup grated Parmesan cheese
⅓ cup whipping cream
¼ cup chopped parsley
¼ cup chopped fresh basil leaves or 2 tablespoons dry basil
3 cloves garlic, minced or pressed
1½ cups diced cooked chicken
1 to 2 tablespoons butter or margarine

Stir pine nuts in a wide frying pan over medium-low heat until lightly browned (about 3 minutes). Remove from pan and set aside in a large bowl. Increase heat to medium; add bacon to pan and cook until brown (about 7 minutes). Lift out bacon; place in bowl with nuts. Reserve drippings in pan.

In a 5- to 6-quart pan, cook linguine in 3 quarts boiling water just until tender to bite (8 to 10 minutes for dry pasta, 1 to 2 minutes for fresh); or cook according to package directions. Drain well.

While pasta is cooking, add eggs, cheese, cream, parsley, basil, garlic, and chicken to bacon and pine nuts. Beat until well mixed.

To reserved bacon drippings in frying pan, add enough butter to make ¼ cup; melt butter in drippings over medium heat. Add linguine, then egg mixture. Mix lightly, using 2 forks, just until linguine is well coated and heated through. Makes 4 servings.

Per serving: 662 calories, 40 g protein, 49 g carbohydrates, 35 g total fat, 306 mg cholesterol, 444 mg sodium

*Brighten the family dinner table with Spaghetti
with Turkey Parmesan (recipe on facing page): juicy, herb-
seasoned turkey patties, topped with two cheeses and
served with a simple tomato sauce and plenty of
hot pasta. Emerald-green steamed broccoli
is good alongside.*

Chicken Livers with Garlic Pasta

Preparation time: About 10 minutes

Cooking time: About 10 minutes

When time is short, try this robust dish. Hot linguine, pungent with garlic, makes a bold partner for buttery-rich sautéed chicken livers.

- 6 tablespoons butter or margarine
- 1 pound chicken livers, drained, cut into halves
- 8 ounces dry linguine or 1 package (9 oz.) fresh linguine
- 3 large cloves garlic, minced or pressed
- ½ cup finely chopped parsley
- ½ teaspoon dry oregano leaves
- ½ cup grated Parmesan cheese (optional)

Melt 2 tablespoons of the butter in a wide frying pan over medium-high heat. Add livers and cook, turning once, until firm and browned on outside but still pink in center; cut to test (5 to 7 minutes *total*). Keep warm.

While livers are cooking, in a 5- to 6-quart pan, cook linguine in 3 quarts boiling water just until tender to bite (8 to 10 minutes for dry pasta, 1 to 2 minutes for fresh); or cook according to package directions. Drain well.

While linguine is cooking, melt remaining ¼ cup butter in a medium-size frying pan over medium heat. Add garlic and stir until it turns opaque (1 to 2 minutes); mix in parsley and oregano.

Divide pasta among 4 warm dinner plates; drizzle with butter mixture. Arrange livers alongside. Serve with cheese, if desired. Makes 4 servings.

Per serving: 511 calories, 28 g protein, 48 g carbohydrates, 22 g total fat, 545 mg cholesterol, 270 mg sodium

Pictured on facing page

Spaghetti with Turkey Parmesan

Preparation time: About 15 minutes

Cooking time: About 50 minutes

Made with ground turkey, this colorful dish is delicious, easy to make, and certain to please the whole family.

Tomato-Onion Sauce (recipe follows)
- 1 egg
- ½ cup soft bread crumbs
- 1⅓ cups (about 7 ozs.) grated Parmesan cheese
- ½ teaspoon poultry seasoning
- 1 pound ground turkey
- 1 tablespoon butter or margarine
- 1 tablespoon olive oil
- 4 slices mozzarella cheese (3 oz. *total*)
- 8 ounces dry spaghetti
  Italian (flat-leaf) parsley sprigs (optional)

Prepare Tomato-Onion Sauce; keep warm over lowest heat.

In a medium-size bowl, beat egg until blended. Add bread crumbs, ⅓ cup of the Parmesan cheese, and poultry seasoning; stir until blended. Add turkey; mix lightly until well combined. Shape turkey mixture into 4 patties, each about 4 inches in diameter.

Melt butter in oil in a wide frying pan over medium-high heat. Add turkey patties and cook, turning once, until browned on both sides (about 8 minutes *total*). Transfer patties to a shallow rimmed baking pan or broiler pan. Spread each patty with 2 tablespoons of the Tomato-Onion Sauce; then top each with 1 slice of the mozzarella cheese and 1 tablespoon of the remaining Parmesan cheese.

Just before broiling patties, in a 5- to 6-quart pan, cook spaghetti in 3 quarts boiling water just until tender to bite (10 to 12 minutes); or cook according to package directions. Meanwhile, broil turkey patties about 4 inches below heat until cheese is melted and lightly browned (3 to 4 minutes).

Drain spaghetti well and transfer to a warm deep platter; spoon remaining Tomato-Onion Sauce over spaghetti, then top with turkey patties. Garnish with parsley sprigs, if desired. Serve with remaining ¾ cup Parmesan cheese to add to taste. Makes 4 servings.

Tomato-Onion Sauce. Heat 2 tablespoons **olive oil** or salad oil in a 2-quart pan over medium heat. Add 1 medium-size **onion,** finely chopped, 2 teaspoons **dry oregano leaves,** 1 **dry bay leaf,** and 1 large clove **garlic,** minced or pressed. Cook, stirring often, until onion is soft but not browned (about 5 minutes). Stir in 1 large can (15 oz.) **tomato sauce.** Cover, reduce heat, and simmer for 20 minutes, stirring occasionally.

Per serving: 759 calories, 47 g protein, 57 g carbohydrates, 38 g total fat, 171 mg cholesterol, 1,383 mg sodium

It isn't pasta, but the coarsely ground cornmeal called *polenta* is nonetheless comparable to the macaroni family in many respects. Like pasta, cooked polenta is a perfect mild-tasting foil for all kinds of flavorful sauces; next time you're hungry for simple Italian food, try topping hot polenta with Garlic Veal Stew (page 518) or the Turkey Marinara sauce on page 508.

Polenta is a staple in certain areas of northern Italy, particularly around Venice and in the regions of Piedmont and Lombardy. In rural markets, you may see flaring, bell-shaped copper or brass pots specifically designed for cooking polenta. Old-time cooks stirred the slowly bubbling mush with a wooden spoon or stick until it was thick enough to pull from the sides of the pan—and to hold the spoon firmly upright!

Today, though, there's more than one way to cook traditional-tasting polenta. You can still use the old-fashioned method, of course—but if you'd rather not stand over the polenta, stirring it constantly, try our microwaved or baked versions of the standard recipe. We also offer some fresh new ways to present polenta—in rich, cheese-dappled cakes to accompany grilled sausages or chops, for example, or as the crust of a savory cheese tart to serve with a crisp green salad.

Stove-top Polenta

3½ cups regular-strength chicken broth or water
1 cup polenta (Italian-style corn-meal) or yellow cornmeal
Salt and pepper

In a deep 4- to 5-quart pan, bring 2 cups of the broth to a boil over high heat. Meanwhile, mix polenta with remaining 1½ cups broth. Stir polenta

Polenta, Plain & Fancy

mixture into boiling broth. Return mixture to a boil, stirring often. When spatters of polenta cannot be stirred down, reduce heat so mixture boils very slowly. Cook until reduced to about 3 cups, stirring constantly to prevent scorching as polenta thickens. Total cooking time is 15 to 20 minutes, starting from the time polenta first boils. Season to taste with salt and pepper.

To serve as is, spoon into a mound on a board or platter; let stand for 5 to 10 minutes to firm up slightly, then cut or slice to serve. Or use in the following recipes. Makes 4 to 6 servings.

Per serving: 103 calories, 3 g protein, 19 g carbohydrates, 2 g total fat, 0 mg cholesterol, 586 mg sodium

Gorgonzola Polenta Cakes

3 tablespoons olive oil
1 small onion, finely chopped
1 clove garlic, minced or pressed
2 tablespoons finely chopped parsley
Stove-top Polenta (at left)
¼ cup grated Parmesan cheese
⅓ cup crumbled Gorgonzola or other blue-veined cheese
1 egg, beaten just to blend

Heat 1 tablespoon of the oil in a wide frying pan over medium heat. Add onion and cook, stirring often, until soft but not brown (about 5 minutes). Add garlic and stir until opaque. Remove pan from heat and stir in parsley; set aside.

Prepare Stove-top Polenta, but omit salt. Into warm polenta, stir

onion mixture, Parmesan cheese, and Gorgonzola cheese. Let stand for at least 5 minutes to firm up slightly. Blend in egg.

Heat remaining 2 tablespoons oil in a wide nonstick frying pan over medium heat. Scoop out polenta, using a scant ½ cup for each portion, and slide into oil; flatten slightly to make round patties. Don't crowd pan (you can cook about 4 patties at a time). Cook patties, turning carefully once, until browned on both sides (10 to 12 minutes total). Makes 8 patties (4 to 8 servings).

Per patty: 165 calories, 5 g protein, 15 g carbohydrates, 9 g total fat, 33 mg cholesterol, 572 mg sodium

Polenta Cheese Tart

½ recipe Stove-top Polenta (at left)
1¼ cups (about 6 oz.) crumbled goat cheese, such as Bûcheron or Montrachet, or 1 cup (about 4 oz.) ½-inch cubes cream cheese
1 cup (about 4 oz.) crumbled blue-veined cheese or shredded pro-volone cheese
1 cup (4 oz.) shredded mozzarella cheese
⅓ cup thinly sliced green onions (including tops)

Prepare Stove-top Polenta, using 1¾ cups broth or water and ½ cup polenta (start with 1 cup of the broth in a 2- to 3-quart pan; mix polenta with remaining ¾ cup broth). Cook until reduced to 1 to 1½ cups (7 to 10 minutes). Omit salt.

Pour polenta into a greased 7½- to 8-inch tart pan with a removable bottom. Let stand until just cool enough to touch; with fingers, press polenta evenly over bottom and up pan sides. Mix goat, blue, and mozzarella cheeses (or cream, provolone, and mozzarella cheeses) with onions; spoon into polenta shell. Bake, uncovered, in a 350° oven until mozzarella cheese is melted (about 30 minutes). Carefully remove pan sides and cut tart into wedges. Makes 6 servings.

Per serving: 276 calories, 15 g protein, 13 g carbohydrates, 18 g total fat, 55·mg cholesterol, 802 mg sodium

Microwave Polenta

2 cups regular-strength chicken broth or water
½ cup polenta (Italian-style cornmeal) or yellow cornmeal
1 tablespoon butter or margarine
Salt (optional)
¼ to ⅓ cup grated Parmesan cheese

In a 2-quart microwave-safe measuring cup or bowl, stir together broth, polenta, and butter. Microwave, uncovered, on **HIGH (100%)** for 12 to 15 minutes or until polenta is tender and liquid has been absorbed, stirring at 5-minute intervals. Spoon polenta into a serving dish; season to taste with salt, if desired. Serve with cheese to add to taste. Makes about 3 servings.

Per serving: 175 calories, 7 g protein, 20 g carbohydrates, 8 g total fat, 16 mg cholesterol, 853 mg sodium

Baked Polenta

5 cups regular-strength chicken broth
1½ cups polenta (Italian-style cornmeal) or yellow cornmeal
1 small onion, finely chopped
¼ cup butter or margarine, diced
½ to ¾ cup grated Parmesan cheese

In a greased 9- by 13-inch baking dish (rectangular or oval), stir together

broth, polenta, onion, and butter. Bake, uncovered, in a 350° oven until liquid has been absorbed (45 to 50 minutes). Serve with cheese to add to taste. Makes 6 servings.

Per serving: 261 calories, 8 g protein, 30 g carbohydrates, 12 g total fat, 27 mg cholesterol, 1,072 mg sodium

Baked Polenta & Sausages

5 medium-size red bell peppers (about 1¾ lbs. *total*), seeded and cut into large slices
12 ounces mushrooms, sliced about ¼ inch thick
1½ pounds mild or hot Italian sausages
Baked Polenta (at left)
2 cups (8 oz.) shredded jack cheese

Spread bell peppers and mushrooms in a shallow 9- by 13-inch baking dish (rectangular or oval). Pierce each sausage in several places with a fork; lay sausages atop vegetables. Bake, uncovered, in a 350° oven for 10 to 15 minutes.

Meanwhile, stir together Baked Polenta mixture in its own greased baking dish.

When sausage mixture has baked for 10 to 15 minutes, stir vegetables to moisten with pan drippings and add polenta to oven. Bake until sausages are lightly browned and no longer pink in center (cut to test) and polenta has absorbed liquid (45 to 50 more minutes). Sprinkle polenta with jack cheese (omit Parmesan cheese called for in Baked Polenta recipe).

Serve polenta and sausage mixture from baking dishes; or spoon polenta into center of a warm deep platter and surround with sausage mixture. Makes 6 servings.

Per serving: 837 calories, 36 g protein, 39 g carbohydrates, 60 g total fat, 147 mg cholesterol, 2,109 mg sodium

Saucy Chicken & Baked Polenta

8 chicken thighs (2 to 2½ lbs. *total*)
1 small onion, finely chopped
1 small green bell pepper (about 4 oz.), seeded and chopped
1 can (14½ oz. to 1 lb.) stewed tomatoes
1 can (8 oz.) tomato sauce
½ cup dry red wine
2 teaspoons dry oregano leaves
1 teaspoon dry basil
Baked Polenta (at left)
¼ to ⅓ cup grated Parmesan cheese

Rinse chicken pieces, pat dry, and arrange slightly apart in a 9- by 13-inch baking pan. Broil about 4 inches below heat, turning once, until browned on both sides (12 to 14 minutes *total*). Lift chicken from pan and set aside. To pan, add onion, bell pepper, tomatoes, tomato sauce, wine, oregano, and basil; mix well.

Stir together Baked Polenta mixture in a greased 9-inch square baking pan or baking dish, using 3½ cups broth and 1 cup polenta; omit onion and butter.

Place baking pans with vegetable mixture and polenta in a 450° oven. Bake, uncovered, stirring both mixtures once or twice, until vegetables are very soft and have formed a thick sauce and polenta liquid is almost absorbed (35 to 40 minutes).

Place chicken pieces in vegetable sauce. Sprinkle cheese over polenta. Continue to bake both mixtures, uncovered, until chicken is no longer pink near bone; cut to test (about 10 more minutes). Serve chicken and sauce over portions of polenta. Makes 4 to 8 servings.

Per serving: 552 calories, 30 g protein, 39 g carbohydrates, 31 g total fat, 128 mg cholesterol, 1,561 mg sodium

Turkey Marinara with Perciatelli

Preparation time: About 20 minutes

Cooking time: About 1¾ hours

The flavor of this thick, chunky tomato sauce will satisfy any traditionalist, but it's made with browned ground turkey (not beef) and a host of fresh vegetables. Serve it over *perciatelli*—long, thin pasta tubes.

- 2 tablespoons olive oil
- 1 medium-size onion, finely chopped
- 1 medium-size green bell pepper (about 5 oz.), seeded and finely chopped
- 2 medium-size carrots (about 4 oz. *total*), finely shredded
- 4 ounces mushrooms, thinly sliced
- 2 tablespoons chopped parsley
- 1 clove garlic, minced or pressed
- 2 teaspoons dry basil leaves
- 1 teaspoon *each* dry rosemary and dry oregano leaves
- 1 pound ground turkey
- 2 large cans (28 oz. *each*) pear-shaped tomatoes
- 1 large can (12 oz.) tomato paste
- ¼ cup dry red wine
- 1 dry bay leaf
  Salt and pepper
- 1 pound dry perciatelli or spaghetti
  About 1 cup (about 5 oz.) grated Parmesan cheese

Heat oil in a 4- to 5-quart pan over medium-high heat. Add onion, bell pepper, carrots, mushrooms, parsley, garlic, basil, rosemary, and oregano. Cook, stirring often, until vegetables are tender to bite (about 15 minutes). Lift vegetables from pan, transfer to a bowl, and set aside.

Crumble turkey into pan; cook over medium-high heat, stirring constantly, until juices have evaporated. Return vegetables to pan and continue to cook, stirring, until turkey is lightly browned. Add tomatoes (break up with a spoon) and their liquid, tomato paste, wine, and bay leaf, stirring to scrape up browned bits from bottom of pan.

Increase heat to high and bring mixture to a boil; reduce heat to medium-low, cover, and boil gently, stirring often, for 30 minutes. Then uncover and continue to cook, stirring occasionally, until sauce is reduced to 8 to 10 cups (40 to 50 more minutes). Season to taste with salt and pepper.

Shortly before sauce is done, in a 6- to 8-quart pan, cook perciatelli in 4 quarts boiling water just until tender to bite (12 to 15 minutes); or cook according to package directions. Drain well and transfer to a warm large serving bowl. Top with sauce and mix lightly, using 2 spoons. Serve with cheese to add to taste. Makes 8 to 10 servings.

Per serving: 419 calories, 23 g protein, 57 g carbohydrates, 12 g total fat, 41 mg cholesterol, 805 mg sodium

Pictured on facing page

Turkey with Tortellini & Oranges

Preparation time: About 25 minutes

Cooking time: About 20 minutes

When you're lucky enough to have plenty of cold roast turkey, dice or shred some of it to use in this elegant pasta dish. Turkey and tortellini are bathed in a sour cream sauce and garnished with gleaming orange slices.

- 3 large oranges (about 1½ lbs. *total*)
- 7 cups regular-strength chicken broth
- 1½ pounds fresh cheese- or meat-filled plain or spinach tortellini
- 3 cups diced or shredded cooked turkey
- 2 teaspoons celery seeds
- 2 cups sour cream
- ¼ cup chopped chives

Using a vegetable peeler, cut a strip of peel (colored part only) 6 inches long and about 1 inch wide from one of the oranges. Cut strip into long, thin shreds and set aside. Then completely peel all 3 oranges, discarding peel and all white membrane. Cut each orange crosswise into 6 slices; set slices aside.

In a 5- to 6-quart pan, bring broth to a boil. Add tortellini and cook just until tender to bite (4 to 6 minutes; or cook according to package directions). With a slotted spoon, lift out tortellini and transfer to a warm platter; keep warm.

To broth in pan, add turkey, celery seeds, and orange peel shreds; cook just until turkey is heated through. Lift out turkey and spoon over tortellini. Place sour cream in a small pan, then stir in 3 tablespoons of the chives and ½ cup of the hot broth (reserve remaining broth for other uses). Stir broth–sour cream mixture over low heat just until hot, then spoon over turkey. Sprinkle with remaining 1 tablespoon chives; arrange orange slices around turkey and pasta. Makes 6 servings.

Per serving: 706 calories, 45 g protein, 71 g carbohydrates, 28 g total fat, 150 mg cholesterol, 1,772 mg sodium

*Plump little cheese-filled pasta rings and fresh
orange slices give leftover poultry a sophisticated new
look. When you make Turkey with Tortellini & Oranges
(recipe on facing page), take your choice of green
or golden pasta.*

Cavatappi

Pea Pod & Turkey Pasta

Preparation time: About 10 minutes

Cooking time: About 10 minutes

Here's a quick pasta combination that can be made on the range or in the microwave with equally delicious results.

- 1 package (9 oz.) fresh fettuccine
- 1 can (14½ oz.) regular-strength chicken broth
- 1 cup whipping cream
- ⅛ teaspoon ground nutmeg
- 2 cups diced cooked turkey
- 1 package (6 oz.) frozen Chinese pea pods, thawed and drained
- 2 cups (8 oz.) shredded Swiss cheese
  Salt and pepper

In a 5- to 6-quart pan, cook fettuccine in 3 quarts boiling water until not quite tender to bite (about 3 minutes); or cook for about 1 minute less than time specified in package directions. Drain well.

While pasta is cooking, combine broth, cream, and nutmeg in a wide frying pan. Bring to a full boil over high heat. Boil, stirring often, until mixture is reduced to 1½ cups (6 to 8 minutes). Reduce heat to medium and add turkey, pea pods, and pasta; mix lightly, using 2 forks. Sprinkle evenly with cheese. Heat without stirring just until cheese is melted (2 to 3 minutes). Season to taste with salt and pepper. Makes 4 to 6 servings.

Per serving: 580 calories, 39 g protein, 34 g carbohydrates, 32 g total fat, 198 mg cholesterol, 555 mg sodium

■ *To Microwave:* Spread fettuccine in a shallow 2- to 2½-quart microwave-safe casserole. Pour broth and cream over fettuccine; sprinkle with nutmeg. Microwave, covered, on **HIGH (100%)** for about 9 minutes or until pasta is tender to bite, stirring every 3 minutes. Mix in turkey and microwave, uncovered, on **HIGH (100%)** for 2 minutes. Add pea pods and cheese; mix lightly, using 2 forks, until blended. Microwave, covered, on **HIGH (100%)** for 1 to 2 minutes or just until cheese is melted. Season to taste with salt and pepper.

Turkey alla Cacciatora

Preparation time: About 30 minutes

Cooking time: 1¾ to 2¼ hours

In Italian cooking, the word *cacciatora* refers to poultry or meat cooked "hunter's style"—with the bold flavors preferred for preparing game. To make our sturdy dish, however, you need only hunt down a few pounds of dark meat turkey parts, such as thighs, drumsticks, or hindquarters.

- 4 pounds turkey thighs, drumsticks, or hindquarters
- 2 tablespoons olive oil
- 3 large onions, chopped
- 4 cloves garlic, minced or pressed
- 2 medium-size green bell peppers (10 to 12 oz. *total*), seeded and chopped
- 8 ounces mushrooms, sliced
- 2 tablespoons all-purpose flour
- 1 can (8 oz.) tomato sauce
- 1 can (14½ oz. to 1 lb.) tomatoes
- ½ cup *each* dry red wine and regular-strength chicken broth
- ½ teaspoon salt
- 1 teaspoon *each* dry basil, dry thyme leaves, and dry oregano leaves
- 1 tablespoon sugar
- ⅛ teaspoon ground allspice
- 2 dry bay leaves
- 1 pound dry spaghetti or vermicelli (not coil vermicelli)
- 2 tablespoons butter or margarine, melted
- 2 tablespoons finely chopped parsley
  About 1 cup (about 5 oz.) grated Parmesan cheese

Rinse turkey pieces and pat dry. Heat oil in a wide, heavy 6- to 8-quart pan over medium-high heat. Add turkey; cook, turning as needed, until browned on all sides. Lift out and set aside.

Add onions to pan and cook, stirring often, until soft but not brown (8 to 10 minutes). Stir in garlic, bell peppers, and mushrooms; continue to cook, stirring, until almost all liquid has evaporated. Sprinkle flour over vegetable mixture, then stir in well. Add tomato sauce, tomatoes (break up with a spoon) and their liquid, wine, broth, salt, basil, thyme, oregano, sugar, allspice, and bay leaves. Bring to a boil, stirring often.

Return turkey to pan, pushing pieces down into sauce. Reduce heat, cover, and simmer for 30 minutes. Then uncover and continue to cook, stirring occasionally and adjusting heat so mixture barely bubbles, until turkey is very tender when pierced (1 to 1½ more hours).

About 15 minutes before turkey is done, in a 6- to 8-quart pan, cook spaghetti in 4 quarts boiling water just until tender to bite (10 to 12 minutes); or cook according to package directions. Drain well, then transfer to a warm large serving bowl; mix lightly with butter and parsley.

Spoon turkey and sauce over spaghetti. Sprinkle with ⅓ cup of the cheese. Serve with remaining cheese to add to taste. Makes 8 servings.

Per serving: 654 calories, 46 g protein, 59 g carbohydrates, 25 g total fat, 137 mg cholesterol, 795 mg sodium

Barbecued Quail with Pappardelle in Mushroom Sauce

Preparation time: About 20 minutes

Cooking time: About 30 minutes

Grilling time: 8 to 10 minutes

Look for fresh or frozen quail in the poultry section of your supermarket. The little all-dark-meat birds grill to sizzling perfection in about 10 minutes; while they cook, you boil the ribbonlike pasta to serve with fresh tomato-mushroom sauce.

If you prefer, you can use Rock Cornish game hens in place of quail, allowing one or two halves for each serving (see *Note* below).

- 2 ounces sliced pancetta or bacon, diced
- 6 tablespoons olive oil
- 1 medium-size onion, thinly sliced
- 8 ounces mushrooms, quartered
- 2 cloves garlic, minced or pressed
- 6 medium-size pear-shaped (Roma-type) tomatoes (about 12 oz. *total*), chopped
- ¼ cup slivered fresh sage leaves or 2 teaspoons dry sage
- 1 cup dry white wine
- 8 quail (3 to 4 oz. *each*), thawed if frozen
  Coarsely ground pepper
- 1 package (8½ oz.) dry pappardelle (wide fettuccine), 10 to 12 ounces fresh pappardelle, or 8 ounces dry extra-wide egg noodles
  Salt
  Fresh sage sprigs
  Lemon wedges (optional)

In a wide frying pan, cook pancetta over medium heat until crisp. Lift out, drain, and set aside. To pan drippings, add ¼ cup of the oil, then onion and

mushrooms. Increase heat to medium-high and cook, stirring often, until mushrooms are lightly browned (about 5 minutes). Stir in garlic, tomatoes, slivered sage, and wine. Adjust heat so mixture boils gently. Cook, uncovered, stirring occasionally, until tomatoes are soft and sauce is slightly thickened (10 to 15 minutes).

Meanwhile, cut through backbone of each quail with poultry shears or a knife. Place quail, skin side up, on a flat surface; press down firmly, cracking bones slightly, until birds lie flat. Rinse quail, pat dry, and brush well on all sides with remaining 2 tablespoons oil; sprinkle with pepper.

Place birds, skin side up, on a lightly greased grill 4 to 6 inches above a solid bed of hot coals. Cook, turning occasionally, until skin is browned and breast meat is still pink at bone; cut to test (8 to 10 minutes *total*). Remove from grill and keep warm.

In a 5- to 6-quart pan, cook pasta in 3 quarts boiling water just until barely tender to bite (3 to 4 minutes for dry pappardelle, about 2 minutes for fresh pappardelle, 4 to 6 minutes for noodles); or cook according to package directions. Drain well.

Add pancetta to tomato sauce; season to taste with salt. Add pasta and mix lightly, using 2 spoons. Transfer to a warm large platter. Surround pasta with grilled quail. Garnish with sage sprigs and lemon wedges, if desired. Makes 4 servings.

Per serving: 874 calories, 46 g protein, 52 g carbohydrates, 53 g total fat, 66 mg cholesterol, 207 mg sodium

Note: To prepare with Rock Cornish game hens, use 2 or 4 hens (1¼ to 1½ lbs. *each*). Remove necks and giblets; reserve for other uses, if desired. Rinse hens and pat dry. Cut each hen in half, cutting through backbone and breastbone. Brush with olive oil and season with pepper as directed for quail. Grill over medium (not hot) coals. Cook, turning several times, until meat near thighbone is no longer pink; cut to test (30 to 40 minutes). Surround pasta mixture with grilled game hen halves.

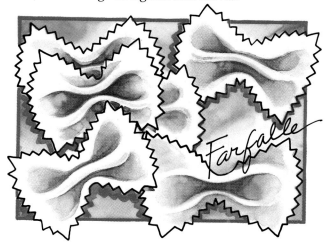

Farfalle

Tender round steak swirled around a filling of raisins,
parsley, garlic, and cheese makes the savory centerpiece
for hearty Braciola & Meatballs with Fusilli
(recipe on facing page).

512

Meats

By some quirk of cultural migration, pasta reached the New World from Italy in the form of spaghetti and meatballs—a match-up far less common on its supposed home ground than its popularity here would suggest. But as anyone who first discovered spaghetti in that guise will attest, it's an inspired combination. Equally captivating, though, are many other pairings of meat and pasta. Serve jaunty bow-shaped noodles with a braised pot roast of beef as a change from the usual potatoes; accompany a vibrant veal stew with plump agnolotti or ravioli. Stir up a speedy sausage sauce to spoon over thin strands of vermicelli. Or bake a casserole of tender pork chops layered with a dressing of tiny pasta stars and colorful vegetables.

Pictured on facing page

Braciola & Meatballs with Fusilli

Preparation time: About 30 minutes

Cooking time: About 2 hours and 20 minutes

Three kinds of meat—sausages, raisin-studded meatballs, and a savory rolled steak—are simmered in a rich red sauce, then served over hot fusilli or spaghetti in this pasta extravaganza. The recipe serves 8 to 12 people generously.

> Braciola (page 514)
> Raisin Meatballs (page 514)
> 1 pound mild Italian sausages (optional)
> About ¼ cup salad oil
> 1 small onion, finely chopped
> 2 cloves garlic, minced or pressed
> 1 large can (15 oz.) tomato sauce
> 3 cups water
> 1 large can (12 oz.) tomato paste
> 3 dry bay leaves
> ¼ teaspoon crushed dried hot red chiles
> 2 tablespoons coarsely chopped fresh basil or 1 tablespoon dry basil
> Salt
> 1½ pounds long fusilli or spaghetti
> Fresh herb sprigs, such as parsley, thyme, and oregano (optional)

Prepare Braciola and Raisin Meatballs; set aside.

If using Italian sausages, prick each several times with a fork; then cut each in half (or into 3-inch lengths). Then place in a 6-quart or larger pan over medium heat; brown on all sides and remove from pan. Add 1 to 2 tablespoons of the oil, if needed; then add Braciola and brown well on all sides. Remove from pan. Then brown meatballs, about half at a time, adding more oil as needed; remove meatballs from pan as they are browned.

Add onion and garlic to pan; cook, stirring often, until soft. Stir in tomato sauce, 3 cups water, tomato paste, bay leaves, and chiles. Return Braciola to pan. Reduce heat, cover, and simmer for 1 hour. Then add meatballs, sausages, and basil; continue to simmer, covered, until Braciola is tender when pierced (about 1 more hour). Season sauce to taste with salt.

When meat is almost tender, in an 8- to 10-quart pan, cook fusilli in 5 quarts boiling water just until tender to bite (12 to 15 minutes); or cook according to package directions. Drain well.

Lift meats from sauce. Remove cord from Braciola and cut meat crosswise into thick slices. Arrange slices in center of a warm large, deep platter. Surround with fusilli. Arrange sausages and meatballs over fusilli. Pour about a fourth of the sauce over meats and fusilli. Garnish with a bouquet of herb sprigs, if desired. Serve remaining sauce to add to taste. Makes 8 to 12 servings.

Braciola. Remove and discard fat and bone from 1 **round steak** (about 1½ lbs.). Using the flat side of a mallet, pound meat between 2 pieces of plastic wrap until flattened to about ½ inch thick. Spread with 1 tablespoon **butter** or margarine (at room temperature). Sprinkle with ½ cup chopped **parsley,** 2 tablespoons grated **Parmesan cheese,** 2 cloves **garlic** (minced or pressed), **pepper** to taste, and ½ cup **raisins.** Starting with a short edge, roll meat up jelly roll style. Tie with cord at about 1½-inch intervals.

Raisin Meatballs. In a medium-size bowl, beat 1 **egg.** Add 1 pound **lean ground beef,** 1 small **onion** (finely chopped), ½ cup chopped **parsley,** 2 cloves **garlic** (minced or pressed), and ½ cup **raisins.** Mix lightly, then shape into 1½-inch balls.

Per serving: 607 calories, 32 g protein, 74 g carbohydrates, 21 g total fat, 89 mg cholesterol, 629 mg sodium

Wine-braised Chuck Roast with Bow Ties

Preparation time: About 15 minutes

Baking time: 2½ to 3 hours

Cooking time: About 20 minutes

A boneless beef roast bakes to moist tenderness in a spicy tomato sauce that's also delicious with the accompanying pasta. Sprinkle fresh mint over all just before serving.

> 2 tablespoons olive oil or salad oil
> 1 large onion, finely chopped
> 4 cloves garlic, slivered
> 1 cup *each* dry red wine and water
> 1 can (8 oz.) tomato sauce
> 2 tablespoons red wine vinegar
> 1 dry bay leaf
> 5 whole allspice
> 1 cinnamon stick (about 3 inches long)
> 1 teaspoon cumin seeds
> ½ teaspoon *each* salt and pepper
> 1 boneless beef chuck roast (3 to 3½ lbs.), trimmed of fat
> 12 ounces dry bow-shaped pasta
> 2 to 3 tablespoons chopped fresh mint leaves

Heat oil in a wide frying pan over medium heat. Add onion and garlic; cook, stirring often, until onion is soft but not brown (6 to 8 minutes). Stir in wine, water, tomato sauce, vinegar, bay leaf, allspice, cinnamon stick, cumin seeds, salt, and pepper. Increase heat to high and bring mixture to a boil; then remove from heat.

Place roast in a 9- by 13-inch baking pan; pour sauce over it. Cover with foil and bake in a 325° oven until meat is very tender when pierced (2½ to 3 hours). Slice roast and arrange in center of a warm deep platter; keep warm. Skim and discard fat from sauce; remove and discard bay leaf and cinnamon stick. Transfer sauce to a 2- to 3-quart pan. Bring to a boil over high heat; boil, stirring often, until reduced to 2 cups (about 10 minutes).

Meanwhile, in a 6- to 8-quart pan, cook pasta in 4 quarts boiling water just until tender to bite (about 10 minutes); or cook according to package directions. Drain well and spoon around meat; pour sauce over pasta and meat, then sprinkle mint over all. Makes 6 to 8 servings.

Per serving: 539 calories, 40 g protein, 41 g carbohydrates, 23 g total fat, 158 mg cholesterol, 491 mg sodium

Lasagne with Spinach

Preparation time: About 15 minutes

Cooking time: About 15 minutes

Baking time: About 1 hour and 10 minutes

This hearty entrée can be put together especially quickly, since the pasta cooks as the lasagne bakes—there's no need to boil it before you assemble the casserole.

- 8 ounces lean ground beef
- 3 cans (15 oz. *each*) marinara sauce
- ½ cup *each* water and dry red wine
- ¼ teaspoon *each* dry basil and dry oregano leaves
- 1 package (10 oz.) frozen chopped spinach, thawed
- 8 ounces ricotta cheese
- ¾ cup grated Parmesan cheese
- 2 eggs
- ⅛ teaspoon ground nutmeg
  Salt and pepper
- 8 ounces dry lasagne
- 12 ounces mozzarella cheese, sliced

Crumble beef into a wide frying pan over medium heat; cook, stirring, until browned (5 to 8 minutes). Spoon off and discard excess fat. Stir in marinara sauce, water, wine, basil, and oregano. Bring to a boil; boil gently, uncovered, stirring often, for 5 minutes. Set aside.

Squeeze as much liquid as possible from spinach. In a food processor or blender, combine spinach, ricotta cheese, ½ cup of the Parmesan cheese, eggs, and nutmeg; whirl until well combined. Season to taste with salt and pepper.

To assemble casserole, rinse dry lasagne well. Then spoon about a fifth of the meat sauce into a 9- by 13-inch baking dish. Cover with a third of the lasagne. Add another fifth of the meat sauce, half the remaining lasagne, and another fifth of the meat sauce. Cover with half of the mozzarella slices; spread with spinach mixture and top with remaining mozzarella slices. Add half the remaining sauce, remaining lasagne, and remaining sauce.

Cover and bake in a 375° oven for 1 hour. Uncover, sprinkle with remaining ¼ cup Parmesan cheese, and continue to bake, uncovered, until lasagne is tender when pierced (about 10 more minutes). Let stand for several minutes before cutting. Makes 8 servings.

Per serving: 491 calories, 28 g protein, 42 g carbohydrates, 25 g total fat, 118 mg cholesterol, 1,396 mg sodium

Agnolotti

Beef-Mushroom Spaghetti in Barbecue Sauce

Preparation time: About 20 minutes

Cooking time: 20 to 25 minutes

If it's too late in the year for outdoor cooking but you still have a bottle of barbecue sauce lingering in the fridge, you're in luck. You can use it to make this easy spaghetti sauce with ground beef and plenty of mushrooms.

- 1 pound lean ground beef
  Salad oil (optional)
- 12 ounces mushrooms, sliced
- 2 medium-size onions, finely chopped
- 1 medium-size green bell pepper (about 5 oz.), seeded and finely chopped
- 1 teaspoon dry oregano leaves
- 8 ounces dry spaghetti
- 1¼ cups prepared tomato-based barbecue sauce
  Chopped parsley

Crumble beef into a wide 3- to 4-quart pan over medium heat; cook, stirring, until browned (10 to 15 minutes). Add up to 2 tablespoons oil, if necessary; or spoon off and discard all but 2 tablespoons of the fat. Add mushrooms, onions, bell pepper, and oregano; cook, stirring often, until onion is soft and lightly browned (about 10 minutes).

Meanwhile, in a 5- to 6-quart pan, cook spaghetti in 3 quarts boiling water just until tender to bite (10 to 12 minutes); or cook according to package directions. Drain well.

Add spaghetti and barbecue sauce to beef mixture; mix lightly, using 2 forks, just until heated through. Sprinkle with parsley. Makes 6 servings.

Per serving: 436 calories, 20 g protein, 53 g carbohydrates, 17 g total fat, 51 mg cholesterol, 888 mg sodium

Pictured on facing page

Spicy Mediterranean Meatballs

Preparation time: About 45 minutes

Cooking time: About 1 hour and 20 minutes

Fresh mint, cilantro, and a blend of sweet spices give meatballs in tomato sauce a Mediterranean character.

> Herbed Meatballs (recipe follows)
> 3 tablespoons salad oil
> 2 medium-size onions, finely chopped
> 3 cloves garlic, minced or pressed
> 1 teaspoon *each* minced fresh ginger and ground cumin
> 1 tablespoon paprika
> ¼ cup finely chopped fresh cilantro (coriander) or parsley
> 3 tablespoons red wine vinegar
> 2 large tomatoes (about 12 oz. *total*), peeled and chopped
> 1 can (14½ oz.) regular-strength beef broth
> 1 beef bouillon cube
> 1 can (6 oz.) tomato paste
> 1 pound dry spaghetti
> 1 cup (about 5 oz.) grated Parmesan cheese

Prepare Herbed Meatballs and set aside.

Heat oil in a wide frying pan over medium-high heat. Add onions and cook, stirring, until they begin to soften (about 5 minutes). Stir in garlic, ginger, cumin, paprika, cilantro, vinegar, tomatoes, broth, and bouillon cube. Increase heat to high and cook, stirring, until mixture comes to a boil. Add meatballs; reduce heat, cover, and simmer for 1 hour.

Lift meatballs carefully from sauce and keep warm. Add tomato paste to sauce; increase heat to high and cook, stirring often, until sauce is thickened (about 10 more minutes).

Meanwhile, in a 6- to 8-quart pan, cook spaghetti in 4 quarts boiling water just until tender to bite (10 to 12 minutes); or cook according to package directions. Drain well, transfer to a warm deep platter, and top with meatballs. Spoon sauce over spaghetti and meatballs. Serve with cheese to add to taste. Makes 8 servings.

Herbed Meatballs. Crumble 1½ pounds **lean ground beef** into a large bowl. Add ¼ cup **fine dry bread crumbs,** 3 **eggs,** and 1 large **onion,** finely chopped; mix well. Sprinkle with ¼ cup finely chopped **fresh cilantro** (coriander) or parsley, ¼ cup finely chopped **fresh mint,** 1 tablespoon **paprika,** 1 teaspoon **salt,** ½ teaspoon **pepper,** and ¼ teaspoon **ground cloves;** mix lightly until thoroughly combined. Shape into 1-inch balls.

Per serving: 620 calories, 32 g protein, 56 g carbohydrates, 29 g total fat, 152 mg cholesterol, 1,026 mg sodium

Norwegian Meatballs with Gjetost Sauce

Preparation time: About 20 minutes

Baking time: About 15 minutes

Cooking time: About 10 minutes

Here's an unusual version of pasta and meatballs. The delicately flavored sauce features *gjetost*, a firm, caramel-colored Norwegian cheese with a distinctive, rather sweet flavor. Look for 8-ounce bricks of gjetost in the supermarket dairy case.

> 1 egg
> ¼ cup all-purpose flour
> 1 pound ground veal or lean ground beef (or 8 oz. of *each* meat)
> 1 cup regular-strength chicken broth
> ½ cup half-and-half or milk
> ¾ cup shredded gjetost cheese
> ½ cup sour cream
> 1 tablespoon chopped fresh dill or ½ teaspoon dry dill weed
> Salt and ground white pepper
> 1 package (9 oz.) fresh linguine

In a medium-size bowl, beat egg with flour. Lightly mix in veal and ½ cup of the broth until well combined. Shape mixture into 1-inch balls; place slightly apart in a greased shallow baking pan. Bake, uncovered, in a 450° oven until well browned (about 15 minutes). Using a spatula, loosen meatballs from pan; set aside in pan and keep warm.

In a wide frying pan, combine half-and-half and remaining ½ cup broth; bring to steaming over medium heat (do not boil). Add cheese and stir until melted. Reduce heat to low and stir in sour cream and dill until smooth. Lightly mix in meatballs and any pan drippings; season to taste with salt and white pepper. Keep warm over lowest heat.

In a 5- to 6-quart pan, cook linguine in 3 quarts boiling water just until tender to bite (1 to 2 minutes); or cook according to package directions. Drain well, divide among warm dinner plates, and top with meatballs in sauce. Makes 4 servings.

Per serving: 604 calories, 37 g protein, 53 g carbohydrates, 27 g total fat, 245 mg cholesterol, 533 mg sodium

The dish may look familiar, but the flavor's far from traditional! Spicy Mediterranean Meatballs (recipe on facing page) forego the typical oregano and basil for ginger, cumin, cilantro, cloves, and plenty of fresh mint.

517

Green Lasagne Donatello

Preparation time: About 20 minutes

Cooking time: About 1 hour

Baking time: 50 minutes; 1 hour and 5 minutes if refrigerated

Your own homemade spinach pasta, a subtly flavored cream sauce, and a thick tomato-veal sauce add up to a delectable and unusual dish.

    1   recipe Spinach Pasta (page 444)
    2   tablespoons butter or margarine
    2   tablespoons olive oil
    ½   cup *each* finely chopped onion, celery, and carrot
    1   pound ground veal
    1   cup dry white wine
    1   can (14½ oz.) pear-shaped tomatoes
    2   tablespoons tomato paste
    ½   cup whipping cream
        Cream Sauce (recipe follows)
    1   cup (about 5 oz.) grated Parmesan cheese
    8   ounces mozzarella cheese, thinly sliced

After rolling out Spinach Pasta, cut strips so they are about as long as a shallow 3-quart casserole or 9- by 13-inch baking dish; cover lightly and set aside.

Melt butter in oil in a wide frying pan over medium heat. Add onion, celery, and carrot; cook, stirring often, until onion is soft but not brown (about 10 minutes). Crumble in veal and continue to cook, stirring, until meat loses its pink color. Add wine; bring to a boil and cook, stirring often, until liquid has evaporated. Add tomatoes (break up with a spoon) and their liquid, tomato paste, and cream; continue to cook, uncovered, until sauce is reduced to 1 quart (about 15 minutes).

Prepare Cream Sauce and set aside.

In a 6- to 8-quart pan, cook pasta, 2 strips at a time, in 4 quarts boiling water just until tender to bite (2 to 3 minutes). As pasta is cooked, lift it from pan and transfer to a bowl of ice water to cool.

Drain pasta strips, one at a time; pat dry. Arrange a third of the strips, overlapping slightly, in casserole. Spread with a third of the Cream Sauce, then a third of the veal sauce; sprinkle with a third of the Parmesan cheese, then layer on half the mozzarella cheese. Add another layer of pasta, Cream Sauce, veal sauce, and Parmesan cheese. Then add remaining ingredients in this order: pasta, veal sauce, mozzarella cheese, Cream Sauce, and Parmesan cheese. (At this point, you may cover and refrigerate for up to 1 day.)

Bake, uncovered, in a 400° oven until lightly browned and heated through (about 50 minutes; about 1 hour and 5 minutes if refrigerated). Let stand for several minutes before cutting. Makes 10 servings.

Cream Sauce. Melt ½ cup (¼ lb.) **butter** or margarine in a 2-quart pan over medium heat. Blend in ½ cup **all-purpose flour**; stir until bubbly. Remove from heat; gradually stir in 2 cups *each* **regular-strength chicken broth** and **half-and-half**. Return to heat; cook, stirring, until sauce boils and thickens. Season to taste with **ground nutmeg**.

Per serving: 585 calories, 27 g protein, 32 g carbohydrates, 39 g total fat, 171 mg cholesterol, 853 mg sodium

Garlic Veal Stew & Agnolotti

Preparation time: About 30 minutes

Cooking time: About 1¾ hours

The name means "fat little lambs," but *agnolotti* look more like plump semicircular ravioli. Typically filled with spinach and cheese, they were once difficult to find outside northern Italy, but now they're sold in the refrigerator case of most supermarkets. If you can't find fresh agnolotti, use fresh ravioli; either pasta is good with this pungent veal stew.

    2   to 3 tablespoons olive oil or salad oil
    2   pounds boneless veal shoulder, cut into 1½-inch cubes
    1   large onion, finely chopped
   12   cloves garlic, halved
   1½   pounds pear-shaped (Roma-type) tomatoes, peeled, seeded, and chopped
    1   cup tomato juice
    ½   cup dry white wine
    ⅓   cup small ripe olives
    1   or 2 small dried hot red chiles
    2   packages (9 oz. *each*) fresh agnolotti or ravioli
        Salt and pepper

Heat 2 tablespoons of the oil in a heavy 3- to 4-quart pan over medium-high heat. Add about half the veal and brown on all sides; remove meat from pan as it is browned. Repeat to brown remaining veal. Set all veal aside. Then add onion and about 1 tablespoon more oil (if needed) to pan; cook, stirring often, until onion is soft and lightly browned (6 to 8 minutes). Stir in garlic, tomatoes, tomato juice, wine, olives, and chiles.

Return meat to pan. Bring to a boil; then reduce heat, cover, and simmer until meat is tender when pierced (about 1 hour). Uncover and continue to cook, adjusting heat so stew boils gently, until sauce is thickened (about 15 more minutes).

Shortly before stew is done, in a 6- to 8-quart pan, cook agnolotti in 4 quarts boiling water just until tender to bite (5 to 6 minutes); or cook according to package directions.

While agnolotti are cooking, discard chiles from stew; skim and discard fat. Season to taste with salt and pepper. Drain agnolotti well; transfer to a warm rimmed platter. Spoon stew over agnolotti. Makes 6 servings.

Per serving: 519 calories, 46 g protein, 36 g carbohydrates, 21 g total fat, 197 mg cholesterol, 766 mg sodium

Pasta & Sausage in Madeira Cream

Preparation time: About 15 minutes

Cooking time: About 25 minutes

Madeira or sherry mellows the flavor of Italian sausage, helping the spicy meat blend smoothly with a mushroom cream sauce. Serve the rich mixture over spinach pasta.

- 1 **pound mild Italian sausages, casings removed**
- 12 **ounces dry bite-size spinach pasta twists or spirals, such as rotelle or fusilli**
- 4 **ounces mushrooms, sliced**
- 2 **large cloves garlic, minced or pressed**
- ¼ **cup Madeira or dry sherry**
- 1 **cup whipping cream**
- 1 **teaspoon ground white pepper**
- ¼ **teaspoon ground nutmeg**
- ½ **to ¾ cup grated Parmesan cheese**

Crumble sausages into a wide frying pan over medium-high heat; cook, stirring often, until well browned (10 to 15 minutes). Lift out sausage and set aside. Discard all but 2 tablespoons of the drippings.

In a 6- to 8-quart pan, cook pasta in 4 quarts boiling water just until tender to bite (about 10 minutes); or cook according to package directions.

Meanwhile, add mushrooms and garlic to drippings in frying pan; cook, stirring often, until mushrooms are brown (8 to 10 minutes). Add Madeira, stirring to scrape up browned bits from pan. Return sausage to pan; then add cream, white pepper, and nutmeg. Increase heat to high, bring to a boil, and boil until large, shiny bubbles form and sauce is slightly thickened (1 to 2 minutes).

Drain pasta and transfer to a warm serving bowl. Top with sausage sauce; mix lightly, using 2 forks. Serve with cheese to add to taste. Makes 4 to 6 servings.

Per serving: 717 calories, 29 g protein, 54 g carbohydrates, 43 g total fat, 180 mg cholesterol, 847 mg sodium

Italian Sausage & Pasta with Basil

Preparation time: About 15 minutes

Cooking time: About 20 minutes

The combination of robust sausages and green bell peppers at once recalls the boisterous bustle of an Italian street fair. To re-create that festive atmosphere any time, whip up this quick entrée: sautéed sausages, onions, peppers, and tomatoes, served over vermicelli and topped with cheese.

- 1 **pound mild Italian sausages, casings removed**
- 1 **large onion, coarsely chopped**
- 1 **large green bell pepper (about 8 oz.), seeded and coarsely chopped**
- 2 **cloves garlic, minced or pressed**
- 1 **can (14½ oz. to 1 lb.) tomatoes**
- 12 **ounces dry vermicelli (not coil vermicelli) or spaghettini**
- 2 **to 3 tablespoons dry basil**
- ¼ **cup chopped parsley**
- ¾ **to 1 cup grated Parmesan cheese**
- ¼ **cup olive oil**

Crumble sausages into a wide frying pan over medium-high heat. Cook, stirring often, until meat begins to brown. Add onion and bell pepper; continue to cook, stirring, until onion is soft but not brown (about 5 minutes). Spoon off and discard excess fat. Stir in garlic, then tomatoes (break up with a spoon) and their liquid. Bring to a boil; reduce heat and boil gently, uncovered, stirring often, until slightly thickened (about 10 minutes).

Meanwhile, in a 6- to 8-quart pan, cook vermicelli in 4 quarts boiling water just until tender to bite (8 to 10 minutes); or cook according to package directions. Drain well.

In a warm large serving bowl, combine basil, parsley, ½ cup of the cheese, and oil. Add vermicelli and mix lightly, using 2 forks. Top with sausage-tomato sauce. Serve with remaining ¼ to ½ cup cheese to add to taste. Makes 6 servings.

Per serving: 558 calories, 25 g protein, 52 g carbohydrates, 28 g total fat, 52 mg cholesterol, 848 mg sodium

Minced vegetables and tiny stelline make a savory
dressing for these Star-studded Baked Pork Chops (recipe
on facing page). Alongside, offer a room-temperature
stir-fry of multicolored bell pepper strips dressed
with olive oil, garlic, and herbs.

Star-studded Baked Pork Chops

Pictured on facing page

Preparation time: 15 to 20 minutes

Cooking time: About 20 minutes

Baking time: 25 to 30 minutes

To make a simplified version of stuffed pork chops, alternate browned chops with spoonfuls of pasta-vegetable dressing in a casserole, then bake.

- ½ cup (2½ to 3 oz.) dry tiny star-shaped pasta
- 1 egg
- 2 tablespoons butter or margarine
- 6 rib or loin pork chops (2 to 2½ lbs. *total*), about ¾ inch thick
- 1 cup *each* finely chopped celery and onion
- 1 clove garlic, minced or pressed
- 1 medium-size carrot (about 2 oz.), coarsely shredded
- ¼ cup chopped parsley
- ¾ teaspoon salt
- ½ teaspoon *each* pepper, dry sage leaves, and dry thyme leaves

In a 3-quart pan, cook pasta in 1½ quarts boiling water just until still slightly chewy (6 to 8 minutes); or cook a little less than time specified in package directions. Drain, rinse with cold water, and drain well again. In a medium-size bowl, beat egg; mix in pasta and set aside.

Melt butter in a wide frying pan over medium-high heat. Add pork chops and cook, turning once, just until browned on both sides (about 4 minutes *total*). Remove from pan and set aside. Reduce heat to medium and add celery, onion, garlic, and carrot; cook, stirring often, until vegetables are soft but not brown (6 to 8 minutes). Remove from heat and stir in parsley, salt, pepper, sage, and thyme. Then lightly stir vegetable mixture into pasta mixture.

Place a pork chop at one end of a greased 7- by 11-inch baking dish; spoon about a fifth of the pasta mixture over chop. Place another chop over pasta, overlapping it slightly. Continue alternating pasta and chops, ending with a pork chop. Spoon any remaining pasta mixture around chops. Cover and bake in a 350° oven just until chops are no longer pink in center; cut to test (25 to 30 minutes). Serve a portion of the pasta mixture with each chop. Makes 6 servings.

Per serving: 283 calories, 27 g protein, 13 g carbohydrates, 13 g total fat, 105 mg cholesterol, 396 mg sodium

Polish Sausage, Zucchini & Rigatoni

Preparation time: About 15 minutes

Cooking time: About 20 minutes

This hearty one-pan entrée combines chunky pasta, juicy sausages, and tender-crisp zucchini; fresh, peppery watercress provides a stylish final touch.

- 3 ounces (about 1 cup) dry rigatoni or elbow macaroni
- 3 tablespoons red wine vinegar
- 1 tablespoon *each* Dijon mustard and dry basil
- 12 ounces Polish sausage (kielbasa), cut into ¼-inch-thick slices
- 1 medium-size red onion, thinly sliced
- 3 small zucchini (about 8 oz. *total*), thinly sliced
- 1 bunch watercress (about 6 oz.), washed and crisped

In a wide frying pan, cook rigatoni in 1 inch boiling water just until tender to bite (10 to 15 minutes; or time according to package directions). Drain well and set aside.

While pasta is cooking, in a small bowl, stir together vinegar, mustard, and basil; set aside.

Rinse and dry pan; add sausage slices and stir over medium-high heat for 1 minute. Add onion and stir until softened (about 3 minutes). Add cooked pasta and vinegar mixture; stir until heated through (1 to 2 minutes). Stir in zucchini and cook just until tender-crisp to bite (about 3 minutes). Garnish in pan with bouquet of watercress and serve at once. Makes 4 servings.

Per serving: 384 calories, 17 g protein, 22 g carbohydrates, 25 g total fat, 60 mg cholesterol, 878 mg sodium

Rigatoni

It's an exceptional pasta dish that doesn't need some last-minute attention, but the two Italian recipes on this page finish baking entirely unattended. They're noteworthy in another respect, too: they feature the unusual combination of creamy pasta enclosed in tender-crisp puff pastry.

Tortellini Pasta Pie

- 2 **packages (12 oz. *each*) frozen meat-filled tortellini**
- 2 **cups whipping cream**
- 1 **cup (about 5 oz.) grated Parmesan cheese**
- 1 **package (17¼ oz.) frozen puff pastry, thawed according to package directions**
- ½ **cup chopped parsley**

In a 6- to 8-quart pan, cook tortellini in 4 quarts boiling water just until tender to bite (15 to 20 minutes); or cook according to package directions. Drain well. In a bowl, combine tortellini, cream, and cheese. Let stand until cool (or for up to 1 hour), stirring occasionally.

Meanwhile, on a lightly floured surface, separately roll out each sheet of pastry to make a 14-inch square. Ease one of the squares into a 9-inch spring-form pan, letting excess pastry drape over rim.

Stir parsley into tortellini mixture; pour mixture into pastry-lined pan. Top with second square of pastry. Trim excess pastry about ¼ inch from pan rim; set scraps aside. Pinch edges of pastry together and fold under, then crimp edge to seal. If desired, cut pastry scraps into decorative shapes, moisten undersides, and place atop pie. Slash top crust in about 6 places to allow steam to escape.

Creamy Pasta Pies

Bake on lowest rack of a 425° oven until pastry is richly browned (about 45 minutes). Let pie cool in pan on a rack for 15 minutes; then carefully remove pan sides. Let pie stand for at least 15 minutes (or up to 30 minutes); then cut into wedges to serve. Makes 6 to 8 servings.

Per serving: 840 calories, 26 g protein, 74 g carbohydrates, 49 g total fat, 142 mg cholesterol, 1,011 mg sodium

Venetian Pasta & Veal Pie

- 2 **tablespoons butter or margarine**
- ½ **cup *each* chopped onion and carrots**
- 8 **ounces ground veal**
- 4 **ounces mushrooms, chopped**
- ½ **teaspoon dry thyme leaves**
- ¼ **cup dry white wine**
- ¼ **cup regular-strength chicken broth**
- 2 **tablespoons tomato paste**
- 6 **ounces dry slender pasta tubes, such as bucatini or perciatelli**
- 1 **cup frozen tiny peas**
  Béchamel Sauce (recipe follows)
- 1 **package (17¼ oz.) frozen puff pastry, thawed according to package directions**

Melt butter in a wide frying pan over medium heat. Add onion and carrots; cook, stirring often, until onion is very soft (about 10 minutes). Crumble in veal and cook, stirring, until no longer pink. Stir in mushrooms, thyme, and wine. Reduce heat and simmer, uncovered, stirring often, until liquid has evaporated (about 15 minutes). Add broth and tomato paste; cook, stirring often, until thick (about 5 minutes). Let cool.

In a 5- to 6-quart pan, cook pasta in 3 quarts boiling water just until tender to bite (about 10 minutes); or cook according to package directions. Drain well.

In a bowl, combine meat mixture, pasta, and peas. Prepare Béchamel Sauce; stir warm sauce gently into pasta mixture.

Following directions given for Tortellini Pasta Pie (at left), roll out pastry, line spring-form pan, fill with pasta mixture, top with remaining pastry, finish edge, and decorate and slash top.

Bake on lowest rack of a 425° oven until pastry is richly browned (about 45 minutes). Let pie cool in pan on a rack for 15 minutes; then carefully remove pan sides. Let pie stand for at least 15 minutes (or up to 30 minutes); then cut into wedges to serve. Makes 6 to 8 servings.

Béchamel Sauce. Melt 3 tablespoons **butter** or margarine in a 1- to 1½-quart pan over medium heat. Blend in 3 tablespoons **all-purpose flour** and cook, stirring constantly, until bubbly. Remove from heat and gradually stir in ¾ cup *each* **regular-strength chicken broth** and **whipping cream;** return to heat and continue to cook, stirring, until sauce boils and thickens. Let cool slightly.

Per serving: 631 calories, 16 g protein, 53 g carbohydrates, 39 g total fat, 77 mg cholesterol, 672 mg sodium

Country-style Pappardelle

Preparation time: About 30 minutes

Baking time: 1¼ to 1½ hours

Cooking time: About 1 hour and 5 minutes

Italians prepare a richly flavored dish like this one with wild boar (*cinghiale*); we find country-style spareribs a reasonable (and more widely available!) substitute.

- 1 teaspoon dry rosemary
- ½ teaspoon coarsely ground pepper
- 3 cloves garlic, minced or pressed
- 3 tablespoons olive oil
- 2 to 2½ pounds country-style spareribs
- 1 medium-size red onion, thinly sliced
- 2 stalks celery, thinly sliced
- 1 medium-size carrot (about 2 oz.), finely chopped
- ¼ teaspoon whole cloves
- ½ cup dry red wine
- 1 can (6 oz.) tomato paste
- 1 can (14½ oz.) diced tomatoes
- 1 can (14½ oz.) regular-strength beef broth
- 2 packages (8½ oz. *each*) dry pappardelle (wide fettuccine), 1¼ pounds fresh pappardelle, or 1 pound dry extra-wide egg noodles
  Salt
- 1 to 2 tablespoons red wine vinegar
- ½ to ¾ cup grated Parmesan cheese

Mix rosemary, pepper, a third of the garlic, and 1 tablespoon of the oil. Coat spareribs with oil mixture on all sides. Place, fat side down, in a shallow baking pan. Bake, uncovered, in a 450° oven for 15 minutes; reduce oven temperature to 325° and continue to bake until meat is tender when pierced (1 to 1¼ more hours). Remove from oven and set aside.

Meanwhile, heat remaining 2 tablespoons oil in a 3½- to 4-quart pan over medium heat. Add onion, celery, and carrot; cook, stirring often, until onion is soft but not brown (6 to 8 minutes). Stir in remaining garlic, cloves, wine, tomato paste, tomatoes and their liquid, and 1½ cups of the broth. Bring to a boil; then reduce heat, cover, and simmer for 30 minutes. Uncover pan and adjust heat so mixture boils gently; cook, stirring occasionally, until thickened (about 20 minutes).

Remove spareribs from baking pan; pour off and discard fat from pan. Pour remaining ¼ cup broth into baking pan and stir to loosen browned drippings; add mixture to tomato-vegetable sauce.

Pull sparerib meat from bones in bite-size shreds; discard bones and fat. Stir shredded meat into sauce. (At this point, you may cover and refrigerate for up to 1 day.)

In an 8- to 10-quart pan, cook pasta in 5 quarts boiling water just until tender to bite (3 to 4 minutes for dry pappardelle, about 2 minutes for fresh pappardelle, 4 to 6 minutes for noodles); or cook according to package directions. Drain well.

While pasta is cooking, reheat sauce, if necessary. Season to taste with salt and vinegar. Place pasta in a large, wide serving bowl; add sauce. Mix lightly, using 2 spoons. Serve with cheese to add to taste. Makes 6 to 8 servings.

Per serving: 604 calories, 25 g protein, 60 g carbohydrates, 29 g total fat, 120 mg cholesterol, 688 mg sodium

Straw & Hay Pasta

Preparation time: About 5 minutes

Cooking time: 10 to 12 minutes

"Straw" and "hay"—golden and green pastas—are a classic duo. In this interpretation of the traditional dish, the sauce is a little lighter than you might expect.

- 8 ounces dry yellow and green tagliarini or 4½ ounces (half of a 9-oz. package) *each* fresh yellow and green linguine
- 1¼ cups half-and-half
- ⅓ to ½ cup julienne strips of thinly sliced cooked ham
- ⅓ cup frozen tiny peas
- ⅔ to ¾ cup grated Parmesan cheese

In a 5- to 6-quart pan, cook pasta in 3 quarts boiling water just until tender to bite (6 to 7 minutes for dry pasta, 1 to 2 minutes for fresh); or cook according to package directions.

Meanwhile, in a wide frying pan, combine half-and-half, ham, and peas; stir over medium heat until steaming (do not boil). Reduce heat to low. Drain pasta well and add to half-and-half mixture. Mix lightly, using 2 forks, until pasta has absorbed most of the liquid (2 to 3 minutes). Sprinkle with ⅓ cup of the cheese; mix lightly. Serve with remaining cheese to add to taste. Makes 4 servings.

Per serving: 407 calories, 19 g protein, 47 g carbohydrates, 16 g total fat, 73 mg cholesterol, 515 mg sodium

Mostaccioli & Swiss Cheese Casserole

Preparation time: 10 to 15 minutes

Cooking time: About 20 minutes

Baking time: About 30 minutes

In this new version of macaroni and cheese, *mostaccioli*—a pasta named for its fancied resemblance to little mustaches—mingles with Swiss cheese, spinach, and slivered ham in a mustardy sauce.

- 8 ounces dry mostaccioli or other small tube-shape pasta, such as penne
- ¼ cup butter or margarine
- ¼ cup all-purpose flour
- 2 cups milk
- ¼ teaspoon liquid hot pepper seasoning
- 1 tablespoon Dijon mustard
- 3 cups (12 oz.) shredded Swiss cheese
- 8 ounces cooked ham, cut into thin bite-size slivers
- 1 package (10 oz.) frozen chopped spinach, thawed

  Salt and pepper

In a 5- to 6-quart pan, cook mostaccioli in 3 quarts boiling water just until tender to bite (10 to 12 minutes); or cook according to package directions. Drain, rinse, and drain well again; set aside.

Melt butter in same pan over medium heat; stir in flour and cook, stirring, until bubbly. Remove from heat and gradually blend in milk. Increase heat to medium-high and cook, stirring constantly, until sauce comes to a boil. Add hot pepper seasoning, mustard, and 2 cups of the cheese; stir until cheese is melted. Remove from heat.

Add mostaccioli and ham to sauce; mix gently. Squeeze as much liquid as possible from spinach; then stir spinach into mostaccioli mixture. Spread in a shallow 2-quart casserole, then cover and bake in a 350° oven for 20 minutes. Uncover, sprinkle with remaining 1 cup cheese, and continue to bake until cheese is melted and mixture is bubbly (about 10 more minutes). Season to taste with salt and pepper. Makes 6 servings.

Per serving: 571 calories, 34 g protein, 40 g carbohydrates, 30 g total fat, 107 mg cholesterol, 949 mg sodium

---

Pictured on facing page

Linguine with Prosciutto & Olives

Preparation time: About 15 minutes

Cooking time: 8 to 10 minutes

The fragrance and sweet-salty flavor of premium-priced prosciutto permeate this dish—yet you need just 2 ounces of the meat to serve four. Cut into thin strips, the prosciutto mingles with stuffed olives, ribbons of linguine, and bright cherry tomatoes.

- 8 ounces dry linguine or 1 package (9 oz.) fresh linguine
- ¼ cup olive oil
- 2 ounces thinly sliced prosciutto, cut into ¼-inch-wide strips
- ½ cup thinly sliced green onions (including tops)
- 1 jar (3 oz.) pimento-stuffed olives, drained
- 1 cup cherry tomatoes, cut into halves
- ½ to ⅔ cup grated Parmesan cheese

In a 5- to 6-quart pan, cook linguine in 3 quarts boiling water just until tender to bite (8 to 10 minutes for dry pasta, 1 to 2 minutes for fresh); or cook according to package directions. Drain well and transfer to a warm serving bowl.

While linguine is cooking, heat oil in a medium-size frying pan over medium-high heat; add prosciutto and cook, stirring often, until lightly browned (3 to 4 minutes). Add onions and stir just until they begin to soften. Add olives and tomatoes; shake pan often until olives are hot (about 2 minutes). Pour prosciutto mixture over linguine; mix lightly, using 2 forks. Serve with cheese to add to taste. Makes 4 servings.

Per serving: 444 calories, 16 g protein, 45 g carbohydrates, 22 g total fat, 18 mg cholesterol, 1,059 mg sodium

■ *To Microwave:* Cook linguine as directed above. Meanwhile, arrange prosciutto strips in a 2-quart microwave-safe casserole. Microwave, covered, on **HIGH (100%)** for 2 to 2½ minutes or until prosciutto is lightly browned, stirring once. Stir in oil and onions. Microwave, covered, on **HIGH (100%)** for 2 to 3 minutes or until oil is hot and onions begin to soften. Lightly mix in olives and tomatoes. Microwave, covered, on **HIGH (100%)** for 1 to 2 minutes or until heated through. Let stand, covered, while draining linguine. Add linguine to prosciutto mixture; mix lightly, using 2 forks. Serve with cheese to add to taste.

For the speediest of main dishes, toss together vivid Linguine with Prosciutto & Olives (recipe on facing page), then serve with country-style Italian bread and a salad of cooked vegetables in a vinaigrette dressing.

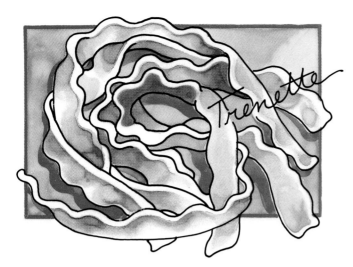

Bacon & Egg Carbonara

Preparation time: About 10 minutes

Cooking time: About 10 minutes

Those reliable staples, bacon and eggs, are supported by a thin pasta such as capellini or vermicelli to make an irresistible entrée for a casual supper.

- 8 ounces sliced bacon (about 10 slices), cut into 1-inch squares
- 8 ounces dry thin pasta such as capellini or vermicelli; or 1 package (9 oz.) fresh angel hair pasta
- 2 cups sour cream
- ¼ cup chopped chives or thinly sliced green onions (including tops)
- 4 egg yolks
- 1 cup (about 5 oz.) grated Parmesan cheese

In a wide frying pan, cook bacon over medium heat until crisp. Spoon off and discard all but 3 tablespoons of the drippings; keep pan with bacon warm over lowest heat.

In a 5- to 6-quart pan, cook pasta in 3 quarts boiling water just until tender to bite (about 3 minutes for dry capellini, 8 to 10 minutes for dry vermicelli, 1 to 2 minutes for fresh angel hair pasta); or cook according to package directions. After adding pasta to boiling water, spoon ½ cup of the sour cream into each of 4 wide, shallow bowls; place bowls in a 200° oven while completing cooking.

Drain pasta well; add pasta and chives to bacon in pan. Mix lightly, using 2 forks. Spoon an equal portion of pasta mixture into each warm bowl. Make a nest in center of each; slip in an egg yolk. Mix each portion individually and sprinkle with cheese. Makes 4 servings.

Per serving: 839 calories, 33 g protein, 50 g carbohydrates, 56 g total fat, 312 mg cholesterol, 1,031 mg sodium

Baked Trenette with Prosciutto & Radicchio

Preparation time: About 15 minutes

Cooking time: About 20 minutes

Baking time: About 20 minutes

Trenette (*trinette*) are long, flat, medium-wide noodles, sometimes ruffle-edged in their dry form. Fresh trenette is the first choice to serve with pesto on its home ground of Liguria. In this recipe, though, we use the dried pasta, baking it with slivered radicchio in a creamy-rich cheese sauce.

- 8 ounces dry trenette or dry fettuccine
- 3 tablespoons butter or margarine
- 2 small heads radicchio (6 to 8 oz. *total*), cored and coarsely slivered
- 4 ounces sliced prosciutto, cut into strips
- 1½ cups whipping cream
- ¼ teaspoon *each* ground nutmeg and ground white pepper
- ⅓ cup dry white wine
- 1½ cups (6 oz.) shredded fontina cheese
- ¾ cup grated Parmesan cheese

In a 5- to 6-quart pan, cook trenette in 3 quarts boiling water just until tender to bite (8 to 10 minutes); or cook according to package directions. Drain well; transfer to a greased shallow 2-quart baking dish.

While trenette is cooking, melt butter in a wide frying pan over medium heat. Add radicchio and prosciutto; cook, stirring constantly, until radicchio is wilted and prosciutto begins to brown.

Lift radicchio mixture from pan, add to trenette in baking dish, and mix lightly. Then add cream, nutmeg, white pepper, and wine to pan. Increase heat to high and bring to a boil; boil, stirring often, until reduced to 1¼ cups. Remove from heat and add fontina cheese; stir over medium heat until cheese is melted. Mix in ½ cup of the Parmesan cheese, then pour sauce over trenette mixture. Sprinkle with remaining ¼ cup Parmesan cheese.

Bake, uncovered, in a 400° oven until heated through (about 20 minutes). Makes 4 servings.

Per serving: 854 calories, 34 g protein, 47 g carbohydrates, 59 g total fat, 254 mg cholesterol, 1,027 mg sodium

Super-rich Fettuccine

Preparation time: About 5 minutes

Cooking time: 8 to 10 minutes

This luscious dish combines two classics—fettuccine Alfredo and pasta carbonara—with sublime results.

    6 slices bacon (about 5 oz.)
    ½ cup (¼ lb.) unsalted butter or margarine
    3 cloves garlic, minced or pressed
    1 egg
    1 cup whipping cream
    1 cup (about 5 oz.) grated Parmesan cheese
    ¼ teaspoon dry oregano leaves
   12 ounces fresh fettuccine or 10 ounces dry
       fettuccine
    3 tablespoons minced parsley
       Salt and pepper

In a wide frying pan, cook bacon over medium heat until crisp. Lift out, drain, crumble, and set aside; discard drippings. Melt butter in pan; add garlic and cook, stirring often, until garlic turns opaque (1 to 2 minutes). Remove from heat and add bacon.

In a small bowl, beat egg with cream, cheese, and oregano. Add egg mixture to bacon mixture and stir over medium heat until sauce is slightly thickened.

Meanwhile, in a 6- to 8-quart pan, cook fettuccine in 4 quarts boiling water just until tender to bite (3 to 4 minutes for fresh pasta, 8 to 10 minutes for dry); or cook according to package directions. Drain well and transfer to a warm serving bowl.

Add sauce and parsley to pasta; mix lightly, using 2 forks, until pasta is well coated. Season to taste with salt and pepper. Makes 4 to 6 servings.

Per serving: 691 calories, 25 g protein, 41 g carbohydrates, 48 g total fat, 254 mg cholesterol, 700 mg sodium

Stovetop Moussaka with Green Fettuccine

Preparation time: About 25 minutes

Draining time: 30 minutes to 1 hour

Cooking time: About 45 minutes

Moussaka is usually baked, but there's a faster way to cook this favorite lamb and eggplant dish—combine the familiar elements in a wide frying pan over direct heat. Before serving, spoon hot pasta around the edges of the skillet to share the cooking juices.

    1   large eggplant (about 2 lbs.), unpeeled, cut
         into 1-inch cubes
    1½   teaspoons salt
    2   tablespoons olive oil
    1   pound lean ground lamb
    1   medium-size onion, finely chopped
    2   cloves garlic, minced or pressed
    4   large pear-shaped (Roma-type) tomatoes
         (about 12 oz. *total*), peeled, seeded, and
         chopped
    1   can (8 oz.) tomato sauce
    3   tablespoons minced parsley
    1½   teaspoons cumin seeds
    1   teaspoon crushed dried hot red chiles
    8   ounces dry green fettuccine or 1 package
         (9 oz.) fresh green fettuccine
    1   package (10 oz.) frozen pearl onions, thawed
    ½   to 1 cup plain yogurt or sour cream

Mix eggplant with salt; transfer to a colander and let drain for 30 minutes to 1 hour. Rinse with cold water, drain, and pat dry.

Heat oil in a wide frying pan over medium-high heat. Add eggplant and cook, turning often with a wide spatula, until lightly browned (6 to 8 minutes). Add 2 tablespoons water; stir and turn eggplant, then quickly cover pan. At 1-minute intervals, add 2 tablespoons more water, turning eggplant and covering again after each addition; cook until eggplant is very soft when pressed (about 6 minutes *total*). Transfer to a bowl and set aside.

Crumble lamb into pan and stir in chopped onion. Increase heat to high and cook, stirring often, until meat is very well browned (about 8 minutes). Stir in garlic; then stir in eggplant and any accumulated juices, tomatoes, tomato sauce, parsley, cumin seeds, and chiles. Reduce heat to medium, cover, and boil gently until tomatoes are very soft (about 20 minutes).

Meanwhile, in a 5- to 6-quart pan, cook fettuccine in 3 quarts boiling water just until tender to bite (8 to 10 minutes for dry pasta, 3 to 4 minutes for fresh); or cook according to package directions. Drain well.

When lamb mixture is done, add pearl onions and gently stir until heated through (1 to 2 minutes). Gently push lamb mixture to one side or to center of pan; add fettuccine next to or around lamb. Serve with yogurt to add to taste. Makes 6 servings.

Per serving: 473 calories, 23 g protein, 42 g carbohydrates, 25 g total fat, 105 mg cholesterol, 526 mg sodium

First oven-browned, then simmered to tenderness
in a rich red sauce, succulent lamb ribs make a hearty
meal for a chilly day. If you can't find the distinctive
pasta called rustici, just substitute bow ties (farfalle);
Rustic Lamb Spareribs with Eggplant Sauce (recipe
on facing page) are delicious either way.

Rustic Lamb Spareribs with Eggplant Sauce

Preparation time: About 15 minutes

Cooking time: About 1¾ hours

Baking time: 30 to 40 minutes

Rustici, an unusual dry pasta with a homemade look, complements this dish of tender lamb spareribs in a spicy, eggplant-thickened tomato sauce.

   2 **tablespoons olive oil**
   1 **small eggplant (8 to 10 oz.), unpeeled, diced**
   4 **cloves garlic, minced or pressed**
   1 **can (14½ oz.) pear-shaped tomatoes**
   1 **large can (15 oz.) tomato sauce**
   ½ **cup port wine**
   1 **tablespoon firmly packed brown sugar**
1½ **teaspoons dry oregano leaves**
   1 **dry bay leaf**
   1 **cinnamon stick (about 3 inches long)**
   ⅓ **cup chopped parsley**
      Salt and pepper
   2 **to 2½ pounds lamb spareribs**
   ⅓ **cup water**
   8 **ounces dry rustici or bow-shaped pasta**

Heat oil in a 3- to 4-quart pan over medium-high heat. Add eggplant and cook, stirring often, until eggplant is very soft (8 to 10 minutes). Stir in garlic, tomatoes (break up with a spoon) and their liquid, tomato sauce, port, sugar, oregano, bay leaf, cinnamon stick, and all but 1 tablespoon of the parsley. Bring to a boil; then reduce heat, partially cover, and simmer until very thick (about 30 minutes). Season to taste with salt and pepper.

Meanwhile, arrange lamb spareribs, fat side up, in a single layer in a shallow baking pan. Bake, uncovered, in a 450° oven until well browned (30 to 40 minutes). Lift lamb from baking pan, cut between bones to separate, and transfer to pan with tomato-eggplant sauce.

Pour off and discard fat in baking pan. Then pour in ⅓ cup water, stirring to dissolve browned bits. Add water mixture to ribs in sauce; cover and simmer over low heat until lamb is very tender when pierced (about 1 hour). Skim and discard fat from sauce.

When lamb is almost tender, in a 5- to 6-quart pan, cook rustici in 3 quarts boiling water just until tender to bite (10 to 12 minutes); or cook according to package directions. Drain well and transfer to a warm deep platter; spoon sauce and ribs over pasta. Sprinkle with remaining 1 tablespoon parsley. Makes 4 servings.

Per serving: 720 calories, 37 g protein, 66 g carbohydrates, 34 g total fat, 163 mg cholesterol, 901 mg sodium

Lamb & Orzo, Mediterranean Style

Preparation time: About 10 minutes

Cooking time: About 25 minutes

A crisp green salad and a warm loaf of crusty bread are superb, simple accompaniments for this one-pan meal of ground lamb and rice-shaped pasta.

   ½ **teaspoon salt**
   1 **pound lean ground lamb**
   1 **large onion, finely chopped**
   2 **cloves garlic, minced or pressed**
   1 **can (14½ oz. to 1 lb.) tomatoes**
   1 **chicken bouillon cube**
1½ **cups hot water**
   ½ **teaspoon dry oregano leaves**
   ¼ **teaspoon pepper**
   1 **cup (about 8 oz.) dry rice-shaped pasta**
   1 **package (10 oz.) frozen chopped spinach, thawed**
   ½ **to ¾ cup grated Parmesan cheese**

Sprinkle salt into a wide frying pan over medium-high heat. Crumble lamb into pan and cook, stirring often, until meat begins to brown (3 to 5 minutes). Reduce heat to medium, stir in onion, and continue to cook, stirring, until onion is soft but not brown (about 5 minutes). Spoon off and discard excess fat. Add garlic, tomatoes (break up with a spoon) and their liquid, bouillon cube, water, oregano, and pepper. Bring mixture to a boil, stirring to dissolve bouillon cube; then stir in pasta. Reduce heat, cover, and boil gently, stirring once or twice, until pasta is just tender to bite (10 to 12 minutes; or time according to package directions).

Meanwhile, squeeze as much liquid as possible from spinach. Stir spinach into pasta mixture just until heated through. Serve with cheese to add to taste. Makes 4 servings.

Per serving: 644 calories, 35 g protein, 54 g carbohydrates, 32 g total fat, 93 mg cholesterol, 1,046 mg sodium

Risotto: Italian Rice

Risotto, Italy's celebrated creamy rice, resembles pasta in a couple of ways: it's usually served as the course preceding the main dish, and it can accommodate a seemingly infinite variety of seasonings and added ingredients. Try it in its basic form, or savor it dressed up with vegetables, herbs, and mushrooms. Plain or fancy, it's good served before or alongside roasted or grilled meats or poultry.

Risotto enjoys its greatest popularity in northern Italy (rice is grown in the valley of the Po River), where it turns up in regional versions from the Adriatic to the Mediterranean coasts; saffron-hued *risotto alla milanese* is a deserved classic.

The recipes presented here can be made with short-grain rice (such as pearl) or with medium-grain rice, including Italian arborio. Because risotto simmers uncovered, the flavor of the cooking liquid will be concentrated—so if you use salted canned broth, dilute it with water so the finished risotto won't be too salty.

Basic Risotto

3 tablespoons butter or margarine
1 medium-size onion, finely chopped
1 cup short- or medium-grain white rice
1¾ cups regular-strength chicken or beef broth
1¼ to 1¾ cups water
¼ to ½ cup grated Parmesan cheese

Melt butter in an 10- to 12-inch frying pan over medium heat. Add onion and cook, stirring, until onion is translucent (about 5 minutes). Add rice and stir until opaque (about 2 minutes). Add broth and water (use 1¼ cups water for short-grain rice, 1½ cups water for medium-grain rice).

Increase heat to high and bring to a boil. Reduce heat and boil very gently, uncovered, just until rice is tender to bite (20 to 25 minutes); stir occasionally at first, then more frequently as liquid is almost absorbed. Add more broth or water, ¼ cup at a time, if needed to prevent sticking.

Just before serving, stir in cheese to taste. Makes about 5 servings.

Per serving: 251 calories, 6 g protein, 34 g carbohydrates, 10 g total fat, 23 mg cholesterol, 550 mg sodium

Porcini Mushroom Risotto

1 ounce dried porcini mushrooms (cèpes)
1½ cups hot water
1¾ cups regular-strength chicken or beef broth
3 tablespoons butter or margarine
1 tablespoon olive oil
1 medium-size onion, finely chopped
1 clove garlic, minced or pressed
1 cup short- or medium-grain white rice
¾ to 1 cup grated Parmesan cheese

Place mushrooms in a bowl, add hot water, and let stand until mushrooms are soft (20 to 30 minutes). Lift out mushrooms (reserve soaking liquid) and rinse well, using your fingers to work out any grit; squeeze mushrooms gently to remove excess liquid. Chop mushrooms coarsely; set aside.

Pour soaking liquid through a fine strainer (do not disturb sediment on bottom of bowl) into a 1-quart measuring cup. Add broth; if necessary, add water to make 3 cups total.

Melt butter in oil in an 10- to 12-inch frying pan over medium heat. Add onion and cook, stirring, until onion is translucent (about 5 minutes). Then add garlic and rice; stir until rice is opaque (about 2 minutes). Add mushrooms and soaking liquid–broth mixture, then continue cooking as directed for Basic Risotto (at left).

Just before serving, stir in ¼ to ½ cup of the cheese; serve with remaining.cheese to add to taste. Makes about 5 servings.

Per serving: 311 calories, 9 g protein, 38 g carbohydrates, 14 g total fat, 29 mg cholesterol, 313 mg sodium

Radicchio or Endive Risotto

Pictured on page 532

1 tablespoon olive oil
3 cups shredded radicchio (about 6 oz.) or Belgian endive (about 12 oz.)
1 tablespoon lemon juice (omit if using endive)
Basic Risotto (at left)
1 small clove garlic, minced or pressed
1 tablespoon butter or margarine
Whole radicchio or Belgian endive leaves, washed and crisped
Lemon wedges
Italian (flat-leaf) parsley sprigs

Heat oil in a 3- to 4-quart pan over high heat. Add shredded radicchio and lemon juice; stir just until radicchio is wilted (about 2 minutes). Lift out and set aside.

In same pan, prepare Basic Risotto, adding garlic with rice; when you add cheese, gently stir in cooked radicchio and the 1 tablespoon butter. Serve in a warm bowl lined with radicchio leaves; or place leaves on individual plates and spoon risotto into leaves. Garnish with lemon wedges and parsley sprigs. Makes 4 to 6 servings.

Per serving: 302 calories, 7 g protein, 36 g carbohydrates, 15 g total fat, 30 mg cholesterol, 576 mg sodium

Green Risotto with Sautéed Liver

2 **medium-size leeks (about 8 oz. total)**
5 **tablespoons butter or margarine**
½ **cup finely chopped parsley**
2 **teaspoons dry basil**
1 **cup short- or medium-grain white rice**
1¾ **cups regular-strength chicken or beef broth**
1¼ **to 1¾ cups water**
1 **pound chicken livers, drained and cut into halves; or 1 pound calf's liver, cut into ¼-inch-wide bite-size strips**
2 **tablespoons dry sherry**
¼ **to ½ cup grated Parmesan cheese Parsley sprigs**

Trim and discard roots and tough parts of green tops from leeks; cut leeks in half lengthwise, rinse well, and slice thinly crosswise.

Melt 3 tablespoons of the butter in a 12- to 14-inch frying pan over medium heat. Add leeks, chopped parsley, and basil. Cook, stirring, until

leeks are tender to bite (about 5 minutes). Add rice and stir until opaque (about 2 minutes); add broth and water and continue cooking as directed for Basic Risotto (facing page).

Meanwhile, melt remaining 2 tablespoons butter in a wide frying pan over high heat. Add half the livers. Cook, turning, until browned on outside but still pink in center; cut to test (1 to 2 minutes). Remove to a warm bowl and keep warm while cooking remaining livers. Return all livers to pan, add sherry, and stir gently just until heated through.

To serve, stir cheese into risotto. Then top risotto with livers; garnish with parsley sprigs. Makes 4 servings.

Per serving: 527 calories, 29 g protein, 51 g carbohydrates, 23 g total fat, 544 mg cholesterol, 859 mg sodium

Pan-grilled Risotto with Mozzarella & Basil

Basic Risotto (facing page)
1 **clove garlic, minced or pressed**
8 **ounces mozzarella cheese, diced**
2 **tablespoons minced fresh basil leaves or 2 teaspoons dry basil**
¾ **to 1 cup grated Parmesan cheese About ¼ cup butter or margarine**

Prepare Basic Risotto, but add garlic with rice and omit Parmesan cheese called for.

When risotto is done, remove from heat and let cool for 25 to 30 minutes. Then stir in mozzarella cheese, basil, and ½ cup of the Parmesan cheese. Line a 9- by 13-inch pan with foil. Spread risotto evenly in foil-lined pan. Cover and refrigerate until firm (at least 2 hours) or for up to 3 days.

Invert risotto onto a board; carefully peel off and discard foil. Cut risotto into 3-inch squares, then cut each square diagonally in half.

Melt 1 tablespoon of the butter in a wide nonstick frying pan over medium-high heat. Add several risotto triangles (do not crowd pan); cook, turning once, until golden brown on both sides (5 to 6 minutes *total*). As triangles are cooked, arrange them in a single layer on a heatproof platter and keep warm in a 300° oven. Cook remaining triangles, adding remaining butter as needed.

Serve hot, with remaining ¼ to ½ cup Parmesan cheese to add to taste. Makes about 6 servings.

Per serving: 416 calories, 15 g protein, 30 g carbohydrates, 26 g total fat, 75 mg cholesterol, 802 mg sodium

The most colorful member of the endive family takes the spotlight in Radicchio Risotto (recipe on page 530). Sliver the purple-red radicchio leaves and blend them with hot, creamy rice; then spoon the melange into cuplike whole leaves for a handsome presentation. Complete the meal with grilled Italian sausages.

Sunset

Low-Fat Italian Cookbook

By the Editors of Sunset Books

Sunset Publishing Corporation • Menlo Park, CA

C o n t e n t s

Roasted Garlic (recipe on page 568)

Buon Appetito!

Farm-fresh vegetables and fruits, splendidly seasoned sauces, pasta in every shape and size, satisfying polenta and risotto—all these are characteristic of Italian cooking. And all are well-suited for lean meals. In fact, dining Italian style and cutting fat are so compatible that you can enjoy many favorite dishes with remarkably little alteration—sometimes, none at all. A suppertime standard such as tender-firm linguine or sturdy polenta topped with a brilliant combination of Roma tomatoes, sweet peppers, garlic, and zippy fresh basil (see page 549) would earn any nutritionist's blessing. When you do need to alter the classic recipes, it may be enough just to decrease the quantity of oil or butter, reduce the cheese from a shower to a light sprinkle, or adjust your favorite pasta dishes to include a little more pasta and a little less sauce.

A look through this book will show you how simple it is to prepare lean dishes with authentic Italian flavor. Take focaccia (pages 592–593), for example. The traditional bread base is already low in fat, so all you need to do is devise a similarly streamlined topping. That means going easy on the cheese and meat, opting instead for lots of vegetables (or even fruits). Risotto (see page 547) is another easily slimmed-down classic. The traditional slow simmering of rice in broth captures the creamy-rich texture of the original, and the lavish addition of vegetables such as mushrooms and pungent greens lends so much appeal you won't miss the butter and cheese we've left out. Even an all-time favorite like Eggplant Parmesan (page 598) can suit a light menu nicely. We baked the crumb-coated eggplant slices instead of frying them, cut down on the mozzarella cheese, and added lots of flavor with a double dose of tomatoes—sliced ripe ones in the casserole, plus a zesty herb-and-garlic tomato sauce to bind all the ingredients together.

Italian-style desserts, too, can be perfect for low-fat meals. As always, start by choosing those that are already lean: intensely flavored ices (pages 619 and 620), crunchy biscotti (pages 616–617), and dense, fruity Panforte (page 622) come to mind. But even emphatically luxurious treats such as Tiramisu (page 612) don't have to remain out of reach in high-fat heaven. Our version uses the classic brandy-soaked ladyfingers as the base, but lightens up the filling by cutting down on the super-rich mascarpone and supplementing it with non-fat cream cheese and whipped topping. The result, though fluffier than genuine *tiramisù*, provides just as luscious a "pick-me-up" with a hot cup of espresso.

Shopping for Ingredients

If you buy the foods you normally would for Italian cooking, you've already stocked up on much of what you need for low-fat Italian meals: poultry, lean meats, and seafood, the best produce, pasta (both fresh and dried), short- or medium-grain rice, polenta, olive oil, Parmesan and mozzarella cheeses, and canned goods such as tomatoes, garbanzos, and cannellini beans. You may want to pay extra attention to seasonings and condiments, though, since adding more flavor is a great way to make up for using less fat. Fresh herbs, aromatic balsamic and wine vinegars, and pungent spices and seeds really make simple dishes sing. Other flavor-boosters include rich, tangy dried tomatoes, silky roasted peppers, and sweet oven-roasted garlic (see pages 568–569). Olives, delicate toasted pine nuts, and fragrant pesto sauces (see page 600) make marvelous accents too—but since these are high in fat, be sure you use them sparingly.

When a recipe calls for dairy products, we typically specify nonfat, low-fat, or reduced-fat choices. Among cheeses, we also favor modest amounts of whole-milk type such as Gorgonzola, provolone, fontina, and Parmesan; these are all so assertive that a small amount makes a significant contribution to a recipe's flavor. Another favorite is smoked mozzarella; stronger tasting than the plain cheese, it lends a wonderful savor to dishes such as Pasta & Cheese Pie (page 556).

An easy way to decrease the percentage of calories from fat in any meal is to include pasta, rice, or polenta on the menu. Where Italian cooking is concerned, of course, this tactic almost goes without saying, since so many dishes are based on pasta. But think about combinations beyond the familiar pair of pasta-and-sauce: serve grilled lamb chops with polenta, for example (see page 587), or present broiled chicken breasts on a bed of flavorful risotto.

Cooking Techniques

Baking, broiling, grilling, and steaming are the standard low-fat cooking methods, and all are represented in this book. Many of our recipes also feature braise-deglazing, a lean version of sautéing used to develop a flavorful base of cooked onions or other vegetables for a variety of dishes. To braise-deglaze, you simply omit some or all of the fat you'd typically use for pan-frying, instead adding a little water or broth to the vegetables you want to cook. Stir the mixture over medium-high to medium heat until the vegetables begin to brown and the liquid is gone; then stir in a bit more liquid, gently scraping free any browned bits sticking to the pan bottom. Repeat the process until the vegetables are as soft and browned as you like. Although braise-deglazing doesn't brown foods as quickly as sautéing

does, you'll find that vegetables cooked in this way have every bit as much deep, rich flavor and color as those cooked in fat.

Using Our Recipes

When you follow our recipes, you may want to make substitutions to achieve the flavor you like. In some cases, you may decide to use products higher in fat or sodium than those we specify; perhaps you prefer part-skim ricotta cheese to the nonfat version, or regular canned broth to the reduced-sodium type. Just be aware that such substitutions will boost the fat or sodium content of the finished dish.

Another point to consider is that low-fat does not always mean low-calorie. If you're trying to lose weight on a calorie-controlled diet, be aware of your daily limit and select foods accordingly. Many of the recipes in this book will fit right into your plan, but some are high enough in calories to qualify as occasional treats.

Remember that the preparation and cooking times given in our recipes are guides, not absolutes. Actual times will vary, depending on your level of expertise, the type of heat source and cookware you have, the ripeness or firmness of the fruits and vegetables you use, and so on.

A Word About Our Nutritional Data

For our recipes, we provide a nutritional analysis stating calorie count; percentage of calories from fat; grams of total fat and saturated fat; milligrams of cholesterol and sodium; grams of carbohydrates, fiber, and protein; and milligrams of calcium and iron. Generally, the analysis applies to a single serving, based on the number of servings given for each recipe and the amount of each ingredient. If a range is given for the number of servings and/or the amount of an ingredient, the analysis is based on the average of the figures given.

The nutritional analysis does not include optional ingredients or those for which no specific amount is stated. If an ingredient is listed with a substitution, the information was calculated using the first choice.

Baked Fennel with Gorgonzola
(recipe on page 540)

Side Dishes

Fresh, nutritious vegetables and fruits play a big part in any low-fat diet, and lean Italian cuisine is no exception. Accompaniments such as Roasted Vegetable Medley, Poached Leeks with Hazelnuts, and elegant Fruited Spinach Purée offer delicious, colorful ways to dress up and round out the simplest of meals. Of course, favorite Italian side dishes include more than just vegetable specialties. You'll find pasta and polenta in this chapter too, from hot, hearty choices like Polenta with Fresh Tomato Sauce to cool salads such as Pastina with Peas.

•

Baked Fennel with Gorgonzola

Braised fresh fennel with a baked-on blue cheese topping is a nice accompaniment for your favorite fish fillets or steaks.

- ½ cup (50 g) fine dry bread crumbs
- 4 large heads fennel (about 3 lbs./1.35 kg *total*)
- 1¾ cups (420 ml) fat-free reduced-sodium chicken broth
- 3 tablespoons packed crumbled Gorgonzola, cambozola, or other blue-veined cheese
  Salt and pepper

Preparation time: 15 minutes
Cooking time: about 50 minutes
Pictured on page 538

1. Sprinkle three-fourths of the bread crumbs over bottom of a rectangular baking dish (about 8 by 12 inches/20 by 30 cm). Set aside.

2. Trim stems from fennel, reserving about 1 cup (30 g) of the feathery green leaves. Trim and discard any bruised areas from fennel; then cut each fennel head in half lengthwise. Lay fennel halves in a wide frying pan. Pour broth into pan and bring to a boil over high heat; then reduce heat, cover, and simmer until fennel is tender when pierced (about 25 minutes). With a slotted spoon, transfer fennel halves to baking dish, arranging them in a single layer with cut side up.

3. Bring cooking broth to a boil over high heat; boil until reduced to ½ cup (120 ml), about 10 minutes. Stir in half the reserved fennel leaves. Spoon mixture over fennel halves in baking dish.

4. In a small bowl, mash cheese with remaining bread crumbs and 1 teaspoon water; dot mixture evenly over fennel. Bake in a 375°F (190°C) oven until topping begins to brown and fennel is heated through (about 15 minutes). Tuck remaining fennel leaves around fennel halves. Season to taste with salt and pepper. Makes 8 servings.

Per serving: 74 calories (28% calories from fat), 2 g total fat, 1 g saturated fat, 5 mg cholesterol, 416 mg sodium, 9 g carbohydrates, 2 g fiber, 4 g protein, 113 mg calcium, 2 mg iron

Baked Zucchini with Mushrooms

Delicious with roast pork, this hearty casserole will remind you of an oven-baked frittata.

- 1 pound (455 g) mushrooms, thinly sliced
- 1 medium-size onion, chopped
  About 1⅓ cups (320 ml) canned vegetable broth
- 3 large eggs
- 4 large zucchini (about 2 lbs./905 g *total*), shredded
- ½ cup (50 g) fine dry bread crumbs
- ¼ cup (20 g) grated Parmesan cheese
- ¼ teaspoon *each* pepper and dried oregano
- 2 tablespoons thinly sliced green onion

Preparation time: 20 minutes
Cooking time: About 1 hour

1. In a wide nonstick frying pan, combine mushrooms, chopped onion, and ½ cup (120 ml) water. Cook over medium-high heat, stirring often, until liquid has evaporated and vegetables are beginning to brown. To deglaze, add ⅓ cup (80 ml) of the broth and stir to scrape browned bits free from pan bottom. Then continue to cook, stirring occasionally, until vegetables begin to brown again. Repeat deglazing and browning steps 2 or 3 more times, using ⅓ cup (80 ml) broth each time; onion should be golden brown (about 15 minutes *total*). Remove pan from heat.

2. In a large bowl, beat eggs to blend; stir in mushroom mixture, zucchini, bread crumbs, cheese, pepper, and oregano.

3. Pour egg mixture into a greased 9- by 13-inch (23- by 33-cm) baking dish; spread out evenly. Bake in a 325°F (165°C) oven until casserole appears set in center when dish is gently shaken (about 45 minutes). Let stand for 5 to 10 minutes; then sprinkle with green onion and serve. Makes 8 servings.

Per serving: 112 calories (30% calories from fat), 4 g total fat, 1 g saturated fat, 82 mg cholesterol, 306 mg sodium, 14 g carbohydrates, 2 g fiber, 7 g protein, 85 mg calcium, 2 mg iron

Sautéed mushrooms laced with sherry and balsamic vinegar embellish these tender-crisp green beans.

....

- 1 **tablespoon butter or margarine**
- 1 **small onion, finely chopped**
- 1 **pound (455 g) mushrooms, finely chopped**
- ½ **cup (120 ml) dry sherry**
- 1 **tablespoon (15 ml) reduced-sodium soy sauce**
- 2 **tablespoons (30 ml) balsamic vinegar**
- 1 **teaspoon *each* cornstarch and Oriental sesame oil**
- 3 **pounds (1.35 kg) green beans, ends trimmed**

Green Beans with Sautéed Mushrooms

....

Preparation time: 20 minutes
Cooking time: About 30 minutes

1. Melt butter in a wide nonstick frying pan over medium-high heat. Add onion and cook, stirring often, until soft. Add mushrooms, ¼ cup (60 ml) of the sherry, and ¼ cup (60 ml) water; cook, stirring often, until almost all liquid has evaporated and mushrooms are lightly browned (about 15 minutes).

2. In a small bowl, stir together remaining ¼ cup (60 ml) sherry, ½ cup (120 ml) water, soy sauce, vinegar, cornstarch, and oil. Add to mushroom mixture and cook, stirring, until sauce boils and thickens slightly. Remove from heat and keep warm.

3. In a 5- to 6-quart (5- to 6-liter) pan, bring 3 quarts (2.8 liters) water to a boil over high heat. Add beans; cook, uncovered, until just tender to bite (4 to 6 minutes). Drain well, arrange on a platter, and top with mushroom-onion mixture. Makes 12 servings.

....

Per serving: 70 calories (21% calories from fat), 2 g total fat, 0.7 g saturated fat, 3 mg cholesterol, 69 mg sodium, 10 g carbohydrates, 2 g fiber, 3 g protein, 42 mg calcium, 2 mg iron

---

A lemon-sherry vinaigrette flavors fennel, green beans, and chunks of russet potato in a dish that's just right for a buffet.

....

- 2 **large heads fennel (about 1½ lbs./680 g *total*)**
- 1 **pound (455 g) slender green beans, ends trimmed**
- 2 **tablespoons (30 ml) olive oil**
- 2 **very large russet potatoes (about 1½ lbs./680 g *total*), peeled and cut into 1-inch (2.5-cm) chunks**
- 1 **teaspoon *each* mustard seeds, cumin seeds, and fennel seeds**
- ⅓ **cup (80 ml) sherry vinegar**
- ⅓ **cup (80 ml) Gewürztraminer or orange juice**
- 1 **tablespoon grated lemon peel**

....

1. Trim stems from fennel, reserving some of the feathery green leaves

Roasted Potatoes, Fennel & Green Beans with Sherry Dressing

....

Preparation time: 25 minutes
Cooking time: 50 to 60 minutes

for garnish. Trim and discard any bruised areas from fennel; then cut fennel into ¾-inch (2-cm) chunks. Transfer to a large, shallow baking pan. Add beans and 4 teaspoons (20 ml) of the oil; stir to coat vegetables. In a 9-inch-square (23-cm-square) baking pan, mix potatoes and remaining 2 teaspoons oil.

2. Bake all vegetables in a 475°F (245°C) oven, stirring occasionally,

until richly browned (about 45 minutes for fennel and beans, 50 to 60 minutes for potatoes). Watch carefully to prevent scorching. As pieces brown, remove them and keep warm; add water, ¼ cup (60 ml) at a time, if pans appear dry.

3. While vegetables are baking, stir mustard seeds, cumin seeds, and fennel seeds in a small frying pan over medium heat until fragrant (2 to 5 minutes). Remove pan from heat and stir in vinegar, Gewürztraminer, and lemon peel; set aside.

4. Transfer fennel, beans, and potatoes to a large rimmed serving bowl; add dressing and mix gently to coat vegetables. Garnish with reserved fennel leaves. Makes 4 to 6 servings.

....

Per serving: 210 calories (27% calories from fat), 6 g total fat, 0.7 g saturated fat, 0 mg cholesterol, 126 mg sodium, 33 g carbohydrates, 5 g fiber, 5 g protein, 99 mg calcium, 3 mg iron

Sautéed Chard with Pine Nuts

Crisp pine nuts top this colorful combination of chard, red bell pepper, and currants.

Preparation time: 15 minutes
Cooking time: About 10 minutes

- 1½ pounds (680 g) Swiss chard
- 1 tablespoon pine nuts
- 1 teaspoon olive oil
- 2 cloves garlic, minced or pressed
- 1 large red bell pepper (about 8 oz./230 g), seeded and cut into slivers about 2 inches (5 cm) long
- ⅓ cup (50 g) dried currants

1. Cut off and discard coarse stem ends of chard. Rinse and drain chard. Then thinly slice stems crosswise up to base of leaves; set sliced stems aside. Use a few whole leaves to line a large rimmed serving dish; coarsely chop remaining leaves. Set aside serving dish and all chard.

2. Toast pine nuts in a wide nonstick frying pan over medium heat until golden (about 3 minutes), stirring often. Pour out of pan and set aside. Heat oil in pan over medium-high heat. Add garlic, chard stems, and 1 tablespoon (15 ml) water; cook, stirring, until stems are softened (about 2 minutes). Stir in chopped leaves, bell pepper, and currants. Cover and cook until leaves are wilted (about 5 minutes), stirring occasionally.

3. With a slotted spoon, lift chard mixture from pan and arrange in serving dish. Sprinkle with pine nuts. Makes 4 servings.

Per serving: 105 calories (20% calories from fat), 3 g total fat, 0.3 g saturated fat, 0 mg cholesterol, 336 mg sodium, 20 g carbohydrates, 2 g fiber, 4 g protein, 99 mg calcium, 4 mg iron

Roasted Artichokes with Vinaigrette

A zesty vinaigrette dresses up these tender whole artichokes.

Preparation time: 30 minutes
Cooking time: About 1¼ hours
Chilling time: At least 2 hours
Pictured on facing page

- 4 large artichokes (*each* 4 to 4½ inches/10 to 11 cm in diameter)
- 2 cups (470 ml) fat-free reduced-sodium chicken broth
- 1 teaspoon *each* dried rosemary, dried oregano, dried thyme, and mustard seeds
- ¼ cup (60 ml) balsamic vinegar
- 1 pound (455 g) pear-shaped (Roma-type) tomatoes, seeded and chopped
- ⅓ cup (35 g) sliced green onions
- 2 tablespoons chopped Italian or regular parsley

1. Break small, coarse outer leaves from artichokes. With a sharp knife, cut off thorny tops; with scissors, snip any remaining thorny tips from leaves. With knife, peel stems and trim bases. Immerse artichokes in water and swish up and down to rinse well; lift out and, holding by stem end, shake to remove water.

2. Place artichokes in a 9- by 13-inch (23- by 33-cm) baking pan. Mix broth, 1 cup (240 ml) water, rosemary, oregano, thyme, and mustard seeds; pour into pan. Cover very tightly with foil and bake in a 450°F (230°C) oven until artichoke bottoms are tender when pierced (about 50 minutes). Uncover and continue to bake until artichokes are just tinged with brown (about 8 more minutes).

3. With a slotted spoon, lift artichokes from pan. Hold briefly above pan to drain; transfer to a rimmed dish. Reserve juices in pan. When artichokes are cool enough to touch, ease center of each open; using a spoon, scoop out a few of the tiny center leaves and the choke.

4. Boil pan juices over high heat until reduced to ½ cup (120 ml), about 10 minutes. Remove from heat, stir in vinegar, and pour over artichokes. Cover; refrigerate for at least 2 hours or until next day, spooning marinade over artichokes occasionally.

5. With a slotted spoon, transfer artichokes to individual plates. Stir tomatoes, onions, and parsley into artichoke marinade; spoon mixture around artichokes and into their centers. Makes 4 servings.

Per serving: 96 calories (7% calories from fat), 0.9 g total fat, 0.1 g saturated fat, 0 mg cholesterol, 441 mg sodium, 19 g carbohydrates, 8 g fiber, 7 g protein, 85 mg calcium, 3 mg iron

Roasted Artichokes with Vinaigrette
(recipe on facing page)

Roasted Sausage & Onion with Pita Breads

Preparation time: 15 minutes
Cooking time: About 45 minutes

- 12 ounces (340 g) mild turkey Italian sausages, cut diagonally into 1-inch (2.5-cm) lengths
- 2 large onions, cut into wedges about ½ inch (1 cm) thick
- 5 tablespoons (75 ml) balsamic vinegar
- 12 miniature pita breads (*each* about 3 inches/8 cm in diameter), cut into halves

1. In a 9- by 13-inch (23- by 33-cm) baking pan, combine sausages, onions, and ¼ cup (60 ml) of the vinegar. Bake in a 425°F (220°C) oven until sausage is well browned and almost all liquid has evaporated (about 45 minutes); stir occasionally and add water, ¼ cup (60 ml) at a time, if drippings begin to scorch.

2. Remove pan from oven and add 1 tablespoon (15 ml) water and remaining 1 tablespoon (15 ml) vinegar. Let stand for about 3 minutes; then stir to scrape browned bits free from pan bottom.

3. Transfer sausage-onion mixture to a serving dish and keep hot. To serve, spoon mixture into pita bread halves. Makes 12 servings.

Per serving: 140 calories (22% calories from fat), 3 g total fat, 0.9 g saturated fat, 15 mg cholesterol, 339 mg sodium, 20 g carbohydrates, 1 g fiber, 8 g protein, 39 mg calcium, 2 mg iron

Chili Shrimp

Preparation time: 15 minutes
Cooking time: 15 to 20 minutes

- 1 bottle or can (about 12 oz./340 g) beer
- ½ cup (85 g) finely chopped onion
- ¾ teaspoon celery seeds
- 1 dried bay leaf
- 1 pound (455 g) large raw shrimp (31 to 35 per lb.), shelled and deveined
- ½ cup (120 ml) tomato-based chili sauce
- 1 tablespoon (15 ml) honey-flavored mustard
  About 20 large fresh spinach leaves, rinsed and crisped
- 2 tablespoons drained capers

1. In a wide frying pan, combine beer, onion, celery seeds, and bay leaf. Bring to a boil over high heat; boil for 2 minutes.

Add shrimp. Reduce heat, cover, and simmer, stirring occasionally, until shrimp are just opaque in center; cut to test (about 3 minutes). With a slotted spoon, lift shrimp from pan and transfer to a large bowl.

2. Bring shrimp cooking liquid to a boil over high heat; then boil until reduced to ⅓ cup (80 ml). Remove and discard bay leaf. Add chili sauce and mustard to reduced liquid; blend well. Serve; or cover shrimp and dressing separately and refrigerate until cool (at least 1 hour) or until next day.

3. To serve, line 4 individual plates with spinach leaves; top equally with shrimp, then with dressing. Sprinkle with capers. Makes 4 servings.

Per serving: 171 calories (10% calories from fat), 2 g total fat, 0.3 g saturated fat, 140 mg cholesterol, 731 mg sodium, 17 g carbohydrates, 1 g fiber, 21 g protein, 100 mg calcium, 4 mg iron

Pickled Vegetables

Preparation time: 15 minutes
Cooking time: About 15 minutes
Chilling time: At least 1 day
Pictured on page 594

- 8 ounces (230 g) small carrots (*each* 4 to 5 inches/10 to 12.5 cm long)
- 1 package (about 10 oz./285 g) frozen tiny onions, thawed
- 1 large red bell pepper (about 8 oz./230 g), seeded and cut into strips about ½ inch (1 cm) wide
- 1 package (about 9 oz./255 g) frozen artichoke hearts, thawed
- 2 cups (470 ml) white wine vinegar
- ¾ cup (150 g) sugar
- 2 tablespoons drained capers
- 2 small dried hot red chiles
- 2 cloves garlic, peeled and crushed

1. In a 2- to 3-quart (1.9- to 2.8-liter) pan, bring 4 cups (950 ml) water to a boil over high heat. Add carrots and boil, uncovered, until barely tender when pierced (about 3 minutes); drain well.

2. In a clean, dry widemouth 1½- to 2-quart (1.4- to 1.9-liter) jar (or in two 1-quart jars), layer carrots, onions, bell pepper, and artichokes. Set aside.

3. In pan used to cook carrots, stir together vinegar, sugar, capers, chiles, and garlic. Bring to a boil over high heat, stirring until sugar is dissolved. Pour hot vinegar mixture

over vegetables. Cover and refrigerate for at least 1 day or up to 2 weeks. To serve, lift vegetables from marinade. Makes about 6 cups (1.4 liters).

Per ¼ cup (60 ml): 42 calories (2% calories from fat), 0.1 g total fat, 0 g saturated fat, 0 mg cholesterol, 28 mg sodium, 10 g carbohydrates, 0.9 g fiber, 0.5 g protein, 10 mg calcium, 0.2 mg iron

Wild Mushroom Polenta Boards

Preparation time: 1 hour
Cooking time: About 1 hour

- ½ cup (60 g) all-purpose flour
- ½ cup (70 g) polenta or yellow cornmeal
- ¼ cup (30 g) instant nonfat dry milk
- 1½ teaspoons baking powder
- 1 tablespoon butter or margarine
- 2 tablespoons (30 ml) olive oil or salad oil
- 1 medium-size head garlic (3 oz./85 g)
- 8 ounces (230 g) *each* fresh shiitake, chanterelle, and oyster mushrooms
- 1 tablespoon *each* chopped fresh rosemary and chopped fresh sage; or 1 teaspoon *each* dried rubbed sage and dried rosemary
- 2 teaspoons cornstarch mixed with ¾ cup (180 ml) fat-free reduced-sodium chicken broth
- 2 tablespoons grated Parmesan cheese
  Rosemary and sage sprigs

1. In a food processor or a medium-size bowl, whirl or stir together flour, polenta, dry milk, and baking powder. Add butter; whirl or rub with your fingers until mixture resembles coarse crumbs. Add ⅓ cup (80 ml) water; whirl or stir with a fork until dough begins to form a ball. Turn dough out onto a lightly floured board and pat into a ball; then knead briefly, just until dough holds together smoothly.

2. Divide dough into 6 equal portions; cover with plastic wrap. Flour board well; then, working with one piece of dough at a time, roll each piece into an irregular 6- to 7-inch (15- to 18-cm) round. As rounds are shaped, arrange them, slightly apart, on large baking sheets; cover with plastic wrap. When all rounds have been shaped, remove plastic wrap and bake polenta boards in a 350°F (175°C) oven until lightly browned (12 to 14 minutes). If made ahead, let cool completely on racks; then store airtight until next day.

3. Pour 1 tablespoon (15 ml) of the oil into a small baking pan. Cut garlic head in half crosswise (through cloves). Place garlic, cut side down, in pan; bake in a 350°F (175°C) oven until cut side is golden brown (about 45 minutes). Using a thin spatula, lift garlic from pan and transfer to a rack; let stand until cool enough to touch (about 10 minutes). Squeeze garlic cloves from skins into a small bowl; mash garlic thoroughly.

4. While garlic is baking, trim and discard stems from shiitake mushrooms. Thinly slice shiitake mushroom caps and whole chanterelles. Place sliced shiitake and chanterelle mushrooms and whole oyster mushrooms in a 5- to 6-quart (5- to 6-liter) pan; add remaining 1 tablespoon (15 ml) oil, chopped rosemary, and chopped sage. Cover and cook over medium-high heat until mushrooms are juicy (about 8 minutes). Uncover; cook, stirring often, until almost all liquid has evaporated and mushrooms are browned (15 to 20 more minutes). Add cornstarch mixture and mashed garlic; stir until mixture boils and thickens slightly.

5. Lay polenta boards, side by side, on 2 large baking sheets. Spoon hot mushroom sauce into center of each; sprinkle evenly with cheese. Broil 4 to 6 inches (10 to 15 cm) below heat until sizzling (about 2 minutes). With a spatula, transfer to individual plates; garnish with rosemary and sage sprigs. Makes 6 servings.

Per serving: 202 calories (30% calories from fat), 7 g total fat, 2 g saturated fat, 7 mg cholesterol, 276 mg sodium, 29 g carbohydrates, 3 g fiber, 7 g protein, 160 mg calcium, 3 mg iron

Cherry Pepper Shooters

Preparation time: 20 minutes

- 2 jars (about 1 lb./455 g *each*) mild cherry peppers, drained
- 1 can (about 8 oz./230 g) pineapple chunks packed in juice, drained
- 2 ounces (55 g) thinly sliced prosciutto, cut into 1½-inch (3.5-cm) squares

1. Cut off and discard pepper stems. With a small spoon, scoop out and discard seeds.

2. Cut each pineapple chunk in half; wrap each half in a piece of prosciutto. Stuff wrapped pineapple chunks into peppers. Makes 12 servings.

Per serving: 44 calories (13% calories from fat), 0.7 g total fat, 0.2 g saturated fat, 4 mg cholesterol, sodium information not available, 8 g carbohydrates, 0.1 g fiber, 1 g protein, 3 mg calcium, 1 mg iron

Italian Greens Risotto
(recipe on facing page)

Broccoli rabe (also called rapini) is a pungent, bitter green that's very popular in Italy. In this recipe, it combines with fresh asparagus in a satisfying risotto.

- 12 ounces (340 g) broccoli rabe (rapini)
- 12 ounces (340 g) asparagus, tough ends snapped off
- 4 teaspoons (20 ml) olive oil
- 1 large onion, finely chopped
- 1 cup (200 g) short- or medium-grain white rice
- 3 cups (710 ml) fat-free reduced-sodium chicken broth
- ½ cup (120 ml) dry white wine
- ½ cup (40 g) grated Parmesan cheese

1. Cut off and discard any coarse stem ends from broccoli rabe; discard any bruised or yellow leaves. If any stems are thicker than ⅜ inch (1 cm), cut them in half lengthwise. Rinse and drain broccoli rabe.

Italian Greens Risotto

Preparation time: 15 minutes
Cooking time: About 45 minutes
Pictured on facing page

2. Chop or thinly slice half each of the broccoli rabe and asparagus. Leave remaining asparagus spears and broccoli rabe leaves and flowerets whole.

3. In a wide nonstick frying pan, combine chopped broccoli rabe, chopped asparagus, and 1 tablespoon (15 ml) of the oil. Cook over medium-high heat, stirring, until vegetables are just tender to bite (about 4 minutes). Remove from pan and set aside. To pan, add ½ cup (120 ml) water, whole asparagus spears, and whole broccoli rabe leaves and flowerets. Cover and

cook, turning vegetables often with a wide spatula, until vegetables are just tender to bite (about 4 minutes). Lift from pan; set aside.

4. In same pan, combine remaining 1 teaspoon oil and onion; cook over medium-high heat, stirring often, until onion is tinged with brown (5 to 8 minutes). Add rice and stir until opaque (3 to 4 minutes). Stir in broth and wine. Bring to a boil, stirring often. Then reduce heat and simmer, uncovered, until rice is tender to bite and almost all liquid has been absorbed (about 25 minutes); stir occasionally at first, more often as mixture thickens. Stir in sautéed chopped vegetables and cheese. Spoon onto a platter; surround with whole vegetables and serve immediately. Makes 6 servings.

Per serving: 237 calories (22% calories from fat), 5 g total fat, 2 g saturated fat, 5 mg cholesterol, 480 mg sodium, 35 g carbohydrates, 3 g fiber, 10 g protein, 154 mg calcium, 3 mg iron

---

Bold with onions and Gorgonzola cheese, this mushroom risotto is good with juicy steaks or chops.

- 1 teaspoon olive oil
- 8 ounces (230 g) mushrooms, thinly sliced
- 1 large onion, chopped
- 1 clove garlic, minced
- 1 cup (200 g) short- or medium-grain white rice
- ¼ teaspoon *each* dried thyme, dried marjoram, and dried rubbed sage
- 3 cups (790 ml) fat-free reduced-sodium chicken broth
- ½ cup (125 g) packed crumbled Gorgonzola or other blue-veined cheese

Risotto with Mushrooms

Preparation time: 15 minutes
Cooking time: About 45 minutes

- 1 teaspoon dry sherry (or to taste)

1. Heat oil in a wide nonstick frying pan over medium heat. Add mushrooms, onion, and garlic. Cook, stirring often, until vegetables are soft and are beginning to stick to pan bottom (about 15 minutes); add water, 1 tablespoon (15 ml) at a

time, if pan drippings begin to scorch.

2. Add rice, thyme, marjoram, and sage; stir until rice is opaque (3 to 4 minutes). Stir in broth. Bring to a boil, stirring often. Then reduce heat and simmer, uncovered, until rice is tender to bite and almost all liquid has been absorbed (about 25 minutes); stir occasionally at first, more often as mixture thickens.

3. Remove rice mixture from heat and stir in cheese and sherry. Makes 4 to 6 servings.

Per serving: 230 calories (19% calories from fat), 5 g total fat, 3 g saturated fat, 10 mg cholesterol, 450 mg sodium, 38 g carbohydrates, 2 g fiber, 8 g protein, 76 mg calcium, 2 mg iron

Here's risotto in a new guise: it's formed into patties, pan-fried until crisp, and served with a tomato-basil purée.

Risotto Cakes with Tomato Purée

Preparation time: 25 minutes
Cooking time: About 1¼ hours

2 tablespoons (30 ml) olive oil; or 2 tablespoons butter

1¼ cups (244 g) short- or medium-grain white rice

1¾ cups (420 ml) fat-free reduced-sodium chicken broth

5 to 6 ounces (140 to 170 g) mozzarella cheese, shredded

¼ cup (20 g) grated Parmesan cheese

4 green onions, finely chopped

1 can (about 14½ oz./415 g) diced tomatoes

¼ cup (60 ml) plain nonfat yogurt

¼ cup (10 g) coarsely chopped fresh basil

Basil sprigs

1. Heat 1 tablespoon (15 ml) of the oil in a 3- to 4-quart (2.8- to 3.8-liter) pan over medium-high heat. Add rice and stir until opaque (3 to 4 minutes). Stir in broth and 1½ cups (360 ml) water. Bring to a boil, stirring often. Then reduce heat and simmer, uncovered, until rice is tender to bite and almost all liquid has been absorbed (25 to 30 minutes); stir occasionally at first, more often as mixture thickens. Remove from heat and stir in mozzarella cheese, Parmesan cheese, and onions. Let cool uncovered. (At this point, you may cover and refrigerate until next day.)

2. In a food processor or blender, combine tomatoes and their liquid, yogurt, and chopped basil. Whirl until smoothly puréed; set aside.

3. Divide rice mixture into 12 equal portions; shape each portion into a cake about ¾ inch (2 cm) thick. Heat 1 teaspoon of the oil in a wide nonstick frying pan over medium-high heat. Add risotto cakes to pan, a portion at a time (do not crowd pan); cook, turning once, until golden on both sides (about 20 minutes). Add remaining 2 teaspoons oil to pan as needed. As cakes are cooked, arrange them in a single layer in a large, shallow baking pan; cover loosely with foil and keep warm in a 300°F (150°C) oven until all cakes have been cooked.

4. To serve, arrange cakes on individual plates; top with tomato purée and garnish with basil sprigs. Makes 6 servings.

Per serving: 286 calories (28% calories from fat), 9 g total fat, 3 g saturated fat, 12 mg cholesterol, 507 mg sodium, 38 g carbohydrates, 1 g fiber, 13 g protein, 313 mg calcium, 3 mg iron

---

Tangy dried tomatoes and sliced mushrooms dot this lively pilaf.

Dried Tomato Pilaf

Preparation time: 15 minutes
Cooking time: 35 to 45 minutes

1 tablespoon (15 ml) olive oil

8 ounces (230 g) portabella or button mushrooms, sliced

1 medium-size onion, chopped

1 cup (185 g) long-grain white rice

2½ cups (590 ml) fat-free reduced-sodium chicken broth

¾ cup (about 1½ oz./43 g) dried tomatoes (not packed in oil), chopped

¼ cup (10 g) chopped cilantro

Salt and pepper

1. Heat oil in a 3- to 4-quart (2.8- to 3.8-liter) pan over medium-high heat. Add mushrooms and onion; cook, stirring often, until almost all liquid has evaporated and vegetables are lightly browned (10 to 12 minutes).

2. Add rice and stir until opaque (3 to 4 minutes). Add broth and tomatoes. Bring to a boil; then reduce heat, cover, and simmer until rice is tender to bite (20 to 25 minutes). Stir in cilantro. Season to taste with salt and pepper. Makes 6 servings.

Per serving: 181 calories (13% calories from fat), 3 g total fat, 0.4 g saturated fat, 0 mg cholesterol, 280 mg sodium, 34 g carbohydrates, 3 g fiber, 6 g protein, 17 g calcium, 2 mg iron

Red Bell Peppers Stuffed with Caper Rice

Preparation time: 20 minutes
Cooking time: 35 to 40 minutes

If you can't find small peppers, just cut medium-size ones down: slice the tops off the peppers as directed, then trim the cut edges of both top and bottom pieces so the whole peppers will be just 2 to 3 inches tall when reassembled.

- 10 to 12 very small red, yellow, or orange bell peppers (*each 2 to 3 inches/5 to 8 cm tall*)
- 1 cup (200 g) short- or medium-grain white rice
- 4 teaspoons grated lemon peel
- 8 ounces (230 g) sliced bacon, crisply cooked, drained, and crumbled
- ¼ cup (43 g) drained capers
- ¼ cup (60 ml) seasoned rice vinegar

1. Cut off the top third of each pepper. With a small spoon, scoop out seeds and white membranes from pepper bases and tops; rinse and drain both bases and tops. If needed, trim pepper bases (without piercing them) so they will sit steadily.

2. In a 2- to 3-quart (1.9- to 2.8-liter) pan, combine rice, lemon peel, and 2½ cups (590 ml) water. Bring to a boil over high heat. Reduce heat, cover, and simmer until rice is tender to bite and almost all liquid has been absorbed (about 20 minutes). Remove from heat. With a fork, stir in bacon, capers, and vinegar.

3. Set pepper bases upright, spacing them slightly apart, in a shallow 10- by 15-inch (25- by 38-cm) baking pan. Mound rice mixture equally in pepper bases; set pepper tops in place. Bake in a 450°F (230°C) oven until peppers are blistered and rice mixture is hot in center (8 to 12 minutes). Makes 10 to 12 servings.

Per serving: 131 calories (21% calories from fat), 3 g total fat, 1 g saturated fat, 5 mg cholesterol, 263 mg sodium, 22 g carbohydrates, 2 g fiber, 4 g protein, 12 mg calcium, 1 mg iron

---

Polenta with Fresh Tomato Sauce

Preparation time: 25 minutes
Cooking time: About 20 minutes

Creamy polenta is enhanced by an easy sauce based on fresh tomatoes, yellow bell peppers, and basil.

- 3 pounds (1.35 kg) pear-shaped (Roma-type) tomatoes, peeled (if desired) and coarsely chopped
- 2 large yellow bell peppers (about 1 lb./455 g *total*), seeded and chopped
- 1 cup (40 g) lightly packed slivered fresh basil or ¼ cup (8 g) dried basil
- 2 cloves garlic, minced
- 2 cups (470 ml) low-fat (2%) milk
- ½ cup (120 ml) canned vegetable broth
- 1 cup (138 g) polenta or yellow cornmeal
- 1 teaspoon chopped fresh sage or ¼ teaspoon ground sage
- ½ teaspoon salt
- ½ cup (40 g) grated Parmesan cheese
- Basil sprigs

1. In a 3- to 4-quart (2.8- to 3.8-liter) pan, combine two-thirds each of the tomatoes and bell peppers, half the slivered basil, and all the garlic. Cook over medium-high heat, stirring often, until tomatoes begin to fall apart (15 to 20 minutes).

2. Meanwhile, in a 4- to 5-quart (3.8- to 5-liter) pan, bring milk and broth just to a boil over medium-high heat. Stir in polenta, sage, and salt. Reduce heat and simmer, uncovered, stirring often and scraping bottom of pan with a long-handled spoon (mixture will spatter), until polenta tastes creamy (about 15 minutes). Remove pan from heat; stir in cheese. Keep warm.

3. Working quickly, stir remaining tomatoes, bell peppers, and slivered basil into sauce. Divide polenta equally among deep individual bowls and top with sauce. Garnish with basil sprigs. Makes 4 servings.

Per serving: 346 calories (19% calories from fat), 7 g total fat, 4 g saturated fat, 18 mg cholesterol, 681 mg sodium, 58 g carbohydrates, 8 g fiber, 16 g protein, 414 mg calcium, 5 mg iron

Toasted hazelnuts and crisp, hazelnut-seasoned crumbs flavor these simple poached leeks.

....

¼ cup (34 g) hazelnuts

3 slices sourdough sandwich bread (about 3 oz./85 g *total*), torn into pieces

2 cloves garlic, minced or pressed

¼ teaspoon dried thyme

1 teaspoon hazelnut oil or olive oil

8 medium-size leeks (about 4 lbs./ 1.8 kg *total*)

Balsamic vinegar

....

1. Spread hazelnuts in a single layer in a shallow baking pan. Bake in a 375°F (190°C) oven until nuts are golden beneath skins (about 10 minutes). Let nuts cool slightly; then

Poached Leeks with Hazelnuts

....

Preparation time: 25 minutes
Cooking time: 20 to 25 minutes

pour into a towel, fold to enclose, and rub to remove as much of loose skins as possible. Let cool; then coarsely chop and set aside.

2. While nuts are toasting, in a food processor or blender, whirl bread to form fine crumbs. Pour crumbs into a medium-size nonstick frying pan and add garlic and thyme. Drizzle with oil and 1 tablespoon (15 ml) water. Then stir over medium-high heat until crumbs are lightly browned (5 to 7 minutes). Remove

from pan and set aside.

3. Trim and discard roots and tough tops from leeks; remove and discard coarse outer leaves. Split leeks lengthwise. Thoroughly rinse leek halves between layers; tie each half with string to hold it together.

4. In a 5- to 6-quart (5- to 6-liter) pan, bring 8 cups (1.9 liters) water to a boil over high heat. Add leeks; reduce heat, cover, and simmer until tender when pierced (5 to 7 minutes). Carefully transfer leeks to a strainer; let drain. Snip and discard strings; arrange leeks on a platter. Sprinkle with crumb mixture, then hazelnuts; offer vinegar to add to taste. Makes 4 to 6 servings.

....

Per serving: 185 calories (25% calories from fat), 5 g total fat, 0.5 g saturated fat, 0 mg cholesterol, 134 mg sodium, 31 g carbohydrates, 3 g fiber, 5 g protein, 115 mg calcium, 4 mg iron

---

For a colorful side dish, present this quintet of richly browned roasted vegetables.

....

1 large beet (about 8 oz./230 g), peeled

2 small red thin-skinned potatoes (about 8 oz./230 g *total*)

1 medium-size sweet potato or yam (about 8 oz./230 g), peeled

2 large carrots (about 8 oz./ 230 g *total*)

1 small red onion (about 8 oz./ 230 g)

5 teaspoons (25 ml) olive oil

2 tablespoons *each* chopped fresh oregano and chopped fresh basil; or 2 teaspoons *each* dried oregano and dried basil

1 or 2 cloves garlic, minced or pressed

Roasted Vegetable Medley

....

Preparation time: 30 minutes
Cooking time: About 45 minutes
Pictured on facing page

¼ cup (20 g) grated Parmesan cheese

Oregano and basil sprigs

Salt

....

1. Cut beet, unpeeled thin-skinned potatoes, and sweet potato into ¾-inch (2-cm) chunks. Cut carrots diagonally into ½-inch (1-cm) pieces; cut onion into ¾-inch (2-cm) wedges. Combine all vegetables in a shallow 10- by 15-inch (25- by 38-cm) baking pan; drizzle with oil

and toss to coat vegetables evenly with oil.

2. Bake in a 475°F (245°C) oven until vegetables are richly browned and tender when pierced (35 to 45 minutes), stirring occasionally. Watch carefully to prevent scorching. As pieces brown, remove them and keep warm; add water, ¼ cup (60 ml) at a time, if pan appears dry.

3. Transfer vegetables to a platter or serving dish and sprinkle with chopped oregano, chopped basil, garlic, and a little of the cheese. Garnish with oregano and basil sprigs. Season to taste with salt and remaining cheese. Makes 6 servings.

....

Per serving: 162 calories (28% calories from fat), 5 g total fat, 1 g saturated fat, 3 mg cholesterol, 104 mg sodium, 26 g carbohydrates, 4 g fiber, 4 g protein, 87 mg calcium, 1 mg iron

Roasted Vegetable Medley
(recipe on facing page)

Soups

Shell & Bean Soup

Preparation time: 20 minutes
Cooking time: About 20 minutes

····································

- 1 **small red onion (about 8 oz./230 g), chopped**
- 1 **teaspoon olive oil**
- 1 **cup (120 g) chopped celery**
- 4 **cloves garlic, chopped**
- 10 **cups (2.4 liters) fat-free reduced-sodium chicken broth**
- 1½ **cups (173 g) dried small pasta shells**
- 3 **to 4 cups (555 to 740 g) cooked or canned white beans, drained and rinsed**
- 1 **cup (110 g) shredded carrots**
- 1 **package (about 10 oz./285 g) frozen tiny peas**
- ½ **cup (40 g) grated Parmesan cheese**

····································

1. Set aside ⅓ cup (57 g) of the chopped onion. In a 6- to 8-quart (6- to 8-liter) pan, combine remaining onion, oil, celery, and garlic. Cook over medium-high heat, stirring often, until onion is lightly browned (5 to 8 minutes). Add broth and bring to a boil. Stir in pasta and beans; reduce heat, cover, and simmer until pasta is almost tender to bite (5 to 7 minutes). Add carrots and peas; bring to a boil.

2. Ladle soup into individual bowls; sprinkle equally with cheese and reserved onion. Makes 6 to 8 servings.

····································

Per serving: 324 calories (9% calories from fat), 3 g total fat, 1 g saturated fat, 5 mg cholesterol, 1,113 mg sodium, 53 g carbohydrates, 7 g fiber, 22 g protein, 194 mg calcium, 5 mg iron

Roasted Vegetable & Cheese Soup

Preparation time: 25 minutes
Cooking time: About 30 minutes

····································

- 2 **medium-size leeks (about 1 lb./455 g)**
- 1 **large ear corn (about 10 inches/ 25 cm long), husk and silk removed**
- 1 **small red onion (about 8 oz./230 g), cut in half**
- 1 **large red bell pepper (about 8 oz./ 230 g)**
- 1 **large yellow or green bell pepper (about 8 oz./230 g)**
- 2 **cloves garlic, peeled**
- 4 **cups (950 ml) fat-free reduced-sodium chicken broth**
- 1 **cup (about 4 oz./ 115 g) shredded reduced-fat sharp Cheddar cheese**
- ¼ **cup (60 ml) nonfat sour cream**

····································

1. Trim and discard roots and tough tops from leeks; remove and discard coarse outer leaves. Split leeks lengthwise; thoroughly rinse leek halves between layers. In a large, shallow baking pan, arrange leeks, corn, onion halves, and whole bell peppers.

2. Broil 4 to 6 inches (10 to 15 cm) below heat, turning vegetables as needed to brown evenly, for 10 minutes. Add garlic. Continue to broil, turning as needed, until vegetables are well charred (about 5 more minutes); remove vegetables from pan as they are charred. Cover vegetables loosely with foil and let stand until cool enough to handle (about 10 minutes).

3. With a sharp knife, cut corn kernels from cob. Remove and discard skins, seeds, and stems from bell peppers. Coarsely chop peppers, leeks, onion, and garlic.

4. In a 4- to 5-quart (3.8- to 5-liter) pan, combine vegetables and broth. Bring to a boil over high heat; then reduce heat, cover, and simmer for 10 minutes to blend flavors. Ladle soup into individual bowls; sprinkle with cheese, top with sour cream, and serve. Makes 4 servings.

····································

Per serving: 231 calories (22% calories from fat), 6 g total fat, 4 g saturated fat, 30 mg cholesterol, 901 mg sodium, 30 g carbohydrates, 5 g fiber, 18 g protein, 331 mg calcium, 2 mg iron

Minestrone with Parsley Pesto

Preparation time: 25 minutes
Cooking time: About 30 minutes

....

- 3 quarts (2.8 liters) fat-free reduced-sodium chicken broth
- 2 ounces (55 g) thinly sliced prosciutto or bacon, chopped
- 2 tablespoons salted roasted almonds
- 2 cups (120 g) lightly packed Italian or regular parsley sprigs
- 2 tablespoons (30 ml) *each* olive oil and white wine vinegar
- 2 teaspoons honey
- 1 clove garlic, peeled
- 1 tablespoon drained capers
- ⅛ to ¼ teaspoon crushed red pepper flakes
- 1½ cups (225 g) diced unpeeled red thin-skinned potatoes
- 1 cup (120 g) sliced celery
- 1 large zucchini (about 8 oz./230 g), cut into ½-inch (1-cm) slices
- 10 ounces (285 g) fresh Italian green beans, cut into 1-inch (2.5-cm) lengths; or 1 package (about 10 oz./285 g) frozen Italian green beans, thawed
- 1 large red or yellow bell pepper (about 8 oz./230 g), seeded and cut into ½-inch (1-cm) chunks
- ¾ cup (85 g) dried salad or elbow macaroni
- 1 cup (53 g) lightly packed shredded radicchio or red Swiss chard
- ½ cup (50 g) thinly sliced green onions

....

1. In a 5- to 6-quart (5- to 6-liter) pan, combine broth and prosciutto. Bring to a rolling boil over high heat (10 to 12 minutes).

2. Meanwhile, in a food processor or blender, combine almonds, parsley sprigs, oil, vinegar, honey, garlic, capers, red pepper flakes, and 1 tablespoon (15 ml) water. Whirl until coarsely puréed; scrape sides of container as needed and add 1 to 2 tablespoons (15 to 30 ml) more water if pesto is too thick. Transfer pesto to a small bowl and set aside.

3. Add potatoes to boiling broth; reduce heat, cover, and simmer for 10 minutes. Add celery, zucchini, beans, bell pepper, and pasta; cover and simmer until potatoes and pasta are tender to bite (about 5 more minutes).

4. Stir in radicchio and onions; simmer until radicchio is limp but still bright red (about 4 minutes). Serve immediately; offer parsley pesto to spoon into individual servings. Makes 8 servings.

Per serving: 180 calories (29% calories from fat), 6 g total fat, 0.9 g saturated fat, 6 mg cholesterol, 1,172 mg sodium, 22 g carbohydrates, 3 g fiber, 11 g protein, 66 mg calcium, 3 mg iron

....

Tomato Fava Soup

Preparation time: 25 minutes
Cooking time: About 30 minutes

....

- 2 tablespoons (30 ml) olive oil
- 1 large onion, chopped
- 1½ pounds (680 g) ripe tomatoes, quartered
- 2 tablespoons finely chopped fresh savory or 1 teaspoon dried savory
- ¾ teaspoon sugar
- ¼ teaspoon pepper
- 2 cups shelled fava beans (about 2 lbs./905 g in the pod); see Note at right
- 4 cups (950 ml) fat-free reduced-sodium chicken broth

....

1. Heat oil in a 3- to 4-quart (2.8- to 3.8-liter) pan over medium-high heat. Add onion and cook, stirring often, until it begins to brown (5 to 10 minutes). Add tomatoes, savory, sugar, and pepper. Bring to a boil; then reduce heat and simmer, uncovered, until tomatoes are very soft when pressed (about 15 minutes).

2. Meanwhile, in a 2- to 3-quart (1.9- to 2.8-liter) pan, bring 4 cups (950 ml) water to a boil over high heat. Add beans and simmer, uncovered, until just tender when pierced (3 to 5 minutes). Drain, then let stand until cool enough to touch. With your fingers, slip skins from beans; discard skins and set beans aside.

3. In a food processor or blender, whirl tomato mixture until coarsely puréed. Return to pan and add broth; stir over high heat until hot. Ladle soup into individual bowls; sprinkle beans equally over each serving. Makes 6 servings.

Note: A few people, typically of Mediterranean descent, have a severe allergic reaction to fava beans and their pollen. If favas are new to you, check your family history before eating them.

....

Per serving: 261 calories (19% calories from fat), 6 g total fat, 0.8 g saturated fat, 0 mg cholesterol, 447 mg sodium, 39 g carbohydrates, 9 g fiber, 17 g protein, 70 mg calcium, 4 mg iron

Pesto Pasta Salad
(recipe on facing page)

Fragrant pesto dressing flavors a good-looking pasta salad dotted with dried tomatoes.

Pesto Pasta Salad

Preparation time: 20 minutes
Cooking time: About 15 minutes
Pictured on facing page

1 cup (about 2 oz./55 g) dried tomatoes (not packed in oil)

2 tablespoons pine nuts

1 pound (455 g) dried medium-size pasta shells or elbow macaroni

1 cup (45 g) firmly packed chopped fresh spinach

3 tablespoons dried basil

1 or 2 cloves garlic, peeled

⅓ cup (30 g) grated Parmesan cheese

¼ cup (60 ml) olive oil

1 teaspoon Oriental sesame oil

Salt and pepper

1. Place tomatoes in a small bowl and add boiling water to cover. Let stand until soft (about 10 minutes), stirring occasionally. Drain well; gently squeeze out excess liquid. Cut tomatoes into thin slivers and set aside.

2. While tomatoes are soaking, toast pine nuts in a small frying pan over medium heat until golden (about 3 minutes), stirring often. Pour out of pan and set aside.

3. In a 6- to 8-quart (6- to 8-liter) pan, bring 4 quarts (3.8 liters) water to a boil over medium-high heat; stir in pasta and cook until just tender to bite, 8 to 10 minutes. (Or cook pasta according to package directions.) Drain, rinse with cold water until cool, and drain well again. Pour into a large serving bowl.

4. In a food processor or blender, whirl spinach, basil, garlic, cheese, olive oil, sesame oil, and 1 teaspoon water until smoothly puréed; scrape sides of container as needed and add a little more water if pesto is too thick.

5. Add tomatoes and spinach pesto to pasta; mix well. Sprinkle with pine nuts; season to taste with salt and pepper. Makes 8 servings.

Per serving: 332 calories (28% calories from fat), 10 g total fat, 2 g saturated fat, 3 mg cholesterol, 78 mg sodium, 49 g carbohydrates, 3 g fiber, 11 g protein, 98 mg calcium, 3 mg iron

---

For a refreshing side dish, serve this combination of tiny pasta beads, sweet peas, and mint-lemon dressing.

Pastina with Peas

Preparation time: 15 minutes
Cooking time: About 20 minutes

2 ounces (55 g) thinly sliced prosciutto or bacon, cut into thin strips

1½ cups (340 g) dried orzo or other tiny rice-shaped pasta

1 package (about 1 lb./455 g) frozen tiny peas

¼ cup (25 g) thinly sliced green onions

¼ cup (10 g) chopped fresh mint

¼ cup (60 ml) olive oil

1 teaspoon finely shredded lemon peel

2 tablespoons (30 ml) lemon juice

Mint sprigs

Pepper

1. In a wide nonstick frying pan, cook prosciutto over medium-high heat, stirring often, just until crisp (about 3 minutes). Remove from pan and set aside.

2. In a 5- to 6-quart (5- to 6-liter) pan, bring about 3 quarts (2.8 liters) water to a boil over medium-high heat; stir in pasta and cook until just tender to bite, about 8 minutes. (Or cook pasta according to package directions.) Drain, rinse with cold water until cool, and drain well again. Pour pasta into a large serving bowl; add peas, onions, and chopped mint. Mix gently.

3. In a small bowl, beat oil, lemon peel, and lemon juice until blended. Add to pasta mixture; mix gently but thoroughly. Sprinkle with prosciutto and garnish with mint sprigs. Season to taste with pepper. Makes 6 servings.

Per serving: 364 calories (28% calories from fat), 12 g total fat, 2 g saturated fat, 8 mg cholesterol, 282 mg sodium, 52 g carbohydrates, 4 g fiber, 14 g protein, 29 mg calcium, 3 mg iron

Pasta & Cheese Pie

Preparation time: 25 minutes
Cooking time: About 35 minutes

Smoked mozzarella or Gouda cheese gives this vegetable-pasta pie an especially savory flavor.

- 8 ounces (230 g) mushrooms, thinly sliced
- 1 large red bell pepper (about 8 oz./230 g), seeded and coarsely chopped
- 1 large onion, chopped
- 4 cloves garlic, minced
- ½ cup (120 ml) low-fat (2%) milk
- 2 teaspoons cornstarch
- 2 large eggs
- 6 large egg whites
- ¾ cup (85 g) shredded smoked part-skim mozzarella or smoked Gouda cheese
- ¼ cup (20 g) grated Parmesan cheese
- 2 tablespoons chopped fresh thyme or 1½ teaspoons dried thyme
- ¼ teaspoon salt
- ⅛ teaspoon crushed red pepper flakes
- 3 cups (405 g) cold cooked spaghetti
- 1 teaspoon olive oil
  Thyme sprigs

1. In a wide nonstick frying pan, combine mushrooms, bell pepper, onion, garlic, and ⅓ cup (80 ml) water. Cook over medium-high heat, stirring occasionally, until mushrooms are soft and almost all liquid has evaporated (about 10 minutes). Remove from pan.

2. In a large bowl, blend milk and cornstarch. Add eggs and egg whites and beat well. Stir in mozzarella cheese, Parmesan cheese, chopped thyme, salt, and red pepper flakes. Add pasta and mushroom mixture to egg mixture; lift with 2 forks to mix well. Set aside.

3. Place a 9-inch-round (23-cm-round) baking pan (do not use a nonstick pan) in oven while it heats to 500°F (260°C). When pan is hot (after about 5 minutes), carefully remove it from oven and pour in oil, tilting pan to coat. Mix pasta mixture again; then transfer to pan and press lightly to make an even layer.

4. Bake on lowest rack of oven until top of pie is tinged with brown and center feels firm when lightly pressed (about 20 minutes). To serve, cut pie into 6 wedges; transfer each wedge to an individual plate and garnish with thyme sprigs. Makes 6 servings.

Per serving: 248 calories (25% calories from fat), 7 g total fat, 3 g saturated fat, 85 mg cholesterol, 309 mg sodium, 31 g carbohydrates, 3 g fiber, 16 g protein, 201 mg calcium, 2 mg iron

Asparagus with Garlic Crumbs

Preparation time: 15 minutes
Cooking time: About 25 minutes

Crisp, garlicky bread crumbs enhance cooked, cooled spring asparagus in this easy dish.

- 3 slices sourdough sandwich bread (about 3 oz./85 g *total*), torn into pieces
- 2 teaspoons olive oil
- 2 cloves garlic, minced or pressed
- 36 thick asparagus spears (about 3 lbs./1.35 kg *total*), tough ends snapped off
  Salt and pepper

1. In a blender or food processor, whirl bread to form fine crumbs. Pour crumbs into a wide nonstick frying pan; add oil and garlic. Cook over medium-high heat, stirring often, until crumbs are lightly browned (5 to 7 minutes). Remove from pan and set aside.

2. Trim ends of asparagus spears so that spears are all the same length (reserve scraps for soups or salads). For the sweetest flavor and most tender texture, peel spears with a vegetable peeler.

3. In frying pan, bring about 1 inch (2.5 cm) water to a boil over medium-high heat. Add a third of the asparagus and cook, uncovered, until just tender when pierced (about 4 minutes). Lift from pan with a slotted spoon and place in a bowl of ice water to cool. Repeat with remaining asparagus, cooking it in 2 batches.

4. Drain cooled asparagus well; then arrange on a large platter. Sprinkle with crumb mixture; season to taste with salt and pepper. Makes 8 servings.

Per serving: 70 calories (20% calories from fat), 2 g total fat, 0.3 g saturated fat, 0 mg cholesterol, 68 mg sodium, 11 g carbohydrates, 2 g fiber, 5 g protein, 39 mg calcium, 1 mg iron

This silky, basil-seasoned purée of sautéed spinach and pears is particularly good with roast leg of lamb.

- 1 **package (about 10 oz./285 g) prewashed spinach leaves**
- 1 **teaspoon olive oil**
- 4 **large Anjou pears (about 2 lbs./905 g *total*), peeled, cored, and thinly sliced**
- ¼ **cup (60 ml) half-and-half**
- 1 **tablespoon dried basil**
- ½ **teaspoon *each* grated lemon peel and Oriental sesame oil**
- **About ¼ teaspoon salt (or to taste)**
- 1 **to 2 teaspoons finely shredded lemon peel**

1. Discard coarse stems and any yellow or bruised leaves from spinach.

Fruited Spinach Purée

Preparation time: 15 minutes
Cooking time: About 10 minutes

Rinse remaining spinach leaves, drain, and set aside.

2. Heat ½ teaspoon of the olive oil in a wide nonstick frying pan over medium-high heat. Add pears and cook, stirring occasionally, until almost tender when pierced (3 to 5 minutes). Transfer pears and any pan juices to a food processor or blender; keep warm.

3. Heat remaining ½ teaspoon olive oil in pan. Add spinach, a handful at a time, and cook, stirring, just until wilted; add water, 1 table-spoon (15 ml) at a time, if pan appears dry. As spinach is cooked, transfer it to a bowl; keep warm. When all spinach has been cooked, press it with the back of a wooden spoon to remove excess liquid; discard as much liquid as possible.

4. At once, transfer spinach to food processor with pears and whirl until mixture is coarsely puréed. Add half-and-half, basil, grated lemon peel, sesame oil, and salt. Whirl just until smooth but still firm enough to mound on a plate (do not overprocess). Spoon purée onto individual plates, garnish with shredded lemon peel, and serve immediately. Makes 4 to 6 servings.

Per serving: 138 calories (21% calories from fat), 4 g total fat, 1 g saturated fat, 4 mg cholesterol, 146 mg sodium, 28 g carbohydrates, 5 g fiber, 2 g protein, 92 mg calcium, 2 mg iron

---

Served at room temperature, this easy-to-assemble side dish is appealingly simple: just roasted eggplant, bell peppers, and garlic, dressed with a splash of balsamic vinegar.

- 2 **large red bell peppers (about 1 lb./455 g *total*)**
- 3 **large heads garlic (about 12 oz./340 g *total*)**
- 1 **medium-size eggplant (about 1 lb./ 455 g), unpeeled, cut into 2-inch (5-cm) pieces**
- 2 **teaspoons olive oil**
- 3 **tablespoons (45 ml) balsamic vinegar**
- 2 **tablespoons chopped Italian or regular parsley**
- **Salt and pepper**

1. Cut bell peppers lengthwise into

Roasted Eggplant with Bell Peppers

Preparation time: 25 minutes
Cooking time: 30 to 40 minutes

halves and arrange, cut side down, in a shallow baking pan. Broil 4 to 6 inches (10 to 15 cm) below heat until skins are charred (about 8 minutes). Cover loosely with foil and let stand until cool enough to handle (about 10 minutes).

2. Meanwhile, separate garlic heads into cloves; peel garlic cloves. Place garlic in a shallow 10- by 15-inch (25- by 38-cm) baking pan; add eggplant and oil. Mix to coat vegetables with oil. Bake in a 475°F (245°C) oven until eggplant is richly browned and soft when pressed, and garlic is tinged with brown (20 to 30 minutes). Watch carefully to prevent scorching; remove pieces as they brown and add water, ¼ cup (60 ml) at a time, if pan appears dry.

3. While eggplant is cooking, remove and discard skins, seeds, and stems from bell peppers. Cut peppers into chunks, place in a large serving bowl, and set aside.

4. Add eggplant, garlic, and vinegar to bowl with peppers; mix gently but thoroughly. Sprinkle with parsley; season to taste with salt and pepper. Serve at room temperature. Makes 4 to 6 servings.

Per serving: 149 calories (13% calories from fat), 2 g total fat, 0.3 g saturated fat, 0 mg cholesterol, 16 mg sodium, 30 g carbohydrates, 4 g fiber, 5 g protein, 148 mg calcium, 2 mg iron

Tomato Compote with Seeded Vinaigrette

Try this rosy, piquant dish with smoky grilled fish or chicken.

Preparation time: 20 minutes, plus 20 to 30 minutes to crisp onion
Cooking time: About 5 minutes
Marinating time: 20 minutes

1 small red onion (about 8 oz./230 g), thinly sliced

¼ cup (60 ml) red wine vinegar

1 small European cucumber (about 12 oz./340 g)

1¼ pounds (565 g) firm-ripe pear-shaped (Roma-type) tomatoes, peeled, cut into chunks, and drained well

1 can (about 15 oz./425 g) cannellini (white kidney beans), drained and rinsed

½ cup (120 ml) balsamic vinegar

3 tablespoons firmly packed brown sugar

1½ tablespoons drained capers

½ teaspoon *each* coriander seeds and mustard seeds

¼ teaspoon fennel seeds

2 tablespoons chopped Italian or regular parsley

1. Place onion in a medium-size bowl and add enough water to cover. Squeeze onion with your hands to bruise slightly; drain. Add 4 cups (455 g) ice cubes, 2 cups (470 ml) water, and wine vinegar. Let stand until onion is crisp (20 to 30 minutes). Drain well; discard any unmelted ice cubes.

2. While onion is soaking, cut cucumber in half lengthwise; then set halves cut side down and thinly slice crosswise. Place cucumber in a large bowl; add tomatoes and beans. Set aside.

3. In a medium-size pan, combine balsamic vinegar, sugar, capers, coriander seeds, mustard seeds, and fennel seeds. Bring to a boil over high heat; immediately pour over vegetables in bowl. Let stand for 20 minutes, stirring gently once or twice. Just before serving, stir in onion and parsley. Makes 6 to 8 servings.

Per serving: 105 calories (6% calories from fat), 0.8 g total fat, 0.1 g saturated fat, 0 mg cholesterol, 137 mg sodium, 21 g carbohydrates, 4 g fiber, 5 g protein, 43 mg calcium, 1 mg iron

---

Garbanzo Beans with Olive Pesto

Garbanzos in a ripe-olive pesto taste great atop juicy sliced tomatoes.

Preparation time: 15 minutes
Cooking time: 15 to 20 minutes
Pictured on facing page

4 slices sourdough sandwich bread (about 4 oz./115 g *total*), cut into ½-inch (1-cm) cubes

5 large tomatoes (about 2½ lbs./1.15 kg *total*), thinly sliced

1 cup (113 g) pitted ripe olives, drained

3 tablespoons drained capers

4 teaspoons (20 ml) lemon juice

2 teaspoons *each* Oriental sesame oil and Dijon mustard

1 tablespoon (15 ml) honey (or to taste)

2 or 3 cloves garlic, peeled

¼ cup (10 g) finely chopped fresh basil

3 tablespoons grated Parmesan cheese

2 cans (about 15 oz./425 g *each*) garbanzo beans, drained and rinsed

Basil sprigs

1. Spread bread cubes in a single layer in a shallow baking pan. Bake in a 325°F (165°C) oven, stirring occasionally, until crisp and lightly browned (15 to 20 minutes). Set aside.

2. Arrange tomato slices, overlapping if necessary, in a large, shallow serving bowl. Set aside.

3. In a food processor or blender, combine olives, capers, lemon juice, oil, mustard, honey, and garlic; whirl until coarsely puréed, scraping sides of container as needed. With a spoon, stir in chopped basil and cheese. Transfer olive pesto to a large bowl; add beans and two-thirds of the croutons. Mix gently but thoroughly.

4. Spoon bean salad over tomatoes; sprinkle with remaining croutons. Garnish with basil sprigs. Makes 4 to 6 servings.

Per serving: 286 calories (29% calories from fat), 10 g total fat, 2 g saturated fat, 2 mg cholesterol, 803 mg sodium, 41 g carbohydrates, 9 g fiber, 11 g protein, 147 g calcium, 5 mg iron

Garbanzo Beans with Olive Pesto
(recipe on facing page)

Mixed Greens with Pesto Dressing

Preparation time: 20 minutes
Cooking time: About 15 minutes

1 tablespoon pine nuts

2 teaspoons Oriental sesame oil

1 clove garlic, minced or pressed

3 slices Italian or sourdough sandwich bread (about 3 oz./85 g *total*), cut into ½-inch (1-cm) cubes

¼ cup (10 g) chopped fresh basil

¼ cup (15 g) chopped Italian or regular parsley

1 cup (240 ml) nonfat sour cream

1 tablespoon (15 ml) white wine vinegar

1 teaspoon honey

1 or 2 cloves garlic, peeled

Salt and pepper

8 ounces/230 g (about 8 cups) mixed salad greens, rinsed and crisped

1. Toast pine nuts in a wide nonstick frying pan over medium heat until golden (about 3 minutes), stirring often. Pour out of pan and set aside. In same pan (with pan off heat), combine 1 teaspoon of the oil, garlic, and 1 tablespoon (15 ml) water. Add bread cubes and toss gently to coat. Place pan over medium heat; cook, stirring occasionally, until croutons are crisp and tinged with brown (about 10 minutes). Remove from pan and set aside.

2. In a food processor or blender, combine basil, parsley, sour cream, vinegar, honey, remaining 1 teaspoon oil, and garlic; whirl until smoothly puréed. Season to taste with salt and pepper; set aside.

3. Place greens in a large bowl; add dressing and mix gently but thoroughly. Add croutons and mix again. Sprinkle with pine nuts. Makes 4 servings.

Per serving: 154 calories (26% calories from fat), 4 g total fat, 0.9 g saturated fat, 0 mg cholesterol, 177 mg sodium, 20 g carbohydrates, 2 g fiber, 8 g protein, 156 mg calcium, 2 mg iron

Wilted Spinach & Prosciutto Salad

Preparation time: 20 minutes
Cooking time: About 5 minutes

⅔ cup (about 1⅓ oz./ 38 g) dried tomatoes (not packed in oil)

1 jar (about 6 oz./ 170 g) marinated artichoke hearts

3 green onions

1 package (about 10 oz./ 285 g) prewashed spinach leaves, coarse stems and any yellow or bruised leaves discarded, remaining leaves rinsed and crisped

½ teaspoon olive oil

2 ounces (55 g) thinly sliced prosciutto, chopped

2 cloves garlic, minced

½ teaspoon dried rosemary

1 can (about 14 oz./ 400 g) artichoke hearts packed in water, drained and quartered

¼ cup (60 ml) balsamic vinegar

1 to 2 tablespoons firmly packed brown sugar

1. Place tomatoes in a small bowl and add boiling water to cover. Let stand until soft (about 10 minutes), stirring occasionally. Drain well; gently squeeze out excess liquid. Cut tomatoes into thin slivers; set aside.

2. While tomatoes are soaking, drain marinated artichokes, reserving marinade. Cut artichoke pieces lengthwise into halves; set aside. Cut onions into 2-inch (5-cm) lengths; then sliver each piece lengthwise. Tear spinach into bite-size pieces. Place onions and spinach in a large bowl; set aside.

3. Heat oil in a wide nonstick frying pan over medium-high heat. Add prosciutto, garlic, and rosemary. Cook, stirring often, until prosciutto is crisp and lightly browned (about 3 minutes); add water, 1 tablespoon (15 ml) at a time, if pan appears dry.

4. To pan, add tomatoes, marinated artichokes, artichoke marinade, quartered canned artichokes, vinegar, and sugar. Mix gently, stirring to scrape browned bits free from pan bottom. Pour artichoke mixture over spinach mixture; toss until spinach is slightly wilted and coated with dressing. Serve at once. Makes 4 servings.

Per serving: 170 calories (29% calories from fat), 6 g total fat, 1 g saturated fat, 11 mg cholesterol, 536 mg sodium, 22 g carbohydrates, 4 g fiber, 10 g protein, 92 mg calcium, 3 mg iron

Autumn Pear Salad

Preparation time: 20 minutes

- ¼ cup (60 ml) red wine vinegar
- 2 tablespoons (30 ml) extra-virgin olive oil
- 1 tablespoon drained capers
- 1 tablespoon (15 ml) lemon juice
- ¼ teaspoon *each* pepper and honey
- 4 large firm-ripe red pears (about 2 lbs./ 905 g *total*)
- 1 package (about 10 oz./285 g) pre-washed spinach leaves, coarse stems and any yellow or bruised leaves discarded, remaining leaves rinsed and crisped
- 8 ounces (230 g) mushrooms, thinly sliced
- ¾ cup (68 g) dried cranberries
- 4 ounces (115 g) sliced pancetta or bacon, crisply cooked, drained, and crumbled

1. In a large bowl, combine vinegar, oil, capers, lemon juice, pepper, and honey; beat until well blended. Set aside.

2. Core pears and cut each into about 16 wedges. As pears are cut, transfer them to bowl with dressing; mix gently to coat with dressing. Add spinach, mushrooms, and cranberries; mix until coated with dressing. Then divide salad among individual plates and sprinkle with pancetta. Makes 8 servings.

Per serving: 160 calories (29% calories from fat), 6 g total fat, 1 g saturated fat, 5 mg cholesterol, 163 mg sodium, 27 g carbohydrates, 4 g fiber, 3 g protein, 39 mg calcium, 1 mg iron

Melon, Basil & Bacon Salad

Preparation time: 25 minutes
Cooking time: About 20 minutes

- 6 ounces (170 g) sliced bacon
- 1½ tablespoons firmly packed brown sugar
- 8 cups (1.4 kg) peeled, seeded melon wedges (*each* about ¾ inch by 2 inches/2 cm by 5 cm); use any soft, aromatic melon, such as honeydew, cantaloupe, and/or crenshaw
- ¼ cup (60 ml) lime juice
- ⅓ cup (15 g) finely slivered fresh basil
  Basil sprigs

1. Line a shallow 10- by 15-inch (25- by 38-cm) baking pan with foil. Arrange bacon in pan in a single layer; bake in a 350°F (175°C) oven for 10 minutes. Spoon off and discard drippings. Evenly pat sugar onto bacon; bake until bacon is deep golden (about 10 more minutes).

2. Lift bacon to a board; let cool slightly, then cut diagonally into ½-inch (1-cm) slices. In a large, shallow bowl, combine melon, lime juice, and slivered basil. Top with bacon; garnish with basil sprigs. Makes 4 servings.

Per serving: 210 calories (26% calories from fat), 7 g total fat, 2 g saturated fat, 10 mg cholesterol, 226 mg sodium, 36 g carbohydrates, 3 g fiber, 6 g protein, 66 mg calcium, 1 mg iron

Fennel & Orange Salad

Preparation time: 20 minutes

- 2 large heads fennel (about 1½ lbs./ 680 g *total*)
- ¼ cup (60 ml) seasoned rice vinegar
- 2 tablespoons (30 ml) olive oil
- 1 tablespoon grated orange peel
- 1 teaspoon anise seeds
- 4 large oranges (about 2½ lbs./ 1.15 kg *total*)
  Seeds from 1 pomegranate (about 3½ inches/ 8.5 cm in diameter)
  Salt

1. Trim stems from fennel, reserving the feathery green leaves. Trim and discard any bruised areas from fennel; then cut each fennel head into thin slivers. Place slivered fennel in a large bowl.

2. Finely chop enough of the fennel leaves to make 1 tablespoon (reserve remaining leaves); add to bowl along with vinegar, oil, orange peel, and anise seeds. Mix well.

3. Cut off and discard peel and all white membrane from oranges. Cut fruit crosswise into slices about ¼ inch (6 mm) thick; discard seeds.

4. Divide fennel mixture among individual plates. Arrange oranges alongside fennel mixture; sprinkle salads equally with pomegranate seeds. Garnish with reserved fennel leaves. Season to taste with salt. Makes 6 servings.

Per serving: 147 calories (29% calories from fat), 5 g total fat, 0.6 g saturated fat, 0 mg cholesterol, 290 mg sodium, 26 g carbohydrates, 4 g fiber, 2 g protein, 110 mg calcium, 1 mg iron

Fig-stuffed Turkey Roast
(recipe on page 564)

Poultry & Seafood

Poultry and seafood have long been staples on Italian dinner tables. Naturally lean and compatible with all sorts of sauces and seasonings, these foods are perfect choices for low-fat entrées. This chapter includes a tempting selection of recipes, some simple, some elegant. For casual meals, try Fish & Fennel Stew or baked Lemon Rosemary Chicken; for dressier occasions, serve impressive Fig-stuffed Turkey Roast or Tuna Steaks with Roasted Peppers & Tuna Sauce.

.

Fig-stuffed Turkey Roast

Preparation time: 15 minutes
Cooking time: About 1¼ hours
Pictured on page 562

Stuffed with figs and seasoned with rosemary and mustard, this turkey roast makes a showy entrée.

- 1 **turkey breast half (about 3½ lbs./1.6 kg), boned and skinned**
- 3 **tablespoons (45 ml) Dijon mustard**
- 1 **tablespoon chopped fresh rosemary or 1 teaspoon dried rosemary**
- 12 **dried Calimyrna or Mission figs, finely chopped**
- 1 **tablespoon (15 ml) honey**
- 1 **tablespoon (15 ml) olive oil**
- 2 **cloves garlic, minced**
  Pepper
  Rosemary sprigs

1. Rinse turkey and pat dry. Then slice lengthwise down middle, cutting meat almost but not quite through. Push cut open and press turkey to make it lie as flat as possible. Spread turkey with mustard and sprinkle with half the chopped rosemary; set aside.

2. In a bowl, mix figs with honey. Mound fig mixture evenly down center of turkey. Starting from a long side, lift turkey and roll over filling to enclose. Tie roll snugly with cotton string at 2- to 3-inch (5- to 8-cm) intervals. Rub roll with oil, then with garlic; pat remaining chopped rosemary onto roll and sprinkle generously with pepper.

3. Place roll on a rack in a 9- by 13-inch (23- by 33-cm) baking pan; add ⅓ cup (80 ml) water to pan. Bake in a 375°F (190°C) oven until a meat thermometer inserted in thickest part of roll (insert thermometer in meat, not filling) registers 160° to 165°F (71° to 74°C), about 1¼ hours. Add water, ¼ cup (60 ml) at a time, if pan appears dry.

4. Remove roll from oven and let stand for 10 minutes; then snip and discard strings and cut roll crosswise into thick slices. Garnish with rosemary sprigs. Serve with pan juices, if desired. Makes 6 to 8 servings.

Per serving: 308 calories (10% calories from fat), 3 g total fat, 0.7 g saturated fat, 117 mg cholesterol, 232 mg sodium, 24 g carbohydrates, 3 g fiber, 44 g protein, 67 mg calcium, 3 mg iron

Sautéed Turkey with Provolone & Sage

Preparation time: 15 minutes
Cooking time: About 5 minutes

When time is short, try thin-sliced, sautéed turkey breast topped with cheese and aromatic fresh sage.

- 1 **pound (455 g) thinly sliced turkey breast**
- 2 **teaspoons finely chopped fresh sage or 1 teaspoon dried sage**
- 2 **teaspoons olive oil**
- ⅓ **cup (45 g) finely shredded provolone or part-skim mozzarella cheese**
  Pepper
  Sage sprigs
  Lemon wedges
  Salt

1. Rinse turkey and pat dry. Sprinkle one side of each slice with chopped sage; set aside.

2. Heat 1 teaspoon of the oil in a wide nonstick frying pan over medium-high heat. Add half the turkey, sage-coated side down, and cook until golden on bottom (about 1½ minutes). Then turn pieces over and continue to cook until no longer pink in center; cut to test (30 to 60 more seconds). Transfer cooked turkey to a platter and sprinkle with half the cheese. Cover loosely with foil and keep warm.

3. Immediately cook remaining turkey, using remaining 1 teaspoon oil; add water, 1 tablespoon (15 ml) at a time, if pan appears dry. Transfer turkey to platter.

4. Sprinkle turkey with remaining cheese, then with pepper; garnish with sage sprigs. Serve at once. Season to taste with lemon and salt. Makes 4 servings.

Per serving: 184 calories (30% calories from fat), 6 g total fat, 2 g saturated fat, 78 mg cholesterol, 149 mg sodium, 0.3 g carbohydrates, 0 g fiber, 31 g protein, 94 mg calcium, 1 mg iron

To give tender turkey slices an intriguing flavor, "cure" them briefly in salt and sugar; then rub the meat with herbs and garlic before sautéing.

- 1 tablespoon salt
- 1½ teaspoons sugar
- 1½ pounds (680 g) thinly sliced turkey breast
- ¼ cup (25 g) sliced green onions
- 2 tablespoons finely chopped Italian or regular parsley
- 3 cloves garlic, minced
- 1 teaspoon chopped fresh oregano or ½ teaspoon dried oregano
- ½ teaspoon *each* coarsely ground pepper and grated lemon peel
- 2 teaspoons olive oil
- Italian or regular parsley sprigs
- Lemon wedges

Oregano-rubbed Turkey

Preparation time: 15 minutes
Marinating time: At least 2 hours
Cooking time: About 5 minutes

1. In a large bowl, combine salt and sugar. Rinse turkey and pat dry; then add to bowl and turn to coat evenly with salt mixture. Cover and refrigerate for at least 2 hours or up to 3 hours. Rinse turkey well, drain, and pat dry.

2. In a small bowl, combine onions, chopped parsley, garlic, oregano, pepper, and lemon peel. Rub onion mixture evenly over both sides of each turkey slice.

3. Heat 1 teaspoon of the oil in a wide nonstick frying pan over medium-high heat. Add half the turkey and cook until golden on bottom (about 1½ minutes). Then turn pieces over and continue to cook until no longer pink in center; cut to test (30 to 60 more seconds). Transfer cooked turkey to a platter, cover loosely with foil, and keep warm.

4. Immediately cook remaining turkey, using remaining 1 teaspoon oil; add water, 1 tablespoon (15 ml) at a time, if pan appears dry. Transfer turkey to platter and garnish with parsley sprigs. Serve at once. Season to taste with lemon. Makes 6 servings.

Per serving: 148 calories (14% calories from fat), 2 g total fat, 0.4 g saturated fat, 70 mg cholesterol, 1,155 mg sodium, 2 g carbohydrates, 0.2 g fiber, 28 g protein, 29 mg calcium, 2 mg iron

---

Crisp bread crumbs coat these moist, lemon-seasoned chicken breasts.

- 6 boneless, skinless chicken breast halves (about 2¼ lbs./1.1 kg *total*)
- 1¼ cups (38 g) soft whole wheat bread crumbs
- 2 tablespoons chopped fresh rosemary or 2 teaspoons dried rosemary
- 1 tablespoon chopped Italian or regular parsley
- 1 teaspoon grated lemon peel
- ½ teaspoon pepper
- 1 tablespoon (15 ml) lemon juice
- Lemon wedges
- Salt

Lemon Rosemary Chicken

Preparation time: 15 minutes
Cooking time: About 25 minutes

1. Rinse chicken and pat dry; then arrange, skinned side up, in an oiled shallow 10- by 15-inch (25- by 38-cm) baking pan. Set aside.

2. In a small bowl, mix bread crumbs, rosemary, parsley, lemon peel, and pepper. Moisten top of each chicken piece with lemon juice; press crumb mixture equally over each piece, covering evenly.

3. Bake in a 400°F (205°C) oven until crumb coating is browned and meat in thickest part is no longer pink; cut to test (about 25 minutes). Season chicken to taste with lemon and salt. Makes 6 servings.

Per serving: 185 calories (11% calories from fat), 2 g total fat, 0.5 g saturated fat, 88 mg cholesterol, 133 mg sodium, 3 g carbohydrates, 0.5 g fiber, 36 g protein, 28 mg calcium, 1 mg iron

Just right for special occasions, these split and roasted game hens are served on a bed of saffron-tinted orzo.

....

2   **Rock Cornish game hens (about 1½ lbs./680 g *each*)**

¼   **cup (60 ml) dry white wine or apple juice**

2   **tablespoons (30 ml) *each* Dijon mustard and honey**

1   **tablespoon chopped fresh thyme or 1 teaspoon dried thyme**

3⅓ **cups (790 ml) fat-free reduced-sodium chicken broth**

Large pinch of saffron threads or ⅛ teaspoon ground saffron (or to taste)

1¼ **cups (285 g) dried orzo or other tiny rice-shaped pasta**

¼   **cup (25 g) thinly sliced green onions**

Thyme sprigs

Salt and pepper

Herb-roasted Game Hens with Saffron Orzo

....

Preparation time: 20 minutes
Cooking time: About 25 minutes
Pictured on facing page

1. Reserve game hen necks and giblets for other uses. With poultry shears or a sharp knife, split each hen in half, cutting along backbone and breastbone. Rinse hens and pat dry. In a medium-size bowl, mix wine, mustard, honey, and chopped thyme. Dip hens in marinade and turn to coat; then lift out and drain briefly, reserving marinade. Place hens, skin side up, on a rack in a foil-lined 12- by 15-inch (30- by 38-cm) broiler pan.

2. Bake hens in bottom third of a 425°F (220°C) oven until meat near thighbone is no longer pink; cut to test (about 25 minutes). Halfway through cooking, brush hens with marinade.

3. While hens are baking, bring broth and saffron to a boil in a 2- to 3-quart (1.9- to 2.8-liter) pan over high heat. Stir in pasta. Reduce heat, cover, and simmer, stirring occasionally, until almost all liquid has been absorbed (about 15 minutes); as liquid cooks down, stir more often and watch closely to prevent scorching.

4. Stir onions into pasta; then divide pasta mixture among 4 individual rimmed plates. Place one hen half on each plate; garnish with thyme sprigs. Season to taste with salt and pepper. Makes 4 servings.

....

Per serving: 688 calories (29% calories from fat), 21 g total fat, 6 g saturated fat, 132 mg cholesterol, 847 mg sodium, 63 g carbohydrates, 2 g fiber, 53 g protein, 48 mg calcium, 5 mg iron

Herb-roasted Game Hens with
Saffron Orzo
(recipe on facing page)

Roasted Garlic

White Bean & Roasted Garlic Bruschetta

Preparation time: 20 minutes
Cooking time: About 1¼ hours

1 large head garlic (about 4 oz./115 g)

½ teaspoon olive oil

8 slices crusty bread, such as Italian ciabatta or sourdough (*each about ½ inch/1 cm thick; about 8 oz./230 g total*)

2 cans (about 15 oz./425 g *each*) cannellini (white kidney beans)

½ cup (20 g) lightly packed fresh basil leaves

¼ cup (15 g) chopped Italian or regular parsley

¼ cup (60 ml) lemon juice

4 teaspoons (20 ml) Oriental sesame oil

½ teaspoon salt

1 pound (455 g) pear-shaped (Roma-type) tomatoes, thinly sliced

4 to 6 teaspoons drained capers (or to taste)

Fresh basil leaves

About 12 canned mild cherry peppers, drained (optional)

Pepper

1. Slice ¼ inch (6 mm) off top of garlic head. Then rub garlic with olive oil. Wrap garlic in foil and bake in a 375°F (190°C) oven until soft when pressed (about 1¼ hours). Carefully remove garlic from foil; transfer to a rack and let stand until cool enough to touch (about 10 minutes).

2. Meanwhile, arrange bread slices slightly apart in a large, shallow baking pan. Broil about 6 inches below heat, turning once, until golden on both sides (about 5 minutes). Let cool on a rack.

3. Squeeze garlic cloves from skins into a food processor or blender. Drain beans, reserving liquid. Rinse beans and add to processor along with the ½ cup (20 g) basil leaves, parsley, lemon juice, sesame oil, and salt. Whirl until coarsely puréed. If necessary, add enough of the reserved bean liquid to make mixture spreadable (do not make it too thin). Discard remaining liquid.

4. Top toast slices equally with bean mixture; arrange tomato slices, capers, and basil leaves over bean mixture. Serve with cherry peppers, if desired. Season to taste with pepper. Makes 4 servings.

Per serving: 445 calories (16% calories from fat), 8 g total fat, 1 g saturated fat, 0 mg cholesterol, 1,455 mg sodium, 77 g carbohydrates, 17 g fiber, 19 g protein, 233 mg calcium, 7 mg iron

Garlic Mashed Potatoes

Preparation time: 20 minutes
Cooking time: About 35 minutes

1 tablespoon (15 ml) olive oil

3 or 4 medium-size heads garlic (9 to 12 oz./255 to 340 g *total*)

4 pounds (1.8 kg) russet potatoes

1 large package (about 8 oz./230 g) Neufchâtel cheese, at room temperature

¾ to 1 cup (180 to 240 ml) fat-free reduced-sodium chicken broth

Salt

1. Pour oil into a shallow baking pan. Cut garlic heads in half crosswise through cloves; place, cut side down, in pan. Bake in a 375°F (190°C) oven until cut side is golden brown (about 35 minutes). Using a thin spatula, lift garlic from pan and transfer to a rack; let stand until cool enough to touch (about 10 minutes).

2. While garlic is baking, peel potatoes and cut into 2-inch (5-cm) chunks; place in a 5- to 6-quart (5- to 6-liter) pan and add enough water to cover. Bring to a boil over medium-high heat; reduce heat, cover, and boil gently until potatoes mash very easily when pressed (25 to 30 minutes). Drain potatoes well; transfer to a large bowl and keep warm.

3. Reserve 1 or 2 half-heads of garlic. Squeeze cloves from remaining garlic; add to potatoes along with Neufchâtel cheese. Mash potatoes with a potato masher or an electric mixer, adding broth as needed to make potatoes as soft and creamy as desired. Season to taste with salt and swirl into a shallow serving dish. Garnish with reserved roasted garlic. Makes 8 servings.

Per serving: 304 calories (26% calories from fat), 9 g total fat, 4 g saturated fat, 22 mg cholesterol, 205 mg sodium, 48 g carbohydrates, 4 g fiber, 9 g protein, 80 mg calcium, 2 mg iron

Roasted Green Beans & Garlic

Preparation time: 15 minutes
Cooking time: About 1 hour

1 medium-size head garlic (3 oz./85 g)

1½ teaspoons olive oil

1½ pounds (680 g) slender green beans, ends trimmed

1 ounce (30 g) thinly sliced prosciutto, coarsely chopped

Pepper

1. Slice ¼ inch (6 mm) off top of garlic head. Then rub garlic with ½ teaspoon of the oil. Wrap garlic in foil; set aside. In a shallow 10- by 15-inch (25- by 38-cm) baking pan, combine beans and remaining 1 teaspoon oil.

2. Bake foil-wrapped garlic (on oven rack) and beans in a 375°F (190°C) oven until garlic is very soft when pressed (about 1 hour) and ends of beans are tinged with brown (about 50 minutes; add water, ¼ cup/60 ml at a time, if pan appears dry).

3. Carefully remove garlic from foil; transfer to a rack and let stand until cool enough to touch (about 10 minutes). Gently squeeze or pry garlic cloves from skins (try not to smash cloves). Sprinkle garlic and prosciutto over beans. Return to oven and bake just until prosciutto is tinged with brown (2 to 5 minutes). Season to taste with pepper. Makes 4 to 6 servings.

Per serving: 105 calories (26% calories from fat), 3 g total fat, 0.5 g saturated fat, 5 mg cholesterol, 116 mg sodium, 16 carbohydrates, 3 g fiber, 5 g protein, 86 mg calcium, 2 mg iron

Garlic Chicken

Preparation time: 15 minutes
Cooking time: About 1½ hours

- 1 **large head garlic (about 4 oz./115 g)**
- ½ **teaspoon olive oil**
- 4 **boneless, skinless chicken breast halves (1½ lbs./680 g *total*)**
- 1 **tablespoon chopped fresh thyme or 1 teaspoon dried thyme**
- ¼ **teaspoon coarsely ground pepper**
- ⅛ **teaspoon salt**
- ¼ **cup (28 g) shredded fontina cheese**
- 4 **small thyme sprigs**

1. Slice ¼ inch (6 mm) off top of garlic head. Then rub garlic with oil. Wrap garlic in foil and bake in a 375°F (190°C) oven until very soft when pressed (about 1¼ hours). Carefully remove garlic from foil; transfer to a rack and let stand until cool enough to touch (about 10 minutes).

2. Meanwhile, rinse chicken, pat dry, and sprinkle with chopped thyme and pepper. Place, skinned side up, in a lightly oiled 9-inch (23-cm) baking pan. Bake in a 450°F (230°C) oven until meat in thickest part is no longer pink; cut to test (12 to 15 minutes). Meanwhile, squeeze garlic cloves from skins into a small bowl. Add salt; mash garlic thoroughly with a fork, incorporating salt.

3. Spread a fourth of the garlic mixture over each chicken piece; then sprinkle chicken with cheese. Return to oven; continue to bake just until cheese is melted and bubbly (about 3 more minutes). Press a thyme sprig into cheese on each piece of chicken. Makes 4 servings.

Per serving: 258 calories (18% calories from fat), 5 g total fat, 2 g saturated fat, 107 mg cholesterol, 241 mg sodium, 9 g carbohydrates, 0.5 g fiber, 43 g protein, 112 mg calcium, 2 mg iron

Roasted Garlic Flatbread

Preparation time: 15 minutes
Cooking time: About 1½ hours

- 1 **medium-size head garlic (3 oz./85 g)**
- ¼ **cup (60 ml) olive oil**
- 2 **cups (250 g) all-purpose flour**
- 4 **teaspoons baking powder**
- 1½ **teaspoons sugar**
- ¼ **to ½ teaspoon *each* pepper and salt**
- ¾ **cup (180 ml) nonfat milk**
- ¼ **cup (35 g) yellow cornmeal**
- 1 **large egg white beaten with 1 teaspoon water**
- ½ **teaspoon dried rosemary**
- ⅛ **teaspoon coarsely ground pepper**

1. Roast and cool garlic as directed for Garlic Chicken (at left), using ½ teaspoon of the oil, but roast for only 1 hour. When garlic is cool, squeeze cloves from skins into a small bowl; add remaining oil. Mash garlic thoroughly with a fork, mixing it with oil.

2. In a large bowl, stir together flour, baking powder, sugar, the ¼ to ½ teaspoon pepper, and salt. Add milk and garlic-oil mixture; stir just until dry ingredients are evenly moistened. In bowl, knead dough a few turns with lightly floured fingers.

3. Sprinkle cornmeal over bottom of an 8-inch-square (20-cm-square) nonstick baking pan. Scrape dough into pan and pat it evenly over pan bottom. With your fingers, poke holes liberally in surface of dough. Brush dough with egg white mixture; sprinkle with rosemary and the coarsely ground pepper.

4. Bake in a 400°F (205°C) oven until bread is a rich brown (20 to 25 minutes). Let stand for 3 to 5 minutes; then cut into squares. Serve hot or warm. Makes 6 servings.

Per serving: 291 calories (30% calories from fat), 10 g total fat, 1 g saturated fat, 0.6 mg cholesterol, 441 mg sodium, 44 g carbohydrates, 2 g fiber, 7 g protein, 250 mg calcium, 3 mg iron

Salt-grilled Shrimp
(recipe on facing page)

A honey-sweetened red onion marmalade dresses up these simple baked chicken breasts.

- 6 small boneless, skinless chicken breast halves (1½ to 1¾ lbs./680 to 795 g *total*)
- 3 tablespoons (45 ml) cream sherry
- 2 small red onions (about 6 oz./170 g *each*)
- ½ cup (120 ml) dry red wine
- 1 tablespoon (15 ml) *each* red wine vinegar and honey

  Italian or regular parsley sprigs

  Salt and pepper

1. Rinse chicken, pat dry, and place in a heavy-duty plastic food-storage bag; add 2 tablespoons (30 ml) of

Sherried Chicken with Onion Marmalade

Preparation time: 15 minutes
Marinating time: At least 30 minutes
Cooking time: About 20 minutes

the sherry. Seal bag and rotate to coat chicken with sherry. Refrigerate for at least 30 minutes or up to 6 hours, turning bag over several times.

2. Thinly slice onions; wrap several slices airtight and refrigerate. In a wide frying pan, combine remaining onion slices, wine, vinegar, and honey. Cook over medium-high

heat, stirring often, until liquid has evaporated. Remove from heat and stir in remaining 1 tablespoon (15 ml) sherry. Set aside.

3. Turn chicken and its marinade into a 9- by 13-inch (23- by 33-cm) baking pan; arrange chicken, skinned side up, in a single layer. Bake in a 450°F (230°C) oven until meat in thickest part is no longer pink; cut to test (12 to 15 minutes). With a slotted spoon, transfer chicken to a platter. Top with onion mixture. Garnish with reserved onion slices and parsley sprigs. Season to taste with salt and pepper. Makes 6 servings.

Per serving: 200 calories (9% calories from fat), 2 g total fat, 0.4 g saturated fat, 74 mg cholesterol, 91 mg sodium, 9 g carbohydrates, 0.9 g fiber, 30 g protein, 33 mg calcium, 1 mg iron

---

Smoky grilled shrimp are served with a salad of crisp greens and tiny tomatoes for a quick and appealing main course.

- 1½ pounds (680 g) extra-jumbo raw shrimp (16 to 20 per lb.)

  About 2 tablespoons sea salt or kosher salt

- 5 to 6 ounces (140 to 170 g) Belgian endive, separated into leaves, rinsed, and crisped
- 8 ounces (230 g) small romaine lettuce leaves, rinsed and crisped
- 12 ounces (340 g) tiny red and/ or yellow cherry tomatoes

  About ½ cup (120 ml) balsamic vinegar

- 1 tablespoon (15 ml) extra-virgin olive oil

  Pepper

Salt-grilled Shrimp

Preparation time: 25 minutes
Cooking time: About 8 minutes
Pictured on facing page

1. Insert a wooden pick under back of each shrimp between shell segments; gently pull up to remove vein. If vein breaks, repeat in another place. Rinse and drain deveined shrimp; then roll in salt to coat lightly.

2. Mix endive, lettuce, and tomatoes in a large bowl.

3. Place shrimp on a lightly greased grill 4 to 6 inches (10 to 15 cm) above a solid bed of hot coals.

Cook, turning once, until shrimp are just opaque in center; cut to test (about 8 minutes). Meanwhile, divide salad among individual plates.

4. To serve, arrange shrimp atop salads. To eat, shell shrimp and season to taste with vinegar, oil, and pepper. Makes 4 servings.

Per serving: 213 calories (27% calories from fat), 6 g total fat, 1 g saturated fat, 210 mg cholesterol, 1,325 mg sodium, 9 g carbohydrates, 3 g fiber, 30 g protein, 104 mg calcium, 5 mg iron

Lightly battered and sautéed, plump shrimp sprinkled with capers make a great main dish.

....

- 3 or 4 large lemons, thinly sliced
- 2 large egg whites
- ¾ cup (96 g) cornstarch
- ¼ cup (25 g) fine dry bread crumbs
- 1 teaspoon baking powder
- ¼ teaspoon salt
- 1 tablespoon butter or margarine
- 1 tablespoon (15 ml) olive oil
- 1 pound (455 g) large raw shrimp (31 to 35 per lb.), shelled and deveined
- ¼ teaspoon grated lemon peel
- 1 to 2 tablespoons drained capers (or to taste)

Sautéed Lemon-Caper Shrimp

....

Preparation time: 25 minutes
Cooking time: About 5 minutes

1. Arrange lemon slices on a rimmed platter; cover and set aside.

2. In a large bowl, beat egg whites and ⅓ cup (80 ml) water until blended. Add cornstarch, bread crumbs, baking powder, and salt; stir until smooth.

3. Melt butter in oil in a wide non-stick frying pan over medium-high heat. Meanwhile, dip shrimp in batter. Lift out and drain briefly to let excess batter drip off; discard remaining batter.

4. When butter-oil mixture is hot, add shrimp to pan; sprinkle shrimp with lemon peel. Cook, separating shrimp and turning gently, until shrimp are lightly browned on outside and just opaque in center; cut to test (about 4 minutes). Arrange shrimp over lemon slices on platter and sprinkle with capers. Makes 4 servings.

....

Per serving: 303 calories (23% calories from fat), 9 g total fat, 3 g saturated fat, 147 mg cholesterol, 596 mg sodium, 41 g carbohydrates, 0.5 g fiber, 23 g protein, 206 mg calcium, 4 mg iron

---

Robust yet light, this traditional Italian favorite goes together in less than an hour.

....

- 2 cans (about 6½ oz./185 g *each*) chopped clams
- 1 teaspoon olive oil
- 2 cloves garlic, minced
- 1 can (about 15 oz./425 g) tomato purée
- 2 tablespoons chopped fresh basil or 1 tablespoon dried basil
- 8 ounces (230 g) dried linguine
- 1 large tomato (about 8 oz./ 230 g), finely chopped
- ¼ cup (20 g) grated Parmesan cheese
- Basil sprigs
- Crushed red pepper flakes

....

1. Drain clams, reserving liquid; set clams and liquid aside.

Linguine with Tomato-Clam Sauce

....

Preparation time: 15 minutes
Cooking time: About 25 minutes

2. Heat oil in a 3- to 4-quart (2.8- to 3.8-liter) pan over medium heat. Add garlic and cook, stirring, just until fragrant (about 30 seconds; do not scorch). Add clam liquid, tomato purée, and chopped basil. Bring to a boil over high heat; then reduce heat and simmer, uncovered, until reduced to 2 cups (470 ml), about 20 minutes. Stir often to prevent scorching, scraping bottom of pan as you stir.

3. While sauce is simmering, cook pasta. In a 4- to 5-quart (3.8- to 5-liter) pan, bring about 8 cups (1.9 liters) water to a boil over medium-high heat; stir in pasta and cook until just tender to bite, 8 to 10 minutes. (Or cook pasta according to package directions.) Drain well, transfer to a large serving bowl, and keep warm.

4. Add clams and chopped tomato to sauce; stir just until heated through. Spoon sauce over pasta and sprinkle with cheese. Garnish with basil sprigs. Season to taste with red pepper flakes. Makes 4 servings.

....

Per serving: 380 calories (12% calories from fat), 5 g total fat, 2 g saturated fat, 37 mg cholesterol, 601 mg sodium, 59 g carbohydrates, 5 g fiber, 25 g protein, 189 mg calcium, 17 mg iron

Succulent scallops and pasta seashells in a simple wine-cheese sauce are delightful for casual company gatherings or family meals.

....

2 ounces (55 g) Neufchâtel or cream cheese, at room temperature

2 teaspoons honey

1 teaspoon Dijon mustard

½ teaspoon grated lemon peel

1 pound (455 g) sea scallops

8 ounces (230 g) dried medium-size pasta shells

¾ cup (180 ml) fat-free reduced-sodium chicken broth

¼ cup (15 g) finely chopped Italian or regular parsley

2 teaspoons dry white wine (or to taste)

¼ cup (20 g) grated Parmesan cheese

Scallops & Shells with Lemon Cream

....

Preparation time: 20 minutes
Cooking time: About 15 minutes

....

1. In a food processor or blender, whirl Neufchâtel cheese, honey, mustard, and lemon peel until smooth; set aside. Rinse scallops and pat dry; cut into bite-size pieces, if desired. Set aside.

2. In a 4- to 5-quart (3.8- to 5-liter) pan, bring about 8 cups (1.9 liters) water to a boil over medium-high heat; stir in pasta and cook until just tender to bite, 8 to 10 minutes. (Or cook pasta according to package directions.) Drain well, transfer to a large serving bowl, and keep warm.

3. In a 3- to 4-quart (2.8- to 3.8-liter) pan, bring broth to a boil over high heat. Add scallops and cook until just opaque in center; cut to test (1 to 2 minutes).

4. With a slotted spoon, transfer scallops to bowl with pasta; keep warm. Quickly pour scallop cooking liquid from pan into Neufchâtel cheese mixture in food processor; whirl until smooth. With a spoon, stir in parsley and wine. Pour sauce over scallops and pasta; sprinkle with Parmesan cheese. Serve immediately. Makes 4 servings.

....

Per serving: 393 calories (16% calories from fat), 7 g total fat, 3 g saturated fat, 53 mg cholesterol, 509 mg sodium, 49 g carbohydrates, 2 g fiber, 31 g protein, 138 mg calcium, 3 mg iron

Pink Peppercorn Swordfish

Pink peppercorns poached to softness add an attractive color and a delicately spicy flavor to baked swordfish steaks.

Preparation time: 15 minutes
Cooking time: About 15 minutes
Pictured on facing page

- ⅓ cup (21 g) whole pink peppercorns
- 4 swordfish or halibut steaks (*each* about 1 inch/2.5 cm thick and 5 to 6 oz./140 to 170 g)
- 8 teaspoons (40 ml) honey
- 4 large butter lettuce leaves, rinsed and crisped
- 2 jars (about 6 oz./170 g *each*) marinated artichoke hearts, drained
  Lemon wedges

1. In a 1- to 1½-quart (950-ml to 1.4-liter) pan, combine peppercorns and about 2 cups (470 ml) water. Bring to a boil over high heat; then reduce heat and simmer until peppercorns are slightly softened (about 4 minutes). Drain well.

2. Rinse fish and pat dry. Arrange pieces well apart in a lightly oiled shallow 10- by 15-inch (25- by 38-cm) baking pan. Brush each piece with 2 teaspoons of the honey; then top equally with peppercorns, spreading them in a single layer.

3. Bake in a 400°F (205°C) oven until fish is just opaque but still moist in thickest part; cut to test (about 10 minutes).

4. Place one lettuce leaf on each of 4 individual plates; top lettuce with artichokes. With a wide spatula, lift fish from baking pan and arrange alongside lettuce. Season to taste with lemon. Makes 4 servings.

Per serving: 277 calories (29% calories from fat), 9 g total fat, 2 g saturated fat, 54 mg cholesterol, 361 mg sodium, 21 g carbohydrates, 3 g fiber, 30 g protein, 44 mg calcium, 3 mg iron

Cioppino

Serve this bold seafood stew with plenty of crusty bread to soak up the flavorful broth.

Preparation time: 30 minutes
Cooking time: About 45 minutes

- 1 tablespoon (15 ml) olive oil
- 1 large onion, chopped
- 1 large red bell pepper (about 8 oz./230 g), seeded and chopped
- ⅓ cup (20 g) chopped Italian or regular parsley
- 2 cloves garlic, minced
- 4 or 5 large tomatoes (2 to 2½ lbs./905 g to 1.15 kg *total*), peeled and cut into chunks
- 1 large can (about 15 oz./425 g) tomato sauce
- 1 cup (240 ml) dry red wine
- 1 dried bay leaf
- 1 tablespoon chopped fresh basil or 1 teaspoon dried basil
- 2 teaspoons chopped fresh oregano or ½ teaspoon dried oregano
- 12 small hard-shell clams (suitable for steaming), scrubbed
- 1 pound (455 g) extra-jumbo raw shrimp (16 to 20 per lb.), shelled and deveined
- 1 pound (455 g) firm-textured, white-fleshed fish, such as rockfish, cut into 2-inch (5-cm) chunks
- 2 cooked whole Dungeness crabs (about 2 lbs./905 g *each*), cleaned and cracked
  Salt

1. Heat oil in an 8- to 10-quart (8- to 10-liter) pan over medium-high heat. Add onion, bell pepper, parsley, garlic, and ¼ cup (60 ml) water. Cook, stirring often, until onion is soft (about 5 minutes); add water, 1 tablespoon (15 ml) at a time, if pan appears dry.

2. Stir in tomatoes, tomato sauce, wine, bay leaf, basil, and oregano. Bring to a boil; then reduce heat, cover, and simmer until flavors are blended (about 20 minutes).

3. Gently stir in clams, shrimp, fish, and crabs. Cover tightly and bring to a boil over high heat. Reduce heat and simmer gently until clams pop open and fish is just opaque but still moist in thickest part; cut to test (10 to 15 minutes).

4. Ladle stew into large soup bowls, discarding bay leaf and any unopened clams. Season to taste with salt. Makes 8 servings.

Per serving: 264 calories (18% calories from fat), 5 g total fat, 0.8 g saturated fat, 149 mg cholesterol, 597 mg sodium, 15 g carbohydrates, 3 g fiber, 35 g protein, 126 mg calcium, 5 mg iron

Pink Peppercorn Swordfish
(recipe on facing page)

Fish & Fennel Stew

Sliced fennel lends a refreshing anise flavor to this garlicky stew of fish and Roma tomatoes.

Preparation time: 25 minutes
Cooking time: About 40 minutes

1 large head fennel (about 12 oz./340 g)

1 tablespoon (15 ml) olive oil

1 large onion, chopped

6 cloves garlic, minced

1¼ pounds (565 g) pear-shaped (Roma-type) tomatoes, chopped

2 cups (470 ml) fat-free reduced-sodium chicken broth

1 bottle (about 8 oz./230 g) clam juice

½ cup (120 ml) dry white wine

¼ to ½ teaspoon ground red pepper (cayenne)

1½ pounds (680 g) boneless, skinless firm-textured, light-fleshed fish, such as halibut, swordfish, or sea bass, cut into 1½-inch (3.5-cm) chunks

1. Trim stems from fennel, reserving feathery green leaves. Trim and discard any bruised areas from fennel. Finely chop leaves and set aside; thinly slice fennel head.

2. Heat oil in a 5- to 6-quart (5- to 6-liter) pan over medium heat. Add sliced fennel, onion, and garlic; cook, stirring often, until onion is sweet tasting and all vegetables are browned (about 20 minutes). Add water, ¼ cup (60 ml) at a time, if pan appears dry.

3. Add tomatoes, broth, clam juice, wine, and red pepper. Bring to a boil; then reduce heat, cover, and simmer for 10 minutes. Add fish, cover, and simmer until just opaque but still moist in thickest part; cut to test (about 5 minutes). Stir in fennel leaves. Makes 4 servings.

Per serving: 317 calories (24% calories from fat), 8 g total fat, 1 g saturated fat, 54 mg cholesterol, 628 mg sodium, 16 g carbohydrates, 4 g fiber, 40 g protein, 151 mg calcium, 3 mg iron

Porcini-crusted Salmon

Coarsely ground dried mushrooms make an unusual coating for baked salmon fillets. Serve the fish with fresh asparagus and whimsical pasta bow ties.

Preparation time: 20 minutes
Cooking time: About 15 minutes

¼ ounce/8 g (about ⅓ cup) dried porcini mushrooms

2 tablespoons fine dry bread crumbs

¼ teaspoon salt

8 ounces (230 g) dried farfalle (pasta bow ties)

8 ounces (230 g) asparagus, tough ends snapped off, spears cut diagonally into thin slices

1 to 1¼ pounds (455 to 565 g) boneless, skinless salmon fillet (1 inch/2.5 cm thick), cut into 4 equal pieces

2 tablespoons (30 ml) olive oil

1. In a food processor or blender, whirl mushrooms to make a coarse powder. Add bread crumbs and salt; whirl to mix, then pour into a wide, shallow bowl. Set aside.

2. In a 5- to 6-quart (5- to 6-liter) pan, bring about 3 quarts (2.8 liters) water to a boil over medium-high heat. Stir in pasta and cook for 5 minutes; then add asparagus and cook, stirring occasionally, until pasta and asparagus are just tender to bite (3 to 5 more minutes).

3. While pasta is cooking, rinse fish and pat dry; then turn fish in mushroom mixture, pressing to coat well all over. Lay fish pieces, flatter side down and well apart, in a shallow 10- by 15-inch (25- by 38-cm) baking pan. Pat any remaining mushroom mixture on fish; drizzle evenly with oil. Bake in a 400°F (205°C) oven until fish is just opaque but still moist in thickest part; cut to test (about 10 minutes).

4. When pasta mixture is done, drain it well and divide among 4 shallow individual bowls; keep warm. With a wide spatula, lift fish from baking pan; set in bowls atop pasta. Drizzle pan juices over pasta and fish. Makes 4 servings.

Per serving: 483 calories (30% calories from fat), 16 g total fat, 2 g saturated fat, 71 mg cholesterol, 226 mg sodium, 48 g carbohydrates, 2 g fiber, 35 g protein, 48 mg calcium, 4 mg iron

Fresh tuna is delicious served rare—but if you use fish that has not been previously frozen, freeze it at 0°F (-18°C) for at least 7 days to destroy any potentially harmful organisms it may contain. Thaw the fish in the refrigerator before cooking.

5½ cups (1.3 liters) fat-free reduced-sodium chicken broth

½ cup (65 g) finely chopped dried apricots

1 pound (455 g) dried orzo or other tiny rice-shaped pasta

1 can (about 6⅛ oz./174 g) tuna packed in water

1 large egg yolk or 1 tablespoon (15 ml) pasteurized egg substitute

¼ teaspoon grated lemon peel

2 tablespoons (30 ml) lemon juice

4 teaspoons (20 ml) balsamic vinegar

1 teaspoon honey

½ teaspoon Dijon mustard

½ teaspoon salt (or to taste)

¼ cup (60 ml) *each* olive oil and salad oil

3 canned anchovy fillets, drained

1 cup (240 ml) nonfat sour cream

2 tablespoons fennel seeds

1 tablespoon whole white peppercorns

1½ teaspoons coriander seeds

2 large egg whites

4 tuna (ahi) steaks (*each* about 1 inch/2.5 cm thick and about 7 oz./200 g)

1 teaspoon olive oil

Tuna Steaks with Roasted Peppers & Tuna Sauce

Preparation time: 35 minutes
Cooking time: About 20 minutes

½ cup (120 ml) bottled clam juice

1 jar roasted red peppers (about 12 oz./340 g), drained and patted dry

3 tablespoons drained capers (or to taste)

Lemon slices

Italian or regular parsley sprigs

1. In a 4- to 5-quart (3.8- to 5-liter) pan, bring broth and apricots to a boil over high heat; stir in orzo. Reduce heat, cover, and simmer, stirring occasionally, until almost all liquid has been absorbed (about 20 minutes); as liquid cooks down, stir more often and watch closely to prevent scorching. Remove from heat and keep warm.

2. While orzo is cooking, drain can of tuna, reserving ¼ cup (60 ml) of the liquid from can. Set tuna and liquid aside.

3. In a food processor or blender, combine egg yolk, lemon peel, lemon juice, vinegar, honey, mustard, and ¼ teaspoon of the salt (or to taste); whirl until blended. With motor running, slowly pour in the ¼ cup (60 ml) olive oil and salad oil in a thin, steady stream. Whirl until well blended. Add canned tuna, reserved tuna liquid, 1 tablespoon (15 ml) water, and anchovies; whirl until smoothly puréed. With a spoon or whisk, stir in sour cream; set aside.

4. Wash and dry food processor or blender; then combine fennel seeds, peppercorns, coriander seeds, and remaining ¼ teaspoon salt in processor or blender. Whirl until finely ground; transfer to a wide, shallow bowl. In another wide, shallow bowl, beat egg whites to blend. Rinse tuna steaks and pat dry; then cut each in half. Dip pieces, one at a time, in egg whites; drain briefly, then coat on both sides with seed mixture. Pat any remaining seed mixture on fish.

5. Heat the 1 teaspoon olive oil in a wide nonstick frying pan over medium-high heat. Add fish and cook, turning once, until browned on both sides. Add clam juice. Reduce heat and cook until fish is still pale pink in center; cut to test (about 5 minutes).

6. Spoon pasta onto a rimmed platter; fluff with a fork. With a slotted spoon, lift fish from pan and place atop pasta; arrange red peppers decoratively around fish. Top with half the tuna sauce and sprinkle with capers. Garnish with lemon slices and parsley sprigs. Offer remaining tuna sauce to add to taste. Makes 8 servings.

Per serving: 562 calories (29% calories from fat), 18 g total fat, 3 g saturated fat, 77 mg cholesterol, 1,201 mg sodium, 60 g carbohydrates, 2 g fiber, 39 g protein, 115 mg calcium, 5 mg iron

Roast Beef with Prunes & Port
(recipe on page 580)

Meats

Red meat is rich-tasting, succulent, satisfying—and a natural for low-fat Italian meals. Just choose well-trimmed cuts of beef, lamb, pork, or veal; then keep the portion sizes modest and the seasonings and accompaniments lean, as we do in Roast Beef with Prunes & Port, Skewered Lamb with Blackberry-Balsamic Glaze, and the other superb dishes in this chapter. Even zesty Italian sausage has a place on lean menus, as Sausage Calzones deliciously prove.

•

To make this Italian version of all-American roast beef, you baste the meat with a port marinade and serve it with poached prunes.

....

- 1 **beef triangle tip (tri-tip) or top round roast (about 2 lbs./905 g), trimmed of fat**
- 1¾ **cups (420 ml) port**
- ⅓ **cup (73 g) firmly packed brown sugar**
- 1 **can (about 14½ oz./400 g) beef broth**
- 2½ **cups (about 1 lb./455 g) pitted prunes**
- 2 **packages (about 10 oz./285 g *each*) frozen tiny onions, thawed**
- 1 **pound (455 g) dried farfalle (pasta bow ties)**
- 2 **cloves garlic, minced**
- 2 **tablespoons chopped fresh oregano or 2 teaspoons dried oregano**
  Oregano sprigs
  Salt and pepper

....

1. Set beef in a 9- by 13-inch (23- by 33-cm) baking pan. Set aside. In a 3- to 4-quart (2.8- to 3.8-liter) pan, combine port and sugar; stir over medium heat just until sugar is dissolved. Remove from heat and let

Roast Beef with Prunes & Port

....

Preparation time: 20 minutes
Cooking time: About 50 minutes
Pictured on page 578

cool slightly; then measure out ⅓ cup (80 ml) of the port mixture to use for basting and set it aside. Add broth, prunes, and onions to port mixture remaining in pan; set aside.

2. Roast meat in a 450°F (230°C) oven, basting 4 times with the ⅓ cup (80 ml) port mixture, until a meat thermometer inserted in thickest part registers 135°F (57°C) for rare (about 35 minutes). After 25 minutes, check temperature every 5 to 10 minutes. If pan appears dry, add water, 4 to 6 tablespoons (60 to 90 ml) at a time, stirring to scrape browned bits free from pan bottom; do not let drippings scorch.

3. While meat is roasting, bring prune mixture to a boil over high heat. Then reduce heat and boil gently, uncovered, until prunes and onions are very soft (about 30 minutes). Remove from heat; keep warm.

4. When meat is done, transfer to a carving board, cover loosely, and let stand for about 15 minutes. Meanwhile, in a 6- to 8-quart (6- to 8-liter) pan, bring about 4 quarts (3.8 liters) water to a boil over medium-high heat; stir in pasta and cook until just tender to bite, 8 to 10 minutes. (Or cook pasta according to package directions.) Drain pasta well; then transfer to a large rimmed platter, mix in garlic and chopped oregano, and keep warm.

5. Pour any meat drippings from baking pan into prune mixture; also add any meat juices that have accumulated on board. With a slotted spoon, ladle prunes and onions over and around pasta; transfer cooking liquid to a small pitcher.

6. To serve, thinly slice meat across the grain and arrange over pasta mixture. Garnish with oregano sprigs. Offer cooking liquid to pour over meat and pasta and season to taste with salt and pepper. Makes 8 servings.

....

Per serving: 581 calories (8% calories from fat), 5 g total fat, 1 g saturated fat, 65 mg cholesterol, 427 mg sodium, 99 g carbohydrates, 6 g fiber, 36 g protein, 87 mg calcium, 7 mg iron

Plump dried cherries poached in Cabernet accompany this herb-rubbed beef roast.

....

1½ teaspoons *each* whole black peppercorns, dried thyme, and grated orange peel

½ teaspoon *each* dried oregano and coriander seeds

¼ teaspoon ground cinnamon

⅛ teaspoon ground allspice

4 cloves garlic, minced or pressed

1 trimmed, tied center-cut beef tenderloin (about 5 lbs./2.3 kg)

3½ cups (830 ml) beef broth

1¾ cups (420 ml) Cabernet Sauvignon

3 cups (about 15 oz./425 g) dried pitted tart cherries

¼ cup (60 ml) red currant jelly

2 tablespoons cornstarch blended with ¼ cup (60 ml) cold water

6 large oranges (about 3 lbs./1.35 kg *total*), thinly sliced

Salt and pepper

....

1. In a small bowl, mix peppercorns, thyme, orange peel, oregano,

Beef Tenderloin with Cabernet-Cherry Sauce

....

Preparation time: 25 minutes
Cooking time: 35 to 50 minutes
Standing time: 15 minutes

coriander seeds, cinnamon, allspice, and garlic. Rub mixture over beef; then set beef in a 10- by 15-inch (25- by 38-cm) roasting pan. Roast in a 450°F (230°C) oven until a meat thermometer inserted in thickest part registers 135°F (57°C) for rare (35 to 40 minutes), 140°F (60°C) for medium (about 50 minutes). Starting about 10 minutes before meat is done, check temperature every 5 to 10 minutes. If pan appears dry, add water, 4 to 6 tablespoons (60 to 90 ml) at a time, stirring to scrape browned bits free from pan bottom; do not let drippings scorch.

2. Meanwhile, in a 3- to 4-quart (2.8- to 3.8-liter) pan, combine

2 cups (470 ml) of the broth, wine, cherries, and jelly; bring to a boil over high heat. Then reduce heat, cover, and simmer until cherries are softened (15 to 20 minutes). Remove from heat.

3. When meat is done, transfer it to a large platter. Snip and discard strings. Cover meat loosely and let stand for about 15 minutes. Meanwhile, add remaining 1½ cups (360 ml) broth to roasting pan; place over medium heat and stir to scrape browned bits free from pan bottom. Pour broth mixture into cherry mixture; bring to a boil, stirring often. Add cornstarch mixture and stir until sauce boils and thickens slightly. Pour into a bowl and keep warm.

4. Garnish meat with orange slices. To serve, slice meat across the grain and offer sauce to spoon over it; season to taste with salt and pepper. Makes about 16 servings.

....

Per serving: 362 calories (30% calories from fat), 11 g total fat, 4 g saturated fat, 88 mg cholesterol, 440 mg sodium, 30 g carbohydrates, 2 g fiber, 30 g protein, 45 mg calcium, 4 mg iron

Each slice of this big special-occasion meat loaf sports a colorful spiral of herb-and-cheese filling.

....

1 cup (about 2 oz./55 g) dried tomatoes (not packed in oil)

2 tablespoons (30 ml) Marsala

1 teaspoon olive oil

1 large red onion (about 12 oz./ 340 g), chopped

5 slices sourdough sandwich bread (about 5 oz./140 g *total*), torn into pieces

1½ pounds (680 g) lean ground beef

4 ounces (115 g) reduced-fat or regular mild Italian sausage, casings removed and meat crumbled

1 large jar (about 4 oz./115 g) diced pimentos, drained

1 large egg

2 large egg whites

2 cloves garlic, minced or pressed

½ teaspoon dried thyme

¼ teaspoon ground sage

⅓ cup (20 g) chopped Italian or regular parsley

¼ cup (20 g) grated Parmesan cheese

¼ teaspoon pepper

1⅓ cups (193 g) dried currants

1¼ cups (50 g) lightly packed fresh basil leaves

1 ounce (28 g) thinly sliced prosciutto, coarsely chopped

¼ cup (28 g) shredded fontina cheese

¼ cup (35 g) yellow cornmeal

Italian or regular parsley sprigs

Spiral Stuffed Meat Loaf

....

Preparation time: 35 minutes
Cooking time: About 1½ hours
Pictured on facing page

1. Place tomatoes in a small bowl and add boiling water to cover. Let stand until soft (about 10 minutes), stirring occasionally. Drain well; gently squeeze out excess liquid. Finely chop tomatoes and return to bowl. Drizzle with Marsala and set aside.

2. Heat oil in a wide nonstick frying pan over medium-high heat. Add onion and cook, stirring often, until it begins to brown (about 10 min-

utes); add water, ¼ cup (60 ml) at a time, if pan appears dry. Transfer onion to a large bowl and let cool slightly.

3. In a food processor or blender, whirl bread to form fine crumbs. Add crumbs to onion in bowl. Add beef, sausage, pimentos, egg, egg whites, garlic, thyme, sage, chopped parsley, Parmesan cheese, and pepper; mix until very well blended.

4. On a large sheet of parchment paper or wax paper, pat meat mixture into a 10- by 15-inch (25- by 38-cm) rectangle. Distribute chopped tomatoes, currants, basil leaves, prosciutto, and fontina cheese over meat in even layers to within 1 inch (2.5 cm) of edges. Using paper to help you, lift narrow end of rectangle nearest you over filling; then carefully roll up meat to form a cylinder. Pinch seam and ends closed. Dust a 9- by 13-inch (23- by 33-cm) baking dish with cornmeal; using 2 wide spatulas, transfer loaf to dish.

5. Bake in a 350°F (175°C) oven until loaf is well browned on top (about 1¼ hours); add water, ¼ cup (60 ml) at a time, if dish appears dry. With wide spatulas, carefully transfer loaf to a platter. Serve hot or cold. Garnish with parsley sprigs. Makes 8 to 10 servings.

....

Per serving: 369 calories (30% calories from fat), 13 g total fat, 5 g saturated fat, 82 mg cholesterol, 384 mg sodium, 39 g carbohydrates, 4 g fiber, 27 g protein, 183 mg calcium, 5 mg iron

Spiral Stuffed Meat Loaf
(recipe on facing page)

The Essence of Olive Oil

In this book, our cooking fat of choice is often olive oil—for two reasons. First, this monounsaturated oil is widely used in Italy; second, recent research suggests that it may carry some health benefits, possibly helping to reduce cholesterol levels.

Which olive oil should you use? In the market, you'll find extra-virgin, virgin, pure, even "light" oils. On this page, we tell you how these oils are made—and what characterizes each type.

What Gives Olive Oil Its Flavor?

An olive oil's character and quality are determined by the variety of fruit and by how it is cultivated, harvested, handled (olives are fragile), and pressed.

Olives for oil can be harvested over several months. Mature green fruit picked in early fall yields oil that is typically green in color, with a raw, sharp flavor often described as acrid, beany, bell pepperish, grassy, herbaceous, leafy, or woodsy. Riper fruit, harvested from early winter to early spring, yields proportionally more oil than greener olives. The oil is usually golden; it's fruitier, smoother, and more velvety in flavor and mouth feel than early-harvest oils.

If an olive oil was made exclusively from a specific harvest period, the label may provide that information. But producers often make oil from several harvests through a season, then blend them to yield oils combining the vigor of early-harvest oils with the softness of late-harvest ones.

How Is It Made?

Olives are crushed with their pits to make a thick paste called mash, which is either pressed or centrifuged to separate the oil from the rest of the mash. The oil rises to the top of the mixture and is then skimmed off; if the mash was centrifuged, the oil, too, is centrifuged a second time. Finally, the oil is aged for 3 to 6 months to mellow its natural bitterness.

Grades of Olive Oil

The International Olive Oil Council in Madrid sets the legal definitions for olive oil grades. Oil is evaluated by two subjective measures—smell and taste—and by one objective measure, namely, the level of free oleic acids (the predominant fatty acid in olive oil). Differences in grade are based on the latter measure: the lower the percentage of free oleic acids, the higher the oil quality.

Oils with 1% or less free oleic acids are *extra-virgin*— the top grade. Those with over 1% but no more than 3.3% of these acids are *virgin* olive oils. *Pure* olive oil is a blend with no more than 3.3% acidity. Any oils with over 3.3% free oleic acids are refined using heat, a process that makes them neutral in color, flavor, and aroma. To give such oils more personality, producers blend them with extra-virgin or virgin oil and sell them as "pure olive oil" or, more frequently, as just "olive oil."

You'll also encounter olive oils with "light" on the label. These are refined specifically to make them taste like mild vegetable oils; despite the word "light," they have the same fat and calorie content as any other olive oil.

Because extra-virgin oil delivers the best flavor, it commands the highest price. Be aware, though, that high grades of olive oil don't always live up to their label: due to the fact that there is no regulatory agency to enforce the official definitions, many manufacturers dilute extra-virgin oil with refined oils, yet still label the product "extra-virgin." Your best tactic is to sample different brands until you find an extra-virgin oil with the flavor you want.

Buying & Storing Olive Oil

For the clearest impression of an oil's flavor, dip a chunk of bread into the oil and taste it. For seasoning salads, vegetables, sauces, and breads, any oil with a flavor you like is fine. For cooking, pure or refined olive oil works well; using extra-virgin oil is extravagant, as heat lessens its flavor.

Good-quality olive oil is quite stable compared with polyunsaturated oils. If bottled airtight and stored in a cool, dark place, unopened olive oil stays fresh-tasting for up to 2 years. If refrigerated, it turns cloudy and solidifies; once returned to room temperature, it will clear again, but frequent chilling and warming start a breakdown that leads rapidly to rancidity.

Even after opening, olive oil keeps longer than polyunsaturated oils. Stored in a tightly closed container in a cool, dark place, it should stay fresh for 6 months to a year.

For a quick meal, try these sausage-topped, sautéed veal scallops, served with a lemony mustard sauce made from the pan drippings.

- 6 very thin slices capocollo (or coppa) sausage (about 1½ oz./43 g *total*)
- 6 slices veal scaloppine (about 1 lb./455 g *total*)
- 1 teaspoon olive oil
- 4 green onions, thinly sliced diagonally
- 2 cloves garlic, minced
- ¼ cup (60 ml) beef broth
- 2 tablespoons (30 ml) Dijon mustard
- 1 tablespoon (15 ml) lemon juice
- 1½ teaspoons chopped fresh basil or ½ teaspoon dried basil

  Lemon slices and basil sprigs

Veal Capocollo

Preparation time: 20 minutes
Cooking time: About 10 minutes

1. Lay a slice of sausage on each veal slice, pressing lightly so that meat and sausage stick together. Set aside.

2. Heat oil in a wide nonstick frying pan over medium heat. Add onions and garlic; stir often until onions are soft but still bright green (about 3 minutes). Push onion mixture aside; place veal in pan, overlapping slices as little as possible. Cook, turning once, just until veal is no longer pink in center; cut to test (about 3 minutes). With a slotted spatula, transfer veal slices, sausage side up, to a platter; keep warm.

3. Working quickly, add broth, mustard, lemon juice, and chopped basil to pan; stir to blend. Cook over medium-high heat, stirring, until mixture boils and thickens slightly. Drizzle sauce over meat; garnish with lemon slices and basil sprigs. Makes 4 servings.

Per serving: 172 calories (22% calories from fat), 4 g total fat, 1 g saturated fat, 94 mg cholesterol, 509 mg sodium, 6 g carbohydrates, 0.4 g fiber, 27 g protein, 45 mg calcium, 2 mg iron

---

Marinated in a blend of purple jam, vinegar, and mustard, this lamb cooks quickly on the grill.

- ½ cup (120 ml) blackberry jam
- ⅓ cup (80 ml) balsamic vinegar
- 1 tablespoon (15 ml) Dijon mustard
- 1 tablespoon chopped fresh rosemary or 1 teaspoon dried rosemary
- 1½ pounds (680 g) lean boneless lamb (such as leg or loin), trimmed of fat and cut into 1-inch (2.5-cm) cubes

  Salt

1. In a large bowl, stir together jam, vinegar, mustard, and rosemary.

Skewered Lamb with Blackberry-Balsamic Glaze

Preparation time: 20 minutes
Marinating time: At least 1 hour
Cooking time: About 8 minutes

Pour a third of the mixture into a small container; cover and refrigerate. Add lamb to remaining jam mixture in bowl. Stir well, cover, and refrigerate for at least 1 hour or until next day.

2. Lift meat cubes from bowl and thread equally on four to six 12- to 14-inch (30- to 35.5-cm) metal skewers; discard marinade left in bowl. Place skewers on a lightly oiled grill 4 to 6 inches (10 to 15 cm) above a solid bed of medium-hot coals. Cook, turning and basting with reserved jam mixture, until meat is evenly browned and done to your liking; cut to test (about 8 minutes for medium-rare).

3. Push meat from skewers onto plates. Season to taste with salt. Makes 4 servings.

Per serving: 324 calories (28% calories from fat), 10 g total fat, 4 g saturated fat, 114 mg cholesterol, 168 mg sodium, 20 g carbohydrates, 0.4 g fiber, 37 g protein, 19 mg calcium, 3 mg iron

Stuffed Lamb Chops with Creamy Polenta
(recipe on facing page)

Tangy blue cheese and toasted pine nuts fill these grilled lamb chops. Serve them with hot polenta studded with corn kernels.

························

8 small lamb rib chops (*each about 1 inch/2.5 cm thick; about 2 lbs./905 g total*), trimmed of fat

½ small onion, cut into chunks

¼ cup (60 ml) reduced-sodium soy sauce

2 tablespoons firmly packed brown sugar

2 tablespoons (30 ml) lemon juice

1 large clove garlic, peeled

¼ cup (65 g) pine nuts or slivered almonds

¼ cup (62 g) packed crumbled blue-veined cheese
Pepper

2 cups (470 ml) low-fat (1%) milk

½ cup (120 ml) beef broth

1 cup (138 g) polenta or yellow cornmeal

1 large can (about 15 oz./425 g) cream-style corn

1 teaspoon chopped fresh thyme or ¼ teaspoon dried thyme

½ teaspoon salt

1 cup (about 8 oz./230 g) nonfat ricotta cheese

¼ cup (20 g) grated Parmesan cheese
Thyme sprigs

Stuffed Lamb Chops with Creamy Polenta

························

Preparation time: 30 minutes
Marinating time: At least 30 minutes
Cooking time: About 25 minutes
Pictured on facing page

1. With a sharp knife, cut a horizontal 1½-inch-wide (3.5-cm-wide) pocket in each lamb chop, starting from meaty side and cutting through to bone. Set chops aside.

2. In a food processor or blender, combine onion, soy sauce, sugar, lemon juice, and garlic. Whirl until smoothly puréed. Pour into a heavy-duty resealable plastic food-storage bag. Add chops; seal bag and rotate to coat chops with marinade. Refrigerate for at least 30 minutes or up to 6 hours, turning bag over occasionally.

3. Toast pine nuts in a small frying pan over medium heat until golden (about 3 minutes), stirring often; then pour into a small bowl and let cool slightly. Add blue-veined cheese and mix well. Season to taste with pepper, cover, and refrigerate until ready to use.

4. When you are almost ready to grill chops, prepare polenta. In a 4- to 5-quart (3.8- to 5-liter) pan, bring milk and broth just to a boil over medium-high heat. Stir in polenta, corn, chopped thyme, and salt. Reduce heat and simmer, uncovered, stirring often and scraping pan bottom with a long-handled spoon (mixture will spatter), until polenta tastes creamy (about 15 minutes). Stir in ricotta cheese; then remove pan from heat, stir in Parmesan cheese, and keep warm.

5. Lift chops from bag; drain, reserving marinade. Using a spoon, stuff an eighth of the cheese–pine nut filling deep into pocket of each chop. Place chops on a greased grill 4 to 6 inches (10 to 15 cm) above a solid bed of hot coals. Cook, basting twice with marinade and turning once, until chops are evenly browned and done to your liking; cut in thickest part to test (6 to 8 minutes for medium-rare).

6. To serve, divide polenta among 4 individual plates; arrange 2 chops on each plate alongside polenta. Garnish with thyme sprigs. Makes 4 servings.

························

Per serving: 660 calories (30% calories from fat), 22 g total fat, 8 g saturated fat, 94 mg cholesterol, 1,823 mg sodium, 68 g carbohydrates, 4 g fiber, 48 g protein, 604 mg calcium, 5 mg iron

Originating in Naples, calzone is reminiscent of a stuffed pizza. These individual calzones have a zesty sausage and cheese filling.

Sausage Calzones

Preparation time: 35 minutes
Rising time: 45 to 60 minutes
Cooking time: 25 to 30 minutes

1 package active dry yeast

1 cup (240 ml) warm water (about 110°F/43°C)

About 2½ cups (310 g) all-purpose flour

About ½ cup (70 g) yellow cornmeal

1 tablespoon sugar

½ teaspoon salt

3 tablespoons (45 ml) olive oil

1 pound (455 g) reduced-fat or regular mild Italian sausage, casings removed and meat crumbled

1 large onion, chopped

¼ teaspoon *each* dried marjoram, dried rubbed sage, and dried thyme

1 large tomato (about 8 oz./230 g), chopped

1 carton (about 15 oz./425 g) nonfat ricotta cheese

½ cup (50 g) fine dry bread crumbs

⅓ cup (30 g) grated Romano cheese

⅓ cup (20 g) chopped Italian or regular parsley

2 tablespoons drained capers (or to taste)

1. In a small bowl, sprinkle yeast over warm water; let stand until foamy (about 5 minutes). In a large bowl, mix 2½ cups (310 g) of the flour, ½ cup (70 g) of the cornmeal, sugar, and salt. Add yeast mixture and 2 tablespoons (30 ml) of the oil. Stir until dough is evenly moistened. *To knead by hand*, scrape dough onto a lightly floured board and knead until smooth and springy (about 10 minutes), adding more flour as needed to prevent sticking. *To knead with a dough hook,* beat dough on medium speed until it pulls cleanly from sides of bowl and is springy (5 to 7 minutes); if dough is sticky, add more flour, 1 tablespoon at a time.

2. Place dough in a greased bowl; turn over to grease top. Cover bowl with plastic wrap; let dough rise in a warm, draft-free place until almost doubled (45 to 60 minutes). Or let rise in refrigerator until next day.

3. Meanwhile, in a wide nonstick frying pan, combine sausage, onion, marjoram, sage, and thyme. Cook over medium-high heat, stirring often, until meat is tinged with brown (10 to 15 minutes); add water, 1 tablespoon (15 ml) at a time, if pan appears dry. Transfer mixture to a large bowl; let cool slightly. Stir in tomato, ricotta cheese, bread crumbs, Romano cheese, parsley, and capers; set aside.

4. Punch dough down, turn out onto a lightly floured board, and knead briefly to release air. Divide dough into 6 equal balls; roll each ball into an 8-inch (20-cm) round. Spoon a sixth of the sausage filling over half of each dough round, spreading it to within ½ inch (1 cm) of edge; fold plain half of round over filling and pinch edges firmly to seal.

5. Dust 2 greased large baking sheets with cornmeal. With a wide spatula, transfer calzones to baking sheets. Prick tops of calzones with a fork; brush lightly with remaining 1 tablespoon (15 ml) oil.

6. Bake in a 425°F (220°C) oven until richly browned (about 15 minutes), switching positions of baking sheets halfway through baking. Let cool for at least 5 minutes before serving; serve hot or warm. Makes 6 servings.

Per serving: 595 calories (30% calories from fat), 20 g total fat, 5 g saturated fat, 26 mg cholesterol, 1,062 mg sodium, 70 g carbohydrates, 4 g fiber, 33 g protein, 472 mg calcium, 5 mg iron

Served over pasta ribbons and topped with cheese, this sturdy three-meat stew is delightful for supper on a chilly day.

- 1 tablespoon (15 ml) olive oil
- 1 pound (455 g) *each* boneless pork, beef, and veal stew meat, trimmed of fat and cut into ½-inch (1-cm) cubes
- 1 large onion, chopped
- 1 large carrot (about 4 oz./115 g), chopped
- 8 ounces (230 g) mushrooms, thinly sliced
- 1 cup (120 g) thinly sliced celery
- 1 large can (about 28 oz./795 g) tomatoes
- 1 can (about 15 oz./425 g) tomato purée
- ½ cup (120 ml) dry red wine
- 1 tablespoon chopped fresh rosemary or 1 teaspoon dried rosemary
- ⅛ to ¼ teaspoon fennel seeds
- 2 pounds (905 g) dried fettuccine
- 1 cup (about 3 oz./85 g) grated Parmesan cheese

  Salt and crushed red pepper flakes

Pork, Beef & Veal Ragout with Fettuccine

Preparation time: 30 minutes
Cooking time: About 1½ hours

1. Heat oil in a 4- to 5-quart (3.8- to 5-liter) pan over medium-high heat. Add pork, beef, and veal, a portion at a time (do not crowd pan). Cook, stirring often, until meat is tinged with brown (about 5 minutes). As meat is browned, use a slotted spoon to transfer it to a large bowl; set aside.

2. Add onion, carrot, mushrooms, celery, and 1 tablespoon (15 ml) water to pan. Cook, stirring often, just until vegetables are soft (about 15 minutes). Return meat (and any juices that have accumulated in bowl) to pan; then add tomatoes (break up with a spoon) and their liquid, tomato purée, wine, rosemary, and fennel seeds. Bring to a boil over high heat, stirring often. Then reduce heat, cover, and sim-

mer until meat is tender when pierced (about 1 hour); stir occasionally at first, then more often near end of cooking time, watching closely to prevent scorching.

3. About 20 minutes before stew is done, bring about 6 quarts (6 liters) water to a boil in an 8- to 10-quart (8- to 10-liter) pan over medium-high heat; stir in pasta and cook until just tender to bite, 8 to 10 minutes. (Or cook pasta according to package directions.) Drain pasta well and divide among wide individual bowls; top with stew. Sprinkle with cheese. Season to taste with salt and red pepper flakes. Makes 10 servings.

Per serving: 638 calories (23% calories from fat), 16 g total fat, 5 g saturated fat, 192 mg cholesterol, 594 mg sodium, 77 g carbohydrates, 5 g fiber, 45 g protein, 198 mg calcium, 8 mg iron

Start by browning veal shanks in a very hot oven, then cover and bake. When the meat is tender enough to pull apart, make risotto the easy way: stir rice into the pan juices and continue to bake, letting the grains absorb the flavorful liquid.

Osso Buco with Risotto

Preparation time: 20 minutes
Cooking time: About 2½ hours
Pictured on facing page

- 2 tablespoons (30 ml) olive oil
- 5 to 6 pounds (2.3 to 2.7 kg) meaty veal shanks (*each about 2 inches/5 cm thick*)
- 1 cup (240 ml) dry red wine
- 4 cups (950 ml) beef broth
- 2 tablespoons grated lemon peel
- 1 teaspoon *each* dried thyme and dried basil
- 2 cups (390 g) medium- or short-grain white rice
- 1 cup (130 g) chopped carrots
- ¼ cup (15 g) chopped Italian or regular parsley
- 2 cloves garlic, minced or pressed
- 1 cup (130 g) chopped zucchini
- 1 cup (150 g) chopped red bell pepper
- ½ cup (40 g) grated Parmesan cheese
- Lemon wedges
- Italian or regular parsley sprigs

1. Place oil in an 11- by 17-inch (28- by 43-cm) roasting pan. Heat in a 475°F (245°C) oven until hot (about 1 minute). Lay veal shanks in pan in a single layer. Bake, uncovered, for 30 minutes; then turn meat over and continue to bake until browned (about 10 more minutes).

2. Remove pan from oven and add wine; stir to scrape browned bits free from pan bottom. Then stir in broth, 1 tablespoon of the lemon peel, thyme, and basil; stir again, scraping browned bits free. Cover pan tightly with foil and bake until meat is tender enough to pull apart easily (about 1½ hours).

3. Uncover pan; stir 2½ cups (590 ml) water, rice, and carrots into pan juices. Bake, uncovered, stirring rice and turning meat over occasionally, until liquid has been absorbed and rice is tender to bite (20 to 25 minutes). If rice begins to dry out, add more water, about ½ cup (120 ml) at a time.

4. In a small bowl, mix remaining 1 tablespoon lemon peel, chopped parsley, and garlic. Remove meat from pan, transfer to a large platter, and sprinkle with parsley mixture. Stir zucchini and bell pepper into rice mixture; spoon rice mixture onto platter alongside meat, then sprinkle with cheese. Garnish with lemon wedges and parsley sprigs. Makes 4 to 6 servings.

Per serving: 581 calories (18% calories from fat), 11 g total fat, 3 g saturated fat, 134 mg cholesterol, 770 mg sodium, 69 g carbohydrates, 2 g fiber, 47 g protein, 155 mg calcium, 6 mg iron

Osso Buco with Risotto
(recipe on facing page)

Focaccia

Grape-studded Focaccia

Preparation time: 25 minutes
Rising time: 1½ to 2 hours
Cooking time: 30 to 35 minutes

....

Focaccia Dough
(recipe follows); or
2 loaves (about 1 lb./
455 g *each*) frozen
white bread dough,
thawed and kneaded
together

1 tablespoon (15 ml)
olive oil

40 to 50 seedless red
grapes (6 to 8 oz./
170 to 230 g *total*)

1 tablespoon chopped
fresh rosemary or
1 teaspoon dried
rosemary

Coarse salt and
coarsely ground
pepper

3 ounces (85 g)
pancetta or bacon,
coarsely chopped

....

1. Prepare Focaccia
Dough. When dough is
almost doubled, punch it
down, turn out onto a
lightly floured board, and
knead briefly to release
air. Roll dough into a 9-
by 12-inch (23- by 30-cm)
rectangle about ½ inch (1
cm) thick. Fold rectangle
loosely in half; transfer to
an oiled shallow 10- by
15-inch (25- by 38-cm)
baking pan and unfold.

Press and stretch dough
to cover pan evenly. If
dough is too elastic, let it
rest for about 5 minutes,
then press again. Cover
dough lightly with plastic
wrap and let rise in a
warm, draft-free place
until almost doubled
(45 to 60 minutes).

2. Brush oil lightly over
dough. With your finger-
tips, gently press dough
down all over, giving surface a dimpled look. Also
press dough gently into
corners of pan. Press
grapes in even rows into
dimpled dough, spacing
them about 1 inch (2.5 cm)
apart. Sprinkle with rosemary, then with salt and
pepper.

3. Bake in a 400°F (205°C)
oven until focaccia is well
browned at edges and on
bottom (30 to 35 min-
utes); after 20 minutes,
sprinkle with pancetta.
If topping is browned
before bread is done,
cover loosely with foil.
Serve hot or warm.
Makes 12 servings.

Focaccia Dough. In a
large bowl, sprinkle 1
package **active dry yeast**
over 1½ cups (360 ml)
warm water (about
110°F/43°C); let stand
until foamy (about 5 min-
utes). Stir in ½ teaspoon
salt and 2 tablespoons

(30 ml) **olive oil**. Add 2½
cups (310 g) **all-purpose
flour;** stir to blend. Beat
with an electric mixer on
high speed until dough is
glossy and stretchy (3 to
5 minutes). Stir in 1⅓ cups
(165 g) more **all-purpose
flour.**

To knead by hand, scrape
dough onto a lightly
floured board and knead
until smooth and springy
(about 10 minutes), adding
more flour as needed to
prevent sticking.

*To knead with a dough
hook*, beat dough on medium speed until it pulls
cleanly from sides of
bowl and is springy (5 to
7 minutes); if dough is
sticky, add more flour,
1 tablespoon at a time.

Place dough in a
greased bowl and turn
over to grease top. Cover
bowl with plastic wrap;
let dough rise in a warm,
draft-free place until
almost doubled (45 to 60
minutes). Or let rise in
refrigerator until next day.

....

Per serving: 214 calories
(27% calories from fat), 6 g total
fat, 1 g saturated fat, 4 mg cholesterol, 167 mg sodium, 33 g
carbohydrates, 1 g fiber, 5 g protein, 10 mg calcium, 2 mg iron

Pear & Pepper Focaccia

Preparation time: 25 minutes
Rising time: 45 to 60 minutes
Cooking time: About 30 minutes

....

1 loaf (about 1 lb./455 g)
frozen white bread
dough, thawed

3 tablespoons (45 ml)
lemon juice

3 medium-size firm-
ripe pears (about
18 oz./510 g *total*)

1½ cups (90 g) firmly
packed Italian or
regular parsley sprigs

3 tablespoons (45 ml)
olive oil

1 tablespoon grated
lemon peel

2 tablespoons sugar

½ to 1 teaspoon coarse-
ly ground pepper

⅓ cup (30 g) grated
Parmesan cheese

....

1. Place dough in a non-
stick or lightly oiled shallow 10- by 15-inch (25- by
38-cm) baking pan; press
and push to cover pan
evenly. If dough is too
elastic, let it rest for a few
minutes, then press again.
Cover dough lightly with
plastic wrap and let rise

in a warm, draft-free place until almost doubled (45 to 60 minutes).

2. Meanwhile, pour lemon juice into a medium-size bowl. Core pears and thinly slice into bowl, turning fruit to coat with juice. Also make parsley pesto: in a blender or food processor, combine parsley sprigs, oil, and lemon peel. Whirl until smoothly puréed, scraping sides of container as needed.

3. With your fingertips, gently press dough down all over, giving surface a dimpled look; also press dough gently into corners of pan. Spread pesto evenly over dough. Arrange pear slices on dough and press in gently. Mix sugar and pepper and sprinkle over pears.

4. Bake in a 400°F (205°C) oven until focaccia is well browned at edges and on bottom (about 30 minutes); after 20 minutes, sprinkle with cheese. If topping is browned before bread is done, cover loosely with foil. Serve hot or warm. Makes 12 servings.

Per serving: 176 calories (30% calories from fat), 6 g total fat, 1 g saturated fat, 4 mg cholesterol, 227 mg sodium, 27 g carbohydrates, 1 g fiber, 4 g protein, 58 mg calcium, 1 mg iron

Eggplant & Onion Focaccia

Preparation time: 30 minutes
Rising time: 1½ to 2 hours
Cooking time: 55 to 60 minutes

Focaccia Dough (recipe on facing page); or 2 loaves (about 1 lb./455 g *each*) frozen white bread dough, thawed and kneaded together

2 medium-size eggplants (about 2 lbs./905 g *total*), unpeeled, cut into ¾-inch (2-cm) cubes

1 small red onion (about 8 oz./230 g), cut into ¾-inch (2-cm) cubes

2 tablespoons (30 ml) olive oil

1½ cups (about 6 oz./170 g) shredded smoked or plain part-skim mozzarella cheese (or use smoked Gouda cheese)

2 tablespoons chopped Italian or regular parsley

1. Prepare Focaccia Dough. When dough is almost doubled, punch it down, turn out onto a lightly floured board, and knead briefly to release air. Roll dough into a 9- by 12-inch (23- by 30-cm) rectangle about

½ inch (1 cm) thick. Fold rectangle loosely in half; transfer to an oiled shallow 10- by 15-inch (25- by 38-cm) baking pan and unfold. Press and stretch dough to cover pan evenly. If dough is too elastic, let it rest for about 5 minutes, then press again. Cover dough lightly with plastic wrap and let rise in a warm, draft-free place until almost doubled (45 to 60 minutes).

2. Meanwhile, place eggplant and onion in a large, shallow baking pan. Drizzle with 1 tablespoon (15 ml) of the oil and mix gently; then spread vegetables out evenly. Bake in a 450°F (230°C) oven, stirring occasionally, until eggplant is lightly browned and beginning to soften (about 25 minutes); add water, ¼ cup (60 ml) at a time, if pan appears dry. Remove vegetables from pan and set aside.

3. Brush remaining 1 tablespoon (15 ml) oil lightly over dough. With your fingertips, gently press dough down all over, giving surface a dimpled look. Also press dough gently into corners of pan. Evenly sprinkle cheese over dimpled dough; distribute eggplant mixture over cheese.

4. Bake in a 400°F (205°C) oven until focaccia is well browned at edges and on bottom (30 to 35 minutes). If topping is browned before bread is done, cover loosely with foil. Sprinkle with parsley. Serve hot or warm. Makes 12 servings.

Per serving: 266 calories (30% calories from fat), 9 g total fat, 3 g saturated fat, 20 mg cholesterol, 261 mg sodium, 38 g carbohydrates, 3 g fiber, 9 g protein, 114 mg calcium, 3 mg iron

Portabella Mushroom Sandwiches
(recipe on page 596)

Meatless Main Dishes

For meatless Italian-style meals that are low in fat and naturally great tasting, focus on popular pasta, grains, and legumes. Choices such as Polenta Pepper Torte, Linguine with Lentils, and Orecchiette with Broccoli Rabe & Pine Nuts provide great nutrition and delicious dining, too. And don't forget egg- or cheese-based dishes such as frittata and ricotta pancakes. With a few adjustments, these too can become low-fat favorites.

•

Big portabella mushrooms pan-fried in a cornmeal batter make wholesome, hearty sandwiches. Serve them in crusty rolls spread with chard-and-herb cream cheese; offer Pickled Vegetables (recipe on page 544) alongside.

Portabella Mushroom Sandwiches

Preparation time: 25 minutes
Cooking time: About 20 minutes
Pictured on page 594

- 4 crusty rolls (about 4 oz./115 g *each*), split into halves
- 1 package (about 10 oz./285 g) frozen chopped Swiss chard, thawed and squeezed dry
- 1 large package (about 8 oz./230 g) nonfat cream cheese, at room temperature
- ¾ cup (85 g) shredded smoked mozzarella or smoked Gouda cheese
- 2 tablespoons (30 ml) nonfat mayonnaise
- 1 teaspoon Dijon mustard
- ½ teaspoon dried rubbed sage
  About ¼ cup (60 ml) balsamic vinegar
  Pepper
- 3 large egg whites
- ¾ cup (104 g) yellow cornmeal
- ⅓ cup (40 g) all-purpose flour
- ¼ teaspoon salt
- 4 large portabella mushrooms (about 3 oz./85 g *each*), stems removed
- 2 tablespoons (30 ml) olive oil
- 4 to 8 green or red leaf lettuce leaves
- 4 to 8 large tomato slices

1. If needed, pull bread from base and top of each roll to make a shell about ¼ inch (6 mm) thick; reserve bread scraps for other uses, if desired. Arrange roll halves, cut side up, in a broiler pan; broil about 6 inches below heat until lightly toasted (1½ to 2 minutes). Set aside.

2. In a food processor or blender, combine chard, cream cheese, mozzarella cheese, mayonnaise, mustard, and sage. Whirl until chard is finely chopped, scraping sides of container as needed. Brush cut side of roll bottoms lightly with vinegar and sprinkle with pepper. Set aside about a fourth of the chard mixture; divide remaining mixture equally among roll bottoms (you need about ⅓ cup/80 ml per roll). With a spatula, spread chard mixture to fill hollows in rolls evenly.

3. In a wide, shallow bowl, beat egg whites and 2 tablespoons (30 ml) water to blend. In another wide, shallow bowl, stir together cornmeal, flour, and salt. Dip mushrooms in egg white mixture; drain briefly, then dip in cornmeal mixture and press to coat well all over.

4. Heat 1 tablespoon (15 ml) of the oil in a wide nonstick frying pan over medium-high heat. Add 2 of the mushrooms; cook, turning once, until mushrooms are golden on both sides and tender when pierced (5 to 7 minutes). Remove from pan and keep warm. Repeat to cook remaining 2 mushrooms, using remaining 1 tablespoon (15 ml) oil.

5. Working quickly, place 1 or 2 lettuce leaves on each roll bottom; then top each with one hot mushroom and 1 or 2 tomato slices. Spoon reserved chard mixture over tomato slices. Brush cut side of roll tops lightly with vinegar and sprinkle with pepper; close sandwiches and serve immediately. Makes 4 servings.

Per serving: 709 calories (24% calories from fat), 19 g total fat, 5 g saturated fat, 36 mg cholesterol, 1,553 mg sodium, 101 g carbohydrates, 5 g fiber, 33 g protein, 436 mg calcium, 8 mg iron

Because it isn't layered like the traditional dish, this lasagne goes together quickly.

....

12 ounces (340 g) dried lasagne

2½ cups (590 ml) low-fat (2%) milk

¼ cup (32 g) cornstarch

1½ teaspoons dried basil

½ teaspoon *each* dried rosemary and salt

¼ teaspoon ground nutmeg

1 cup (about 8 oz./230 g) nonfat ricotta cheese

2 packages (about 10 oz./285 g *each*) frozen chopped Swiss chard, thawed and squeezed dry

2 large ripe tomatoes (about 1 lb./ 455 g *total*), chopped

2 cups (about 8 oz./230 g) shredded mozzarella cheese

Three-cheese Lasagne with Chard

....

Preparation time: 20 minutes
Cooking time: About 1 hour

⅓ cup (30 g) grated Parmesan cheese

....

1. In a 5- to 6-quart (5- to 6-liter) pan, bring about 3 quarts (2.8 liters) water to a boil over medium-high heat; stir in pasta and cook until just barely tender to bite, about 8 minutes. Drain pasta well and lay out flat; cover lightly.

2. In pasta-cooking pan, smoothly blend milk, cornstarch, basil, rosemary, salt, and nutmeg. Stir over medium-high heat until mixture boils and thickens slightly (about 5 minutes). Stir in ricotta cheese, chard, tomatoes, and half the mozzarella cheese. Gently stir in pasta.

3. Transfer mixture to a 9- by 13-inch (23- by 33-cm) baking pan; gently push pasta down to cover it with sauce. Sprinkle with remaining mozzarella cheese, then with Parmesan cheese. Bake in a 375°F (190°C) oven until lasagne is bubbly in center (about 40 minutes). Let stand for about 5 minutes before serving. Makes 8 servings.

....

Per serving: 362 calories (24% calories from fat), 10 g total fat, 5 g saturated fat, 33 mg cholesterol, 531 mg sodium, 48 g carbohydrates, 3 g fiber, 22 g protein, 499 mg calcium, 3 mg iron

---

Creamy cannellini beans are the base of this easy vegetable stew.

....

6 slices Italian sandwich bread (about 6 oz./ 170 g *total*), cut into ½-inch (1-cm) cubes

2 teaspoons olive oil

2 large onions, chopped

4 cloves garlic, minced

½ teaspoon *each* dried rubbed sage, dried thyme, and dried marjoram

¼ cup (10 g) chopped fresh basil

4 large tomatoes (about 2 lbs./ 905 g *total*), chopped

3 cans (about 15 oz./425 g *each*) cannellini (white kidney beans), drained and rinsed

1 cup (240 ml) canned vegetable broth

1 tablespoon (15 ml) red wine vinegar

Tuscan Bean Stew

....

Preparation time: 25 minutes
Cooking time: About 45 minutes

¼ cup (20 g) grated Parmesan cheese

....

1. Toast bread cubes as directed for Garbanzo Beans with Olive Pesto (page 558). Set aside.

2. Heat oil in a 4- to 5-quart (3.8- to 5-liter) pan over medium-high heat. Add onions, garlic, sage, thyme, marjoram, and ¼ cup (60 ml) water. Cook, stirring often, until onions are soft (about 5 minutes). Add water, 1 tablespoon (15 ml) at a time,

if pan appears dry. Stir in basil and half the tomatoes. Cook, stirring often, just until tomatoes are soft (about 3 minutes). Remove from heat and let cool slightly.

3. Transfer onion mixture to a food processor or blender; whirl until smoothly puréed. Return purée to pan and add beans, broth, and vinegar. Bring to a boil over medium-high heat; then reduce heat, cover, and simmer for 15 minutes.

4. Stir croutons into bean stew; spoon stew into individual bowls. Sprinkle remaining tomatoes around edge of each bowl. Sprinkle with cheese and serve at once. Makes 4 servings.

....

Per serving: 505 calories (12% calories from fat), 7 g total fat, 2 g saturated fat, 4 mg cholesterol, 1,716 mg sodium, 89 g carbohydrates, 25 g fiber, 25 g protein, 260 mg calcium, 7 mg iron

Sure to become a family favorite, this layered eggplant-tomato casserole is a satisfying choice for casual company meals as well.

....

3 large egg whites

3 tablespoons (45 ml) Marsala

1 cup (100 g) fine dry bread crumbs

½ cup (40 g) shredded Parmesan cheese

1 tablespoon chopped fresh thyme or ½ teaspoon dried thyme

½ teaspoon salt

2 medium-size eggplants (about 2 lbs./905 g *total*)

¼ cup (35 g) yellow cornmeal

¾ cup (180 ml) nonfat sour cream

2 cloves garlic, peeled

2 teaspoons cornstarch

1 teaspoon honey

3 cans (about 14½ oz./410 g *each*) diced tomatoes, drained well

1 tablespoon chopped fresh basil or ½ teaspoon dried basil

2 large tomatoes (about 1 lb./455 g *total*), very thinly sliced

1 cup (about 4 oz./115 g) shredded mozzarella cheese

Thyme sprigs

Eggplant Parmesan

....

Preparation time: 30 minutes
Cooking time: About 1 hour
Pictured on facing page

1. In a wide, shallow bowl, beat egg whites and Marsala to blend. In another wide, shallow bowl, combine bread crumbs, ¼ cup (20 g) of the Parmesan cheese, chopped thyme, and salt; set aside.

2. Cut unpeeled eggplants crosswise into slices about ¼ inch (6 mm) thick. Dip slices in egg white mixture; drain briefly, then dip in crumb mixture and press to coat lightly all over. Arrange eggplant slices on 2 or 3 greased large baking sheets; pat any remaining crumb mixture on slices.

3. Bake in a 400°F (205°C) oven, turning once, until golden brown on both sides (about 30 minutes); switch positions of baking sheets halfway through baking. If any slices begin to brown excessively, remove them and set aside.

4. Meanwhile, sprinkle cornmeal over bottom of a greased 9- by 13-inch (23- by 33-cm) baking pan; set aside. In a food processor or blender, whirl sour cream, garlic, cornstarch, honey, and two-thirds of the canned tomatoes until smoothly puréed. Stir in remaining canned tomatoes and basil.

5. Spoon a third of the tomato sauce over cornmeal in pan; top evenly with a third of the tomato slices. Arrange half the eggplant slices over tomatoes; sprinkle with half the mozzarella cheese. Top evenly with half each of the remaining tomato sauce and tomato slices, then with remaining eggplant. Top with remaining tomato sauce, tomato slices, and mozzarella cheese. Sprinkle with remaining ¼ cup (20 g) Parmesan cheese.

6. Cover and bake in a 400°F (205°C) oven for 15 minutes. Then uncover and continue to bake until sauce is bubbly and casserole is golden on top and hot in center (15 to 20 more minutes). Garnish with thyme sprigs. Makes 6 servings.

....

Per serving: 337 calories (27% calories from fat), 10 g total fat, 4 g saturated fat, 20 mg cholesterol, 938 mg sodium, 44 g carbohydrates, 6 g fiber, 17 g protein, 390 mg calcium, 4 mg iron

Eggplant Parmesan
(recipe on facing page)

Pesto

Originating in Genoa, pesto is an uncooked sauce featuring a variety of crushed or chopped ingredients. On this page, you'll find several versions, including the familiar basil pesto as well as a few more innovative choices.

Though pesto tends to derive over 30% of its calories from fat, it still fits into lean menus. Just use it sparingly, in combination with low-fat ingredients such as pasta, cooked vegetables, or even warm breadsticks.

If you make pesto in advance, cover and chill it, then use within 4 hours. After that, it may darken and (if made with garlic) taste too strongly garlicky.

Basil Pesto

Preparation time: 10 minutes

- 2 cups (80 g) lightly packed fresh basil leaves
- ½ cup (40 g) grated Parmesan cheese
- ⅓ cup (80 ml) olive oil
- ¼ cup (31 g) walnut pieces
- 2 cloves garlic, peeled

1. In a food processor or blender, whirl basil, cheese, oil, walnuts, and garlic until smoothly puréed. Makes about 1 cup (240 ml).

Per tablespoon: 69 calories (80% calories from fat), 6 g total fat, 1 g saturated fat, 2 mg cholesterol, 48 mg sodium, 2 g carbohydrates, 0.1 g fiber, 2 g protein, 84 mg calcium, 1 mg iron

Mixed Herb Pesto

Preparation time: 15 minutes

- 2 cups (80 g) lightly packed fresh basil leaves
- ½ cup (50 g) thinly sliced green onions
- ⅓ cup (15 g) lightly packed fresh oregano leaves
- ¼ cup (20 g) grated Parmesan cheese
- ¼ cup (60 ml) red wine vinegar
- 2 tablespoons fresh rosemary leaves
- 2 tablespoons (30 ml) olive oil
- ¼ to ½ teaspoon pepper

1. In a food processor or blender, whirl basil, onions, oregano, cheese, vinegar, rosemary, oil, and pepper until smoothly puréed. Makes about 1 cup (240 ml).

Per tablespoon: 29 calories (62% calories from fat), 2 g total fat, 0.5 g saturated fat, 1 mg cholesterol, 25 mg sodium, 2 g carbohydrates, 0.1 g fiber, 0.9 g protein, 74 mg calcium, 1 mg iron

Mint Pesto

Preparation time: 10 minutes
Cooking time: About 3 minutes

- ½ cup (65 g) pine nuts
- 1 cup (40 g) lightly packed fresh mint leaves
- 3 cloves garlic, peeled
- 3 tablespoons (45 ml) olive oil
- ¼ cup (20 g) grated Parmesan cheese

1. Stir pine nuts in a wide frying pan over medium heat until golden (about 3 minutes). Pour into a food processor or blender; let cool slightly.

2. To pine nuts, add mint, garlic, oil, and cheese. Whirl until smoothly puréed. Makes about ¾ cup (180 ml).

Per tablespoon: 71 calories (81% calories from fat), 7 g total fat, 1 g saturated fat, 1 mg cholesterol, 31 mg sodium, 1 g carbohydrates, 0.7 g fiber, 2 g protein, 29 mg calcium, 0.8 mg iron

Red Pepper Pesto

Preparation time: 10 minutes

- 1 jar (12 oz./340 g) roasted red peppers, drained, patted dry
- 1 cup (40 g) lightly packed fresh basil leaves
- 1 clove garlic, peeled
- ⅓ cup (30 g) grated Parmesan cheese

Salt and pepper

1. In a food processor or blender, whirl peppers, basil, garlic, and cheese until basil is finely chopped. Season to taste with salt and pepper. Makes about 1½ cups (360 ml).

Per tablespoon: 14 calories (25% calories from fat), 0.4 g total fat, 0.2 g saturated fat, 0.9 mg cholesterol, 51 mg sodium, 2 g carbohydrates, 0 g fiber, 0.7 g protein, 47 mg calcium, 0.8 mg iron

Pistachio Pesto

Preparation time: 15 minutes

- ¼ cup (30 g) shelled salted roasted pistachio nuts
- 1 cup (60 g) firmly packed Italian or regular parsley sprigs
- ¼ cup (60 ml) white wine vinegar
- ¼ cup (60 ml) canned vegetable broth
- 2 tablespoons (30 ml) olive oil

1. In a food processor or blender, whirl pistachios, parsley, vinegar, broth, and oil until smoothly puréed. Makes about ¾ cup (180 ml).

Per tablespoon: 40 calories (77% calories from fat), 4 g total fat, 0.5 g saturated fat, 0 mg cholesterol, 36 mg sodium, 2 g carbohydrates, 0.4 g fiber, 0.8 g protein, 17 mg calcium, 0.8 mg iron

This tempting casserole will remind you of a savory bread pudding. While it bakes, prepare a sweet-tart relish of dried figs, dried cranberries, and fresh pears to serve alongside.

1 package (about 10 oz./285 g) frozen chopped spinach, thawed and squeezed dry

3 large eggs

4 large egg whites

2 tablespoons cornstarch

2 cloves garlic, peeled

1½ teaspoons *each* chopped fresh oregano, fresh marjoram, and fresh sage; or ½ teaspoon *each* dried oregano, dried marjoram, and dried rubbed sage

2 cups (470 ml) half-and-half

8 slices egg or whole wheat sandwich bread (about 8 oz./ 230 g *total*), torn into large pieces

¾ cup (85 g) shredded fontina or mozzarella cheese

1 large firm-ripe pear such as Anjou or Bartlett (about 8 oz./ 230 g), peeled, cored, and finely chopped

⅓ cup (73 g) firmly packed brown sugar

⅓ cup (80 ml) red wine vinegar

Spinach Torta with Fig Relish

Preparation time: 30 minutes
Cooking time: About 1½ hours

1½ cups dried figs (about 8 oz./ 230 g), stems removed and fruit quartered

¾ cup (68 g) dried cranberries or raisins

¾ cup (180 ml) canned vegetable broth

⅛ teaspoon *each* pepper, ground cinnamon, and ground nutmeg

2 teaspoons Marsala (or to taste)

¼ cup (25 g) thinly sliced green onions

1. In a food processor or blender, combine spinach, eggs, egg whites, cornstarch, garlic, oregano, marjoram, and sage. Whirl until smoothly puréed. Transfer to a large bowl and whisk in half-and-half. Add bread and cheese; mix gently but thoroughly. Let stand until bread is softened (about 5 minutes), stirring occasionally.

2. Transfer mixture to an 8-inch-square (20-cm-square) nonstick or greased regular baking pan. Set pan in a larger baking pan; then set on center rack of a 325°F (165°C) oven. Pour boiling water into larger pan up to level of spinach mixture. Bake until top of torta is golden brown and center no longer jiggles when pan is gently shaken (about 1 hour and 35 minutes).

3. Meanwhile, in a wide nonstick frying pan, mix pear, sugar, and vinegar. Add figs, cranberries, broth, pepper, cinnamon, and nutmeg. Bring to a boil over medium-high heat. Then cook, uncovered, stirring often, until almost all liquid has evaporated (about 20 minutes); as mixture thickens, watch carefully and stir more often to prevent scorching. Remove pan from heat and stir in Marsala and onions.

4. To serve, spoon torta from pan; offer fig relish alongside. Makes 6 servings.

Per serving: 549 calories (30% calories from fat), 19 g total fat, 10 g saturated fat, 172 mg cholesterol, 570 mg sodium, 79 g carbohydrates, 6 g fiber, 18 g protein, 338 mg calcium, 4 mg iron

Fettuccine Alfredo
(recipe on facing page)

Fettuccine Alfredo

Alfredo aficionados will enjoy this variation on an Italian classic. Artichoke hearts enhance the tender pasta and its creamy two-cheese sauce.

Preparation time: 15 minutes
Cooking time: About 25 minutes
Pictured on facing page

2 cans (about 14 oz./400 g *each*) artichoke hearts packed in water, drained and quartered

3 tablespoons chopped Italian or regular parsley

3 tablespoons thinly sliced green onions

12 ounces (340 g) dried fettuccine

1 tablespoon butter or olive oil

3 cloves garlic, minced

1 tablespoon all-purpose flour

1½ cups (360 ml) low-fat (2%) milk

1 large package (about 8 oz./230 g) nonfat cream cheese, cut into small chunks

1½ cups (about 4½ oz./130 g) shredded Parmesan cheese

⅛ teaspoon ground nutmeg (optional)

Pepper

1. In a medium-size bowl, combine artichokes, parsley, and onions. Set aside.

2. In a 5- to 6-quart (5- to 6-liter) pan, bring about 3 quarts (2.8 liters) water to a boil over medium-high heat; stir in pasta and cook until just tender to bite, 8 to 10 minutes. (Or cook pasta according to package directions.) Drain well, return to pan, and keep hot.

3. Melt butter in a wide nonstick frying pan over medium heat. Add garlic and cook, stirring, until fragrant (about 30 seconds; do not scorch). Whisk in flour until well blended, then gradually whisk in milk. Cook, whisking constantly, until mixture boils and thickens slightly (about 5 minutes). Whisk in cream cheese, 1 cup (about 3 oz./85 g) of the Parmesan cheese, and nutmeg (if desired). Continue to cook, whisking constantly, until cheese is melted and evenly blended into sauce.

4. Working quickly, pour hot sauce over pasta and lift with 2 forks to mix. Spoon pasta into center of 4 shallow individual bowls. Then quickly arrange artichoke mixture around pasta. Sprinkle with remaining ½ cup (40 g) Parmesan cheese, then with pepper. Serve immediately (sauce thickens rapidly and is absorbed quickly by pasta). Makes 4 servings.

Per serving: 641 calories (24% calories from fat), 17 g total fat, 9 g saturated fat, 126 mg cholesterol, 924 mg sodium, 82 g carbohydrates, 4 g fiber, 39 g protein, 753 mg calcium, 6 mg iron

Linguine with Lentils

Simmered in herb-seasoned broth, nutritious lentils make a great topping for linguine.

Preparation time: 20 minutes
Cooking time: About 35 minutes

1 cup (190 g) lentils

2 cups (470 ml) canned vegetable broth

1 teaspoon dried thyme

⅓ cup (80 ml) lemon juice

3 tablespoons chopped fresh basil

2 tablespoons (30 ml) olive oil

1 teaspoon honey (or to taste)

2 cloves garlic, minced

12 ounces (340 g) dried linguine

1 large tomato (about 8 oz./230 g), chopped and drained

¾ cup (60 g) grated Parmesan cheese

1. Rinse and sort lentils, discarding any debris; drain lentils. In a 1½- to 2-quart (1.4- to 1.9-liter) pan, bring broth to a boil over high heat; add lentils and thyme. Reduce heat, cover, and simmer just until lentils are tender to bite (25 to 30 minutes). Drain and discard any remaining cooking liquid; keep lentils warm.

2. While lentils are cooking, combine lemon juice, chopped basil, oil, honey, and garlic in a small bowl; set aside. Also bring about 3 quarts (2.8 liters) water to a boil in a 5- to 6-quart (5- to 6-liter) pan over medium-high heat; stir in pasta and cook until just tender to bite, 8 to 10 minutes. (Or cook pasta according to package directions.)

3. Working quickly, drain pasta well and transfer to a large serving bowl. Add basil mixture, lentils, and tomato. Lift with 2 forks to mix. Sprinkle with cheese and serve immediately. Makes 6 servings.

Per serving: 426 calories (19% calories from fat), 9 g total fat, 3 g saturated fat, 8 mg cholesterol, 531 mg sodium, 66 g carbohydrates, 5 g fiber, 21 g protein, 185 g calcium, 6 mg iron

Pungent, mildly bitter greens and butter-toasted pine nuts combine with tender-firm pasta for a satisfying supper dish. Use any favorite pasta shape; we like orecchiette ("little ears").

Orecchiette with Broccoli Rabe & Pine Nuts

Preparation time: 30 minutes
Cooking time: 20 to 25 minutes

- 1 **pound (455 g) broccoli rabe (rapini)**
- 12 **ounces (340 g) dried orecchiette or other medium-size pasta shapes**
- 1 **tablespoon butter**
- 1 **tablespoon (15 ml) olive oil**
- ½ **cup (85 g) finely chopped onion**
- ⅓ **cup (43 g) pine nuts**
- 1 **or 2 small fresh hot red chiles, seeded and thinly sliced**
- 4 **to 6 cloves garlic, minced or pressed**
- 1½ **cups (360 ml) canned vegetable broth**
- 3 **tablespoons chopped Italian or regular parsley**
  Salt

1. Cut off and discard any coarse stem ends from broccoli rabe; discard any bruised or yellow leaves. Rinse and drain broccoli rabe; then cut stems and leaves into 1-inch (2.5-cm) lengths. Leave flowerets whole. Place stems on a steamer rack over about 1 inch of gently boiling water. Cover and steam for 2 to 3 minutes. Add leaves and flowerets; continue to steam until stems are tender-crisp to bite (2 to 3 more minutes). Remove from rack and set aside.

2. In a 5- to 6-quart (5- to 6-liter) pan, bring about 3 quarts (2.8 liters) water to a boil over medium-high heat; stir in pasta and cook until just tender to bite, 8 to 10 minutes.

(Or cook pasta according to package directions.)

3. Meanwhile, melt butter in oil in a wide nonstick frying pan over medium heat. Add onion and pine nuts; cook, stirring often, until onion is translucent but not browned and pine nuts are light golden (about 3 minutes). Add water, 1 tablespoon (15 ml) at a time, if pan appears dry. Add chiles and garlic; cook, stirring often, until fragrant (about 30 seconds; do not scorch). Add all broccoli rabe; cook, stirring often, for 2 minutes. Stir in broth and bring to a boil over medium-high heat. Reduce heat to low and simmer for 1 minute.

4. Working quickly, drain pasta well and transfer to a large serving bowl; top with vegetable mixture. Lift with 2 forks to mix. Sprinkle with parsley; season to taste with salt. Makes 4 servings.

Per serving: 484 calories (26% calories from fat), 14 g total fat, 3 g saturated fat, 8 mg cholesterol, 473 mg sodium, 75 g carbohydrates, 7 g fiber, 18 g protein, 118 mg calcium, 7 mg iron

Great any time of day, this attractive frittata can be served straight from the pan—there's no need for a serving dish.

- **1 teaspoon olive oil**
- **½ teaspoon dried rosemary**
- **1 pound (455 g) red thin-skinned potatoes, scrubbed and cut into ¼-inch (6-mm) cubes**
- **1 small red onion (about 8 oz./ 230 g), thinly sliced and cut into 1-inch (2.5-cm) slivers**
- **4 ounces (115 g) green beans (ends trimmed), cut into 1-inch (2.5-cm) pieces**
- **⅓ cup (80 ml) canned vegetable broth**
- **1 tablespoon cornstarch**
- **¼ teaspoon salt**
- **4 large eggs**
- **4 large egg whites**
- **⅔ cup (60 g) dried cranberries**
- **½ cup (55 g) shredded part-skim mozzarella cheese**
- **1 large red bell pepper (about 8 oz./230 g), seeded and chopped**
- **⅛ teaspoon crushed red pepper flakes (or to taste)**

Potato, Green Bean & Bell Pepper Frittata

Preparation time: 25 minutes
Cooking time: About 30 minutes

1. Pour oil into a wide frying pan with an ovenproof handle. Heat oil over medium-high heat; then add rosemary and cook, stirring, just until fragrant (about 30 seconds; do not scorch). Add potatoes, onion, beans, and ½ cup (120 ml) water. Cover, reduce heat to medium, and cook, stirring occasionally, just until potatoes are tender when pierced (about 12 minutes). Add water, about ¼ cup (60 ml) at a time, if pan appears dry.

2. Meanwhile, whisk broth, cornstarch, and salt in a large bowl until smoothly blended. Add eggs and egg whites; whisk until blended. Stir in cranberries and cheese. Set aside.

3. Uncover pan and add half the bell pepper. Cook, stirring, until all liquid has evaporated from vegetable mixture. Whisk egg mixture and pour over vegetables; stir gently to combine. Reduce heat to low; cook until eggs begin to set at pan rim (about 6 minutes). Then broil about 6 inches (15 cm) below heat until frittata feels set when lightly pressed (4 to 6 minutes). Sprinkle with remaining bell pepper and red pepper flakes. Spoon from pan to serve. Makes 4 servings.

Per serving: 329 calories (23% calories from fat), 8 g total fat, 3 g saturated fat, 217 mg cholesterol, 426 mg sodium, 47 g carbohydrates, 5 g fiber, 17 g protein, 170 mg calcium, 2 mg iron

Brilliant red peppers accent this golden combination of polenta, eggs, and cream-style corn in a mildly sweet polenta crust.

- ⅔ **cup (85 g) all-purpose flour**
- 1⅓ **cups (183 g) polenta or yellow cornmeal**
- ¼ **cup (50 g) sugar**
- ½ **teaspoon salt**
- 5 **tablespoons (71 g) butter or margarine, cut into chunks**
- 1 **jar (about 7 oz./200 g) roasted red peppers, rinsed and patted dry**
- 1 **large can (about 15 oz./425 g) cream-style corn**
- ½ **cup (120 ml) nonfat sour cream**
- 1 **large egg**
- 5 **large egg whites**
- 2 **tablespoons cornstarch**
- ¼ **cup (28 g) shredded fontina or mozzarella cheese**
- 1 **tablespoon chopped fresh oregano or 1 teaspoon dried oregano**
  Oregano sprigs

Polenta Pepper Torte

Preparation time: 25 minutes
Cooking time: About 1 hour
Pictured on facing page

1. In a food processor or a large bowl, whirl or stir together flour, ⅔ cup (92 g) of the polenta, sugar, and ¼ teaspoon of the salt. Add butter and 1 tablespoon (15 ml) water; whirl or rub together with your fingers until mixture resembles coarse crumbs. If pastry is too dry, add a little more water.

2. Press pastry firmly over bottom and about 1 inch (2.5 cm) up sides of a 9-inch (23-cm) nonstick or well-greased regular cheesecake pan with a removable rim. Prick all over with a fork to prevent puffing. Bake in a 350°F (175°C) oven until crust is tinged with gold and feels slightly firmer when pressed (about 15

minutes). Let cool on a rack for 5 minutes.

3. Cut any very large pieces of red peppers into smaller pieces. Arrange peppers in baked crust. In food processor, whirl remaining ⅔ cup (92 g) polenta, corn, sour cream, egg, egg whites, cornstarch, and remaining ¼ teaspoon salt until smooth. Pour egg mixture over peppers in crust. Sprinkle with cheese.

4. Return torte to oven and bake until filling is golden and a knife inserted in center comes out clean (about 45 minutes). Let cool on a rack for about 10 minutes. To serve, sprinkle with chopped oregano and garnish with oregano sprigs. Remove pan rim; then cut torte into wedges with a very sharp knife. Makes 6 servings.

Per serving: 498 calories (28% calories from fat), 15 g total fat, 9 g saturated fat, 80 mg cholesterol, 809 mg sodium, 76 g carbohydrates, 3 g fiber, 14 g protein, 65 mg calcium, 3 mg iron

Polenta Pepper Torte
(recipe on facing page)

Polenta Berry Muffins

Preparation time: 15 minutes
Cooking time: 20 to 25 minutes

- 1 cup (125 g) all-purpose flour
- 1 cup (138 g) polenta or yellow cornmeal
- 2 tablespoons sugar
- 1 teaspoon baking powder
- ¼ teaspoon salt
- 1 large egg
- 1 cup (240 ml) low-fat (2%) milk
- 1 tablespoon butter or margarine, melted
- 1 cup (123 g) fresh raspberries or blueberries

1. In a large bowl, stir together flour, polenta, sugar, baking powder, and salt. In a medium-size bowl, beat egg, milk, and butter to blend. Add egg mixture to flour mixture; stir just until dry ingredients are evenly moistened. Gently mix in berries.

2. Spoon batter equally into 12 lightly oiled 2½-inch (6-cm) nonstick or regular muffin cups. Bake in a 425°F (220°C) oven until muffins are brown (20 to 25 minutes). Let cool in pans on a rack for about 5 minutes, then turn out of pans and serve warm. Makes 12 muffins.

Per muffin: 123 calories (19% calories from fat), 3 g total fat, 1 g saturated fat, 22 mg cholesterol, 111 mg sodium, 21 g carbohydrates, 1 g fiber, 3 g protein, 54 mg calcium, 1 mg iron

Mushroom, Ham & Cheese Calzones

Preparation time: 25 minutes
Cooking time: About 35 minutes

- 5 to 6 ounces (140 to 170 g) mushrooms, sliced
- 1 very large onion (about 10 oz./285 g), thinly sliced
- 2 cloves garlic, minced
- 2 tablespoons minced fresh basil or 2 teaspoons dried basil
- ½ cup (120 ml) fat-free reduced-sodium chicken broth
- 1 tablespoon all-purpose flour
- 2 cups (280 g) chopped cooked ham
- 1 loaf (about 1 lb./455 g) frozen white bread dough, thawed
- ¾ cup (85 g) shredded fontina cheese
- 1 large egg yolk beaten with 1 tablespoon (15 ml) water

1. In a wide frying pan, combine mushrooms, onion, garlic, basil, and ¼ cup (60 ml) of the broth. Cook over medium-high heat, stirring often, until vegetables brown and begin to stick to pan bottom (about 8 minutes). To deglaze pan, stir in remaining ¼ cup (60 ml) broth and stir to scrape browned bits free from pan bottom. Continue to cook, stirring, until almost all liquid has evaporated. Stir in flour and ham; remove from heat.

2. On a lightly floured board, divide dough into 4 equal pieces; shape each into a ball. To shape each calzone, roll one ball into a 5- to 6-inch (12.5- to 15-cm) round; then flatten it with your hands until it is 7 to 8 inches (18 to 20 cm) in diameter.

3. Spoon a fourth of the ham filling over half each round, spreading it to within ½ inch (1 cm) of edge. Sprinkle filling with a fourth of the cheese. Brush edge of dough round with water; fold plain half of round over filling and press edges firmly together to seal. With a fork, prick top several times.

4. Transfer calzones to a lightly oiled 12- by 15-inch (30- by 38-cm) baking sheet. Brush with egg yolk mixture. Bake in a 425°F (220°C) oven until richly browned (about 20 minutes). Let cool slightly before serving. Makes 4 servings.

Per serving: 571 calories (30% calories from fat), 19 g total fat, 7 g saturated fat, 12 mg cholesterol, 1,656 mg sodium, 67 g carbohydrates, 2 g fiber, 32 g protein, 201 mg calcium, 4 mg iron

Breakfast Bruschetta

Preparation time: 20 minutes
Cooking time: About 5 minutes

- ¼ cup (25 g) chopped dried apricots
- 3 tablespoons (45 ml) fresh orange juice
- 8 slices crusty bread, such as Italian ciabatta or French bread (about 8 oz./230 g *total*)
- 2 cups (246 g) mixed fresh berries, such as raspberries, blueberries, and blackberries
- 1 tablespoon chopped fresh mint
  About 1 teaspoon sugar (or to taste)
- 1 cup (about 8 oz./230 g) nonfat ricotta cheese
- 3 tablespoons (45 ml) honey
- ½ teaspoon ground coriander

1. In a small bowl, soak apricots in orange juice until soft (about 10 minutes), stirring occasionally.

2. Meanwhile, arrange bread slices slightly apart in a shallow 10- by 15-inch (25- by 38-cm) baking pan. Broil about 6 inches (15 cm) below heat,

turning once, until golden on both sides (about 5 minutes). Let cool on a rack.

3. In a medium-size bowl, combine berries, mint, and sugar; mix gently and set aside. In a food processor or blender, combine apricot mixture, ricotta cheese, honey, and coriander; whirl until smoothly blended.

4. Top toast slices equally with ricotta mixture, then berries. Makes 4 servings.

Per serving: 322 calories (6% calories from fat), 2 g total fat, 0.5 g saturated fat, 5 mg cholesterol, 389 mg sodium, 62 g carbohydrates, 5 g fiber, 15 g protein, 357 mg calcium, 2 mg iron

Ricotta Pancakes with Lemon-Maple Syrup

Preparation time: 20 minutes
Cooking time: 10 to 15 minutes

½ **cup (120 ml) pure maple syrup**

½ **teaspoon grated lemon peel**

1 **teaspoon lemon juice**

2 **large eggs**

⅔ **cup (152 g) nonfat ricotta cheese**

¼ **cup (50 g) sugar**

¼ **cup (60 ml) half-and-half**

1 **teaspoon vanilla**

½ **cup (60 g) all-purpose flour**

¼ **teaspoon baking powder**

2 **large egg whites**

¼ **teaspoon cream of tartar**

⅛ **teaspoon salt**

2 **tablespoons (30 ml) salad oil**

1. In a small pan, combine syrup, ¼ teaspoon of the lemon peel, and lemon juice. Stir over medium heat until steaming (3 to 5 minutes); keep warm over very low heat.

2. In a food processor or blender, combine eggs, ricotta cheese, 2 tablespoons of the sugar, half-and-half, vanilla, and remaining ¼ teaspoon lemon peel; whirl until smooth. Add flour and baking powder; whirl until flour is evenly moistened. Transfer batter to a medium-size bowl.

3. In a large, deep bowl, beat egg whites and 1 tablespoon (15 ml) water with an electric mixer on high speed until frothy. Beat in cream of tartar and salt. Add remaining 2 tablespoons sugar, 1 tablespoon at a time, beating until mixture holds stiff, moist peaks. Stir about a third of the egg white mixture into batter to lighten it; then fold batter into remaining egg white mixture.

4. Heat 1 tablespoon (15 ml) of the oil on each of 2 nonstick griddles over medium heat (or heat oil in wide nonstick frying pans). For each pancake, measure out ⅓ cup (80 ml) batter, scooping it up from bottom of bowl; pour onto griddle and spread out slightly. Cook until tops of pancakes are bubbly and almost dry (2 to 3 minutes); turn over and cook until browned on bottoms (about 2 more minutes). Serve with warm syrup. Makes about 12 pancakes (4 servings).

Per serving: 379 calories (27% calories from fat), 11 g total fat, 3 g saturated fat, 115 mg cholesterol, 209 mg sodium, 56 g carbohydrates, 0.4 g fiber, 14 g protein, 289 mg calcium, 2 mg iron

Orange Polenta Cakes

Preparation time: 20 minutes
Cooking time: About 20 minutes

½ **teaspoon grated orange peel**

2½ **cups (590 ml) fresh orange juice**

½ **teaspoon salt**

1 **cup (138 g) polenta or yellow cornmeal**

2 **tablespoons butter or margarine**

About ¼ cup (60 ml) honey

½ **cup (60 g) slivered almonds**

1½ **cups (360 ml) plain nonfat yogurt**

About 2 cups (330 g) sliced fresh fruit

1. In a 2- to 2½-quart (1.9- to 2.4-liter) pan, bring orange peel, orange juice, and salt to a boil over medium-high heat.

Gradually add polenta, stirring until blended. Reduce heat and boil gently, uncovered, stirring often and scraping bottom of pan with a long-handled spoon (mixture will spatter), until polenta is thick (about 10 minutes). Reduce heat to low; continue to stir until polenta stops flowing after spoon is drawn across pan bottom (3 to 5 more minutes). Stir in butter and ¼ cup (60 ml) of the honey.

2. Divide hot polenta among 4 greased ¾-cup (180-ml) custard cups; with the back of a spoon, press polenta solidly into cups. Let cool for at least 5 minutes or up to 30 minutes.

3. Meanwhile, toast almonds in a wide frying pan over medium heat until golden (about 3 minutes), stirring often. Pour out of pan and set aside. Sweeten yogurt to taste with honey.

4. To serve, run a knife around edge of each cup; invert polenta cakes onto individual plates. Sprinkle cakes with almonds; accompany with sweetened yogurt and fruit. Makes 4 servings.

Per serving: 522 calories (26% calories from fat), 16 g total fat, 5 g saturated fat, 17 mg cholesterol, 402 mg sodium, 87 g carbohydrates, 5 g fiber, 13 g protein, 258 mg calcium, 3 mg iron

Tiramisu
(recipe on page 612)

Desserts

Indulge yourself—enjoy one of our low-fat desserts! Espresso Cheesecake, Pistachio Ice Cream, and Amaretto Soufflé are all as rich and sweet as you could wish, perfect conclusions to your lean Italian meals. For other fitting finales, try our fruit specialties, from simple poached pears to an apricot-studded almond torte to an unusual tart filled with tender sliced apples, currants, and fennel.

•

A perfect partner for hot coffee at any time of day, popular tiramisu features a filling of sweet, creamy cheese spooned over ladyfingers soaked in brandy and espresso. Garnish the dessert with chocolate curls and a dusting of cocoa before serving.

Tiramisu

Preparation time: 25 minutes
Cooking time: About 5 minutes
Chilling time: At least 3 hours
Pictured on page 610

- 20 ladyfingers (about 5 oz./140 g total)
- ⅔ cup (67 g) sifted powdered sugar
- 6 ounces (170 g) nonfat cream cheese, at room temperature
- 2 ounces (55 g) mascarpone cheese, at room temperature
- 2 cups (470 ml) frozen reduced-calorie whipped topping, thawed
- 9 tablespoons (108 g) granulated sugar
- 3 large egg whites
- ¼ teaspoon cream of tartar
- 1 tablespoon instant espresso powder
- 2 tablespoons (30 ml) brandy, coffee-flavored liqueur, or orange juice
- About 2 tablespoons unsweetened cocoa powder
- Semisweet chocolate curls

1. Split ladyfingers into halves. Arrange half the ladyfinger halves, cut side up, over bottom of an 8-inch-square (20-cm-square) dish or pan; overlap ladyfingers as needed to fit. Set aside.

2. In a food processor or a large bowl, combine powdered sugar, cream cheese, and mascarpone cheese. Whirl or beat with an electric mixer until smooth. Gently fold in 1 cup (240 ml) of the whipped topping; cover and refrigerate.

3. In a large metal bowl, combine ½ cup (100 g) of the granulated sugar, ¼ cup (60 ml) water, egg whites, and cream of tartar. Beat with an electric mixer on low speed until foamy. Nest bowl over a pan of simmering water (do not let bowl touch water) and beat on high speed until mixture holds stiff peaks. Lift bowl from pan; stir about a fourth of the egg white mixture into cheese mix-ture to lighten it, then gently but thoroughly fold in remaining egg white mixture. Set aside.

4. Working quickly, stir together ½ cup (120 ml) hot water, remaining 1 tablespoon sugar, instant espresso, and brandy in a small bowl. Drizzle half the hot espresso mixture even-ly over ladyfingers in dish. Top with half the cheese mixture, spreading mixture level. Top with remaining ladyfinger halves (cut side up), espresso mixture, and cheese mix-ture. Cover with remaining 1 cup (240 ml) whipped topping and smooth top.

5. Cover dessert airtight (do not let cover touch topping) and refrigerate until cold (at least 3 hours) or until next day. Spoon out of dish or cut to serve. Sift cocoa over individual servings and garnish with chocolate curls. Makes 8 servings.

Per serving: 261 calories (25% calories from fat), 7 g total fat, 3 g saturated fat, 77 mg cholesterol, 153 mg sodium, 40 g carbohy-drates, 0.3 g fiber, 7 g protein, 71 mg calcium, 0.8 mg iron

Filled with smooth, luscious hazelnut spread and topped with chocolate–cream cheese frosting, this fancy dessert gets a quick start with a purchased loaf cake.

....

2 tablespoons hazelnuts

1 purchased nonfat chocolate loaf cake (about 15 oz./425 g)

½ cup (120 ml) purchased hazelnut-cocoa spread

1 small package (about 6 oz./ 170 g) semisweet chocolate chips

2 cups (200 g) sifted powdered sugar

1 large package (about 8 oz./ 230 g) Neufchâtel cheese, cut into chunks

½ cup (43 g) unsweetened cocoa powder

¼ cup (60 ml) nonfat sour cream

2 teaspoons vanilla

Chocolate Hazelnut Cake

....

Preparation time: 25 minutes
Cooking time: About 15 minutes
Chilling time: At least 2 hours

....

1. Toast and coarsely chop hazelnuts as directed for Espresso Biscotti (page 624). Set aside.

2. Cut cake in half horizontally. Set bottom half, cut side up, on a serving plate. Stir hazelnut-cocoa spread to soften, if necessary; then spread evenly over cake to within about ½ inch (1 cm) of edges. Place top half of cake, cut side down, over filling; press lightly.

3. Place chocolate chips in a metal bowl nested over a pan of hot (not boiling) water. Stir often until

chocolate is melted and smooth. Remove from heat and transfer to a food processor or blender; let stand for 2 to 3 minutes to cool slightly. Add powdered sugar, Neufchâtel cheese, cocoa, sour cream, and vanilla; whirl until smooth, scraping sides of container often. Let frosting cool slightly; it should be spreadable, but not too soft.

4. Generously spread frosting over sides and top of cake. Cover cake with a cake cover or an inverted bowl (don't let cover touch frosting); refrigerate until cold (at least 2 hours) or until next day. Sprinkle with hazelnuts, pressing them lightly into frosting. Cut into slices to serve. Makes 10 servings.

....

Per serving: 401 calories (29% calories from fat), 13 g total fat, 6 g saturated fat, 11 mg cholesterol, 324 mg sodium, 67 g carbohydrates, 2 g fiber, 7 g protein, 66 mg calcium, 2 mg iron

---

A touch of olive oil enriches this easy make-ahead dough. Serve the delicate anise-flavored cookies with milk, coffee, or sweet dessert wine.

....

About 2 cups (200 g) sifted powdered sugar

1 cup (125 g) all-purpose flour

1 teaspoon baking powder

¼ teaspoon ground cinnamon

1 tablespoon (15 ml) olive oil

1 large egg, beaten

2 tablespoons (30 ml) anisette liqueur; or 1 teaspoon anise extract (or to taste) blended with 5 teaspoons (25 ml) water

1 teaspoon vanilla

Anise Poofs

....

Preparation time: 25 minutes
Standing time: 8 to 24 hours
Cooking time: About 8 minutes

....

1. In a large bowl, stir together 2 cups (200 g) of the powdered sugar, flour, baking powder, and cinnamon. Add oil, egg, liqueur, and vanilla; stir until well blended. Turn dough out onto a board lightly dusted with powdered sugar; knead until smooth, about 4 turns.

2. Cut dough into 6 pieces. Roll each piece into a rope 20 inches

(50 cm) long and about ½ inch (1 cm) wide. Cut each rope into 2-inch (5-cm) lengths. Place pieces about 1½ inches (3.5 cm) apart on lightly oiled large baking sheets. Let cookies stand, uncovered, for 8 to 24 hours. (*Do not* omit standing time; if dough does not stand, cookies will not puff.) Then bake in a 325°F (165°C) oven until pale golden (about 8 minutes). Immediately transfer cookies to racks and let cool. Makes 5 dozen cookies.

....

Per cookie: 27 calories (18% calories from fat), 0.5 g total fat, 0.1 g saturated fat, 4 mg cholesterol, 9 mg sodium, 5 g carbohydrates, 0 g fiber, 0.3 g protein, 5 mg calcium, 0.1 mg iron

Tender almond-flavored cake studded with sliced fresh apricots makes a pretty company dessert. Serve it with a silky, orange-accented apricot sauce.

Apricot-Amaretto Torte

Preparation time: 25 minutes
Cooking time: About 25 minutes
Pictured on facing page

- 1 tablespoon (15 ml) lemon juice
- 5 medium-size apricots (about 1 lb./455 g *total*)
- ¼ cup (30 g) slivered almonds
- 2 large eggs
- 1 cup (200 g) sugar
- 4 to 5 tablespoons (60 to 75 ml) almond-flavored liqueur
- ½ teaspoon almond extract
- ¾ cup (95 g) all-purpose flour
- 2 teaspoons baking powder
- ⅛ teaspoon salt
- ¼ cup (55 g) butter or margarine, melted and cooled slightly
- 4 teaspoons cornstarch
- 1 cup (240 ml) apricot nectar
- ½ cup (120 ml) fresh orange juice
- ½ teaspoon vanilla

1. Pour lemon juice into a medium-size bowl. Quarter and pit apricots; add to bowl and turn to coat with juice. Set aside.

2. In a food processor, whirl almonds until finely ground. (Or finely chop almonds with a knife, then place in a large bowl.) To almonds, add eggs, ½ cup (100 g) of the sugar, 1 tablespoon (15 ml) of the liqueur, and almond extract; whirl or beat with an electric mixer until thick and well blended. Add flour, baking powder, salt, and butter; whirl or beat until well blended. Spread batter in a greased, floured 9-inch (23-cm) cake pan with a removable rim. Decoratively arrange apricots in batter, overlap-ping as needed; press fruit lightly into batter.

3. Bake in a 375°F (190°C) oven until cake just begins to pull away from side of pan and a wooden pick inserted in center comes out clean (about 25 minutes; pierce cake, not fruit). Let cool slightly on a rack.

4. While cake is cooling, stir together cornstarch and 6 tablespoons (72 g) of the sugar in a small pan. Whisk in apricot nectar and orange juice; cook over medium-high heat, whisking constantly, until mixture boils and thickens slightly (about 2 minutes). Remove from heat and stir in vanilla and remaining 3 to 4 tablespoons (45 to 60 ml) liqueur; keep warm.

5. Sprinkle cake with remaining 2 tablespoons sugar. Remove pan rim and cut cake into wedges; serve with apricot-orange sauce. Makes 8 servings.

Per serving: 340 calories (28% calories from fat), 10 g total fat, 4 g saturated fat, 69 mg cholesterol, 240 mg sodium, 54 g carbohydrates, 1 g fiber, 5 g protein, 100 mg calcium, 1 mg iron

Apricot-Amaretto Torte
(recipe on facing page)

Lemon Poppy Seed Biscotti

Preparation time: 25 minutes
Cooking time: About 25 minutes

- 5 tablespoons (71 g) butter or margarine, at room temperature
- ½ cup (100 g) granulated sugar
- 2 teaspoons grated lemon peel
- 2 large eggs
- 1 teaspoon vanilla
- 2 tablespoons poppy seeds
- 2 cups (250 g) all-purpose flour
- 2 teaspoons baking powder
- 1½ cups (150 g) sifted powdered sugar
- About 5 teaspoons (25 ml) lemon juice

1. In a large bowl, beat butter, granulated sugar, and 1½ teaspoons of the lemon peel until well blended. Add eggs, one at a time, beating well after each addition. Stir in vanilla; then mix in poppy seeds. In a medium-size bowl, stir together flour and baking powder; add to butter mixture and stir until well blended.

2. Divide dough in half. On a lightly floured board, shape each portion into a long roll about 1½ inches (3.5 cm) in diameter. Place rolls on a large nonstick or greased regular baking sheet, spacing them 3 inches (8 cm) apart. Flatten rolls to make ½-inch-thick (1-cm-thick) loaves. Bake in a 350°F (175°C) oven until loaves feel firm to the touch (about 15 minutes).

3. Remove baking sheet from oven and let loaves cool for 3 to 5 minutes; then cut crosswise into slices about ½ inch (1 cm) thick. Tip slices cut side down on baking sheet (at this point, you may need another sheet to bake biscotti all at once). Return to oven and continue to bake until biscotti look dry and are lightly browned (about 10 minutes); if using 2 baking sheets, switch their positions halfway through baking. Transfer biscotti to racks and let cool.

4. Meanwhile, in a small bowl, combine powdered sugar, remaining ½ teaspoon lemon peel, and 5 teaspoons (25 ml) of the lemon juice; stir until icing is easy to spread, adding a little more lemon juice as needed.

5. Spread icing over about 1½ inches (3.5 cm) of one end of each cooled cookie. Let stand until icing is firm before serving. Makes about 3½ dozen cookies.

Per cookie: 66 calories (28% calories from fat), 2 g total fat, 1 g saturated fat, 14 mg cholesterol, 43 mg sodium, 11 g carbohydrates, 0.2 g fiber, 1 g protein, 22 mg calcium, 0.3 mg iron

Cornmeal–Pine Nut Biscotti

Preparation time: 30 minutes
Cooking time: About 35 minutes

- 2 tablespoons butter or margarine, at room temperature
- ¼ cup (50 g) sugar
- 1 teaspoon fennel seeds
- 2 teaspoons dry sherry or water
- 2 large egg whites
- ¾ cup (95 g) all-purpose flour
- ⅓ cup (45 g) yellow cornmeal
- 1 tablespoon cornstarch
- ½ teaspoon baking powder
- 2 to 3 tablespoons pine nuts

1. In a large bowl, beat butter, sugar, fennel seeds, and sherry until well blended. Add egg whites and beat until well blended. In a small bowl, stir together flour, cornmeal, cornstarch, and baking powder; add to butter mixture and stir until well blended. Mix in pine nuts. Dough will be soft.

2. Scrape dough out onto a large nonstick or greased regular baking sheet. With heavily floured fingers, shape dough into a loaf about 15 inches (38 cm) long and 1½ inches (3.5 cm) in diameter. Bake in a 375°F (190°C) oven until loaf feels firm to the touch (about 20 minutes).

3. Remove baking sheet from oven and let loaf cool for 3 to 5 minutes; then cut crosswise into slices about ½ inch (1 cm) thick. Tip slices cut side down on baking sheet (at this point, you may need another sheet to bake biscotti all at once).

4. Reduce oven temperature to 350°F (175°C). Return baking sheet(s) to oven and continue to bake until biscotti look dry and are lightly browned (about 15 minutes); if using 2 baking sheets, switch their positions halfway through baking. Transfer biscotti to racks and let cool. Makes about 2 dozen cookies.

Per cookie: 46 calories (29% calories from fat), 1 g total fat, 0.7 g saturated fat, 3 mg cholesterol, 25 mg sodium, 7 g carbohydrates, 0.3 g fiber, 1 g protein, 8 mg calcium, 0.4 mg iron

Anise Biscotti

Preparation time: 25 minutes
Cooking time: About 25 minutes

- 5 tablespoons (71 g) butter or margarine, at room temperature
- 11 tablespoons (132 g) sugar
- 1½ teaspoons anise seeds (or to taste)
- 2 large eggs
- 2 teaspoons vanilla
- 2 cups (250 g) all-purpose flour
- 2 teaspoons baking powder
- 2 large egg whites

1. In a large bowl, beat butter, ½ cup (100 g) of the sugar, and anise seeds until well blended. Add eggs, one at a time, beating well after each addition. Stir in vanilla. In a medium-size bowl, stir together flour and baking powder; add to butter mixture and stir until well blended.

2. Divide dough in half. On a lightly floured board, shape each portion into a long roll about 1½ inches (3.5 cm) in diameter. Place rolls on a large nonstick or greased regular baking sheet, spacing them 3 inches (8 cm) apart. Flatten rolls to make ½-inch-thick (1-cm-thick) loaves.

3. In a small bowl, whisk egg whites with 1 tablespoon (15 ml) water until blended; brush some of the mixture lightly over loaves. Bake in a 350°F (175°C) oven until loaves feel firm to the touch (about 15 minutes).

4. Remove baking sheet from oven and let loaves cool for 3 to 5 minutes; then cut crosswise into slices about ½ inch (1 cm) thick. Tip slices cut side down on baking sheet (at this point, you may need another sheet to bake biscotti all at once). Brush slices with remaining egg white mixture and sprinkle with remaining 3 tablespoons sugar.

5. Return to oven and bake until biscotti look dry and are lightly browned (about 10 minutes); if using 2 baking sheets, switch their positions halfway through baking. Transfer biscotti to racks and let cool. Makes about 4 dozen cookies.

Per cookie: 45 calories (29% calories from fat), 1 g total fat, 0.8 g saturated fat, 12 mg cholesterol, 38 mg sodium, 7 g carbohydrates, 0.1 g fiber, 0.9 g protein, 14 mg calcium, 0.3 mg iron

Chocolate Biscotti

Preparation time: 25 minutes
Cooking time: 35 to 40 minutes

- ¼ cup (55 g) butter or margarine, at room temperature
- ½ cup (100 g) granulated sugar
- 4 large egg whites
- 2 cups (250 g) all-purpose flour
- ⅓ cup (29 g) unsweetened cocoa powder
- 2 teaspoons baking powder
- ⅓ cup (33 g) sifted powdered sugar
- About 2 teaspoons low-fat (1%) milk

1. In a large bowl, beat butter and granulated sugar until fluffy. Add egg whites and beat until well blended. In a medium-size bowl, stir together flour, cocoa, and baking powder; add to butter mixture and stir until well blended.

2. Turn dough out onto a large nonstick or lightly greased regular baking sheet. Shape dough down length of sheet into a loaf about 2½ inches (6 cm) wide and ⅝ inch (2 cm) thick. Bake in a 350°F (175°C) oven until crusty and firm to the touch (about 20 minutes).

3. Remove baking sheet from oven and let loaf cool for 3 to 5 minutes; then cut diagonally into slices about ½ inch (1 cm) thick. Tip slices cut side down on baking sheet. Return to oven and continue to bake until biscotti feel firm and dry (15 to 20 minutes). Transfer to racks and let cool.

4. In a small bowl, stir together powdered sugar and 2 teaspoons of the milk, or enough to make a pourable icing. Using a spoon, drizzle icing decoratively over biscotti. Let stand until icing is firm before serving. Makes about 1½ dozen cookies.

Per cookie: 112 calories (25% calories from fat), 3 g total fat, 2 g saturated fat, 7 mg cholesterol, 97 mg sodium, 19 g carbohydrates, 0.8 g fiber, 3 g protein, 36 mg calcium, 0.9 mg iron

Port Ice
(recipe on facing page)

For a cooling conclusion to a special meal, serve a simple, vividly colored ice made from a blend of port wine, orange juice, and aromatic bitters.

½ cup (100 g) sugar

1 cup (240 ml) port or cream sherry

¼ cup (60 ml) fresh orange juice

1 teaspoon aromatic bitters

Port Ice

Preparation time: 10 minutes
Cooking time: About 5 minutes
Chilling & freezing time: About 5 hours
Pictured on facing page

1. In a 1- to 2-quart (950-ml to 1.9-liter) pan, combine sugar and 1½ cups (360 ml) water. Bring to a boil over high heat, stirring until sugar is dissolved. Remove from heat and let cool; then stir in port, orange juice, and bitters. Cover and refrigerate until cold (about 1 hour).

2. Pour port mixture into a metal pan 8 to 9 inches (20 to 23 cm) square; cover and freeze until solid (about 4 hours) or for up to 3 days.

3. To serve, break mixture into chunks with a heavy spoon, transfer to a blender or food processor, and whirl until slushy; then spoon into bowls and serve at once. (Or pour cold port mixture into container of a self-refrigerated ice cream machine and freeze according to manufacturer's instructions.) Makes 6 to 8 servings.

Per serving: 114 calories (0% calories from fat), 0 g total fat, 0 g saturated fat, 0 mg cholesterol, 3 mg sodium, 19 g carbohydrates, 0 g fiber, 0.1 g protein, 4 mg calcium, 0.1 mg iron

Smooth, creamy, and studded with pistachios, this easy ice cream is sure to be a family favorite.

2 jars (about 7 oz./200 g *each*) marshmallow fluff (marshmallow creme)

1 large package (about 8 oz./ 230 g) Neufchâtel cheese, at room temperature

½ cup (120 ml) low-fat buttermilk

2 teaspoons vanilla

1 large carton (about 1 lb./ 455 g) nonfat sour cream

½ cup (60 g) shelled salted roasted pistachio nuts

Pistachio Ice Cream

Preparation time: 15 minutes
Chilling time: About 1 hour
Freezing time: Depends on ice cream machine

1. In a food processor or blender, combine marshmallow fluff, Neufchâtel cheese, buttermilk, and vanilla. Whirl until smooth. Stir in sour cream.

2. Transfer mixture to a large bowl; cover and refrigerate until cold (about 1 hour) or until next day. Stir in pistachios.

3. Transfer mixture to container of a self-refrigerated ice cream machine and freeze according to manufacturer's instructions. Makes about 12 servings.

Per serving: 217 calories (30% calories from fat), 7 g total fat, 3 g saturated fat, 15 mg cholesterol, 146 mg sodium, 32 g carbohydrates, 0 g fiber, 7 g protein, 85 mg calcium, 0.5 mg iron

This refreshing ice of sweet vermouth and astringent Campari is a welcome hot-weather dessert—or an unusual starter for a special meal.

½ cup (100 g) sugar

1 cup (240 ml) sweet vermouth or fresh orange juice

2 tablespoons (30 ml) Campari or 2 teaspoons aromatic bitters

1 tablespoon (15 ml) lime juice

Thin lime slices

1. In a 1- to 2-quart (950-ml to 1.9-liter) pan, combine sugar and

Campari Ice

Preparation time: 10 minutes
Cooking time: About 5 minutes
Chilling & freezing time: About 5 hours

1½ cups (360 ml) water. Bring to a boil over high heat, stirring until sugar is dissolved. Remove from heat and let cool; then stir in vermouth, Campari, and lime juice. Cover mixture and refrigerate until cold (about 1 hour).

2. Pour mixture into a metal pan 8 to 9 inches (20 to 23 cm) square;

cover and freeze until solid (about 4 hours) or for up to 3 days.

3. To serve, break mixture into chunks with a heavy spoon, transfer to a blender or food processor, and whirl until slushy; then spoon into bowls and serve at once. (Or pour cold port mixture into container of a self-refrigerated ice cream machine and freeze according to manufacturer's instructions.) Garnish individual servings with lime slices. Makes 6 to 8 servings.

Per serving: 120 calories (0% calories from fat), 0 g total fat, 0 g saturated fat, 0 mg cholesterol, 4 mg sodium, 20 g carbohydrates, 0 g fiber, 0 g protein, 3 mg calcium, 0.1 mg iron

---

This soufflé owes its intense almond flavor to crushed amaretti cookies, amaretto liqueur, and almond extract.

½ cup (64 g) coarsely crushed amaretti cookies (about ten 1½-inch/4-cm cookies)

¾ cup (180 ml) low-fat (2%) milk

3 large egg yolks

6 tablespoons (72 g) granulated sugar

¼ cup (30 g) all-purpose flour

¼ cup (60 ml) almond-flavored or other nut-flavored liqueur

⅛ teaspoon almond extract

5 large egg whites

½ teaspoon cream of tartar

⅛ teaspoon salt

About 1 tablespoon sifted powdered sugar

1. Sprinkle crushed cookies over bottom of a greased 1½- to 1¾-quart (1.4- to 1.7-liter) soufflé dish. Place dish in a larger pan (at least 2 inches/5 cm deep); set aside.

Amaretto Soufflé

Preparation time: 25 minutes
Cooking time: About 35 minutes

2. Bring milk to a boil in a medium-size nonstick pan over medium heat (about 5 minutes), stirring often. Remove from heat and let cool slightly.

3. In a large bowl, whisk egg yolks and 3 tablespoons of the granulated sugar until thick and lemon-colored. Add flour and whisk until smoothly blended. Whisk in a little of the warm milk, then whisk egg yolk mixture back into warm milk in pan. Return to heat and stir constantly (be careful not to scratch pan) just until mixture boils and thickens slightly. Return to large bowl and whisk in liqueur and almond extract; let cool completely.

4. In a clean large, deep bowl, beat egg whites and 1 tablespoon (15 ml) water with an electric mixer on high

speed until frothy. Beat in cream of tartar and salt. Then beat in remaining 3 tablespoons granulated sugar, 1 tablespoon at a time; continue to beat until mixture holds stiff, moist peaks. Stir about a third of the egg white mixture into yolk mixture; then fold all of yolk mixture into egg white mixture.

5. Gently spoon soufflé batter into prepared dish. Set pan with dish on middle rack of a 350°F (175°C) oven. Pour boiling water into larger pan up to level of soufflé batter. Bake until soufflé is richly browned and center jiggles only slightly when dish is gently shaken (about 25 minutes); if top begins to brown excessively, carefully cover dish with foil. As soon as soufflé is done, sprinkle it with powdered sugar and serve immediately. Makes 6 servings.

Per serving: 198 calories (21% calories from fat), 4 g total fat, 1 g saturated fat, 109 mg cholesterol, 115 mg sodium, 29 g carbohydrates, 0.1 g fiber, 6 g protein, 51 mg calcium, 0.5 mg iron

Here's a lovely autumn dessert: poached whole pears served in a glistening port-citrus syrup spiced with nutmeg.

··

2 cups (470 ml) port

½ cup (100 g) sugar

1 tablespoon shredded orange peel

¼ teaspoon ground nutmeg

4 large firm-ripe pears (about 2 lbs./905 g *total*)

1 tablespoon (15 ml) lemon juice

2 teaspoons finely shredded orange peel

··

1. In a 3- to 4-quart (2.8- to 3.8-liter)

Poached Pears with Ruby Citrus Syrup

··

Preparation time: 15 minutes
Cooking time: 30 to 45 minutes

pan, combine port, sugar, the 1 tablespoon orange peel, and nutmeg. Stir over medium heat until sugar is dissolved; then bring to a boil, stirring often.

2. Add whole pears to hot syrup. Reduce heat, cover, and simmer

until pears are very tender when pierced (20 to 30 minutes), turning fruit over a few times. With a slotted spoon, transfer pears to a wide bowl or rimmed platter; set aside.

3. Bring cooking liquid to a boil over high heat; then boil, uncovered, until liquid is thickened and reduced to about ½ cup (120 ml), 10 to 12 minutes. Stir in lemon juice; then pour syrup over pears. Garnish with the 2 teaspoons orange peel. Serve warm or at room temperature. Makes 4 servings.

··

Per serving: 282 calories (3% calories from fat), 0.9 g total fat, 0.1 g saturated fat, 0 mg cholesterol, 12 mg sodium, 72 g carbohydrates, 5 g fiber, 1 g protein, 38 mg calcium, 0.8 mg iron

---

For a luxurious dessert, stir a hot froth of Marsala wine, sugar, and egg yolks into whipped topping; then spoon over poached dried fruits.

··

1 package (about 12 oz./340 g) mixed dried fruit (whole or halved fruits, not dried fruit bits)

1½ cups (360 ml) white grape juice

¼ to ½ teaspoon ground cinnamon

3 whole cloves

6 large egg yolks

3 tablespoons sugar

½ cup (120 ml) Marsala

2 cups (470 ml) frozen reduced-calorie whipped topping, thawed

··

1. Cut large pieces of fruit into bite-size chunks; set fruit aside. In a

Zabaglione Cream over Warm Fruit Compote

··

Preparation time: 15 minutes
Cooking time: About 40 minutes

medium-size pan, combine grape juice, cinnamon, and cloves; bring to a boil over high heat. Stir in fruit; then reduce heat, cover, and simmer until fruit is plump and tender when pierced (about 30 minutes). Remove from heat and keep warm.

2. In the top of a double boiler, combine egg yolks and sugar. Beat with an electric mixer on high speed or with a whisk until thick

and lemon-colored. Beat in Marsala. Set double boiler over (not in) gently simmering water; beat mixture constantly just until it is thick enough to retain a slight peak briefly when beater or whisk is withdrawn (3 to 6 minutes).

3. Working quickly, pour warm egg mixture into a large bowl. Fold in about a third of the whipped topping to lighten egg mixture; then fold in remaining whipped topping. Serve immediately.

4. To serve, lift fruit from pan with a slotted spoon and divide among six 8-ounce (240-ml) stemmed glasses; discard cooking liquid or reserve for other uses. Top with zabaglione cream. Makes 6 servings.

··

Per serving: 346 calories (22% calories from fat), 8 g total fat, 4 g saturated fat, 213 mg cholesterol, 24 mg sodium, 61 g carbohydrates, 3 g fiber, 4 g protein, 48 mg calcium, 2 mg iron

Thin fennel slices add a licorice-flavored surprise to this unusual apple tart.

½ cup (75 g) dried currants

¾ cup plus 2 teaspoons (100 g) all-purpose flour

½ cup (40 g) regular rolled oats

¼ cup (55 g) butter or margarine, cut into chunks

1 large egg white

⅓ cup (70 g) granulated sugar

1 teaspoon ground cinnamon

2 cups (220 g) sliced apples such as Newtown Pippin (cut slices ¼ inch/6 mm thick)

1½ cups (148 g) sliced fennel (cut slices ¼ inch/6 mm thick)

2 teaspoons lemon juice

About 2 tablespoons sifted powdered sugar

Apple-Fennel Tart

Preparation time: 30 minutes
Cooking time: About 1¼ hours
Pictured on facing page

1. Place currants in a small bowl and add enough water to cover. Let stand until currants are softened (about 10 minutes), stirring occasionally. Drain well; set aside.

2. In a food processor, combine ¾ cup (95 g) of the flour, oats, and butter. Whirl until mixture resembles fine crumbs. Add egg white; whirl until dough holds together. Press dough evenly over bottom and sides of an 8-inch (20-cm) tart pan with a removable rim.

3. In a large bowl, mix remaining 2 teaspoons flour, granulated sugar, cinnamon, and currants. Add apples, fennel, and lemon juice; mix well. Pour fruit mixture into pan; pat to make level.

4. Bake on lowest rack of a 425°F (220°C) oven until top of filling begins to brown (about 45 minutes). Drape tart with foil; continue to bake until juices begin to bubble (about 30 more minutes).

5. Remove pan rim; slide a wide spatula under hot tart to release crust (leave tart in place). Serve warm or cool; dust with powdered sugar before serving. Makes 6 servings.

Per serving: 268 calories (27% calories from fat), 8 g total fat, 5 g saturated fat, 21 mg cholesterol, 116 mg sodium, 46 g carbohydrates, 3 g fiber, 4 g protein, 38 mg calcium, 2 mg iron

---

A cross between candy and fruit-cake, panforte ("strong bread") is loaded with fruits and nuts.

1 cup (130 g) salted roasted almonds, coarsely chopped

1 cup (about 5 oz./140 g) dried pitted tart cherries

1 cup (185 g) *each* candied orange peel and candied lemon peel, finely chopped

1 teaspoon *each* grated lemon peel and ground cinnamon

½ teaspoon ground coriander

¼ teaspoon *each* ground cloves and ground nutmeg

½ cup (60 g) all-purpose flour

¾ cup (150 g) granulated sugar

¾ cup (180 ml) honey

2 tablespoons butter or margarine

½ cup (50 g) sifted powdered sugar

Panforte

Preparation time: 25 minutes
Cooking time: About 1¼ hours

1. In a large bowl, combine almonds, cherries, candied orange peel, candied lemon peel, grated lemon peel, cinnamon, coriander, cloves, nutmeg, and flour. Mix until nuts and fruit pieces are thoroughly coated with flour; set aside.

2. In a deep medium-size pan, combine granulated sugar, honey, and butter. Cook over high heat, stirring often, until mixture registers 265°F/129°C (hard-ball stage) on a candy thermometer. Working quickly, pour hot syrup over fruit mixture and mix thoroughly. Immediately scrape mixture into a

heavily greased, floured 8- to 9-inch (20- to 23-cm) cake pan.

3. Bake in a 300°F (150°C) oven for 1 hour; if cake begins to brown excessively, drape it loosely with foil (don't let foil touch cake). Let cool completely in pan on a rack.

4. Sprinkle a work surface with half the powdered sugar. Using a slender knife and spatula, loosen sides and bottom of cake from pan, then invert cake (prying gently, if needed) onto sugared surface. Sprinkle and pat sugar over entire cake. Then dust cake with remaining powdered sugar to coat completely. Transfer to a platter. To serve, cut into wedges. Makes 12 servings.

Per serving: 370 calories (24% calories from fat), 10 g total fat, 2 g saturated fat, 5 mg cholesterol, 131 mg sodium, 71 g carbohydrates, 2 g fiber, 4 g protein, 37 mg calcium, 0.9 mg iron

Apple-Fennel Tart
(recipe on facing page)

Espresso Chocolate Cake with Orange Sauce

Preparation time: 35 minutes
Cooking time: 35 to 40 minutes
Pictured on page 626

- 2 tablespoons butter or margarine, at room temperature
- 1 cup (220 g) firmly packed brown sugar
- 1 large egg
- 3 large egg whites
- 1 cup (240 ml) nonfat sour cream
- 1 teaspoon vanilla
- ¾ cup (95 g) all-purpose flour
- ⅓ cup (29 g) unsweetened cocoa powder
- 1 tablespoon instant espresso powder
- 1½ teaspoons baking powder
- 6 or 7 large oranges (about 8 oz./230 g *each*)
- 6 tablespoons (72 g) granulated sugar
- 4 teaspoons cornstarch
- 1½ teaspoons instant espresso powder (or to taste)
- 1½ cups (360 ml) fresh orange juice
- 2 tablespoons (30 ml) orange-flavored liqueur (or to taste)
- 2 tablespoons unsweetened cocoa powder
- Mint sprigs

1. In a food processor or a large bowl, combine butter and brown sugar; whirl or beat with an electric mixer until well blended. Add egg, egg whites, sour cream, and vanilla; whirl or beat until well blended. Add flour, the ⅓ cup (29 g) cocoa, the 1 tablespoon instant espresso, and baking powder; whirl or beat just until combined. Spread batter in a greased 8-inch-square (20-cm-square) nonstick or regular baking pan. Bake in a 350°F (175°C) oven until cake begins to pull away from pan sides and center springs back when lightly pressed (35 to 40 minutes).

2. While cake is baking, finely shred enough peel (colored part only) from oranges to make 1 to 2 teaspoons for sauce; cover and set aside. Cut off and discard remaining peel and all white membrane from oranges. Cut between membranes to release segments. Cover orange segments and set aside.

3. In a small pan, combine granulated sugar, cornstarch, and the 1½ teaspoons instant espresso. Whisk in orange juice and the reserved shredded orange peel; cook over medium-high heat, stirring constantly, until sauce boils and thickens slightly (about 1 minute). Remove from heat and stir in liqueur.

4. Just before serving, sift the 2 tablespoons cocoa over cake. Cut cake into diamonds, triangles, or squares; transfer to individual plates. Arrange orange segments alongside. Drizzle sauce over oranges. Garnish with mint sprigs. Makes 8 servings.

Per serving: 361 calories (12% calories from fat), 5 g total fat, 2 g saturated fat, 34 mg cholesterol, 187 mg sodium, 74 g carbohydrates, 5 g fiber, 8 g protein, 189 mg calcium, 2 mg iron

Espresso Biscotti

Preparation time: 35 minutes
Cooking time: About 35 minutes
Pictured on page 626

- ½ cup (68 g) hazelnuts
- 5 tablespoons (71 g) butter or margarine, at room temperature
- ½ cup (100 g) granulated sugar
- 2½ teaspoons instant espresso powder
- 1 large egg
- 2 large egg whites
- 1 teaspoon vanilla
- 2 cups (250 g) all-purpose flour
- 2 teaspoons baking powder
- 1½ cups (150 g) sifted powdered sugar

1. Spread hazelnuts in a single layer in a shallow baking pan. Bake in a 375°F (190°C) oven until nuts are golden beneath skins (about 10 minutes). Let nuts cool slightly; then pour into a towel, fold to enclose, and rub to remove as much of loose skins as possible. Let cool; chop coarsely and set aside. Reduce oven temperature to 350°F (175°C).

2. In a large bowl, beat butter, granulated sugar, and 1½ teaspoons of the instant espresso until well blended. Add egg and egg whites, beating until well blended. Stir in vanilla. In a medium-size bowl, stir together flour and baking powder; add to butter mixture and stir until well blended. Mix in hazelnuts.

3. Divide dough in half. On a lightly floured board, shape each portion into a long roll about 1½ inches (3.5 cm) in diameter. Place rolls on a large nonstick or greased regular baking sheet, spacing them 3 inches (8 cm) apart. Flatten rolls to make ½-inch-thick (1-cm-thick) loaves. Bake in a 350°F (175°C) oven until loaves feel firm to the touch (about 15 minutes).

4. Remove baking sheet from oven and let loaves

cool for 3 to 5 minutes; then cut crosswise into slices about ½ inch (1 cm) thick. Tip slices cut side down on baking sheet (at this point, you may need another sheet to bake biscotti all at once). Return to oven and continue to bake until biscotti look dry and are lightly browned (about 10 minutes); if using 2 baking sheets, switch their positions halfway through baking. Transfer biscotti to racks and let cool.

5. Meanwhile, in a small bowl, dissolve remaining 1 teaspoon instant espresso in 4 teaspoons (20 ml) very hot water. Stir in powdered sugar; if needed, add more hot water, 1 teaspoon at a time, to make icing easy to spread.

6. Spread icing over 1 to 1½ inches (2.5 to 3.5 cm) of one end of each cooled cookie. Let stand until icing is firm before serving. Makes about 4 dozen cookies.

Per cookie: 60 calories (30% calories from fat), 2 g total fat, 0.7 g saturated fat, 7 mg cholesterol, 35 mg sodium, 10 g carbohydrates, 0.2 g fiber, 1 g protein, 15 mg calcium, 0.3 mg iron

Chocolate-Espresso Sauce

Preparation time: 10 minutes
Cooking time: About 5 minutes
....

½ cup (110 g) firmly packed brown sugar

¼ cup (22 g) unsweetened cocoa powder

4 teaspoons cornstarch

1 teaspoon instant espresso powder

2 tablespoons (30 ml) light corn syrup

1 teaspoon coffee-flavored liqueur

½ teaspoon vanilla
....

1. In a small pan, mix sugar, cocoa, cornstarch, and instant espresso. Add corn syrup and ½ cup (120 ml) water; stir until smooth. Cook over medium-high heat, stirring constantly and scraping sides of pan often, until sauce comes to a rapid boil and thickens slightly (about 5 minutes).

2. Remove pan from heat and stir in liqueur and vanilla. Serve warm; just before serving, stir well. If made ahead, let cool; then cover and refrigerate for up to 1 week. Before serving, bring to a gentle boil over medium-low heat, stirring often. Makes about 1 cup (240 ml).

Per tablespoon: 40 calories (4% calories from fat), 0.2 g total fat, 0.1 g saturated fat, 0 mg cholesterol, 6 mg sodium, 10 g carbohydrates, 0.4 g fiber, 0.3 g protein, 8 mg calcium, 0.3 mg iron

Espresso Cheesecake

Preparation time: 25 minutes
Cooking time: 1½ to 1¾ hours
Cooling & chilling time:
At least 4½ hours
Pictured on page 626
....

1 package (about 9 oz./255 g) chocolate wafer cookies

¼ cup (55 g) butter or margarine, melted and cooled slightly

1 tablespoon instant espresso powder

½ teaspoon vanilla

4 large packages (about 8 oz./230 g *each*) nonfat cream cheese, at room temperature

1 cup (200 g) sugar

3 large eggs

2 large egg whites

2 cups (470 ml) nonfat sour cream

3 tablespoons (45 ml) coffee-flavored liqueur

1 tablespoon sugar

1 tablespoon unsweetened cocoa powder

Chocolate-covered espresso beans or mocha candy beans
....

1. In a food processor, whirl cookies to form fine crumbs. Add butter, instant espresso, and vanilla; whirl just until crumbs are evenly moistened. Press crumb mixture firmly over bottom and about 1 inch (2.5 cm) up sides of a greased 9-inch (23-cm) cheesecake pan with a removable

rim. Bake in a 350°F (175°C) oven until crust feels slightly firmer when pressed (about 15 minutes).

2. In clean food processor or in a large bowl, combine cream cheese, the 1 cup (200 g) sugar, eggs, egg whites, 1 cup (240 ml) of the sour cream, and liqueur. Whirl or beat with an electric mixer until smooth.

3. Pour cheese filling into baked crust. Return to oven and bake until filling is golden on top and jiggles only slightly in center when pan is gently shaken (1¼ to 1½ hours).

4. Gently run a slender knife between cheesecake and pan rim; then let cheesecake cool in pan on a rack for 30 minutes. Meanwhile, in a small bowl, gently stir together remaining 1 cup (240 ml) sour cream and the 1 tablespoon sugar; cover and refrigerate.

5. Spread cooled cheesecake with sour cream topping. Cover and refrigerate until cold (at least 4 hours) or until next day. Just before serving, sprinkle with cocoa; then remove pan rim. Garnish with chocolate-covered espresso beans. Makes 12 to 16 servings.

Per serving: 276 calories (23% calories from fat), 7 g total fat, 3 g saturated fat, 62 mg cholesterol, 492 mg sodium, 37 g carbohydrates, 0.7 g fiber, 15 g protein, 239 mg calcium, 0.9 mg iron

Espresso Cheesecake, Espresso Biscotti, and Espresso
Chocolate Cake with Orange Sauce
(recipes on pages 624–625)

Sunset
Wok
COOK BOOK

Recipes in this book were previously published
as part of the *Sunset Complete Wok Cook Book*.

By the Editors of

Sunset Books

and Sunset Magazine

Lane Publishing Co. ■ *Menlo Park, California*

Contents

Special Features

Wok Cooking

When you think of wok cooking, you probably think first of stir-frying—of quickly tossing and stirring bite-size pieces of meat and vegetables in a little hot oil, letting them barely touch the sides of the steel bowl. You think of Asian dishes, of foods with crisp textures and fresh flavors.

But Oriental stir-fries are by no means the only recipes a wok can handle. Though it may not be the universal utensil with as many uses as a Swiss army knife, this simple pan is undeniably versatile. It doubles as a deep-fryer; it's a perfect steamer for seafood, dumplings, delicate pâtés, even puddings. And stainless steel woks and those with a nonstick finish are ideal for stewing and braising.

Thanks to its unique shape, the wok is also a model of efficiency: the sloping sides and rounded bottom heat up quickly and evenly, and provide the greatest possible surface for cooking. Whether you use an electric or a gas range, you'll find that wok cookery saves you time and energy.

Choosing & caring for your wok

Woks are available in two basic shapes and a variety of sizes. The traditional wok has a rounded bottom, reflecting its original use—it was designed to be suspended in a brazier over a hot fire. The curved shape is as efficient as ever today, but the brazier has been replaced by a perforated ring stand that holds the wok steady on the range top.

A fairly recent introduction is the flat-bottomed wok, intended to sit directly atop burner or element. You'll need to purchase this style if you can't get a round-bottomed wok close enough to the heat source (see "Using a wok on your range," facing page).

Woks typically have two handles, one on each side. Some models are equipped with wooden handle covers; if yours lacks this feature, you'll need to protect your hands with potholders when you cook. Woks with a single long wooden handle are also available. They're easy to maneuver when you stir-fry—but when you want to lift a one-handled wok full of food or oil, be sure to lift it from *both* sides.

Woks range from 9 to 30 inches in diameter, but the 14-inch size is usually the best choice for home cooks: it's ample in capacity, yet simple to manage. Obviously, a wok of this size is also easier to store than a really big one would be—but all woks take up a fair amount of shelf space, and round-bottomed types tend to wobble instead of sitting flat. Many cooks find it more convenient to hang woks from pot hooks than to keep them in a cupboard.

In addition to selecting the wok shape and size, you'll need to choose the best material for your needs. Woks were originally made of cast iron, but today the most commonly used metal is heavy-gauge rolled *carbon steel*. Carbon steel woks conduct heat well, making them great for stir-frying, but they do require seasoning and proper care to keep the surface in good condition and prevent rusting.

Seasoning a carbon steel wok is a simple procedure. Before the first use, wash the wok with mild soapy water, then dry it directly over medium heat on your range until no moisture remains. Next, rub the inside with a paper towel dampened with about 2 teaspoons of salad oil; wipe off any excess oil with a clean paper towel. After each use, wash the wok with sudsy water, using a dishwashing or bamboo brush to scrub out any sticking food; then rinse well and dry again on the range. If not kept completely dry between uses, carbon steel woks will rust.

Aluminum and *stainless steel* woks—often with copper bottoms and sides to improve heat conduction—are also available. They need no seasoning; they won't rust, so you can simply clean them as you would any other aluminum or stainless pan. These woks are particularly good for steaming and stewing; they're fine for stir-frying, too, though they don't distribute heat as evenly as carbon steel woks do.

Top choice for tabletop cooking are *electric* woks. You'll find them especially suitable for poaching foods in hot broth, such as in Mizutaki (page 650). They also work well for steaming and deep-frying, but because they tend to recover heat rather slowly after food is added, they aren't always successful for stir-frying.

Clean and care for your electric wok according to the manufacturer's directions, always removing the heat element before washing. And if you've chosen a nonstick model, be sure not to use sharp utensils for stirring.

Wok accessories

Purchasing a wok doesn't mean re-outfitting your kitchen with dozens of new accessories. Though you can certainly buy specially designed wok tools if you wish, you'll be just as successful using basic utensils you already own.

The most useful wok accessory is a *long-handled spatula* with a wide, curved edge (a regular spatula will do). The handle is often tipped with wood to prevent it from getting too hot to touch during cooking.

A dome-shaped *wok lid* is helpful in stir-frying and braising, and necessary for steaming unless you use lidded *stacking bamboo* baskets. Also required for steaming is a metal or bamboo *rack* to hold food above boiling water (use a round cake rack, if you like).

When steaming or deep-frying, you'll find a *ring stand* with slanting sides helpful for balancing the wok over the range burner or element. Other accessories for deep-frying include a *wire skimmer* or slotted spoon for removing bits of food from the oil, a semicircular wire *draining rack* that attaches to the top of the wok, and a *deep-frying thermometer*.

Using a wok on your range

Woks can be used on either gas or electric ranges. Flat-bottomed woks are designed to rest directly on the cooking element of either kind of range, but round-bottomed types may need to be set in a ring stand. Before you start to cook in a round-bottomed wok, experiment with an empty wok to find the arrangement that works best for the sort of cooking you want to do.

To cook on a gas range. If you're planning to stir-fry, you can simply place the wok directly on the metal burner support above the flame; it should rest fairly steadily. For deep-frying or steaming, you'll probably need to stabilize the wok on a ring stand (see photograph on page 633): place the ring stand on the range, then set the work on top. The bottom of the wok should be within 1 inch of the flame. If it's too far away, turn the ring stand over to bring the wok

closer to the burner; or remove the burner support and place the ring stand directly on the range top.

To cook on an electric range. For stir-frying, set the wok directly on the element. A more stable arrangement is necessary when deep-frying or steaming; though: invert the ring stand over the electric element, then suspend the wok in the stand so that it rests directly on the element or no more than 1 inch above it.

Cooking in a wok

Once you have the wok set up on your range, you're ready to cook. Stir-frying, deep-frying, and steaming are the three techniques for which the wok is best suited; we've focused on these methods in the following pages, but you'll also find a few braised dishes. Each chapter concentrates on one technique and offers menu selections from appetizers to desserts. Although particular attention is paid to the foods of Asia, recipes from other cuisines are presented.

Stir-frying in a wok. The one cooking method that is uniquely Asian, but adaptable to many different foods, is stir-frying, the technique basic to the recipes in the first chapter of this book.

As the name implies, stir-frying is an active method that involves plenty of stirring. Foods aren't really fried, though: they're flash-cooked in a little hot oil, constantly tossed and lifted to bring every side of each piece in contact with the hot wok and to seal in juices and flavors.

Stir-frying isn't difficult to master, though you will have to learn to work with higher-than-usual heat. It's easiest to use one hand to hold the wok, the other hand to stir; this lets you move the wok on and off the heat as needed to control the temperature. The one utensil you'll need is a long-handled spatula.

The stir-frying technique is outlined step by step on page 637, but a few general pointers are worth repeating here. The first unbreakable rule is to have everything ready to go before you begin, since there's no time to assemble ingredients once you start cooking. Cut up meat and vegetables as the recipe directs (see also "Slicing & chopping tips," page 632); mix up any cooking sauces.

With all ingredients ready at hand, set your clean, dry wok over high heat (or as the recipe directs). When the wok is hot, add the oil—always salad oil, since it can withstand high temperatures without burning. When the oil is hot enough to ripple when the wok is tilted from side to side (but not smoking hot), begin cooking, adding ingredients as directed. If you need to add more oil at any point, bring it to rippling hot before adding more food. *Note:* If a recipe specifies butter, heat should be reduced to, at the most, medium-high. If your stir-fry contains firm vegetables such as carrots or asparagus, you may need to add water and cover the wok for a few minutes to let the vegetables steam tender. Let the recipe be your guide, and use the chart on page 638 for additional information on stir-frying vegetables.

Braising & stewing in a wok.

The wok shape is fine for braising and stewing, and we've included a few simmered dishes. It's important, though, to make your soups and stews in a stainless steel wok or one with a nonstick finish. Foods simmered for any length of time in a carbon steel wok often take on a metallic taste.

To braise in a wok, follow the same initial steps for stir-frying: brown the meat in oil and cook any vegetables briefly; then add liquid and simmer, covered, until the meat is tender. If you're using a round-bottomed wok and a large amount of liquid, you'll need to set the wok in a ring stand.

Deep-frying in a wok.

If you have a wok, you can easily make fried onions, crispy chicken, fritters—or anything else you'd make in a deep-fryer. The two basic utensils you'll need are a wire skimmer or large slotted spoon and a deep-frying thermometer; if you're using a regular round-bottomed wok, you'll also need a ring stand to hold the wok steady when it's filled with oil.

The details of deep-frying in a wok are covered on page 693. At least two rules apply to deep-frying in any pan, though. First, remember that successful results depend on keeping the oil at the right temperature. To prevent the oil from cooling too much when food is added, keep the wok over high heat (unless otherwise instructed) and add food just a few pieces at a time. Second, always be careful when you deep-fry: slide or lower foods into oil to minimize

spattering, lift a wok full of oil with *both* hands, and let the oil cool before pouring it out of the wok.

Steaming in a wok.

Steaming foods in a wok is so easy and gives such good results that you may want to use this technique for some of your regular cooking tasks. For example, steaming fish or chicken breasts for a salad takes no longer than cooking these foods in simmering water, and there's less flavor loss. And you can easily enhance the flavors of foods while they steam: sprinkle them with salt, pepper, or herbs; surround with slices of onion, lemon, or ginger; or drizzle with soy.

As far as equipment is concerned, you'll need only a ring stand, a lid, and a metal rack—one made especially for the wok, or just a round cake rack—to turn your wok into a steamer. Also available are stacking bamboo baskets (see photo on page 633) that let you steam several different foods (on different tiers) at once. Basket lids are sold separately; if you buy one, you'll be able to steam in your wok even if you don't have a wok lid. The main advantage of a bamboo lid, though, is that it minimizes condensation by absorbing moisture. If you use a metal wok lid, drops of water will form on it, then drip into the food; you may want to protect some foods (such as custards) with wax paper.

For the how-to's of steaming in a wok, see page 709. Additional information on steaming fresh vegetables is on page 718.

Slicing & chopping tips

Uniform cutting means uniform cooking. That's true no matter what method you use. But cutting pieces of equal size is particularly important for stir-frying; because this technique is so fast, there's no time for differences in size and shape to even out. If you don't cut ingredients evenly, the finished dish may

To diagonally slice fibrous vegetables, such as celery, cut crosswise on the diagonal into ⅛- to ¼-inch-thick slanting slices.

To slice meat, such as flank steak, cut while partially frozen, across the grain, at a 45° angle.

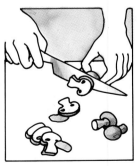

To thinly slice food, such as mushrooms, cut straight down at a right angle.

To cut food, such as zucchini, into julienne strips, first cut vegetable into 2- to 3-inch lengths. Then cut into ⅛-inch-thick slices, stack 2 or 3 slices at a time, and cut slices into ⅛-inch-thick strips.

To dice food, such as potatoes, cut as directed for julienne strips, then cut crosswise into small squares. For larger dice, start with thicker strips.

Wok options and accessories include (clockwise from lower right):
electric wok with lid; round-bottomed wok with skimmer and steamer rack;
stainless steel wok with copper lid and bottom, set in a ring stand; spatula
and cleaver; bamboo steaming baskets; wok lid; flat-bottomed wok with
long wooden handle; semicircular wire draining rack; and chopsticks.

well end up as a blend of undercooked, overdone, and just right.

Cutting into slanting or diagonal slices is a very effective way to cut through fibrous vegetables (such as celery) and meat (such as flank steak) to tenderize them and to expose the greatest possible area to the heated wok sides. Our recipes usually call for ⅛- to ¼-inch-thick slanting slices (see illustration on page 632). Use a very sharp knife or cleaver, and cut meat across the grain at a 45° angle; you'll find that meat is easier to slice if it's partially frozen.

If a recipe simply calls for foods to be thinly sliced, it usually means cutting straight down, not at a slant (see illustration on page 632). Julienne strips should be about the size of a wooden matchstick; diced foods should be cut into small cubes. Such consistent chopping and slicing contribute to both the preparation and presentation of any dish—one that tastes good and looks good, too.

Planning meals for wok cooking

Though the wok is an Asian invention, you don't have to use it exclusively for Oriental-style recipes. In fact, you may find yourself reaching for your wok to fry chicken or boil pasta! Keep in mind, though, that a wok can't do everything at once. If you want to steam one dish, braise another, and stir-fry a third, you'll need to use more than one wok or choose alternate pans. And no matter how many woks you have, preparing several stir-fries at once is difficult—unless you have extra range tops and kitchen help!

Wok cookery & sodium

If you frequently use your wok for Oriental-style cooking, you should think about the amount of sodium you may be consuming. Soy sauce is a basic seasoning in many of these recipes, and that can mean high levels of sodium.

It's not too difficult to reduce the sodium content of most dishes, though. First, you can use low-sodium soy sauce and substitute homemade low-salt chicken broth (see page 683) for the canned or reconstituted variety; you can also season foods to taste with salt rather than automatically adding the amount specified. You can simply cut down on serving sizes and round out the meal with plenty of plain rice or noodles. In China, rice is actually the bulk of the meal; some 250 pounds per person are consumed annually, compared to 10 pounds per person in the United States. A generous helping of steamed rice or boiled noodles serves another purpose, too—to soothe the palate when the main course is extra spicy.

Stir-frying

What could be simpler? A wok, a spatula, and a few minutes of your time—these, plus fresh ingredients, are the elements of stir-frying. Understandably, it's a popular technique with time-conscious cooks. But beyond its efficiency, stir-frying also brings out the best of good food. It seals in juices and flavors, along with vitamins and minerals; it intensifies colors. Vegetables become crisp, meats silken and tender. Measure, chop, and organize all ingredients before you start, because stir-frying goes very quickly.

Stir-frying Chinese Chicken & Zucchini *(Recipe on facing page)*

1 Soak dried mushrooms in warm water for 30 minutes. Cut off and discard hard stems; cut caps into ¼-inch-thick slices.

2 Cut boned chicken breasts into bite-size pieces. Then add chicken to soy marinade flavored with garlic, ginger, and fermented black beans; stir to coat and let marinate for 15 minutes.

3 Roll-cut zucchini by making a diagonal slice straight down through squash, giving it a quarter turn, and slicing again. Cut pepper into 1-inch squares; cut bamboo shoot into small pieces.

4 When vegetables are tender-crisp, return cooked chicken to pan and toss to heat through.

5 Add cooking sauce, pouring it in around edges of pan so it will heat quickly. Cook, stirring constantly, until sauce thickens (about 30 seconds).

6 Stir-fried vegetables have bright color, crisp texture; chicken morsels are tender and juicy. To serve the meal Chinese style, provide each diner with an individual bowl of rice.

How to stir-fry in a wok

When you stir-fry, you don't really fry; you cook foods quickly by stirring and tossing them in a small amount of hot fat. This kind of flash-cooking seals in juices and keeps flavors fresh; it's a technique you can use to make dishes of every kind, from appetizers to desserts. All stir-fry recipes follow the same basic steps; once you've mastered the method, you can easily create recipes of your own.

In addition to your wok, the only tool you need for successful stir-frying is a long-handled spatula with a wide, curved edge. You'll also need to keep these pointers in mind:

- Do all your cutting in advance. Foods should be cut into small, uniform pieces or thin slices.

- Prepare any seasonings and sauce mixtures in advance. Once you start to cook, you won't have time to stop and create a sauce.

- Assemble the cut-up meat and/or vegetables, seasonings, sauce mixture, and salad oil or other fat near the range.

- Place a clean, dry wok over the heat specified in the recipe—typically high heat, sometimes medium or medium-high. When the wok is hot, add the fat as directed. Heat oil until it's hot enough to ripple when the wok is tilted from side to side; heat butter until it's foamy.

- Add any seasonings (garlic or ginger, for example). Holding the wok handle in one hand and a wide spatula in the other, stir and toss the seasonings until lightly browned.

  Now add meat, if used. (Never add more than about 1 pound at a time; if you have more, cook it in batches.) Spread the pieces evenly over the wok's surface; stir and toss until lightly browned all over. Turn meat out of wok.

- Add 1 to 2 tablespoons more oil (or other fat). When oil is hot, add vegetables, one variety at a time. Start with the type that has the longest cooking time (see page 638); stir-fry just until tender-crisp to bite, lifting and tossing vegetables to coat them with oil. Turn out of wok; repeat to cook remaining vegetables. (Or simply add all vegetables in sequence, timing your additions so all will be done at the same time.) For dense or fibrous vegetables such as broccoli or asparagus, you may need to add a little water, then cover the wok and steam the vegetable slightly, stirring often.

- Return meat and vegetables to wok. Stir cooking sauce to reblend cornstarch; pour into wok. Stir until sauce boils and thickens. Serve.

NOTE: Use the cooking times given in our recipes as guides, not absolutes. Actual cooking time will vary, depending upon the kind of wok you use and the intensity of the heat source.

(Pictured on facing page)

Chinese Chicken & Zucchini

Preparation time: About 20 minutes, plus 30 minutes to soak mushrooms

Marinating time: 15 minutes

Cooking time: About 10 minutes

Follow the step-by-step photos on the facing page to make this classic stir-fry of crisp vegetable chunks and spicy chicken.

- 5 **dried Oriental mushrooms**
- 2 **teaspoons** *each* **soy sauce, cornstarch, dry sherry, and water**
  Dash of white pepper
- 1 **clove garlic, minced**
- ½ **teaspoon minced fresh ginger**
- 2 **teaspoons fermented salted black beans, rinsed, drained, and finely chopped**
- 1½ **pounds chicken breasts, skinned and boned**
- 3½ **tablespoons salad oil**
  Cooking Sauce (recipe on page 663, right)
- ½ **pound zucchini**
- 1 **whole bamboo shoot, cut into small pieces, or ½ cup sliced bamboo shoots**
- 1 **red or green bell pepper, seeded and cut into 1-inch squares**

Soak mushrooms in warm water to cover for 30 minutes, then drain. Cut off and discard stems; squeeze caps dry, thinly slice, and set aside.

In a bowl, mix soy, cornstarch, sherry, water, pepper, garlic, ginger, and beans. Cut chicken into bite-size pieces; add to marinade and stir to coat, then stir in 1½ teaspoons of the oil. Let marinate for 15 minutes. Meanwhile, prepare Cooking Sauce; set aside. Roll-cut zucchini as shown on facing page.

Place a wok over high heat. When wok is hot, add 2 tablespoons of the oil. When oil is hot, add chicken mixture and stir-fry until meat is no longer pink in center; cut to test (about 3 minutes). Remove from wok and set aside.

Pour remaining 1 tablespoon oil into wok. When oil is hot, add mushrooms, bamboo shoots, zucchini, and bell pepper. Stir-fry for 1 minute, then add 2 tablespoons water, cover, and cook until zucchini and bell pepper are tender-crisp to bite (about 3 more minutes). Return chicken to wok. Stir Cooking Sauce, pour into wok, and stir until sauce boils and thickens. Makes 3 or 4 servings.

Per serving: 296 calories, 29 g protein, 12 g carbohydrates, 15 g total fat, 65 mg cholesterol, 836 mg sodium

Stir-frying Fresh Vegetables

Perfect stir-fried vegetables are bright, colorful, and naturally sweet in flavor, with a texture that's crisp yet tender to the bite. They're quick to fix, too—most types cook in 5 minutes or less.

To stir-fry:

1) Cut vegetables into slices or small pieces, as directed in chart below.

2) Place wok over high heat. When wok is hot, add specified amount of oil; when oil is hot, add vegetables all at once and stir-fry, uncovered, for time noted in chart.

3) Add designated amount of liquid (regular-strength chicken or beef broth or water); cover and cook for remaining time. As vegetables cook, all or most of liquid will evaporate; because there's no cooking liquid to drain off and discard, vitamins and minerals are retained.

Remember that the times noted below should be used as guides. Actual times will vary, depending on the freshness and maturity of the vegetables and on individual preference. Taste after the minimum cooking time; if you prefer a softer texture, continue cooking, tasting often, until vegetables are done to your liking.

If you'd like to cook a medley of several vegetables, add the firmest kind to the wok first; cook for the time indicated, adding the more tender vegetables near the end of the cooking time. Or cook each vegetable separately, then combine them all for reheating and blending of flavors.

A final pointer for success: never crowd the wok. Cook no more than 5 cups of cut-up vegetables in a 12- to 14-inch wok. To prepare more servings than you can cook at once, just cut up the total quantity of vegetables you'll need, then cook them in two or more batches. Stir-frying is so fast that you can keep the first portions warm, without flavor loss, while the others cook.

Vegetable *4 to 5 cups cut-up vegetable*	Tablespoons salad oil	Minutes to stir-fry uncovered	Tablespoons broth or water	Minutes to cook covered
Asparagus. Cut into ½-inch slanting slices	1	1	1–2	2–3
Beans, green, Italian, wax. Cut into 1-inch pieces	1	1	4	4–7
Bok choy. See Swiss chard				
Broccoli. Cut into ¼-inch slices	1	1	3–5	3–5
Cabbage, green, red, Savoy. Shredded	1	1	2	3–4
Cabbage, napa. Cut white part into 1-inch slices; shred leaves and add during last 2–3 minutes of cooking time	1	1–2	2	4–5
Carrots. Cut into ¼-inch slices	1	1	2–3	3–5
Cauliflower. Flowerets, cut into ¼-inch slices	1	1	3–4	4–5
Celery. Cut into ¼-inch slices	1	1	1–2	1–3
Fennel. Cut into ¼-inch slices	1	2–3	No liquid necessary	Not necessary
Leeks, white part only. Cut into ¼-inch slices	1	1	3–4	3
Mushrooms. Cut into ¼-inch slices	1	3–4	No liquid necessary	Not necessary
Onions, dry. Cut into ¼-inch slices	1	1	No liquid necessary	3–4
Parsnips. Cut into ¼-inch slices	2	1	6–8	4–6
Pea pods, Chinese.	1	3	1	½
Peas, green. Shelled	1	1	3–4	2–3
Peppers, green or red bell. Cut into 1-inch pieces	1	1	2–3	3–5
Rutabagas. Cut into ¼-inch slices	1	1	4–5	5–6
Spinach. Leaves, whole or coarsely chopped	1	½	No liquid necessary	2–3
Sprouts, bean.	1	1	1	½–1½
Squash, summer (crookneck, pattypan, zucchini). Cut into ¼-inch slices	1	1	2–4	3–4
Swiss chard. Cut stems into ¼-inch slices; shred leaves and add during last 2–3 minutes of cooking time	1	1	1	3½–4½
Turnips. Cut into ¼-inch slices	1	1	4–5	4–5

Appetizers

Meatballs with Ginger Glaze

Preparation time: About 25 minutes

Cooking time: About 45 minutes (about 10 minutes/batch)

A sweet and sour sauce that's nippy with fresh ginger coats these small meatballs. If you prepare the dish in an electric wok, you can serve it right in the cooking pan.

Ginger Glaze (recipe follows)
1 can (about 8 oz.) water chestnuts, drained and finely chopped
1 cup chopped green onions (including tops)
2 pounds lean ground pork
2 tablespoons soy sauce
2 eggs
¾ cup fine dry bread crumbs
About 1 tablespoon salad oil

Prepare Ginger Glaze; set aside.

In a bowl, combine water chestnuts, onions, pork, soy, eggs, and bread crumbs. Mix thoroughly with a fork or your hands, then shape mixture into ¾-inch balls (you should have about 72).

Place a wok over medium-high heat; when wok is hot, add 1 tablespoon of the oil. When oil is hot, add 24 meatballs and stir-fry until well browned (about 10 minutes). Remove from wok and set aside. Repeat to brown remaining meatballs, adding more oil as needed. Clean wok.

Place wok over high heat; when wok is hot, pour in Ginger Glaze and stir until glaze boils vigorously. Add meatballs and simmer for about 10 minutes. If using an electric wok, serve in wok; otherwise, transfer to a chafing dish. Provide wooden picks for spearing meatballs. Makes about 6 dozen meatballs (10 to 12 servings).

Ginger Glaze. In a large bowl, smoothly blend ½ cup **water** and ¼ cup **cornstarch.** Add 1 cup *each* **unsweetened pineapple juice** and **regular-strength beef broth,** ½ cup **cider vinegar,** ⅓ cup **sugar,** 1 tablespoon **soy sauce,** and 2 tablespoons minced **fresh ginger.**

Per serving: 233 calories, 17 g protein, 19 g carbohydrates, 9 g total fat, 97 mg cholesterol, 447 mg sodium

Quick Pot Stickers

Preparation time: About 1 hour

Cooking time: About 1 hour (about 15 minutes/batch)

Traditional pot stickers (page 640) are delicious, but they do take time to make. It isn't hard to speed up the preparation, though—instead of using home-made wrappers, just start with the purchased ones (*gyoza*) sold in some grocery stores and Asian markets.

2 small whole chicken breasts (about ¾ lb. *each*), skinned, boned, and split
¼ cup sesame oil
1 cup finely chopped celery
½ cup chopped green onions (including tops)
3 tablespoons dry sherry
2 tablespoons cornstarch
1 teaspoon sugar
½ teaspoon salt
1 package (14 oz.) pot sticker wrappers (*gyoza*) or won ton skins
¼ cup salad oil
1 cup water
Rice wine vinegar, soy sauce, and chili oil

Rinse chicken and pat dry, then chop finely. Place in a bowl and stir in sesame oil, celery, onions, sherry, cornstarch, sugar, and salt.

Set out 6 to 8 wrappers at a time; keep remaining wrappers tightly covered. Mound 2 teaspoons of the filling on each wrapper. To shape each pot sticker, fold dough in half over filling. Pinch about ½ inch of curved edge closed; continue to pinch closed, forming 3 tucks along dough edge, until entire curve is sealed. Set pot sticker down firmly, seam side up, so it will sit flat. Cover lightly until all pot stickers are shaped. (At this point, you may freeze pot stickers as directed on page 640. Cook without thawing as directed below.)

Place a wok over medium heat; when wok is hot, add 1 tablespoon of the salad oil. When oil is hot, add 12 pot stickers, seam side up. Cook until bottoms are golden brown (5 to 7 minutes). Pour in ¼ cup of the water; reduce heat to low, cover, and cook until liquid is absorbed (6 to 10 more minutes). Remove from wok and keep warm. Repeat to cook remaining pot stickers, using remaining salad oil and water.

Offer pot stickers with vinegar, soy, and chili oil on the side for dipping. Makes about 4 dozen pot stickers (about 10 servings).

Per serving: 273 calories, 14 g protein, 24 g carbohydrates, 13 g total fat, 54 mg cholesterol, 151 mg sodium

(Pictured on facing page)

Pot Stickers

Preparation time: About 1½ hours, plus 30 minutes to let dough rest

Cooking time: About 1¾ hours (about 25 minutes/batch)

These savory filled dumplings—called *guotie* in Chinese—make a tasty and substantial first course for parties or everyday meals. They freeze well, so you can make them well in advance.

    Shrimp Filling (recipe follows)
 3 cups all-purpose flour
 ¼ teaspoon salt
 1 cup boiling water
 ¼ cup salad oil
    About 1⅓ cups regular-strength chicken
    broth
    Soy sauce, rice wine vinegar, and chili oil

Prepare filling; cover and refrigerate.

In a bowl, combine flour and salt; mix in water until dough is evenly moistened and begins to hold together. On a lightly floured board, knead dough until very smooth and satiny (about 5 minutes). Cover and let rest at room temperature for 30 minutes.

Divide dough into 2 equal portions. Keep 1 portion covered; roll out other portion about ⅛ inch thick (or thinner). Cut dough into 3½- to 4-inch circles with a round cookie cutter or a clean, empty can with both ends removed. Repeat with scraps and remaining dough.

Mound 2 teaspoons of the filling on each circle. To shape each pot sticker, fold dough in half over filling. Pinch about ½ inch of curved edge closed; continue to pinch closed, forming 3 tucks along dough edge, until entire curve is sealed. Set pot sticker down firmly, seam side up, so it will sit flat. Cover lightly until all pot stickers are shaped. (At this point, you may place pot stickers in a single layer on a baking sheet and freeze until hard, then transfer to a heavy plastic bag, seal, and return to freezer for up to 1 month. Cook without thawing as directed below.)

Place a wok over medium heat; when wok is hot, add 1 tablespoon of the salad oil. When oil is hot, add 12 pot stickers, seam side up. Cook until bottoms are golden brown (8 to 10 minutes). Pour in ⅓ cup of the broth and immediately cover wok tightly. Reduce heat to low and cook for 10 minutes (15 minutes if frozen). Uncover and continue to cook until all liquid is absorbed. Remove from wok and keep warm. Repeat to cook remaining pot stickers, using remaining salad oil and broth.

Offer pot stickers with soy, vinegar, and chili oil on the side for dipping. Makes about 4 dozen pot stickers (about 10 servings).

Shrimp Filling. Shell, devein, and finely chop ½ pound **medium-size raw shrimp.** Combine shrimp with ½ pound **lean ground pork,** 1 cup finely shredded **cabbage,** ¼ cup minced **green onions** (including tops), ¼ cup chopped **mushrooms,** 1 clove **garlic** (minced or pressed), ½ teaspoon **salt,** and 2 tablespoons **oyster sauce** or soy sauce. Mix well.

Per serving: 253 calories, 13 g protein, 30 g carbohydrates, 9 g total fat, 42 mg cholesterol, 497 mg sodium

Beef Chiang Mai

Preparation time: About 10 minutes

Cooking time: About 15 minutes

Warm, spicy beef wrapped in cool lettuce leaves makes a tempting appetizer; the dish is traditional in northern Thailand. If you like, you can wash and crisp the lettuce leaves a day ahead.

 ¼ cup short-grain rice (such as pearl) or
    long-grain rice
 1 pound lean ground beef
 1 teaspoon *each* sugar and crushed red
    pepper
 ½ cup *each* thinly sliced green onions
    (including tops) and chopped fresh mint
 2 tablespoons chopped fresh cilantro
    (coriander)
 ¼ cup lemon juice
 1½ tablespoons soy sauce
    Small inner leaves from 2 large or 3 small
    heads butter lettuce
    About 36 fresh mint sprigs

Place a wok over medium heat. When wok is hot, add rice and stir-fry until golden (about 5 minutes). Remove from heat and transfer to a blender or food processor; whirl until finely ground. Set aside.

Return wok to medium heat; when wok is hot, crumble in beef and cook, stirring, just until meat begins to lose its pinkness (about 3 minutes). Add ground rice, sugar, red pepper, onions, chopped mint, cilantro, lemon juice, and soy; stir until well combined. Pour into a serving dish and surround with lettuce leaves and mint sprigs.

To eat, spoon beef mixture onto lettuce leaves, top with a mint sprig, roll up, and eat out of hand. Makes about 12 servings.

Per serving: 123 calories, 7 g protein, 5 g carbohydrates, 8 g total fat, 28 mg cholesterol, 157 mg sodium

Golden brown Pot Stickers (recipe on facing page) are an ever-popular appetizer, first course, or light entrée. Let guests dip these dumplings into soy, vinegar, and chili oil, combined or served in individual bowls.

Ginger Chicken Wings

Preparation time: About 15 minutes

Cooking time: About 25 minutes

Like the ginger-glazed meatballs on page 639, these hearty chicken wings feature a snappy fresh-ginger sauce. Serve them hot or at room temperature.

Cooking Sauce (recipe follows)
- 12 chicken wings (about 2¼ lbs. *total*)
- 5 tablespoons salad oil
- 2 tablespoons *each* soy sauce and minced fresh ginger
- 2 teaspoons *each* cornstarch and sugar
- ¼ cup regular-strength chicken broth
- ⅓ cup sliced green onions (including tops), optional

Prepare Cooking Sauce; set aside.

Cut off and discard tips of chicken wings, then cut wing sections apart at the joint. Rinse and pat dry.

In a bowl, stir together 2 tablespoons of the oil, soy, ginger, cornstarch, and sugar. Add chicken pieces; stir to coat.

Place a wok over high heat; when wok is hot, add remaining 3 tablespoons oil. When oil is hot, add chicken mixture and cook, uncovered, stirring occasionally, until chicken is browned (about 5 minutes). Stir in broth. Reduce heat to medium, cover, and cook until chicken pulls easily from bone (15 to 20 minutes).

Stir Cooking Sauce, then add to chicken wings. Cook, stirring, until sauce boils and thickens. If made ahead, let cool, then cover and refrigerate for up to 3 days.

Serve chicken wings hot or at room temperature. To serve, arrange wings on a dish; sprinkle with onions, if desired. Makes 4 to 6 servings.

Cooking Sauce. Stir together ¼ cup **regular-strength chicken broth,** 2 teaspoons **cornstarch,** and 2 tablespoons *each* **oyster sauce** and **dry sherry.**

Per serving: 335 calories, 18 g protein, 6 g carbohydrates, 26 g total fat, 71 mg cholesterol, 733 mg sodium

Tequila-Lime Ice with Shrimp

Preparation time: About 45 minutes

Freezing time: 4 to 6 hours

Cooking time: About 5 minutes

A refreshingly tart, super-simple ice perfectly sets off the sweetness of stir-fried shrimp. Make the ice early in the day (or up to a month ahead); cook the shrimp just 30 minutes in advance.

- 1½ teaspoons grated lime peel
- 1 cup sugar
- 2 cups lime juice (about 14 fresh limes; or use bottled juice)
- ½ cup tequila
- 1 cup water
  Stir-fried Shrimp (recipe follows)
  Lime peel strips (optional)

In a 9- by 13-inch pan, stir together grated lime peel, sugar, lime juice, tequila, and water until sugar is dissolved; cover. Freeze until firm (4 to 6 hours) or for up to 1 month.

About 30 minutes before serving, prepare shrimp and set aside; also place 5 to 8 small bowls in the freezer.

With a heavy spoon, break lime ice into chunks. Whirl in a food processor or beat with an electric mixer until a thick, icy slush forms. Immediately spoon into chilled bowls; garnish with strips of lime peel, if desired. Accompany with shrimp. Makes 4 cups ice (5 to 8 first-course servings).

Stir-fried Shrimp. Shell and devein 1 pound **large raw shrimp.** Place a wok over high heat; when wok is hot, add 2 tablespoons **salad oil.** When oil is hot, add shrimp and stir-fry until pink (about 3 minutes). Stir in 2 tablespoons **tequila;** carefully ignite with a match (not beneath an exhaust fan or near flammable items) and shake wok until flames die down. Add 2 tablespoons **lime juice.** Serve at room temperature.

Per serving: 226 calories, 10 g protein, 31 g carbohydrates, 4 g total fat, 65 mg cholesterol, 97 mg sodium

Crunchy Indian Snack

Preparation time: About 10 minutes

Cooking time: About 30 minutes

Spicy Bombay *chiura,* a crunchy Indian snack, is a mixture of legumes, nuts, sesame seeds, and sweet raisins. Serve it in a bowl, as finger food.

- ¼ cup *each* uncooked lentils, long-grain rice, and dried split peas
- 3 cups water
- 2 tablespoons salad oil
- 1 tablespoon sesame seeds
- 1 teaspoon *each* ground coriander and ground cumin
- ½ teaspoon ground turmeric
- ½ cup *each* salted roasted peanuts and cashews
- ¼ cup raisins
- ⅛ to ¼ teaspoon ground red pepper (cayenne)
- ¼ teaspoon ground cloves
- 1 teaspoon salt

Rinse lentils, rice, and peas; drain well. Place in a 2- to 3-quart pan and add 3 cups water; bring to a boil over high heat. Boil for 1 minute; then remove from heat, cover, and set aside for 10 minutes. Drain, rinse under cold water, and drain again; spread on paper towels and pat dry.

Place a wok over medium-high heat; when wok is hot, add oil. When oil is hot, add lentils, rice, peas, sesame seeds, coriander, cumin, and turmeric. Cook, stirring, until mixture is toasted (5 to 10 minutes). Remove from heat and stir in peanuts, cashews, raisins, red pepper, cloves, and salt. Let cool. If made ahead, store airtight for up to 1 week. Makes 2 cups.

Per ¼ cup: 215 calories, 7 g protein, 20 g carbohydrates, 13 g total fat, 0 mg cholesterol, 371 mg sodium

Cold Spiced Cabbage

Preparation time: About 10 minutes

Cooking time: 3 minutes

Chilling time: About 4 hours

Garlic, sesame, and crushed red pepper season this simple cold relish. It's a fine addition to an appetizer tray as well as a good complement for a richly seasoned main course.

- 1 small head napa cabbage (about 1½ lbs.)
- 2 tablespoons salad oil
- 2 cloves garlic, minced
- ⅓ cup water
- 3 tablespoons *each* sugar and white wine vinegar
- ½ teaspoon salt
- 1½ teaspoons sesame oil
- ¼ to ½ teaspoon crushed red pepper

Cut cabbage into 2-inch pieces. Place a wok over high heat. When wok is hot, add salad oil. When oil begins to heat, add garlic and stir once. Then add cabbage and stir-fry for 30 seconds. Add water, cover, and cook, stirring occasionally, until cabbage is just barely wilted (about 1½ minutes). Remove from heat and pour off any excess liquid. Stir sugar, vinegar, salt, sesame oil, and red pepper into cabbage. Let cool, then cover and refrigerate until cold (about 4 hours) or for up to 1 week. Serve cold. Makes about 2½ cups.

Per ¼ cup: 57 calories, .85 g protein, 6 g carbohydrates, 4 g total fat, 0 mg cholesterol, 116 mg sodium

Spiced Pecans

Preparation time: About 5 minutes

Cooking time: About 3 minutes

Pecans, a favorite in the South, are sautéed in a pungent spice mixture in this Creole-style snack. Your guests will find them hard to resist!

- ½ teaspoon *each* salt, paprika, and ground red pepper (cayenne)
- 1 teaspoon white pepper
- 1 tablespoon fresh or dry rosemary
- 2 tablespoons butter or margarine
- 1 tablespoon olive oil
- 10 ounces (about 2½ cups) pecan halves
- 1 tablespoon Worcestershire
- ½ teaspoon liquid hot pepper seasoning

Combine salt, paprika, red pepper, white pepper, and rosemary. Set aside.

Place a wok over high heat; when wok is hot, add butter and oil. When butter is melted, add pecans and stir-fry until nuts are well coated with butter and oil and slightly darker in color (about 1 minute). Add Worcestershire, hot pepper seasoning, and spice mixture; continue to stir-fry until pecans are deep brown (about 1½ more minutes; be careful not to scorch nuts). Let cool. If made ahead, store airtight for up to 2 days. Makes 2½ cups.

Per ¼ cup: 225 calories, 2 g protein, 6 g carbohydrates, 23 g total fat, 6 mg cholesterol, 156 mg sodium

Hot chiles, characteristic of Szechwan province, boldly accent
lean, tender strips of sirloin in Szechwan Beef (recipe on facing page).
Slender carrot ribbons and sliced bamboo shoots contribute
color and crispness.

Beef & Pork

(Pictured on facing page)

Szechwan Beef

Preparation time: About 10 minutes

Cooking time: About 10 minutes

Tender beef, crisp carrots, and a handful of hot chiles go into this stir-fry. Use small dried chiles or larger ones, as you prefer.

     Cooking Sauce (recipe follows)
1 **pound lean boneless beef steak (such as top round, flank, or sirloin)**
2 **tablespoons salad oil**
16 **dried hot red chiles**
2 **large carrots, cut into about 3-inch-long julienne strips**
1 **can (about 8 oz.) sliced bamboo shoots, drained (and thinly sliced, if desired)**
     Fresh cilantro (coriander) leaves (optional)

Prepare Cooking Sauce and set aside.

Cut beef with the grain into 1½-inch-wide strips; then cut each strip across the grain into ⅛-inch-thick slanting slices. Set aside.

Place a wok over high heat; when wok is hot, add oil. When oil is hot, add chiles and cook, stirring, until chiles just begin to char. Remove chiles from wok; set aside.

Add beef to wok and stir-fry until browned (1½ to 2 minutes); remove from wok and set aside. Add carrots to wok and stir-fry until tender-crisp to bite (about 3 minutes). Add bamboo shoots and stir-fry for 1 more minute.

Return meat and chiles to wok; stir Cooking Sauce and add. Stir until sauce boils and thickens. Garnish with cilantro, if desired. Makes 4 servings.

Cooking Sauce. Stir together 2 tablespoons **soy sauce,** 1 tablespoon **dry sherry,** 2 teaspoons **sugar,** and ½ teaspoon **cornstarch.**

Per serving: 349 calories, 31 g protein, 26 g carbohydrates, 17 g total fat, 65 mg cholesterol, 602 mg sodium

Beef with Napa Cabbage

Preparation time: About 15 minutes

Marinating time: 10 minutes

Cooking time: About 8 minutes

Red bell pepper and green napa cabbage give this entrée its bright, fresh look and flavor. Napa cabbage is sold in most supermarkets; sometimes called Chinese or celery cabbage, it has a sweeter taste and a more tender texture than the familiar head cabbage.

½ **to ¾ pound lean boneless beef steak (such as top round, flank, or sirloin)**
1 **teaspoon cornstarch**
1 **tablespoon soy sauce**
½ **teaspoon minced fresh ginger**
     Cooking Sauce (recipe follows)
     About ¾ pound napa cabbage (about ½ small head)
¼ **cup salad oil**
1 **clove garlic, minced or pressed**
1 **red bell pepper, seeded and cut into 1-inch squares**
2 **green onions (including tops), thinly sliced**

Cut beef with the grain into 1½-inch-wide strips; then cut each strip across the grain into ⅛-inch-thick slanting slices. In a bowl, stir together cornstarch, soy, and ginger. Add beef and stir to coat well. Let marinate for 10 minutes.

Meanwhile, prepare Cooking Sauce and set aside. Also cut cabbage crosswise into ¾-inch slices.

Place a wok over high heat. When wok is hot, add 2 tablespoons of the oil. When oil is hot, add meat mixture. Stir-fry until meat is browned (1½ to 2 minutes); set aside.

Add remaining 2 tablespoons oil to wok. When oil is hot, add garlic and bell pepper. Stir-fry for about 30 seconds. Add cabbage and stir-fry until cabbage is bright green and tender-crisp to bite (about 2 minutes).

Return meat mixture to wok. Stir Cooking Sauce and add, then stir until sauce boils and thickens. Mix in onions. Makes 2 or 3 servings.

Cooking Sauce. Stir together 1 tablespoon *each* **corn-starch** and **sugar,** ½ cup **regular-strength beef broth,** and 1 tablespoon *each* **soy sauce** and **dry sherry.**

Per serving: 386 calories, 29 g protein, 14 g carbohydrates, 23 g total fat, 65 mg cholesterol, 912 mg sodium

Beef with Bok Choy

Preparation time: *About 10 minutes*

Marinating time: *15 minutes*

Cooking time: *About 12 minutes*

Crisp bok choy and sweet sesame seeds complement strips of steak in this simple entrée. As you prepare the bok choy, remember to keep stems and leaves separate—they go into the wok at different times.

- **Cooking Sauce (recipe follows)**
- ¾ **pound lean boneless beef steak (such as top round, flank, or sirloin)**
- 1 **tablespoon soy sauce**
- 1 **medium-size head bok choy**
- 2 **to 3 teaspoons sesame seeds**
- ¼ **cup salad oil**
- 1 **clove garlic, minced or pressed**
- ¼ **cup water**

Prepare Cooking Sauce and set aside.

Cut beef with the grain into 1½-inch-wide strips; then cut each strip across the grain into ⅛-inch-thick slanting slices. Place meat in a bowl, stir in soy, and let marinate for 15 minutes.

Meanwhile, cut bok choy leaves from stems. Cut stems diagonally into ¼-inch slices; coarsely shred leaves. Set stems and leaves aside separately; you should have 6 to 8 cups *total* lightly packed stems and leaves.

Place a wok over medium heat. When wok is hot, add sesame seeds and stir until golden (about 2 minutes); remove from wok and set aside. Increase heat to high. Add 2 tablespoons of the oil to wok; when oil is hot, add garlic and bok choy stems. Stir-fry for 1 to 2 minutes. Add water, then cover and cook for 2 minutes; add bok choy leaves and cook, uncovered, stirring occasionally, just until leaves and stems are tender to bite (1 to 2 more minutes). Remove from wok and set aside.

Pour remaining 2 tablespoons oil into wok. When oil is hot, add meat; stir-fry until browned (1½ to 2 minutes). Return bok choy to wok. Stir sauce and add, then add sesame seeds. Cook, stirring, until sauce boils and thickens. Makes 2 or 3 servings.

Cooking Sauce. Stir together ¾ cup **regular-strength chicken broth,** 4 teaspoons **cornstarch,** 2 teaspoons **soy sauce,** 1 teaspoon minced **fresh ginger** or ½ teaspoon ground ginger, and 2 tablespoons **dry sherry.**

Per serving: 407 calories, 32 g protein, 14 g carbohydrates, 26 g total fat, 65 mg cholesterol, 1,081 mg sodium

Oyster Beef

Preparation time: *About 15 minutes, plus 30 minutes to soak mushrooms*

Marinating time: *15 minutes*

Cooking time: *About 7 minutes*

This tasty beef dish gains subtle flavor from oyster sauce—a thick brown sauce sold in Asian markets and well-stocked supermarkets.

- 6 **medium-size dried Oriental mushrooms**
- ¾ **pound lean boneless beef steak (such as top round, flank, or sirloin)**
- 1 **tablespoon *each* dry sherry and soy sauce**
- 2 **tablespoons water**
- ¼ **teaspoon sugar**
- 2 **teaspoons cornstarch**
- 3½ **tablespoons salad oil**
- **Cooking Sauce (recipe follows)**
- 1 **clove garlic, minced**
- ½ **teaspoon minced fresh ginger**
- ½ **cup sliced bamboo shoots**
- **Salt**

Soak mushrooms in warm water to cover for 30 minutes, then drain. Cut off and discard stems; squeeze caps dry, thinly slice, and set aside.

Cut beef with the grain into 1½-inch-wide strips; then cut each strip across the grain into ⅛-inch-thick slanting slices. In a bowl, stir together sherry, soy, 1 tablespoon of the water, sugar, and cornstarch. Add beef and stir to coat, then stir in 1½ teaspoons of the oil and let marinate for 15 minutes.

Meanwhile, prepare Cooking Sauce and set aside.

Place a wok over high heat; when wok is hot, add 2 tablespoons of the oil. When oil begins to heat, add garlic and ginger and stir once. Add beef mixture and stir-fry until meat is browned (1½ to 2 minutes); remove from wok and set aside.

Pour remaining 1 tablespoon oil into wok. When oil is hot, add bamboo shoots and mushrooms; stir-fry for 1 minute. Add remaining 1 tablespoon water, cover, and cook for 2 minutes. Return meat mixture to wok. Stir Cooking Sauce, add to wok, and stir until sauce boils and thickens. Season to taste with salt. Makes 4 servings.

Cooking Sauce. Stir together 2 tablespoons **oyster sauce,** 1 tablespoon **cornstarch,** and ½ cup **regular-strength chicken broth.**

Per serving: 268 calories, 22 g protein, 9 g carbohydrates, 16 g total fat, 49 mg cholesterol, 787 mg sodium

Asparagus Beef

Follow directions for **Oyster Beef,** but substitute 1 pound **asparagus** for mushrooms and bamboo shoots. To prepare asparagus, snap off and discard tough ends of spears, then cut spears into ½-inch slanting slices.

Two-Onion Beef

Follow directions for **Oyster Beef,** but substitute 1 large **onion** and 12 **green onions** (including tops) for mushrooms and bamboo shoots. Cut onion in half, then thinly slice; cut green onions into 1½-inch lengths. After removing beef from wok, stir-fry sliced onion for 1 minute. Then add green onions and stir-fry for 30 seconds before returning beef to wok.

Beef & Broccoli

Preparation time: About 20 minutes

Marinating time: 15 minutes

Cooking time: About 15 minutes

Ginger and ground red pepper heat up the hearty sauce that coats beef strips and tender broccoli. Make the cooking sauce while the beef marinates.

- ¾ **pound broccoli**
- 1 **pound lean boneless beef steak (such as top round, flank, or sirloin)**
- 2 **tablespoons soy sauce**
- 1 **clove garlic, minced or pressed**
  Cooking Sauce (recipe follows)
- ¼ **cup salad oil**
- 2 **tablespoons water**

Cut off and discard tough ends of broccoli stalks; peel stalks, if desired. Cut tops into small flowerets; slice stalks ¼ inch thick. Set aside.

Cut beef with the grain into 1½-inch-wide strips, then cut each strip across the grain into ¼-inch-thick slanting slices. In a bowl, mix beef, soy, and garlic. Let marinate for 15 minutes. Meanwhile, prepare Cooking Sauce and set aside.

Place a wok over high heat; when wok is hot, add 1 tablespoon of the oil. When oil is hot, add half the meat mixture and stir-fry until meat is browned (2 to 3 minutes); remove from wok and set aside. Repeat to brown remaining meat, using 1 tablespoon more oil.

Pour remaining 2 tablespoons oil into wok. When oil is hot, add broccoli and stir-fry for about 1 minute. Add water, cover, and cook, stirring fre-

quently, until broccoli is tender-crisp to bite (about 3 more minutes). Stir Cooking Sauce, then add to wok along with meat; stir until sauce boils and thickens. Makes 3 or 4 servings.

Cooking Sauce. Stir together 1½ tablespoons **cornstarch,** ¼ teaspoon **ground ginger,** a dash of **ground red pepper** (cayenne), 2 tablespoons **dry sherry,** and 1¼ cups **regular-strength beef broth.**

Per serving: 318 calories, 29 g protein, 8 g carbohydrates, 19 g total fat, 65 mg cholesterol, 879 mg sodium

Steak Paprikash

Preparation time: About 10 minutes

Cooking time: About 15 minutes

A traditional slow-simmered dish from central Europe is easily adapted to stir-frying—with delicious results (and a considerable savings of time).

- 6 **slices bacon**
- 1½ **pounds lean boneless beef steak (such as top round, flank, or sirloin), cut across the grain into ¼-inch-thick slices**
- 1 **large onion, thinly sliced**
- 1 **small head green cabbage (about 1½ lbs.), coarsely shredded**
- 1 **tablespoon paprika**
- 2 **tablespoons water**
- 1 **cup *each* sour cream and plain yogurt**
- 2 **tablespoons all-purpose flour**
- 2 **tablespoons minced parsley**

Place a wok over medium heat; when wok is hot, add bacon. Cook, turning as needed, until crisp (about 3 minutes). Lift from wok, drain, crumble, and set aside. Pour off and discard all but 2 tablespoons of the drippings.

Place wok with bacon drippings over high heat. When fat is hot, add half the beef and stir-fry just until browned (2 to 3 minutes); with a slotted spoon, transfer meat to a bowl. Repeat to brown remaining beef.

Add onion, cabbage, and paprika to wok. Stir-fry for 1 minute; then add water, cover, and cook for 4 more minutes.

Stir together sour cream, yogurt, and flour; then stir into cabbage mixture. Add meat and any juices and stir just until hot. Top with bacon and parsley. Makes 4 servings.

Per serving: 565 calories, 50 g protein, 23 g carbohydrates, 31 g total fat, 138 mg cholesterol, 375 mg sodium

Tomato Beef

(Pictured on facing page)

Preparation time: *About 20 minutes*

Marinating time: *15 minutes*

Cooking time: *About 7 minutes*

Tender strips of beef and crisply cooked vegetables are tossed with a curry-flavored sauce for this easy Cantonese dish.

¾ **pound lean boneless beef steak (such as top round, flank, or sirloin)**

2 **teaspoons** *each* **cornstarch and soy sauce**

1 **tablespoon** *each* **dry sherry and water**

¼ **cup salad oil**
   Cooking Sauce (recipe follows)

½ **teaspoon minced fresh ginger**

1 **clove garlic, minced**

2 **large stalks celery, cut into ¼-inch-thick slanting slices**

1 **medium-size onion, cut into wedges, layers separated**

1 **green bell pepper, seeded and cut into 1-inch squares**

3 **medium-size tomatoes,** *each* **cut into 6 wedges**
   Salt

Cut beef with the grain into 1½-inch-wide strips; then cut each strip across the grain into ⅛-inch-thick slanting slices. In a bowl, stir together cornstarch, soy, sherry, and water. Add meat and stir to coat, then stir in 1½ teaspoons of the oil and let marinate for 15 minutes.

Meanwhile, prepare Cooking Sauce and set aside.

Place a wok over high heat; when wok is hot, add 2 tablespoons of the oil. When oil begins to heat, add ginger and garlic and stir once. Add meat mixture and stir-fry until meat is browned (1½ to 2 minutes); remove from wok and set aside.

Pour remaining 1½ tablespoons oil into wok. When oil is hot, add celery and onion and stir-fry for 1 minute. Add bell pepper and stir-fry for 1 minute, adding a few drops of water if wok appears dry. Add tomatoes and stir-fry for 1 minute. Return meat to wok. Stir Cooking Sauce, pour into wok, and stir until sauce boils and thickens. Season to taste with salt. Makes 4 servings.

Cooking Sauce. Stir together 1 tablespoon *each* **soy sauce, Worcestershire,** and **cornstarch;** 3 tablespoons **catsup;** 1 teaspoon **curry powder;** and ½ cup **water.**

Per serving: 308 calories, 22 g protein, 16 g carbohydrates, 18 g total fat, 48 mg cholesterol, 679 mg sodium

Beef with Snow Peas

Preparation time: *About 25 minutes*

Marinating time: *2 hours*

Cooking time: *About 8 minutes*

This spicy stir-fry of beef and snow peas owes its complex flavors to a meat marinade of soy, sherry, sesame oil, hoisin sauce, and Tientsin preserved vegetables. You'll find the preserved vegetables—called *chong choy*— in Asian markets.

1 **pound lean boneless beef steak (such as top round, flank, or sirloin)**
   Spicy Marinade (recipe follows)

¼ **cup salad oil**

¾ **pound Chinese pea pods (also called snow or sugar peas) or sugar snap peas, ends and strings removed; or 2 packages (6 oz.** *each***) frozen Chinese pea pods, thawed and drained**

1 **tablespoon water**

1 **tablespoon soy sauce**

1 **teaspoon sugar**

1 **small onion, cut into slivers**

Cut beef into 1-inch chunks. With a mallet, pound each piece to a thickness of about ¼ inch. Prepare marinade; stir in beef, then cover and refrigerate for at least 2 hours or until next day.

Place a wok over high heat; when wok is hot, add 2 tablespoons of the oil. When oil is hot, add fresh pea pods. Stir-fry for about 3 minutes; add water, cover, and cook until pea pods are tender-crisp to bite—about 30 seconds. (If using frozen pea pods, simply stir-fry for 30 seconds *total*.) Transfer to a serving dish. Return wok to heat and add remaining 2 tablespoons oil; when oil is hot, add beef and marinade. Stir-fry until meat is browned (2 to 3 minutes). Stir in soy, sugar, and onion; cook for 1 more minute. Makes about 4 servings.

Spicy Marinade. Stir together 2 tablespoons **salad oil** and 1 tablespoon *each* **soy sauce, catsup, dry sherry, cornstarch, hoisin sauce,** and **sesame oil.** If desired, stir in 1 tablespoon **Tientsin preserved vegetables.** Then stir in 1 teaspoon **Worcestershire** and 1 clove **garlic,** minced or pressed.

Per serving: 436 calories, 29 g protein, 14 g carbohydrates, 29 g total fat, 65 mg cholesterol, 764 mg sodium

A visual feast of appetizing color, Tomato Beef
(recipe on facing page) shows off the wok's magic with
fresh ingredients. A touch of curry gives the spicy
sauce memorable flavor.

The Tabletop Wok

If your guests like to participate in making a meal, you'll want to introduce them to these easy and delicious variations on the popular Asian hot-pot tradition. To present the meal, you'll need one electric wok (or a regular wok with a portable heat source) for every six guests. If serving more than six, set up a second table and wok. Set the wok in the middle of the table and fill it with boiling broth, then offer trays of cut-up meats and vegetables and let guests choose and cook their own portions.

Mizutaki

1½ **pounds lean boneless beef sirloin, trimmed of excess fat and cut across the grain into ¼-inch-thick slanting slices**

6 **chicken thighs (1½ to 2 lbs. *total*) or 3 whole chicken breasts (about 1 lb. *each*), skinned, boned, and cut across the grain into ¼-inch-thick slices**

1 **pound carrots, cut into ¼-inch-thick slanting slices**

¾ **pound cauliflower (about ½ head), cut into flowerets, each floweret sliced in half lengthwise**

6 **to 8 green onions (including tops), cut into 2-inch lengths**

½ **pound fresh shiitake or button mushroom caps, cut into ¼-inch-thick slices**

1 **pound spinach or watercress, stems and any yellow or wilted leaves removed, green leaves rinsed well**

½ **pound medium or firm tofu (bean curd), drained and cut into ½-inch cubes**

Mizutaki Sauce (recipe follows)

6 **to 8 cups hot cooked rice**

8 **cups regular-strength beef broth**

Arrange beef, chicken, vegetables, and tofu on trays. Place next to wok in center of table.

Prepare Mizutaki Sauce; pour into 6 small bowls (1 for each diner). Fill 6 more small bowls with rice.

Place an electric wok in center of table. Pour broth into wok and bring to a boil; adjust heat to keep broth simmering. Let guests fill wok with some of each food, starting with the slower-cooking carrots and cauliflower and ending with meats. Cover wok. Let foods simmer until chicken is no longer pink in center; cut to test (3 to 5 minutes).

Uncover wok; let guests remove portions with chopsticks, tongs, or strainer ladles, a bite at a time. Dip each bite in Mizutaki Sauce, then eat with rice. As wok is emptied, let guests add more food and cook it to taste.

At the end of the meal, add the enriched broth to sauce cups; stir broth and sauce together, then sip mixture as soup. Makes 6 servings.

Mizutaki Sauce. In a blender or food processor, combine 1 **egg,** 2 tablespoons **rice wine vinegar** or white wine vinegar, and ¼ teaspoon **dry mustard;** whirl until blended. With motor running, pour in 1 cup **salad oil** in a slow, steady stream. Pour mixture into a bowl; stir in ½ cup **sour cream,** 2 tablespoons **soy sauce,** 2 tablespoons **mirin** (sweet sake) or dry sherry, and ⅓ cup **regular-strength beef broth.** Makes about 2 cups.

Chicken & Vegetable One-pot Meal

Mushroom Bundles (directions follow)

Carrot Bundles (directions follow)

Spinach Rolls (directions follow)

Peanut Sauce (recipe follows)

1½ **to 2 pounds skinned, boned chicken breasts**

1½ **to 2 pounds mustard greens, tough stems removed, leaves rinsed well and chilled**

2 **large cans (49½ oz. *each*) regular-strength chicken broth**

½ **cup finely chopped green onions (white part only)**

2 **limes, *each* cut into 4 wedges**

1 **tablespoon crushed dried hot red chiles**

Prepare Mushroom Bundles, Carrot Bundles, Spinach Rolls. Prepare Peanut Sauce and set aside.

Rinse chicken, pat dry, and cut into 1- by 2-inch strips no thicker than 1 inch. Arrange chicken, mustard greens, Mushroom Bundles, Carrot Bundles, and Spinach Rolls on trays.

Place an electric wok in center of table. Pour half the broth into wok and bring to a boil; adjust heat to keep broth simmering. Place trays of foods alongside. Place onions, limes, chiles, and Peanut Sauce in separate containers for each guest. Guests add foods to broth, removing vegetables when hot (about 1 minute) and chicken when no longer pink in center, cut to test (2 to 4 minutes). Add remaining broth as needed.

Let guests flavor their portions of Peanut Sauce to taste with onions, a squeeze of lime, and chiles. Dip vegetables and chicken into sauce to eat. At the end of the meal, ladle hot broth into cups, add Peanut Sauce to taste, and sip broth. Makes 6 servings.

Mushroom Bundles. Divide 2 bags (3½ oz. *each*) **enoki mushrooms** into 6 equal portions, laying mushrooms parallel.

Cut 6 green stems (tops) from about 2 **green onions;** reserve white part to chop for flavoring Peanut Sauce. Immerse stems in **boiling water** until limp (about 30 seconds); drain and let cool. Tie each portion of mushrooms with an onion stem. Cut off and discard brown, woody ends of mushrooms.

Carrot Bundles. Peel 2 medium-size **carrots;** trim off ends. Cut each carrot crosswise into thirds; cut each third into thin sticks. Divide sticks into 12 equal portions, laying them parallel. Cut 12 green stems (tops) from about 4 **green onions;** reserve white part to chop for flavoring Peanut Sauce. Immerse stems in **boiling water** until limp (about 30 seconds); drain and let cool. Tie each portion of carrots with an onion stem.

Spinach Rolls. Discard stems and any yellow or wilted leaves from 2 pounds **spinach;** rinse green leaves well and set aside. Cut 4 large outer **napa cabbage** leaves, *each* 9 to 10 inches long. Immerse cabbage leaves in **boiling water** until limp (about 2 minutes). Lift from water; drain, lay flat, and pat dry. Trim thick part of rib from center of each leaf, making a V-shaped cut.

Add spinach to boiling water and cook until limp (about 2 minutes); drain. Let cool; firmly squeeze out moisture with your hands.

On a muslin cloth, lay 2 cabbage leaves side by side (stems in opposite directions), with edges overlapping by several inches. Lay half the spinach along outer edge of cabbage leaves. Form a roll by lifting cloth with 1 hand (from spinach side); smooth roll with other hand. Make roll tight so it will hold its shape when heated in broth. Form another roll with remaining cabbage and spinach. Cut rolls crosswise into 1½-inch slices.

Peanut Sauce. Blend ⅔ cup **creamy peanut butter,** 2 tablespoons **soy sauce,** 4 teaspoons **distilled white vinegar,** and 2 teaspoons **sugar.** Slowly whisk in 1 cup **regular-strength chicken broth.** Makes 1¾ cups.

Udon-suki

Pork Balls (recipe follows)
Prepared vegetables (suggestions follow)
12 **small live hard-shell clams, scrubbed well, rinsed in cold water**
3 **packages (about 7 oz. *each*) fresh udon noodles or about 6 ounces dried udon or spaghetti**
Boiling salted water
1 **tablespoon salad oil**
2 **large cans (49½ oz. *each*) regular-strength chicken broth**

Prepare Pork Balls and vegetables. Set aside with clams.

Shortly before serving, immerse fresh noodles in boiling salted water until tender to bite (2 to 3 minutes); drain. (Or cook dried noodles according to package directions; drain.) Mix noodles with oil and place in a bowl.

Place an electric wok in center of table. Pour half the broth plus pan juices from Pork Balls into wok; bring to a boil. Place half the clams in broth. Cover and cook until broth returns to a boil; reduce heat and simmer for 3 minutes. Then

add about half the Pork Balls and half the vegetables; continue to simmer until clams pop open. Let guests remove cooked ingredients and noodles to individual bowls; then ladle some of the hot broth into each bowl. Repeat to prepare second servings. Makes 4 to 6 servings.

Pork Balls. Toast ¼ cup **pine nuts** in a small frying pan over medium heat until golden (about 4 minutes), shaking pan frequently. Place in a bowl and add 1 pound **lean ground pork,** 1 **egg,** 2 tablespoons **all-purpose flour,** 1 tablespoon **soy sauce,** and ½ teaspoon grated **fresh ginger.** Mix well. Shape into balls, using about 1 tablespoon meat mixture for each; arrange slightly apart on a rimmed baking sheet. Bake in a 475° oven until no longer pink in center; cut to test (about 15 minutes). Reserve any pan juices to add to broth. Makes about 3 dozen meatballs.

Prepared vegetables. You'll need a total of 6 to 8 cups vegetables.

■ *Carrots or celery.* Cut into ¼-inch-thick slanting slices. Immerse in boiling water until tender to bite (about 5 minutes); drain.

■ *Daikon or turnips.* Peel and cut crosswise into ¼-inch-thick slices. Immerse in boiling water until tender to bite (3 minutes for daikon, 4 minutes for turnips); drain.

■ *Chinese pea pods* (also called snow or sugar peas) or sugar snap peas. Remove and discard ends and strings. Immerse in boiling water until tender to bite (about 30 seconds); drain.

■ *Dried Oriental mushrooms or fresh button mushrooms.* Soak dried mushrooms in warm water to cover for 30 minutes; drain. Cut off and discard stems; squeeze caps dry and leave whole. Cut fresh mushrooms lengthwise into ¼-inch-thick slices.

Fajitas in a wok? Yes—when you make this hearty
stir-fried version of the Southwestern barbecue classic. Fun, delicious,
and quick, Fajitas Stir-fry (recipe on facing page)
is sure to become a favorite.

Fajitas Stir-fry

(Pictured on facing page)

Preparation time: About 30 minutes

Cooking time: About 7 minutes

In this quick version of fajitas, the steak is stir-fried instead of grilled. You wrap the meat in warm flour tortillas—or crisp iceberg lettuce leaves.

- 1 **pound lean boneless beef steak (such as top round, flank, or sirloin)**
- 2 **tablespoons salad oil**
- 2 **cloves garlic, minced or pressed**
- 1 **large onion, thinly sliced and separated into rings**
- 2 **or 3 fresh jalapeño chiles, seeded and minced**
- 1 **large red bell pepper, seeded and cut into thin strips**
- 2 **teaspoons ground cumin**
- 3 **tablespoons lime juice**
- 1 **teaspoon cornstarch**
- 2 **medium-size Roma-type tomatoes, diced**
  Salt and pepper
  Lime wedges
  Sour cream (optional)
- 1 **large ripe avocado, pitted, peeled, and diced**
- 8 **warm flour tortillas (8-inch diameter); or 8 large iceberg lettuce leaves, chilled**
  Homemade or purchased salsa (optional)

Cut beef with the grain into 1-inch-wide strips; then cut each strip across the grain into ⅛-inch-thick slices. Set aside.

Place a wok over high heat; when wok is hot, add 1 tablespoon of the oil. When oil is hot, add meat. Stir-fry until meat is browned (1½ to 2 minutes); transfer meat to a bowl with a slotted spoon.

Add remaining 1 tablespoon oil to wok, then add garlic, onion, chiles, and bell pepper. Stir-fry until onion is soft (about 3 minutes). Stir together cumin, lime juice, and cornstarch; add to wok. Return meat to wok, add tomatoes, and stir until mixture is hot and juices boil. Season to taste with salt and pepper, then pour fajitas into a serving dish; garnish with lime wedges. Offer sour cream (if desired) and avocado in separate dishes.

Spoon meat mixture onto tortillas or lettuce leaves; add sour cream, avocado, and a squeeze of lime to taste. Fold up and eat out of hand. Accompany with salsa, if desired. Makes 4 servings.

Per serving: 612 calories, 34 g protein, 49 g carbohydrates, 32 g total fat, 65 mg cholesterol, 76 mg sodium

Simple Sauerbraten

Preparation time: 15 minutes

Marinating time: 15 minutes

Cooking time: About 10 minutes

Traditional sauerbraten is a tasty but time-consuming dish to prepare. Slicing the meat and stir-frying cuts down on the cooking time without sacrificing the familiar tangy flavor. Accompany this spicy sweet-and-sour main course with broccoli and butter noodles.

- 1 **pound lean boneless beef steak (such as top round, flank, or sirloin)**
- ¼ **cup *each* dry white wine and white vinegar**
- 1 **tablespoon brown sugar**
- 1 **dry bay leaf**
- ¼ **teaspoon *each* pepper and ground cloves**
- 2 **tablespoons salad oil**
- 1 **red onion, thinly sliced**
- 1 **cup thinly sliced carrots**
- ½ **cup thinly sliced celery**
- 1 **clove garlic, minced or pressed**
- 2 **tablespoons water**
- ¼ **cup crushed gingersnaps**
  Sour cream (optional)

Cut beef with the grain into 2-inch-wide strips; then cut each strip across the grain into ⅛-inch-thick slanting slices. In a bowl, mix wine, vinegar, brown sugar, bay leaf, pepper, and cloves; stir in meat and let marinate for about 30 minutes. Drain meat, reserving marinade, and remove bay leaf.

Place a wok over high heat; when wok is hot, add oil. When oil is hot, add meat and stir-fry until meat is browned (1½ to 2 minutes). Remove meat from wok; set aside. Immediately add red onion and carrots to wok and stir-fry for 1 minute. Add celery and garlic; stir-fry for 1 more minute. Add water, cover, and cook until carrots and celery are tender-crisp to bite (about 3 more minutes).

Return meat to wok and add marinade and gingersnaps. Stir until sauce thickens slightly. Serve with a dollop of sour cream, if desired. Makes 4 servings.

Per serving: 283 calories, 27 g protein, 15 g carbohydrates, 12 g total fat, 67 mg cholesterol, 123 mg sodium

Sirloin Tips & Vegetables

Preparation time: About 10 minutes

Marinating time: About 30 minutes

Cooking time: About 8 minutes

Thin sirloin strips and vegetables, enhanced with ginger and hoisin, are served over spinach for an outstanding entrée. A red wine marinade both flavors and tenderizes the meat. You may use either fresh or frozen spinach; cook it just before you start to stir-fry.

> About 1 pound sirloin tips
> ¼ cup dry red wine
> 2 tablespoons soy sauce
> 1 clove garlic, minced or pressed
> 1 teaspoon minced fresh ginger
> 2 tablespoons salad oil
> 1 cup thinly sliced celery
> ½ pound mushrooms, thinly sliced
> 1 can (about 8 oz.) water chestnuts, drained and sliced
> ½ cup thinly sliced green onions (including tops)
> 2 tablespoons hoisin sauce
> Hot cooked spinach

Cut beef across the grain into ⅛-inch-thick strips and place in a shallow dish. Stir together wine, soy, garlic, and ginger; pour over meat and let marinate for about 30 minutes.

Place a wok over high heat; when wok is hot, add oil. When oil is hot, add meat mixture and stir-fry until meat is browned (1½ to 2 minutes). Remove meat from wok and set aside. Immediately add celery, mushrooms, water chestnuts, onions, and hoisin. Stir-fry until celery is tender-crisp to bite (2 to 3 minutes). Return meat to wok; stir until heated through. Serve immediately over spinach. Makes 4 servings.

Per serving: 305 calories, 25 g protein, 14 g carbohydrates, 16 g total fat, 68 mg cholesterol, 352 mg sodium

Burgundy Beef

Preparation time: About 10 minutes

Marinating time: About 15 minutes

Cooking time: About 7 minutes

Nobody would describe *boeuf bourguignon* as a classic stir-fry—but this bold beef dish can in fact be made quite successfully in a wok. Wine and herbs flavor the distinctive sauce.

> 1 pound lean boneless beef steak (such as top round, flank, or sirloin)
> ¼ pound mushrooms, thinly sliced
> ½ cup dry red wine
> 2 tablespoons salad oil
> ¼ teaspoon *each* dry chervil, dry tarragon, and salt
> ⅛ teaspoon dry marjoram leaves
> 1½ tablespoons all-purpose flour

Cut beef with the grain into 2-inch-wide strips; then cut each strip across the grain into ⅛-inch-thick slanting slices. Combine meat and mushrooms in a bowl; stir in wine and let marinate at room temperature for about 15 minutes (or cover and refrigerate for up to 3 hours).

Drain meat and mushrooms, reserving marinade. Place a wok over high heat; when wok is hot, add oil. When oil begins to heat, add chervil, tarragon, salt, and marjoram. Then add meat and mushrooms and stir-fry just until meat is browned (1½ to 2 minutes).

Sprinkle meat mixture with flour, then blend in reserved marinade. Stir until sauce is slightly thickened. Makes 4 servings.

Per serving: 235 calories, 27 g protein, 4 g carbohydrates, 12 g total fat, 65 mg cholesterol, 197 mg sodium

Picadillo

Preparation time: About 5 minutes

Marinating time: 15 minutes

Cooking time: About 15 minutes

Picadillo is a South American specialty—"minced meat" (here, ground beef) served with a sweet and sour sauce and such traditional ingredients as olives, raisins, and bell peppers.

> 1 pound lean ground beef
> 1½ tablespoons distilled white vinegar
> 1 clove garlic, minced or pressed
> 1 teaspoon ground cumin
> 2 tablespoons salad oil
> 1 small onion, chopped
> 1 small green bell pepper, seeded and cut into thin strips
> 1 can (8 oz.) tomato sauce
> ½ cup water
> ½ teaspoon cracked bay leaves
> 6 pimento-stuffed green olives, sliced
> 1 tablespoon raisins
> Salt and pepper
> 1 can (4 oz.) shoestring potatoes

In a bowl, combine beef, vinegar, garlic, and cumin; mix well and let stand for 15 minutes.

Place a wok over medium-high heat; when wok is hot, add 1 tablespoon of the oil. When oil is hot, add meat mixture; cook, stirring, until meat is browned (about 3 minutes). Lift out and set aside; spoon out and discard any fat.

Pour remaining 1 tablespoon oil into wok; when oil is hot, add onion and bell pepper and stir-fry until onion is soft (about 4 minutes). Stir in tomato sauce, water, bay leaves, olives, and raisins. Bring to a boil; then reduce heat and simmer, uncovered, until slightly reduced (about 5 minutes). Add meat mixture and cook until heated through (about 2 more minutes). Season to taste with salt and pepper. Mound on a rimmed platter; surround with potatoes. Makes 4 servings.

Per serving: 378 calories, 22 g protein, 16 g carbohydrates, 26 g total fat, 69 mg cholesterol, 525 mg sodium

Lettuce Tacos

Preparation time: About 25 minutes

Cooking time: 8 to 10 minutes

Crisp lettuce leaves make a light, cool, change-of-pace wrapper for this spicy meat and vegetable mixture.

- 1 **medium-size head iceberg lettuce (about 1 lb.)**
- 1 **tablespoon salad oil**
- 2 **medium-size carrots, coarsely chopped**
- 1 **large zucchini (7 to 8 inches long), cut into ¼-inch cubes**
- 1 **cup fresh corn kernels cut from cob or 1 cup frozen whole-kernel corn, thawed and drained**
- 1 **pound lean ground beef**
- 2 **cloves garlic, minced or pressed**
- 1 **tablespoon chili powder**
- 1 **teaspoon ground cumin**
- 1 **cup thinly sliced green onions (including tops)**
- 1 **can (6 oz.) spicy tomato cocktail**
- 1 **tablespoon cornstarch**
  Salt
- ½ **cup shredded jack cheese**

Separate leaves from lettuce; rinse and shake dry. Arrange on a serving plate, cover, and refrigerate.

Place a wok over high heat; when wok is hot, add oil. When oil is hot, add carrots; stir-fry for 1 minute. Add zucchini and corn; stir-fry for 1 more minute, then remove vegetables with a slotted spoon and set aside.

Crumble beef into wok; cook, stirring, until browned (2 to 3 minutes). Spoon off and discard all but 1 tablespoon of the fat. Then add garlic, chili powder, cumin, and onions to meat; cook, stirring, just until onions begin to soften. Return carrot mixture to wok and stir until heated through.

Mix tomato cocktail and cornstarch; add to wok and cook, stirring, until sauce boils and thickens. Season to taste with salt. Transfer to a serving bowl; sprinkle with cheese.

To serve, spoon beef mixture onto chilled lettuce leaves. Makes 4 servings.

Per serving: 451 calories, 28 g protein, 24 g carbohydrates, 28 g total fat, 85 mg cholesterol, 342 mg sodium

Five-spice Pork & Potatoes

Preparation time: About 10 minutes

Cooking time: About 25 minutes

Russet potatoes and thin, tender pork strips soak up the fragrance and flavor of Chinese five-spice. The bottled spice blend is sold in many markets, but if you can't find it, you can easily make your own.

- 3 **large russet potatoes (about 1½ lbs. *total*)**
- 2 **tablespoons salad oil**
- 1 **pound lean boneless pork (such as shoulder or butt), trimmed of excess fat and cut into ¼- by 1- by 3-inch strips**
- 2 **cloves garlic, minced or pressed**
- 1½ **cups water**
- 3 **tablespoons soy sauce**
- 2 **teaspoons sugar**
- 1¼ **teaspoons Chinese five-spice; or ½ teaspoon ground ginger, ¼ teaspoon *each* ground cinnamon and crushed anise seeds, and ⅛ teaspoon *each* ground allspice and ground cloves**
- ⅓ **cup thinly sliced green onions (including tops)**

Peel potatoes and cut crosswise into ½-inch-thick slices; cut large slices in half. Set aside.

Place a wok over high heat; when wok is hot, add oil. When oil is hot, add pork and garlic. Stir-fry until pork is browned (2 to 3 minutes). Add potatoes, water, soy, sugar, and five-spice. Bring to a boil; then reduce heat, cover, and simmer, stirring occasionally, until potatoes are tender when pierced (about 20 minutes). Garnish with onions. Makes 3 or 4 servings.

Per serving: 359 calories, 26 g protein, 28 g carbohydrates, 16 g total fat, 76 mg cholesterol, 867 mg sodium

Twice-cooked Pork

(Pictured on facing page)

Preparation time: About 5 minutes

Cooking time: About 45 minutes to simmer; about 6 minutes to stir-fry

The pork in this spicy Szechwan dish really is cooked twice—first simmered, then stir-fried (if you like, you can even do the cooking on different days). Sweet and hot bean sauces add a distinctive flavor—but if you can't find them, you may use hoisin sauce and chiles with equally tasty results.

1 pound lean boneless pork (such as shoulder or butt), in 1 piece
1 tablespoon dry sherry
1 thin, quarter-size slice fresh ginger, crushed with the side of a cleaver
3 green onions (including tops)
2 teaspoons hot bean sauce; or 2 small dried hot red chiles, crumbled
4 teaspoons sweet bean sauce or hoisin sauce
1 tablespoon soy sauce
1 teaspoon sugar
2 small green bell peppers or 1 *each* small green and red bell pepper
3 tablespoons salad oil
½ teaspoon salt
2 cloves garlic, minced
1 teaspoon minced fresh ginger

Place pork, sherry, and ginger slice in a 2-quart pan. Cut 1 of the green onions in half crosswise and add to pork, then add enough water to barely cover meat. Bring to a simmer; cover and simmer until meat is tender when pierced (about 45 minutes).

Lift meat from broth and refrigerate until cold. Then cut into 1½-inch-square pieces about ⅛ inch thick. (The fatty parts of the meat are considered a delicacy, but remove them if you wish.)

In a bowl, combine hot bean sauce, sweet bean sauce, soy, and sugar. Seed bell peppers and cut into 1-inch squares; cut remaining 2 green onions into 1-inch lengths.

Place a wok over high heat; when wok is hot, add 2 tablespoons of the oil. When oil is hot, add bell peppers and stir-fry for 1½ minutes, adding a few drops of water if wok appears dry. Sprinkle with salt and stir once, then remove peppers from wok. Add remaining 1 tablespoon oil to wok. When oil begins to heat, add garlic and minced ginger and stir once; then add pork and stir-fry for 1 minute. Add bean sauce mixture and toss until pork is coated

with sauce. Return bell peppers to wok along with onion. Stir for 30 seconds to heat through. Makes 3 or 4 servings.

Per serving: 302 calories, 24 g protein, 8 g carbohydrates, 20 g total fat, 76 mg cholesterol, 790 mg sodium

Hawaiian Pork

Preparation time: About 15 minutes

Cooking time: About 20 minutes

Emerald-green snow peas and bright bell peppers add color and crisp texture to this richly flavored version of sweet and sour pork.

Sweet-Sour Sauce (recipe follows)
2 pounds lean boneless pork (such as shoulder or butt), trimmed of excess fat and cut into ¾-inch cubes
1 egg, beaten
   About ½ cup cornstarch
   About 6 tablespoons salad oil
1 *each* small green and red bell pepper, seeded and cut into 1-inch squares
1 small onion, cut into wedges, layers separated
¼ pound Chinese pea pods (also called snow or sugar peas) or sugar snap peas, ends and strings removed; or 1 package (6 oz.) frozen Chinese pea pods, thawed and drained

Prepare Sweet-Sour Sauce; set aside.

Dip pork cubes in beaten egg, drain briefly, and roll in cornstarch to coat lightly; shake off excess.

Place a wok over high heat; when wok is hot, add 2 tablespoons of the oil. When oil is hot, add half the pork; stir-fry until evenly browned (5 to 7 minutes). Lift pork from wok and set aside. Repeat to brown remaining meat, adding more oil as needed.

Add remaining oil (about 2 tablespoons) to wok. Add bell peppers and onion; stir-fry until vegetables are tender-crisp to bite (about 2 minutes). Add pea pods; then stir sauce and add. Stir until sauce boils and thickens; return pork to wok and stir until heated through. Makes 6 to 8 servings.

Sweet-Sour Sauce. Stir together ½ cup *each* **cider vinegar,** firmly packed **brown sugar,** and **catsup;** ¼ cup *each* **cornstarch** and **unsweetened pineapple juice;** and 2 tablespoons **soy sauce.**

Per serving: 408 calories, 24 g protein, 33 g carbohydrates, 20 g total fat, 110 mg cholesterol, 535 mg sodium

Instead of going out for Chinese food, you'll soon choose to
stay home and dine on spicy Twice-cooked Pork (recipe on
facing page). It really does involve double-cooking the pork,
but the flavor is well worth the extra time.

Pork Tenderloin Normandy

Preparation time: About 15 minutes

Cooking time: About 10 minutes

Apple slices, onion, and sliced pork mingle in a creamy sauce sparked with Dijon mustard. A sprinkle of raisins adds a sweet finishing touch.

- ½ teaspoon *each* salt and dry oregano leaves
- ⅛ teaspoon pepper
- 3 tablespoons all-purpose flour
  About ¾ pound pork tenderloin, cut into ⅛-inch-thick, 1½-inch-wide slices
- ¼ cup butter or margarine
- 1 large onion, chopped
- 1 large Golden Delicious apple, cored and thinly sliced
- 2 tablespoons Dijon mustard
- 1 cup milk
- 2 tablespoons raisins
  Chopped parsley

Combine salt, oregano, pepper, and flour. Dredge pork in flour mixture; shake off excess. Set remaining flour mixture aside.

Place a wok over medium-high heat; when wok is hot, add 2 tablespoons of the butter. When butter is melted, add pork and stir-fry until browned (2 to 3 minutes); remove pork from wok and set aside.

Add remaining 2 tablespoons butter to wok; when butter is melted, add onion and stir-fry until soft (about 3 minutes). Add apple, then sprinkle in remaining flour mixture; stir-fry for about 1 minute. Stir in mustard and milk; bring to a boil, then return meat to wok and stir-fry for about 2 minutes. Stir in raisins and sprinkle with parsley. Makes 3 or 4 servings.

Per serving: 318 calories, 21 g protein, 22 g carbohydrates, 16 g total fat, 95 mg cholesterol, 686 mg sodium

Pork with Baby Corn

Preparation time: About 20 minutes

Marinating time: 15 minutes

Cooking time: About 8 minutes

Baby sweet corn is a treat in this quick Cantonese entrée. Sold canned or bottled, the tiny, tender ears of corn are available in Asian markets and in the imported food section of most supermarkets.

- 1 teaspoon *each* cornstarch and soy sauce
- 1 tablespoon dry sherry
- ¼ teaspoon pepper
- 1 pound lean boneless pork (such as shoulder or butt), trimmed of excess fat and cut into ⅛- by 1- by 2-inch strips
- ¼ cup salad oil
  Cooking Sauce (recipe follows)
- 2 cloves garlic, minced
- 1 small onion, cut into wedges, layers separated
- ¼ pound mushrooms, thinly sliced
- 1 can (about 1 lb.) whole baby sweet corn, drained
- 8 green onions (including tops), cut into 2-inch lengths

In a bowl, stir together cornstarch, soy, sherry, and pepper. Add pork and stir to coat. Stir in 1 teaspoon of the oil. Let marinate for 15 minutes. Meanwhile, prepare Cooking Sauce and set aside.

Place a wok over high heat; when wok is hot, add 2 tablespoons of the oil. When oil begins to heat, add garlic and stir once. Then add half the pork mixture and stir-fry until meat is lightly browned (1½ to 2 minutes); remove from wok. Repeat to brown remaining meat, using 1 tablespoon more oil.

Pour remaining 2 teaspoons oil into wok. When oil is hot, add onion pieces and mushrooms and stir-fry for 1 minute, adding a few drops of water if wok appears dry. Return meat mixture to wok, then add corn and green onions; stir-fry for 30 seconds. Stir Cooking Sauce, add to wok, and stir until sauce boils and thickens. Makes 4 servings.

Cooking Sauce. Stir together 1½ tablespoons **cornstarch,** 1 teaspoon *each* **sugar** and **vinegar,** ¼ teaspoon **salt,** 1 tablespoon **soy sauce,** and ¾ cup **regular-strength chicken broth** or water.

Per serving: 435 calories, 27 g protein, 32 g carbohydrates, 24 g total fat, 76 mg cholesterol, 1,064 mg sodium

Yu-shiang Pork

Preparation time: About 15 minutes

Marinating time: 15 minutes

Cooking time: About 8 minutes

Yu-shiang pork doesn't taste like fish—but because the seasonings used are typical of Szechwan fish cookery, the dish is often called fish-flavored pork.

1 teaspoon cornstarch
¼ teaspoon salt
 Dash of white pepper
1 tablespoon dry sherry
¾ pound lean boneless pork (such as shoulder or butt), trimmed of excess fat and cut into matchstick pieces
3½ tablespoons salad oil
 Cooking Sauce (recipe follows)
2 cloves garlic, minced
1 teaspoon minced fresh ginger
3 or 4 small dried hot red chiles
⅔ cup sliced bamboo shoots, cut into matchstick pieces
10 green onions (including tops), cut into 2-inch lengths

In a bowl, combine cornstarch, salt, white pepper, and sherry. Add pork and stir to coat; then stir in 1½ teaspoons of the oil. Let marinate for 15 minutes. Meanwhile, prepare Cooking Sauce; set aside.

Place a wok over high heat. When wok is hot, add 2 tablespoons of the oil. When oil begins to heat, add garlic, ginger, and chiles; stir once. Add pork mixture and stir-fry until meat is lightly browned (2 to 3 minutes); remove from wok.

Pour remaining 1 tablespoon oil into wok. When oil is hot, add bamboo shoots and onions and stir-fry for 1 minute. Return pork mixture to wok. Stir Cooking Sauce, pour into wok, and stir until sauce boils and thickens. Makes 4 servings.

Cooking Sauce. Stir together 1 tablespoon *each* **sugar, vinegar,** and **dry sherry;** 2 tablespoons **soy sauce;** 3 tablespoons **regular-strength chicken broth** or water; and 2 teaspoons **cornstarch.**

Per serving: 299 calories, 19 g protein, 13 g carbohydrates, 17 g total fat, 57 mg cholesterol, 766 mg sodium

Sweet & Sour Pork

Preparation time: About 15 minutes

Cooking time: About 25 minutes

Here's one Chinese dish that's familiar to just about everybody. Crisp, juicy chunks of pork and a colorful medley of vegetables and fruit combine in a tangy, ginger-spiked sauce.

 Sweet & Sour Sauce (recipe follows)
2 pounds lean boneless pork (such as shoulder or butt), trimmed of excess fat and cut into 1-inch cubes
1 egg, beaten
 About ½ cup cornstarch

 About 5 tablespoons salad oil
1 medium-size onion, cut into 1-inch cubes
2 medium-size carrots, cut into ¼-inch-thick slanting slices
1 clove garlic, minced or pressed
2 tablespoons water
1 green bell pepper, seeded and cut into 1-inch squares
½ cup fresh or drained canned pineapple chunks
2 medium-size tomatoes, cut into 1-inch cubes

Prepare Sweet & Sour Sauce; set aside.

Dip pork cubes in beaten egg, drain briefly, and roll in cornstarch to coat lightly; shake off excess.

Place a wok over medium-high heat. When wok is hot, add 3 tablespoons of the oil. When oil is hot, add half the pork and stir-fry until evenly browned (about 7 minutes); lift pork from wok and set aside. Repeat to brown remaining meat, adding more oil as needed.

Scrape away and discard any browned particles from sides and bottom of wok, but leave oil in wok. If necessary, add more oil to wok to make about 2 tablespoons total. Place wok over high heat. When oil is hot, add onion, carrots, and garlic; stir-fry for about 1 minute. Add water and bell pepper; cover and cook, stirring frequently, for about 2 minutes. Add pineapple, tomatoes, and pork; stir Sweet & Sour Sauce, then add. Stir until mixture boils and thickens (about 1 minute). Makes 6 servings.

Sweet & Sour Sauce. Stir together 1 tablespoon **cornstarch** and ⅓ cup firmly packed **brown sugar.** Then stir in ½ teaspoon minced **fresh ginger** or ¼ teaspoon ground ginger, 1 tablespoon *each* **soy sauce** and **dry sherry,** and ¼ cup *each* **wine vinegar** and **regular-strength chicken or beef broth.**

Per serving: 474 calories, 32 g protein, 31 g carbohydrates, 25 g total fat, 147 mg cholesterol, 358 mg sodium

Rich flavors mingle in Papaya & Sausage Sauté
(recipe on facing page). Brought together in a spicy honey glaze,
hearty bites of Italian sausage and smooth papaya slices
make an exquisite entrée.

Sausage Etouffée

Preparation time: About 25 minutes

Cooking time: About 35 minutes

Extra-rich, spicy, and filling! This Cajun entrée starts with a "black roux": a blend of flour and oil cooked until deep brown, then blended with minced vegetables.

- 1 **cup Black Roux (recipe follows)**
- ½ **pound bacon, chopped**
- 1 **medium-size eggplant (¾ to 1 lb.), cut into ½-inch cubes**
- ½ **cup** *each* **chopped onion, chopped green bell pepper, and chopped celery**
- 1 **clove garlic, minced or pressed**
- 1 **pound kielbasa (Polish sausage), cut into ½-inch-thick slices**
- ½ **teaspoon black pepper**
- ⅛ **teaspoon ground red pepper (cayenne)**
- 1½ **cups water**
  Salt
- ½ **cup sliced green onions (including tops)**

Prepare roux; set aside.

Place a wok over medium heat; when wok is hot, add bacon and cook until crisp (about 3 minutes). Lift out with a slotted spoon and set aside; spoon out and discard all but 3 tablespoons of the drippings. Add eggplant to wok; stir often until eggplant is soft when pressed (about 5 minutes). Add bacon, chopped onion, bell pepper, celery, and garlic; stir-fry until onion is soft (about 4 minutes). Add sausage and stir-fry until hot. Mix in roux, black pepper, red pepper, and water; bring to a boil over high heat. Season to taste with salt, sprinkle with green onions, and serve. Makes 4 to 6 servings.

Black Roux. In a bowl, mix 1 cup **salad oil** and 1 cup **all-purpose flour** until smoothly blended. Place a wok over medium-high heat; when wok is hot, add oil-flour mixture. Using a spoon with a long wooden or heat-resistant handle, stir until mixture is dark brown to red-brown in color and smells darkly toasted (about 15 minutes); if it begins to smell burned, immediately remove wok from heat, let cool, discard roux, and start again.

All at once add ¾ cup *each* finely chopped **onion** and finely chopped **green bell pepper** and ⅓ cup finely chopped **celery** to hot roux. Then remove wok from heat and stir until roux is no longer bubbly (2 to 3 minutes).

Per serving: 791 calories, 18 g protein, 26 g carbohydrates, 69 g total fat, 67 mg cholesterol, 884 mg sodium

(Pictured on facing page)

Papaya & Sausage Sauté

Preparation time: About 10 minutes

Cooking time: About 12 minutes

If you like meat and fruit together, be sure to try this unusual dish: succulent papaya slices and sausage rounds tumbled in a spicy honey glaze. When papayas aren't in season (or if you can't find them at the market), try making the sauté with apples instead.

- 1¼ **pounds mild Italian sausages, cut into ½-inch-thick slices**
- 2 **tablespoons** *each* **lemon juice and honey**
- ½ **teaspoon** *each* **ground ginger, ground coriander, and curry powder**
- 2 **medium-size papayas (about 1 lb.** *each***), peeled, seeded, and cut lengthwise into ½-inch-thick slices**
  Green onions (roots and any wilted tops trimmed) and minced green onion tops (optional)

Place a wok over high heat; when wok is hot, add sausage. Stir-fry until browned (about 3 minutes). Discard all but 3 tablespoons of the drippings. Push sausage to side of wok; stir lemon juice, honey, ginger, coriander, and curry powder into drippings at bottom of wok. Then push sausage into spice mixture and toss to coat; transfer to a serving plate and keep warm.

Add papayas to wok. Cook over high heat, turning occasionally, until fruit is glazed and light brown (3 to 5 minutes). Arrange papayas around sausage. Garnish with whole and minced green onions, if desired. Makes about 4 servings.

Per serving: 499 calories, 22 g protein, 26 g carbohydrates, 35 g total fat, 88 mg cholesterol, 1,012 mg sodium

Apple & Sausage Sauté

Follow directions for **Papaya & Sausage Sauté,** but substitute 2 large **green-skinned apples,** cored and cut into ½-inch-thick slices, for papayas. Add ½ cup **toasted whole blanched almonds** along with apples.

Chicken & Turkey

Sweet & Sour Chicken in Pineapple Shells

Preparation time: About 30 minutes

Cooking time: About 10 minutes

Pineapple shells make attractive individual serving dishes for hot rice and a stir-fry of chicken, pepper strips, and juicy pineapple chunks.

  2 **small pineapples (about 3 lbs.** *each***)**
     Sweet & Sour Sauce (recipe follows)
  3 **tablespoons salad oil**
  1 **clove garlic, minced or pressed**
  1¾ **pounds chicken breasts, skinned, boned, and cut into ½- by 2-inch strips**
  1 **medium-size onion, thinly sliced**
  1 **medium-size green bell pepper, seeded and cut into thin strips**
     About 4 cups hot cooked rice
     Fresh cilantro (coriander) sprigs (optional)

Cut each pineapple in half lengthwise, cutting through crown. With a curved, serrated knife, such as a grapefruit knife, cut fruit from peel, leaving shells intact; turn shells upside down to drain. Trim away core from fruit, then cut fruit into chunks about ½ inch thick. You'll need 3 cups pineapple chunks; reserve any remaining fruit for another use.

Just before cooking, drain the 3 cups pineapple chunks; reserve juice for another use. Also prepare Sweet & Sour Sauce and set aside.

Place a wok over high heat; when wok is hot, add 1 tablespoon of the oil. When oil is hot, add garlic and half the chicken and stir-fry until chicken is no longer pink in center; cut to test (about 3 minutes). Remove from wok and set aside. Repeat to cook remaining chicken, adding 1 tablespoon more oil.

Pour remaining 1 tablespoon oil into wok. When oil is hot, add onion and bell pepper; stir-fry until tender-crisp to bite (about 2 minutes). Return chicken to wok. Stir sauce; add to wok with pineapple chunks. Stir until sauce boils and thickens.

Spoon equal portions of the chicken mixture into each pineapple shell, mounding mixture at 1 end. Spoon about 1 cup of the rice alongside chicken in each shell. Garnish with cilantro, if desired. Pour any extra chicken mixture into a serving bowl; offer at the table. Makes 4 servings.

Sweet & Sour Sauce. Stir together 4 teaspoons **cornstarch;** ¼ cup *each* **sugar, wine vinegar,** and **regular-strength chicken broth;** 2 tablespoons minced **fresh cilantro** (coriander) or 1½ teaspoons dry cilantro leaves; 2 tablespoons **catsup;** 1 tablespoon *each* **soy sauce** and **dry sherry;** ½ teaspoon **ground ginger;** and ¼ teaspoon *each* **salt** and **crushed red pepper.**

Per serving: 603 calories, 36 g protein, 85 g carbohydrates, 13 g total fat, 75 mg cholesterol, 634 mg sodium

Hot & Sour Chicken

Preparation time: About 15 minutes

Cooking time: About 10 minutes

Peppery-hot foods are favored in the Chinese province of Hunan—a preference reflected in this spicy dish. Season the sauce with purchased red pepper flakes, if you like, or use crushed whole dried chiles (remove the seeds for a milder flavor).

     Cooking Sauce (recipe follows)
  2 **teaspoons** *each* **cornstarch, dry sherry, and salad oil**
  ¼ **teaspoon pepper**
  1½ **to 1¾ pounds chicken breasts, skinned, boned, and cut into ¾-inch cubes**
  2 **to 3 tablespoons salad oil**
  1 **tablespoon finely chopped garlic**
  2 **teaspoons finely chopped fresh ginger**
  1 **tablespoon fermented salted black beans, rinsed, drained, and patted dry**
  1 **green bell pepper, seeded and cut into 1-inch squares**
  1 **carrot, thinly sliced**
  1 **can (about 8 oz.) sliced bamboo shoots, drained**

Prepare Cooking Sauce and set aside. In a bowl, stir together cornstarch, sherry, the 2 teaspoons oil, and pepper. Add chicken and stir to coat.

Place a wok over high heat; when wok is hot, add 2 tablespoons of the oil. When oil is hot, add chicken mixture; stir-fry for 2 minutes. Add 1 tablespoon more oil, if needed; then add garlic, ginger, and black beans. Stir-fry until chicken is lightly browned (about 2 more minutes). Then add bell pepper, carrot, and bamboo shoots; stir-fry for 2 minutes. Stir sauce and add; stir until sauce boils and thickens. Makes 4 servings.

Cooking Sauce. Stir together 2 teaspoons **cornstarch,** ½ teaspoon **crushed dried hot red chiles,** 2 tablespoons **soy sauce,** 2½ tablespoons **white wine vinegar,** and ½ cup **regular-strength chicken broth.**

Per serving: 302 calories, 32 g protein, 9 g carbohydrates, 15 g total fat, 75 mg cholesterol, 843 mg sodium

Kung Pao Chicken

Preparation time: About 10 minutes

Marinating time: 15 minutes

Cooking time: About 10 minutes

If you're fond of Chinese food and fiery flavors, you're almost certain to enjoy this Szechwan specialty. Chinese chefs often leave the charred whole chiles in the dish, but you can remove them if you prefer.

- **1** tablespoon *each* **dry sherry and cornstarch**
- **½** teaspoon **salt**
- **⅛** teaspoon **white pepper**
- **1½** **pounds chicken breasts, skinned, boned, and cut into ½-inch chunks**
- **¼** **cup salad oil**
  Cooking Sauce (recipe follows)
- **4** to 6 **small dried hot red chiles**
- **½** **cup salted peanuts**
- **1** teaspoon *each* **minced garlic and grated fresh ginger**
- **2** **green onions (including tops), cut into 1½-inch lengths**

In a bowl, stir together sherry, cornstarch, salt, and white pepper. Add chicken and stir to coat, then stir in 1 tablespoon of the oil and let marinate for 15 minutes. Meanwhile, prepare Cooking Sauce and set aside.

Place a wok over medium heat; when wok is hot, add 1 tablespoon of the oil. When oil is hot, add chiles and peanuts and stir until chiles just begin to char. (If chiles become completely black, discard them. Remove peanuts from wok and set aside; repeat with new oil and chiles.) Remove peanuts and chiles from wok; set aside.

Pour 1 tablespoon more oil into wok and increase heat to high. When oil begins to heat, add garlic and ginger and stir once, then add half the chicken mixture. Stir-fry until meat is no longer pink in center; cut to test (about 3 minutes). Remove from wok and set aside. Repeat to cook remaining chicken, adding remaining 1 tablespoon oil.

Return all chicken to wok; add peanuts, chiles, and onions. Stir Cooking Sauce and pour into wok; stir until sauce boils and thickens. Makes 4 servings.

Cooking Sauce. Stir together 2 tablespoons **soy sauce,** 1 tablespoon *each* **white wine vinegar** and **dry sherry,** 3 tablespoons **regular-strength chicken broth** or water, and 2 tablespoons *each* **sugar** and **cornstarch.**

Per serving: 425 calories, 32 g protein, 21 g carbohydrates, 25 g total fat, 65 mg cholesterol, 1,069 mg sodium

Chicken & Snow Peas

Preparation time: About 20 minutes, plus 30 minutes to soak mushrooms

Marinating time: About 15 minutes

Cooking time: About 10 minutes

Use either thin, flat Chinese pea pods (often sold as snow or sugar peas) or the thicker, crisper sugar snap peas in this classic Cantonese dish.

- **4** **dried Oriental mushrooms**
- **2** teaspoons *each* **soy sauce, cornstarch, dry sherry, and water**
  Dash of white pepper
- **1½** **pounds chicken breasts, skinned, boned, and cut into bite-size pieces**
- **3½** **tablespoons salad oil**
  Cooking Sauce (recipe follows)
- **1** **small clove garlic, minced or pressed**
- **½** **cup sliced bamboo shoots**
- **¼** **pound Chinese pea pods (also called snow or sugar peas) or sugar snap peas, ends and strings removed; or 1 package (6 oz.) frozen Chinese pea pods, thawed and drained**

Soak mushrooms in warm water to cover for 30 minutes, then drain. Cut off and discard stems; squeeze caps dry, thinly slice, and set aside.

In a bowl, mix soy, cornstarch, sherry, water, and white pepper. Add chicken and stir to coat, then stir in 1½ teaspoons of the oil. Let marinate for 15 minutes. Prepare Cooking Sauce; set aside.

Place a wok over high heat; when wok is hot, add 1 tablespoon of the oil. When oil begins to heat, add garlic and stir once. Add half the chicken mixture and stir-fry until meat is no longer pink in center; cut to test (about 3 minutes). Remove chicken from wok and set aside. Repeat to cook remaining chicken, adding 1 tablespoon more oil.

Pour remaining 1 tablespoon oil into wok. When oil is hot, add mushrooms and bamboo shoots. Stir-fry for 1 minute, adding a few drops of water if wok appears dry. Add pea pods and stir-fry for 3 minutes (30 seconds if using frozen pea pods), adding a few drops more water if wok appears dry. Return chicken to wok. Stir Cooking Sauce, pour into wok, and stir until sauce boils and thickens. Makes 3 or 4 servings.

Cooking Sauce. Stir together ½ cup **water,** 1 tablespoon **dry sherry,** 2 tablespoons **oyster sauce** or soy sauce, ¼ teaspoon **sugar,** 1 teaspoon **sesame oil,** and 1 tablespoon **cornstarch.**

Per serving: 294 calories, 28 g protein, 12 g carbohydrates, 15 g total fat, 65 mg cholesterol, 604 mg sodium

Thai Chicken & Basil Stir-fry

Preparation time: 10 to 15 minutes, plus 30 minutes to soak mushrooms

Cooking time: About 15 minutes

An unusual combination of coconut milk, aromatic fish sauce, and fresh basil enhances chicken strips and succulent mushrooms. When you buy fish sauce, look for the Thai variety, labeled *nam pla;* the Vietnamese version, *nuoc mam,* is somewhat stronger-tasting.

- 6 **dried Oriental mushrooms,** *each* **2 to 3 inches in diameter**
  Cooking Sauce (recipe follows)
- 2 **to 3 tablespoons salad oil**
- 1 **medium-size onion, thinly sliced**
- 3 **cloves garlic, minced or pressed**
- 2 **tablespoons minced fresh ginger**
- 2 **pounds chicken breasts, skinned, boned, and cut into ¼-inch-wide strips**
- 1½ **cups lightly packed slivered fresh basil leaves**
- 5 **green onions (including tops), cut into 1-inch lengths**

Soak mushrooms in warm water to cover for 30 minutes, then drain. Cut off and discard stems; squeeze caps dry, cut into ¼-inch slivers, and set aside.

Prepare Cooking Sauce and set aside.

Place a wok over high heat; when wok is hot, add 2 tablespoons of the oil. When oil is hot, add sliced onion, garlic, and ginger; stir-fry until onion is soft (about 4 minutes). Remove vegetables from wok and set aside.

Add half the chicken to wok and stir-fry until meat is tinged with brown (about 3 minutes). Remove from wok; set aside with cooked onion mixture. Repeat to brown remaining chicken, adding 1 tablespoon more oil if needed.

Pour Cooking Sauce into wok and boil until reduced by a third. Return onion mixture and chicken to wok. Add basil, mushrooms, and green onions; stir to heat through. Makes 4 or 5 servings.

Cooking Sauce. Stir together ¾ cup **canned or thawed frozen coconut milk,** 3 tablespoons *each* **soy sauce** and **rice wine vinegar,** 1½ tablespoons **fish sauce** (*nam pla*) or soy sauce, and ½ to 1 teaspoon **crushed dried hot red chiles.**

Per serving: 321 calories, 31 g protein, 12 g carbohydrates, 17 g total fat, 68 mg cholesterol, 1,011 mg sodium

(Pictured on facing page)

Chicken in Tomato Sauce

Preparation time: About 15 minutes

Cooking time: About 30 minutes

Cut into 2-inch chunks, chicken cooks quickly in a rich, brandied tomato sauce. Serve on a bed of zucchini sticks (just follow directions for Zucchini Sticks on page 61, cutting zucchini into noodle-thin strips, reducing cooking time to 2 minutes).

To make easy work of cutting the chicken, use a well-sharpened heavy knife or cleaver.

- 1 **frying chicken (3 to 3½ lbs.), cut up**
- 2 **tablespoons salad oil**
  Salt and pepper
- 2 **tablespoons brandy**
- 1 **small onion, finely chopped**
- ¼ **pound mushrooms, sliced**
- 1 **fresh rosemary sprig (2 to 3 inches long) or 1 teaspoon dry rosemary**
- 1 **tablespoon all-purpose flour**
- ½ **cup dry white wine**
- 1 **can (about 14 oz.) pear-shaped tomatoes**
  Fresh rosemary sprigs (optional)

Pull off and discard all visible fat from chicken pieces, then rinse chicken and pat dry. With a heavy knife or cleaver, cut each chicken piece through bones into 2-inch lengths.

Place a wok over medium-high heat; when wok is hot, add oil. When oil is hot, add thickest dark-meat pieces of chicken and cook, turning, until browned on both sides (about 5 minutes). Add remaining chicken. Continue to cook, turning, until pieces are well browned on both sides and meat near thighbone is no longer pink; cut to test (about 15 more minutes). Season to taste with salt and pepper.

Add brandy; when liquid bubbles, carefully ignite (not beneath an exhaust fan or near flammable items), then shake wok until flames die down. Lift out chicken pieces. Spoon off and discard all but about 1 tablespoon of the drippings.

Add onion, mushrooms, and 1 rosemary sprig (or 1 teaspoon dry rosemary) to drippings in wok; stir-fry until onion is soft (about 4 minutes). Sprinkle in flour and stir until golden. Blend in wine and bring to a boil. Add tomatoes (break up with a spoon) and their liquid; bring to a simmer. Return chicken to wok and stir gently just until heated through. Garnish with rosemary, if desired. Makes 4 servings.

Per serving: 518 calories, 50 g protein, 8 g carbohydrates, 31 g total fat, 154 mg cholesterol, 308 mg sodium

A rosemary sprig tops robust Italian-inspired Chicken in
Tomato Sauce (recipe on facing page). This speedy version of classic
chicken *cacciatore* can be ready in just half an hour. If you like,
serve it atop low-calorie zucchini instead of pasta.

Garlic Celebration Chicken

Preparation time: About 20 minutes

Cooking time: About 1¼ hours

Simmered in white wine and vermouth and seasoned with basil and plenty of garlic, this hearty entrée is a good choice for a cool-weather meal. Wedges of ripe tomato make a pretty, fresh-tasting garnish.

- 1 **frying chicken (3 to 3½ lbs.), cut up**
- 4 **slices bacon, chopped**
- 2 **medium-size onions, chopped**
- 5 **cloves garlic, minced or pressed**
- 1 **cup dry white wine**
- ¼ **cup dry vermouth or dry white wine**
- 1 **tablespoon dry basil**
- 1 **teaspoon poultry seasoning**
  Salt and pepper
- 1 **tablespoon** *each* **cornstarch and water, stirred together**
- 2 **medium-size tomatoes, cut into wedges**

Rinse chicken and pat dry; set aside.

Place a wok over medium-high heat; when wok is hot, add bacon and stir-fry until crisp (about 2 minutes). Lift out bacon with a slotted spoon, leaving drippings in wok; drain bacon and set aside.

Add half the chicken to wok; cook, turning, until browned on all sides (about 15 minutes). Remove from wok and set aside. Repeat to brown remaining chicken.

Add onions and garlic to wok and stir-fry until onions are soft (about 4 minutes). Spoon off and discard any fat from wok; add wine, vermouth, basil, poultry seasoning, bacon, and chicken pieces. Bring to a boil over high heat. Then reduce heat, cover, and simmer, turning once, until meat near thighbone is no longer pink; cut to test (about 35 minutes).

Arrange chicken on a platter; keep warm. Skim and discard fat from pan juices, then season to taste with salt and pepper. Stir cornstarch-water mixture into pan juices; continue to stir until sauce is thickened. Garnish chicken with tomatoes; pass sauce at the table. Makes about 4 servings.

Per serving: 505 calories, 51 g protein, 12 g carbohydrates, 27 g total fat, 159 mg cholesterol, 256 mg sodium

Indian Pan-roasted Chicken

Preparation time: About 10 minutes

Cooking time: About 35 minutes

Despite the name, this handsome, spice-fragrant whole chicken isn't really roasted; it's braised in a broth seasoned with cumin, cardamom, cinnamon, and pepper. Garnish the bird with juicy orange slices and sprigs of fresh cilantro.

- **Seasoned Broth (recipe follows)**
- 1 **frying chicken (3 to 3½ lbs.)**
  Pepper
- 3 **tablespoons salad oil**
- 2 **dry bay leaves**
- 1 **cinnamon stick (about 3 inches long)**
- 6 **whole cloves**
- 5 **whole black peppercorns**
- 3 **cloves garlic, minced or pressed**
  Orange slices
  Fresh cilantro (coriander) sprigs

Prepare Seasoned Broth and set aside.

Remove chicken neck and giblets; reserve for other uses, if desired. Remove and discard skin from entire chicken; pull off and discard lumps of fat. Rinse chicken inside and out, pat dry, and sprinkle lightly with pepper. Tie ends of drumsticks together.

Place a wok over medium-high heat; when wok is hot, add oil. When oil is hot, add bay leaves, cinnamon stick, cloves, and peppercorns; then add chicken and cook, uncovered, turning occasionally with long-handled tongs, until browned on all sides (about 10 minutes). Stir in Seasoned Broth and garlic; bring to a boil. Then reduce heat, cover, and simmer, turning chicken occasionally, until meat near thighbone is no longer pink; cut to test (20 to 25 more minutes).

Transfer chicken to a serving dish. Skim and discard any fat from pan juices; pour juices over chicken. Garnish with orange slices and cilantro. Makes about 4 servings.

Seasoned Broth. In a bowl, combine 1 cup **regular-strength chicken broth**, 2 teaspoons *each* **soy sauce** and **Worcestershire**, 1 teaspoon **ground cumin**, ¼ teaspoon **ground red pepper** (cayenne), and ⅛ teaspoon **ground cardamom.**

Per serving: 530 calories, 49 g protein, 3 g carbohydrates, 35 g total fat, 154 mg cholesterol, 596 mg sodium

Turkey Chili

Preparation time: About 15 minutes

Cooking time: About 45 minutes

An alternative to traditional beef chili is this version made with chunks of turkey. At the table, offer lime wedges, cheese, chopped tomato, and green onions to embellish individual servings.

- 2 tablespoons salad oil
- 1 onion, chopped
- 1 small green bell pepper, seeded and chopped
- 1 clove garlic, minced or pressed
- 1½ pounds turkey breast, skinned, boned, and cut into bite-size chunks
- 1 small can (about 8 oz.) tomatoes, drained and chopped
- 2 cans (about 15 oz. *each*) kidney beans, drained
- 1 can (15 oz.) tomato sauce
- 2 tablespoons soy sauce
- 1½ tablespoons chili powder
- ½ teaspoon *each* ground cumin, dry sage leaves, and dry thyme leaves
  Garnishes (suggestions follow)

Place a wok over medium-high heat; when wok is hot, add oil. When oil is hot, add onion, bell pepper, and garlic; stir-fry until onion is soft (about 4 minutes). Remove from wok and set aside.

Increase heat to high. Add half the turkey and stir-fry until no longer pink in center; cut to test (about 3 minutes). Remove from wok and set aside. Repeat to cook remaining turkey.

Return all turkey and vegetables to wok. Then add tomatoes, beans, tomato sauce, soy, chili powder, cumin, sage, and thyme. Bring to a boil; reduce heat, cover, and simmer until chili is thick and flavors are well blended (about 30 minutes; uncover for last 5 minutes).

To serve, ladle hot chili into bowls; offer garnishes to embellish individual servings. Makes 4 servings.

Garnishes. Offer **lime wedges,** sliced **green onions** (including tops), shredded **jack or Cheddar cheese,** and chopped **tomatoes.**

Per serving: 476 calories, 47 g protein, 50 g carbohydrates, 11 g total fat, 84 mg cholesterol, 2,074 mg sodium

Turkey & Green Bean Stir-fry

Preparation time: About 15 minutes

Cooking time: About 15 minutes

Readily available turkey breast is a nice alternative to chicken in stir-fry dishes; though not as velvety-textured as chicken, it's every bit as tasty. This easy-to-prepare dish features turkey with fresh green beans and celery; if you like, offer toasted almonds or sesame seeds to sprinkle on top.

- Cooking Sauce (recipe follows)
- 1 egg white
- 2 tablespoons soy sauce
- 2 pounds turkey breast, skinned, boned, and cut into ¼- by 2-inch strips
- ¼ cup salad oil
- ½ pound green beans (ends removed), cut into 2-inch pieces
- ½ cup thinly sliced celery
- ½ cup thinly sliced onion, separated into rings
- 6 tablespoons water or dry sherry
- 1 or 2 cloves garlic, minced or pressed

Prepare Cooking Sauce; set aside.

In a bowl, beat together egg white and soy; add turkey and stir to coat. Set aside. Place a wok over high heat; when wok is hot, add 2 tablespoons of the oil. When oil is hot, add beans, celery, and onion; stir-fry for about 1 minute, then add water. Cover and cook, stirring occasionally, until beans are tender-crisp to bite (about 4 minutes).

Remove vegetables from wok, then add remaining 2 tablespoons oil. When oil is hot, add garlic and half the turkey. Stir-fry until meat is no longer pink in center; cut to test (about 3 minutes). Remove from wok. Repeat to cook remaining turkey; return all turkey to wok along with green bean mixture. Stir Cooking Sauce, pour into wok, and stir until sauce boils and thickens. Makes 4 servings.

Cooking Sauce. Mix 1 tablespoon *each* **cornstarch** and **soy sauce,** 2 tablespoons **dry sherry,** ½ teaspoon **ground ginger,** and ½ cup **water.**

Per serving: 376 calories, 45 g protein, 10 g carbohydrates, 17 g total fat, 111 mg cholesterol, 922 mg sodium

Ready in minutes from your wok, Sweet & Sour Fish
(recipe on facing page) is a seafood lover's symphony of contrasts.
Nuggets of fish, onion, green pepper, and tomato
harmonize in a tangy sauce.

Fish & Shellfish

(Pictured on facing page)

Sweet & Sour Fish

Preparation time: About 15 minutes

Cooking time: 12 minutes

Sweet-sour sauce is just as good with fish as it is with pork or chicken. Here, the familiar red sauce enhances a combination of bell pepper squares, tomato, and chunks of turbot or halibut.

Sweet-Sour Sauce (recipe follows)
About ⅓ cup **cornstarch**
2 pounds **turbot or halibut fillets,** cut into ½-inch squares
About 6 tablespoons **salad oil**
1 clove **garlic,** minced or pressed
1 **onion,** cut into 1-inch cubes
1 medium-size **green bell pepper,** seeded and cut into ½-inch thick strips
1 medium-size **tomato,** cut into 1-inch cubes
Fresh **cilantro (coriander)** or Italian **parsley** (optional)

Prepare Sweet-Sour Sauce and set aside.

Place cornstarch in a bag, add fish pieces, and shake to coat completely; shake off excess.

Place a wok over medium-high heat; when wok is hot, add 2 tablespoons of the oil. When oil is hot, add some of the fish; stir-fry until fish is browned on all sides and flakes when prodded (about 2 minutes). Remove from wok and keep warm. Repeat to cook remaining fish, adding about 2 tablespoons more oil.

Increase heat to high and pour 2 tablespoons more oil into wok. When oil is hot, add garlic, onion, and bell pepper; stir-fry for 2 minutes. Stir Sweet-Sour Sauce; pour into wok and stir in tomato. Bring to a boil, stirring. Return fish and any accumulated juices to wok; stir to combine. Garnish with cilantro, if desired. Makes 4 servings.

Sweet-Sour Sauce. Stir together 1 tablespoon **cornstarch** and ¼ cup **sugar.** Stir in 2 tablespoons *each* **soy sauce** and **catsup,** ¼ cup **distilled white vinegar,** and ½ cup **regular-strength chicken broth.**

Per serving: 736 calories, 35 g protein, 31 g carbohydrates, 52 g total fat, 104 mg cholesterol, 915 mg sodium

Lemony Fish with Asparagus

Preparation time: About 10 minutes

Cooking time: About 5 minutes

Bright green asparagus and delicate white-fleshed fish are flavored with fresh lemon in this simple and speedy entrée.

1 pound **asparagus**
2 teaspoons *each* **cornstarch, lemon juice, and salad oil**
¾ pound **orange roughy, sea bass,** or **halibut fillets,** *each* about ½ inch thick, cut into 1- by 3-inch strips
3 tablespoons **salad oil**
1 large clove **garlic,** minced or pressed
2 tablespoons **regular-strength chicken broth** or **water**
2 tablespoons **lemon juice**

Snap off and discard tough ends of asparagus; cut spears into ½-inch slanting slices. Set aside.

In a bowl, stir together cornstarch, the 2 teaspoons lemon juice, and the 2 teaspoons oil. Add fish and stir gently until evenly coated.

Place a wok over medium-high heat; when wok is hot, add 2 tablespoons of the oil. When oil is hot, add fish and stir-fry until opaque (about 2 minutes); remove fish from wok and set aside.

Pour remaining 1 tablespoon oil into wok. When oil begins to heat, add garlic and stir-fry for about 30 seconds. Then add asparagus and stir-fry for 1 minute. Stir together broth and the 2 tablespoons lemon juice; pour into wok, cover, and cook, stirring often, until asparagus is tender-crisp to bite (2 to 3 more minutes). Return fish and any accumulated juices to wok and stir just until heated through. Makes 3 or 4 servings.

Per serving: 199 calories, 16 g protein, 4 g carbohydrates, 13 g total fat, 40 mg cholesterol, 294 mg sodium

Lemony Fish with Fennel

Follow directions for **Lemony Fish with Asparagus,** but substitute 1 large **fennel** bulb for asparagus. To prepare fennel, trim off and discard stalks, reserving a few of the feathery leaves for garnish. Cut away and discard base; cut bulb in half lengthwise, then thinly slice crosswise. (Fennel may need to cook for a few more minutes than asparagus.) Garnish dish with reserved fennel leaves.

Lime & Chile Monkfish with Corn

Preparation time: About 10 minutes

Cooking time: 10 minutes

Often called "poor man's lobster," monkfish is valued for its delicate flavor and lean, firm flesh. Monkfish fillets are encased in a tough membrane; you can have the membrane removed at the fish market or do the job yourself.

     Lime-Chile Sauce (recipe follows)
1½ pounds monkfish fillets
  3 tablespoons salad oil
  1 cup fresh corn cut from cob or 1 cup frozen whole-kernel corn, thawed and drained
  2 tablespoons chopped fresh cilantro (coriander)

Prepare Lime-Chile Sauce; set aside.

   Remove and discard membrane from fish. Rinse fish and pat dry, then cut into 1-inch chunks. Place a wok over high heat; when wok is hot, add 2 tablespoons of the oil. When oil is hot, add half the fish; stir-fry until fish flakes when prodded (about 2 minutes). Remove from wok and set aside. Repeat to cook remaining fish, adding remaining 1 tablespoon oil.

   Pour Lime-Chile Sauce into wok and bring to a boil, stirring constantly. Add corn and stir until heated through (2 to 3 minutes). Return fish and any accumulated juices to wok; mix gently to heat. Pour onto a warm platter and sprinkle with cilantro. Makes 4 servings.

Lime-Chile Sauce. Stir together ⅓ cup **lime juice;** 3 tablespoons **regular-strength chicken broth;** 1 clove **garlic,** minced or pressed; 1 **small fresh Fresno or jalapeño chile,** minced; ½ teaspoon *each* **ground cumin, pepper,** and **sugar;** and 1 teaspoon **cornstarch.**

Per serving: 268 calories, 26 g protein, 11 g carbohydrates, 13 g total fat, 43 mg cholesterol, 88 mg sodium

Teriyaki Monkfish

Follow directions for **Lime & Chile Monkfish with Corn,** but omit Lime-Chile Sauce. Instead, use this teriyaki sauce: stir together ¼ cup **regular-strength chicken or beef broth,** 2 tablespoons *each* **dry sherry** and **soy sauce,** 2 teaspoons **sugar,** and 1 teaspoon **cornstarch.** Also omit corn; instead, use 1 cup **cooked fresh shelled peas** or 1 cup frozen peas, thawed and drained.

Squid & Pea Stir-fry

Preparation time: About 30 minutes

Cooking time: 7 minutes

Its flavor is sweet and delicate—but squid quickly toughens if it's cooked too long. To eliminate the risk of overcooking, start by scoring the squid; the cross-hatched cuts permit rapid cooking.

     Pan-fried Noodles (recipe follows)
  1 pound squid
  2 tablespoons salad oil
  ½ teaspoon minced fresh ginger
  1 cup shelled peas (about 1 lb. unshelled)
  ½ cup regular-strength chicken broth
  1 teaspoon soy sauce
  1 tablespoon oyster sauce
  ¼ teaspoon sugar
  2 teaspoons cornstarch and 1 tablespoon water, stirred together

Prepare Pan-fried Noodles and keep warm.

   To clean each squid, gently pull on body to separate it from hood. Then pull out and discard long, clear quill from hood. Scoop out and discard contents of hood; rinse out hood. Set aside.

   With a sharp knife, sever body between eyes and tentacles. Discard eyes and attached material. Pop out and discard hard black beak in center of tentacles. Rinse and drain tentacles; pat dry and set aside.

   Pull off and discard thin, speckled membrane from hood; rinse and drain hood. Slit hood lengthwise and open flat. Make ½-inch-wide diagonal cuts across inside of hood. Repeat in opposite direction. Cut scored hood in about 2-inch-square pieces.

   Place a wok over medium-high heat; when wok is hot, add 1 tablespoon of the oil. When oil begins to heat, add ginger; stir once. Add squid; stir-fry until edges of squares curl (1½ to 2 minutes). Remove from wok.

   Pour remaining 1 tablespoon oil into wok. When oil is hot, add peas and stir-fry for 1 minute. Add broth, soy, oyster sauce, and sugar; bring to a boil and boil for 1 minute. Stir cornstarch-water mixture; pour into wok and stir until sauce boils and thickens. Return squid to wok, stir, and serve at once, over Pan-fried Noodles. Makes 3 or 4 servings.

Pan-fried Noodles. Heat 2 tablespoons **salad oil** in a frying pan over medium-high heat. Spread 8 ounces **Chinese wheat flour noodles,** cooked and drained, in pan in a layer 1 inch thick. Cook until brown on bottom. Turn noodles over in 1 piece; add 1 tablespoon more **salad oil** and cook until browned on other side. Serve whole or in wedges.

Per serving: 473 calories, 27 g protein, 49 g carbohydrates, 19 g total fat, 49 mg cholesterol, 458 mg sodium

Shrimp Pesto Stir-fry

Preparation time: 15 minutes

Cooking time: 12 minutes

Shrimp teams well with a pesto sauce redolent of basil. Make the pesto from fresh basil if you can find it or use our quick version made with dried herbs.

> Quick Pesto Sauce (recipe follows) or 2 tablespoons Fresh Pesto (page 678)
> 3 tablespoons butter or margarine
> 1 carrot, cut into ¼-inch-thick slices
> 1 small onion, cut into 1-inch squares
> 1 small zucchini, cut into ¼-inch-thick slices
> 8 to 10 small mushrooms, sliced
> ½ small green bell pepper, seeded and sliced lengthwise
> ½ small red bell pepper, seeded and sliced lengthwise
> ¾ pound medium-size raw shrimp, shelled and deveined
> Fresh basil sprigs (optional)
> Grated Parmesan cheese (optional)
> Hot cooked rice (optional)

Prepare Quick Pesto Sauce; set aside.

Place a wok over medium-high heat; when wok is hot, add 1 tablespoon of the butter. When butter is melted, add carrot and onion and stir-fry for 2 minutes. Add 1 tablespoon more butter, zucchini, mushrooms, and green and red bell peppers; stir-fry just until carrot is tender-crisp to bite (about 2 more minutes). Remove vegetables from wok and keep warm.

Add remaining 1 tablespoon butter to wok; when butter is melted, stir in Quick Pesto Sauce. Add shrimp and stir-fry until pink (3 to 4 minutes). Return vegetables to wok and stir until vegetables are hot and coated with sauce.

Turn shrimp-vegetable mixture into a shallow serving dish; garnish with basil and sprinkle with cheese, if desired. Serve with rice, if desired. Makes 2 servings.

Quick Pesto Sauce. Stir together 1 tablespoon grated **Parmesan cheese,** 2 teaspoons *each* **dry basil** and **parsley flakes,** and 1 tablespoon **olive oil** or salad oil.

Per serving: 415 calories, 31 g protein, 11 g carbohydrates, 28 g total fat, 259 mg cholesterol, 444 mg sodium

Scallop Pesto Stir-fry

Follow directions for **Shrimp Pesto Stir-fry,** but in place of shrimp, use ½ to ¾ pound **scallops** (thawed if frozen). Rinse scallops and pat dry, then cut into ¼-inch-thick slices. Cook scallops until opaque throughout; cut to test (3 to 4 minutes).

Scallops in Garlic Butter

Preparation time: About 10 minutes

Cooking time: About 10 minutes

Toasted almonds add a little crunch to a super-simple stir-fry of scallops seasoned with lemon peel and plenty of garlic.

> 1 to 1½ pounds scallops (thawed if frozen)
> 3 tablespoons sliced almonds
> ¼ cup butter
> 5 large cloves garlic, minced or pressed
> 2 tablespoons chopped parsley
> 1 teaspoon grated lemon peel

Rinse scallops and pat dry; then cut any large scallops in half. Set aside.

Place a wok over medium heat; when wok is hot, add almonds and stir until golden (about 2 minutes). Pour out of wok and set aside.

Add butter; when butter is melted, add garlic, parsley, and lemon peel and stir for about 1 minute. Add scallops (a portion at a time, if necessary) and stir-fry just until opaque throughout; cut to test (3 to 4 minutes). Transfer scallop mixture to a platter, top with almonds, and serve immediately. Makes 4 servings.

Per serving: 290 calories, 31 g protein, 6 g carbohydrates, 15 g total fat, 94 mg cholesterol, 393 mg sodium

Crab in Black Bean Sauce

Preparation time: About 15 minutes

Cooking time: 5 minutes

If you cook crab in its shell, the meat stays especially succulent—and the preparation time stays brief. Like our Crab Curry (at right), this is finger food; it's a good choice for an informal meal.

  1 **large cooked crab in shell (1½ to 2 lbs.), cleaned and cracked**
  2 **tablespoons salad oil**
  1½ **tablespoons fermented salted black beans, rinsed, drained, and finely chopped**
  1 **large clove garlic, minced or pressed**
  ¾ **teaspoon minced fresh ginger**
  1 **green bell pepper, seeded and cut into 1-inch squares**
  1 **tablespoon** *each* **soy sauce and dry sherry**
  2 **green onions (including tops), cut into 1-inch lengths**
  ⅓ **cup regular-strength chicken broth**

Cut crab body into quarters; leave legs and claws whole. Set aside.

Place a wok over high heat; when wok is hot, add oil. When oil begins to heat, add black beans, garlic, and ginger and stir once. Add bell pepper and stir-fry for 1 minute. Add crab, soy, sherry, onions, and broth; stir until crab is heated through (about 3 minutes). Makes 2 servings.

Per serving: 328 calories, 22 g protein, 7 g carbohydrates, 24 g total fat, 114 mg cholesterol, 1,248 mg sodium

Crab in Tomato-Garlic Sauce

Follow directions for **Crab in Black Bean Sauce,** but increase garlic to 3 cloves and omit black beans and ginger. Add 2 large **tomatoes,** peeled, seeded, and chopped, along with bell pepper. Omit soy, sherry, and broth; instead, use ½ cup **dry white wine.**

Crab in Cream Sauce

Follow directions for **Crab in Black Bean Sauce,** using 1 tablespoon minced **shallots** and 1 **red bell pepper,** seeded and cut into 1-inch squares, in place of the black beans, ginger, and green bell pepper. Substitute ¼ cup **whipping cream,** 2 tablespoon **dry white wine,** 1 teaspoon **Dijon mustard,** and 1 tablespoon chopped **parsley** for the soy, sherry, green onions, and broth.

(Pictured on facing page)
Crab Curry

Preparation time: About 15 minutes

Cooking time: 10 minutes

This mild Cantonese curry of crab and vegetables is appealing to the eye and fun to eat, too. Finger food can be messy, though, so pass a basket of damp cloths around the table at the end of the meal.

  Cooking Sauce (recipe follows)
  1 **teaspoon** *each* **salt and sugar**
  4 **teaspoons curry powder**
  ¼ **pound lean boneless pork (such as shoulder or butt), trimmed of excess fat and finely chopped or ground**
  1 **large cooked crab in shell (1½ to 2 lbs.), cleaned and cracked**
  3 **tablespoons salad oil**
  1 **large clove garlic, minced**
  1 **medium-size onion, cut into wedges, layers separated**
  1 **medium-size green bell pepper, seeded and cut into 1-inch squares**
  1 **egg, lightly beaten**

Prepare Cooking Sauce and set aside. Sprinkle salt, sugar, and curry powder over pork; mix well and set aside. Cut crab body into quarters; leave legs and claws whole. Set crab aside.

Place a wok over high heat. When wok is hot, add oil. When oil begins to heat, add garlic and stir once; then add seasoned pork and stir-fry until no longer pink (about 2 minutes). Add onion and bell pepper and stir-fry for 1 minute. Add crab and stir often until heated through (about 3 minutes). Stir Cooking Sauce, pour into wok, and stir until sauce boils and thickens. Add egg; stir just until egg begins to set (about 30 seconds). Makes 3 or 4 servings.

Cooking Sauce. Stir together ¾ cup **regular-strength chicken broth** and 1 tablespoon *each* **cornstarch, soy sauce,** and **dry sherry.**

Per serving: 252 calories, 18 g protein, 8 g carbohydrates, 16 g total fat, 145 mg cholesterol, 1,155 mg sodium

Shrimp Curry

Follow directions for **Crab Curry,** but use 1 pound **medium-size raw shrimp,** shelled and deveined, in place of crab. Stir-fry shrimp until they turn pink (about 3 minutes).

Use fingers—not forks or chopsticks—to enjoy Crab Curry
(recipe on facing page). Once you get started, it's hard to stop until
the last bite of this Cantonese specialty has disappeared! Pass around a
basket of hot, damp cloths after the meal.

Noodles, Rice & Tofu

Asian-style Pasta Primavera

Preparation time: About 20 minutes, plus 30 minutes to soak mushrooms

Cooking time: 30 minutes

Linguine is tossed with asparagus and favorite Asian vegetables in this light dish. You can adjust the recipe to suit available ingredients: Swiss chard can substitute for the bok choy, and button mushrooms can take the place of shiitakes.

- 3 tablespoons sesame seeds
- 8 large dried Oriental or fresh shiitake mushrooms (about 3 inches in diameter); or ½ pound fresh button mushrooms
- ½ pound *each* asparagus and bok choy
- 6 ounces dried linguine
  Boiling salted water
- 2 tablespoons salad oil
- 2 cloves garlic, minced or pressed
- 1 tablespoon very finely chopped fresh ginger
- ½ pound Chinese pea pods (also called snow or sugar peas) or sugar snap peas, ends and strings removed; or 1 package (6 oz.) frozen Chinese pea pods, thawed and drained
- ¼ cup dry sherry
- 1 cup regular-strength chicken broth
- 2 tablespoons soy sauce
- 1 teaspoon *each* sugar and white wine vinegar

Place a wok over medium heat; when wok is hot, add sesame seeds and stir until golden (about 2 minutes). Pour out of wok and set aside.

If using dried mushrooms, soak in warm water to cover for 30 minutes, then drain. Cut off and discard stems; squeeze caps dry and thinly slice. Or trim any tough stems from fresh shiitake mushrooms; thinly slice caps. (Simply slice fresh button mushrooms thinly.)

Snap off and discard tough ends of asparagus; cut asparagus spears and bok choy stems and leaves into ½-inch slanting slices. Set vegetables aside.

Following package directions, cook linguine in boiling salted water until barely tender to bite; drain well. Place in a large, shallow serving bowl and keep warm.

Place wok over high heat; when wok is hot, add oil. When oil is hot, add garlic and ginger; stir-fry until lightly browned (about 30 seconds). Add mushrooms, asparagus, bok choy, fresh pea pods, and sherry. Cover and cook, stirring once or twice, until vegetables are bright green and tender-crisp to bite (about 2 minutes; if using frozen pea pods, add for last 30 seconds). Spoon over noodles.

Add broth, soy, sugar, and vinegar to wok; bring to a boil, stirring. Pour over noodles and vegetables. Sprinkle with sesame seeds, then mix lightly. Serve immediately. Makes 4 servings.

Per serving: 347 calories, 12 g protein, 51 g carbohydrates, 12 g total fat, 0 mg cholesterol, 806 mg sodium

Fried Rice with Ham & Peanuts

Preparation time: About 10 minutes

Cooking time: About 10 minutes

Fried rice is a classic quick meal, easily embellished with leftover meat and your favorite vegetables. For best success, start with *cold* cooked rice; if it's warm or hot, the grains will stick together.

- 2 cups cold cooked long-grain white rice
- 2 eggs
- ¼ teaspoon salt
- ¼ cup salad oil
- 1 small onion, chopped
- 1 clove garlic, minced or pressed
- 1 medium-size green bell pepper, seeded and diced
- ¼ pound mushrooms, chopped
- ½ pound cold cooked ham, chicken, turkey, or pork, diced (about 1½ cups)
- ½ cup salted roasted peanuts
- 2 tablespoons soy sauce
  Tomato wedges and cucumber slices

Rub cooked rice with wet hands so all grains are separated; set aside. In a small bowl, lightly beat together eggs and salt.

Place a wok over medium heat; when wok is hot, add 1 tablespoon of the oil. When oil is hot, add eggs and cook, stirring occasionally, until soft curds form; remove from wok and set aside.

Increase heat to medium-high; add 1 tablespoon more oil to wok. When oil is hot, add onion and garlic. Stir-fry until onion is soft; then add bell pepper, mushrooms, ham, and peanuts. Stir-fry until heated through (about 2 minutes). Remove from wok and set aside.

Pour remaining 2 tablespoons oil into wok. When oil is hot, add rice and stir-fry until heated through (about 2 minutes); stir in ham mixture and soy. Add eggs; stir mixture gently until eggs are in small pieces. Garnish with tomato and cucumber. Makes 4 servings.

Per serving: 467 calories, 24 g protein, 25 g carbohydrates, 31 g total fat, 170 mg cholesterol, 1,616 mg sodium

Cajun Dirty Rice

Preparation time: About 10 minutes

Cooking time: About 15 minutes

This rice may be "dirty," but it's delicious! It's one of the most popular dishes in Louisiana. Vary the spiciness by adding cayenne to taste; real Cajuns like it fiery.

- ¼ **pound chicken giblets, including liver**
- ¼ **cup salad oil**
- ½ **pound lean ground beef**
- 2 **stalks celery, chopped**
- 1 **red bell pepper, seeded and chopped**
- 1 **medium-size onion, chopped**
- 2 **teaspoons all-purpose flour**
- ½ **to 2 teaspoons ground red pepper (cayenne)**
- 2 **teaspoons paprika**
- 1½ **teaspoons dry oregano leaves**
- 1 **cup regular-strength chicken broth**
- 3 **cups cold cooked white rice**
- 2 **green onions (including tops), thinly sliced**
  Salt and black pepper

Using a sharp knife, trim giblets of any hard membranes or connective tissue. Finely chop giblets or grind them in a food processor.

Place a wok over high heat; when wok is hot, add 2 tablespoons of the oil. When oil is hot, add giblets and beef and cook, stirring, until no longer pink (about 4 minutes). Using a slotted spoon, transfer to a small bowl and set aside.

Pour remaining 2 tablespoons oil into wok; when oil is hot, add celery, bell pepper, and chopped onion. Stir-fry until vegetables are soft (about 7 minutes). Sprinkle in flour, red pepper, paprika, and oregano; cook until flour is browned (about 1 minute). Pour in broth, bring to a boil, and stir in giblets and beef. Add rice and stir-fry until heated through (about 3 minutes); stir in green onions. Season to taste with salt and black pepper. Makes 6 servings.

Per serving: 315 calories, 13 g protein, 23 g carbohydrates, 19 g total fat, 78 mg cholesterol, 221 mg sodium

Tofu & Vegetable Stir-fry

Preparation time: about 15 minutes

Cooking time: 6 minutes

For a speedy vegetarian meal, try Vietnamese *rau xao*. The dish is made in countless variations; this one features vegetables readily available in North American markets.

- ½ **pound medium-firm tofu (bean curd), cut into ½-inch cubes**
- 3 **tablespoons soy sauce**
- 1 **teaspoon rice wine vinegar or white vinegar**
- ¼ **teaspoon ground cumin**
- 2 **cloves garlic, minced or pressed**
- ½ **teaspoon grated fresh ginger or ⅛ teaspoon ground ginger**
- 3 **tablespoons peanut oil or salad oil**
- 1 **large carrot, chopped**
- 2 **cups thinly sliced broccoli stems and bite-size flowerets**
- 1 **cup *each* bean sprouts and sliced mushrooms**
- ½ **cup thinly sliced green onions (including tops)**
- 3 **tablespoons minced fresh cilantro (coriander)**

Place tofu in a shallow bowl. In another bowl, mix soy, vinegar, cumin, garlic, and ginger; drizzle over tofu. Set aside.

Place a wok over high heat. When wok is hot, add oil. When oil is hot, add carrot and stir-fry for 1 minute; add broccoli and stir-fry for 2 more minutes. Then mix in bean sprouts, mushrooms, and onions; stir-fry for 30 more seconds.

Reduce heat to medium-high. Add tofu mixture and stir gently just until tofu is heated through but vegetables are still crisp (1 to 2 minutes). Garnish with cilantro. Makes 4 servings.

Per serving: 181 calories, 7 g protein, 11 g carbohydrates, 13 g total fat, 0 mg cholesterol, 800 mg sodium

Start this extraordinary main dish by stir-frying strips of marinated beef.
Then spoon the sizzling meat over cool, crisp watercress and onions
to create Hot Beef & Watercress Salad (recipe on facing page).
Add fresh tangerines for dessert.

676

Salads

(Pictured on facing page)
Hot Beef & Watercress Salad

Preparation time: About 10 minutes

Marinating time: 30 minutes

Cooking time: About 3 minutes

Hot, garlicky stir-fried beef strips top chilled watercress dressed with a light vinaigrette in this unusual salad. Marinate the meat for about half an hour before cooking or, if you like, marinate it overnight in the refrigerator.

- ½ **pound lean boneless beef steak (such as top round, flank, or sirloin), cut about 1 inch thick**
- 4 **cloves garlic, minced or pressed**
- 2 **teaspoons soy sauce**
- 1 **teaspoon sugar**
- 1 **tablespoon salad oil**
- 2 **tablespoons white wine vinegar**
- ¼ **teaspoon pepper**
- 1 **small white onion, thinly sliced and separated into rings**
  About ½ pound watercress

Cut beef with the grain into 3-inch-wide strips; then cut each strip across the grain into ⅛-inch-thick slanting slices. In a bowl, stir together garlic, soy, ½ teaspoon of the sugar, and 1 teaspoon of the oil. Add beef; stir to coat. Cover and refrigerate for at least 30 minutes or until next day.

In another bowl, stir together remaining ½ teaspoon sugar, remaining 2 teaspoons oil, vinegar, and pepper. Add onion and mix lightly. Cover and refrigerate for at least 30 minutes or until next day.

Remove and discard tough watercress stems; rinse sprigs thoroughly and pat dry. Then measure 3 cups sprigs, lightly packed. Shortly before serving, add watercress to onion mixture, mixing lightly to coat. Arrange on 2 dinner plates.

Place a wok over high heat. When wok is hot, add beef mixture and stir-fry until meat is browned (1½ to 2 minutes). Arrange meat evenly atop watercress salads. Makes 2 servings.

Per serving: 258 calories, 29 g protein, 8 g carbohydrates, 12 g total fat, 65 mg cholesterol, 449 mg sodium

Hot Chicken & Fruit Salad Platter

Preparation time: 30 minutes

Cooking time: 7 minutes

Here's an extra-pretty whole-meal salad: cantaloupe chunks and warm stir-fried chicken tumbled in a sweet-sour lime sauce, then mounded atop hot rice and ringed with golden pineapple wheels.

- **Sweet Lime Sauce (recipe follows)**
- 1 **small cantaloupe (about 1½ lbs.)**
- 2 **whole chicken breasts (about 1 lb. *each*), skinned and boned**
- 1 **small pineapple (about 3 lbs.)**
- 8 **to 10 large romaine lettuce leaves**
  About 1 tablespoon salad oil
- ¼ **cup lightly packed chopped fresh mint leaves**
- 4 **cups hot cooked rice**
  Fresh mint sprigs (optional)

Prepare Sweet Lime Sauce; set aside.

Seed and peel cantaloupe. Cut fruit into bite-size chunks; set aside. Cut chicken breasts across the grain into ¼-inch-thick strips; set aside.

Peel pineapple. Cut fruit crosswise into 8 equal slices; trim core from each slice, if desired. On a large platter (at least 12 inches in diameter), arrange romaine leaves with tips extending beyond rim of platter. Arrange pineapple on leaves around edge of platter. (At this point, you may cover and refrigerate sauce, cantaloupe, chicken, and salad platter separately for up to 4 hours.)

Place a wok over high heat; when wok is hot, add 1 tablespoon of the oil. When oil is hot, add half the chicken. Stir-fry until meat is no longer pink in center; cut to test (about 3 minutes). Lift out chicken with a slotted spoon and set aside. Repeat to cook remaining chicken, adding more oil as needed.

Stir sauce and pour into wok; bring to a boil, stirring. Remove wok from heat. Add chicken, cantaloupe, and chopped mint; gently turn meat and melon in sauce to coat.

Mound rice on platter atop lettuce. Spoon chicken mixture over rice; garnish with mint sprigs, if desired. Serve hot. Makes 6 servings.

Sweet Lime Sauce. Stir together ½ cup **white wine vinegar,** ¼ cup **sugar,** 1 teaspoon grated **lime peel,** 3 tablespoons **lime juice,** 2 tablespoons **soy sauce,** 1 tablespoon **cornstarch,** and ¼ teaspoon **ground red pepper** (cayenne).

Per serving: 379 calories, 21 g protein, 64 g carbohydrates, 4 g total fat, 42 mg cholesterol, 400 mg sodium

Chile Shrimp & Corn Salad

Preparation time: About 20 minutes

Cooking time: 11 minutes

Chilling time: 1 to 4 hours

The salad is cold, but its flavor is *hot*: corn, bell peppers, and juicy shrimp are stir-fried in a zippy chile-infused oil. Before serving, you toss the chilled stir-fry with fresh spinach and leaf lettuce.

¼ cup olive oil or salad oil
3 small dried hot red chiles
½ teaspoon pepper
2 cups fresh corn kernels, cut from about 3 large ears of corn; or 1 package (10 oz.) frozen whole-kernel corn, thawed and drained
1 medium-size red bell pepper, seeded and diced
1 pound medium-size raw shrimp, shelled and deveined
1 tablespoon soy sauce
⅔ cup cider vinegar
1 pound spinach, stems and any tough or wilted leaves removed, green leaves washed and crisped
1 pound green leaf lettuce, washed and crisped

Place a wok over medium heat; when wok is hot, add oil. When oil is hot, add chiles and stir until lightly browned (about 4 minutes). Add pepper, corn, and bell pepper. Increase heat to high; stir-fry until bell pepper is tender to bite (about 3 minutes). Add shrimp; stir-fry just until shrimp turn pink (about 3 minutes).

Remove wok from heat. Stir in soy and vinegar, then spoon shrimp mixture into a small bowl. Let cool, then cover and refrigerate until shrimp are cold (at least 1 hour) or for up to 4 hours.

Meanwhile, tear spinach and lettuce into bite-size pieces; you should have about 4 quarts, lightly packed. Place torn greens in a large salad bowl;

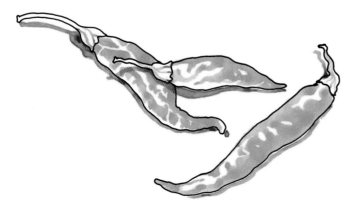

spoon shrimp mixture over greens. Use chiles as garnish or remove and discard. Toss salad and serve. Makes 6 to 8 servings.

Per serving: 172 calories, 13 g protein, 14 g carbohydrates, 9 g total fat, 65 mg cholesterol, 269 mg sodium

Calamari Salad al Pesto

Preparation time: About 15 minutes

Cooking time: 7 minutes

Chilling time: At least 3 hours

Julienne strips of squid and crunchy toasted walnuts go into this delicious and attractive salad. The dressing's a homemade pesto sauce you whirl together in your blender.

Fresh Pesto (recipe follows)
¼ cup olive oil
1 small onion, finely diced
2 cloves garlic, minced or pressed
3 tablespoons chopped walnuts
1 pound tenderized giant squid (calamari) steaks, cut into ¼-inch-wide strips
2 tablespoons dry sherry
1 medium-size red bell pepper, seeded and diced
¼ cup diced celery
1 tablespoon chopped parsley
¼ cup cider vinegar
1 tablespoon lemon or lime juice
Salt and pepper
About 4 cups shredded iceberg lettuce

Prepare Fresh Pesto and set aside.

Place a wok over medium heat; when wok is hot, add oil. When oil is hot, add onion, garlic, and walnuts. Stir-fry until onion is soft and walnuts are toasted (about 5 minutes). Add squid and sherry and stir-fry just until squid turns an opaque chalky white (about 1 minute); do not overcook. With a slotted spoon, transfer contents of wok to a bowl.

To squid mixture, add bell pepper, celery, parsley, Fresh Pesto, vinegar, and lemon juice; mix well. Season to taste with salt and pepper. Cover and refrigerate for at least 3 hours or until next day. Serve over lettuce. Makes 4 to 6 servings.

Fresh Pesto. In a blender or food processor, whirl until smoothly puréed ¼ cup **olive oil**, ¼ cup lightly packed **fresh basil leaves**, 2 tablespoons **pine nuts**, 1 clove **garlic**, and 1 teaspoon **dry white wine** (optional).

Per serving: 284 calories, 15 g protein, 7 g carbohydrates, 23 g total fat, 42 mg cholesterol, 67 mg sodium

Sesame Noodle Salad

Preparation time: About 10 minutes, plus 30 minutes to soak dried mushrooms

Cooking time: 5 minutes

Chilling time: At least 2 hours

Al dente vermicelli combined with tender-crisp vegetables and a light, sweet-tart dressing makes a delightful chilled salad. For a perfect summer meal, serve it with cold roast chicken and fresh fruit in season.

Sesame Dressing (recipe follows)
8 medium-size fresh shiitake or dried Oriental mushrooms; or 8 large button mushrooms
8 ounces dried vermicelli
    Boiling salted water
    About 3 tablespoons salad oil
2 teaspoons minced fresh ginger
¼ pound green beans (ends removed), cut into ¼-inch slanting slices
2 medium-size carrots, peeled and cut into julienne strips
2 medium-size crookneck squash, cut into julienne strips
1 tablespoon *each* soy sauce and dry sherry
    Salt

Prepare Sesame Dressing; set aside.

If using dried mushrooms, soak in warm water to cover for 30 minutes, then drain. Cut off and discard stems; squeeze caps dry. If using fresh mushrooms, trim any tough stems from shiitake mushrooms. Then set shiitake or button mushroom caps aside; cut stems into julienne strips.

Meanwhile, following package directions, cook vermicelli in boiling salted water until barely tender to bite. Drain, rinse with cold water, and drain again. Place in a large bowl and set aside.

Place a wok over high heat; when wok is hot, add 2 tablespoons of the oil. When oil is hot, add ginger, beans, carrots, squash, and julienned mushroom stems. Stir-fry just until vegetables are barely tender-crisp to bite (about 1½ minutes). Remove from wok; add to noodles.

To wok, add remaining 1 tablespoon oil, soy, sherry, and mushroom caps. Reduce heat to medium; cover wok if using dried mushrooms (leave uncovered if using fresh mushrooms). Cook, turning occasionally, until mushrooms have absorbed all liquid (about 2 minutes). Pour into a small bowl, cover, and refrigerate.

Mix dressing with noodles and vegetables. Season to taste with salt. Cover and refrigerate, stirring occasionally, for at least 2 hours or until next day.

To serve, garnish salad with mushroom caps. Makes 4 to 6 servings.

Sesame Dressing. In a wok, combine ¼ cup **salad oil** and 3 tablespoons **sesame seeds.** Stir over medium-low heat until seeds are golden (2 to 3 minutes). Remove from heat and let cool. Stir together ⅓ cup **sugar,** ½ cup **distilled white vinegar,** and 2 tablespoons **dry sherry** until sugar is dissolved. Mix in cooled sesame seed mixture.

Per serving: 402 calories, 7 g protein, 52 g carbohydrates, 19 g total fat, 0 mg cholesterol, 185 mg sodium

Soy-braised Eggplant Salad

Preparation time: 20 minutes

Cooking time: About 30 minutes

Flavored with vinegar, ginger, chiles, and soy, tender braised eggplant is equally good as an appetizer or an accompaniment to barbecued meats.

1 medium-size eggplant (¾ to 1 lb.)
3 tablespoons salad oil
1 cup water
¼ cup soy sauce
5 thin, quarter-size slices fresh ginger
2 cloves garlic, minced or pressed
1 teaspoon sugar
3 tablespoons red wine vinegar
⅓ cup coarsely chopped fresh cilantro (coriander)
2 teaspoons minced fresh ginger
¼ to ½ teaspoon crushed dried hot red chiles

Remove stem from eggplant, then peel eggplant and cut lengthwise into 1-inch-thick slices. Cut slices into 1-inch strips.

Place a wok over medium-high heat; when wok is hot, add oil. When oil is hot, add eggplant and stir-fry for 3 minutes. (Eggplant will soak up oil immediately; stir constantly to prevent burning.)

Add water, soy, ginger slices, garlic, and sugar. Reduce heat to low, cover, and simmer, stirring occasionally, until eggplant is tender when pierced (about 15 minutes). Add vinegar. Let cool, turning eggplant occasionally. (At this point, you may cover and refrigerate until next day.)

Transfer eggplant and sauce to a serving dish, then sprinkle with cilantro, minced ginger, and chiles. Serve cold or at room temperature. Makes 4 servings.

Per serving: 232 calories, 3 g protein, 11 g carbohydrates, 21 g total fat, 0 mg cholesterol, 1035 mg sodium

Vegetables

Cantonese Vegetable Medley

Preparation time: About 10 minutes, plus 30 minutes to soak fungus

Cooking time: 5 minutes

Meaty "cloud ears" combine with crisp carrots, broccoli, and water chestnuts in this colorful Cantonese dish. Be sure to allow an extra half hour or so to soak the black fungus.

- ½ **cup dried black fungus (also called cloud or tree ears)**
- 1 **tablespoon** *each* **cornstarch, water, and soy sauce**
- 1 **cup regular-strength chicken broth**
- 2 **tablespoons salad oil**
- ½ **teaspoon minced fresh ginger**
- 1 **small clove garlic, minced or pressed**
- 1½ **cups** *each* **broccoli flowerets and thinly sliced carrots**
- ⅓ **cup sliced water chestnuts**

Soak fungus in warm water to cover for 30 minutes; drain. Pinch out and discard hard, knobby centers; cut remaining fungus into bite-size pieces.

In a small bowl, stir together cornstarch, water, and soy; stir in broth and set aside.

Place a wok over high heat; when wok is hot, add oil. When oil is hot, add ginger, garlic, broccoli, carrots, and fungus. Stir-fry for 1 minute. Stir cornstarch mixture; add to vegetables along with water chestnuts. Stir until sauce boils and thickens. Makes 4 to 6 servings.

Per serving: 93 calories, 2 g protein, 11 g carbohydrates, 5 g total fat, 0 mg cholesterol, 190 mg sodium

(Pictured on facing page)

Sesame-topped Vegetables

Preparation time: 10 minutes

Cooking time: 8 minutes

Malaysian *achar*, a colorful tumble of sweet-and-sour vegetables, provides a cooling contrast to any spicy entrée. Serve warm or at room temperature.

- ½ **English or European cucumber**
- 3 **large carrots**
- 3 **cups cauliflowerets**
- ½ **cup sesame seeds**
- ⅓ **cup salad oil**
- 2 **cloves garlic, minced or pressed**
- ½ **cup minced shallots**
- ½ **cup distilled white vinegar**
- ¼ **cup sugar**
  Soy sauce
  Arugula leaves (optional)

Cut cucumber and carrots into thin, about 6-inch-long slivers. Break cauliflowerets into smaller flowerets. Set vegetables aside.

Place a wok over medium heat. When wok is hot, add sesame seeds and stir until golden (2 to 3 minutes). Pour out of wok and set aside.

Pour oil into wok. When oil is hot, add garlic and shallots; stir-fry until shallots are soft. Increase heat to high and add vinegar, sugar, cauliflowerets, and carrots. Stir-fry until vegetables are tender-crisp to bite; add cucumber and stir-fry until hot. Season to taste with soy. Transfer to a serving plate; sprinkle with sesame seeds. Garnish with arugula, if desired. Makes 6 to 8 servings.

Per serving: 192 calories, 3 g protein, 17 g carbohydrates, 14 g total fat, 0 mg cholesterol, 22 mg sodium

Chinese Ginger-Garlic Asparagus

Preparation time: About 10 minutes

Cooking time: About 5 minutes

Crisp stir-fried asparagus is especially tasty when accented with garlic and fresh ginger; broccoli benefits from the same treatment.

- 1 **pound asparagus**
- 2 **tablespoons salad oil**
- 1 **large clove garlic, minced or pressed**
- ½ **to 1 teaspoon grated fresh ginger**
- 2 **tablespoons water**

Snap off and discard tough ends of asparagus, then cut spears into ¼-inch slanting slices.

Place a wok over high heat; when wok is hot, add oil. When oil begins to heat, add garlic and ginger and stir once; then add asparagus and stir-fry for 1 minute. Add water; cover and cook until asparagus is tender-crisp to bite (2 to 3 minutes). Makes 4 servings.

Per serving: 75 calories, 2 g protein, 3 g carbohydrates, 7 g total fat, 0 mg cholesterol, 1 mg sodium

Bright carrot and cucumber slivers, cauliflowerets, and sweet-sour flavorings
come together in these Sesame-topped Vegetables from Malaysia
(recipe on facing page). Garnish with arugula leaves and a delicate fan
of paper-thin cucumber slices.

A Light Technique

Stir-frying is widely appreciated for its bright, fresh-tasting results. But not everyone realizes that those rich colors and peak flavors can be enjoyed for a surprisingly small investment of calories. The following hearty entrées, for example, weigh in at just 226 to 274 calories per serving.

If it's salt that you wish to reduce, use a low-sodium soy sauce. We also recommend using your own homemade unsalted chicken broth in these and other stir-fries; you and your guests can add salt to taste at the table.

Lamb with Spring Onions

- 1 **pound boneless leg of lamb**
- ½ **teaspoon Chinese five-spice**
- 1 **egg white**
- 2 **cloves garlic, slivered**
- 4 **thin, quarter-size slices fresh ginger or ⅛ teaspoon ground ginger**
- 1 **tablespoon cornstarch**
- 5 **teaspoons soy sauce**
- 6 **tablespoons dry sherry**
- 2 **tablespoons water**
- 10 **green onions (including tops)**
- 2 **tablespoons salad oil**

Trim and discard fat from lamb; cut meat into bite-size strips ⅛ inch thick. In a bowl, mix lamb, five-spice, egg white, garlic, ginger, 1 teaspoon of the cornstarch, and 1 teaspoon of the soy. Let stand for 10 minutes.

Meanwhile, blend sherry, water, remaining 2 teaspoons cornstarch, and remaining 4 teaspoons soy in a small bowl. Cut off white part of each onion, then cut each of these pieces in half. Cut two 1½-inch-long sections from each green top; discard remainder of green tops.

Place a wok over high heat; when wok is hot, add oil. When oil is hot, add meat mixture and stir-fry until lightly browned (2 to 3 minutes). Return to bowl.

To wok, add sherry mixture and white part of onions. Cook, stirring, until mixture is thickened. Add meat mixture and onion tops and cook, stirring, just until heated through (1 to 2 minutes). Makes 4 servings.

Per serving: 226 calories, 21 g protein, 8 g carbohydrates, 12 g total fat, 66 mg cholesterol, 511 mg sodium

Beef & Vegetable Sauté

- ⅓ **cup firmly packed brown sugar**
- 2 **tablespoons cornstarch**
- ¼ **cup cider vinegar**
- 3 **tablespoons soy sauce**
- 1½ **pounds top round or flank steak, cut ½ to ¾ inch thick**
- 2 **tablespoons butter or margarine**
- 1 **large onion, thinly sliced**
- 1½ **cups thinly sliced carrots**
- 1 **cup green beans, in 1-inch lengths**
- 1 **cup water**
- 1½ **cups thinly sliced zucchini**

In a small bowl, stir together sugar, cornstarch, vinegar, and soy until cornstarch is dissolved. Set aside.

Trim and discard fat from meat. Cut meat into slanting slices ⅛ to ¼ inch thick.

Place a wok over medium heat; when wok is hot, add 1 tablespoon of the butter. When butter is melted, add meat strips, a few at a time, and stir-fry until well browned, adding remaining 1 tablespoon butter as needed. As meat is browned, lift out and set aside.

When all meat has been cooked, add onion, carrots, beans, and ½ cup of the water to wok; stir well, cover, and cook, stirring often, for 8 minutes. Stir in zucchini and remaining ½ cup water; cook, uncovered, just until all vegetables are tender to bite (about 2 more minutes).

Stir cornstarch mixture and add to vegetables along with meat; stir until sauce boils and thickens. Serve immediately. Makes 6 servings.

Per serving: 274 calories, 26 g protein, 23 g carbohydrates, 9 g total fat, 71 mg cholesterol, 628 mg sodium

Shrimp with Peking Sauce

- **Peking Stir-fry Sauce (recipe follows)**
- 2 **tablespoons salad oil**
- 1 **pound medium-size raw shrimp, shelled and deveined**

1 large red onion, slivered

2 cups broccoli flowerets

1 red bell pepper, seeded and cut into long strips

1 green or yellow bell pepper, seeded and cut into long strips

2 to 4 tablespoons water

2 teaspoons cornstarch

Prepare Peking Stir-fry Sauce; set aside.

Place a wok over high heat; when wok is hot, add 1 tablespoon of the oil. When oil is hot, add shrimp. Stir-fry just until shrimp turn pink (about 2 minutes). Remove shrimp from wok.

Add remaining 1 tablespoon oil, onion, broccoli, all bell peppers, and 1 tablespoon of the water. Stir-fry, adding more water as needed, until broccoli is barely tender to bite (2 to 4 minutes).

Blend cornstarch into prepared sauce. Add to wok and stir just until sauce is thickened and clear. Add shrimp; stir just until heated through. Serve immediately. Makes 4 servings.

Peking Stir-fry Sauce. Stir together 2 cloves **garlic,** minced or pressed; 2 tablespoons minced **fresh ginger** or 1 teaspoon ground ginger; ½ cup **water;** ¼ cup **hoisin sauce;** 2 tablespoons **soy sauce;** 1 tablespoon **rice wine vinegar;** and 2 teaspoons **sugar.**

Per serving: 246 calories, 23 g protein, 19 g carbohydrates, 9 g total fat, 140 mg cholesterol, 1179 mg sodium

Asparagus Chicken Stir-fry

½ cup Homemade Chicken Broth (recipe follows) or regular-strength chicken broth

8 green onions (including tops)

1 pound asparagus

½ pound mushrooms

1 tablespoon *each* cornstarch, dry sherry, and soy sauce

3 tablespoons sesame oil or salad oil

1 tablespoon minced fresh ginger or ½ teaspoon ground ginger

2 cloves garlic, minced or pressed

1½ pounds chicken breasts, skinned, boned, and cut into ½- by 1-inch strips

Prepare Homemade Chicken Broth and set aside.

Cut onions diagonally into 1-inch pieces. Snap off and discard tough ends of asparagus; cut spears into 1-inch slanting slices. Thinly slice mushrooms. Combine cornstarch, sherry, soy, and broth; stir until cornstarch is dissolved.

Place a wok over high heat; when wok is hot, add oil. When oil is hot, add ginger, garlic, and chicken. Stir-fry until chicken is no longer pink in center; cut to test (about 2 minutes). Lift chicken from wok and set aside.

To wok, add onions, asparagus, and mushrooms; stir-fry for 1 minute. Add chicken; stir broth mixture and add. Bring to a boil, stirring; stir for 1 more minute. Makes 4 servings.

Per serving: 268 calories, 30 g protein, 10 g carbohydrates, 12 g total fat, 65 mg cholesterol, 343 mg sodium

Homemade Chicken Broth. Rinse 5 pounds **bony chicken pieces** (wings, backs, necks, carcasses); place in a 6- to 8-quart pan. Add 2 large **onions,** cut into chunks; 2 large **carrots,** cut into chunks; 6 to 8 **parsley sprigs;** ½ teaspoon **whole black peppercorns;** and 3½ quarts **water.** Bring to a boil; then reduce heat, cover, and simmer for 3 hours. Let cool.

Strain broth into a bowl. Discard scraps. Cover broth and refrigerate until fat solidifies (at least 4 hours)

or for up to 2 days. Lift off and discard fat. To store, freeze in 1-cup to 4-cup portions. Makes about 10 cups.

Vegetable & Bulgur Stir-fry

2 tablespoons salad oil

1 cup bulgur

1 tablespoon sesame seeds

2 medium-size carrots, thinly sliced

1 *each* medium-size zucchini and crookneck squash, thinly sliced

¼ pound mushrooms, thinly sliced

1 clove garlic, minced or pressed

½ teaspoon *each* dry basil, dry marjoram leaves, and dry oregano leaves

⅛ teaspoon pepper

1¾ cups water

2 cups broccoli flowerets

½ cup shredded jack cheese

½ cup sliced green onions (including tops)

3 pocket breads, halved and warmed (optional)

Lemon wedges

Place a wok over medium-high heat; when wok is hot, add 1 tablespoon of the oil. When oil is hot, add bulgur, sesame seeds, and carrots; stir-fry for 2 minutes. Add remaining 1 tablespoon oil, zucchini, crookneck squash, mushrooms, and garlic; stir-fry for 2 more minutes. Add herbs, pepper, and water; reduce heat, cover, and simmer until liquid is absorbed (about 10 minutes).

Add broccoli; cover and cook for 2 minutes. Stir in cheese. Sprinkle with onions and spoon into pocket bread, if desired. Serve with lemon wedges. Makes 6 servings.

Per serving: 231 calories, 8 g protein, 32 g carbohydrates, 9 g total fat, 9 mg cholesterol, 78 mg sodium

In all their golden glory, Sweet & Sour Carrots (recipe on facing page)
show off the Chinese cook's artistry with humble ingredients.
Covered cooking in a wok preserves the vegetable's intense color
and sweet flavor.

Broccoli with Gorgonzola & Walnuts

Preparation time: About 10 minutes

Cooking time: About 15 minutes

Gorgonzola is a creamy blue-veined cheese from a small Italian town of the same name; if you can't find the Italian product, use one of the delicious American Gorgonzolas or any other blue-veined cheese.

- 1¼ **pounds broccoli**
- ¼ **cup butter or margarine**
- ¾ **cup walnut pieces**
- ½ **cup regular-strength chicken broth**
- 1 **small onion, finely chopped**
- 1 **teaspoon cornstarch**
- 1 **tablespoon white wine vinegar**
- ½ **teaspoon pepper**
- 1 **cup (about 4 oz.) crumbled Gorgonzola or other blue-veined cheese**

Cut off broccoli flowerets and slash their stems; discard broccoli stalks or reserve for another use. You should have about 4½ cups flowerets.

Place a wok over medium-high heat; when wok is hot, add 1 tablespoon of the butter. When butter is melted, add walnuts and stir-fry until browned (about 1½ minutes). Transfer to a bowl; set aside.

Wipe wok clean and add 2 tablespoons more butter; when butter is melted, add broccoli and stir-fry for 3 minutes. Add ¼ cup of the broth, cover, and cook until tender-crisp to bite (about 5 more minutes). Transfer broccoli to bowl with walnuts.

Wipe wok clean again and add remaining 1 tablespoon butter; when butter is melted, add onion and stir-fry until golden brown (about 3 minutes). Mix cornstarch with remaining ¼ cup broth, add to wok, bring to a boil, and boil for 30 seconds. Reduce heat to low; stir in vinegar, pepper, broccoli, and walnuts and cook until heated through (about 2 minutes). Add cheese and stir until partially melted. Makes 2 or 3 servings.

Per serving: 536 calories, 20 g protein, 20 g carbohydrates, 46 g total fat, 70 mg cholesterol, 901 mg sodium

Spicy Napa Cabbage

Preparation time: About 5 minutes

Cooking time: 4 minutes

Spiced with ground red pepper, mild-flavored napa cabbage turns zesty—and makes a good companion dish for roast pork or ham.

- 2 **tablespoons white wine vinegar**
- 2 **tablespoons sugar**
- 1 **tablespoon soy sauce**
- ¼ **teaspoon ground red pepper (cayenne)**
- 3 **tablespoons salad oil**
- 1 **small head napa cabbage (1¼ to 1½ lbs.), cut into 2-inch pieces**

In a small bowl, stir together vinegar, sugar, soy, and red pepper; set aside.

Place a wok over high heat; when wok is hot, add oil. When oil is hot, add cabbage and stir-fry until cabbage begins to wilt (2 to 3 minutes). Add vinegar mixture and mix well. Serve warm or at room temperature. Makes 4 to 6 servings.

Per serving: 137 calories, 2 g protein, 11 g carbohydrates, 10 g total fat, 0 mg cholesterol, 362 mg sodium

(Pictured on facing page)

Sweet & Sour Carrots

Preparation time: About 10 minutes

Cooking time: 8 minutes

A simple, not-too-sweet sauce intensifies the natural sweetness of carrots. The sauce enhances cauliflower and green beans, too.

- ¼ **cup regular-strength chicken broth**
- 2 **tablespoons *each* vinegar and firmly packed brown sugar**
- 1 **tablespoon cornstarch**
- 1 **tablespoon salad oil**
- 1 **pound carrots (about 4 medium-size), cut into ¼-inch-thick slanting slices**
- 1 **small onion, cut in half, then cut crosswise into ¼-inch-thick slices**
- 3 **tablespoons regular-strength chicken broth**
  Salt
  Minced parsley (optional)

In a bowl, stir together the ¼ cup broth, vinegar, sugar, and cornstarch. Set aside.

Place a wok over high heat; when wok is hot, add oil. When oil is hot, add carrots and onion and stir-fry for 1 minute. Add the 3 tablespoons broth and reduce heat to medium; cover and cook until carrots are tender-crisp to bite (about 4 minutes). Increase heat to high. Stir cornstarch mixture, pour into wok, and stir until sauce boils and thickens. Season to taste with salt. Sprinkle with parsley, if desired. Makes 4 servings.

Per serving: 114 calories, 1 g protein, 20 g carbohydrates, 4 g total fat, 0 mg cholesterol, 147 mg sodium

Sesame-blacked Carrots

Preparation time: About 10 minutes

Cooking time: About 10 minutes

Sold in Asian markets, black sesame seeds cost and taste the same as the familiar yellow or white seeds—but they look a lot more dramatic. Here, they're toasted and blended with gingery stir-fried carrots.

> ¼ **cup black sesame seeds**
> 1 **tablespoon olive oil or salad oil**
> 1 **small onion, thinly sliced**
> 2 **tablespoons butter or margarine**
> 1½ **pounds carrots (about 6 medium-size), peeled and shredded**
> 1 **tablespoon minced crystallized ginger**
> **Salt and pepper**

Place a wok over medium heat; when wok is hot, add sesame seeds and stir often until seeds taste toasted and the few light-colored seeds among the black turn golden (about 2 minutes). Pour seeds out of wok and set aside.

Add oil to wok and increase heat to medium-high. When oil is hot, add onion and stir-fry until soft (about 4 minutes). Add butter, carrots, and ginger; stir-fry until carrots are tender-crisp to bite (about 3 minutes). Stir in sesame seeds and season to taste with salt and pepper. Makes 4 to 6 servings.

Per serving: 143 calories, 2 g protein, 14 g carbohydrates, 9 g total fat, 10 mg cholesterol, 77 mg sodium

Acapulco Corn Medley

Preparation time: About 15 minutes

Cooking time: About 10 minutes

Enjoy this red, green, and yellow side dish in any season—you can use either fresh or frozen corn, and the other ingredients are available year round. If you'd like to tone down the snappy flavor, cut back on the hot pepper seasoning and chili powder.

> 2 **tablespoons butter or margarine**
> 1 **medium-size onion, chopped**
> 1 **red or green bell pepper, seeded and chopped**
> 1 **pound zucchini, cut into ½-inch cubes**
> 1 **canned whole green chile, seeded and chopped**
> 1½ **cups fresh corn kernels, cut from about 2 large ears of corn; or 1½ cups frozen whole-kernel corn, thawed and drained**

> 1 **can (about 14 oz.) pear-shaped tomatoes**
> ¼ **teaspoon liquid hot pepper seasoning**
> 1 **teaspoon paprika**
> ½ **teaspoon chili powder**

Place a wok over medium heat; when wok is hot, add butter. When butter is melted, add onion and bell pepper; stir-fry until vegetables are soft (about 5 minutes).

Stir in zucchini, chile, corn, tomatoes (break up with a spoon) and their liquid, hot pepper seasoning, paprika, and chili powder. Increase heat to high; stir often until almost all liquid has evaporated and zucchini is tender to bite (about 5 minutes). Makes 4 to 6 servings.

Per serving: 102 calories, 3 g protein, 15 g carbohydrates, 7 g total fat, 10 mg cholesterol, 209 mg sodium

Green Beans with Garlic

Preparation time: About 10 minutes

Cooking time: About 15 minutes

Those familiar Asian seasonings of soy, sherry, ginger, and garlic enhance just about any food; here, they accent tender-crisp green beans. Sesame seeds add extra crunch.

> 4 **teaspoons soy sauce**
> 1 **teaspoon sugar**
> 1 **tablespoon dry sherry or water**
> 1 **tablespoon sesame seeds**
> 1½ **tablespoons salad oil**
> 3 **cloves garlic, minced or pressed**
> 1 **tablespoon minced fresh ginger**
> 1 **pound green beans (ends removed), cut diagonally into 2-inch lengths**

In a small bowl, stir together soy, sugar, and sherry; set aside.

Place a wok over medium heat; when wok is hot, add sesame seeds and stir until golden (about 2 minutes). Pour out of wok and set aside.

Increase heat to medium-high and pour oil into wok. When oil is hot, add garlic, ginger, and beans; stir-fry for 1½ minutes. Stir in soy mixture; reduce heat to medium, cover, and cook until beans are tender-crisp to bite (4 to 7 more minutes).

Uncover, increase heat to high, and boil, stirring, until almost all liquid has evaporated (1 to 3 minutes). Pour onto a warmed platter and sprinkle with sesame seeds. Makes 4 servings.

Per serving: 105 calories, 3 g protein, 11 g carbohydrates, 6 g total fat, 0 mg cholesterol, 448 mg sodium

Hominy Fry Delight

Preparation time: About 10 minutes

Cooking time: 4 minutes

Plump grains of white or yellow hominy look like tiny dumplings among the vegetables in this dish. Lemon pepper adds a pleasantly tangy accent.

2 tablespoons salad oil
1 medium-size carrot, thinly sliced
1 medium-size red or green bell pepper, seeded and cut into thin, short strips
1 medium-size zucchini, thinly sliced
1 can (about 1 lb.) white or yellow hominy, drained
½ teaspoon lemon pepper
3 green onions (including tops), sliced
1 tablespoon Worcestershire

Place a wok over high heat; when wok is hot, add oil. When oil is hot, add carrot, bell pepper, zucchini, hominy, and lemon pepper. Stir-fry until vegetables are tender-crisp to bite (about 3 minutes). Stir in onions and Worcestershire; serve. Makes about 4 servings.

Per serving: 148 calories, 2 g protein, 20 g carbohydrates, 7 g total fat, 0 mg cholesterol, 467 mg sodium

Parsnip & Carrot Sauté with Tarragon

Preparation time: About 10 minutes

Cooking time: About 5 minutes

A sprinkling of tarragon is a perfect accent for sweet, tender carrots and parsnips in this easy side dish.

3 *each* medium-size parsnips and carrots (about 1½ lbs. *total*)
5 tablespoons butter or margarine
1 tablespoon minced shallot or onion
⅓ cup regular-strength chicken broth
1 tablespoon fresh tarragon leaves, chopped, or 1½ teaspoons dry tarragon
2 tablespoons minced parsley

Peel parsnips and carrots and cut into matchstick pieces. Set aside.

Place a wok over medium-high heat; when wok is hot, add butter. When butter is melted, add shallot and stir once. Add carrots and parsnips; stir-fry just

until tender-crisp to bite (about 2 minutes). Add broth, cover, and cook until tender to bite (2 to 3 more minutes). Stir in tarragon and parsley; serve. Makes 4 servings.

Per serving: 223 calories, 2 g protein, 22 g carbohydrates, 15 g total fat, 39 mg cholesterol, 262 mg sodium

Zucchini Sticks

Preparation time: About 10 minutes

Cooking time: 4 minutes

For a simple side dish that's also light on calories, cut zucchini into strips, then stir-fry in a bit of oil. Season simply with garlic, pepper, and Parmesan cheese.

4 medium-size zucchini (about 1½ lbs. *total*)
1 tablespoon olive oil or salad oil
2 cloves garlic, minced or pressed
Pepper
Enoki mushrooms and red bell pepper strips (optional)
Grated Parmesan cheese (optional)

Cut zucchini in half lengthwise. Then cut each half lengthwise into thirds.

Place a wok over medium heat; when wok is hot, add oil. When oil is hot, add zucchini and garlic and stir-fry gently until zucchini is tender-crisp to bite (about 3 minutes). Season to taste with pepper and serve immediately. If desired, garnish with mushrooms and bell pepper and offer cheese to sprinkle atop individual servings. Makes 4 servings.

Per serving: 61 calories, 2 g protein, 7 g carbohydrates, 4 g total fat, 0 mg cholesterol, 2 mg sodium

Matchstick Zucchini with Marinara Sauce

Place a wok over medium-high heat; when hot, add 2 tablespoons **olive oil.** When oil is hot, add 1 clove **garlic,** minced or pressed, and 1 **onion,** finely chopped; stir-fry until golden (about 3 minutes). Add ¼ cup **fresh basil leaves,** finely chopped, and 1½ pounds **tomatoes,** peeled, cored, and finely chopped. Cook, stirring occasionally, for 15 minutes. Add ½ teaspoon **sugar** and season to taste with **salt** and **pepper.** Keep warm while preparing zucchini.

Follow directions for **Zucchini Sticks,** but cut zucchini lengthwise into thin slices; then cut slices into 4- or 5-inch long julienne strips and reduce cooking time to 2 minutes. Omit mushrooms and red bell pepper; serve with sauce and cheese.

Eggs

Silver Thread Stirred Eggs

Preparation time: About 10 minutes, plus 30 minutes to soak bean threads and mushrooms

Cooking time: 8 minutes

Thin, near-transparent bean threads, also sold as cellophane or shining noodles, are made from ground mung beans. They have a neutral flavor and a slippery texture; here, they add a bouncy lightness to scrambled eggs, meat, and vegetables.

- 2 **ounces dried bean threads**
- 4 **dried Oriental mushrooms**
- 2 **teaspoons soy sauce**
- 6 **eggs**
- ½ **teaspoon salt**
- ⅛ **teaspoon white pepper**
- 2 **tablespoons salad oil**
- 1 **clove garlic, minced**
- ¼ **pound cooked ham, cut into match-stick pieces**
- 1 **stalk celery, thinly sliced**
- ¼ **cup sliced bamboo shoots**
- 2 **green onions (including tops), thinly sliced**

Soak bean threads in warm water to cover for 30 minutes, then drain and cut into 4-inch lengths. Also soak mushrooms in ¾ cup warm water for 30 minutes. Remove mushrooms from water. Pour ½ cup of the soaking water into a bowl; stir in soy. Cut off and discard mushroom stems; squeeze caps dry and thinly slice. Set mushrooms and bean threads aside.

In a bowl, beat eggs with salt and white pepper; set aside.

Place a wok over high heat; when wok is hot, add oil. When oil begins to heat, add garlic and stir once; then add ham and mushrooms and stir-fry for 1 minute. Add celery and bamboo shoots and stir-fry for 2 minutes. Add bean threads and mushroom water and cook until liquid is absorbed. Add onions and cook for 30 seconds.

Reduce heat to medium. Pour eggs into wok. Cook, turning eggs occasionally with a wide spatula, until eggs are set but still soft and creamy. Makes 4 servings.

Per serving: 297 calories, 17 g protein, 17 g carbohydrates, 18 g total fat, 428 mg cholesterol, 984 mg sodium

(Pictured on facing page)

Huevos Revueltos Rancheros

Preparation time: About 10 minutes

Cooking time: 25 minutes

A treat to the eye as well as the palate, these scrambled eggs are topped with a spicy tomato-sausage sauce.

- ½ **pound chorizo sausage, casings removed**
- ½ **cup thinly sliced green onions**
- 1 **large firm-ripe tomato, seeded and diced**
- ½ **cup diced tomatillos**
- 1 **can (4 oz.) diced green chiles**
- 10 **eggs**
- 3 **tablespoons water**
- 2 **tablespoons butter or margarine**
  Sliced radishes, sour cream, fresh cilantro (coriander) sprigs (optional)
  Salt and pepper

Place a wok over medium heat; when wok is hot, crumble in sausage. Stir-fry until sausage is browned (about 7 minutes); spoon off and discard fat. Stir in onions, tomato, tomatillos, and chiles. Then stir occasionally until almost all liquid in sauce has evaporated and vegetables are soft (about 10 minutes). Pour into a bowl and keep warm; clean and dry wok.

Beat eggs with water until blended. Place wok over medium heat; when wok is hot, add butter. When butter is melted, pour in eggs and stir gently until eggs are set to your liking. Transfer eggs to individual plates, spoon sausage mixture over eggs; garnish with radishes, sour cream, and cilantro, if desired. Season to taste with salt and pepper. Makes 5 servings.

Per serving: 408 calories, 18 g protein, 6 g carbohydrates, 34 g total fat, 591 mg cholesterol, 632 mg sodium

Eggs, chorizo, tomatoes, tomatillos, chiles, radishes,
and cilantro contribute zest to Huevos Revueltos Rancheros
(recipe on facing page). Who would expect such a
fiesta from the wok?

Desserts

Apple-Blueberry Delight

Preparation time: About 10 minutes

Cooking time: About 10 minutes

Use crisp, tart apples for this sweet and spicy dessert. For a special treat, cover the hot fruit with cold whipped cream before serving.

- 2 **tablespoons sugar**
- 1 **teaspoon ground cinnamon**
- ¼ **teaspoon ground nutmeg**
  Juice and grated peel of 2 large oranges
- 4 **tart green-skinned apples (such as Granny Smith)**
- 2 **tablespoons butter or margarine**
- 1 **tablespoon orange-flavored liqueur**
- 1 **pint blueberries**
  Whipped cream (optional)

In a small bowl, mix sugar, cinnamon, and nutmeg; set aside.

In a large bowl, mix orange juice and peel. Peel, core, and thinly slice apples; toss with juice.

Place a wok over medium heat; when wok is hot, add butter. When butter is melted, add sugar mixture and cook, stirring constantly, for about 1 minute.

Add apple mixture to wok and stir-fry until apples are soft (about 3 minutes). Add liqueur, bring to a boil, and boil for about 1 minute. Add blueberries and stir-fry until sauce is thickened. Serve hot, topped with whipped cream, if desired. Makes 4 to 6 servings.

Per serving: 157 calories, 1 g protein, 35 g carbohydrates, 5 g total fat, 10 mg cholesterol, 43 mg sodium

Bananas Managua

Preparation time: About 10 minutes

Cooking time: 6 minutes

Here's a tropical delicacy that's decidedly elegant, yet quick and easy to prepare. If you'd like to top it with homemade Mexican Cream, be sure to start a few days ahead; the cream needs plenty of time to thicken and develop its tangy flavor.

- ¾ **cup sour cream or Mexican Cream (recipe follows)**
- 3 **large firm-ripe bananas**
- ⅓ **cup orange juice**
- 6 **tablespoons firmly packed brown sugar**
- 1 **teaspoon ground cinnamon**
- 3 **tablespoons butter or margarine**
- 2 **tablespoons lime or lemon juice**

If using Mexican Cream, prepare 2 days ahead.

Peel bananas and cut into ¼-inch-thick slanting slices. Pour orange juice into a small, shallow bowl. Mix sugar and cinnamon in another bowl.

Place a wok over medium heat; when wok is hot, add 1 tablespoon of the butter. When butter is melted, dip a third of the banana slices into orange juice and then into sugar mixture. Add to wok and cook until lightly browned and glazed on both sides (about 1 minute). Spoon into 2 shallow dessert dishes. Repeat with remaining bananas, using remaining 2 tablespoons butter and filling 4 more dessert dishes.

When all bananas have been cooked, add lime juice and any remaining orange juice and sugar mixture to wok. Cook over medium heat, stirring, until mixture boils and becomes syrupy (this happens quickly). Pour evenly over bananas. Top each serving with a dollop of sour cream or Mexican Cream. Serve immediately. Makes 6 servings.

Mexican Cream. In a small pan, warm 1 cup **whipping cream** to between 90° and 100°F; add 1 tablespoon **buttermilk** or sour cream, mixing well. Cover and let stand at room temperature (68° to 72°F—or put in a yogurt maker) until mixture starts to thicken (12 to 16 hours).

Refrigerate for at least 24 hours before using to allow acid flavor to develop and cream to thicken further; cream should be of almost spreadable consistency. Store in refrigerator for up to 2 weeks or as long as taste is tangy but fresh. Makes 1 cup.

Per serving: 258 calories, 2 g protein, 32 g carbohydrates, 15 g total fat, 49 mg cholesterol, 77 mg sodium

Deep-frying

C risp golden morsels that disappear almost as soon as you serve them can result from deep-frying in a wok. Success is easy if you understand the technique. Keep the oil continuously at the correct temperature. Don't add too much food at once, because this will lower the temperature. Check the thermometer often, adjusting the heat level as needed. Also, remember that oil and water don't mix and that dangerous spattering can occur when moist foods hit hot oil. Carefully pat dry all meat, fish, poultry, and vegetables before cooking. Make sure that no water clings to utensils before you put them in the wok.

Deep-frying Oriental Chicken Salad (Recipe on facing page)

1 To test temperature of oil, drop 1 bean thread into pan—it should expand at once. When oil is ready, drop in bean threads, a handful at a time.

2 As soon as bean threads hit hot oil, they start to expand. To ensure even cooking, push them down into oil with a wire skimmer or slotted spoon; then turn entire mass over and press down into oil.

3 Cook chicken in same pan of oil (test oil temperature with a bean thread before adding chicken). Cook chicken until well browned on all sides; drain.

4 Chicken cuts most easily when still slightly warm. Anchor chicken with fork; then cut meat and skin off bones. Chicken and bean threads can be prepared a day in advance.

5 Accompanied with fresh fruit and tea, Oriental Chicken Salad makes a satisfying meal. Dressing softens crisp bean threads quickly, so serve salad immediately after tossing.

How to deep-fry in a wok

Anything that can be cooked in a deep-fryer can also be done in a wok, and often with less oil. You'll need just a few extra utensils. A deep-frying thermometer is essential for checking the oil temperature; a wire skimmer or slotted spoon is handy for lifting out cooked foods and removing browned bits before they scorch. Another useful accessory is a semi-circular wire draining rack that attaches to the top of the wok. And unless you have an electric or flat-bottomed wok, you'll need to use a ring stand to support the wok over the burner or element and prevent it from tipping.

Almost any kind of salad oil will work well for deep-frying; peanut and safflower oils are particularly good. Avoid olive oil, since it burns at a very low temperature. To reuse oil for frying, let it cool completely; then strain it through several layers of cheesecloth into a wide-mouthed jar and refrigerate it (chilled oil will turn cloudy, then clear again when returned to room temperature). You can generally recycle oil three or four times; discard it when it begins to develop an off odor. Keep in mind that the oil will darken slightly and increase in saturated fat content with each use.

To deep-fry, place your wok over the heat source, pour in oil to the specified depth, and heat it to the temperature indicated in the recipe. Then carefully add the food, remembering that moist foods will spatter. Cook just a few pieces at a time, since crowding the wok will lower the oil temperature and give you greasy, soggy results. As you fry, check your deep-frying thermometer often and adjust the heat as needed to maintain the correct oil temperature.

(Pictured on facing page)

Oriental Chicken Salad

Preparation time: About 35 minutes

Cooking time: About 25 minutes

Start by deep-frying bean threads and chicken; then combine the crisp noodles and sliced meat with salad greens, onions, crunchy peanuts, and a tangy dressing. The process is shown, step by step, on the facing page.

- ¼ cup all-purpose flour
- ½ teaspoon *each* Chinese five-spice and salt
  Dash of pepper
- 1 whole chicken breast (about 1 lb.), split
- 2 chicken thighs (about ½ lb. *total*)
- 3 ounces dried bean threads
  Salad oil
- ½ cup sesame seeds
  Soy-Lemon Dressing (recipe follows)
- 4 cups finely shredded iceberg lettuce
- 3 green onions (including tops), thinly sliced
- 1 large bunch fresh cilantro (coriander), washed, stemmed, drained, and finely chopped
- 1 cup coarsely chopped salted roasted peanuts

Place flour, five-spice, salt, and pepper on a large plate; stir together. Rinse chicken and pat dry, then dredge in flour mixture until well coated on all sides; shake off excess. Set chicken aside.

Break bean threads into sections. Set a wok in a ring stand. Pour oil into wok to a depth of 1½ inches and heat to 375°F on a deep-frying thermometer (when a bean thread dropped into oil expands immediately, oil is ready).

Drop a handful of bean threads into oil. As they puff and expand, push them down into oil with a wire skimmer or slotted spoon; then turn over entire mass. When bean threads stop crackling (about 30 seconds), remove them with skimmer and drain on paper towels. Repeat until all are cooked. After cooking each batch, skim and discard any bits of bean threads from oil. (At this point, you may let bean threads cool completely, then package airtight and store at room temperature until next day.)

Add chicken to hot oil and cook, turning as needed, until well browned (about 10 minutes for breasts, 12 minutes for thighs); adjust heat as needed to maintain oil temperature at 375°F. Drain on paper towels; set aside and let cool.

Meanwhile, clean and dry wok. Place wok over medium heat; when wok is hot, add sesame seeds and stir until golden (about 2 minutes). Set aside.

Prepare Soy-Lemon Dressing; set aside. Cut cooled chicken and skin off bones, then cut into bite-size pieces.

Place lettuce in a large bowl; top with onions, cilantro, and chicken. Sprinkle with sesame seeds and peanuts. Stir dressing, then drizzle over salad and toss. Add bean threads, lightly crushing some of them with your hands; toss lightly. Serve immediately. Makes 4 servings.

Soy-Lemon Dressing. Stir together ¾ teaspoon **dry mustard**, 1 teaspoon *each* **sugar** and grated **lemon peel**, 1 tablespoon *each* **soy sauce** and **lemon juice**, and ¼ cup **salad oil**.

Per serving: 935 calories, 43 g protein, 40 g carbohydrates, 70 g total fat, 96 mg cholesterol, 796 mg sodium

Appetizers

Chicken Wings with Garlic Sauce

Preparation time: About 25 minutes

Cooking time: About 20 minutes

To make this traditional Thai appetizer, you cut chicken wings apart at the joints, then deep-fry them and serve the crisp results with a sweet-sour garlic sauce. You won't need the wingtips for this recipe; save them for making stock or for other uses, if you like.

   Garlic Sauce (recipe follows)
12 chicken wings (about 2¼ lbs. *total*)
   Salad oil
 2 eggs
   All-purpose flour

Prepare Garlic Sauce; set aside. Rinse chicken and pat very dry. Cut wings apart at joints; reserve wingtips for other uses, if desired.

Set a wok in a ring stand. Pour oil into wok to a depth of 1½ inches; heat to 350°F on a deep-frying thermometer. Meanwhile, in a shallow pan, beat eggs; dip wings in beaten egg, then in flour to coat lightly. Lower chicken into oil, 4 to 6 pieces at a time. Cook, turning, until meat near bone is no longer pink; cut to test (about 5 minutes). Adjust heat as needed to maintain oil temperature at 350°F.

Lift out cooked chicken with tongs and drain on paper towels; keep warm until all chicken has been cooked. Serve with sauce for dipping. Makes 2 dozen pieces (4 to 6 appetizer servings, 2 or 3 entrée servings).

Garlic Sauce. In a 1- to 2-quart pan, stir together ½ cup **sugar,** ¼ cup **water,** ⅓ cup **distilled white vinegar,** ¼ teaspoon **salt,** and 15 cloves **garlic,** minced or pressed. Cover and cook over medium-low heat until garlic is translucent (about 10 minutes). Mix 1½ teaspoons **cornstarch** with 2 teaspoons **water.** Stir into garlic mixture; cook, stirring, until mixture boils.

In a blender or food processor, combine garlic mixture, 8 more cloves **garlic,** and 1 small **fresh hot chile,** cut up; whirl until puréed.

Per appetizer serving: 414 calories, 20 g protein, 25 g carbohydrates, 20 g total fat, 162 mg cholesterol, 183 mg sodium

Meat-filled Fried Rice Balls

Preparation time: About 1 hour

Cooking time: About 1¼ hours

Seedless raisins and pine nuts add texture and a light crunch to the beef filling for these egg-shaped rice balls.

 6 cups water
   Salt
1½ cups long-grain white rice
 ½ teaspoon grated lemon peel
 ½ pound lean ground beef
 1 small onion, chopped
 1 clove garlic, minced or pressed
 ½ teaspoon *each* ground cinnamon and allspice
 ¼ teaspoon ground cumin
 ¼ cup *each* raisins and pine nuts
 2 tablespoons chopped parsley
   Salad oil

In a heavy 3-quart pan, bring water and 1½ teaspoons salt to a boil. Stir in rice. Reduce heat to low, cover, and simmer until water is absorbed (about 40 minutes; rice will be sticky). Uncover, stir in lemon peel, and let cool.

While rice is cooking, place a wok over medium heat. When wok is hot, crumble in beef, then add onion and garlic. Cook, stirring, until meat is no longer pink (about 3 minutes). Stir in cinnamon, allspice, and cumin; mix in raisins, pine nuts, and parsley. Season to taste with salt. Transfer meat mixture to a bowl; clean and dry wok.

To shape each ball, place about ⅓ cup of the cooked rice in your palm and flatten into a thin patty. Top with 1 heaping tablespoon of the meat filling. Cup your hand, then top with additional rice. Press together into an egg shape. If rice is too sticky to handle easily, moisten hands lightly with water.

Set wok in a ring stand. Pour oil into wok to a depth of 2 inches and heat to 375°F on a deep-frying thermometer. With a slotted spoon, lower 1 rice ball at a time into oil. Cook, turning often, until golden brown on all sides (about 5 minutes); adjust heat as needed to maintain oil temperature at 375°F. Lift out and drain on paper towels; keep warm until all rice balls have been cooked.

If made ahead, let cool, then cover and refrigerate until next day. To reheat, place on a baking sheet and heat in a 375° oven until heated through (about 25 minutes). Makes 12 to 14 balls (6 servings).

Per serving: 391 calories, 12 g protein, 46 g carbohydrates, 18 g total fat, 28 mg cholesterol, 30 mg sodium

Beef & Pork

Picadillo Turnovers

Preparation time: About 45 minutes

Cooking time: About 25 minutes

Picadillo (page 654) is a satisfying entrée all on its own, but it's also a tasty filling for the flaky fried turnovers called *empanadas*.

- 1 teaspoon butter or margarine
- ½ pound *each* lean ground beef and lean ground pork; or 1 pound lean ground beef
- 1 large clove garlic, minced or pressed
- ½ cup *each* tomato purée and raisins
- ¼ cup dry sherry
- 2 teaspoons ground cinnamon
- ½ teaspoon ground cloves
- 2 tablespoons distilled white vinegar
- 1 tablespoon sugar
  Salt
- ¾ cup slivered almonds
  Pastry for a double-crust 9-inch pie
  Salad oil

Place a wok over medium heat; when wok is hot, add butter. When butter is melted, crumble in meat and cook, stirring, until meat is no longer pink (3 to 5 minutes). Spoon off and discard fat. Stir in garlic, tomato purée, raisins, sherry, cinnamon, cloves, vinegar, and sugar. Cook, uncovered, until almost all liquid has evaporated (about 10 minutes). Season to taste with salt, then stir in almonds; transfer to a bowl and let cool. Clean and dry wok.

On a floured board, roll out pastry about ⅛ inch thick and cut into 4-inch circles. Spoon filling evenly on 1 side of each pastry circle; moisten edges of pastry, fold over, and seal.

Set wok in a ring stand. Pour oil into wok to a depth of 1½ inches; heat to 375°F on a deep-frying thermometer. Add 4 turnovers at a time and cook until browned on both sides (about 5 minutes); adjust heat as needed to maintain oil temperature at 375°F. Lift out cooked turnovers and drain on paper towels; keep warm until all turnovers have been cooked. Makes about 16 turnovers (about 8 servings).

Per turnover: 264 calories, 7 g protein, 19 g carbohydrates, 18 g total fat, 16 mg cholesterol, 154 mg sodium

Japanese Pork Cutlets

Preparation time: About 50 minutes

Cooking time: About 10 minutes

A popular dish in Japan today, *tonkatsu* appeals to Western diners as well. Both tonkatsu sauce and *pan ko*—the coarse bread crumbs used to coat the meat—are available in many well-stocked markets, but it's easy to make your own.

- 1 to 1½ cups coarse dry bread crumbs (*pan ko*), homemade (directions follow) or purchased
  Tonkatsu Sauce, homemade (recipe follows) or purchased
- 1 to 1½ pounds pork chops or steaks, cut ½ inch thick
- 1 egg
- 1 tablespoon water
  Salt and pepper
  About 2 tablespoons all-purpose flour
  Salad oil
- 2 cups finely shredded cabbage
- ½ cup shredded carrot

Prepare bread crumbs and Tonkatsu Sauce; set aside.

Trim and discard fat and bones from pork. Place meat between sheets of wax paper and pound with a mallet until about ¼ inch thick (overlap any small pieces and pound together into a single piece).

In a shallow bowl, lightly beat egg with water. Spread crumbs on a piece of wax paper. Sprinkle each cutlet lightly with salt and pepper; dust with flour, then shake off excess. Dip cutlets into egg, let drain briefly, and press into crumbs to coat thickly all over. Set aside for 10 minutes to dry slightly.

Set a wok in a ring stand. Pour oil into wok to a depth of 1½ inches and heat to 360°F on a deep-frying thermometer. Add 1 or 2 cutlets at a time and cook, turning as needed, until golden brown on both sides (about 2 minutes); adjust heat as needed to maintain oil temperature at 360°F. Drain briefly on paper towels. Serve with cabbage, carrot, and Tonkatsu Sauce. Makes 3 or 4 servings.

Coarse dry bread crumbs. Trim crusts from 10 slices **firm-textured white or whole wheat bread;** cut bread into cubes. Whirl cubes, a few at a time, in a blender or food processor until evenly coarse crumbs form. Spread crumbs in a shallow rimmed baking pan; bake in a 325° oven, stirring often, until completely dry but not brown (15 to 20 minutes). Makes about 4 cups.

Tonkatsu Sauce. Stir together ½ cup **catsup** and 2 tablespoons *each* **Worcestershire** and **soy sauce.**

Per serving: 512 calories, 34 g protein, 45 g carbohydrates, 22 g total fat, 140 mg cholesterol, 1,331 mg sodium

China's Edible Nest

Golden "phoenix nests"— baskets of deep-fried vegetable shreds— make handsome showcases for many stir-fried dishes. After eating the contents, you break the nest apart with your fingers and nibble the crisp pieces.

Making these decorative nests is surprisingly easy. In addition to your wok, the only utensils you'll need are two sieves of the same size: one to act as a form for shaping the shredded vegetable and one to hold the shreds in place as they cook. *To determine how much oil to use,* place an empty sieve in your wok, then pour in enough oil to cover at least three-fourths of the sieve.

Because the nests have an open, meshlike structure, it's best to fill them with lightly sauced stir-fries like the Green Pepper Beef featured here.

Potato Phoenix Nest

Peel 2 medium-size **white thin-skinned potatoes** and shred them lengthwise (you should have 2 cups). Squeeze shreds to remove liquid; then place in a bowl. Sprinkle 1 tablespoon **cornstarch** over potatoes and toss to distribute cornstarch and loosen shreds. Arrange a handful of shreds in a latticework inside a 4-inch-diameter sieve, covering bottom of sieve and extending at least halfway up sides. Fit a second sieve inside first one.

Set a wok in a ring stand. Heat appropriate amount of **salad oil** (see above) to 325°F on a deep-frying thermometer. Place sieve in oil and cook until nest is golden brown (3 to 4 minutes). Remove from oil and lift off top sieve. Loosen edges of nest with tip of a sharp knife, then gently remove nest and drain on paper towels. Repeat, adjusting heat as necessary, to maintain oil temperature at 325°F.

If made ahead, let cool; stack nests, separating them with paper towels, and seal in plastic bags. Store at room temperature for up to 2 days. Makes 4 or 5 nests, each about 4 inches in diameter.

Per nest: 162 calories, .92 g protein, 9 g carbohydrates, 14 g total fat, 0 mg cholesterol, 3 mg sodium

(Pictured on facing page)

Sweet Potato or Yam Nest

Follow directions for **Potato Phoenix Nest,** but substitute 2 cups shredded **sweet potatoes** or yams for potatoes and increase oil temperature to 350°F. Cook sweet potato nests until golden brown (3 to 4 minutes); cook yam nests until a light pumpkin color (4 to 5 minutes).

(Pictured on facing page)

Green Pepper Beef

About ¾ **pound lean boneless beef steak (such as top round, flank, or sirloin)**
1 tablespoon *each* **dry sherry and soy sauce**
2 tablespoons **water**
¼ teaspoon *each* **salt and sugar**
2 teaspoons **cornstarch**
3½ tablespoons **salad oil**
   Cooking Sauce (recipe follows)
1 clove **garlic, minced**
½ teaspoon **minced fresh ginger**
2 small **green bell peppers, seeded and cut into ¼-inch-wide strips**

Cut beef with the grain into 1½-inch-wide strips; then cut each strip across the grain into ⅛-inch-thick slanting slices. In a bowl, combine sherry, soy, 1 tablespoon of the water, salt, sugar, and cornstarch. Add beef and stir to coat, then stir in 1½ teaspoons of the oil and let marinate for 15 minutes.

Meanwhile, prepare Cooking Sauce and set aside.

Place a wok over high heat; when wok is hot, add 2 table-spoons of the oil. When oil begins to heat, add garlic and ginger and stir once. Add beef mixture and stir-fry until meat is browned (about 2 minutes); remove from wok.

Pour remaining 1 tablespoon oil into wok; when oil is hot, add bell peppers and stir-fry for 30 seconds. Add remaining 1 tablespoon water, cover, and cook for 1 minute. Return meat to wok. Stir Cooking Sauce, pour into wok, and stir until sauce boils and thickens. Makes 4 servings.

Cooking Sauce. Stir together 1½ teaspoons *each* **soy sauce** and **cornstarch** and ¼ cup **regular-strength chicken broth** or water. *(If you don't plan to serve the stir-fry in a phoenix nest, double this sauce recipe.)*

Per serving: 249 calories, 21 g protein, 5 g carbohydrates, 16 g total fat, 49 mg cholesterol, 692 mg sodium

Spoon savory Green Pepper Beef (recipe on facing page)
into individual-size phoenix nests made from shredded yams
(recipe on facing page). Guests enjoy the filling first, then break apart
and eat its crisp container.

Chicken

Seasoned Fried Chicken

Preparation time: *About 20 minutes*

Marinating time: *About 30 minutes*

Cooking time: *About 30 minutes*

These crumb-coated chicken cubes are marinated in ginger, soy, and lemon juice before frying. Leftover marinade makes a simple dip.

- ½ cup soy sauce
- 1 tablespoon grated or minced fresh ginger
- 1 tablespoon lemon juice
- 2 tablespoons sake or dry sherry
- 3 whole chicken breasts (about 1 lb. *each*), skinned, boned, and cut into 1-inch chunks
- 1½ cups coarse dry bread crumbs (*pan ko*), purchased or homemade (page 695)
- 6 tablespoons all-purpose flour
- 2 tablespoons cornstarch
- 2 eggs
  Salad oil

In a bowl, combine soy, ginger, lemon juice, and sake. Add chicken and stir to coat; let marinate for about 30 minutes, stirring occasionally. Drain chicken and pat dry; reserve marinade.

Spread bread crumbs in a pie pan or rimmed plate. In another pie pan, combine flour and cornstarch. In a third pie pan, lightly beat eggs. Dredge chicken in flour mixture; shake off excess. Dip into eggs, then roll in crumbs to coat.

Meanwhile, set a wok in a ring stand. Pour oil into wok to a depth of 2 inches and heat to 375°F on a deep-frying thermometer. Add as many pieces of chicken at a time as will fit without crowding. Cook, turning occasionally, until coating is browned on all sides and meat is no longer pink in center; cut to test (about 2 minutes). Adjust heat as needed to maintain oil temperature at 375°F.

Lift out cooked chicken with a slotted spoon, drain briefly on paper towels, and serve at once; offer reserved marinade in a small bowl for dipping. Makes 4 to 6 servings.

Per serving: 464 calories, 42 g protein, 30 g carbohydrates, 19 g total fat, 178 mg cholesterol, 1,677 mg sodium

Chicken with Plum Sauce

Preparation time: *About 20 minutes*

Marinating time: *15 minutes*

Cooking time: *About 15 minutes*

A flavorful sweet-sour plum sauce laced with strips of pickled ginger makes this dish distinctive.

  Plum Sauce (recipe follows)
- 1½ pounds chicken breasts or thighs, skinned, boned, and cut into about 1½-inch-square pieces
- 2 tablespoons soy sauce
- 1 tablespoon *each* cornstarch and water
- ¼ teaspoon sesame oil
  Dash of white pepper
  Salad oil
- 1 cup all-purpose flour
- ¼ cup cornstarch
- 1½ teaspoons baking powder
- 1 cup water

Prepare Plum Sauce and set aside.

In a bowl, mix soy, cornstarch, water, sesame oil, and white pepper. Add chicken; stir to coat. Stir in 1 tablespoon salad oil; marinate for 15 minutes. In another bowl, mix flour, the ¼ cup cornstarch, and baking powder. Blend in water and 1 tablespoon salad oil. Let batter stand for 10 minutes.

Set a wok in a ring stand. Pour salad oil into wok to a depth of 1½ inches and heat to 350°F on a deep-frying thermometer. Dip each piece of chicken in batter, then lower into oil; add as many pieces as will fit without crowding. Cook, turning occasionally, until crust is golden brown and meat is no longer pink in center; cut to test (about 2 minutes for breast pieces, about 4 minutes for thigh pieces). Adjust heat as needed to maintain oil temperature at 350°F.

Lift out cooked chicken with a slotted spoon and drain on paper towels. Serve at once with Plum Sauce. Makes 3 or 4 servings.

Plum Sauce. In a bowl, stir together ¾ cup **water**, 1½ teaspoons **cornstarch**, 2 teaspoons **sugar**, 1 teaspoon **soy sauce**, and ¼ cup **canned plum sauce.**

Heat 1 tablespoon **salad oil** in a small pan over medium-high heat. Add 2 tablespoons thinly sliced **pickled red ginger;** stir-fry for 30 seconds. Pour in plum sauce mixture; cook, stirring, until sauce boils and thickens slightly (about 2 minutes). Let cool to room temperature. Makes 1 cup sauce.

Per serving chicken: 427 calories, 20 g protein, 50 g carbohydrates, 17 g total fat, 41 mg cholesterol, 703 mg sodium

Per tablespoon sauce: 17 calories, .03 g protein, 4 g carbohydrates, 0 g total fat, 0 mg cholesterol, 24 mg sodium

Fish & Shellfish

Trout on a Spinach Bed

Preparation time: About 15 minutes, plus 30 minutes to soak mushrooms

Cooking time: About 20 minutes

Trout, pork, and spinach make an unusual but savory combination in this dish for two. The fried trout is presented on a bed of cooked spinach, then topped with a pork and mushroom sauce.

6 medium-size dried Oriental mushrooms
  Cooking Sauce (recipe follows)
  About 1 pound spinach
2 cleaned trout (about ½ lb. *each*)
  Salt
  Cornstarch
  Salad oil
2 cloves garlic, minced or pressed
½ pound lean boneless pork (such as shoulder or butt), trimmed of excess fat and cut into ⅛- by 1- by 2-inch strips
1 teaspoon grated fresh ginger
2 green onions (including tops), thinly sliced

Soak mushrooms in warm water to cover for 30 minutes, then drain. Cut off and discard stems; squeeze caps dry and cut into thin strips. Set aside.

While mushrooms are soaking, prepare Cooking Sauce and set aside. Also remove and discard tough stems and any yellow or wilted leaves from spinach; rinse remaining leaves thoroughly. Set aside.

Rinse trout and pat dry. Sprinkle each fish lightly with salt and coat with cornstarch; shake off excess.

Place a wok in a ring stand. Pour oil into wok to a depth of about 1 inch and heat to 400°F on a deep-frying thermometer. Add fish and cook, turning as needed, until crisp and browned on both sides (about 5 minutes); adjust heat as needed to maintain oil temperature at 400°F. Lift out, drain on paper towels, and keep warm.

Carefully pour off oil from wok and wipe any remaining bits of browned fish from wok. Place wok over high heat. When wok is hot, add 1 tablespoon oil. When oil is hot, add spinach and half the garlic. Stir-fry just until spinach is wilted (about 30 seconds). Turn into a shallow serving dish.

Pour 2 tablespoons more oil into wok. When oil is hot, add remaining garlic, pork, and ginger. Stir-

fry until pork is browned (about 4 minutes); then add mushrooms. Stir Cooking Sauce and add; stir until sauce boils and thickens (about 1 minute).

Arrange fish on spinach. Pour pork sauce over fish and sprinkle with onions. Makes 2 servings.

Cooking Sauce. Stir together 1 tablespoon *each* **cornstarch, soy sauce,** and **dry sherry;** ¼ teaspoon **salt;** ⅛ teaspoon **pepper;** and ¾ cup **regular-strength chicken broth.**

Per serving: 560 calories, 52 g protein, 25 g carbohydrates, 29 g total fat, 142 mg cholesterol, 1,431 mg sodium

Phoenix-tail Shrimp

Preparation time: About 20 minutes

Cooking time: About 20 minutes

A puffy, crunchy batter coats the shrimp in this simply prepared dish. Shell the shrimp but leave the tail sections on; use them as handles for dipping the shrimp in your favorite cocktail sauce.

1 pound medium-size or large raw shrimp
1 cup all-purpose flour
2½ teaspoons baking powder
¼ teaspoon salt
  Dash of white pepper
1 cup water
  Salad oil

Shell shrimp, but leave tail sections on for handles. Devein, rinse, and pat dry. In a bowl, combine flour, baking powder, salt, and white pepper. Add water and stir until batter is smooth.

Set a wok in a ring stand. Pour oil into wok to a depth of 1½ inches and heat to 375°F on a deep-frying thermometer. Hold each shrimp by tail and dip into batter so batter covers shrimp but not tail; then lower into hot oil. Add as many shrimp at a time as will fit without crowding; cook, turning occasionally, until crisp and golden (2 to 3 minutes). Adjust heat as necessary to maintain oil temperature at 375°F.

Remove cooked shrimp from oil with a slotted spoon, drain on paper towels, and keep warm until all shrimp have been cooked. Makes 4 servings.

Per serving: 303 calories, 22 g protein, 25 g carbohydrates, 12 g total fat, 140 mg cholesterol, 538 mg sodium

The striking flavor of fragile Crisp-fried Leaves
(recipe on facing page) enhances simple foods, from plain baked potatoes
to the Brie and quail eggs shown here. Choose spinach,
watercress, mint, or other greens.

Fried Fresh Leaves

Deep-fried leaves? A bit outlandish, perhaps, but surprisingly delicious. Dropped into hot oil, leaves of spinach, mustard, watercress, cilantro, mint, and parsley very quickly turn brittle, translucent, and intensely green. Fragile and shattery-crisp, they're a striking complement to simply cooked seafood, eggs, meat, or composed salads; they also make an intriguing garnish for baked potatoes or hot melted cheese appetizers like the one featured below.

Wash and dry leaves thoroughly before frying. Even carefully dried leaves tend to spatter as they hit the hot oil, though, so be sure to wear an apron and stand back from the wok as you work.

Fried leaves stay crisp for several days. Add to dishes just before serving; as soon as they touch a liquid or moist food, they go limp.

(Pictured on facing page)
Crisp-fried Leaves

Remove and discard thick stems from 2 ounces **spinach,** mustard greens (small leaves work best), watercress, fresh cilantro (coriander), parsley (flat-leaf or curly), or mint. Wash leaves thoroughly, drain well, and pat dry. If you like, cut spinach leaves and mustard greens across the grain into ¼-inch-wide strips.

Wrap leaves loosely in towels and enclose in a plastic bag. Refrigerate for at least 1 hour or until next day to dry thoroughly.

Set a wok in a ring stand. Pour **salad oil** into wok to a depth of about 2 inches and heat to 370°F on a deep-frying thermometer. Fry greens a handful at a time (stand back, because oil may spatter). Turn leaves with a slotted spoon until they take on a brighter green color and are at least partly translucent (5 to 20 seconds); leaves may not turn completely translucent in oil, but will become more translucent as they stand. If leaves turn a darker green and begin to scorch, they're overcooked.

Lift leaves from oil with a slotted spoon; drain on paper towels. Serve hot or at room temperature. If made ahead, store airtight at room temperature in a paper towel–lined container for up to 3 days. Makes about 2 cups.

Per ¼ cup: 31 calories, .14 g protein, .17 g carbohydrate, 3 g total fat, 0 mg cholesterol, 4 mg sodium

(Pictured on facing page)
Quail Eggs in Crisp-fried Nest

About 2 cups whole or shredded Crisp-fried Leaves (recipe at left)
12 to 18 quail eggs
1 tablespoon sesame seeds
Salt

Prepare Crisp-fried Leaves; set aside.

Fill a 1- to 2-quart pan with about 2 inches of water; add eggs. Bring water to a boil; then reduce heat and simmer, uncovered, for 5 minutes. Drain and cover with cold water. Let stand until cool. Carefully shell eggs. (At this point, you may cover and refrigerate until next day.)

Toast sesame seeds in a small frying pan over medium heat until golden (about 2 minutes), shaking pan often. Set aside.

Pat eggs dry with a towel. Place fried leaves in a basket or bowl and nest eggs in leaves. Sprinkle sesame seeds and salt to taste over eggs and greens. Eat with fingers, picking up some of the greens with each egg. Makes 4 to 6 appetizer servings.

Per serving: 93 calories, 4 g protein, .69 g carbohydrate, 8 g total fat, 228 mg cholesterol, 6 mg sodium

(Pictured on facing page)
Melted Cheese with Crisp-fried Leaves

Place 1 small wheel (8 oz.) **Brie or Camembert cheese** in a 6- to 7-inch shallow pan or heatproof dish. Bake, uncovered, in a 350° oven just until cheese begins to melt (12 to 15 minutes).

Set hot cheese on a tray. Place alongside in separate baskets or bowls about 2 cups **Crisp-fried Leaves** (recipe at left; use watercress, mint, cilantro, or parsley) and 1 **baguette** (8 oz.), thinly sliced and toasted.

To eat, spread hot cheese on a toasted baguette slice and sprinkle with fried leaves. Makes 12 appetizer servings.

Per serving: 138 calories, 6 g protein, 11 g carbohydrates, 8 g total fat, 19 mg cholesterol, 230 mg sodium

Salads

Crispy Shrimp Salad

Preparation time: About 30 minutes

Marinating time: 30 minutes

Cooking time: About 5 minutes

Crisp deep-fried shrimp top a light cabbage and carrot salad in this Vietnamese-inspired entrée.

- 1 **medium-size onion, thinly sliced**
- 3 **tablespoons** *each* **sugar and distilled white vinegar**
- ¼ **teaspoon white pepper**
- ¾ **pound medium-size raw shrimp, shelled and deveined**
- ¼ **cup lime juice**
- 2 **tablespoons soy sauce**
- 2 **tablespoons fish sauce (***nam pla***)**
- 1 **clove garlic, minced or pressed**
  Salad oil
- 4 **cups finely shredded green cabbage**
- 2 **cups shredded carrots**
- ¼ **cup cornstarch**
- ⅓ **cup thinly slivered fresh mint leaves**
- 3 **tablespoons unsalted peanuts, chopped**

In a bowl, mix onion, sugar, vinegar, and white pepper. Cover; refrigerate for 30 minutes.

In another bowl, combine shrimp, 2 tablespoons of the lime juice, and soy; toss well and set aside at room temperature until ready to use.

Stir remaining 2 tablespoons lime juice, fish sauce, garlic, and ¼ cup oil into marinated onion; toss onion mixture with cabbage and carrots.

Set a wok in a ring stand. Pour oil into wok to a depth of 1 inch and heat to 350°F on a deep-frying thermometer. Working quickly, lift shrimp, 1 at a time, from marinade and dip into cornstarch to coat; shake off excess, then add shrimp to oil (you can cook 5 to 7 at a time). Cook until golden brown (about 30 seconds); adjust heat as needed to maintain oil temperature at 350°F. Remove cooked shrimp with a slotted spoon, drain on paper towels, and keep warm until all have been cooked.

Spread cabbage-onion mixture on a platter and top with hot shrimp. Sprinkle with mint and peanuts; serve at once. Makes 4 to 6 servings.

Per serving: 176 calories, 12 g protein, 21 g carbohydrates, 6 g total fat, 70 mg cholesterol, 778 mg sodium

Spinach Salad with Warm Feta & Crisp Chiles

Preparation time: About 15 minutes

Cooking time: About 7 minutes

Wonderful flavors come to life in this unusual combination of tender spinach, tangy feta, and spicy fried chiles.

- 1 **pound spinach**
  Lime Dressing (recipe follows)
- 3 **large dried red New Mexico or California chiles**
- 1 **medium-size red onion, thinly sliced**
- 2 **large ripe avocados**
  Salad oil
- 1 **egg**
- 1 **tablespoon water**
- 1 **cup fine dry bread crumbs**
- 8 **ounces feta cheese, drained and cut into 1-inch cubes**

Remove tough spinach stems and any yellow or wilted leaves. Rinse remaining spinach well; drain. Wrap in paper towels, enclose in plastic bags, and refrigerate until chilled. Prepare Lime Dressing; set aside. Cut chiles crosswise with scissors into thin strips; discard stems and seeds. Set aside.

Pinch off and discard stems from chilled spinach leaves; tear or cut leaves into small pieces and toss in a serving bowl with onion. Pit and peel avocados; dice and add to spinach mixture.

Set a wok in a ring stand. Pour oil into wok to a depth of 2 inches and heat over medium heat to 300°F on a deep-frying thermometer. Meanwhile, beat together egg and water in a shallow dish; spread bread crumbs in another shallow dish.

Add chiles all at once to oil and cook until just crisp (about 10 seconds). Remove with a slotted spoon and drain on paper towels. Increase heat; when oil reaches 375°F, quickly dip feta pieces in egg, then coat with bread crumbs. Add cheese cubes to oil, a portion at a time, and cook until crisp and brown on the outside and just melted on the inside (about 30 seconds); adjust heat as needed to maintain oil temperature at 375°F. As cheese cubes are cooked, remove from oil with a slotted spoon and drain.

Toss spinach mixture with Lime Dressing and chiles. Spoon onto individual plates and top with cheese cubes. Serve at once. Makes 4 to 6 servings.

Lime Dressing. Whisk together ¼ cup **lime juice,** ½ teaspoon **Dijon mustard,** and ⅓ cup **salad oil** until smooth. Season to taste with **pepper,** if desired.

Per serving: 501 calories, 11 g protein, 24 g carbohydrates, 42 g total fat, 80 mg cholesterol, 582 mg sodium

Vegetables

Corn Fritters

Preparation time: 50 to 55 minutes

Cooking time: 45 minutes

Use your food processor or blender to prepare these Indonesian corn and shrimp fritters.

   5 or 6 large ears corn, husked
   ¼ to ½ pound raw shrimp, shelled, deveined, and finely chopped
   1 egg
   1 green onion (including top), finely chopped
   ½ medium-size onion, finely chopped
   1 clove garlic, minced or pressed
   ¼ cup finely chopped celery leaves or fresh cilantro (coriander)
   ⅛ teaspoon pepper
   1 tablespoon ground coriander
   1 teaspoon sugar
      About 1 teaspoon salt
   ½ to ¾ cup all-purpose flour
      Salad oil

Cut corn off cob, then scrape cob with knife to remove pulp and "milk"; you should have 4 cups corn in all. In a food processor or blender, whirl corn, half at a time, until mixture is creamy but has some pieces of coarsely chopped corn; scrape down sides of processor bowl often.

Pour puréed corn into a bowl and add shrimp, egg, green onion, onion, garlic, celery leaves, pepper, coriander, sugar, salt, and ½ cup of the flour. Set aside for about 10 minutes.

Set a wok in a ring stand. Pour oil into wok to a depth of 2 inches and heat to 350°F on a deep-frying thermometer. Scoop up a rounded tablespoon of batter and carefully drop into oil; if this test fritter falls apart, stir more flour into batter, 1 tablespoon at a time, until a test fritter will hold together.

When batter has the correct consistency, add 4 or 5 fritters to oil, using a rounded tablespoon of batter for each. As fritters come to surface, turn as needed until evenly browned (about 5 minutes). Adjust heat as needed to maintain oil temperature at 350°F; skim and discard browned bits of batter frequently.

Lift out cooked fritters, drain on paper towels, and keep warm until all fritters have been cooked.

Serve warm or at room temperature. Makes about 3½ dozen fritters (6 to 10 appetizer or vegetable servings).

Per serving: 179 calories, 7 g protein, 20 g carbohydrates, 8 g total fat, 55 mg cholesterol, 264 mg sodium

Eggplant with Sesame Sauce

Preparation time: About 10 minutes

Cooking time: About 20 minutes

Japanese eggplant aren't exclusively from Japan—but the Japanese may have the best method of cooking them. Quick frying in oil produces soft and creamy eggplant that absorbs almost no fat.

   8 Japanese eggplants, *each* about 6 inches long and 2 inches in diameter (about 2 lbs. *total*)
   1 tablespoon sesame seeds
      Salad oil
   ¼ cup *each* regular-strength chicken broth and soy sauce
   ½ teaspoon grated fresh ginger

Trim and discard ends from eggplant. In each one, make four ⅓-inch-deep lengthwise slashes, extending to within ½ inch of ends and spaced evenly around eggplant. Place a wok over medium heat; when wok is hot, add sesame seeds and stir until golden (about 2 minutes). Pour out of wok.

Set wok in a ring stand. Pour oil into wok to a depth of 1½ inches and heat to 350°F on a deep-frying thermometer. Slip several eggplant at a time into oil. Cook, turning occasionally, until soft when pressed (about 4 minutes); adjust heat as needed to maintain oil temperature at 350°F. Lift out cooked eggplant, drain on paper towels, and keep warm until all eggplant have been cooked.

Mix broth, soy, ginger, and sesame seeds. Spoon over eggplant. Makes 4 servings.

Per serving: 206 calories, 5 g protein, 16 g carbohydrates, 15 g total fat, 0 mg cholesterol, 1,102 mg sodium

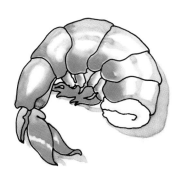

Bread & Cheese

Navajo Fry Bread

Preparation time: About 20 minutes

Cooking time: About 20 minutes

These chewy breads—also called Papago popovers—are great for tostada bases. Or try them as a snack, sprinkled with sugar or drizzled with honey.

> **About 2 cups all-purpose flour**
> ½ **cup instant nonfat dry milk**
> 1 **tablespoon baking powder**
> ½ **teaspoon salt**
> 2 **tablespoons lard or solid vegetable shortening**
> ¾ **cup water**
> **Salad oil**

In a bowl, stir together 2 cups of the flour, dry milk, baking powder, and salt. With your fingers, crumble in lard until mixture is like cornmeal. Add water; stir with a fork just until dough clings together. Turn out onto a floured board and knead until smooth and satiny (about 5 minutes).

Divide dough into 6 portions; shape each into a ball. On a floured board, press out 1 ball to a 6- to 7-inch round; cover loosely. Repeat with remaining dough.

Set a wok in a ring stand. Pour oil into wok to a depth of 1 inch and heat to 350°F on a deep-frying thermometer. To fry each bread, place it on a wide spatula; lower into oil. Cook, turning often, until golden brown on both sides (1½ to 2 minutes); adjust heat as needed to maintain oil temperature at 350°F. Drain breads on paper towels and serve hot. Makes 6 fry breads.

Per bread: 252 calories, 6 g protein, 35 g carbohydrates, 9 g total fat, 5 mg cholesterol, 427 mg sodium

Spicy Fry Bread

Follow directions for **Navajo Fry Bread** adding 1 teaspoon **chili powder,** 1 teaspoon **paprika,** ½ teaspoon **ground cumin,** ¼ teaspoon **ground coriander,** and ⅛ teaspoon **ground red pepper (cayenne)** to flour mixture.

Mozzarella in Carrozza (Italian Cheese Sandwiches)

Preparation time: About 15 minutes

Cooking time: About 20 minutes

"Mozzarella in a carriage" is a tasty dish from southern Italy; we've given it a new lightness by deep-frying it without the traditional egg coating and topping it with a zesty tomato sauce. Serve the hot fried cheese sandwiches with steamed zucchini for a satisfying meatless supper.

> **Quick Tomato Sauce (recipe follows)**
> 4 **slices mozzarella cheese,** *each* ¼ **inch thick (about 4 oz.** *total***)**
> 8 **slices French or Italian bread,** *each* ½ **inch thick, crusts removed**
> ½ **cup milk**
> ⅓ **cup all-purpose flour**
> **Salad oil**

Prepare Quick Tomato Sauce, cover, and keep warm.

Trim cheese slices to make them just slightly smaller than bread slices. Assemble sandwiches, using 2 bread slices and 1 cheese slice for each. Gently pinch together edges of bread to seal. Place milk in a shallow dish; place flour in another shallow dish.

Set a wok in a ring stand. Pour oil into wok to a depth of 2 inches and heat to 375°F on a deep-frying thermometer. Cook sandwiches 1 at a time: dip each first in milk, then in flour; then place in wok and cook, turning once, until golden brown and crisp on both sides (about 2 minutes). Adjust heat as needed to maintain oil temperature at 375°F. Remove from oil with a slotted spoon and drain on paper towels.

Quickly reheat tomato sauce. Transfer mozzarella "carriages" to a warm platter; spoon sauce over and around them. Serve immediately. Makes 4 servings.

Quick Tomato Sauce. Heat 2 tablespoons **salad oil** in a medium-size frying pan over medium heat. Add 1 small **onion,** chopped, and 1 clove **garlic,** minced or pressed; cook, stirring, just until onion is soft. Add 1 can (about 1 lb.) **tomatoes** (break up with a spoon) and their liquid; stir in ½ teaspoon **dry marjoram or oregano leaves.** Bring sauce to a boil, stirring frequently; then reduce heat and simmer, uncovered, until slightly thickened (about 5 minutes). Season to taste with **salt** and **pepper,** if desired.

Per serving: 607 calories, 15 g protein, 54 g carbohydrates, 37 g total fat, 24 mg cholesterol, 712 mg sodium

A showy dessert, Caramel Fried Apples (recipe on page 706)
arrive hot at the table, then get a quick dip in ice water to cool and harden
their sweet coating. Banana slices are every bit as delicious as apples
in this Chinese treat.

Desserts

(Pictured on page 705)

Caramel Fried Apples

Preparation time: *About 10 minutes*

Cooking time: *About 30 minutes*

Caramelizing the sugar for this show-stopper dessert calls for split-second timing; it goes so quickly that you don't have time to use a candy thermometer. You may want to practice this step once before making the whole dessert.

- ½ **cup all-purpose flour**
- 2 **tablespoons cornstarch**
- ¾ **teaspoon baking powder**
- ½ **cup water**
- 2 **Golden Delicious apples or 2 bananas**
  Salad oil
  Ice cubes
- ⅔ **cup sugar**
- ⅓ **cup warm water**
- 2 **teaspoons sesame seeds**

In a bowl, mix flour, cornstarch, and baking powder. Add the ½ cup water and stir until smooth. Peel and core apples; cut each into 8 wedges. (If you use bananas, peel, then cut diagonally into ½-inch slices.) Place fruit in batter and turn to coat evenly.

Set a wok in a ring stand. Pour oil into wok to a depth of about 1½ inches and heat to 350°F on a deep-frying thermometer. Lift fruit, a piece at a time, from batter. Let excess batter drip off; then lower fruit into oil (cook several pieces at a time; do not crowd wok). Cook until coating is golden brown (about 2 minutes); adjust heat as needed to maintain oil temperature at 350°F. Remove with a slotted spoon and drain on paper towels.

When all fruit has been cooked, generously oil a shallow pan or flat serving dish. Fill a serving bowl to the brim with ice cubes; add water to cover.

To make the caramel coating, place sugar, the ⅓ cup warm water, and 1 tablespoon oil in a 10-inch frying pan; stir to blend. Place pan over high heat. When mixture begins to bubble (about 1 minute), shake pan continuously to prevent burning. Continue cooking and shaking pan until syrup *just* turns a pale straw color (about 9 minutes). Immediately remove from heat, add sesame seeds, and swirl to mix. (Syrup will continue to cook after you remove it from heat and will turn to a golden color in a few seconds.) Drop a few pieces of fruit into syrup and swirl to coat evenly. Using 2 spoons, immediately remove each piece of fruit; arrange on oiled pan (pieces should not touch). Repeat with remaining fruit. At the table, dip fruit in ice to harden coating and cool fruit. Makes 6 servings.

Per serving: 204 calories, 1 g protein, 39 g carbohydrates, 5 g total fat, 0 mg cholesterol, 54 mg sodium

Ricotta Puffs

Preparation time: *About 10 minutes*

Cooking time: *About 30 minutes*

In flavor and appearance, these tempting puffs can pass for doughnuts—but they're plumped up with protein rather than calories.

- 8 **ounces (1 cup) ricotta cheese**
- 3 **eggs**
- ¼ **cup granulated sugar**
- 1 **cup all-purpose flour**
- 4 **teaspoons baking powder**
- ¼ **teaspoon salt**
  Salad oil
  Powdered sugar

In a large bowl, beat ricotta cheese, eggs, and granulated sugar until blended and smooth. In another bowl, stir together flour, baking powder, and salt; add to ricotta mixture, beating until batter is smooth.

Set a wok in a ring stand. Pour oil into wok to a depth of about 1½ inches; heat to 360°F on a deep-frying thermometer. For each puff, drop a rounded teaspoon of batter into oil (cook several puffs at a time; do not crowd wok). Cook, turning occasionally, until golden brown (about 1½ minutes); adjust heat as needed to maintain oil temperature at 360°F. Lift out cooked puffs with a slotted spoon; drain well on paper towels.

If made ahead, let cool, then wrap airtight and refrigerate. To reheat, arrange puffs in a single layer on a rimmed baking sheet; place in a 350° oven until heated through (about 10 minutes).

Dust with powdered sugar and serve hot. Makes about 3½ dozen puffs.

Per puff: 48 calories, .74 g protein, 5 g carbohydrates, 3 g total fat, 20 mg cholesterol, 59 mg sodium

Steaming

A delicate and healthful technique, steaming in a wok helps to retain vitamins and minerals. It also requires less fat, if any. So, it's clearly the choice of fitness-aware cooks. But steaming offers much more than good nutrition alone. It allows flavors to mingle more thoroughly than other methods. And it produces moist, tender results that you can serve directly from the steaming basket. Avoid peeking under the lid during steaming, because this lets valuable moisture and heat escape, which slows the cooking. Also, hot steam can burn, so be careful whenever you do lift the lid.

Steaming Lemon Chicken with Fermented Black Beans *(Recipe on facing page)*

1 Cut rinsed and dried chicken into 1- to 1½-inch lengths, pressing down firmly on cleaver to cut through bones.

2 In a heatproof dish that will fit inside a steamer basket or wok, arrange black bean-coated chicken pieces snugly; top with lemon slices.

3 Lay a wax-paper round on dish to catch drips from lid of wok (use outside rim of dish as a template for cutting wax paper).

4 Steam chicken in basket or on a rack directly over, but not touching, water. Cut to test for doneness; meat near bone should not be pink.

5 Steaming gives succulent, flavorful results. Serve chicken with steamed rice and, for an elegant presentation, garnish with sliced green onions, lemon, and parsley.

How to steam in a wok

You can steam anything in a wok—from seafood to poultry, desserts to breads—and master the technique in no time.

To convert your wok to a steamer, you'll need a ring stand (unless you have a flat-bottomed wok), a lid, and a metal rack. Steaming racks made just for the wok are readily available (see photo on page 633), but a regular round metal cake rack works well, too. Also available are stacking bamboo steaming baskets with lids. If you invest in two or more of these baskets, you'll be able to cook more than one food at a time, and, because the basket lids absorb moisture, you needn't be concerned about condensed steam dripping into the food during cooking.

To steam, place the wok in a ring stand over the heat source. Pour in 1½ to 2 inches of hot water; set the rack in place. Check the water level; food arranged on the rack should be directly above the water, but not touching it. Cover the wok and bring the water to a boil. Then place the food on the rack or set it on a shallow plate or in a steaming basket atop the rack. To ensure that the steam can circulate freely, be careful not to cover all the holes in the rack. If you're not using a steaming basket, it's a good idea to drape some foods (such as custards) with wax paper, so drops of water won't fall from the inside of the wok lid into the dish.

Cover the wok, adjust the heat to keep the water at a boil, and steam for the time specified in your recipe or in the chart for steaming vegetables (see page 718). In general, you can allow about the same amount of time for steaming foods as you would for boiling them. Throughout the cooking time, check the water level periodically and add more water as needed to keep the wok from boiling dry; when you lift the wok lid, remember to keep an eye out for moisture dripping form the lid into the food.

Remove cooked food from the steaming rack carefully, using a single large spatula or two spatulas placed at right angles to each other.

(Pictured on facing page)

Lemon Chicken with Fermented Black Beans

Preparation time: About 15 minutes

Cooking time: About 30 minutes

The photos on the facing page show you just how easy it is to steam this flavorful entrée in your wok. Tender chicken pieces, cut into short lengths for faster cooking, are seasoned with black beans, garlic, and tangy lemon.

2	teaspoons sugar
¼	cup cornstarch
2	teaspoons sesame oil
3	tablespoons soy sauce
2	tablespoons dry sherry
¼	cup fermented salted black beans, rinsed, drained, and patted dry
1	clove garlic
	About 2½ pounds chicken thighs and legs
2	lemons
4	green onion tops, thinly sliced (optional)
	Thin lemon slices (optional)
	Fresh cilantro (coriander) sprigs (optional)

In a large bowl, smoothly blend sugar, cornstarch, oil, soy, and sherry. In a small bowl, mash black beans with garlic; add to cornstarch paste.

Rinse chicken and pat dry. With a heavy cleaver or knife, cut each piece through bones into 1- to 1½-inch lengths. Add chicken to cornstarch mixture; stir to coat well. (At this point, you may cover and refrigerate for up to 4 hours. Stir well before continuing.)

Arrange chicken evenly in a 10- to 11-inch-wide rimmed heatproof serving dish that will fit inside your wok. Cut 1 of the lemons in half; squeeze juice over chicken. Trim ends from remaining lemon; then slice lemon and cut each slice in half. Arrange half-slices over chicken.

Set dish on a rack in wok over 1½ to 2 inches of boiling water. Cover and steam until meat near bone is no longer pink; cut to test (about 30 minutes). Garnish with onion, lemon slices, and cilantro, if desired. Makes 4 servings.

Per serving: 420 calories, 40 g protein, 12 g carbohydrates, 23 g total fat, 130 mg cholesterol, 1805 mg sodium

Western-Style Lemon Chicken

Follow directions for **Lemon Chicken with Fermented Black Beans,** but omit sesame oil and black beans. Press garlic and mix into cornstarch paste. Garnish the finished dish with 1 small firm-ripe **avocado,** pitted, peeled, and sliced.

Appetizers

Pork-stuffed Clams

Preparation time: About 30 minutes

Cooking time: About 20 minutes

Small clam shells filled with a savory pork and clam mixture are an attractive appetizer. Present them three or four to a plate, with small forks for scooping out the filling.

We suggest steaming the clams as a first step, but you can also simmer them in a cup of water for about 5 minutes, then drain off the cooking liquid to use in seafood soups or stews.

- 2 **pounds small live hard-shell clams, scrubbed**
- ½ **pound lean boneless pork (such as shoulder or butt), trimmed of excess fat and finely chopped or ground**
- ¼ **cup finely chopped water chestnuts**
- 1 **green onion (including top), minced**
- 1 **tablespoon** *each* **soy sauce, dry sherry, and cornstarch**
- ½ **teaspoon** *each* **salt and minced fresh ginger**
- 1 **teaspoon sugar**
  Dash of white pepper

Place clams in a heatproof serving bowl (at least 1 inch deep) that will fit in your wok. Place bowl on a rack in wok over 1½ to 2 inches of boiling water. Cover and steam until clam shells open (about 10 minutes); discard any unopened clams.

Remove clams from shells; finely chop meat. Separate each shell into 2 halves; turn upside down to drain. In a bowl, mix chopped clams with pork, water chestnuts, onion, soy, sherry, cornstarch, salt, ginger, sugar, and white pepper.

Mound about 4 teaspoons of the clam mixture in each half-shell. Arrange shells, filled side up, on 2 heatproof plates that will fit inside your wok. (At this point, you may cover and refrigerate for up to 8 hours; bring to room temperature before steaming.)

To steam each plate, set on a rack in wok over 1½ to 2 inches of boiling water. Cover and steam until meat is no longer pink in center; cut to test (about 20 minutes). Makes about 20 appetizers.

Per appetizer: 29 calories, 3 g protein, 1 g carbohydrates, 1 g total fat, 10 mg cholesterol, 118 mg sodium

Shrimp-stuffed Mushrooms

Preparation time: 20 minutes, plus 30 minutes to soak dried mushrooms

Cooking time: About 10 minutes

Succulent mushroom caps make flavorful containers for a light shrimp filling dotted with crunchy water chestnuts. If you like, substitute rich-tasting dried mushrooms for the fresh ones; in either case, you'll need even-sized, well-shaped mushrooms.

- 16 **fresh button mushrooms,** *each* **about 2 inches in diameter, or medium-size Oriental mushrooms**
- ½ **teaspoon** *each* **salt and sugar**
- 1 **tablespoon soy sauce**
- 1 **cup regular-strength chicken broth Shrimp Filling (recipe follows)**
- 1 **jar (2 oz.) sliced pimentos, drained (optional)**
  Parsley leaves

Remove stems from fresh mushrooms; place caps in a pan with salt, sugar, soy, and broth. Simmer in broth mixture for 10 minutes. (If using dried mushrooms, soak in warm water to cover for 30 minutes, then drain. Cut off and discard stems. Squeeze caps dry, then simmer in broth mixture for 30 minutes.)

While mushrooms are simmering, prepare Shrimp Filling; set aside.

Remove mushrooms from broth, drain, and let cool slightly.

Mound about 2 teaspoons of the filling in each mushroom. Arrange mushrooms, filled side up, on 1 or 2 serving plates that will fit inside your wok. (At this point, you may cover and refrigerate for up to 8 hours; bring to room temperature before steaming.)

To steam each plate, place on a rack in wok over 1½ to 2 inches of boiling water. Cover and steam until filling is cooked through (about 10 minutes). If you cook mushrooms on 2 plates, serve the first portion while the second is cooking. Garnish with pimentos and parsley, if desired. Makes 16 appetizers.

Shrimp Filling. In a bowl, beat 1 **egg white** until foamy. Blend 2 teaspoons *each* **dry sherry** and **cornstarch,** then stir into egg white along with ½ teaspoon *each* **salt** and grated **fresh ginger.** Add ¼ cup finely chopped **water chestnuts** and ½ pound **raw shrimp,** shelled, deveined, and finely chopped; mix well.

Per appetizer: 31 calories, 3 g protein, 4 g carbohydrates, .35 g total fat, 17 mg cholesterol, 284 mg sodium

Beef, Veal & Pork

Beef-stuffed Cabbage Leaves in Tomato Sauce

Preparation time: About 40 minutes

Cooking time: About 35 minutes

Stuffed cabbage leaves are traditionally baked in sauce, but this version of the familiar dish is a bit different. You steam the beef- and rice-filled leaves, then top them with a simple tomato sauce (easily made while the leaves are cooking).

- 1 large head green cabbage (about 2 lbs.)
- ¾ pound lean ground beef
- 1 medium-size onion, chopped
- 1 cup cooked rice
- 2 tablespoons butter or margarine, melted
- ½ cup fine dry bread crumbs
- ¾ teaspoon salt
- ¼ teaspoon *each* pepper and dry rubbed sage
  Tomato Sauce (recipe follows)

Cut out and discard core from cabbage. Place cabbage, cored end down, on a rack in a wok over 1½ inches of boiling water. Cover and steam until leaves are bright green and limp throughout (about 8 minutes). Remove cabbage with tongs; let cool slightly, then peel off leaves. You will need about 15 leaves. Set aside 3 of the largest leaves for lining the wok rack; use remaining 12 leaves for stuffing.

In a bowl, combine beef, onion, rice, butter, bread crumbs, salt, pepper, and sage.

To fill leaves, mound some of the meat mixture near base of each leaf—3 to 4 tablespoons for larger leaves, 2 to 3 tablespoons for smaller leaves. With base of leaf toward you, fold leaf up over meat and roll toward tip. Hold roll with seam underneath and fold outer edges of leaf under, making a pillow-shaped roll. (At this point, you may cover and refrigerate until next day.)

Line rack in wok with the 3 reserved leaves, leaving some of rack exposed. Carefully place cabbage rolls on top of leaves. Cover and steam over 1½ to 2 inches of boiling water until filling is no longer pink in center; cut to test (about 35 minutes; 45 minutes if refrigerated). Meanwhile, prepare Tomato Sauce.

Serve cabbage rolls with hot sauce. Makes about 12 rolls (4 servings).

Tomato Sauce. Melt ¼ cup **butter** or margarine in a small pan. Add ½ teaspoon **chili powder** and 2 tablespoons **all-purpose flour.** Stir to make a smooth paste; then bring to a boil over high heat, stirring. Remove from heat and gradually stir in 2 cups **tomato juice.** Return to heat and stir until sauce boils and thickens. Season to taste with **salt.**

Per serving: 566 calories, 21 g protein, 41 g carbohydrates, 36 g total fat, 111 mg cholesterol, 1,486 mg sodium

Gingered Veal Loaf

Preparation time: About 30 minutes

Cooking time: About 50 minutes

Standing time: 30 minutes

Meat loaf boring? Not if you add garlic and ginger to ground veal before steaming.

- 2 tablespoons butter, margarine, or salad oil
- 1 medium-size onion, finely chopped
- 2 stalks celery, finely chopped
- 1 clove garlic, minced or pressed
- 2 pounds ground veal
- 1 egg
- 1 cup fine dry bread crumbs
- ½ cup milk
- 1 tablespoon minced fresh ginger
  Salt and pepper
  Tomato Sauce (recipe above)

Place a wok over medium-high heat. When wok is hot, add butter or oil. When butter is melted (or oil is hot), add onion, celery, and garlic. Stir-fry until onion is soft; then let cool.

In a large bowl, combine onion mixture, veal, egg, bread crumbs, milk, and ginger. Mix well with your hands or a heavy spoon. Season to taste with salt and pepper. Clean and dry wok.

Firmly and evenly pat veal mixture in a loaf pan (about 4½ by 8½ inches). Cover pan tightly with foil. Set pan on a rack in wok over 1½ to 2 inches of boiling water. Cover and steam until loaf feels firm in center when pressed through foil (about 50 minutes). Let stand for at least 30 minutes before serving. Meanwhile, prepare Tomato Sauce.

To unmold, remove foil; invert loaf onto a serving dish, and accompany with Tomato Sauce. Makes 6 to 8 servings.

Per serving loaf: 303 calories, 26 g protein, 13 g carbohydrates, 16 g total fat, 125 mg cholesterol, 231 mg sodium

Pork & Yams with Rice Crumbs

Preparation time: About 25 minutes

Marinating time: 4 hours

Cooking time: About 40 minutes

Rice powder is a traditional ingredient in this recipe, but because it's hard to find, we've substituted toasted cream of rice cereal. Combined with sherry, soy sauce, and seasonings, the cereal makes a fluffy coating for pork cubes and yams.

- 3 tablespoons cream of rice cereal
- 1½ tablespoons *each* dry sherry, soy sauce, and salad oil
- 1 tablespoon sweet bean sauce or hoisin sauce
- 1 teaspoon *each* minced fresh ginger and minced garlic
- 1 teaspoon hot bean sauce or ¼ teaspoon liquid hot pepper seasoning
- ¼ teaspoon sesame oil
  Dash of white pepper
- 1 pound lean boneless pork (such as shoulder or butt), trimmed of excess fat and cut into ½-inch cubes
- 2 medium-size yams (about 1 lb. *total*)
- ¼ teaspoon salt
- 1 tablespoon dry sherry
- 2 green onions (including tops), thinly sliced

In a small frying pan, toast cereal over medium heat until lightly browned (about 5 minutes), shaking pan occasionally. Let cool.

In a bowl, combine the 1½ tablespoons sherry, soy, salad oil, sweet bean sauce, ginger, garlic, hot bean sauce, sesame oil, white pepper, and 2 tablespoons of the toasted cereal. Add pork and stir to coat. Cover and refrigerate for at least 4 hours or until next day.

Peel yams and cut into ½-inch-thick slices. Blend remaining 1 tablespoon toasted cereal with salt and the 1 tablespoon sherry; mix with yams.

Arrange pork cubes in a heatproof 1-quart casserole that will fit inside your wok. Distribute yam mixture on top. Place casserole on a rack in wok over 1½ to 2 inches of boiling water. Cover and steam until pork and yams are tender when pierced (about 40 minutes). Remove casserole from wok and let stand for a few minutes, then invert onto a serving plate. Scatter onions over top. Makes 4 or 5 servings.

Per serving: 318 calories, 20 g protein, 30 g carbohydrates, 13 g total fat, 62 mg cholesterol, 597 mg sodium

Beef with Rice Crumbs

Follow directions for **Pork & Yams with Rice Crumbs,** but substitute 1 pound **flank steak,** cut into 1-inch squares, for pork. Omit yams with their coating of sherry, salt, and cream of rice. Steam meat until tender when pierced (about 40 minutes); then invert onto a plate lined with **lettuce leaves** before sprinkling with onions.

(Pictured on facing page)

Black Bean Spareribs

Preparation time: About 15 minutes

Marinating time: 15 minutes

Cooking time: About 1 hour

A good choice to include in a Chinese meal of several courses, these spareribs require no last-minute attention. You'll need to have the ribs cut for you at the meat market; they're first sawed through the bones into 1½-inch strips, then cut apart between the bones.

- 2 tablespoons fermented salted black beans, rinsed, drained, and finely chopped
- 2 cloves garlic, minced or pressed
- 1 teaspoon chopped fresh ginger
- 1 tablespoon *each* cornstarch, dry sherry, and soy sauce
- ½ teaspoon *each* salt and sugar
- 1½ pounds spareribs, cut 1½ inches long, then cut apart between bones
- 2 tablespoons salad oil
  Thinly sliced green onion tops

In a bowl, stir together black beans, garlic, ginger, cornstarch, sherry, soy, salt, and sugar. Add ribs and turn until well coated; let marinate for 15 minutes.

Place a wok over high heat; when wok is hot, add oil. When oil is hot, add meat and cook, turning once, until browned on both sides (about 4 minutes). Transfer to an 8- or 9-inch round heatproof bowl.

Rinse wok. Place bowl on a rack in wok over 1½ to 2 inches of boiling water. Cover and steam until meat is tender when pierced (about 1 hour). Skim fat from sauce; sprinkle meat with onions. Makes 2 or 3 servings.

Per serving: 329 calories, 17 g protein, 6 g carbohydrates, 26 g total fat, 66 mg cholesterol, 1,050 mg sodium

Though they start with the same cut of meat, these Black Bean Spareribs (recipe
on facing page) bear little resemblance to their Texan counterpart.
But they're just as wonderful to eat, either on their own or
combined with other courses.

Chicken & Turkey

Chicken with Ginger Sauce

Preparation time: About 15 minutes

Cooking time: About 1½ hours

Lightly seasoned with ginger, a steamed whole chicken is a succulent entrée. Serve hot, with a sauce made from the cooking juices; or chill and slice to use in salads and sandwiches.

- 2 **tablespoons dry sherry**
- 1 **tablespoon soy sauce**
- 1½ **teaspoons minced fresh ginger**
- 1 **large clove garlic, minced or pressed**
- 1 **frying chicken (3 to 3½ lbs.)**
- 1 **tablespoon** *each* **cornstarch and water, stirred together**
- ¼ **cup thinly sliced green onions (including tops)**
  Salt and pepper

In a small bowl, combine sherry, soy, ginger, and garlic. Set aside.

Remove chicken neck and giblets and reserve for other uses. Pull off and discard lumps of fat. Rinse chicken inside and out; pat dry. Place chicken, breast down, on a sheet of heavy-duty foil large enough to enclose it. Bring foil up around all sides of chicken, then pour sherry mixture over chicken. Enclose bird in foil, folding foil over on top so package can be opened easily.

Place foil-wrapped chicken, seam side up, on a rack in a wok over 1½ to 2 inches of boiling water. Cover and steam until meat near thighbone is no longer pink; cut to test (1 to 1¼ hours). Open foil and transfer chicken to a platter, draining juices back into foil container; keep chicken warm.

Skim and discard fat from juices, then measure; you need 1¼ cups. (If you have more, boil to reduce; if you have less, add water.) In a 1- to 2-quart pan, mix juices and cornstarch-water mixture. Stir over medium heat, stirring, until sauce boils and thickens. Stir in onions; season to taste with salt and pepper. Spoon some of sauce over chicken; pass remaining sauce at the table. Makes about 4 servings.

Per serving: 435 calories, 48 g protein, 4 g carbohydrates, 24 g total fat, 154 mg cholesterol, 402 mg sodium

Turkey Breast with Herb Mayonnaise

Preparation time: About 15 minutes

Cooking time: 1 to 2 hours, depending on size of turkey breast

Chilling time: 1½ to 4 hours for turkey, 30 minutes for mayonnaise

When you need a simple, easy-to-cook meal for a crowd, consider this juicy steamed turkey breast. You just top the meat with parsley and onion, wrap it in foil, and steam it for an hour or two. Serve the chilled, sliced meat with a fresh-tasting sauce of minced green herbs mixed with mayonnaise.

- 1 **whole or half turkey breast (3 to 6 lbs.)**
- 6 **parsley sprigs**
- 1 **small onion, sliced**
  Green Herb Mayonnaise (recipe follows)

Rinse turkey and pat dry. Then place turkey on a sheet of heavy-duty foil large enough to enclose it. Insert a meat thermometer into thickest part of breast (not touching bone). Top breast with parsley and onion; enclose in foil, shaping foil around thermometer on top.

Place foil-wrapped turkey on a rack in a wok over 1½ to 2 inches of boiling water. Cover and steam until thermometer registers 165°F (or until meat near bone is no longer pink; cut to test). For a 3- to 4-pound breast, allow 1 to 1½ hours; for 4½ to 6 pounds, allow 1½ to 2 hours.

Remove turkey from wok. Open foil; discard parsley and onion and save juices for other uses. When turkey is cool enough to handle, remove and discard skin and bones. Cover meat and refrigerate until cold (1½ to 4 hours) or for up to 2 days. Meanwhile, prepare Green Herb Mayonnaise.

To serve, slice breast across the grain and serve with mayonnaise. Makes 12 to 24 servings (4 servings per pound).

Green Herb Mayonnaise. In a food processor, combine 1 cup lightly packed **watercress** (coarse stems removed), 1 cup lightly packed **parsley sprigs,** ⅓ cup sliced **green onions** (including tops), 1 clove **garlic** (chopped), and ¼ teaspoon **dry rosemary.** Whirl until greens are finely chopped. Blend in ½ cup **mayonnaise;** cover and refrigerate for at least 30 minutes or up to 2 days. Makes enough for a 4-pound turkey breast; if breast is over 4 pounds, double this sauce recipe. Makes about ¾ cup.

Per serving turkey: 148 calories, 22 g protein, .27 g carbohydrate, 6 g total fat, 57 mg cholesterol, 49 mg sodium

Per tablespoon mayonnaise: 69 calories, .32 g protein, .85 g carbohydrate, 7 g total fat, 5 mg cholesterol, 55 mg sodium

Fish & Shellfish

Soft-shell Crabs

Preparation time: 30 to 45 minutes, depending on sauce used

Cooking time: About 10 minutes

A soft-shell crab's shell isn't just soft, it's edible—and the combination of crackly parchmentlike shell and sweet, moist meat is unusually delicious. Serve hot or chilled, with your choice of sauces.

Ginger Sauce or Cayenne Sauce (recipes follow)

6 fresh or thawed frozen soft-shell crabs (about 2 oz. *each*)

Prepare your choice of sauce and set aside. (If you intend to serve crabs chilled, wait to prepare Cayenne Sauce until shortly before serving.)

If using live crabs, first kill them by holding claws away from you and snipping off shell ¼ inch behind eyes. Lift up flexible back shell on each side of crab; pull off and discard soft gills. Also pull off and discard triangular flap of shell on belly of crab. Rinse crabs and pat dry.

Lay crabs, backs up, in a single layer on a rack in a wok over 1½ to 2 inches of boiling water. Cover and steam until crabs are opaque in center of body; cut to test (about 8 minutes). Serve hot or chilled with sauce. Makes 2 or 3 servings.

Ginger Sauce. Stir together ⅓ cup **rice wine vinegar,** 1 to 2 tablespoons sliced **green onion** (including top), 1½ tablespoons minced **fresh ginger,** and 1 teaspoon **sugar.** Makes about ¾ cup.

Cayenne Sauce. In a 6- to 8-inch frying pan, combine ¼ cup **dry white wine,** 3 tablespoons chopped **shallots,** 2 tablespoons **red wine vinegar,** and ¼ to ½ teaspoon **ground red pepper** (cayenne). Bring to a boil over high heat; boil, uncovered, until liquid is reduced to about 1 tablespoon. Scrape mixture into a blender; add 2 **egg yolks.** Whirl until blended; then, with motor running, slowly add ¾ cup (¼ lb. plus ¼ cup) hot melted **butter** or margarine. Serve hot or at room temperature; do not reheat. Makes 1¼ cups.

Per serving: 98 calories, 20 g protein, .83 g carbohydrate, 1 g total fat, 67 mg cholesterol, 335 mg sodium

Per tablespoon Ginger Sauce: 3 calories, .02 g protein, .72 g carbohydrate, 0 g total fat, 0 mg cholesterol, .13 mg sodium

Per tablespoon Cayenne Sauce: 69 calories, .37 g protein, .34 g carbohydrate, 7 g total fat, 46 mg cholesterol, 71 mg sodium

Fish & Clams in Black Bean Sauce

Preparation time: 10 to 15 minutes

Cooking time: About 15 minutes

Calorie-conscious diners will delight in this succulent combination of fish and clams in a pungent sauce.

1 rockfish or cod fillet (about 1 lb.), about 1 inch thick

1½ tablespoons fermented salted black beans, rinsed, drained, and patted dry

2 cloves garlic

1 tablespoon *each* soy sauce and dry sherry

2 green onions (including tops)

3 thin, quarter-size slices fresh ginger

12 small live hard-shell clams, scrubbed

2 tablespoons salad oil

Rinse fish and pat dry. Place in a heatproof dish (at least 1 inch deep) that will fit inside your wok.

Mince or mash black beans and garlic; add soy and sherry. Drizzle mixture over fish. Cut 1 of the onions into thirds; place cut onion and ginger on top of fish. Cut remaining onion into 2-inch lengths; cut lengths into thin shreds and set aside. Arrange clams around fish.

Place dish on a rack in wok over 1½ to 2 inches of boiling water. Cover and steam until fish flakes when prodded in thickest part (about 10 minutes). If clams open before fish is done, remove them and continue to cook fish for a few more minutes; then return clams to dish.

Lift dish from wok. Discard ginger and onion pieces from top of fish. Sprinkle onion slivers over fish. Heat oil in a small pan until it ripples when pan is tilted; pour over fish (oil will sizzle). Makes 2 or 3 servings.

Per serving: 166 calories, 13 g protein, 26 g carbohydrates, 2 g total fat, 35 mg cholesterol, 940 mg sodium

A specialty of the Southwest, mild-mannered Green Corn Tamales
(recipe on facing page) are wrapped in green corn husks and gently steamed.
Enriched with a little chile and some cheese, these bite-size tamales
are a great partner for grilled meats.

Vegetables

(Pictured on facing page)

Green Corn Tamales with Cheese & Chiles

Preparation time: About 1½ hours

Cooking time: About 1 hour

Like delicate corn pudding enclosed in fresh green corn husks, these *tamalitos* are a tasty accompaniment to barbecued meats. The mild, slightly sweet filling gets a little zip from Longhorn Cheddar cheese and green chiles.

> 5 or 6 large ears corn in husks (about 5 lbs. *total*)
> ¼ cup lard, melted
> 2 teaspoons sugar
> Salt
> ¾ cup shredded Longhorn Cheddar cheese
> ⅓ cup (half of a 4-oz. can) canned diced green chiles

With a sharp, heavy knife or cleaver, cut through husk, corn, and cob of each ear of corn, removing about ¼ inch of cob on both ends of each ear.

Peel off husks without tearing them; rinse if soiled. To keep moist, put in plastic bags and seal; set aside. Pull and discard silk from corn. Rinse corn.

With a knife or a corn scraper, cut kernels from cobs; you need 4 cups, lightly packed. Put corn through a food chopper fitted with a fine blade (or whirl in a food processor until finely ground). Mix ground corn with lard and sugar, then season to taste with salt. Stir cheese and chiles into corn.

To shape each tamale, center 1⅓ tablespoons of the cheese-corn filling near stem (firmer) end of a large single husk. Fold 1 side of husk over to completely cover filling, then fold other side over top. Fold up flexible end to seal in filling. Gently stack tamales, folded ends down, in a steamer; support them against other tamales so ends stay shut. Tamales should be loosely fitted into steamer so air can circulate.

Set steamer on a rack in a wok over 1½ to 2 inches of boiling water. Cover and steam until tamales in center of steamer are firm to touch, not runny; pull a tamale out and unwrap to test (about 1 hour).

Serve tamales, or keep warm over hot water for several hours. To freeze, let cool completely; place in a single layer on baking sheets and freeze until firm, then transfer to plastic bags and return to freezer for up to 6 months. To reheat, let thaw, then steam as directed above until hot through (about 15 minutes).

Makes about 3 dozen tamales (3 to 6 servings).

Per serving: 217 calories, 6 g protein, 20 g carbohydrates, 14 g total fat, 23 mg cholesterol, 149 mg sodium

Marinated Broccoli & Mushrooms

Preparation time: About 20 minutes

Cooking time: About 3 minutes

Marinating time: 1 to 2 hours

Serve this fresh-tasting dish cold on a hot day. You start by steaming broccoli, then mix in celery, green onions, mushrooms, and a sweet-sour vinaigrette.

> About 1½ pounds broccoli
> ¾ pound mushrooms, thinly sliced
> 1 cup *each* thinly sliced green onions (including tops) and thinly sliced celery
> ¼ cup sugar
> ⅓ cup cider vinegar
> 1 teaspoon *each* paprika and celery seeds
> 1 cup salad oil
> Salt and pepper

Cut off and discard tough ends of broccoli stalks. Cut flowerets into bite-size pieces; peel stalks, then cut into ¼-inch-thick slanting slices. Arrange broccoli on a rack in a wok over 1½ to 2 inches of boiling water; cover and steam until barely tender-crisp to bite (2 to 3 minutes). Immerse in cold water; when cool, drain well. In a large bowl, combine broccoli, mushrooms, onions, and celery.

Stir together sugar and vinegar until sugar is dissolved. Stir in paprika, celery seeds, and oil. Pour over vegetable mixture; stir to coat. Cover and refrigerate for 1 to 2 hours, stirring occasionally. Season to taste with salt and pepper. Makes 6 to 8 servings.

Per serving: 299 calories, 3 g protein, 13 g carbohydrates, 28 g total fat, 0 mg cholesterol, 30 mg sodium

Steaming Fresh Vegetables

Steaming is one of the best techniques you can choose for cooking vegetables. Colors stay bright, flavors sweet and fresh; and because the vegetables cook in swirling steam rather than boiling water, there's no loss of vitamins and minerals into cooking liquid.

To steam vegetables, place a steaming rack in your wok (you can also use a collapsible metal steaming basket). Pour in water to a depth of 1 to 1½ inches, making sure the water doesn't touch the bottom of the rack. Bring water to a boil over high heat; then place the vegetable on the rack. Cover the wok, reduce heat to medium, and begin timing. The water should boil throughout the cooking time; adjust the heat as needed and add boiling water to the wok as necessary to maintain the level at 1 to 1½ inches.

Total cooking time will depend on the freshness and maturity of the vegetables—and on personal taste. Test after the minimum cooking time; if necessary, continue to cook, testing frequently, until vegetables are done to your liking. Most cooked vegetables should be just tender when pierced; whole potatoes should be tender throughout. Leafy vegetables should appear wilted and have bright color.

Vegetable	Amount to buy for 4 servings	Steaming time (in minutes)	Test for doneness
Artichokes. Whole	4 medium to large	30–45	Stem end tender when pierced
Asparagus. Spears	1½–2 pounds	8–12	Tender when pierced
Slices (½ to 1 inch)	1½–2 pounds	5–7	Tender when pierced
Beans, green, Italian, wax. Whole	1 pound	5–10	Tender-crisp to bite
Pieces (1 to 2 inch)	1 pound	4–7	Tender-crisp to bite
Broccoli. Spears	1–1½ pounds	15–20	Stalks tender when pierced
Pieces (1 inch)	1–1½ pounds	8–15	Tender when pierced
Cabbage. Wedges	1–1½ pounds	9–14	Tender when pierced
Carrots. Whole, baby	1 pound	8–12	Tender when pierced
Slices (¼ inch)	1 pound	5–10	Tender when pierced
Cauliflower. Flowerets	1½ pounds	10–18	Stem end tender when pierced
Slices (¼ inch)	1½ pounds	7–12	Tender-crisp to bite
Celery. 1-inch slices	1½ pounds	8–10	Tender when pierced
Celery hearts.	1½ pounds	10–14	Tender when pierced
Okra. Whole	1 pound	15–20	Tender when pierced
Onions. Small white boiling (whole, 1- to 1½-inch diameter)	1 pound	20–25	Tender when pierced
Parsnips. Whole	1 pound	15–25	Tender when pierced
Potatoes, red or white. Thin-skinned ½-inch slices	4 medium to large	8–10	Tender when pierced
Potatoes, sweet (or yams). Whole, 3-inch diameter	4 medium to large	30–40	Tender throughout when pierced
Snow peas.	1 pound	3–5	Tender-crisp to bite
Spinach. Whole leaves	1½ pounds	3–5	Wilted appearance, bright color
Squash, summer. ¼-inch slices	1–1½ pounds	4–7	Tender when pierced
Squash, winter. ½-inch slices	1½–2 pounds	9–12	Tender when pierced
Sunchokes. ¼- to ½-inch slices	1–1½ pounds	12–15	Tender when pierced
Swiss chard. Stems, leaves	1¼–2 pounds	Stems 3 minutes; add leaves and steam for 2–4 more minutes	Tender when pierced

Desserts

(Pictured on page 720)
Carrot Pudding

Preparation time: About 15 minutes

Cooking time: 3 to 3¼ hours

Cooling time: 10 to 15 minutes

Shredded carrots contribute to the moist texture of this rich, spicy dessert. The pudding shown on page 720 was steamed for about 3 hours in a 5-inch-deep 6-cup mold partially submerged in boiling water; puddings made in shallower 6- to 8-cup molds can be steamed on a rack above 1½ to 2 inches of boiling water for about the same length of time.

- ½ cup (¼ lb.) butter or margarine, at room temperature
- ½ cup *each* sugar and dark molasses
- ¼ cup dark rum
- 1½ cups all-purpose flour
- 1 teaspoon *each* ground ginger and cinnamon
- ½ teaspoon *each* baking soda, ground nutmeg, ground cloves, and ground allspice
- 1½ cups shredded carrots (about 2 large or 3 medium-size)
- 1 cup raisins
- ¾ cup chopped walnuts
  Carrot curls and mint leaves (optional)
  Half-and-half or light cream

In large bowl of an electric mixer, beat butter, sugar, and molasses until smoothly blended; mix in rum. Stir together flour, ginger, cinnamon, baking soda, nutmeg, cloves, and allspice; beat into butter mixture. Add carrots, raisins, and walnuts; mix well.

Thoroughly butter a 6- to 8-cup tube mold or deep 6- to 8-cup metal bowl. Scrape batter into mold or bowl. Butter a piece of foil and place, buttered side down, over batter; crimp foil tightly against edges of mold (including center hole) or bowl. Set mold in wok on a low rack or canning jar ring. Pour in boiling water to reach halfway up mold. Cover and cook at a gentle boil until edges of pudding spring back when lightly pressed (3 to 3¼ hours; center may feel slightly sticky).

Remove pudding from wok and let cool for 10 to 15 minutes. Run a knife blade around edges of mold to loosen pudding, then invert onto a plate. Rap top of mold to loosen. Garnish pudding with carrot curls and mint, if desired. Serve warm or at room temperature; add half-and-half to taste.

If made ahead, let cool, then wrap pudding airtight and refrigerate for up to 2 weeks; freeze for longer storage. To reheat, thaw if frozen, then seal in foil and steam as directed above for about 45 minutes. Makes 6 to 8 servings.

Per serving pudding: 417 calories, 5 g protein, 61 g carbohydrates, 17 g total fat, 31 mg cholesterol, 200 mg sodium

Apples with Cinnamon Dumplings

Preparation time: 10 to 15 minutes

Cooking time: About 40 minutes

Typical apple dumplings are whole apples enclosed in pastry, but this version of the old-fashioned dessert is more like a cobbler. The dumplings are much like drop biscuits; sweet, spicy, and vanilla-scented, they crown a cinnamony apple filling.

- 4 large tart apples, peeled, cored, and sliced (5 to 6 cups)
  Juice and grated peel of 1 lemon
- ⅔ cup sugar
- 1 tablespoon all-purpose flour
- ¼ teaspoon ground cinnamon
- ⅛ teaspoon ground nutmeg
  Dumpling Dough (recipe follows)
  Half-and-half or light cream

Mix apples, lemon juice, lemon peel, sugar, flour, cinnamon, and nutmeg in an 8- or 9-inch round baking dish. Place dish on a rack in a wok over 1½ to 2 inches of boiling water. Cover and steam until apples are tender when pierced (18 to 20 minutes). Meanwhile, prepare Dumpling Dough.

Using a large spoon, scoop out dough in 6 spoonfuls; drop on top of fruit in a circle around edge of dish. Cover wok and steam for 15 minutes. Remove from wok and let stand for 5 minutes. To serve, spoon dumplings onto dessert plates; top with apples and sauce. Offer half-and-half to pour on top. Makes 6 servings.

Dumpling Dough. Stir together 1 cup **all-purpose flour,** 2 teaspoons **baking powder,** ⅛ teaspoon **salt,** ¼ cup firmly packed **brown sugar,** ½ teaspoon **ground cinnamon,** and ¼ teaspoon **ground nutmeg.** Combine ⅓ cup **milk** and ½ teaspoon **vanilla;** add to dry mixture, stirring just until blended.

Per serving: 271 calories, 2 g protein, 60 g carbohydrates, 4 g total fat, 2 mg cholesterol, 243 mg sodium

Converting your wok to a steamer is easy—
and that makes it simple to prepare old-fashioned steamed puddings
like this one. The recipe for our spicy Carrot Pudding is
on page 719.

Cookies
STEP-BY-STEP TECHNIQUES

By the Editors of Sunset Books
and Sunset Magazine

Sunset Publishing Corporation • Menlo Park, California

Contents

*Temptation at its best—a jar full of plump,
chewy Oatmeal Raisin Cookies (page 728)*

Special Features

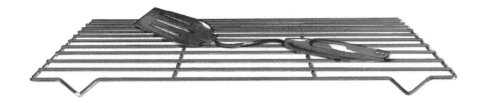

Cookie Craftsmanship

Trends in food come and go, but the popularity of cookies never wanes—easy to make, easy to eat, and appropriate for so many occasions, they're favorites with everyone.

The key to successful cookie baking is a thorough understanding of the ingredients, equipment, and techniques used in the process. The following tips will help you bake with confidence, turning out perfect cookies every time.

Ingredients

The ingredients used in cookie baking certainly aren't mysterious; butter, sugar, eggs, flour, leavenings, spices, and vanilla and other flavorings are familiar and widely available items. There are, however, a few things the baker should know when composing a shopping list.

For the shortening in most of our recipes, we call for butter *or* margarine. Butter gives cookies better flavor, but margarine may be substituted for dietary reasons. Some recipes—Spritz and Scottish Shortbread, for example—call for butter only; the flavor of butter is important in these cookies, and margarine should not be used.

When we call for brown sugar, we mean light (or "golden") brown sugar unless otherwise specified. If a recipe calls for honey, choose a mild-flavored variety such as clover or sage. Our recipes were tested using large eggs, and with real vanilla rather than imitation.

Many of our cookies call for peanut butter; you can use crunchy or creamy, unless the recipe indicates one style or the other. "Coconut" means packaged sweetened coconut; if unsweetened coconut is needed, the recipe specifically requests it. If you see "nuts" in an ingredient list, use almonds, walnuts, pecans, hazelnuts—whatever you have on hand or like best.

We use all-purpose flour in most of our cookies; either bleached or unbleached is fine. When rolled oats are called for, you can use either regular or quick-cooking unless the recipe indicates otherwise.

Techniques

In most of the recipes in this book, we use a standard technique for mixing cookie dough. You begin by beating butter and sugar until creamy, then beat in eggs, flavoring, and any liquid. Next, flour, leavening, salt, and any spices are stirred together and gradually beaten into the butter mixture. Nuts, chocolate chips, and other chunky ingredients are usually mixed in last of all, by hand.

Beating the butter and sugar until creamy is important for three reasons: to combine these ingredients thoroughly, to help the sugar start to dissolve, and to incorporate air into the dough for a light product. To achieve these goals, you must start with softened butter. Leave butter out of the refrigerator—or soften it in a microwave oven—until it reaches room temperature. (On the other hand, if the recipe calls for cutting the butter into dry ingredients, you'll need to use firm butter.)

Stir dry ingredients together in a bowl; it isn't necessary to sift them unless the recipe directs you to do so. It is important, however, to measure your dry ingredients carefully and accurately. Measure them in metal or plastic cups intended for dry ingredients, and use the cup that holds the exact amount called for in the recipe. Gently spoon the ingredient into the cup, piling it high and light; don't shake or pack it down. Then level off the top of the cup with a metal spatula or knife. Brown sugar is the exception to this rule; to measure it, pack it firmly into the cup with your fingers until it's even with the rim.

When you're ready to bake, always start out with cool baking sheets. If they're warm, the fat in the dough will begin to melt before the dough starts to bake, resulting in flat cookies. And don't grease sheets unless the recipe tells you to do so. Some cookies can't keep their "footing" on a greased sheet—they spread out and lose their shape as the grease melts.

Always preheat your oven before baking cookies. It's also a good idea to use an oven thermometer to make sure you're baking at the correct temperature. For best results, bake one sheet of cookies at a time, placing the baking sheet in the center of the oven and leaving at least an inch of space between the sides of the sheet and the oven wall.

After baking, transfer cookies to a rack to cool. Arrange them in a single layer, never stacked or overlapped; this lets air circulate around the hot cookies, allowing steam to evaporate and preventing cookies from becoming soggy. Let cookies cool completely before moving them.

Equipment

For mixing your cookie dough, an electric mixer is invaluable—though you can mix most doughs by hand, it takes much more time and effort. A mixer is a particularly worthwhile investment if you do a lot of baking; either a heavy-duty standing model or a small hand-held unit will give good service. You'll also want a rubber scraper and a sturdy wooden spoon to help in the mixing process. For grinding nuts, you'll need a blender or food processor.

To ensure accuracy, it's very important to have good measuring equipment. You'll need at least one set of measuring spoons, and separate measuring cups for liquid and dry ingredients.

For shaping the dough, have on hand a rolling pin, cookie cutters, and a sharp knife or pastry wheel. Some cookies require more specialized equipment, such as a cookie press, pastry bag, or cookie irons. For some recipes, you'll need wax paper, parchment paper, or plastic wrap.

Shiny, unrimmed baking sheets give the most evenly baked and browned cookies. Dark metal sheets retain heat, giving cookies dark (or even burned) bottoms; rimmed sheets make it harder for oven heat to reach cookies on all sides. You may also wish to try insulated baking sheets, made of two sheets of aluminum joined together with an air space in between. These do an especially good job of reducing the risk of burning.

A cooling rack (or racks) of wire or wood is a must for your finished cookies. Also have on hand a wide spatula for transferring cookies to the rack from baking sheets. Finally, you'll need utensils for decorating your cookies: a small spatula for spreading icing, a wire strainer or sifter for powdered sugar, a soft pastry brush for painting on melted chocolate and some glazes—and, occasionally, a pastry bag fitted with decorating tips.

Storage of Cookies

To preserve the freshly baked flavor and texture of your homemade cookies, store them airtight. This way, the moisture in the air won't soften crisp cookies, and soft cookies won't dry out. Unless otherwise specified in the recipe, cookies in this book will keep for about a week when stored airtight—depending, of course, on the climate and on what type of cookies they are.

What does airtight mean? Sealed plastic bags, tins, cookie jars with screw tops or gasket lids, rigid plastic storage containers, and sealed foil packets are all fine; separate layers with wax paper if the cookies are very moist or sticky. (If a recipe instructs you to store "covered" rather than "airtight," just cover cookies with plastic wrap or foil, making sure to secure the wrapping firmly around the edges of the plate or pan.)

Don't store cookies on loosely covered plates, in paper bags, or in boxes—these all allow air to circulate freely. And never store crisp cookies and soft cookies in the same container.

If you wish to keep your cookies for longer than a few days, consider freezing them. Cookies freeze beautifully, and will maintain oven-fresh quality for months if wrapped airtight first to prevent drying and freezer burn. If you freeze cookies that are frosted or glazed, be sure to thaw them unwrapped; otherwise, the icing may stick to the wrapping. (If possible, freeze the cookies unfrosted, then thaw and frost just before serving.) You can also freeze cookie dough, shaped or unshaped, for baking at a later time.

Heat-sealing offers a neat and attractive way of packaging cookies airtight; try it for large cookies that you want to give away as gifts or offer at a bake sale. To heat-seal, line a baking sheet with paper towels; put in a 325° oven. Wrap each cookie firmly in plastic wrap, taping at the back if necessary. Place cookies slightly apart on warm baking sheet without removing it from the oven; heat for about 2 minutes or until plastic shrinks tightly over cookies. Remove from oven and let cool.

Drop Cookies

So called because the dough is "dropped" by spoonfuls onto the baking sheets, drop cookies are generally simple, old-fashioned, and homey creations such as oatmeal raisin and chocolate chip. In fact, the very first cookie was a drop cookie—a small spoonful of cake batter, baked before the cake so that the cook could judge the oven temperature and the flavor and texture of the batter. The very word "cookie" comes from the Dutch *koekje,* meaning "little cake."

Today, drop cookies take a variety of forms. Though they're most often simple mounds studded with nuts or raisins or chocolate, they sometimes strike a more sophisticated pose—as in Chocolate-covered Almond Macaroons (page 735) and Florentines (page 736), for example.

Photo at left *presents a tempting collection of drop cookies. From top to bottom: Coconut-Macadamia Cookies (page 730); Blueberry Lemon Drops (page 733); Chocolate Cream Cushions (page 730); Mint Meringues (page 736); Brownie Date Drops (far left and far right; page 732); Coconut Macaroons (left and right center; page 735); Big Oatmeal Chocolate Chip Cookie (center; page 729); Mint Meringues, Chocolate Cream Cushions, Blueberry Lemon Drops, and Coconut-Macadamia Cookies.*

Oatmeal Raisin Cookies

(Pictured on page 723)

Oatmeal raisin drops are an ever-popular choice for lunchboxes, picnics, and after-school snacks. These are plump, chewy, and delightfully pebbled with oats, raisins, and nuts.

       1 cup (½ lb.) butter or margarine, softened
       2 cups firmly packed brown sugar
       2 eggs
       3 tablespoons lemon juice
       2 cups all-purpose flour
       1 teaspoon *each* salt and baking soda
       3 cups quick-cooking rolled oats
    1½ cups raisins
       1 cup chopped walnuts

In large bowl of an electric mixer, beat butter and sugar until creamy; then beat in eggs and lemon juice. In another bowl, stir together flour, salt, and baking soda; gradually add to butter mixture, blending thoroughly. Add oats, raisins, and walnuts and stir until well combined.

Drop dough by rounded tablespoonfuls onto ungreased baking sheets, spacing cookies about 2 inches apart. Bake in a 350° oven for 18 to 20 minutes or until edges are golden brown. Transfer to racks and let cool. Store airtight. Makes about 4 dozen.

Cream Cheese Gems

Creamy flavor and chewy texture distinguish these extravagantly rich little cookies.

    ½ cup (¼ lb.) butter or margarine, softened
       4 ounces cream cheese, softened
       1 cup sugar
    ½ teaspoon *each* vanilla and grated lemon peel
       1 cup all-purpose flour

In large bowl of an electric mixer, beat butter, cream cheese, and sugar until creamy; beat in vanilla and lemon peel. Gradually add flour, blending thoroughly.

Drop dough by rounded teaspoonfuls onto ungreased baking sheets, spacing cookies about 2 inches apart. Bake in a 350° oven for about 12 minutes or until edges are golden. Transfer to racks and let cool. Store airtight. Makes about 3½ dozen.

Addendum Cookies

Here's a drop cookie recipe with unlimited personality. After you make the basic dough, you stir in your choice of additions to decide the flavor and texture of the finished cookies. Since you divide the dough in half, you can make two distinctly different kinds of cookies from one batch.

       1 cup (½ lb.) butter or margarine, softened
       1 cup *each* granulated sugar and firmly packed brown sugar
       2 eggs
       2 teaspoons vanilla
    2½ cups all-purpose flour
       1 teaspoon baking soda
    ½ teaspoon salt
       Addenda (suggestions follow)

In large bowl of an electric mixer, beat butter, granulated sugar, and brown sugar until creamy; then beat in eggs and vanilla. In another bowl, stir together flour, baking soda, and salt; gradually add to butter mixture, blending thoroughly. Divide dough in half and mix one addendum into each portion; or double an addendum and mix it into the entire batch of dough.

Drop dough by rounded teaspoonfuls onto ungreased baking sheets, spacing cookies 2 inches apart. Bake in a 350° oven for 12 to 15 minutes or until just set in center when lightly touched. Transfer to racks and let cool. Store airtight. Makes 8 to 10 dozen.

Addenda. Stir one of the following into each half of the dough:

- 2 ounces **unsweetened chocolate,** melted and cooled, and ½ cup finely crushed **hard peppermint candy.**

- 2 ounces **unsweetened chocolate,** melted and cooled, 1½ teaspoons **rum flavoring,** and ½ cup crushed **peanut brittle** or chopped salted peanuts.

- ¼ cup **sour cream,** 1 teaspoon **ground nutmeg,** and ½ cup dry-roasted **sunflower seeds.**

- 1 cup **rolled oats**, 1 teaspoon grated **orange peel**, ¼ cup **orange juice**, and ½ cup **raisins** or snipped pitted dates.

- ½ cup **applesauce**, ½ cup **wheat germ** or crushed ready-to-eat cereal flakes, ½ cup chopped **nuts**, and 1 teaspoon **pumpkin pie spice** or ground cinnamon.

- 1 cup **granola-style cereal** (break up any large lumps before measuring), 1 cup snipped **pitted dates** or dried apricots, 1 teaspoon **ground cinnamon**, and ¼ cup **milk**.

Peanut Butter Platters

To give these giant peanut butter cookies the traditional crisscrossed tops of their smaller cousins, you can score them before baking with the tines of a fork or with a cake rack.

>   1 cup (½ lb.) **butter** or margarine, softened
>   1 cup crunchy **peanut butter**
>   2 cups firmly packed **brown sugar**
>   2 **eggs**
>   2½ cups **all-purpose flour**
>   1½ teaspoons **baking soda**
>   1 teaspoon **baking powder**
>   1 cup chopped salted **peanuts** (optional)
>   Granulated **sugar**

In large bowl of an electric mixer, beat butter, peanut butter, and brown sugar until creamy; beat in eggs. In another bowl, stir together flour, baking soda, and baking powder; gradually add to butter mixture, blending thoroughly. Stir in peanuts, if desired.

To shape each cookie, spoon dough into a ½-cup measure, level off, and turn out onto a greased baking sheet. Space cookies at least 6 inches apart and 2½ inches from edge of baking sheet. Lightly grease the bottom of a pie pan, dip in granulated sugar, and use to flatten each cookie into a 5½-inch circle. If necessary, press cookies lightly with your fingers to give them an even thickness. If desired, make a crisscross pattern on top of cookies by lightly scoring with fork tines or pressing with a wire cake rack.

Bake in a 350° oven for about 14 minutes or until edges are lightly browned. Let cool on baking sheets for about 5 minutes; then transfer to racks and let cool completely. Store airtight. Makes 10 or 11.

Big Oatmeal Chocolate Chip Cookies

(Pictured on page 726)

Oversized cookies, often best-sellers at fund-raising events, are easy to make at home. Our Big Oatmeal Chocolate Chip Cookies, like our Peanut Butter Platters (preceding), reach a diameter of about 7 inches—enough cookie to last all day! For variety, you can use butterscotch-flavored chips instead of chocolate, or try the cinnamon-spiced raisin variation (see below).

>   1 cup (½ lb.) **butter** or margarine, softened
>   1½ cups firmly packed **brown sugar**
>   2 **eggs**
>   1 teaspoon **vanilla**
>   1½ cups **all-purpose flour**
>   2 teaspoons **baking soda**
>   1 teaspoon **salt**
>   2⅓ cups **rolled oats**
>   1 large package (12 oz.) **semisweet chocolate** or **butterscotch-flavored chips**
>   1½ cups chopped **nuts**
>   Granulated **sugar**

In large bowl of an electric mixer, beat butter and brown sugar until creamy; then beat in eggs and vanilla. In another bowl, stir together flour, baking soda, and salt; gradually add to butter mixture, blending thoroughly. Add oats, chocolate chips, and nuts; stir until well combined.

To shape each cookie, spoon dough into a ½-cup measure, level off, and turn out onto a greased baking sheet. Space cookies at least 6 inches apart and 2½ inches from edge of baking sheet. Lightly grease the bottom of a pie pan, dip in granulated sugar, and use to flatten each cookie into a 5½-inch circle. If necessary, press cookies lightly with your fingers to give them an even thickness.

Bake in a 350° oven for about 15 minutes or until edges are lightly browned. Let cool on baking sheets for about 5 minutes; then transfer to racks and let cool completely. Store airtight. Makes about 1 dozen.

Big Oatmeal Raisin Cookies

Follow directions for **Big Oatmeal Chocolate Chip Cookies,** but add 1 teaspoon **ground cinnamon** and ½ teaspoon **ground nutmeg** with flour. Omit chocolate chips and add 1½ cups **raisins.**

Chocolate Chip Cookies at Their Best

(Pictured on facing page)

The cook who invented these special cookies was obviously following William Blake's dictum, "the road to excess leads to the palace of wisdom"— they're large and chock-full of chocolate and nuts. Bake them one way if you like your cookies soft and chewy, another way if you prefer them crisp.

>   1 cup (½ lb.) butter or margarine, softened
>   ½ cup solid vegetable shortening
>   1⅓ cups granulated sugar
>   1 cup firmly packed brown sugar
>   4 eggs
>   1 tablespoon vanilla
>   1 teaspoon lemon juice
>   3 cups all-purpose flour
>   2 teaspoons baking soda
>   1½ teaspoons salt
>   1 teaspoon ground cinnamon (optional)
>   ½ cup rolled oats
>   2 large packages (12 oz. *each*) semisweet chocolate chips
>   2 cups chopped walnuts

In large bowl of an electric mixer, beat butter, shortening, granulated sugar, and brown sugar on high speed until very light and fluffy (about 5 minutes). Add eggs, one at a time, beating well after each addition. Beat in vanilla and lemon juice. In another bowl, stir together flour, baking soda, salt, cinnamon (if used), and oats. Gradually add to butter mixture, blending thoroughly. Stir in chocolate chips and walnuts.

Use a scant ¼ cup of dough for each cookie. Drop dough onto lightly greased baking sheets, spacing cookies about 3 inches apart. For soft cookies, bake in a 325° oven for 17 to 19 minutes or until light golden brown; for crisp cookies, bake in a 350° oven for 16 to 18 minutes or until golden brown. Transfer to racks and let cool. Store airtight. Makes about 3 dozen.

Coconut-Macadamia Cookies

(Pictured on page 726)

Follow directions for **Chocolate Chip Cookies at Their Best**, but use ⅔ cup granulated sugar and 1⅔ cups firmly packed brown sugar; increase flour to 3½ cups and omit cinnamon and oats. Omit chocolate chips and walnuts; instead, stir in 2½ cups **shredded coconut** and 1½ cups very coarsely chopped **macadamia nuts.** Bake in a 325° oven for 22 to 25 minutes or until golden brown.

Chocolate Cream Cushions

(Pictured on page 726)

Depending on what flavor you fancy, you can fill these soft chocolate sandwich cookies with vanilla, peppermint, or peanut buttercream.

>   6 tablespoons butter or margarine, softened
>   1 cup sugar
>   1 egg
>   1 teaspoon vanilla
>   2 cups all-purpose flour
>   1¼ teaspoons baking soda
>   ¼ teaspoon salt
>   5 tablespoons unsweetened cocoa
>   1 cup milk
>   Buttercream (recipes follow)

In large bowl of an electric mixer, beat butter and sugar until creamy; beat in egg and vanilla. In another bowl, stir together flour, baking soda, salt, and cocoa; add to butter mixture alternately with milk, beating just until smooth.

Drop dough by rounded teaspoonfuls onto greased baking sheets, spacing cookies about 2 inches apart. Bake in a 400° oven for 10 minutes or until firm when lightly touched. Transfer to racks and let cool completely. Meanwhile, prepare your choice of buttercream.

Spread bottoms of half the cooled cookies with buttercream; top with remaining cookies, top side up. Store airtight. Makes about 2½ dozen.

Vanilla buttercream. In small bowl of an electric mixer, beat until smooth: ¾ cup (¼ lb. plus 4 tablespoons) **butter** or margarine (softened), ¾ cup **powdered sugar**, 6 tablespoons **marshmallow creme,** and 1 teaspoon **vanilla.**

Peppermint buttercream. Follow directions for **Vanilla buttercream,** but use 1 teaspoon **peppermint extract** in place of vanilla.

Peanut buttercream. Follow directions for **Vanilla buttercream,** but substitute ½ cup **peanut butter** for ½ cup of the butter. Omit vanilla.

Chocolate Chip Cookies at Their Best *(Recipe on facing page)*

1 Beat sugar mixture until very light and fluffy to combine thoroughly, and to incorporate air.

2 Chop nuts with a large knife, lifting heel of knife in up-and-down movements and steadying tip of blade with other hand.

3 Chopped nuts and chocolate chips are stirred in by hand after other ingredients are well combined.

4 For each cookie, drop a scant ¼ cup dough onto lightly greased baking sheet.

Brownie Date Drops

(Pictured on page 726)

Chewy and chocolaty as a brownie, these soft drops are studded with dates and walnuts for extra-special flavor and texture.

- ½ cup (¼ lb.) butter or margarine, softened
- 1 cup sugar
- 2 eggs
- 1 teaspoon vanilla
- 2 ounces unsweetened chocolate, melted and cooled
- 1 cup all-purpose flour
- 1 teaspoon baking powder
- ½ teaspoon salt
- 1 cup *each* snipped pitted dates and chopped walnuts

In large bowl of an electric mixer, beat butter and sugar until creamy; beat in eggs and vanilla, then chocolate. In another bowl, stir together flour, baking powder, and salt; gradually add to butter mixture, blending thoroughly. Stir in dates and walnuts.

Drop dough by level tablespoonfuls onto greased baking sheets, spacing cookies about 1 inch apart. Bake in a 350° oven for 13 minutes or until tops are dry and just set when lightly touched (cookies will be soft; do not overbake). Transfer to racks and let cool. Store airtight. Makes about 3 dozen.

Clove Cookies

One doesn't often find drop cookies of the crisp, buttery variety, but these clove-spiced morsels are just that. Serve them with hot tea on a winter's afternoon—or with lemonade in summer.

- ½ cup (¼ lb.) butter
- 1 cup sugar
- 1 teaspoon vanilla
- 1 egg
- 1 cup all-purpose flour
- 1 teaspoon ground cloves

Melt butter in a small pan over medium heat. Remove from heat and stir in sugar until well com-

bined; then stir in vanilla. Add egg and beat until mixture is smooth. In a small bowl, stir together flour and cloves; gradually add to butter mixture, blending thoroughly.

Drop dough by level teaspoonfuls onto well-greased baking sheets, spacing cookies 2½ to 3 inches apart. Bake in a 350° oven for 12 to 14 minutes or until edges are golden brown and puffy tops start to crinkle and collapse. Immediately transfer cookies to racks and let cool. Store airtight. Makes about 4 dozen.

Frosted Apple Drops

A plateful of these soft, frosted apple cookies is sure to please on an autumn afternoon—or any other time. The spicy cookies are studded with raisins and chunks of apple.

- ½ cup (¼ lb.) butter or margarine, softened
- 1⅓ cups firmly packed brown sugar
- 1 egg
- 2 cups all-purpose flour
- 1 teaspoon *each* baking soda and ground cinnamon
- ½ teaspoon *each* salt, ground cloves, and ground nutmeg
- ¼ cup apple juice or milk
- 1 cup *each* raisins and peeled, finely chopped apples
- Apple frosting (recipe follows)

In large bowl of an electric mixer, beat butter and sugar until creamy; beat in egg. In another bowl, stir together flour, baking soda, cinnamon, salt, cloves, and nutmeg. Add flour mixture to butter mixture alternately with apple juice, mixing well after each addition; stir in raisins and apples.

Drop dough by level tablespoonfuls onto well-greased baking sheets, spacing cookies about 2 inches apart. Bake in a 400° oven for about 10 minutes or until golden brown. Transfer to racks. Prepare apple frosting and spread over cookies while they're still slightly warm. Let cool completely. Store airtight. Makes about 4½ dozen.

Apple frosting. In a bowl, beat 2 tablespoons **butter** or margarine (softened) and 1½ cups sifted **powdered sugar** until creamy. Beat in ¼ teaspoon **vanilla**, a dash of **salt**, and enough **apple juice** or milk (about 2 tablespoons) to obtain a good spreading consistency.

Maple Graham Crisps

Graham cracker crumbs and maple flavoring give these golden cookies their warm, sweet flavor. They're rich and buttery, with an appealingly crisp texture—good cookies to serve with a glass of cold milk. Use purchased cracker crumbs or whirl your own in a food processor or blender.

> 1 cup (½ lb.) butter or margarine, softened
> 1 cup sugar
> 1 egg
> 1 teaspoon maple flavoring
> 1¼ cups fine graham cracker crumbs (about 20 squares)
> 1 cup all-purpose flour

In large bowl of an electric mixer, beat butter and sugar until creamy; then beat in egg and maple flavoring. Gradually add graham cracker crumbs and flour, blending thoroughly. Cover tightly with plastic wrap and refrigerate until firm (at least 1 hour).

Drop dough by rounded teaspoonfuls onto ungreased baking sheets, spacing cookies about 2 inches apart. (Keep any remaining dough refrigerated until you're ready to use it.) Bake in a 325° oven for 16 to 18 minutes or until firm when lightly touched. Let cool on baking sheets for 1 to 2 minutes, then transfer to racks and let cool completely. Store airtight. Makes about 4 dozen.

Bourbon Chews

These cookies are spirited in more ways than one. Molasses and ginger provide part of their spicy character; bourbon whiskey does the rest.

> 1 cup all-purpose flour
> ½ cup sugar
> 1 teaspoon ground ginger
> ¼ teaspoon salt
> ⅓ cup light molasses
> ½ cup (¼ lb.) butter or margarine
> 3 tablespoons bourbon whiskey
> ¼ cup chopped almonds or walnuts

In a small bowl, stir together flour, sugar, ginger, and salt; set aside. In a 1-quart pan, bring molasses to a boil over high heat; add butter and stir until melted. Remove from heat and stir in flour mixture, bourbon, and almonds until batter is smooth and well combined.

Drop batter by level tablespoonfuls onto greased baking sheets, spacing cookies about 3 inches apart; then spread each into a 2-inch circle with the back of a spoon. Bake in a 300° oven for 8 to 10 minutes or until cookies look dry and are no longer sticky to the touch. Let cool on baking sheets for about 3 minutes, then transfer to racks and let cool completely. Store airtight. Makes about 2 dozen.

Blueberry Lemon Drops

(Pictured on page 726)

Here's a summertime treat made with fresh blueberries—a sugar-dusted drop cookie that resembles a blueberry muffin in its soft, cakelike appeal. The cookies are at their prime of fragrance and juiciness while still warm, so plan to eat them soon after baking. If you like, you can prepare the dough in advance and refrigerate it, then bake the cookies at the last minute.

> ½ cup (¼ lb.) butter or margarine, softened
> 1 cup granulated sugar
> 1½ teaspoons grated lemon peel
> 1 egg
> 2 cups all-purpose flour
> 2 teaspoons baking powder
> ½ teaspoon salt
> ¼ cup milk
> 1 cup fresh blueberries
> Powdered sugar

In large bowl of an electric mixer, beat butter until creamy; gradually add granulated sugar, beating until smoothly blended. Beat in lemon peel and egg. In another bowl, stir together flour, baking powder, and salt; add to butter mixture alternately with milk, blending thoroughly. Gently stir in blueberries.

Drop dough by rounded tablespoonfuls onto greased baking sheets, spacing cookies about 2 inches apart. Bake in a 375° oven for about 15 minutes or until golden brown. Transfer to racks and let cool for 5 minutes; then sift powdered sugar lightly over tops. Serve warm, or let cool completely and store airtight for up to 3 days. Makes about 3 dozen.

Chocolate-covered Almond Macaroons *(Recipe on facing page)*

1 Fold ground almond mixture, a third at a time, into beaten egg whites.

2 Use a spoon, a small rubber scraper, or a finger to nudge batter onto parchment-lined baking sheets.

3 Spread chocolate buttercream over flat bottom of each macaroon; then refrigerate until buttercream is firm.

4 Dip buttercream side of each cookie into chocolate. Refrigerate until coating is set.

Chocolate-covered Almond Macaroons

(Pictured on facing page)

In Swedish *konditorier* (pastry shops), you'll find a rich and irresistible confection: almond macaroons topped with chocolate buttercream and dipped in semisweet chocolate. Though they take a little more time to make than the average cookie, these elegant morsels are well worth the trouble when the occasion calls for something special—and you can make them well in advance, then refrigerate or freeze them.

> **Almond macaroons (recipe follows)**
> **Chocolate buttercream (recipe follows)**
> 5 **ounces semisweet chocolate**
> 1 **tablespoon plus 2 teaspoons
> solid vegetable shortening**

Prepare macaroons and let cool completely. Prepare buttercream and spread one tablespoonful over bottom of each cooled cookie. Then place cookies, buttercream side up, in a single layer on a pan or plate and refrigerate until buttercream is firm (at least 15 minutes).

Meanwhile, place chocolate and shortening in the top of a double boiler over simmering water; stir just until melted. Transfer chocolate mixture to a small, shallow bowl for easier handling and let cool, stirring occasionally, until lukewarm (80° to 85° F).

Hold each cookie buttercream side down and dip in chocolate to coat buttercream. Then place cookies on a pan or plate, chocolate side up, and refrigerate until chocolate coating is set (at least 10 minutes). When chocolate is firm, cover cookies lightly and store in the refrigerator for up to 3 days. (Freeze for longer storage; let thaw in refrigerator for at least 3 hours before serving.) Makes about 1½ dozen.

Almond macaroons. In a blender or food processor, whirl 1½ cups **whole blanched almonds** until finely ground. Place in a bowl and add 1½ cups sifted **powdered sugar**; stir until mixture is free from lumps.

Separate 3 eggs. Reserve yolks for buttercream; place **egg whites** in a bowl and beat just until moist, stiff peaks form. Then sprinkle almond mixture over egg whites, a third at a time, folding in each addition until blended.

Drop mixture by rounded tablespoonfuls onto baking sheets lined with parchment paper, spacing cookies about 1 inch apart. Bake in a 350° oven for 15 to 18 minutes or until lightly browned. Let cool on baking sheets for about 5 minutes, then transfer to racks with a wide spatula. Let cool.

Chocolate buttercream. In a small pan, stir together 7 tablespoons *each* **sugar** and **water**. Bring to a boil over high heat; continue to boil until syrup reaches 230° to 234° F on a candy thermometer (or until syrup spins a 2-inch thread when dropped from a fork or spoon).

In small bowl of an electric mixer, beat 4 **egg yolks** until blended. Beating constantly, slowly add hot syrup in a thin, steady stream; beat until mixture is thick and lemon-colored and has cooled to room temperature. Then beat in ⅔ cup **butter** (softened), a tablespoon at a time, just until blended. Stir in 4 teaspoons **unsweetened cocoa.** (If mixture gets dark and runny from overbeating, refrigerate it, then beat again.)

Coconut Macaroons

(Pictured on page 726)

Traditionally, macaroons are made from egg whites, sugar, and ground almonds (see preceding recipe) or almond paste (see Swiss Almond Macaroons, page 775). Sometimes, however, coconut makes an appearance to provide a rich and chewy variation. If you'd like to enjoy the flavor of both almond and coconut in the same macaroon, try substituting almond extract for the vanilla in this recipe; that way, you can enjoy the best of both worlds.

> 4 **egg whites**
> ¼ **teaspoon salt**
> ⅔ **cup sugar**
> 1 **teaspoon vanilla**
> ¼ **cup all-purpose flour**
> 3 **cups lightly packed flaked coconut**

In large bowl of an electric mixer, beat egg whites until foamy; beat in salt, sugar, vanilla, and flour. Add coconut and stir until well combined.

Drop batter by rounded teaspoonfuls onto well-greased baking sheets, spacing cookies about 1 inch apart. Bake in a 325° oven for 20 to 25 minutes or until lightly browned. Let cool briefly on baking sheets, then transfer to racks and let cool completely. Store airtight. Makes about 3 dozen.

Mint Meringues

(*Pictured on page 726*)

These light, dainty cookies are flavored with mint and studded with chocolate chips. If you like, you can give them a festive holiday look by tinting them with green or red food color.

    2 egg whites
    ½ cup sugar
    ½ teaspoon peppermint or spearmint extract
    6 to 8 drops green or red food color
       (optional)
    1 package (6 oz.) semisweet chocolate chips

In large bowl of an electric mixer, beat egg whites until foamy. With mixer on high speed, gradually add sugar, about a tablespoon at a time, beating well after each addition, until whites hold stiff, glossy peaks. Add peppermint extract and food color (if used); beat for 1 more minute. Fold in chocolate chips.

Drop meringue mixture by rounded teaspoonfuls onto well-greased baking sheets, spacing cookies about 1 inch apart. Bake in a 200° oven for 1 hour or until outside is dry and set; cookies should not turn brown. Let cool on baking sheets for about 5 minutes, then transfer to racks and let cool completely. Store airtight. Makes about 3½ dozen.

Date-nut Meringues

If you've got a couple of extra egg whites, put them to delicious use in these chewy little datenut nuggets.

    2 egg whites
       Dash of salt
    ½ cup sugar
    1 teaspoon vanilla
    1 cup *each* snipped pitted dates and finely
       chopped walnuts

In large bowl of an electric mixer, beat egg whites until foamy. With mixer on high speed, beat in salt; then gradually add sugar, about a tablespoon at a time, beating well after each addition, until whites hold stiff, glossy peaks. Add vanilla and beat for 1 more minute. Fold in dates and walnuts.

Drop meringue mixture by rounded teaspoonfuls onto well-greased baking sheets, spacing cookies about 1 inch apart. Bake in a 200° oven for 1 hour or until outside is dry and set; cookies should not turn brown. Let cool on baking sheets for about 5 minutes, then transfer to racks and let cool completely. Store airtight. Makes about 3½ dozen.

Florentines

Rich and chewy Florentines are truly a dessert cookie, best served in the evening with coffee or tea. They're flavored with almonds and candied orange peel, and painted on one side with semisweet chocolate.

    1 cup sliced almonds
    ¼ cup whipping cream
    ⅓ cup sugar
    4 tablespoons butter or margarine
    ½ cup candied orange peel, finely chopped
    2 tablespoons all-purpose flour
    4 ounces semisweet chocolate
    4 teaspoons solid vegetable shortening

In a blender or food processor, whirl ½ cup of the almonds until finely ground. Set aside.

Combine cream, sugar, and butter in a medium-size pan and cook over low heat, stirring occasionally, until butter is melted. Increase heat to medium-high and bring mixture to a boil; then remove from heat and stir in ground almonds, remaining ½ cup sliced almonds, orange peel, and flour. Batter will be very thin.

Drop batter by level tablespoonfuls onto lightly greased and flour-dusted baking sheets, spacing cookies 3 inches apart; then spread each into a 2-inch circle with the back of a spoon. Bake in a 350° oven for 10 to 12 minutes or until edges are lightly browned (centers will still be bubbling). Let cool on baking sheets for 1 to 2 minutes, then carefully transfer to racks with a wide spatula and let cool completely.

Turn cooled cookies upside down on a piece of wax paper. Place chocolate and shortening in top of a double boiler over simmering water; stir until melted. With a soft pastry brush, paint a thin layer of chocolate over bottom of each cookie. Refrigerate until chocolate has hardened; then cover lightly and store in the refrigerator for up to 3 days. Makes about 15.

Packing & Sending Cookies

Sending homemade cookies to friends and loved ones in faraway places is a sure way of showing your affection, no matter what the occasion. Birthdays, holidays, and college exam weeks are perhaps the most popular times for sending cookie gifts, but why wait for a special event? Cookies are a welcome sight any time.

Which Cookies to Send

Make sure you select cookies that are good travelers. They must be sturdy enough to make the journey, and must keep well enough to stay fresh until they arrive at their destination. Don't choose anything fragile (Krumkake, for example), or it may be crushed in transit. Also avoid sticky cookies or those with moist icings or frostings. Crisp cookies are fine if they're not too delicate or crumbly, but the most reliable travelers are firm but not brittle cookies.

The cookies listed below are especially good candidates for mailing.

Wrapping, Packing & Mailing

Cookies can be wrapped for travel in several ways. You can wrap them in foil—either individually, in pairs (flat sides together), or in small stacks. Or layer the cookies in containers, such as pretty tins, rigid plastic containers, or attractively wrapped foil loaf or pie pans. Separate layers with wax paper, and pack the cookies securely so they won't jostle about and damage each other in transit. If the container you've chosen isn't airtight, seal it in a plastic bag.

However you wrap your cookies, be sure to pack soft and crisp ones separately to preserve their textures.

To pack the cookies for mailing, you'll need a stout box lined with foil or wax paper, and plenty of filler for insulation. For filler, use tightly crumpled newspaper or other paper (colored tissue paper gives a festive appearance) or styrofoam packing material. Pad the bottom of the box with several inches of filler; then start adding cookies, making sure to insulate well with filler between packages and around the sides of the box. Add several inches of filler on top of the cookies before closing the box.

The post office requires that all packages be sealed securely with reinforced packing tape; don't use masking tape or transparent tape or tie your package with string. Send the package first-class so that your cookies will arrive promptly.

Bar Cookies

Sometimes chewy, sometimes cakey, and sometimes crisp and crunchy, bar cookies are always popular—and because they're quick to prepare, they're often favorites with the cook, too. The key to their speedy preparation is the fact that they're spread in a pan and baked all at once, rather than being individually shaped. This also makes them good candidates for taking to picnics and parties—you can wrap and carry them easily, right in their baking pans.

The recipes in this chapter run the gamut from classics like Fudge Brownies (page 741) to more unusual creations such as Bee Sting Bars (page 744) and Cheesecake Squares (page 749). For best results, always use the pan size specified in the recipe: we most often call for 8 or 9-inch square, 9 by 13-inch, or 10 by 15-inch. After baking, the cookies may be cut into squares, rectangles, or triangles—or, in some cases, just broken into irregular chunks.

Photo at right displays a mosaic of delectable bar cookies. Separating the sections: Dream Bars (page 749). Others, clockwise from upper right: Fudge Brownies (page 741), Buttery Lemon Bars (page 740), Banana Squares (page 740), Chocolate Oatmeal Peanut Bars (page 741), and Bee Sting Bars (page 744)

Banana Squares

(Pictured on page 739)

Paired with cold milk, these banana-flavored treats are the perfect thing to satisfy after-school appetites. Each square is studded with butterscotch chips (or raisins, if you prefer).

- 6 tablespoons butter or margarine, softened
- 1 cup firmly packed brown sugar
- 1 egg
- ½ teaspoon vanilla
- 1 large banana, mashed
- 1¾ cups all-purpose flour
- 1½ teaspoons baking powder
- ½ teaspoon salt
- ½ cup chopped walnuts
- 1 package (6 oz.) butterscotch-flavored chips or 1 cup raisins

In large bowl of an electric mixer, beat butter and sugar until creamy; beat in egg, vanilla, and banana. In another bowl, stir together flour, baking powder, and salt; gradually add to butter mixture, blending thoroughly. Stir in walnuts and butterscotch chips.

Spread batter evenly in a greased 9-inch square baking pan. Bake in a 350° oven for 35 to 40 minutes or until golden brown. Let cool in pan on a rack, then cut into 2¼-inch squares. Store airtight. Makes 16.

Buttery Lemon Bars

(Pictured on page 739)

These luscious bars will remind you of lemon meringue pie—minus the meringue topping, and with a cookie crust instead of pie pastry.

- 1 cup (½ lb.) butter or margarine, softened
- ½ cup powdered sugar
- 2⅓ cups all-purpose flour
- 4 eggs
- 2 cups granulated sugar
- 1 teaspoon grated lemon peel
- 6 tablespoons lemon juice
- 1 teaspoon baking powder
- Powdered sugar

In large bowl of an electric mixer, beat butter and the ½ cup powdered sugar until creamy; beat in 2 cups of the flour, blending thoroughly. Spread mixture evenly over bottom of a well-greased 9 by 13-inch baking pan. Bake in a 350° oven for 20 minutes.

Meanwhile, in small bowl of mixer, beat eggs until light. Gradually add granulated sugar, beating until mixture is thick and lemon-colored. Add lemon peel, lemon juice, remaining ⅓ cup flour, and baking powder; beat until smooth and well combined.

Pour lemon mixture over baked crust and return to oven; bake for 15 to 20 minutes or until topping is pale golden. Place on a rack to cool; while still warm, sift powdered sugar lightly over top. To serve, cut into bars about 2¼ by 2½ inches. Store airtight. Makes about 20.

Lemon-Coconut Dessert Bars

A buttery coconut crumb crust conceals the piquant lemon filling of these rich bars. They belong to a versatile group of desserts somewhere between cookies and cake—you can cut them into cookie-size pieces to eat out of hand, or serve larger portions on small plates, to eat with forks.

- 2 cups all-purpose flour
- 1 cup sugar
- 1 teaspoon *each* baking powder and grated lemon peel
- 9 tablespoons (¼ lb. plus 1 tablespoon) firm butter or margarine, cut into pieces
- 1 cup flaked coconut
- 2 egg yolks
  Lemon filling (recipe follows)

In a large mixing bowl, stir together flour, sugar, baking powder, and lemon peel. Add butter and rub in with your fingers until mixture resembles cornmeal. Add coconut and egg yolks and blend thoroughly.

Spoon a little more than half the coconut mixture into a lightly greased 9-inch square baking pan. Press gently and evenly over bottom of pan. Bake in a 350° oven for 15 minutes. Meanwhile, prepare lemon filling.

Remove pan from oven; pour lemon filling over crust and spread to edges of pan. Sprinkle remaining coconut mixture evenly over top; spread with a fork to level, then pat down gently. Return to oven and bake for 20 to 25 minutes or until lightly browned. Let cool completely in pan on a rack; then cut into bars about 1¾ by 3 inches. Store, covered, for up to 4 days. Makes about 15.

Lemon filling. In a small pan, stir together ½ cup **sugar** and 2½ tablespoons **cornstarch.** Gradually stir in 1 cup **water.** Bring to a full boil over medium-high heat, stirring; cook, stirring constantly, for 1 minute (mixture will be very thick). Remove from heat; add 2 tablespoons **butter** or margarine, ⅓ cup **lemon juice,** and 1½ teaspoons grated **lemon peel.** Stir until butter is melted.

Chocolate Oatmeal Peanut Bars

(Pictured on page 739)

Chocolate and peanuts are a tempting combination, especially in these chewy, candylike bar cookies. They feature a creamy topping of chocolate and peanut butter over an oatmeal crust; a sprinkling of chopped peanuts makes a decorative crowning touch.

- ⅔ **cup butter or margarine, softened**
- ½ **cup firmly packed brown sugar**
- ½ **cup light corn syrup**
- 2 **teaspoons vanilla**
- 4 **cups quick-cooking rolled oats**
- 1 **package (6 oz.) semisweet chocolate chips**
- ⅔ **cup creamy peanut butter**
- ⅓ **cup chopped dry-roasted peanuts**

In large bowl of an electric mixer, beat butter and sugar until creamy; stir in corn syrup, vanilla, and oats, blending thoroughly. Pat dough evenly over bottom of a greased 9 by 13-inch baking pan. Bake in a 350° oven for about 20 minutes or until golden around edges; let cool in pan on a rack, then cover and refrigerate until cold.

Meanwhile, place chocolate chips and peanut butter in a 1½ to 2-quart pan. Stir over very low heat until melted and smooth. Spread mixture evenly over baked crust; sprinkle with peanuts. Refrigerate until topping firms slightly (about 15 minutes); then cut into bars about 1 by 2 inches. Store, covered, in refrigerator. Makes about 4½ dozen.

Fudge Brownies

(Pictured on page 739)

Brownies are always winners, and this fudgy version will keep you coming back for more.

- ½ **cup (¼ lb.) butter or margarine**
- 4 **ounces unsweetened chocolate**
- 2 **cups sugar**
- 1½ **teaspoons vanilla**
- 4 **eggs**
- 1 **cup all-purpose flour**
- ½ **to 1 cup coarsely chopped walnuts**

In a 2 to 3-quart pan, melt butter and chocolate over medium-low heat, stirring until well blended. Remove from heat and stir in sugar and vanilla. Add eggs, one at a time, beating well after each addition. Stir in flour; then mix in walnuts.

Spread batter evenly in a greased 9-inch square baking pan. Bake in a 325° oven for about 35 minutes or until brownie feels dry on top. Let cool in pan on a rack, then cut into 2¼-inch squares. Store airtight. Makes 16.

Butterscotch Brownies

Sometimes called "blondies," these chewy squares are made with butter and brown sugar for a rich flavor and a handsome golden hue.

- 4 **tablespoons butter or margarine**
- 1 **cup firmly packed brown sugar**
- 1 **egg**
- 1 **teaspoon vanilla**
- 1 **cup all-purpose flour**
- 1 **teaspoon baking powder**
- ½ **teaspoon salt**
- ¼ **cup chopped walnuts or pecans**

Melt butter in a medium-size pan over medium heat. Remove from heat and stir in sugar; add egg and vanilla and beat until well combined. Stir in flour, baking powder, salt and walnuts.

Spread batter evenly in a greased 8-inch square baking pan; bake in a 375° oven for 20 to 25 minutes or until golden brown. Let cool in pan on a rack, then cut into 2-inch squares. Store airtight. Makes 16.

Triple-layered Brownie Squares *(Recipe on facing page)*

1 In the top of a double boiler over simmering water, melt chocolate and butter.

2 Turn brownie batter into a lightly greased 9-inch square baking pan. Spread out in an even layer.

3 Spread vanilla frosting evenly over baked and cooled brownie to make second layer.

4 Drizzle chocolate glaze over frosting and tilt pan so chocolate covers surface evenly.

Triple-layered Brownie Squares

(Pictured on facing page)

Gilding the lily may not be good taste in art, but for a brownie the standards are different. Dieters beware: here you bake a thin, nut-laden brownie, spread a vanilla frosting over it, and then top it all with a dark chocolate icing. For variety, you may also want to try our mint variation (below).

> 2 ounces unsweetened chocolate
> ¾ cup (¼ lb. plus 4 tablespoons) butter or margarine
> 1 egg
> ½ cup granulated sugar
> ¼ cup all-purpose flour
> 1 cup chopped almonds or pecans
> 2 cups powdered sugar
> ½ teaspoon vanilla
> 2 to 3 tablespoons whipping cream

For the first layer, place 1 ounce of the chocolate and 4 tablespoons of the butter in the top of a double boiler over simmering water (or in a small pan over lowest possible heat). Stir until melted.

In a small mixing bowl, beat egg and granulated sugar, then gradually beat in chocolate mixture. Stir in flour and almonds. Spread batter evenly in a lightly greased 9-inch square baking pan; bake in a 350° oven for 20 to 25 minutes or until brownie feels dry on top. Let cool completely in pan on a rack.

For the second layer, place 4 tablespoons of the butter, powdered sugar, and vanilla in small bowl of an electric mixer. Beat together; then beat in enough cream to make frosting spreadable. Spread evenly over cooled brownie.

For the third layer, combine remaining 1 ounce chocolate and remaining 4 tablespoons butter in the top of a double boiler over simmering water (or in a small pan over lowest possible heat). Stir until melted. Drizzle over frosting layer; tilt pan so chocolate covers surface evenly. Refrigerate until chocolate is hardened (about 15 minutes). Cut into 2¼-inch squares. Store, covered, in refrigerator. Makes 16.

Mint-layered Brownie Squares

Follow directions for **Triple-layered Brownie Squares,** but add 1 teaspoon **peppermint extract** to frosting (second layer).

Applesauce-Raisin Brownies

Not all brownies are dark and chocolaty, as this recipe proves. It produces old-fashioned "brownies" that are much like spice cake—light-textured, dotted with raisins and nuts, and flavored with cinnamon and nutmeg. Applesauce makes them moist; an orange butter frosting lends a special, fancy touch.

If you have a citrus zester, you can use it to make fine strands of orange peel for decorating the brownies.

> 6 tablespoons butter or margarine
> 1¼ cups firmly packed brown sugar
> ½ cup applesauce
> 1 egg
> 1 teaspoon vanilla
> 1¼ cups all-purpose flour
> 1 teaspoon baking powder
> ½ teaspoon *each* salt and ground cinnamon
> ¼ teaspoon *each* baking soda and ground nutmeg
> ½ cup *each* raisins and chopped nuts
> Orange frosting (optional; recipe follows)
> Orange zest (optional)

Melt butter in a small pan over medium-low heat. Remove from heat and stir in sugar; then stir in applesauce, egg, and vanilla. In a bowl, stir together flour, baking powder, salt, cinnamon, baking soda, and nutmeg; add applesauce mixture and blend thoroughly. Add raisins and nuts; stir until well combined.

Spread batter evenly in a greased 9 by 13-inch baking pan. Bake in a 350° oven for 25 minutes or until a pick inserted in center comes out clean. Let cool completely in pan on a rack. If desired, prepare orange frosting and spread over cooled brownie; then garnish with orange zest. Cut into bars (about 1½ by 3 inches) or squares (about 2¼ by 2¼ inches). Store covered. Makes about 2 dozen.

Orange frosting. In small bowl of an electric mixer, beat together until smooth: 1¾ cups **powdered sugar;** 2½ tablespoons **butter** or margarine, softened; 2 tablespoons **milk;** and ½ teaspoon **vanilla.** Beat in ½ teaspoon grated **orange peel.** If necessary, beat in a few more drops milk to make a good spreading consistency.

English Toffee Squares

When you need a dessert for a large gathering, you'll appreciate this recipe. With little effort, you can produce six dozen delicious and easily portable toffee-flavored bar cookies.

> 1 cup (½ lb.) butter or margarine, softened
> 1 cup sugar
> 1 egg
> 2 cups all-purpose flour
> 1 teaspoon ground cinnamon
> 1 cup chopped pecans or walnuts

In large bowl of an electric mixer, beat butter and sugar until creamy. Separate egg. Beat yolk into butter mixture; cover and reserve white.

In another bowl, stir together flour and cinnamon; add to butter mixture, using your hands if necessary to blend thoroughly.

With your hands, spread dough evenly over bottom of a greased 10 by 15-inch rimmed baking pan. Beat egg white lightly, then brush over dough to cover evenly. Sprinkle pecans over top; press in lightly.

Bake in a 275° oven for 1 hour or until firm when lightly touched. While still hot, cut into 1½-inch squares. Let cool in pan on a rack. Store airtight. Makes about 6 dozen.

Bee Sting Bars

(Pictured on page 739)

These fancifully named honey-almond bars come from Germany, where they're known as *Bienenstich.*

> 1 cup (½ lb.) firm butter or margarine
> ¾ cup sugar
> 2 tablespoons *each* honey and milk
> 1 cup chopped or slivered almonds
> 1 teaspoon almond extract
> 1¾ cups all-purpose flour
> 2 teaspoons baking powder
> ¼ teaspoon salt
> 1 egg

In a small pan, combine ½ cup of the butter, ¼ cup of the sugar, honey, milk, almonds, and almond

extract. Bring to a rolling boil over medium-high heat, stirring; set aside.

In a mixing bowl, stir together flour, remaining ½ cup sugar, baking powder, and salt. Cut remaining ½ cup butter into pieces and, with a pastry blender or 2 knives, cut into flour mixture until mixture is very crumbly and no large particles remain. Add egg and mix with a fork until dough holds together.

Press dough evenly over bottom of an ungreased 10 by 15-inch rimmed baking pan. Pour almond mixture over dough, spreading evenly. Bake in a 350° oven for 20 to 25 minutes or until topping is deep golden. Let cool in pan on a rack. Cut into 2-inch squares; for smaller cookies, cut each square diagonally into 2 triangles. Store airtight. Makes about 3 dozen squares or about 6 dozen triangles.

Italian Crumb Cookie

A specialty of Veneto, Italy, this giant break-apart cookie starts as a pile of buttery crumbs. In its native land, it's known as *torta fregolotti.* You let it stand for a day after baking, then break it into irregular chunks to serve alongside fruit.

> 1 cup blanched almonds, ground
> 2⅔ cups all-purpose flour
> 1 cup sugar
> Pinch of salt
> 1 teaspoon grated lemon peel
> 1 cup (½ lb.) plus 2 tablespoons firm butter or margarine, cut into pieces
> 2 tablespoons lemon juice
> 1 tablespoon brandy or water

In a mixing bowl, stir together almonds, flour, sugar, salt, and lemon peel. With a pastry blender or 2 knives, cut in butter until mixture resembles coarse crumbs. Sprinkle with lemon juice and brandy and mix lightly with a fork until blended. Mixture should be crumbly.

Spread mixture in a greased and flour-dusted 12-inch pizza pan or a 9 by 13-inch baking pan; do not press into pan. Bake in a 350° oven for 50 to 60 minutes or until browned. Let cool completely in pan on a rack.

When cookie is cooled, wrap well (either in or out of pan) and let stand for at least a day. To serve, break into chunks. Store airtight. Makes 2 to 3 dozen pieces.

Cookie Tortes

When you want a dessert with all the charm of a cookie—and a little extra pizzazz—try these special tortes. They start with extra-large round cookies; but when those plain cookies are dressed up with fillings and toppings, cut into wedges, and served with a plate and fork, you'd hardly recognize them. They make a perfect company dessert when your guests are confirmed cookie-lovers.

Chocolate Rum Custard Torte

        Rum custard filling (recipe follows)
    6 tablespoons solid vegetable shortening
    6 tablespoons butter or margarine, softened
    1 cup sugar
    2 eggs
    ½ teaspoon vanilla
    3 ounces unsweetened chocolate, melted and cooled
    2½ cups all-purpose flour
    1 teaspoon *each* baking powder and salt
        Toasted sliced almonds

Prepare rum custard filling and refrigerate. In large bowl of an electric mixer, beat shortening, butter, and sugar until creamy; beat in eggs, vanilla, and chocolate. In another bowl, stir together flour, baking powder, and salt; gradually add to chocolate mixture, blending thoroughly. Cover tightly with plastic wrap and refrigerate for about 1 hour.

Divide dough into 4 equal portions. Press each portion evenly over bottom of a greased and flour-dusted 9-inch round cake pan with a removable bottom. Bake layers in a 375° oven, 2 at a time, for 15 minutes or until cookies pull away from pan sides. Let cool in pans on racks for 10 minutes; then remove pan sides and slide cookies onto racks. Let cool completely.

To assemble torte, place one cookie layer on a serving plate. Top with a fourth of the filling and spread evenly to within ¼ inch of edge. Repeat layers, ending with filling on top. Invert a large bowl over torte (or place a cake cover over it) and refrigerate for at least 24 hours or for up to 3 days. To serve, sprinkle top with toasted sliced almonds and cut into wedges. Makes 8 to 10 servings.

Rum custard filling. In a 2 to 3-quart pan, stir together ¾ cup **all-purpose flour,** ⅔ cup **sugar,** and ¼ teaspoon **salt.** Gradually stir in 2½ cups **milk** until smooth. Cook over medium heat, stirring constantly, until mixture boils and thickens. Remove from heat.

In a small bowl, lightly beat 3 **egg yolks.** Stir a small amount of hot milk mixture into egg yolks; then slowly return mixture to pan, stirring until well incorporated. Return to heat and cook for 1 more minute. Remove from heat and stir in 1 teaspoon **vanilla** and 2 tablespoons **rum.** Let custard cool, then refrigerate until very thick (3 to 4 hours). Beat ⅓ cup **whipping cream** until stiff; fold into cold custard.

Chocolate Cherry Custard Torte

Prepare **Chocolate Rum Custard Torte** as directed above, but omit rum in custard filling; instead, use 2 tablespoons **kirsch.** Thaw and drain one bag (16 oz.) **frozen pitted red cherries;** cut cherries in half and pat dry with paper towels. Divide cherries into 3 equal portions.

To assemble torte, place one cookie layer on a serving plate. Top with a fourth of the filling and spread evenly to within ¼ inch of edge; then scatter a third of the cherries evenly over filling. Repeat layers, using cherries only on the first three layers and ending with filling on top.

Refrigerate as directed above. Before serving, top with **grated semisweet chocolate** instead of toasted sliced almonds.

Scottish Shortbread

(Pictured on facing page)

Were you to take tea in the highlands, you might be served Scotland's famous shortbread, a butter-rich cookie of delightful simplicity. If you like your shortbread a bit more dressed up, try our ginger variation—or sample Orange-Walnut Shortbread (following), Coconut Shortbread Cookies (page 788), Brown Sugar Shortbread (page 773), or Nutty Whole Wheat Shortbread (page 794).

1¼ **cups all-purpose flour**
3 **tablespoons cornstarch**
¼ **cup sugar**
½ **cup (¼ lb.) firm butter, cut into pieces**
Sugar

In a mixing bowl, stir together flour, cornstarch, and the ¼ cup sugar. Rub in butter with your fingers until mixture is very crumbly and no large particles remain. With your hands, gather mixture into a ball; place in an ungreased 8 or 9-inch round baking pan with a removable bottom, or in a 9-inch spring-form pan. Firmly press out dough into an even layer.

With the tines of a fork, make impressions around edge of dough; then prick surface evenly. Bake in a 325° oven for about 40 minutes or until pale golden brown. Remove from oven and, while hot, cut with a sharp knife into 8 to 12 wedges. Sprinkle with about 1 tablespoon sugar. Let cool completely; then remove sides of pan and lift out cookies. Store airtight. Makes 8 to 12.

Ginger Shortbread

Follow directions for **Scottish Shortbread,** but substitute ½ teaspoon **ground ginger** for cornstarch. After rubbing in butter, stir in 2 tablespoons minced **candied ginger.**

Orange-Walnut Shortbread

This orange-flavored shortbread is sprinkled with walnuts and drizzled with an orange glaze while still warm, then cut into tiny squares for bite-size enjoyment with coffee or tea.

1¼ **cups all-purpose flour**
¼ **cup sugar**
⅛ **teaspoon salt**
2 **teaspoons grated orange peel**
½ **cup (¼ lb.) firm butter, cut into pieces**
1 **cup finely chopped walnuts**
1 **tablespoon orange juice**
Orange glaze (recipe follows)

In a mixing bowl, stir together flour, sugar, salt, and orange peel. Rub in butter with your fingers until mixture is very crumbly and no large particles remain. Mix in ¾ cup of the walnuts and orange juice. Place mixture in a greased 7 by 11-inch baking pan and press firmly into an even layer.

Bake in a 325° oven for 40 to 45 minutes or until pale golden brown. Meanwhile, prepare orange glaze. Let shortbread cool slightly; then sprinkle with remaining ¼ cup walnuts and drizzle evenly with glaze. Cut into about 1¼-inch squares. Let cool completely in pan on a rack; lift from pan and store airtight. Makes about 4½ dozen.

Orange glaze. In a bowl, stir together ½ cup **powdered sugar,** ½ teaspoon grated **orange peel,** and 2 tablespoons **orange juice** until smooth.

Buttery Cookie Brittle

This delectable confection—part cookie, part candy—is studded with bits of almond brickle.

½ **cup (¼ lb.) butter or margarine, softened**
¾ **teaspoon vanilla**
1 **cup all-purpose flour**
½ **cup sugar**
1 **package (6 oz.) almond brickle bits**

In large bowl of an electric mixer, beat butter and vanilla until creamy. Blend in flour and sugar, then stir in brickle bits (mixture will be quite crumbly).

Spread mixture evenly over bottom of an ungreased 9 by 13-inch baking pan. Lay a piece of wax paper on top and press firmly to pack crumbs evenly. Discard paper.

Bake in a 375° oven for 15 to 20 minutes or until golden around edges. Let brittle cool in pan on a rack for 10 minutes; then loosen with a wide spatula, turn out onto rack, and let cool completely. Break into pieces. Store airtight for up to 2 days; freeze for longer storage. Makes about 3 dozen 1½ by 2-inch chunks.

Scottish Shortbread (Recipe on facing page)

1 Rub butter into flour mixture until very crumbly and no large particles remain.

2 Press dough out firmly into an even layer in an 8 or 9-inch round baking pan with a removable bottom.

3 With tines of a fork, make impressions around edge of dough; then prick surface evenly.

4 Cut baked shortbread into wedges while still warm; for best results, use a ruler as a guide.

Persimmon Bars

After an autumn walk, try serving these soft, spicy bar cookies with glasses of apple cider. Their special flavor comes from bright orange persimmons; a tangy lemon glaze adds extra sparkle.

When preparing the persimmon purée, be sure to use the type of persimmons that become very soft when ripe; you'll recognize them by their pointed tips.

       1 **cup persimmon purée (directions follow)**
       1 **teaspoon baking soda**
       1 **egg**
       1 **cup sugar**
    ½ **cup salad oil**
       1 **package (8 oz.) pitted dates (about 1½ cups lightly packed), finely snipped**
    1¾ **cups all-purpose flour**
       1 **teaspoon** *each* **salt, ground cinnamon, and ground nutmeg**
    ¼ **teaspoon ground cloves**
       1 **cup chopped walnuts or pecans**
         Lemon glaze (recipe follows)

Prepare persimmon purée; measure out 1 cup and stir in baking soda. Set aside. In a large bowl, lightly beat egg; then stir in sugar, oil, and dates.

In another bowl, stir together flour, salt, cinnamon, nutmeg, and cloves; add to date mixture alternately with persimmon mixture, stirring just until blended. Stir in walnuts. Spread batter evenly in a lightly greased, flour-dusted 10 by 15-inch rimmed baking pan. Bake in a 350° oven for 25 minutes or until top is lightly browned and a pick inserted in center comes out clean.

Let cool in pan on a rack for 5 minutes. Prepare lemon glaze and spread over cookies. Let cool completely; then cut into 2 by 2½-inch bars. Store covered. Makes 2½ dozen.

Persimmon purée. You'll need fully ripe pointed-tip **persimmons**—pulp should be soft and jellylike. Cut fruits in half and scoop out pulp with a spoon. Discard skin, seeds, and stem. In a blender or food processor, whirl pulp, a portion at a time, until smooth (you'll need 2 or 3 medium-size persimmons for 1 cup purée). For each cup purée, thoroughly stir in 1½ teaspoons **lemon juice**. To store, freeze in 1-cup batches in rigid containers; thaw, covered, at room temperature.

Lemon glaze. In a small bowl, stir together 1 cup **powdered sugar** and 2 tablespoons **lemon juice** until smooth.

Pineapple-Coconut Bars

Transport yourself to the islands with these tropical-tasting bar cookies—they're the next best thing to being on a beach under a palm tree.

    ½ **cup (¼ lb.) butter or margarine, softened**
       1 **cup firmly packed brown sugar**
       2 **eggs**
    ¼ **teaspoon almond extract**
    ¾ **cup all-purpose flour**
    ¾ **teaspoon baking powder**
    ½ **teaspoon salt**
    ¾ **cup flaked coconut**
       1 **can (8 oz.) crushed pineapple packed in its own juice, drained well**

In large bowl of an electric mixer, beat butter and sugar until creamy; beat in eggs and almond extract. In another bowl, stir together flour, baking powder, and salt; gradually add to butter mixture, blending thoroughly. Stir in coconut and pineapple.

Spread mixture evenly in a greased and flour-dusted 9-inch square baking pan. Bake in a 350° oven for 25 to 30 minutes or until top springs back when lightly touched. Let cool in pan on a rack, then cut into 1 by 2¼-inch bars. Store airtight. Makes 3 dozen.

Apple Butter Crumb Bars

Between top and bottom layers of oats and nuts, there's one of dark, flavorful apple butter. These bars can be served as cookies, or cut into bigger pieces and topped with ice cream for a more substantial dessert.

    1½ **cups all-purpose flour**
       1 **teaspoon baking soda**
    ½ **teaspoon ground cinnamon**
    2½ **cups quick-cooking rolled oats**
    ½ **cup chopped nuts**
       1 **cup firmly packed brown sugar**
       1 **cup (½ lb.) firm butter or margarine, cut into pieces**
       1 **jar (16 oz.) apple butter or 1½ cups homemade apple butter**

In a mixing bowl, stir together flour, baking soda, cinnamon, oats, nuts, and brown sugar until thoroughly blended. With a pastry blender or 2 knives, cut in butter until mixture is crumbly and no large particles remain.

Spread half the oat mixture evenly over bottom of an ungreased 9 by 13-inch baking pan and press down lightly. Spread apple butter evenly over crumb layer, then sprinkle remaining oat mixture over top; press down lightly.

Bake in a 400° oven for about 25 minutes or until golden brown. Let cool completely in pan on a rack. Cut into bars (about 1½ by 2 inches) or squares (about 2¼ by 2¼ inches). Store covered. Makes 2 to 3 dozen.

Cheesecake Squares

Here's a cookie just for cheesecake lovers. Like cheesecake, the crumb-topped squares are sumptuously creamy—but they're easier to make and more convenient to serve.

- ⅓ cup butter or margarine, softened
- ⅓ cup firmly packed brown sugar
- 1 cup all-purpose flour
- ½ cup finely chopped walnuts
- ¼ cup granulated sugar
- 1 large package (8 oz.) cream cheese, softened
- 1 egg
- ½ teaspoon vanilla
- 2 tablespoons milk
- 1 tablespoon lemon juice

In large bowl of an electric mixer, beat butter and brown sugar until creamy. With a fork, blend in flour until mixture resembles fine crumbs. Stir in walnuts. Reserve 1 cup crumb mixture for topping; then press remainder firmly and evenly over bottom of a greased 8-inch square baking pan. Bake in a 350° oven for 12 to 15 minutes or until lightly browned.

Meanwhile, in small bowl of mixer, beat granulated sugar and cream cheese until fluffy. Add egg, vanilla, milk, and lemon juice; beat until smooth. Pour cream cheese mixture over baked crust; sprinkle evenly with remaining crumb mixture.

Return to oven and bake for about 20 minutes or until top is lightly browned. Let cool in pan on a rack, then cut into 2-inch squares. Store, covered, in refrigerator. Makes 16.

Dream Bars

(Pictured on page 739)

Of all the cookies that have made a hit over the years, "dream bars" are certainly one of the leaders. Their rich, coconutty filling and buttery crust explain their enduring popularity. Our version of dream bars includes a sweet orange frosting; some cookie connoisseurs wouldn't dream of skipping it, while the purists among us generally prefer our dream bars plain.

- ⅓ cup butter or margarine, softened
- 1½ cups firmly packed brown sugar
- 1 cup plus 2 tablespoons all-purpose flour
- 2 eggs
- 1 teaspoon vanilla
- ½ teaspoon salt
- 1 teaspoon baking powder
- 1½ cups shredded coconut
- 1 cup chopped nuts
  Orange butter frosting (optional; recipe follows)

In large bowl of an electric mixer, beat butter and ½ cup of the sugar until creamy. With a fork, blend in 1 cup of the flour until mixture resembles fine crumbs. Press mixture firmly over bottom of a greased 9 by 13-inch baking pan, forming an even layer. Bake in a 375° oven for 10 minutes; let cool in pan on a rack.

Wash and dry mixer bowl. Place eggs in bowl and beat until light and lemon-colored; then gradually beat in remaining 1 cup sugar. Beat in vanilla, remaining 2 tablespoons flour, salt, and baking powder. Stir in coconut and nuts until thoroughly combined.

Pour coconut mixture over baked crust, spreading evenly. Return to oven and bake for 20 minutes or until topping is golden; then let cool in pan on a rack for 10 to 15 minutes. Meanwhile, prepare orange butter frosting, if desired. Cut partially cooled cookies into bars (about 1½ by 3 or 1½ by 2 inches), but do not remove from pan. Spread frosting over cookies and let cool completely in pan on rack. (Don't frost cookies *before* cutting them—if you do, frosting will crack when cookies are cut.) Store covered. Makes 2 to 3 dozen.

Orange butter frosting. In small bowl of an electric mixer, beat 4 tablespoons **butter** or margarine, softened, and 2 cups **powdered sugar** until creamy. Add 1 teaspoon *each* **vanilla** and grated **orange peel.** Beat in enough **orange juice** (about 2 tablespoons) to make a good spreading consistency.

Hand-molded Cookies

When you fashion cookie dough with your hands, you'll be rewarded with a variety of shapes: crescents, balls, pretzels, and more. Hand-molded cookies tend to be fancy, simply because there's so much you can do to the pliable doughs they're made from. They can be rolled in sugar or nuts before baking, filled with jam or jelly, flattened with fork tines in a crisscross pattern—the possibilities are almost endless.

Included in our collection of hand-molded cookies are recipes for special cookies—such as pirouettes and fortune cookies—that are shaped *after* baking, while they're still warm. These take a little extra skill, but once you've practiced on a few, you'll be surprised at how quickly you become proficient.

Hand-molded cookies are often time-consuming to shape, since each morsel of dough must be individually crafted. Most bakers consider them a labor of love, though, and enjoy the shaping process almost as much as the results.

Photo at left shows the variety of cookie shapes you can create with your hands. From top to bottom: Favorite Peanut Butter Cookies (page 752), Italian Fruit Cookies (page 761), Peanut Blossom Cookies (page 752), Pirouettes (page 762), Norwegian Kringle (page 757), Finnish Ribbon Cakes (page 759), Chocolate Chews (page 760), Almond Crescents (page 752), and Chocolate-dipped Hazelnut Bonbons (page 760).

Favorite Peanut Butter Cookies

(Pictured on page 750)

Among the best-known and best-loved of cookies are these traditional treats with crisscrossed tops.

  1 cup (½ lb.) butter or margarine, softened
  1 cup peanut butter
  1 cup firmly packed brown sugar
  1 cup granulated sugar
  2 eggs
  1 teaspoon vanilla
  3½ cups all-purpose flour
  1 teaspoon baking soda

In large bowl of an electric mixer, beat butter until creamy. Gradually beat in peanut butter, then brown sugar, then granulated sugar. Beat in eggs, then vanilla.

In another bowl, stir together flour and baking soda; gradually add to butter mixture, blending thoroughly. Roll dough into 1-inch balls and place 2 inches apart on greased baking sheets. Press balls down with a fork, making a crisscross pattern on top of each with fork tines.

Bake in a 375° oven for 10 to 12 minutes or until golden brown. Let cool on baking sheets for about a minute, then transfer to racks and let cool completely. Store airtight. Makes about 7 dozen.

Peanut Blossom Cookies

(Pictured on page 750)

Each of these thick, chewy peanut butter cookies has a chocolate candy kiss on top.

  ½ cup *each* solid vegetable shortening and peanut butter
  ½ cup *each* granulated sugar and firmly packed brown sugar
  1 egg
  1 teaspoon vanilla
  1⅓ cups all-purpose flour
  1 teaspoon baking soda
  ½ teaspoon salt
  ¼ cup granulated sugar
  2½ to 3 dozen chocolate candy kisses

In large bowl of an electric mixer, beat shortening, peanut butter, the ½ cup granulated sugar, and brown sugar until creamy; beat in egg and vanilla. In another bowl, stir together flour, baking soda, and salt; gradually add to shortening mixture, blending thoroughly.

Place the ¼ cup granulated sugar in a small bowl. Roll dough into 1-inch balls, then roll in sugar to coat. Place balls 2 inches apart on greased baking sheets.

Bake in a 350° oven for 10 minutes; meanwhile, unwrap chocolate kisses. Remove cookies from oven and quickly top each with a kiss, pressing down until cookie cracks around edges. Return to oven and bake for 3 to 5 more minutes or until cookies are lightly browned and firm to the touch. Transfer to racks and let cool completely. Store airtight. Makes 2½ to 3 dozen.

Almond Crescents

(Pictured on page 750)

A snowy mantle of powdered sugar cloaks these buttery, brandy-spiked nut cookies. Called *kourabiedes*, they're a Greek specialty—but they have close cousins in other cuisines, such as Mexican wedding cakes, Russian teacakes, and Viennese nut crescents.

  ½ cup ground almonds
  1 cup (½ lb.) unsalted butter or margarine, softened
  1 egg yolk
  2 tablespoons powdered sugar
  1 tablespoon brandy or ½ teaspoon vanilla
  2 cups all-purpose flour
  ½ teaspoon baking powder
    Whole cloves (optional)
  1½ to 2 cups powdered sugar

Spread almonds in a shallow pan and toast in a 350° oven for 6 to 8 minutes or until lightly browned. Let cool completely.

In large bowl of an electric mixer, beat butter until creamy. Add egg yolk and the 2 tablespoons powdered sugar, mixing well. Stir in brandy and almonds. In another bowl, stir together flour and baking powder. Gradually add to butter mixture, blending thoroughly.

Pinch off dough in 1-inch balls and roll each into a 3-inch rope. Place ropes about 2 inches apart on ungreased baking sheets; shape into crescents. Insert a whole clove in each crescent, if desired. Bake in a 325° oven for 30 minutes or until very lightly browned. Place baking sheets on racks and let cookies cool for 5 minutes.

Sift about half the 1½ to 2 cups powdered sugar over a sheet of wax paper. Transfer cookies to paper, placing them in a single layer. Sift remaining powdered sugar over cookies to cover. Let stand until cool. Store airtight; remove clove (if used) from each cookie before eating. Makes about 2½ dozen.

Caramel Almond Wafers

German pastry shops offer an impressive array of tempting treats, from fabulous tortes to cookies of every kind. These rich butter wafers come from the city of Bremen; they're crowned with a caramelized almond topping that sinks into the cookies as they bake.

½ cup (¼ lb.) butter or margarine, softened
1 cup sugar
1 teaspoon vanilla
1 egg
1⅔ cups all-purpose flour
2 teaspoons baking powder
   Sugar
⅔ cup whipping cream
2 teaspoons sugar
1 cup sliced almonds

In large bowl of an electric mixer, beat butter and the 1 cup sugar until creamy; add vanilla and egg and beat until smooth. In another bowl, stir together flour and baking powder; add to butter mixture, blending thoroughly. Wrap dough in plastic wrap and refrigerate for at least 2 hours or until next day.

Roll dough into 1-inch balls and place 2½ to 3 inches apart on greased baking sheets. Grease bottom of a glass, dip in sugar, and flatten each ball to a thickness of about ¼ inch.

In a 2-quart pan, bring cream and the 2 teaspoons sugar to a boil; continue to boil until reduced by half. Remove from heat and stir in almonds. Spread about 1 teaspoon of the almond mixture on top of each cookie.

Bake in a 325° oven for 12 to 15 minutes or until golden brown. Transfer cookies to racks and let cool. Store airtight. Makes about 4 dozen.

Chinese Almond Cookies

It's hard to imagine a Chinese meal without fortune cookies (page 762)—but these almond-crowned tidbits are actually a more authentic Chinese dessert. Even if you're not serving them with Chinese food you'll enjoy them as a rich, nutty snack or everyday dessert. If you'd like to vary the recipe, try topping the cookies with pine nuts (used in northern Chinese cooking) or peanuts instead of almonds—or make our sesame-seed variation (below).

1 cup (½ lb.) lard or solid vegetable shortening
½ cup granulated sugar
¼ cup firmly packed brown sugar
1 egg
1 teaspoon almond extract
2¼ cups all-purpose flour
⅛ teaspoon salt
1½ teaspoons baking powder
   About 5 dozen whole blanched almonds
1 egg yolk
2 tablespoons water

In large bowl of an electric mixer, beat lard with granulated sugar and brown sugar until creamy. Add whole egg and almond extract; beat until well blended. In another bowl, stir together flour, salt, and baking powder; add to creamed mixture, blending thoroughly.

To shape each cookie, roll about 1 tablespoon dough into a ball. Place balls 2 inches apart on ungreased baking sheets, then flatten each slightly to make a 2-inch round. Gently press an almond into center of each round. Place egg yolk and water in a small bowl; beat together lightly with a fork. Brush mixture over top of each cookie with a pastry brush.

Bake in a 350° oven for 10 to 12 minutes or until lightly browned. Transfer to racks and let cool. Store airtight. Makes about 5 dozen.

Chinese Sesame Cookies

Follow directions for **Chinese Almond Cookies,** but substitute about ¼ cup **sesame seeds** for almonds. Press each ball in the palm of your hand to make a 2-inch round. Brush egg mixture on one side of each round, then dip coated side in sesame seeds. Place cookies, seeded side up, on ungreased baking sheets. Bake as for **Chinese Almond Cookies.**

Thumbprint Cookies

(Pictured on facing page)

A sweet "jewel" of jelly sparkles in the center of each of these nutty morsels. It rests in a small indentation made by your thumb—or the tip of a spoon, if you prefer.

> 1 cup (½ lb.) butter or margarine, softened
> ½ cup firmly packed brown sugar
> 2 eggs
> ½ teaspoon vanilla
> 2½ cups all-purpose flour
> ¼ teaspoon salt
> 1½ cups finely chopped walnuts
> 3 to 4 tablespoons red currant jelly or raspberry jam

In large bowl of an electric mixer, beat butter and sugar until creamy. Separate eggs. Place whites in a small bowl, lightly beat, and set aside; then beat yolks and vanilla into butter mixture. In another bowl, stir together flour and salt. Gradually add to butter mixture, blending thoroughly.

To shape and fill cookies, follow steps 1 through 4 on facing page. Bake in a 375° oven for 12 to 15 minutes or until lightly browned. Let cool on baking sheets for about a minute, then transfer to racks and let cool completely. Store airtight. Makes about 3½ dozen.

Almond Pillows

These crisp brown sugar cookies, each topped with a whole almond, are shaped like little pillows. They're a good choice if you want to bake in quantity, since shaping is quick and easy.

> ½ cup (¼ lb.) butter or margarine, softened
> ½ cup *each* granulated sugar and firmly packed brown sugar
> 1 egg
> 1 teaspoon vanilla
> 2 cups all-purpose flour
> ½ teaspoon salt
> 1 teaspoon baking powder
> ¾ teaspoon ground cardamom
> 1 teaspoon ground cinnamon
> 5 dozen whole blanched almonds

In large bowl of an electric mixer, beat butter, granulated sugar, and brown sugar until creamy. Add egg and vanilla and beat until combined.

In another bowl, stir together flour, salt, baking powder, cardamom, and cinnamon; gradually add to butter mixture, blending thoroughly. Turn mixture out onto a lightly floured board and divide into 4 equal portions.

Roll each portion into a 15-inch rope. Cut each rope into 1-inch pieces and gently press an almond into each piece. Place cookies 2 inches apart on ungreased baking sheets. Bake in a 350° oven for 15 minutes or until lightly browned. Let cool on baking sheets for about a minute, then transfer to racks and let cool completely. Store airtight. Makes 5 dozen.

Pine Nut Crescents

These generously proportioned crescents, studded with pine nuts, are typical of cookies sold in the *pâtisseries* of Provence, France. A honey glaze subtly complements the faintly resinous flavor of the nuts; a touch of orange flower water adds a special, sweet fragrance. (Orange flower water is a concentrated, nonalcoholic flavoring that's available at most liquor stores.)

> 1 cup (½ lb.) butter or margarine, softened
> ⅔ cup firmly packed brown sugar
> 3 egg yolks
> 1 teaspoon *each* orange flower water and grated orange peel
> ½ teaspoon vanilla
> 2¾ cups all-purpose flour
> About ½ cup pine nuts
> 3 tablespoons honey

In large bowl of an electric mixer, beat butter and sugar until creamy. Beat in egg yolks, one at a time; beat in orange flower water, orange peel, and vanilla. Add flour and stir until well blended.

To make each cookie, roll about 1 tablespoon dough between lightly floured hands into a 2½-inch rope. Place ropes about 2 inches apart on greased baking sheets; shape into crescents. Scatter pine nuts over cookies and press in firmly. Heat honey over low heat until it liquefies completely, then brush liberally over cookies.

Bake in a 325° oven for 15 to 20 minutes or until golden. Transfer to racks and let cool. Store airtight. Makes about 3½ dozen.

Thumbprint Cookies *(Recipe on facing page)*

1 With your hands, roll dough into balls about 1 inch in diameter.

2 Dip each ball in egg whites, then roll in finely chopped walnuts to coat. Place on greased baking sheets, spacing 1 inch apart.

3 With your thumb or the tip of a spoon, make an indentation in the center of each ball.

4 Neatly fill each indentation with about ¼ teaspoon red currant jelly or raspberry jam.

Cookie Sculpture

Making these whimsical cookies is child's play—you just press, pinch, mold, cut, or roll dough into whatever shapes you like. It's an engrossing family project for a rainy day, or a good party activity for kids—and best of all, it results in an assortment of edible sculptures for enjoying at home or giving away. To package the cookies as gifts, wrap in clear or colored cellophane and tape shut, or heat-seal in plastic wrap as directed on page 5.

Honey-Lemon Sculpture Cookies

5½ cups all-purpose flour
3 teaspoons baking soda
1¾ cups sugar
¼ teaspoon salt
¼ cup honey
2 teaspoons vanilla
3 teaspoons grated lemon or orange peel
1 cup (½ lb.) butter or margarine, melted
½ cup boiling water
1 egg, lightly beaten

In a large bowl, combine flour and baking soda; set aside. In another large bowl, combine sugar, salt, honey, vanilla, and lemon peel; add butter and water and beat until sugar is dissolved. Gradually stir in flour mixture to form a stiff dough.

Use dough immediately, or cover tightly with plastic wrap and refrigerate for up to 2 days. For longer storage, wrap in plastic wrap and freeze. Bring dough to room temperature before shaping (let frozen dough thaw in its wrapping).

To shape dough, use any of the following techniques—or devise your own methods.

Cookie-cutter composites. On a floured board, roll out dough to a thickness of ⅛ to ¼ inch. Cut with floured cookie cutters. Arrange cutouts on greased baking sheets, combining shapes and overlapping edges to build decorative images. Be sure completed cookies are spaced at least 1 inch apart.

Cutouts with appliqués. Roll dough out on a floured board to a thickness of ⅛ to ¼ inch (for large cookies, roll directly on a greased unrimmed baking sheet). Cut out shapes with floured cutters—or design paper patterns, place them on dough, and cut around edges with a sharp knife. Space cookies at least 1 inch apart on a greased baking sheet.

To make appliqués, shape small pieces of dough into dabs, dots, narrow ropes, or whatever other forms you like, and press these lightly onto the cookie base. For best results, don't build up cookies thicker than ¾ inch.

Rolled ropes. Roll small pieces of dough on a floured board or between your hands to form even ropes ¼ to ½ inch thick. Make these into letters or numbers, or appliqué onto other dough forms to make arms or legs. Place cookies at least 1 inch apart on greased baking sheets.

Freeform sculptures. Pinch or press dough to make shapes, or roll it out and cut it freehand with a sharp knife. Place cookies at least 1 inch apart on greased baking sheets.

To bake cookies, brush with beaten egg. Bake in a 300° oven for 20 to 30 minutes or until golden at edges. Let cool on baking sheets for at least 10 minutes; then transfer to racks and let cool completely.

Wrap cookies airtight and store at room temperature for up to 2 weeks, or freeze for longer storage. Makes 1½ to 2 dozen large cookies.

Snickerdoodles

Delicately crisp outside, soft and cakelike inside, these old-fashioned cookies with their cinnamon-sugar coating make dainty nibbling with a cup of tea.

1 cup (½ lb.) butter or margarine, softened
1⅓ cups sugar
2 eggs
1 teaspoon vanilla
3 cups all-purpose flour
1 teaspoon *each* baking soda and cream of tartar
¼ teaspoon salt
2 teaspoons ground cinnamon
3 tablespoons sugar

In large bowl of an electric mixer, beat butter and the 1⅓ cups sugar until creamy. Beat in eggs and vanilla. In another bowl, stir together flour, baking soda, cream of tartar, and salt; gradually add to butter mixture, blending thoroughly.

In a small bowl, combine cinnamon and the 3 tablespoons sugar. Roll dough into 1-inch balls, then roll in cinnamon-sugar mixture to coat. Place at least 2 inches apart on greased baking sheets. Bake in a 375° oven for about 12 minutes or until lightly browned. Let cool on baking sheets for about a minute, then transfer to racks and let cool completely. Store airtight. Makes about 4½ dozen.

Norwegian Kringle

(Pictured on page 750)

Hard-cooked egg yolks lend extra richness to the dough for *kringle*, Norway's pretzel-shaped butter cookies.

1 cup (½ lb.) butter, softened
1 cup sugar
1 egg
2 hard-cooked egg yolks, finely mashed
1 teaspoon vanilla
3 cups all-purpose flour
¼ teaspoon salt
1 egg white, lightly beaten
    Granulated sugar or coarsely crushed sugar cubes

In large bowl of an electric mixer, beat butter and the 1 cup sugar until creamy; beat in egg, egg yolks, and vanilla until well combined. In another bowl, stir together flour and salt; gradually add to butter mixture, blending thoroughly. Wrap dough in plastic wrap and refrigerate for at least 1 hour or until next day.

Pinch off 1-inch balls of dough and roll each into a 6-inch-long strand. Form each strand into a pretzel shape on greased baking sheets, spacing pretzels about an inch apart. Using a pastry brush, brush cookies with egg white; then sprinkle with sugar.

Bake in a 350° oven for 12 to 15 minutes or until pale golden brown. Transfer to racks and let cool completely. Store airtight. Makes about 4 dozen.

Orange Coconut Crisps

The coconut is native to the tropics, where it's used in hundreds of different ways. Cooks in cooler climates have developed lots of delectable coconut recipes, too—such as these crisp cookies. They combine coconut with a subtle touch of orange for extra-tempting flavor.

1 cup (½ lb.) butter or margarine, softened
1 cup sugar
1 egg
1 teaspoon *each* grated orange peel and vanilla
1½ cups all-purpose flour
1 cup cornstarch
1 teaspoon baking powder
¼ teaspoon salt
1⅓ cups flaked or shredded coconut

In large bowl of an electric mixer, beat butter and sugar until creamy; beat in egg, orange peel, and vanilla. In another bowl, stir together flour, cornstarch, baking powder, and salt. Gradually add to butter mixture, blending thoroughly. Add coconut and mix until well combined. Cover dough tightly with plastic wrap and refrigerate for about 2 hours.

Roll dough into 1 to 1¼-inch balls and arrange about 2 inches apart on greased baking sheets. With tines of a fork, flatten each ball to a thickness of about ¼ inch. Bake in a 375° oven for 8 to 10 minutes or until lightly browned. Let cool for about a minute on baking sheets, then transfer to racks and let cool completely. Store airtight. Makes about 4 dozen.

Koulourakia *(Recipe on facing page)*

1 Pinch off balls of dough about 1 inch in diameter, then roll each into a 7-inch strand.

2 Fold strand in half lengthwise. With one end in each hand, twist ends of folded strand in opposite directions.

3 Brush twists lightly with egg yolk mixture. This helps sesame seeds stick and gives finished cookies a rich golden color.

4 Sprinkle cookies with sesame seeds before baking; you'll need 2 to 3 tablespoons.

Koulourakia

(Pictured on facing page)

At Eastertime in Greece, these sesame-topped cookies are enjoyed by the dozen. Like shortbread, they're crunchy, buttery, and not too sweet.

  ½ **cup (¼ lb.) butter or margarine, softened**
  ½ **cup sugar**
  3 **egg yolks**
  ¼ **cup half-and-half (light cream)**
  2¼ **cups all-purpose flour**
  1 **teaspoon baking powder**
  ¼ **teaspoon salt**
  2 **to 3 tablespoons sesame seeds**

In large bowl of an electric mixer, beat butter and sugar until creamy. Beat in 2 of the egg yolks, one at a time. Mix in 3 tablespoons of the half-and-half. In another bowl, stir together flour, baking powder, and salt; gradually add to butter mixture, blending thoroughly.

To shape cookies, pinch off 1-inch balls of dough; roll each into a 7-inch strand. Bring ends together and twist (see photo 2 on facing page) or form into a pretzel shape. Place slightly apart on greased baking sheets. Beat remaining egg yolk with remaining 1 tablespoon half-and-half; brush lightly over cookies and sprinkle with sesame seeds. Bake in a 350° oven for about 15 minutes or until golden. Transfer to racks and let cool completely. Store airtight. Makes about 2½ dozen.

White Chocolate Chip Cookies

This variation on a favorite American cookie uses white chocolate instead of dark. You'll find white chocolate in candy stores and gourmet shops.

  1 **cup (½ lb.) butter or margarine, softened**
  1½ **cups sugar**
  2 **teaspoons baking soda**
  1 **egg**
  1 **cup all-purpose flour**
  2 **cups quick-cooking rolled oats**
  6 **ounces (1¼ cups) white chocolate, coarsely chopped**

In large bowl of an electric mixer, beat butter, sugar, and baking soda until creamy; beat in egg. Gradually add flour and oats, blending thoroughly. Stir in chocolate.

Roll dough into ¾-inch balls and place 2 inches apart on ungreased baking sheets. Bake in a 350° oven for 10 to 12 minutes or until light golden. Let cool on baking sheets until firm to the touch, then transfer to racks and let cool completely. Store airtight for up to 3 days. Makes about 5 dozen.

Finnish Ribbon Cakes

(Pictured on page 750)

For holiday (or everyday) entertaining, offer a platter of assorted Scandinavian cookies: Swedish Spritz (page 775), Norwegian Kringle (page 757), and these fancy Finnish morsels.

  1 **cup (½ lb.) butter or margarine, softened**
  ½ **cup sugar**
  1 **egg yolk**
  1 **teaspoon vanilla**
  ½ **teaspoon grated lemon peel**
  2½ **cups all-purpose flour**
  ¼ **teaspoon salt**
     About 6 tablespoons raspberry or apricot jam
  ½ **cup powdered sugar mixed with 1 tablespoon water**

In large bowl of an electric mixer, beat butter and sugar until creamy; beat in egg yolk, vanilla, and lemon peel. In another bowl, stir together flour and salt. Gradually add to butter mixture, blending thoroughly.

Shape dough into ropes about ¾ inch in diameter and as long as your baking sheets; place them about 2 inches apart on ungreased baking sheets. With the side of your little finger, press a long groove down the center of each rope (don't press all the way down to baking sheets). Bake cookies in a 375° oven for 10 minutes.

Remove cookies from oven and spoon jam into the grooves. Return to oven for 5 to 10 minutes or until cookies are firm to touch and light golden brown. While cookies are hot, drizzle them with powdered sugar mixture (or spread mixture along sides of cookies). Then cut at a 45° angle into 1-inch lengths. Let cool briefly on baking sheets; transfer to racks and let cool completely. Store airtight. Makes about 4 dozen.

Old-fashioned Molasses Chews

How to glorify a glass of milk? Enjoy it with a plateful of these big, spicy molasses cookies. Their tops are sugary and crinkled, their interiors moist and chewy.

- ¾ cup salad oil
- ¼ cup dark molasses
- 1¼ cups sugar
- 2 eggs
- 2¾ cups all-purpose flour
- 1½ teaspoons baking soda
- 1 teaspoon *each* ground cinnamon and ginger
- ¼ teaspoon ground cloves

In a large bowl, stir together oil, molasses, and 1 cup of the sugar. Add eggs and beat until smooth. In another bowl, stir together flour, baking soda, cinnamon, ginger, and cloves; gradually add to molasses mixture, beating until well combined. Cover tightly with plastic wrap and refrigerate for at least 1 hour or until next day.

Place remaining ¼ cup sugar in a small bowl. Roll dough into 1½-inch balls, then roll in sugar to coat. Place 3 inches apart on greased baking sheets. Bake in a 350° oven for 10 to 12 minutes or until lightly browned. Transfer to racks and let cool completely. Store airtight. Makes about 2½ dozen.

Chocolate Chews
(Pictured on page 750)

Satisfying a chocolate lover is never easy, but these dark, sugary cookies can help. Their crinkly tops and chewy texture will remind you of Old-fashioned Molasses Chews (above).

- 1 package (6 oz.) semisweet chocolate chips
- ½ cup (¼ lb.) butter or margarine, softened
- 1¼ cups sugar
- 2 eggs
- 2 cups all-purpose flour
- ¼ teaspoon salt
- ½ teaspoon *each* baking powder and baking soda

In top of a double boiler over simmering water or in a small pan over lowest possible heat, stir chocolate chips just until melted; set aside. In large bowl of an electric mixer, beat butter and 1 cup of the sugar until creamy; beat in eggs and melted chocolate. In another bowl, stir together flour, salt, baking powder, and baking soda; gradually add to butter mixture, blending thoroughly.

Place remaining ¼ cup sugar in a small bowl. Roll dough into 1-inch balls and roll in sugar to coat; place at least 2 inches apart on greased baking sheets. Bake in a 350° oven for 12 to 14 minutes or until tops appear dry. Let cool on baking sheets for about a minute, then transfer to racks and let cool completely. Store airtight. Makes about 3½ dozen.

Chocolate-dipped Hazelnut Bonbons
(Pictured on page 750)

Add variety to a cookie tray with these chewy, no-bake bonbons made from toasted hazelnuts. If you prefer, you can use whole blanched almonds in place of hazelnuts; you'll need 3 cups.

- 1 pound (3½ cups) hazelnuts (filberts), whole or in large pieces
- 2 cups powdered sugar
- 5 to 6 tablespoons egg whites (whites of about 3 large eggs)
- About 6 ounces semisweet chocolate chips

Spread hazelnuts in a 10 by 15-inch rimmed baking pan. Bake in a 350° oven for 10 to 15 minutes or until pale golden beneath skins, shaking pan occasionally. (If using almonds, toast for 8 to 10 minutes.) Pour nuts into a dishcloth and fold cloth to enclose; rub briskly to remove as much of skins as possible (see photo on page 795; omit this step if using almonds). Lift nuts from cloth and let cool.

Coarsely chop nuts. In a food processor or blender, finely grind nuts, about ⅓ at a time, until mealy.

Return all nuts to food processor and add sugar and 5 tablespoons egg whites. Process until a paste forms, adding more egg whites if needed. (Or mix ground nuts with egg whites and sugar with a heavy-duty mixer on low speed; or knead by hand until mixture sticks together.) If mixture is too soft to shape, wrap in plastic wrap and refrigerate for about 1 hour.

Roll nut paste into 1-inch balls; set 1 inch apart on wax-paper-lined rimmed baking pans, pressing balls down to flatten bottoms slightly.

In top of a double boiler over simmering water or in a small pan over lowest possible heat, stir chocolate chips just until melted. Dip each ball (by hand) into chocolate to cover top half; return to paper-lined pan, chocolate side up. Refrigerate, uncovered, until chocolate is set (about 30 minutes). Serve at once, or cover and refrigerate for up to 1 week; let stand at room temperature for about 15 minutes before serving. Makes 3 to 4 dozen.

Italian Nut Cookies

An Italian inclination is to dunk a cookie into wine or coffee before eating it, so it comes as no surprise that Italian cookies are often firm in texture. These rusk-type cookies are studded with nuts and flavored with anise; you bake them twice, to a toasty crunchiness.

> 2 cups sugar
> 1 cup (½ lb.) butter or margarine, melted
> ¼ cup anise seeds
> ¼ cup anisette or other anise-flavored liqueur
> 3 tablespoons whiskey, or 2 teaspoons vanilla and 2 tablespoons water
> 6 eggs
> 5½ cups all-purpose flour
> 3 teaspoons baking powder
> 2 cups coarsely chopped almonds or walnuts

In a large bowl, stir together sugar, butter, anise seeds, anisette, and whiskey. Beat in eggs. In another bowl, stir together flour and baking powder; gradually add to sugar mixture, blending thoroughly. Mix in almonds. Cover tightly with plastic wrap and refrigerate for 2 to 3 hours.

Directly on greased baking sheets, shape dough with your hands to form flat loaves about ½ inch thick, 2 inches wide, and as long as baking sheets. Place loaves parallel and 4 inches apart. Bake in a 375° oven for 20 minutes or until lightly browned.

Remove loaves from oven and let cool on baking sheets until you can touch them; then cut diagonally into ½ to ¾-inch-thick slices. Place slices close together, cut sides down, on baking sheets; bake in 375° oven for 15 more minutes or until lightly toasted. Transfer to racks to cool. Store airtight. Makes about 9 dozen.

Italian Fruit Cookies

(Pictured on page 750)

Follow directions for **Italian Nut Cookies,** but in place of almonds use 1½ cups diced **mixed candied fruit** and ½ cup **pine nuts** or slivered almonds. Second baking will take 12 to 15 minutes.

German Oatmeal Lace Cookies

Fragile, snowflake prettiness isn't usually expected of oatmeal cookies, but these lacy German treats have just that. When warm, they're flexible enough to be curved, rolled, folded, or bent into various shapes—or you can just leave them flat. The cooled cookies are crisp and brittle, almost like candy.

> ⅔ cup quick-cooking rolled oats
> ¼ cup all-purpose flour
> ¼ teaspoon *each* salt, ground cloves, and ground ginger
> ½ cup sugar
> ½ cup (¼ lb.) butter or margarine
> 2 tablespoons whipping cream

In a small pan, combine all ingredients. Cook over medium heat, stirring, until mixture begins to bubble. Remove from heat and stir well. Drop dough, 1 level teaspoonful at a time, onto lightly greased baking sheets (they must be flat, not warped), allowing 3 or 4 cookies per sheet.

Bake in a 375° oven for 5 to 7 minutes or until evenly browned (bake only one sheet at a time if you wish to shape cookies; they cool quickly). Place baking sheet on a rack and let cookies cool until firm enough to lift from pan with a spatula but still soft enough to shape—less than a minute. (For flat cookies, leave cookies on baking sheets until firm, then transfer to racks and let cool completely.)

To shape cookies, wrap them around metal pastry tubes or cones that are at least ½ inch in diameter (or make your own forms from several thicknesses of foil). Let cool on racks, then remove forms. Or drape cookies over horizontally suspended wooden spoon handles or a broomstick and let stand until completely cool. If cookies become too stiff to shape, you can restore their flexibility by returning them briefly to the oven. Store airtight. Makes 3 to 4 dozen.

Fortune Cookies

(Pictured on facing page)

Fortune cookies: A traditional sweet made from an ancient Chinese recipe? Hardly. Fortune cookies aren't really Chinese at all—they're the innovation of an enterprising Los Angeles baker in the 1920s. But they taste good, and they're always popular with Chinese food or as snacks.

Making fortune cookies at home is easy once you get the hang of it. You bake the batter in flat circles, and then shape each cookie while it's hot, enclosing a fortune inside. Wear trim-fitting cotton gloves to protect your hands, and work quickly— each cookie must be formed within 15 seconds. After that, it begins to harden.

For the fortunes, consult books of poetry or proverbs, or rely on your own wit. Original messages are a good way to provide entertainment, and fate has a curious way of matching people to appropriate fortunes.

>   1 cup all-purpose flour
>   2 tablespoons cornstarch
>   ½ cup sugar
>   ½ teaspoon salt
>   ½ cup salad oil
>   ½ cup egg whites (whites of about
>   4 large eggs)
>   1 tablespoon water
>   2 teaspoons vanilla

Type or print fortunes, allowing a ½ by 3-inch area of paper for each. Then cut paper into strips, separating individual fortunes; place near oven. Also have ready a saucepan or straight-sided bowl for shaping and a muffin pan for cooling the cookies. In a bowl, stir together flour, cornstarch, sugar, and salt. Add oil and egg whites and beat until smooth; beat in water and vanilla.

Drop batter by level tablespoonfuls on a well-greased baking sheet and spread out evenly with the back of a spoon into 4-inch circles. (Bake only 1 or 2 cookies per sheet at first, then increase to 4 per sheet as your shaping speed improves.) Bake in a 300° oven for about 14 minutes or until light golden brown; if underbaked, cookies will tear during shaping.

With a wide spatula, remove one cookie at a time from oven. Working quickly, follow steps 1 through 4 on facing page. If cookie hardens too fast, you can restore its flexibility by returning it to the oven for about a minute. Repeat for remaining batter, using a cold, well-greased baking sheet for each batch. Store airtight. Makes about 2½ dozen.

Giant Fortune Cookies

Type or print fortunes, allowing a 1 by 3-inch area of paper for each. Cut paper into strips, separating individual fortunes. Prepare batter as directed for **Fortune Cookies**.

Bake 1 cookie at a time: drop a level 1/3 cup of batter onto a greased baking sheet and spread evenly into a 10-inch circle. Bake as directed. Immediately remove cookie from baking sheet and shape as for **Fortune Cookies** (see steps 1 through 4 at right), but crease cookie by hand and hold it for a minute or two to maintain its shape as it cools (giant cookies are too big to crease over a pan edge or cool in a muffin pan). Repeat until all batter is used. Makes 6.

Pirouettes

(Pictured on page 750)

These delicate, lemon-scented cookies are rolled into graceful scrolls while still warm. They make an elegant addition to a platter of teatime fancies; you might also try serving them as a crisp and pretty accompaniment to chocolate mousse or fruit sorbet.

>   6 tablespoons butter or margarine, softened
>   1 cup powdered sugar
>   ⅔ cup all-purpose flour
>   ½ teaspoon grated lemon peel
>   1 teaspoon vanilla
>   4 egg whites

In small bowl of an electric mixer, beat butter and sugar until creamy. Gradually add flour and lemon peel and beat until well combined; then add vanilla and egg whites and beat until batter is smooth.

Bake cookies 4 at a time. First, drop four 1½-teaspoon portions well apart on a well-greased baking sheet; then spread each thinly with a spatula or knife to make an oblong about 3 by 4 inches. Bake in a 425° oven for 3 minutes or until edges begin to brown.

Remove from oven and quickly roll each cookie lengthwise around a wooden spoon handle or chopstick to form a scroll. (If your fingers are sensitive to heat, wear trim-fitting cotton gloves to protect them.) Slide cookie off spoon handle and let cool on a rack. Repeat baking and rolling until all batter is used. Store airtight. Makes about 3 dozen.

Fortune Cookies *(Recipe on facing page)*

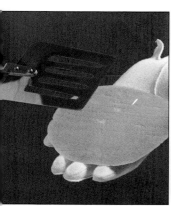

1 Reach into oven with a wide spatula, remove one cookie, and flip it over into gloved hand.

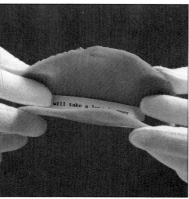

2 Hold prepared fortune in center of cookie while you fold it in half; work quickly.

3 Grasp ends of cookie and draw gently down over the edge of a pan or bowl to crease.

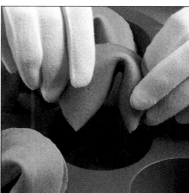

4 To ensure that cookies hold their shape as they finish cooling, place them, ends down, in muffin pans.

Cookies & Ice Cream

Cookies and ice cream go well together, offering appealing contrasts in flavor and texture. You can always enjoy this compatible combination simply by serving a few crisp wafers alongside a dish of ice cream; but when you're in the mood for something more elaborate, try one of the following presentations.

Our first cookies-and-cream specialty is a chocolate-covered ice cream sandwich made with chewy homemade oatmeal cookies and your favorite ice cream. The second is a crisp, lacy cookie "basket" that holds ice cream and your choice of fresh fruit for a special summer dessert. And the third is a homemade ice cream cone, made from an almond-flavored cookie batter that bakes in a waffle iron. True devotees of cookies and ice cream will want to try all three.

Ice Cream Sandwiches

    ¾ cup solid vegetable shortening
    1 cup firmly packed brown sugar
    ½ cup granulated sugar
    1 egg
    ¼ cup water
    1 teaspoon vanilla
    1 cup all-purpose flour
    1 teaspoon salt
    ½ teaspoon baking soda
    3 cups rolled oats
    1 cup chopped nuts
    ½ gallon brick-packed ice cream (vanilla, coffee, peppermint, or other)
    3 packages (6 oz. each) plain or mint-flavored semisweet chocolate chips
    5 tablespoons solid vegetable shortening

In large bowl of an electric mixer, beat together the ¾ cup shortening, brown sugar, and granu-lated sugar until creamy. Beat in egg, water, and vanilla until well combined. In another bowl, stir together flour, salt, and baking soda; gradually add to sugar mixture, blending thoroughly. Stir in oats and nuts.

Divide batter between 2 greased 10 by 15-inch rimmed baking pans. Spread batter evenly over bottom of one pan; bake in a 350° oven for 12 minutes or until surface is just dry (don't overbake, or cookies won't be chewy). While first pan bakes, spread batter evenly over bottom of second pan.

Remove first pan from oven. Using a sharp knife and a ruler, immediately cut into 16 rectangles, each 2½ by 3¾ inches. Remove cookies from pan while warm; let cool completely on racks. Bake the second pan while cutting cookies from the first; cut into 16 more rectangles, transfer to racks, and let cool completely before assembling sandwiches.

To assemble sandwiches: Cut 8 crosswise slices, each ½ to ¾ inch thick, from brick of ice cream; cut each slice in half. Sandwich each ice cream slice between 2 cookies. Place on a baking sheet and freeze, uncovered, until firm (about 4 hours).

To coat sandwiches: Place chocolate chips in top of a double boiler with the 5 tablespoons shortening. Place over simmering water; stir until melted and smooth (temperature should be 100°F to 110°F). If overheated, chocolate becomes too thick; to thin it, remove from heat and stir a few times until it cools. To reheat, place over simmering water and stir until melted and smooth again.

Coat sandwiches a few at a time. Take from freezer; trim off any uneven cookie edges, if desired. With a new paintbrush or a soft pastry brush, coat ice cream edges with chocolate, then place sandwiches on a baking sheet and coat tops. Freeze, uncovered, until firm (about 45 minutes).

Reheat chocolate. Turn sandwiches over and coat remaining side. Freeze again, uncovered, until firm (about 45 minutes). Wrap each sandwich in foil and store in freezer. Makes 16.

Cookie Baskets

- 4 tablespoons butter or margarine
- ¼ cup *each* firmly packed brown sugar and light corn syrup
- 3½ tablespoons all-purpose flour
- ½ cup finely chopped nuts
- 1 teaspoon vanilla
  Vanilla or nut ice cream
- 1½ to 2 cups fresh fruit, cut into bite-size pieces if necessary (optional)

In a 1 to 2-quart pan, melt butter over low heat. Add sugar and corn syrup. Increase heat to high; bring mixture to a boil, stirring constantly. Remove from heat, add flour and nuts, and stir until blended. Stir in vanilla.

Grease and flour-dust 2 baking sheets (they must be flat, not warped). For each cookie, use a 2 to 3-tablespoon portion of batter; drop portions about 8 inches apart on sheets. (Depending on baking sheet size and cookie size, you'll only be able to bake 1 or 2 cookies on each sheet.) If the batter has cooled and does not flow easily, evenly press or spread it out to a 3 to 4-inch circle.

Bake in a 325° oven for about 12 minutes or until a rich golden brown all over. (You can bake 2 sheets of cookies at a time, staggering sheets in oven and switching their positions halfway through baking to ensure even browning.) Place baking sheets on racks and let cool until cookie edges are just firm enough to lift (about 1 minute). Cookie should be hot, flexible, and somewhat stretchy, but cooled enough to be moved without pulling apart.

Loosen edges with a wide spatula, then slide spatula under entire cookie to remove. Turn cookie over and drape over an inverted glass that measures about 2 inches across the bottom. With your hand, gently cup cookie around the glass; make bottom flat and flare out cookie at sides.

If cookies become too firm to shape, return to oven for a few minutes or until pliable.

Let shaped cookies cool until firm (about 2 minutes). Gently remove from glasses. Repeat, using remaining batter and greasing and reflouring baking sheets each time.

Use baskets at once. Or store airtight in rigid containers at room temperature for up to 1 week; or freeze for longer storage. To serve, place a small scoop of ice cream in each basket and top with fruit, if desired. Break off pieces of cookie to eat along with ice cream and fruit. Makes 4 to 6.

Cookie Cones

- 3 eggs
- ⅔ cup sugar
- ⅔ cup butter or margarine, melted
- 2 teaspoons vanilla
- 1 teaspoon almond extract
- 1 cup all-purpose flour

In a medium-size bowl, beat together eggs, sugar, butter, vanilla, and almond extract. Add flour and stir until smoothly blended. Place flat griddle plates on an electric waffle iron and preheat to medium-hot.

Cone forms should be about 7 inches long, with a 2½-inch top opening. Use purchased metal cream horn forms or purchased pointed sugar cones wrapped with foil; or make your own forms out of lightweight cardboard. You'll need only 1 or 2 forms.

For each 5-inch cone (maximum size for most rectangular griddles), use 1½ tablespoons of batter; for a 7 to 8-inch cone, use 3 to 4 tablespoons. Pour batter onto center of hot griddle (lightly grease griddle for first few cookies, if necessary); close tightly to flatten. Let bake until golden brown (1½ to 2 minutes).

Quickly lift off cookie with a fork or spatula and place on a flat surface. Immediately wrap cookie around cone form, holding it firmly at tip to make a sharp point. (If your fingers are sensitive to heat, wear trim-fitting cotton gloves.) Place cookie on a rack, seam side down, and let cool until firm (about 2 minutes). Remove cone form to use again.

If made ahead, carefully stack and store airtight in rigid containers for up to 1 week; freeze for longer storage. Makes about 1½ dozen small cones, about 9 large cones.

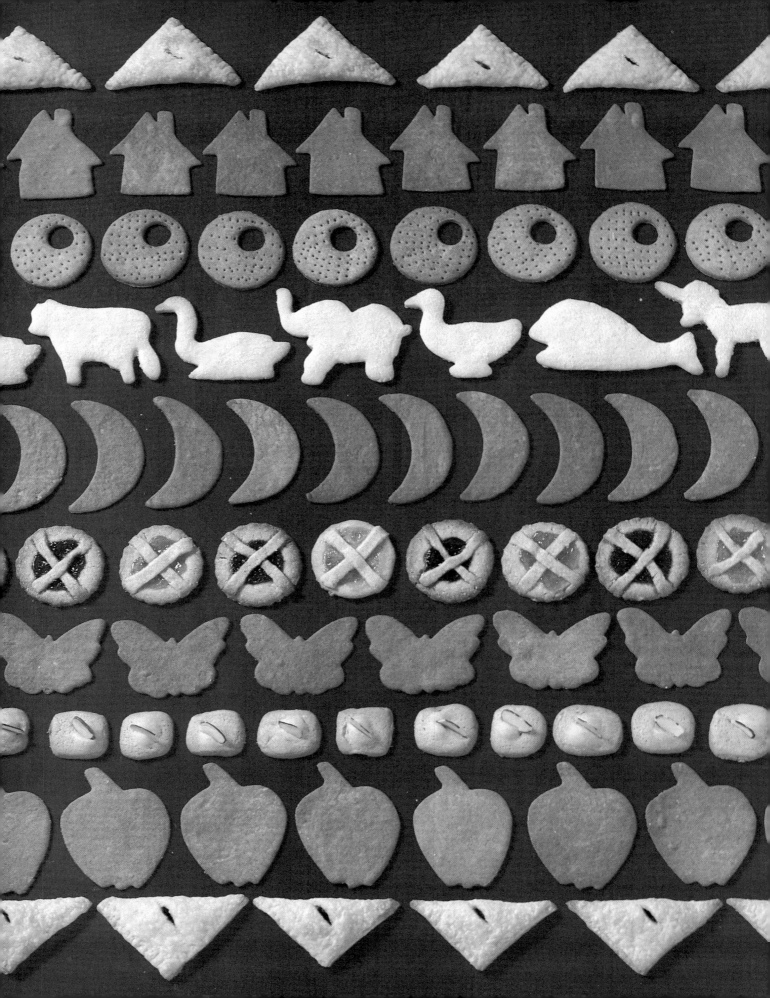

Cut-out & Specialty Cookies

These cookies get their distinct, well-defined shapes from special tools. Cut-out cookies, as most bakers know, are made by rolling out the dough with a rolling pin, then cutting it into plain or fancy shapes with cookie cutters. You can also use a knife as a cutting tool; or use a pastry wheel to obtain a pretty, fluted edge (see Crisp-fried Knots, page 770). Once the cookies are cut, they may be filled in various ways to produce turnovers, horns, and other fancy creations.

Another type of cookie shaped with special equipment is the pressed cookie, which is made by forcing a soft dough through a cookie press or pastry bag to yield such treats as Spritz (page 775) and Ladyfingers (page 776). We also include a half-dozen recipes for cookie-iron cookies, which get their patterned surfaces from gadgets, resembling waffle irons; for examples, see pages 778 to 781.

Photo at left *presents a procession of cut-out cookies on parade. From top to bottom: Flaky Fruit Turnovers (page 776); Swedish Ginger Thins (page 769); Finnish Rye Cookies (page 768); Sugar Cookies (page 770); Swedish Ginger Thins; Viennese Jam Rounds (page 778); Swedish Ginger Thins; Almond Ravioli Cookies (page 777); Swedish Ginger Thins; and Flaky Fruit Turnovers.*

Cut-out Cookies

For these cookies, you'll need a rolling pin and a flat surface. How the dough is cut varies from recipe to recipe; while most use cookie cutters, a few call for knives or pastry wheels. Our collection of cut-out cookies includes a variety of types—some plain, some sugared or frosted, and one that's colorfully painted with water-color brushes and food color "paints."

Anise Cookies

The secret of these cookies' flavor is anise sugar: plain granulated sugar that has been mixed with anise seeds, then allowed to stand for a day. When you make the cookies, you can add the seeds to the dough along with the sugar, or sift them out first for a subtler flavor.

    ¾ cup sugar
    2 teaspoons anise seeds
    1 cup (½ lb.) butter or margarine, softened
    1 egg
    2 tablespoons brandy or 1 tablespoon *each* lemon juice and water
    3 cups all-purpose flour
    1 teaspoon baking powder
    ½ teaspoon salt
    ½ teaspoon ground cinnamon

Combine sugar and anise seeds; cover tightly and let stand for about 24 hours. Sift out and discard seeds, if desired.

In large bowl of an electric mixer, beat butter and ½ cup of the anise sugar until creamy. Beat in egg and brandy. In another bowl, stir together flour, baking powder, salt, and cinnamon; gradually add to butter mixture, blending thoroughly. Gather dough into a ball, wrap tightly in plastic wrap, and refrigerate until firm (about 1 hour) or for up to 3 days.

Roll out dough on a lightly floured board to a thickness of ⅛ inch. Cut out with cookie cutters (about 2½ inches in diameter) and place 1 inch apart on lightly greased baking sheets. Sift and discard seeds from remaining ¼ cup anise sugar (if you haven't already done so) and sprinkle sugar evenly over cookies.

Bake in a 350° oven for about 12 minutes or until golden brown. Transfer to racks and let cool. Store airtight. Makes about 5 dozen.

Nutmeg Crisps

Made from a buttermilk dough and flavored with ground nutmeg, these simple cookies go well with tea or coffee. For extra-fresh nutmeg flavor, try buying whole nutmeg and grating it yourself.

    1   cup (½ lb.) butter or margarine, softened
    1   cup sugar
    1   egg
    3½   cups all-purpose flour
    ⅛   teaspoon salt
    1   teaspoon *each* ground nutmeg and baking soda
    ½   cup buttermilk

In large bowl of an electric mixer, beat butter and sugar until creamy; beat in egg until well combined. In another bowl, stir together flour, salt, nutmeg, and baking soda; add to butter mixture alternately with buttermilk, beating thoroughly after each addition. Gather dough into a ball, wrap tightly in plastic wrap, and refrigerate until firm (2 to 3 hours) or for up to 3 days.

On a well-floured board, roll out dough, a portion at a time, to a thickness of about ⅛ inch (keep remaining portions refrigerated). Cut out with cookie cutters (about 2½ inches in diameter) and place slightly apart on ungreased baking sheets.

Bake in a 350° oven for about 10 minutes or until lightly browned. Transfer to racks and let cool. Store airtight. Makes about 7 dozen.

Finnish Rye Cookies

(Pictured on page 766)

Rye flour gives these cookies their unusual nutty flavor. The shape is a bit unusual, too—each thin round has a small, off-center hole cut in it. In Finland, where they're a Christmas tradition, the cookies are known as *ruiskakut.*

    1   cup rye flour
    ½   cup all-purpose flour
    ¼   teaspoon salt
    ½   cup sugar
    ½   cup (¼ lb.) firm butter or margarine, cut into pieces
    4   tablespoons milk

In a bowl, stir together rye flour, all-purpose flour, salt, and sugar. Add butter and rub in with your fingers until mixture forms fine, even crumbs. Add milk, 1 tablespoon at a time, stirring with a fork until a stiff dough is formed. Gather dough into a ball, wrap tightly in plastic wrap, and refrigerate for 1 hour.

On a floured board, roll out dough, a portion at a time, to a thickness of about ⅛ inch. Cut out with a round cookie cutter (about 2½ inches in diameter). Then cut a hole slightly off center in each cookie, using a tiny round cutter about ½ inch in diameter (you can use the cap from a vanilla or other extract bottle). Place slightly apart on lightly greased baking sheets; prick each cookie several times with a fork.

Bake in a 375° oven for 8 to 10 minutes or until cookies are lightly browned and firm to the touch (you can bake the little cut-out holes, too—or reroll them to make more cookies). Transfer baked cookies to racks and let cool. Store airtight. Makes about 2½ dozen.

Buttery Cornmeal Wafers

Yellow cornmeal is the surprise ingredient in these tender, delicately sweet butter cookies accented with lemon. Added to the dough along with the flour, it gives the cookies a special crunch and a nutlike flavor.

- 1 cup (½ lb.) butter or margarine, softened
- 1 cup sugar
- 2 egg yolks
- 1 teaspoon grated lemon peel
- 1½ cups all-purpose flour
- 1 cup yellow cornmeal

In large bowl of an electric mixer, beat butter and sugar until creamy. Add egg yolks and lemon peel and beat well. In another bowl, stir together flour and cornmeal; gradually add to butter mixture, blending thoroughly. Gather dough into a ball, wrap tightly in plastic wrap, and refrigerate just until firm (about 1 hour).

Roll out dough on a well-floured board to a thickness of about ¼ inch. Cut out with cookie cutters (about 2½ inches in diameter) and place about 1 inch apart on lightly greased baking sheets. Bake in a 350° oven for 10 to 12 minutes or until edges are golden. Transfer to racks and let cool. Store airtight. Makes about 3 dozen.

Swedish Ginger Thins

(Pictured on page 766)

Very spicy, very dark, very thin, and very crisp— these are the words to describe *pepparkakor,* Sweden's version of gingersnaps. They can be cut into fancy shapes and decoratively iced for the holidays, if you like; or, if you prefer a plainer cookie, just cut them into rounds and leave them unfrosted.

- ⅔ cup butter or margarine
- ⅓ cup *each* granulated sugar and firmly packed brown sugar
- 2 tablespoons dark corn syrup
- 2 teaspoons *each* ground ginger and cloves
- 3 teaspoons ground cinnamon
- 2 teaspoons baking soda
- ¼ cup water
- 2½ cups all-purpose flour
  Royal icing (recipe follows) or purchased decorating icing in a tube or aerosol can (optional)

In a medium-size pan, combine butter, granulated sugar, brown sugar, and corn syrup; place over medium heat and stir until butter is melted. Remove from heat, stir in ginger, cloves, and cinnamon, and let cool slightly. Stir baking soda into water and add to butter mixture, blending thoroughly. Then stir in flour until well combined (dough will be quite soft). Cover tightly with plastic wrap and refrigerate until firm (2 to 3 hours) or for up to 3 days.

On a floured board, roll out dough, a portion at a time, to a thickness of about 1/16 inch. Cut out with cookie cutters (about 2½ inches in diameter). If necessary, dip cutters in flour to prevent dough from sticking to them. Place cookies slightly apart on ungreased baking sheets. Bake in a 325° oven for 10 to 12 minutes or until slightly darker brown and firm to the touch. Transfer to racks and let cool completely.

If desired, prepare royal icing. Press icing through a decorating tube with a plain tip, making swirls and outline designs on cookies. Let icing dry before storing cookies. Store airtight. Makes about 5 dozen.

Royal icing. In small bowl of an electric mixer, beat 1 **egg white** with ⅛ teaspoon **cream of tartar** and a dash of **salt** for 1 minute at high speed. Add 2 cups sifted **powdered sugar** and beat slowly until blended; then beat at high speed until very stiff (3 to 5 minutes).

Sugar Cookies

(Pictured on page 766)

Why do children love sugar cookies? Maybe it's because of their flavor, and maybe it's because they can be cut into such fancy shapes. If your youngsters like to help make sugar cookies as well as eat them, try our Easy-to-Cut Cookies—they allow the children to create their own shapes and choose decorative toppings.

>   ¾ cup (¼ lb. plus 4 tablespoons) butter or
>   margarine, softened
>   1 cup sugar
>   2 eggs
>   1 teaspoon vanilla
>   2¾ cups all-purpose flour
>   1 teaspoon *each* baking powder and salt
>   Sugar

In large bowl of an electric mixer, beat butter and the 1 cup sugar until creamy; beat in eggs and vanilla. In another bowl, stir together flour, baking powder, and salt; gradually add to butter mixture, blending thoroughly, to form a soft dough. Cover tightly with plastic wrap and refrigerate until firm (at least 1 hour) or for up to 3 days.

On a floured board, roll out dough, a portion at a time, to a thickness of ⅛ inch (keep remaining portions refrigerated). Cut out with cookie cutters (about 2½ inches in diameter) and place slightly apart on ungreased baking sheets. Sprinkle generously with sugar.

Bake in a 400° oven for 8 to 10 minutes or until edges are lightly browned. Transfer to racks and let cool completely before handling. Store airtight. Makes about 4 dozen.

Easy-to-Cut Cookies

Let children choose one or more fairly simple cookie shapes—block letters, numbers, or shapes such as triangles, squares, and circles. Then trace or draw shapes on sturdy cardboard (about 1/16 inch thick), making each one about 3 by 5 inches. Cut out patterns with scissors, making sure edges are smooth.

Prepare dough as directed for **Sugar Cookies;** divide into 12 equal portions. On a floured board or directly on a lightly floured baking sheet, roll out each portion to a thickness of ⅛ inch. Let children cut around patterns with a dull knife; then lift off excess dough and set aside to reroll for additional cookies. Offer toppings such as **raisins, chocolate chips,** whole or chopped **nuts,** sun-flower seeds, and **flaked coconut** for embellishing cookies. Bake as directed for **Sugar Cookies.** Makes about 2 dozen.

Crisp-fried Knots

(Pictured on facing page)

Cookies aren't always baked. Several cuisines feature deep-fried cookies; Italian *crespelle* and Swedish *fattigmands bakkels* are just two examples. Here's a third—*hrustule,* Yugoslavia's contribution to the collection. To Yugoslavian families, *hrustule* are special-occasion cookies, often prepared for Christmas or to celebrate festive events such as weddings. To make them, you tie strips of anise-flavored dough into loose knots, then deep-fry them to a golden crunch and dust them with powdered sugar while still warm.

>   2 eggs
>   ¼ cup granulated sugar
>   2½ tablespoons brandy
>   2½ tablespoons butter or margarine, melted
>   ¼ teaspoon salt
>   2 teaspoons anise seeds
>   ½ teaspoon grated lemon peel
>   About 2 cups all-purpose flour
>   Salad oil
>   Powdered sugar

In large bowl of an electric mixer, beat eggs and granulated sugar until lemon-colored. Mix in brandy, butter, salt, anise seeds, and lemon peel. Gradually stir in 1½ cups of the flour. Spread ⅓ cup more flour on a board; turn dough out onto board and knead until smooth. Wrap tightly in plastic wrap and let rest at room temperature for 30 minutes.

Work with ⅓ of the dough at a time. On a well-floured board, roll out each portion to a 6 by 30-inch rectangle (dough will be paper thin). With a pastry wheel or knife, cut into 1 by 6-inch strips; tie strips into loose knots.

Into a deep 3 to 4-quart pan, pour oil to a depth of 1 inch and heat to 360°F on a deep-frying thermometer. Add several cookies at a time and cook, turning once, until golden brown all over (about 1 minute total). Lift out cookies with a slotted spoon and let drain on paper towels. While warm, sift powdered sugar generously over tops. Serve immediately or store airtight for up to 3 days. Makes 7½ dozen.

Crisp-fried Knots *(Recipe on facing page)*

1 Roll dough into a paper-thin rectangle and cut with a pastry wheel or knife into 1 by 6-inch strips.

2 Tie each strip into a loose knot, being careful not to tear dough.

3 Fry cookies, a few at a time, until golden—it takes only about a minute.

4 Drain cookies on paper towels. While still warm, sift powdered sugar generously over tops.

Cookie Canvases

These sturdy cookies make perfect canvases for food-coloring artists of all ages. Offer them as a diverting at-home project or as party entertainment, letting guests take home their "edible masterpieces."

You'll need to bake the cookies ahead of time, since they're coated with a glaze that must dry for 8 to 24 hours. When it's time to paint, provide several sizes of water-color brushes, clear water for rinsing them, and small cups of food color—undiluted for bright colors, slightly diluted with water for lighter colors. To prevent colors from bleeding together, let each color dry briefly before painting another over it.

        2 cups (1 lb.) butter or margarine, softened
        2 cups granulated sugar
        2 teaspoons vanilla
        5 cups all-purpose flour
        1 to 1½ pounds powdered sugar
        6 to 9 tablespoons warm water
           Assorted food colors

In large bowl of an electric mixer, beat butter, granulated sugar, and vanilla until creamy. Beat in flour until thoroughly combined. With a floured stockinet-covered rolling pin, roll out enough dough on an ungreased unrimmed baking sheet to cover sheet in a ¼ to ⅜-inch-thick layer.

For rectangular or square cookies, use a sharp knife and a ruler to cut away a 1-inch strip of dough on all sides of baking sheet; make no other cuts. For round or decorative shapes, use large floured cookie cutters (or use a coffee can or tuna can with both ends removed). Cut shapes, leaving at least 1 inch between cookies and lifting away excess dough.

Combine trimmings with remaining dough; then repeat rolling and cutting until all dough is used. Bake in a 300° oven for 25 to 30 minutes or until cookies are pale gold and centers are firm to the touch.

Meanwhile, place powdered sugar in a large bowl. Gradually add water (you'll need about 6 tablespoons per pound), beating constantly, until glaze is smooth and thick; mixture should flow smoothly but set quickly.

Remove cookies from oven. If making rectangles or squares, cut while still hot, using a sharp knife and a ruler; trim to straighten edges. Let cookies of all shapes cool on baking sheets until just warm to the touch (about 7 minutes).

With a wide spatula, transfer cookies to a flat foil-covered surface. Quickly spread each cookie with enough glaze to make a very smooth surface. Do not cover or move cookies until glaze is dry to the touch (8 to 24 hours).

Paint with food colors. Or stack unpainted cookies between pieces of foil and wrap airtight; store at room temperature for up to 4 days, or freeze for longer storage. (If frozen, unwrap and let thaw at room temperature before painting.) Makes about 1 dozen 6-inch cookies or 2 dozen 3 to 4-inch cookies.

Puzzle Cookies

Not one fragment of cookie dough becomes a scrap with this ingenious recipe, inspired by a jigsaw puzzle. You roll the dough directly onto the baking sheet and bake it as one huge, solid cookie; then, while it's still warm, you cut it into interlocking elephants and owls. (If you fancy yourself a designer, try puzzling out other cookie patterns.)

        2 cups (1 lb.) butter or margarine, softened
        1 pound powdered sugar
        2 eggs
        1 teaspoon vanilla
       5½ cups all-purpose flour
           Purchased decorating icing (in a
           tube or aerosol can)

In large bowl of an electric mixer, beat butter and sugar until creamy; beat in eggs and vanilla. Gradually add flour, blending thoroughly (dough will be soft).

Divide dough into 3 equal portions. Place each on an ungreased unrimmed 12 by 15-inch baking sheet. With a well-floured stockinet-covered rolling pin, roll dough out to edges of baking sheet in an even layer. As bits of dough extend beyond sheet, pinch them off and pat into open areas. When baking sheet is covered, use a wide spatula to push dough back about ¼ inch from unrimmed sides, forming a slight ridge; then press ridge level with fingertips.

Bake, one baking sheet at a time, in a 300° oven for about 20 minutes or until edges are lightly browned. Remove from oven; if necessary, trim off any dough that has spread beyond edges of sheet. Then, using a small pointed knife, immediately cut cookie into 2, 4, 8, 12, or 16 rectangles of similar proportions (depending on the size cookies you desire). Cut a lopsided "Z" freehand down middle of each rectangle to create the two elephants (see illustration below). Then make U-shaped cuts to delineate legs; the cutouts become owls. Leave cookies on baking sheet until slightly cooled.

With a wide spatula, lift (or guide) each rectangle to a flat surface. Carefully separate elephants, taking care not to break trunks; then remove owls. Transfer carefully to racks and let cool completely. When cool, force icing through a plain tip to make toes, eyes, and ears on elephants, and eyes, beaks, and folded wings on owls. Store airtight. Makes at least 12 large elephants and 12 owls, or 96 small elephants and 96 owls.

Cut a lopsided "Z" down middle of each rectangle to create 2 elephants. Then make U-shaped cuts to delineate legs; the cutouts become owls. Icing turns the cookies into fanciful animal friends.

Sour Cream Spice Cookies

Ground coriander lends a warm, sweet spiciness to these cut-out sour cream cookies. For variety, you can top the cutouts with pine nuts and a sprinkling of sugar.

    ½ **cup (¼ lb.) butter or margarine, softened**
    1 **cup sugar**
    1 **egg**
    ½ **teaspoon** *each* **vanilla and almond extract**
    ½ **teaspoon baking soda**
    ½ **cup sour cream**
    3 **cups all-purpose flour**
    1½ **teaspoons baking powder**
    ½ **teaspoon** *each* **salt and ground coriander**

In large bowl of an electric mixer, beat butter and sugar until creamy; beat in egg, vanilla, and almond extract. Stir baking soda into sour cream, then beat into butter mixture. In another bowl, stir together flour, baking powder, salt, and coriander; gradually add to butter mixture, blending thoroughly. Wrap dough tightly in plastic wrap and refrigerate until firm (about 1 hour) or for up to 3 days.

On a lightly floured board, roll out half the dough to a thickness of about ⅛ inch. Cut out with cookie cutters (about 2½ inches in diameter) and place slightly apart on ungreased baking sheets. Repeat with remaining dough. Bake in a 400° oven for 8 to 10 minutes or until golden. Transfer to racks and let cool. Store airtight. Makes about 5 dozen.

Pine Nut Sugar Cookies

Prepare dough and cut out cookies as directed for **Sour Cream Spice Cookies,** but place on greased baking sheets. Beat 1 **egg** with 1 teaspoon **water** and brush over cookies; then press **pine nuts** into surface of cookies (you'll need about ½ cup). Sprinkle cookies lightly with **sugar** and bake in a 375° oven for about 10 minutes or until edges are golden.

Brown Sugar Shortbreads

You need just four ingredients to make these buttery brown sugar cookies. As they cool, they acquire an appealing crunch.

    1 **cup (½ lb.) butter or margarine, softened**
    1¼ **cups firmly packed brown sugar**
    1 **teaspoon vanilla**
    2½ **cups all-purpose flour**

In large bowl of an electric mixer, beat butter and sugar until creamy. Add vanilla; then gradually beat in flour, blending thoroughly. Gather dough into a ball, wrap tightly in plastic wrap, and refrigerate until firm (about 1 hour) or for up to 3 days.

On a lightly floured board, roll out dough to a thickness of ¼ inch. Cut out with cookie cutters (about 2½ inches in diameter) and place slightly apart on lightly greased baking sheets. Bake in a 300° oven for 35 to 40 minutes or until firm to the touch (press very lightly to test). Transfer to racks and let cool. Store airtight. Makes about 3 dozen.

Spritz *(Recipe on facing page)*

1 Assemble press according to manufacturer's directions, selecting design plate(s) you wish to use. Fill press with dough, packing it in firmly.

2 For snowflakes, stand press on baking sheet; turn handle to shape dough. To release cookie, turn handle slightly in reverse direction and lift press.

3 For rosettes, use star plate. Hold press at an angle and release dough in a spiral, working from the center out.

4 For ribbons, use ridged plate to form long strips of dough. Cut into 2½-inch lengths; separate lengths slightly. Press down gently to release any air bubbles.

Pressed Cookies

Pressed cookies are made from soft doughs or batters that are forced through a cookie press or pastry bag to make fancy shapes. Perhaps more than any other technique in cookiedom, this one yields professional-looking results—though you may need to practice a little before you can turn out perfect cookies with ease. Cookie presses and pastry bags are available in cookware shops and some hardware stores, and often through mail-order catalogues.

Spritz

(Pictured on facing page)

Buttery, almond-flavored Swedish spritz are probably the best known pressed cookies. Though they're often baked for the holidays, they're just as good at any other time of year. You can make spritz in a variety of fancy shapes, depending on which design plate you choose, and dress them up with candied fruit, colored sugar, silver dragées, or other decorations.

> 1 cup (½ lb.) butter, softened
> ¾ cup sugar
> 2 egg yolks
> 1 teaspoon vanilla
> ½ teaspoon almond extract
> 2½ cups all-purpose flour
> ½ teaspoon baking powder
> ⅛ teaspoon salt
> Decorations (suggestions follow)

In large bowl of an electric mixer, beat butter until creamy. Gradually add sugar, beating until fluffy. Add egg yolks, one at a time, and beat until smooth. Beat in vanilla and almond extract. In another bowl, stir together flour, baking powder, and salt; gradually add to butter mixture, blending thoroughly.

Place dough in a cookie press fitted with a design plate, packing it in firmly and evenly. Force out onto ungreased baking sheets, spacing cookies about 1 inch apart. If kitchen is very warm and dough is soft and sticky, refrigerate until firm enough to press easily. Decorate as desired.

Bake in a 350° oven for 12 to 15 minutes or until edges are lightly browned. Transfer to racks and let cool. Store airtight. Makes about 4 dozen.

Decorations. Before baking, top cookies with halved **candied cherries;** or sprinkle with finely chopped **nuts, colored sugar, nonpareils, silver dragées,** or **chocolate sprinkles.** Or brush baked cookies with this chocolate glaze: in top of a double boiler over simmering water, melt together 4 ounces **semisweet chocolate** and ½ teaspoon **solid vegetable shortening.** Apply with a pastry brush. Refrigerate glazed cookies for 10 minutes to harden glaze.

Swiss Almond Macaroons

Snowy with powdered sugar, these Swiss-style macaroons have a crisp surface and a chewy, lemon-flavored center. To get the crackled surface that marks the Swiss touch, let the unbaked cookies dry at room temperature for 8 to 24 hours; then pinch tops and bake.

> 8 ounces almond paste
> 1 cup plus 2 tablespoons granulated sugar
> 1 teaspoon grated lemon peel
> About ⅓ cup egg whites (whites of about 3 large eggs)
> About ½ cup powdered sugar

In large bowl of an electric mixer, beat almond paste, granulated sugar, and lemon peel until mixture resembles very fine crumbs. Gradually drizzle in egg whites, blending well after each addition, until batter just barely holds soft peaks.

Stand a pastry bag fitted with a plain tip (#6 size) in a drinking glass; then fill it with batter. Pipe onto baking sheets lined with parchment paper or brown wrapping paper, making 1¼-inch circles spaced 2 inches apart. (If batter is so thin that it runs out of bag, spoon it onto baking sheets by rounded teaspoonfuls.)

Sift powdered sugar generously over each round to cover completely. Let unbaked cookies stand, uncovered, until they're dry enough to develop a slight crust (at least 8 hours or up to 24 hours).

Pinch top of each round simultaneously with thumb and forefinger of both hands, making 4 indentations. Bake on center rack in a 350° oven for 12 to 15 minutes or until richly golden. Slide parchment and macaroons off baking sheet onto a damp towel and let cool. Run a spatula under cookies to loosen from parchment. Store airtight. Makes about 3½ dozen.

Ladyfingers

Feathery-light and luscious, ladyfingers are among the world's daintiest cookies. They make a lovely accompaniment for a cup of tea, and can also be used in the preparation of classic desserts such as charlottes.

    Cornstarch
    ¾ cup plus 1 tablespoon all-purpose flour
       Dash of salt
    ⅔ cup sugar
    4 eggs
    1 teaspoon vanilla

Grease 2 baking sheets, then dust with cornstarch and set aside.

Sift flour, measure, and sift again with salt and ⅓ cup of the sugar; set aside.

Separate eggs. In large bowl of an electric mixer, beat whites until stiff, beating in remaining ⅓ cup sugar, 1 tablespoon at a time. In small bowl of mixer, beat yolks with vanilla until thick and lemon-colored. Fold yolk mixture into beaten whites. Sift flour mixture over eggs; carefully fold in.

Stand a pastry bag fitted with a plain tip (#7 size) in a drinking glass; fill with batter. Pipe batter onto prepared baking sheets, forming fingers about 1 by 4 inches; space fingers about 1 inch apart. (Or spoon batter into greased and cornstarch-dusted ladyfinger pans.)

Bake in a 350° oven for 9 to 10 minutes or until lightly browned. Let cool on baking sheets (or in pans) for about a minute, then transfer to racks and let cool completely. Store airtight. Makes 2½ dozen.

Filled Cookies

To make these elaborate treats, you begin by rolling out dough with a rolling pin as you would for cut-out cookies (page 768). Then, however, you wrap it around a filling, using cutting and shaping techniques that vary from recipe to recipe. What you end up with might be anything from a horn to a turnover—or even a special little cookie that looks like ravioli.

If you like making filled cookies, you might also want to try Fruit Bars (page 799), Date Tarts (page 800), and Raspberry-Nut Valentines (page 804).

Flaky Fruit Turnovers

(Pictured on page 766)

A rich butter pastry distinguishes these tender, triangular turnover cookies; tucked inside is a dried-fruit filling made of apricots or dates. The cookies freeze well, so consider baking a batch of each kind and putting some away.

    2 cups all-purpose flour
    ¼ cup sugar
    1 cup (½ lb.) firm butter or margarine,
       cut into pieces
    ⅓ cup milk
       Apricot or date filling (recipes follow)

In a bowl, combine flour and sugar. Add butter; with your fingers or a pastry blender, rub or cut mixture until it forms fine, even crumbs. Gradually add milk, mixing with a fork until dough holds together. Cover tightly with plastic wrap and refrigerate for 30 minutes to 1 hour. Meanwhile, prepare filling of your choice.

Divide dough in half; form each half into a ball. On a well-floured board, roll out one ball into a 12-inch square, then cut it into sixteen 3-inch squares (press straight down with a long-bladed knife to make neat cookies). Mound a scant teaspoon of filling in the center of each square. Fold each over into a triangle and seal by running a pastry wheel around edges or crimping them with the tines of a fork. Repeat with remaining dough.

Transfer cookies to ungreased baking sheets. If desired, use a small, sharp knife to cut a small slash in each cookie to expose filling. Bake in a 350° oven for 18 to 20 minutes or until golden brown. Transfer to racks and let cool. Store airtight. Makes 32.

Apricot filling. In a small pan, combine ½ cup firmly packed chopped **dried apricots,** ⅔ cup **water,** and ¼ cup firmly packed **brown sugar.** Cook over medium heat, stirring constantly and mashing with a spoon, until mixture forms a smooth, thick paste (about 10 minutes). Let cool to room temperature.

Date filling. In a small pan, combine ½ cup firmly packed snipped **pitted dates,** ½ teaspoon grated **lemon peel,** 3 tablespoons **lemon juice,** ½ cup **water,** and ¼ cup firmly packed **brown sugar.** Cook over medium heat, stirring constantly and mashing with a spoon, until mixture forms a smooth, thick paste (about 10 minutes). Let cool to room temperature.

Russian Walnut Horns

A cinnamon-spiced ground walnut filling rests snugly inside these "horns" of sweet yeast pastry. Powdered sugar lends a bakeshop-fancy finish.

- 2¾ **cups all-purpose flour**
- ¼ **teaspoon salt**
- 1 **cup (½ lb.) firm butter or margarine, cut into pieces**
- 1 **package active dry yeast**
- ¼ **cup warm water (about 110°F)**
- 2 **eggs**
- ½ **cup sour cream**
  Walnut filling (recipe follows)
  About ⅓ cup *each* all-purpose flour and granulated sugar
  Powdered sugar

In a large mixing bowl, stir together the 2¾ cups flour and salt. With a pastry blender or 2 knives, cut in butter until mixture resembles cornmeal; set aside.

Dissolve yeast in warm water. Separate eggs; set whites aside and beat yolks until light and lemon-colored. Add dissolved yeast and ¼ cup of the sour cream to yolks, stirring until blended; stir yolk mixture into flour mixture.

In another bowl, using clean, dry beaters, beat egg whites until stiff but not dry. Fold remaining ¼ cup sour cream into whites, then add to flour mixture, blending thoroughly (dough will be sticky). Cover tightly with plastic wrap and refrigerate until firm (2 to 3 hours). Meanwhile, prepare walnut filling; cover and set aside.

Stir together the ⅓ cup flour and granulated sugar; sprinkle enough of the mixture over a board to coat generously. Divide dough into portions about the size of baseballs. Roll out one portion to a rectangle about ⅛ inch thick (keep remaining portions refrigerated). With a pastry wheel or sharp knife, cut into 2-inch squares. For tender cookies, handle the dough as little as possible.

Place a scant teaspoon of filling in the center of each square. Fold 2 opposite corners of square into center, overlapping dough and pinching firmly to seal. Place horns slightly apart on ungreased baking sheets. Repeat with remaining dough, sprinkling board with more flour-sugar mixture as necessary.

Bake in a 350° oven for 15 minutes or until lightly browned. Transfer to racks and let cool slightly; while still warm, sift powdered sugar over cookies to cover lightly. Store airtight. Makes about 8 dozen.

Walnut filling. Stir together 1⅓ cups ground **walnuts** (whirled fine in a food processor or blender), ⅔ cup **sugar,** ¾ teaspoon **ground cinnamon,** and 4 teaspoons **melted butter.** Add **milk,** a few drops at a time, just until mixture binds together loosely (you'll need 1 to 2 teaspoons).

Almond Ravioli Cookies

(Pictured on page 766)

We borrowed a technique from Italian cooking to make these little almond-filled bites.

- 1 **cup (½ lb.) butter or margarine, softened**
- 1½ **cups powdered sugar**
- 1 **egg**
- 1 **teaspoon vanilla**
- 2½ **cups all-purpose flour**
- 1 **teaspoon *each* baking soda and cream of tartar**
  About ⅔ cup (6 oz.) almond paste
  About ⅓ cup sliced almonds

In large bowl of an electric mixer, beat butter and sugar until creamy; beat in egg and vanilla. In another bowl, stir together flour, baking soda, and cream of tartar; gradually add to butter mixture, blending thoroughly. Divide dough in half. Wrap each half tightly in plastic wrap and refrigerate until firm (2 to 3 hours) or for up to 3 days.

Place one portion of dough between 2 pieces of wax paper and roll out into a 10 by 15-inch rectangle. Peel off and discard top paper.

With a pastry wheel or a long-bladed knife, lightly mark dough into 1-inch squares. Place a small ball of almond paste (use a scant ¼ teaspoon for each) in the center of each square; refrigerate while rolling top layer.

Repeat rolling procedure for second portion of dough. Peel off and discard top paper. Invert sheet of dough onto almond-paste-topped dough. Peel off and discard paper. Gently press top layer of dough around mounds of filling.

Flour a pastry wheel or sharp knife and cut filled dough into 1-inch squares, then run pastry wheel around outer edges to seal (or press with fingers). Place cookies about 1 inch apart on ungreased baking sheets. Push a sliced almond diagonally into the center of each cookie.

Bake in a 350° oven for 10 to 12 minutes or until golden. Transfer to racks and let cool. Store airtight. Makes about 12½ dozen.

Viennese Jam Rounds

(Pictured on page 766)

These fancy cookies resemble stained-glass windows; before baking, each one is crowned with a bit of jam and two crisscrossed dough strips.

    1   cup (½ lb.) butter or margarine, softened
    1   cup sugar
    2   egg yolks
    1   teaspoon grated lemon peel
    2   cups all-purpose flour
    ¼   teaspoon salt
    ¾   teaspoon ground cinnamon
    ¼   teaspoon ground cloves
    1   cup ground almonds
        About ½ cup raspberry or apricot jam

In large bowl of an electric mixer, beat butter and sugar until creamy. Beat in egg yolks and lemon peel. In another bowl, stir together flour, salt, cinnamon, and cloves; gradually add to butter mixture, blending thoroughly. Stir in almonds (dough will be very stiff). Gather dough into a ball, wrap tightly in plastic wrap, and refrigerate for 1 hour.

Divide dough in half. Roll each half between 2 pieces of wax paper to a thickness of ⅛ inch. Cut out with a 2-inch round cookie cutter and place about 2 inches apart on ungreased baking sheets. Top each cookie with about ½ teaspoon jam, spreading to within about ½ inch of edges. Cut dough scraps (reroll, if necessary) into ¼ by 2-inch strips; cross 2 strips over top of each cookie and press ends down lightly.

Bake in a 375° oven for about 12 minutes or until edges are browned. Let cool for about a minute on baking sheets, then transfer to racks and let cool completely. Store airtight. Makes about 4 dozen.

Cookie-iron Cookies

Cookies shaped with cookie irons are specialty items indeed. Scandinavian rosettes and *krumkake*, French *gaufrettes*, Italian *pizelle*, and the Dutch *siroop wafel* all belong to this category.

Rosettes must be made with a rosette iron, a long-handled metal mold with a decorative shape. The other cookies are all made in hinged waffle-type irons—so, though each type has its own special iron, you can use recipes and irons interchangeably. Just be sure to adjust the amount of batter to suit the size iron you're using.

New waffle-type irons that don't have a nonstick fluorocarbon finish must be seasoned before you make cookies. To season an iron, place it directly over medium heat (on a gas or electric range) until water dripped inside sizzles. Open and brush generously with salad oil, then close and heat just until oil smokes. Remove from heat; let cool in the open position. Wipe clean.

Even if your iron does have a nonstick finish, brush it with melted butter before baking the first few cookies in each batch.

Krumkake

(Pictured on facing page)

Traditionally prepared in a round cookie iron, our *krumkake* take advantage of a decorative rectangular iron.

    3   eggs
    ½   cup sugar
    6   tablespoons butter or margarine, melted
    ½   teaspoon lemon extract
    ½   teaspoon ground cardamom (optional)
    ⅔   cup all-purpose flour
        Melted butter or margarine
        Whipped cream (optional)

In a bowl, beat eggs with sugar, the 6 tablespoons butter, lemon extract, and cardamom (if used). Add flour and stir until mixture is smooth.

Place a seasoned iron (5 or 6 inches in diameter) directly over medium-high heat. Alternately heat both sides of iron until water dripped inside sizzles. Open and brush lightly with melted butter. Reduce heat to medium.

Spoon batter down center of iron (you'll need 1 to 3 tablespoons, depending on size of iron). Close and squeeze handles together; scrape off and discard any batter that flows out. Bake, turning about every 20 seconds and opening often to check doneness, until cookie is light golden brown. Remove iron from heat and lift out cookie with a fork, spatula, or tongs.

Working quickly, shape hot cookie into a cone or roll into a cylinder (or leave flat, if you prefer). Place on a rack to cool. Return iron to heat and repeat with remaining batter. Store cookies airtight; serve plain or fill with whipped cream just before serving. Makes about 1½ dozen 5-inch cookies.

Krumkake (Recipe on facing page)

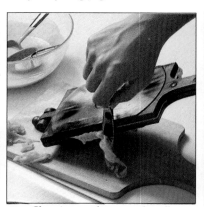

1 Spoon batter down center of iron; you'll need 1 to 3 table-spoons per cookie, depending on size of iron.

2 Close iron and squeeze handles together. Remove from heat and scrape off any batter that flows out.

3 Return to heat and bake, turning iron about every 20 seconds. When cookie is golden, lift out of iron with a fork, spatula, or tongs.

4 Working quickly, shape hot cookie into a cone—or leave flat, if you prefer. Let cool on a rack.

Pizelle

Italian *pizelle* start with a dough that you shape by hand before baking it in an iron. The baked cookies have a star design and a lemon-anise flavor.

> 3 eggs
> ¾ cup sugar
> ¾ cup (¼ lb. plus 4 tablespoons) butter or margarine, melted
> 1 teaspoon lemon extract
> ¾ teaspoon *each* baking powder and anise seeds
> 3½ cups all-purpose flour
> Melted butter or margarine

Beat eggs until thick. Add sugar, the ¾ cup butter, lemon extract, baking powder, anise seeds, and flour; mix well.

Place a seasoned pizelle iron (about 5 inches in diameter) directly over medium-high heat. Alternately heat both sides of iron until water dripped inside sizzles. Open and brush lightly with melted butter.

Shape dough into balls, using 2 to 4 tablespoons for each, depending on size of iron. Place a ball of dough in center of iron (roll into a rope if using a rectangular iron). Close and squeeze handles together; turn iron. Bake, turning about every 20 seconds and opening often to check doneness, until cookie is light golden brown. Quickly lift out cookie with a fork or spatula; place flat on a rack to cool. Return iron to heat and repeat with remaining dough. Store cookies airtight. Makes about 1½ dozen.

Gaufrettes

A tiny wafflelike pattern is characteristic of French *gaufrettes*. After baking, each cookie is cut in half to make two little squares, which happen to make excellent ice cream sandwiches—just place a slice of your favorite ice cream in between.

> ½ pint (1 cup) whipping cream
> 1 cup all-purpose flour
> ¾ cup powdered sugar
> 2 teaspoons vanilla
> ¼ teaspoon salt
> Melted butter or margarine

In small bowl of an electric mixer, beat cream just until it begins to thicken; then add flour, sugar, vanilla, and salt and blend until mixture is smooth.

Place a seasoned gaufrette iron directly over medium-high heat. Alternately heat both sides of iron until water dripped inside sizzles. Open and brush lightly with melted butter.

Spoon batter down center of iron (you'll need 1 to 3 tablespoons, depending on size of iron). Close and squeeze handles together; scrape off and discard any batter that flows out. Bake, turning about every 20 seconds and opening often to check doneness, until cookie is light golden brown. Remove iron from heat and lift out cookie with a fork, spatula, or tongs. While cookie is still hot, cut in half crosswise and place on a rack to cool. Repeat with remaining batter. Store cookies airtight. Makes about 2 dozen.

Rosettes

With a rosette iron, you can produce unusual deep-fried batter cookies with an airy snowflake design. You preheat the iron in hot oil, dip it in batter, and then plunge it back into the oil until the cookie turns golden—it takes only a few seconds. The irons are available in cookware shops; most come with interchangeable molds, so you can vary the shape of the cookies.

> ½ cup cornstarch
> 2 tablespoons all-purpose flour
> 2 teaspoons granulated sugar
> 1 teaspoon ground cinnamon or 1½ teaspoons ground cardamom
> ½ teaspoon salt
> 1 egg
> ¼ cup milk
> Salad oil
> Powdered sugar

In a bowl, stir together cornstarch, flour, granulated sugar, cinnamon, and salt. Beat egg lightly, combine with milk, and add to dry ingredients. Stir until batter is smooth.

Into a deep, heavy pan about 6 inches in diameter, pour oil to a depth of about 1½ inches and heat to 375°F on a deep-frying thermometer. For each rosette, preheat iron in oil; then dip hot iron into batter nearly up to (but not over) top. If batter does not adhere to iron, temperature of iron or oil is too hot or too cold.

Lower iron into oil for about 10 seconds or until rosette is lightly browned. Remove from oil, gently loosen rosette from iron with a fork, and drain on paper towels. Repeat with remaining batter. When rosettes are completely cooled, sift powdered sugar over them. Store airtight. Makes about 1½ dozen.

Gouda Syrup Waffles

The same Dutch community that gives Gouda cheese its name also has a cookie to its credit: the syrup waffle (*stroop* or *siroop wafel* in Dutch). It's made of vanilla wafers baked in a cookie iron, then sandwiched around a thick, golden caramel filling for a cookie that's crisp on the outside, chewy on the inside.

In Gouda and some other Dutch cities, mainly on national holidays and at fairs, street vendors bake the cookies while you watch; warm and freshly made, they're a true delight. More typically, however, you buy the syrup waffles packaged in cellophane or cans at pastry shops or grocery stores. In Dutch homes, syrup waffles are served for birthdays and feast days, or as a special treat with morning coffee.

You can make syrup waffles at home, using any waffle-type cookie iron to bake the wafers. A gaufrette iron gives the most authentic appearance, but pizelle and krumkake irons work well, too.

> 2 cups all-purpose flour
> ½ cup sugar
> 1½ teaspoons baking powder
> ¼ teaspoon salt
> 4 tablespoons butter or margarine, melted
> 2 eggs, lightly beaten
> 1 teaspoon vanilla
> Melted butter or margarine
> Caramel syrup (recipe follows)

In a large mixing bowl, stir together flour, sugar, baking powder, and salt. Add the 4 tablespoons butter, eggs, and vanilla; with a wooden spoon or your hands, work dough until well blended. Form into a ball, wrap tightly in plastic wrap, and refrigerate until firm (at least 1 hour).

Divide dough into 50 equal portions; roll each into a ball. Place a seasoned gaufrette iron or other waffle-type cookie iron directly over medium-high heat. Alternately heat both sides of iron until water dripped inside sizzles. Open and brush lightly with melted butter. Place a ball of dough in iron; close. Bake, turning about every 20 seconds and opening often to check doneness, until cookie is golden brown (about 1 minute). Quickly lift out cookie with a fork or spatula and transfer to a rack to cool. Repeat with remaining dough.

Prepare caramel syrup. To assemble syrup waffles, spread warm syrup on one wafer, then top with another; gently press together. Store airtight. Makes 25 filled wafers.

Caramel syrup. In a 2-quart pan, combine ½ pint (1 cup) **whipping cream,** 1 cup firmly packed **brown sugar,** and ¼ cup **light corn syrup.** Boil over medium-high heat, uncovered, stirring occasionally, until a candy thermometer registers 238°F. Let cool briefly (just until thick enough to spread). If caramel becomes too thick, set pan in hot water and stir until spreadable.

Cookies for Young Bakers

Children love to eat cookies any time, but especially when they've helped in the baking. The cookies listed below are good choices for those times when you have a small pair of helping hands in the kitchen; they involve techniques that children enjoy and can manage easily.

Icebox Cookies

For the baker whose time is limited, icebox cookies are a boon indeed, offering make-ahead ease and adaptability. Sometimes called refrigerator cookies or slice-and-bake cookies, they're made by forming the dough into long rolls or logs, refrigerating it until firm, and then slicing it crosswise into cookies ready for baking. This method is appealing to many because the dough can be prepared days or even weeks in advance (it freezes well); slicing and baking take little time and can be done at your convenience.

The icebox technique generally yields uniform, waferlike cookies with a crisp texture. If you want cookies with decorated edges, just roll the log of dough in sugar or nuts before chilling. Or adapt the technique to produce more elaborate results; by rolling the dough around a filling or stacking different kinds of dough, you can turn out fancy treats such as pinwheels (pages 786, 788, and 789) and two-toned striped cookies (page 786).

Photo at left offers a look at our galaxy of icebox cookies. From inside out: Danish Sugar Cookies (page 784), Spiced Almond Thins (page 785), Lemon-Pecan Wafers (page 785), Peanut Pinwheels (page 789), Coconut Shortbread Cookies (page 788), Poppy Seed Nut Slices (page 785), Date-Oatmeal Cookies (page 789), and Danish Sugar Cookies.

Danish Sugar Cookies

(Pictured on page 782)

Denmark is well known for the quality of her pastry and cookies, and these little treats will show you why. Crisp, sugary edges and a ground-almond dough make them special.

> 1 cup sugar
> ½ cup (¼ lb.) firm butter, cut into pieces
> ½ cup whole blanched almonds, finely ground
> 1 teaspoon vanilla
> 1 cup all-purpose flour
> Sugar

Place the 1 cup sugar in a large bowl; cut in butter with a pastry blender or 2 knives until mixture forms fine particles. Stir in almonds and vanilla. Blend in flour, mixing with your hands if necessary, until well combined. Shape dough into a roll 1½ inches in diameter. Sprinkle a little sugar (1 to 2 tablespoons) on a sheet of wax paper; then place roll of dough on paper and wrap snugly, coating outside of roll with sugar. Refrigerate until firm (at least 2 hours) or for up to 3 days.

Unwrap dough. Using a sharp knife, cut into ⅛-inch-thick slices. Place slices slightly apart on ungreased baking sheets. Bake in a 375° oven for 8 to 10 minutes or until lightly browned. Let cool on baking sheets for about a minute, then transfer to racks and let cool completely. Store airtight. Makes about 5 dozen.

French Butter Wafers

Crisp and fragile butter wafers, accented only with vanilla, are elegant in their simplicity. Since the butter provides much of their delicate flavor, it's best not to substitute margarine in this recipe.

> 1 cup (½ lb.) butter, softened
> 1¼ cups powdered sugar
> 1 egg
> 1 teaspoon vanilla
> 2 cups all-purpose flour
> 1 teaspoon *each* baking soda and cream of tartar
> ⅛ teaspoon salt

In large bowl of an electric mixer, beat butter until creamy. Beat in sugar; add egg and vanilla and beat well. In another bowl, stir together flour, baking soda, cream of tartar, and salt; gradually add to butter mixture, blending thoroughly. Shape dough into a roll 1½ inches in diameter; wrap in wax paper and refrigerate until firm (at least 2 hours) or for up to 3 days.

Unwrap dough. Using a sharp knife, cut into ⅜-inch-thick slices; place slices 2 inches apart on ungreased baking sheets. Bake in a 350° oven for 10 to 12 minutes or until golden. Let cool on baking sheets for about a minute, then transfer to racks and let cool completely. Store airtight. Makes about 4 dozen.

Candied Ginger Crisps

Tiny nuggets of candied ginger are a piquant surprise in these dark, spicy coconut cookies. They're especially delicious alongside fruit salad or ice cream. Candied ginger (sometimes called crystallized ginger) is available in most well-stocked supermarkets.

> ½ cup (¼ lb.) butter or margarine, softened
> ½ cup solid vegetable shortening
> 1 cup sugar
> ½ cup light molasses
> 3 cups all-purpose flour
> 1 teaspoon *each* baking soda, ground ginger, and ground cinnamon
> ½ teaspoon ground cloves
> 1 cup flaked coconut
> ½ cup finely chopped candied ginger

In large bowl of an electric mixer, beat butter, shortening, and sugar until creamy; beat in molasses. In another bowl, stir together flour, baking soda, ground ginger, cinnamon, and cloves; gradually add to butter mixture, blending thoroughly. Add coconut and candied ginger and mix until well combined. Shape dough into 2 or 3 rolls, each 1½ inches in diameter; wrap in wax paper and refrigerate until firm (at least 4 hours) or for up to 3 days.

Unwrap dough. Using a sharp knife, cut into ¼-inch-thick slices; place slices about 1 inch apart on lightly greased baking sheets. Bake in a 350° oven for 10 minutes or until edges are lightly browned. Transfer to racks and let cool. Store airtight. Makes about 7 dozen.

Lemon-Pecan Wafers

(Pictured on page 782)

Here's a good summertime cookie. Though rich with butter and nuts, it has a refreshing, lemony sparkle.

- ½ cup (¼ lb.) butter or margarine, softened
- 1 cup sugar
- 1 egg
- 1 tablespoon *each* grated lemon peel and lemon juice
- 2 cups all-purpose flour
- ⅛ teaspoon salt
- 1 teaspoon baking powder
- 1 cup chopped pecans

In large bowl of an electric mixer, beat butter and sugar until creamy; beat in egg, lemon peel, and lemon juice. In another bowl, stir together flour, salt, and baking powder; gradually add to butter mixture, blending thoroughly. Stir in pecans, mixing with your hands if necessary to distribute nuts evenly. Shape dough into 2 rolls, each 1½ inches in diameter; wrap in wax paper and refrigerate until firm (at least 2 hours) or for up to 3 days.

Unwrap dough. Using a sharp knife, cut into ⅛-inch-thick slices; place slices about 1 inch apart on greased baking sheets. Bake in a 350° oven for 12 minutes or until edges are lightly browned. Transfer to racks and let cool. Store airtight. Makes about 6 dozen.

Spiced Almond Thins

(Pictured on page 782)

Sour cream, brown sugar, cinnamon, and nutmeg combine in a crisp spice wafer with an appealing old-fashioned flavor. Crunchy bits of almond give the cookies a pebbly appearance.

- 1 cup (½ lb.) butter or margarine, softened
- 1 cup firmly packed brown sugar
- 2 cups all-purpose flour
- 2 teaspoons ground cinnamon
- ½ teaspoon ground nutmeg
- ¼ teaspoon baking soda
- ¼ cup sour cream
- ½ cup slivered blanched almonds

In large bowl of an electric mixer, beat butter and sugar until creamy. In another bowl, stir together flour, cinnamon, and nutmeg. Stir baking soda into sour cream; add to butter mixture alternately with flour mixture, blending thoroughly. Stir in almonds until well combined. Shape dough into a 2½-inch-thick rectangular log; wrap in wax paper and refrigerate until firm (at least 2 hours) or for up to 3 days.

Unwrap dough. Using a sharp knife, cut into ⅛-inch-thick slices; place slices about 1 inch apart on ungreased baking sheets. Bake in a 350° oven for 10 minutes or until golden brown. Let cool for about a minute on baking sheets, then transfer to racks and let cool completely. Store airtight. Makes about 5 dozen.

Poppy Seed Nut Slices

(Pictured on page 782)

Hazelnuts and poppy seeds team up to give these crunchy little cookies their distinctive flavor. If you like hazelnuts, you might also enjoy the chocolate-dipped bonbons on page 760 and the nut shortbread on page 794.

- 1 cup (½ lb.) butter or margarine, softened
- 1 cup sugar
- 1 egg
- 1 teaspoon vanilla
- 2½ cups all-purpose flour
- ⅓ cup poppy seeds
- ½ teaspoon ground cinnamon
- ¼ teaspoon *each* salt and ground ginger
- 1½ cups coarsely chopped hazelnuts (filberts)

In large bowl of an electric mixer, beat butter and sugar until creamy; beat in egg and vanilla. In another bowl, stir together flour, poppy seeds, cinnamon, salt, and ginger; gradually add to butter mixture, blending thoroughly. Add hazelnuts, mixing with your hands if necessary to distribute nuts evenly. Shape dough into 2 or 3 rolls, each 1½ inches in diameter; wrap in wax paper and refrigerate until firm (at least 2 hours) or for up to 3 days.

Unwrap dough. Using a sharp knife, cut into ¼-inch-thick slices; place slices about 1 inch apart on ungreased baking sheets. Bake in a 350° oven for 12 to 15 minutes or until edges are golden. Transfer to racks and let cool. Store airtight. Makes about 7 dozen.

Cinnamon Pinwheels

In their buttery flavor and crisp, flaky texture, these cookies resemble puff pastry. They're made from slices of yeast dough swirled with sweet cinnamon filling; each slice is rolled out into a large, thin circle and sprinkled generously with sugar before baking.

    3   cups all-purpose flour
    ½   teaspoon salt
    1   teaspoon ground cardamom (optional)
    2   tablespoons sugar
    1   cup (½ lb.) firm butter or margarine,
        cut into pieces
    1   package active dry yeast
    ¼   cup warm water (about 110°F)
    ½   cup milk
    1   egg, lightly beaten
    3   tablespoons salad oil
        Cinnamon filling (recipe follows)
        Sugar

In a large mixing bowl, combine flour, salt, cardamom (if used), and the 2 tablespoons sugar. With a pastry blender or 2 knives, cut butter into flour mixture until particles are about the size of peas.

Dissolve yeast in water; then stir in milk, egg, and oil. With a fork, stir yeast mixture into flour mixture just until flour is moistened. Cover tightly with plastic wrap and refrigerate until cold (about 2 hours). Meanwhile, prepare cinnamon filling and set aside.

Turn dough out onto a lightly floured board; knead gently, 4 times only. Roll out to an 11 by 18-inch rectangle, keeping sides straight. Sprinkle filling evenly over surface to within ¼ inch of each edge. Starting with a long edge, roll up jelly roll style; pinch seam to seal. Wrap in wax paper and refrigerate until firm (at least 2 hours) or for up to 3 days.

Cut filled and rolled dough crosswise into fourths; return 3 rolls to refrigerator. Using a sharp knife, cut remaining portion into ½-inch-thick slices. On a well-floured board, roll each slice out with a floured rolling pin into a circle about 5 inches in diameter, adding more flour as needed to prevent sticking. (If kitchen is warm, keep unrolled slices in refrigerator until needed.)

Place circles close together on ungreased baking sheets and sprinkle generously with sugar. Bake in a 350° oven for 15 minutes or until golden brown. Transfer to racks and let cool. Repeat with remaining dough. Store airtight. Makes 3 dozen.

Cinnamon filling. In a bowl, stir together ¼ cup firmly packed **brown sugar** and 2 tablespoons *each* **granulated sugar** and **ground cinnamon**.

Black & White Slices
(Pictured on facing page)

Jaunty stripes of vanilla and chocolate-flavored dough give these little squares a festive appearance. If you like, you can experiment with combining the doughs in other shapes—try making checkerboards, pinwheels, or half moons.

    ½   cup (¼ lb.) butter or margarine, softened
    ½   cup sugar
    1   egg yolk
    1½ cups all-purpose flour
    1½ teaspoons baking powder
    ⅛   teaspoon salt
    3   tablespoons milk
    ½   teaspoon vanilla
    1   square (1 oz.) unsweetened chocolate

In large bowl of an electric mixer, beat butter and sugar until creamy; beat in egg yolk. In another bowl, stir together flour, baking powder, and salt. In a small cup, combine milk and vanilla. Add dry ingredients to butter mixture alternately with milk mixture, blending thoroughly after each addition.

In top of a double boiler over simmering water or in a small pan over lowest possible heat, melt chocolate, stirring constantly; let cool slightly. Divide dough in half; take 1 tablespoon dough from one half and add it to the other half. Stir chocolate into smaller portion of dough, blending until well combined.

Shape each portion of dough into a roll 1½ inches in diameter. Wrap each in wax paper; flatten sides to make square logs. Refrigerate until firm (at least 2 hours) or for up to 3 days.

Unwrap dough. Using a sharp knife, slice each log lengthwise into fourths. Then reassemble logs, using 2 dark slices and 2 light slices for each, alternating colors to make stripes. Gently press layers together to eliminate interior air pockets.

Cut logs crosswise into ⅛-inch-thick slices (if layers start to separate, refrigerate until dough is firmer). Place slices about 1 inch apart on greased baking sheets. Bake in a 350° oven for about 10 minutes or until light golden. Transfer to racks and let cool. Store airtight. Makes about 4 dozen.

Black & White Slices (Recipe on facing page)

1 Form each portion of dough into a roll and wrap in wax paper; flatten sides to make square logs. Chill until firm.

2 Unwrap chilled logs and slice lengthwise into quarters, using a sharp knife.

3 Reassemble logs, alternating dark and light portions to make stripes. Press layers together gently as you work.

4 With a sharp knife, cut logs crosswise into ⅛-inch-thick slices; place on greased baking sheets.

Coconut Shortbread Cookies

(Pictured on page 782)

Is it possible to improve on traditional Scottish shortbread? One taste of these meltingly rich cookies may convince you to answer "yes." Lots of coconut is added to a basic shortbread dough for an irresistible cross-cultural treat.

   1 cup (½ lb.) butter, softened
   ¼ cup granulated sugar
   1 teaspoon vanilla
   2 cups all-purpose flour
   ¼ teaspoon salt
   2 cups flaked coconut
     About 1 cup powdered sugar

In large bowl of an electric mixer, beat butter until creamy; add granulated sugar and beat until smooth. Mix in vanilla. In another bowl, stir together flour and salt; gradually add to butter mixture, blending thoroughly. Add coconut and mix until well combined. Shape dough into a roll about 1½ inches in diameter; wrap in wax paper and refrigerate until firm (at least 2 hours) or for up to 3 days.

Unwrap dough. Using a sharp knife, cut into ¼-inch-thick slices; place slices slightly apart on ungreased baking sheets. Bake in a 300° oven for 20 minutes or until cookies are firm to the touch and lightly browned on bottoms. Transfer to racks and let cool for 5 minutes. Sift half the powdered sugar onto wax paper and transfer cookies to it in a single layer; sift additional powdered sugar on top to cover cookies lightly. Let cookies cool completely. Store airtight. Makes about 4 dozen.

Peanut Butter & Jam Cookies

Kids will love these jam-filled cookies as a warm-from-the-oven snack or a lunchbox dessert. You make them by sandwiching a spoonful of your favorite preserves between two slices of refrigerator dough, then crimping the edges to seal the filling inside.

For variety, try substituting five or six semisweet chocolate, butterscotch, or peanut butter-flavored chips for the jam in each cookie.

  1½ cups all-purpose flour
   ½ cup sugar
   ½ teaspoon baking soda
   ¼ teaspoon salt
   ½ cup *each* solid vegetable shortening and peanut butter
   ¼ cup light corn syrup
   1 tablespoon milk
     About ½ cup jam (strawberry, raspberry, apricot, or other fruit flavor)

In a large mixing bowl, combine flour, sugar, baking soda, and salt. With a pastry blender or 2 knives, cut in shortening and peanut butter until mixture forms moist, even crumbs. Stir in corn syrup and milk until blended. Shape dough into a roll 2 inches in diameter; wrap in wax paper and refrigerate until firm (at least 3 hours) or for up to 3 days.

Unwrap dough. Using a sharp knife, cut into ⅛-inch-thick slices. Place half the slices slightly apart on ungreased baking sheets and top each with ½ teaspoon jam. Place another slice of dough on top of each and press down lightly to mold dough around filling. Then lightly crimp edges with tines of a fork to seal.

Bake in a 350° oven for 8 to 10 minutes or until lightly browned. Let cool for about 5 minutes on baking sheets, then transfer to racks and let cool completely. Store airtight. Makes about 4 dozen.

Date Pinwheel Cookies

Swirling date filling through a simple brown sugar dough produces a spiral of contrasting color and rich, sweet flavor. Before slicing, be sure to chill the dough thoroughly.

   1 cup whole pitted dates, snipped
   2 cups firmly packed brown sugar
   ½ cup water
   ⅔ cup solid vegetable shortening
   2 eggs
   1 teaspoon vanilla
   4 cups all-purpose flour
   1 teaspoon baking soda
   ¼ teaspoon cream of tartar
   ½ teaspoon salt

In a pan, combine dates, ½ cup of the sugar, and water. Bring to a boil over high heat; then reduce heat and simmer, stirring constantly and mashing with a spoon, until mixture is thick and smooth (about 8 minutes). Remove from heat and let cool completely.

In large bowl of an electric mixer, beat shortening and remaining 1½ cups sugar until creamy; beat in eggs and vanilla. In another bowl, stir together flour, baking soda, cream of tartar, and salt; gradually add to shortening mixture, blending thoroughly to make a stiff dough.

Divide dough in half. Roll out each portion on a floured board, making an 8 by 10-inch rectangle about ¼ inch thick. On each rectangle, spread half the filling to within ½ inch of edges. Then roll up jelly roll style, starting with a long edge. Wrap rolls in wax paper and refrigerate until very firm (at least 12 hours) or for up to 3 days.

Unwrap dough. Using a sharp knife, cut into ¼-inch-thick slices. Place slices slightly apart on ungreased baking sheets. Bake in a 400° oven for 8 to 10 minutes or until lightly browned. Transfer to racks and let cool. Store airtight. Makes about 7 dozen.

Date-Oatmeal Cookies

(Pictured on page 782)

When you bite into these cookies, you'll find a delectable combination of flavors: oats, nuts, dates, and a subtle touch of cinnamon.

- 1 cup (½ lb.) butter or margarine, softened
- 1 cup sugar
- 1 teaspoon vanilla
- 2 eggs
- 1¾ cups all-purpose flour
- 1 teaspoon *each* baking powder and ground cinnamon
- ¾ teaspoon baking soda
- ½ teaspoon salt
- 2 cups quick-cooking rolled oats
- 1 package (8 oz.) whole pitted dates (about 1½ cups lightly packed)
- 1 cup chopped pecans or walnuts

In large bowl of an electric mixer, beat butter and sugar until creamy. Beat in vanilla; then beat in eggs, one at a time. In another bowl, stir together flour, baking powder, cinnamon, baking soda, and salt; gradually add to butter mixture, blending

thoroughly. Stir in oats, dates, and pecans, mixing well and distributing dates evenly through dough. Shape dough into 2 or 3 rolls, each 1¾ inches in diameter; wrap in wax paper and refrigerate until firm (at least 4 hours) or for up to 3 days.

Unwrap dough. Using a sharp knife, cut into ¼-inch-thick slices; place slices about 1 inch apart on ungreased baking sheets. Bake in a 375° oven for 10 to 12 minutes or until edges are golden. Transfer to racks and let cool. Store airtight. Makes about 6½ dozen.

Peanut Pinwheels

(Pictured on page 782)

In this recipe, a ribbon of chocolate winds its way through the center of a crisp peanut butter cookie.

- ½ cup (¼ lb.) butter or margarine, softened
- ½ cup creamy peanut butter
- ½ cup *each* granulated sugar and firmly packed brown sugar
- 1 egg
- 1¼ cups all-purpose flour
- ½ teaspoon *each* baking soda, salt, and ground cinnamon
- 1 package (6 oz.) semisweet chocolate chips

In large bowl of an electric mixer, beat butter, peanut butter, granulated sugar, and brown sugar until creamy; beat in egg. In another bowl, stir together flour, baking soda, salt, and cinnamon; gradually add to butter mixture, blending thoroughly. Cover tightly with plastic wrap and refrigerate until firm (about 2 hours).

In top of a double boiler over simmering water or in a small pan over lowest possible heat, melt chocolate chips, stirring constantly. Let cool slightly. On wax paper, pat chilled dough out into a 12-inch square. Spread chocolate evenly over dough to within ½ inch of edges. Roll up jelly roll style; then cut in half crosswise. Wrap each roll in wax paper and refrigerate until firm (at least 2 hours) or for up to 3 days.

Remove one roll from refrigerator. Unwrap; using a sharp knife, cut into ¼-inch-thick slices. Place slices about 1 inch apart on ungreased baking sheets. Bake in a 375° oven for about 10 minutes or until lightly browned. Let cool on baking sheets for 2 to 3 minutes, then transfer to racks and let cool completely. Repeat with second roll of dough. Store airtight. Makes about 4 dozen.

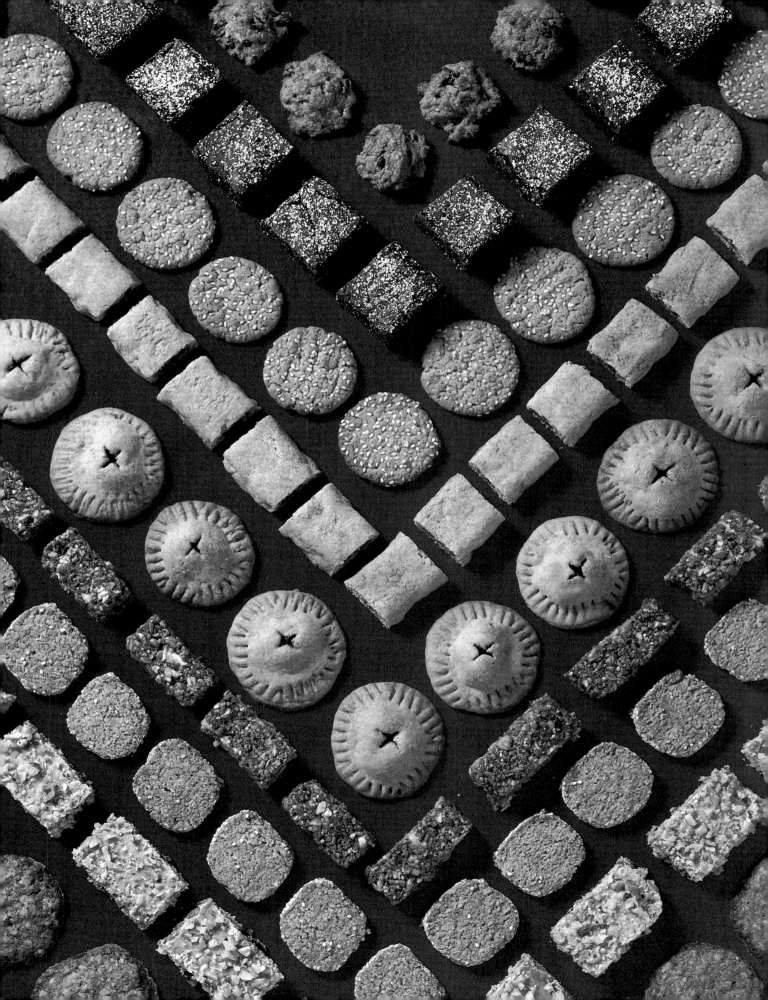

Wholesome Cookies

Cookies that are packed full of nutritious ingredients are the best kind for Scout meetings, school lunches, backpacking, and even for breakfast—especially when they taste wonderful, too. The cookies in this chapter owe their wholesomeness to ingredients such as whole wheat flour, wheat germ, seeds, nuts, dried fruits, and vegetables. Made by the same techniques as other cookies in this book—drop, bar, hand-molded, cut-out, and icebox—they're generally higher in protein, vitamins and minerals, and fiber.

Most of the supplies you'll need to make our wholesome cookies are available in supermarkets, but you may have to visit a health food store for a few ingredients: carob powder, carob chips, granulated fructose, tahini, and unsweetened coconut, for example.

Photo at left reveals a profusion of good-for-you delights. From top to bottom: Half-cup Cookies (page 792), Quick Carob Brownies (page 792), Tahini Cookies (page 793), Fruit Bars (page 799), Date Tarts (page 800), Branapple Bars (page 797), Orange Wheat Cookies (page 796), Zucchini Bars (page 796), and Oatmeal Chews (page 797).

Half-cup Cookies

(Pictured on page 790)

These chunky, down-to-earth drop cookies get their name from the nine (count 'em!) ingredients they include in one-half-cup quantity.

> ½ cup (¼ lb.) butter or margarine, softened
> ½ cup *each* peanut butter and firmly packed brown sugar
> 2 eggs
> ½ cup honey
> ¼ cup milk
> ½ teaspoon vanilla
> 2 cups whole wheat flour
> 1 teaspoon *each* baking powder and ground cinnamon
> ¾ teaspoon salt
> ½ cup *each* semisweet chocolate chips or carob chips; chopped roasted cashews, toasted almonds, or walnut pieces; unsweetened flaked coconut; raisins; and granola-style cereal

In large bowl of an electric mixer, beat butter, peanut butter, and sugar until creamy; beat in eggs, honey, milk, and vanilla. In another bowl, stir together flour, baking powder, cinnamon, and salt; gradually add to butter mixture, blending thoroughly. Mix in chocolate chips, nuts, coconut, raisins, and granola until well combined.

Drop dough by rounded tablespoonfuls onto lightly greased baking sheets, spacing cookies about 1 inch apart. Bake in a 375° oven for about 10 minutes or until golden brown. Transfer to racks and let cool. Store airtight. Makes about 5 dozen.

Carob Chip Cookies

Nutrition-minded cooks favor carob as a substitute for chocolate. Though its flavor, color, and aroma are all reminiscent of light chocolate, carob is lower in fat and contains no caffeine. Both roasted carob powder (see Quick Carob Brownies, following) and carob chips can be used in baking; both are sold in natural food stores and some supermarkets.

These honey-sweetened whole wheat cookies are generously studded with carob chips and sunflower seeds; rolled oats make them chewy (and even more nutritious).

> 1 cup solid vegetable shortening
> ½ cup firmly packed brown sugar
> 2 eggs
> ¾ cup honey
> 1 teaspoon vanilla
> 2¼ cups whole wheat flour
> 1 teaspoon baking soda
> ¾ teaspoon salt
> ½ cup raw sunflower seeds
> 1 cup quick-cooking rolled oats
> 8 ounces carob chips (about 1½ cups)

In large bowl of an electric mixer, beat shortening and sugar until creamy; beat in eggs, honey, and vanilla. In another bowl, stir together flour, baking soda, and salt; gradually add to shortening mixture, blending thoroughly. Add sunflower seeds, oats, and carob chips and stir until well combined.

Drop dough by rounded teaspoonfuls onto greased baking sheets, spacing cookies about 2 inches apart. Bake in a 375° oven for about 9 minutes or until golden. Carefully transfer to racks and let cool. Store airtight. Makes about 8 dozen.

Quick Carob Brownies

(Pictured on page 790)

Though it's relatively unfamiliar to many in the United States, carob has been around for a long time. In the Mediterranean area, the carob tree's native environment, carob pods have been a food source for centuries. Carobs also grow in parts of California and Arizona.

When ground and roasted, carob pods yield a brown powder that can be used in baking as a stand-in for unsweetened cocoa—as in these quick-to-mix brownies. Serve the brownies dusted with powdered sugar, or dress them up with a fluffy carob frosting.

> 6 tablespoons butter or margarine
> 2 eggs
> 1 cup granulated sugar
> ½ teaspoon vanilla
> ¾ cup all-purpose flour
> ½ cup roasted carob powder
> 1 teaspoon baking powder
> ½ teaspoon salt
> Powdered sugar or Fluffy carob frosting (recipe follows)

Place butter in an 8-inch square baking pan; set pan in oven while oven preheats to 325°. When butter is melted, remove pan from oven and set aside.

In large bowl of an electric mixer, beat eggs, granulated sugar, and vanilla until thick and lemon-colored; pour in butter and stir until blended (set baking pan aside unwashed). In another bowl, stir together flour, carob powder, baking powder, and salt; sift into egg mixture and stir just until smoothly blended.

Spread batter in baking pan and bake in a 325° oven for 25 minutes or until a pick inserted in center comes out clean. Place pan on a rack and let cool completely. Sift powdered sugar lightly over top or prepare fluffy carob frosting and spread on cooled brownies. Cut into 2-inch squares. Store airtight. Makes 16.

Fluffy carob frosting. In small bowl of an electric mixer, lightly beat 1 **egg white.** Add 3 tablespoons **butter** or margarine, softened; a dash of **salt;** ¼ cup **roasted carob powder;** and ¼ teaspoon **vanilla.** Beat until blended. Gradually add 1 cup sifted **powdered sugar,** beating until frosting is smooth and fluffy.

Tahini Cookies

(Pictured on page 790)

The sesame-seed paste called *tahini* is a staple in Middle Eastern cooking, adding rich, nutty flavor to a variety of dishes. Here, we use it in crisp whole wheat cookies topped with toasted sesame seeds.

You'll find tahini in Middle Eastern markets and natural food stores, and also in some well-stocked supermarkets. It keeps almost indefinitely—but, like unhomogenized nut butters, it separates on standing, so stir until smooth and well blended before using.

 ½ cup *each* granulated sugar and firmly packed brown sugar
 ½ cup tahini (stir before measuring)
 4 tablespoons butter or margarine, softened
 ¼ cup solid vegetable shortening
 1 egg
 1⅓ cups whole wheat flour
 ¾ teaspoon baking soda
 ½ teaspoon baking powder
 About 3 tablespoons sesame seeds

In large bowl of an electric mixer, beat granulated sugar, brown sugar, tahini, butter, and shortening until creamy. Beat in egg. In another bowl, stir together flour, baking soda, and baking powder; gradually add to tahini mixture, blending thoroughly. Cover tightly with plastic wrap and refrigerate until easy to handle (about 2 hours) or until next day.

Meanwhile, in a small frying pan over medium heat, toast sesame seeds, shaking pan frequently, until golden (about 2 minutes). Let cool.

Roll dough into 1-inch balls. Dip balls into toasted sesame seeds and press down so seeds adhere to dough; then place balls, seeded side up, about 3 inches apart on ungreased baking sheets. Flatten each ball with a fork dipped in flour, making a crisscross pattern with fork tines.

Bake in a 375° oven for 8 to 10 minutes or until lightly browned. Let cool on baking sheets for 2 minutes; then transfer to racks and let cool completely. Store airtight. Makes about 5 dozen.

Peanut Raisin Honeys

Here's a honey-flavored cookie that makes a good energy-booster on any occasion, from morning coffee to late-night snack.

 1 cup (½ lb.) butter or margarine, softened
 ½ cup crunchy peanut butter
 1 cup firmly packed brown sugar
 2 eggs
 1 cup honey
 2 cups *each* whole wheat flour and rolled oats
 1 cup toasted unsweetened wheat germ
 1 cup *each* unsweetened flaked coconut, raisins, and chopped salted peanuts

In large bowl of an electric mixer, beat butter, peanut butter, and sugar until creamy. Beat in eggs, one at a time, beating well after each addition, until mixture is fluffy. Mix in honey, flour, oats, and wheat germ, blending thoroughly; add coconut, raisins, and peanuts and mix to distribute evenly.

Drop dough by level tablespoonfuls onto greased baking sheets, spacing cookies about 2 inches apart. Bake in a 375° oven for 10 to 12 minutes or until golden and firm to the touch. Transfer to racks and let cool. Store airtight. Makes about 7 dozen.

Graham Crackers

These crisp, slightly sweet grahams have hearty whole-grain flavor—and they're easy to make. Serve them as is with a glass of milk or a cup of coffee, or top with nutty caramel to make easy graham cracker pralines.

  ¾ cup (¼ lb. plus 4 tablespoons) butter or margarine, softened
  ¼ cup honey
  ½ cup firmly packed brown sugar
  1 teaspoon vanilla
  3 cups whole wheat flour
  ½ cup toasted unsweetened wheat germ
  1 teaspoon *each* salt and ground cinnamon
  ½ teaspoon baking powder
  ¾ cup water

In large bowl of an electric mixer, beat butter, honey, brown sugar, and vanilla until creamy. In another bowl, stir together flour, wheat germ, salt, cinnamon, and baking powder. With mixer on low speed, add flour mixture to butter mixture alternately with water, blending well after each addition. Cover tightly with plastic wrap and refrigerate until easy to handle (at least 1 hour) or for up to 3 days.

Divide dough into 2 equal portions; return one portion to refrigerator. On a lightly floured board, pat out other portion into a ½-inch-thick rectangle. Place on a lightly greased unrimmed 12 by 15-inch baking sheet and roll out with a floured rolling pin until dough completely covers baking sheet and is an even ⅛ inch thick. Trim edges with a knife. (If dough becomes too soft, refrigerate again until firm.)

Using a floured pastry wheel or knife, cut dough into 3-inch squares (to obtain straight edges, use a ruler as a guide). Prick each 3 times with a fork. Bake in a 325° oven for about 30 minutes or until very lightly browned; remove crackers around edges of baking sheet if they brown more quickly than center crackers. Transfer crackers to racks and let cool. Repeat with remaining dough. Store airtight. Makes 40.

Cracker Pralines

Place 20 baked **Graham Crackers** close together on a baking sheet; set aside.

In a heavy 1½-quart pan, combine ½ cup firmly packed **brown sugar** and ½ cup (¼ lb.) **butter** or margarine. Bring to a boil over medium heat, stirring constantly. Boil gently (reduce heat if necessary), stirring, for 5 minutes. Remove from heat and stir in ½ cup chopped **walnuts** or almonds, ½ teaspoon **vanilla,** and ¼ teaspoon **ground cinnamon.**

Working quickly, immediately drizzle mixture over crackers and spread evenly with a small spatula. Bake in a 275° oven for 10 minutes, then carefully transfer to racks and let cool. Store airtight. Makes 20.

Nutty Whole Wheat Shortbread

(Pictured on facing page)

The flavor of toasted hazelnuts or almonds makes these whole wheat shortbread cookies almost irresistible. Eat them plain for a sweet snack, or serve alongside a bowl of frozen yogurt or a fruit salad for a nutritious dessert.

  ¾ cup (about ¼ lb.) hazelnuts (filberts) or whole blanched almonds
  ½ cup (¼ lb.) butter, softened
  ½ cup sugar
  1 cup whole wheat flour

Spread hazelnuts in a shallow rimmed baking pan and toast in a 350° oven for 10 to 15 minutes or until golden beneath skins; shake pan occasionally. Let cool. (If using almonds, toast for only 8 to 10 minutes.) Pour hazelnuts into a clean dishcloth, fold to enclose, and rub briskly to remove skins. (Omit this step if using almonds.) Whirl nuts in a blender or food processor until finely ground.

In large bowl of an electric mixer, beat butter and sugar until creamy; beat in ground nuts. Gradually add flour, blending thoroughly.

Gather dough into a ball and transfer to a lightly floured board. Roll out to a straight-edged rectangle ¼ inch thick. Cut rectangle lengthwise into thirds; then cut each third into triangles (see photograph on facing page). Or roll out dough free-form, keeping it an even ¼ inch thick, and cut out with cookie cutters (about 2 inches in diameter). Place cookies slightly apart on ungreased baking sheets. Bake in a 350° oven for 10 to 12 minutes or until golden brown. Let cool on baking sheets for 5 minutes, then transfer to racks and let cool completely. Store airtight. Makes about 2 dozen.

Nutty Whole Wheat Shortbread *(Recipe on facing page)*

1 Toast nuts on a rimmed baking sheet until skins have cracked and meat underneath has turned golden.

2 Rub nuts briskly in a towel to remove as much of skins as possible.

3 In a blender or food processor, whirl nuts until finely and evenly ground.

4 Cut rectangle of dough lengthwise into thirds, then cut each third into triangles.

Lemon Carrot Cookies

Shredded carrots add vitamins and natural sweetness to these lemon-flavored drop cookies.

> 1 cup (½ lb.) butter or margarine, softened
> ¾ cup sugar
> 1 teaspoon lemon extract
> ½ teaspoon vanilla
> 1 egg
> 1 cup finely shredded carrots (about 2 medium-size)
> 1 cup *each* all-purpose flour and whole wheat flour
> 2 teaspoons baking powder
> ¼ teaspoon *each* salt and baking soda
> 1½ cups chopped walnuts

In large bowl of an electric mixer, beat butter and sugar until creamy; beat in lemon extract, vanilla, and egg. Stir in carrots. In another bowl, stir together all-purpose flour, whole wheat flour, baking powder, salt, and baking soda; gradually add to butter mixture, blending thoroughly. Mix in walnuts.

Drop dough by level tablespoonfuls onto greased baking sheets, spacing cookies about 2 inches apart. Bake in a 375° oven for 12 minutes or until edges are browned. Transfer to racks and let cool. Store airtight. Makes about 6 dozen.

Orange Wheat Cookies

(Pictured on page 790)

A crunchy, decorative rim of sesame seeds adds interest to these icebox wafers. Daintier than most whole wheat cookies, they have a pleasing crispness and a delicate orange flavor.

> 1 cup (½ lb.) butter or margarine, softened
> 1 cup firmly packed brown sugar
> 1 egg
> 1 teaspoon grated orange peel
> 2¼ cups whole wheat flour
> 1½ cups quick-cooking rolled oats
> ¼ cup sesame seeds

In large bowl of an electric mixer, beat butter and sugar until creamy; beat in egg and orange peel.

Gradually add flour and oats, blending thoroughly. Shape dough into 2 rolls, each about 1½ inches in diameter. Evenly sprinkle 2 tablespoons of the sesame seeds on each of 2 sheets of wax paper. Roll each portion of dough in seeds to coat on all sides; then wrap in wax paper and refrigerate until firm (at least 2 hours) or for up to 3 days.

Unwrap dough. Using a sharp knife, cut into ¼-inch-thick slices; place slices about 1 inch apart on ungreased baking sheets. Bake in a 350° oven for 12 to 15 minutes or until lightly browned. Transfer to racks and let cool. Store airtight. Makes about 5 dozen.

Zucchini Bars

(Pictured on page 790)

Coarse shreds of zucchini, bits of dried fruit, and coconut make these bar cookies extra moist and chewy. They're topped with chopped walnuts for a crunchy finishing touch.

> ¾ cup (¼ lb. plus 4 tablespoons) butter or margarine, softened
> ½ cup *each* granulated sugar and firmly packed brown sugar
> 2 eggs
> 2 teaspoons vanilla
> 1¾ cups all-purpose flour
> ½ teaspoon salt
> 1½ teaspoons baking powder
> ¾ cup *each* unsweetened flaked coconut, snipped pitted dates, and raisins
> 2 cups unpared, coarsely shredded zucchini
> 1 tablespoon butter or margarine, melted
> 2 tablespoons milk
> ¼ teaspoon ground cinnamon
> 1 cup powdered sugar
> 1 cup finely chopped walnuts

In large bowl of an electric mixer, beat the ¾ cup butter, granulated sugar, and brown sugar until creamy; beat in eggs and 1 teaspoon of the vanilla. In another bowl, stir together flour, salt, and baking powder; gradually add to butter mixture, blending thoroughly. Mix in coconut, dates, raisins, and zucchini until well combined.

Spread batter evenly in a greased 10 by 15-inch rimmed baking pan. Bake in a 350° oven for 35 to 40 minutes or until a pick inserted in center comes out clean. Place on a rack and let cool slightly.

In a small bowl, beat together the 1 tablespoon butter, milk, remaining 1 teaspoon vanilla, cinnamon, and powdered sugar. Drizzle glaze over warm cookies, then spread evenly; sprinkle walnuts on top. Let cool completely, then cut into 1½ by 2-inch bars. Store airtight. Makes about 4 dozen.

Oatmeal Chews

(Pictured on page 790)

Oatmeal cookies have long been considered a nutritious snack or lunchbox treat. This delightfully chewy version includes whole wheat flour, chopped walnuts, and wheat germ for a fine toasty flavor that will please children and help nourish them, too.

 1 cup (½ lb.) butter or margarine, softened
 1 cup firmly packed brown sugar
 ¼ cup granulated sugar
 2 eggs
 1 teaspoon vanilla
 1 cup whole wheat flour
 ½ cup toasted unsweetened wheat germ
 1 teaspoon *each* baking soda and
     ground cinnamon
 ½ teaspoon salt
 1½ cups rolled oats
 1 cup chopped walnuts
     Granulated sugar

In large bowl of an electric mixer, beat butter, brown sugar, and the ¼ cup granulated sugar until creamy; beat in eggs and vanilla. In another bowl, stir together flour, wheat germ, baking soda, cinnamon, and salt; gradually add to butter mixture, blending thoroughly. Mix in oats and walnuts. Cover tightly with plastic wrap and refrigerate until easy to handle (about 2 hours) or for up to 3 days.

For each cookie, shape about 1 tablespoon dough into a ball. Place balls about 4 inches apart on well-greased baking sheets. Generously grease the bottom of a glass or jar (one with a wide, flat base). For each cookie, dip glass in granulated sugar; then press ball of dough to flatten it to a thickness of about ¼ inch.

Bake in a 375° oven for 5 to 6 minutes or until lightly browned. Let cool on baking sheets for about a minute, then transfer to racks and let cool completely. Store airtight. Makes about 4½ dozen.

Branapple Bars

(Pictured on page 790)

In recent years, dietary fiber has been recognized as an important component of good nutrition. Perhaps the best source of fiber in our diets is bran—the outer layer of a kernel of wheat (or other grain). Bran is sold in its natural, unprocessed state; it's used in breads and a number of high-fiber breakfast cereals.

These no-bake cookies are made with bran cereal for an extra-high fiber content. Like the "health food candy bars" sold in many markets, they're moist, chewy, and packed with good things—apples, nuts, seeds, peanut butter, and wheat germ, as well as the bran cereal. Served with milk or fruit juice, they make a nutritious snack or breakfast treat.

 1 package (6 oz.) dried apple rings or slices
 3 cups boiling water
 ½ cup sesame seeds
 4 cups whole bran cereal
 ¼ cup toasted unsweetened wheat germ
 ½ cup roasted unsalted sunflower seeds
 ½ cup chopped walnuts or almonds
 1 cup honey
 1½ cups peanut butter
 2 tablespoons butter or margarine
 1 teaspoon ground cinnamon

Place dried apples in a medium-size bowl and pour boiling water over them. Let stand for 20 minutes. Meanwhile, in a wide frying pan over medium heat, toast sesame seeds, shaking pan frequently, until golden (about 2 minutes). Let cool; then place in a large mixing bowl and stir in bran cereal, wheat germ, sunflower seeds, and walnuts. Drain apples well; then whirl in a food processor until finely ground (or put through a food chopper fitted with a fine blade). Add to cereal mixture.

In a 2½ to 3-quart pan, cook honey over medium heat until it reaches 230°F on a candy thermometer; stir in peanut butter, butter, and cinnamon. Cook, stirring, until mixture returns to 230°F. Remove from heat and pour over cereal mixture. Stir with a wooden spoon until thoroughly blended.

Turn mixture into a well-greased 10 by 15-inch rimmed baking pan and press down firmly to fill pan evenly. Cover and refrigerate until firm (about 2 hours); then cut into 2 by 2½-inch bars. Wrap bars individually in foil and store in refrigerator for up to 2 weeks. Makes 2½ dozen.

Fruit Bars *(Recipe on facing page)*

1 Use your fingers and a ruler to form dough into a straight-edged rectangle with square corners.

2 Cut rectangle lengthwise into thirds. Spread dried fruit filling (in this case, prune) evenly down center of each strip.

3 Fold sides over filling to overlap slightly on top. Cut strips in half crosswise and invert onto greased baking sheets.

4 After baking, let cookies cool slightly; then cut each strip into 4 pieces.

Fruit Bars

(Pictured on page 790 and on facing page)

If you like fruit-filled cookies, you'll want to make these moist bars. Our recipe presents a choice of four fruit fillings; use either figs, prunes, apricots, or dates. The cookies keep well, becoming softer and more flavorful after they've stood at least a day.

- ½ cup (¼ lb.) butter or margarine, softened
- ½ cup *each* granulated sugar and firmly packed brown sugar
- 2 eggs
- ½ teaspoon vanilla
- 1 cup whole wheat flour
- 1¼ cups all-purpose flour
- ¼ cup toasted unsweetened wheat germ
- ¼ teaspoon *each* salt and baking soda
  Fruit filling (recipes follow)

In large bowl of an electric mixer, beat butter, granulated sugar, and brown sugar until creamy. Beat in eggs and vanilla. In another bowl, stir together whole wheat flour, all-purpose flour, wheat germ, salt, and baking soda; gradually add to butter mixture, blending thoroughly.

Cover dough tightly with plastic wrap and refrigerate until easy to handle (at least 1 hour) or until next day. Meanwhile, prepare fruit filling of your choice; set aside.

Divide dough into 2 equal portions. Return one portion to refrigerator. On a floured board, roll out other portion to a straight-edged 9 by 15-inch rectangle; cut lengthwise into three strips.

Divide cooled fruit filling into 6 equal portions and evenly distribute one portion down center of each strip, bringing it out to ends. Use a long spatula to lift sides of each dough strip over filling, overlapping edges slightly on top. Press together lightly. Cut strips in half crosswise; lift and invert onto greased baking sheets (seam side should be down). Brush off excess flour. Refrigerate for about 15 minutes. Meanwhile, repeat rolling and filling with remaining dough.

Bake in a 375° oven for 15 to 20 minutes or until browned. Let cool on baking sheets on a rack for about 10 minutes; then cut each strip crosswise into 4 pieces. Transfer cookies to racks and let cool completely. Store covered. Makes 4 dozen.

Fig filling. Using a food processor or a food chopper fitted with a medium blade, grind together 1 pound **dried figs** (about 2 cups lightly packed) and ½ cup **walnuts** or almonds. Turn into a medium-size pan and add ⅓ cup **sugar**, ½ cup **water**, 1 teaspoon grated **lemon peel**, and 2 tablespoons **lemon juice**. Place over medium heat and cook, stirring, until mixture boils and becomes very thick (5 to 8 minutes). Let cool completely.

Prune filling. Follow directions for **Fig filling**, but substitute 2 cups lightly packed **moist-pack pitted prunes** for figs and add ¾ teaspoon **ground cinnamon** with sugar.

Apricot filling. Follow directions for **Fig filling**, but substitute 3 cups lightly packed **dried apricots** for figs and use 1 teaspoon grated **orange peel** in place of lemon peel.

Date filling. Follow directions for **Fig filling**, but substitute 1 pound **pitted dates** for figs and increase lemon peel to 2 teaspoons.

Chewy Granola Brownies

Not all brownies are dark and chocolaty, as this version proves. Its golden color and rich flavor come from brown sugar and crunchy granola-style cereal.

- ½ cup (¼ lb.) butter or margarine
- 1¾ cups firmly packed brown sugar
- 2 eggs, lightly beaten
- 1 teaspoon vanilla
- ¾ cup *each* all-purpose flour and whole wheat flour
- 2 teaspoons baking powder
- ¾ teaspoon salt
- 1½ cups granola-style cereal (break up any large lumps before measuring)
- ½ cup chopped nuts (optional)

Melt butter in a medium-size pan over medium heat. Remove from heat and mix in sugar. Stir in eggs and vanilla; set aside.

In a mixing bowl, stir together all-purpose flour, whole wheat flour, baking powder, and salt. Add sugar mixture and stir until well combined. Stir in granola, then nuts (if used). Spread batter in a greased 9 by 13-inch baking pan.

Bake in a 350° oven for 25 minutes or until a pick inserted in center comes out clean (do not overbake). Let cool in pan on a rack, then cut into 1½ by 3-inch bars. Store airtight. Makes about 2 dozen.

Date Tarts

(Pictured on page 790)

Dates have a history of cultivation that goes back 4,500 years, to the Middle East and North Africa. In these regions, the fruit was so important a food source that it was known as "bread of the desert." Though dates taste as sugary-sweet as candy, they're quite nutritious, containing relatively large amounts of potassium, iron, and niacin, as well as some protein and fiber.

Here, the sun-ripened fruits lend their rich flavor and wholesomeness to a fancy filled cookie. We've called it a "date tart" because of its resemblance to a plump little pie.

> ½ cup (¼ lb.) butter or margarine, softened
> 1 cup firmly packed brown sugar
> 2 eggs
> 1 teaspoon vanilla
> 2 cups all-purpose flour
> ½ cup toasted unsweetened wheat germ
> ½ teaspoon *each* salt and ground nutmeg
> ¼ teaspoon baking soda
> Date filling (recipe follows)

In large bowl of an electric mixer, beat butter and sugar until creamy; beat in eggs and vanilla. In another bowl, stir together flour, wheat germ, salt, nutmeg, and baking soda; gradually add to butter mixture, blending thoroughly. Cover dough tightly with plastic wrap and refrigerate until easy to handle (at least 2 hours) or for up to 3 days. Meanwhile, prepare date filling.

Take out a third of the dough, leaving remaining dough in refrigerator. On a well-floured board, roll out dough to a thickness of ¹⁄₁₆ inch; cut out with a 3-inch round cookie cutter. Repeat with remaining dough, rolling and cutting one portion at a time.

Place half the cookies slightly apart on greased baking sheets; spoon a heaping teaspoonful of filling onto each. Cover each with another cookie and press edges together with a floured fork. Decoratively slash top, if desired. Bake in a 350° oven for 12 to 15 minutes or until lightly browned. Transfer to racks and let cool. Store airtight. Makes about 2½ dozen.

Date filling. In a small pan, combine 1½ cups lightly packed **pitted dates,** ½ cup **water,** and 2 tablespoons **honey.** Cook over medium heat, stirring and mashing with a spoon, until mixture is thick and smooth. Stir in ½ teaspoon **vanilla.** Let cool; then cover and refrigerate.

Apricot Bran Chews

Breakfast from a cookie jar? Why not, when the cookies are as wholesome as these. Paired with a glass of milk, they offer quick, easily handled nourishment to start the day—a boon to those whose schedules demand on-the-go meals.

> ⅓ cup whole bran cereal
> ¼ cup water
> ¾ cup (¼ lb. plus 4 tablespoons) butter or margarine, softened
> ¼ cup firmly packed brown sugar
> 1 egg
> ¼ cup honey
> 1 teaspoon vanilla
> 1 cup all-purpose flour
> 1 teaspoon baking powder
> ¼ teaspoon *each* salt and baking soda
> ¼ cup instant nonfat dry milk
> 1 cup rolled oats
> ¾ cup chopped walnuts
> 1 cup finely chopped dried apricots

Combine bran cereal and water in a small bowl; set aside. In large bowl of an electric mixer, beat butter and sugar until creamy; add egg and beat until fluffy. Mix in honey, vanilla, and cereal mixture. In another bowl, stir together flour, baking powder, salt, baking soda, dry milk, oats, walnuts, and apricots; gradually add to butter mixture, blending thoroughly.

Drop dough by level tablespoonfuls onto greased baking sheets, spacing cookies about 2 inches apart. Bake in a 375° oven for 10 minutes or until golden brown and firm to the touch. Transfer to racks and let cool. Store airtight. Makes 3 to 4 dozen.

Fructose Spice Cookies

All of us are familiar with sucrose—ordinary table sugar. But fructose, a sugar found in many fruits and vegetables, is becoming increasingly available in supermarkets and natural food stores. Sold in granulated form, it looks and tastes like sucrose, but it's up to 1½ times sweeter, depending on how it's used. You can often use less fructose than sucrose for the same degree of sweetness.

Baked goods made with fructose are moister and brown more readily than those made with sucrose. If you'd like to try baking with fructose, it's best to use recipes specifically designed for it—such as this one, for soft, chewy spice cookies.

1 cup granulated fructose
½ cup (¼ lb.) butter or margarine, melted
2 eggs, lightly beaten
1 teaspoon grated lemon peel
2 teaspoons vanilla
1 cup *each* all-purpose flour and whole wheat flour
1 teaspoon cream of tartar
½ teaspoon baking soda
1½ teaspoons ground cinnamon
¼ teaspoon *each* ground nutmeg and salt
⅛ teaspoon ground cloves

In a large bowl, stir together fructose and butter; mix in eggs, lemon peel, and vanilla. In another bowl, stir together all-purpose flour, whole wheat flour, cream of tartar, baking soda, cinnamon, nutmeg, salt, and cloves; add to egg mixture and stir until blended. Cover dough tightly with plastic wrap and refrigerate until firm (about 2 hours).

Force dough through a cookie press to form round shapes, spacing cookies about 1½ inches apart on greased baking sheets. (Or drop rounded teaspoonfuls of dough 1½ inches apart.) Bake in a 350° oven for 10 to 12 minutes or until firm to the touch. Transfer to racks and let cool. Store airtight. Makes 4 to 5 dozen.

Tutti Frutti Oat Bars

Apple juice and three kinds of dried fruit—raisins, apricots, and dates—go into the filling for these oat-topped treats.

Fruit filling (recipe follows)
½ cup (¼ lb.) butter or margarine, softened
1 cup firmly packed brown sugar
1½ cups all-purpose flour
½ teaspoon *each* baking soda and salt
1½ cups rolled oats
2 tablespoons water

Prepare fruit filling; set aside.

In large bowl of an electric mixer, beat butter and sugar until creamy. In another bowl, stir

together flour, baking soda, and salt; gradually add to butter mixture, blending thoroughly. Add oats and water and mix until well combined and crumbly.

Pat half the crumb mixture firmly into a greased 9 by 13-inch baking pan. Spread with cooled fruit filling. Spoon remaining crumb mixture evenly over filling; pat down firmly. Bake in a 350° oven for about 35 minutes or until lightly browned. Let cool in pan on a rack, then cut into 1½ by 2½-inch bars. Store covered. Makes about 2½ dozen.

Fruit filling. In a small pan, combine ¼ cup **sugar** and 1 tablespoon **cornstarch.** Stir in 1 cup **unsweetened apple juice,** 1 teaspoon grated **lemon peel,** 1 tablespoon **lemon juice,** 1 cup **raisins,** and ½ cup *each* finely chopped, lightly packed **dried apricots** and lightly packed snipped **pitted dates.** Cook over medium heat, stirring, until mixture boils and thickens; let cool.

Lunchbox Cookies

Freshly baked cookies make an excellent addition to a lunchbox, adding a little touch of home to a meal eaten elsewhere. When deciding on cookies to tuck into someone's lunch, choose ones that are sturdy enough to pack and carry well. Here are a dozen suggestions; for more, see "Which Cookies to Send," page 737.

Holiday Cookies

olidays and cookies go together naturally—festive occasions just seem to call for a bite of something sweet. Christmas, of course, is the holiday most often associated with baking, but Valentine's Day and Halloween are often celebrated with special cookies of their own.

The Christmas cookies in this chapter include a number of traditional favorites, such as Gingerbread Boys (page 812), Nürnberger Lebkuchen (page 812), and Speculaas (page 813). In addition, we present recipes for some really unusual holiday treats: cookie ornaments with candy centers that resemble stained glass, almond cookies that you shape into little partridges and pears, and a gingerbread log cabin that would make a showstopping buffet centerpiece.

Many of the cookies in this chapter are good gift candidates; some of the Christmas cookies can also be hung on a tree or tied with ribbons to gift packages.

Photo at right celebrates three holidays with a fanfare of festive cookies. In center: Kiss-me Cookies (page 804). Im corners: Halloween Cookie Pops (page 807). Others, from top to bottom: Fruitcake Cookie Cups (page 807); Candy Cane Crisps (page 810); Nürnberger Lebkuchen (page 812); Glazed Mincemeat Drops (page 809); Speculaas (page 813) Glazed Mincemeat Drops; Nürnberger Lebkuchen; Candy Cane Crisps; and Fruitcake Cookie Cups.

Küss
mich

Valentine's Day

What better way to say "Happy Valentine's Day" than with a gift of freshly baked cookies? Whether you're expressing your affection for the gang at the office, some very special children, or your one and only, cookies make a declaration of love that Cupid himself couldn't resist.

Kiss-me Cookies

(Pictured on page 803)

Vendors at German festivals sell big, spicy cookie hearts, decorated with sentimental messages written in icing. The hearts are tied onto ribbons so they can be worn as badges of affection—many a hopeful lad has draped one about the neck of a pretty Fräulein.

To make these hearts at home, you start with a traditional lebkuchen dough, cutting it into large hearts with the aid of a paper pattern; use purchased icing to inscribe your message. Any language will do, but these German phrases are most authentic: *Liebling* (darling), *Mein Schatz* (my treasure), *Küss mich* (kiss me), *Du bist mein Alles* (you are my everything), *Alte Liebe rostet nicht* (old love never rusts), *Nur du* (only you), *Du bist mein Traum* (you are my dream), *Ich liebe dich* (I love you), *Liebst du mich?* (do you love me?), *Bist du mein?* (are you mine?), *Heute oder nie* (today or never), *Bleib mir treu* (stay true to me).

- ¾ cup honey
- ⅔ cup firmly packed brown sugar
- 1 teaspoon grated lemon peel
- 4 tablespoons butter or margarine
- 2 eggs
- 3¾ cups all-purpose flour
- ½ teaspoon baking soda
- ¼ teaspoon salt
- ½ cup almonds, ground
- 1 teaspoon ground ginger
- ½ teaspoon ground cinnamon
- ¼ teaspoon ground nutmeg
- ½ cup minced candied orange peel
- 1 egg yolk beaten with 1 tablespoon water
  Purchased decorating icing (in tubes or aerosol cans)

In a small pan, combine honey, sugar, lemon peel, and butter; stir over medium heat until butter is melted. Let cool to lukewarm. In a large mixing bowl, beat eggs until foamy; stir in honey mixture. In another bowl, stir together flour, baking soda, salt, almonds, ginger, cinnamon, nutmeg, and orange peel; gradually add to egg mixture, blending thoroughly.

To make cookie pattern, cut as large a heart shape as possible from a 7 by 8-inch rectangle of heavy paper. Divide dough into 8 equal portions; dust with flour and shake off excess. On a lightly floured board, roll out one portion of dough until just slightly larger than pattern. Transfer dough to a greased baking sheet and place pattern on top; cut around pattern with a knife and remove scraps.

Repeat with remaining dough, spacing cookies slightly apart on baking sheets. Combine scraps and re-roll to make 1 or 2 additional hearts. Brush cookies with egg yolk mixture. Bake in a 350° oven for 12 to 15 minutes or until lightly browned. Transfer to racks and let cool completely.

Decorate cookies with icing, making a decorative border around edges and writing messages in center (white icing and a plain tip are best for writing). Let dry, uncovered, until icing is firm (several hours or until next day). Wrap each cookie snugly in plastic wrap, joining overlaps on back (tape, if necessary). With an ice pick or metal skewer, make 2 evenly spaced holes near the top of each heart; then force a piece of narrow ribbon through plastic and cookie. Tie ribbon ends, making loop long enough to fit over a head. Store airtight for up to 2 weeks. Makes 8 to 10.

Raspberry-Nut Valentines

Rich, European-style nut cookies cut into heart shapes are the foundation for these fancy jam-filled sandwiches. A shower of powdered sugar provides a pastry-shop finish.

- 1 cup (½ lb.) butter or margarine, softened
- ⅔ cup granulated sugar
- ½ teaspoon vanilla
- 1⅓ cups pecans, ground
- 2 cups all-purpose flour
  Powdered sugar
  About ¼ cup raspberry jam

In large bowl of an electric mixer, beat butter and granulated sugar until creamy; beat in vanilla. Gradually add pecans and flour, blending thoroughly. Cover tightly with plastic wrap and refrigerate until easy to handle (1 to 2 hours) or for up to 3 days.

On a floured board, roll out dough to a thickness of 1/8 inch. Cut out with a 2-inch heart-shaped cookie cutter and transfer to ungreased baking sheets, spacing about 1 inch apart. Cut out a hole in center of half of the cookies, using a tiny round cutter about 1/2 inch in diameter (you can use the cap from a vanilla or other extract bottle). Bake in a 375° oven for about 12 minutes or until lightly browned. Transfer to racks and let cool completely.

Sift powdered sugar over tops of cookies with holes; then spread bottom sides of remaining cookies with jam. Place a sugar-topped cookie on each jam-topped cookie to form a sandwich. Store airtight. Makes about 3 dozen.

Lemon Hearts

"Sweets for the sweet" is an appropriate announcement on February 14, when you present your valentine with a basketful of these crisp, buttery lemon cookies. Each is sprinkled with sugar before baking and crowned with half a candied cherry.

- 1 cup (1/2 lb.) butter or margarine, softened
- 1 cup sugar
- 1 egg yolk
- 3 teaspoons grated lemon peel
- 2 cups all-purpose flour
- 1/2 cup ground blanched almonds
  Sugar
  About 20 candied cherries, cut in half

In large bowl of an electric mixer, beat butter and the 1 cup sugar until creamy; beat in egg yolk and lemon peel. Gradually add flour, blending thoroughly; stir in almonds. Gather dough into a ball with your hands.

On a lightly floured board, roll out dough to a thickness of 1/4 inch. Cut out with a 2 to 3-inch heart-shaped cookie cutter; transfer cookies to greased baking sheets, spacing about 1 inch apart. Sprinkle cookies lightly with sugar. Place half a cherry, cut side down, in center of each and press in lightly.

Bake in a 325° oven for about 20 minutes or until edges are golden. Transfer to racks and let cool completely. Store airtight. Makes about 3½ dozen.

Halloween

When the wind whistles, the back door creaks, and you seem to hear an owl hooting in the distance, ward off the witches with these delicious Halloween cookies.

Pumpkin Bars

These pumpkin spice bars are ideal for Halloween parties; you might also serve them at Thanksgiving as an alternative to pumpkin pie.

- 4 eggs
- 3/4 cup salad oil
- 2 cups sugar
- 1 can (about 15 oz.) pumpkin
- 2 cups all-purpose flour
- 2 teaspoons ground cinnamon
- 3/4 teaspoon *each* ground ginger, cloves, and nutmeg
- 3/4 teaspoon salt
- 2 teaspoons baking powder
- 1 teaspoon baking soda
  Orange cream cheese frosting (recipe follows)
  About 72 whole unblanched almonds (optional)

In large bowl of an electric mixer, beat eggs lightly; beat in oil, sugar, and pumpkin. In another bowl, stir together flour, cinnamon, ginger, cloves, nutmeg, salt, baking powder, and baking soda; gradually add to pumpkin mixture, blending thoroughly.

Pour batter into a greased and flour-dusted 10 by 15-inch rimmed baking pan. Bake in a 350° oven for about 35 minutes or until edges begin to pull away from pan sides and center springs back when lightly touched. Let cool in pan on a rack. Prepare orange cream cheese frosting and spread over cooled cookies; cut into 1 by 2-inch bars. If desired, top each bar with an almond. Store covered. Makes about 6 dozen.

Orange cream cheese frosting. In small bowl of an electric mixer, beat 1 small package (3 oz.) **cream cheese** (softened) and 2 tablespoons **butter** or margarine (softened) until fluffy. Beat in 1½ teaspoons **milk,** ½ teaspoon **vanilla,** and ¾ teaspoon grated **orange peel.** Gradually sift in enough **powdered sugar** (about 2 cups) to make a spreadable icing.

Halloween Cookie Pops *(Recipe on facing page)*

1 Lay homemade patterns on rolled-out dough; cut around patterns with a small, sharp knife.

2 Gently insert sticks 1½ to 2 inches into base of each cookie before baking. If dough is too soft, cover and refrigerate briefly.

3 Tint icing as desired; spread over each baked and cooled cookie.

4 Add decorations before icing sets; let children choose from an assortment of colored candies.

Halloween Cookie Pops

(Pictured on page 803)

These delightful cookies-on-sticks make fine Halloween treats for your favorite little goblins.

- ⅔ **cup solid vegetable shortening**
- ⅔ **cup butter or margarine, softened**
- ¾ **cup** *each* **granulated sugar and firmly packed brown sugar**
- 2 **eggs**
- 2 **teaspoons vanilla**
- 3½ **cups all-purpose flour**
- 2 **teaspoons baking powder**
- 1 **teaspoon salt**
- 4 **teaspoons pumpkin pie spice or 1 teaspoon** *each* **ground allspice, cinnamon, ginger, and nutmeg**
  Confectioner's icing (recipe follows)
  Assorted candy decorations

In large bowl of an electric mixer, beat shortening, butter, granulated sugar, and brown sugar until creamy; beat in eggs and vanilla. In another bowl, stir together flour, baking powder, salt, and pumpkin pie spice; gradually add to butter mixture, blending thoroughly. Cover tightly with plastic wrap and refrigerate for 1 to 2 hours.

Meanwhile, cut cookie patterns from lightweight cardboard, choosing simple Halloween shapes and making them 5 to 6 inches wide at the widest point. Also have ready 4½ to 5½-inch Popsicle sticks or tongue depressors.

Using a stockinet-covered or floured rolling pin, roll out dough, a portion at a time, on a floured board to a thickness of about ⅜ inch. (Keep remaining dough refrigerated until ready to roll.) Place patterns on dough and cut around edges with a knife. Remove patterns; use a wide spatula to transfer cookies carefully to ungreased baking sheets, spacing them about 2 inches apart. Insert Popsicle sticks 1½ to 2 inches into the base of each.

Bake in a 375° oven for 12 to 15 minutes or until very lightly browned. Transfer to racks and let cool completely. Prepare confectioner's icing and spread on cooled cookies; decorate with candies as desired. Let icing dry thoroughly, then wrap cookies individually in plastic wrap. Store in a single layer on a flat surface. Makes about 1 dozen.

Confectioner's icing. In a bowl, stir together 2 cups sifted **powdered sugar** and enough **milk** (about 3 tablespoons) to make a spreadable icing. Tint with **food color** as desired.

Christmas

Christmas is the time when many home bakers like to display their talents, producing batch after batch of festive cookies to delight family and friends. Our Christmas cookie collection includes some familiar old standbys and some new ideas; elsewhere in this book, you'll find more treats for your holiday cookie tray—try Norwegian Kringle, page 757; Finnish Ribbon Cakes, page 759; Italian Fruit Cookies, page 761; Swedish Ginger Thins, page 769; Spritz, page 775; Almond Ravioli Cookies, page 777; and Mint Meringues, page 736.

Fruitcake Cookie Cups

(Pictured on pages 803 and 814)

Like miniature Christmas fruitcakes, these moist cookies age well. You bake them in little paper bonbon cups, available in cookware shops.

- 4 **tablespoons butter or margarine, softened**
- ½ **cup firmly packed brown sugar**
- ¼ **cup apple or red currant jelly**
- 2 **eggs**
- 1 **teaspoon vanilla**
- 1½ **cups all-purpose flour**
- 2 **teaspoons baking soda**
- ½ **teaspoon** *each* **ground allspice, cloves, cinnamon, and nutmeg**
- 1 **cup chopped walnuts or pecans**
- 1 **cup currants or raisins**
- 1 **cup chopped candied cherries or mixed candied fruit**

In large bowl of an electric mixer, beat butter and sugar until creamy; beat in jelly, eggs, and vanilla. In another bowl, stir together flour, baking soda, allspice, cloves, cinnamon, and nutmeg. Blend half the flour mixture into butter mixture. Add walnuts, currants, and cherries to remaining flour mixture; then stir into butter mixture, blending thoroughly.

Spoon 1½ to 2 teaspoons batter into each paper bonbon cup and place about 1 inch apart on baking sheets; or drop batter by rounded teaspoonfuls directly onto lightly greased baking sheets, spacing cookies about 2 inches apart. Bake in a 300° oven for 17 to 20 minutes or until centers spring back when lightly touched. Let cool on racks. Store airtight. Makes about 6 dozen.

Partridge & Pear Cookies

Three French hens, two turtle doves—any child could complete the line, especially if he or she saw your tree decorated with partridges and pears made of almond cookie dough. Whole cloves provide stems for the pears, eyes for the birds, and hangers for both; a lightly tinted egg white glaze lends a blush of color.

>   1 cup (½ lb.) butter or margarine, softened
>   8 ounces almond paste
>   ¾ cup sugar
>   1 egg
>   3 cups all-purpose flour
>   Whole cloves
>   Egg white glaze (recipe follows)

In large bowl of an electric mixer, beat butter, almond paste, and sugar until creamy; beat in egg. Gradually add flour, blending thoroughly.

Shape just a few cookies at a time, keeping remaining dough covered. For each cookie, use about 2 tablespoons of dough; flatten and shape into a partridge or pear. Insert cloves and prick partridge cookies as shown in illustrations below. Transfer cookies to ungreased baking sheets, spacing about 1 inch apart.

Bake in a 325° oven for about 20 minutes or until lightly browned on bottoms. Transfer to racks and let cool. Prepare egg white glaze; use a watercolor brush or soft pastry brush to apply a thin wash of color to cookies. Store airtight. Makes about 3½ dozen.

Egg white glaze. Beat 1 **egg white** until frothy; beat in ½ cup sifted **powdered sugar.** Divide glaze into portions and tint lightly with yellow, red, and/or orange **food color.**

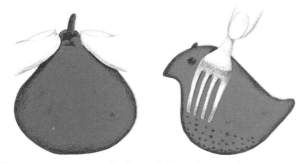

For stem of pear, insert bud end of clove; shape and press dough firmly around it. Partridge has clove hanger and eye; prick with a fork to simulate speckled breast.

Stained-glass Cookies

(Pictured on page 814)

Shimmering red or green candy centers accent these crisp cut-out cookies. Each one has a loop of ribbon attached, so you can hang them on your Christmas tree or tie them to gifts as edible decorations. The cookies are made from a sour cream dough flavored with nutmeg—but if you prefer, you can substitute the dough used for our gingerbread Log Cabin (page 810).

For shaping, you'll need a 4-inch round cookie cutter (or a tuna can with ends removed) and some smaller cutters for making the center cutouts. Also have ready about 7½ yards of ¼-inch ribbon for hanging.

Though these ornaments are quite durable, their candy centers may run if you hang them near a hot light or where humidity is high. To prevent this, we recommend heat-sealing the cookies in plastic wrap (directions follow).

>   ½ cup (¼ lb.) butter or margarine, softened
>   ½ cup solid vegetable shortening
>   1½ cups sugar
>   ½ cup sour cream
>   1 teaspoon vanilla
>   1 egg
>   3¾ cups all-purpose flour
>   1 teaspoon ground nutmeg
>   ½ teaspoon *each* baking soda and salt
>   2 cups sugar
>   1 cup light corn syrup
>   ½ cup water
>   Red or green food color
>   ½ to 1 teaspoon flavoring, such as raspberry, peppermint, or pineapple

In large bowl of an electric mixer, beat butter, shortening, and the 1½ cups sugar until creamy; beat in sour cream, vanilla, and egg. In another bowl, stir together flour, nutmeg, baking soda, and salt; gradually add to butter mixture, blending thoroughly. Cover dough tightly with plastic wrap and refrigerate until next day.

Divide dough into quarters. Work with one portion at a time; keep remaining dough refrigerated until ready to roll. Roll out on a floured board to a thickness of ⅛ inch. Cut out with a 4-inch round cookie cutter and transfer to greased baking sheets, spacing cookies about 1 inch apart. Refrigerate sheets. When cookies are cold, cut out centers with a smaller cutter. Refrigerate scraps to re-roll with remaining dough.

Bake cookies in a 375° oven for 6 to 7 minutes or just until firm but not yet browned around edges. Let cool on baking sheets for 5 minutes; transfer to a flat surface and let cool completely.

Cut ¼-inch ribbon into 8-inch lengths. Loop a piece of ribbon through center of each cooled cookie; tie securely at top. Arrange cookies, right side up, on greased baking sheets.

For candy centers, place two 1-cup glass measuring cups in a 375° oven to preheat. Combine the 2 cups sugar, corn syrup, and water in a 2-quart pan. Cook over medium-high heat, stirring, until sugar is dissolved. Then cook without stirring until syrup reaches 280°F (hard crack stage) on a candy thermometer. Remove from heat; stir in your choice of food color and flavoring.

Remove one measuring cup from oven; fill with half the syrup (keep remaining syrup over low heat). As soon as syrup in cup stops bubbling, hold cup with a potholder and pour syrup in a thin stream to fill cookie centers. Repeat, using second cup and remaining syrup. Let cookies cool completely; twist gently to loosen, then slide off sheets. Store airtight in a single layer in a cool, dry place, or heat-seal in plastic wrap (see below). Makes about 2½ dozen.

To heat-seal, lay a piece of brown paper (or a piece of paper bag) on a baking sheet. Set sheet in oven and heat to 300°. Tear plastic wrap into 8-inch lengths. Wrap each cookie; secure with cellophane tape. Place about 4 cookies at a time, right sides up, on paper; close oven door for 20 seconds. Remove and let cool.

Brandy Balls

The flavor of brandy enlivens these rich and nutty holiday nuggets.

1¼ cups (½ lb. plus 4 tablespoons) butter or margarine, softened
½ cup granulated sugar
1 egg yolk
2 teaspoons brandy flavoring
3 cups all-purpose flour
¼ teaspoon salt
1 cup finely chopped pecans or walnuts
Powdered sugar

In large bowl of an electric mixer, beat butter and granulated sugar until creamy; beat in egg yolk and brandy flavoring. In another bowl, stir to-

gether flour and salt; gradually add to butter mixture, blending thoroughly. Stir in pecans until well combined.

Roll dough into 1-inch balls and place about 1 inch apart on lightly greased baking sheets. Bake in a 350° oven for about 25 minutes or until firm to the touch and very light golden. Transfer to racks and let cool slightly; while still warm, roll in powdered sugar to coat. Let cool completely. Store airtight. Makes about 4 dozen.

Glazed Mincemeat Drops

(Pictured on page 803)

Old-fashioned mincemeat recipes usually call for beef and suet. These holiday drop cookies are made with purchased mincemeat, which contains mainly fruit and sweeteners with little or no meat—but they still boast traditional spicy flavor and festive seasonal appeal.

1 cup (½ lb.) butter or margarine, softened
1½ cups firmly packed brown sugar
3 eggs
3 cups all-purpose flour
½ teaspoon *each* baking powder and salt
1 teaspoon *each* baking soda and ground cinnamon
1 cup rolled oats
2 cups prepared mincemeat
1 cup chopped walnuts
Spicy glaze (recipe follows)

In large bowl of an electric mixer, beat butter and sugar until creamy; beat in eggs. In another bowl, stir together flour, baking powder, salt, baking soda, cinnamon, and oats. Gradually add to butter mixture, blending thoroughly. Stir in mincemeat and walnuts.

Drop dough by level tablespoonfuls onto greased baking sheets, spacing cookies 3 inches apart. Bake in a 400° oven for 8 to 10 minutes or until golden brown.

Transfer cookies to racks. Prepare spicy glaze and spread over tops of cookies while they're still warm; let cool completely. Store airtight. Makes 6 to 7 dozen.

Spicy glaze. In a bowl, stir together 3 cups **powdered sugar,** ¾ teaspoon **ground cinnamon,** and 3 tablespoons *each* **brandy** and **water** (or 6 tablespoons water) until smooth.

Gingerbread Log Cabin

(Pictured on facing page)

This sugary, snow-covered log cabin is easily as-sembled from gingerbread "logs" cut out with homemade cardboard patterns; you'll also need a 12-inch square of stiff cardboard for a "founda-tion." Complete the edible winter wonderland with decorative details cut from leftover dough. Or use your favorite holiday decorations—tiny Christ-mas trees, figurines, toy reindeer, and the like.

> ¾ cup solid vegetable shortening
> ¾ cup granulated sugar
> ¾ cup molasses
> 2 tablespoons water
> 3¼ cups all-purpose flour
> 1 teaspoon *each* salt, baking soda, and ground ginger
> ¼ teaspoon *each* ground nutmeg and allspice
> Icing (recipe follows)
> About 4 cups powdered sugar

In large bowl of an electric mixer, beat shortening and granulated sugar until creamy; beat in mo-lasses and water. In another bowl, stir together flour, salt, baking soda, ginger, nutmeg, and all-spice; gradually add to shortening mixture, blend-ing thoroughly. Cover tightly with plastic wrap and refrigerate until firm (about 2 hours).

Meanwhile, prepare foundation for cabin by covering a 12-inch square of stiff cardboard with foil. Also prepare patterns for cutting logs: cut lightweight cardboard into a 4 by 6-inch rectangle (for the roof); ½-inch-wide strips that are 2, 3½, and 6 inches long (for logs); and a ½-inch square (for spacers).

With a floured rolling pin, roll out a third of the dough on a floured board to a thickness of ⅛ inch (keep remaining dough refrigerated). Make 2 roof sections by cutting around roof pattern with a sharp knife; transfer carefully to a lightly greased baking sheet.

Roll out scraps and all remaining dough to a thickness of ⅜ inch. Then cut out eight 2-inch-long logs, two 3½-inch-long logs, seventeen 6-inch-long logs, and 30 spacers (½-inch squares). Transfer cookies to lightly greased baking sheets (bake sep-arately from roof sections), arranging about 1 inch apart. From remaining dough, cut out trees or other decorative details. Extra spacers can be used for chimney and stepping stones.

Bake in a 350° oven for 12 to 15 minutes or until just firm to the touch (cookies will harden as they cool). As soon as roof section is baked, lay pattern on each section and evenly trim one long edge (where the 2 sections will meet). Let cookies cool briefly on baking sheets, then transfer to racks and let cool completely. If not assembling cabin at once, package airtight; freeze if desired.

Prepare icing. With a pastry brush, paint foil-covered foundation with icing, then sift some of the powdered sugar over icing to cover lightly. Assemble cabin, following steps 1 through 4 at right and using icing as glue wherever logs join. Decorate as desired with extra shapes.

In most dry climates, cabin will keep for about 1 week. In humid areas, cookies may absorb mois-ture and start to sag, so plan to keep cabin for only 2 or 3 days before eating.

Icing. In a bowl, beat together 2 cups **powdered sugar** and ¼ cup **water** until smooth.

Candy Cane Crisps

(Pictured on page 803)

The month of December is punctuated with occa-sions calling for cookies, and these crisp morsels suit the season perfectly.

> 1 cup (½ lb.) butter or margarine, softened
> About 1¼ cups powdered sugar
> 1½ teaspoons vanilla
> 1⅓ cups all-purpose flour
> 1 cup rolled oats
> ½ teaspoon salt
> About ¾ cup coarsely crushed candy canes

In large bowl of an electric mixer, beat butter and 1 cup of the sugar until creamy; beat in vanilla. In another bowl, stir together flour, oats, and salt; gradually add to butter mixture, blending thor-oughly. Add ¼ cup of the crushed candy canes and mix until well combined.

Roll dough into ¾-inch balls, then roll in re-maining sugar (about ¼ cup) to coat. Place balls about 2 inches apart on greased and flour-dusted baking sheets. Flatten cookies with a fork, making a crisscross pattern with fork tines. Sprinkle each with about ½ teaspoon crushed candy canes.

Bake in a 325° oven for 18 to 20 minutes or until edges are lightly browned. Let cool on baking sheets for 2 to 3 minutes, then transfer to racks and let cool completely. Store airtight. Makes about 4 dozen.

Gingerbread Log Cabin *(Recipe on facing page)*

1 Start with a 6-inch log in back, two 2-inch logs in front. Top with 6-inch logs on sides, letting ends extend. Continue building, using spacers at inner edges of 2-inch logs.

2 Fourth layer uses 6-inch logs all around. Add 3 spacers across doorway; then top with 6-inch logs across front and back.

3 Using spacers and 3½ and 2-inch logs, build up gables on front and back of cabin. Place a spacer on top of each gable.

4 Ice and sugar roof pieces; ice top logs and spacers. Set roof in place, trimmed edges together.

Nürnberger Lebkuchen

(Pictured on pages 803 and 814)

In Nürnberg, Germany, Christmas baking begins in November with the preparation of *lebkuchen* — spicy, cakelike honey cookies that need to age for several weeks to become soft and chewy.

   1 **cup honey**
   ¾ **cup firmly packed dark brown sugar**
   1 **egg, lightly beaten**
   1 **tablespoon lemon juice**
   1 **teaspoon grated lemon peel**
2⅓ **cups all-purpose flour**
   1 **teaspoon ground cinnamon**
   ½ **teaspoon** *each* **ground allspice, cloves, and nutmeg**
   ½ **teaspoon** *each* **salt and baking soda**
   ⅓ **cup** *each* **finely chopped candied citron and finely chopped almonds**
      About 24 candied cherries, cut in half
   6 **to 8 ounces whole blanched almonds**
      Glaze (recipe follows)

Heat honey in a small pan over medium-high heat just until it begins to bubble. Remove from heat and let cool slightly. Stir in sugar, egg, lemon juice, and lemon peel; let cool to lukewarm.

In a large mixing bowl, stir together flour, cinnamon, allspice, cloves, nutmeg, salt, and baking soda. Add honey mixture, citron, and chopped almonds; stir until well blended (dough will be soft). Cover tightly with plastic wrap and refrigerate for at least 8 hours or for up to 2 days.

Work with a fourth of the dough at a time, keeping remaining dough refrigerated. On a heavily floured board, roll out dough with a floured rolling pin to a thickness of ⅜ inch. Cut dough with a 2½-inch round cookie cutter; place cookies 2 inches apart on baking sheets lined with lightly greased parchment paper.

Press a cherry half into center of each cookie; surround with 3 almonds arranged like flower petals. Bake in a 375° oven for 12 to 15 minutes or until golden brown. Meanwhile, prepare glaze. Remove cookies from oven and immediately brush glaze over tops with a pastry brush; transfer to racks and let cool. As soon as top glaze dries, turn cookies over and brush glaze over bottoms.

When cookies are completely cooled and dry, pack into airtight containers and store at room temperature for at least 2 weeks or for up to 3 months. If cookies get slightly hard, add a thin slice of apple to each container; cover tightly and store until cookies are moist again (about 1 day), then discard apple. Makes about 4 dozen.

Glaze. Stir together 1 cup **powdered sugar** and 5 tablespoons **rum** or water until very smooth.

Gingerbread Boys

(Pictured on page 814)

Full of personality, crisp gingerbread boys hang like holiday puppets on your Christmas tree.

   ½ **cup (¼ lb.) butter or margarine, softened**
   1 **cup firmly packed brown sugar**
1½ **cups light molasses**
   ⅔ **cup water or apple juice**
6½ **cups all-purpose flour**
   2 **teaspoons** *each* **baking soda and salt**
   1 **teaspoon** *each* **ground cinnamon, ginger, cloves, and allspice**
      Raisins
   1 **egg white, lightly beaten**
      Purchased decorating icing (in tubes or aerosol cans)

In large bowl of an electric mixer, beat butter and sugar until creamy. Add molasses and beat until blended, then mix in water. In another bowl, stir together flour, baking soda, salt, cinnamon, ginger, cloves, and allspice. Gradually add to butter mixture, blending to form a stiff dough. Cover tightly with plastic wrap and refrigerate for several hours or until next day.

On a floured board, roll out dough, a portion at a time, to a thickness of 3/16 inch. Cut out with a 4 to 6-inch gingerbread boy cutter and, with cutter still in place, transfer cookie and cutter with a wide spatula to a lightly greased baking sheet. Lift off cutter and repeat. If desired, insert a short length of plastic drinking straw into each cookie near the top to make a hole for hanging; press straw all the way through to baking sheet.

Dip raisins in egg white and press them firmly into dough to make buttons (use about 3 per cookie). Move arms and legs to animate the figures.

Bake in a 350° oven for 10 to 15 minutes or until lightly browned. Transfer cookies to racks, remove straws (if used), and let cool completely. Draw faces on cooled cookies with icing. Tie ribbon or thread through holes for hanging, if desired. Store airtight. Makes about 4 dozen.

Speculaas

(Pictured on page 803)

Cookies are to the Netherlands as *Wienerbrød* is to Denmark and *Torten* are to Austria—a specialty of the country. As long ago as the 17th century, some Dutch bakers produced cookies exclusively. The very word "cookie" is our phonetic approximation of the Dutch *koekje* (little cake).

In Dutch homes, cookies are baked in profusion for *Sinterklaas avond* (the eve of St. Nicholas Day). Perhaps the best known of these holiday treats are crisp and spicy *speculaas*, traditionally shaped by pressing the dough into elaborately carved wooden molds. If you have a speculaas mold (they're sometimes sold in cookware shops), you'll be able to make cookies with old-fashioned embossed designs; if you don't, you can just roll out the dough and cut it with your favorite holiday cookie cutters.

    2 cups all-purpose flour
    2 teaspoons ground cinnamon
    ½ teaspoon *each* baking powder and ground nutmeg
    1 teaspoon ground cloves
    ⅛ teaspoon salt
    ¼ cup ground blanched almonds
    1 cup firmly packed brown sugar
    ¾ cup (¼ lb. plus 4 tablespoons) firm butter or margarine, cut into pieces
    2 tablespoons milk

In a large bowl, stir together flour, cinnamon, baking powder, nutmeg, cloves, and salt. Blend in almonds and sugar until well combined. With a pastry blender or 2 knives, cut in butter until mixture resembles cornmeal; stir in milk. Work dough with your hands until you can form it into a smooth ball.

For molded cookies: Press dough firmly and evenly into a floured wooden speculaas mold; invert onto an ungreased baking sheet and release cookie by tapping back of mold (ease cookies out with the point of a knife, if necessary). Space cookies about 1 inch apart.

For rolled cookies: On a lightly floured board, roll out dough to a thickness of about ¼ inch. Cut out with 2 to 3-inch cookie cutters. Transfer to ungreased baking sheets, spacing cookies about 1 inch apart.

Bake in a 300° oven for 20 to 25 minutes or until lightly browned. Let cool briefly on baking sheets; transfer to racks and let cool completely. Store airtight. Makes about 4 dozen.

Anise Pretzels

(Pictured on page 814)

The attractive shape of these anise-flavored holiday cookies makes them a good choice for gifts, parties, or hanging on the tree. The anise flavor may remind you of *springerle*, an old-fashioned German cookie—and if you wish, you can shape the dough as you would for springerle, using the traditional carved rolling pin to produce little square cookies with embossed patterns.

    1 cup (½ lb.) butter or margarine, softened
    ½ cup sugar
    2 eggs
    1½ teaspoons anise extract
    3½ cups all-purpose flour
    1 egg beaten with 1 tablespoon water (omit if shaping dough with a springerle rolling pin)
    1 to 2 tablespoons anise seeds

In large bowl of an electric mixer, beat butter and sugar until creamy; beat in the 2 eggs, one at a time, beating until well combined after each addition. Beat in anise extract. Gradually add flour, blending thoroughly.

Divide dough in half. For pretzels, roll each half into a log 2 inches in diameter. For picture cookies, shape each half into a rectangular slab. Wrap tightly in plastic wrap and refrigerate until easy to handle (at least 1 hour).

For pretzels: Cut logs of dough into ⅜-inch-thick slices. Roll each slice into a rope about 14 inches long, then twist into a pretzel shape. Place on greased baking sheets, spacing at least 1 inch apart. Brush with egg-water mixture, then sprinkle lightly with anise seeds. Bake in a 325° oven for about 20 minutes or until light golden and firm to the touch. Transfer to racks and let cool. Store airtight. Makes about 2 dozen.

For picture cookies: On a lightly floured board, roll out dough, half at a time, to form a ¼-inch-thick rectangle slightly wider than your springerle rolling pin. Pressing down firmly, roll springerle rolling pin once over dough so that designs are sharply imprinted. With a sharp knife, cut pictures into squares, following lines made by springerle rolling pin.

Sprinkle each of 2 greased baking sheets with about 1 tablespoon anise seeds. Set cookies about 1 inch apart on seeds. Bake in a 325° oven for 15 to 18 minutes or until bottoms are golden and tops are firm to the touch but still white. Transfer to racks and let cool. Store airtight. Makes about 3½ dozen.

Dear Santa Claus,
I would like a
dollhouse and a kitten
and a pony for
christmas.
Thank you.
Love, Alexandra

Santa is sure to feel welcome when he sees the tree
decorated with Anise Pretzels (page 813), Gingerbread Boys (page 812), and Stained-glass Cookies
(page 808). A plate of Nürnberger Lebkuchen
(page 812) and Fruitcake Cookie Cups (page
807)—with hot cocoa to sip alongside—might
tempt him to stay until New Year's Day!

Index

Muffins, 300, 305
  freezing, 176
  polenta berry, 608
Mulled apple-ginger sparkler, 91
Munchies, make-ahead, 26–27
Mushroom(s)
  almond pâté, 233
  baked zucchini with, 540
  blue cheese & walnut salad, 234
  -broccoli Stroganoff, 277
  bundles, 651
  cabbage rolls, 280
  canning, 128
  -cheese sauce, tortellini with, 474
  -crust quiche, 262
  drying, 213
  fettuccine with dried tomatoes &, 206
  fingers, cheese-, 35
  Florentine, 67
  freezing, 188
  garlic-buttered, 66
  ham & cheese calzones, 608
  heavenly, 66
  marinated broccoli &, 717
  miso grilled, 66
  pâté, fresh, 30
  portabella, sandwiches, 596
  risotto with, 547
  risotto, porcini, 530
  sauce, double, linguine with, 474
  sauce, pappardelle in, barbecued quail
    with, 511
  sautéed, green beans with, 541
  shiitake & cheese cannelloni, 498
  shiitake, sautéed squid &, 60
  shrimp-stuffed, 67, 710
  soup, double, 247
  spaghetti, beef-, in barbecue sauce, 515
  -tomato sauce, 499
  wild, polenta boards, 545
Mussel(s)
  & clam appetizer, 57
  garlic, on the half shell, 57
Mustard
  chicken, apricot Dijon-, 357
  chicken chunks with vermicelli, 366
  chicken & pasta, 384
  chicken, rooster crests with, 495
  crust, game hens with, 350
  dressing, 241, 395
  eggs, 25
  marinade, 47, 402
  sauce, sliced pepper steak in, 47
  seed chutney, ginger &, 31
  wings & ribs, grilled, 402

N

Nachos, super, 34
Napa cabbage
  beef with, 645
  spicy, 685
Navajo fry bread, 704
Nectarines
  canning, 113
  drying, 209
  freezing, 181
Needles in a haystack, 83
Neoclassic cheese fondue, 59
Nests
  crisp-fried, quail eggs in, 701
  potato phoenix, 696
  sweet potato, 696
  yam, 696
Nippy cheese puffs, 36
No-cook freezer jam, 140
Noodle(s)
  chicken &, with pimentos, 328, 496
  green, scallops &, 491
  pan-fried, 670
  salad, chicken, Chinese hot & sour, 432
  salad, Chinese, with five-spice chicken, 358
  salad, sesame, 462, 679
  stir-fried, grilled swordfish with, 487

Noodle(s) *(continued)*
  toasted cabbage with, 480
  wide, in tomato-cheese sauce, 468
  yogurt soup, chicken-, 450
Norwegian kringle, 757
Norwegian meatballs with gjetost sauce, 516
Nuggets, roasted Thai, 334
Nürnberger lebkuchen, 812
Nut cookies, Italian, 761
Nutmeg crisps, 768
Nut
  & cheese-filled fruits, 95
  cookies, Italian, 761
  meringues, date-, 736
  slices, poppy seed, 785
  -studded garlic-herb cheese, 23
  valentines, raspberry-, 804
Nutritional data, 7, 228–229, 231, 323, 443
Nutty whole wheat shortbread, 794

O

Oat bars, tutti frutti, 801
Oatmeal
  bread, pebble-top, 293
  chews, 797
  chocolate chip cookies, big, 729
  cookies, date-, 789
  lace cookies, German, 761
  pancakes, 304
  pastry, 307
  peanut bars, chocolate, 741
  raisin cookies, 728, 729
Okra
  canning, 128
  drying, 213
  freezing, 188
Old-fashioned molasses chews, 760
Olive oil, facts about, 584
Olive(s)
  chèvre &, tagliarini with, 479
  orange-fennel, 94
  -pecan chicken slaw, 429
  pesto, garbanzo beans with, 558
  & pine nuts, chicken with, 384
  prosciutto &, linguine with, 524
  purée, 31
  relish poor boy sandwich loaf, 43
  terrine, veal &, 78
Omelets, 257–258
Onion(s)
  in basil-Parmesan butter, 58
  -cheese spread, 31
  crisp-fried, 67
  -dill spaghetti squash, 483
  drying, 213
  focaccia, eggplant &, 593
  freezing, 188
  glazed, with corn, peppers & shrimp, 68
  green, garlic-, vinegar, 158
  knots with peanut sauce, 92
  marmalade, sherried chicken with, 571
  peppers & pasta with, 478
  pickled Maui, 162
  pink, 42
  -potato blintzes, 276
  roast chicken with beets, squash &, 326
  roasted sausage &, with pita breads, 544
  sauce, tomato-, 505
  spread, sweet & sour, 31
  spring, lamb with, 682
  & sprouts, sun-gold, 290
  sweet, & creamy eggs, 262
  tarts, 36
  triangles, egg &, 42
  two-, beef, 647
Orange(s)
  canning, 113
  -carob cake, 308
  coconut crisps, 757
  conserve, peach-pineapple-, 145
  -fennel olives, 94
  freezing, 181
  froth, 303

Orange(s) *(continued)*
  -herb sauce, 370
  jam, cranberry-, 137
  jam, peach-, 134
  polenta cakes, 609
  preserves, quince &, 147
  salad, fennel &, 561
  sauce, espresso chocolate cake with, 624
  sauce, whole cranberry-, 166
  tortellini &, turkey with, 437, 508
  vinaigrette, 390
  -walnut shortbread, 746
  wheat cookies, 796
  yogurt waffles, 305
Orecchiette
  with broccoli rabe & pine nuts, 604
  with spinach & garlic, 477
Oregano
  -peppercorn-basil vinegar, 158
  -rubbed turkey, 565
Oriental chicken salad, 692, 693
Orzo
  & chard stuffing, 494
  lamb &, Mediterranean style, 529
  saffron, herb-roasted game hens with, 566
  -stuffed roast chicken & vegetables, 494
  sweet spice chicken &, 408
Osso buco with risotto, 590
Oven-barbecued chicken, 330
Oven-browned eggplant, 407
Oven chicken & linguine, 496
Oven drying, 197
  fruits, 201
  vegetables, 210
Oven-fried buttermilk chicken legs, 382
Oven-fried chicken, easy, 344
Oven-fried turkey wings, 403
Oven pancake, filled, 264
Oyster beef, 646
Oyster(s)
  boats, bell pepper &, 86
  smoked, cherry tomatoes with, 86

P

Packaging
  for dried foods, 198
  for frozen foods, 172, 179, 185
Packets, lasagne, 475
Packing methods for canned fruits &
    vegetables, 104, 105, 108–109, 116,
    124–125
Packing & sending cookies, 737
Paella, brown rice, 389
Pancakes
  cottage cheese, with applesauce, 304
  filled oven, 264
  oatmeal, 304
  ricotta, with lemon-maple syrup, 609
  walnut wheat, 304
Panforte, 622
Pan-fried noodles, 670
Pan-grilled risotto with mozzarella & basil, 531
Paniolo beef jerky, 216
Papaya
  butter, 139
  ice, 182
  -plum chutney, 167
  & sausage sauté, 661
  -tomatillo relish, 165
Pappardelle
  country-style, 523
  in mushroom sauce, barbecued quail
    with, 511
Paprikash, steak, 647
Parchment, seafood in, 488
Parmesan
  butter, basil-, onions in, 58
  chicken eggplant, 407
  chicken wings, basil, 400
  eggplant, 598
  -pepper pastry, 438
  pesto, chicken breasts with, 349
  sour cottage sauce, 289

Acknowledgments

PHOTOGRAPHERS
Victor Budnik: 497, 665, 676. **Glenn Christiansen:** 469. **Peter Christiansen:** 489. **Norman A. Plate:** 716. **Allan Rosenberg:** 2, 535, 538, 543, 546, 551, 554, 559, 562, 567, 570, 575, 578, 583, 586, 591, 594, 599, 602, 607, 610, 615, 618, 623, 626. **Kevin Sanchez:** 361, 364, 369, 412. **Darrow M. Watt:** 40, 633, 636, 692, 723, 726, 731, 734, 739, 742, 747, 750, 755, 758, 763, 766, 771, 774, 779, 782, 787, 790, 795, 798, 803, 806, 811, 814. **Tom Wyatt:** 5, 8, 13, 16, 21, 24, 29, 32, 45, 48, 53, 72, 77, 93, 103, 106, 111, 114, 119, 122, 127, 130, 135, 138, 143, 146, 151, 154, 159, 178, 183, 186, 191, 194, 199, 202, 207, 230, 235, 238, 243, 246, 251, 254, 259, 270, 275, 278, 283, 286, 291, 294, 299, 324, 329, 332, 337, 340, 345, 353, 356, 372, 377, 380, 385, 388, 393, 396, 401, 404, 409, 417, 425, 428, 433, 517, 673, 697. **Nikolay Zurek:** 37, 56, 61, 64, 69, 80, 85, 88, 96, 321, 348, 420, 436, 439, 445, 448, 453, 456, 461, 464, 473, 476, 481, 484, 492, 501, 504, 509, 512, 520, 525, 528, 532, 641, 644, 649, 652, 657, 660, 668, 681, 684, 689, 700, 705, 708, 713, 720.

ASSOCIATE PHOTOGRAPHER
Allen V. Lott: 535, 538, 543, 546, 551, 554, 559, 562, 567, 570, 575, 578, 583, 586, 591, 594, 599, 602, 607, 610, 615, 618, 623, 626.

PHOTO STYLISTS
Sandra Griswold: 535, 538, 543, 546, 551, 554, 559, 562, 567, 570, 575, 578, 583, 586, 591, 594, 599, 602, 607, 610, 615, 618, 623, 626. **Susan Massey:** 5, 8, 13, 16, 21, 29, 32, 45, 48, 53, 61, 64, 72, 77, 85, 88, 93, 103, 106, 111, 114, 119, 122, 127, 130, 135, 138, 143, 146, 151, 154, 159, 178, 183, 186, 191, 194, 199, 202, 207, 321, 361, 364, 369, 412, 324, 329, 332, 337, 340, 345, 348, 353, 356, 372, 377, 380, 385, 388, 393, 396, 401, 404, 409, 417, 420, 425, 428, 433, 436, 439, 445, 448, 453, 456, 461, 464, 473, 476, 481, 484, 492, 501, 504, 509, 512, 520, 525, 528, 532. **Evelyn Newell:** 230, 235, 238, 243, 246, 251, 254, 259, 270, 275, 278, 283, 286, 291, 294, 299. **Lynne B. Tremble:** 37, 40, 56, 69, 497, 723, 726, 731, 734, 739, 742, 747, 750, 755, 758, 763, 766, 771, 774, 779, 782, 787, 790, 795, 798, 803, 806, 811, 814. **JoAnn Masaoka Van Atta:** 24, 80, 96, 517, 641, 644, 649, 652, 657, 660, 665, 676, 673, 697, 668, 681, 684, 689, 700, 705, 708, 713, 720.

FOOD STYLISTS
Judith A. Gaulke: 641, 644, 649, 652, 657, 660, 665, 676, 673, 697, 668, 681, 684, 689, 700, 705, 708, 713, 720. **Heidi Gintner:** 535, 538, 543, 546, 551, 554, 559, 562, 567, 570, 575, 578, 583, 586, 591, 594, 599, 602, 607, 610, 615, 618, 623, 626.

ASSISTANT FOOD & PHOTO STYLIST
Elizabeth C. Davis: 535, 538, 543, 546, 551, 554, 559, 562, 567, 570, 575, 578, 583, 586, 591, 594, 599, 602, 607, 610, 615, 618, 623, 626.